R. Gupta's®

POPULAR MASTER GUIDE

National Testing Agency (NTA)

UGC-NET/JRF

Junior Research Fellowship & Assistant Professor Eligibility Exam

Physical Education

PAPER II

by

Dr. K.N. Jha

2027
EDITION

RAMESH PUBLISHING HOUSE, NEW DELHI

Published by

O.P. Gupta *for* Ramesh Publishing House

Admin. Office

12-H, New Daryaganj Road, Opp. Officers' Mess,
New Delhi-110002 ✆ 23275224, 23245124

E-mail: info@rameshpublishinghouse.com
For Online Shopping: www.rameshpublishinghouse.com

Showroom

- Balaji Market, Nai Sarak, Delhi-110006 ✆ 23282525 📱 9354373464
- 4457, Nai Sarak, Delhi-110006

Book Code: R-979

ISBN: 978-93-87604-60-5

Price: ₹ 590

Printed at: B.K. Offset, Delhi

CONTENTS

Previous Years' Paper

National Testing Agency (NTA)

UGC-NET Junior Research Fellowship & Assistant Professor Eligibility Exam

PHYSICAL EDUCATION, JANUARY-2026

(Exam held on 07-01-2026)

PAPER-II

1. Which International Federation won the IOC climate action award for the year 2024?
1. World Sailing
2. The International Basketball Federation
3. The International Hockey Federation
4. The International Cricket Council

2. The curriculum of the Philanthropinium was guided by:
1. Philosophy of Naturalism
2. Philosophy of Pragmatism
3. Philosophy of Humanism
4. Philosophy of Idealism

3. Which of the following is a potential negative social aspect of competition in sports?
1. Promotion of teamwork
2. Reinforcement of aggression and hostility
3. Encouragement of social harmony
4. Development of leadership skills

4. Which of the following statements about the common teaching style in physical education is true?
1. It is effective for teaching new and complex skills
2. It is rarely used in skill acquisition
3. It encourages maximum learner autonomy
4. It fosters open-ended exploration

5. Acclimatization to exercise in cold environments involves all of the following except.
1. Increased peripheral vasoconstriction
2. Enhanced shivering thermogenesis
3. Improved insulation via subcutaneous fat
4. Elevated sweat gland sensitivity

6. Which physiological response is most likely to occur during the early phase of rehabilitation following immobilization?
1. Decreased muscle cross-sectional area and increase connective tissue proliferation.
2. Enhanced mitochondrial density in muscle fibres.
3. Increased synovial fluid viscosity.
4. Hyperplasia of type II b muscle fibres.

7. What is another name for the autonomic nervous system?
1. Somatic nerves
2. Non-visceral nervous system
3. Voluntary nerves
4. Vegetative nerves

8. The transmitter norepinephrine is inactivated by:
1. Chalinesterare
2. Catechol-o-methyl transferase
3. Acetylcholine
4. Acromegaly

9. Which factor most significantly increases drag force experienced by a cyclist according to the drag equation?

1. Doubling the cyclist's velocity.
2. Doubling the cyclist's mass.
3. Decreasing air density.
4. Halving the cyclist's frontal area.

10. Which exercise is most effective for collecting excessive lumbar lordosis?

1. Stretching the gluteus maximus
2. Strengthening the erector spinae
3. Stretching the quardriceps
4. Strengthening the hamstrings and abdominal muscles.

11. Which of the following is a correct calculation for mechanical advantage in a lever system?

1. MA = effort arm/load arm
2. MA = load arm/effort arm
3. MA = (effort arm + load arm)/fulcrum
4. MA = fulcrum/(load arm – effort arm)

12. Ability to manage the angular momentum of your body at discrete angle is called as:

1. Mobility
2. Manoeuvrability
3. Change of direction
4. Multidirectional speed

13. Which corrective exercise is most appropriate for addressing genu valgum deformity?

1. Strengthening the hip abductors and vastus medialis.
2. Strengthening the hip adductors
3. Stretching the iliotibial band
4. Strengthening the gastrocnemius

14. During a pull-up, which muscle acts as the prime mover for elbow flexion and what is its insertion?

1. Triceps brachii; olecranon process of the ulna.
2. Brachialis; scapular spine
3. Deltoid: deltoid tuberosity
4. Biceps brachii: radial tuberosity

15. Who have a goal-directed orientation toward life?

1. Apathetic individuals
2. Fun loving individuals
3. Telic-dominant individuals
4. Paratelic-dominant individuals

16. In sports training, negative transfer most commonly occurs when

1. Skills involve identical motor patterns
2. Athletes train in highly specific environments
3. Two tasks share similar movements but require different responses
4. Skills involve completely different movement patterns

17. Which players are keen to find out if the drills they have practiced have helped them improve their skills during a competitive game?

1. The goal oriented
2. The performance oriented
3. The ego oriented
4. The task oriented

18. Which of the following is a key principle of curriculum planning that ensures continuity and sequence in physical education learning experiences?

1. Fragmentation
2. Randomization
3. Stammering
4. Articulation

19. Which of the following situations best illustrates the application of diagnostic assessment in physical education?

1. Providing feedback during a gymnastic routine to help students improve.
2. Using a pre-test to identify students who need additional support in learning the Tennis serve.
3. Grading students based on their performance in the final handball match.
4. Assigning homework to reinforce concepts taught in class.

20. Which of the following statements about the Rashtriya Khel protsahan puraskar is incorrect?

1. The award is open to both organisations and individuals.
2. It includes recognition for contributions to sports welfare measures.
3. It is given exclusively for achievements in Olympic sports.
4. It is distinct from the Arjuna and Dronacharya Awards.

21. Which of the following best illustrates a Pedagogical responsibility specific to primary level physical education teacher?

1. Coaching school-level athletes
2. Supervising laboratory based research
3. Introducing basic motor skills through play
4. Introducing basic cognitive skills

22. Sperm cell moves with the help of _____.

1. Circumcision 2. Syphilis
3. Corpus luteum 4. Flagellum

23. Which of the following is not an example of a primary prevention measure?

1. Immunization
2. Water sanitation
3. Health education
4. Cardiac rehabilitation

24. Which anatomical structure is most directly compressed during Heimlich maneuver to expel a foreign object from the airway?

1. The trachea 2. The oesophagus
3. The diaphragm 4. The larynx

25. Which of the following is the most critical step in the first-aid management of a chemical burn?

1. Immediately wash the area with copious amounts of water.
2. Apply ice packs to the affected area
3. Neutralize the chemical with an opposite substance
4. Cover the burn with butter or oil

26. In Resistance training, the amount of work accomplished is called as:

1. Intensity 2. Frequency
3. Volume 4. Set

27. Which of the following is not a phase that compose the stretch-shortening cycle?

1. Eccentric 2. Concentric
3. Amortization 4. Deceleration

28. Which type of fatigue impacts the whole body irrespective of where or how it was generated?

1. Local fatigue
2. Systemic fatigue
3. Axial fatigue
4. Muscular specific fatigue

29. A linear periodization model is characterized by:

1. Randomized training sessions
2. Constant training load throughout
3. Gradually increase in intensity with decrease in volume.
4. Frequent changes in load and intensity

30. Which of the following is the valid variable name in SPSS?

1. Arm strength
2. Arm-Strength
3. Armstrength
4. "Arm-strength"

31. Which research design lacks randomization but manipulates variables?

1. True experiment 2. Cross sectional
3. Longitudinal 4. Quasi experiment

32. In research, asking athletes to train at dangerous intensities without proper safety monitoring would violate which ethical principle?

1. Autonomy
2. Beneficence
3. Non-maleficence
4. Justice

33. Which type of validity refers to the degree to which a measure obviously involves the performance being measured?

1. Construct validity
2. Logical validity
3. Content validity
4. Criterion validity

34. To find out VO_2 max _____ formula used in cooper 12 minute Run/walk Test:

1. VO_2 max (ml.kg^{-1}.min^{-1}) = 3.5 + (438 ÷ time in minutes)
2. VO_2 max (ml.kg^{-1}.min^{-1}) = (Distance – 0.3138) ÷ 0.0278
3. VO_2 max (ml.kg^{-1}.min^{-1}) = 108.94 – 8.41 (time) – 0.38 (time^2)
4. VO_2 max (ml.kg^{-1}.min^{-1}) = –32.678 + 6.592 (maximal speed)

35. Which is the only site you can use to assess body composition in AAHPERD-HRPF(1984)?

1. Triceps Skinfold
2. Abdominal Skinfold
3. Subscapular Skinfold
4. Suprailium Skinfold

36. Which year softball throw test item was deleted from the AAHPER youth fitness test?

1. 1988 2. 1976
3. 1932 4. 1995

37. What does the ponderal index measure?

1. Body weight relative to height cubed
2. Body mass per unit height
3. Lean body mass
4. Body fat percentage

38. Which of the following is not a type of budget in sports?

1. Performance budget
2. Random budget
3. Capital budget
4. Zero-based budget

39. In sports management efficiency primarily refers to:

1. Achieving organisational goals regardless of cost
2. Focusing only on financial profit
3. Maximising outcomes with minimum use of resources
4. Ensuring players satisfaction at all times

40. Which one of the following is not related to leadership theories?

1. Behavioural theories
2. Trait theories
3. Situational and contingency theories
4. Hierarchy of need theories

41. Given below are two statements : one is labelled as Assertion (A) and the other is labelled as Reason (R).

Assertion (A): Philosophy of idealism emphasises moral and spiritual development through physical education.

Reason (R): Idealistic philosophy believes that the human body is more important than the mind.

In the light of the above statements, choose the ***most appropriate*** answer from the options given below:

1. Both (A) and (R) are correct and (R) is the correct explanation of (A)
2. Both (A) and (R) are correct, but (R) is NOT the correct explanation of (A)
3. (A) is correct, but (R) is not correct
4. (A) is not correct, but (R) is correct

42. Given below are two statements : one is labelled as Assertion (A) and the other is labelled as Reason (R).

Assertion (A): All of the energy used by the human body is ultimately derived from the chemical energy in the foods that we eat.

Reason (R): This chemical energy may be used immediately or it may be stored for later use.

In the light of the above statements, choose the ***most appropriate*** answer from the options given below:

1. Both (A) and (R) are correct and (R) is the correct explanation of (A)
2. Both (A) and (R) are correct, but (R) is NOT the correct explanation of (A)
3. (A) is correct, but (R) is not correct
4. (A) is not correct, but (R) is correct

43. Given below are two statements : one is labelled as Assertion (A) and the other is labelled as Reason (R).

Assertion (A): Deep breathing is an effective psychological skill for reducing anxiety in athletes.

Reason (R): Deep breathing increases oxygen supply to muscles and enhances their strength.

In the light of the above statements, choose the ***most appropriate*** answer from the options given below:

1. Both (A) and (R) are correct and (R) is the correct explanation of (A)
2. Both (A) and (R) are correct, but (R) is NOT the correct explanation of (A)
3. (A) is correct, but (R) is not correct
4. (A) is not correct, but (R) is correct

44. Given below are two statements : one is labelled as Assertion (A) and the other is labelled as Reason (R).

Assertion (A): Intramural sports competitions promote mass student participation in educational institutions.

Reason (R): Mass student participation in sport activities helps in identifying hidden talents.

In the light of the above statements, choose the ***most appropriate*** answer from the options given below:

1. Both (A) and (R) are correct and (R) is the correct explanation of (A)
2. Both (A) and (R) are correct, but (R) is NOT the correct explanation of (A)
3. (A) is correct, but (R) is not correct
4. (A) is not correct, but (R) is correct

45. Given below are two statements : one is labelled as Assertion (A) and the other is labelled as Reason (R).

Assertion (A): Eutrophication caused by water pollution can lead to the death of aquatic organisms.

Reason (R): Excess algae growth reduces oxygen levels in the water.

In the light of the above statements, choose the ***most appropriate*** answer from the options given below:

1. Both (A) and (R) are correct and (R) is the correct explanation of (A)
2. Both (A) and (R) are correct, but (R) is NOT the correct explanation of (A)
3. (A) is correct, but (R) is not correct
4. (A) is not correct, but (R) is correct

46. Given below are two statements : one is labelled as Assertion (A) and the other is labelled as Reason (R).

Assertion (A): Ballistic stretching is considered really safe and suitable for beginners.

Reason (R): Balistic stretching involves bouncing movements which may cause muscle strain if not done properly.

In the light of the above statements, choose the ***most appropriate*** answer from the options given below:

1. Both (A) and (R) are correct and (R) is the correct explanation of (A)
2. Both (A) and (R) are correct, but (R) is NOT the correct explanation of (A)
3. (A) is correct, but (R) is not correct
4. (A) is not correct, but (R) is correct

47. Given below are two statements : one is labelled as Assertion (A) and the other is labelled as Reason (R).

Assertion (A): The tennis serve accuracy test is used to evaluate a player's footwork and movements.

Reason (R): The test involves serving balls into target zone of the service court.

In the light of the above statements, choose the ***most appropriate*** answer from the options given below:

1. Both (A) and (R) are correct and (R) is the correct explanation of (A)
2. Both (A) and (R) are correct, but (R) is NOT the correct explanation of (A)
3. (A) is correct, but (R) is not correct
4. (A) is not correct, but (R) is correct

48. Given below are two statements : one is labelled as Assertion (A) and the other is labelled as Reason (R).

Assertion (A): Sports management involves planning, organizing, directing, controlling and evaluating sports events.

Reason (R): Sports management ensures that only elite level athletes are allowed to participate in sports events.

In the light of the above statements, choose the ***most appropriate*** answer from the options given below:

1. Both (A) and (R) are correct and (R) is the correct explanation of (A)
2. Both (A) and (R) are correct, but (R) is NOT the correct explanation of (A)
3. (A) is correct, but (R) is not correct
4. (A) is not correct, but (R) is correct

49. Given below are two statements : one is labelled as Assertion (A) and the other is labelled as Reason (R).

Assertion (A): To compare the means of the levels of the test factor, a measure of the variation between the level, the MS (factor), will be compared with a measure of the variation within the level, the MS (error).

Reason (R): If MS (factor) is not significantly larger than MS (error), we will not be able to reject the null hypothesis that all means are equal.

In the light of the above statements, choose the ***most appropriate*** answer from the options given below:

1. Both (A) and (R) are correct and (R) is the correct explanation of (A)
2. Both (A) and (R) are correct, but (R) is NOT the correct explanation of (A)
3. (A) is correct, but (R) is not correct
4. (A) is not correct, but (R) is correct

50. Given below are two statements : one is labelled as Assertion (A) and the other is labelled as Reason (R).

Assertion (A): The coefficient of restitution is the absolute value of the ratio of the velocity of separation to the velocity of approach.

Reason (R): The velocity of separation and approach are the difference between the velocities of the two colliding objects just after and before the collision respectively.

In the light of the above statements, choose the ***most appropriate*** answer from the options given below:

1. Both (A) and (R) are correct and (R) is the correct explanation of (A)
2. Both (A) and (R) are correct, but (R) is NOT the correct explanation of (A)
3. (A) is correct, but (R) is not correct
4. (A) is not correct, but (R) is correct

51. Arrange the following games in chronological order based on the year their first editions were held.

A. Commonwealth E-sport Championship
B. Commonwealth Youth Games
C. Commonwealth Winter Games
D. Commonwealth Paraplegic Games

Choose the ***correct*** answer from the options given below:

1. D, C, B, A
2. A, C, B, D
3. B, A, C, D
4. C, D, B, A

52. Arrange the distinct phases of the cardiac cycle in a sequential order.

A. Isovolumetric contraction
B. Isovolumetric relaxation
C. Ventricular ejection
D. Ventricular filling

Choose the ***correct*** answer from the options given below:

1. A, C, D, B 2. D, A, C, B
3. C, A, D, B 4. B, D, A, C

53. Choose the correct sequential order of skeletal muscle fiber type classification based on fatigue resistance (low to high)

A. Type I fibers
B. Type II a fibers
C. Type II b fibers
D. Type II x fibers

Choose the ***correct*** answer from the options given below:

1. D, B, C, A 2. A, B, C, D
3. C, D, B, A 4. B, C, A, D

54. Choose the correct sequential order of neural impulse pathway from external stimulus to muscle fibers.

A. Motor Neuron B. Sensory Neuron
C. Interneuron D. Stimulus

Choose the ***correct*** answer from the options given below:

1. A, B, C, D 2. B, C, A, D
3. C, A, D, B 4. D, B, C, A

55. Arrange the levels of motivation from lowest to highest self-determination.

A. Intrinsic motivation
B. External regulation
C. Amotivation
D. Identified regulation

Choose the ***correct*** answer from the options given below:

1. A, C, D, B 2. C, B, D, A
3. C, D, B, A 4. A, B, D, C

56. Arrange the stages of the stress process in the correct order.

A. Stress response
B. Coping with stress
C. Environmental demand
D. Individual's perception of demand

Choose the ***correct*** answer from the options given below:

1. C, D, A, B 2. B, D, A, C
3. A, B, D, C 4. D, C, B, A

57. Find the correct sequential order of stages of infection:

A. Illness B. Convalescence
C. Incubation D. Prodromal

Choose the ***correct*** answer from the options given below:

1. C, D, A, B 2. A, D, B, C
3. D, C, A, B 4. B, A, D, C

58. Find the correct sequential order of the stages of healing.

A. Inflammation B. Injury
C. Remodeling D. Repair

Choose the ***correct*** answer from the options given below:

1. A, B, C, D 2. D, C, A, B
3. B, C, A, D 4 B, A, D, C

59. Write the correct sequential stages of strength development in training.

A. General strength base
B. Maximal strength development
C. Maintenance phase
D. Conversion to specific strength

Choose the ***correct*** answer from the options given below:

1. A, B, C, D 2. C, D, A, B
3. A, B, D, C 4. A, C, B, D

60. What is the correct sequence in the progression of plyometric training from basic to advanced.

A. Depth jumps
B. Bounding

C. Hopping
D. Double foot jump in place
Choose the ***correct*** answer from the options given below:
1. B, C, A, D 2. A, C, D, B
3. C, B, D, A 4. D, C, B, A

61. Write the correct sequential order of steps in the scientific method of problem solving.
A. Gather data
B. Define and delimit the problem
C. Form a hypothesis
D. Analysing and interpreting results
Choose the ***correct*** answer from the options given below:
1. B, C, A, D 2. C, A, B, D
3. A, C, B, D 4. C, D, A, B

62. Choose the correct sequential order to sum the 'T'-score.
A. Sum the T-score for each student
B. Assign each student a T-score in each of the tests
C. Develop T-score norms for each test
D. Assign final grade
E. Develop final letter-grade standards
Choose the ***correct*** answer from the options given below:
1. B, A, E, D, C 2. C, B, A, E, D
3. A, E, D, C, B 4. B, C, A, E, D

63. Find the correct sequential order of types of evaluation based on when they are conducted in physical education.
A. Norm-Referenced evaluation
B. Formative evaluation
C. Summative evaluation
D. Diagnostic evaluation
Choose the ***correct*** answer from the options given below:
1. D, B, C, A 2. B, A, C, D
3. A, C, B, D 4. D, C, B, A

64. Identify the correct sequential step of the control process in management.
A. Evaluating deviations
B. Measuring actual performance
C. Establishing performance standards
D. Taking corrective action
Choose the ***correct*** answer from the options given below:
1. B, C, A, D 2. C, B, A, D
3. D, B, A, C 4. A, B, D, C

65. Find the correct sequential order of qualitative biomechanical analysis.
A. Observation B. Evaluation
C. Description D. Instruction
Choose the ***correct*** answer from the options given below:
1. A, B, C, D 2. C, A, B, D
3. B, A, C, D 4. C, B, A, D

66. What are the Olympic values?
A. Excellence B. Sustainability
C. Friendship D. Respect
Choose the ***correct*** answer from the options given below:
1. A, B, C only 2. A, C, D only
3. B, C only 4. A, C only

67. An increase in the blood's oxygen carrying capacity provides the most important longer-term adjustment to altitude exposure which factors account for this adaptation?
A. Initial decrease in plasma volume
B. Increase in erythrocytes
C. Increase in hemoglobin synthesis
D. Initial increase in plasma volume
Choose the ***correct*** answer from the options given below:
1. A, B, C only 2. B, C, D only
3. A, C only 4. B, D only

68. The non-axial motion is also known as:
A. Rotary motion
B. Gliding motion
C. Translation motion
D. Sliding motion

Choose the ***correct*** answer from the options given below:

1. A, B only
2. C, D only
3. B, C, D only
4. A, B, D only

69. Which of the following are examples of tangible reinforcers?

A. Medal
B. Cash Prize
C. Public acknowledgement
D. Verbal Praise

Choose the ***correct*** answer from the options given below:

1. A, D only
2. B, C only
3. A, B, C only
4. A, B only

70. The role of the National Council for Teacher Education in Professional Physical Education courses includes:

A. Accreditation of institutions offering BPEd, MPEd programs.
B. Determining curriculum frame works for physical education teacher training.
C. Organizing AIU sports tournaments
D. Setting eligibility criteria for all higher education degree programs in India.

Choose the ***correct*** answer from thc options given below:

1. A, B, D only
2. A, B only
3. B, D only
4. B, C, D only

71. Diseases caused by bacteria are:

A. Cholera
B. Gastric ulcers
C. Legionellosis
D. Histoplasmosis
E. Rabies

Choose the ***correct*** answer from the options given below:

1. C, D, E only
2. B, C, D only
3. A, B, C only
4. A, D, E only

72. Myogenic adaptations to resistance training are:

A. Increased neural drive
B. Stretch reflex potentiation
C. Increased muscle cross sectional area
D. Increased number of myofibrils

Choose the ***correct*** answer from the options given below:

1. C, D only
2. A, B, C only
3. B, C, D only
4. A, C only

73. What are the types of formal experimental designs?

A. Randomized block design
B. Factorial designs
C. Latin Square design
D. Before and after with control design

Choose the ***correct*** answer from the options given below:

1. A, C, D only
2. A, B, C only
3. B, C, D only
4. A, B only

74. Skill tests are most useful for the evaluation of learning, they can also be used for:

A. Diagnosis
B. Prediction
C. Winning
D. Positional placement

Choose the ***correct*** answer from the options given below:

1. A, B and C only
2. A, B and D only
3. B, C and D only
4. B and A only

75. Management in Physical Education and sports primarily involves:

A. Planning and organizing activities
B. Random decision making
C. Directing and motivating participants
D. Evaluating outcomes

Choose the ***correct*** answer from the options given below:

1. A, B only
2. A, B, D only
3. A, C, D only
4. A, D only

76. Match the List-I with List-II.

List-I (*Arjuna Award Winner 2024)*	List-II (*Sports Discipline*)
A. Jyothi Yarraji	I. Boxing
B. Saweety Boora	II. Chess
C. Vantika Agrawal	III. Athletics
D. Sajan Prakash	IV. Swimming

Choose the ***correct*** answer from the options given below:

1. A-II, B-I, C-III, D-IV
2. A-III, B-I, C-II, D-IV
3. A-IV, B-II, C-I, D-III
4. A-III, B-IV, C-II, D-I

77. Match the List-I with List-II.

List-I (*Normal Curve*)	List-II
A. If SAT score $\sigma = 100$	I. equal to 1
B. Total area	II. $\overline{X} = 0$
C. In a distribution if σ is 1	III. $\overline{X} = 100$
D. In Binet intelligence scale score $\sigma = 16$	IV. $\overline{X} = 500$

Choose the ***correct*** answer from the options given below:

1. A-I, B-III, C-IV, D-II
2. A-II, B-IV, C-I, D-III
3. A-III, B-II, C-IV, D-I
4. A-IV, B-I, C-II, D-III

78. Match the List-I with List-II.

List-I (*Category*)	List-II (*Monark Ergometer Setting*)
A. Children	I. 0.10 × Body weight in kg
B. Adult women	II. 0.075 × Body weight in kg
C. Adult men	III. 0.086 × Body weight in kg
D. Athletes	IV. 0.087 × Body weight in kg

Choose the ***correct*** answer from the options given below:

1. A-IV, B-I, C-II, D-III
2. A-III, B-IV, C-I, D-II
3. A-I, B-II, C-III, D-IV
4. A-II, B-III, C-IV, D-I

79. Match the List-I with List-II.

List-I (*Leadership styles*)	List-II (*Characteristics in Sports Management*)
A. Autocratic	I. Decisions made collectively
B. Democratic	II. Coach gives complete freedom
C. Laissez-faire	III. Strict authority and control
D. Transformational	IV. Inspires players with vision

Choose the ***correct*** answer from the options given below:

1. A-III, B-I, C-II, D-IV
2. A-II, B-I, C-IV, D-III
3. A-III, B-II, C-I, D-IV
4. A-IV, B-III, C-II, D-I

80. Match the List-I with List-II.

List-I (*Method*)	List-II (*Weakness*)
A. Isometric	I. Difficult to find 1-RM
B. Isotonic	II. Measuring intensity is more complex
C. Isokinetic	III. Velocity of movement affect torque output
D. Plyometric	IV. Only one joint angle is tested

Choose the ***correct*** answer from the options given below:

1. A-III, B-I, C-II, D-IV
2. A-IV, B-II, C-III, D-I
3. A-IV, B-I, C-III, D-II
4. A-I, B-II, C-III, D-IV

81. Match the List-I with List-II.

List-I (*Speed Ability*)	List-II (*Determining Factors*)
A. Reaction ability	I. Mobility of CNS
B. Movement speed	II. Explosive strength
C. Locomotor ability	III. Functional capacity
D. Speed endurance	IV. Aerobic capacity

Choose the ***correct*** answer from the options given below:

1. A-I, B-II, C-III, D-IV
2. A-IV, B-III, C-II, D-I
3. A-III, B-II, C-I, D-IV
4. A-II, B-I, C-III, D-IV

82. Match the List-I with List-II.

List-I (*Test Situation*)	List-II (*Parametric Test*)
A. One Mean	I. p-value 0.474
B. Two Independent mean	II. p-value 0.703
C. Two dependent mean	III. p-value 0.550
D. Correlation (Pearson's)	IV. p-value 0.564

Choose the ***correct*** answer from the options given below:

1. A-III, B-IV, C-II, D-I
2. A-II, B-III, C-IV, D-I
3. A-I, B-IV, C-III, D-II
4. A-I, B-IV, C-II, D-III

83. Match the List-I with List-II.

List-I (*Virus*)	List-II (*Disease*)
A. Herpes varicella -zoster	I. Common cold
B. Epstein-Barr	II. Hemorrhagic fever
C. Rhinoviruses	III. Chickenpox
D. Ebola Viruses	IV. Mononucleosis

Choose the ***correct*** answer from the options given below:

1. A-III, B-I, C-IV, D-II
2. A-II, B-III, C-I, D-IV
3. A-IV, B-I, C-III, D-II
4. A-III, B-IV, C-I, D-II

84. Match the List-I with List-II.

List-I	List-II
A. Pivot joint	I. Ginglymus joint
B. Condyloid joint	II. Trochoid joint
C. Saddle joint	III. Ovoid joint
D. Hinge joint	IV. Sellar joint

Choose the ***correct*** answer from the options given below:

1. A-II, B-III, C-IV, D-I
2. A-IV, B-III, C-II, D-I
3. A-I, B-II, C-III, D-IV
4. A-III, B-II, C-IV, D-I

85. Match the List-I with List-II.

List-I (*Stage*)	List-II (*Event*)
A. Prophase	I. The centromeres now divide
B. Metaphase	II. The spindle fibers contract and pull the chromosomes
C. Telophase	III. The nuclear membrane disappear
D. Anaphase	IV. A nuclear membrane re-farms around each of chromosomes

Choose the ***correct*** answer from the options given below:

1. A-II, B-I, C-IV, D-III
2. A-IV, B-III, C-II, D-I
3. A-III, B-I, C-IV, D-II
4. A-III, B-IV, C-II, D-I

86. Match the List-I with List-II.

List-I	List-II
A. Compression	I. Twisting force around a longitudinal axis
B. Tension	II. Force pressing or squeezing axially
C. Shear	III. Force acting parallel to a surface
D. Torsion	IV. Pulling force along the axis of structure

Choose the ***correct*** answer from the options given below:

1. A-III, B-II, C-I, D-IV
2. A-II, B-I, C-III, D-IV
3. A-IV, B-II, C-III, D-I
4. A-II, B-IV, C-III, D-I

87. Match the List-I with List-II.

List-I (*Arousal Performance Theory*)	List-II (*Principle*)
A. Drive Theory	I. Performance collapses when cognitive anxiety is high
B. Catastrophe Model	II. Athletes have unique optimal zones
C. Inverted-U-Hypothesis	III. Best performance at moderate arousal
D. Individualized zone of optimal functioning (IZOF)	IV. High arousal boosts performance if well-learned

Choose the ***correct*** answer from the options given below:

1. A-II, B-III, C-I, D-IV
2. A-III, B-I, C-IV, D-II
3. A-IV, B-I, C-III, D-II
4. A-III, B-IV, C-I, D-II

88. Match the List-I with List-II.

List-I (*Teaching Aid*)	List-II (*Benefit*)
A. Wearable fitness devices	I. Provides clear demonstrations of techniques
B. Sports Equipment	II. Enhances skill development through hands-on practice
C. Videos and Animations	III. Tracks individual fitness progress
D. Instructional diagrams	IV. Helps in injury prevention and safety awareness

Choose the ***correct*** answer from the options given below:

1. A-III, B-II, C-I, D-IV
2. A-II, B-I, C-IV, D-III
3. A-I, B-II, C-III, D-IV
4. A-IV, B-III, C-II, D-I

89. Match the List-I with List-II.

List-I (*Terms*)	List-II (*Meaning*)
A. Epidemiology	I. An unexpectedly large number of cases of disease in a particular population.
B. Epidemic	II. A disease that occurs regularly in a population as a matter of course.
C. Endemic disease	III. An outbreak of disease over a wide geographical area such as a continent.
D. Pandemic	IV. The distribution and determinants of diseases and injury in human populations.

Choose the ***correct*** answer from the options given below:

1. A-II, B-III, C-I, D-IV
2. A-IV, B-I, C-II, D-III
3. A-III, B-I, C-IV, D-II
4. A-IV, B-I, C-III, D-II

90. Match the List-I with List-II.

List-I (*Types of variable*)	List-II (*Meaning*)
A. Extraneous Variable	I. A factor that could possibly influence the results and that is kept out of the study.
B. Dependent Variable	II. A kind of independent variable such as age, sex that cannot be manipulated.
C. Control Variable	III. A factor that could affect the relationship between the independent and dependent variables but that is not included or controlled.
D. Moderator Variable	IV. The effect of the independent variable.

Choose the ***correct*** answer from the options given below:

1. A-II, B-IV, C-III, D-I
2. A-I, B-II, C-III, D-IV
3. A-III, B-I, C-II, D-IV
4. A-III, B-IV, C-I, D-II

Directions (Qs. No. 91 to 95): *Read the following paragraph and answer the questions:*

There are basically two kinds of variables: Variables that results in qualitative information and variables that results quantitative informations. Qualitative variable that characterizes an element of a population or incorporates ordered position. The quantitative variable that can assume a countable number of values or can assume uncountable number of values. For a research a sample of four hair-salon customers was surveyed for their "hair colour" (White, Brown and Black) "Hometown" (Village, Urban and Town) and "Level of satisfaction", (Very satisfied, satisfied and somewhat satisfied) with the results of their salon treatment. Don't let the appearance of the data fool you in regard to their type. Qualitative variable are not always easy to recognize: Sometimes they appear as numbers. The sample of hair colour could be coded: 1 = White, 2 = Brown and 3 = Black. The sample data would then appear as [2, 3, 1, 3], but they are still attribute or qualitative data. In many cases, the two types of quantitative variables can be distinguished by deciding whether the variables are related to a count or a measurement. The variable number of courses for which you are currently registered for a semester and the variable weight of books and supplies you are carrying as you attend class today. When trying to determine whether a variable is quantitative remember to look at the variable and think about the values that might occur.

91. "Hair colour" is an example of _____ variable.

1. Nominal
2. Ordinal
3. Discrete
4. Continuous

92. The courses currently registered is an example of _____ variable.

1. Nominal
2. Ordinal
3. Discrete
4. Continuous

93. The "Level of satisfaction" is an example of _____ variable.

1. Nominal
2. Ordinal
3. Discrete
4. Continuous

94. The weight of books and supplies are an example of _____ variable.

1. Nominal
2. Ordinal
3. Discrete
4. Continuous

95. The "Hometown" is an example of _____ variable.

1. Nominal
2. Ordinal
3. Discrete
4. Continuous

Directions (Qs. No. 96 to 100): *Read the following paragraph and answer the questions:*

It is common experience that physical overexertion results in pain. Evidence for structural damage is now available for investigators showing bio-chemical, histological and ultrastructural changes in muscle soreness (DOMS). The mechanical trauma theory for DOMS proposes a model in which the original caused factor is the disruption of muscle tissue due to high mechanical forces required during exercise, particularly in eccentric contraction. The deterioration of the Sarcolemma results in diffusion of inter cellular components into the tissue fluids and plasma and results in the sensation of DOMS. Acute inflammation theory is based on the similarities between inflammation and DOMS. The WBC and monocytes emigrates to the injured area after exercise. They are present in large number at 24 hours, peak in number of 48 hours and are generally no longer seen at 72 hours. The local ischemia theory for DOMS proposes a model in which muscle overuse causes increased tissue pressure and significantly decreased muscle blood flow. As per the spasm theory localized soreness that occurs after unaccustomed exercise is caused tonic, localized spasm of motor units. The pain brings reflex tonic muscle contraction.

96. Which type of exercise is most associated with mechanical trauma leading to DOMS?

1. Concentric
2. Eccentric
3. Isometric
4. Aerobic

97. According to the mechanical trauma theory, muscle soreness is caused by:

1. Micro-tear in muscle fibres
2. Lactic acid accumulation
3. Nerve compression
4. Decreased oxygen supply

98. The acute inflammatory response in DOMS usually peaks at:

1. Immediately after exercise
2. 12-24 hours post exercise
3. 48-72 hours post exercise
4. 72 hours post-exercise

99. Local ischemia in exercising muscle is caused by:

1. Vasodialation of blood vessels
2. Compression of blood vessels during sustained contraction
3. Excess oxygen supply
4. Increased heart rate

100. According to spasm theory, the main cause of DOMS is:

1. Overactivation of mitochondria
2. Accumulation of lactic acid
3. Structural micro-tear muscle fibres
4. Reflex muscle spasm reducing blood flow

ANSWERS

1	2	3	4	5	6	7	8	9	10
3	1	2	1	4	1	4	2	1	4
11	**12**	**13**	**14**	**15**	**16**	**17**	**18**	**19**	**20**
1	2	1	4	3	3	4	4	2	1, 3
21	**22**	**23**	**24**	**25**	**26**	**27**	**28**	**29**	**30**
3	4	4	3	1	3	4	2	3	3
31	**32**	**33**	**34**	**35**	**36**	**37**	**38**	**39**	**40**
4	3	2	2	1	2	1	2	3	4
41	**42**	**43**	**44**	**45**	**46**	**47**	**48**	**49**	**50**
3	2	3	1	1	4	4	3	1	1
51	**52**	**53**	**54**	**55**	**56**	**57**	**58**	**59**	**60**
4	2	3	4	2	1	1	4	3	4
61	**62**	**63**	**64**	**65**	**66**	**67**	**68**	**69**	**70**
1	2	1	2	2	2	1	3	4	2
71	**72**	**73**	**74**	**75**	**76**	**77**	**78**	**79**	**80**
3	1	2	2	3	2	4	4	1	3
81	**82**	**83**	**84**	**85**	**86**	**87**	**88**	**89**	**90**
3	1	4	1	3	4	3	1	2	4
91	**92**	**93**	**94**	**95**	**96**	**97**	**98**	**99**	**100**
1	3	2	4	1	2	1	3	2	4

EXPLANATORY ANSWERS

1. The International Hockey Federation won the IOC Climate Action Award for the year 2024 in the International Federation category. This award was given for its climate-related work, especially in reducing water use in elite hockey through dry turf technology. World Sailing, International Basketball Federation, and International Cricket Council were not the correct winners in this specific 2024 International Federation category. The question asks specifically which International Federation won the IOC climate action award for 2024, so the correct option is The International Hockey Federation. It directly matches the required International Federation winner for the IOC climate action award in 2024.

2. The curriculum of the Philanthropinium was guided by the philosophy of Naturalism. The Philanthropinium was associated with Basedow and the educational ideas influenced by Rousseau's naturalistic approach. It emphasized learning according to nature, practical experiences, physical activity, observation, and child-centred education. This makes Naturalism more suitable than Pragmatism, Humanism, or Idealism for this question. The curriculum's focus on natural development and practical learning fits the philosophy of Naturalism.

3. A potential negative social aspect of competition in sports is reinforcement of aggression and hostility. Competition can develop positive qualities like teamwork, leadership, motivation, and discipline when properly guided. However, excessive or poorly controlled competition may increase hostile attitudes, over-aggressiveness, rivalry, and unsporting behaviour. Promotion of teamwork, social harmony, and leadership skills are positive social outcomes rather than negative ones. The option "reinforcement of aggression and hostility" is the negative social aspect asked in the question.

4. The common teaching style in physical education is generally teacher-directed and is useful when students need clear demonstration, instruction, correction, and control. It is especially helpful when learners are being introduced to a new skill because the teacher can explain the correct technique step by step. For complex skills also, structured teaching helps reduce confusion and allows students to practise safely and correctly. It does not mainly encourage maximum learner autonomy or open-ended exploration, because those are features of learner-centred styles. The statement that it is effective for teaching new and complex skills is the true statement about the common teaching style.

5. Acclimatization to exercise in cold environments does not mainly involve elevated sweat gland sensitivity. Cold adaptation usually involves responses such as better conservation of body heat, increased peripheral vasoconstriction, and improved shivering thermogenesis. Improved insulation through subcutaneous fat may also help in maintaining body temperature in cold conditions. Elevated sweat gland sensitivity is more closely related to heat acclimatization, where sweating begins earlier and becomes more efficient. It is the exception among the listed responses for acclimatization to exercise in cold environments.

6. Decreased muscle cross-sectional area and increase connective tissue proliferation: During the early phase of rehabilitation after immobilization, muscle wasting and stiffness are commonly seen. Immobilization causes disuse atrophy, so the muscle cross-sectional area decreases due to reduced muscle activity and loading. Connective tissue proliferation may also increase around joints and soft tissues, contributing to reduced mobility and stiffness. Enhanced mitochondrial density and hyperplasia of type II b fibres are not expected early effects after immobilization. Increased synovial fluid viscosity may occur with reduced movement, but the option combining muscle atrophy with connective tissue proliferation best fits the early rehabilitation condition.

7. The autonomic nervous system is also called the vegetative nervous system. It controls

involuntary functions of the body such as heart rate, digestion, blood vessel diameter, glandular secretion, and smooth muscle activity. It is not called the somatic nervous system because somatic nerves mainly control voluntary skeletal muscle movements. It is also not called voluntary nerves, because the autonomic nervous system works largely without conscious control. The term vegetative nerves fits because this system regulates the automatic internal functions necessary for life.

8. The transmitter norepinephrine is inactivated partly by the enzyme catechol-O-methyl transferase. Norepinephrine is a catecholamine neurotransmitter, and catechol-O-methyl transferase helps metabolize catecholamines. Cholinesterase is mainly associated with the breakdown of acetylcholine, not norepinephrine. Acetylcholine is itself a neurotransmitter and not the enzyme that inactivates norepinephrine. Acromegaly is an endocrine disorder related to excess growth hormone and has no role in norepinephrine inactivation.

9. According to the drag equation, drag force increases with the square of velocity. This means that if the cyclist's velocity is doubled, the drag force becomes four times greater, assuming other factors remain constant. Doubling the cyclist's mass does not directly increase aerodynamic drag in the drag equation. Decreasing air density would reduce drag force rather than increase it. Halving the cyclist's frontal area would also reduce drag force, so velocity is the most significant factor among the given options.

10. Excessive lumbar lordosis is commonly associated with weak abdominal muscles and weak hip extensors such as the hamstrings. Strengthening the abdominal muscles helps posteriorly tilt and stabilize the pelvis, reducing excessive lumbar curvature. Strengthening the hamstrings also assists in controlling anterior pelvic tilt, which is often linked with increased lumbar lordosis. Stretching the gluteus maximus would not be the most effective correction because the gluteals usually need strengthening rather than stretching. Strengthening the erector spinae may worsen excessive lordosis, while stretching quadriceps alone does not directly address the main muscular imbalance.

11. Mechanical advantage in a lever system is calculated by dividing the effort arm by the load arm. The effort arm is the distance from the fulcrum to the point where effort is applied. The load arm is the distance from the fulcrum to the point where resistance or load acts. When the effort arm is longer than the load arm, the mechanical advantage is greater than one and less effort is needed. The formula MA = effort arm/load arm directly represents the correct relationship in a lever system.

12. The ability to manage the angular momentum of the body at discrete angles is called manoeuvrability. Manoeuvrability refers to controlling body movement effectively while changing position, direction, or body orientation. It is especially important in sports where the body must be controlled through turns, cuts, pivots, and angular adjustments. Mobility refers more to range of motion, while change of direction and multidirectional speed are broader performance abilities. The specific ability to manage angular momentum of the body at discrete angles fits the term manoeuvrability.

13. Genu valgum deformity refers to knock-knees where the knees move inward toward the midline Strengthening the hip abductors helps contro excessive inward movement of the femur anc improves lower-limb alignment. Strengthening th vastus medialis helps improve patellar trackin and medial knee stability. Strengthening hi adductors may worsen the inward pull, an gastrocnemius strengthening does not directl correct the main deformity. Stretching th iliotibial band may be useful in some cases, bu strengthening hip abductors and vastus mediali is the most appropriate corrective approach.

14. During a pull-up, elbow flexion is strong assisted by the biceps brachii, especially whe the forearm is supinated or partially supinate The biceps brachii flexes the elbow and al helps in supination of the forearm during pullin actions. Its main insertion is on the radi tuberosity of the radius through the biceps tendo

The triceps brachii is an elbow extensor, not the prime mover for elbow flexion. Brachialis is an elbow flexor, but the given insertion "scapular spine" is incorrect, making biceps brachii with radial tuberosity the correct option.

15. Telic-dominant individuals have a goal-directed orientation toward life. In reversal theory, the telic state is associated with seriousness, planning, achievement, and future-oriented behaviour. Such individuals usually prefer purposeful activity and tend to focus on outcomes, targets, and long-term goals. Paratelic-dominant individuals are more play-oriented, spontaneous, and focused on immediate enjoyment. Apathetic and fun-loving individuals do not specifically describe the goal-directed orientation asked in the question.

16. Negative transfer in sports training most commonly occurs when two skills or tasks appear similar but require different movement responses or decision responses. Because the movement pattern looks familiar, the athlete may mistakenly apply the old response to the new task. This can interfere with correct learning and reduce performance efficiency in the new skill. Identical motor patterns usually produce positive transfer, not negative transfer. Completely different movement patterns are less likely to interfere because the athlete can recognize them as separate skills.

17. Task-oriented players are keen to find out whether the drills they have practised have helped them improve their skills during a competitive game. They focus on mastery, learning, personal improvement, and correct execution of skills rather than only winning or defeating others. Such players judge success by whether their own performance has improved as a result of practice and training. Ego-oriented players mainly compare themselves with others, while performance-oriented players may focus more on external results or showing ability. The description in the question best fits task-oriented players because they want to know whether practice drills have actually improved their skill performance in competition.

18. Articulation is a key principle of curriculum planning that ensures continuity and proper sequence in physical education learning experiences. It helps connect learning experiences from one level, class, or stage to the next in a systematic manner. Through articulation, skills and concepts are arranged progressively so that earlier learning supports later learning. Fragmentation and randomization would break the learning sequence and reduce continuity. Stammering is not a principle of curriculum planning in physical education.

19. Diagnostic assessment is used before or at the beginning of instruction to identify learners' strengths, weaknesses, and learning needs. A pre-test in the tennis serve helps the teacher find out which students already know the skill and which students need extra support. This allows the teacher to plan suitable instruction, correction, and practice according to student needs. Providing feedback during performance is formative assessment, while grading a final match is summative assessment. Assigning homework may reinforce learning but does not directly diagnose the learner's initial difficulty.

20. The award is open to both organisations and individuals; It is given exclusively for achievements in Olympic sports: The incorrect statements are options 1 and 3. Rashtriya Khel Protsahan Puraskar is mainly meant for corporate entities, sports control boards, NGOs, and sports bodies that contribute to sports promotion and development. So, the statement that it is open to both organisations and individuals is not correct in the present scheme sense, because individual sportsperson-type achievement is not the main eligibility basis of this award. The statement that it is given exclusively for achievements in Olympic sports is also incorrect, because this award is not restricted to Olympic sports or Olympic achievements. It recognizes contribution in areas such as sports promotion, development, encouragement through CSR, talent identification, employment of sportspersons, sports welfare measures, and sports for development. It is distinct from the Arjuna Award and Dronacharya Award, and recognition for sports welfare measures is one of its valid areas. so options 2 and 4 are correct statements.

21. A pedagogical responsibility specific to a primary level physical education teacher is introducing basic motor skills through play. At the primary level, children need development of fundamental movements such as running, jumping, hopping, throwing, catching, balancing, and simple coordination activities. These skills are best taught through playful, age-appropriate, enjoyable, and activity-based learning experiences. Coaching school-level athletes is more suitable for higher-level sports training, while laboratory-based research is not a primary physical education teaching responsibility. Introducing basic cognitive skills is not as specific to physical education as introducing basic motor skills through play.

22. A sperm cell moves with the help of a flagellum. The flagellum is the tail-like structure of the sperm that produces whip-like movements. These movements help the sperm swim through the female reproductive tract toward the ovum. Circumcision is a surgical removal of the foreskin and is not related to sperm movement. Syphilis is a sexually transmitted infection, and corpus luteum is an ovarian structure formed after ovulation.

23. Cardiac rehabilitation is not an example of a primary prevention measure. Primary prevention aims to prevent disease before it occurs through measures such as immunization, sanitation, and health education. Immunization prevents infectious diseases before they develop, while water sanitation reduces exposure to disease-causing organisms. Health education helps people adopt healthy behaviours and avoid risk factors before illness develops. Cardiac rehabilitation is used after heart disease or a cardiac event has already occurred, so it belongs to secondary or tertiary prevention rather than primary prevention.

24. During the Heimlich maneuver, abdominal thrusts are applied below the rib cage and above the navel to force the diaphragm upward. This sudden upward pressure increases air pressure in the lungs and helps expel the foreign object from the airway. The trachea and larynx are parts of the airway involved in obstruction, but they are not the structure most directly compressed by the abdominal thrust. The oesophagus is part of the digestive tract and is not the target structure for expelling an airway obstruction. The diaphragm is the anatomical structure most directly affected by the upward abdominal compression.

25. The most critical first-aid step in managing a chemical burn is immediate irrigation with large amounts of water. Washing the affected area dilutes and removes the chemical from the skin, reducing the duration and severity of tissue damage. The contaminated clothing or accessories should also be removed carefully while flushing continues, when safe to do so. Applying ice packs can worsen tissue injury, and using butter or oil can trap the chemical and delay proper treatment. Neutralizing with an opposite chemical is unsafe because it may cause heat production or further chemical reaction on the skin.

26. In resistance training, the amount of work accomplished is called volume. Training volume usually refers to the total quantity of exercise performed in a session, week, or training phase. It may be calculated through factors such as sets, repetitions, and load lifted during resistance training. Intensity refers to how heavy or difficult the exercise is, not the total amount of work completed. Frequency means how often training is performed, and set is only one unit within the total training volume.

27. Deceleration is not one of the main phases that compose the stretch-shortening cycle. The stretch-shortening cycle is commonly divided into the eccentric phase, amortization phase, and concentric phase. The eccentric phase involves rapid muscle lengthening before the movement changes direction. The amortization phase is the brief transition period between eccentric loading and concentric action. The concentric phase uses stored elastic energy and reflex contribution to produce powerful shortening of the muscle.

28. Systemic fatigue is the type of fatigue that impacts the whole body irrespective of where or how it was generated. It affects general physical performance, energy level, coordination, concentration, and overall ability to continue exercise. Local fatigue is limited to a particular muscle or muscle group that has been stressed during activity. Muscular specific fatigue refers to fatigue in a particular muscle function or region rather than the whole body. Systemic fatigue is broader because it involves the entire body system and not only one working muscle group.

29. A linear periodization model is characterized by gradual increase in training intensity along with a decrease in training volume. In this model, training usually begins with higher volume and lower intensity during the early phase. As the training program progresses, the load or intensity increases while the total volume is reduced. This structure helps athletes move from general preparation toward more specific strength, power, or peak performance phases. Randomized sessions and frequent changes in load and intensity are more related to non-linear or undulating periodization.

30. Armstrength is a valid variable name in SPSS because it has no spaces, hyphen, or quotation marks. SPSS variable names must begin with a letter and should not contain blank spaces or special characters such as hyphens. "Arm strength" is invalid because it contains a space between the words. "Arm-Strength" is invalid because a hyphen is not allowed in a normal SPSS variable name. "Arm-strength" with quotation marks and a hyphen is also not a valid SPSS variable name.

31. A quasi-experimental research design manipulates an independent variable but lacks true randomization of subjects or groups. In this design, the researcher may apply a treatment or intervention, but participants are not randomly assigned in the strict experimental sense. This makes it different from a true experiment, where both manipulation and randomization are important features. Cross-sectional and longitudinal designs are mainly observational or time-based research designs and do not necessarily involve manipulation of variables. Quasi experiment best fits the condition where variables are manipulated but randomization is absent.

32. Asking athletes to train at dangerous intensities without proper safety monitoring would violate the ethical principle of non-maleficence. Non-maleficence means that the researcher must not cause harm or expose participants to unnecessary risk. Dangerous training intensities without safety supervision may lead to injury, exhaustion, cardiac risk, or other harmful outcomes. Autonomy is related to informed choice, beneficence is related to promoting benefit, and justice is related to fairness in participant treatment. The main ethical violation in this situation is the risk of harm to athletes.

33. Logical validity refers to the degree to which a measure obviously involves the performance or ability being measured. It is based on the logical and apparent relationship between the test item and the specific skill or performance under assessment. For example, a test that directly requires the same movement or performance being evaluated has strong logical validity. Construct validity deals with whether a test measures an abstract concept, while criterion validity compares a test with an accepted standard. Content validity concerns whether the test adequately covers the full content area, not merely whether it obviously involves the measured performance.

34. In the Cooper 12-minute run/walk test, VO_2 max can be estimated from the distance covered in 12 minutes. The formula using miles is VO_2 max = (Distance in miles – 0.3138) ÷ 0.0278. This equation converts the 12-minute performance distance into an estimated aerobic capacity value. The other given equations belong to different fitness tests or different prediction methods and do not match the Cooper 12-minute run/walk test. The option with distance minus 0.3138 divided by 0.0278 is the correct Cooper test formula among the choices.

35. In AAHPERD-HRPF (1984), the body composition assessment in the given single-site question is represented by the triceps skinfold. The triceps skinfold is commonly used as a practical field measure of subcutaneous fat in school-based health-related fitness testing. Among the given options, abdominal, subscapular, and suprailium are not the expected answer for the only site asked in this version of the question.

Although some AAHPERD-related discussions may include more than one skinfold site in broader contexts, this specific question asks for the only site to assess body composition in AAHPERD-HRPF (1984). Thus, within the provided options and wording, triceps skinfold is the best-fitting answer.

36. The softball throw test item was deleted from the AAHPER Youth Fitness Test in 1976. The original AAHPER Youth Fitness Test included the softball throw as one of the test items for assessing throwing distance and related motor ability. In the 1976 revision, the softball throw was removed because it was considered more of a skill-based item than a pure physical fitness item. The same revision also modified the sit-up test and included alternative distance-run options. Among the given options, 1976 is the correct year for deletion of the softball throw test item.

37. The ponderal index measures body weight relative to height cubed. It is an anthropometric index used to describe body build or body proportionality in relation to height. Unlike body mass index, which uses height squared, the ponderal index uses height cubed in its calculation. It does not directly measure lean body mass or body fat percentage. The option "body weight relative to height cubed" best matches the meaning of ponderal index.

38. Random budget is not a recognized type of budget in sports management. Sports organizations may prepare different types of budgets such as performance budget, capital budget, operating budget, and zero-based budget. A capital budget is used for long-term assets or major facilities and equipment. A zero-based budget starts from a fresh base and requires justification for each expense. Random budget is not a standard or systematic budgeting method in sports administration.

39. In sports management, efficiency primarily means achieving maximum results with minimum use of available resources. Resources may include money, time, facilities, equipment, human effort, and administrative support. An efficient sports manager tries to reduce waste while maintaining or improving performance and organizational output. Achieving goals regardless of cost may show effectiveness, but it does not show efficiency. Focusing only on financial profit or player satisfaction alone does not fully define management efficiency.

40. Hierarchy of need theory is not directly a leadership theory. It is primarily a motivation theory associated with human needs, usually arranged from basic physiological needs to higher-level self-actualization needs. Trait theories, behavioural theories, and situational or contingency theories are major approaches used to explain leadership. Trait theories focus on qualities of leaders, behavioural theories focus on leader actions, and contingency theories focus on matching leadership style with the situation. Hierarchy of needs may influence motivation in management, but it is not classified as a leadership theory.

41. Assertion (A) is correct because the philosophy of idealism emphasizes moral, spiritual, mental, and character development through education and physical education. In idealism, physical education is not limited to physical fitness alone, but is also used for developing discipline, self-control, values, and higher ideals.

Reason (R) is not correct because idealism does not believe that the human body is more important than the mind. Idealism gives greater importance to mind, soul, ideas, values, and spiritual development rather than the superiority of the body.

The assertion correctly represents idealism, while the reason gives an incorrect statement about idealistic philosophy.

42. Assertion (A) is correct because the energy used by the human body is ultimately derived from the chemical energy present in food. Carbohydrates, fats, and proteins obtained from food are broken down and converted into usable energy for body functions and physical activity.

Reason (R) is also correct because this chemical energy may be used immediately by the body or stored for later use as glycogen or fat. However, Reason (R) only describes the use and storage of chemical energy after food energy is available in the body.

It does not directly explain why all body energy is ultimately derived from food, so both statements are correct but Reason (R) is not the correct explanation of Assertion (A).

43. Assertion (A) is correct because deep breathing is an effective psychological skill for reducing anxiety in athletes. Deep breathing helps control arousal, reduce tension, calm the nervous system, and improve emotional control before or during performance.

Reason (R) is not correct because deep breathing does not reduce anxiety by enhancing muscle strength. Its main role in anxiety control is relaxation and regulation of breathing, not increasing the strength of muscles.

The assertion is correct, but the reason gives an incorrect explanation for the anxiety-reducing effect of deep breathing.

44. Assertion (A) is correct because intramural sports competitions are organized within educational institutions and are designed to encourage maximum student participation. They provide opportunities for a large number of students to take part in sports activities, not only selected or highly skilled athletes.

Reason (R) is also correct because mass participation allows teachers, coaches, and instructors to observe many students in activity situations. Through such wide participation, students with hidden sporting ability, skill, or potential can be identified within the institution.

Reason (R) correctly explains the value and purpose of promoting mass student participation through intramural sports competitions.

45. Assertion (A) is correct because eutrophication caused by water pollution can lead to the death of aquatic organisms. Eutrophication occurs when excess nutrients enter water bodies and cause rapid growth of algae and other aquatic plants.

Reason (R) is correct because excessive algal growth reduces dissolved oxygen levels in water. When algae die and decompose, oxygen is consumed, creating oxygen-deficient conditions for aquatic life.

The reason correctly explains how eutrophication can cause the death of fish and other aquatic organisms.

46. Assertion (A) is not correct because ballistic stretching is not considered really safe and suitable for beginners. Ballistic stretching uses rapid, jerky, bouncing movements that force the muscle beyond its normal range of motion. Beginners usually lack adequate flexibility, control, and technique, so this type of stretching may increase the risk of injury.

Reason (R) is correct because ballistic stretching does involve bouncing movements. These bouncing movements may cause muscle strain or soft-tissue injury if the exercise is not performed properly.

47. Assertion (A) is not correct because the tennis serve accuracy test is used to evaluate serving accuracy, not footwork and movement ability. The main purpose of the test is to assess how accurately a player can serve the ball into specified target areas. Footwork and movement are assessed through different tennis skill or agility tests, not primarily through a serve accuracy test.

Reason (R) is correct because the test involves serving balls into target zones of the service court. Serving into marked target areas directly measures the accuracy and control of the tennis serve.

48. Assertion (A) is correct because sports management includes planning, organizing, directing, controlling, and evaluating sports events and activities. These functions are needed for proper administration, coordination, resource use, event conduct, and successful completion of sports programmes. Sports management applies to many levels, including school, college, community, recreational, amateur, and elite sports.

Reason (R) is not correct because sports management does not ensure that only elite level athletes are allowed to participate. Participation may be organized for different groups depending on the purpose of the event, not only for elite athletes.

49. Assertion (A) is correct because in ANOVA, comparison of the means of different levels of a factor is done by comparing variation between the levels with variation within the levels. The variation between the levels is represented by MS (factor), while the variation within the levels is represented by MS (error).

Reason (R) is also correct because if MS (factor) is not significantly larger than MS (error), the calculated F-ratio will not be statistically significant. When the F-ratio is not significant, the null hypothesis that all group means are equal cannot be rejected.

Reason (R) directly explains why MS (factor) is compared with MS (error), so option 1 is the correct answer.

50. Assertion (A) is correct because the coefficient of restitution is the absolute value of the ratio of velocity of separation to velocity of approach. It describes how elastic a collision is by comparing the relative velocity after collision with the relative velocity before collision.

Reason (R) is correct because velocity of separation is the difference between velocities of the two colliding objects just after collision. Velocity of approach is the difference between velocities of the two colliding objects just before collision.

The reason correctly explains the terms used in the formula for coefficient of restitution.

51. The correct chronological order is Commonwealth Winter Games, Commonwealth Paraplegic Games, Commonwealth Youth Games, and Commonwealth E-sport Championship.

C. Commonwealth Winter Games came first, with its first edition held in 1958.

D. Commonwealth Paraplegic Games came next, with its first edition held in 1962.

B. Commonwealth Youth Games followed later, with its first edition held in 2000.

A. Commonwealth E-sport Championship came last, with its first edition held in 2022.

52. The correct sequential order of the distinct phases of the cardiac cycle is ventricular filling, isovolumetric contraction, ventricular ejection, and isovolumetric relaxation.

D. Ventricular filling occurs first, when blood enters the ventricles during diastole.

A. Isovolumetric contraction follows, when ventricles contract while all valves are closed.

C. Ventricular ejection comes next, when blood is pumped out into the arteries.

B. Isovolumetric relaxation occurs after ejection, when ventricles relax while all valves are closed.

53. The correct sequential order of skeletal muscle fibre types based on fatigue resistance from low to high is Type II b, Type II x, Type II a, and Type I.

C. Type II b fibres have the lowest fatigue resistance and fatigue very quickly during high-intensity activity.

D. Type II x fibres also fatigue quickly but are generally placed above Type II b in fatigue resistance.

B. Type II a fibres have moderate fatigue resistance because they have both fast and oxidative characteristics.

A. Type I fibres have the highest fatigue resistance due to their oxidative capacity and endurance nature.

54. The correct sequential order of the neural impulse pathway from external stimulus to muscle fibres is stimulus, sensory neuron, interneuron, and motor neuron.

D. Stimulus is the starting point because an external change is first detected by receptors.

B. Sensory neuron carries the impulse from the receptor toward the central nervous system.

C. Interneuron processes and relays the impulse within the central nervous system.

A. Motor neuron carries the command from the central nervous system to the muscle fibres for response.

55. The correct order of motivation from lowest to highest self-determination is amotivation, external regulation, identified regulation, and intrinsic motivation.

C. Amotivation is the lowest level because there is no clear intention or motivation to act.

B. External regulation comes next because behaviour is controlled by rewards, punishment, or external pressure.

D. Identified regulation is higher because the person values the activity and accepts its importance.

A. Intrinsic motivation is the highest level because the activity is performed out of genuine interest and enjoyment.

56. The correct order of the stress process is environmental demand, individual's perception of demand, stress response, and coping with stress.

C. Environmental demand comes first because a stressful situation or demand arises in the environment.

D. Individual's perception of demand comes next because the person evaluates or interprets whether the demand is threatening or challenging.

A. Stress response follows when the body and mind react physiologically and psychologically to the perceived demand.

B. Coping with stress comes after the response, when the individual uses strategies to manage, reduce, or adapt to the stress.

57. The correct sequential order of stages of infection is incubation, prodromal, illness, and convalescence.

C. Incubation is the first stage, when the pathogen enters the body but symptoms are not yet clearly visible.

D. Prodromal stage follows, when early general symptoms such as tiredness, mild fever, or discomfort may begin.

A. Illness stage comes next, when the disease symptoms are fully developed and most evident.

B. Convalescence is the final stage, when symptoms decline and the body gradually recovers from infection.

58. The correct sequential order of the stages of healing is injury, inflammation, repair, and remodeling.

B. Injury occurs first because tissue damage starts the healing process.

A. Inflammation follows, bringing protective responses such as swelling, pain, heat, and increased blood flow.

D. Repair comes next, when new tissue formation and collagen deposition help restore the damaged area.

C. Remodeling is the final stage, when the repaired tissue reorganizes, strengthens, and matures over time.

59. The correct sequential stages of strength development in training are general strength base, maximal strength development, conversion to specific strength, and maintenance phase.

A. General strength base comes first because athletes need a broad foundation of strength before more intense work.

B. Maximal strength development follows, where the aim is to improve the highest level of force production.

D. Conversion to specific strength comes next, when general and maximal strength are changed into sport-specific strength or power.

C. Maintenance phase is last, where the developed strength is preserved during competition or later training phases.

60. The correct progression of plyometric training from basic to advanced is double foot jump in place, hopping, bounding, and depth jumps.

D. Double foot jump in place is the basic starting exercise because it has lower complexity and allows controlled landing practice.

C. Hopping is progressed after basic jumping because it increases single-leg demand and balance requirements.

B. Bounding is more advanced because it involves greater horizontal force, coordination, and dynamic movement.

A. Depth jumps are the most advanced among these because they create high landing forces and require strong eccentric control.

61. The correct sequential order of steps in the scientific method of problem solving is define and delimit the problem, form a hypothesis, gather data, and analyse and interpret results.

B. Define and delimit the problem comes first because the researcher must clearly identify what is to be studied and set the limits of the problem.

C. Form a hypothesis comes next because a tentative answer or expected relationship is framed after the problem is clearly stated.

A. Gather data follows because relevant information and observations are collected to test the hypothesis.

D. Analysing and interpreting results comes last because the collected data must be studied to reach a meaningful conclusion.

62. The correct sequential order to sum the T-score is develop T-score norms for each test, assign each student a T-score in each of the tests, sum the T-score for each student, develop final letter-grade standards, and assign final grade.

C. Develop T-score norms for each test comes first because norms are needed before individual scores can be converted into T-scores.

B. Assign each student a T-score in each of the tests comes next after the norms are available.

A. Sum the T-score for each student follows because individual test T-scores are added to obtain a total score.

E. and D. Final letter-grade standards are then developed, and the final grade is assigned according to those standards.

63. The correct sequential order of types of evaluation based on when they are conducted in physical education is diagnostic evaluation, formative evaluation, summative evaluation, and norm-referenced evaluation.

D. Diagnostic evaluation is conducted first, usually before teaching or training, to identify strengths, weaknesses, and learning needs.

B. Formative evaluation is conducted during the teaching-learning process to monitor progress and provide feedback.

C. Summative evaluation is conducted at the end of a unit, course, or programme to judge final achievement.

A. Norm-referenced evaluation compares performance with a norm group and is placed last among the given sequence options.

64. The correct sequential steps of the control process in management are establishing performance standards, measuring actual performance, evaluating deviations, and taking corrective action.

C. Establishing performance standards comes first because expected results or criteria must be fixed before control can take place.

B. Measuring actual performance comes next because real performance must be observed or recorded.

A. Evaluating deviations follows by comparing actual performance with the established standards.

D. Taking corrective action is the final step when deviations are found and improvement or adjustment is required.

65. The correct sequential order of qualitative biomechanical analysis is description, observation, evaluation, and instruction.

C. Description comes first because the movement skill or performance pattern must be clearly described before analysis begins.

A. Observation follows because the performer's actual movement is then watched carefully.

B. Evaluation comes next because the observed movement is judged against the desired technique or mechanical principles.

D. Instruction is last because feedback and corrective teaching are given after the movement has been evaluated.

66. The Olympic values are Excellence, Friendship, and Respect.

A. Excellence is an Olympic value because athletes are encouraged to give their best effort in sport and life.

C. Friendship is an Olympic value because sport promotes understanding, unity, and cooperation among people and nations.

D. Respect is an Olympic value because athletes, officials, opponents, rules, and fair play must be honoured.

B. Sustainability is important in modern sports administration and Olympic planning, but it is not one of the three core Olympic values.

67. The increase in the blood's oxygen-carrying capacity during altitude exposure is associated with initial decrease in plasma volume, increase in erythrocytes, and increase in hemoglobin synthesis.

A. Initial decrease in plasma volume causes hemoconcentration, which temporarily increases the concentration of red blood cells and hemoglobin in blood.

B. Increase in erythrocytes occurs because altitude stimulates erythropoietin release, leading to greater red blood cell production.

C. Increase in hemoglobin synthesis improves the blood's ability to transport oxygen to working tissues.

D. Initial increase in plasma volume is not the correct adaptation because plasma volume usually decreases initially during altitude exposure.

68. Non-axial motion is also known as gliding motion, translation motion, or sliding motion.

B. Gliding motion is non-axial because the movement occurs without rotation around a fixed axis.

C. Translation motion is also non-axial because the body or surface moves from one place to another without angular movement around an axis.

D. Sliding motion is another term used for this type of movement where surfaces move over each other.

A. Rotary motion is not non-axial because rotary movement occurs around an axis.

69. Tangible reinforcers are material or physical rewards that can be touched or possessed.

A. Medal is a tangible reinforcer because it is a physical reward given for performance or achievement.

B. Cash prize is also a tangible reinforcer because it is a material reward with monetary value.

C. Public acknowledgement is a social reinforcer, not a tangible reinforcer.

D. Verbal praise is also a social or verbal reinforcer, not a tangible reinforcer.

70. The role of the National Council for Teacher Education in professional physical education courses includes accreditation or recognition of institutions offering B.P.Ed. and M.P.Ed. programmes and determining curriculum frameworks for teacher training.

A. Accreditation or recognition of institutions offering B.P.Ed. and M.P.Ed. programmes is related to NCTE because these are professional teacher education courses.

B. Determining curriculum frameworks, norms, and standards for physical education teacher training is also part of NCTE's role.

C. Organizing AIU sports tournaments is not the role of NCTE, as AIU tournaments are related to the Association of Indian Universities.

D. Setting eligibility criteria for all higher education degree programmes in India is not the role of NCTE, because NCTE is concerned with teacher education, not all higher education degrees.

71. Diseases caused by bacteria among the given options are cholera, gastric ulcers, and legionellosis.

A. Cholera is caused by the bacterium *Vibrio cholerae* and mainly affects the intestine through contaminated food or water.

B. Gastric ulcers may be caused by the bacterium *Helicobacter pylori,* which damages the stomach lining and contributes to ulcer formation.

C. Legionellosis is caused by *Legionella* bacteria and may produce a severe form of pneumonia known as Legionnaires' disease.

D. Histoplasmosis is caused by a fungus, not by bacteria.

E. Rabies is caused by a virus, not by bacteria.

72. Myogenic adaptations to resistance training are adaptations that occur within the muscle tissue itself.

C. Increased muscle cross-sectional area is a myogenic adaptation because resistance training causes hypertrophy of muscle fibres.

D. Increased number of myofibrils is also a myogenic adaptation because contractile protein content and myofibrillar structure increase with training.

A. Increased neural drive is a neural adaptation, not a myogenic adaptation.

B. Stretch reflex potentiation is also related more to neuromuscular or neural mechanisms rather than direct muscle structural adaptation.

73. Formal experimental designs include randomized block design, factorial design, and Latin square design.

A. Randomized block design is a formal experimental design used to control variability by grouping similar subjects before random assignment.

B. Factorial design is a formal experimental design used to study two or more independent variables and their interaction effects.

C. Latin square design is also a formal experimental design used to control two sources of extraneous variation.

D. Before and after with control design is generally classified under quasi-experimental or pre-experimental style arrangements rather than the standard formal experimental designs listed here.

74. Skill tests are useful for evaluation of learning and can also be used for diagnosis, prediction, and positional placement.

A. Diagnosis is possible because skill tests help identify strengths, weaknesses, and specific areas needing correction.

B. Prediction is possible because skill test scores may help estimate future performance or potential in a sport.

D. Positional placement is also possible because test results can help place players in suitable roles or playing positions.

C. Winning is not a direct evaluative use of skill tests, because tests measure ability and learning rather than guarantee competition victory.

75. Management in physical education and sports primarily involves planning and organizing activities, directing and motivating participants, and evaluating outcomes.

A. Planning and organizing activities are basic management functions needed for arranging programmes, events, facilities, personnel, and schedules.

C. Directing and motivating participants are important for guiding students, athletes, coaches, and staff toward desired goals.

D. Evaluating outcomes is necessary to judge effectiveness, identify problems, and improve future sports programmes.

B. Random decision making is not a proper function of management because sports management requires systematic, planned, and purposeful decisions.

76. The correct matching is Jyothi Yarraji—Athletics, Saweety Boora—Boxing, Vantika Agrawal—Chess, and Sajan Prakash—Swimming.

A. Jyothi Yarraji — III. Athletics: Jyothi Yarraji is associated with athletics, especially hurdling events, so she matches with Athletics.

B. Saweety Boora — I. Boxing: Saweety Boora is associated with boxing, so she correctly matches with Boxing.

C. Vantika Agrawal — II. Chess: Vantika Agrawal is associated with chess, so she correctly matches with Chess.

D. Sajan Prakash — IV. Swimming: Sajan Prakash is associated with swimming, so he correctly matches with Swimming.

77. The correct matching is SAT score $\sigma = 100 - \overline{X} = 500$, Total area—equal to 1, In a distribution if σ is $1 - \overline{X} = 0$, and Binet intelligence scale score $\sigma = 16 - \overline{X} = 100$.

A. If SAT score $\sigma = 100$ – IV. $\overline{X} = 500$

In the SAT score distribution, the standard deviation is commonly taken as 100 and the mean is 500.

B. Total area — I. equal to 1

In a normal curve, the total area under the curve is equal to 1, representing the complete probability distribution.

C. In a distribution if σ is 1 – II. $\overline{X} = 0$

In the standard normal distribution, the standard deviation is 1 and the mean is 0.

D. In Binet intelligence scale score $\sigma = 16$ – III. $\overline{X} = 100$

In the Binet intelligence scale; the standard deviation is taken as 16 and the mean is 100.

78. The correct matching of Monark ergometer settings is Children—0.075 × body weight, Adult women—0.086 × body weight, Adult men—0.087 × body weight, and Athletes—0.10 × body weight.

A. Children — II. 0.075 × Body weight in kg: Children are matched with the lower Monark ergometer resistance setting of 0.075 × body weight in kg.

B. Adult women — III. 0.086 × Body weight in kg: Adult women are matched with 0.086 × body weight in kg as the given ergometer setting.

C. Adult men — IV. 0.087 × Body weight in kg: Adult men are matched with 0.087 × body weight in kg in the given list.

D. Athletes — I. 0.10 × Body weight in kg: Athletes are matched with the higher resistance setting of 0.10 × body weight in kg.

79. The correct matching is Autocratic—Strict authority and control, Democratic—Decisions made collectively, Laissez-faire—Coach gives complete freedom, and Transformational—Inspires players with vision.

A. Autocratic — III. Strict authority and control: Autocratic leadership is based on strong control, command, and decision-making authority by the leader.

B. Democratic — I. Decisions made collectively: Democratic leadership involves group participation and collective decision-making.

C. Laissez-faire — II. Coach gives complete freedom: Laissez-faire leadership gives players or group members a high level of freedom with minimum direct control.

D. Transformational — IV. Inspires players with vision: Transformational leadership motivates and inspires players through vision, encouragement, and personal influence.

80. The correct matching is Isometric—Only one joint angle is tested, Isotonic—Difficult to find 1-RM, Isokinetic—Velocity of movement affects torque output, and Plyometric—Measuring intensity is more complex.

A. Isometric — IV. Only one joint angle is tested: Isometric testing measures force at a fixed joint angle, so its weakness is that only one joint angle is tested.

B. Isotonic — I. Difficult to find 1-RM: Isotonic strength testing often uses one-repetition maximum, and finding true 1-RM can be difficult or risky for some participants.

C. Isokinetic — III. Velocity of movement affect torque output: In isokinetic testing, torque output varies with movement velocity, so velocity affects the measured torque.

D. Plyometric — II. Measuring intensity is more complex: Plyometric training intensity is harder to quantify because it depends on jump height, contact time, speed, body mass, and landing forces.

81. The correct matching is Reaction ability—Functional capacity, Movement Speed—Explosive Strength, Locomotor ability—Mobility of CNS, and Speed endurance—Aerobic capacity.

A. Reaction ability — III. Functional capacity: Reaction ability depends on the functional capacity of the sensory organs and nervous system to receive, process, and respond quickly to a stimulus.

B. Movement Speed — II. Explosive Strength: Movement speed is strongly influenced by explosive strength because rapid force production helps execute movement in minimum time.

C. Locomotor ability — I. Mobility of CNS: Locomotor ability requires quick and coordinated cyclic movement, which depends on the mobility and quick functioning of the central nervous system.

D. Speed endurance — IV. Aerobic capacity: Speed endurance depends on the ability to maintain speed and resist fatigue, for which aerobic capacity supports recovery and sustained performance.

82. The correct matching is One Mean—p-value 0.550, Two Independent mean—p-value 0.564, Two dependent mean—p-value 0.703, and Correlation Pearson's—p-value 0.474.

A. One Mean — III. p-value 0.550: One mean is tested by a one-sample parametric test, and in the given matching set it corresponds to p-value 0.550.

B. Two Independent mean — IV. p-value 0.564: Two independent means are compared by an independent-samples parametric test, and in the given matching set it corresponds to p-value 0.564.

C. Two dependent mean — II. p-value 0.703: Two dependent means are compared by a paired-samples parametric test, and in the given matching set it corresponds to p-value 0.703.

D. Correlation Pearson's — I. p-value 0.474: Pearson's correlation is the parametric test used for correlation, and in the given matching set it corresponds to p-value 0.474.

83. The correct matching is Herpes varicella zoster—Chickenpox, Epstein-Barr—Mononucleosis, Rhinoviruses—Common cold, and Ebola Viruses—Hemorrhagic fever.

A. Herpes varicella zoster — III. Chickenpox: Herpes varicella zoster virus causes chickenpox as its primary infection.

B. Epstein-Barr — IV. Mononucleosis: Epstein-Barr virus is the virus classically associated with infectious mononucleosis.

C. Rhinoviruses — I. Common cold: Rhinoviruses are common viral agents responsible for the common cold.

D. Ebola Viruses — II. Hemorrhagic fever: Ebola viruses cause Ebola virus disease, which is a severe viral hemorrhagic fever.

84. The correct matching is Pivot joint—Trochoid joint, Condyloid joint—Ovoid joint, Saddle joint—Sellar joint, and Hinge joint—Ginglymus joint.

A. Pivot joint — II. Trochoid joint: A pivot joint is also called a trochoid joint because it permits rotational movement around a longitudinal axis.

B. Condyloid joint — III. Ovoid joint: A condyloid joint is also called an ovoid joint because one oval articular surface fits into another.

C. Saddle joint — IV. Sellar joint: A saddle joint is also called a sellar joint because the opposing articular surfaces are saddle-shaped.

D. Hinge joint — I. Ginglymus joint: A hinge joint is also called a ginglymus joint because it allows movement mainly in one plane, such as flexion and extension.

85. The correct matching from the given options is Prophase—The nuclear membrane disappear, Metaphase—The centromeres now divide, Telophase—A nuclear membrane re-forms around each of chromosomes, and Anaphase—The spindle fibers contract and pull the chromosomes.

A. Prophase — III. The nuclear membrane disappear: In prophase, the chromosomes condense and the nuclear membrane disappears as the cell prepares for chromosome separation.

B. Metaphase — I. The centromeres now divide: In the given option pattern, metaphase is matched with centromere division as the stage after chromosome arrangement at the equatorial region.

C. Telophase — IV. A nuclear membrane re-forms around each of chromosomes: In telophase, nuclear membranes re-form around the separated chromosome groups at opposite poles.

D. Anaphase — II. The spindle fibers contract and pull the chromosomes: In anaphase, spindle fibres contract and pull sister chromatids toward opposite poles of the cell.

86. The correct matching is Compression—Force pressing or squeezing axially, Tension—Pulling force along the axis of structure, Shear—Force acting parallel to a surface, and Torsion—Twisting force around a longitudinal axis.

A. Compression — II. Force pressing or squeezing axially: Compression acts when a structure is pressed, squeezed, or shortened along its axis.

B. Tension — IV. Pulling force along the axis of structure: Tension acts when a structure is stretched or pulled apart along its long axis.

C. Shear — III. Force acting parallel to a surface: Shear force acts parallel to a surface and tends to make one part of a structure slide over another part.

D. Torsion — I. Twisting force around a longitudinal axis: Torsion is produced when a structure is twisted around its long axis.

87. The correct matching is Drive Theory—High arousal boosts performance if well-learned, Catastrophe Model—Performance collapses when cognitive anxiety is high, Inverted-U Hypothesis—Best performance at moderate arousal, and IZOF—Athletes have unique optimal zones.

A. Drive Theory — IV. High arousal boosts performance if well-learned: Drive theory states that increased arousal improves performance when the skill is well learned or dominant response is correct.

B. Catastrophe Model — I. Performance collapses when cognitive anxiety is high: Catastrophe theory explains that performance may suddenly drop when physiological arousal is high along with high cognitive anxiety.

C. Inverted-U-Hypothesis — III. Best performance at moderate arousal: The inverted-U hypothesis states that performance is best at a moderate level of arousal and declines at very low or very high arousal.

D. Individualized zone of optimal functioning — II. Athletes have unique optimal zones: IZOF explains that each athlete has an individual arousal or emotional zone in which best performance is likely.

88. The correct matching is Wearable fitness devices—Tracks individual fitness progress, Sports Equipment—Enhances skill development through hands-on practice, Videos and Animations—Provides clear demonstrations of techniques, and Instructional diagrams—Helps in injury prevention and safety awareness.

A. Wearable fitness devices — III. Tracks individual fitness progress: Wearable fitness devices can monitor activity, heart rate, steps, distance, and other indicators of personal fitness progress.

B. Sports Equipment — II. Enhances skill development through hands-on practice: Sports equipment allows learners to practise skills directly and improve performance through active participation.

C. Videos and Animations — I. Provides clear demonstrations of techniques: Videos and animations help learners see correct movement patterns, techniques, and skill execution clearly.

D. Instructional diagrams — IV. Helps in injury prevention and safety awareness: Instructional diagrams can show safe positions, correct technique, and precautions to reduce injury risk.

89. The correct matching is Epidemiology—Distribution and determinants of diseases and injury in human populations, Epidemic—Unexpectedly large number of cases in a population, Endemic disease—Disease occurring regularly in a population, and Pandemic—Outbreak over a wide geographical area.

A. Epidemiology — IV. The distribution and determinants of diseases and injury in human populations: Epidemiology studies how diseases and injuries are distributed and what factors influence them in populations.

B. Epidemic — I. An unexpectedly large number of cases of disease in a particular population: An epidemic occurs when disease cases rise above the expected level in a particular population or area.

C. Endemic disease — II. A disease that occurs regularly in a population as a matter of course: An endemic disease is constantly or regularly present in a particular population or region.

D. Pandemic — III. An outbreak of disease over a wide geographical area such as a continent: A pandemic is an epidemic that spreads across countries, continents, or large geographical regions.

90. The correct matching is Extraneous Variable—Factor that could affect the relationship but is not included or controlled, Dependent Variable—Effect of the independent variable, Control Variable—Factor kept out or controlled in the study, and Moderator Variable—Kind of independent variable such as age or sex that cannot be manipulated.

A. Extraneous Variable — III. A factor that could affect the relationship between the independent and dependent variables but that is not included or controlled: An extraneous variable is an outside factor that may influence the result if it is not properly controlled.

B. Dependent Variable — IV. The effect of the independent variable: The dependent variable is the outcome or result that changes because of the independent variable.

C. Control Variable — I. A factor that could possibly influence the results and that is kept out of the study: A control variable is managed, held constant, or kept out so that it does not disturb the result of the study.

D. Moderator Variable — II. A kind of independent variable such as age, sex that cannot be manipulated: A moderator variable may influence the strength or direction of the relationship between variables and may include factors such as age or sex.

91. Hair colour is an example of a nominal variable. It classifies customers into categories such as White, Brown, and Black. These categories are names or labels and do not have a natural order or ranking. Even if hair colour is coded as 1, 2, and 3, the numbers only represent categories. So hair colour remains qualitative nominal data, not discrete or continuous quantitative data.

92. The number of courses currently registered is an example of a discrete variable. It is quantitative because it is expressed as a count. A student may be registered for 1, 2, 3, 4, or more courses, but not for fractional values such as 2.5 courses in the usual counting sense. Discrete variables take countable separate values. So the courses currently registered represent a discrete quantitative variable.

93. Level of satisfaction is an example of an ordinal variable. It includes ordered categories such as very satisfied, satisfied, and somewhat satisfied. These responses are qualitative categories, but they have a meaningful ranking from higher satisfaction to lower satisfaction. The exact numerical distance between the categories is not fixed or measurable. So level of satisfaction is ordinal because it shows order without equal measurable intervals.

94. The weight of books and supplies is an example of a continuous variable. It is quantitative because weight is measured numerically. Weight can take many possible values, including fractional or decimal values such as 2.5 kg or 3.75 kg. Continuous variables are based on measurement rather than simple counting. So the weight of books and supplies is a continuous quantitative variable.

95. Hometown is an example of a nominal variable. It classifies customers into categories such as Village, Urban, and Town. These categories are labels used to identify the type or place of residence. They do not form a true numerical scale and do not have a necessary measurable order. So hometown is a qualitative nominal variable, not ordinal, discrete, or continuous.

96. Eccentric exercise is most associated with mechanical trauma leading to DOMS. During eccentric contraction, the muscle lengthens while producing force, which places high mechanical stress on muscle fibres. This high mechanical force can disrupt muscle tissue and damage structures such as the sarcolemma. The paragraph specifically states that mechanical trauma occurs particularly during eccentric contraction. So eccentric exercise is the exercise type most directly linked with mechanical trauma in DOMS.

97. According to the mechanical trauma theory, muscle soreness is caused by disruption or micro-tear in muscle fibres. The paragraph explains that high mechanical forces during exercise cause disruption of muscle tissue. This damage allows intracellular components to diffuse into tissue fluids and plasma. Such structural damage contributes to the pain and soreness experienced in DOMS. Lactic acid accumulation, nerve compression, and decreased oxygen supply are not the main explanation under mechanical trauma theory.

98. The acute inflammatory response in DOMS usually peaks at 48 hours and is generally no longer seen at 72 hours. The paragraph states that WBCs and monocytes migrate to the injured area after exercise. They are present in large numbers at 24 hours after exercise. Their number peaks at 48 hours and they are generally no longer seen by 72 hours. So the best option given is 48-72 hours post exercise.

99. Local ischemia in exercising muscle is caused by reduced blood flow due to increased tissue pressure and vascular compression. The paragraph states that local ischemia theory proposes increased tissue pressure and significantly decreased muscle blood flow. During sustained contraction or overuse, pressure inside the muscle can compress blood vessels. This compression reduces blood supply to the working or sore muscle area. Vasodilation, excess oxygen supply, and increased heart rate do not explain local ischemia in this context.

100. According to spasm theory, DOMS is mainly caused by reflex tonic muscle spasm after unaccustomed exercise. The paragraph states that localized soreness is caused by tonic, localized spasm of motor units. Pain then brings reflex tonic muscle contraction, creating a cycle of soreness and spasm. Such muscle spasm can reduce local blood flow and contribute to continued pain. Overactivation of mitochondria, lactic acid accumulation, and structural micro-tear are not the main explanation under spasm theory.

◊◊◊◊◊◊◊◊◊◊◊◊◊◊◊◊◊◊◊◊◊◊◊◊◊◊◊◊◊◊

YOUR SPACE

Previous Years' Paper

National Testing Agency (NTA)

UGC-NET Junior Research Fellowship & Assistant Professor Eligibility Exam

PHYSICAL EDUCATION, JUNE-2025

(Exam held on 28-06-2025)

PAPER-II

1. Recreation theory was proposed by

1. G. Stanley Hall
2. Karl Groos
3. Friedrich Schiller
4. Moritz Lazarus & Patrick

2. The meaning of Recapitulation theory of Play is:

1. Children play to release the excess energy in their body
2. Through play children can let go of unnecessary instincts which are ingrained in us
3. Through play children get a chance to practice skills they will need in the future
4. Children play to restore energy that has been depleted after doing labour work

3. International Olympic Committee (IOC) officially approved in 2021 Olympic motto is Citius, Altius, Fortius, ______:

1. Suburbanite 2. Commuter
3. Communiter 4. Combination

4. In Event 4X400 Meter Mixed Relay the order of Legs is:

1. Male-Female-Male-Female
2. Female-Male-Female-Male
3. Male-Female-Female-Male
4. Female-Male-Male-Female

5. Match LIST-I with LIST-II.

LIST-I (Name)	LIST-II (Place)
A. Franz Nachtegall	I. Sweden
B. Per Henrik Ling	II. Greece
C. Johan Bernhard Basedow	III. Denmark
D. Galen	IV. Germany

Choose the ***correct*** answer from the options given below:

1. A-III, B-IV, C-II, D-I
2. A-III, B-I, C-IV, D-II
3. A-III, B-IV, C-I, D-II
4. A-IV, B-III, C-II, D-I

6. Match List-I with List-II.

LIST-I (Terms)	LIST-II (Explanation)
A. Meta Physics	I. Explores the nature of beauty art and taste
B. Axiology	II. An inquiry into the ultimate reality
C. Epistemology	III. Study of values and the nature of value judgement
D. Aesthetics	IV. Exposition of truth

Choose the ***correct*** answer from the options given below:

1. A-III, B-IV, C-I, D-II
2. A-III, B-I, C-IV, D-II
3. A-II, B-III, C-I, D-IV
4. A-II, B-III, C-IV, D-I

7. Which of the following group of disorders in female athlete is termed as "Female Athlete Triad"?

1. Amenorrhea, Hormonal imbalance and Osteoporosis
2. Disordered Eating, Low Energy availability and Low Bone Density
3. Irregular Mensuration, Low Estrogen Level and Disordered Eating
4. Amenorrhea, Osteoporosis and Disordered Eating

8. Which of the following is called basic functional unit of a Skeletal Muscle?

1. Sarcomere
2. Sarcoplasmic Reticulum
3. Actin Filaments
4. Myosin Filaments

9. Which of the following is also known as the direct source of energy for muscular contraction?

1. Phospho-creatine
2. Glycogen
3. Adenosine Triphosphate
4. Calcium Ions

10. ______ are the primary source of blood supply to the heart muscles?

1. Coronary Arteries
2. Pulmonary Arteries
3. Renel Arteries
4. Carotid Arteries

11. Which of the following is NOT a contraindication for Cryotherapy?

1. Raynaud's disease
2. Peripheral Vascular disease
3. Hyperthermia
4. Ischemia

12. Arrange the following events of sensory-Motor Integration in a correct sequence.

A. The CNS interprets in sensory information and reflexively initiate a motor response
B. The motor action potential is transmitted to muscle and response occurs
C. The Sensory action potential is transmitted along sensory neurons to CNS
D. A Sensory stimulus is received by sensory receptors
E. The action potential for the response is transmitted from CNS along alpha motor neurons

Choose the ***correct*** answer from the options given below:

1. C, D, A, E, B
2. D, C, A, E, B
3. E, C, D, A, B
4. D, A, C, B, E

13. Which of the following health risks are associated with high altitude training?

A. Hyperthermia
B. Pulmonary Edema
C. Frost Bite
D. Hypoxia
E. Cerebral Edema

Choose the ***correct*** answer from the options given below:

1. B, D, E only
2. A, B, D only
3. B, C, D only
4. A, D, E only

14. The causes of fatigue are ______.

A. Phospho Creatine depletion
B. Decrease in Hydrogen Ion level
C. Decrease in body core temperature
D. Glycogen depletion
E. Accumulation of lactic acid

Choose the ***most appropriate*** answer from the options given below:

1. A, B, E only
2. A, D, E only
3. B, D, E only
4. B, C, E only

15. Match List-I with List-II.

LIST-I (Component)	LIST-II (Location)
A. Myelin Sheath	I. Muscle cell
B. Troponin and Tropomyosin	II. Brain
C. Basal Ganglia	III. Axon
D. Sarcolemma	IV. Actin Filaments

Choose the ***correct*** answer from the options given below:

1. A-IV, B-II, C-I, D-III
2. A-III, B-II, C-IV, D-I
3. A-IV, B-III, C-I, D-II
4. A-III, B-IV, C-II, D-I

16. Match List-I with List-II.

LIST-I (Condition)	LIST-II (Explanation)
A. Bradycardia	I. Resting Heart Rate > 60 bpm
B. Atherosclerosis	II. Temporary deficiency in blood supply in a particular body part
C. Ischemia	III. Irregular heart beat
D. Arrhythmia	IV. Progressive narrowing of Arteries

Choose the ***correct*** answer from the options given below:

1. A-III, B-I, C-IV, D-II
2. A-I, B-IV, C-II, D-III
3. A-III, B-IV, C-II, D-I
4. A-I, B-III, C-II, D-IV

17. When clearing the bar in a High Jump or Pole Vault competition:

1. The centre of mass must pass over the bar
2. The centre of mass must reach a height equal to the height of the bar
3. A successful bar clearance may not require the centre of mass to be higher than the bar
4. The centre of mass is only required to be higher than the bar at the clearance mid-point

18. If an object is projected from a point higher than landing then the optimum projection angle will be:

1. less than the object is projected from the ground
2. greater than the object is projected from the ground
3. the same as the object is projected from the ground
4. not the same as the object is projected from the ground

19. If a women's weight is 556N, the surface area of the spike heel is 4 cm^2, and the surface area of the court shoe is 175 cm^2, how much pressure is exerted by each shoe?

1. 139 N/cm^2 & 3.18 N/cm^2
2. 135 N/cm^2 & 3.05 N/cm^2
3. 130 N/cm^2 & 2.95 N/cm^2
4. 138 N/cm^2 & 3.10 N/cm^2

20. If the runners speed at the 10 m mark is 5.9 $m.s^1$ and it took 1.8 s to get there, then the average acceleration would be:

1. 5.5 $m.s^{-2}$ 2. 5.3 $m.s^{-2}$
3. 3.5 $m.s^{-2}$ 4. 3.3 $m.s^{-2}$

21. A vector is defined by its;

A. Speed B. Magnitude
C. Distance D. Direction
E. Displacement

Choose the ***correct*** answer from the options given below:

1. B, C, D only 2. B, D, E only
3. A, B, E only 4. A, B, C only

22. Rolling friction is influenced by;

A. Normal reaction force
B. Coefficient of restitution
C. Radius of rolling object
D. Centripetal and Centrifugal forces
E. Deformation of the surfaces and their coefficient of friction

Choose the ***correct*** answer from the options given below:

1. B, D, E only 2. A, C, D only
3. A, C, E only 4. B, C, D only

23. The important characteristics of force are;

A. Centre of gravity
B. Point of application
C. Line of application
D. Base of support
E. Force sense

Choose the ***most appropriate*** answer from the options given below:

1. A, C, D only 2. B, C, D only
3. B, C, E only 4. A, D, E only

24. Match List-I with List-II.

LIST-I	LIST-II
A. Objects seems bigger or slower as they move towards or Away from the camera	I. Parallel axes theorem
B. Objects size and shape seems to change as it moves across the camera	II. Radius of gyration
C. Total Inertia	III. Perspective error
D. Distribution of mass relative to the centre of rotation	IV. Parallax error

Choose the ***correct*** answer from the options given below:

1. A-IV, B-III, C-I, D-II
2. A-III, B-IV, C-II, D-I
3. A-III, B-IV, C-I, D-II
4. A-IV, B-III, C-II, D-I

25. Match List-I with List-II.

LIST-I	LIST-II
A. Walking	I. Propelling oneself forward by alternatively setting each foot on the ground
B. Running	II. Propelling oneself upward off the ground by using muscles in Own legs
C. Jumping	III. Propelling an object using one's arm or hand
D. Throwing	IV. Propelling oneself forward by moving both feet rapidly and continuously

Choose the ***correct*** answer from the options given below:

1. A-IV, B-I, C-II, D-III
2. A-I, B-IV, C-III, D-II
3. A-I, B-IV, C-II, D-III
4. A-IV, B-I, C-III, D-II

26. Which one of the following is the objective of a sports Psychologist?

1. To win in any condition
2. To deal with athletes only when in trouble
3. Ensure every sports participant reach his/her potential
4. Suggest medicine to overcome mental issues

27. In Sports Psychology, the hypothesis that exercise encourages and generates positive thoughts and feelings that serve to counteract negative mood states is referred as:

1. Social Interaction Hypothesis
2. Distraction Hypothesis
3. Endorphin Hypothesis
4. Cognitive Behavioral Hypothesis

28. Concept of looking world through a multicultural lens to promote group cohesion is referred as:

1. Enculturation 2. Feminism
3. Accreditation 4. Acculturation

29. A theory of arousal that results in sudden and sharp decline in performance is referred as:

1. Inverted-U Theory
2. Multi-dimensional Theory
3. Catastrophe Theory
4. Reversal Theory

30. List the correct sequence as per Harter's theory of achievement motivation which lead to Youth Sports Development:

A. Fewer mastery attempts
B. Dropout
C. Unsuccessful performance
D. Negative Affects
E. Low competence motivation

Choose the *correct* answer from the options given below:

1. A, C, D, E, B
2. E, A, C, D, B
3. C, D, E, A, B
4. D, E, C, A, B

31. List the correct sequence of Cognitive Affective Processing System (CAPS) proposed by Smith:

A. Stimuli are encoded and represented in memory
B. Competencies and self-regulation skills determine behaviour
C. Individual personality interacts with situation
D. Pre-determined expectations and beliefs confer meaning on events
E. Emotions influence behaviour

Choose the *correct* answer from the options given below:

1. A, E, B, C, D
2. C, A, D, E, B
3. A, C, E, B, D
4. C, B, A, E, D

32. Find the key words from the definition of personality as "consistant ways in which behaviour of one person differs from that of others, especially in social situations"

A. Stable B. Unique
C. Group D. Competition
E. Training

Choose the *correct* answer from the options given below:

1. B, C, D only 2. A, B, C only
3. B, C, E only 4. A, B, E only

33. Which of the following are important concern of Sports Psychologists for superior athletic performance?

A. Strength B. Self Control
C. Motivation D. Confidence
E. Endurance

Choose the ***most appropriate*** answer from the options given below:

1. C, D, E only 2. A, B, C only
3. A, C, D only 4. B, C, D only

34. Match List-I with List-II.

LIST-I	LIST-II
A. Task cohesion	I. Applied Sports Psychology
B. Trait	II. Ethics
C. Bruce Ogilvie	III. Personality
D. Client Consent	IV. Group Dynamics

Choose the *correct* answer from the options given below:

1. A-I, B-II, C-III, D-IV
2. A-II, B-I, C-III, D-IV
3. A-III, B-IV, C-II, D-I
4. A-IV, B-III, C-I, D-II

35. Match List-I with List-II.

LIST-I	LIST-II
A. Imagery	I. Motivation
B. Hostile and Instrumental	II. Anxiety
C. Zone of Optimal Functioning (ZoF)	III. Aggression
D. Introjected Regulation	IV. Psychological Skill Training

Choose the *correct* answer from the options given below:

1. A-IV, B-III, C-II, D-I
2. A-III, B-II, C-I, D-IV
3. A-IV, B-I, C-III, D-II
4. A-I, B-II, C-III, D-IV

36. Which is the following discipline in physical education is concerned with preparing teachers to provide services for individuals with disabilities.

1. Sports Medicine
2. Sports Management
3. Adapted Physical Education
4. Sports Sociology

37. According to NEP-2020, the school curriculum framework 5-3-3-4 refers to:

1. Preparatory Stage, Foundation Stage, Middle Stage, Secondary Stage
2. Foundation Stage, Preparatory Stage, Middle Stage, Senior Secondary Stage
3. Preparatory Stage, Middle Stage, Secondary Stage, Senior Secondary Stage
4. Foundation Stage, Preparatory Stage, Middle Stage, Secondary Stage

38. Select the organization which regulates Physical Education Teacher Education program in India?

1. A.I.C.T.E
2. N.C.T.E
3. N.A.A.C
4. U.G.C

39. According to Muska Mosston's anatomy of teaching style, Guided Discovery style comprises of:

1. Teacher Centered decision
2. Combined approach of teacher and student-centered decision
3. Student centered decision
4. Evaluation centered design

40. Sequencing the cognitive domain of learning in acending order of complexity as suggested by Bloom (1950)

A. Understanding
B. Analysis
C. Remembering
D. Application
E. Evaluation

Choose the ***correct*** answer from the options given below:

1. A, C, B, D, E
2. A, C, D, B; E
3. C, A, D, B, E
4. C, A, B, D, E

41. Arrange the following steps involved in curriculum construction in appropriate sequence:

A. Understanding of Education Philosophy and Policies
B. Determining age-based needs of children
C. Evaluation of program and feedback
D. Selection of appropriate activities
E. Formulating objectives

Choose the ***correct*** answer from the options given below:

1. A, E, B, D, C
2. E, A, B, D, C
3. A, E, D, C, B
4. E, B, A, C, D

42. Which of the following are the objectives of physical education program at foundation stage of School Physical Education Program.

A. Development of Spatial Awareness
B. Development of Gross Motor Skills
C. Development of Fine Motor Skills
D. Development of Leadership Skills
E. Development of Sports Specific Skills

Choose the ***correct*** answer from the options given below:

1. B, C, D only
2. C, D, E only
3. A, C, D only
4. A, B, C only

43. The professional prepration program should provide:

A. Opportunities to think about the proper justification for the profession
B. Devotion for the profession
C. Incentives
D. Concern of the state
E. Loyalty for the profession

Choose the ***most appropriate*** answer from the options given below:

1. A, C, D only
2. A, B, E only
3. B, C, E only
4. B, C, D only

44. Match List-I with List-II.

LIST-I	LIST-II
A. L.C.P.E, Gwalior	I. 1914
B. H.V.P.M, Amravati	II. 1920
C. National Sports University, Imphal	III. 1957
D. Y.M.CA Madras	IV. 2018

Choose the ***correct*** answer from the options given below:

1. A-III, B-IV, C-I, D-II
2. A-III, B-I, C-II, D-IV
3. A-III, B-I, C-IV, D-II
4. A-III, B-II, C-I, D-IV

45. Which of the following to be avoided while giving First Aid for Burns?

1. Applying Ice
2. Removing Restricted items from body
3. Covering the burn
4. Providing pain relief medication

46. Which of the following is NOT recommended by the School Health Committee for Mid-day Meal program?

1. It should be based on "No Profit No Loss" basis
2. It should provide atleast one energy drink on daily basis
3. It should provide one-third of daily calorie requirement
4. It should provide half of daily protein requirement

47. Which of the following is not a Hereditary disorder?

1. Thalassaemias
2. Haemophilia
3. Ascariasis
4. Sickle Cell Anaemia

48. Which of the following Index is NOT used for the assessment of obesity?

1. Body Mass Index
2. Ponderal Index
3. Brocca Index
4. Relative Autonomy Index

49. Arrange in proper sequence the basic steps of conducting a Randomized controlled trials for treatment and prevention of disease

A. Randomization
B. Manipulation or Intervention
C. Drawing up a protocol
D. Selecting Reference and Population for trial
E. Follow-up and assessment of outcome

Choose the ***correct*** answer from the options given below:

1. C, D, A, B, E
2. A, C, D, B, E
3. C, A, D, E, B
4. D, C, A, B, E

50. Arrange the main steps of Health Education Planning in an appropriate sequence.

A. Collecting information and identifying the problem
B. Assessment of resources
C. Deciding priorities and setting goals and objectives
D. Monitoring and evaluating the program
E. Preparing and Implementing plan of action

Choose the ***correct*** answer from the options given below:

1. A, B, C, E, D
2. C, A, B, E, D
3. A, C, B, E, D
4. C, B, A, D, E

51. Which of the following are the zoonotic disease:

A. Rabies B. Anthrax
C. Influenza D. Plague
E. Typhoid

Choose the ***correct*** answer from the options given below:

1. A, C, D only
2. B, C, D only
3. A, B, D only
4. A, D, E only

52. Which of the following are water borne disease?

A. Hepatitis A B. Bronchitis
C. Amoebiasis D. Typhoid
E. Emphysema

Choose the ***correct*** answer from the options given below:

1. B, C, D only 2. A, C, D only
3. A, B, E only 4. C, D, E only

53. Match List-I with List-II.

LIST-I (Health Program)	LIST-II (Year of Launch)
A. Swachh Bharat Abhiyan	I. 2018
B. National AIDS Control Program	II. 2014
C. Ayushman Bharat Programme	III. 1953
D. National Malaria Control Program	IV. 1987

Choose the ***correct*** answer from the options given below:

1. A-I, B-III, C-II, D-IV
2. A-II, B-IV, C-I, D-III
3. A-IV, B-I, C-II, D-III
4. A-II, B-III, C-I, D-IV

54. The ability to determine and change the position and movement of the body in time and space in relation to a definite field of action is known as ______.

1. Coupling ability
2. Differentiation ability
3. Orientation ability
4. Adaptation ability

55. ______ is the development of maximal force in minimal time, typically used an index of explosive strength

1. Stretch Shortening Cycle (SSC)
2. Rate of Force Development (RFD)
3. Ratings of Perceived Exertion (RPE)
4. General Adaptation Syndrome (GAS)

56. While recording the training plan the coach must record the exercises, number of sets, number of repetitions and training load as follows:

1. $\frac{\text{\% of IRM}}{\text{Session}} \times \text{Sets}$
2. $\frac{\text{\% of IRM}}{\text{Sets}} \times \text{Session}$
3. $\frac{\text{\% of IRM} \times \text{Sets}}{\text{Number of repetition}}$
4. $\frac{\text{\% of IRM}}{\text{Number of repetition}} \times \text{sets}$

57. In which of the following training, athlete complete a combination of task of some added resistance, some assisted and then under normal conditions:

1. Complex Training
2. Cross Training
3. Contrast Training
4. Continuous Training

58. Find the correct sequential order of learning the technique

A. Conscious Competence
B. Conscious Incompetence
C. Reflective Competence
D. Unconscious Competence
E. Unconscious Incompetence

Choose the ***correct*** answer from the options given below:

1. E, B, A, D, C
2. B, E, A, D, C
3. A, D, C, B, E
4. D, A, C, B, E

59. Arrange in correct sequence the anatomical adaptation of periodization of strength:

A. Maintenance Phase
B. Conversion to Specific Strength Phase
C. Compensation Phase
D. Maximum Strength Phase
E. Cessation Phase

Choose the ***correct*** answer from the options given below:

1. B, D, A, C, E
2. B, D, C, A, E
3. D, A, B, E, C
4. D, B, A, E, C

60. Which of the following components are used to calculate the training load?

A. Intensity of Load
B. Density of Load
C. Training and Competition
D. Frequency of Load
E. Training and Performance

Choose the ***correct*** answer from the options given below:

1. A, B, E only 2. A, B, D only
3. A, C, E only 4. A, B, C only

61. Match List-I with List-II.

List-I (Component)

A. Relative Density
B. Index of Overall Demand
C. Overall Intensity
D. Partial Intensity

LIST-II (Formulae)

I. $\dfrac{\sum(\text{Partial intensity} \times \text{Volume of exercises})}{\sum(\text{Volume of exercises})}$

II. $\dfrac{\text{OI} \times \text{AD} \times \text{AV}}{10{,}000}$

III. $\dfrac{\text{Absolute volume} \times 100}{\text{Relative volume}}$

IV. $\dfrac{\text{HR}_\text{P} \times 100}{\text{HR max}}$

Choose the ***correct*** answer from the options given below:

1. A-III, B-IV, C-I, D-II
2. A-III, B-II, C-I, D-IV
3. A-III, B-IV, C-II, D-I
4. A-III, B-II, C-IV, D-I

62. ______ is a range of values within which the analyst can declare, with same confidence, the population parameters lies.

1. Interval Estimate
2. Point Estimate
3. Population Estimate
4. Declarative Estimate

63. A study in which either the quantitative or qualitative component goes first and then is followed by the other component is known as:

1. Parallel Mixed Method
2. Sequential Mixed Method
3. Concurrent Method
4. Narrative Method

64. Establishing the age or Authorship of documents comes under:

1. External Criticism
2. Internal Criticism
3. Experimental Research
4. Descriptive Research

65. Inclination of a rater to consider behaviours to be more nearly the same when they are united close together on a scale than when they are separated by some distance refers to:

1. Observer Bias Error
2. Type-I Error
3. Proximity Error
4. Scaled Error

66. Arrange the following steps of developing skills in computer data analysis in a proper sequence:

A. Storing the data in the computer
B. Selection of appropriate software package
C. Data Organisation and coding
D. Selection of appropriate statistical measures/techniques
E. Execution of the computer program

Choose the ***correct*** answer from the options given below:

1. C, A, B, D, E
2. A, C, B, D, E
3. C, A, D, B, E
4. C, B, A, D, E

67. Identify the correct sequential order of steps for developing a sample design:

A. Parameters of Interest
B. Budgetary Constraint
C. Type of Universe & Sampling Unit
D. Sampling Procedure
E. Source list & Size of Sample

Choose the ***correct*** answer from the options given below:

1. E, C, B, A, D
2. C, E, A, D, B
3. C, E, A, B, D
4. C, E, B, A, D

68. Which of the following terms are associated with cohort studies ?

A. Follow-up studies
B. Exploratory studies
C. Prospective studies
D. Case studies
E. Longitudinal studies

Choose the *correct* answer from the options given below:

1. A, C, E only
2. A, B, D only
3. B, D, E only
4. B, C, E only

69. Which of the following are considered as a part of True Experimental Design?

A. Randomized Group Design
B. One-Group Pre-Test Post-Test Design
C. Non Equivalent control Group Design
D. Pretest-Post-test Randomized Group Design
E. Soloman Four Group Design

Choose the ***most appropriate*** answer from the options given below:

1. A, D, E only
2. A, B, D only
3. B, C, E only
4. B, D, E only

70. Match List-I with List-II.

	LIST-I (Purpose)		**LIST-II (Statistic)**
A.	Comparison of two independent data points	I.	Chi-Square & Kruskal-Wallis
B.	Comparison of two non-independent data points	II.	Cochran Q Test & Friedman analysis of variance
C.	Comparison of more than two independent data points for one experimental variable	III.	Chi-Square & Mann-Whitney
D.	Comparison of more than two non-independent data points for one experimental variable	IV.	Wilcoxin test & Sign test

Choose the ***correct*** answer from the options given below:

1. A-II, B-III, C-I, D-IV
2. A-II, B-III, C-IV, D-I
3. A-III, B-IV, C-II, D-I
4. A-III, B-IV, C-I, D-II

71. According to ______ theory if enough related test are given, some of them will be measures of the skill in question.

1. Motor Integration theory
2. Dynamic action theory
3. Action theory
4. Buck shot theory

72. Physical Educators (McCloy & Young 1954) call ______ as "agility that does not involves running".

1. Dynamic Flexibility
2. Static Flexibility
3. Quickness
4. Balance

73. ______ was the first to propose a system for classifying students on their age and size dimensions into homogenous groups for instruction.

1. Larson and Yocom
2. Metheny
3. McCloy
4. Gire & Espenschade

74. Which of the following test aim to judge the playing ability of potential varsity basketball players using peer evaluations?

1. Harrison Basketball Battery
2. Antrim Basketball Skill Test
3. Mitchell Balloting Scale
4. Stubbs Ball Handling Test

75. Identify the correct sequential order of steps that must be followed in selecting a published test:

A. Locating suitable and appropriate test
B. Narrowing the choice
C. Defining the needs of testing
D. Using a test evaluation form
E. Reviewing test material

Choose the *correct* answer from the options given below:

1. C, A, B, D, E
2. C, B, A, E, D
3. A, C, B, D, E
4. C, A, B, E, D

76. Arrange the following in correct sequential order of duties after testing:

A. Converting raw scores
B. Collecting score cards
C. Constructing norms and Interpreting results
D. Using results and the follow-up
E. Comparing test results with norms and constructing a profile

Choose the *correct* answer from the options given below:

1. B, A, C, E, D
2. B, A, E, D, C
3. B, A, E, C, D
4. B, A, D, C, E

77. What three test items does the Hicks Batminton Test measure?

A. Drop B. Clear
C. Lob D. Smash
E. Strategy

Choose the *correct* answer from the options given below:

1. A, C, D only 2. A, B, D only
3. B, C, E only 4. B, D, E only

78. The process of evaluation comprises of:

A. Collecting suitable data
B. Judging the values of data
C. Generalisation
D. Making decision based on data
E. Establish results

Choose the *correct* answer from the options given below:

1. A, C, E only 2. A, B, E only
3. B, C, D only 4. A, B, D only

79. Which of the following uses major categories of ETS taxonomy?

A. Remembering
B. Application
C. Understanding
D. Knowledge
E. Thinking

Choose the ***most appropriate*** answer from the options given below:

1. A, C, E only 2. A, B, D only
3. A, D, E only 4. B, C, E only

80. Match List-I with List-II.

LIST-I (Test)	LIST-II (Test Items)
A. Barrow Motor Ability Test	I. 04
B. Schilling Body Coordination Test	II. 07
C. AAPHER Youth Fitness Test	III. 03
D. North Carolina Motor Fitness Battery	IV. 05

Choose the *correct* answer from the options given below:

1. A-III, B-IV, C-I, D-II
2. A-III, B-I, C-II, D-IV
3. A-II, B-IV, C-I, D-III
4. A-II, B-IV, C-III, D-I

81. Which one of the following sport event management functions is described as the "Nuts and Bolts" of an event?

1. Registration
2. Volunteer Management
3. Hospitality
4. Tournament Operation

82. The financial success of an organization is dependent on the difference between Revenue and Expenditure. It is referred to as;

1. Debt
2. Profit
3. Equity
4. Asset

83. Which of the following dimension of Sports promotion involves working with business to generate added revenue for sports programme?

1. Manager
2. Corporate Partner
3. Athlete
4. Governing Body

84. List the correct sequence of sports event planning stages:

A. Detail plan and time scale
B. Determine aim and objective
C. Establish control system
D. Formulate Policy
E. Compile Budget

Choose the ***correct*** answer from the options given below:

1. E, C, B, D, A
2. E, A, C, B, D
3. B, D, E, A, C
4. B, E, A, C, D

85. List the correct sequence of human resource Management in sports organization:

A. Recruitment
B. Training and Development
C. Selection and Screening
D. Planning
E. Orientation and Induction

Choose the ***correct*** answer from the options given below:

1. A, B, C, D, E
2. E, D, C, B, A
3. C, E, B, D, A
4. D, A, C, E, B

86. Media is often considered to provide three broad functions in a society;

A. Competition
B. Information
C. Relationship
D. Education
E. Entertainment

Choose the ***correct*** answer from the options given below:

1. B, D, E only
2. A, B, C only
3. B, C, D only
4. C, D, E only

87. Primary dimension of organisational structure involves;

A. Marketing
B. Departmentalisation
C. Work Specialisation
D. Span of Control
E. Advertising

Choose the ***correct*** answer from the options given below:

1. B, C, D only
2. A, B, C only
3. C, D, E only
4. A, D, E only

88. Key aspects of directing effective physical education and sports program in Institutions includes:

A. Defined chain of commands
B. Authoritarian Approach
C. Clarity of Delegation
D. Advertising
E. Fixed Responsibilities

Choose the ***most appropriate*** answer from the options given below:

1. A, B, C only
2. B, C, D only
3. B, C, E only
4. A, C, E only

89. Match List-I with List-II

LIST-I	LIST-II
A. Assigning responsibilities	I. Recruitment
B. Reporting system	II. Planning
C. Staffing	III. Directing
D. Forecasting	IV. Controlling

Choose the ***correct*** answer from the options given below:

1. A-III, B-IV, C-I, D-II
2. A-I, B-III, C-IV, D-II
3. A-IV, B-II, C-I, D-III
4. A-II, B-IV, C-III, D-I

90. Match List-I with List-II.

LIST-I	LIST-II
A. Indoor Sports Facility	I. Appraisal
B. Financial Management	II. Image
C. Public Relations	III. Auditing
D. Personnel Management	IV. Arena

Choose the *correct* answer from the options given below:

1. A-IV, B-III, C-II, D-I
2. A-III, B-IV, C-I, D-II
3. A-IV, B-I, C-II, D-III
4. A-II, B-III, C-I, D-IV

Directions (Qs. No. 91 to 95): *Read the following paragraph and answer the questions:*

Mental training in sports is an essential aspect that often goes unnoticed compared to physical training. Athletes face tremendous pressure during competition and their mental resilience can significantly influence their performance. Mental training involves visualization, concentration and relaxation techniques that helps athletes to enhance their focus, manage stress and maintain a positive mindset. By incorporating mental training in their regular routine, athlete can improve their confidence and develop stronger mental abilities which are crucial for achieving peak performance. Visualization is one of the most effective mental training technique. Athlete mentally rehearse their performance, envisioning themselves executing the skills flawlessly. This practice not only prepares them for the actual competition but also helps in reducing anxiety. Concentration technique such as mindfulness, Tratak (yoga) enables athletes to stay present and focused, minimizing distractions that can hinder the performance. Additionally relaxation strategies, including progressive relaxation, deep breathing and meditation, helps athletes to manage stress and recover mentally after intense training session or competition. Mental Training is a vital component of athletes overall preparation. By prioritizing mental resilience alongside physical training, athletes can unlock their full potential and achieve their ultimate goal in sports.

91. What is the main focus of Mental Training in sports?

1. Mental Concentration
2. Mental Attention
3. Mental Resilience
4. Mental Rehearsal

92. Which of following Mental Training technique involves rehearsing the performances mentally?

1. Progressive Relaxation Technique
2. Visualization Technique
3. Imagery Technique
4. Bio-feedback

93. What does Mindfulness help athletes with?

1. Building cohesion with co athletes and coach.
2. Improving Self Efficacy.
3. Staying in present and focused.
4. Improve social well being.

94. Which of the following is a relaxation strategy?

1. Imagery training 2. Practicing tratak
3. Deep breathing 4. Visualization

95. Why is Mental Training in Sports is often unnoticed?

1. It is less important than physical training.
2. It is less time consuming.
3. It is not as visible as physical training.
4. It is easier to implement.

Directions (Qs. No. 96 to 100): *Read the following paragraph and answer the questions:*

Inclusive Physical Education (IPE) is an educational approach, which aims that all students, regardless of their physical abilities or disabilities, have equal access to physical education program and meaningful participation in them. The approach not only promotes physical fitness but also fosters social interactions, teamwork and personal development among students. By implementing adaptive strategies and modifications, educator can cater to the diverse needs of the students, ensuring that everyone can engage in meaningful physical activities. In an Inclusive Physical Education setting, teachers are encouraged to use variety of teaching methods and tools to accommodate different skill levels and abilities. For instance, activities can be modified to allow students with mobility challenges to participate alongside their peers. Additionally, peer support and collaborations are vital component of Inclusive Physical Education, as they encourage students to work together, learn from each other and build sense of community. The emphasis on inclusivity not only benefits the students with disability but also enriches the experience of all students, promoting empathy, respect and understanding. Inclusive Physical Education also aligns with the broader educational goals, such as promoting lifelong well-being. By instilling positive attitudes towards physical activity, Inclusive Physical Education helps to break barriers and stereotypes associated with disabilities.

96. What is the primary goal of Inclusive Physical Education?
1. To focus on making students with disability participate in appropriate physical activities.
2. To ensure equal access and meaningful participation of all, in Physical Education Program.
3. To develop sympathy towards students with disabilities.
4. To prepare Para-Athletes.

97. Which of the following is the key component of Inclusive Physical Education?
1. Adherence to the indigenous and traditional sports.
2. Fitness and skill training for all.
3. Foster peer support and collaboration among students.
4. Special and separate activities for students with disabilities.

98. In Inclusive Physical education, how a teacher can accommodate different learning levels of students?
1. By modifying activities and using adaptive strategies.
2. By encouraging individual performances.
3. By using same activities for different group.
4. By eliminating existing physical activities from the program.

99. What is the benefit of Inclusive Physical Education for all students?
1. Promotes individual participation and development.
2. Fosters empathy, understanding and teamwork.
3. Prioritizes competition over participation.
4. Develops sympathetic attitude towards student with disabilities.

100. How does, Inclusive Physical Education aligns with broader educational goals?
1. By promoting cognitive development.
2. By focusing on psychomotor developments.
3. By emphasizing on individual achievements.
4. By promoting lifelong well-being.

ANSWERS

1	2	3	4	5	6	7	8	9	10
4	2	3	1	2	4	4	1	3	1
11	**12**	**13**	**14**	**15**	**16**	**17**	**18**	**19**	**20**
3	2	1	2	4	2	3	1	1	4
21	**22**	**23**	**24**	**25**	**26**	**27**	**28**	**29**	**30**
2	3	3	3	3	3	4	4	3	3

31	32	33	34	35	36	37	38	39	40
2	2	4	4	1	3	4	2	2	3
41	**42**	**43**	**44**	**45**	**46**	**47**	**48**	**49**	**50**
1	4	2	3	1	2	3	4	1	3
51	**52**	**53**	**54**	**55**	**56**	**57**	**58**	**59**	**60**
3	2	2	3	2	4	3	1	4	2
61	**62**	**63**	**64**	**65**	**66**	**67**	**68**	**69**	**70**
2	1	2	1	3	1	3	1	1	4
71	**72**	**73**	**74**	**75**	**76**	**77**	**78**	**79**	**80**
4	1	3	3	2	3	4	4	1	2
81	**82**	**83**	**84**	**85**	**86**	**87**	**88**	**89**	**90**
4	2	2	3	4	1	1	4	1	1
91	**92**	**93**	**94**	**95**	**96**	**97**	**98**	**99**	**100**
3	2	3	3	3	2	3	1	2	4

EXPLANATORY ANSWERS

1. Recreation theory was proposed by Moritz Lazarus and Patrick, who believed that play functions mainly as a means of relaxation and refreshment after hard work. According to this theory, individuals become physically and mentally tired after engaging in strenuous activities or routine labour. To overcome this fatigue, they seek recreational activities such as play, games, or leisure pursuits. These activities help restore energy, reduce stress, and bring back efficiency. Thus, play is not just for enjoyment but also for recharging the body and mind to maintain overall well-being.

2. The meaning of Recapitulation theory of Play is that through play children can let go of unnecessary instincts which are ingrained in us. This theory was proposed by G. Stanley Hall and is based on the idea that a child's development reflects the evolutionary stages of human history. According to this view, children express primitive instincts through play, such as hunting or fighting games. As they grow, these instincts gradually disappear. Play, therefore, helps children eliminate outdated and unnecessary behaviours that are no longer useful in modern life.

3. The International Olympic Committee (IOC) officially approved the updated Olympic motto in 2021 as "Citius, Altius, Fortius, Communiter." The original motto meant "Faster, Higher, Stronger," and the word "Communiter" was added to reflect unity and togetherness. It emphasizes that sports should promote cooperation among athletes and nations. This change was made to highlight the importance of solidarity, especially in challenging global times. The motto now encourages collective progress rather than just individual excellence.

4. In the 4 × 400 Meter Mixed Relay event, the order of legs is Male-Female-Male-Female. This sequence is commonly adopted to ensure a balanced competition between teams. The presence of both male and female runners makes this event unique and more strategic. Teams plan their runners carefully to maximize speed and performance. The order allows fair participation and smooth alternation of gender roles. This format has been standardized in international competitions, including the Olympics and World Championships.

5. Let's correctly match the contributors to Physical Education (List I) with their respective countries (List II):

A. **Franz Nachtegall → III. Denmark** – He is regarded as the father of Danish gymnastics and played a key role in introducing systematic physical training in Denmark.

B. **Per Henrik Ling → I. Sweden** – He developed the Swedish system of gymnastics and laid the foundation of scientific physical education in Sweden.

C. **Johan Bernhard Basedow → IV. Germany** – A German educational reformer who emphasized physical training as an essential part of holistic education.

D. **Galen → II. Greece** – A renowned Greek physician whose ideas greatly influenced physical culture, health, and anatomy in ancient Greece.

6. Let's correctly match the Philosophical Terms (List I) with their correct Explanations (List II):

A. **Meta Physics → II. An inquiry into the ultimate reality** – It deals with the nature of existence and the fundamental structure of reality.

B. **Axiology → III. Study of values and the nature of value judgement** – It focuses on ethics, morals, and value systems.

C. **Epistemology → IV. Exposition of truth** – It is concerned with the nature, source, and validity of knowledge.

D. **Aesthetics → I. Explores the nature of beauty, art and taste** – It studies how beauty and artistic expression are perceived and appreciated.

7. The "Female Athlete Triad" is a medical condition commonly seen in physically active women and athletes. It consists of three interrelated components that negatively affect health and performance. These include disordered eating, amenorrhea (absence of menstruation), and osteoporosis (low bone density). The condition mainly occurs due to inadequate calorie intake compared to energy expenditure. This imbalance affects hormonal levels, leading to menstrual disorders and weakened bones. Therefore, the correct combination representing the Female Athlete Triad is clearly identified below.

8. The basic functional unit of a skeletal muscle is responsible for muscle contraction and relaxation. It is the smallest segment of a muscle fiber that performs the contractile function. This unit contains actin and myosin filaments arranged in a specific pattern that allows muscles to shorten and produce movement. The repeated arrangement of these units gives muscles their striated appearance. Hence, the correct answer is the structural unit that directly controls contraction.

9. The direct source of energy for muscular contraction is Adenosine Triphosphate (ATP). During muscle activity, ATP breaks down into ADP and releases energy required for muscle fibers to contract. This energy powers the sliding mechanism of actin and myosin filaments. While glycogen and phosphocreatine help in producing ATP, ATP itself is the immediate energy source. Thus, muscles rely directly on ATP for movement.

10. The heart muscle requires a continuous and rich supply of oxygenated blood to function effectively. This blood supply is provided by the coronary arteries, which branch from the aorta and surround the heart. They deliver oxygen and nutrients essential for the contraction and relaxation of cardiac muscles. Any blockage in these arteries can lead to serious heart conditions. Therefore, they are the primary source of blood supply to the heart.

11. Cryotherapy is the therapeutic use of cold to reduce pain, swelling, and inflammation in injured tissues. However, certain medical conditions make the use of cryotherapy unsafe. Raynaud's disease, peripheral vascular disease, and ischemia are all contraindications because cold can further restrict blood flow and cause tissue damage. Hyperthermia, on

the other hand, refers to an abnormally high body temperature and is actually a condition where cold therapy can be helpful. Therefore, hyperthermia is NOT a contraindication for cryotherapy and can safely be treated using cold applications under proper supervision.

12. Let's correctly arrange the events of Sensory–Motor Integration in their proper physiological sequence:

D. A sensory stimulus is received by sensory receptors – The process begins when receptors detect a change in the internal or external environment.

C. The sensory action potential is transmitted along sensory neurons to CNS – The detected stimulus is carried as a nerve impulse to the central nervous system.

A. The CNS interprets the sensory information and reflexively initiates a motor response – The brain or spinal cord processes the information and decides on an appropriate response.

E. The action potential for the response is transmitted from CNS along alpha motor neurons – The motor command is sent from the CNS to the effector muscle.

B. The motor action potential is transmitted to muscle and response occurs – The muscle contracts and the final response is produced.

13. Let's correctly identify the health risks associated with high altitude training:

B. Pulmonary Edema – Due to reduced oxygen pressure, fluid can accumulate in the lungs causing High Altitude Pulmonary Edema (HAPE), leading to breathing difficulty.

D. Hypoxia – At high altitudes, the low availability of oxygen results in inadequate oxygen supply to body tissues, which can impair physical and mental performance.

E. Cerebral Edema – Swelling of the brain caused by lack of oxygen is known as High Altitude Cerebral Edema (HACE), a serious and life-threatening condition.

Hyperthermia is not associated with high altitude as temperatures are generally low, and frostbite is more related to extreme cold exposure rather than altitude itself in this context.

14. Let's identify the true causes of fatigue during physical activity:

A. Phospho Creatine depletion – When phospho-creatine stores are exhausted, immediate energy supply reduces, contributing to fatigue.

D. Glycogen depletion – The depletion of glycogen reserves reduces energy availability, leading to decreased performance and tiredness.

E. Accumulation of lactic acid – The build-up of lactic acid increases muscle acidity, causing discomfort and fatigue.

A decrease in hydrogen ion level and decrease in core body temperature are not causes of fatigue; rather, fatigue is linked to increased hydrogen ions and increased body temperature.

15. Let's correctly match the components with their respective locations:

A. Myelin Sheath → III. Axon – The myelin sheath is a fatty insulating layer that surrounds the axon and helps in faster transmission of nerve impulses.

B. Troponin and Tropomyosin → IV. Actin Filaments – These regulatory proteins are found on actin filaments and play a vital role in muscle contraction.

C. Basal Ganglia → II. Brain – The basal ganglia are groups of nuclei located in the brain and are involved in movement control and coordination.

D. Sarcolemma → I. Muscle cell – The sarcolemma is the cell membrane that encloses a muscle fiber and maintains its structure.

16. Let's correctly match the medical conditions with their explanations:

A. Bradycardia → I. Resting Heart Rate > 60 bpm – Bradycardia refers to an abnormally slow heart rate under resting conditions.

B. Atherosclerosis → IV. Progressive narrowing of Arteries – This condition occurs due to plaque buildup in arteries, reducing blood flow.

C. Ischemia → II. Temporary deficiency in blood supply in a particular body part – It occurs when blood flow is restricted, leading to oxygen shortage in tissues.

D. Arrhythmia → III. Irregular heart beat – This condition involves abnormal heart rhythm, either too fast, too slow, or uneven.

17. This question relates to the biomechanics of high jump and pole vault. During bar clearance, the athlete uses body positioning techniques such as the Fosbury Flop to manipulate the path of the centre of mass. By arching the body over the bar, the athlete can allow different body parts to pass over while the centre of mass travels below the bar. This makes the clearance more efficient and requires less vertical force. Therefore, a successful clearance does not always require the centre of mass to rise above the height of the bar. This principle explains how elite jumpers clear remarkably high bars with optimal technique.

18. This question is based on the principles of projectile motion. When an object is projected from a height greater than the landing point, the angle required for maximum horizontal distance changes. In such a case, the optimum projection angle becomes less than 45 degrees, unlike when projected from ground level. This is because gravity acts over a longer descending phase, allowing the object to travel further horizontally at a lower angle. Hence, the projection angle is smaller compared to ground-level projection.

19. This question is solved using the pressure formula in mathematical form:

$$\text{Pressure} = \frac{\text{Force}}{\text{Area}}$$

Given:

Force (Weight) = 556 N

For Spike Heel:

$$P_1 = \frac{556}{4} = 139 \text{ N/cm}^2$$

For Court Shoe:

$$P_2 = \frac{556}{175} = 3.18 \text{ N/cm}^2$$

This clearly shows that the spike heel produces much more pressure due to its smaller surface area, while the court shoe distributes the force over a large area resulting in lower pressure.

20. This question is solved using the mathematical formula for average acceleration:

$$a = \frac{v - u}{t}$$

Where

a = acceleration

v = final velocity = 5.9 m/s

u = initial velocity = 0 m/s (runner starts from rest)

t = time = 1.8 s

Substituting the values:

$$a = \frac{5.9 - 0}{1.8}$$

$$a = \frac{5.9}{1.8} = 3.27 \approx 3.3 \text{ m/s}^2$$

This shows that the runner's average acceleration during the first 10 meters is approximately 3.3 m/s^2.

21. Let's correctly identify the factors that define a vector quantity:

B. Magnitude – Every vector must have a definite size or amount, which indicates how large the quantity is.

D. Direction – A vector always acts in a specific direction, which distinguishes it from scalar quantities.

E. Displacement – Displacement is a vector quantity because it represents change in position along with direction.

Speed and distance are scalars as they only represent quantity without direction. Therefore, the correct defining properties of a vector are magnitude, direction, and displacement.

22. Let's identify the factors that influence rolling friction:

A. Normal reaction force – Greater normal force increases contact pressure and affects rolling resistance.

C. Radius of rolling object – The size of the rolling body influences friction, as larger radii generally reduce resistance.

E. Deformation of the surfaces and their coefficient of friction – Surface compression and frictional properties play a major role in determining rolling friction.

Coefficient of restitution and centripetal/centrifugal forces do not directly affect rolling friction. Hence, the correct influencing factors are listed below.

23. Let's correctly identify the important characteristics of force:

B. Point of application – This refers to the exact point on the body where the force is applied, which greatly affects the outcome of the force.

C. Line of application – Also known as the line of action, it indicates the direction along which the force acts through the point of application.

E. Force sense – This describes the direction in which the force is acting (push or pull), which is essential in determining its effect.

Centre of gravity and base of support are concepts related to stability, not direct characteristics of force. Therefore, the correct characteristics of force are listed below.

24. Let's correctly match the visual and mechanical concepts with their appropriate terms:

A. Objects seem bigger or smaller as they move towards or away from the camera → III. Perspective error – This occurs because the apparent size of an object changes based on its distance from the observer or camera, which is a natural effect of perspective projection.

B. Objects size and shape seem to change as it moves across the camera → IV. Parallax error – This results from the apparent shift in position of an object when viewed from different angles or lines of sight.

C. Total Inertia → I. Parallel axes theorem – This theorem is used to determine the total moment of inertia of a body when the axis of rotation is shifted from the centre of mass.

D. Distribution of mass relative to the centre of rotation → II. Radius of gyration – It represents how the mass of a body is spread around its axis of rotation.

25. Let's correctly match the physical movements with their correct definitions:

A. Walking → I. Propelling oneself forward by alternatively setting each foot on the ground – Movement occurs in a steady, rhythmic manner.

B. Running → IV. Propelling oneself forward by moving both feet rapidly and continuously – Both feet leave the ground during running.

C. Jumping → II. Propelling oneself upward off the ground by using muscles in own legs – Movement is vertical and powered by leg muscles.

D. Throwing → III. Propelling an object using one's arm or hand – Force is applied to move an external object.

26. A sports psychologist focuses on the mental development and well-being of athletes to improve their performance and overall growth. Their role includes enhancing confidence, concentration, motivation, and emotional control. They work with athletes not only when problems arise but also to prevent issues and build strong mental skills. They do not aim to win at any cost or prescribe medication, as their focus is psychological training. The ultimate goal is to help every sportsperson achieve their maximum potential.

27. The hypothesis that exercise encourages and generates positive thoughts and feelings that counteract negative mood states is known as the Cognitive Behavioral Hypothesis. This hypothesis proposes that physical activity improves mood by positively influencing cognitive processes and emotional responses. Exercise develops a sense of achievement, self-confidence, mastery, and self-efficacy in individuals. These positive experiences promote constructive self-talk and better emotional control. As a result, negative moods such as stress, anxiety, and depression are effectively reduced through improved thinking patterns.

28. Acculturation refers to the process of adapting to and understanding different cultures while promoting social harmony. It involves viewing the world through a multicultural perspective to encourage unity and cooperation among diverse groups. This concept helps individuals integrate and respect cultural differences. It plays a vital role in strengthening group cohesion in multicultural environments.

29. Catastrophe Theory states that performance does not decline gradually when arousal exceeds the optimal level. Instead, performance drops sharply and suddenly, especially when anxiety is also high. This explains why athletes sometimes fail dramatically under extreme pressure. The theory highlights the dangerous effects of excessive stress on performance.

30. Let's correctly arrange the sequence as per Harter's theory of achievement motivation leading to youth sports dropout:

C. Unsuccessful performance – The process begins when the young athlete repeatedly fails to perform successfully.

D. Negative Affects – These failures lead to negative emotions such as frustration, anxiety, and low self-esteem.

E. Low competence motivation – The athlete begins to feel incapable and loses belief in their own abilities.

A. Fewer mastery attempts – Due to low motivation and confidence, the athlete makes fewer efforts to improve or master skills.

B. Dropout – Finally, the continuous negative cycle results in complete withdrawal from sports participation.

31. Let's correctly arrange the sequence of Cognitive Affective Processing System (CAPS) proposed by Smith:

C. Individual personality interacts with situation – The process starts when a person's personality traits respond to a specific situation.

A. Stimuli are encoded and represented in memory – The individual processes the information and stores it mentally.

D. Pre-determined expectations and beliefs confer meaning on events – Personal beliefs and past experiences shape interpretation of the situation.

E. Emotions influence behaviour – These interpretations generate emotional responses that affect actions.

B. Competencies and self-regulation skills determine behaviour – Finally, behavioural response is controlled by one's skills and ability to regulate themselves.

32. Let's correctly identify the key words from the definition of personality:

A. Stable – Personality reflects consistent or stable patterns of behaviour over time.

B. Unique – It highlights how one person's behaviour differs from others, making each individual distinct.

C. Group – The definition mentions differences especially in social situations, which involve groups of people.

Competition and training are not core keywords in the given definition of personality. Therefore, the correct key terms are stable, unique, and group.

33. Let's identify the important concerns of Sports Psychologists for superior athletic performance:

B. Self Control – Helps athletes regulate emotions and behaviour during pressure situations.

C. Motivation – Drives athletes to train consistently and pursue excellence.

D. Confidence – Enables athletes to believe in their abilities and perform at their best.

Strength and endurance are mainly physical components, not primary psychological concerns. Therefore, the correct psychological factors are listed below.

34. Let's correctly match the concepts with their related fields in Sports Psychology:

A. Task cohesion → IV. Group Dynamics – Task cohesion refers to the degree to which team members work together to achieve common goals, which is a core element of group dynamics.

B. Trait → III. Personality – A trait is a stable characteristic or quality that forms an important part of an individual's personality.

C. Bruce Ogilvie → I. Applied Sports Psychology – He is regarded as one of the pioneers of applied sports psychology and contributed significantly to its development.

D. Client Consent → II. Ethics – Client consent is a fundamental ethical requirement in professional psychological practice.

35. Let's correctly match the psychological concepts with their relevant categories:

A. Imagery → IV. Psychological Skill Training – Imagery is a mental technique used to enhance performance and is a key component of psychological skill training.

B. Hostile and Instrumental → III. Aggression – These are two recognized forms of aggression seen in sports behaviour.

C. Zone of Optimal Functioning (ZoF) → II. Anxiety – This concept explains the ideal level of anxiety at which an athlete performs best.

D. Introjected Regulation → I. Motivation – This type of regulation is linked to internalised motivation driven by feelings of guilt or pressure.

36. Adapted Physical Education is the branch of physical education specifically designed to meet the needs of individuals with disabilities. It focuses on modifying physical activities, teaching methods, and equipment so that persons with physical, intellectual, or sensory impairments can participate safely and effectively. This discipline prepares teachers and professionals to develop inclusive programs that enhance motor skills, physical fitness, and social development. The goal is to provide equal opportunities for participation in physical activities despite limitations. Therefore, this field directly concerns preparing teachers to serve individuals with disabilities.

37. According to the National Education Policy (NEP) 2020, the 5-3-3-4 structure represents a new school curriculum framework designed to support holistic development. This includes the Foundation Stage (5 years), Preparatory Stage (3 years), Middle Stage (3 years), and Secondary Stage (4 years). The framework focuses on age-appropriate learning, conceptual understanding, and skill development. It aims to replace the old 10+2 system with a more flexible and learner-centric approach. Hence, the correct sequence of stages is clearly identified.

38. In India, the regulation and recognition of Physical Education Teacher Education programs are handled by the National Council for Teacher Education (NCTE). This statutory body ensures proper standards, quality, and uniformity in teacher education across the country. It approves institutions, frames norms, and monitors the functioning of teacher training programs, including B.P.Ed and M.P.Ed courses. Other bodies like AICTE, NAAC, and UGC have different roles, but the specific authority for teacher education lies with NCTE. Therefore, the correct regulatory organization is NCTE.

39. According to Muska Mosston's Anatomy of Teaching Styles, the Guided Discovery style involves a shared decision-making process between teacher and students. In this style, the teacher presents a sequence of questions or problems, and the students discover the correct responses through logical thinking. The teacher guides the learning process, while students actively participate in finding solutions. This makes it neither fully teacher-centered nor entirely student-centered but a balanced combination of the two. Hence, Guided Discovery reflects a combined approach.

40. Let's correctly arrange the cognitive domain of learning in ascending order of complexity as suggested by Bloom:

C. Remembering – The most basic level, involving recall of facts and information.

A. Understanding – Comprehending the meaning of learned material and interpreting it.

D. Application – Using the acquired knowledge in practical or real-life situations.

B. Analysis – Breaking information into parts to understand structure and relationships.

E. Evaluation – Making judgments based on criteria and evidence.

This sequence represents the progression from simple to complex mental processes.

41. Let's correctly arrange the steps involved in curriculum construction in appropriate sequence:

A. Understanding of Education Philosophy and Policies – The process begins with clarity about the guiding principles and goals of education.

E. Formulating objectives – Specific aims and outcomes of the curriculum are then defined.

B. Determining age-based needs of children – Learners' developmental needs are considered to make the curriculum relevant.

D. Selection of appropriate activities – Suitable content and learning experiences are chosen to meet objectives.

C. Evaluation of program and feedback – Finally, the curriculum is assessed and improved through feedback.

This sequence ensures systematic and effective curriculum planning.

42. Let's correctly identify the objectives of Physical Education at the foundation stage of School Physical Education Program:

A. Development of Spatial Awareness – Helps children understand body positioning and movement in space.

B. Development of Gross Motor Skills – Focuses on large muscle activities such as running, jumping, and balancing.

C. Development of Fine Motor Skills – Enhances control of smaller muscles needed for precise movements.

Leadership skills and sports-specific skills are more appropriate for higher stages of development, not the foundation stage. Therefore, the correct objectives are spatial awareness, gross motor skills, and fine motor skills.

43. Let's identify what a professional preparation program should provide:

A. Opportunities to think about the proper justification for the profession – Encourages critical thinking and understanding of professional purpose.

B. Devotion for the profession – Builds commitment and dedication among professionals.

E. Loyalty for the profession – Strengthens ethical responsibility and professional integrity.

Incentives and concern of the state are not core elements of professional preparation, as the focus is on developing professional values and attitudes. Hence, the most appropriate components are listed below.

44. Let's correctly match the Physical Education institutions with their respective year of establishment:

A. L.C.P.E, Gwalior → III. 1957 – The Lakshmibai College of Physical Education was established in 1957 and is one of the premier institutions in physical education in India.

B. H.V.P.M, Amravati → I. 1914 – Hanuman Vyayam Prasarak Mandal was founded in 1914 and played a major role in promoting indigenous physical culture.

C. National Sports University, Imphal → IV. 2018 – This university was established in 2018 as India's first National Sports University to strengthen sports education and research.

D. Y.M.C.A Madras → II. 1920 – YMCA Madras was founded in 1920 and contributed significantly to physical education and sports development in South India.

45. While giving first aid for burns, certain actions must be avoided as they can worsen the injury. Applying ice directly to a burn can cause further tissue damage and delay healing because extreme cold restricts blood flow and harms sensitive skin. Removing restricted items, covering the burn with a clean cloth, and providing pain relief medication are all appropriate first-aid measures when done correctly. The correct burn care focuses on cooling with running water, protecting the area, and preventing infection. Therefore, applying ice is the action that should be avoided.

46. The School Health Committee has laid down specific guidelines for the Mid-day Meal program to ensure proper nutrition for school children. The meal should be provided on a "No Profit No Loss" basis and should supply one-third of the daily calorie requirement along with half of the daily protein requirement. These measures help promote balanced growth and development in children. However, providing an energy drink daily is not included in the recommendations, as emphasis is on wholesome, nutritious food rather than commercial beverages.

47. Hereditary disorders are conditions that are passed from parents to children through genes. Thalassaemias, Haemophilia, and Sickle Cell Anaemia are all genetic blood disorders inherited from family lineage. Ascariasis, on the other hand, is a parasitic infection caused by roundworms and is spread through contaminated food or water, not through heredity. Therefore, it is not a hereditary disease.

48. The assessment of obesity is carried out using various body measurement indices that help determine body fat and weight status. Body Mass Index (BMI) is the most commonly used index to evaluate obesity by comparing weight and height. The Ponderal Index and Brocca Index are also used to assess body composition and ideal body weight. However, the Relative Autonomy Index is a psychological measure used in motivation studies and has no connection with body weight or obesity assessment. Therefore, it is not used for evaluating obesity.

49. Let's correctly arrange the basic steps involved in conducting a Randomized Controlled Trial (RCT) for treatment and disease prevention:

C. Drawing up a protocol – The process begins with preparing a detailed research plan outlining objectives and methodology.

D. Selecting reference and population for trial – Suitable participants and control groups are chosen for the study.

A. Randomization – Participants are randomly assigned to experimental and control groups.

B. Manipulation or Intervention – The treatment or preventive measure is applied to the experimental group.

E. Follow-up and assessment of outcome – Finally, results are observed, recorded, and analyzed over time.

50. Let's correctly arrange the main steps of Health Education Planning in an appropriate sequence:

A. Collecting information and identifying the problem – The planning process begins with gathering data, identifying health needs, and defining the problem to be addressed.

C. Deciding priorities and setting goals and objectives – Based on the identified problems, priorities are fixed and clear objectives are formulated.

B. **Assessment of resources** – Available resources such as manpower, funds, materials, and community support are evaluated to ensure feasibility.

E. **Preparing and implementing plan of action** – Suitable strategies and activities are designed and the plan is put into practice.

D. **Monitoring and evaluating the program** – The final step involves tracking progress and assessing effectiveness for future improvement.

51. Let's identify the diseases that are zoonotic in nature:

A. **Rabies** – A viral disease transmitted from animals to humans through bites or saliva.

B. **Anthrax** – A bacterial disease that spreads from infected animals or animal products to humans.

D. **Plague** – A serious infection transmitted through fleas carried by rodents and other animals.

Influenza and typhoid are primarily human-to-human or water-borne diseases, not strictly zoonotic in this context. Therefore, the correct zoonotic diseases are listed below.

52. Let's correctly identify the water-borne diseases:

A. **Hepatitis A** – A viral infection transmitted through contaminated water and food, commonly linked to poor sanitation.

C. **Amoebiasis** – Caused by Entamoeba histolytica, it spreads through consumption of contaminated water.

D. **Typhoid** – A bacterial disease spread through unsafe drinking water and contaminated food.

Bronchitis and emphysema are respiratory diseases and are not transmitted through water. Therefore, the correct water-borne diseases are listed below.

53. Let's correctly match the Health Programs with their Year of Launch:

A. **Swachh Bharat Abhiyan → II. 2014** – Launched to promote cleanliness, sanitation, and hygiene across India.

B. **National AIDS Control Program → IV. 1987** – Initiated to prevent and control the spread of HIV/AIDS in India.

C. **Ayushman Bharat Programme → I. 2018** – Introduced as a major health insurance and wellness scheme for the poor.

D. **National Malaria Control Program → III. 1953** – Started to control and reduce malaria cases in the country.

54. Orientation ability refers to the capacity of an individual to determine and adjust the position and movement of the body in time and space in relation to a specific field of action. It helps a person understand where their body is in relation to objects, opponents, or surroundings. This ability is especially important in sports that require quick directional changes, spatial awareness, and precise positioning. Hence, the correct term describing this skill is orientation ability.

55. Rate of Force Development (RFD) refers to how quickly an individual can produce maximum force, and it is commonly used as an index of explosive strength. It is crucial in activities like sprinting, jumping, and throwing where rapid force production is required. A higher RFD indicates better explosive power. Therefore, the correct term associated with this definition is Rate of Force Development.

56. The training load represents the total work performed by an athlete during a training session. It depends on:

- Intensity → expressed as percentage of 1RM (% of 1RM)
- Volume → expressed as number of sets and repetitions

Hence, the accepted mathematical expression for the training load in this question is:

$$\text{Training Load} = \left(\frac{\%\text{ of 1RM}}{\text{Number of Repetitions}}\right) \times \text{Sets}$$

This formula shows that training load increases when:

- the intensity (% of 1RM) increases
- the number of sets increases

and it is adjusted relative to the number of repetitions performed.

Therefore, this equation best represents how coaches record and monitor workload during resistance training.

57. Contrast Training is a method where the athlete performs exercises with added resistance, followed by assisted movements, and then under normal conditions. This combination enhances neuromuscular efficiency and improves speed and power by stimulating the muscles in different ways. It is commonly used to develop explosive strength and performance. Hence, the training method described in the question is contrast training.

58. Let's correctly arrange the sequential order of learning a technique:

E. Unconscious incompetence – The learner is unaware of their lack of skill or knowledge.

B. Conscious incompetence – The learner becomes aware of their inability and realizes the need for improvement.

A. Conscious competence – The learner can perform the skill correctly but only with deliberate effort and focus.

D. Unconscious competence – The skill is performed automatically without conscious thought.

C. Reflective competence – The learner can perform the skill and also analyze, refine, and improve it through reflection.

59. Let's correctly arrange the anatomical adaptation phases of periodization of strength:

D. Maximum Strength Phase – This phase focuses on developing absolute strength and forms the foundation for higher-level performance.

B. Conversion to Specific Strength Phase – The general strength developed is converted into power and sport-specific strength patterns.

A. Maintenance Phase – Strength levels are preserved during the competitive period while emphasis shifts to performance.

E. Cessation Phase – Training load is significantly reduced or temporarily stopped, usually after competition.

C. Compensation Phase – The body enters a recovery and regeneration phase, allowing physical and psychological restoration before the next cycle.

60. Let's correctly identify the components used to calculate training load:

A. Intensity of Load – Refers to the level of effort or difficulty, often expressed as % of 1RM or training zone.

B. Density of Load – Indicates the relationship between work and rest periods during training.

D. Frequency of Load – Represents how often the training sessions are performed within a given time period.

Training and competition, and training and performance are not direct components used in calculating training load. Therefore, the correct components are intensity, density, and frequency.

61. Let's correctly match the training load components with their respective formulas:

A. Relative Density →

III. $\frac{\text{Absolute Volume} \times 100}{\text{Relative Volume}}$

This formula expresses how much work is performed in relation to the total volume, showing the density of training.

B. Index of Overall Demand →

II. $\frac{\text{OI} \times \text{AD} \times \text{AV}}{10,000}$

This formula combines overall intensity, absolute duration, and absolute volume to calculate total training demand.

C. Overall Intensity →

I. $\frac{\sum(\text{Partial Intensity} \times \text{Volume of exercises})}{\sum(\text{Volume of exercises})}$

This gives the average intensity of the entire training session.

D. Partial Intensity → IV. $\frac{HR_p \times 100}{HR_{max}}$

This represents exercise intensity based on heart rate as a percentage of maximum heart rate.

These formulas accurately describe how training load and intensity values are measured and calculated.

62. Interval Estimate refers to a range of values within which the population parameter is expected to lie with a certain level of confidence. It provides lower and upper limits and expresses the uncertainty of an estimate more effectively than a single value. This is commonly used in inferential statistics to make population predictions based on sample data. Hence, it best fits the given definition.

63. In research methodology, when a study is designed so that one component (either quantitative or qualitative) is conducted first and the other follows afterward, it is referred to as a Sequential Mixed Method. In this approach, the findings of the first phase help inform, expand, or refine the second phase. This allows researchers to explore a topic more deeply by building one type of data upon the other in a structured sequence. Unlike parallel or concurrent methods, the components do not occur at the same time. Therefore, the correct term for this type of research design is Sequential Mixed Method.

64. Establishing the age or authorship of historical documents is done through External Criticism. This method focuses on verifying the authenticity of a document by examining its origin, date, authorship, handwriting, and material used. It ensures that the document is genuine before analyzing its content. Internal criticism, on the other hand, deals with the accuracy and credibility of the information within the document. Hence, the process of determining age or authorship clearly falls under external criticism.

65. Proximity Error refers to the tendency of a rater to judge behaviours as more similar when they appear close together on a rating scale. This occurs because the rater subconsciously links adjacent traits or performances, reducing accurate differentiation. As a result, distinct behaviours may receive almost identical ratings simply due to their closeness on the scale. This psychological bias affects the objectivity and reliability of evaluation. Therefore, the error described in the question is known as Proximity Error.

66. Let's correctly arrange the steps involved in developing skills in computer data analysis:

C. **Data Organisation and coding** – Raw data is first arranged, classified, and coded systematically.

A. **Storing the data in the computer** – The organized data is then entered and saved in the computer system.

B. **Selection of appropriate software package** – Suitable statistical software is chosen for analysis.

D. **Selection of appropriate statistical measures/techniques** – Proper statistical tools are selected based on the nature of data.

E. **Execution of the computer program** – Finally, the program is run to analyze and generate results.

This sequence ensures efficient and accurate data processing.

67. Let's correctly identify the sequential order of steps for developing a sample design:

C. **Type of Universe & Sampling Unit** – The process begins by clearly defining the population and identifying the unit from which samples will be selected.

E. **Source list & Size of Sample** – Next, a proper sampling frame (source list) is prepared and the size of the sample is determined.

A. **Parameters of Interest** – The key variables or characteristics to be measured in the study are then identified.

B. **Budgetary Constraint** – Financial limitations are considered to ensure the design is practical and feasible.

D. **Sampling Procedure** – Finally, the appropriate method of sampling is selected and applied.

This order ensures a logical and systematic approach to sample design.

68. Let's identify the terms associated with cohort studies:

A. **Follow-up studies** – Cohort studies involve observing a group over a period of time to track outcomes.

C. **Prospective studies** – They often move forward in time, examining how exposure affects future outcomes.

E. **Longitudinal studies** – Cohort studies collect data repeatedly over extended periods, making them longitudinal in nature.

Exploratory and case studies are different research designs and are not specifically characteristic of cohort studies.

69. Let's identify the designs that are considered part of a True Experimental Design:

A. **Randomized Group Design** – This design uses random assignment of subjects into experimental and control groups, which is a core feature of true experimental research.

D. **Pretest-Posttest Randomized Group Design** – In this design, participants are randomly assigned and tested both before and after the experiment, ensuring strong internal validity.

E. **Solomon Four Group Design** – This advanced true experimental design combines pretesting and randomization in four groups to control for testing effects.

One-Group Pre-Test Post-Test Design and Non-Equivalent Control Group Design are quasi-experimental designs because they lack proper randomization or control.

70. Let's correctly match the purpose of comparison with the appropriate statistical tests:

A. **Comparison of two independent data points → III. Chi-Square & Mann-Whitney**

These tests are used when two separate and independent groups are being compared.

B. **Comparison of two non-independent data points → IV. Wilcoxon test & Sign test**

These are applied when the same subjects are measured twice or when data sets are related.

C. **Comparison of more than two independent data points for one experimental variable → I. Chi-Square & Kruskal-Wallis**

These tests are suitable for comparing three or more independent groups.

D. **Comparison of more than two non-independent data points for one experimental variable → II. Cochran Q Test & Friedman analysis of variance**

These are used when multiple related or repeated measures are compared.

This matching correctly aligns each research purpose with the suitable statistical method.

71. Buck Shot Theory states that if a large number of related tests are administered, some of them will naturally measure the specific skill in question due to overlapping characteristics. This theory compares skill testing to firing a shotgun, where multiple pellets increase the chance of hitting the target. It suggests that broad testing increases the probability of accurately assessing a particular motor skill. The theory emphasizes quantity and variety of tests rather than precision in a single test.

72. Physical educators McCoy and Young (1954) referred to "agility that does not involve running" as Dynamic Flexibility. This term describes the ability to move joints and muscles smoothly and efficiently through their full range of motion during active movement without rapid locomotion. It involves controlled, coordinated body movements such as twisting, bending, or stretching while maintaining balance and posture. Unlike running-based agility, this focuses on fluid body coordination and mobility in changing positions. Therefore, the correct term for this concept is Dynamic Flexibility.

73. McCloy was the first to propose a system for classifying students based on their age and body size to form homogeneous groups for instruction. This system aimed to improve teaching effectiveness by grouping students with similar physical characteristics. It allowed better planning of physical activities and reduced performance disparities among students. His contribution played a significant role in developing organized physical education instruction methods.

74. The test designed to judge the playing ability of potential varsity basketball players using peer evaluations is the Mitchell Balloting Scale. This scale relies on teammates' judgments to evaluate a player's overall basketball ability, making it distinctly different from skill-based performance tests such as shooting or dribbling. Peer evaluation is the core feature of the Mitchell Balloting Scale, which aims to identify players with strong game sense, team value, and overall playing ability.

75. Let's correctly arrange the steps that must be followed in selecting a published test:

C. Defining the needs of testing – The process begins by clearly stating the objectives, target group, and testing requirements.

B. Narrowing the choice – Based on these needs, the range of possible tests is reduced to a manageable list.

A. Locating suitable and appropriate test – Specific tests are then searched from professional sources and literature that fit the narrowed criteria.

E. Reviewing test material – The manuals, sample items, and technical details of the selected tests are carefully examined.

D. Using a test evaluation form – Finally, a structured evaluation form is used to judge the test in terms of validity, reliability, and practicality.

76. Let's correctly arrange the sequential order of duties after testing:

B. Collecting score cards – The process begins by gathering all the recorded performance data from participants.

A. Converting raw scores – These raw scores are then transformed into standard or meaningful scores for evaluation.

E. Comparing test results with norms and constructing a profile – The converted scores are compared with established norms to form an individual performance profile.

C. Constructing norms and interpreting results – Based on comparison, results are analyzed and interpreted to draw conclusions.

D. Using results and the follow-up – Finally, the results are applied for decision-making and necessary follow-up actions are taken.

77. Let's identify the test items measured by the Hicks Badminton Test:

B. Clear – Measures the player's ability to hit the shuttle deep into the opponent's court with accuracy.

D. Smash – Evaluates the power and effectiveness of attacking shots.

E. Strategy – Assesses the player's tactical awareness and ability to apply game plans during play.

Drop and Lob are not included as test items in the Hicks Badminton Test. Therefore, the correct components measured are Clear, Smash, and Strategy.

78. Let's identify the components involved in the process of evaluation:

A. Collecting suitable data – Relevant and accurate information is gathered for assessment.

B. Judging the values of data – The collected data is analyzed and its worth or significance is determined.

D. Making decision based on data – Final decisions are taken based on the interpretation of the evaluated data.

Generalisation and establishing results are not the core steps in evaluation. Therefore, the correct components are collecting data, judging its value, and making decisions.

79. Let's identify the major categories used in the ETS Taxonomy:

A. Remembering – Refers to the ability to recall facts, terms, and basic information from memory.

C. Understanding – Involves comprehending the meaning of information and interpreting concepts beyond simple recall.

E. Thinking – Represents higher-order mental processes such as reasoning, analysis, evaluation, and problem-solving.

Application and Knowledge are more closely aligned with other taxonomic models and are not listed as the core categories in ETS taxonomy. Therefore, the correct major categories are Remembering, Understanding, and Thinking.

80. Let's correctly match the tests with their respective number of test items:

A. Barrow Motor Ability Test → III. 03

This test includes three items: standing broad jump, zig-zag run, and medicine ball put.

B. Schilling Body Coordination Test → I. 04

It comprises four coordination items such as walking backward on a balance beam and two-legged jumping.

C. AAPHER Youth Fitness Test → II. 07

This test includes seven items such as pull-ups, sit-ups, shuttle run, standing broad jump, 50-yard dash, softball throw, and 600-yard run/walk.

D. North Carolina Motor Fitness Battery → IV. 05

This battery contains five motor fitness items including sit-ups, side stepping, squat thrusts, broad jump, and pull-ups (for boys).

Thus, the correct matching aligns with the given test structures and item counts.

81. The term "Nuts and Bolts" of a sport event refers to the core operational activities that ensure the smooth execution of the competition. This includes scheduling matches, arranging officials, managing equipment, ensuring rule enforcement, coordinating venues, and handling all on-field procedures. These technical and functional aspects form the backbone of the event and directly affect its success. Among the given options, Tournament Operation best represents these essential operational functions that keep the event running effectively.

82. The financial success of an organization is determined by the difference between its total revenue and total expenditure. When revenue exceeds expenditure, the organization is said to have made a profit. Profit indicates efficient financial management and organizational growth. Debt, equity, and assets represent other financial terms but do not specifically describe the net financial gain. Therefore, the correct term for this difference is profit.

83. The dimension of sports promotion that involves working with businesses to generate additional revenue for sports programmes is the Corporate Partner. Corporate partners contribute through sponsorships, advertising, endorsements, and strategic collaborations that provide financial support and enhance the visibility of sports events. This relationship helps in funding infrastructure, promoting events, and ensuring sustainability of sports programmes. Managers, athletes, and governing bodies play important roles, but direct revenue generation through business collaboration is primarily the responsibility of corporate partners.

84. Let's correctly arrange the stages of sports event planning in their proper sequence:

B. Determine aim and objective – The planning process starts by clearly defining what the event intends to achieve.

D. **Formulate Policy** – Guidelines and operational policies are then established to provide direction.

E. **Compile Budget** – Financial planning is carried out to estimate expenses and resources.

A. **Detail plan and time scale** – A detailed action plan and scheduling timeline are prepared.

C. **Establish control system** – Finally, monitoring and control mechanisms are developed to ensure smooth execution.

This logical progression ensures effective and systematic event planning.

85. Let's correctly arrange the sequence of Human Resource Management in a sports organization:

D. **Planning** – The process begins by identifying manpower needs and determining the type and number of personnel required.

A. **Recruitment** – Suitable candidates are then attracted through various recruitment methods.

C. **Selection and Screening** – Applicants are evaluated, shortlisted, and the most suitable individuals are selected.

E. **Orientation and Induction** – Newly selected staff are introduced to the organization, its policies, and work environment.

B. **Training and Development** – Finally, employees are provided with skill enhancement and professional development opportunities.

This sequence ensures systematic and effective management of human resources in sports organizations.

86. Let's identify the three broad functions of media in society:

B. **Information** – Media provides news and updates that keep the public informed about current events and important issues.

D. **Education** – It plays a key role in spreading knowledge and creating awareness through informative content.

E. **Entertainment** – Media offers recreation and relaxation through sports, films, music, and shows.

Competition and relationship are not recognized as core functions of media. Therefore, the correct functions are Information, Education, and Entertainment.

87. Let's identify the primary dimensions of organisational structure:

B. **Departmentalisation** – Refers to grouping activities and responsibilities into organized units or departments.

C. **Work Specialisation** – Involves dividing work into specific tasks to improve efficiency and expertise.

D. **Span of Control** – Indicates the number of employees a manager can effectively supervise.

Marketing and Advertising are operational activities, not structural dimensions. Hence, the correct primary dimensions are departmentalisation, work specialisation, and span of control.

88. Let's identify the key aspects of directing an effective Physical Education and Sports Program:

A. **Defined chain of commands** – Ensures clear flow of authority and communication within the organization.

C. **Clarity of delegation** – Helps in assigning duties systematically so everyone understands their role.

E. **Fixed responsibilities** – Specifies accountability and ensures smooth coordination of activities.

Authoritarian approach and advertising are not essential principles of effective program direction. Therefore, the correct aspects include defined command structure, clear delegation, and fixed responsibilities.

89. Let's correctly match List-I with List-II:

A. **Assigning responsibilities → III. Directing**

This involves guiding and instructing individuals by allocating duties and tasks.

B. **Reporting system → IV. Controlling**
Reporting helps in monitoring performance and ensuring activities follow planned standards.

C. **Staffing → I. Recruitment**
Staffing includes the process of recruiting and appointing suitable personnel.

D. **Forecasting → II. Planning**
Forecasting predicts future needs and conditions, forming the basis of planning.

90. Let's correctly match List-I with List-II:

A. **Indoor Sports Facility → IV. Arena**
An arena is a structured indoor space designed for sports activities.

B. **Financial Management → III. Auditing**
Auditing ensures proper financial control and accountability.

C. **Public Relations → II. Image**
Public relations focuses on building and maintaining the organization's image.

D. **Personnel Management → I. Appraisal**
Appraisal is used to evaluate employee performance.

91. Mental training mainly emphasizes strengthening the athlete's ability to cope with pressure, maintain focus, manage stress, and stay psychologically strong during competition. These factors together contribute to enhancing an athlete's mental strength and emotional stability. The paragraph repeatedly highlights the importance of developing the psychological toughness needed for peak performance. Therefore, the primary focus is mental resilience.

92. Visualization is described in the passage as imagining oneself executing skills perfectly before actual competition. This mental rehearsal prepares athletes for real situations and reduces anxiety. Hence, the technique that involves mental rehearsal of performance is visualization.

93. Mindfulness allows athletes to remain mentally present and fully focused on the task at hand. It helps reduce distractions and improves concentration during competition and training. Therefore, its primary benefit is helping athletes stay in the present and focused.

94. Relaxation strategies listed in the passage include progressive relaxation, deep breathing, and meditation. Among the given options, deep breathing clearly belongs to this category.

95. The passage explains that mental training is overshadowed by physical training because it is not as easily observable. Unlike physical exercises, mental techniques are internal and less visible to others. Therefore, it often remains unnoticed.

96. The passage clearly states that Inclusive Physical Education aims to provide equal access and meaningful participation to all students, irrespective of their physical abilities or disabilities. It focuses on ensuring that every student can actively engage in physical education programs without discrimination. Therefore, the main objective is inclusion and equal participation for all.

97. The paragraph highlights that peer support and collaboration help students work together, learn from one another, and build a sense of community. This cooperative interaction promotes inclusivity and enhances the learning environment. Therefore, fostering peer support and collaboration is a core element of IPE.

98. Teachers adapt activities and apply flexible strategies to meet the diverse needs of students. This ensures that all students, including those with mobility challenges, can participate meaningfully. Hence, modifying activities and using adaptive strategies is the correct approach.

99. IPE promotes empathy, respect, understanding, and teamwork among students by encouraging interaction and cooperation. This enriches the overall learning experience and strengthens social bonds. Therefore, fostering empathy and teamwork is the key benefit.

100. The passage explains that IPE supports lifelong well-being by encouraging positive attitudes towards physical activity and removing barriers associated with disabilities. This promotes holistic development and healthy living habits. Therefore, it aligns with the goal of lifelong well-being.

YOUR SPACE

Choose the ***correct*** answer from the options given below:

	(*a*)	(*b*)	(*c*)	(*d*)
A.	IV	I	II	III
B.	I	II	III	IV
C.	II	IV	I	III
D.	IV	II	III	I

7. Arrange in ascending order of there establishment:

(*a*) Christian College of Physical Education, Lucknow

(*b*) HVPM, Amrawati

(*c*) YMCA, Madras

(*d*) LCPE, Gwalior

Choose the ***correct*** answer from the options given below:

A. (*a*), (*d*), (*c*), (*b*)

B. (*b*), (*c*), (*a*), (*d*)

C. (*c*), (*a*), (*b*), (*d*)

D. (*d*), (*c*), (*a*), (*b*)

8. Oxford method is associated with:

A. High resistance method

B. Circuit training

C. Progressive - Regressive

D. Decreasing Resistance - Constant repetitions

9. Match the List-I with List-II.

List-I (Vaccine)	List-II (Adverse Effect)
(*a*) Measles	I. Sudden infant death syndrome
(*b*) Diphtheria	II. Diabetes
(*c*) Haemophilus influenzae Type-B	III. Multiple Sclerosis
(*d*) Hepatitis-B	IV. Autism

Choose the ***correct*** answer from the options given below:

	(*a*)	(*b*)	(*c*)	(*d*)
A.	I	III	II	IV
B.	IV	I	II	III
C.	III	II	I	IV
D.	II	III	IV	I

10. Which among the options is not the elements of cognition?

A. Perception B. Attention

C. Concentration D. Emotion

11. Which among the following falls under the Laws of Heredity?

A. Law of Regression

B. Law of Continuity

C. Law of Progression

D. Law of Readiness

12. What is the validity coefficient of Johnson Basket ball test?

A. .78 B. .75

C. .87 D. .88

13. Several Problems adversly affect repeated-measures designs, including the following:

(*a*) Carryover effects

(*b*) Interpersonal effects

(*c*) Fatigue

(*d*) Sensitization

(*e*) Factorial effects

Choose the ***correct*** answer from the options given below:

A. (*a*), (*b*), (*c*) only

B. (*b*), (*d*), (*e*) only

C. (*a*), (*c*), (*d*) only

D. (*b*), (*c*), (*d*) only

14. The major diagnose which should not be done at the time of medical examination is:

A. Present Health Status

B. Prolonged Illness Record

C. Environmental Record

D. Family Health Status

15. Sequence adopted during the opening ceremony.

(*a*) Tribune of honor to president of games

(*b*) The Olympic oath.

(*c*) March past of the Athletes

(*d*) Arrival of the president of the games

(*e*) Declaration as opening games by the president

Previous Years' Paper

National Testing Agency (NTA)

UGC-NET Junior Research Fellowship & Assistant Professor Eligibility Exam

PHYSICAL EDUCATION, January-2025

(Exam held on 09-01-2025)

PAPER-II

1. Who among the following received the Arjun Award 2023 in Table Tennis?

A. Ms R. Vaishali
B. Ms Ayhika Mukherjee
C. Ms Nasreen
D. Ms Divyakriti Singh

2. Which class of lever is associated with most of the body movements?

A. First Class Lever
B. Second Class Lever
C. Combination of (A) & (B)
D. Third Class Lever

3. Sleep walking is also known as:

A. Sleep apnea
B. Schizophrenia
C. Somnambulism
D. Insomnia

4. The test for evaluation of Endurance are:

(*a*) Astrand Treadmill Test
(*b*) Conconi Test
(*c*) Cunningham and Faulker Test
(*d*) Cannadian Crunch Test
(*e*) Multistage Fitness Test

Choose the ***correct*** answer from the options given below:

A. (*a*), (*b*), (*c*), (*d*) only
B. (*a*), (*b*), (*c*), (*e*) only
C. (*b*), (*d*), (*e*) only
D. (*b*), (*c*), (*d*), (*e*) only

5. Match the List-I with List-II.

List-I	List-II
(*a*) Gluconeogenesis	I. Incomplete breakdown of glycogen
(*b*) Glycogenesis	II. Breakdown of glycogen to glucose
(*c*) Glycogenolysis	III. Manufacturing of glycogen from glucose
(*d*) Glycolysis	IV. Manufacturing of carbohydrate from non-carbohydrate source

Choose the ***correct*** answer from the options given below:

	(*a*)	(*b*)	(*c*)	(*d*)
A.	I	II	IV	III
B.	IV	III	II	I
C.	III	IV	II	I
D.	I	II	III	IV

6. Match the List-I with List-II.

List-I	List-II
(*a*) V_{O2}	I. Fractional Concentration of O_2 in inspired gas
(*b*) F_{IO_2}	II. Mean capillary O_2 pressure
(*c*) $\bar{P}_{EO_2}$	III. Alveolar O_2 pressure
(*d*) P_{AO_2}	IV. O_2 Consumption per minute

Choose the ***correct*** answer from the options given below:

A. (*d*), (*a*), (*b*), (*e*), (*c*)
B. (*d*), (*c*), (*a*), (*b*), (*e*)
C. (*d*), (*a*), (*c*), (*e*), (*b*)
D. (*d*), (*c*), (*e*), (*b*), (*a*)

16. Which muscles are NOT primary flexor of knee:

(*a*) Gastrocnemius
(*b*) Plantaris
(*c*) Vastus Medialis
(*d*) Rectus Femoris
(*e*) Vastus Lateralis

Choose the ***correct*** answer from the options given below:

A. (*a*), (*c*), (*d*) only
B. (*a*), (*d*), (*e*) only
C. (*a*) and (*b*) only
D. (*c*), (*d*), (*e*) only

17. Which was the first Indian University to recognize physical education as an degree course?

A. Vikram University
B. Jiwaji University
C. Dr. Hari Singh Gour University
D. Devi Ahilya University

18. Match the List-I with List-II.

List-I (Terminology)	List-II (Meaning)
(*a*) Accounting	I. Properties of value owned by an individual
(*b*) Assets	II. The recording interpreting of financial data
(*c*) Book Value	III. Debt owned to others and the equity of creditors in business firm
(*d*) Liability	IV. The value of an assets-appears on the balance sheet

Choose the ***correct*** answer from the options given below:

	(*a*)	(*b*)	(*c*)	(*d*)
A.	III	II	I	IV
B.	II	I	IV	III
C.	I	II	III	IV
D.	IV	III	II	I

19. Identify the correct sequential order of steps for the process of staffing

(*a*) Placement of manpower's
(*b*) Assessing manpower requirements
(*c*) Recruitment selection and training
(*d*) Determination of employs remuneration
(*e*) Development promotion, transfer and appraisal

Choose the ***correct*** answer from the options given below:

A. (*a*), (*c*), (*b*), (*e*), (*d*)
B. (*b*), (*c*), (*a*), (*e*), (*d*)
C. (*b*), (*a*), (*d*), (*e*), (*c*)
D. (*d*), (*a*), (*b*), (*c*), (*e*)

20. "Physical education is an education of and through human movement where many of the educational objectives are achieved by means of big muscle activities involving sports games, gymnastics dance and exercise" is defined by:

A. J.B. Nash
B. Harold M Barrow
C. Charles A Bucher
D. J.P. Thomas

21. Name the energy utilized to change the state of motion or shape of an object?

A. Kinetic Energy B. Potential Energy
C. Static Energy D. Force

22. Carbohydrate Loading leads to:

(*a*) Increase muscle glycogen by 25 gm/kg of muscle weight
(*b*) One gram of muscle glycogen is stored with 3-4 gm of water
(*c*) One gram of muscle glycogen is stored with 8-9 gm of water
(*d*) A total of 1-2 kg extra water stored in body

Choose the ***correct*** answer from the options given below:

A. (*a*), (*c*), (*d*) only
B. (*b*), (*c*), (*d*) only
C. (*a*), (*b*), (*d*) only
D. (*a*), (*b*), (*c*) only

23. Identify the correct sequential order of a typical fatigue cause.

(*a*) Warming up period
(*b*) Initial Spurt
(*c*) Familiarization and practice
(*d*) End spurt
(*e*) Fatigue

Choose the ***correct*** answer from the options given below:

A. (*a*), (*b*), (*d*), (*c*), (*e*)
B. (*b*), (*a*), (*c*), (*e*), (*d*)
C. (*b*), (*a*), (*c*), (*d*), (*e*)
D. (*b*), (*c*), (*a*), (*d*), (*e*)

24. Match the List-I with List-II.

List-I	List-II
(*a*) Time Table	I. Course of study offered by an institution
(*b*) Syllabus	II. A documents including all the learning experience provide to the students
(*c*) Curriculum	III. Out Lines of contents
(*d*) Professional Ethics	IV. A document showing what to be done by who and at what time

Choose the ***correct*** answer from the options given below:

	(*a*)	(*b*)	(*c*)	(*d*)
A.	IV	III	I	II
B.	IV	II	I	III
C.	III	IV	II	I
D.	III	I	IV	II

25. Match the List-I with List-II.

List-I (Theories)	List-II (Proposed By)
(*a*) Close-Loop theory	I. Lincoln Guba
(*b*) Schema theory	II. Adams
(*c*) Grounded theory	III. R.A. Schmidt
(*d*) Concept of credibility	IV. Glaser & Strauss

Choose the ***correct*** answer from the options given below:

	(*a*)	(*b*)	(*c*)	(*d*)
A.	I	II	IV	III
B.	III	I	II	IV
C.	II	III	IV	I
D.	I	III	II	IV

26. What are the areas of maintenance management?

(*a*) Safety
(*b*) Cleanliness
(*c*) Quality
(*d*) Finance
(*e*) Amenities

Choose the ***correct*** answer from the options given below:

A. (*a*), (*b*), (*c*), (*d*) only
B. (*a*), (*b*), (*d*) only
C. (*a*), (*b*), (*c*), (*e*) only
D. (*a*), (*c*), (*d*), (*e*) only

27. "The application of the principles of Physical and Behavioral Science to make the educational process more effective" is defined by:

A. Prof. S.S. Krishan
B. Urwin
C. Ludwig
D. Nixon

28. Find out the correct sequential order of stages for clinical manifestation of lymphatic filariasis:

(*a*) Stages of chronic obstructive lesions
(*b*) Asymptomatic microfilaremia
(*c*) Stage of acute manifestations
(*d*) Asymptomatic microfilaremia

Choose the ***correct*** answer from the options given below:

A. (*a*), (*b*), (*c*), (*d*)
B. (*b*), (*c*), (*d*), (*a*)
C. (*c*), (*d*), (*a*), (*b*)
D. (*d*), (*b*), (*a*), (*c*)

29. Who was the first president of International Olympic Committee?

A. Baren De Coubertin
B. Dimitrias Vikelas
C. Henry Brundale
D. Comte De Boillet

30. In which term the health of population is measured?

A. Applied Statistics
B. Vital Statistics
C. Descriptive Statistics
D. Inferential Statistics

31. Which is a metabolic product of glycolysis during exercise?

A. Glucose B. Glycogen
C. Phosphate D. Lactate

32. List the correct sequential order of Motivated activity for motivation.

(*a*) Goal (*b*) Need
(*c*) Sore Activity (*d*) Satisfaction
(*e*) Drive

Choose the ***correct*** answer from the options given below:

A. (*a*), (*b*), (*c*), (*e*), (*d*)
B. (*b*), (*c*), (*a*), (*d*), (*e*)
C. (*c*), (*b*), (*d*), (*a*), (*e*)
D. (*b*), (*e*), (*c*), (*a*), (*d*)

33. Match the List-I with List-II.

List-I (Asian Games)	**List-II (Year)**
(*a*) New Delhi	I. 1962
(*b*) Tehran	II. 1951
(*c*) Jakarta	III. 1994
(*d*) Hiroshima	IV. 1974

Choose the ***correct*** answer from the options given below:

	(*a*)	(*b*)	(*c*)	(*d*)
A.	II	IV	I	III
B.	II	IV	III	I
C.	IV	I	II	III
D.	III	IV	II	I

34. Find the correct sequential order of inductive reasoning according to R.L. Hoenes 1975.

(*a*) Hypothesis
(*b*) Theory
(*c*) Observation
(*d*) General Explanation
(*e*) Tie hypotheses together

Choose the ***correct*** answer from the options given below:

A. (*a*), (*e*), (*b*), (*c*), (*d*)
B. (*c*), (*a*), (*e*), (*d*), (*b*)
C. (*c*), (*e*), (*a*), (*d*), (*b*)
D. (*a*), (*c*), (*d*), (*b*), (*e*)

35. Match the List-I with List-II.

List-I	**List-II**
(*a*) Heat Stroke	I. Water & salt depletion
(*b*) Heat Exhaustion	II. General weakness and hypotension
(*c*) Heat Syncopc	III. Muscle spasms
(*d*) Heat Cramp	IV. Temperature may rise to 105°F

Choose the ***correct*** answer from the options given below:

	(*a*)	(*b*)	(*c*)	(*d*)
A.	I	III	IV	II
B.	IV	I	II	III
C.	III	II	IV	I
D.	II	IV	I	III

36. Which of the following are considered as threats to external validity? According to Campbell and Stanley (1963).

(*a*) Interactive effects of testing
(*b*) Statistical regression

(*c*) Interaction of selection bias and experimental treatment
(*d*) Instrumentation process
(*e*) Reactive effects of experimental arrangement

Choose the ***correct*** answer from the options given below:

A. (*a*), (*c*), (*d*) only
B. (*a*), (*c*), (*e*) only
C. (*a*), (*b*), (*d*) only
D. (*a*), (*d*), (*e*) only

37. Mention correct type of class formation during teaching practice.

(*a*) Spoke Formation (*b*) Rank Formation
(*c*) Rope Formation (*d*) File Formation
(*e*) Tree Formation

Choose the ***correct*** answer from the options given below:

A. (*a*), (*b*), (*d*) only
B. (*a*), (*d*), (*e*) only
C. (*b*), (*d*), (*c*) only
D. (*e*), (*d*), (*c*) only

38. Which law states that "The greater the initial length of the cardiac muscle fiber, the stronger the myocardium contraction".

A. Boyles law of the heart
B. Pavlov law of the heart
C. Starling's law of the heart
D. Mendel's law of the heart

39. A rejection of null hypothesis when the null hypothesis is true, called as:

A. Type II error
B. Type I error
C. Level of significance
D. Standard error

40. The ability to increase maximal oxygen consumption is limited due to which factor?

A. Genetical
B. Environmental
C. Training
D. Overload

41. The magnitude of type II error is determined by:

A. Beta B. Alpha
C. Gama D. Theta

42. "Teaching is a system of action intended to induce learning" is defined by:

A. B.O. Smith
B. Clarke
C. Israel Sheffler
D. Yoakum and Simpson

43. In the year 1971, Adams proposed a theory of motor skill learning is known as:

A. Schema Theory
B. Closed-Loop Theory
C. Avis Effected Theory
D. Placebo Theory

44. The main factors which affects growth and development:

(*a*) Genetic Factor
(*b*) Spiritual Factor
(*c*) Environmental Factor
(*d*) Nutritional Factor
(*e*) Movement Factor

Choose the ***correct*** answer from the options given below:

A. (*e*), (*c*), (*a*) only
B. (*d*), (*c*), (*b*) only
C. (*e*), (*a*), (*d*) only
D. (*a*), (*c*), (*d*) only

45. Arrange the following in ascending order of their existence:

(*a*) Epic Period (*b*) British Period
(*c*) Buddhist Period (*d*) Vedic Period
(*e*) Rajput Period

Choose the ***correct*** answer from the options given below:

A. (*d*), (*b*), (*a*), (*c*), (*e*)
B. (*d*), (*e*), (*c*), (*a*), (*b*)
C. (*d*), (*c*), (*e*), (*b*), (*a*)
D. (*d*), (*a*), (*c*), (*e*), (*b*)

46. Who introduced Liberal attitude regarding education and sports in Germany?

A. John Basedow B. Niels Buck

C. Adolph John D. Ronald Joseph

47. Choose the parametric sampling methods among the following:

(*a*) Quasi Random Sampling

(*b*) Bayesian Sampling (MCMC)

(*c*) Multistage Sampling

(*d*) Bootstrap Sampling

(*e*) Cluster Sampling

Choose the ***correct*** answer from the options given below:

A. (*a*), (*b*), (*d*), (*e*) only

B. (*a*), (*b*), (*c*), (*e*) only

C. (*b*), (*c*), (*d*), (*e*) only

D. (*a*), (*c*), (*d*), (*e*) only

48. Match the List-I with List-II.

List-I (White Blood Cell Type)	List-II (Life Spam)
(*a*) Neutrophil	I. Days to years
(*b*) Eosinophil	II. Hours to 3 days
(*c*) Monocyte	III. 8 to 12 days
(*d*) B-Lymphocyte	IV. Days to months

Choose the ***correct*** answer from the options given below:

	(*a*)	(*b*)	(*c*)	(*d*)
A.	II	III	IV	I
B.	I	II	III	IV
C.	III	IV	II	I
D.	IV	I	III	II

49. Match the List-I with List-II.

List-I	List-II
(*a*) Ischemia	I. Irregularity in force and rhythm of Heart
(*b*) Fibrillation	II. An excitatory neurotransmitter
(*c*) Hemolysis	III. Local and temporary deficiency of blood and oxygen
(*d*) Serotonin	IV. The rupture of cell

Choose the ***correct*** answer from the options given below:

	(*a*)	(*b*)	(*c*)	(*d*)
A.	I	III	IV	II
B.	II	IV	III	I
C.	III	I	IV	II
D.	IV	III	II	I

50. Which is not a type of curriculum development models?

A. Subject Centered Design

B. Evaluation Centered Design

C. Learner Centered Design

D. Problem Centered Design

51. Who is the Learning Disable Children?

(*a*) Generally Slow

(*b*) Specifically Slow

(*c*) High Intelligent Quotient

(*d*) Mentally Retarded

(*e*) Socially Well-Adjusted

Choose the ***correct*** answer from the options given below:

A. (*b*), (*c*), (*d*) only

B. (*a*), (*b*), (*e*) only

C. (*c*), (*d*), (*e*) only

D. (*a*), (*c*), (*d*) only

52. Match the List-I with List-II.

List-I (Auto Immune Disease)	List-II (Tissue Effected)
(*a*) Hashimoto's Disease	I. Joints
(*b*) Chronic Hepatitis	II. Connective Tissue
(*c*) Scleroderma	III. Thyroid
(*d*) Rheumatoid arthritis	IV. Liver

Choose the ***correct*** answer from the options given below:

	(*a*)	(*b*)	(*c*)	(*d*)
A.	IV	III	II	I
B.	I	II	III	IV
C.	III	IV	II	I
D.	II	III	I	IV

53. Which Vitamins are classed as antioxidants?

(*a*) Vitamin A (*b*) Vitamin D
(*c*) Vitamin E (*d*) Vitamin K
(*e*) Vitamin C

Choose the ***correct*** answer from the options given below:

A. (*a*), (*b*), (*c*) only
B. (*b*), (*c*), (*d*) only
C. (*b*), (*d*), (*e*) only
D. (*a*), (*c*), (*e*) only

54. Match the List-I with List-II.

List-I	List-II
(*a*) Iso-Kinetic Method	I. Intensity more than 100%
(*b*) Fartlek Method	II. Effective for the improvement of speed endurance
(*c*) Repetition Method	III. Method effective for swimming, rowing
(*d*) Dynamic Eccentric Method	IV. Training is not pre-planned

Choose the ***correct*** answer from the options given below:

	(*a*)	(*b*)	(*c*)	(*d*)
A.	III	IV	II	I
B.	IV	I	II	III
C.	I	II	III	IV
D.	II	I	IV	III

55. Stress on kinesthetic perception should be given in which phase of technique training?

A. First phase B. Second phase
C. Third phase D. Forth phase

56. Match the List-I with List-II.

List-I	List-II
(*a*) Progressive Regressive Procedure	I. 5 × 80%, 4 × 85%, 3 × 90%, 2 × 95%, 1 × 100%
(*b*) Progressive Procedure	II. 5 × 80%, 3 × 90%, 1 × 100%, 3 × 90%, 5 × 80%
(*c*) High Resistance Method	III. 20 × 50%, 20 × 50%, 20 × 50%
(*d*) Low Resistance Method	IV. 2 × 95%, 2 × 95%, 2 × 95%, 2 × 95%

Choose the ***correct*** answer from the options given below:

	(*a*)	(*b*)	(*c*)	(*d*)
A.	I	II	IV	III
B.	IV	II	III	I
C.	II	I	IV	III
D.	III	II	IV	I

57. Sequence of technique training in 3rd phase:

(*a*) Practice under difficult and different condition.
(*b*) Increased participation in competition.
(*c*) Ideo-motor training.
(*d*) Accurate and precise feedback.
(*e*) Development of movement concept.

Choose the ***correct*** answer from the options given below:

A. (*e*), (*a*), (*b*), (*c*), (*d*)
B. (*a*), (*c*), (*e*), (*d*), (*b*)
C. (*c*), (*b*), (*d*), (*e*), (*a*)
D. (*a*), (*e*), (*d*), (*b*), (*c*)

58. Heterochronicity of recovery means:

A. Faster pace of recovery of limbs
B. Different pace of recovery for different organs
C. Slower pace - of recovery of body parts and organs
D. Relentless pace of recovery of organs

59. Choose the correct sequential orders for the basics of scientific management.

(*a*) Select the worker and train them
(*b*) Distribute the gains between employers and employees
(*c*) Study the work scientifically
(*d*) Match Job and workers properly

Choose the ***correct*** answer from the options given below:

A. (*c*), (*a*), (*d*), (*b*)
B. (*a*), (*c*), (*b*), (*d*)
C. (*a*), (*b*), (*c*), (*d*)
D. (*d*), (*c*), (*b*), (*a*)

60. Match the List-I with List-II.

List-I	List-II
(*a*) Thirty or more	I. Range
(*b*) Discrete	II. Scale
(*c*) Interval measurement	III. Large Group
(*d*) Dispersion	IV. Type of Data

Choose the ***correct*** answer from the options given below:

	(*a*)	(*b*)	(*c*)	(*d*)
A.	I	II	III	IV
B.	I	III	IV	II
C.	III	IV	I	II
D.	III	IV	II	I

61. Arrange the following Joints according to order of greater range of motion:

(*a*) Neck Joint (*b*) Shoulder Joint
(*c*) Elbow Joint (*d*) Skull Joint

Choose the ***correct*** answer from the options given below:

A. (*c*), (*b*), (*d*), (*a*)
B. (*b*), (*c*), (*a*), (*d*)
C. (*c*), (*a*), (*b*), (*d*)
D. (*b*), (*a*), (*c*), (*d*)

62. Which among the following are phyto-chemicals?

(*a*) Anthocyanidins (*b*) Capsaicin
(*c*) Calcipherol (*d*) Flavanones
(*e*) Phylloquinone

Choose the ***correct*** answer from the options given below:

A. (*a*), (*c*), (*d*) only
B. (*b*), (*c*), (*d*) only
C. (*a*), (*b*), (*d*) only
D. (*c*), (*d*), (*e*) only

63. Which is considered as a speech disorder?

A. Semantic Transformation
B. Form Perception
C. Articulation Problems
D. Visual Closure

64. What are the types of Attention?

(*a*) Enforced (*b*) Awareness
(*c*) Concentration (*d*) Voluntary
(*e*) Habitual

Choose the ***correct*** answer from the options given below:

A. (*a*), (*d*), (*e*) only
B. (*b*), (*c*) only
C. (*a*), (*b*), (*d*), (*e*) only
D. (*b*), (*c*), (*d*), (*e*) only

65. What are the statistical software for data analysis?

(*a*) Minitab
(*b*) Python
(*c*) SPSS (Statistical Package for the Social Science)
(*d*) Jamovi
(*e*) G * Power

Choose the ***correct*** answer from the options given below:

A. (*a*), (*b*), (*c*), (*e*) only
B. (*b*), (*c*), (*d*), (*e*) only
C. (*a*), (*b*), (*c*), (*d*) only
D. (*a*), (*c*), (*d*), (*e*) only

66. Risk of injury is heightened when joint flexibility is

(*a*) Extremely low
(*b*) Rigid
(*c*) Extremely high
(*d*) Significant imbalance between dominant and non-dominant sides of the body
(*e*) Medium

Choose the ***correct*** answer from the options given below:

A. (*b*), (*c*), (*d*) only
B. (*a*), (*c*), (*d*) only
C. (*b*), (*d*), (*e*) only
D. (*c*), (*d*), (*e*) only

67. Which city is hosting 2032 Para Olympic Games?

A. Tokyo, Japan
B. Paris, France
C. Los Angeles, United States of America
D. Brisbane, Australia

68. What are the models of situational Leadership theory of management?

(*a*) Fiedler's contingency model
(*b*) Path-goal model
(*c*) Situational Leadership model
(*d*) Scientific leadership model
(*e*) Full range of leadership model

Choose the ***correct*** answer from the options given below:

A. (*a*), (*b*), (*c*), (*e*) only
B. (*a*), (*c*), (*d*) only
C. (*a*), (*b*), (*c*) only
D. (*b*), (*c*), (*d*), (*e*) only

69. Which form of stress produces a serious long-lasting psychological conditions?

A. Pre-traumatic stress disorder
B. Post-traumatic stress disorder
C. Preventive-traumatic stress disorder
D. Prior-traumatic stress disorder

70. Proximal attachment of ______ muscles is between posterior and anterior gluteal lines on the posterior ilium.

A. Gluteus Maximus B. Rectus Femoris
C. Gluteus Medius D. Sartorius

71. Sequence of Recovery is:

(*a*) Anabolic in nature
(*b*) Re-synthesis of ATP and glycogen
(*c*) Neutralization of Lactic acid
(*d*) Restoration of Homeostasis

Choose the ***correct*** answer from the options given below:

A. (*a*), (*b*), (*c*), (*d*)
B. (*b*), (*c*), (*d*), (*a*)
C. (*c*), (*d*), (*a*), (*b*)
D. (*d*), (*a*), (*b*), (*c*)

72. As an when individual gets older there is decline in the following components:

(*a*) Muscle Size
(*b*) Percent Body Fat
(*c*) Muscular Strength
(*d*) Blood Pressure
(*e*) Lean Body Weight

Choose the ***correct*** answer from the options given below:

A. (*a*), (*b*), (*c*) only
B. (*b*), (*c*), (*e*) only
C. (*a*), (*c*), (*e*) only
D. (*a*), (*b*), (*e*) only

73. Which nerve plays most important role in the automatic adjustment of the heart during body movement?

A. Trigeminal nerve B. Vestibular nerve
C. Facial nerve D. Spinal nerve

74. Hypertrophy of muscles involves more:

(*a*) Myofibrils
(*b*) Actin and myosin filaments
(*c*) Sarcoplasm
(*d*) Tendon
(*e*) Lipids

Choose the ***correct*** answer from the options given below:

A. (*a*), (*b*), (*e*) only
B. (*a*), (*b*), (*c*) only
C. (*a*), (*b*), (*d*) only
D. (*a*), (*c*), (*e*) only

75. Match the List-I with List-II.

List-I	List-II
(*a*) "German Gymnastics"	I. Per Hanrik Ling
(*b*) "Primitive Gymnastics"	II. Guts Muths
(*c*) "Swedish Gymnastics"	III. Archibald Maclaren
(*d*) "A system of physical education-Theoretical and practical"	IV. Niels Bukh

Choose the ***correct*** answer from the options given below:

	(*a*)	(*b*)	(*c*)	(*d*)
A.	II	I	IV	III
B.	II	III	I	IV
C.	II	IV	III	I
D.	II	IV	I	III

76. Which method is mostly used in survey research to collect opinions on specific topic to gain consensus?

A. Delphi Method
B. Cross Sectional Method
C. Interview Method
D. Trend Study Method

77. Match the List-I with List-II.

List-I	List-II
(*a*) Body mass index	I. Height (cm) – 100
(*b*) Ponderal index	II. $\frac{\text{Weight (kg)}}{\text{Height}^2\text{ (m)}}$
(*c*) Broca index	III. Height (cm) – $\frac{\text{Height(cm)} - 150}{2\text{(Women) or }4\text{(Men)}}$
(*d*) Lorentz's formula	IV. $\frac{\text{Height (cm)}}{\text{Cube root of body Weight (kg)}}$

Choose the ***correct*** answer from the options given below:

	(*a*)	(*b*)	(*c*)	(*d*)
A.	IV	III	II	I
B.	III	IV	II	I
C.	I	II	III	IV
D.	II	IV	I	III

78. The part of experiment that the researcher is manipulated is called:

A. Dependent Variable
B. Third Variable
C. Treatment Variable
D. Extraneous Variable

79. Critical speed does not include:

A. Anaerobic threshold
B. 90-100% of V_{O_2} max
C. 75-80% of V_{O_2} max
D. Heart rate is between 175-180 beats

80. The Sterno-Clavicular Joint is also known as:

A. Hing Joint
B. Condyloid Joint
C. Gliding Joint
D. Pivot Joint

81. Which animal was sacrificed before commencement of Ancient Olympic games?

A. Lamb
B. Bufflow
C. Horse
D. Pig

82. Match the List-I with List-II.

List-I	List-II
(*a*) Cronbach alpha coefficient	I. Internal Validity
(*b*) Halo effect	II. Reliability
(*c*) Ancova	III. Criterion Validity
(*d*) Concurrent Validity	IV. Distractor Variable

Choose the ***correct*** answer from the options given below:

	(*a*)	(*b*)	(*c*)	(*d*)
A.	I	III	IV	II
B.	II	I	IV	III
C.	II	III	I	IV
D.	I	II	III	IV

83. Match the List-I with List-II.

List-I	List-II
(*a*) Surplus Energy Theory	I. G. Stanley Hall
(*b*) Recapitulatory Theory	II. Carl Groos
(*c*) Cathartic Theory	III. Van Schiller and Herbert
(*d*) Anticipatory Theory	IV. Aristotle

Choose the ***correct*** answer from the options given below:

	(*a*)	(*b*)	(*c*)	(*d*)
A.	III	IV	II	I
B.	III	I	IV	II
C.	III	II	I	IV
D.	III	I	II	IV

84. Match the List-I with List-II.

List-I	**List-II**
(*a*) Phlegmatic	I. Unstable Introvert
(*b*) Sanguine	II. Unstable Extrovert
(*c*) Melancholic	III. Stable Introvert
(*d*) Choleric	IV. Stable Extrovert

Choose the ***correct*** answer from the options given below:

	(*a*)	(*b*)	(*c*)	(*d*)
A.	IV	I	II	III
B.	II	III	IV	I
C.	I	II	III	IV
D.	III	IV	I	II

85. During exercise up to 40 to 60 per cent of maximal capacity of cardiac output in trained athlete may increase up to ______.

A. 100 liters B. 40 liters
C. 10 liters D. 15 liters

86. Which is considered as a type of stressful situation?

A. Environmental Situation
B. Mental Situation
C. Harm-and-Loss Situation
D. Conditional Situation

87. Which is a pain control system of brain?

A. Analgesia B. Cortex
C. Spinal Chord D. Axon

88. Which of the following threat to internal validity was identified by Ronsenthal in 1966?

A. Maturation
B. Instrumentation
C. Expectancy
D. Experimental Mortality

89. Meaning of Eustress:

A. Exhilaration B. Fear
C. Apprehension D. Anger

90. Which of the following categories are included in H. McCloy classification index?

(*a*) High School Boys
(*b*) High School
(*c*) College Men
(*d*) College
(*e*) Elementry School

Choose the ***correct*** answer from the options given below:

A. (*a*), (*b*), (*c*) only
B. (*b*), (*d*), (*e*) only
C. (*b*), (*c*), (*e*) only
D. (*a*), (*d*), (*e*) only

Directions (Qs. No. 91 to 95): *Read the passage and answer on the basis of the following passage:*

Extraneous variables are factors that could affect relationship between the independent and dependent variables but are not includes.

The independent variable in the experimental or treatment variable, it is cause. The dependent variables is measures to assess the effects of independent variables. A categorical variable sometime called a moderator variables, for example gender or race.

An experiment was done on the effect of synchronous and asynchronous movement to music on endure performance. One group with synchronized music, one group with not synchronized music and one group with no music separately for men and women were taken with same intensity of workload. It was speculated that same different in the performance of men and women might be due to the women's reluctance to exhibit maximum effort in the presence of male.

The decision to include or exclude some variable depends on several consideration such as whether the variable is closely related to the theoretical model and how likely there is to be an interaction.

91. In all experimental research, it should have control variable?

A. Always
B. Never
C. Sometime
D. Decision of Researcher

92. The difference performance of men and women is an example of:

A. Independent Variable
B. Dependent Variable
C. Categorical Variable
D. Extraneous Variable

93. Which of variable cannot be manipulated?

A. Categorical Variable
B. Extraneous Variable
C. Independent Variable
D. Discrete Variable

94. Doing exercise with background music that was not synchronized is an examples of:

A. Continuous Variable
B. Dependent Variable
C. Moderate Variable
D. Independent Variable

95. Which type of variable is mainly responsible to affect the internal validity of any experiment?

A. Moderator Variable
B. Dependent Variable
C. Extraneous Variable
D. Independent Variable

Directions (Qs. No. 96 to 100): *Read the passage and answer on the basis of the following passage:*

A hormone is chemical substance secreted into the body fluids by an endocrine gland and has a specific effect on the activities of other organs (target organs). An endocrine gland is ductless and secrets a hormone directly on to the blood or lymph's. The actions of hormones are target organs include: (1) Activation of enzymes systems. (2) Alterations of cell membrane permeability. (3) Muscular contraction or relaxation. (4) Protein Synthesis, or (5) Cellular Secretion. This actions are brought about through a mechanism referred to as the cyclic AMP mechanism. Some hormones have an effect only on specific target organ. The predominant hormonal control system is negative feedback mechanism. The nervous system is also involved in the control of hormone secretion. The hormones and their endocrine glands, include the following: 1. The Pituitary Gland: ADH, Oxytocin, GH, TSH, ACTH, FSH, LH and prolactin. 2. The Adrenal Glands: The catecholamine, epinephrine and non-epinephrine, mineralocorticoids, glucocorticoids and endogens. 3. Pancreas: Insulin and Glycogen. 4. The Thyroid Gland: Thyroxin, triiodothyronine and calcitonin. 5. The Para-Thyroid gland: PTH. 6. Ovaries and Testes: Androgen.

Blood level of hormones known to increase with exercise include: GH, catecholamine, ACTH, Glucocorticoids, Mineralocorticoids, Glucagon, Testosterone, Estrogen, Progesterone, TSH, Thyroxin and triode thyroxine. Blood level of Luteinizing hormone do not change with exercise whereas insulin decreases during exercise.

96. Which hormone do not change with exercise?

A. ACTH B. LH
C. FSH D. ADH

97. What is negative feedback mechanism?

A. Predominant hormonal control
B. Specificity of hormone receptor
C. Muscular Contraction or relaxation
D. Imbalanced pancreatic function

98. Which of the following hormones increase with exercise?

A. Calcitonin B. Insulin
C. TSH D. FSH

99. Thyroid Gland Secrets ______?

A. Testosterone B. Estrogen
C. ACTH D. FSH

100. Which of the following is NOT a part of cyclic AMP mechanism?

A. Alteration of cell membrane permeability
B. Nervous Stimulation
C. Activation of enzymes systems
D. Protein Synthesis

ANSWERS

1. **(B):** Ayhika Mukherjee was conferred the Arjuna Award in 2023 for her achievements in Table Tennis. She has represented India at various international levels and notably contributed to India's performance at the Asian Games 2022 (held in 2023), where she was part of the Indian women's team that won a historic bronze medal in women's doubles along with Sutirtha Mukherjee. Her consistent performance and dedication to the sport earned her this prestigious recognition by the Government of India.

2. **(D):** Most of the body movements in the human musculoskeletal system involve third-class levers, where:

   The effort is applied between the fulcrum and the load.

   Common examples include:

   Biceps curl: The elbow is the fulcrum, the biceps apply the effort in the middle, and the weight in the hand is the load.

   Kicking a ball using the quadriceps.

   This lever type allows greater speed and range of motion, which is advantageous in most athletic and daily movements.

   Though mechanically less efficient, the third-class lever system is designed to favour mobility over force.

3. **(C):** Sleepwalking, medically termed Somnambulism, is a parasomnia that typically occurs during deep non-REM sleep (stage 3 or 4). Characteristics include:

   The person may walk, sit up, or perform activities while remaining in a sleep state.

   It usually occurs in children more than adults and is often harmless, though it can lead to injury.

   It is different from Insomnia (inability to sleep), Sleep apnea (breathing disorder), and Schizophrenia (a mental disorder).

   Sleepwalking affects approximately 1% to 15% of the general population at some point in life.

4. **(B):** The following tests are used for evaluation of endurance:

   (*a*) Astrand Treadmill Test: Submaximal test to estimate aerobic endurance ($V_{O_2\ max}$).

   (*b*) Conconi Test: Determines anaerobic threshold, used in endurance sports.

   (*c*) Cunningham and Faulker Test: A treadmill-based test to evaluate anaerobic capacity and endurance.

   (*e*) Multistage Fitness Test (Beep Test): Progressive aerobic cardiovascular endurance test.

   (*d*) Canadian Crunch Test is not a test of endurance; it's a muscular strength/endurance test but limited to abdominal strength, hence less suitable for evaluating overall endurance.

5. **(B):** (*a*) Gluconeogenesis – IV: Refers to the formation of glucose (a carbohydrate) from non-carbohydrate sources like amino acids and glycerol, primarily in the liver. This process is vital during fasting.

   (*b*) Glycogenesis – III: It is the process of synthesizing glycogen from glucose, stored in liver and muscles.

   (*c*) Glycogenolysis – II: Breakdown of glycogen to glucose, especially during physical activity or fasting, to supply immediate energy.

   (*d*) Glycolysis – I: The anaerobic breakdown of glucose to pyruvate or lactate, producing ATP. It involves an incomplete breakdown of glucose, especially under anaerobic conditions.

6. **(A):** (*a*) V_{O_2} – IV: Refers to the volume of oxygen consumed per minute, a key indicator of aerobic fitness. It is measured in ml/kg/min and commonly assessed in $V_{O_2\ max}$ tests.

   (*b*) F_{IO_2} – I: Stands for Fraction of Inspired Oxygen, indicating the concentration of oxygen in the inhaled air. In atmospheric air, F_{IO_2} is typically around 20.93% (0.2093).

   (*c*) $\bar{P}_{EO_2}$ – II: Refers to mean capillary oxygen pressure, representing the oxygen partial pressure in expired air, useful in assessing gas exchange efficiency.

(*d*) P_{AO_2} – III: Stands for Alveolar Oxygen Pressure, indicating the partial pressure of oxygen in the alveoli, calculated using the alveolar gas equation.

7. (B): (*b*) HVPM, Amravati (1914): Founded as Hanuman Vyayam Prasarak Mandal, it is one of the oldest physical education institutes in India.

(*c*) YMCA, Madras (1920): Established soon after HVPM, contributed significantly to early physical education training.

(*a*) Christian College of Physical Education, Lucknow (1931): Played a vital role in spreading physical education in northern India.

(*d*) LCPE, Gwalior (1957): Laxmibai National College of Physical Education was later upgraded to LNIPE, a premier institute in India.

Ascending order of establishment based on years is thus: 1914 → 1920 → 1931 → 1957.

8. (D): The Oxford method is a strength training technique involving:

- A reverse pyramid structure.
- Starting with the heaviest weight and decreasing the load in subsequent sets.
- The repetitions remain constant, typically 10 reps per set.
- This method was developed during World War II for rehabilitation purposes and is the reverse of the DeLorme (Progressive) technique.

Hence, Oxford method is associated with Decreasing Resistance – Constant repetitions.

9. (*)

10. (D): Cognition includes mental processes involved in acquiring knowledge and understanding:

- Perception: Recognizing sensory input.
- Attention: Focusing cognitive resources.
- Concentration: Sustained attention on a task.

Emotion, however, is part of the affective domain, not the cognitive domain.

It involves feelings and mood, which influence cognition but are not themselves cognitive processes.

Hence, Emotion is not an element of cognition.

11. (A): The Law of Regression is one of the classical Laws of Heredity, originally studied and formulated by Sir Francis Galton. It explains how offspring tend to regress towards the mean of a particular trait found in the population, especially when the parents show extreme forms of that trait. For example, very tall parents are likely to have children shorter than themselves, and very short parents may have taller children — both moving closer to the average. This statistical concept is a key principle in understanding hereditary variation and predictability.

12. (D): The validity coefficient of the Johnson Basketball Test is .88, which indicates a very high level of validity. Validity refers to the degree to which the test measures what it is intended to measure — in this case, basketball playing ability. The Johnson test evaluates components such as passing, shooting, and dribbling skills, and a coefficient of .88 means that it has strong predictive capability and correlates well with actual basketball performance.

13. (C): In repeated-measures designs, where the same participants are tested across multiple conditions or time points, several methodological issues can arise:

(*a*) Carryover effects: Performance in one condition may affect performance in the next.

(*c*) Fatigue: Participants may become tired over time, influencing later responses.

(*d*) Sensitization: Repeated exposure can make participants more aware or sensitive, altering their responses. Interpersonal effects and factorial effects are not typical problems associated directly with repeated-measures designs.

14. (C): During a medical examination, the focus should be on personal health data, such as:

- Current health status
- Family medical history
- Past illnesses or chronic conditions

Environmental record, though important for public health studies, is not a direct medical diagnostic concern at the time of individual examination. It deals with the surrounding environmental factors like pollution, living conditions, etc., and is thus considered irrelevant to immediate personal diagnosis during physical check-ups.

15. (C): The correct sequence of the opening ceremony in major international games such as the Olympic Games is as follows:

(*d*) Arrival of the president of the games: The official host arrives and is welcomed.

(*a*) Tribune of honour to president of games: The president takes position on the ceremonial stand.

(*c*) March past of the Athletes: All participating teams parade in the stadium.

(*e*) Declaration as opening games by the president: Official declaration of the event being open.

(*b*) The Olympic oath: Taken by a representative athlete on behalf of all competitors, pledging fair competition.

This order is based on established Olympic protocol and observed international traditions.

16. (D): The primary flexors of the knee joint include muscles like biceps femoris, semitendinosus, semimembranosus, gastrocnemius, and plantaris. However:

(*c*) Vastus Medialis, (*d*) Rectus Femoris, and (*e*) Vastus Lateralis are part of the quadriceps femoris group, whose primary function is knee extension, not flexion.

Rectus Femoris also assists in hip flexion. Hence, these three are not primary flexors of the knee joint.

17. (A): Vikram University, Ujjain (Madhya Pradesh), was the first Indian university to recognize Physical Education as a degree course. This pioneering step helped institutionalize the subject as an academic discipline in higher education in India, laying the foundation for professional physical education programs in the country.

18. (B): (*a*) Accounting – II: It is the process of recording, classifying, and interpreting financial data, essential for business decision-making.

(*b*) Assets – I: These are resources or properties owned by an individual or entity that have economic value.

(*c*) Book Value – IV: Refers to the value of an asset as recorded in the company's balance sheet, typically the original cost minus depreciation.

(*d*) Liability – III: Represents debts or obligations owed to outsiders (creditors), and the equity of creditors in the firm.

19. (B): The correct sequence for staffing process is:

(*b*) Assessing manpower requirements: First step to determine the number and type of personnel needed.

(*c*) Recruitment, selection and training: Attracting and preparing suitable candidates for the job.

(*a*) Placement of manpower: Assigning selected candidates to appropriate roles.

(*e*) Development, promotion, transfer and appraisal: Ensuring growth, performance evaluation, and internal mobility.

(*d*) Determination of employee remuneration: Deciding salary and benefits based on role and performance.

20. (B): The given definition – "Physical education is an education of and through human movement where many of the educational objectives are achieved by means of big muscle activities involving sports games, gymnastics, dance and exercise" – was given by Harold M. Barrow. He emphasized that physical education not only focuses on physical development but also contributes to emotional, intellectual, and social growth through structured physical activity. This holistic view supports the integration of physical education in general education systems.

21. (D): Force is the correct answer because it is the external energy or influence that causes a change in the state of motion or shape of an object. According to Newton's First Law of Motion, an object remains at rest or in uniform motion unless acted upon by a net external force. Kinetic and potential energy are forms of energy possessed by the object, but they do not themselves cause the motion or deformation — force is the cause, while kinetic energy is a result of motion.

22. (C): (*a*) Increase muscle glycogen by 25 gm/kg of muscle weight: Carbohydrate loading increases muscle glycogen content significantly, often reaching up to 20–25 gm/kg of muscle tissue.

(*b*) One gram of muscle glycogen is stored with 3–4 gm of water: This is scientifically accurate. Glycogen is a hydrophilic molecule, and for every gram of stored glycogen, 3–4 grams of water are retained.

(*d*) A total of 1–2 kg extra water stored in body: Due to the water stored with glycogen, the body can retain 1-2 kg of additional water, which is often seen as a side effect of carb loading.

(*c*) is incorrect: It overestimates the water stored per gram of glycogen. The correct range is 3-4 gm, not 8-9 gm.

23. (B): The correct sequential order of events related to fatigue in performance is:

(*b*) Initial spurt: Sudden burst of energy and effort at the beginning of activity.

(*a*) Warming up period: Body gradually adjusts and reaches optimal working conditions.

(*c*) Familiarization and practice: Performer gets into rhythm and refines technique.

(*e*) Fatigue: Due to prolonged exertion, energy levels begin to drop.

(*d*) End spurt: A final burst of energy often fueled by motivation or nearing completion. This order represents a typical performance-fatigue cycle.

24. (A): (*a*) Time Table – IV: A structured document indicating what to be done, by whom, and at what time, used in educational institutions to organize activities.

(*b*) Syllabus – III: A brief outline of the contents of a subject, generally prescribed by a university or educational board.

(*c*) Curriculum – I: Refers to the comprehensive course of study, including syllabus, activities, materials, and pedagogy offered by an institution.

(*d*) Professional Ethics – II: Represents the learning experiences or values expected to be followed by professionals, forming part of education and conduct norms.

25. (C): (*a*) Closed-Loop Theory – II (Adams): Proposed by Jack Adams, this theory explains motor learning through feedback and error correction during the performance of a skill.

(*b*) Schema Theory – III (R.A. Schmidt): Introduced by Richard Schmidt, it suggests that movement is controlled by generalized motor programs developed from past experiences.

(*c*) Grounded Theory – IV (Glaser & Strauss): A qualitative research methodology involving the generation of theory through data collection and analysis.

(*d*) Concept of Credibility – I (Lincoln & Guba): Refers to trustworthiness and authenticity in qualitative research, as emphasized by Yvonna Lincoln and Egon Guba.

26. (C): The key areas of maintenance management in physical or institutional settings include:

(*a*) Safety: Ensuring that all infrastructure and equipment do not pose any hazard to users.

(*b*) Cleanliness: Regular maintenance of hygiene in all facilities.

(*c*) Quality: Maintaining the standard and durability of services and equipment.

(*e*) Amenities: Proper upkeep of facilities provided for comfort and usability, such as restrooms, drinking water, etc.

Finance is a broader administrative domain, not directly a maintenance activity, hence not included under the core areas of maintenance management.

27. (A): The definition – "The application of the principles of Physical and Behavioural Science to make the educational process more effective" – was given by Prof. S.S. Krishan.

He emphasized the role of scientific principles, including psychology, physiology, and education theory, in improving teaching-learning methods, especially in the context of physical education. The approach aims at integrating human behaviour understanding with physical activity to enhance educational outcomes.

28. (*)

29. (B): The first president of the International Olympic Committee (IOC) was Dimitrios Vikelas of Greece.

- He served from 1894 to 1896.
- He played a crucial role in organizing the first modern Olympic Games in Athens in 1896.
- Pierre de Coubertin, who later became president, had nominated Vikelas initially to gain support for the revival of the Games in Greece.

30. (B): The term used to measure the health of a population is Vital Statistics. These include:

- Birth rate

- Death rate
- Infant mortality rate
- Life expectancy
- Fertility rate

These data help governments and health agencies monitor population trends and plan health programs. They are considered a core component of public health surveillance and planning.

31. (D): Lactate is a key metabolic product of glycolysis during exercise, especially under anaerobic conditions when oxygen is insufficient to fully metabolize glucose through the aerobic pathway. In such cases:

- Glucose is broken down into pyruvate through glycolysis.
- In the absence of oxygen, pyruvate is converted into lactate by the enzyme lactate dehydrogenase.
- This helps regenerate NAD^+ needed for continued glycolysis and short-term energy production.
- Lactate accumulation in muscles leads to the burning sensation during intense exercise.

32. (D): The correct sequential order of motivated activity is:

(*b*) Need: A deficiency or lack that initiates motivation.

(*e*) Drive: Internal force or energy aroused due to unmet needs.

(*c*) Sore Activity: Action taken to reduce the drive or fulfill the need.

(*a*) Goal: The desired outcome or target of the activity.

(*d*) Satisfaction: Achievement of the goal leads to relief of the need and psychological satisfaction. This sequence is aligned with motivational theories like Hull's Drive Reduction Theory.

33. (A): (*a*) New Delhi – II (1951): Hosted the 1st Asian Games, marking the beginning of this multi-sport event in Asia.

(*b*) Tehran – IV (1974): Hosted the 7th Asian Games in Iran.

(*c*) Jakarta – I (1962): Hosted the 4th Asian Games in Indonesia.

(*d*) Hiroshima – III (1994): Hosted the 12th Asian Games, the first Asian Games in Japan. This matching aligns with the correct historical hosting years of the Asian Games.

34. (B): As per R.L. Hoenes (1975), the correct sequence of inductive reasoning is:

(*c*) Observation: Collection of facts or data from specific instances.

(*a*) Hypothesis: A tentative explanation formed based on the observed data.

(*e*) Tie hypotheses together: Integration of related hypotheses to see common patterns.

(*d*) General Explanation: Deriving a broader understanding or generalization.

(*b*) Theory: Formation of a theory that explains the observed phenomena consistently. This method reflects how inductive reasoning progresses from specific observations to general theories.

35. (B): (*a*) Heat Stroke – IV: A life-threatening condition with core body temperature rising up to 105°F (40.5°C) or higher, often without sweating.

(*b*) Heat Exhaustion – I: Involves water and salt depletion, causing fatigue, dizziness, and nausea.

(*c*) Heat Syncope – II: Characterized by temporary loss of consciousness (fainting) due to hypotension and blood pooling.

(*d*) Heat Cramp – III: Involves muscle spasms due to electrolyte imbalance, typically from heavy sweating during intense exercise. Each condition reflects a different severity and physiological cause within heat-related illnesses.

36. (B): According to Campbell and Stanley (1963), the following are considered threats to external validity:

(*a*) Interactive effects of testing: When prior testing interacts with the treatment and influences the outcome, limiting generalizability.

(*c*) Interaction of selection bias and experimental treatment: If specific groups are selected for treatment, the effect might not apply to other populations.

(*e*) Reactive effects of experimental arrangement: When participants behave differently due to awareness of being in an experiment (Hawthorne effect), it threatens applicability to real-world scenarios.

Whereas (*b*) statistical regression and (*d*) instrumentation are considered threats to internal validity, not external validity.

37. (A): The correct types of class formations commonly used during teaching practice, especially in physical education, include:

(*a*) Spoke Formation: Students form spokes around a central point or instructor, ideal for demonstration.

(*b*) Rank Formation: Students stand in horizontal lines, useful for large group instructions.

(*d*) File Formation: Vertical lines useful for moving in an orderly manner or warming up.

(*c*) and (*e*) (Rope and Tree formations) are not standard class formations in teaching practice.

38. (C): Starling's Law (also known as the Frank-Starling mechanism) states that:

"The greater the initial length of the cardiac muscle fibers (i.e., the greater the end-diastolic volume), the more forcefully the heart contracts."

This physiological principle helps maintain balance between the volume of blood entering and leaving the heart and plays a crucial role in cardiac output regulation during exercise or stress.

39. (B): A Type I error occurs when the null hypothesis (H_0) is rejected even though it is actually true. It is also known as:

- False positive
- Represented by alpha (α), often set at 0.05 or 5% This error leads the researcher to conclude that an effect or difference exists, when in reality, it does not.

40. (A): The ability to increase maximal oxygen consumption ($V_{O_2\ max}$) is strongly influenced by genetic factors, which:

- Determine the efficiency of the cardiovascular and respiratory systems
- Influence muscle fiber type distribution
- Set the upper ceiling for aerobic performance Although training, environment, and overload contribute to improvements, the genetic makeup ultimately limits how much $V_{O_2\ max}$ can increase. Studies suggest genetics may account for 20%-40% of the variability in $V_{O_2\ max}$ responses.

41. (A): The magnitude of Type II error is denoted by Beta (β).

- A Type II error occurs when a false null hypothesis is not rejected — i.e., failing to detect a real effect.
- The value of β represents the probability of making this error.
- The power of a test is defined as 1 – β, which indicates the ability of the test to detect an actual effect.
- The magnitude of β depends on sample size, effect size, and significance level (α), but it is β specifically that quantifies Type II error.

42. (A): The definition – "Teaching is a system of action intended to induce learning" – was given by B.O. Smith, a renowned educationist and philosopher.

He viewed teaching as a purposeful, structured, and dynamic system where the teacher's actions are designed to produce learning.

This approach emphasizes that teaching is not merely instruction, but a deliberate system of organized interaction between teacher, learner, and content aimed at cognitive, affective, and psychomotor development.

43. (B): In 1971, Jack A. Adams proposed the Closed-Loop Theory of motor skill learning.

According to this theory, movements are controlled through a system that relies on feedback to correct errors during the performance.

It emphasizes the role of sensory feedback (especially proprioception) in comparing the performed movement with the intended movement.

Especially applicable to slow and precise motor skills, the theory laid the foundation for later development of Schema Theory by R.A. Schmidt.

44. (D): The main factors that affect growth and development are:

(*a*) Genetic Factor: Determines inherited traits, such as height, body structure, and intellectual potential.

(*c*) Environmental Factor: Includes living conditions, social surroundings, pollution, etc., which influence both physical and mental growth.

(*d*) Nutritional Factor: Affects both growth rate and immune strength; poor nutrition can lead to stunted growth and developmental delays.

Spiritual and movement factors may influence certain aspects but are not considered core biological determinants of growth and development.

45. (D): The correct ascending historical order of the listed periods is:

(*d*) Vedic Period (1500–600 BCE): Origin of early Hindu scriptures and social structure.

(*a*) Epic Period (circa 1000–500 BCE): Time of Mahabharata and Ramayana.

(*c*) Buddhist Period (6th century BCE onwards): Emergence of Buddhism and Jainism; emphasis on moral and spiritual education.

(*e*) Rajput Period (7th–12th century CE): Known for warrior clans and regional kingdoms.

(*b*) British Period (1757–1947): Colonial rule in India, introduction of Western education. This order reflects the chronological development of Indian civilization and educational traditions.

46. (A): John Basedow was a German educator who introduced a liberal and reformative attitude towards education and sports in Germany during the 18th century.

He emphasized naturalism in education, integrating physical activities, games, and gymnastics as essential parts of the school curriculum.

He founded the Philanthropinum School in Dessau, which promoted education in tune with natural development and emphasized practical and physical education over purely theoretical learning.

His approach marked a significant shift from traditional authoritarian education systems to a more holistic and liberal model.

47. (B): The following are considered parametric sampling methods:

(*a*) Quasi Random Sampling: Approximates true randomness while still maintaining probabilistic properties.

(*b*) Bayesian Sampling (MCMC): A parametric method relying on probability distributions and model-based assumptions.

(*c*) Multistage Sampling: A form of probability sampling where the selection process occurs in stages, maintaining parametric structure.

(*e*) Cluster Sampling: Involves selection of groups (clusters) and is widely used in parametric statistical designs.

(*d*) Bootstrap Sampling is non-parametric, relying on resampling with replacement, hence not included.

48. (A): (*a*) Neutrophil – II (Hours to 3 days): These are the most abundant white blood cells and are short-lived, providing immediate immune response.

(*b*) Eosinophil – III (8 to 12 days): These survive longer and play a role in allergic reactions and defense against parasites.

(*c*) Monocyte – IV (Days to months): These circulate in blood briefly but can survive longer in tissues as macrophages.

(*d*) B-Lymphocyte – I (Days to years): Can persist in the body for long periods, especially as memory B-cells, contributing to long-term immunity.

49. (C): (*a*) Ischemia – III: Refers to a temporary and localized deficiency of blood and oxygen to tissues, often causing pain or damage (e.g., angina).

(*b*) Fibrillation – I: It is the irregular contraction of heart muscle fibers, disrupting normal rhythm and force of heartbeat.

(*c*) Hemolysis – IV: Involves the rupture of red blood cells, leading to the release of hemoglobin into the blood plasma.

(*d*) Serotonin – II: A neurotransmitter that plays a major role in mood regulation, sleep, and gut function; it is excitatory in nature.

50. (B): Among the options, Evaluation Centered Design is not a recognized model of curriculum development.

The widely accepted curriculum development models are:

(A) Subject Centered Design: Focuses on content and subject matter.

(C) Learner Centered Design: Emphasizes students' needs, interests, and learning styles.

(D) Problem Centered Design: Oriented around solving real-world problems, promoting critical thinking. Evaluation is an integral component of all models, but not a standalone model of curriculum design.

51. (*)

52. (C): (*a*) Hashimoto's Disease – III (Thyroid): An autoimmune disorder where the immune system attacks the thyroid gland, leading to hypothyroidism.

(*b*) Chronic Hepatitis – IV (Liver): Autoimmune hepatitis targets the liver tissues, causing chronic inflammation.

(*c*) Scleroderma – II (Connective Tissue): Affects skin and connective tissues, resulting in thickening and tightening of the skin.

(*d*) Rheumatoid Arthritis – I (Joints): Immune system attacks the synovial membranes of the joints, causing inflammation and deformities.

53. (D): The following vitamins are classified as antioxidants:

(*a*) Vitamin A: Helps protect cells from oxidative damage, especially in vision and immune function.

(*c*) Vitamin E: A fat-soluble antioxidant that protects cell membranes from free radicals.

(*e*) Vitamin C: A water-soluble antioxidant, plays a key role in collagen synthesis and neutralizing free radicals. Vitamins D and K do not primarily act as antioxidants; they are involved in calcium metabolism and blood clotting, respectively.

54. (A): (*a*) Iso-Kinetic Method – III: Effective in resistance training involving constant speed, used in sports like swimming, rowing.

(*b*) Fartlek Method – IV: A Swedish term for "speed play", where training is not pre-planned but varies with terrain and pace.

(*c*) Repetition Method – II: Used to develop speed and anaerobic endurance, involving high-intensity efforts with rest.

(*d*) Dynamic Eccentric Method – I: Involves controlled muscle lengthening under load, often performed at intensities >100% of 1RM, effective for hypertrophy and strength.

55. (B): In technique training, the second phase emphasizes kinesthetic perception, where the athlete becomes aware of:

- The correct body positions
- Muscle coordination
- Movement precision: This phase comes after the initial cognitive understanding and focuses on internal sensory feedback for motor learning and movement control. Developing this sense improves performance quality and efficiency.

56. (C): (*a*) Progressive-Regressive Procedure – II: This involves gradually increasing and then decreasing the intensity. The pattern 5 × 80%, 3 × 90%, 1 × 100%, 3 × 90%, 5 × 80% clearly represents this format.

(*b*) Progressive Procedure – I: Follows a pattern of continuously increasing intensity such as 5 × 80%, 4 × 85%, 3 × 90%, 2 × 95%, 1 × 100%.

(*c*) High Resistance Method – IV: Repeated efforts at near maximal intensities like 2 × 95%, 2 × 95%, 2 × 95%, 2 × 95% indicate use of heavy loads suitable for strength gains.

(*d*) Low Resistance Method – III: Light loads performed with high repetitions such as 20 × 50%, 20 × 50%, 20 × 50%, suitable for muscular endurance training.

57. (D): The correct sequence of technique training in the 3rd phase is:

(*a*) Practice under difficult and different conditions: Simulates competition variability.

(*e*) Development of movement concept: Helps athletes refine strategy and spatial awareness.

(*d*) Accurate and precise feedback: Essential for correcting technique and reinforcing learning.

(*b*) Increased participation in competition: To apply skills in actual performance situations.

(*c*) Ideo-motor training: Mental rehearsal of movement after physical patterns are well-established.

This stage focuses on refining skills, adaptability, and mental preparation.

58. (B): Heterochronicity of recovery refers to the variation in recovery time among different body systems and organs after exertion.

For example, the central nervous system may take longer to recover than muscles, and the cardiovascular system may recover faster than endocrine functions.

This concept is critical in periodization and recovery planning, ensuring that training loads consider organ-specific recovery timelines.

59. (A): The correct sequential order for basics of scientific management is:

(*c*) Study the work scientifically: Analyze tasks and methods using scientific techniques.

(*a*) Select the worker and train them: Find the right person and provide systematic training.

(*d*) Match job and workers properly: Ensure that worker capabilities align with job requirements.

(*b*) Distribute the gains between employers and employees: Share the productivity gains fairly to maintain motivation.

This approach was part of Frederick Taylor's principles of scientific management.

60. (D): (*a*) Thirty or more - III (Large Group): A group size of 30 or more is statistically considered a large sample, often enabling parametric tests.

(*b*) Discrete - IV (Type of Data): Discrete data refers to countable values such as number of goals, players, etc.

(*c*) Interval measurement - II (Scale): Interval scale has equal units, e.g., temperature in Celsius, but no true zero.

(*d*) Dispersion - I (Range): Dispersion is the spread of data, and range is one of the simplest measures of dispersion (max. - min.).

61. (B): The joints arranged in descending order of range of motion are:

(*b*) Shoulder Joint: A ball-and-socket joint, it offers the greatest range of motion in all planes - flexion, extension, abduction, adduction, rotation, and circumduction.

(*c*) Elbow Joint: A hinge joint, allows mainly flexion and extension, with limited rotation.

(*a*) Neck Joint: Formed by cervical vertebrae; allows rotation, flexion, and extension, but not as wide-ranging as shoulder or elbow.

(*d*) Skull Joint: Refers to cranial sutures, which are immovable (synarthrotic) in adults

Hence, the order from greatest to least mobility is: Shoulder → Elbow → Neck → Skull.

62. (C): Phytochemicals are bioactive compounds found in plants that have health benefits. The following are phytochemicals:

(*a*) Anthocyanidins: Found in berries and grapes, provide colour and antioxidant properties.

(*b*) Capsaicin: Present in chili peppers, known for anti-inflammatory and metabolism-boosting effects.

(*d*) Flavanones: Found in citrus fruits, contribute to antioxidant and cardiovascular benefits.

Whereas:

(*c*) Calcipherol (Vitamin D) and (*e*) Phylloquinone (Vitamin K1) are vitamins, not phytochemicals, even though they may be present in plant sources.

63. (C): Articulation problems are a type of speech disorder, where individuals have difficulty:

- Producing certain sounds correctly
- Forming clear and intelligible speech Examples include lisping, mispronouncing "r" as "w", etc.

This condition affects speech production, whereas options like semantic transformation (meaning), form perception, and visual closure relate more to language or visual processing disorders, not directly to speech articulation.

64. (A): The types of attention include:

(*a*) Enforced Attention: When attention is maintained due to external demands or pressure (e.g., exam).

(*d*) Voluntary Attention: Conscious focusing of mental resources on a task (e.g., studying).

(*e*) Habitual Attention: Automatic attention that develops through repeated exposure or habit.

Whereas:

(*b*) Awareness is a broader concept involving consciousness.

(*c*) Concentration is a feature or outcome of attention but not a type of attention by itself.

65. (C): The following are statistical software/tools used for data analysis:

(*a*) Minitab: Popular for teaching and industrial statistics.

(*b*) Python: A programming language with powerful libraries (Pandas, NumPy, SciPy, StatsModels) for statistical computing.

(*c*) SPSS: A GUI-based software widely used in social sciences for statistical analysis.

(*d*) Jamovi: A user-friendly, open-source alternative to SPSS.

(*e*) G*Power is specifically used for power analysis, not general statistical data analysis. Hence, it's excluded in this option.

66. (B): Risk of injury increases when joint flexibility is:

(*a*) Extremely low: Poor flexibility limits range of motion, leading to muscle strain or ligament tears during physical activity.

(*c*) Extremely high: Hyperflexibility can lead to joint instability, making joints more susceptible to dislocations and overuse injuries.

(*d*) Significant imbalance between dominant and non-dominant sides of the body: Muscle imbalances can result in uneven stress on joints, increasing the likelihood of injury during movement or athletic performance. Medium flexibility is considered ideal for both mobility and stability, while rigidity and imbalances are risk factors.

67. (D): The 2032 Paralympic Games will be hosted in Brisbane, Australia, following the Olympic Games which will also be held in the same city.

- The International Olympic Committee (IOC) announced Brisbane as the official host on 21 July 2021.
- Brisbane will be the third Australian city to host the Olympic and Paralympic Games after Melbourne (1956) and Sydney (2000).
- The Games are scheduled for 24 August to 5 September 2032.

68. (A): The models under Situational Leadership Theory of management include:

(*a*) Fiedler's Contingency Model: Leadership effectiveness depends on the match between leader's style and situational favorableness.

(*b*) Path-Goal Theory: Leaders adjust behaviour to help subordinates reach goals, influenced by task and environmental factors.

(*c*) Situational Leadership Model (Hersey-Blanchard): Emphasizes adapting leadership style based on follower readiness and maturity.

(*e*) Full Range Leadership Model: Includes transformational, transactional, and laissez-faire styles, covering a wide spectrum of leadership behaviour.

(*d*) Scientific Leadership Model is not a recognized situational model.

69. (B): Post-Traumatic Stress Disorder (PTSD) is a serious long-term psychological condition resulting from experiencing or witnessing a traumatic event such as war, assault, accident, or disaster.

- Symptoms include flashbacks, nightmares, emotional numbness, hypervigilance, and anxiety.
- It is recognized in DSM-5 (Diagnostic and Statistical Manual of Mental Disorders) and requires clinical intervention.
- Unlike stress before or during trauma, PTSD develops after the event, making it a chronic form of psychological distress.

70. (C): The proximal attachment of the Gluteus Medius muscle is located between the anterior and posterior gluteal lines on the outer surface of the ilium.

It plays a crucial role in hip abduction and stabilization of the pelvis during walking or running.

In contrast:

(A) Gluteus Maximus attaches posterior to posterior gluteal line.

(B) Rectus Femoris originates from anterior inferior iliac spine, not the ilium surface.

(D) Sartorius originates from the anterior superior iliac spine. Thus, only Gluteus Medius originates in the region specified.

71. (B): The correct sequence of recovery after physical exertion is:

(*b*) Re-synthesis of ATP and glycogen: This is the immediate priority post-exercise to restore energy reserves.

(*c*) Neutralization of lactic acid: Lactic acid accumulated due to anaerobic metabolism is cleared via conversion to pyruvate or glucose.

(*d*) Restoration of homeostasis: After the immediate needs are met, body systems begin restoring internal balance (e.g., temperature, pH, hormonal levels).

(*a*) Anabolic in nature: Finally, anabolic processes such as protein synthesis and tissue repair occur, contributing to adaptation and performance improvement.

72. (C): As individuals age, they typically experience:

(*a*) Decline in muscle size (atrophy), particularly without regular strength training.

(*c*) Reduced muscular strength, due to both neural and muscular degeneration.

(*e*) Decrease in lean body weight, as fat mass increases and muscle mass declines.

On the contrary:

(*b*) Percent body fat tends to increase, not decline.

(*d*) Blood pressure often increases with age due to vascular stiffness and lifestyle factors.

73. (B): The vestibular nerve, part of the vestibulocochlear nerve (Cranial Nerve VIII), plays a major role in:

- Postural adjustments
- Balance and coordination

Influences autonomic regulation of heart rate via its connection with vestibulo-cardiovascular reflexes during changes in body position and movement. It automatically helps the body adapt the heart's response to movement without conscious control.

74. (B): Muscle hypertrophy involves:

(*a*) Increase in myofibrils: These are the contractile units that thicken and multiply, leading to muscle growth.

(*b*) Increase in actin and myosin filaments: These proteins form the structure of myofibrils, and their accumulation contributes to strength and mass.

(*c*) Increase in sarcoplasm: Especially in sarcoplasmic hypertrophy, the volume of the muscle cell's fluid component increases.

(*d*) Tendons do not hypertrophy in the same manner, and (*e*) lipids are not contributors to muscle hypertrophy.

75. (D): (*a*) German Gymnastics – II: Guts Muths: Known as the grandfather of German gymnastics, introduced systematic physical training.

(*b*) Primitive Gymnastics – IV: Niels Bukh: Developed a more dynamic and expressive form of gymnastics emphasizing natural movement.

(*c*) Swedish Gymnastics – I: Per Henrik Ling: Introduced medical and therapeutic gymnastics with a scientific approach.

(*d*) "A system of physical education – theoretical and practical" – III: Archibald Maclaren: A British pioneer in integrating physical training into education and military systems.

76. (A): The Delphi Method is a structured communication and forecasting technique that:

- Involves a panel of experts.
- Uses multiple rounds of questionnaires to collect opinions.

Is designed to reach consensus on complex topics or predictions. It is especially useful in survey research for building agreement on specific issues through controlled feedback and anonymity.

77. (D): Matching each index with its correct formula:

(*a*) Body Mass Index (BMI) – II:

Formula: Weight (kg)/Height^2 (m)

BMI is used to assess whether a person is underweight, normal, overweight, or obese based on height and weight.

(*b*) Ponderal Index – IV:

Formula: Height (cm)/Cube root of body weight (kg)

This index is similar to BMI but takes into account the three-dimensional nature of the body. It is especially used in pediatric and neonatal studies.

(*c*) Broca Index – I:

Formula: Height (cm) – 100

A simple way to estimate ideal body weight primarily used in the past.

(*d*) Lorentz's Formula – III:

Formula: Height (cm) – [150/2 (women) or 4 (men)]

Lorentz's formula refines Broca's index by adjusting based on gender.

78. (C): The part of the experiment that the researcher manipulates is called the Treatment Variable, also known as the Independent Variable.

It is intentionally changed to observe its effect on the dependent variable.

For example, in a study testing the effect of different training methods on performance, the type of training is the treatment variable.

79. (C): Critical speed is the maximum speed an athlete can maintain over a prolonged period without fatigue, closely associated with the anaerobic threshold and typically:

- Involves 90–100% of $V_{O_2\ max}$
- Is associated with heart rates around 175–180 bpm

Does not include 75–80% of $V_{O_2\ max}$, which represents moderate intensity, below the threshold required to define critical speed.

80. (C): The Sterno-Clavicular joint is a saddle-type synovial joint but functionally behaves similar to a gliding joint, allowing movement in multiple planes:

- It connects the sternum and the clavicle.
- Allows elevation, depression, protraction, retraction, and limited rotation.
- Among the options given, Gliding Joint is the most functionally accurate classification.

81. (D)

82. (B): (*a*) Cronbach alpha coefficient – II (Reliability): Measures internal consistency reliability of a test.

(*b*) Halo Effect – I (Internal Validity): A bias where the perception of one trait influences the judgment of other traits, impacting internal validity.

(*c*) ANCOVA – IV (Distractor Variable): Used to control the effect of extraneous variables, often referred to as covariates or distractor variables.

(*d*) Concurrent Validity – III (Criterion Validity): Reflects how well a test correlates with a criterion measure taken at the same time.

83. (B): (*a*) Surplus Energy Theory – III (Van Schiller and Herbert): Suggests play is the result of excess energy not used for survival activities.

(*b*) Recapitulatory Theory – I (G. Stanley Hall): Proposes that play recapitulates the evolutionary development of the human species.

(*c*) Cathartic Theory – IV (Aristotle): Views play and drama as means for emotional release (catharsis).

(*d*) Anticipatory Theory – II (Carl Groos): States that play prepares children for future adult roles and responsibilities.

84. (D): (*a*) Phlegmatic – III (Stable Introvert): Calm, thoughtful, reliable; emotionally stable and reserved.

(*b*) Sanguine – IV (Stable Extrovert): Sociable, outgoing, and lively with stable emotions.

(*c*) Melancholic – I (Unstable Introvert): Anxious, quiet, pessimistic, emotionally unstable.

(*d*) Choleric – II (Unstable Extrovert): Aggressive, impulsive, and active but emotionally unstable.

This classification is based on Eysenck's model of personality involving introversion/extroversion and stability/instability.

85. (B): In highly trained athletes, cardiac output (amount of blood pumped by the heart per minute) can rise to as much as 40 liters/min during intense exercise.

- At rest: ~5 liters/min
- Untrained during max exercise: ~20–25 liters/min
- Trained athlete: up to 40 liters/min due to higher stroke volume and heart efficiency.

86. (C): This is a recognized type of stressful situation, where:

- An individual experiences or anticipates damage (physical or psychological).
- Examples: loss of a loved one, injury, failure.

It is emotionally impactful and typically triggers coping mechanisms. Environmental and mental situations describe contexts, not specific types. Conditional situation is not a recognized category in stress theory.

87. (A): Analgesia is the brain's internal pain control system, where the body reduces or suppresses pain perception.

- Involves endogenous opioids like endorphins and enkephalins.
- Controlled by structures like the periaqueductal gray and descending pain-inhibition pathways.
- Can be activated naturally (e.g., during extreme exertion or stress) or via medication.

88. (C): In 1966, Robert Rosenthal identified Expectancy as a threat to internal validity, also called the "experimenter expectancy effect".

- Occurs when the researcher's expectations influence the participants' behaviour or the interpretation of results.
- Leads to bias and distortion of actual outcomes. Other threats like maturation, instrumentation, and mortality were identified by Campbell and Stanley, not Rosenthal.

89. (A): Eustress is defined as positive stress, which:

- Enhances motivation, focus, and perfor-mance.
- Creates feelings of exhilaration and fulfillment.

Examples include preparing for a competition, performing on stage, or facing a challenge with excitement. It is distinct from distress, which is harmful and overwhelming.

90. (B): H. McCloy's classification index included:
(*b*) High School (not specifically boys)
(*d*) College (broader than "college men")
(*e*) Elementary School This classification was based on age and educational level, not gender-specific categories.

Hence options like (*a*) High School Boys and (*c*) College Men are not aligned with the original classification system.

91. (D): Whether to include a control variable in experimental research is not an absolute requirement in every case but is based on the decision of the researcher.

- The inclusion depends on research design, theoretical framework, and potential confounding factors.
- If a variable is likely to influence the dependent variable but is not of primary interest, the researcher may choose to control, ignore, or account for it.

92. (D): The observed difference in performance between men and women is considered an extraneous variable because it was not the primary variable manipulated in the experiment. The passage mentions that the difference might be due to women's reluctance to exhibit maximum effort in the presence of men, which could unintentionally influence the results. Since this factor is outside the controlled variables yet has the potential to affect the dependent variable (performance), it fits the definition of an extraneous variable, which threatens the internal validity of the study if not accounted for.

93. (A): Categorical variables like gender, race, or blood group represent fixed categories and cannot be manipulated by the researcher.

- They are used to group data, often for comparison or moderation analysis.
- In contrast, independent variables are manipulated, and extraneous variables may or may not be controlled.

94. (D): In the experiment, background music (synchronized or not) is a factor being manipulated by the researcher, making it the independent (treatment) variable.

The goal is to assess its effect on endurance performance, which is the dependent variable.

95. (C): Extraneous variables are factors that may influence the dependent variable but are not part of the planned experimental design.

If not controlled, they threaten internal validity, making it difficult to isolate the true effect of the independent variable.

96. (B): According to the passage, Luteinizing Hormone (LH) does not change with exercise, whereas others like GH, ACTH, glucagon, and thyroid hormones increase.

LH is involved in reproductive processes, and its levels remain unchanged during physical activity.

97. (A): The negative feedback mechanism is the main regulatory system for hormone levels.

- When the level of a hormone rises above the desired range, the endocrine system reduces further secretion, thus maintaining balance.
- It is the body's auto-regulatory hormonal control system.

98. (C): The passage lists Thyroid Stimulating Hormone (TSH) among those that increase with exercise.

- It stimulates the thyroid gland to secrete thyroxine and triiodothyronine, which are vital for metabolic regulation.
- Insulin decreases with exercise, and FSH and Calcitonin are not mentioned as increasing.

99. (*)

100. (B): Among the given options, Nervous Stimulation is not part of the cyclic AMP mechanism.

The cyclic AMP mechanism includes:

- Activation of enzymes
- Changes in cell membrane permeability
- Protein synthesis

Although the nervous system plays a role in hormone secretion, it is not directly a component of the cyclic AMP hormone action pathway.

Previous Years' Paper

National Testing Agency (NTA)

UGC-NET Junior Research Fellowship & Assistant Professor Eligibility Exam

PHYSICAL EDUCATION, September-2024

(Exam held on 02-09-2024)

PAPER-II

1. In which Olympiad of the ancient Olympic games Pankration event was included?

1. 14th Olympiad 2. 18th Olympiad
3. 25th Olympiad 4. 30th Olympiad

2. What was the theme of the 10th International Yoga day?

1. Yoga for Vasudhaiva Kutumbakam
2. Yoga for Humanity
3. Yoga for Self and Society
4. Yoga for Wellness

3. Which Country boycotted the winter Olympic games 1980?

1. France 2. China
3. Taiwan 4. Russia

4. Which clock determines the number of times a cell can divide?

1. Telomere 2. Mitvey
3. Biological 4. Nares

5. Which is the predominant cell type in the growing cartilage?

1. peritoneusblasts 2. merocrine
3. mesothelium 4. chondroblasts

6. What occurs when ionic compounds are formed?

1. Oxidation reactions
2. Exergonic reactions
3. Helix Beta pleated reactions
4. Redox reactions

7. Who developed the mercury barometer, an instrument that permits the accurate measurement of atmospheric pressure?

1. Pascal 2. Barode
3. E. Lavoisier 4. Torricelli

8. Children often hold a larger bat closer to the center of the bat. This makes it easier to swing because:

1. The centre of mass is reduced
2. The radius of gyration is reduced
3. The effective mass is increased
4. The radius of gyration is increased

9. We apply a force against the ground in running, but the force that propels us, the ground reaction force, is directed upwards. This principle is consistent with Newton's:

1. Law of Inertia
2. Law of Acceleration
3. Law of Action-reaction
4. Law of Gravitation

10. By what amount does the Kinetic energy of an object change if its velocity triples?

1. It increases 3 times
2. It decreases 3 times
3. It increases 9 times
4. It decreases 9 times

11. During running, the legs predominately move in which plane?

1. Frontal 2. Coronal
3. Transverse 4. Sagittal

12. A footballer committing a professional foul to avoid a conceding a goal is an example of ______.

1. Unsanctioned aggression
2. Hostile aggression
3. Instrumental aggression
4. Assertive aggression

13. According to ______, the success of leadership depends on the characteristics of leaders and the situation in which they are leading.

1. Instinct theory
2. Trait theory
3. Contingency theory
4. Self-perception theory

14. Execute backstroke with firm wrist and with elbow pointed down is an example of which type of goal?

1. Outcome goal 2. Performance goal
3. Process goal 4. Measurable goal

15. The experience of physiological changes associated with anxiety is called ______.

1. Somatic anxiety 2. Cognitive anxiety
3. Trait anxiety 4. State anxiety

16. An evaluation that takes place during the activity is called ______.

1. Formative evaluation
2. Preformative evaluation
3. Summative evaluation
4. Planning evaluation

17. A skill containing a single unit of activity with a clear beginning and end is known as ______.

1. Discrete skill
2. Continuous skill
3. Serial skill
4. Linear skill

18. Which is not an example of an invasion game?

1. Team Handball 2. Soccer
3. Tennis 4. Hockey

19. When urban malaria scheme was launched?

1. 1972 2. 1974
3. 1971 4. 1970

20. ______ is a colourless gas with a sharp odour.

1. Hydrocarbon 2. Cadmium
3. Sulphur dioxide 4. Hydrogen sulphide

21. Which is the most dangerous cancer?

1. Carcinoma 2. Melanoma
3. Alopecia 4. Sebum

22. Which loading process is often classified as a short term overloading?

1. Conjugated sequence loading
2. Concentrated Loading
3. Flat Loading
4. Linear Loading

23. The ability to rapidly switch from an eccentric contraction to a concentric contraction is known as:

1. Starting strength
2. Speed strength
3. Elastic reactive strength
4. Stabilisation strength

24. The retention of change by systematic workloads beyond a certain time period after the cessation of training is called ______.

1. The acute training effect
2. The immediate training effect
3. The residual training effect
4. The delayed training effect

25. Who introduced the modern theory of periodisation?

1. Ron Clarke
2. L.P. Matveyer
3. T.D. Noakes
4. Gundlach

26. If mean of x, $x + 4$, $x + 7$, $2x + 5$, $x + 10$ is 10 then which is the mean of last four scores?

1. 11 2. 12.5
3. 9.5 4. 11.5

27. If N = 10 and rank order correlation (ρ, rho) = 0.80, then, which is the value of $\in d^2$?

1. 32 2. 33
3. 34 4. 36

28. A cricket coach compared 3 training groups having 10 players in each group by using one way Analysis of Variance (ANOVA). Results revealed sum of squares between groups $(ss)_b$ = 134.6 and sum of squares within groups $(ss)_w$ = 110.1. Which is the value of F-ratio?

1. 15.60 2. 16.60
3. 16.05 4. 16.50

29. An unscientific method of problem solving is ______.

1. Ethnographic 2. Tenacity
3. Naturalistic 4. Reductionism

30. Which of the following is not a Analytical Research?

1. Philosophical 2. Historical
3. Case studies 4. Reviews

31. In standard normal distribution of a normal curve has a mean of ______ and a standard deviation of ______.

1. 1 and 0 2. 0 and 0
3. 1 and 1 4. 0 and 1

32. When the null hypothesis is accept and symbolically we can express as:

1. $\mu = \mu_{H0}$ 2. $\mu \neq \mu_{H0}$
3. $\mu > \mu_{H0}$ 4. $\mu < \mu_{H0}$

33. Scramble is a test item of which test?

1. Newton Motor Ability Test
2. Scott Motor Ability Test
3. Indiana Motor Fitness Test
4. Barrow Motor Ability Test

34. Which of the following refers to the degree to which performances on a test correspond to the abilities or traits that the test purports to measure?

1. Differential validity
2. Content validity
3. Concurrent validity
4. Construct validity

35. Which evaluation is usually based on specific objectives and utilizes criterion referenced standards?

1. Subjective evaluation
2. Objective evaluation
3. Summative evaluation
4. Formative evaluation

36. If in a test of 50 items with mean of 30 and standard deviation of 6, which will be the reliability of the test?

1. 0.86
2. 0.69
3. 0.78
4. 0.68

37. Which types of leaders use contingent reinforcement in management?

1. Transactional Leaders
2. Transformational Leaders
3. Bureaucratic Leaders
4. Democratic Leaders

38. Effectively integrating various human, financial and material resources to accomplish a plan is known as:

1. Planning
2. Organizing
3. Directing
4. Evaluating

39. Amount of resources used as considered in relation to the organizations level of goal attainment is called ______.

1. Organizational efficiency
2. Organizational effectiveness
3. Organizational achievement
4. Organizational leadership

40. First line managers are also known as:

1. Top-Level managers
2. Middle-Level managers
3. Supervisory-Level managers
4. Executive-Level managers

41. As altitude increases the decrease in air Temperature is accompanied by:

A. Water loss decrease
B. Increase sweat evaporation
G. Increased respiratory water loss
D. Dehydration through increased insensible water loss

Choose the ***correct*** answer from the options given below:

1. B, C, D Only
2. B, C Only
3. A, C Only
4. A, B, D Only

42. The rotator cuff is a hood like convergency of tendons around the head of humerus from which of the following muscles?

A. Subscapularis
B. Teres minor
C. Supraspinatus
D. Lattissimus dorsi
E. Infraspinatus

Choose the ***correct*** answer from the options given below:

1. A, B, E Only
2. A, B, D Only
3. A, B, D, E Only
4. A, B, C, E Only

43. Which of the following parameters influence the form drag?

A. Relative mass
B. Form drag coefficient
C. Relative velocity
D. Frontal surface area
E. Squared relative velocity

Choose the ***correct*** answer from the options given below:

1. A, B, D Only
2. A, C, E Only
3. B, D, E Only
4. A, B, C Only

44. Which of the following equations used to assess the projectile motion?

A. $V = u + at$
B. $V^2 = u^2 + 2as$
C. $S = ut + ½at$
D. $V = \Delta s + \Delta t$
E. $m_1v_1 = m_2v_2$

Choose the ***correct*** answer from the options given below:

1. A, B Only
2. A, B, C Only
3. A, B, C, D Only
4. A, B, C, D, E

45. Which of the following examples in sport psychology are related to social psychology approach?

A. Aggression
B. Motivation
C. Team Cohesion
D. Imagery
E. Skill acquisition

Choose the ***correct*** answer from the options given below:

1. A, C, E Only
2. A, C Only
3. B, C, D Only
4. C, E Only

46. Which types of factors affect the cohesiveness of a team according to carron?

A. Individual factors
B. Situational factors
C. Team factors
D. Coaching style
E. Leadership

Choose the ***correct*** answer from the options given below:

1. A, B, C Only
2. B, C, E Only
3. C, D, E Only
4. A, B, C, E Only

47. Examples of psychological skills include:

A. Self talk
B. Goal setting
C. Self confidence
D. Mental toughness
E. Anxiety control

Choose the *correct* answer from the options given below:

1. A, C, D Only 2. C, D, E Only
3. A, B, E Only 4. B, D, E Only

48. Purpose of curricular evaluation includes:

A. Program effectiveness
B. To identify program omissions
C. Program justification
D. Employment opportunity of the program
E. Reduce the evaluation cost money

Choose the *correct* answer from the options given below:

1. A, C, D Only 2. A, B, C Only
3. C, D, E Only 4. A, B, E Only

49. The advantage of ground water are:

A. It usually requires no treatment
B. It is high in mineral content
C. It is likely to be free from pathogenic agents
D. It requires pumping to lift the water

Choose the *correct* answer from the options given below:

1. B, C, D Only 2. A, B, C Only
3. A, B Only 4. A, C Only

50. Which of the following are zoonotic diseases?

A. Plague B. Chikungunya fever
C. SARS D. Rabies
E. Yellow Fever

Choose the *correct* answer from the options given below:

1. A, C, D, E Only
2. A, C, D Only
3. A, B, D, E Only
4. A, B, D Only

51. Which of the following training effects are part of the cooper's training effect categories?

A. Involution B. Overreaching
C. Minor D. Maintenance
E. Positive

Choose the *correct* answer from the options given below:

1. A, B, C Only 2. C, D, E Only
3. C, B, A Only 4. B, C, D Only

52. What are the three types of mesocycle-blocks given by Issurin & Kaverin?

A. Developmental B. Accumulation
C. Transformation D. Realization
E. Restorative

Choose the *correct* answer from the options given below:

1. A, C, E Only
2. B, C, E Only
3. B, C, D Only
4. A, B, C Only

53. Which of the following statements are correct about Multiple Correlation?

A. Multiple correlation can be used to select the test battery which is composed of the test items that correlate lowest to the criterion and highest with one another.
B. Test item that correlate highly with another one is considered to be measuring the same thing and is therefore superfluous.
C. If two test items are formed to be highly related, the one that correlates lowest with the criterion is selected.
D. If these are considerable number of test items multiple correlation process select least no. of items to comprise the test battery.
E. Regression equations can also be used to predict an individual performance based on the scores on the selected items.

Choose the *correct* answer from the options given below:

1. B, D, E Only
2. A, C, D, E Only
3. B, C, D, E Only
4. A, B, D, E Only

54. Which of the following are correct about the characteristics of Normal Curve?

A. The curve is asymptotic towards the base line.
B. The Quartile deviation of normal distribution is 3/2.
C. The point of inflexion of the curve is given by $\sigma \pm \mu$.
D. Total area of normal curve is considered to be 100%.
E. Limit of $\mu - \sigma$ to $\mu + \sigma$ covers 68.26% area.

Choose the ***correct*** answer from the options given below:

1. A, C, E Only
2. A, B, D, E Only
3. A, C, D, E Only
4. A, D, E Only

55. Which of the following are comes under informal design?

A. Before-and-after without control
B. After-only control
C. Latin square design
D. Before-and-after with control
E. Completely randomized

Choose the ***correct*** answer from the options given below:

1. B, C, E Only
2. A, B, C Only
3. C, D, E Only
4. A, B, D Only

56. The characteristics involves to solve a research problems are:

A. Reductive B. Replicable
C. Empirical D. Delimitation
E. Limitation

Choose the ***correct*** answer from the options given below:

1. A, B, C Only
2. B, C, D Only
3. C, D, E Only
4. A, D, E Only

57. In SPSS "Variable views" of the data editor the columns has the following label.

A. Name B. Width
C. Transform D. Decimals
E. Add-one

Choose the ***correct*** answer from the options given below:

1. A, B, C Only 2. A, B, D Only
3. A, B, E Only 4. B, D, E Only

58. Which of the following statements are correct for standard scores?

A. Mean of standard scores is 0.
B. Standard deviation of standard scores is 1.
C. Standard scores is free from units.
D. Limits of standard scores are ± 2.
E. Standard scores are always positive.

Choose the ***correct*** answer from the options given below:

1. A, B, C, E Only
2. A, B, C Only
3. B, C, D Only
4. A, B, D Only

59. Which of the following statements are not correct?

A. Norm referenced standard is concerned with the degree to which a student has a level of competence.
B. Criterion referenced standard is based on statistical procedures.
C. Criterion referenced standard is not used to judge an individual's performance in relation to others of the same age, sex and ability level.
D. In criterion referenced standard the coach would motivate the player to strive for the highest percentile before the next testing.

Choose the ***correct*** answer from the options given below:

1. B, C, D Only 2. A, C, D Only
3. A, B, D Only 4. A, B, C Only

60. Which of the following are correct about Sports Anxiety Scale-2 (SAS-2, 2006)?

A. SAS-2 consists of 21 items.

B. SAS-2 items assess somatic anxiety, worry and concentration disruption.

C. All items are scored on a 4 point scale.

D. No item has reverse scoring.

E. SAS-2 has seven items for each scale.

Choose the *correct* answer from the options given below:

1. A, B, C, E Only
2. A, B, E Only
3. B, C, E Only
4. B, C, D Only

61. Find the correct sequential rank order of teams in the Khelo India Winters Games in 2024.

A. Uttarakhand B. Karnataka

C. Indian Army D. Maharashtra

E. Himachal Pradesh

Choose the *correct* answer from the options given below:

1. A, E, C, D, B
2. B, D, C, A, E
3. C, B, D, E, A
4. E, A, D, C, B

62. Arrange the host states of Khelo India Youth Games in ascending order.

A. Maharashtra B. Haryana

C. Assam D. New Delhi

Choose the *correct* answer from the options given below:

1. A, B, C, D 2. B, D, A, C
3. C, A, B, D 4. D, A, C, B

63. Arrange the stages in endochondral ossification occurring in a long bone.

A. Cartilage in the center of the diaphysis calcifies and then cavities

B. The periosteal bud invades the internal cavities and spongy bone forms

C. The epiphyses ossify

D. Formation of bone collar around hyaline cartilage model

E. The diaphysis elongates and medullary cavity forms

Choose the *correct* answer from the options given below:

1. D, A, B, E, C
2. A, B, E, D, C
3. D, C, A, B, E
4. C, D, B, A, E

64. Write the steps of a qualitative Bio-mechanical analysis.

A. Observation B. Instruction

C. Description D. Evaluation

Choose the *correct* answer from the options given below:

1. B, D, A, C 2. C, D, B, A
3. C, A, D, B 4. A, B, D, C

65. Find the correct sequence of stages in learning of behaviour proposed by Bandura.

A. Reproduction B. Retention

C. Attention D. Reinforcement

Choose the *correct* answer from the options given below:

1. C, B, D, A 2. B, C, A, D
3. C, D, B, A 4. C, B, A, D

66. Find the correct order of a five stage model of athlete self-regulation developed by Kirschenbaum.

A. Problem identification

B. Execution

C. Commitment

D. Generalization

E. Environmental management

Choose the *correct* answer from the options given below:

1. B, C, A, D, E
2. A, C, B, E, D
3. A, B, E, C, D
4. C, A, B, E, D

67. Identify the correct sequential order of the skill theme approach in Physical Education.

A. Skill in contexts
B. Combinations
C. Basic skill
D. Culminating activity

Choose the ***correct*** answer from the options given below:

1. B, C, A, D
2. C, D, B, A
3. A, B, C, D
4. C, B, A, D

68. Write the first aid steps followed for snake bite as per the Government of India protocol 2007.

A. Do not give alcoholic beverages
B. Immobilize
C. Do not manipulate the bitten site
D. Do not apply any compression
E. Transport the patient to a medical facility

Choose the ***correct*** answer from the options given below:

1. A, C, D, B, E
2. B, D, A, C, E
3. B, A, C, D, E
4. C, A, B, D, E

69. Write the correct sequential order of training factors in the bottom up approach of a training factors pyramid.

A. Technical training
B. Tactical training
C. Physical training
D. Psychological and mental training

Choose the ***correct*** answer from the options given below:

1. B, C, A, D
2. D, A, B, C
3. C, A, B, D
4. C, B, A, D

70. Write the steps while developing Sampling design.

A. Size of sample
B. Sampling unit
C. Source list
D. Parameter of interest
E. Types of universe

Choose the ***correct*** answer from the options given below:

1. E, B, C, A, D
2. B, C, A, D, E
3. C, A, D, E, B
4. A, D, E, B, C

71. Write the correct sequence for developing likert-type scale.

A. Five point scale for sourcing
B. Trail Test
C. Correlated statement in instrument
D. Large number of statement
E. Find statement have high discriminatory power

Choose the ***correct*** answer from the options given below:

1. A, E, B, D, C
2. D, B, A, E, C
3. D, E, B, A, C
4. B, A, D, E, C

72. Find the correct sequence of the following sports skill tests in ascending order according to the year in which these were constructed/ published.

A. Poole Badminton test
B. Hewitt Tennis achievement test
C. AAHPER volleyball test
D. French short serve test
E. Knox Basketball test

Choose the ***correct*** answer from the options given below:

1. D, E, C, B, A
2. D, B, E, C, A
3. E, D, B, C, A
4. D, E, B, C, A

73. Sequentially arrange the following steps of item analysis:

A. Separate answer sheets into upper, lower and middle groups

B. Record No. of frequencies in upper and lower groups
C. Calculate Index of difficulty
D. Score the tests
E. Arrange answer sheets from high to low scores

Choose the *correct* answer from the options given below:

1. D, C, E, A, B
2. D, E, A, C, B
3. D, A, E, B, C
4. D, E, A, B, C

74. Write the correct sequential order of steps in the control process used by sports managers.

A. Reinforcing performance at or above expectations
B. Analyzing and correcting deviation from the standards
C. Accurately measuring performance
D. Establishing performance standards
E. Comparing performance with the established standards

Choose the *correct* answer from the options given below:

1. A, B, C, D, E
2. D, C, E, B, A
3. E, C, A, D, B
4. C, A, D, B, E

75. Find the correct sequential order of speed ability involved in sprinting events.

A. Acceleration ability
B. Locomotor ability
C. Reaction ability
D. Speed endurance
E. Movement speed

Choose the *correct* answer from the options given below:

1. A, E, B, D, C
2. E, B, D, A, C
3. C, E, A, B, D
4. C, A, E, B, D

76. Match the List-I with List-II.

List-I (Olympic Games opened by)	**List-II (Host city)**
A. H.M. King Albert I	I. Sydney (2000)
B. Sir William Deane	II. Seoul (1988)
C. President Roh tae woo	III. Antwerp (1920)
D. President hu Jinto	IV. Beijing (2008)

Choose the *correct* answer from the options given below:

1. A-I, B-II, C-III, D-IV
2. A-III, B-II, C-IV, D-I
3. A-III, B-I, C-II, D-IV
4. A-II, B-IV, C-I, D-III

77. Match the List-I with List-II.

List-I (Philosophical terms)	**List-II (Focus)**
A. Existentialism	I. Self actualization and the development of value are emphasized
B. Humanism	II. The individual more important than society
C. Realism	III. Individual experiences determined what is true
D. Naturalism	IV. Science reveals the truth

Choose the *correct* answer from the options given below:

1. A-I, B-II, C-III, D-IV
2. A-III, B-I, C-IV, D-II
3. A-IV, B-II, C-III, D-I
4. A-II, B-I, C-IV, D-III

78. Match the List-I with List-II.

List-I (Organs)	List-II (Sympathetic effects)
A. Liver	I. Cause vasodilation
B. Lungs	II. Stimulate secretion of epinephrine and norepinephrine
C. Adrenal glands	III. Cause bronchodilation
D. Heart: Coronary blood vessels	IV. Stimulates glucose release

Choose the ***correct*** answer from the options given below:

1. A-I, B-II, C-III, D-IV
2. A-III, B-II, C-I, D-IV
3. A-II, B-III, C-IV, D-I
4. A-IV, B-III, C-II, D-I

79. Match the List-I with List-II.

List-I (Variable)	List-II (Equation)
A. Kinetic energy	I. ½ mv^2
B. Potential energy	II. μR
C. Momentum	III. m × v
D. Friction	IV. m × g × h

Choose the ***correct*** answer from the options given below:

1. A-IV, B-III, C-II, D-I
2. A-I, B-IV, C-III, D-II
3. A-II, B-I, C-IV, D-III
4. A-III, B-IV, C-I, D-II

80. Match the List-I with List-II.

List-I (Name of the muscle)	List-II (Origin)
A. Levatores costarum	I. T_{12} & L_1 to L_5
B. Serratus posterior superior	II. C_7 & T_1 to T_{11}
C. Serratus posterior inferior	III. C_7 & T_1 to T_3
D. Psoas	IV. T_{11}-T_{12} & L_1 to L_3

Choose the ***correct*** answer from the options given below:

1. A-I, B-II, C-III, D-IV
2. A-II, B-III, C-IV, D-I
3. A-III, B-IV, C-I, D-II
4. A-IV, B-I, C-II, D-III

81. Match the List-I with List-II.

List-I	List-II
A. A broad attentional focus	I. A cricket batsman directs attention to a ball
B. A narrow attentional focus	II. A Baseball batter prepares to swing at a pitch
C. An external attentional focus	III. A Soccer player dribbling the ball upfield
D. An internal attentional focus	IV. A high jumper prepares to start her run-up

Choose the ***correct*** answer from the options given below:

1. A-II, B-III, C-IV, D-I
2. A-IV, B-III, C-II, D-I
3. A-II, B-III, C-I, D-IV
4. A-III, B-II, C-I, D-IV

82. Match the List-I with List-II.

List-I	List-II
A. Personality	I. The force within the individual that drives a person to confront and overcome adversity.
B. Personality profile	II. All the consistent ways in which the behaviour of one person differs from that of others, especially in social situations.
C. Personality trait	III. The plotting of an athlete's standardized personality scores on a line or bar graph
D. Resilience	IV. A disposition to exhibit certain personality characteristics.

Choose the *correct* answer from the options given below:

1. A-II, B-III, C-IV, D-I
2. A-III, B-IV, C-I, D-II
3. A-IV, B-III, C-II, D-I
4. A-II, B-I, C-IV, D-III

83. Match the List-I with List-II.

List-I (Assessments)	**List-II (Meaning/ Explanation)**
A. Skill tests	I. An assessment in which students present a scenario and then demonstrate how they would react in that situation
B. Role play	II. Collections of artifacts that typically are used to show students competency of a subject area
C. Journals	III. An assessment that provides students opportunity to reflect and write on events or topics in class
D. Portfolios	IV. Assessment of students physical ability usually done in a closed environment

Choose the *correct* answer from the options given below:

1. A-IV, B-I, C-III, D-II
2. A-II, B-III, C-I, D-IV
3. A-IV, B-III, C-II, D-I
4. A-I, B-IV, C-III, D-II

84. Match the List-I with List-II.

List-I (Essential fatty acids)	**List-II (Dietary source)**
A. Linoleic acid	I. Fish oil
B. Arachidonic acid	II. Leafy greens
C. Linolenic acid	III. Milk
D. Eichosapentaenoic acid	IV. Corn oil

Choose the *correct* answer from the options given below:

1. A-III, B-I, C-II, D-IV
2. A-IV, B-I, C-II, D-III
3. A-III, B-IV, C-I, D-II
4. A-IV, B-III, C-II, D-I

85. Match the List-I with List-II.

List-I (Arjuna Awards (2023) Name of the Sportsperson)	**List-II (Discipline)**
A. Shri Anush Agarwalla	I. Kabaddi
B. Shri Pawan Kumar	II. Equestrian
C. Ms. Nasreen	III. Para Canoeing
D. Ms. Prachi Yadav	IV. Kho-Kho

Choose the *correct* answer from the options given below:

1. A-II, B-I, C-IV, D-III
2. A-III, B-I, C-IV, D-II
3. A-IV, B-III, C-I, D-II
4. A-II, B-I, C-III, D-IV

86. Match the List-I with List-II.

List-I (Training Terms)	**List-II (Meaning)**
A. Intensity	I. A quantitative element of training that can be measured as time or duration of training
B. Volume	II. The qualitative element of training such as speed, power
C. Density of training	III. Intensity determined by dividing the total volume load by the total number of repetitions
D. Training intensity	IV. The frequency of training within a given time frame

Choose the *correct* answer from the options given below:

1. A-I, B-III, C-II, D-IV
2. A-II, B-I, C-IV, D-III
3. A-IV, B-III, C-II, D-I
4. A-II, B-IV, C-I, D-III

87. Match the List-I with List-II.

List-I	List-II
A. Plagiarism	I. Protection of Human participants
B. Outlier	II. Using ideas of other
C. Copyright	III. An unrepresentative score
D. Informed consent	IV. Seek permission

Choose the *correct* answer from the options given below:

1. A-I, B-II, C-III, D-IV
2. A-II, B-III, C-IV, D-I
3. A-I, B-II, C-IV, D-III
4. A-III, B-II, C-IV, D-I

88. Match the List-I with List-II.

List-I (Research Design)	List-II (Descriptive study)
A. Sampling design	I. Pre-planned
B. Statistical design	II. Structured
C. Observational design	III. Probability
D. Operational design	IV. Advanced decisions

Choose the *correct* answer from the options given below:

1. A-II, B-III, C-IV, D-I
2. A-III, B-II, C-IV, D-I
3. A-III, B-I, C-II, D-IV
4. A-I, B-II, C-III, D-IV

89. Match the List-I with List-II.

List-I	List-II
A. Competitive State Anxiety Inventory-2 (CSAI-2)	I. Robin S. Vealy (1986)
B. Sports Confidence Inventory	II. Dishman and Ickes (1981)
C. Group Environment Questionnaire	III. Craft, Magyar, Becker and Feltz (2003)
D. Self-Motivation Inventory	IV. Carron, Widmeyar and Brawley (1985)

Choose the *correct* answer from the options given below:

1. A-IV, B-I, C-III, D-II
2. A-III, B-I, C-II, D-IV
3. A-III, B-I, C-IV, D-II
4. A-IV, B-I, C-II, D-III

90. Match the List-I with List-II.

List-I (Somatotype)	List-II (Body Build Classification)
A. Extreme ectomorph	I. 2-6-4
B. Extreme endomorph	II. 1-7-1
C. Extreme mesomorph	III. 7-1-1
D. Ectomorphic mesomorph	IV. 1-1-7

Choose the *correct* answer from the options given below:

1. A-IV, B-III, C-II, D-I
2. A-IV, B-III, C-I, D-II
3. A-III, B-IV, C-II, D-I
4. A-III, B-IV, C-I, D-II

Direction (Qs. No. 91 to 95): *Read the following passage carefully and answer the questions based on it:*

Validity and reliability are a constant point of confusion and concern for many researchers. They are three types such as external, instrument and internal. The results of external validity and reliability can applies to population and further. The instrument validity and reliability consider only on instruments. To enhance instrument reliability the researcher can use a test-retest or a split-half methods. Finally internally validity and reliability focuses on how the study was conducted and the difference or relationship observed are the result of the variables being studied. The relationship between validity and reliability are either directly or indirectly associated. For an example, if the golfers are trying to sink the ball in the hole, but the golfers are in a random pattern all over the green area and the golfers made an second try still cannot sink the ball but their putting is consistent and tight cluster. Further the golfers made the third attempt and have achieved every ball hit has landed in the hole. The relationship between validity and reliability is an important one that must be received in research studies.

91. The split-half method is used to improve ______.

1. External validity
2. External reliability
3. Instrument validity
4. Instrument reliability

92. The outcome of ______ can be generalize beyond the sample.

1. External validity
2. Instrument validity
3. Internal validity
4. Relationship observed

93. The Golf balls are in a random pattern all over the green area is an example of ______.

1. No validity and No reliability
2. Low validity and Low reliability
3. Low validity and High reliability
4. High validity and High reliability

94. The golfers are putting the ball consistent and tight cluster is an example of ______.

1. No validity and No reliability
2. Low validity and Low reliability
3. Low validity and High reliability
4. High validity and High reliability

95. The golfers every hit, the ball has landed in the hole is an example of ______.

1. No validity and No reliability
2. Low validity and Low reliability
3. Low validity and High reliability
4. High validity and High reliability

Direction (Qs. No. 96 to 100): *Read the following passage carefully and answer the questions based on it:*

High altitude training is a technique used by athletes to enhance their performance by training at elevations typically above 2,400 meters (8,000 feet). At these heights, the oxygen levels are significantly lower than the sea level, which forces the body to adapt to the reduced availability of oxygen. The physiological adaptation is an elevated production of erythropoietin, a harmone stimulates the production of red blood cells. This increase in red blood cells enhances the oxygen carrying capacity of the blood, which can improve endurance and performance when the athlete returns to lower altitudes, other physiological changes include increased capillary density, improved buffering capacity of muscles, and enhanced efficiency of respiratory muscles. These adaptations collectively enhance the body's ability to utilize oxygen more effectively. Moreover, high altitude training can lead to improved mitochondrial density' and function, further boosting the energy production capacities of muscle cells. However, it is important to note that the benefits of high altitude training can vary among individuals and not all athletes may experience the same level of performance enhancement. Athletes often use a strategy known as "Live high, train low," where they live at high altitudes to gain the physiological benefits but train at lower altitudes to maintain training intensity. This method maximizes the advantages of high altitude acclimatization while minimizing the potential downsides, such as reduced training intensity due to lower oxygen availability.

96. What primary physiological adaptation taken place at altitude training?

1. Increased muscle mass
2. Increased erythropoietin
3. Decreased lung capacity
4. Decreased Heart rate

97. Which of the following is not a physiological change due to altitude training?

1. More number of capillary
2. Increased pH balance
3. Effective pulmonary function
4. Reduced Power-house density

98. What is the "Live high, train low" strategy?

1. Living and training at high altitudes
2. Living at high altitudes but training at lower altitudes
3. Living at sea level and training at high altitudes
4. Living and training at sea level

99. How the altitude training influences the pulmonary muscle?

1. Increasing number
2. Increasing size
3. Increasing efficiency
4. Increasing diameter

100. If an long distance runner adopt "Live high, train low" strategy, why to reduce training intensity at altitude?

1. Decreased blood volume
2. Decreased HbO_2
3. Decreased atmosphere O_2
4. Decreased Anaerobic metabolism

ANSWERS

1. (*)

2. (3): The theme of the 10th International Yoga Day, held on 21st June 2024, was "Yoga for Self and Society". This theme emphasized the holistic benefits of yoga not only for individual well-being but also for creating a healthier and more harmonious society. It highlighted yoga's role in balancing personal physical and mental health, which ultimately contributes to societal wellness. The event saw mass participation across the globe, including a grand session at the United Nations headquarters led by India's Prime Minister.

3. (3): Taiwan (officially the Republic of China) boycotted the 1980 Winter Olympic Games held in Lake Placid, USA, due to a dispute with the International Olympic Committee (IOC) over the use of its name, flag, and anthem. The IOC had decided to recognize the People's Republic of China as the official representative of China, which led Taiwan to withdraw in protest. The political tension around the issue of "One China" policy led Taiwan to boycott both the Winter and Summer Olympics of 1980. Later, Taiwan competed under the name "Chinese Taipei" starting from 1984.

4. (1): Telomeres are the protective caps at the ends of chromosomes that serve as a kind of biological clock determining how many times a cell can divide. Each time a cell divides, a small portion of the telomere is lost. Eventually, the telomeres become too short to protect the chromosomes, triggering cellular senescence or apoptosis. This process is a major factor in aging and cellular lifespan. Telomeres are composed of repetitive DNA sequences (TTAGGG in humans) and are maintained by the enzyme telomerase in certain cell types like stem cells and cancer cells.

5. (4): Chondroblasts are the predominant cell type in growing cartilage. These cells are responsible for secreting the extracellular matrix components such as collagen type II and proteoglycans that form the cartilage tissue. As the cartilage matures, chondroblasts become embedded in the matrix and differentiate into chondrocytes, which maintain the cartilage structure. Growing cartilage, especially during development and at epiphyseal growth plates, is rich in active chondroblasts involved in cartilage formation and repair.

6. (4): When ionic compounds are formed, they involve redox (reduction-oxidation) reactions. In such reactions, one atom loses electrons (oxidation) and another gains electrons (reduction). For example, in the formation of sodium chloride (NaCl), sodium loses an electron (gets oxidized) to become Na^+, and chlorine gains that electron (gets reduced) to become Cl^-. This transfer of electrons leads to the formation of ions, which then attract each other to form an ionic bond.

7. (4): Evangelista Torricelli, an Italian physicist and mathematician, developed the mercury barometer in 1643. This instrument was the first accurate method for measuring atmospheric pressure. He filled a glass tube with mercury and inverted it into a dish, observing that the mercury level dropped slightly, leaving a vacuum at the top. The height of the mercury column was affected by atmospheric pressure, which led to the fundamental understanding of barometric pressure and the invention of the barometer.

8. (2): When children hold a larger bat closer to its center, it reduces the radius of gyration, which is the distance from the axis of rotation to the point where the mass of the object can be considered to be concentrated. A smaller radius of gyration means the moment of inertia is reduced, making it easier to rotate or swing the bat. Thus, by gripping the bat closer to the center, children reduce the resistance to angular motion, allowing for easier and faster swings.

9. (3): The statement reflects Newton's Third Law of Motion, which is the law of action-reaction. It states: "For every action, there is an equal and opposite reaction". When we run, we push backward and downward against the ground (action), and the ground exerts an equal and opposite force — forward and upward (reaction). This ground reaction force propels us forward during locomotion.

10. (3): Kinetic energy (KE) is given by the formula

$$KE = (1/2)mv^2,$$

where m is mass and v is velocity.

If the velocity triples, i.e., becomes 3v, then:

$$\text{New KE} = (1/2)\ m/(3v)^2$$
$$= (1/2)\ m/(9v^2)$$
$$= 9 \times (1/2)\ mv^2.$$

Thus, the kinetic energy becomes 9 times greater than before.

11. (4): The sagittal plane is the anatomical plane that divides the body into left and right halves. Movements in this plane involve forward and backward motions, such as flexion and extension.

- During running, the primary movements of the legs (hip flexion, knee flexion, hip extension, and knee extension) all occur in the sagittal plane.
- For example, when the thigh swings forward, it's hip flexion; when it drives backward, it's hip extension — both of which are sagittal movements.
- Similarly, the arms also move forward and backward during running in this same plane to assist with balance and momentum.
- In contrast, the frontal plane involves side-to-side motion, and the transverse plane involves rotational movement — both of which are less prominent during straight-line running.

12. (3): Instrumental aggression is a form of aggressive behaviour aimed at achieving a specific goal or reward, not necessarily driven by anger or intent to harm.

In the context of sports, this might involve a calculated or strategic foul to prevent an opponent's advantage — such as a footballer committing a foul to prevent a goal-scoring opportunity.

This is different from hostile aggression, which is emotionally driven and intended to cause harm.

Instrumental aggression is:

- Purposeful
- Often seen as part of competitive strategies
- Not based on emotional outburst

It is typically penalized in sport, but it highlights the tension between competitive drive and sportsmanship.

13. (3): The Contingency Theory of leadership proposes that there is no single best way to lead; rather, the success of a leader depends on how well their leadership style matches the specific context or situation.

Introduced primarily by Fred Fiedler, the theory assesses:

- Leader's personality and style (task-oriented or relationship-oriented)
- The characteristics of the group (e.g., team dynamics, experience level)
- The nature of the task (structured vs. unstructured)

For example, a task-oriented leader might succeed in a crisis but not in a creative environment, while a relationship-oriented leader might thrive in team-building or collaborative tasks.

Hence, leadership effectiveness is "contingent" on these situational factors aligning properly with the leader's traits.

14. (3): A process goal focuses on the technique, form, or strategy used to perform a task rather than the outcome or performance level.

The statement "Execute backstroke with firm wrist and with elbow pointed down" describes specific mechanical actions involved in swimming technique.

Characteristics of process goals:

- They help in refining skill acquisition and execution
- Emphasis is on how the action is performed, not whether the action wins or achieves a specific result
- Ideal for practice and training environments

Compared to outcome goals (e.g., winning a race) or performance goals (e.g., improving time by 2 seconds), process goals are essential for building foundational skills and improving consistency.

15. (1): Somatic anxiety refers to the physical symptoms of anxiety that occur when an individual is under stress or pressure, especially in performance contexts like sports.

Common symptoms include:

- Increased heart rate
- Rapid breathing
- Muscle tension
- Sweating
- Shaking or butterflies in the stomach

It is one part of the multi-dimensional theory of anxiety, which separates anxiety into:

- Cognitive anxiety: mental worry, fear of failure
- Somatic anxiety: physiological arousal

In athletes, somatic anxiety usually peaks just before competition and may decline once the performance begins.

Managing somatic anxiety through relaxation techniques, breathing control, or progressive muscle relaxation can help improve performance.

16. (1): Formative evaluation is an assessment conducted during the process of an activity or program, with the aim of monitoring progress and making real-time improvements.

In the context of education, sports, or training programs, formative evaluation provides ongoing feedback to instructors and participants.

Its purpose is diagnostic, allowing for timely adjustments to improve performance or understanding.

Examples include:

- Quizzes during a course
- Coach feedback during practice
- Peer assessments mid-way through a project

Unlike summative evaluation, which occurs at the end to assess overall achievement, formative evaluation is integral to guiding learning and development during the process.

17. (1): A discrete skill is a single-unit movement with a clearly defined beginning and end, often performed in a short time frame.

These skills are not continuous or repetitive and are usually simple motor tasks.

Examples include:

- A golf swing
- A basketball free throw
- A punch in boxing

Discrete skills contrast with continuous skills, which have no clear start or end (e.g., cycling or swimming), and serial skills, which are combinations of discrete movements performed in sequence (e.g., gymnastics routine or triple jump).

18. (3): Tennis is not an example of an invasion game.

Invasion games involve two teams trying to invade the opponent's territory to score points, often requiring strategic movement, positioning, and teamwork.

Examples of invasion games include:

- Soccer
- Hockey
- Team Handball

In contrast, tennis is a net/wall game, where players or teams are separated by a net and aim to score by hitting the ball into the opponent's side of the court.

The focus is not on territory invasion but on rallying and outmanoeuvring the opponent within set boundaries.

19. (3): The Urban Malaria Scheme (UMS) was launched in the year 1971 by the Government of India.

This initiative was aimed at controlling malaria in urban areas, particularly in regions with high population density and poor sanitation, which created favourable conditions for mosquito breeding.

Key features:

- Vector surveillance and control
- Health education and awareness campaigns
- Indoor residual spraying and use of larvicides

UMS complemented earlier rural-centric programs like the National Malaria Eradication Programme (NMEP), addressing the rising concern of urban malaria outbreaks due to rapid urbanization.

20. (3): Sulphur dioxide (SO_2) is a colourless gas with a sharp, irritating odour, commonly associated with burning fossil fuels, especially coal and oil in power plants and industrial processes.

Characteristics:

- Pungent smell, often compared to a burnt match
- Heavier than air and can form toxic concentrations at ground level
- It is a major air pollutant and contributes to acid rain

Exposure to SO_2 can cause respiratory problems, particularly in individuals with asthma or other lung conditions.

Other options like hydrocarbons are typically a group of compounds, cadmium is a metal, and hydrogen sulphide (H_2S), though also with a sharp odour (rotten eggs), is not the correct match for the given description.

21. (2): Melanoma is considered one of the most dangerous types of cancer, especially among skin cancers, because of its high potential to spread (metastasize) rapidly to other organs if not detected early.

It originates in the melanocytes, the cells responsible for producing melanin, the pigment that gives skin its color.

While less common than carcinomas, melanomas are far more aggressive.

Key reasons for its danger include:

- It can spread quickly to lymph nodes and distant organs.
- If not treated early, it becomes difficult to manage.
- It accounts for a majority of skin cancer-related deaths despite being less prevalent than basal cell or squamous cell carcinomas.

Early detection through changes in moles or unusual skin patches is critical for survival.

22. (2): Concentrated loading refers to a type of short-term overloading, typically used in advanced training programs to create a supercompensation effect by accumulating fatigue over a short period, followed by rest or tapering.

This method involves high-intensity or high-volume workloads applied over a short cycle, such as a few days or a week.

Purpose:

- Temporarily depress performance to trigger long-term adaptation.
- Improve strength, power, or endurance after recovery.

It is different from linear or flat loading, which involve gradual or consistent workload increases, and from conjugated loading, which trains multiple traits simultaneously.

23. (3): Elastic reactive strength refers to the ability to quickly switch from an eccentric contraction (muscle lengthening under tension) to a concentric contraction (muscle shortening).

This quality is essential for plyometric movements, such as jumping, bounding, or sprinting.

It utilizes the stretch-shortening cycle (SSC) of muscle actions:

- Eccentric phase stores elastic energy.

- A rapid transition to concentric action allows efficient force release.

Examples:

- Depth jumps
- Sprinting acceleration
- Hurdle take-offs

Enhancing elastic reactive strength improves explosiveness and athletic performance in dynamic sports.

24. (3): The residual training effect is the phenomenon where the effects of a specific type of training continue to be retained in the body for a certain period after the training stimulus has stopped. This is particularly important in periodisation and long-term planning, as it informs when and how often a certain quality (e.g., strength, endurance) needs to be re-stimulated.

Duration of residual effects (approximate):

- Aerobic endurance: up to 30 days
- Maximal strength: ~30 days
- Anaerobic capacity: ~18 days
- Speed/Power: ~5–10 days

Understanding residual effects helps coaches to prevent detraining and optimize performance peaking.

25. (2): L.P. Matveyev, a Soviet sports scientist, is widely credited with introducing the modern theory of periodisation in the 1950s.

Periodisation refers to the systematic planning of athletic training to achieve optimal performance at a specific time.

Matveyev's model included:

- Macrocycles, mesocycles, and microcycles
- Progressive variation in training load
- Balanced development of training components (volume, intensity, recovery)

His work laid the foundation for modern sports training, and his principles are still used worldwide in the design of training programs for elite and amateur athletes.

26. (4): We are given five terms:

$x,\ x + 4,\ x + 7,\ 2x + 5,\ x + 10$

Their mean is 10, so we write:

$$\frac{x+(x+4)+(x+7)+(2x+5)+(x+10)}{5} = 10$$

$$\frac{6x+26}{5} = 10$$

Multiply both sides by 5:

$$6x + 26 = 50$$

$$\Rightarrow \quad 6x = 24 \Rightarrow x = 4$$

Now substitute $x = 4$ into the last four scores:

$$x + 4 = 8$$
$$x + 7 = 11$$
$$2x + 5 = 13$$
$$x + 10 = 14$$

Mean of these four:

$$\frac{8+11+13+14}{4} = \frac{46}{4} = 11.5.$$

27. (2): We use the formula for Spearman's rank correlation coefficient:

$$\rho = 1 - \frac{6\sum d^2}{N(N^2-1)}$$

Given: $\rho = 0.80$, $N = 10$

$$0.80 = 1 - \frac{6\sum d^2}{10(100-1)}$$

$$= 1 - \frac{6\sum d^2}{990}$$

Rearranging:

$$\frac{6\sum d^2}{990} = 0.20$$

$$\Rightarrow \quad \sum d^2 = \frac{0.20 \times 990}{6}$$

$$= \frac{198}{6} = 33.$$

28. (4): In One-Way ANOVA,

df between groups $= k - 1$

$= 3 - 1 = 2$

df within groups $= N - k$

$= 30 - 3 = 27$

Mean Square Between (MSB)

$$= \frac{SS_b}{df_b} = \frac{134.6}{2} = 67.3$$

Mean Square Within (MSW)

$$= \frac{SS_w}{df_w} = \frac{110.1}{27} \approx 4.0778$$

$$\text{F-ratio} = \frac{\text{MSB}}{\text{MSW}} = \frac{67.3}{4.0778} \approx 16.50.$$

29. (2): Tenacity is an unscientific method of problem solving where a belief is held stubbornly without evidence or despite contradictory facts.

It relies on habit, tradition, or superstition, not objective reasoning or empirical validation.

For example, someone might believe in a specific health remedy "just because it has always worked" even if there's no scientific proof.

In contrast:

- Ethnographic and naturalistic methods involve systematic observation.
- Reductionism is a philosophical scientific approach breaking down complex systems.

30. (3): Case studies are not considered analytical research; they fall under descriptive research, which provides in-depth analysis of a single case or limited number of cases.

They focus on what is happening, not necessarily why through statistical or logical analysis.

In contrast:

- Philosophical, historical, and reviews involve critical, logical, and comparative approaches, fitting within analytical research.

Analytical research involves examining available information in detail to understand cause-effect relationships or patterns.

31. (4): In a standard normal distribution, the mean is 0 and the standard deviation is 1.

This is a normalized version of the normal distribution (also called the Z-distribution), used for statistical purposes like calculating probabilities and comparing different data sets.

Characteristics:

- Symmetrical bell-shaped curve
- Total area under the curve = 1
- Mean = 0 (center of the curve)
- Standard Deviation = 1 (spread of data)

Z-scores are calculated using this distribution to express how many standard deviations a data point is from the mean.

32. (1)

33. (1): The Scramble test is one of the test items included in the Newton Motor Ability Test, which is designed to evaluate motor fitness and coordination in children and adolescents.

The test includes multiple components, such as:

- Scramble test (measuring agility and coordination)
- Other agility or strength-based tasks

It assesses general motor ability, and the results are used in physical education and talent identification contexts.

34. (4): Construct validity refers to the degree to which a test accurately measures the theoretical construct or trait it claims to measure.

For example, a test designed to measure intelligence should accurately capture the multifaceted nature of intelligence (e.g., reasoning, memory, problem-solving).

It involves empirical and theoretical justification:

- How well test results align with expected behaviour patterns
- Whether it correlates appropriately with other related constructs

It's considered the most comprehensive and critical type of validity for psychological and educational tests.

35. (4): Formative evaluation is typically based on specific instructional or performance objectives and often uses criterion-referenced standards to assess progress.

It is conducted during the learning or training process to provide ongoing feedback.

Criterion-referenced standards are pre-defined performance benchmarks (e.g., scoring 8 out of 10 to demonstrate mastery).

Formative evaluation helps:

- Identify areas for improvement
- Modify instruction
- Track incremental progress toward goals

It differs from summative evaluation, which is conducted at the end and is often norm-referenced.

36. (4): First, note that a common way to estimate the reliability of a dichotomous (right/wrong) test with items of similar difficulty is by using the Kuder-Richardson 20 (KR-20) formula:

$$r_{KR20} = \frac{k}{k-1}\left[1 - \frac{\sum p_i q_i}{\sigma^2_{total}}\right]$$

where:

k = total number of items (here k = 50)

p_i = proportion of students who answered item i correctly

$q_i = 1 - p_i$

σ^2_{total} = variance of the total test scores

Given information

Number of items (k): 50

Mean of total scores: 30

This suggests that on average, test takers got 30 out of 50 items correct.

Standard deviation of total scores: 6

Hence, the variance $\sigma^2_{\text{total}} = 6^2 = 36$.

Simplifying assumptions

A common simplifying assumption (especially if no item-level data are given) is that each item has similar difficulty, so:

$$p_i \approx \frac{\text{Mean score}}{k} = \frac{30}{50} = 0.6,$$

$$q_i = 1 - p_i = 0.4.$$

Then, for each item i,

$$p_i q_i \approx 0.6 \times 0.4 = 0.24.$$

Since there are 50 items, we sum across all itmes:

$$\Sigma p_i q_i \approx 50 \times 0.24 = 12.$$

Applying the KR-20 formula

Now, $r_{KR20} = \frac{k}{k-1}\left[1 - \frac{\sum p_i q_i}{\sigma^2_{total}}\right]$

$$= \frac{50}{49}\left[1 - \frac{12}{36}\right].$$

Computer the fraction inside the brackets:

$$\frac{12}{26} = 0.3333...$$

So,

$1 - 0.3333... \approx 0.6667.$

Multiply by $\frac{50}{49} \approx 1.204$:

$$r_{KR20} = 1.0204 \times 0.6667 \approx 0.68.$$

Thus, the estimated reliability (KR-20) is approximately 0.68.

37. (1): Transactional leaders are known for using contingent reinforcement as a primary tool in managing teams and individuals.

In transactional leadership, the relationship between leader and follower is based on a clear exchange:

- Rewards for performance
- Punishments for failure

This style relies heavily on performance-based incentives, and leadership is exercised through structured tasks and supervision.

Common in military, corporate, and bureaucratic settings where short-term goals and task completion are prioritized.

38. (2): The process of effectively integrating various human, financial, and material resources to execute a plan is called organizing.

It involves:

- Grouping tasks into departments
- Assigning responsibilities
- Allocating resources
- Establishing lines of authority

Organizing follows planning, setting the framework through which the planned objectives can be operationalized effectively.

39. (1): Organizational efficiency is the measure of how well an organization uses its resources (human, financial, physical) to achieve its goals.

It refers to:

- Minimizing waste
- Maximizing output with the least input

Efficiency is about doing things right — using minimal resources to achieve objectives.

It is different from effectiveness, which is about doing the right things, i.e., achieving the desired outcomes regardless of resource usage.

40. (3): First-line managers are also known as supervisory-level managers.

They are the lowest level of management in an organization and directly oversee day-to-day operations and non-managerial employees.

Their responsibilities include:

- Assigning tasks
- Monitoring performance
- Implementing the plans developed by higher management

Examples: shift supervisors, office managers, foremen, department heads.

They act as a bridge between workers and middle-level management.

41. (1): As altitude increases, the atmosphere becomes thinner, resulting in several physiological changes affecting water balance and thermoregulation.

B. Increase sweat evaporation: At higher altitudes, air is typically drier, which increases the rate of sweat evaporation, even though actual sweating may decrease.

C. Increased respiratory water loss: Breathing cold, dry air at altitude increases the loss of water vapor through respiration.

D. Dehydration through increased insensible water loss: Together, sweat evaporation and respiratory loss lead to increased insensible (non-observable) water loss, contributing to dehydration.

A. Water loss decrease is incorrect, as overall water loss typically increases due to the above factors.

42. (4): The rotator cuff is a group of four muscles and their tendons that stabilize the shoulder joint by forming a cuff around the head of the humerus. These muscles are:

A. Subscapularis (anterior)

B. Teres minor (posterior)

C. Supraspinatus (superior)

E. Infraspinatus (posterior)

These muscles converge at the shoulder joint and are crucial for shoulder mobility and stability.

43. (3): Form drag is the resistance created by the shape and size of an object moving through a fluid, such as air or water. It is affected by:

B. Form drag coefficient: A dimensionless number indicating how much drag a shape produces.

D. Frontal surface area: Larger surface area results in more drag.

E. Squared relative velocity: Drag increases proportionally to the square of relative velocity.

A. Relative mass does not influence form drag directly.

C. Relative velocity matters, but its square is the actual factor in the formula for drag:

$$\text{Form Drag} \propto \frac{1}{2} \cdot \rho \cdot C_d \cdot A \cdot v^2$$

44. (2): These three kinematic equations are used to analyze projectile motion, assuming constant acceleration (like gravity):

A. $V = u + at$

B. $V^2 = u^2 + 2as$

C. $s = ut + \frac{1}{2}at^2$

These equations calculate velocity, displacement, and time in projectile trajectories.

D. $V = \Delta s + \Delta t$ is incorrect and not a recognized motion equation.

E. $m_1V_1 = m_2v_2$ is the equation for conservation of momentum, not for projectile motion.

45. (2): Social psychology in sports focuses on how group dynamics and social interactions affect behaviour and performance.

A. Aggression: Influenced by crowd behaviour, competition, or group dynamics.

C. Team cohesion: Strongly linked to social psychology, studying how team members relate and function together.

Other options:

B. Motivation is more individual-centered (part of cognitive psychology).

D. Imagery is related to mental skills training, not social psychology.

E. Skill acquisition falls under motor learning, not social behaviour.

46. (4): According to Carron's model of group cohesion, team cohesiveness is influenced by the following four key factors:

A. Individual factors: These include personal characteristics such as motivation, personality, and satisfaction with the team.

B. Situational factors: These are environ-mental aspects such as team size, time spent together, and geographic location.

C. Team factors: Group roles, norms, and the team's history of success or failure impact cohesion.

E. Leadership: The behaviour and communication style of leaders and captains significantly affect group unity.

D. Coaching style, though related to leadership, is not listed separately in Carron's core model but is considered under leadership.

Hence, the correct grouping is A, B, C, and E.

47. (2): Psychological skills are techniques used to manage mental aspects of performance, especially in sports and high-pressure environments.

C. Self-confidence: Belief in one's own abilities; crucial for optimal performance.

D. Mental toughness: Ability to stay focused, resilient, and composed under pressure.

E. Anxiety control: Managing both somatic and cognitive anxiety to maintain performance.

48. (2): The purpose of curricular evaluation is to assess the quality and effectiveness of educational programs. Key objectives include:

A. Program effectiveness: Evaluating how well the curriculum meets its goals.

B. Identify program omissions: Finding gaps or missing components in the curriculum.

C. Program justification: Providing data to support the continuation or revision of a program.

D. Employment opportunity is more of a career planning concern, not a core curricular evaluation goal.

E. Reducing evaluation cost money is a financial/ logistical issue, not a purpose of evaluation.

49. (4): The advantages of groundwater include:

A. It usually requires no treatment: Groundwater is naturally filtered as it passes through soil layers, making it generally clean and safe.

C. Likely to be free from pathogenic agents: Due to natural filtration, it has low biological contamination, especially when tapped from deep aquifers.

B. High mineral content can be a disadvantage, especially if it leads to hardness.

D. Requires pumping is also a limitation, not an advantage, as it increases cost and infrastructure needs.

50. (3): Zoonotic diseases are diseases that are transmitted from animals to humans. The following are zoonotic:

A. Plague: Caused by Yersinia pestis, transmitted via fleas from rats.

B. Chikungunya fever: Though mainly mosquito-borne, it originated from non-human primates.

D. Rabies: Transmitted through the saliva of infected animals (dogs, bats, etc.).

E. Yellow fever: A viral zoonotic disease, transmitted by mosquitoes after infecting primates.

C. SARS: Though zoonotic in origin (likely bats via civet cats), it is primarily human-to-human in later transmission, and its classification as zoonotic is context-dependent.

Thus, A, B, D, and E are clearly zoonotic.

51. (4): Cooper's training effect categories describe the different types of physiological adaptations and responses to training. The three valid categories from the given list are:

B. Overreaching: A short-term increase in training load that can lead to temporary performance decrements but may enhance performance after adequate recovery.

C. Minor: Refers to small, short-term training effects that contribute to general fitness improvements.

D. Maintenance: Training designed to maintain the current level of fitness or performance rather than improve it.

Other options:

A. Involution: This term refers to decline or regression in training outcomes, often due to detraining — not a positive training effect.

E. Positive is a general description but not a specific category in Cooper's framework.

52. (3): According to Issurin & Kaverin, the three mesocycle blocks in Block Periodization are:

B. Accumulation: Focuses on general preparation and building base abilities like aerobic endurance or basic strength.

C. Transformation: Converts general abilities into sport-specific qualities; includes more intense and specific training.

D. Realization: A peaking phase aimed at achieving maximum performance; includes tapering and competition preparation.

Other options:

(A) Developmental and (E) Restorative may be descriptive, but they are not the specific blocks defined in the block periodization model by Issurin & Kaverin.

53. (1): Multiple correlation is used in test construction to analyze how well a combination of test items predicts a criterion. The correct statements are:

B. Test items that correlate highly with one another are redundant, indicating they measure the same trait; thus, one can be eliminated.

D. When many test items are available, multiple correlation helps to select the least number of most effective items to form a concise, efficient test battery.

E. Regression equations can be derived from multiple correlation analysis to predict performance based on scores from selected test items.

Incorrect statements:

A. It incorrectly suggests choosing items lowest to the criterion, which is the opposite of the actual aim.

C. Preference is always for the test item with higher correlation with the criterion, not lower.

54. (4): The characteristics of a normal curve (bell curve) are:

A. The curve is asymptotic: It never touches the baseline, approaching it infinitely on both sides.

D. Total area = 100%: The total probability distribution under the curve equals 1 or 100%.

E. $\mu - \sigma$ to $\mu + \sigma$ covers 68.26% area: This is a fundamental property of the normal distribution.

Incorrect:

B. Quartile deviation of a normal distribution is not 3/2.

C. The points of inflection occur at $\mu \pm \sigma$, not $\sigma \pm \mu$ (the latter is incorrectly phrased, though it likely meant the same). Still, since the expression is miswritten, it's considered incorrect.

55. (4): Informal designs are less rigid and often lack full experimental control. The correct options are:

A. Before-and-after without control: Measures change in one group, lacks a control group.

B. After-only control: Compares two groups after treatment, no pre-test data.

D. Before-and-after with control: Includes pre and post-testing for both experimental and control groups but often lacks full randomization.

56. (1): The core characteristics involved in solving a research problem are:

A. Reductive: Research aims to simplify complex phenomena by reducing them into understandable components or theories.

B. Replicable: A good study must be repeatable by other researchers to confirm findings and ensure consistency.

C. Empirical: Research is based on observations and evidence, not just theory or logic; it relies on data gathered through systematic investigation.

Other options:

(D) Delimitation and (E) Limitation are components of research design, but they are not intrinsic characteristics of problem-solving in research itself.

57. (2): In SPSS, the Variable View tab provides metadata for each variable. The relevant columns include:

A. Name: Assigns a unique name to each variable.

B. Width: Specifies the number of characters or digits the variable can display.

D. Decimals: Controls how many decimal places will be shown for numeric variables.

Incorrect options:

C. Transform: This is a menu option, not a column in Variable View.

E. Add-one: This is not a valid SPSS column in Variable View.

58. (2): Standard scores (often called Z-scores) are a way to describe a value's position relative to the mean in a standard normal distribution. Correct statements:

A. Mean of standard scores is 0: This is the defining center of the Z-distribution.

B. Standard deviation of standard scores is 1: Standard scores normalize the spread of data.

C. Standard scores are unit-free: Because they are calculated in terms of standard deviations, they have no physical units.

Incorrect:

D. Limits of standard scores are ± 2: This is false — while about 95.44% of values lie within ± 2 SDs, standard scores are not limited to this range.

E. Standard scores are always positive: Incorrect — they can be positive or negative depending on whether a score is above or below the mean.

59. (3): Let's identify which statements are not correct:

A. Incorrect. Norm-referenced standards compare a person's performance to others, not to a fixed competence level — that's the job of criterion-referenced standards.

B. Incorrect. Criterion-referenced standards are not based on statistics but on predetermined performance levels.

D. Incorrect. In criterion-referenced testing, the aim is to meet specific standards — not necessarily to strive for a percentile rank.

(C) is correct: Criterion-referenced assessments do not compare performance to others but to defined standards.

60. (4): The Sports Anxiety Scale-2 (SAS-2) is a validated instrument for assessing sports-related anxiety in youth. Correct statements:

B. SAS-2 evaluates somatic anxiety, worry, and concentration disruption — the three subscales.

C. All items are scored on a 4-point Likert scale, ranging from "not at all" to "very much."

D. There is no reverse scoring in SAS-2, making it easier to administer and interpret.

Incorrect:

A. SAS-2 has 15 items, not 21.

E. It includes 5 items per subscale, not 7 — totaling 15 items.

61. (3): In the Khelo India Winter Games 2024, the correct sequential rank order of teams based on medal tally was:

C. Indian Army – 1st position with the highest number of medals due to dominance in snow and ice sports.

B. Karnataka – performed exceptionally in skating and ice hockey.

D. Maharashtra – consistent performer with a balanced medal tally.

E. Himachal Pradesh – strong in winter sports but behind the top three.

A. Uttarakhand – lower rank compared to others.

Hence, the correct order is C, B, D, E, A.

62. (4): The Khelo India Youth Games were hosted in the following chronological (ascending) order:

D. New Delhi – 2018 (1st edition)

A. Maharashtra – 2019 (2nd edition)

C. Assam – 2020 (3rd edition)

B. Haryana – 2021 (4th edition, held in 2022 due to COVID-19)

So, the correct ascending order of host states is D, A, C, B.

63. (1): The correct sequential order of events in endochondral ossification (bone formation from cartilage) is:

D. Formation of bone collar around hyaline cartilage model – begins the ossification process.

A. Cartilage in the center of the diaphysis calcifies and then cavities – as the cartilage dies, it leaves spaces.

B. The periosteal bud invades the internal cavities and spongy bone forms – blood vessels, nerves, and osteoblasts enter.

E. The diaphysis elongates and medullary cavity forms – long bone growth begins.

C. The epiphyses ossify – ossification centers appear at the ends.

Correct sequence: D, A, B, E, C

64. (3): The steps of qualitative biomechanical analysis are:

C. Description – understanding the ideal technique or movement to analyze.

A. Observation – watching and recording the actual performance.

D. Evaluation – comparing observed performance to the ideal to identify errors.

B. Instruction – providing feedback or corrections to improve performance.

So, the correct sequence is C, A, D, B.

65. (4): According to Albert Bandura's Social Learning Theory, learning through observation involves four key stages:

C. Attention – observing the model's behaviour.
B. Retention – mentally storing the observed behaviour.
A. Reproduction – physically replicating the behaviour.
D. Reinforcement – receiving feedback or rewards that affect the likelihood of repeating the behaviour.

Thus, the correct order is C, B, A, D.

66. (2): The five-stage model of athlete self-regulation by Kirschenbaum outlines how athletes take control of their own development and performance. The stages are:

A. Problem Identification: Recognizing a need for change or improvement in performance.
C. Commitment: Making a firm decision and setting a goal to change or improve.
B. Execution: Implementing strategies and behaviours to reach the goal.
E. Environmental Management: Modifying surroundings to support the behavioural change (e.g., managing distractions, setting routines).
D. Generalization: Applying the newly learned behaviour to various situations, maintaining consistency.

Correct sequence: A, C, B, E, D.

67. (4): The Skill Theme Approach in physical education promotes skill development in a progressive manner. The correct instructional sequence is:

C. Basic Skill: Initial learning of fundamental movement skills (e.g., throwing, kicking).
B. Combinations: Combining two or more basic skills (e.g., dribbling and passing).
A. Skill in Contexts: Applying learned skills in modified games or realistic settings.
D. Culminating Activity: Final activity that integrates all learned skills in a game or complex setting.

Correct sequence: C, B, A, D.

68. (2): According to Government of India protocol (2007) for first aid after a snakebite, the proper sequential steps are:

B. Immobilize: Keep the affected limb still and below heart level to slow venom spread.
D. Do not apply any compression: No tourniquets or tight bands should be used.
A. Do not give alcoholic beverages: Alcohol can worsen the effects of venom.
C. Do not manipulate the bitten site: No cutting, sucking, or massage.
E. Transport the patient to a medical facility: Immediate medical attention is essential.

Correct sequence: B, D, A, C, E.

69. (3): In the bottom-up approach of the training factors pyramid, athletes must first develop foundational abilities before moving to complex ones. The correct sequence is:

C. Physical Training: Base level involving strength, endurance, speed, flexibility.
A. Technical Training: Developing sport-specific skills (e.g., strokes, kicks).
B. Tactical Training: Learning strategies and decision-making in competition.
D. Psychological and Mental Training: Focus on motivation, focus, stress handling, and resilience.

Correct sequence: C, A, B, D.

70. (1): The correct sequence for developing a sampling design involves logical steps for effective sampling in research:

E. Types of Universe: Identify the overall population type (finite/infinite, real/hypothetical).
B. Sampling Unit: Determine the basic unit to be selected (individual, group, institution).
C. Source List: Prepare the sampling frame – a list from which units will be selected.
A. Size of Sample: Decide how many units will be included.
D. Parameter of Interest: Define what specific characteristic (mean, proportion) is to be measured.

Correct sequence: E, B, C, A, D.

71. (2): The correct sequence for developing a Likert-type scale follows a systematic method of identifying and refining attitudinal statements, which includes:

D. Large number of statement: Initially, a large pool of attitudinal statements is created, covering the full range of opinions on the topic.
B. Trial test: These statements are tested on a sample population to observe responses and item behaviour.

A. Five point scale for scoring: A standard Likert scale format (usually 5-point) is used during the trial for response collection (e.g., Strongly agree to Strongly disagree).

E. Find statements with high discriminatory power: After trial, statistical analysis is conducted to select items that best differentiate among different levels of agreement or attitude.

C. Correlated statement in instrument: Finally, the selected high-quality items are assembled into a finalized instrument ensuring internal consistency (e.g., through Cronbach's alpha or inter-item correlations).

72. (4): The correct chronological (ascending) order according to the year of construction/publication of the sports skill tests is:

D. French Short Serve Test – Introduced in 1940, designed to evaluate badminton short-serve accuracy.

E. Knox Basketball Test – Developed in 1944 to assess basketball fundamentals.

B. Hewitt Tennis Achievement Test – Released in 1960 for tennis performance analysis.

C. AAHPER Volleyball Test – Developed in the 1960s by the American Alliance for Health, Physical Education, Recreation.

A. Poole Badminton Test – Published in 1969, used to measure badminton performance skills.

Thus, the correct sequence based on years is: D, E, B, C, A.

73. (4): The correct sequential steps in item analysis (a process in test construction to evaluate the quality of test items) are:

D. Score the tests: Initially, all test responses are scored.

E. Arrange answer sheets from high to low scores: Once scored, answer sheets are sorted from highest to lowest total scores to classify performance.

A. Separate answer sheets into upper, lower and middle groups: The top and bottom 27% of scorers are typically chosen for comparative item analysis.

B. Record number of frequencies in upper and lower groups: The number of correct responses for each item is tallied for both high and low performers.

C. Calculate Index of Difficulty: The difficulty level (proportion of students who answered correctly) is calculated along with discrimination index to assess item quality.

74. (2): In the control process used by sports managers (and in general management), the correct sequence is as follows:

D. Establishing performance standards: Begin by defining clear, measurable expectations or benchmarks for performance.

C. Accurately measuring performance: Gather data on actual performance using appropriate methods.

E. Comparing performance with the established standards: Identify any gaps between expected and actual outcomes.

B. Analyzing and correcting deviation from the standards: Investigate causes of discrepancies and take corrective action.

A. Reinforcing performance at or above expectations: Provide motivation and recognition for those who meet or exceed expectations to maintain or enhance performance.

This sequence ensures continuous improvement and accountability in sports or organizational settings.

75. (3): The correct sequential order of speed abilities in sprinting events aligns with neuromuscular and biomechanical progression. These are:

C. Reaction Ability: The initial response to a stimulus (e.g., starting gun in sprints).

E. Movement Speed: Quick limb movement in the initial acceleration phase.

A. Acceleration Ability: The athlete's capacity to increase velocity quickly after the start.

B. Locomotor Ability: The efficiency and control of movement mechanics during full-speed running.

D. Speed Endurance: The ability to maintain near-maximal speed over the duration of the event, crucial in longer sprints like 200 m or 400 m.

This progression reflects how sprinters develop and apply different speed components during race phases.

76. (3): This question matches the Olympic Games with the dignitary who officially opened them and the corresponding host cities.

A. H.M. King Albert I – III. Antwerp (1920): King Albert I of Belgium opened the 1920 Antwerp Olympic Games after World War I.

B. Sir William Deane – I. Sydney (2000): He was the Governor-General of Australia and formally opened the Sydney Olympics in 2000.

C. President Roh Tae-woo – II. Seoul (1988): He opened the Games as the sitting President of South Korea.

D. President Hu Jintao – IV. Beijing (2008): Hu Jintao was the President of the People's Republic of China when the Olympics were held in Beijing.

Hence, the correct matching is: A-III, B-I, C-II, D-IV.

77. (2): The question deals with matching philosophical schools with their focus or emphasis.

A. Existentialism – III. Individual experiences determine what is true: Existentialism emphasizes individual freedom, experience, and personal responsibility.

B. Humanism – I. Self-actualization and the development of value are emphasized: Humanism values personal growth, self-concept, and achieving one's full potential.

C. Realism – IV. Science reveals the truth: Realism sees the world as objectively existing and believes in scientific reasoning to discover truths.

D. Naturalism – II. The individual is more important than society: Naturalism emphasizes the importance of natural development and that humans should be free to develop without societal constraints.

Therefore, the correct order is: A-III, B-I, C-IV, D-II.

78. (4): This question relates to sympathetic nervous system effects on specific organs.

A. Liver – IV. Stimulates glucose release: Sympathetic activation triggers glycogenolysis in the liver to provide quick energy.

B. Lungs – III. Cause bronchodilation: To increase airflow and oxygen supply during fight or flight.

C. Adrenal glands – II. Stimulate secretion of epinephrine and norepinephrine: These hormones intensify sympathetic effects.

D. Heart: Coronary blood vessels – I. Cause vasodilation: Increases blood flow to heart muscles during stress or activity.

So, correct matches are: A-IV, B-III, C-II, D-I.

79. (2): This question tests knowledge of formulas for physical quantities in mechanics.

A. Kinetic energy – I. $\frac{1}{2} mv^2$: The energy due to motion.

B. Potential energy – IV. $m \times g \times h$: The energy an object has due to its position in a gravitational field.

C. Momentum – III. $m \times v$: The product of mass and velocity.

D. Friction – II. μR: Frictional force equals the coefficient of friction multiplied by the normal reaction force.

Thus, the correct formula matching is: A-I, B-IV, C-III, D-II.

80. (2): This question focuses on muscle origin anatomy.

A. Levatores costarum – II. C_7 & T_1 to T_{11}: These small muscles originate from the transverse processes of C_7 to T_{11} vertebrae and assist in rib elevation.

B. Serratus posterior superior – III. C_7 & T_1 to T_3: Originates from these vertebrae to help elevate ribs during inspiration.

C. Serratus posterior inferior – IV. T_{11}-T_{12} & L_1 to L_3: It assists in depressing the ribs during exhalation.

D. Psoas – I. T_{12} & L_1 to L_5: This deep hip flexor muscle originates from the lumbar vertebrae.

Hence, the correct matching is: A-II, B-III, C-IV, D-I.

81. (4): This matching is based on types of attentional focus in sports psychology, as described by Nideffer.

A. A broad attentional focus – III. A soccer player dribbling the ball upfield: Broad focus involves attention to multiple cues simultaneously, such as teammates, opponents, and the ball.

B. A narrow attentional focus – II. A baseball batter prepares to swing at a pitch: Narrow focus refers to concentration on one specific cue, such as the ball.

C. An external attentional focus – I. A cricket batsman directs attention to a ball: External focus is directed toward the environment or external objects.

D. An internal attentional focus – IV. A high jumper prepares to start her run-up: Internal focus involves thoughts, feelings, or body positioning before action.

Thus, correct matches are: A-III, B-II, C-I, D-IV.

82. (1): This question relates to key terms in sports psychology and personality theory.

A. Personality – II. All the consistent ways in which the behaviour of one person differs from that of others: This is the general definition of personality.

B. Personality profile – III. The plotting of an athlete's standardized personality scores: This refers to graphical representation of different traits or scores.

C. Personality trait – IV. A disposition to exhibit certain personality characteristics: Traits are enduring patterns in behaviour or thought.

D. Resilience – I. The force within the individual that drives a person to confront and overcome adversity: Resilience is crucial in high-pressure sports scenarios.

Correct matches: A-II, B-III, C-IV, D-I.

83. (1): These are different types of assessments used in educational and physical activity contexts.

A. Skill tests – IV. Assessment of students' physical ability usually done in a closed environment: Often involves standardized testing for motor skills.

B. Role play – I. An assessment in which students present a scenario and demonstrate their reaction: Used for interpersonal or situational judgment.

C. Journals – III. Opportunity to reflect and write on class-related events or feelings: Promotes critical thinking and personal expression.

D. Portfolios – II. Collections of artifacts that show competency in a subject area: Used to document learning over time.

Correct matches: A-IV, B-I, C-III, D-II.

84. (4): Matching essential fatty acids with their dietary sources.

A. Linoleic acid – IV. Corn oil: An omega-6 fatty acid commonly found in vegetable oils.

B. Arachidonic acid – III. Milk: Found in animal products like meat, eggs, and milk.

C. Linolenic acid – II. Leafy greens: An omega-3 fatty acid found in green leafy vegetables, flaxseeds, etc.

D. Eicosapentaenoic acid (EPA) – I. Fish oil: A long-chain omega-3 fatty acid mainly found in cold-water fish.

Correct matches: A-IV, B-III, C-II, D-I.

85. (1): Matching Arjuna Awardees (2023) with their respective sports disciplines.

A. Shri Anush Agarwal – II. Equestrian: Recognized for his performance in horse-riding sports.

B. Shri Pawan Kumar – I. Kabaddi: Awarded for excellence in the national sport of kabaddi.

C. Ms. Nasreen – IV. Kho-Kho: Honoured for her achievements in the traditional Indian game.

D. Ms. Prachi Yadav – III. Para Canoeing: A para-athlete excelling in the water sport of canoeing.

Correct matches: A-II, B-I, C-IV, D-III.

86. (2): This question deals with key training terms and their definitions:

A. Intensity – II. The qualitative element of training such as speed, power: Intensity refers to how hard an athlete trains, often indicated by weight lifted, speed, or level of exertion.

B. Volume – I. A quantitative element of training that can be measured as time or duration: Volume refers to the total amount of work done (e.g., sets × reps × weight).

C. Density of training – IV. The frequency of training within a given time frame: Density measures how often training sessions occur or how compactly work is done in time.

D. Training intensity (alternative form) – III. Intensity determined by dividing the total volume load by the total number of repetitions: This is a calculated form of intensity to evaluate training load per rep.

Correct match: A-II, B-I, C-IV, D-III.

87. (2): These are common research-related concepts and their meanings:

A. Plagiarism – II. Using ideas of others: Plagiarism is the unethical use of someone else's work without proper acknowledgment.

B. Outlier – III. An unrepresentative score: An outlier is a data point that differs significantly from other observations in the dataset.

C. Copyright – IV. Seek permission: Copyright laws protect original works and often require permission for reproduction or use.

D. Informed consent – I. Protection of human participants: This ensures participants are fully aware of the nature of the research before agreeing to participate.

Correct match: A-II, B-III, C-IV, D-I.

88. (3): This relates to types of research designs in descriptive studies:

A. Sampling design – III. Probability: Sampling design involves methods for selecting participants, typically using probability or non-probability techniques.

B. Statistical design – I. Pre-planned: Statistical design involves pre-planning data analysis methods including selecting appropriate tests.

C. Observational design – II. Structured: Observational studies require a structured plan to record and analyze behaviours or phenomena.

D. Operational design – IV. Advanced decisions: It outlines all steps of research implementation, requiring detailed advance planning for execution.

Correct match: A-III, B-I, C-II, D-IV.

89. (3): This question connects psychological inventories to their developers:

A. Competitive State Anxiety Inventory-2 (CSAI-2) – III. Craft, Magyar, Becker and Feltz (2003): Measures cognitive and somatic anxiety in athletes.

B. Sports Confidence Inventory – I. Robin S. Vealey (1986): Measures an athlete's confidence in performance.

C. Group Environment Questionnaire – IV. Carron, Widmeyer and Brawley (1985): Assesses team cohesion.

D. Self-Motivation Inventory – II. Dishman and Ickes (1981): Evaluates an individual's internal motivation for maintaining physical activity.

Correct match: A-III, B-I, C-IV, D-II.

90. (1): This is based on Sheldon's somatotyping system, which classifies body types using a three-number rating: endomorphy (fat), mesomorphy (muscle), ectomorphy (thinness):

A. Extreme ectomorph – IV. 1-1-7: Very thin and linear physique.

B. Extreme endomorph – III. 7-1-1: Rounded and soft body type with high fat.

C. Extreme mesomorph – II. 1-7-1: Muscular and well-built physique.

D. Ectomorphic mesomorph – I. 2-6-4: Primarily muscular with slight ectomorphic traits.

Correct match: A-IV, B-III, C-II, D-I.

91. (4): The split-half method is a technique used to assess and enhance the reliability of an instrument, specifically how consistently it measures a concept.

- It involves dividing the test into two equal halves and correlating the scores of both halves.
- If the correlation is high, the instrument is said to have good internal consistency reliability.
- The passage clearly mentions: "To enhance instrument reliability, the researcher can use a test-retest or a split-half method", indicating its role is confined to instrument reliability, not external aspects or validity.

92. (1): External validity refers to how well the results of a study can be generalized to populations beyond the sample used in the study.

- The passage states: "The results of external validity and reliability can apply to population and further", confirming that external validity deals with generalization beyond the specific research setting.
- It ensures that findings hold true in real-world settings or different contexts, beyond the controlled experimental conditions.

93. (2): The example from the passage describes golf balls being placed in a random pattern all over the green, and golfers failing even on a second try.

- This represents inconsistency (low reliability) and also missing the target (low validity).
- The placement lacks both aim and repeatability, symbolizing a scenario where neither the measurements are accurate (valid) nor consistent (reliable).

94. (3): In this case, the putting is consistent and in a tight cluster, but not reaching the hole, i.e., the target.

- This indicates high reliability (the shots are closely grouped) but low validity (they are consistently wrong).
- The example is a classic illustration in research where a measurement tool gives consistent results that are not accurate.

95. (4): Here, every ball lands in the hole, indicating that the outcome is both accurate (valid) and consistent (reliable).

- High validity: Because the goal (sinking the ball) is achieved.
- High reliability: Because the result is achieved every time, showing consistency in measurement or action.
- This scenario is the ideal in research — where an instrument or method yields accurate and consistent results.

96. (2): The primary physiological adaptation during high altitude training is the increased production of erythropoietin (EPO), a hormone secreted by the kidneys.

- EPO stimulates the production of red blood cells, enhancing the blood's oxygen-carrying capacity.
- The passage states: "The physiological adaptation is an elevated production of erythropoietin, a hormone that stimulates the production of red blood cells."
- This adaptation is crucial for improving aerobic performance and endurance after returning to lower altitudes.

97. (4): A reduction in powerhouse (mitochondrial) density is not a physiological change caused by high altitude training. In fact, the opposite occurs.

- The passage mentions: "High altitude training can lead to improved mitochondrial density and function".
- Mitochondria are the energy powerhouses of cells, and improved mitochondrial function enhances aerobic energy production.
- The other options—increased capillary number, better pH (buffering) balance, and improved pulmonary function—are all valid adaptations to altitude training.

98. (2): The "Live high, train low" strategy involves:

- Living at high altitudes to stimulate the physiological adaptations associated with low oxygen (e.g., increased EPO and red blood cell count).
- Training at lower altitudes where oxygen availability is higher, enabling higher-intensity training.
- As per the passage: "Live at high altitudes to gain the physiological benefits but train at lower altitudes to maintain training intensity."
- This hybrid approach maximizes adaptation without compromising the quality of workouts.

99. (3): Altitude training enhances the efficiency of respiratory (pulmonary) muscles.

- The passage states: "...enhanced efficiency of respiratory muscles."
- It doesn't suggest an increase in number, size, or diameter of these muscles, but rather how effectively they function in extracting and utilizing oxygen under reduced availability.
- Improved efficiency leads to better ventilation and oxygen uptake under stress, aiding endurance.

100. (3): The reduced oxygen availability at higher altitudes (due to decreased atmospheric O_2) is the primary reason for lower training intensity at altitude.

- At high elevations, the partial pressure of oxygen is lower, making it harder for the body to uptake oxygen, which in turn affects energy production and exercise intensity.
- That's why athletes prefer to train at lower altitudes, where oxygen levels are sufficient to sustain high-intensity training, while still living at high altitude for adaptation.
- This principle is central to the "Live high, train low" model.

UGC-NET/JRF
PHYSICAL EDUCATION

UNIT-I

MEANING AND DEFINITIONS OF PHYSICAL EDUCATION

Physical Education – A Preview

Evolution of human life started with the movement. Human beings have been very active and creative by nature and physical activity has been part of their life all along since evolution. For primitive man, search for food and shelter was the first activity. This first physical activity was necessitated by his instinct for survival. Physical activity was also the first mode of communication, it was also a means of expression. As human beings evolved culturally, emotionally, and socially, physical activity also evolved. As the society became more and more complex leading towards the modern age, physical activity came to be recognized as an organized and supervised form of education, and was termed as physical education.

The importance of physical education and activity was recognized by Plato when he said "Lack of activity destroys the good conditions of every human being, while movement and methodical physical exercise save it and preserve it." When human movement is combined with the universal drive of play, the combination forms one of the most powerful education media – the physical education.

Meaning

Physical education is a component of education that takes place through movement. It creates the opportunity for individuals to learn and understand academic applications for healthy lives. In physical education, as in all academic areas, students must learn the basic skills which require practice and refinement in physical education settings. Students integrate and apply these skills in everyday life. Through regular participation in physical activity, students will have the opportunity to develop a pattern of life-enhancing and self-rewarding experiences that contribute to their potential to be healthier members of society. Physical education and athletic programmes have different purposes. The purpose of physical education is for all students:

— to learn and develop fundamental movement skills

— to become physically fit to participate regularly in physical activity

— to know the implication of and the benefits from involvement in physical activities

— to appreciate the value of physical activity and its contributions to a healthy lifestyle.

In contrast, athletic programmes are essentially designed for students who desire to specialise in one or more sports and refine their talents in order to compete with others of similar interests and abilities. Developmentally appropriate physical education programmes are designed for every child from the physically gifted to the physically challenged.

The intent is to provide students of all abilities and interests with a foundation of movement experiences that will eventually lead to active and healthy lifestyles. Physical education provides educational experiences that are movement based and that contribute to a students's comprehensive health status as well as other areas of academic performance and achievement.

Definitions change with the ideas that express people's notions of values, of importance, of measures, and of life. It is therefore not possible to give one definition of physical education. Different physical educationists have given different definitions. Few are mentioned below :

Physical education is a way of education through physical activities which are selected and carried on with full regard to values in human growth, development, and the behaviour.

— Physical Education platform, American Association for Health, Physical Education, Recreation

Physical education is the sum of the changes in the individual caused by experiences centering on motor activity.

– Rosalind Cassidy

Physical education is the social process of change in the behaviour of the human organism, originating primarily from the stimulus.of social - large - muscle - play and related activities.

– Chaver C Co well

Physical education is that phase of the school programme which is concerned largely with the growth and development of children through the medium of big-muscle activities.

– The society of State Directors of Physical Education & Health

Physical education is that phase of education which is concerned, first, with the organisation and leadership of children in big-muscle activities to gain the development and adjustment inherent in the activities according to social standards and second, with the control of health or growth, continues naturally, associated with the leadership of the activities so that the educational process may go on without growth handicaps.

– Clark W. Heterington

Physical education is the accumulation of wholesome experiences through participation in large-muscle activities that promote optimum growth and development.

– Brown well

Physical education is an indispensable part of health programmes. Its various activities should be so planned as to develop the physical and mental health of the students, cultivate recreational interest and skills, and promote the spirit of team work, sportsmanship and respect of others. Physical education is, therefore, much more than drill or a series of regulated exercises. It includes all forms of physical activities and games which promote the development of the body and the mind.

– Secondary Education Commission Report

Physical education is that part of education that has to do with the development and training of the whole individual through physical activities.

– A.R Wayman

Physical education is education. It is education through physical activities for the development of the total personality of the child, to its fullness and perfection in body, mind and spirit. Immediately, it is concerned with the development of physical fitness. In striving for such fitness, however, physical education has to train the child's mental, moral and social qualities, arouse its awareness of environment and develop alertness, presence of mind, resourcefullness, discipline, co-operation and the spirit of respect, sympathy and generosity towards others – qualities that are essential for a happy and well adjusted life in a free and democratic world. Physical education can thus, make a very valuable contribution to our national life.

– A National Plan for Physical Education and Recreation, A Report by Ministry of Education, Govt. of India

Physical education is that phase of the whole process of education which is concerned with vigorous muscular activities and related responses, and with the modification in the individual resultant from these responses.

– Nixon and Cozen

Physical education, as understood, is such a cultivation of power and capabilities of student as will enable him to maintain his bodily condition in the best working order, providing at the same time for the greatest efficiency of his intellectual and spiritual life.

— Edward Hitch Cock

Physical education should aim to improve the mass of students and to give them as much health strength and stamina as possible to enable them to perform the duties that awards them after they leave the college.

— Dudley A. Sergent

Physical education is the accumulation of wholesome experiences through participation in large muscle activities that promote optimum growth and development —

Brownhill l& Hagman

Physical education is that part of education which proceeds by means of or predominantly through physical activity.

Physical education is an education through human movement where many of the educational objectives are achieved by means of big muscle activities involving sport, games, gymnastics, dance and exercises.

– Harold M. Barrow

Physical education, an integral part of the total education process, is a field of endeavour that has as its aim the improvement of human performance through the medium of physical activities that have been selected with a view to realizing this outcome.

– Charles A Bucher.

Physical education is the sum of those experiences which come to the individual through movement.

– Delbert Oberteuffer

Physical education is the sum of man's physical activities selected as a kind and conducted as to outcomes.

– Jesse Feiring Williams

Physical education is that phase of the whole field of education that deals with big muscle activities and their related responses.

– Jay B Nash

Later on modified as :

Physical education is a way of education through motor activities and related experiences and its subject matter is primarily ways of behaving.

– William H Kilpatrick

The great thought in physical education is not the education of the physical nature, but the relation of physical training to complete education.

– Thomas wood

Physical education is the process by which changes in the individual are brought about through his movement experiences.

– Edward F. Voltmer & Arthur, A. Esstinger

Physical education is education through physical activities for the development of total personality of the child and its fulfillment and perfection in body, mind and spirit.

– J.P. Thomas

Physical education is that part of the general education programme which is concerned with the growth, development and education of children through the medium of big muscle activities. It is education of the whole child by means of physical activities. Physical activities are the tools. They are so selected and conducted as to influence every aspect of child's life, physically, mentally, emotionally, and morally

– H.C. Buck

AIMS OF PHYSICAL EDUCATION

According to National Plan of Physical Education and Recreation, "The aim of the physical education must be to make every child physically, mentally and emotionally fit and also to develop in him such personal and social qualities as will help him to live happily with others and build him as a good citizen." The main aims of physical education are:

1. It understands that physical activity provides opportunities for enjoyment, challenge, self expression and social interaction.
2. It demonstrates understanding and respect for differences among people in physical activity settings.
3. It applies movement concepts and principles to the learning and development of motor skills.
4. It demonstrates responsible personal and social behaviour in physical activity settings.
5. It achieves and maintains a health enhancing level of physical fitness.
6. It exhibits a physically active lifestyle.

According to J.R., Sherman "The aim of physical education is to influence the experiences of persons to the extent that each individual within the limits of his capacity may be helped to adjust successfully in society, to increase and improve his wants, and to develop the ability to satisfy his wants." It can thus be said that aim of physical education is to provide experiences so that the man is able to adjust in the society and live a quality of life.

Another definition of aim by Nixon and Cozen states "Organised physical education should aim to make the maximum contribution to the development of an individual's potentialities in all phases of life by placing him in an environment, as favourable as possible, to the promotion of such muscular and related responses or activities as will best contribute to this purpose.

Probably one of the most concise aim of physical education was stated by Book Walters, "the aim of physical education is the optimum development of the physically, socially, and mentally integrated and adjust individual through guided instruction and participation in selected total – body sports, rhythmic and gymnastic activities conducted according to social and hygienic standards."

The definitions stated above emphasize the holistic concept by providing ample opportunities and sufficient facilities for development of an integrated and adjusted individual so that he may live an enriched, radiant, and abundant life. In nutshell, the aim of physical education is the wholesome development of human personality for complete living.

Objectives of Physical Education

The objectives of physical education, enlisted by various authors are being mentioned below:

According to **Charles A. Bucher,** the objectives listed by various physical educationists may be incorporated under four headings:

1. Physical development objective
2. Motor and movement development objective
3. Cognitive and mental development objective
4. Social development objective

In 1934, the committee on **objectives of the American Physical Education Association,** listed five objectives:

1. Physical fitness
2. Mental health and efficiency
3. Social-moral character
4. Emotional expression and control
5. Appreciation

In 1948, J.B. Nash listed four development objectives:

1. Organic development
2. Neuromuscular development
3. Interpretive development
4. Emotional development

Cowell and Schein classified the objectives of physical education into five groups:

1. Organic power
2. The ability to maintaing adaptive effeort
3. Neuro muscular development
4. Personal and social attitudes and adjustments
5. Interpretive, intellectual and emotional responsiveness.

In 1947, Agnes Stoodly reviewing the literature of various authors categorized the objectives under five heads :

1. health, physical, or organic development,
2. mental – emotional development,
3. neuromuscular development,
4. social development, and
5. intellectual development.

In 1950 a Joint Committee of the American Association for Health, Physical Education and Recreation and Society of State Directors of Health, Physical Education, and Recreation formulated four objectives :

1. to develop and maintain minimum physical efficiency,
2. to develop useful skills,
3. to conduct one self in socially useful ways, and
4. to enjoy wholesome recreation.

Later on, in 1965 the American Association for Health, Physical Education and Recreation listed five major objectives :

1. To help children learn to move skillfully and effectively not only in exercises, games,

sports, and dances but also in all active life situations.

2. To develop understanding of voluntary movements and the ways in which individuals may organize their own movement to accomplish the significant purposes of their lives.
3. To enrich understanding of space, time, mass energy relationships and related concepts
4. To extend understanding of socially approved pattern of personal behaviour with particular reference to the interpersonal interactions of games and sports, and
5. To condition the heart, lungs, muscles and other organic systems to respond to increased demands by imposing progressively greater demands upon them.

Obteruffer and Ulrich categorised the objectives under two headings:

1. Immediate objectives (skill in an activity organic values and funda-mental amusement)
2. Long range objectives (psychological characteristics and social control)

Cowell and Schein classified the objectives into five groups :

1. Organic power,
2. The ability to maintain adaptive effort,
3. Neuro muscular development,
4. Personal and social attitudes and adjustments,
5. Interpretive and intellectual and emotional responsiveness.

J.R. Sherman listed six objectives :

1. To provide opportunities for controlled participation in physical activities that will result in educative experiences
2. To develop theoretic system of the body.
3. To develop skills in activities and favourable attitudes towards play.
4. To develop desirable social attitude and conduct.
5. To dcvclop correct health habits, and
6. To develop emotionally and intellectually.

According to *Charles A. Bucher* the objectives listed by various physical educationists may be incorporated under four headings :

1. Physical development objective,
2. Motor and movement development objective,
3. Cognitive and mental development objective, and
4. Social development objective.

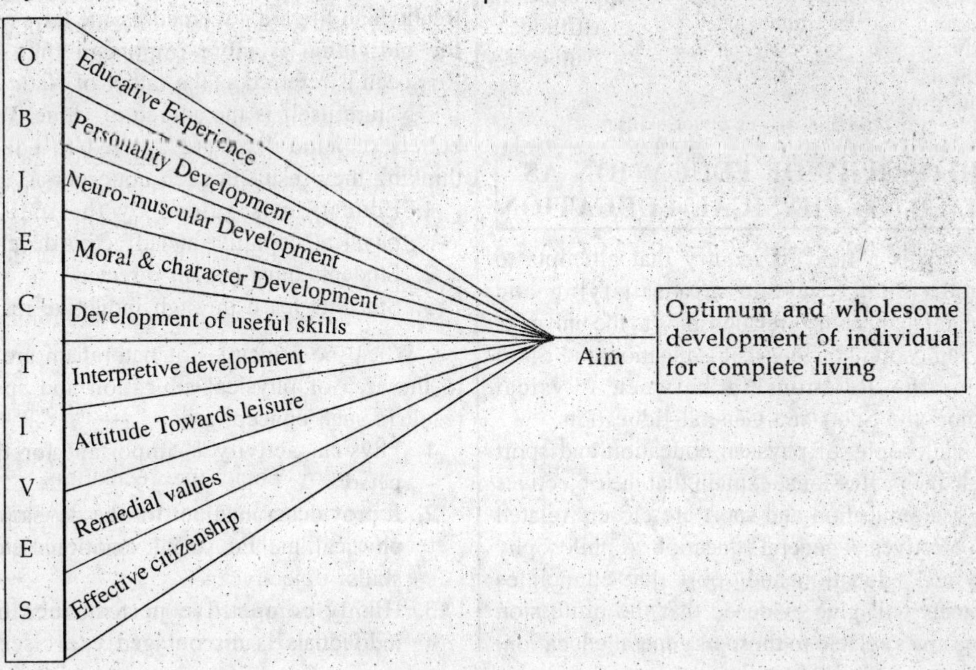

Edward F. Volmer et al after reviewing related literature, also suggested four objectives :

1. Physical development objective,
2. Motor development objective,
3. Knowledge and understanding objective, and
4. Social and emotional development objective.

Bloom and Krathwohl and associates had summarized the objectives under three inter dependent domains to effectively communicate the nature and scope of the objectives :

1. the cognitive,
2. the affective and
3. the psychomotor.

Harold M. Barrow after reviewing the objectives listed by various authors including Hetherington, J.B. Nash, J.F. Williams and others, also considered these three domains suggested by Bloom et al as appropriate.

A new Look at Objectives : The Three Domains

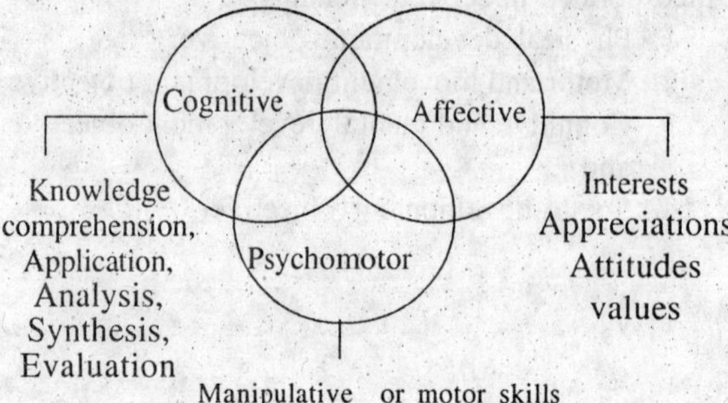

PHILOSOPHY OF EDUCATION AS APPLIED TO PHYSICAL EDUCATION

Philosophy is a field of inquiry that attempts to help individuals evaluate in a satisfying and meaningful manner their relationships to the universe.

A Philosophy of Physical Education and Sport explains the Relationship between Physical Education and Sport and General Education.

A Philosophy of physical education and sport will help the professional explain that the objectives of physical education and sport are closely related to the objectives of general education. A philosophy of physical education and sport that enunciates basic goals will give evidence that the profession has objectives related to those of general education.

Idealism

This interprets events and creates reality, truth and values are absolute and universally shared. The Greek philosopher Plato is referred as the father of idealism.

As a philosophy, idealism emphasizes the mind as central to understanding. It encompasses that, the mind is the focus of person's being. In the scheme of the universe, people are more important than nature because nature is interpreted by the mind. An individual exercises free will in choosing between right and wrong. Reasoning and intuition help individuals arrive at the truth.

When these basic principles of idealism are applied to educational thinking, they result in such concept as: Education develops the personality and character particularly the moral and spiritual values of the individual.

When these principles are applied to the area of physical education and sport, they result in such concept as physical education and sport involves more than the "Physical". The teacher is a role model for the students.

Naturalism

Reality and life are governed by the laws of nature, the individual is more important than society. Rossoeau is referred as the father of Naturalism.

Nature itself is the source of value. When the beliefs of naturalism are applied to educational thinking they result in such concepts as:

1. Education is guided by the individual's physical, cognitive and affective development.
2. Students must be self directed.
3. Students learn through inductive reasoning.

When the principles of naturalism are applied to the area of physical education and sport they result in such concept as:

1. Physical activity is important for the total person.
2. It provides a medium for the development of physical, mental, social, emotional and moral skills.
3. Highly competitive performance between individuals is discouraged.

Realism

The physical world is the real world and it is governed by the nature; science reveals the truths. It deals with the concept as:

1. Nature is in control.
2. The truth can best be determined through the scientific method.
3. People's sense and experiences also help people to understand nature.

When the general principles of realism are applied to education they result in:

1. Education develops one's reasoning power and ability to apply the scientific method to interpret the real things in life; this is essential for life long learning.

When these general principles are applied to the area of physical education and sport they result in :

1. Education is for life.
2. Physical education and sport is valuable because of its contribution to health.
3. A healthy person can lead a life and be more productive.

Pragmatism

Reality is determined by all individual's life experiences — the individual learns the truth through experiences.

It emphasizes experience was a key to life. It deals with concept such as:

1. Truth is based on one's experiences because individuals experience is different under different conditions and situations, reality changes in pragmatism.
2. Truth is situational.
3. Social responsibility is important. When the general principles of pragmatism are applied to education they result in concept such as :
   (*a*) The individual learns through experience.
   (*b*) Problem solving is the primary educational method and is a necessary skill for coping with an ever solving method.

Existentialism

Reality is based on human existence. Individual experiences determine what is true.

It deals with such concept as :

1. Human existence is the only true reality.
2. An individual's experiences and choices are unique, affecting their perception of reality.

When the general principles on existentialism are applied to educational thinking they result in concept such as:

1. Education is all individual process.
2. The teacher serves as a stimulator in the educational process.

When these principles of existentialism are applied to the area of physical education and sport such as:

1. Each student is free to choose from a variety of activities within the curriculum.
2. Individual activities provide oppor-tunities for students to develop self awareness and self-responsibility.

Humanism

It may be defined as a revolt against depersonalization and as the emergence of the belief that a human being is all individual and should be treated as such rather than as a part of a larger group. Humanism encourages total involvement and participation in all that is going on around us.

The humanistic teacher must encourage students towards self actualization and self-fulfillment.

1. Expressing open, genuine feelings.
2. Placing a value on humanity and the individual.
3. Being creative and independent and encouraging the same in students.

BIOLOGICAL BASIS OF PHYSICAL ACTIVITY

Traditionally nature and nurture have been understood to be antagonistic and two separate factors that determine the behaviour of indivi-duals.

In the light of scientific advancements in genetics, the exclusive character of one's influence or the other has been challenged. No doubt nature provides a strong basis for human structure and function, but the environmental influences too play a key role in consolidating and modifying behaviour of individuals. For example it is necessary for an individual to inherit a fairly good organised structure for efficient functioning which is without genetic handicaps, but if this structure is not nurtured carefully it can degenerate gradually into a non functional unit. This is perhaps one of the biggest problems of mankind because human beings have become less active due to mechanisation and scientific and technological advancements. This has led to numerous physical problems. The basic difference between human life and animal life compels to understand the role of environment in shaping our lives. Human beings are said to possess highest form of life only because they have learnt in the environment to modify, strengthen, weaken or at times completely check their drives, urges and impulses bestowed on them by nature. Biological and Cultural evolution has far reaching implications for the physical educators today, which can be summed up as follows :

1. Physical activity which was a biological compulsion in the primitive society where a man had to run for hunting food and survive against natural calamities, formed his basis of existence. Today man needs to keep himself fit even in this highly mechanised world just to sustain his biological posture.
2. Physical activity is necessary not only to keep oneself fit but is an effective means of emotional and mental outlet.
3. Biological evolution has brought an inheritance of structure and function that require care and attention. Because the artificial conditions created by modern civilization not only would result in physical degeneration but also affect mental processes negatively. Sound mind would require a sound body.

GROWTH AND DEVELOPMENT

More often 'Growth' and Development' are used interchangeably. Without going into the detailed meaning of them, it is enough to say that growth is an aspect of development. In other words, we can say that development is much wider term than growth. More specifically it is true in the light of fact that development continues from the first day of life till the death, whereas growth terminates at specific age.

Generally it is difficult to separate growth and development since both the processes are interrelated and interdependent on each other. But the scholars in the field of Biology and Psychology have made earnest effort to differentiate these two terms.

Growth

Growth refers to the process through which body increases in size and shape. Growth is a biological process. In other words growth means increase in mass. From the time conception takes place in the mothers womb, the process of growth starts. The fertilized egg continues to grow and after birth this process goes on till complete physical maturity is obtained. Growth is thus a quantitative increase in size and shape. Physical growth refers to these changes in size and shape of different organs of the body each of which normally proceeds at a different rate. Growth, therefore, is a tangible biological process in which the organ gains in size, volume, height and weight. There is enlargement of cells, muscles, bones and elongation of the skeleton and structure. It is quantitative change which is perceptible, concrete and solid.

Development

Development on the other hand is related with advancement and a progressive series of qualitative changes towards greater maturity. It is rather a qualitative change in the structural, the functional, and the behavioural aspects of the human being. Development processes have greater factors such as nutrition, activity protection from disease, other cultural and social influences are well ensured. More specifically development can be defined as the emerging and expanding of capabilities of the individual to provide greater facility in functioning such as development of motor ability from uncertain step to proficiency in games. Development, as a matter of fact is achieved through growth and forms the basis for the development of functional capacities of the child. Without proper growth probably, required level of development may not be achieved at a given stage. Development refers to mental, intellectual, emotional and social aspects. Acquisition of skills and knowledge indicate development process. Growth and Development are complementary. Although growth comes to an end at some stage of life, development continues.

Maturation

It is a stage of physiological development which is qualitative in nature and occurs as a biological function. This stage leads the vital organs of the body to function efficiently in a more mature way as compared to childhood.

Learning

Learning is a process of acquiring new skills of awareness as a result of certain experiences. Learning is a process of modification in behaviour.

As the child grows, becomes heavier and taller, process of development also starts which increases his capacities and abilities to understand complex functions. At the same time, he is maturing i.e. his systems are becoming better adapted to handle various situations. Also he continues to learn consciously or unconsciously as a result of his interaction with environment. It is obvious that all these processes are not fully independent, but they are intricately and intimately interdependent. To conclude we can say that growth, maturation and learning all contribute to the development of the child.

Motor Development

It refers to the development of general body control, fine motor skills and large muscle movements such as running, jumping and throwing.

Sensory, perceptual, cognitive development (Mental Development)refers to the process of development which increases abilities to discriminate weight, depth and distance perception, learning imagination and creativity reasoning ability and so on.

Social Development

Social development of qualitative human behaviour such as social qualities of cooperation adjustment and leadership

GENERAL PRINCIPLES OF GROWTH AND DEVELOPMENT

A careful analysis of growth and development reveals that this process is guided by certain principles which have far- reaching effects on the formulation of programmes in Physical Education:

1. Growth and development is the result of interaction between the germ plasm (heredity)) and the environment.
2. Growth and development (behaviour) follow a specific sequence e.g. a child has to pass through the various stages such as infancy, childhood, puberty, adolescence and adulthood. During these stages the growth and development moves from simple to complex.
3. Growth and development is a gradual and long process because longer the life span of a species the more gradual and long the process of growth and development.
4. Growth and development is a creative process. Right from the time of conception, the human child develops in such a manner that something is added to it both physiologically and psychologically. In other words as the child grows in years, it shows changes in functional and behavioural characteristics.
5. Growth and development are inevitable but they are definitely affected by the quality of genes and environmental factors.
6. Growth and development proceeds at different rate speed. The physical, the mental, the emotional, the intellectual and the social aspect of growth and development though

thickly related, have different pace of movement in different individuals, because each individual grows in his own way depending upon genetic and environmental factors.

7. Growth is determined by heredity because heredity sets the limits. Even if ideal environmental factors are available, individual would not grow beyond limits.
8. Growth proceeds rapidly in the early year. As the child advances in years the rate of his growth declines notwithstanding the sequence of developmental stages e.g., childhood puberty and adolescence etc.

DIFFERENCES BETWEEN GROWTH AND DEVELOPMENT

Growth	Development
1. Growth is visible	1. Development is invisible
2. Growth can be measured directly in terms of size, volume, and weight of the body.	2. Development cannot be measured directly for instance measurement of speed, strength, mental ability, and academic achievement and so on.
3. Growth continues upon certain age of an individual.	3. Development continues from the birth till death.
4. The limits of the growth are set by the heredity of an individual.	4. The development is more affected by the environment available to the person.

FACTORS AFFECTING GROWTH AND DEVELOPMENT

There are four main factors which affect growth and development of an individual. These are:

- Genetic Factors
- Environmental Factors
- Nutritional Factors
- Specific Programmes of Physical Education

Genetic Factors

Genetics is the branch of biology which deals with the heredity. There are some traits and characteristics which are passed on from the parents to the children through the genes. Genes are the most powerful of living forces because they control the patterns of growth from one generation to another. The traits which can be transferred to the next generation are height, body built, speed, agility, intelligence temperaments, physiological functioning and so on. Besides, some weak inherited organs predispose an individual to certain diseases.

Environmental Factors

Environmental factors include, geographical conditions, healthy traditions, culture, social codes, religious practices, education, knowledge of health and diseases, health related facilities, socio economic conditions etc.

Nutritional Factors

Well balanced diet keeping in view the climatic conditions, occupation, and stages of growth and development ensures growth and development to its optimum limits.

Specific Prgorammes of Physical Education

The programme of physical education in the curriculum of schools and colleges should be specific to the need of the students. Any deviation in the programme of their specific need will produce negative results.

NEED OF STUDY OF GROWTH AND DEVELOPMENT FOR A TEACHER

A teacher has to deal with children of different socio–economic, culture, religion, heredity, environment, gender, race and caste etc. backgrounds. These factors constitute a wide variety of individual differences among the children at different age levels. These differences in them play an important role in education. The teacher must know potentialities and capacities of each and every student of his class so that he may exploit them to the maximum for the benefit of the individual and society. He must know the basic principles of growth and development and the characteristics which emerge at different age-levels in various developmental dimensions to provide effective guidance for harmonious development of children. Also, he must know the basic factors affecting growth and development of a child such as heredity and environment. The teacher is an effective agent of the society who is responsible to bring desirable changes in the behaviour of children. In return, the children may shoulder the responsibilities of a good citizen to contribute and accelerate the process of national development. The other reason to have the knowledge of growth and development of a child is its continuity from the past to the present and present can be understood in terms of his past history.

AGE AND SEX DIFFERENCES IN RELATION TO PHYSICAL ACTIVITIES AND SPORTS

Physical education teachers should be aware of the fact that some differences in boys and girls are of great importance. Up to puberty boys and girls are hardly distinguished but as they cross this stage, marked differences become evident in their sexes. These differences are important in structuring and formulating activity programme for both sexes. These differences are not only biologically prominent, but social factors also impinge upon as men and women have to take up different roles. So while activity programme it is necessary that marked differences in boys and girls are taken into consideration not again saying the fact that there should be separate programmes.

The above mentioned differences between male and female with regard to their structures and functions put the later at a biologically disadvantageous position. For example, wider pelvis and a marked obliquity of femur gives her mechanical disadvantage which interferes with the running ability. Similarly female is weaker as compared to her counter part in events where strength is an important component. Since the arm strength of girls after puberty is less and shoulder girdle weak, the programme of physical education should avoid such activities that may put unnecessary strain on the shoulder girdle. To summarize physical education programmes should take into consideration age and sex differences among males and females in order to provide most suitable programmes to them.

EFFECT OF HEREDITY AND ENVIRONMENT ON GROWTH AND DEVELOPMENT

Heredity, environment of an individual are influenced by both biological and psychological factors. In this connection there is a difference of opinion between two schools of thought. The school belonging to biological scientists firmly advocates in favour of inherited qualities for the all round development of an individual. They say we remain whatever we are though to a great extent the behaviour of an individual at school, on the athletic stadium and in general public is greatly influenced by the teachers and trainers. Yet the value of certain innate qualities such as aggression, self preservation and so on are not to be under estimated when the question of all round development of an individual arise. These qualities are biological, inherited and their strength has far reaching effects on the individual's personality. For example, an athlete who does not possess the basic qualities such as speed, agility and killing instinct may never prove to be outstanding competitor.

On the other hand the social psychologists belonging to nations like Germany and U.S.S.R. and so on do not accept the superiority of inherited traits in comparison to environmental factors. They firmly believe that athletes are produced and not born. Vigorous training, scientific coaching, diet controls, proper motivation etc. can produce athletes in quality as well as in quantity.

ANATOMICAL AND PHYSIOLOGICAL DIFFERENCES BETWEEN MALE AND FEMALE

Female	Male
1. Girls grow faster up to the age of early adolescence and slow down after the age of 14 years.	1. Before the adolescence age, growth in boys is slow and they grow faster after the age of 14 -16 years.
2. Girls are smaller in size i.e. height and they attain maturity in early age.	2. Boys are generally taller in size i.e. height and maturity comes in the late stage.
3. Female has broader and shallow pelvis which causes difficulty in running.	3. Male has narrow pelvis (Hips). They can perform better in running events.
4. Women have large body for swimming.	4. Man has shorter trunk and long legs. Their centre of gravity is high; this results in unstable position.They are more frequent in shifting exercise and jumping but have disadvantage in balancing events as gymnastics.
5. Female's shoulders are weaker in strength and narrow, their bones and cartilages are also weak. They have disadvantage in throwing events, lifting activities, and hanging movements in gymnastics.	5. Male has broader and strong shoulders with strong bones and cartilages. They can perform better throwing events, rope climbing, pole vault, and circling activities e.g. Roman rings in Gymnastics.
6. Female stops growing in height around the age of 18 to 20 years.	6. Boys generally continue to grow until the age of about 20 to 23 years.
7. Their muscular strength is less because of different structure of muscles and thereby comparatively cannot improve muscle power even with weight training and cannot perform better in pulling, pushing, punching and lifting activities.	7. Men have more muscle power, due to their muscle structure, they have better ability in performing, slapping, putting, puslading, pushing, striking, kicking and squeezing activities.
8. Women have smaller heart and faster pulse rate resulting in more rapid increase in pulse rate at the beginning of the exercise and recovery is much slow after the exercise.	8. Man has large heart because of more muscle tissues, circulation is better and the pulse rate is slow.
9. Women have slower reaction time and movement time.	9. Man has better reaction time and movement time.
10. Women are emotionally weak; the effect of defeat, victory, accident and injury on them is for longer time and they cannot recover from the shocks easily.	10. Men are emotionally stronger; defeat, victory, accident etc. do not have much effect on them. They overcome such shocks easily.
11. Menstruation in women is a biological activity, and has little effect on physical activists. It is more psychological than physiological, hard training should be avoided.	11. Men do not have such biological activity and can perform any type of activity.
12. Women breathe more shallowly with the upper part of the chest.	12. Men tend to breathe deeper and hence more diagragmatically.

A careful analysis of both the schools reveals that they have adopted an extreme approach in favour of heredity and environment. It is safe to conclude that man is actually the product of heredity and environment. Since sports is a biological necessity and a social institution, a sportsman is a beautiful blend of the both. If he possesses distinctive biological potentiality he is also subjected to certain fairable sociological forces, he can grow and develop to the desired level. The type of children, their manners, behaviour, type of school, social practices, religious attitudes and political pressure do have their part to play in the development of an individual. Similarly the physical education teachers, the coach, the trainer, the team mates and so on are not only responsible for grooming an athlete into a skilled performer but also guiding him in personal matter such as morality ethics, etc. From the concluding point of view it can be safely said that one cannot alter genetic make up of an individual but he can provide cordial environment in which the inherited potentialities can develop to an optimum level. This is how the heredity and environment affect the growth and development of the individual.

CHRONOLOGICAL AGE, ANATOMICAL AGE, PHYSIOLOGICAL AGE AND MENTAL AGE

Various aspects of growth do not proceed at the same rate; there are fluctuations. We have to deal with all sorts of children even in a particular class. Some children at the same age are slender, some short, some tall, some heavy, some light, some physiologically advance and some psychologically mature and so on. This definitely create problems of handling, disciplining and teaching children. Growth and development indicates that a child develops through various stages and each stage is characteristically different from the one preceding or succeeding it. An infant is not like a child and an adolescent is what an adult is not. To deal with these there are various ways and means to group or to classify students by using various criteria, taking into consideration the activities, capacities, capabilities of children at various levels. It is not difficult to know the age of an individual in years, months and days. The record is available in the school registers. The difficulty arises when the exact date of birth of a child is not available. In such situation, the developmental characteristics are taken into account with the Biologists who call anatomical and physiological age and the psychologists call mental age.

Chronological Age

Chronological age means the age of person recorded in years, months, and days. It beings from the day when a child is born and is calculated till one dies. Chronological age is a legal criterion of classifying a person as a child, or an adolescent, a major or a minor, his qualification for taking up some job, in getting admission to a school and even in competing in many sports events as a junior or a senior player. At the age of 17 years, almost 95% of the growth has already taken place and after the age of 17 years there is little or no effect on the developmental processes. At the school level, classifying pupils on the basis of chronological age has been found to be preposterous because of the development effects. Development of each child is not always the same with his advancement in years. Individual rate of growth, even the rate of growth of his various organs, differs considerably as a result of which some children are stouter, healthier, stronger or faster at a particular age while others are not. Similarly, some are mentally more mature than others. It is because of this that sports scientists advise the use of chronological age as a singular criterion for classification of pupil. However this will differ from activity to activity.

Anatomical Age

Anatomical age refers to the growth and development of the skeletal system. The quality of the bone structure or ossification of the bone is a major factor in determining the anatomical age of a person. Through X-Ray, the development in the skeletal system can easily be determined.Nutrition affects the quality of the skeletal development of a child. Anatomical age is also calculated by dentition, the number of teeth a child has at a particular age. In sports competitions for juniors or sub-juniors where it becomes necessary to refer the age cases, to a medical practitioner, it is through dentition test that the age of the participant is determined. Consideration of anatomical age is very important because it helps the sports person to find out whether heavy weight exercise should be given to the participants or not. Children with soft or green skeleton must not be burdened with heavy exercise work outs.

Physiological Age

The age is related to physiological capacities and capacities of children.Normally it is related to puberty. Secretion of hormones forms various glands and functional condition of the organs is taken into account while calculating the age of a child. This age may be determined to some extent by the growth of hair in the armpit in boys and onset of menstruation in case of girls. Determination of the age helps the sports persons to make work-schedules according to the physiological capacities and capabilities of the participants. It has been noticed that some children, though advance in chronological age, are still physiologically immature, this obstructs the planning of physical activity programmers. Activity loads cannot be worked out without taking into account physiological age of children. Activities which suit the physiological age of the different groups of children should be managed. Children like to play with the children of their physiological age.

Mental Age

Mental age is related to the mental development of the child i.e. mental maturation. Physical maturity and mental maturity are two different things. Many boys who have grown in years or in bodily characteristics are yet childish and immature. Their mental faculties have not developed fully. The mental age is usually detected through psychological tests.

Growing up in body does not necessarily make the child mature mentally. There are late matures and early matures. Through psycho-logical test, one can determine the mental age of boys and girls. This will not only help the teacher, a coach to adjust his methods and techniques of teaching training but also give him an insight into their intelligence, memory, retention etc.

In accordance with the structure, standard and objectives of an activity, the.age groups should be formed.In classifying pupils, the principle of homogeneity should be followed. It is harmful to drive all children with the same stick.Children of varying groups should not be made to play together nor allowed to compete against each other. Proper matching builds up confidence in learners and they do not face the risk of injury.

TYPES OF BODY

All individuals have different physical characteristics because of different biological, psychological, sociological, cultural and racial backgrounds. The concept that an individual's body type is related to his health, immunity from disease, physical performance and personality characteristic have developed from ancient times. On the basis of this concept, number of scholars have made attempts to describe the body types into two or three categories and proved to be inadequate in many respects. However, one thing is common in the result of research studies that physique pattern is significant to an under-standing of individual relation physically, mentally, emotionally and socially. For a teacher of Physical Education and coach it is very important to have knowledge of the physique pattern of students.This body of knowledge will help in many ways to understand his student/players for imparting physical fitness training/conditioning, teaching of a skill, choosing particular sports grouping or practical /theoretical instruction class, to control the behaviour of the student, to maintain discipline and finally to take best out of him with naturally available bodily qualities with the student.

For the student of Physical Education of undergraduate classes, it is thought to be appropriate to rely upon the information related to physique types give by Sheldon and his associates. They believed that human beings could not be classified into just two/ three physique types because nearly all individuals are mixtures. However they did designate three primary components of body build that are the best criteria for differentiating individuals, such as:

- Endomorph
- Mesomorphy
- Ectomorph

Endomorph

1. They have better digestive system and can digest hard food. This gives them more energy.
2. They have large roundhead with broad face square jaw and small ears.
3. Their abdomen is large ,full above the navel.
4. They have short and thick neck, chest with fatty breasts.
5. Their palms are broad with short fingers.
6. Their feet are also broad with low arch.
7. They have thick and hairy type of skin.
8. They act first and think after wards.
9. They are less secretive and are fond of making speeches in public places.
10. They have heavy buttocks and heavy legs.
11. They are very social and like social gathering.Ready to help the people when they are in trouble.
12. They always overestimate their abilities.
13. They remain in relaxed mood and do not feel irritated over small issues.
14. They have butterfly tendencies and cannot stick to their day to day affairs.
15. In games and sports they take up the activities such as power-lifting, heavy-weight wrestling, throwing events and even short distance running.

Mesomorphy

1. They are medium type of individuals and known as athletic type persons.
2. They are heavy, hard and rectangular in outlilne with large and prominent bones.
3. Their face bones are prominent and long and has the shape of a long oval.
4. Their neck is strong and long, shoulders are broad with heavy and prominent clavicle bones.
5. Their abdomen is large with low waist.
6. They have heavy buttocks with heavy fore legs.
7. Their skin is rough and the complexion is not so good.
8. They are quite dominant, assertive, energetic and action packed, and love to take risks.
9. They are bold, brave and take actions quickly whenever they face any problem.
10. They are courageous and open-minded and show directness in any kind of work.

Ectomorph

1. They have poor digestive system and the energy output is also less.
2. They have delicate body structure.
3. Their face is small, forehead and chin is pointed and nose is sharp.
4. They have long slender neck, long narrow thorax, drooping and hanging shoulders with long arms.
5. Their abdomen is flat with hollow above navel.
6. They have thin buttock and log thin legs.
7. Their hands are small but fingers and toes are long.
8. Their feet are also long with high arch.
9. They are tall and thin built with poor vital capacity
10. Their skin is soft but with more hairy growth.
11. Their reflections are quick but actions are very slow.
12. They always under estimate their abilities but want to lead an ambitious life.
13. They feel irritated, over-tensed and excited whenever they face any trouble and want to be left alone.
14. They are very submissive and one track minded and solve their problems more at the mental level with less use of energy.
15. They take up sports activities like basket ball, volley ball, and even long duration events.

It is suggested that the above mentioned body types do not always provide authentic information. Therefore, other factors such as age, physical maturity, interest aptitude, skill, strength, physical fitness combined with understanding of body types may be used in making judgments.

PSYCHOLOGICAL CHARACTERISTICS OF AN ADOLESCENT

The terms adolescence, adolescent age, adolescent period, or teen-age phase of development are used variously to designate the period of transition from dependence upon adult at direction and protection to self dependence and self determination. This is that period of life when the individual is in the process of transfer from the dependent, irresponsible age of childhood to the self-reliant, responsible age of adulthood. Psychologically, this is a period of adjustment to the physical and social changes which distinguish childhood behaviour from adult behaviour.

Adolescence is essentially the age of adventure and experiment. From time to time every normal adolescent will behave in a way that is contrary to accepted as adult standards. Some adolescents in their early teens seem naturally to begin planning their lives far into the future, planning in general terms of the life goals. Others live for the pleasure of the moment, they fail to mature psychologically in keeping with the passage of years. The former have a better chance of avoiding delinquency and maladjustment because they are developing a mature concept of life before they are thrust into it. Such a concept of life is one of the psychological structures adolescents need to build as an essential part of their development into adulthood. Many problems appear at this stage. Some people have misunderstood the appearance of these problems and refer to the adolescent period as a problem's age or problem's group. It is more correct to say that individuals at this age are faced with many problems. Adolescents who fail to make the normal transition to adulthood become misfits, delinquents, criminals and their problems spill over onto their children.

As in the case of younger children, the adolescent who is overprotected, provided immunity from normal ill results of his misbehaviour or poor judgment, is being carefully prepared for future trouble or tragedy. If he had been given a reasonable amount of responsibility during this period and even during past few years, and if he had been given the opportunity to exercise his own thinking without too much hindrance from adults, he would be better prepared to face the task of growing up when reaches the adulthood. Adolescent requires the experiences of accepting both the growing adult opportunities for self determination and the responsibility for the result of the use of those opportunities. The adolescent is particularly apt to be handicapped by lack of skills and habits. Adolescence appears to be a period of many "firsts", many new situations. And a new situation is a situation in which the individual finds his previously established habits inadequate. Since the "teen" years represent period in an individual's life of finding himself as a person, there is likely to be, more or less, a struggle within the maturing adolescent as he attempts to determine his rights and responsibilities in his relationships with adults and with his peer groups. Adolescence is not necessarily a period of constant stress and strain. Some young people are helped to experience a gradual, relatively peaceful and successful continuum of development from early childhood to adulthood. The future is theirs. What they will make of that future is the society's responsibility as well as theirs.

This period can be classified in three stages : Preadolescence, early adolescence and late adolescence.

Preadolescence is the period when the childhood personality is broken up and the modifications reaching up to adult personality starts. It is a period of hyperactivity, rebelliousness, moodiness and irritability. These are the manifestations of the way in which the individual is coping with the disorganization of his childhood personality. The boys as well as girls are restless and hyperactive in this period. Tapping pencils, manipulating objects in their pockets, playing with their hair etc, indicate the same. Emotionally, the main task is to develop appropriate ways of adjusting to new feeling evoked by the bodily changes. Another task is to change one's perceptions regarding the parents, the peers and the self. Boys and girls at this stage may respond to their elders with irritation, distrust and suspicion. They are easily offended and are quick to complain that the adults do not understand them or that they do not treat them fairly. They are highly sensitive and self conscious. Sometimes they may be over-powered by their emotions of anger, fear or love.

They have yet to develop the social skills to get along with their peers. Many of their frustrations arise out of conflicts with parents and peers. Conflicts with parents may arise over his manners of dress, the friends he chooses, the way he spends his time, the condition of his table and his room, the lack of respect and consideration for others. He resists these demands and expectations by asserting his independence. As the boys and girls now spend more time with their friends, they constantly strive to conform to the peer groups in matters of dress, language, behaviour and values. This may give rise to conflicts with the parents when there is great discrepancy between the values cherished at home and the values of the peer group. The preadolescents have a strong idealism and sense of justice and fair play. They develop a strong conscience and may often experience intense feelings of guilt. They are also likely to be very critical of the people who do not live up to their ideals. They are also very keen on exposure to the mass media, particularly the movies, the radio, the television and cable network programmes. Thus, the preadolescents are more oriented to people, events and phenomena of the outside world compared to the children of earlier age. Peer group activities and group games become very important for them.

Early adolescence extends upto fifteen years age. The early adolescent has to incorporate into his self-concept the new feelings, the new body image and the new conceptions about his role. They are more and more concerned about their body, their stature and size. The rapid physical changes during adolescence produce a rapid change in body image. This generally leads to a self rejection. Often the adolescent finds it difficult to accept his physical self-height, weight, complexion and problems like pimples etc. The boys are concerned about their muscular strength and are eager to go to the gymnasium to develop their strength. The girls are concerned with their shapeliness, their facial features and their complexion. The hair styling, clothing fads, etc. may be the attempts on the part of the adolescent to develop a consistent and acceptable body image. The physical attractiveness is the chief criterion of social acceptability in adolescence and young adulthood.

They now need information about sex matter and seek it among their peers. Lack of informations makes them anxious and overcurious and misinformed. Strong friendship ties with members of their own sex continue to grow but there is also an increased awareness about the members of the opposite sex. One of the most important development tasks for them is the search for and the achievement of a sense of identity. Becoming independent of parents and gaining acceptance of peers are important steps in achieving a sense of personal identity. The choice of and preparation for a career is another step in the process.

The late adolescence is the period by which time most of them have entered into their career or are engaged in higher professional studies. By this time they achieve a great measure of independence from the parents though the parents continue to be important person. They are high idealistic and seek to abolish inequalities in society and build up a more perfect world.

Growth into late adolescence is especially characterized by changed attitudes towards member of the opposite sex. Boys and girls who were indifferent to the opposite sex just a few years ago are not anxious to secure approval from members of that sex. This affects changes in their ways of behaving and presents new problems to teachers and parents. Most children begin showing signs of modesty and often times timidity in the presence of the opposite sex during this period. Mental maturity is reached during late adolescence, though the age at which an individual becomes emotionally and socially mature varies.

Late adolescence has often been described as a period of heightened social consciousness. The desire for stands and social acceptability, though important in varying degrees throughout life ,is given a special attention by adolescents because at this age, status and acceptance among members of opposite sex and among adults are much to be desired. The desire for acceptance and status is so basic that it will be reflected in many other motives. There is perhaps no period in an individual's life when he does not have desire to be popular among his peers, but this desire is dominant during adolescent years. If the adolescent is to secure and maintain a well-adjusted personality, he must develop out of his early egocentric nature into a social being who recognizes and appreciates the personality of others, and who is eager to become a part of his peer group. The expectations and demands of the various social groups of which one is a member influence one's behaviour. The parents as well as others keep shifting in their demands and expectations.Sometimes they look upon the adolescent as a child, but when he responds with that behaviour he is called childish. When he behaves like an adult, his parents and others ridicule him saying so you have grown older. In such circumstances the adolescent has a problem in getting his role clearly defined. This creates problems with respect to his identity i. e the identity crisis of adolescents. The three chief problems faced by the adolescent in his quest for identity are the changed body image, the changed social role and the changed sex role.

With increasing independence from parents, the adolescent can no longer accept ready–made values he has received from them. Then hero worship of pre-adolescence may give place to certain cynicism. As a result the achievement of autonomy during adolescence involves a certain amount of friction between the adolescence and his parents regarding the values and attitudes. Generally, this transitional period of defiance is far more salient in boys than in girls. Boys show more defiance over the imposition of parental rules that restricts them than the girls. He now questions, considers and arrives at his own decisions, he does not just accept what he is told. This is an important feature of the adolescent's search of identity and maturity. He makes comparisons, contrast and evaluations and arrives at ways of behaving which gives satisfaction to his self-concept and to the society in which he has to live and function.

Not only is the young person beset by compelling new physiologically based drives from within, but he also finds himself on the threshold of a complex, inconsistent, and confusing adult world on the outside world with which he has had little involvement or concern before.

PROBLEMS OF AN ADOLESCENT

The seeds of adult troubles are often sown in early life and not a few of them germinate during adolescence. At this stage they are more readily amenable to treatment than they are in their fully established state. It is therefore, important to try to recognize the signs of psychological problems in the adolescent and to take early measures to correct the same. Some of the problems accruing during adolescence are mentioned below:

1. **Identity crisis:** Quests for identity is another major problem faced by the adolescents. He asserts for his own identity as an individual whereas in many situations, he is not considered by his parents and peers competent enough for it. Over exposure to popular media like TV, network, etc further confound his problems. There is wide gap between his desires and ambitions, and his ability to achieve the same, and unless they are helped to acquire some objective in self understanding their day by day attempts for self assertion may be unrealistic.
2. **Problem Connected with the Future:** The adolescence is a period when the individual is not a child. He has emerged from the safe and protected life of child- hood. He has now to decide as to what course of life he has to follow. Though he is expected to make decision regarding giving direction to his life, he has not yet matured enough to take intelligent decisions. The problems connected

with their future put a lot of psychological stress and strain on them.

3. **Desire for Independence:** Achieving independence from home and family ties is one of the major problems faced by adolescents. This problem is made more difficult by the failure of many parents to realize that the boys and girls are advancing towards maturity. Among adolescents the desire for self determination and independence (to be accepted as a mature, responsible, self directing adult) is perhaps the most important problem faced by them. The three types of home problems most frequently noted are : (i) those indicating a lack of understanding between parents and adolescents (ii) those involving a limitation of their freedom and (iii) problems involving money or finances.
4. **Problems Relating to Physical Development:** The pubescent spurt of growth does not occur simultaneously for the different parts of the body. The variations in body build and variations in the outsent of pubescence become sources of disturbances to many adolescent. Boys in particular are disturbed over conditions that may cause them not to look masculine. Any condition that may cause the girl to be looked upon as less feminine becomes a problem for her. Even temporary deviations from the "sex appropriate physique" may produce significant adjustment problems for boys and girls.
5. **Problems Related to Physiological Growth:** The physical changes associated with adolescence present conditions and problems that the adolescent has not met upto this time and in many cases is ill prepared to meet them when they appear. The period of first menarche may be a real problem for girls if she has not been properly prepared for it. Problems of skin blemishes and acne disturb many boys and girls at this age. The appearance of auxiliary hair is, in some cases, a source of disturbance for girls, while the lack of the appearance of hair on the arms, legs and chest has been regarded by many boys as weakness in the development of a masculine type. These problems are inextricably related to the sex roles to be played by the adolescent boys and girls. Any condition that interferes with development and assertion of the masculine role on the part of boys is likely to be a source of difficulty conversely, any condition that interferes with the development and assertion of the feminine role on part of the girls is likely to be a source of difficulty for them.
6. **School problems of Adolescents:** Adjustments to different aspects of the school environment present problems at all age levels. The pre adolescents and adolescents are required to adjust to a number of different teachers having different personalities, they may be expected to obey and follow the dictates of an authoritarian teacher at one time, had then later participate in the planning under a teacher with more democratic moods and concepts. Many situations in the traditional schools involve competitions. The adolescents must learn to adjust to failures and successes in these activities. Fear of failure, fear of disapproval of his teacher fear of disapproval of his peers, and many other fears may loom large at this stage.
7. **Social demands upon Adolescents:** The development into adolescence brings forth impulses relating to the sex drive and more sensitized social reactions. The changed physiological self causes individual to take a different attitude towards members of the opposite sex. At this stage, the individual must learn to adapt to a society in which his role is complementary to that of the opposite sex. New demands are made upon him. A few years ago, he was excused for any acts because he was immature.Now he is expected to assume the role of an adult on many occasions, even though he is inexperienced in living and participating as an adult in an adult society. There is perhaps no period of life when individuals are so frequently misunderstood as they are in the adolescent period, the transitional stage of life.

8. **Problem of Adherence to Codes and Ideals:** Much of our behaviour is guided by principles of "right" and "wrong". As a person grows, he makes the standards and norms of his particular culture his own, and in this way a need to conform to the society's demands becomes a personal need. An adolescent's habitual ways of behaving and habitual attitude may not be appropriate to the new social life in which he now finds himself. He is faced with special problems involving readjustments of ideals and behaviours related thereto.
9. **Confusion Between Adolescent's Role Status:** Unfortunately, neither the adolescent's role nor his status is clear-cut in this society. A boy may be treated like a man in many situations outside but like a child in his own home. He continues to be bossed like a child but no longer enjoys the protected status of childhood. Because of such inconsistencies in the role and status, the adolescent finds himself as hanging in between. This in–between status constitutes a sort of limbo in which adults-in- the making remain suspended. By the time he is sure that he is no longer a child, he is beginning to wonder- but isn't yet sure-whether or not he is an adult. Such vagueness hardly permits clear definition of his current responsibilities.
10. **Behaviour Related Problems:** Adolescence is a period of restlessness, hyperactivity, rebelliousness, moodiness and irritability which cause many behaviour related problems. An adolescent is troubled by personal fears and vague feelings of insecurity. He is trying to learn many new causes to adult behaviour. He feels the need to establish his personal identity and recognition by his peer and many a time due to his behavioural inconsistencies he may come into conflict with them.

Other problems of relatively frequent occurrence include those in the areas of conduct and morals, educational and vocational choices, personal adjustment, recreation, social relations with the opposite sex and problems concerning religion. A careful study of all these problems will show that an individual fortified with affection, security and a feeling of personal worth during childhood will be better prepared as an adolescent to meet and solve these problems. If the developmental progress, is to be socially acceptable and effective a young person's transition from childhood to adult status must proceed gradually under guidance of self disciplined adults.Too much and too suddenly gained liberty leads to adolescent's confusion. At the same time overprotection or dominance may arouse in them strong feeling of resentment, or result in retarded personal and social development.

THE ROLE OF PHYSICAL EDUATION AND SPORTS IN SOLVING THE PROBLEMS OF AN ADOLESCENT

Like any other healthy adult, the adolescent also takes a delight in physical activity. Though the physical benefits derived from this activity are self evident, it is conducive to the general development of the personality as well. The field of physical education and sports provide ample opportunities to the adolescent to engage himself in physical activities for his own benefit and for the benefit of the society of which he is an integral part.

- Self-confidence and self control are in their fullest sense, qualities of the 'whole man' and not just qualities of the mind. The first step towards a fuller self- confidence may well be taken by the mastery of some physical skill. All sports and games contribute to some extent to this end. The degree to which they do will vary with the complexity of the skills that adolescents involve themselves, and the amount of application that it takes to acquire those skills. The activities that offer a definite challenge to courage and endurance have a special contribution to make towards knowledge of self.
- Everyone inherits from his ancestors certain definitely aggressive instincts. Unless these instincts can find expression in action, these will be repressed and will exert a distorting

influence on adolescent's personality. Many sports and games give outlets of aggression. In the absence of such legitimate outlets, uncontrolled aggression will commonly appear in the form of delinquency. This principle, to a certain extent, is true of both sexes though it is much more apparent in the boys than in the girls. Any keenly competitive activity will absorb a certain amount of aggression. It will be surprising to see how a young thug or bully can be civilized by taking up boxing seriously. He reserves his aggression for the ring, and out of it he is content to live at peace with his fellows.

- Man is a social animal and his social instincts must have it fling if he is to acquire emotional balance. Loyalty and unselfishness are indispensable social virtues, and the team games afford a convenient and pleasant training ground for the same. These games, therefore, rightly take a prominent place in any programme of adolescent sport. Membership of an athletic club or gymnasium is often safeguard against recruitment into antisocial gangs.
- Physical activities, apart from the direct physical benefits that they confer, will also give opportunities for the acquisition of deep aesthetic satisfaction. Hiking, cycling, field sports and sailing, all bring the participants into close contact with nature and may awake an interest in their ways that will give lifelong pleasure. Few will deny that these aesthetic contributions are valuable influences in the development of the adolescent's personality.
- Physical education and sports also encourage an adolescent to take up some sport which will develop a trait in which he is thought to be lacking. For example, to inculcate a virtue of patience he may be encouraged to take part in games like rifle shooting, chess, archery etc, This will go a long way in moulding his personality for adjustment in his life.
- In almost every sport, adolescents will show a degree of aptitude that will justify an ambition to pursue that sport at its highest competitive level. This ambition can be of great importance as it enables them to avid frustration, and can lead to achievement that contributes considerably in the formation of a self determined and self sufficient personality.
- Participation of an adolescent in physical activities and games contribute greatly towards the development of his total personality. He emerges as a physio-logically healthy individual. This will enable him to overcome the problems associated with irritability, rebelliousness, moodiness etc which are common to adolescent's behaviour.
- There are a number of adolescents who are physically incompetent due to weakness or lack of coordination. This incompetence can often give rise to deep discouragement and feeling of inferiority which affect the whole of an adolescent's approach to life. Physical education and sports can do much to help these cases. Such child can be introduced to a porgressive course of training which works in two ways. In the first place it corrects in time the basic weakness or lack of coordination. In the second place it enables him to compete effectively against himself instead of ineffectively against his fellows. Suitable tests can be administered at intervals that will give objective evidence of his improving performance. This will often light the spark of physical ambition and before long he will be able to hold of his own on the ladder of general adolescent physical accomplishment. This achievement can often have a very significant effect on his performance in other fields.
- There are certain body functions that we take very much for granted. The way in which we sit or stand, the way in which we walk or run, even the way in which we breathe are all matters of unconscious habits. Bad habits can develop particularly during adolescence. Bad habits of posture or function interfere with the mechanics of the body and cause various organs to work at disadvantage. While this

may produce few symptoms during the adaptable period of adolescent, it may often sow seeds of trouble in later life. The detection and correction of these habits is, therefore important. Their treatment lies within the sphere of the remedial and rehabilitative programmes of physical education. If such remedial measures were applied more widely in adolescence we should see less of the "bad feet" slipped disc" and chronic respiratory troubles..

- Adolescence is the age of adventure and thrill. Taking part in physical activities and sports involving adventure and thrill like paragliding, diving, etc. provide an outlet to adolescents for getting rid of undue anxiety and fear, though it carries a special liability to injury. Modern methods of rehabilitation provided through physical education can do a lot to help the adolescents to be back in the normal life with ease.
- Some adolescents suffer from permanent physical disabilities as a result of accident, disease or congenital defect. The body may be crippled but the mind retains its normal need for physical activity, and special physical education and sports programmes cater for their need to the maximum degree possible.

Thus the importance of physical education and sports in solving the problems of an adolescent cannot be over emphasized. It plays a very significant role in disciplining the feelings, in controlling the emotions, in channelizing the energy and in stimulating and motivating an adolescent to form a constructive approach to life.

PSYCHOLOGICAL BASIS OF PHYSICAL EDUCATION

Human beings and animals are product of a long process of biological evolution. Their activities are highly complex in nature and directed from within. Since ancient times, philosophers have tried to understand why human being and other animals behave as they do.

The origin of psychology is often traced to the Greek Philosophers. The term 'psychology' is derived from two Greek words psyche; and logos'. Herein psyche means the soul or mind, and the meaning of logos is to talk about, or science or study. Thus, the literal meaning of psychology is the science or study of soul. Greek philosophers believed that soul was responsible for various mental activities such as learning, thinking, feeling etc.It was believed that soul was the essence or true being of an organism, the cause and the principles of life. As the relation of soul to the body and the functions of soul could be explained, some philosophers tried to define psychology as a science of mind.

In 1590, Rudolf Goeckel used the word psychology for the first time as a study of the mind. As the word mind could not be defined clearly, questions arose; what is mind? How can it be studied? And consequently, this view was also rejected. For centuries psychologists tried hard to understand the human actions and thoughts and to disentangle the body-soul dichotomy. French philosopher Rene Descartes described the body and mind as two separate structures that strongly influence each other.

In the mid – 1800's two German scientists Muller and Helmholtz established that the physical processes underlying mental activity could be studied scientifically. In 1875, Whilhelm Wundt founded probably the worlds first psychology laboratory and defined psychology as a science of consciousness. In 1879, he also published the first journal of psychology. During the same period William James also defined psychology as 'description and explanation of state of consciousness'. The works of William James and Wundt marked the beginning of psychology as a distinct field separate from philosophy. Wundt tried to understand the 'conscious mind' by breaking down such mental processes as sensation, perception, reaction tie, etc. into their basic elements and to analyse their inter relationships through a method called introspection. This approach did not find much favour and was rejected for not taking into account sub-conscious and unconscious activities of mind and the introspection method also proved to be the most subjective and unscientific method.

These problems prompted John B. Watson and his followers to concentrate on the observable aspect of behaviour in order to know the mind, and psychology came to be defined as "science of behaviour." William Mc Dougall in his book, 'An outline of psychology' stated that "Psychology is a science which is to give us better understanding and control of the behaviour of the organism as a whole". The psychologists also stressed the importance of environment in shaping an individual's behaviour. This behaviourist movement was greatly influenced by the work of Russian psychologist Ivan P. Pavlov and it was realised that the human behaviour could also be hanged by conditioning. At most simultaneously emerged the Gestalt movement which believed that behaviour should be studied as an organised pattern rather than separate incident of stimulus and response, as the German word Gestalt meant pattern form or shape i.e. overall whole. However, as the science of behaviour as defined by Watson did not include mental or psychological process of the individual, it was said to be incomplete.

In early 1900' Sigmund Freud through his psychoanalytical approach, added new dimension to psychology and stated that an individual's overt behaviour could not be understood without reference to his unconscious springs of motivation'. Psychoanalysis was based on the theory that behaviour is determined by powerful inner forces, most of which are buried in the unconscious mind.

Thus it appears that the meaning and concept of psychology has frequently changed its shape, based on its dependence on philosophical views taking into consideration every thing that contributes directly or indirectly to the understanding of behaviour. Modern approaches to psychology are more realistic with greater emphasis placed on concrete aspect of behaviour and thus, a humanistic psychology developed an alternative to behaviourism and psychoanalysis. Humanistic psychologists, Abraham H.Maslow and Carl R.Rogers believed that individuals are controlled by their own values and choices and not merely by the environment. The purpose of humanistic psychology is to help people function effectively and fulfill their own unique potential. Humanistic psychology was followed by Transpersonal psychology. What we think and how do we feel in our altered state of awareness is the subject of Transpersonal psychology — most recent Cognitive psychology. It studies higher cognitive abilities and capacities of human beings for their adaptation to the environment.

Modern psychology has incorporated within itself many of the principles discussed above. Modern psychology, in the words of Desiderato, Howieson and Jackson (1976) " is the instigation of human and animal behaviour, and of the mental and physiological processes associated with the behaviour". Crooks and Stein (1988) defined psychology as "the scientific study of behaviour and mental processes of humans and other animals". Even though techniques and strategies of investigating mind and behaviour have become sophisticated and refined during last century, no substantial change seems to have occurred in the meaning and definition of psychology and consequently it may be concluded that psychology is a science of behaviour or scientific study of the behavioural activities and experiences.

SPORTS PSYCHOLOGY

Sports psychology is concerned with the study of the behaviour of the players and sports personnel in relation to the activities, experiences, situations and environment prevailing in the world of sports. Today, this branch of psychology is playing quite an effective role in bringing desirable improvement in the processes and persons connected with the sports world like bringing improvement in the mental and physical health of the players, inculcating in them the true sports man's feelings and spirits through suitable behaviour modification and group dynamics techniques, providing sufficient motivation and raising their morale at the time of competition, devising techniques of training and coaching the players for their excellence in individual as well as group activities etc.

Sports psychology is an important ingredient of sports training programme and deals with the way in which various psychological states and traits influence sports performance. It is the application of psychology to the issues and problems in the field of sports as the problems of sports persons are quite unique, different, subtle and complex. Therefore, the main purpose of sports psychology is to understand the behaviour of an athlete, to modify it according to the demands of situations, and to optimize the benefits for elite performance and excellence. According to Singer," "sports psychology encompasses various branches of psychology as they are related to our ability to understand athlete performance, how to make it better, and how to improve exercise programmes."

According to Cratty, there are three main sub divisions of sports psychology :

(*i*) **Experimental sports psychology:** It involves research on the psychological variables that effect athlete and his performance, through field as well as experimental studies.

(*ii*) **Educational sports psychology:** The broad goal of this sub-division is to educate coaches, athletes and others concerned with sports regarding factors that are particularly important in sports setting especially those related to sports performance and interpersonal variables that influence the performance of athletes and teams.

(*iii*) **Clinical sports psychology:** It utilizes psychological interventions to improve the performance of athlete and to increase the psychological well- being of the athlete by preventing the problems and by assisting him to solve the problems. Recently another sub-division has emerged i.e. Developmental sports psychology which deals with psychological variables that impose themselves on children and youth of various ages as they engage in competitive sports.

SUB DIVISIONS OF SPORTS PSYCHOLOGY

Sports psychology, in the words of Singer, "encompasses research, counseling/clinical, educational and practical/programmatic activities associated with understanding, explaining and influencing selected behaviours of individuals and

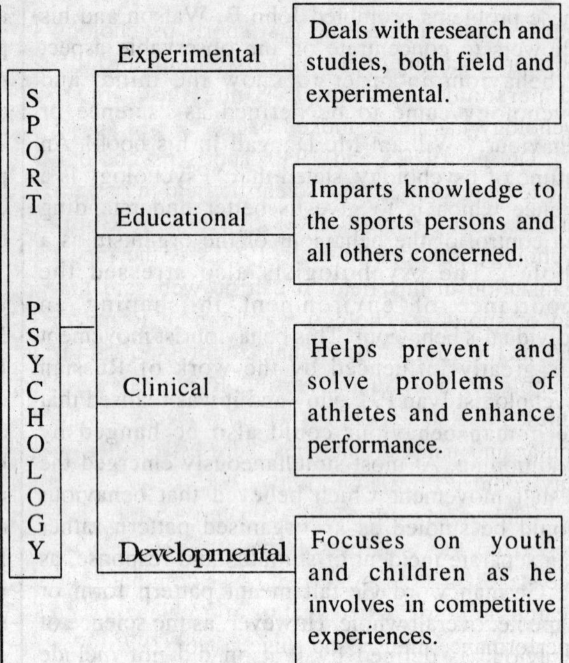

groups involved inching level sports, recreational sport exercise, and other vigorous activities." Sports psychology is striving hard to investigate athletic performance, to stabilize it, and to improve sports performance by seeking an appropriate balance between physiological and psychological dimensions of performance. Sports psychology is a healthy field with a bright future and with physical education, the field continues to grow.

Development of Sports Psychology

The historical development of sports psychology indicates that it began with the application of general principles of psychology to the process of skill acquisition and gradually to other specific areas. Most of the first experimental psychologists focused on movement and motor related factors, and thus a kind of motor psychology preceded the emergence of sports psychology and a broad foundation of movement psychology was established. This resulted in opening of motor learning laboratories where the focus was on physical skill, and skill acquisition. Coleman Griffith is known as father of sports psychology. He organsied and directed the first sports psychology laboratory focusing on learning psycho-motor kills, and personality variables. Since then sports psychology has never looked back.

During 1920's and 1930' sports psychology came to be recognized as a scientific field in Eastern Europe. The International Society of Sport Psychology, founded in early 1960's is the oldest organization in this field. It can be well said that field of sports psychology was born in Rome in 1965 at the first International Congress of Sport Psychology, held just after the Rome Olympic Games. In 1980's sports psychology became very popular and national societies were established in many countries providing impetus to its growth.

The sports psychologist Dani Lander has categorized the progress of sports psychology in three stages first (1950 – 1965) was dominated by research on how the personalities of athletes relate to performance, the second stage (1966-1976) was dominated by the borrowing of then current theories from main stream psychology and to test them in sports setting and the third stage (1976 – to the present) has focused more on developing information and theory directly derived from sports and on developing and refining psychological skill and strategies to enhance sports performance.

PSYCHOLOGICAL FACTORS AFFECTING PHYSICAL PERFORMANCE

Psychological factors affecting Physical performance in sports is no longer dependent on physiological well-being of the athlete. It is well established by now that there are numerous psychological factors which effect and improve the physical performance. The point where physiological response potential reaches the dead end, the psychological process seems to make the athlete click proving the boost or energy to achieve the goal which physiologically seemed impossible that is why psychological training and conditioning are now – a- days a part and parcel of total sports training programmes. Important psychological factors which affect the physical performance are:

1. **Attention and Concentration:** Attention is the concentration of consciousness upon one object rather that upon another.It is the process of getting an object or thought clearly before the mind. It helps in bringing mental alertness and preparedness, and as a result, one becomes alert and alive, and tries to exercise one's mental and physical power as effectively as possible. Giving high quality attention to the skill/ task during sports competition is important for effective performance. Various cognitive strategies and intensive over learning of skills may enhance the capacity to focus attention on the task at hand, resulting in better performance. There are a number of factors which distract and reduce attention and concentration, which in turn will result in poor performance.
2. **Mental Imagery:** Mental ability and imagery help the athletes mould their emotional state, and the way they approach the physical efforts. Such mental activity enables the athlete to improve the execution and precision of the given skill or task by thinking and imagining about it. Mental imagery of critical competitive situations is essential to boost the fighting spirit to help an athlete to organise himself in a better way. Mental rehearsal of competitive situations certainly help in improving athlete's emotional state as well as his physical performance. It also helps in the smooth flow of energy as and when required.
3. **Individual differences among the athletes:** Each athlete is unique to oneself. Apart from physiological differences such as height / weight etc, there are bound to be psychological differences as well. Some athletes may be outgoing and extrovert whereas others may be shy ,introvert and withdrawn, and they may also differ in their levels of perception. Some athletes are born strong psychologically while others have weak dispositions. Athletes with weak dispositions fail to accomplish their task. Thus, individual differences in sports

performance are an inevitable phenomenon and the teacher/coach has to modify his approach according to the nature of each individual athlete.

4. **Personality:** The human personality is a marvellously intricate structure, delicately woven of motives, emotions, habits and thoughts into a pattern that balances the pulls and pushes of the outside world. It is the totality of his being and includes his physical, mental emotional and temperamental make up. His experience perception, memory, imagination instincts, habits, thoughts and sense at times constitute his personality. Therefore, personality differences are inevitable, as to individuals cannot possess similar personality traits. Personality traits are basic to sports excellence. It is necessary to identify and cultivate those personality traits which are most conducive to the performance in sports. Hence personality is an important psychological factor which to a great extent determines the result of new athletic output.

5. **Intelligence:** Intelligence is the aggregate mental capacity or energy of an individual to act purposefully, to think rationally, and to deal effectively with ones environment. Intelligence involves awareness, is goal directed and has value. It is an ability to undertake the activities that are difficult, complex, and which lead to the creation of something new and different. Intelligence of an individual plays an important role in effecting physical performance. The more complex and the more interpretative the movement, the grater the amount of intelligence necessary to comprehend. Sports activities involve complex skilled actions. Since all skilled behaviour is intelligent behaviour, relationship between sports performance and intelligence cannot de denied.

6. **Attitude:** Attitudes are about thoughts and feelings. Attitude is often thought to predict behaviour. Attitudinal responses are also evaluative in nature. They are significant in deciding the kind and extent of the learning that takes place and reflect the likes and dislikes concerning a specified object of action. For example if a child says "I like running ", it reflects his attitude towards running and if a child says," I don't like running" it shows this child's attitude towards running. Attitudes involve knowledge and beliefs. Attitudes are developed through direct experience and inter personal communication. Positive beliefs and values concerning physical activity result in development of good and positive attitudes, enabling the athlete to strive hard for better performance.

7. **Motivation:** Motivation is a force, drive which prompts, compels, and energizes an individual to act or behave in a particular manner, at a particular time, for attaining the specific goal or purpose. In the absence of motivation either there will be no learning, or very little learning, and the learned activity or skill will be forgotten very soon. Motivation is the first requisite of efficient learning. Motivation is basic to overcome the hurdles which otherwise could have influenced the performance negatively. Without proper attention keen interest setting of right attitude, and the resulting optimum level of motivation, many top class athletes have failed to accomplish their task. It is thus necessary to find out ways and means of motivating athletes for better physical performance.

8. **Aggression:** Aggression is a part of human behaviour and is necessary for an individual to live and struggle for higher achievements. Struggle for supremacy, dominance, and excellence in sports obviously involve aggression. Aggression in one form or the other is inevitable and inescapable in sports activities. When hostility takes over aggression, the situation becomes alarming and it becomes an anti social behaviour. Aggression may help into performance of an athlete because it arouses the athlete to put in harder effort for the success of the team.

Athletes must be helped to reduce and control aggression in order to play calmly and perform the best. Appropriate level of aggression as permitted under the rules governing the game tend to improve the skill and enhance the effort and on the other hand, high or low level of aggression will hamper and retard the performance in sports.

9. **Arousal and Activation:** The term arousal reflects the varying degrees of readiness to perform physical intellectually or perceptually. Activation is a short term change of energy mobilization, and implies raising of energy above an individuals arousal, baseline, for a brief period. Arousal and activation are the bodily states and feeling that indicate the degree to which an athlete is physically and emotionally ready to perform. With appropriate levels of activation and arousal athletes tend to see better, think more clearly, and concentrate longer regarding the impending situations.Over excitement, over activation and over- arousal of an athlete may result in reduction of performance, or even in an inability to perform at all ,whereas optimum levels of arousal and activation at the relevant time may definitely help in better performance.It is, therefore, necessary to know what are the real activating forces that push and pull an athlete to move or act for achieving the goal.

10. **Anxiety:** Anxiety means a disturbed state of mind; emotional reactivity; arousal: nervousness; and unrealistic and unpleasant state of mind. Anxiety is an essential ingredient of any competitive situation and without certain level of anxiety is not conducive to sports performance. Adequate level of anxiety produces best results. Unless sports persons learn to cope up with stressful competitive situations by managing anxiety, they would fail to achieve their goal.

11. **Group Dynamics:** A sports team comprises of various individual athletes, each having different orientations and perceptions, and at times, these differences may interfere with performance of the team. Better performance will result if each member of the team merges his personal feelings and abilities into a total team effort. Success of a team depends on adjustment within i.e. how closely the team seems to be working and feeling together. Psychological togetherness among the members of the team does reflect on the outcome of the performance. Group dynamics and performance are thus mutually influential, and are further influenced by the order of the stability of the personnel concerned with the team. It has been found that better group cohesion generally tends to produce better performance.

MOTOR SKILL LEARNING

Motor skill learning is an indispensable and central task in any Physical Education Prgoramme. The acquisition and improvement of motor skills are fundamental and important factors in practising sport of any kind. Psychologists have identified several types of learnings and perhaps one of the simplest kinds of learning is the motor skill learning. Modern life demands high level of skill in motor activity. Speaking, reading, writing, dancing, swimming or playing – all entail a high measure of motor activity. Motor skill is an expression of level of development. As people learn to read and write, to run and jump, to think and talk, they are relying on the coordinated development of the body. The development of motor skill depends not only on neuron muscular maturity but also on environmental opportunities, particularly the availability of equipment, the opportunity to observe and imitate others, and the opportunity to experiment. If a child lacks opportunities of explorations and practice ,or if the parents inhabit activities through over protection, the development of motor ability will be poor.

Effective motor skill learning is based on certain pre-requisite factors including muscular strength, dynamic energy, flexibility, concentration, visual activity and understanding of the mechanics of the activity. Most of the motor activities are closely related to perceptual motor problems involving coordination balance, agility, sense of direction etc. It is through these early motor learning's that a better base for other learnings is established. Motor learning is not completed until the habits are firmly fixed and capable of fluent and accurate performance.

Motor skill learning is the heart of the physical education experience as it results in achievement of general motor ability as well as selective skills. Motor activities in physical education and sports are oriented towards movement education and provide many experiences that contribute to the development of a child's motor skills, is a prerequisite to achieving goals in the filed of sports. Where motor ability stops and other activities like typewriting, creative or a golf swing, is not determinable, yet the motor components of each act are essential for full expression of the activity.

The development of motor skill allows a person to express and enjoy his capabilities in much the same way as verbal skill and quickly enhance his personality. Good things tend to get together, so that those who enjoy superior intellectual, educational, social, emotional and physical development, commonly have atleast adequate motor ability. Usually, this superiority develops into satisfactory motor skills. In motor learning, as in all other learning, maturation and readiness produce awareness. Motor development is based, in part, on many motor learnings, each of which involves the performing person in some degree; full motor development is essential for unhampered self expression.

The traditional, and skill prevailing method of learning a motor–skill is to imitate a good model, compared one's own trials with that of the demonstrator, note the errors, and try to eliminate them by repeated trials. One of the important factors that influence the individual's attempt to acquire a motor skill is his ability to perceive speed, distance, and shape of object. If he encounters difficulty in such activities, the learning of motor skills will also be more difficult. As most motor skill tasks initially involve perception of an object, especially visual perception (as in hitting a ball or striking an object), the interest in perception accompany the development of the interest in skill acquisition. In fact, in many places this field is referred as perceptual motor skills learning also. In motor skill, learning the major focus is on how the nervous system controls the muscular system to produce skilled movement, as all movement must originate on the impulse from the nervous system.

Mental practice does enhance the learning of motor skill. It enables an individual to visualize symbolic rehearsal of the skill, without there being any muscular movement. Motor skill learning involves the management of information coming through the senses. The information coming through the senses is first recognized, discriminated, and then selectively carried to various levels of the brain. This information is processed as to whether it is for current or present use or for future use. Such information is compared, integrated, and stored within the brain on the basis of past experiences. This stored information acts as a constant source of feed back which provides continual means for adjusting and reacting in terms of overt motor behaviour.

The feature of motor skill that makes its learning different from the learning of knowledge is the necessity to correct immediate motor response with cues, and coordinate the responses in time and space. Since motor skills are adjustments of our bodies to the features of social and physical situations, there are two sets of cues by which the adjustments are made. One set comes from the environment; the distance and direction of the spot where we wish to place the ball in tennis, the height of the net, and the kind of the ball we have been served. The other is the sensations we get from our bodies. To some extent we see how we look in playing, but more particularly how it feels to perform the act; the sweeping movements of the left and the right arms in crawl stroke and the scissors movements of the legs in the swimming. These muscular sensations aid the beginner to differentiate the right movement from the wrong ones. When performer becomes more expert, the muscular sensations pass, more or less, into his marginal consciousness and the cues from the environment become the dominating ones, for example in tennis, the adjustment of a chosen play to the location and preparation of the performer's opponent. Motor skill is this immediate motor response to the perceptual cue, or a series of cues, and the response involves organisation of a number of movements, in direction, in order of sequence, and in timings, as well as in many other ways.

Motor learning is learning involving neuro-muscular system of the body. As it can be defined as muscular actions directed towards the achievement of a goal, motor skill learning, therefore, is a relatively permanent change in the performance of a motor skill resulting from experience and practice. The motor skill can be as basic as a young child learning to climb and as complex as a highly trained basketball player performing intricate manoeuvers in a constantly changing game.

Principles of Motor Skill Learning

1. **Need to learn :** Like in case of any other learning, the learning of motor skill will be more effective if the individual feels that there is need to learn is recognised, the learning will be more meaningful and wholesome as the intent to learn would be greater. We cannot force learning on an unwilling learner..
2. **Information regarding objectives :** It has been seen that pace of learning is faster if objectives of the skill are clear to the students. The students should have a clear picture of what constitutes a successful performance. It is, however, necessary that the objective is within the reach of the students, because if they realize that they are unable to attain the objective or the goal, the resultant tension and frustration will tend to decrease the motivation for learning the skill.
3. **Knowledge of Nervous System :** The learner should have elementary knowledge and understanding about the nervous system and its functioning. The very initiation and continuation of any motor skill is controlled by the complicated mechanism of the nervous system, i.e. it is the key to the development of motor skill. Therefore, providing some basic knowledge about the nervous system and its functioning will enhance the capabilities of the learner to learn a motor skill.
4. **Maturity :** We know that maturation is the growth that takes place without any special training, practice or stimulus, and psychological development of an individual is also associated with it. To facilitate the process of motor skill learning it is necessary to take into account the maturation level of the individual, and the type of activity appropriate for him should be determined accordingly. It will not be a wise step to teach tennis to primary grade students, as they would not be ready to understand the skill involved therein.
5. **Individual Differences :** No two individuals are identical in all respects and even the twins too, generally, have some individual differences. Due to such individual differences, there is bound to be differences in their adaptation to learning. Such individual differences must be accepted and recognized if motor learning of any skill is to take place.
6. **Mechanical Knowledge of skills :** Learning any motor skill which involves mechanical principles like laws of motion, gravity, levers etc. is facilitated by providing knowledge to the students regarding these principles. The rationale behind this assertion is that such knowledge will enable the students to learn the desired motor skills with minimum effort and maximum efficiencly.
7. **Mental Rehearsal :** Though it is an accepted fact that the practice develops and maintains the skill, yet the mental rehearsal is also of great value in its learning process. No motor skill act occurs without the assistance of some thought. Mental rehearsal refers to the learner's act of thinking through the motor act, both before and after the performance of the skill. Thinking about past performances provide

thought models by which one can modify the present performance.

8. **Repetition :** Although mental rehearsal guides performance, yet it is not a substitute for actual practice. Skill improves with careful practice, particularly if it is varied. Over learning through repetitive practice also has great value in the acquisition of motor skills. A partially learned skill does not remain in possession of the learner as long as the same is not overlearned. It should be practised until it establishes a pattern in the nervous system. Learning is not completed until the habits are firmly fixed, and capable of fluent and accurate performance. A skill which is properly mastered and continually practised will not be lost to the learner for quite a long time. An appropriate examples of swimming may be referred here. Once we have learnt and mastered the skill of swimming, it remains with us throughout our life.

9. **Learning as a whole :** When possible, it is better to learn the skill as the entity. When a person learns different parts of a skill, and then attempts to integrate the same into a smooth performance, he usually has to relearn the total as a unit, and the prior part learning, very often, interferes in the process. At the same time, there are some skills which are too complex to yield benefits from attempting to learn the same as a total unit. In such circumstances, the complex skills may be broken down into basic parts to facilitate the learning process. It is, however, a well recognized fact that for those activities in which it is possible, learning the total skill is generally, more superior and efficient. For example, when teaching a child how to ride a bicycle, we do not break up the task first into balancing, then steering and finally cycling. Rather, the child has to experience the entire task as a whole.

10. **Imitation of a Model** : The most usual and efficient method of learning a motor skill is to imitate a good model, then to compare one's own trials with that of the model, noting down the errors, and trying to eliminate the same by repeated trials. Verbal comments by the teacher on performance of the skill, lift out the errors more clearly than one's own comparison to oneself and others. In fact, in such comparisons one is often unable to see the difference until it is pointed out.

11. **Speed, Accuracy, Rhythm, Timings :** In motor learning, speed, accuracy, rhythm, timings etc. deserve special attention. For a physical education teacher, it is necessary to find out as to which skill requires speed at the initial stage, and as to which one requires, the accuracy. In case of teaching golf or tennis skills, it is the momentum which is required for successful performance, and emphasis on accuracy will tend to hamper the learning process. Speed and accuracy are frequently not compatible in learning motor skills; the slow performances are usually more accurate. Rhythm helps timing, as do accuracy and speed, but the essence of motor skill lies in the timing itself. A baseball swing in good form has a well defined rhythm, but without timing, the bat does not meet the ball with maximum power. Usually, attention to accuracy, speed and rhythm, will enable the learner to develop the timing necessary for the skill.

12. **Value of Transfer Effect :** The teaching of skill should be so planned that learning of one part or unit of skill has positive transfer effect on the other to be learned. This positive transfer most likely occurs when two tasks have similar part-whole relationship. For example playing racquet games like tennis, badminton etc. have similar part whole involved and in such cases the positive transfer effect is quite obvious.

13. **Context and Setting :** Learning a skill in the setting where it will be used, usually result in greater learning. The same rule applies to practice of motor skill as well. Transferring skills learned in practice sessions to game like situations also has beneficial effects on the perfection of motor skills. It is for this reason

that in a team game, the substitutes imitate the action, of their opponents during practice so that the team gets familiar with the style of the game of their opponents, which may result in improvement of their own skills also.

14. **Feed back :** Feed back is very important for proper and effective learning of any motor skill, more so in case of learners. The beginners are bound to commit mistakes while performing the motor skills. If mistakes and errors are not corrected by proper and effective feedback, such errors will harden into a habit and will be difficult to remove at a later stage. Even for accomplished athletes, feedback enables them to give suitable finer touches to their skills.
15. **Self Appraisal :** Self appraisal of one's abilities and competence is of immense value in the acquisition and improvement of any motor skill. The way in which an athlete appraises his or her motor competence has a strong impact not only on the level of sport participation but also on the development of motors skills.
16. **Progression :** Learning from simple to complex is universally accepted principle of learning and more so in learning any motor skill. Complex skills are, generally, nothing more than a combination of simple ones. Gradually moving from simple to complex, according to the capacity of the learner, makes the learning of motor skill more easier, simplified, and attractive at the same time.
17. **Duration of Practice period :** The duration of practice of any skill should be carefully worked out. It has been observed that practice periods are more profitable when they are short and spread over a period of time. Massed practice or long and continuous periods of practice may be effective only when the learner finds the skill itself highly motivating. Disrupted practice or shorter periods of practice will yield better results in case of learning very tiring, physically and psychologically taxing skills. Continuous and long durations in case of such activity may make it tedious and boring. Apart from it, fatigue will also adversely affect the rate of learning.

SOCIOLOGICAL BASIS OF PHYSICAL EDUCATION-SOCIALIZATION

1. Socialization is a fundamental social process that affects us all because it is a means by which we acquire values, beliefs, behaviour.
2. Socialization has been traditionally important cultural content from one generation to the next.
3. This process involves interaction with others that results in the teaching and learning of skills, dispositions and knowledge that enable us in the society.
4. Socialization is extremely important during childhood. Because, it is the critical period.
5. Because all experiences are new and we learn that our behaviour is influenced by other people and their expectations.
6. For example, as very young children we learned that parents had rules that they expected us to follow, if we did not behave according to their expectations, quite often we were punished. By the same token most of us learned at an early age how to please our parents because they rewarded us when they wanted us to continue behaving in a certain way.
7. Socialization is an interactive process between teacher and learner.
8. An interesting point is what is taught what is learned are not necessarily conscious processes.

Physical Education in Ancient Greece, Rome and Contemporary Germany, Sweden, Denmark and Russia

Physical education as well as sport experiences a "golden age" in ancient Greece. The Greeks strove for physical perfection. It has its influence on the political and educational systems and on painting. No country in history has held physical education or sport in such high respect as did Ancient Greece. Literature such as Homer's Illiad and Odyssey also is a source of this information.

Gymnastics and music were considered the two most important subjects, music for the spirit, and gymnastics for the body. "Exercise for the body and music for the soul" was concern pronouncement.

Gymnasium became the physical, social and intellectual centres of Greece. Although the first use was for physical activity, men such as Plato, Aristotle and Agisthenes were responsible for making gymnasiums such as the Academy, cyceure and kynosarges outstanding intellectual centres as well. Youths usually entered the gymnasium at about 14-16 years of age.

The national festivals were events that were most important in the lives of the Greeks and were also important in laying the foundation for the modern Olympic games. The first and most famous was the Olympia festival in honour of Zeus, the supreme god.

During the time, the games were held a truce was declared by all the city, states in Greece. The contestant had to be a free man; he could not have a criminal record, he had to compete in accordance with the rules. To be crowned a victor in an Olympic event was to receive the highest honour that could be bestowed. The Olympic games were first held in 776 B. C. and continued every fourth year, thereafter abolished by the Romans in AD 394.

Physical Education in Rome

While the Hellenes were settling in the Greecian peninsula about 200 BC, another Indo-European people was settling in the central migrating and southern parts of this country. One of these wandering tribes known then as latins, settled near the Tiber river, a settlement that later became known as Rome.

In respect to physical education and sport the average Roman believed that exercise was for health and military purposes. The Romans lack the drive for clean competition. They did not believe in developing the "body beautiful". The Romans wanted something exciting, bloody, ghastly and sensational. The thermae and the campus inartenns in Rome took the place of the gymnasium in Greece.

Physical Education in Germany

Physical education in Germany during the modern European period is associated with names such as Baredeow, Gutsmutus and Spiess.

Adoleph Spiess (1810-1858) was the founder of school gymnastics in Germany, and more than any other individual in German history he helped to make physical education a part of school life. Physical education should receive the same consideration as the important academic subjects such as mathematics and language. The physical education programme should be progressive, starting with simple exercises and progressing to the more difficult ones. Exercises combined with music offer all opportunity for freer individual expression.

Physical Education in Sweden

The name of Per Henrik Ling (1776-1839) is symbolic of the rise of physical education to a place of importance in Sweden.

Formerly physical education had been conducted mainly on the premise that people believed it was good for the human body because it increased the size of musculature contributed to strength, stamina, endurance an agility and left one exhilarated.

Physical education was necessary for weak persons as well as strong persons that exercises must be prescribed on the basis of individual differences, that the mind and body must function harmoniously together and that teachers of physical education must have a foundational knowledge of the effects of exercise on the human body.

Physical Education in Denmark

Denmark has been one of the leading European countries in the promotion of physical education. Franz Nachtegall (1777-1847) was largely responsible for the early interest in this field. He had a direct influence in introducing physical education into public schools of Denmark and in preparing teachers of this subject.

Physical Education in Russia

1. Physical education in the U. S. S. R. is referred to as physical culture.
2. The significant goal of physical culture as expressed by V. A. Blyakh is "health, strength, dexterity, boldness, presence of mind, quickness of action and discipline all these properties should be developed not only in the Red Angry men but also among the broad masses of the population".
3. Russia spends large sums of money for sports facilities.
4. All sports activities in the U.S.S.R. are exhibited. Speeches are made by leading physical educators.
5. It was in 1952, for the first time Russian athletes participated in the world Olympics.

OLYMPIC MOVEMENT

When we talk about Olympic games or Asian games, we mean participation in inter- continental and international sports competitions. Participation in Sports helps people to know one another. It provides opportunities to the participants to see one another. It unites countries and continents. The Olympic movement, like sport in general, by its very nature opposes the division of the world and promotes rapprochement and friendship among peoples of all continents. Neither distances nor differences in belief must or can prevent mankind from barring the way to the forces of insanity and war. Peace is dear and necessary to all of us. Saving it from the flames of war is every body's moral and sacred duty. Sport participation is very effective vehicle to reach and realize the said goals for the betterment of human beings of the nations. In the light of the aforementioned facts, the importance or significance of sport participation in international and intercontinental competition may be realized through the following salient features of sport :

1. Participation in sport develops unity of mind and body, through which physical beauty and optimum health are achieved.
2. Sports participation helps in promoting social democracy.
3. It promotes social peace and justice.
4. It helps in breaking down barriers not only between social classes but also between nations.

There are some indirect benefits of organizing/ conducting inter-continental/international sport competition, as given below.

1. Enhancement of National Prestige.
2. Stimulation of national interest in sports in the youth of the country.
3. Creation of outstanding physical facilities/ infrastructures.
4. Creating sources of income, jobs, self employment.

Goals of the Olympic Movement

The goals of Olympic movement mentioned in Olympic Charter, 1982, are given below:

1. To promote the development of those physical and moral qualities which are the basis of sport.
2. To educate young people through sports, in a spirit of better understanding between each other and of friendship, there by helping to build a better and more peaceful world.
3. To spread the Olympic principles throughout the world, thereby creating international goodwill.
4. To bring together the athletes of the world in the great four yearly sports festival, the Olympic Games.

The Olympic Spirit

Regarding the Olympic Spirit, this is what the International Olympic Committee has to say:

"To encourage the development of Olympic Spirit among the youth of the world and promote a programme of education for the public and the press on philosophy of amateurism, the National Olympic Committees will keep in mind not to concentrate too much on performance and new records, but more the social education, aesthetic, ethical and spiritual value of amateur sports".

Ancient Olympic Games

Historical Background

The sports was by no means a Greek invention. Despite the severe conditions (rigours) of life at the dawn of history, men found time to enjoy a variety of sports. These were valued as a means of developing hunting skill, of preparing for war, and of placating (pleasing) the angry gods. However, the Greeks' interest in sports apparently dates back to the Bronze Age. Tumbling, bull vaulting, boxing, wrestling, archery, and distance running were all popular spectacles. (Public displays or entertainment) in the ancient Minoan Civilization of Crete (3000 B.C. – 1200 B.C). Building on this concept many of the Greek City States began to organize major athletic festivals, the most famous being that held at Olympia, in honour of the God Zeus.

The simple purity of classical athleticism is well set – out in the eleventh Olympic Ode. "Strength and Beauty are gifts of Zeus ... *natural gifts imply the duty of developing them with God's help by Cost and Toil"*. Such was the importance of the sacred festival that a "pax Olympica" guaranteed all participants safe conduct, irrespective of immediate wars and ideological conflicts. Tradition has it that the first contest (Olympic games) was held in 776 B.C., but some historian trace the games back much further into the mists of legends, linking the festival to either the phaeacian games organized for Odysseus, or an elaborate funeral celebration arranged for the mythical hero Peoples.

Athletes performed naked. This nudity was more likely a concession to the heat and humidity of the Greek mountain valleys. The Olympic itself was strictly a male preserve, but the festival of Bera provided a separate contest for Greek women. The winner of the first Olympics 776 B.C. was Coroebus. Milo, an army Commander-in-Chief and a member of the learned Society of Pythagorean was reputed to have won at least six Olympiads and twenty six other lesser crowns. These games were held regularly once in four years. A sequence of some 293 Olympids was terminated in 394 A.D. by Theodosius the Great. Having embraced Christianity, the Roman Emperors objected strongly to the pagan overtones of the Greek festivals.

Significance of the Ancient Games

The games were held in honour of God Zenus since the games were the greatest religious festival in the life of the Greeks. Messengers (heralds) were sent sufficiently in advance to every part of the Hellenic World to announce the forthcoming Olympic Festival. This month during which the games were held, was considered to be a sacred month. Any wars or disputes that might be taking place among the city states would be stopped at once and a truce would be declared. All competitors or visitors travelling to or from Olympic moved freely without any fear, since any harm done to any one of them was considered to be an act of sacrilege given to the religious festival. The very fact that hostile city states met together at Olympia in healthy and peaceful rivalry even in times of war, was itself a true indication of the remarkable influence, the Olympic festival had on peace and good will among the ancient Greeks.

Rules of Eligibility for Competition

1. The participants should be free born Greeks.
2. The amateurs were allowed to participate.
3. The competition must have at least 10 months of training prior to their participation in the Olympics, the last and the final month being spent at Olympic under the control of the official judges of the games (The Hellanodikai).

Conduct of the Games

1. **Opening Caremony :** The herald announced/ declared/proclaimed the opening of the games. The chief judge or some distinguished person addressed the parpetually. Afterwards the events were conducted. The sacred fire was kept burning perceptually (without stopping/ non stop) at the Altar of Zeus.
2. **Events :** Originally foot race was the only item in Ancient Olympics and it was conducted in a single day. Later on other

events such as foot races, chariot race, horse race, pentathlon (Running, Long jump, discus Throw, Javelin Throw, and wresting) boxing, wrestling, pancratium etc. were added. Because of the addition of more events from time to time the duration of the games was extended to five days.

3. **Assembly :** Before the commencement of the games the competitors, their trainees (coaches), their fathers, their brothers and the judges assembled in the council house in front of the statue of Zeus Horkios (God of Oaths).
4. **Sacrifice :** A pig was sacrificed to Zeus.
5. **Oath :** The competitors took an oath that they would not resort to any unfair means to secure victory. Also they took oath they had ten months of training as per Olympic rules and regulations.It was followed by the Olympic judges who swore that they would be honest and fair in their decisions.
6. **March Past :** The March Past took place in which the Trumpeter, Officials and competitors participated. At the time of march past, as the competitors passed by the herald (announcer / commentator) announced to the spectators the name of each competitor, his father's name and his city and asked whether any one had any charge to make against him. The silence on the part of the spectators was considered as "No Objection" for the concerned competitor.

- The first day was devoted to Religious sacrifice and Oath taking ceremonies. No event of the competition was held.
- On the second day, there was the march past, the introduction of the competitors to the spectators, and the opening of the games. This was followed by the competitive events such chariot-race horse-race and pentathlon.
- The third day morning time was devoted to the official sacrifice of 100 oxen at the altar of Zeus. In the afternoon foot-race, wrestling and boxing were conducted for the boys.
- The fourth day was reserved mainly for the competition in Chief athletic events for men, such as three foot-race, the dual combats (wrestling, boxing and pancratium). The race in armour was conducted at the end of the day's programme.
- The fifth and last day was devoted for celebration through feasting and rejoicing

Note: Originally women were not allowed to compete in the Olympics and married women were not allowed to witness the competition. Further, it is understood that women had their own festival called the Heraca in honour of Hera, wife of God Zenus. In this festival women had athletic competitions. Later on women were allowed to compete in the Olympics in the Chariot – race.

Awards

The winner of the Olympic was highly honoured. It is believed that till the 7th Olympiad, the Olympic winner was given tripods and other valuable objects as prizes. Later on a wreath made out of leaves plucked from sacred Olive tree in the temple Zeus was the only reward given to him by the judges at Olympic stadium. The poets immortalized his name in poems and sculptors carved figure in stones. The concerned Olympiad was named after the name of the winner of the 200 yards race known as stade race. Then the winners were escorted home in triumph by their fellowmen and loaded with honour, with variety of gifts and with privileges. Also it is known that they were received in their cities not through the ordinary gates but through a breach made in the walls of the city. They were even considered demi gods. To be crowned a victor in the Olympics was the highest honour coveted by every Greek.

Decline and Termination of the Olympic Games

The Olympic games continued for several centuries. When Greece came under Roman domination, it was found that the games lost their original significance/ glory; professionalism, corruption and foul play set in. The then Roman Emperor Theodosius I passed a decree and terminated the games in the year 394 A.D. In the history, we trace the glorious past of the Ancient Olympics which lasted for nearly 12 centuries in which 293 Olympic games were conducted.

Modern Olympic Games

The Renaissance and Beyond

Before the revival of Modern Olympic Games the Educationists and other dignitaries of the developed countries began realizing the value of sport activities in one's life and extending its contribution towards the international community. During this period which is considered a link between the dim past and uncertain future of sport competition, a great theologian, Martin Luther observed that a strong body could help the mind in its quest for piety (search for being pious). He also spoke about the recreative and moral values of sport. Educational theorists such as Da Filtre in Italy, Comenius in Czechoslovakia and Mulcaster in England stated the contribution that sport could make to the learning process, both by improving the physical health of the pupils, and also by promoting the development of an integrated personality.

The eighteenth century brought in its turn the age of reason. A great educationist Rosseau (1712-78) preaching a naturalism in education with strong emphasis on health and the unity of mind and body said that games and sports were seen to have real therapeutic value taking from man *"all the dangerous inclinations that spring from idleness"*. So to the nineteenth century, Friedrich restore John sought to national morale through a system of outdoor gymnasia. Unfortunately it was not fully endorsed by the German Govt. However, human ingenuity devised exercises that could be performed in a limited space. Consequently, a strong interest in gymnastics was thus carried to the United States and Canada. The British Govt. also did not like the combination of regimented gymnastics and heavy political discussions. In the same century North Europe also developed strong interest in gymnastics. The pioneers were Salzman (1744-1811) and Ling (1776-1839). Ling became the principal of the world renowned Royal Central Gymnastics Institute in Stockholm in Sweden. The Swedish gymnastics system was less politically oriented than German. The main four objectives of this school were pedagogy, therapy, military preparation and aesthetic development, with an emphasis on free hand exercise rather than on apparatus work.

In Britain, sport continued in socially stratified pattern. The upper class enjoyed hunting, riding, and dancing whereas the people of other classes had to satisfy themselves with the games suitable for village grounds and industrial streets. However, another new feature for the upper middle class was the opening of public Rugby School. In this school sport was pursued with strong idealism; all pupils were taught of fair play and gallant defeat. Barriers of class were maintained in rigid distinctions between amateur and professional players.

The Revival of Modern Olympic Games

Historians may dispute the novelty of the idea. Over the centuries, some Greek villages had continued to hold what were described as Olympic contests. It is on historical record that two Olympic Games were organized by the Greeks and Evangelos Zappas (a Greek living in Romania), in 1859 and 1870 but they were unsuccessful in their mission. But before his death, Zappas donated lot of money to re-establish the Olympic Games in Greece. Equally the '*Parisian Directorie*' had attempted to establish an Olympic celebration on *champs de Mars* at the end of the 18th century.

However, the scope of a wealthy Baron Piere de Coubertin's (1863-1937) plans far outshadowed those of his predecessors. He was stimulated by German success in excavating (making uncover) the Olympic site, conceived the yet more ambitious project of reviving the games. In one of his writings, he writes with nationalistic fervour *"Germany had brought to light what remained of Olympia. Why should not France succeed in restoring its glory?"*

The germ of Baro de Coubertin's idea was conceived when he was twenty three, but at first he moved cautiously, fearing that such an ambitious project would arouse both hostility and scorn. After seven years of patient preparation, a congress was called at Paris in the spring of 1893, under the auspices of the Council of French Athletic Sports Club. The organisers being the Baron and his friends Mr. C Herbert, Secretary of the British Amateur Athletic Association and professor W.M Slone of Princeton University. The prime objective of the trio- was top secret, the confessional reasons for the meeting being (1) the defence of amateur sport against the evil of professionalism and (2) the clarification of the rules governing amateur status.

In June 1894, another International Athletic Congress was held in Paris, with wider representations. Again much time was given to technicalities such as, the definition of an amateur, reasons for suspension, disqualification and re-qualification, the possibility of being a professional in one sport and an amateur in another, and the treatment of the athlete who received a work of art as a prize and promptly sold it to the highest bidder. Further time could not be devoted for a more detailed consideration of the Olympic project.

In the process of pressing for the re-establishment of the games, Baron de Coubertin was strongly influenced by the ideas of Victorian England, the 'Muscular Christianity' of Kingsley, and the use of athletics in moral training, as preached by Dr. Arnold of Rugby School. His speeches continually stressed the search for physical beauty and health through a happy balance of mind and body, the healthy drunkenness flow of the blood nowhere so intense and exquisite as in bodily exercise, and the value of sport in promoting social democracy and international understanding.

To begin with, de Baron included all forms of competitive exercise widely used in the modern world. However, in order to keep the games to a manageable size he proposed excluding certain regional sports such as cricket and baseball. Further, to manage the games economically, he set the ideal size of the games. In any case the number of individual participant, team sportsmen and spectators should not exceed 1200, 200-500 and ten thousands respectively.

De Baron accepted the Greek tradition that the games were in a sense, a religious rite/ ceremony, true religion being found not in the sacrifices made by the athlete at the altar of Zeus, but rather in spiritual preparedness, an inner feeling of devotion to an ideal greater than the athlete himself, as expressed in the Olympic Oath. "Dishonour would not lie in defeat, but in failure to take part."

The games offered also a potential for the promotion of social peace and justice. Further, Baron firmly opined that the Games could break down barriers not only between classes, but also between nations; 'Let us export rowers, runners, and fencers, there is the free- trade of the future.' Equally, differences between rival athletic factions could be resolved – the German could learn to appreciate the finer points of Swedish Gymnastics, and the Englishman could come to enjoy American Football.

The artist in thc Baron insisted that the games should become a true festival, with its solemn ceremonies of oath, hoisting flags, and worthy opening and closing ceremonies. Even the design of grounds should make its contribution to the beauty of the great public display.

THE REVIVED MODERN OLYMPIC GAMES – 1896

As the ancient site at Olympia was not suitable to conduct the games therefore, the first of the revived games was held, naturally enough, in Athens in 1896. The sponsors of the Modern Olypics were hard pressed for money. The Greek-Government gave about 2½ lacs drachmac in addition to the money donated by Zappas. Even this amount was not enough. Fortunately one George Aver off, a merchant of Alexandria gave a princely gift of a million drachmae for renovating the Pan Athletic stadium and conducting the games. Only a few countries took part in this first modern Olympic games. As years passed by, several countries began to participate in the games. At present almost all the nations of the world compete in these games.

Modern Olympics is also held once in four year. But during the two world wars the Olympic games (i.e. VIth, XIIth and XIIIth Olympiads respectively in the year 1916, 1940 and 1944) were not held. It is noteworthy to mention here that in the days of Ancient Olympics such a sanctity was attached to the games that wars were stopped for the conduct of the Olympics. Contrary to the aforementioned evidence, in the days of Modern Olympics, games had to be stopped for the conduct of two world wars.

Governing Body

International Olympic Committee is the supreme controlling body for the modern Olympic games which was formed during the International Athletic Congress held in Paris on June 25th, 1894. The first committee was nominated by Baron de Coubertin on his personal selection of fifteen members in whom he had confidence that they would help in fostering the Olympic Ideals. The headquarters of I.O.C. are located at Campagne Mon Repos, Lausanne (Switzerland).

The I.O.C is a permanent and self elected body which has at least one member from a country where there is a National Olympic Committee. However, the countries that have had once conducted Olympic Games or have made a special contribution to Olympic Movement have the privilege to be represented by two members. From India, Sir Darabji Jamshedji Tata in 1920, Mr. G.D Sondhi in 1932 and Raja Bhalindra Singh in 1947, had the honour of being members of I.O.C.

Functions of the I.O.C

1. The I.O.C. selects the sites and fixes the dates for the Olympic Games. The honour of allotment of site always goes to the city to host the games not to the country.
2. It draws the rules and regulations, for the competition, and programme of the Olympics. However, the technical aspect of a sport is left to International Federation concerned.

Organization and Conduct of the Games

Olympic cycle and duration. The Olympic games should be held in the first year of the Olympiad. If for any reason games cannot be conducted as aforesaid; then the next Olympic games will be conducted in the first years of the next olympiad. As it has happened during the two world wars in 1916, 1940 and 1944. The duration of the games shall not exceed a period of 16 days.

Rules of Eligibility for Competition

The first Olympic Games at Athens in 1896 were merely experimental. The main object was to give the movement a start. There were no hard and fast rules. There was no Olympic Village. Games at Paris in 1900 and those at St. Louis in 1904 were no different. It was only in Olypic held in 1908 in London that the rules were given a definite direction.

1. One who is by birth (native) belonging to a participating country.
2. One who has competed already in the Olympic games for nation, cannot compete in future Olympic games for another nation except in the case of captured country or the creation of a new state confirmed by the Treaty (An agreement made and signed between nations).
3. Every competitor must be an Amateur (A player who plays a game for the love of it not for money).
4. There is no age limit for competitor.
5. There is bar on either sex to compete in the Olympics. However, in some of the sport events the women are not allowed, due to some other technical reasons.

Venue for the Olympic Games

The venue will be fixed by a majority of votes among the members of International Olympic Committee taking into consideration the claims made by the cities to stage the games. The decision of the IOC about the venue is conveyed to the concerned National Olympic Committee through the Mayor of the City to which games are allotted. Then, the National Olympic Committee of the concerned country will take the responsibility for organizing and conducting the games. A high power organizing committee is constituted which will look after all kinds of activity related with the Olympic Games being organized.

Events

The events are fixed by the Organizing Committee in consultation with International Olympic Committee. The approval of the event must be obtained at lest two years before the commencement of the games. Once approved the programme cannot be changed. The sports recognized for the Olympics are athletics, gymnastics, boxing, fencing, shooting, wrestling, canoeing, cycling, rowing, swimming, diving, horse riding events, weightlifting, modern pentathlon, yatching and Fine Arts. Due to the wide popularity other games such as foot ball, hockey, basket ball, handball, volleyball and water polo, have found a permanent place in the Olympic Games programme.

Fine Art Competitions

Many people are under the erroneous impression that the Modern Olympic games are exclusively devoted to games and sports. This is because media give importance only to games and athletic events. On the suggestion of Baron de Coubertin, the first art competition was introduced in the Vth Olympic games at Stockholm in 1912. Since 1949 painting and drawings have been excluded from the award of positions, as it was felt that such awards might encourage professionalism. The fine art items are included in the Olympic programme because the Greeks had them. Moreover sports itself is a Fine Art.

Entries

All entries must be forwarded to the Organising Committee for the Olympic games through the National Olympic Committee.

- The President of the Organising Committee will request the President of the Games to declare it open. The President will declare the games open with the conventional words : *"I declare open the Olympic games of (name of the host city) celebrating the .... Olympiad of the Modern era".*
- Immediately there will be a fanfare of Trumpets and to the tune of the Olympic Hymn the Olympic Flag is hoisted.
- Pigeons will be released as symbolic gesture of peace, followed by a salute of three gun-fires.
- The runner with the Olympic Flame will enter the stadium, run round the track once and then Olympic flame will be lit in bowl constructed for this purpose. The flame will be burning throughout the period of the Olympic games held.
- As soon as Olympic Flame is lit, all the flag-bearers will move forward and stand in semi-circle around the Rostrum facing the Tribune of Honour.
- The Olympic Oath will be taken by the athlete of the host country team, usually the captain. He along with the flag bearers of his country will go up to the Rostrum; he will hold a corner of the flag and then on behalf of all the competitors will take the following Oath : *"We swear that we shall take part in these Olympic Games, respecting and abiding by the rules which govern them, in the true spirit of sportsmanship, for the glory of sport and the honour of our country".*

Revised oath Effective from Sydney Olympics

"In the name of all competitors I promise that we shall take part in these Olympic Games (Name of the Olympiad/Asiad/meet) respecting and abiding by the rules which govern them, without the use of doping and drugs in the true spirit of sportsmanship for the glory of sport and the honour of our teams".

The national Anthem of the host country will be played. Thereafter, the athletes and the officials march out of the stadium through the nearest exit. The opening ceremony will end and the games proper shall then begin.

Awards

As far as possible medals are awarded immediately after the event is over. When the results are announced the three position holders are called to the victory stand. The first place winner will stand in the centre at a higher level. The second place winner will be on his right and the third place winner on his left. The winners will face the Tribune of Honour and receive their medals and certificates either from the President of the I.O.C or his representative authorized by him. The national flag of the winner will be hoisted to the tune of the National Anthem of the winner's country. Gold, Silver and Bronze medals along with certificates are awarded to the competitors who have secured Ist, IInd and IIIrd place respectively. However, those competitors who have secured IVth, Vth and VIth place in each event are awarded only certificates.

Closing Ceremony of the Olympic Games

The closing ceremony of the games is simple but quite impressive, though it is on a smaller scale than the opening ceremony. In the closing ceremony, the flag and banner bearers intermingle with each other, forgetting their colour, caste, creed and nationality. They march into the stadium and assemble in the centre of the field.

Three flags are then hoisted : First the Greek Flag to the tune of the Greek National Anthem. Second the host country's flag with its National Anthem, and third the next country's flag (where the next Olympic will be held) with that country's National Anthem.

After completing the above mentioned procedure the President of the I.O.C. will express his gratitude to the Organisers. He will then declare the games closed and will call upon the youth of various countries to assemble again after four years at the next venue of the games.

Immediately after his declaration the ceremonial Olympic flag will be handed over to the Mayor of the City. He is responsible for keeping the flag safely till the next Olympic Games. Then trumpets will be sounded, the Olympic Flames will be put off. The Olympic Flag will be lowered to the tune of Olympic Hymn.

The lowering of the flag is followed by a salute of five guns. The flag and shield bearers march out of the Stadium while the band present there plays soft music.

THE OLYMPIC FLAG

There are two kinds of flags used by the International Olympic Committee as mentioned below:

1. The Olympic Flag.
2. The ceremonial Olympic Flag.

1. The Olympic Flag

- This Olympic Flag is based on a model designed by Baron de Cubertin in 1914. It was first hoisted in 1920 at Antwerp (Belgium) Olympics.
- It is made of white silk. In the centre of the flag there are five interlocked rings in the spirit of friendship in different five colours. The colours are blue, yellow, black, green and red (one of these colours shall be there in the flags of each continent).
- The five rings are arranged in the shape of a 'W'.
- The blue ring shall be high on the left nearer the flag pole.
- Below the rings appear the Olympic Motto " CITIUS, ALTIUS, FORTIUS", which means "Faster, Higher, Stronger".
- The rings and motto combined constitute the **Olympic Emblem,** which is the exclusive property of the International Olympic Committee.
- The Olympic Emblem cannot be used by commercial concerns as trade marks or for any business propaganda.
- Only this flag is hoisted during the Olympic Games.

2. The Ceremonial Olympic Flag

(*a*) This flag is made of silk.

(*b*) This is bordered with five colours of the rings representing five continents.

(*c*) The colours are blue, yellow, black, green and red.

(*d*) This flag is not used for hoisting purposes.

(*e*) This flag is handed over to the mayor of the City by the President of the International Olympic Committee at the time of closing ceremony. This flag shall be under the custody of the Mayor of the City till the next Olympics.

OLYMPIC TORCH

The Olympic games are full of ceremonies such as marching, flag raising, medal giving, anthem playing, and perhaps the most dramatic is lighting and carrying Olympic torch.

The Torch is used to light the Olympic flame, which burns throughout the games. The flame dates back to the 1928 Olympics. The founder of the modern Olympic Games, Baron Pierre de Coubertin, was too ill to go to Amsterdam (The Netherland) Olympic games. So he sent a message to the athletes, and all others taking part. In this message he urged them to "keep alive the flame of the revived Olympic spirit". And this is what the flame symbolizes.

The Torch ceremony was introduced during Berlin (German)Olympic held in 1936. The special torch is lit by the rays of sun at Olympia, in Greece, where the Ancient Olympic Games were held. It is lit sufficiently in advance of the beginning (commencement) of the Olympic games. This Torch is carried and relayed on foot as far as possible by the runners until it is finally taken to the city where the games are to be conducted. On its way, the particular country through which it passes through shall arrange for the relay of runners to bear the torch. Often, the torch has to be taken aboard ship/ plane to cross the ocean.

The identity of the runner who has the honour of carrying the Torch into the stadium and lighting the flame is kept secret. He might be a former athlete of international repute of the host country or an upcoming young athlete. His arrival with Torch will be synchronized with the opening of the games.

It is believed that the idea of lighting a torch from Olympic at Greece, carrying it all the way to the place of Modern games being conducted might have been innovated by Germans. Since, in the Ancient Olympics the sacred fires were burning continuously at the altar of Zeus at Olympia and the modern Olympic games are not conducted at Olympia, therefore, as a symbolic representation the sacred fires are taken from Olympia to the concerned city where the Olympic games are conducted.

INDIA IN OLYMPICS

It may be recalled that India had figured in the medal tally as early as the 2nd edition of Olympic Games held at Paris in 1900, when a Calcutta-based Anglo–Indian althete Norman G. Prithchard won a silver medal in the 220 yds sprint and finished fifth in the 110M hurdles. Henry Rebello missed a sure medal in his pet event-triple jump due to an unfortunate injury at the London Olympic Games in 1948.

In 1952 Helsinki Olympics, Mr Yadav won bronze medal in wrestling.

In 1960 Rome Olympics "Flying Sikh" Mikha Singh gave a historic performance in the 400m race. When he finished a highly creditable fourth, while talented Gurbanchan Singh Randhawa came fifth in the 110m hurdles in 1964 Tokyo Olympics.

The 1976 Montreal Olympics saw the Indian middle distance runner Sriram Singh at his best in the 800m race, when he made a superlative effort to enter the finals, " The Payyoli express, P.T Usha missed a bronze medal by one hundreadth of a second in the 400m hurdless at the Los-Angeles Olympic Games in 1984, when she was placed fourth in a Photo- finish.

In 1996 Atlanta Olympic Games, Indian ace Lawn Tennis player Leander Paes won bronze medal. In Sydney Olympic Games, held in 2000, the first ever woman Karnam Malleswari got bronze medal in weightlifting. Maj Rajyavardhan Singh Rathod won the Silver medal for Shooting in the Athens Olympics (2004). In Beijing Olympics-2008, **Abhinav Bindra** won India's first individual gold in an Olympics (10m rifle shooting), Sushil Kumar and Vijender Kumar won bronze in 66-kg Freestyle Wrestling and 75-kg boxing respectively.

India competed at the 2012 Summer Olympics in London, from 27 July to 12 August 2012. This was India's most successful Olympics in terms of total medal tally, having won a total of 6 medals (2 silver and 4 bronze), doubling the nation's previous record (3 medals at the 2008 Beijing Olympics). Two medals each were awarded to the athletes in shooting and wrestling. India also set a historical milestone for the female athletes who won two Olympic medals.

India competed at the 2016 Summer Olympics in Rio De Janeiro, Brazil, from 5 to 21 August 2016. India won two medals (One silver; P.V. Sindhu-Badminton and one bronze; Sakshi Malik-Wrestling) in this Olympics.

DIFFERECES AND SIMILARITIES IN THE ANCIENT AND MODERN OLYMPICS

Ancient Olympics	Modern Olympics
1. The Ancient Olympic games were held only at Olympia in Greece.	1. The Modern Olympic games are held at different cities of the world.
2. In ancient Olympic games Oath was taken by all competitors, their trainers, their fathers, their brothers and the judges in front of the statue of Zeus Horkios (God of Oaths) in the council house.	2. In modern Olympic Games, an athlete (a captain) leading the host contingent, takes the oath on behalf of the competitors of all Nations participating in front of the Tribune of Honour at the Olympic Stadium.
3. The competitors who wished to participate in Ancient Olympics must be free born Greeks.	3. The competitors who wish to participate in Modern Olympics shall be the naturally born of a member country.
4. To begin with the married women were not allowed even to witness the games. Later on they were allowed not only to witness but also to participate in the games.	4. In the Modern Olympics, officially women were never banned to participate but they started taking part from 1900 onwards.
5. The men and boys were allowed to participate in competitions in naked form.	5. In the Modern games competitors have to wear a proper uniform as prescribed in the rules of a particular sport.
6. The Ancient Olympic games were a religious festival for the Greeks being held in honour of God Zeus.	6. The modern Olympic Games are an international sports gathering.
7. Sacred fires were burning continuously in the temple of god Zeus at Olympia.	7. The Olympic flame is lit and kept burning at the stadium till the close of games.
8. Ancient Olympic games were held to develop and maintain unity among the Greeks.	8. The modern Olympic Games are held to foster international understanding and brotherhood.
9. Ancient Olympics were conducted for five days.	9 The modern Olympic Games are conducted for sixteen days.
10. In Ancient Olympics only individual sport events were conducted.	10 In modern Olympic Games both individual and team sports are conducted.
11. In ancient Olympics the winners were crowned with sacred olive leave wreaths.	11. In the modern Olympics the winners/position holders are awarded Medals and Diplomas.
12. Each Olympiad was named after the winner of 200 yard race known as stade race.	12 Each Olympiad is called in its serial order, e.g. XIVth Olympiad 1948-52, XVth Olympiad 1952-56 and so on.
13. Wars were stopped for the conduct of Ancient Olympic Games.	13. Games had to be stopped because of wars (World Wars; 1916, 1940 & 1944).
14. There was march past of the participants and officials.	14. There is march past of the participants only.
15. The Ancient Olympics were conducted once in four years.	15. The Modern Olympics are conducted once in four years.
16. Only amateur players were allowed to participate.	16. Only amateurs are allowed to participate.

THE MODERN OLYMPIC GAMES

Year	Olympiad	Venue (City & Country)	Year	Olympiad	Venue (City & Country)
1896	I	Athens, Greece	1948	XIV	London, England
1900	II	Paris, France	1952	XV	Helsinki, Finland
1904	III	St. Louis, USA	1956	XVI	Melbourne, Australia
1908	IV	London England	1960	XVII	Rome, Italy
1912	V	Stockholm, Sweden	1964	XVIII	Tokyo, Japan
1916	VI	Berlin, Germany Olympic Games not held due to World War-I	1968	XIX	Mexico City, Mexico
			1972	XX	Munich, West Germany
			1976	XXI	Montreal, Canada
1920	VII	Antwerp, Belgium	1980	XXII	Moscow, USSR
1924	VIII	Paris, France	1984	XXIII	Los Angeles, USA
1928	IX	Amsterdam, The Netherlands	1988	XXIV	Seoul, South Korea
			1992	XXV	Barcelona, Spain
1932	X	Los Angeles, USA	1996	XXVI	Atlanta, USA
1936	XI	Berlin, Germany	2000	XXVII	Sydney, Australia
1940	XII	Tokyo, Japan London, were cancelled	2004	XXVIII	Athens, Greece
			2008	XXIX	Beijing, China
1944	XIII	England due to World War-II cancelled	2012	XXX	London, England
			2016	XXXI	Rio De Janeiro, Brazil

LIST OF OLYMPIC MASCOTS

Olympiad	Mascot	Character
XIX	Schuss	Stylizedskier
XX	Waldi	Dachshund dog
XXI	Amik	Beaver
XXII	Misha	Bear cub
XXIII	Sam	Bald eagle
XXIV	Hodori	Tiger cub
XXV	Cobi	A Catalan sheep dog
XXVI	Izzy	An abstract figure
XXVII	Olly, Syd, Millie	Kookaburra, Platypus, Echidna
XXVIII	Athena and Phevos	Brother and sister
XXIX	Fuwa	Fish, giant panda, Olympic Flame, Tibetan ontelope, Swallow
XXX	Wenlock	Drops of steel with cameras for eyes
XXXI	Vinicius	The agility of cats, sway of monkeys and grace of birds.

The Olympic Games a Permanent Institution

The Modern Olympic Games have become a part of world events. With the instinct for competition as a nucleus for growth, the Games have expanded in the due course of time. They have crossed their hundredth anniversary and are held every fourth year.

From 1896 to 1960 only fourteen Olympic Games were organized and yet the Tokyo Games are called the eighteenth. Three games in between were not held because of the two World Wars, but they were officially not cancelled. The Olympic records only mention that they were "NOT CELEBRATED". For this reason the 1916, 1940 and 1944 Games are numbered as sixth twelfth and thirteenth respectively.

The Olympic Games were revived with the following three objectives:

1. To spread physical education, games and sports all over the world.
2. To raise the standard of performance in various forms of sports.
3. To promote international understanding and peace.

So far as the first two objectives are concerned the Games have succeeded to a great extent. Regarding the third objective the world had drifted far away from perpetual peace. As long as countries display their national flags, sing their national anthems, stick to their self-centred economic structures, it is doubtful if the Olympic Games will ever succeed in creating an atmosphere of international peace and friendship.In the words of Prof. Toynbee, "NATIONALISM IS MANKIND'S ENEMY NUMBER ONE".

Jack London, who came second in 100 metres in1928 at the Amsterdam Olympic Games, declared that:

"*It is difficult for the athlete who wears the flag of his country on his breast to have any real feeling of sportsmanship in the Olympic Games. It is far too grim an international contest. The only people who benefit by the Olympic Games are the spectators. There is little sportsmanship in the whole affair.*"

In any case it would be wrong to think that the Olympic Games do not foster any spirit of sportsmanship. According to **Aldous Huxley,** '*Games and sports can be used for good or bad ends. The competitive spirit, if turned into a wrong channel, can produce an intensely national complex at the cost of sportsmanship and would be detrimental to international friendship. If turned into a desirable channel it can promote tolerance, sense of fair play, spirit of give and take and even non-attachment.*'

There are various factors which contribute to international peace and friendship, of which games and sports can be one. It is up to the political leaders to decide whether games and sports are to be used to unite nations in friendly competitions or to promote national interest. Much depends on whether people observe the spirit in which Coubertin revived the Olympics.

Olympic Spirit on Decline

The noble objective with which Frenchman Coubertin had started modern Olympic Games, are being forgotten by everyone concerned with it, i.e. the organizers, officials participants, the sponsors, the international federations etc.

During ancient Olympic games war were stopped at the time of Olympic Games/Competitions so that athletes/officials/organizers/spectators could participate directly or indirectly to kindle the spirit of Olympics. On the contrary modern Olympic games were not held due to World wars in 1916, 1940, and 1944. In other words wars were given preference over Olympic games that too at the cost of sports persons/athletes.

Politically motivated acts of *"Poor sportsmanship"* ranges from Hitler's snuffing of "JESSE OWENS" a black super athlete in 1936 Berlin Olympics Games to the murder of eleven Israeli participants by Palestinian terrorists (Palestinian Liberation Organisation) in 1972 Munich Olympics; the boycott of 1976 Montreal Olympic Games by the African nations on account of apartheid; 1980 Moscow Olympic boycott by the United States and its allies on account of invasion of U.S.S.R on Afghanistan and 1984 Los Angeles Olympics boycott by the Socialist countries led by the U.S.S.R. in retaliation to 1980 boycott by the U.S and its allies. Again the hard labour put in by sportspersons to show their talents were spoiled for a life by one decision of boycotting the games. What is the fault of those athletes who belonged to the Olympics boycotting nations?

Professionalism in sports is one of the major reasons of violation of Olympic ideals. Till Avery Brundage, the then President of International Olympic Committee remained at the helm of affairs, professionalism in all sports were kept out of Olympic games and the Olympic spirit was kept intact. The moment he went away from the scene, professionalism invaded Olympic games. Further not only the participants and coaches, even the organisers are now fully professional since lot of money is involved. Nations compete with each other with cut-throat competitions to host the Olympic games or other International competitions with sole aim of earning money and gaining political mileage at the international level. Lots of scams have been unearthed where the members of the International Olympic Committee, who were to vote for the allotment of venue of Olympic, games, had been paid heavy bribes. This kind of practice of getting Olympic venue allotted has polluted the whole atmosphere of fair play and sports-manship. It shows that money has entered in the sports arena in a big way.

Professionalism among sportspersons coaches, federations, national Olympic associations etc. has given birth to another evil i.e doping in sports. Under the prevailing circumstances competitive sports participation no more provides health the primary objective of sports. It has become a health hazard due to excessive use of doping by the sports persons all over the world. All sorts of unethical tricks and tactics are being adopted with sole aim of winning a medal.

In view of the abovementioned facts one can easily draw out inferences that the ancient Olympic games continued for more than 700 years, but it is doubtful of modern Olympic games will survive even 200 years. At present the net result is that Olympic spirit is declining, and no body knows its bottom line.

THE MARATHONE RACE

An interesting but strenuous item covering a distance of 26 miles and 385 yards is the marathon race. This was introduced in 1896 at Athens in order to commemorate the battle of marathon in which the Persians were defeated by the Greek in 490 B.C.

The scene of the battlefield was a plain in marathon over looking the sea and surrounded on three sides by small mountains. The Athenians sent a runner, Pheidippides to Sparta for help. He ran more than a hundred miles and reached Sparta on the second day. The Spartans, in spite of their rivalry with Athens, agree but with characteristic shrewdness took three days to reach the battlefield.

In the meantime the Athenian Army assembled under General Militates on the small mountains of Marathon, and thinking it unwise to wait for Spartan help charged from the top of the mountains, riving the Persians back to their fleet. When the Spartans reached the battle field on the third day they found nothing but dead bodies.

At Athens people were anxious for the news of the battle, so Pheidippides who had taken part in the battle, ran the distance of 26 miles from Marathon to Athens he found a large crowd outside the city gates of Athens waiting for the news. Pheidippides should 'REJOICE, WE CONQUER'. *He then fell down dead.*

It is to commemorate this historical event that the marathon race is now an important event in the Olympic programme.

The First Marathon Race

In the inaugural modern Olympic games held at Athens in 1896, the first Marathon race was conducted on the final day. There were twenty five competitors who left Marathon at 2.00 pm.

Now about the progress of the race was brought to the Stadium from time to time by men on horse backs. The last message that a Greek competitor had taken the lead, produced wild enthusiasm among the spectators. Finally when Spiridon Loues, a Greek shepherd entered the Stadium, he was greeted with tumultuous applause. Two members of the Greek Royal family came down from the Royal

Box and gave him company by flanking him on either side and running till the finishing line, Loues covered the distance, in two hours and forty five minutes.

Forty years later Spiridon Loues was present at the Eleventh Olympics games in Berlin in 1936 at the invitation of Organizing Committee

The Marathon Distance

Since it was difficult to ascertain the exact distance which Pheidippides ran from Marathon to Athens in 490 BC the running distance of the marathon race has undergone fluctuations.

In 1896 the distance covered was 24 miles and 1500 yards. In 1900 it was converted into a round figure of 25 mile. In 1904 it was reverted to 24 miles and 1500 yards. In 1908 London Olympics it took another historical turn. The Organizing Committee decided that the starting point for the marathon race should be on the lawns of the Windsor Castle so that the British Royal Family could see the start of the race. The distance covered by the competitors from the starting line to the finishing line in the Stadium was 26 miles and 385 yards. In 1912 it was reduced to 24 miles 1725 yards and in 1920 it was increased to 26 miles 990 yards. In 1924 the distance was finally fixed at 26 miles 385 yards.

Note : *Extra 385 yards were added in 1908 Olympics so as to finish the race in front of the royal box.*

Marathon Race : A Controversial Item

In view of the long distance and its semi tragic appearance the marathon race has come under severe criticism: it is doubtful whether this race has any scientific reasons for it can hardly be considered useful or healthy to strain the body to such an extent as is required by this long run, particularly if the full distance is run through more than once during a season. In 1908 Dorondo was helped to the finishing line and was disqualified.In 1948 Etienne Gailly reached the Stadium exhausted and was dragging his feet near the finishing line. But despite adverse criticism, the marathon race has a strong spectator appeal and its drama makes newspaper headlines. It has enriched the English language, which now uses the word 'marathon' to describe any action requiring reserves of stamina.

WINTER OLYMPIC GAMES

The winter Olympic Games were introduced in 1924 and are held separately because of geographical and climatic conditions. The programme lasts only ten days. Although the same general rules apply to the winter Olympic Games as to the summer Olympic games, they are never referred to as "Olympiad" and the medals and diplomas are different.

The winter Games are also controlled by international federations so far as the technical matters are considered. Games for which there are no international controlling bodies can also be included in the winter Olympic games programme, but winners in these games are not given any Olympic award or even recognition as winners. Such games are regarded purely as demonstrations. Popular Items in the Winter Olympic Games are Ice-hockey, Skating, Skiing and the Bobsleigh. The summer Olympics and winter Olympics now alternate every two years a practice since 1994.

The Winter Olympic Games started in 1924 AD when the first Games were held at Chamonix, France followed by St. Moritz, Switzerland (1928 & 1948); Lake Placid, New York (1932 & 1980); Garmisch-Partenkirchen, Germany (1936); Oslo, Norway (1952); Cortina d'Amprezzo, Italy (1956); Squaw Valley, California (1960); Innsbruck, Austria (1964 & 1976); Grenoble, France (1968); Sapporo, Japan (1972); Sarajevo, Yugoslavia (1984); Calgary, Canada (1988) and Albertville, France (1992). The XVII Winter Olympic Games were held in Lillehharnmer (Norway) in February 1994. Incidentally, the 1994 Games were the first in accordance with the International Olympic Committee's new cycle of having Winter Games and Summer Games two years apart, instead of in the same year, as had been the tradition since the commencement of these Games in 1924.

The XVII Winter Games were held in Nagano (Japan) from February 7 to February 22, 1998. Germany topped the medal tally with 12 Gold, 9

Silver and 8 Bronze. The host country, Japan ranked 7th with a tally of 10 medals (5 Gold, 1 Silver and 4 Bronze). XIX Winter Olympic Games (February 9-24, 2002) were held in Salt Lake City (USA). Germany topped the Medals Tally winning 35 medals (including 12 Golds) while Norway finished as runner-up bagging 24 medals (11 Golds). The hosts United States of America with 34 medals (10 Golds) were in the third place.

XXI Winter Olympic Games, Vancouver, Canada (February 12-28, 2010): 21st Winter Olympic Games were held in Vancouver, Canada in February, 2010. Approximately 2,600 athletes from 82 nations participated in 86 events in fifteen disciplines. With 14, Canada broke the record for the most gold medals won at a single Winter Olympics, which was 13, set by the former Soviet Union in 1976 and Norway, 2002. United States won the most medals in total, their second time doing so at the Winter Olympics, and broke the record for the most medals won at a single Winter Olympic, with 37, which was held by Germany in 2002 at 36 medals. Athletes from Slovakia and Belarus won the first Winter Olympic gold medals for their nations.

2014 Winter Olympics

Three athletes represented India at the 2014 Winter Olympics in Sochi, Russia from 7 to 23 February 2014. They initially entered the competition as Independent Olympic participants, competing under the Olympic flag, as the Indian Olympic Association had been suspended by the IOC since 2012. However, on 11 February 2014 the IOC reinstated the India's NOC after they held an election, allowing the two athletes that still had competitions planned to compete under the Indian flag rather than as independent athletes. India still has yet to win its first Winter Olympic medal.

Paralympics

Very few people are aware of the fact that these games are the gift of second world war. After the second world war, the patients suffering from war incurred backbone and other serious injuries were treated by Sir Ludwig Gutman. In 1948 he found that majority of the patients have lost their will power and keep remembering the horrors of war all the time. Sir Ludwig started the game organization for such patients.

During London Olympics that year, Sir Ludwig organised competitive games for the soldiers undergoing treatment in various hospitals. In the next decades, this system of treatment of Sir Ludwig was implemented in all the hospitals in Britain that were dealing with problem of the back-bone.

It was named as "**Parallel Olympics**". In this context, the holding of Paralympics at the international level was okayed after 1960 Rome Olympics.

During Rome Olympics, Sir Ludwig collected 400 handicapped athletes and made an essential organization along with Olympics which is still continuing. It is different matter that earlier it was not organized on such a large scale as Olympics.

Shooting was the first game to be introduced for the handicapped people. By this game, the entire back was exercised thoroughly, while sitting on a wheel chair. After 1964 Tokyo Olympics, paralympics were held in Tokyo. After 1968 Mexico Olympics, paralympics were held in Israel. After 1972 Munich Olympics, these games were organised in Heidelberg (Germany). During these games, more than 1000 athletes from over 44 countries participated. In 1976 Toronto Olympics, for the first time competition for medals was partially started for blind athletes. In these games, the number of the athletes increased to 1600. Specially manufactured racing wheel chairs were used for the first time over here. In 1980 during the boycott of the Moscow Olympics by the Western Countries, after the refusal for organizing Paralympics by the organizer, the games were organized at Aanhim (Holland) for 2500 athletes from 42 countries.

For the first time mentally retarted athletes got a chance to show their competence. The Paralympic Games got a new lease of life in the 80's Stock Medwelay (Great Britain) and New York (America) organised United Paralympics. Wheel-chair marathon was included in Paralympics.

South Korea set an example by organizing paralympics in 1988 with great zeal and enthusiasm. After 1992 Barcelona Olympics, Paralympics in which 3500 athletes from 82 countries participated, packed the stadium with teeming enthusiastic spectators, was a great source of inspiration.

Unfortunately at Atlana (1996), Paralympic Organizing Committee did not get any help from Olympic organizers. Most of the handicapped athletes were dissatisfied with the facilities provided at the Olympic Village and the Stadium. At Sydney (2000), athletes from 32 countries were present, for the first time, rugby and wheel-chair basketball was ranked as 'medal sport' in these paralympics.

Athens welcomed the 12th edition of Paralympic Games (2004) in September (17-28), 2004. A total of 3969 athletes from 136 countires participated in the Games. China won the most medals-141 (63 G, 46 S, 32 B) followed by Great Britain-94 (35 G, 30 S, 29 B) and Canada-72 (28 G, 19 S, 25 B).

First Ever Gold for India: India's Devendra created history by winning the first ever gold for the country in Athens Paralympics 2004. He claimed gold in javelin throw.

The 13th edition of Paralympics held in Beijing, China in September (6-17), 2008, in which four thousand athletes from 147 regions and countries took part in 20 sports. In medal-tally, China topped with winning 89 gold and 211 overall. The 14th edition of the Paralympics held in London, United Kingdom from August 29 to September 9, 2012. Girisha Nagarajegowda of India won silver medal in Athletics. The 15th edition of the Paralympics was held in Rio de Janeiro, Brazil from September 7 to 18.

India has sent its largest ever delegation in the history of summer paralympic games *i.e.*, 19 competitors in 5 sports. Also, as far as the games have progressed till now, it has been India's best ever performance in the history of the summer Paralympic games with a total of 4 medals won till now (2 Gold, 1 Silver and 1 Bronze) with Devendra Jhajharia breaking the World Record to win a gold medal at the Paralympics.

HISTORY OF PHYSICAL EDUCATION IN INDIA

The beliefs and experience of physical education today rest on the history of this field endeavour. It is the source of physical education's identity. Many of today's activities have their fore-runners in history. For instance, the first Olympics date back to 776 B.C. in ancient Greece. Yoga and Karate, activities with much recent interest, date back to ancient oriental societies.

Budha's prohibition of games, amusements and exercises in ancient India did not totally prevent participation in such activities. The Indian physical activities such as Chariot races, riding elephants and horse, swordsmanship, wrestling, boxing, kabaddi, kho-kho atyapaty, dancing, dand baithak, malkhamb, lezium, lathi, etc. have been in practice from time immemorial. But neither the names of the inventors of the Indian system of physical culture nor the dates of their origin are known. Yet we are aware of the fact that a scientific system of physical education was in existence in India and was practised by the people. Yoga, an activity common in India and involving exercises of posture and regulated breathing was popular. This disciplining of mind and body required the instruction of experts and a person fully trained in this activity followed routine involving eighty four different postures.

The physical activities were performed in open places and grounds because the Indian system of physical education was such that they needed little or no equipment. Besides, the religious /worship places were the institutes of physical culture where the sages and rishis were the ustads.

The places where Indian physical activities were promoted and practised were generally called as Vyayamashalas / Vyayam Mandirs.

In the physical culture of India, the age old Vedas advocated that non-violence is the best of righteous acts. This can be realized properly in its true spirit only by a strong individual and not by weak ones, because physical weakness may be attributed to cowardice. Further, protection is well assured only by a powerful one. *Moreover, the Great poet Kalidasa has emphasized that physique is the lease indeed for accomplishment of duty. Vedas have emphasized that just as wealth is essential for the appropriate fulfillment of desire, similarly for the salvation of life healthy physique is essential.*

Physical education in the past was part and parcel of daily life, it was not considered merely as a vocational or free time activity. It was considered as the fundamental factor for self realization. *Upanishad as has strongly advocated that the attainment of the powerful soul is not possible for a weak individual.*

The history of India has witnessed that the society was divided into different classes on the basis of their occupation e.g. teachers, warriors, merchants and servants. They were given social status which ultimately broke into rigid caste system bearing the stamps as *Brahmins, Kshtriyas, Vaisyas* and *Sudras*. In all the fields of education the teachers were invariably *Brahmins*. Their workshop included Branayama, Yoga, Namaskar etc. Further, *the Brahmins*, being teachers, had to master the art of handling weapons and missiles. This included archery, sword fighting etc. The Kshatriyas as the future rulers and protectors of the country had to compulsorily learn the science of archery, sword fighting, horse and elephant riding. The *Vaishyas* and *Shudras* practised many physical activities of their will; they were not compelled to learn the particular physical activities. Wrestling was practised by all irrespective of castes ; we also find references about first fighting in Rigveda which indicated the place of Military Science in Indian system of Physical Education. The great epics "The Ramayana" and "The Mahabharata" are full of stories of great warriors depicting their martial qualities. If we just look into the epics we can well understand that physical fitness was considered as an important factor in all warfare and it was promoted by indigenous system of physical education. All war weapons and war tactics were also of indigenous nature. The warriors were well versed in archery, wrestling, sword fighting, horse riding, elephant riding and chariot racing.

Texila University is an example, where training of Archery (Dhanurveda) was of a very high order.

In the last decade of 13th century and during the 15th half century the army of different kings was highly trained in handling the war weapons. The great Rajput kings like Prithviraj, Rana Sangram Singh and Rana Pratap were highly skilled, in using the weapons like lances, swords and horse riding.

In the days of Shivaji, the great Maratha King, the Maratha soldiers were highly skilled in handling weapons even in their war front. During the regime of Shivaji, the love of indigenous physical culture reached its peak.

The Indian system of physical culture in general and military training in particular were rapidly deteriorated under the British Rule. The Indian system of physical culture and military training came to the halt after rulers had passed Arms Act and prohibited the use of indigenous weapons and banned the activities of Akharas and Vyayamshalas.

Further the indigenous weapons disappeared from the curriculum of Indian Military Science in the presence of Guns/ Rifles.

India has faced many foreign invasions and atrocities by Muslim, Portuguese, the French and the British till the dawn of independence. The atrocities of the foreign rulers helped the Indian people to fight well against the foreign domination not in a united manner but in an individual way. Though, the result was not much encouraging yet definitely, the practice in indigenous physical activities increased remarkably and resulted in re-establishing a number of Akharas / Military training centres at almost every village.

The first war of independence in 1857 was pressed and by that time almost the nation was in the strong grip of the British Rulers. Very intelligent rulers attracted the people towards the aristocrat games.

On the other hand the revolutionaries who condemned the foreign rule went under ground and continued their efforts of injecting the fire of patriotism in the minds of the members of the Akharas and they were filled with the spirit of independence and freedom, ultimately they were successful in their mission to attract many more strong and young people who also were infused with the spirit of patriotism and once again Akharas were running to their full swing.

To study the historical development of physical education in India more efficiently we should study the development of physical education from ancient period till this day. Despite our poor cultural habits of not writing history and the fact that in stat concise history of education including field of physical education in India is found written. Pandit Jawahar Lal Nehru has rightly remarked that : "*Unlike the Greeks, Chinese and Arabs, Indians in the past were not historians. This was very unfortunate and it has made difficult for us now to fix dates or make up an accurate chronology*". However in the modern time people have started taking interest in writing articles, books, etc.

In order to study the history of physical education minutely the ancient period is divided into different phases.

Division of Ancient Period

Indus Valley Civilization period.	(3250 B.C.-2500 B.C.)
The Vedic Period	(2500 B.C. – 600 B.C.)
Early Hindu Period	(600 B.C. – 320 A.D.)
Later Hindu Period	(320 A.D. - 1000 A.D.)
Medieval Period	(1000A.D.–1757 A.D.)

Indus valley Civilization Period (3250 B.C. – 2500 B.C.)

There is no record of any physical art or craft during the pre-vedic age. But an idea of the same can be formed from a careful study of the war weapons, tools and implements, seals and sculptures found at Harappan and Mohanjodaro. During this age the objective of physical exercise was achieved through a daily routine of work, games, sports and amusements.

Dancing, particularly community dancing, was the favourite recreation of pre-vedic people as it appears from a bronze dancing girl from Mahanjodaro in the National Museum in Delhi. The most important and interesting thing during the Indus Valley Civilization at Mohanjodaro was the Great Bath, which was similar to modern swimming pool. It was a part of vast dropalhic establishment, which measured 60 mts by 36 mts. The actual swimming pool measuring 18 mts by 7 mts by 2.5 mts, was situated in the middle of a quadrangle having varandahs on all sides. Near the great bath was situated hammam, a kind of hot and cold shower and oil room.

Marbels, balls and dice were used for games. Dicing was a very popular game as it would be evident from a large number of dices unearthed. Both cubical and tubular specimens have been found. It is, however, not certain whether the throwing of dice constituted a game in itself. Most probably dices were used along with board games. Two incomplete specimens of game boards have been found. Animal fighting was another pastime during this civilization. Boxing was also in practice as evident from a seal found.

Vedic Period (2500 B.C. – 600 B.C.)

Suryanamaskara, the origin of which dates back to vedic period was performed more as a religious duty than today a mere physical exercise or training. Now this has developed into a very popular exercise for health. The practice of pranayama was another important development which took place during this period. It was considered beneficial for the lungs and as a means of prolonged life. Military training was also popular during this period, because Aryans were engaged in subjugating non-aryans and establishing their supremacy. As it demanded physical strength, vigour and martial skill they were involved in hand wrestling, use of bow and arrow, dagger fight, sword fight, male fight hurling the discuss and spear. Horse riding, chariot racing, hunting, elephant riding and boxing were also needed in battle.

Ball games were in practice during this period and were played by men as well as women. Game with ball seems to have been the chief outdoor physical exercise. Playing of dice had become very popular. It was played by the young as well as the old. The art of the boxing was known to the Aryans and it was used in battles for defeating the enemies.

Hunting as a sport was also prevalent. Music and dancing was well known. Bird and animal fighting was also popular pastime. Fights were organised in the fair and festivals for amusements. Great emphasis was placed on the culture of physique and strength during the vedic period. Physical strength was emphasised greater than academic learning. Practice of yoga was recommended for the development of spiritual strength.

Early Hindu Period (600 B.C. – 320 A.D.)

Ramayana makes a great deal of reference to physical training and recreation. Dramas and festivals played an important part in the life of citizens during this period. Hunting was very popular which was considered a royal sport. Big dogs were domesticated for the purpose of sport. Enjoying water sports surrounded by female attendants was another diversion for the kings. Dicing and chess were popular games. The game of chess was in fact the invention of some Hindu and this country is considered the original home of this game, which spread throughout the ancient world. Animal combats were also prevalent. Wrestling, male fight, chariot driving, archery and water tactics prevalent during the Mahabharta period, depict the nature of physical culture practice existence at that time. Balrama was a strong man and excelled in wrestling and male fighting. He was an excellent teacher in the art of teaching male fighting. Bhisma was skilled in all the branches of physical culture and weapons and was a mighty bowman. The practice of fighting with animals was prevalent and was considered to be an important feature of this age.

Later Hindu Period (320 A.D. – 1000 A.D.)

Great universities like Taksila an Nalanda developed during this period. There was a happy correlation of the physical, intellectual and aesthetic training at these centers of learning. Wrestling, archery, and mountain climbing were given special attention. At Nalanda University swimming, breathing exercise and yoga formed an essential part of the daily life of the student. During this period physical education was greatly patronized by the Gupta Rulers. People followed the glorious example set by their brave rulers and participated in many sports and physical activities. India during this period was a land of men noted for the excellence of their physique and keenness of their intellect. In the art work of Kusana period of Mathura, several scenes of combats between men and lions can be noticed. Great emphasis was laid on the military and physical art during the Ganga dynasty in Orissa. During this period hunting was very popular pastime of the people. There were 31 ways of hunting known to the people. Cock fighting was another popular sport. There were separate officials to look after each of the eight varieties of cocks which were known to be suitable for fighting. Elephant, buffalo, and partridge fighting was also in existence. There were more than ten swimming pools near Nalanda monastery and every morning a bell was sounded to remind the students of the swimming hours. Bodily health was considered important for the improvement of the spiritual condition. Exercises were encouraged in the monasteries. Great emphasis was laid on the maintenance of sound health and physical fitness which was achieved through regular habits, regulated diet, long walking, physical labour such as collecting of twigs and filling water etc.

Medieval Period (1000 A.D. – 1757 A.D.)

In the 12th century A.D our system of physical education was promoted in the Gurukulas (place of study where the teachers and taught lived together) by our ancient teachers in the gymnasium which enjoyed the high patronage of kings.

During the 1200 to 1525 A.D. kings paid more attention towards the military training which resulted in practice of handling different types of weapons for self defence.

The well known religious prophets like Shree Samarth Ramadas Swamee felt the importance of physical education. He used to practice 1200 Suryanamaskars every day. He travelled throughout the country and inspired people to build gymnasium with a temple of God Hanuman and to practice namaskar everyday. Because of his efforts hundreds of gymnasiums were built in the country. Hence he can be rightly called as the "*Grand Father of Indian Gymnasium Movement*". However, traditionally, the indigenous system of physical education was promoted in the religious places, though very few gymnasiums were in operation or functional. The physical activities in the gymnasium included Suryanamaskars, Dands, Heavy club Swinging, Malkhamb, Wrestling, Sword fight etc. The rulers of the time themselves were lovers of gymnasium work and they patronized several wrestlers.

The art of Malkhamb was revived and a new type of Malkhamb known as Hanging Malkhamb and care Malkhamb were introduced during this period. Horse riding, Javeline throwing, wrestling, hunting, male fighting, and above all archery were extremely popular sports with the Rajputs. The Rajputs were lovers of festivals, music and dance. The Rajput girls were also tough to ride horses without saddle. The tradition of religious fairs in Rajasthan speaks of that glory. The chess was extremely popular recreational activity not only amongst the princes but also among the masses.

Later on the Mughals gained supremacy over the entire sub-continent. The physical education continued to play an important role in the life of the countries and soldiers. Hunting, sword fighting, male fighting, horse riding were preferred to yogic exercises, because physical activity leading to acquisition of war skills was an important aspect of the life of these people. The Mughals were great patrons of wrestling as it served dual purpose as a recreation game as well as suitable actually for war preparedness. They encouraged the wrestling schools and even kept wrestlers in their courts. Often dands and baithaks were used to develop muscular power and elasticity. Massaging was an extremely important aspect of wrestling training. Boxing was another notable activity. Hunting, swimming, animal fight were other activities which were popular during this period. Chogan is considered to be a precursor of polo. This sport was even played at night. Pigeon flying was another pastime very popular during this period. Individual sports competitions especially horse riding and sword fighting were a matter of routine in the courts.

Apart from out door active sporting events the courtiers and the commoners recreated themselves with such activities as chess changer, Pachissi etc. This way the history owes to the Mughal rulers who had great love for games and sports and for construction of great gardens in various parts of the country which are ably regarded as a big source of recreation.

British Period (Till 1947)

After 1825 A.D. the entire system of physical education rapidly deteriorated to the unexpected levels. The events of daily life started moving just in opposite direction to the previous period in the strong grip of British Rule.

During this period the Western civilization influenced the Indian Culture with the result that the youngsters developed an aversion towards the indigenous activities and kept themselves away from Akharas/Vyayamshalas. The main reasons for this change were : (1) The activities introduced by the foreigners were more attractive (2) games had more recreational values than indigenous activities (3) The Western activities were of group type where more people could participate with lesser skill as compared to indigenous ones (4) The indigenous physical activities were not an essential part of the school curriculums.

India has been ruled by many foreign rulers (the Muslims, the Portuguese, the French and the British). They had programme of their own interest which ultimately adversely affected the indigenous physical activities. For instance the Muslim rulers were interested in imparting training in different disciplines such as gymnastics, pole drill, dagger fighting, fire fighting, archery, fight with wild animals, hunting, horse riding, swimming etc. But the training was given to the army personnel only.

Among the foreign rulers it was the British who were successful in establishing their rule in India with great supremacy and ruled for about 200 years. Under the British rule the indigenous physical activities and military training lost their importance, when they passed arms act. Under this act the Indians were prohibited from keeping weapons of war and the activities practised by the Indians on the ancient line, such as sword fighting, dagger–fight, spear fight etc. were banned. It resulted in the degeneration of physical state of the Indian people.

During the British rule the organization and the conduct of athletic activities and cricket were the result of private efforts. Further the German system of Gymnastics was adopted and introduced in the educational institutes but it could not attract masses due to some inborn problem. Drills and calisthenics were also introduced in the schools in order to create greater interests and promote larger participation of the student in these activities, but it was not very successful. At the same time we should not forget the fact that the love for outdoor sports/ games of the British people and their long association with the Indians resulted in the introduction and popularizing of the team games in India for e.g. Cricket, Hockey and Football. Most of the modern games and sports came to India via England. British Government's policy put emphasis on the practice of physical training in schools only for name sake. The real credit for propagating physical education goes to the voluntary organizations. Vyayamashalas, Krida-Mandals and Akharas contributed a great deal in the development of interest in physical activities like Dands, Baithaks, Yogic exercises, Folk dancing, wrestling, lathi exercises and indigenous games like Kho-kho and kabaddi. Those who were good in sports activities, practised these sports in their free time and were given some encouragement from the school authorities. During school hours, some military drill, physical exercises were given to the students by ex-army personnel. The public schools which followed the elite British systems of education had some arrangement of compulsory physical education. In these schools greater attention was paid to the western type of games and sports and not to indigenous activities. Track and field, swimming, horse riding, horse polo, cycle polo etc were popular in these schools.

The organized scientific physical education came to India in 1920 when Mr. H.C. Buck founded the Y.M.C.A. College of Physical Education at Madras. This institution gave a firm foothold to physical education in India. Later on, many more institutions came into being. The teachers passing from these institutions replaced ex-army personnel and gradually lent a new meaning to physical education programmes in schools and community.

The contributions made by the Americans for the development of physical and Sports education in India cannot be over looked. The games of Basketball, and Volley ball are of American origin. These were introduced in India by the Y.M.C.A.

In order to make the indigenous activities more attractive the Hanuman Vyayam Prasarak Mandal, Amravati was formed. The H.V.P Mandal offered a number of courses like certificate course, diploma and degree course in physical education. It was also the first institution to start demonstration–cum–propaganda tours to propagate the cause of indigenous physical education all over India and abroad. The rules of indigenous games like Kabaddi, kho-kho and Atypatya were standaridsed by Akhil Maharashtra Sharirik Shiksha Mandal and they were followed throughout India.

PHYSICAL EDUCATION IN INDIA AFTER 1947

With the achievement of independence in 1947, India made rapid progress in all aspects. For the development of physical education and recreation a number of schemes were floated by the Govt. of India. The first central Government Physical Education Committee called as Tara Chand Committee was set up in the year 1948. This committee made several recommendations for the development of physical education and recreation in the country which included the establishment of central institute of physical education and recreation. The Central Advisory Board of Physical Education was set up in 1950 to advise the Government on all matters pertaining to physical education. In 1951 the first Asian Games were held at Delhi, which encouraged the Indian youth to take part in games and sports at the international level. In the year 1953, the Ministry of Health, Government of India initiated a coaching Scheme for games and sports when the late Rajkumari Amrit Kaur was the Health Minister. The scheme was intended to provide training to athletes in various games and sports. During this time there were no professionally qualified coaches available and 40 systematic programmes of coaching players was in existence. The purpose of the scheme was to streamline the coaching programme for various games and sports by providing services of coaches. Since there were no qualified coaches, the job of doing coaching was entrusted to those who had made mark in their sport of specialization like Dhayan Chand etc. Services of some foreign coaches were also requisitioned on contract basis. In the absence of permanent coaching centres, the camps were held at various places. Short term coaching camps for school and college students also used to be conducted. The scheme was envisaged to be extremely fruit bearing, but it did not yield tangible results. The scheme was named as the Rajkumari Sports Coaching Scheme.

In the year 1954 an All India Council of Sports came into existence. This acted as a liaison between the Government and the National Federations for the various games/ sports and offered financial assistance to these federations. Under the AICS, the State Sports Council and District Sports Council were formed.

To promote and popularize indigenous physical activities a National Plan of Physical Education and Recreation was prepared by the Central Advisory Board of Physical Education in the year 1956.

The Minister of Education established a college of physical education at Gwalior (M.P) in 1957 offering three year degree course. Later on Master's Degree Course of two year duration was introduced in the same college. The college was named as Lakshmibai College of Physical Education in the memory of the famous Rani of Jhansi, the heroine of the first war of Indian independence. In 1954, National Discipline Scheme was started by General Bhonsle who was Deputy Minister of Rehabilitation at the Centre. In 1957 the scheme was handed over to Union Ministry of Education. Directorate of National Discipline Scheme set up Central Training Institute in Alwar (Rajasthan) in 1960 and at Barwaha (M.P) in 1963 to cater to the increasing demand of trained teachers.

In the year 1958 Sports and Youth Welfare Department was opened by the Ministry of Education to promote physical education in the country. In the same year seminars for the Principals of Physical Education Institutions, inspectors of physical education and experts and specialists in indigenous physical activities were sponsored by the Ministry of Education.

To evaluate the standards and status of the physical education and to look into the details of the then existing playground facilities in educational institutions in various states an ad-hoc committee was appointed by the Ministry of Education, Government of India, in the year 1959.

In order to evaluate the physical fitness status of the people the National Physical Efficiency Drive for men, women, boys and girls was started and sponsored by the Ministry of Education in 1959.

In the year 1961 National Institute of Sports was established at Moti Bagh, Patiala, Punjab to produce the qualitative coaches (Experts) in particular games and sports. A southern Coaching centre was established in 1974 at Banglore.

In 1965 a new venture called as National Fitness Corps was set up. This was an amalgamation of physical education. National Discipline Scheme and National Cadet Corps Directorat of N.F.C prepared a hand book of activity programmes for teachers.

In 1970-71 the rural sports tournament scheme was launched by the Central Government with two major objectives:

(*i*) To involve a major segment of the rural youth.

(*ii*) To spot out natural talent.

In 1970-71 Sports Talent Search Scholarship scheme was introduced by the Government of India to enable the young promising and talented boys and girls to develop their talent in sports. The scheme provides National Level and State level Scholarships. Another Scheme was implemented through University Grants Commission which aimed at improving sport standards among college and university youth. This also is in the form of awarding scholarship to talented players. In 1975 national Sports Championship for women was started in order to encourage women participation in games and sports.

In 1982 Asian Games were conducted in India; it was a great step towards promotion of Physical Education and sports in our country. For hosting these games huge infrastructures were built and sports industries were encouraged to manufacture sports goods of top quality. To look after, to maintain and to generate funds from the sports infrastructure, sports Authority of India was established in 1982.

To have an integrated approach towards the development of physical education and sports, in 1982 the Society for National Institutes of Physical Education and Sports was merged with Sports Authority of India. It has two wings i.e., academic wing and sports wing. The academic wing deals with the promotion of Physical Education and sports through institutions of Physical Education and sports which are producing teachers of physical education and sports coaches of high calibre. The sports wing deals with the promotion of sports in the country. Besides the sports wing of SAI, it has many sports promotion schemes covering almost all the sections of the society.

In 1995, the premier Institute of Physical Education, being run by the Central Govt. under the name of L.N.C.P.E. was given the status of "Deemed University" which is now known as: "Lakshmi Bai National Institute of Physical

Education". After conferring the status, it was delinked from the academic wing of SAI. It is the only independent institution (Deemed University) in physical education in the country. It deals with preparing teachers of physical education for schools, colleges and universities, has well established research centre to produce Ph.D's in physical education. The institute also runs an academic staff college of U.G.C. to cater to the needs of college/ university teachers of physical education by conducting orientation /refreshers courses in physical education.

RECOMMENDATIONS OF EDUCATION COMMISSION (KOTHARI COMMISSION 1964)

Physical Education

In the government plan related to physical education it has been noticed that greater stress is laid on good health, physical part of the body and its educational value is being ignored. There is a need to make it clear that physical education not only influences physical health, but also the physical capacity and mental alertness. It helps in the development of fine virtues such as *sportsman spirit, leadership, discipline, spirit of victory and defeat etc. etc.* A satisfactory physical education programme can be worked on the following principles.

1. Physical education programme planning should be made keeping in view the interests and capacities of the people participating in the programme and its results.
2. Greater emphasis should be laid on the traditional sports and physical activities (Indigenous activities) that were developed in our country.
3. The activities that are to be encouraged should be used to awaken the feelings of personal importance and pride in each child.
4. The students should be encouraged to develop the intelligence to provide help in taking on the responsibility in the spirit of democratic cooperation in the playground as well as gymnasium.
5. Whatever plan is formulated, it should not be the only one, but should be additional to other programmes.
6. The programme should not be beyond our financial capacity.
7. The programme should be within reach of everyone and not only a handful of selected people.
8. Special attention should be paid to the students who have the capacity and show keen interest.

Physical education should include developmental exercise, rhythmic activities, sports and games, walking and collective or team activities. All theses activities have both- simple as well as complex aspects. Easy activities should begin in the primary classes and as the boys and girls mature, they should be taught the complex ones.

Small children are not physically and mentally mature to take part in disciplined and tough activities. The basic activities must be developed gradually. Pre-schools and preparatory school education for children should be based on their desire to copy the activities around them, their sportsman spirit, their ability to take part in brave acts, to beat their friends in courageous acts. This age is the most important stage of "*Education Through Movements*". At this stage, the child should perfect the art of walking, running, throwing etc. The higher level of correctness and accuracy should be left for the next age.

On reaching pre-adolescence age, there is a change in the interest and capabilities of the child. Therefore, greater emphasis should be laid on the fundamentals of those activities, simple sports and skills that increase his strength. Students of middle school copy their elders. They should be taught the higher level of games, sports and athletics. The skills learned earlier must be perfected through exercise and guidance. This is the age when boys and girls want to specialize in a particular field. Therefore, the technique of doing the work perfectly should be included in the course of physical education.

Leaving the last two classes aside, all the other classes at the preparatory level can make use of the same course for both the boys and girls. After that, keeping in view their different interests and capabilities, courses should be evolved. Girls are attracted towards the rhythmic activities; badminton, throw-ball etc. which does not involve collision and are less strenuous, are liked by them. More strenuous sports like basketball, net-ball, hockey can be taught later along with exercises of higher level.

While preparing the courses for physical education for all age groups, because of limited facilities, paucity of time and shortage of teachers, we have to see not only what is useful but what is possible. There is a great competition between various national educational policies prepared by special groups on behalf of the Ministry of Education, National Administration System and Sahayak Cadet Corps which have similar activities. A special commission appointed by the Ministry of Education under the leadership of Dr. Hirdyanath Kunjroo recommended that a social scheme should prepare a course in which the good points of various other courses should be included. An effort was made to bring together all the ideas put forth by the enthusiastic supporters of the various schemes of the commission which resulted in mixed programme of physical education titled National Fitness Corp. It is possible that in the practical implementation of the new system, we might forget or overlook the educative programme of physical education. Chunki Compromise Policy has been criticized a lot. So is our suggestion that an enquiry should be commissioned and with the help of the above mentioned principles, a new physical programme be made.

National Policy On Education – 1986

Sports and physical education are an integral part of the learning process, and will be included in the evaluation of performance. A nation wide infrastructure for physical education, sports and games will be built into the educational institution. The infrastructure will consist of playfields, equipment, coaches and teacher of physical education as part of the school Improvement Programme. Available open spaces in urban areas will be reserved for playgrounds, if necessary by legislation. Efforts will be made to establish sports institutions and hostels where specialised attention will be given to sports activities and sports–related studies. along with normal education. Appropriate encouragement will be given to those talented in sports and games. Due stress will be laid on indigenous traditional games.

Yoga

As a system which promotes an integrated development of body and mind, Yoga will receive special attention. Efforts will be made to introduce Yoga in all schools. To this end, it will be introduced in teacher training courses.

Place of Physical Education in the Present System of Education in India

Govt. of India has been setting many commissions with the promotion of physical education and sports as is evident from Kothari Commission, Kunjroo Commission etc. Accordingly established L.N.C.P.E., Gwalior for the promotion of physical education and N.I.S Patiala for the promotion of competitive sports. Later on the Central Govt. sponsored schemes like National Discipline Schemes, National Fitness Corps, National Physical Efficiency Drive/National Physical Fitness Programme etc. also came into being and vanished away in the thin air.

Immediately after 1982 Asian Games held in Delhi, Govt. of India launched Sports Authority of India amalgamating Physical Education College, Gwalior and Sports Institute Patiala with the very ambitious plan of producing better physical educationists and coaches. Sports Authority of India introduced 17 different schemes in the process for the promotion of sports. L.N.C.P.E. Gwalior, L.N.C.P.E. Trivandram, NSNIS Patiala got reduced to schemes, the purpose for which these institutions were established was forgotten totally. Main concentration was focussed on few elite sportspersons with the aim of bringing medals in the Olympic Games, Asian Games and other such

International Competitions. Ill conceived and poorly implemented schemes have resulted in a chaos. Whatever was being achieved prior to 1982 has also gone away. Galib's couplet :

न खुदा ही मिला, न विसाले सनम,
न इधर के रहे, न उधर के रहे।।

is most appropriate for the present scenario of Sports Authority of India. India had been winning a good number of gold, silver and bronze medals from 1951 to 1982 and enjoying the respectable place in the overall champion-ship in the Asian Games. Our only Olympic hope hockey is no-where at the world scene. Similarly, Boxing, Wt. Lifting, Cycling, Football, Volleyball and a number of other games and sports in which Indian sports persons have been achieving respectable positions at Asian Games level have reached the rock bottom.

Scenario in the field of physical education is equally gloomy. There are hundreds of private institutions run by influential politicians / businessmen which can be described as mushroom shops, producing half baked / poorly trained, physical educationists with exception of few reputed institutions like L.N.I.P.E. Gwalior, L.N.C.P.E., Trivandram, H.V.P Mandal Amravati, Punjab Govt. College of Physical Education, Patiala and a few departments of physical education in the universities like Punjab University, Chandigarh, Guru Nanak Dev University, Amritsar. For a population of hundred crore Indians, we need lacs of well trained, knowledgeable physical education personnel to look after the physical education programmes at various levels, specially in the educational institutions.

It is heartening to note that a new national policy for physical education and sports was under the consideration of Ministry of Youth Affairs and Sports under the dynamic leadership of Union Minister of Sports. All the professionals physical educationists and sports- promoters are waiting with their fingers crossed for announcement of the new national sports and physical education policy for the country.

SOME OTHER USEFUL MATTERS

Scenario of Physical Education in Ancient Greece

The level of education and physical education was very high in ancient Greece. Greek period was the golden period for physical education and sports. All great philosophers and thinkers like Aristotle hailed from Greece. Ancient Greece was divided into twenty eight city states with Athens and Sparta being the most important states. Physical education in ancient Greece can be studied under following heads:

(i) **Homeric Period:** (1000 B.C. to 750 B.C.) Most of our knowledge of this period has come to us from Homer and his two epics, Iliad and the Odyssey. Both these epics are full of information about the period of history. The Greeks believed that a perfect body was indeed an offering to God Zeus. Aim of Greeks was to produce soldiers who were physically tough. The individuals learnt fighting skills by themselves, or by imitating their elders.

(ii) **Physical education in Sparta:** The Spartans led extremely disciplined and orderly life. There were military schools in the city state where a student had to spend two years and weapons training used to be given. Dancing and singing was popular among women and men both.

(iii) **Physical Education in Athens:** In Athens, the students were given training in wrestling and other physical activities. Here the children were taught jumping, running, boxing, wrestling, javelin throw and discus etc.

Like in Sparta, military training was imparted to children till 18. The Athenians believed in giving training to the children in arithmetic, gymnastics as well as music.

(iv) **Pan Hellienic Festivals:** Although most of the time, the city-states were engaged in

fighting, still the people of Greece could find time for sports and games. In the beginning, games were part of different religious ceremonies and later they became organized and formal. During Pan Hellenic festivals the competitions were organized in sports like foot races, chariot races, wrestling, swimming, gymnastics etc. Different Pan Hellenic Festivals of Greeks were:

The Pythian Games, in the honour of god Apollo, Isthmian Games in the honour of God Poseidon, Nemean games in the honour of God Zeus and Olympic Games in the honour of God Zeus.

History of Commonwealth Games

Commonwealth games are the second largest festival of sports. These are held once in four years, and are held in countries, which are members of the commonwealth countries. Commonwealth includes those, which were British colonies in the past. The citizens of only Ccommonwealth countries are allowed to participate in these games. The name of Commonwealth games when they first started was "British Empire games." The games have undergone a change of name and expanded into a major multi-racial and cultural event. Specialists argue that these games used to be organized as "Inter Empire Games" and "Pan Britanica Festival". Also competition was organized at crystal place in London. The British colonies took part in these games with great enthusiasm. The idea of organizing these sports competitions was propounded by J. Aslect Cooper who was a resident of Yorkshire, in 1891, in a popular magazine of England named 'Great Britain'. The idea was supported and put into practice by an Australian sportsman named Richard Cumbess. The festival was named 'Inter Empire Games'. Even the then ruler Kind George V also appreciated these games whole-heartedly. In 1928, the British felt the need of globalizing these games. The competitions held only in the games of athletics, swimming, heavy weight boxing and middle weight wrestling. The purpose of bringing the 'Inter Empire Games' to fore front in the world was to give opportunity to all current and past British colonies to participate and develop good relations with the British Empire. Thus in 1930, the first Commonwealth Games were organized at Hamilton, Canada. Total 11 countries participated in these games. In fact in 1958, the name was changed from 'British Empire Games to "Commonwealth Games".

History of Ancient Olympic Games

It is difficult to refer to the exact origin of the Olympic Games, but the first recorded ancient Olympic Games were held in 776 B.C, at 'Olympia' a small village township about 220 miles from 'Athens' capital city of Greece known for its unrivalled architecture, splendor, its stadia, gymnasiums and temples.

In ancient time, the Games formed part of a religious festival dedicated to the God Zeus. Both the sacred rituals and competitive events were regarded as offerings to the Gods. During the period of these games 'truce' was observed among the otherwise belligerent nations. A sacred flame was lit at the altar of God Zeus throughout the duration of games. The contestants fought for honours with purely competitive spirit. The winners were awarded Olive branch rather than medals or money as today. The winners became heroes: Olympic games were banned by Romans in 394 A.D. The monuments, temples, stadiums etc. were destroyed by Romans. They, in fact believed more in bloody battles and their past time was to see more blood. The sportsmanship was not their motto. Ancient Olympic games survived nearly 1200 years.

History of Modern Olympic Games

The credit of reviving Modern Olympic Games goes to French nobleman Baron Pierre-de-Coubertin. He went to Greece with an excavation team and found traces of ancient Olympic games through coins, wall pictures etc. Here, the idea of organizing Olympic games struck to his mind. He thought it as a great opportunity to bring the fighting nations together, through sports and games. He thought of bringing harmony and peace through organization of some mega sports event. During the fifth anniversary of the union of French Athletics and Sports Association in November, 1892, B. P. Coubertin announced his determination to revive the games on international lines with objectives like; wide participation in games and sports, high standard of international achievement in various physical activities and to promote international understanding, peace and friendship through healthy competition. The international congress reached consensus in June, 1994 to revive Olympic games.

Olympic flag: The Olympic flag was created and designed by Pierre de Coubertin in 1913, first displayed at the Olympic congress in 1914 and hoisted for the first time in 7th Olympic Games at Antwerp in 1920. The flag is white in base and five interlinked rings on the flag represent union of five continents Asia, Africa, Europe, North and South America. The white colour of the flag signifies, peace, serenity and purity of spirit.

Olympic Torch: The Olympic torch is lit from the altar of God Zeus in Greece and travels a long distance, passing through many hands ultimately to the venue of Olympic games. A renowned athlete of the host city lights the sacred flame at the stadium, where the Olympics are to be inaugurated. The Olympic flame leaps skywards and it burns throughout the games and is extinguished on the last day after all events have been completed.

Olympic Motto: The Olympic motto inscribed under the emblem consists of three Latin words.

CITIUS- Faster

ALTIUS- Higher

FORTIUS- Stronger

In literal meanings, the words on the Emblem represent athletic goals running faster, jumping as high as possible and throwing more strongly.

Philosophy of Existentialism in Relation with Sports and Physical Education

Literary meaning of existentialism is a philosophical theory emphasizing the existence of the individual person as a free and responsible agent determining his or her own development. This should be conceived as a purely individualization theory aiming at absolute freedom to the individual in all the matters concerning his life. An existentialist thinks that man's existence is the only true reality. A man is what he causes himself to become. He and not the society, should be responsible for his past, present and future. Although education should be individual oriented, certain activities in physical education are not possible without groups. Individual needs to be looked after as a separate identity but the team games in sports and physical education are aimed at developing, inculcating and maintaining the social values of discipline, obedience to law and many other social factors for all round development. So, existentialism with its extreme implications in physical education cannot be implemented as such yet there are many activities, which are done individually and not collectively.

Philosophy of Naturalism

The philosophy of naturalism is concerned with the world of nature as being the only thing that is real. Its earlier teachings came from Democritus. This philosophy rejects any reasoning that claims there is a supernatural power. According to this philosophy physical nature is the hub about which the universe revolves; it is the greatest reality. Whatever man is capable of accomplishing he can do only in so far as he adapts himself to nature.

Relation of Naturalization to physical education

1. Philosophy of naturalization maintains that education should be geared to the natural processes of growth and mental development, should be pleasurable, and should engage the spontaneous self activity of the child. Education of the body is important as well as education of the mind.
2. The physical education teacher as a naturalist must know what the needs of life are. What conditions do children normally lean towards to satisfy their needs. By what processes are these needs met, and what experiences on the playing field, in the gymnasium, or in the pool are best suited to meet their needs.
3. To aid children in reaching their optimum development, the physical activities must be given according to the children's needs and nature.

4. The physical education personnel should accept the fact that the child comes into the world with 'Unlearned cores of behaviour, tendencies to respond, which were once referred to as instincts. All normal children tend to be physically active, to be curious, to explore, to seek excitement and new experiences, to become increasingly gregarious and eventually social, and to play. These forms of behaviour are universal, and all educative efforts must start from such instinctive tendencies.
5. The earliest naturalists, like Rousseau stressed discipline by natural consequences. For example, if the child overeats, let him be sick, if he is slow to walk, let him be left alone. In fact let him suffer the natural results of violating any laws of nature. A child's play and games fall into the above category, for they provided success and failures, risks and thrills, victories and defeats. In games and sports; the child learns not only to control his body by more skilled and graceful movements but he also learns to control his emotions and becomes less clumsy in his social dealing with other children. Thus play is nature's means of education.

Philosophy of Pragmatism and its Relation to Physical Education and Sports

Pragmatism is also called Experi-mentalism. That is so because this kind of philosophy believed in dynamism. It believes that our key to life lies in experience, and experiences of life are ever changing. They are not static. Any idea or law or principle which cannot stand the test of practicability is useless. A pragmatist gives lot of importance to child's social interaction.

Relationship of pragmatism to physical education and sport.

1. A child should be given enough opportunity to participate in a variety of games. He learns more and his learning is more enriched through experiences of participation in varied activities. Every activity gives different rules to be followed in the activity. A child's experiences about the objects and surroundings are different in the outdoor and indoor activities. He learns differently while playing in water and while playing on musical instruments.
2. Physical activities are socializing in nature. Different activities which are organised in groups provide the child, a good experience of interacting with society and influence the peer group. He may be influenced by the peer group. The child learns group cohesion, fellow feeling and learns to cooperate and coordinate in the group activity.
3. The physical education programme should take into account the interests and needs of the learner. The physical education teacher should base his judgement on experiences. He has to see that the child's experience in swimming pool is wholesome so that the child returns to him for training again and again.
4. Pragmatism has success as its criterion. It gives more emphasis on more practice, than on theories and principles. The physical education teacher should not be rigid to rules and standardization is not a part of the programme. A P.E. T. should resort to trial and error method and then train. Training should be mainly practical.

Philosophy of Idealism

Philosophy of idealism believes that there is no matter in the world: all' that exists is the mind, or spirit. The philosophy of idealism originated with the Greeks, particularly so with Aristotle. As the name clearly shows, the philosophy of idealism aims at achieving ideals. There is a tendency to create perfection in everything in life. In other words, we fix up high standards in the matter of eating, drinking, walking dressing up etc. In all matters, we fix up high standards, or ideas, and then try our best to achieve them.

Relation of idealism to physical education: Man on this earth should have an ideal athletic body, knowledge of mathematics (which means all calculations) in his working life .and a very highly developed sense of beauty (Aesthetics). He must combine all three.

1. Physical education involves more than 'Physical'. Plato and Aristotle believed that the human's should possess an 'ideal body' which means harmoniously developed personality. The Greeks believed that both human mind and body should be equally strong and efficient.
2. The ideal of 'body-beautiful' was given by the Greeks. They believed in rearing only the strong new born babies and the weak babies used to be left to die an Mount Tagytus. They believed that ideally the human body should be robust, tough, well built and muscular.
3. The teacher is a model for students. He should be an ideal human being so that he can impart best training to the pupil. The teacher is responsible for the effectiveness of the programme.
4. The programme of physical education should aim at identifying the child's innate potentials. It is the function of a physical education teacher to produce such humans who could meet the ideals set by society.

Development of Physical Education and Sports in India During British Period

The Britishers came to India about two hundred years back. Slowly they began to occupy India and remained here as rulers till 15th August 1947. When East India Company came to India and established itself, the Britisher's introduced a number of games for the entertainment of their own people. It was at this time that the Indians were introduced to Cricket, Hockey, Football and Gymnastics. Development of physical education and sports in India during British period can be divided into four Stages :

1. **The *'Akhara'* Stage:** This period covers early 19th century. The 'Akhara' is place where a Guru imparted training to his disciples (students) in the arts ('wrestling fencing, archery, horse-riding). Some of the prominent gurus of this period were guru Balam Bhat, Dada Deodhar, Guru Damodar, Swami Achyu Nand and Narayan Guru.
2. ***'Vyayamshalla'* Stage:** During this period Lazium, Dand-baithak, Lathi etc. became popular. Prof. Mahak Rao prepared programme for the schools, ('Vyayamshallas' and also for institutions of higher learning. In a way Prof. Rao had transformed the Akharas into Vyayamshallas.
3. ***'Vyayam Prasarak'* Stage:** We can divide this into three parts:

(*i*) **Indigenous type of Vyayamshalla:** The objective was to popularise those exercises which were associated with Vyayamshallas. In Bombay, central provices and Bihar it became very popular. In 1914, Mandal in Amravati was set up. In 1924, the Gujrat VyayamShalla Mandal was set up in Ahamadabad and Vyayam Prasarak Mandal in Bhavnagar and Maharashatra Mandal in 1924.

(*ii*) **Gymnastic Institutions:** (Western Type)- The indigenous physical education institutions also adopted the western exercises like drill, the European games like Hockey, Gymnastics etc. The prominent institutions were Petitie Gymnastic Institution, 1958. These institutions trained teachers in various games.

(*iii*) Summer classes of school of Physical Education! Besides the above mentioned institutions, there were YMCA, YWCA etc. They conducted classes in summer. In 1908, Dr. LH. Grey and later on in 1913, P. C. Wren were running such schools, which became very popular.

Development of Physical Education in the Pre-Independence era in India

Development of Physical Education in the pre-independence period.

1. **Vedic Era:** The vedas are considered to be first ever ancient books. We find the mention of sauna bath and massage in 'rig ved'. In ancient times people observed two different kinds of Physical Education:

(*a*) Asanas

(*b*) Wrestling and Archery.

People observed 'celibacy' or 'Brahmacharya', till around twenty five years of age and did physical exercises like training in archery, dancing etc.

2. **Epic Era:** The Epic period was the period of 'Ramayana' and 'Mahabharata', the two holy epics of the Hindus. Ramayana has the mention of Archery, horse riding and wrestling. Great physical endeavours were made during the fight between 'Ravana' and 'Rama'. Similarly in Mahabharata, there is a mention of wrestling. 'Bhim' was a symbol of body beautiful and immense physical power.
3. **Nalanda Period:** The Chinese travelers in India have thrown some light on the different games played in Nalanda University. We learn that competitions were arranged. Physical exercises occupied an important place in daily life. Taxila was well known for its high degree of military training.
4. **Rajput Period:** Maharana Pratap, the great Rajput warrior was proficient in throwing Bhala, Neza and was perfect horse rider. Rajput Kings used to love hunting, wrestling and fencing tournaments.
5. **Muslim Period:** Muslims destroyed lots of cities made by Hindu kings. They were very active in keeping themselves fit for wars and used to participate in activities like wrestling, chaugan, boxing, swimming, chariot racing, chess, kite flying etc.
6. **British Period:** The Britishers came to India after crushing Muslims and ruled India for 200 years. They were hard task masters. During British rule, Indigenous games of India were forced to take back seat. Although India gave the game of Badminton (Poona) to world, but English took this game from India and gave it the new name 'Badminton' during British period. Games like cricket, hockey, football and gymnastics became very popular. The Britishers influenced the minds of Indian people to a great extent and even today we see many people in India reeling under the impression that foreign games like Rugby, Ice Hockey, Roller Skating, Golf etc., are better than the indigenous sports like Kabaddi, Kho-kho, Malkhamb etc.

EXERCISE

1. In which events, did India win gold medal in Beijing Olympics?
   (*a*) Shooting (*b*) Swimming
   (*c*) Boxing (*d*) Archery
2. How many records were broken at Beijing Olympics?
   (*a*) 35 (*b*) 43
   (*c*) 48 (*d*) 54
3. What rank did India achieve in Beijing Olympics?
   (*a*) 50 (*b*) 45
   (*c*) 62 (*d*) 71
4. How many countries were first-time medal winners among 87 countries who won medals in Beijing Olympics?
   (*a*) 15 (*b*) 5
   (*c*) 12 (*d*) 8
5. The exponent of modern Olympic Games B. P. Coubertin belongs to—
   (*a*) France (*b*) England
   (*c*) USA (*d*) Denamrk
6. Which Indian Captain mounted on the victory stand for first time during Olympics?
   (*a*) Dhyan Chand
   (*b*) Jaipal Singh
   (*c*) K. D. Singh "Babu"
   (*d*) Kapil Dev
7. In which year the National Anthem of India was played for the first time in Olympics?
   (*a*) 1948 (*b*) 1952
   (*c*) 1928 (*d*) 1932
8. "Mesomorphy" is characterized by—
   (*a*) linearity and tallness
   (*b*) roundless of the body

(*c*) muscularity and strength
(*d*) does not relate to any of the above.

9. "Lean Body Mass" is—
(*a*) muscle, bone and other non-fat tissues of the body
(*b*) fatty tissues of the body
(*c*) total body weight
(*d*) none of the above

10. Which of the following is considered for preparing the physical profile of a sports person?
(*a*) Weight (*b*) Height
(*c*) Both (*a*) and (*b*) (*d*) Muscle Strength

11. "Endomorph" is characterized by—
(*a*) thin and lethargic
(*b*) flabby and fat
(*c*) muscular and athletic
(*d*) none of the above

12. Hockey matches in the Olympics were organized for the first time on Astro turf at—
(*a*) Los Angeles (*b*) Montreal
(*c*) Moscow (*d*) Seoul

13. "Altius" in the Olympic motto "Citius Altius Fortius" stands for—
(*a*) faster (*b*) stronger
(*c*) higher (*d*) deeper

14. Who coined the Olympic motto "Citius, Altius, Fortius"?
(*a*) Rousseau (*b*) Arsitotle
(*c*) Plato (*d*) Henry Didion

15. Who are the participants in Special Olympics?
(*a*) Physically handicapped
(*b*) Mentally retarted children and adults
(*c*) Both (*a*) and (*b*)
(*d*) Veterans

16. Which country hosted the first "Special Olympics"?
(*a*) USA (*b*) England
(*c*) India (*d*) Germany

17. Who equalled the Jesse Owens fete of winning four medals in different events in Olympics?
(*a*) Marion Jones (*b*) Michael Johnson
(*c*) Carl Lewis (*d*) Ben Johnson

18. Atlanta Olympics marked—
(*a*) Centenary of modern Olympics
(*b*) First time Olympics in USA
(*c*) Olympics in North America
(*d*) None of the above.

19. "Physical education is a fundamental right of every citizen" is included in—
(*a*) WHO Charter
(*b*) SNIPES Charter
(*c*) HRD Ministry Charter
(*d*) UNESCO Charter

20. The first Olympic Games were held in Olympia (Greece) in the year—
(*a*) 300 BC (*b*) 872 BC
(*c*) 776 BC (*d*) 205 AD

21. Which of the following is a Kretschmer's body classification?
(*a*) Dyplastic (*b*) Mesomorph
(*c*) Ectomorph (*d*) Endomorph

22. Sheldon's body types classification is—
(*a*) endomorph (*b*) mesomorph
(*c*) ectomorph (*d*) all of the above

23. Who started turnverein movement in Germany?
(*a*) Ludwig John
(*b*) Johann Base Dow
(*c*) Fredrick Gutsmuth
(*d*) None of the above

24. Where will the 30th Olympic Games be held in 2012?
(*a*) Canada (*b*) U.K.
(*c*) Japan (*d*) Germany

25. Which country experienced physical education as a "Golden Age"?
(*a*) Rome (*b*) Germany
(*c*) Ancient Greece (*d*) USA

26. Which organisation leads the Olympic Movement within each country?
(*a*) NOC (*b*) IOC
(*c*) IFC (*d*) NGB

27. Who designed the Olympic emblem?
(*a*) Pierre de Coubertin
(*b*) King George
(*c*) Demetrius Vikelas
(*d*) Henri de Baillet

28. Who suggested the idea of Olympic flame?
(*a*) Pierre de Coubertin
(*b*) Theordore Lewald
(*c*) Sondre Nordheim
(*d*) Stein Grubem

29. Which Olympics were the first to be televised live?
(*a*) Berlin, 1936
(*b*) London, 1948
(*c*) Helsinki, 1952
(*d*) Rome, 1960

30. When were the women participants formally admitted to Olympic Games?
(*a*) Berlin, 1936 (*b*) London, 1908
(*c*) St. Louis, 1904 (*d*) Stockholm, 1912

31. The ancient Olympics were abolished by–
(*a*) Greeks (*b*) Romans
(*c*) Germans (*d*) Egyptians

32. The ancient Olympics were abolished in the year–
(*a*) 394 A.D. (*b*) 349 A.D.
(*c*) 341 A.D. (*d*) 350 A.D

33. Who was the founder of School of Gymnastics in Germany?
(*a*) Ling (*b*) Nachtegall
(*c*) Rousseau (*d*) Adoplh Spiess

34. Who is symbolic of the rise of physical education in Sweden?
(*a*) Franz Nachtegall
(*b*) V. A. Blyakh
(*c*) Per Henrik Zing
(*d*) Spiess

35. Who postulated the Surplus energy theory of play?
(*a*) Patricks
(*b*) Lumley
(*c*) Spencer and Schiller
(*d*) G. Stanely Hall

36. Which theory of play maintains that "past is the key to play"?
(*a*) Instinct or Gross theory
(*b*) Inheritance or Recapitulation theory
(*c*) Self Expression theory
(*d*) Recreation theory

37. Who said that "Play is the natural unfolding of germinal leaves of childhood"?
(*a*) William Mcdaughall
(*b*) Roger Caillois
(*c*) Froebel
(*d*) Patricks

38. Social contact theory of play was postulated by–
(*a*) Bernard S. Mason (*b*) G. Stanley Hall
(*c*) Lumley (*d*) Patricks

39. What is chronological age?
(*a*) Age in years, months and days
(*b*) Indicated by bones and dentition
(*c*) Determined by signs of puberty
(*d*) Determined by use of intelligence tests

40. Which age is determined by signs of puberty?
(*a*) Chronological Age
(*b*) Anatomical age
(*c*) Physiological age
(*d*) Mental age

41. The physical growth of the child is most rapid–
(*a*) upto 3 years
(*b*) between 6 and 10 years
(*c*) between 13 and 19 years
(*d*) between 19 and 25 years

42. The growth of females is more rapid than boys in–
(*a*) 6-10 years (*b*) 13-19 years
(*c*) 19-25 years (*d*) above 25 years

43. Which of the following is not the benefit of exercise?
(*a*) Reduce fat
(*b*) Maintain blood pressure
(*c*) Injuries
(*d*) Freedom from diseases

44. Which of the Kretchmer's body type classification means 'thick' in Greek?
(*a*) Pyknic (*b*) Athletic
(*c*) Asthenic (*d*) Dyplastic

45. Which of the following refers to Asthenic body type?
(*a*) Short thick

(b) Muscular
(c) Lean, shallow chested
(d) Abnormal bodies

46. By which of the following means do we acquire values, beliefs and behaviour?
(a) Socialization
(b) Culture
(c) Recreation
(d) Physical Education

47. The ancient Olympics were held in which months?
(a) July-August
(b) August-September
(c) September-October
(d) October-November

48. Which event was the first and the original event for Olympics?
(a) Foot race (b) Chariot race
(c) Boxing (d) Wrestling

49. The first Olympic event lasted for how many days in 776 B. C.?
(a) One day (b) Two days
(c) Three days (d) Four days

50. The festival for women held in honour of the wife of God Zeus was–
(a) Helena (b) Heraca
(c) Horkios (d) Olympics

51. The ancient Olympics were closed down due to a degree passed by–
(a) Theodousis I (b) Augeas
(c) Pelops (d) Heracles

52. There was a break of how many centuries between the modern and ancient Olympics?
(a) 13 centuries (b) 15 centuries
(c) 16 centuries (d) 14 centuries

53. The modern Olympics were revived in–
(a) 1900 AD (b) 1897 AD
(c) 1896 AD (d) 1894 AD

54. The ancient Olympics lasted for how many centuries?
(a) 10 (b) 11
(c) 12 (d) 13

55. How many Olympic games in all were held in ancient Olympic games?
(a) 290 (b) 291
(c) 292 (d) 293

56. The revival of modern Olympics was due to hard work of–
(a) George Averoff
(b) Phedippides
(c) Frenchman
(d) Pierre de Coubertin

57. The first modern Olympics were held in–
(a) Olympia (b) Athens
(c) St. Louis (d) Antwerp

58. The venue of the modern Olympics is fixed by–
(a) International Olympic Committee
(b) National Olympic Committee
(c) International Sports Federations
(d) Participants of various countries.

59. The president of International Olympic Committee is selected for–
(a) Four years (b) Two years
(c) Twelve years (d) Eight years

60. Which of the following is not a rule for eligibility for competition?
(a) To be a native or naturalized subject of a member country.
(b) Onc should play only for one country and not for another country in the next Olympics.
(c) One should be amateur.
(d) One should be below 40.

61. The ceremonial Olympic flag was first used in–
(a) Antwerp, 1920
(b) Paris, 1900
(c) London, 1908
(d) Paris, 1924

62. Match the following years with the venues of Olympic games–

(a)	1948	I	Moscow
(b)	1980	II	London
(c)	1956	III	Rome
(d)	1960	IV	Melbourne

Codes :
(*a*) A-I, B-III, C-IV, D-II
(*b*) A-II, B-I, C-IV, D-III
(*c*) A-II, B-I, C-III, D-IV
(*d*) A-III, B-II, C-IV, D-I

63. Winter Olympics, 2010 were held in—
(*a*) Paris (*b*) Beijing
(*c*) Kuala Lumpur (*d*) Vancouver

64. In which Summer Olympics, did India win gold in individual event?
(*a*) Seoul, 1988 (*b*) Moscow, 1980
(*c*) Beijing, 2008 (*d*) Athens, 2004

65. Who broke Mark Spitz's record of seven gold haul in swimming in Bejing Olympics, 2008?
(*a*) Ian Thorpe (*b*) Michael Phelps
(*c*) Nathan Adrian (*d*) David Walters

66. The winter Olympics were introduced in the year–
(*a*) 1942 (*b*) 1956
(*c*) 1952 (*d*) 1924

67. In Taxila University, training of which sports was at its peak?
(*a*) Chariot racing (*b*) Marathon
(*c*) Archery (*d*) Akharas

68. In which year did All India Council of Sports came into being?
(*a*) 1954 (*b*) 1952
(*c*) 1956 (*d*) 1955

69. In India, National Fitness Corps was set up in–
(*a*) 1954 (*b*) 1971
(*c*) 1959 (*d*) 1965

70. Which of the following body types are characterized by delicate body structure and poor digestive system?
(*a*) Endomorph (*b*) Mesomorph
(*c*) Ectomorph d) Athletic

71. The headquarters of IOC are located in–
(*a*) France (*b*) U.K.
(*c*) U. S. A. (*d*) Switzerland

72. Of the following, which Indian has not been the member of IOC?
(*a*) Sir Darabji Jamshedji Tata
(*b*) G. D. Sondhi
(*c*) S. Randhir Singh
(*d*) Vallabh Bhai Patel

73. In which of the following years, the Olympic games were not cancelled–
(*a*) 1912 (*b*) 1916
(*c*) 1940 (*d*) 1944

74. What is the maximum duration of days for which the Olympic games are held?
(*a*) 12 days (*b*) 14 days
(*c*) 15 days (*d*) 16 days

75. During closing ceremony of Olympic games which of the following flags is not hoisted?
(*a*) Greek flag
(*b*) Host country's flag
(*c*) Winner Country's flag
(*d*) Next country's flag (where next Olympics are held)

76. The torch ceremony in Olympic Games was introduced during–
(*a*) London Olympics, 1948
(*b*) Tokyo Olympics, 1964
(*c*) Seoul Olympics, 1988
(*d*) Berlin Olympics, 1936

77. Asian Games were conceived by–
(*a*) G. D. Sondhi
(*b*) Jawaharlal Nehru
(*c*) Maharaja Yaduvendra Singh
(*d*) M. C. Dhawan

78. The first Asian Games were held in the year–
(*a*) 1949 (*b*) 1951
(*c*) 1950 (*d*) 1952

79. The first Asian Games were held in–
(*a*) Pakistan (*b*) Japan
(*c*) China (*d*) India

80. In 2014, the Asian Games will be held in–
(*a*) India (*b*) Japan
(*c*) Thailand (*d*) South Korea

81. The city 'Olympia" is in –
(*a*) Rome (*b*) Italy
(*c*) Greece (*d*) Germany

82. Olympiad refers to–
(*a*) Olympics
(*b*) Period between two Olympics
(*c*) Place in Greece
(*d*) Olympic medal

83. The Olympic motto 'Fortius' means–
(*a*) higher (*b*) faster
(*c*) stronger (*d*) none

84. Which place in Greece developed into an institution where people engaged in physical activity?
(*a*) Athens (*b*) Olympia
(*c*) Palaestra (*d*) None of the above

85. Which of the following organizations controls the participation of Indian teams in Olympic Games?
(*a*) IOC (*b*) AAFI
(*c*) IOA (*d*) OCA

86. Who is the President of Indian Olympic Association?
(*a*) Milkha Singh
(*b*) B. B. Bhagwat
(*c*) Suresh Kalmadi
(*d*) Raja Bhalindra Singh

87. The highest award given to sports coaches in India is–
(*a*) Arjuna Award
(*b*) Khel Ratna Award
(*c*) Ati Vashisth Jyoti
(*d*) Dronacharya Award

88. National game of India is–
(*a*) Cricket (*b*) Fotoball
(*c*) Kabaddi (*d*) Hockey

89. The term 'Marathon" Race is named after a–
(*a*) person (*b*) place
(*c*) foot race (*d*) chariot race

90. The number of schools of thought associated with philosophy are–
(*a*) one (*b*) two
(*c*) three (*d*) four

91. Which of the following is also called the cognitive learning?
(*a*) Affective Learning
(*b*) Mental Learning
(*c*) Motor learning
(*d*) None of the above

92. The theory of 'conditioned response' was given by–
(*a*) Pavlov (*b*) Freud
(*c*) Skinner (*d*) Jung

93. Who is known as the father of Naturalism?
(*a*) Aristotle (*b*) Pavlov
(*c*) Rossoeau (*d*) Plato

94. Which philosophy of education emphasizes that experience is key to life?
(*a*) Existentialism (*b*) Realism
(*c*) Pragmatism (*d*) Idealism

95. Plato is considered the father of which Philosophy of Education?
(*a*) Idealism (*b*) Naturalism
(*c*) Realism (*d*) Existentialism

96. Which Philosophy of Education defines teacher as a role model of students?
(*a*) Idealism (*b*) Naturalism
(*c*) Realism (*d*) Existentialism

97. When did Russians first participate in World Olympics?
(*a*) 1948 (*b*) 1952
(*c*) 1956 (*d*) 1960

98. Who was the first recorded winner of ancient Olympics?
(*a*) Hera (*b*) Iphitos
(*c*) Koroibos (*d*) Coubertin

99. Which country topped in Medal Tally in XXIX Beijng Olympics, 2008?
(*a*) China (*b*) USA
(*c*) Russia (*d*) Germany

100. The First Olympic winter games were held in–
(*a*) USA (*b*) Germany
(*c*) Norway (*d*) France

101. What is the aim of Physical Education?
(*a*) Physical development
(*b*) A wholesome development of an individual
(*c*) Growth and development
(*d*) All of the above.

102. What is the philosophy of physical education programmes?
(*a*) Realism (*b*) Pragmatism
(*c*) Idealism (*d*) All of the above

103. Who among the following started the custom of carrying the flaming torch from Athens to the site of Olympic Games?
(*a*) Adolf Hitler (*b*) King George – 1
(*c*) Plato (*d*) Aristotle

104. The Olympic flag consists of—
(*a*) white background with no border & Olympic symbol in the centre
(*b*) white background with black border & Olympic symbol in the centre.
(*c*) yellow background with black border & Olympic symbol on the top right corner.
(*d*) grey background with no border & Olympic symbol in the centre.

105. Under whose control were the first Olympic Games held?
(*a*) King George - II
(*b*) King George - I
(*c*) Theodosius
(*d*) Martin Luthar King

106. Which of the following statements about the first modern Olympic Games is true?
(*a*) All the participating members were female
(*b*) All the participating members were Greek
(*c*) All the participating members were male
(*d*) All the participating members were Romans

107. Women had separate competitions in games during Olympics which were held at Olympion in the honour of—
(*a*) God Zeus (*b*) Goddess Hera
(*c*) God Apollo (*d*) None of the above

108. The word "athlete" in Greek means—
(*a*) a city state (*b*) money maker
(*c*) prize seeker (*d*) race

109. In which Olympics was it discovered that drugs are being used for performance enhancement?
(*a*) 1960 Rome (*b*) 1988 Seoul
(*c*) 1992 Barcelona (*d*) 1996 Atlanta

110. What was "Takshashila", in ancient times famous for?
(*a*) Sham battles (*b*) Horse Riding
(*c*) Archery Traning (*d*) Chariot Racing

111. Which Muslim ruler died after falling from his horse while playing "Polo"?
(*a*) Babar (*b*) Qutub din Aibek
(*c*) Jahangir (*d*) Akbar

112. When was the YMCA (Chennai) College of Physical Education formed?
(*a*) 1914 (*b*) 1896
(*c*) 1920 (*d*) 1924

113. Who was the first principal of YMCA College of Physical Education?
(*a*) G. D. Sondhi (*b*) H. C. Buck
(*c*) B. P. Coubertin (*d*) C. A. Bucher

114. Who was the first person to receive "Rajiv Gandhi Khel Ratna" Award?
(*a*) K. Malleshwari
(*b*) Baichung Bhutia
(*c*) Vishwanathan Anand
(*d*) Sachin Tendulkar

115. Olympic rings indicate—
(*a*) five continents (*b*) five rivers
(*c*) five countries (*d*) five mountains

116. "Phillipides" was a—
(*a*) Anthenian Greek (*b*) Spartan Greek
(*c*) Roman (*d*) None of the above

117. Which Mughal emperor was associated with the game of "Polo"?
(*a*) Babar (*b*) Aurangzeb
(*c*) Jahangir (*d*) Akbar

118. "Agoge" was in—
(*a*) Greece (*b*) Rome
(*c*) Iran (*d*) China

119. Who was the pioneer of Medical Gymnastics?
(*a*) Rosseau (*b*) Gestalt
(*c*) Arsitotle (*d*) Hyppocrates

120. In which year were the Winter Olympics held for the first time?
(*a*) 1923 (*b*) 1924
(*c*) 1925 (*d*) 1926

121. When and where was the Olympic flag used for the first time?

(a) 1896, Athens Olympics
(b) 1996, Atlanta Olympics
(c) 1920, Antwerp Olympics
(d) None of the above

122. Indian Olympics Association was formed in the year–
(a) 1927 (b) 1928
(c) 1929 (d) 1930

123. For the first time, who won gold for India in an individual event in Beijing Olympics, 2008?
(a) Sushil Kumar (b) Gagan Narang
(c) Abhinav Bindra (d) Vijender Kumar

124. What is the duration of Summer Olympic Games?
(a) 16 days (b) 17 days
(c) 18 days (d) 19 days

125. In which year, were the ancient Olympic Games banned?
(a) 396 A.D. (b) 394 A.D.
(c) 296 A.D. (d) 334 B.C.

126. "Agoge" in ancient Greece meant—
(a) formal system of education
(b) informal system of education
(c) reading, writing, playing
(d) all of the above.

127. What was "Palaestra" famous for, in the ancient Greece?
(a) It was a wrestling school
(b) It was a music school
(c) It was a stadium
(d) It was a swimming pool

128. "Didascaleum" in the ancient Greece was famous for—
(a) aerobics (b) dance
(c) music (d) weight training

129. Where were the 15th Asian Games held?
(a) Tehran (b) Doha
(c) Tokyo (d) Busan

130. Which of the following Asian countries hosted the first Common Wealth Games?
(a) Malaysia (b) China
(c) Japan (d) Pakistan

131. Which of following games were included in the Asian Games held in 1998?
(a) Basketball and Volleyball
(b) Snooker and Billiards
(c) Squash and Tennis
(d) Kabaddi and Kho-Kho

132. Sports Authority of India was formed in the year—
(a) 1983 (b) 1984
(c) 1985 (d) 1986

133. In ancient Greece, the 'sky god' was—
(a) Poseidon (b) Apollo
(c) Zeus (d) None of the above

134. In ancient Greece, the 'God of sea' was—
(a) Poseidon (b) Apollo
(c) Zeus (d) None of the above

135. In the ancient Greece, 'Apollo" was—
(a) God of Sea (b) God of healing
(c) God of fire (d) God of water

136. Word "Diskos" in Greek meant—
(a) a thing for throwing
(b) a thing for pushing
(c) a thing for eating
(d) a thing for playing

137. The main profession of the Greeks was—
(a) agriculture (b) pottery
(c) playing (d) music

138. A weak child born, used to be left on the "Mount Tygatus" for dying, in—
(a) Athens (b) Rome
(c) Sparta (d) None of the above

139. In Sparta, at the age of 18, the boys were enrolled for in the secret corps known as—
(a) Dedascalum
(b) Palaestra
(c) Crypteia
(d) None of the above.

140. Sports grounds in Sparta were called—
(a) Paedotribes (b) Crypteia
(c) Platanistas (d) Dedascaleum

141. Who were the first to strip naked in the competitions?

(a) Athenians (b) Spartans
(c) Romans (d) None of the above

142. Who invented use of "oil" in the gymnasium?
(a) Romans (b) Athenian
(c) Spartans (d) None of the above

143. The slave tutors who used to teach at home were called—
(a) paedotribes (b) pedagogue
(c) platanistas (d) none of the above

144. "Palaestra" was formed for—
(a) gymnastics (b) music
(c) swimming (d) arithmetic

145. In Athens, the boys were enrolled in Cadet Corps called—
(a) crypteia (b) epheboi
(c) pedagogue (d) ecclesia

146. Lyceum, the public gymnasia was related with—
(a) Rousseau (b) Aristotle
(c) God Zeus (d) None of the above

147. The teachers of ball who worked under the instructions from the paidotribes were called—
(a) Paidogogue (b) Epheboi
(c) Sphairistes (d) Spartans

148. Teachers of Archery in the ancient Greece were known as—
(a) Sphairistes (b) Paido tribes
(c) Ecclesia (d) Toxotes

149. The masseurs in the ancient Greece were known as—
(a) toxotes (b) aleiptae
(c) paido tribes (d) epheboi

150. Mud bath was popular in—
(a) Athens (b) Sparta
(c) Rome (d) None of the above

151. The word "athlete" originated in —
(a) Rome (b) Greece
(c) China (d) India

152. Meaning of word athlete was—
(a) "the contest"
(b) 'the prize'
(c) 'the strong man'
(d) 'the slave'

153. The Greeks emphasized more upon—
(a) individualism
(b) naturalism
(c) professionalism
(d) none of the above

154. What is the motto written on the shrine of God Apollo, in Greece?
(a) Meden Agan
(b) Citius Altius Fortius
(c) Ever onward
(d) None of the above

155. Which of the following games were held in the honour of God Poseidon?
(a) Isthmian (b) Nemean
(c) Pythian (d) Plympics

156. Which games were held in the honour of God Zeus?
(a) Pythian (b) Nemean
(c) Isthmian (d) None of the above

157. Which games were held in the honour of God Apollo?
(a) Nemean Games (b) Isthmian Games
(c) Phythian Games (d) None of the above

158. The ancient Olympic Games were banned by which emperor?
(a) Aristotle (b) Poseidon
(c) Theodoseus (d) None of the above

159. What type of track was made, for foot races, by the Greeks?
(a) Round track (b) Straight track
(c) Oval track (d) Hilly track

160. In "pentathlon' what does 'penta' and 'athlon' stands for?
(a) Five and prize
(b) Six and flower
(c) Five and leaves
(d) Six and individual

161. "Plato" earned proficiency in the game of—
(a) Golf (b) Wrestling
(c) Judo (d) Swimming

162. Who was the founder of 'lyceum'?
(a) Rousseau (b) Aristotle
(c) Galen (d) Plato

163. Who among the following first classified different exercises?
(*a*) Plato (*b*) Galen
(*c*) Aristotle (*d*) Rousseau

164. The principles of physical training were first prescribed by—
(*a*) Galen (*b*) Plato
(*c*) Rousseau (*d*) Aristotle

165. "Palaestra" and "Didascaleum" were famous in—
(*a*) Athens (*b*) Sparta
(*c*) Rome (*d*) Both (*a*) and (*b*)

166. "Palaestra" was famous for—
(*a*) music
(*b*) grammar
(*c*) both (*a*) and (*b*)
(*d*) swimming and bathing

167. "Didascaleum" was a place for—
(*a*) music (*b*) grammar
(*c*) both (*a*) and (*b*) (*d*) none of the above

168. In Rome, training was given to boys—
(*a*) by their fathers
(*b*) by their mothers
(*c*) by their teachers
(*d*) none of the above.

169. "Campus Martius" in the ancient Rome was—
(*a*) a military ground
(*b*) a place for music and grammar
(*c*) a place for swimming and bathing
(*d*) none of the above

170. What was the favourite pastime of Romans?
(*a*) Music
(*b*) Dance
(*c*) Gladiatorial Combats
(*d*) Playing games

171. "Colosseum" in the ancient Rome was famous for—
(*a*) Horse racing
(*b*) Judo
(*c*) Swimming
(*d*) Gladiatorial Comabts

172. Which of the following represents the correct combination of colours of Olympic rings?
(*a*) Blue, Yellow, Black, Green. Red
(*b*) Brown, Blue, Yellow, Black, Red
(*c*) Purple, Green, Red, Pink, Yellow
(*d*) Blue, Yellow, Brown, Green, Purple

173. To which of the following is the hosting of Olympic Games awarded?
(*a*) To the district (*b*) To the country
(*c*) To the city (*d*) To the capital

174. Which Olympics were longest as per their duration in days?
(*a*) 1906 (*b*) 1908
(*c*) 1952 (*d*) 1956

175. How many cities have hosted Olympics more than twice?
(*a*) 2 (*b*) 3
(*c*) 4 (*d*) 5

176. To whom does the Olympic movement in India owe its birth?
(*a*) Pt. Jawahar Lal Nehru
(*b*) Sir Dorabji Tata
(*c*) B. P. Coubertein
(*d*) Maharaja Yadavendra Singh

177. What award was given to the winners in the ancient Olympic Games?
(*a*) Coins
(*b*) Caps
(*c*) Wild Olive leaf crowns
(*d*) Medals

178. Which Indian has the most Olympic appearances to his credit?
(*a*) Dr. Randhir Singh Karni
(*b*) Yadvindra Singh
(*c*) Khazan Singh
(*d*) None of the above.

179. Who inaugurated the first modern Olympic games in 1896?
(*a*) King George II of Greece
(*b*) King George I of Greece
(*c*) Mrs. Margaret Thatcher
(*d*) B. P. Coubertin

180. In which Olympics did women, participate for the first time?
(*a*) 1896, Athens (*b*) 1900, Paris
(*c*) 1920, Antwerp (*d*) None of the above

181. What are events in the modern pentathlon in Olympics?
(*a*) Riding, fencing, shooting, swimming and cross country racing
(*b*) Shooting, swimming, horse racing, fencing and cross country racing
(*c*) javelin, discus, hammer, long jump and high jump
(*d*) None of these

182. How many entries per event are allowed in Olympics?
(*a*) 2 (*b*) 3
(*c*) 4 (*d*) 5

183. In which year were the interim Olympic held?
(*a*) 1896 (*b*) 1906
(*c*) 1908 (*d*) 1916

184. What was the punishment given to the cheaters in the ancient Olympics?
(*a*) They used to be hanged
(*b*) They used to be drowned
(*c*) They used to be beaten with hunters
(*d*) They used to be detained.

185. Which Roman King won prizes in the ancient Olympics by bribing the officials?
(*a*) King George (*b*) Theodosius I
(*c*) King Nero (*d*) Arsitotle

186. In which Olympics were gold medals first given to the winners?
(*a*) 1928, Antwerp (*b*) 1908, London
(*c*) 1900, Paris (*d*) 1896, Athens

187. In which year did B. P. Coubertin, father of Modern Olympics, died?
(*a*) 1937 (*b*) 1938
(*c*) 1939 (*d*) 1940

188. How many countries participated in the first modern Olympics in 1986?
(*a*) 11 (*b*) 12
(*c*) 13 (*d*) 14

189. In which Olympics was the Olympic oath administered for the first time?
(*a*) 1896, Athens (*b*) 1900, Paris
(*c*) 1908, London (*d*) 1920, Antwerp

190. Which of the following has been the highest venue for Olympics?
(*a*) Atlanta (*b*) Mexico
(*c*) Paris (*d*) Los Angeles

191. Iliad and Odyssey were authored by—
(*a*) Homer (*b*) Plato
(*c*) Socrates (*d*) None of the above

192. "Body Beautiful" was the ideal of—
(*a*) Greeks (*b*) Indians
(*c*) Romans (*d*) Egyptians

193. The term "citius" in the Olympic motto denotes—
(*a*) higher (*b*) faster
(*c*) stronger (*d*) all of the above

194. The body which controls the participation of the Indian teams in Olympic games is—
(*a*) A. A. F. I. (*b*) I. O. C.
(*c*) I. O. A. (*d*) O. C. A.

195. Which of the following events constituted pentathlon in ancient Olympics?
(*a*) Running, Jumping, Discus, Javelin and Wrestling
(*b*) Running, Jumping, Discus, Swimming and Chariot Racing
(*c*) Boxing, Wrestling, Running, Jumping and Swimming
(*d*) None of the above

196. Which city/ state emphasized on the training of warriors through education?
(*a*) Peking (*b*) Sparta
(*c*) Athens (*d*) All of the above

197. The aim of Spartan education was to produce—
(*a*) intellectuals (*b*) good citizens
(*c*) warriors (*d*) all of the above

198. What is the name of the stadium where the first modern Olympic games' were held in 1896?
(*a*) Pan Atheniac stadium, Athens
(*b*) Amphitheratre
(*c*) Colosseum
(*d*) Dedascaleum

199. Who suggested modern pentathlon in Olympics?
(*a*) G. D. Sondhi (*b*) J. A. Samaranch
(*c*) B. P. Coubertin (*d*) Bill Clinton

200. Who among the following, declares the Olympic Games closed?
(*a*) Chairman I. O. C.
(*b*) President I. O. C.
(*c*) Secretary I. O. C.
(*d*) Prime Minister of the country

201. In which Paralympics, did India win a gold medal for first-time in javelin throw event?
(*a*) Tokyo, 1964 (*b*) Toronto, 1976
(*c*) Athens, 2004 (*d*) Beijing, 2008

202. The number of members of IOC on its inception were—
(*a*) 12 (*b*) 13
(*c*) 14 (*d*) 15

203. Who was the first IOC President?
(*a*) Pierre de Coubertin
(*b*) Avery Brundage
(*c*) Lord Killanin
(*d*) Demetrius Vikelas

204. Who served as the President of IOC for maximum years?
(*a*) Demetrius Vikelas
(*b*) Avery Brundage
(*c*) Heni de Baillet
(*d*) Pierre de Coubertin

205. 'Come Out And Play' was the anthem of:
(*a*) Olympic Games 2008
(*b*) Asian Games 2010
(*c*) National Games 2010
(*d*) Common Wealth Games 2010

206. What is "a state of complete physical, mental and social well being and not merely the absence of disease and deformity"?
(*a*) Physiology (*b*) Recreation
(*c*) Health (*d*) Growth

207. Physical education as well as sports experienced a 'golden age' in which ancient country?
(*a*) Greece (*b*) Italy
(*c*) Rome (*d*) Germany

208. In which Paralympics, for the first time competition for medals was partially started for blind athletes?
(*a*) Heidelberg, 1972 (*b*) Toronto, 1976
(*c*) Aanhim, 1980 (*d*) Tokyo, 1964

209. Which country topped in medal tally in Bejing Paralympics, 2008?
(*a*) USA (*b*) China
(*c*) Great Britain (*d*) Canada

210. The Olympic games are held every—
(*a*) third year (*b*) fifty year
(*c*) second year (*d*) fourth year

ANSWERS

1	2	3	4	5	6	7	8	9	10
(*a*)	(*b*)	(*a*)	(*b*)	(*a*)	(*b*)	(*a*)	(*c*)	(*a*)	(*c*)
11	**12**	**13**	**14**	**15**	**16**	**17**	**18**	**19**	**20**
(*b*)	(*b*)	(*c*)	(*d*)	(*b*)	(*a*)	(*c*)	(*a*)	(*d*)	(*c*)
21	**22**	**23**	**24**	**25**	**26**	**27**	**28**	**29**	**30**
(*a*)	(*d*)	(*a*)	(*b*)	(*c*)	(*a*)	(*a*)	(*b*)	(*a*)	(*d*)
31	**32**	**33**	**34**	**35**	**36**	**37**	**38**	**39**	**40**
(*b*)	(*a*)	(*d*)	(*c*)	(*c*)	(*b*)	(*c*)	(*c*)	(*a*)	(*c*)
41	**42**	**43**	**44**	**45**	**46**	**47**	**48**	**49**	**50**
(*a*)	(*b*)	(*c*)	(*a*)	(*c*)	(*a*)	(*b*)	(*a*)	(*a*)	(*b*)
51	**52**	**53**	**54**	**55**	**56**	**57**	**58**	**59**	**60**
(*a*)	(*b*)	(*c*)	(*c*)	(*d*)	(*d*)	(*b*)	(*a*)	(*d*)	(*d*)
61	**62**	**63**	**64**	**65**	**66**	**67**	**68**	**69**	**70**
(*a*)	(*b*)	(*d*)	(*c*)	(*d*)	(*d*)	(*c*)	(*a*)	(*d*)	(*c*)
71	**72**	**73**	**74**	**75**	**76**	**77**	**78**	**79**	**80**
(*d*)	(*d*)	(*a*)	(*d*)	(*c*)	(*d*)	(*a*)	(*b*)	(*d*)	(*d*)

81	82	83	84	85	86	87	88	89	90
(*c*)	(*b*)	(*c*)	(*c*)	(*c*)	(*c*)	(*d*)	(*d*)	(*b*)	(*d*)
91	**92**	**93**	**94**	**95**	**96**	**97**	**98**	**99**	**100**
(*b*)	(*a*)	(*c*)	(*c*)	(*a*)	(*a*)	(*b*)	(*c*)	(*a*)	(*d*)
101	**102**	**103**	**104**	**105**	**106**	**107**	**108**	**109**	**110**
(*b*)	(*b*)	(*a*)	(*a*)	(*b*)	(*b*)	(*b*)	(*b*)	(*a*)	(*c*)
111	**112**	**113**	**114**	**115**	**116**	**117**	**118**	**119**	**120**
(*b*)	(*c*)	(*b*)	(*c*)	(*a*)	(*a*)	(*b*)	(*a*)	(*d*)	(*b*)
121	**122**	**123**	**124**	**125**	**126**	**127**	**128**	**129**	**130**
(*c*)	(*a*)	(*c*)	(*a*)	(*b*)	(*a*)	(*a*)	(*c*)	(*b*)	(*a*)
131	**132**	**133**	**134**	**135**	**136**	**137**	**138**	**139**	**140**
(*b*)	(*b*)	(*b*)	(*a*)	(*b*)	(*a*)	(*a*)	(*c*)	(*c*)	(*c*)
141	**142**	**143**	**144**	**145**	**146**	**147**	**148**	**149**	**150**
(*b*)	(*c*)	(*b*)	(*a*)	(*b*)	(*b*)	(*c*)	(*d*)	(*b*)	(*a*)
151	**152**	**153**	**154**	**155**	**156**	**157**	**158**	**159**	**160**
(*b*)	(*a*)	(*a*)	(*a*)	(*a*)	(*b*)	(*c*)	(*c*)	(*b*)	(*c*)
161	**162**	**163**	**164**	**165**	**166**	**167**	**168**	**169**	**170**
(*b*)	(*b*)	(*c*)	(*a*)	(*a*)	(*d*)	(*c*)	(*a*)	(*a*)	(*c*)
171	**172**	**173**	**174**	**175**	**176**	**177**	**178**	**179**	**180**
(*d*)	(*a*)	(*c*)	(*b*)	(*b*)	(*b*)	(*c*)	(*a*)	(*b*)	(*b*)
181	**182**	**183**	**184**	**185**	**186**	**187**	**188**	**189**	**190**
(*a*)	(*b*)	(*b*)	(*c*)	(*c*)	(*b*)	(*a*)	(*c*)	(*b*)	(*b*)
191	**192**	**193**	**194**	**195**	**196**	**197**	**198**	**199**	**200**
(*a*)	(*a*)	(*b*)	(*c*)	(*a*)	(*c*)	(*c*)	(*a*)	(*c*)	(*b*)
201	**202**	**203**	**204**	**205**	**206**	**207**	**208**	**209**	**210**
(*c*)	(*c*)	(*d*)	(*d*)	(*d*)	(*c*)	(*a*)	(*b*)	(*b*)	(*d*)

UNIT-II

PHYSIOLOGY OF MUSCULAR ACTIVITY, NEUROTRANSMISSION AND MOVEMENT MECHANISM

Muscles

All movements of our body inner or outer are made by muscles. Animal life has this peculiar characteristic of movement and this is provided by muscles. Even the tiniest creatures that move have muscles whereas there is no such entity in stones, vegetation or trees.

Muscles control voluntary movements which are under our control and involuntary movements which go on and on which we have no control. In the former category, comes most of the bodily movements as that of limbs. These together with the fat cover the bones. It forms the red flesh. These are also called striped or striated muscles as they appear so under a microscope. In the latter category comes the muscles of our heart and those of stomach which help in digestion, circulation of blood, respiration and secretion. These go on all the time, even during our sleep. These are not under our will. These muscles under microscope appear smooth and regular and therefore, are also called unstriped or nonstriated muscles.

STRUCTURE OF MUSCLES

Voluntary Muscles

Voluntary muscles are responsible for about two fifth of the weight of our body. Bones are clothed by these muscles. They are separated by bundles of flesh. They are of different sizes and lengths and perform independent functions of movement.

Blood vessels and nerves do not pass through the muscles but between them. Each muscle has its own set of blood vessels and nerves. In addition, it has its own set of lymphatics. These vessels contain fluid that is derived from tissue fluid. The tough connective tissues called the fascia, surround each muscle. These tissues also surround blood vessels and organs. Muscles are not connected directly with the bones. These are connected by means of cords called tendons. These tendons are white, shining fibrous tissues forming cords.

Muscles are made of fibres and each fibre is enclosed by a transparent sheet called sarcolemma. Each fibre of muscle consists of fibrillae. These fibres also have dark stripes and for this reason voluntary muscles are called stripped or striated muscle.

Involuntary Muscles

These muscles, unlike the voluntary muscles which consist of fibres, are long and spindle like cells. Unlike the voluntary muscles they are not attached to bones and as such they do not require any tendon to bind them. They have also no cross markings, strips or sarcolemma. As such, they are ribbon like bands and surround hollow fleshy tubes.

Unlike the voluntary muscles, one part of these muscles contracts while the other relaxes at the same time. They also respond to irritation slowly.

These muscles are found in blood vessels, lungs, heart and intestine. These muscles pump the blood in the heart and they drive the blood through the arteries and veins. In the lungs, they are responsible for inhalation and exhalation of air. In the stomach and intestine they keep the food in motion and break it up until it is digested. These activities go on all the time whether we will it or not.

Muscle Fibre Types, Fibres Distribution and Performance

Human skeletal muscle can be classified into three different types of fibre based on biochemical and performance characteristics of the individual muscle cells.

These three groups are often referred to as fast twitch, intermediate and slow twitch fibres. The percentage of the respective fibre types contained in skeletal muscle is genetically determined and play an important role in performance in both power and endurance events.

The classification of fibre types is done by histochemical analysis of a sample of muscle tissue obtained by a needle through biopsy procedure. This procedure involves the insertion of a pencil size needle through small incision in the skin and fascia, under topical anesthesia. The needle is pushed into the muscle and a small window like opening is filled with tissue. An internal cutting blade pulls of the tissue off 20 to 40 mg. it is then thinly sliced, stained and examined under a microscope. Those fibres that stain black in this histochemical method are the slow twitch type (ST). Those fibres which stain slightly and appear in grey colour in staining are fast twitch fibres. Mainly the nerves controlling these fibres determine whether they will be ST or FT.

Slow Twitch Fibres

These slow twitch fibres are otherwise called as slow oxidative, (so) type, I and Red fibres.

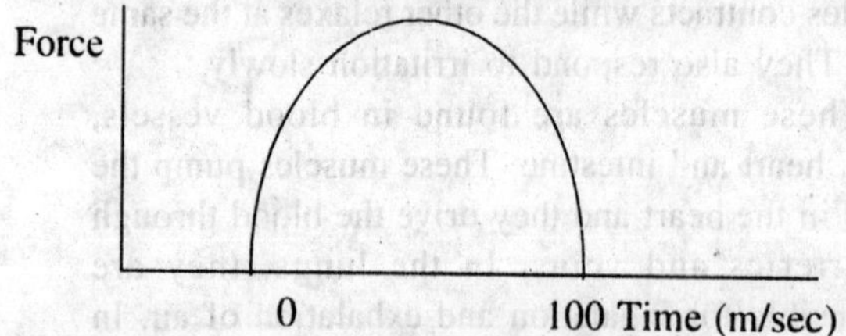

These muscle fibres contain (1) Larger number of mitochondria and are surrounded by (2) more capillaries than fast twitch fibres. In addition slow twitch fibres contain higher concentrations of the (3) red pigments myoglobin than fast twitch fibres. Myoglobin is similar to haemoglobin, in the blood, in that it binds O_2, but it also acts as a 'shuttle' mechanism for O_2 between the cell membrane and the mitochondria. The high concentration of myoglobin, the large number of capillaries and the higher content of mitochondrial enzymes provide slow twitch fibres with a high capacity for aerobic metabolism and a high resistance to fatigue. The rate at which action potentials are conducted along the motor neurons that innervate slow twitch fibres is lesser. That is why slow twitch fibres have a slower contraction time as its name implies.

Size of the neuron innervate in this type of fibres is comparatively small and number of fibres per neuron is 10 to 180.

Fast Twitch Fibres

They are also called as; Fast glycolytic (FG) Type II fibres or white fibres. They have relatively a small number of mitochondria, a limited capacity for aerobic metabolism, and are less resistant to fatigue than slow twitch fibres. However, fast twitch fibres are rich in glycogen, which provide them with a large anaerobic capacity. In addition FT fibres contain more myofilbrils and higher AT pase activity than ST fibres. High AT pase activity in fast twitch fibres results in a fast contraction speed. The high number of myofibrils in fast twitch fibres means that the cell contains many myosin cross bridges and therefore can develop more force compared to a ST fibre. More over the rate at which the action potentials are conducted along the motor neurons the innervate fast twitch fibre is faster than that of slow twitch fibres. The size of the neuron innervate in the fibres is comparatively large and no. of fibres per neuron is 300 to 800.

They are also called as fast oxidative glycolytic (EDG) or type II 'a' fibres. As the name implies these fibres contain biochemical and fatigue characteristics that are somewhere between FT and ST fibres. They are thought to be a mixture of both slow and fast twitch fibre, characteristics. They are not a single fibre type i.e. some of the intermediate fibres may have biochemical and contractile properties similar to FT fibres while other intermediate fibres may exhibit contractile and performance characteristics similar to ST fibres.

The force and speed of contraction difference between three type of fibres.

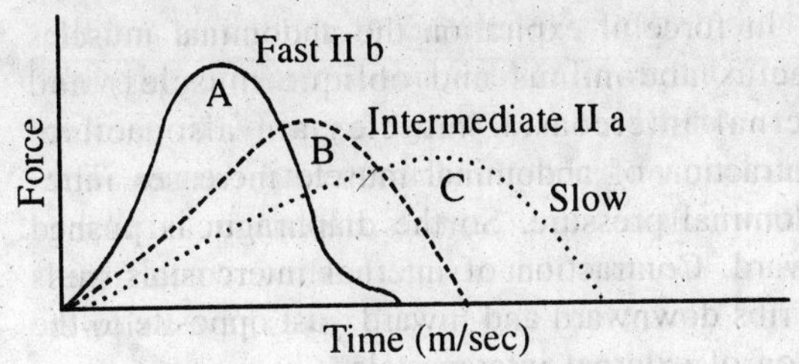

Figure. characteristics of St, Ft, etc.

Athletes who have a high percentage of ST fibres might have an advantage in long, endurance events (aerobic), whereas those athletes with the predominance of FT fibres might better be suited for short, explosive activities. Leg muscles of sprinters are composed principally of FT fibres, whereas elite distance runners has a predominance of ST fibres. Likewise cyclists and swimmers have a slightly higher percentage of ST fibres in their muscles.

An average individual has roughly 50 percent ST, 25 percent FTa and 25 percent FTb fibres in his or her leg muscles. Studies of elite male and female distance runners, revealed that some have calf muscles composed of more than 90% ST Fibres, for example. The calf muscle from a recent world record holder in the marathon was found to have 93% S.T. fibres, 7% FT a fibres and no FTb fibres. In contrast muscles of world class sprinters are composed mostly of FT a fibres. Although there is a marked difference in the composition of fibres in the muscles of sprinters and distance runners, fibre composition alone is not a reliable predictor of distance success.

The percentage of FT, ST fibres is established soon after birth during the process of natural development and remains relatively unchanged throughout life.

Any changes that might occur in the percentage of ST and FT fibres with training is probably small and that too in detraining it will be vanished.

PHYSIOLOGY OF RESPIRATION

The process of inhalation of oxygen and exhalation of carbon dioxide is known as respiration.

The function of the lungs is the interchange of the gases oxygen and carbon dioxide. This exchange of "stale air for fresh air" is accomplished by the mechanical process of breathing.

Breathing consists of two phases; Inspiration (breathing in) during which air flows into the lungs and expiration (breathing out), during which air is expelled from the lungs. The combined actions of the inspiration and expiration constitute the respiratory cycle.

External and Internal Respiration

The delivery of oxygen to the cells and the elimination of carbon dioxide from the body are accomplished in three phases; (*i*) external respiration (*ii*) Transpiration of Gases in the body and (*iii*) internal respiration.

External Respiration

External respiration is the exchange of oxygen and carbon dioxide between the lungs and blood in the 'pulmonary capillaries' via the interstitial fluid. The oxygen diffuses due to pressure gradient, into the blood and at the same time carbon dioxide diffuses in the reverse direction. Thus the blood is changed from "Venous Blood" (low in oxygen) to "Arterial Blood" (higher in oxygen).

Internal Respiration

Internal respiration is the exchange of oxygen and carbon dioxide between blood in the "systemic capillaries" and the cells via the interstitial fluid. Since the metabolis cells constantly consume oxygen and produce carbon dioxide, the concentration of the oxygen will be lower and the carbon dioxide concentration will be higher at the cells than in the arterial blood. Consequently oxygen diffuses out of the blood towards the cells while carbon dioxide diffuses away from the cells towards the blood.

MECHANISM OF RESPIRATION (OR) BREATHING

The lungs are enclosed by the thoracic vertebrae, respiratory muscles and diaphragm. The only means of communication between the lungs and external environment is by way of conducting passages. For air in the lungs to be changed there must be alternate inflow and outflow of air through the conducting passages leading to and from alveoli. The flow of air, like the flow of fluid, require Pressure Gradient. Air flows from an area of high pressure to an area of low pressure.

Since the atmospheric pressure is relatively constant, creation of pressure gradient depends upon the intra-pulmonic pressure being alternately lower and higher than atmospheric pressure. This is accomplished by changing the size (volume) of the thoracic cavity and consequently the intra-pulmic pressure. It is achieved through the combined action of the main respiratory muscles, the diaphragm and external intercostals when the thoracic pressure is lowered, and the pressure on the lungs is decreased conversely. When the thoracic volume is reduced, the intra-thoracic pressure is raised, and the pressure on the lung is increased.

Inspiration

When the diaphragm and external intercoastal muscles contract, quiet inspiration begins. As the dome shaped diaphragm flattens, it descends into the abdominal cavity and the thoracic volume is increased from top to bottom. At the same time contraction of the external intercoastal muscle raises the ribs upward and outward. So the thoracic cavity is increased from front to back and side to side. As the thoracic volume increases, the intra thoracic pressure falls below the atmospheric pressure. As the lungs expand alveoli are enlarged. Thus a pressure gradient is created between atmosphere and alveoli and the air rushes into the lungs untill the intra thoracic pressure equals atmospheric pressure.

Expiration

In expiration, the events are just the opposite of those in inspiration. The diaphragm and external intercoastal muscles relax and return to their original position. As a result, the thoracic volume is decreased, and the pressure on the lungs is increased. The elastic tissue of the lungs, stretched on inspiration, now recoils, and the lungs shrink back. The intra-pulmonic pressure is raised and air is forced out of the lungs.

In forceful expiration the abdominal muscles (Rectus abdominus and oblique muscles) and internal intercoastal muscles are also active. Contraction of abdominal muscle increases intra-abdominal pressure. So the diaphragm is pushed upward. Contraction of internal intercostals pulls the ribs downward and lnward, just opposite to the action of external intercoastals.

PHYSIOLOGY OF BLOOD CIRCULATION

The heart is the chief organ of the circulation of the blood. The course of the blood from the left ventricle through arteries, arterioles and capillaries, returning it to the right atrium by veins is called "systemic circulation". The course from the right ventricle, through the lungs, to the left atrium is the lesser or "pulmonary circulation".

The Systemic Circulation

The oxygenated blood leaves the left ventricle of the heart by the aorta, the largest artery in the body. This breaks upto into smaller arteries which carry the blood to the different parts of the body. These divide and sub-divide until the arterioles are reached. These arterioles, the capillaries have very thin walls so that exchange can take place between the plasma and the interstitial fluid. These capillaries then unite and form larger vessels called venules which in turn become veins and carry the deoxygenated blood back to the heart. The veins unite and reunite again until finally two large venous trunks are formed, the inferior venacava which collects the blood from the trunk and lower extremities and the superior venacava which collects the blood from the head and upper extremities. Both these vessels empty their deoxygenated blood into right atrium of the heart.

Pulmonary Circulation

The deoxygenated blood pumped by the right ventricle passes into the pulmonary artery which divides into two to carry the blood to the right and left lungs. In the lungs each artery breaks up into numerous smaller arteries, then into arterioles and finally into pulmonary capillaries which surround the alveoli in the lung tissue where the deoxygenated blood takes up oxygen and gives off carbon dioxide and becomes oxygenated blood. The pulmonary capillaries then unit until veins which empty into the left ventricles which contracts and pumps it into the aorta to begin the systemic circulation again.

BIO – ENERGETICS

Energy is defined as the ability or capacity to do a work and work is one application of force through distance. There are 6 forms of energy :

1. Chemical
2. Mechanical
3. Heat
4. Light
5. Electrical
6. Nuclear.

All these types of energy cannot be created or destroyed but each can be converted from one form to another.

Food in the presence of O_2 is broken down to CO_2 and H_2O with the liberation of chemical energy by a metabolic process called "Respiration". The metabolic respiration supply the energy we need to carry out such biological processes as the chemical work of growth and the mechanical work of muscular contractions.

- Sun (light energy)
- Photosysnthesis
  Plants (Chemical energy)
- Metabolic respiration chemical work of growth animals.
- Mechanical work of muscular contraction (Biological process)
- The amount of energy taken in by the body shall be spent by the output of the body (Exercise).
- The energy liberated during the break down of food is not directly used to do work. Rather it is used to manufacture another chemical compound called 'adenosine triphosphote' (ATP) which is stored in all muscle cells.
- The structure of ATP consists of a complex component adenosine and 3 phosphate groups.

The bonds between the two terminal phosphate groups are known as high energy, when one mole at this phosphate bonds is broken (is removed from the rest of the molecules) 7 to 12 kilo calories of energy are liberated and adenosine diphosphate (ADP) plus inorganic phosphate (Pi) are formed. This energy released during the break down of ATP represents the immediate source of energy that can be used by the muscle cell to perform its work. The unit of this energy calorie and one kilo calorie is the amount of heat energy required to raise amount of 1 kilogram of water. One thousand calories equal one kilo calorie.

The average energy expenditure of the individual who is engaged in normal daily activity will range from 1,800 to 2700 kilo calories. For athletes in intense daily training this value can be much higher approaching 10,000 kilo calories /day.

SOURCE OF ATP

ATP is the immediate source of energy and break down of ATP releases energy for muscular contraction. But there is limited quantity of ATP in a muscle cell and the ATP and it can give 5.7 to 6.9 kilo calories of energy only.

Regeneration of ATP is required for energy. There are 3 common energy yielding systems for the production of ATP.

1. **ATP-PC system or phosphogen system:** In this energy for resynthesis of ATP comes from only one compound called 'Phopshocreatine' (PC)
2. **Anaerobic or latic acid system:** This provides ATP from practical degradation of glucose or glycogen.
3. **Oxygen system (or) aerobic system:** It has 3 parts in production of ATP.
   1. Aerobic glycolysis
   2. Krebs cycle
   3. Electron transport system

Aerobic Sources of ATP: Aeroabic Metabolism

In this process, in the presence of oxygen 1 mole of glycogen is completely broken to a CO_2 and H_2O releasing sufficient energy to regain the size of 39 moles of ATP. It involves with highly complex chemical reactions enhanced by enzymes called acetylco enzyme, phosphorylase hexokinate phosphortokinase etc.

The reactions of aerobic metabolism occur within the mitochondria. The reactions of aerobic system can be divided into 3 main series:

1. **Aerobic Glycolysis**: The first series of reactions involved in the aerobic breakdown of glycogen to O_2 and H_2O is glycolysis. The presence of oxygen inhibits the accumulation of lactic during the reaction. 1 mole of glycogen is broken down into 2 moles of pyruvic acid releasing through energy for resynthesising 3 mole of ATP with the help of energy called NAD (Nicotinamide Adenine, Dinucletide)

$C_6H_{12}O_6 \rightarrow 2C_3H_4O_3$

Glycogen Energy (Pyruvic acid)

Energy + 3 ADP + 3pi $\rightarrow$ 3 ATP

Glycogen
| (Glycogenlysis)
Glucose
ADP+Pi (Max 3)
ATP

Pyruvic acid (sufficient O_2)

CO_2 H_2O $\rightarrow$ ATP

2. **The Krebs cycle**: The pyruvic acid formed during aerobic glycolysis passes into the mitochondria. It is broken down in a series of reactions called the "Kreb's cycle". It is named after its discoverer 'Sir Hans Kreb". In the Kreb cycle 3 stages of reactions occur.

(*a*) CO_2 produced

(*b*) Oxidation

(*c*) ATP is produced.

In the Kreb cycle the produced CO_2 is removed from pyruvic acid and forms acetyl co-enzyme, after combining with co-enzyme. All the produced CO_2 diffuses into the blood and is carried to the lungs were it is eliminated from the body through respiration.

This production of CO_2 is because of the oxidation of pyruvic acid i.e. when 'H' is removed by oxidation it removes the hydrogen O_2 is formed. In the Kreb Cycle mole of ATP are formed.

3. **Electron Transport System (E. T.S.)**: In this system H_2O is formed from the Hydrogen ions and electron that are removed in the kreb's Cycle and the O_2 we breath in. This is other wise called respiratory chain. Here two major chemical events take place, the hydrogen ions and electrons are transported by electron carriers to the O_2 we breath to form water through a series of enzymatic reactives (2), at the same time ATP is resynthesised in coupled reactions from the energy release totally 39 moles ATP are resynthesised.

$(C_6H_{12})O_6 + 6O_2 \rightarrow 6O_2$ + Energy

(glycogen)

Energy + 39 ATP+ 30 Pi $\rightarrow$ 39 ATP.

$4H^+ + 4e^- + O_2 \rightarrow 2H_2O$ | energy.

The energy released from the break down of food stuffs and phosphocreatine is functionally linked or coupled to the energy needs or resynthesising ATP from ADP Pio. It is the fundamental principle involved in the metabolic production of ATP.

Anaerobic Sources of ATP – Anaerobic Metabolism:

The ATP – PC system (phosphogen system) and anaerobic glycolysis (lactic acid system) are called as 'anaerobic metabolism'. It means the synthesis of ATP through chemical reaction that does not require the presence of O_2 we breath.

(Anaerobic = without oxygen)

1. **ATP – PC system (Phosphogen system):** PC (Phosphogen system) like ATP is stored in muscle cells. ATP and PC contain phosphate groups and they are collectively referred to as "phosphogen system".

Due to the breakdown of PC into Pi and C an energy release occurs that energy is used to resynthesise ATP from ADP and Pi. Hence no need of O_2 for this resynthesis of ATP. So, this energy system is very much essential in the events that require few seconds to complete e.g., spinting in 100 mm. run.

The enzyme that **calayses** (speeds) the break down of pc with the result and formation of ATP is creative kinase.

PC + ADP → ATP + C

The only means by which pc can be reformed from pi and C is the energy released by the break down of ATP. This occurs during recovery from exercise.

2. **Anaerobic glycolysis (Lactic acid system)**
The other anaerobic (anaerobic glycolysis) system in which ATP is resynthesised with the muscle by the incomplete break down of CO_2 (sugar) to lactic acid (that is why the name lactic acid system).
In the body CO_2 is converted to the simple sugar glucose, which is stored in blood as glucose and in liver and muscle as glycogen (cluster of glucose molecules) approximately 350 to 400 of glycogen are stored in the human body)
Glycogen is chemically broken down into lactic acid by a series of chemical reaction enhanced by the enzymes called phosphotructoniase, hexokinase, pyruvatikinase, and arctic dithydrogenase. During aerobic glycolysis only 3 moles of ATP can be resynthesised from 1 mole of glycogen. Glycolysis means splitting of glucose to lactic acid or glycogenysis means splitting of glycogen to glucose.
Anaerobic glycolysis is very important to us during exercise primarily because it provides a relatively rapid supply of ATP exercise that can be performed at maximum rate for 1 to 3 minutes (400 mts. & 800 mts. Run) depend heavily on the phosphogen system and anaerobic glycolysis for ATP formation.

Fat Metabolism

Fat and protein can also be aerobically broken down to CO_2 to releasing the energy for ATP resynthesis. Fat in the form of triglycerides are broken down into 2 compound (A) groups by a series of reactions called beta oxidation (B) before entering into Kreb's cycle and (K.T.S.). The majority of the fat taken by man is stored in the body as *tricyrides* made of 3 mole of faty acid and one mole of glycerol. Each fatty acid molecule is made of 16 or 18 long chains of carbon atoms with the hydrogen atoms attached. When the fatty acid molecules splits off from triglycerides molecules from adipose tissue which diffuses into blood and transported to muscles. There it undergoes chemical transformation called B oxidation, in which fatty acid molecules degraded into *Acytyle* Co. enzyme A and enters into Kreb's cycle etc. Through fat metabolism 147 ATPS are produced.

Fatty Acid

Activated fatty acid oxidation (B)
Acetyle group
Acetyl co-enzyme (NAD)
Kreb's cycle and E.T.S.

Protein Metabolism

Only about 5 to 15% of total body energy is produced by protein. Though proteins are not a common source of fuel, they form an important part of diet used mainly for construction of new body tissues and respiring them. Each protein molecule contains complex chains of carbon, oxygen, hydrogen and and nitrogen atoms, with amino acids, having the basic units. There are different amino acids present in proteins. They are broken down to pyruvic acid and enter kreb's cycle.

ENERGY METABOLISM DURING REST, EXERCISE AND RECOVERY

A. Rest

Metabolism during rest is aerobic, because

1. Oxygen consumption during rest remains constant (approx. 0.25 litres/min.).
2. Blood lactic acid level remains within normal range (10 mg/100 ml)
3. Aerobic breakdown of fats and glucose supplies all the ATP required for the body during rest.

B. Exercise

1. **Short duration, High-Intensity Exercise:** Here activities include swimming events upto 200 mts. Track events upto 800 mts. Jumping, throwing vaulting, cycling, sprinters, weight

lifting, fast breaks in basket ball. The golf swing and some apparatus routine in gymnastic activities.

ATP and glycogen are primary food fuels. Anaerobic metabolism is dominant in short duration exercise where exercises are repeated many times with rest period in between like in football, basket ball and base ball. ATP and CP are reproduced during rest periods at the expense of glycogen, blood glucose and fatty acids. Why aerobic metabolism is not the main source of energy for maximal work of short duration?

For athletes, the oxygen in take capacity is 4.5 litres per minute for females and 6 litres/ minute for males. For untrained the oxygen in take capacity is around 3 litres/ minute for female and 3.5 litres/ minute for males.

Hence a race like 100 mts dash is so fast and short and may require on oxygen consumption of around 45 to 60 litres / minute.

It is clear that the above oxygen con-sumption capacities for both the athlete and non athlete are not adequate to furnish all the ATP molecules needed for this type of event.

2. **High intensity exercises lasting several minutes:**

   In any strenuous exercises of 5 to 10 minutes like middle distance run, swimming, soccer or basket ball, aerobic sources with lactic acid formation the major food fuels are stored ATP, creative phosphate and muscle glycogen.

3. **Long duration exercises:**

   These exercises include channel swimming, cycling, marathon running, recreational jogging, long - distance walking etc. which require constant supply of energy. For this type of work, energy is provided more from aerobic break down of fat, glycogen and glucose with little or no lactic acid formation. When work is prolonged and the glucose supply is reduced, a greater consumption of energy fuel comes from stored fat and fatty acid in blood.

   In the long duration exercises of low intensity like golf leisure walking, lactic acid levels do not go much above resting levels. Blood lactate is found to reach a high of 140 mg / 100 ml blood when a final sprint is preceded (ends with) by 35 minutes of hard work

   After 31 or 32 minutes of exhaustive running, lactic values are found to be round 38 to 47 mg / 100 ml blood. At the end of marathon races (26.2 miles in about 2.5 hours) blood lactic acid levels are found to be only about 3 times at rest (at rest 10 mg/ 100 ml) blood. Fatigue seen during this type of long duration exercise is not due to high blood lactic acid levels, but because of low blood glucose levels and high body temperature brought by loss of HO_2 and .electrolytes. Boredom and more physical heating also add to fatigue.

C. Recovery

Recovery period following exercise is to repay energy stores used during exercise period. This is accomplished solely by aerobic (oxygen) system.

The Oxygen Debt

It is defined as the post-exercise oxygen consumption above the basal oxygen consumption level. This means that the oxygen taken in during recovery over and above that which would have normally been consumed for the same period of repaying the energy stores that were used up during exercise.

During high intensity work (anaerobic) in which a steady state cannot be achieved, the oxygen debt continues to rise until work leases (stops).

The highly trained athlete is able to tolerate a much larger oxygen debt than untrained. In determining oxygen debt, two measurements are needed.

1. Resting oxygen consumption.
2. Oxygen consumed during recovery period.

BLOOD

Introduction

Blood is the life-giving fluid that flows through the human body. We cannot live without it. The heart pumps blood to all our body cells, supplying them with oxygen and food. At the same time, blood carries carbon dioxide and other waste products from the cells. Blood also fights infection, keeps our temperature steady, and carries chemicals that regulate many body functions. Blood even has substances that plug broken blood vessels and so prevent us from bleeding to death.

The amount of blood in our body depends on our size and the altitude at which we live. An adult who weighs 80 kilograms has bout 5 litres of blood. A 40 kilogram child has about half that amount, and a 4- kilogram infant has abut 250 millilitres. People who live at high altitudes, where the air contains less oxygen, may have up to 2 litres more blood than people who live in low regions. The extra blood delivers additional oxygen to body cells.

Functions of Blood

The important functions of the blood are as under:

1. **Maintenance of pH:** The plasma proteins of blood acts as buffer system and therefore prevent any change in pH (acid base balance) of blood.
2. **Chemical coordination:** Organs called endocrine glands produce hormones and release them directly into the blood. The hormones enter the plasma and act as "chemical messenger". When a hormone reaches a part of the body it regulates, it may affect growth, reproductive processes.
3. **Transport of oxygen (O_2) and carbon dioxide (CO_2):** Blood transports oxygen from the respiratory surfaces such as lungs to the tissues and from the tissues to the respiratory surfaces and hence blood helps in respiration.
4. **Transport of food:** Blood carries soluble food (i.e. glucose, amino acids, polypeptides, vitamins, fats, minerals and water) from the intestine, first to the liver and then to the whole of the body tissues where it is required for cellular activities.
5. **Transport of waste products:** Waste products are produced regularly by all the cells of the body, which are harmful to the body and need to be eliminated immediately from the body. Blood transports these wastes to the kidney, lungs, skin and intestine so that they may be eliminated.
6. **Maintenance of water balance:** Blood maintains water balance to a constant level, by bringing about constant exchange of water between circulating blood and tissue cytoplasm.
7. **Regulates body temperature:** All cell activities produce heat. But some cells, particularly those in muscles and glands, create more heat than others. The heat enters our blood stream and travels throughout our body. Excess heat escapes through our skin. If blood did not distribute heat, some body areas would become extremely hot, while others would remain extremely cold. Therefore, blood circulation distributes body heat and regulates body temperature.
8. **Defence against infection:** White blood cells (WBC) play an important role in our immune system, which helps our body resist disease causing substances. The invasion (attack) of a harmful substance activates the white blood cells. They then work to destroy it. Some proteins in the plasma also help to fight diseases.

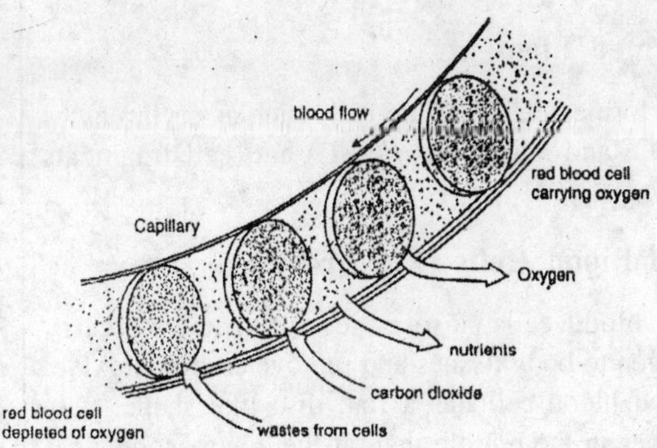

9. **Clotting of blood:** Blood prevents loss of blood in injury as it has power of coagulation.
10. **Support and formation of stable environment:** Blood provides support and a relatively stable environment for the active body cells.

Composition of Blood

Blood is a connective tissue and consists of cells that move about in a watery liquid called plasma. The cells are known as formed elements because they have definite shapes. Three types of cells make up the formed elements :

1. red blood cells,
2. white blood cells, and
3. platelets, A microlitre of blood normally contains about 4 million to 6 million red blood cells, 5,000 to 10,000 white blood cells, and 150, 000 to 500,000 platelets. The red and white blood cells are also called corpuscles. Total blood volume is approximately 5 litres.

Plasma

Plasma is the liquid, straw–coloured part of blood. It makes up about 50 to 60 per cent of the total volume of blood. The formed elements account for the rest. Plasma consists of about 90 per cent water and 9% suspended or dissolved substances. These substances include proteins that enable blood to clot and to fight infection; dissolved nutrients (foods) and waste products. Plasma also carries chemicals called hormones, which control growth and certain other body functions.

Formed Elements

The formed elements are cells such as erythrocytes (RBC) and leukocytes (WBC) and cell fragments (Platelets).

Red Blood Cells (Erythrocytes)

Red blood cells, also called erythrocytes, carry oxygen to body tissues and remove carbon dioxide. A red blood cell has a flat, disc like shape. It is thinner in the middle than at the edges- somewhat like a ring doughnut without the hole.

Red blood cells consist mainly of haemglobin, an oxygen–carrying protein that gives them their red colour. The cells also contain chemicals, particularly enzyme. Enzymes enable the cells to carry out necessary chemical processes more effectively. A flexible membrane surrounds each red blood cell. The membrane is so flexible that the cells can squeeze through the tiniest blood vessels. Most kinds of cells have a nucleus, a central structure that controls many cell activities. But mature red blood cells have no nuclei.

White Blood Cells (Leukocytes)

White blood cells, also called leucocytes, fight infections and harmful substances that attack the body. Most of the cells are round and colourless. They have several sizes, and their nuclei differ in shape. Some kinds of white blood cells kill bacteria by surrounding and digesting them. Other kinds produce antibodies, proteins that destroy bacteria, viruses, and other invaders or make them harmless.

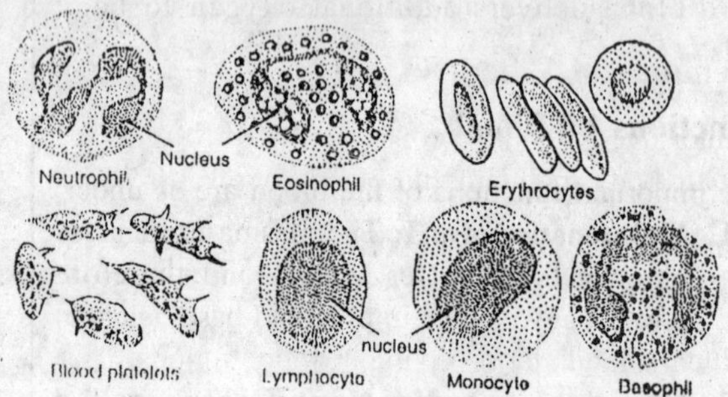

Platelets

Platelets, also known as thrombocytes,are disc like structures that help stop bleeding. They are the smallest formed elements. If a blood vessel is cut platelets stick to the edges of the cut, and to one another, forming a plug. They then release chemicals that react with fibrinogen and certain other plasma proteins,leading to the formation of a blood clot.

Blood Clotting

One may bleed to death from a small cut if blood did not coagulate (clot). An injured blood vessel causes platelets to stick to the damaged surface and to one another, forming a plug. The plasma contains proteins called clotting factors. They normally circulate in an inactive form in the blood. But if a blood vessel suffers damage, the platelet plug and the injured vessel give off chemicals that react with the clotting factors. Eventually, the plasma protein fibrinogen changes into stick strands of fibrin. The strands crisscross one another, create a mesh that holds red blood cells and the platelet plug tightly to the site of bleeding. The fluid is squeezed out, and a solid plug-the clot forms. A clot on the skin surface is a scab.

Sometime, a clot may occur in an undamaged vessel that has no bleeding. Such a clot, called a thrombus, may block the flow of blood to tissues beyond the clot and cut off food and oxygen to those tissues. If a clot blocks an artery that nourishes the heart, a coronary thrombosis results, which may cause a heart attack. If a clot blocks an artery to the brain, a stroke may occur.

Blood contains substances that dissolve clots as well as substances that produce them. The clot dissolving substances are activated when clotting occurs to control its extent and duration.

Maintenance of Blood Supply

We cannot live without a proper supply of healthy blood. Our body maintains its blood supply by:

Regulating the Volume of Blood Components

The volume of each blood component continuously adjusts to meet the body's needs. The plasma proteins (albumin) control the movement of plasma between the capillaries and the cells. Normally, only dissolved substances, such as nutrients pass from the plasma through the capillary walls. But if the amount of albumin (espial protein) falls below normal, plasma may escape into tissues and if the concentration of albumin is high, then water from the tissues enters the plasma.

The volume of red blood cells depends on how much oxygen body tissues require. The kidneys produce a hormone called erythropoietin that stimulates output of the cells. When the tissues need oxygen, the kidneys produce increased amounts of erythropoietin, causing red-cell producing to rise. When oxygen need falls, erythropoietin output drops. Certain diseases also affect the production of red blood cells.

Other haematopoietic growth factors control the number of white blood cells and platelets, which also increase and decrease according to the condition of the body. For example, an infection leads to a rise in the number of germ-fighting white blood cells. Similarly, severe bleeding can cause an increase in the number of platelets, thus improving the blood's ability to clot.

Replacing Worn – Out Blood Components

Each formed element can live only a particular length of time, so our body must continuously replace worn out cells. Red blood cells live about 120 days, and platelets about 10 days. The life period of white blood cells varies greatly from few hours to many years.

The liver and the spleen remove worn–out red blood cells from the blood stream and break them down. The liver uses colouring matter from the old cells in producing a digestive liquid called bile. The body reuses the iron from haemoglobin to make new red blood cells. Worn-out white blood cells migrate to blood tissues, where they die. Platelets probably wear out plugging tiny leaks in blood vessels.

Formation of new Blood Components

The core of human bones is filled with a soft red or yellow substance called marrow. In adults, the red bone marrow produces millions of blood cells per second. Red marrow occurs mostly in flat bones such as the vertebrae, sternum, ribs, and skull. All blood cells begin in the marrow as stem cells. They develop into more mature precursor cells, each of which forms many red blood cells, white blood cells, or platelets.

Controlling Bleeding

An injured blood vessel causes platelets to stick to the damaged surface and to one another, forming a plug. The plasma contains proteins called clotting factors. They normally circulate in an inactive form in the blood. If a blood vessel suffers damage, the platelets plug it as described above in blood clotting.

Blood Groups

The membranes of red blood cells contain proteins called antigens. Based on the presence or absence of particular antigens, scientists have classified human blood into following groups:

A B O Blood Group:

1. Type A blood has A antigens, type B blood has B antigens, type AB blood has A and B antigens, and type O blood has neither A nor B antigens.
2. Type A blood has B antibodies, type B blood has A antibodies, type AB blood has neither A nor B antibodies, and type O blood has both A and B antibodies.
3. Mismatching the A B O blood group can result in transfusion reactions.

Rh Blood Group:

1. Rh-positive blood has Rh antigens, whereas Rh-negative blood does not.
2. Antibodies against the Rh antigen are produced when an Rh negative person is exposed to Rh positive blood.

Globally, type O blood is the most common, followed by type A. Relatively few people have type B, fewer have type AB and rare have Rh.

Doctors prefer to use donor blood of the same A B O type as that of the patient to avoid clumping during a transfusion. But in an emergency, type O blood may be transfused into patients of any blood type. This is why group O blood is known as the *universal donor*. Similarly, type AB patients may be able to receive any A B O blood in an emergency because they have no antibodies to A or B antigens. But even then, hospitals, perform a cross- match to ensure that no clumping will occur. Type A patients should never receive type B blood, and type B patients should never receive type A blood.

Rh Babies

Rh babies is a strange phenomenon arising due to incompatibility between the blood groups of the husband and wife. That is why blood transfusion experts now a days suggest that before a couple gets married they should match their blood groups instead of matching janampatries as in the tradition. Matching of blood at least can save the Rh babies.

According to Prof. J.N. Jolly of PGI, whenever parent's blood group does not match baby's blood gets damaged due to the production of Rh antibodies while still in womb. But this combination can be easily found out before a couple gets married and much before the family has the misfortunate to witness Rh incompatibility disaster in their body.

A bay's blood group is combination of both husband and wife that is why with timely detection mother can be immunized with protective Rh immunoglobul to provide protection against the formation of antibodies. After timely transfusion, the baby starts producing its own RBC's and leads a perfectly normal life. Any delay can cause damages of severe nature to the brain.

Importance of Blood Groups

Blood-group classifications have vital importance in certain medical procedures. Information about

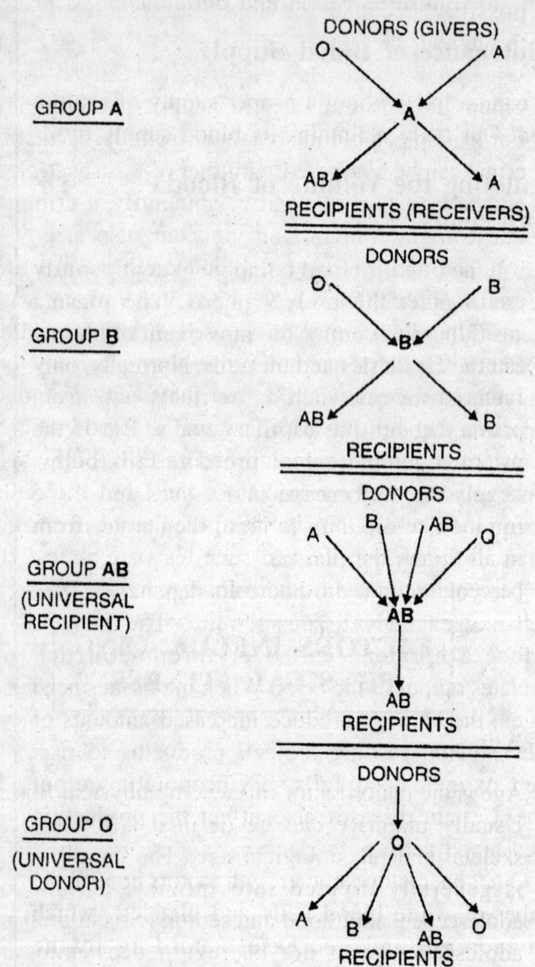

blood groups has also been used in anthropology and law.

In medicine, the main use of blood groups is to determine whether the blood of one person, called a donor, can be transfused into the body of a patient without rejection or serious reaction. The most serious transfusion reaction is the rapid destruction of the transfused red blood cells. This may lead to shock, kidney failure, and sometimes death. Other reactions may include fever, shaking and chills.

In *anthropology*, many anthropologists have used blood group frequencies to separate people into races and subraces. But that method of racial identification has not been successful. Blood-group antigens apparently do not differ among races, possibly because the races have intermarried throughout the ages.

In law, Forensic scientists have used blood groups to help uncover the identity of criminals. For example, a blood specimen from the scene of a crime can be compared with that of a suspect. Such comparison cannot positively identify a criminal, but it might eliminate an innocent suspect.

The antigens on red blood cells are inherited and so blood tests have been used in paternity cases,in which a man is accused of being a child's father. The tests cannot prove that a certain man fathered a certain child, but they can sometimes prove that he did not. The use of blood tests in paternity and other parenthood cases has now been largely replaced by studies of the DNA molecules in blood cells. DNA carries hereditary information in all the body cells, and such tests are almost 100 percent accurate in determining parenthood.

FACTORS INFLUENCING PHYSICAL FITNESS

Age

Age is the major factor influencing physical fitness. Usually maturity can be defined chronological, skeletal and physiological age. The period of life is generally divided into infancy, childhoods, adolescence, adulthood and seniors. So children and adolescence must not be regarded as miniature versions of adults. They are unique at each stage in their development. Their physiological and physical performance in term of physical fitness mainly depends on the growth and development of their bones, muscles, nerves and other organs. As children size increase, their functional capacities along with physical fitness also increase/improve.

The child is physiologically distinct from the adult and must be considered differently while planning fitness programme. The training can improve the physical fitness of the child. Generally youngsters, adapt well to the same type of training used by adults. But training programme for children and adolescents should be specifically prepared for each age group, keeping in mind the developmental factors associated with that age.

Studies have shown that humans tend to decrease their physical activity as they grow older, which affects the physical fitness. When older people participate in training, most of the changes associated with aging are lessened. It is clear that mode and nature of fitness training is an individual matter, which differs from person to person.

Sex

Prior to adolescence boys and girls do not differ substantially in height, weight, girth, bone width and body composition. But at maturity they differ significantly on various parameters. These physically, physiological and anthropometrical differences also affect the physical fitness of male and female. Thus the sex differences affect the type of exercise frequency of participation, duration and intensity of the exercise for developing physical fitness. Due consideration should be given to these factors while preparing a training programme for males and females.

Body Composition

Body composition is the proportion of the lean body mass and depot fat and it is one of the most important morphological features characterizing human organisation. Obesity is defined as that percentage of body fat that begins to increase the chances for cardiovascular disease. Ideal body fat levels for men are 12% to 17% and 18% to 22 % for women. Body fat is essential for certain bodily functions. Sometimes body type, determined genetically, prevents an individual from achieving unrealistic body shaping goals. There are basically three body types. The Endomorph is characterized by a large block shaped body. The Mesomorph is characterized by a solid muscular structure. The Ectomorph is characterized by a frail, slight build and very little fat.

Body composition assessment has revealed that athletes generally have physique characteristics unique to their specific sports. For example, field event athletes have large quantities of lean tissue and a high percent body fat whereas long distance runners have the least amount of lean body and fat weight. Nowadays body composition is considered one of the components of fitness as it plays important role in developing fitness. For athletes, weight gain must be in the form of lean body weight i.e. muscle mass. Strength training seems to increase muscle mass and strength effectively. Actually, individual physiologic variations and training factors affect weight gain. Because of this body weight body fat should be monitored on a regular basis and training programme should be developed accordingly.

Diet

Diet plays an Important role in maintaining physical fitness level. The key to weight control is keeping energy intake (food) and energy output (physical exercises) in balance. When we consume only as many calories as our body needs, our weight will remain constant. If we take in more calories than our body needs, we will put on more fat. If we expand more energy than we take in we will burn excess fat. Diet requirement varies from training to training and from individual to individual. An athlete requires good diet while he is undergoing vigorous training schedules. While planning a physical fitness programme diet factor must also be given due consideration.

Diet and Physical Activities

Do you know that you need to burn off 3,500 calories more than you take into lose just one kg? If you're overweight, eating your usual amount of calories while increasing activity is good for you, but eating fewer calories and being more active is even better. The following chart gives you an idea of the calories used per hour in common activities. Calories burned differ in proportion to body weight. So these figures are averages.

Activity Calories Burned Per Hour Calories burned per hour in different activities has been given in the following Table just for reference.

Calories burned per hour in some Activities

Bicycling 6 mph 240
Bicycling 12 mph 410
Jogging 5.5 mph 740
Jogging 7 mph 920
Jumping rope 750
Running in place 650
Running 10 mph 1,280
Cross- country 700
Swimming 25 yds/min 275
Swimming 50 yds/ min 500
Tennis (singles) 400
Walking 2 mph 240
Walking 4 mph 440

Climate

Physical fitness by and large also gets influenced by different climatic conditions such as winter, summer, humid etc.

When it's Hot or Humid

- Exercise during cooler and /or less humid times of day. Try early morning or late evening.
- Drink plenty of fluids especially water. Avoid alcohol which encourages dehydration.
- Wear light, loose-fitting clothes.
- Stop at the first sign of **Muscle cramping** or dizziness

When it's Cold

- Dress in layers.
- Wear gloves to protect your hands
- Wear a hat or cap. Up to 40% of body heat is lost through your neck and head.

- Adjust the size of your shoes if you need to wear thicker socks.
- Warm up slowly.
- Drink plenty of fluids. You can get dehydrated in the winter, too.
- Stop if you experience **Shivering, drowsiness or disorientation**

SPORTS INJURIES

Introduction

Every day, millions of people (of all ages) in the world participate in games and sports activities, from soccer fields to softball diamonds and kabaddi courts. It's called Playing, but sports activities are more than play. Participation in sports improves physical fitness, coordination, and self discipline, and gives children individuals valuable opportunities to learn teamwork. Games and Sports can also result in injuries some minor, some serious, and still others resulting in lifelong medical problems.

Young athletes/sport persons taking part in games/sports/physical activities are in majority and they are not merely small adults. Their bones, muscles, tendons and ligaments are still growing, which makes them more susceptible to injury. ***Growth plates-the areas of developing cartilage when bone growth occurs in youngsters-are weaker than the nearly ligaments and tendons. What is often a bruise or sprain in an adult can be potentially serious growth plate injury in a young athlete/sportsperson.***

Young sportsperson/athletes of the same age can differ greatly in size and physical maturity. Some youngsters may be physically less mature than their peers and try to perform at levels for which they are not ready. Thus, Coaches, Physical Educators and Parents should try to group youngsters according to skill level and size, not chronological age, particularly during contact sports. If this is not practical, they should modify the sport/game to accommodate the needs of children with varying skill levels.

TYPES OF SPORTS INJURIES

Injuries among sports persons / athletes may be classified into two basic categories :

1. Acute Injuries, and
2. Overuse Injuries

Both types include injuries to the soft tissues (muscles and ligaments) and bones.

Acute Injuries

Acute injuries are caused by a sudden trauma. Common acute injuries among young sports persons/athletes include sprains (a partial or complete tear of a ligament), strains (a partial or complete tear of a muscle or tendon), contusions (Bruises) and fractures.

Overuse Injuries

Not all injuries are caused by a single, sudden twist, fall, or collision. A series of small injuries to immature bodies can cause minor fractures, minimal muscle tears, or progressive bone deformities, known as overuse injuries. As an example, "*Little League Elbow*" is the term used to describe a group of common overuse injuries in young throwers involved in many sports. Other common overuse injuries occur in the heels and knees with tears in the tissue where tendons attach to the leg bone or the heel bone.

Contact sports have inherent dangers that put young athletes/ trainees at special risk for severe injuries. Even with rigorous training and proper safety equipment, youngsters are at risk severe injuries to the neck, spinal cord, and growth plates. However, obeying the rules of the game and using proper equipment can decrease these risks.

Common Sports Injuries

Some of the common sports injuries are sprain, strain, fracture, dislocation, abrasion, and contusion.

Sprain

A sprain is a stretch and / or tear of a ligament, the fibrous band of connective tissue that joints the end of one bone with another. Ligaments stabilize, and support the body's joints. For example, ligaments in the knee connect the upper leg with the lower leg, enabling people to walk and run.

Strain

A strain is a twist, pull and /or tear of a muscle and /or tendon. Tendons are fibrous cords of tissue that attach muscles to bone.

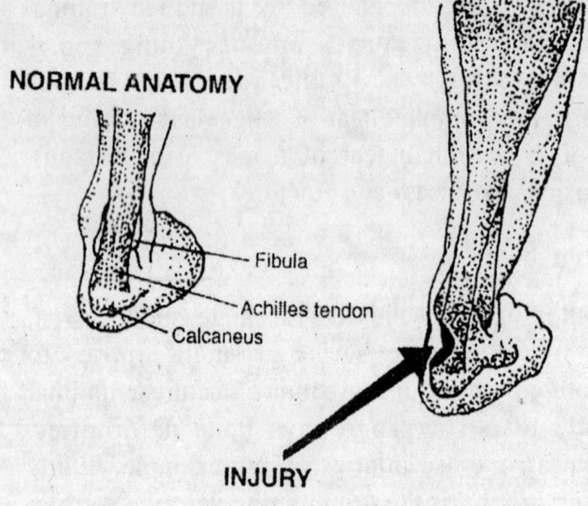

Causes of Sprain and Strains

A sprain is caused by direct or indirect trauma (a fall, a blow to the body, etc) that knocks a joint out of position, and overstretches, and in severe cases, ruptures the supporting ligaments. Typically, this injury occurs when an individual lands on an outstretched arm; slides into a base; jumps up and lands on the side of the foot; or runs on an uneven surface.

Chronic strain are the result of over use - prolonged, repetitive movement - of muscles and tendons. Inadequate rest breaks during intensive training precipitates a strain. Acute strains are caused by a direct blow to the body, overstretching, or excessive muscle contraction.

Sportspersons/athletes and the general public, as well, can sustain this injury. People at risk for the injury have a history of sprains and strains, are overweight, and are in poor physical condition.

WHAT ACTIVITIES MAKE SPORTS PERSONS / ATHLETES MOST SUSCEPTIBLE TO SPRAINS AND STRAINS

All sports and exercises, even walking, carry a risk of sprains. The anatomic areas most at risk for a sprain depend on the specific activities involved. For example, basketball, volleyball, soccer, and other jumping sports share a risk for foot, leg, and ankle **sprains**. Soccer, football, hockey, boxing, wrestling and other contact sports put players/ athletes at risk **for strains**. So do other sports activities that feature quick starts (hurdling, long jump, running etc). Gymnastics, tennis, rowing, golf-sports that require extensive gripping have a high incidence of hand strains. Elbow strains frequently occur in racquet, throwing and contact sports.

Signs of a Sprain

While the intensity varies, pain, bruising, and inflammation are common to **all three categories of sprains, mild, moderate and severe**. The individual will usually feel a tear or pop in the joint. A severe sprain produces acute pain at the moment of injury, as ligament tear completely, or separate from the bone. This loosening makes the joint nonfunctional. **A moderate sprain partially tears the ligament, producing joint instability, and some swelling**. A ligament is stretched in a mild sprain, but there is no joint loosening.

Ankle Sprains

Ankle sprains *(see figure a, b, c)* are among the most commonly experienced sports injuries. Injury or sprain occurs when the stout (strong and thick) ligaments connecting bones of the ankle are either stretched, partially ruptured or completely torn. Sportspersons/Athletes experiencing ankle sprains commonly remark that they felt their ankle turn under. This is associated with an almost immediate onset of swelling along the outside of the ankle and pain. If treated quickly and appropriately ankle sprains can heal well, returning the sports person/ athlete to competition/ training within a few days.

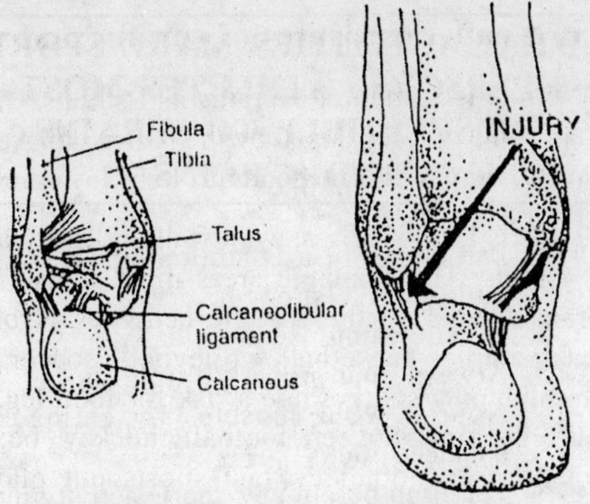

Figure (a) Normal Anatomy

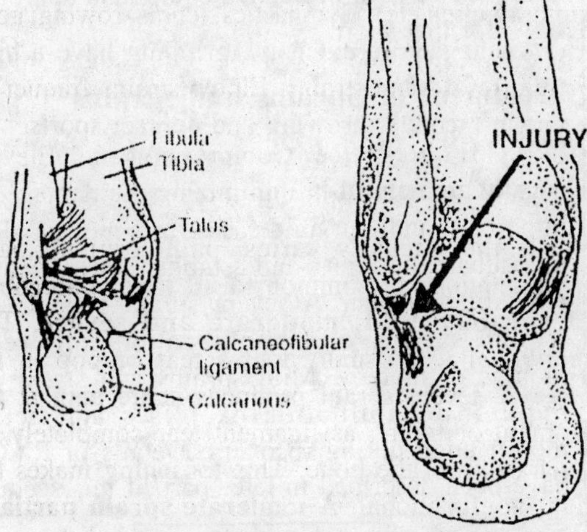

Figure (b) Normal Anatomy

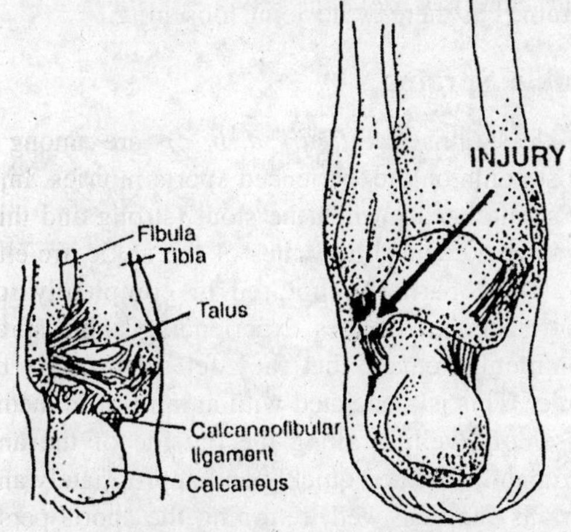

Figure (c) Normal Anatomy

If ankle sprains are ignored enormous swelling occurs keeping the sportsperson / athlete out of competition/ training for weeks to months.

Ankle sprains are graded by health care specialists in terms of degree of severity. The more severe the sprain, the higher the degree and the longer the time to recover. First degree ankle sprains are the most common. In this injury the ligaments including the anterior talofibular ligament (ATFL) are stretched but not completely torn. There is modest swelling but no gross instability.

Second degree sprains involve partial tearing of the anterior talofibular ligament. There is more swelling, more pain and generally longer time to recover. Third degree ankle sprains involve complete rupture of the lateral ankle ligaments beginning with *the anterior talofibular ligament and extending posteriorly to the talocalcaneal ligament.*

Initial treatment for all three degrees of ankle sprains is the same. The ankle should be compressed with an elastic bandage such as an Ice wrap. Ice should be applied and the ankle should be elevated. Sportspersons/Athletes should be placed on crutches allowing weight bearing as soon as comfortable. After taping, icing, elevating and protecting the ankle through the inflammatory stage usually up to three days, taping is continued but work has now begun on range of motion. Once painless motion has been restored to normal, strengthening begins. This may be performed on your own or under the auspices of a coach / trainer or physical therapist. Once strength has returned, sportspersons / athletes may begin walking on their ankle, then jogging, then advancing to sports specific cutting and twisting activities.

If the ankle is allowed to swell initially after the injury, the time taken to recover is markedly delayed making immediate care the most important aspect of ankle injury.

A second type of ankle sprain involves a disruption of the ligaments connecting the two bones, the tibia and fibula, at the ankle. This is a rupture of the syndesmotic ligament commonly known as a high ankle sprain. This injury takes a significantly longer period of time to recover.

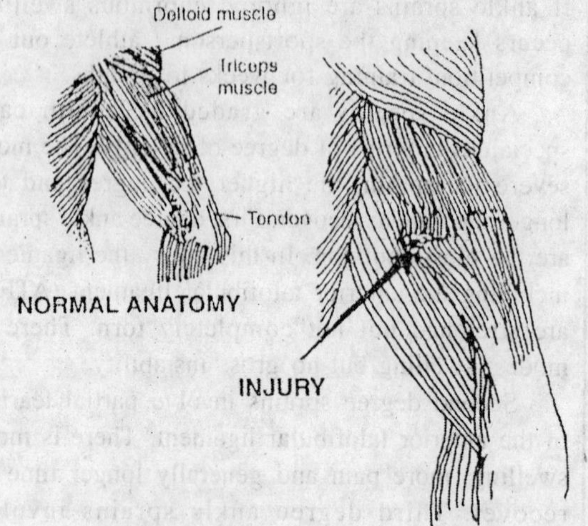

Figure. Arm (Tricepts) Strain

Signs of a Strain

Typical indications include pain, muscle spasm, muscle weakness, swellings inflammation, and cramping. In severe strains, the muscle and/or tendon are partially or completely ruptured, often incapacitating the individual. Some muscle functions will be lost with a moderate strain, where the muscle/ tendon is over stretched and slightly torn. With a mild strain, the muscle / tendon is stretched or pulled, slightly. Some common strains are:

Back Strain

When the muscles that support the spine are twisted, pulled, or torn, the result is a back strain. Players/ Athletes who engage in excessive jumping (during basketball, volleyball, etc) are vulnerable to this injury.

Hamstring Muscle Strain

A hamstring muscle strain is a tear or stretch of a major muscle in the back of the thigh. The injury can sideline a person for up to six months. The likely cause is muscle strength imbalance between the hamstrings and muscles in the front of the thigh, the quadriceps kicking a football, running or leaping to make a basket can pull a hamstring injuries tend to recur.

Preventive measures of sprains and strains

No one is immune to sprains and strains, but here are some tips developed by the **American Academy of Orthopaedic Surgeons** to help in reducing the injury risk:

1. Participate in a conditioning programme to build muscle strength.
2. Do stretching exercises daily.
3. Always wear properly fitting shoes.
4. Nourish your muscles by eating a well-balanced diet.
5. Warm up before any sports activity including practice.
6. Use or wear protective equipment appropriate for that sport.

Treatment of Sprains and Strains

"R.I.C.E." Rest, Ice, Compression and Elevation usually are helpful in minimizing the damage. It is important in all but mild cases for a medical doctor to evaluate the injury and establish a treatment and rehabilitation plan. A severe sprain or strain may require surgery or immobilization followed by months of therapy. Mild sprains and strains may require rehabilitation exercises and activity modification during recovery. Details of R.I.C. E. have been described in later part of this section.

FRACTURE

Fracture is a brokenne.

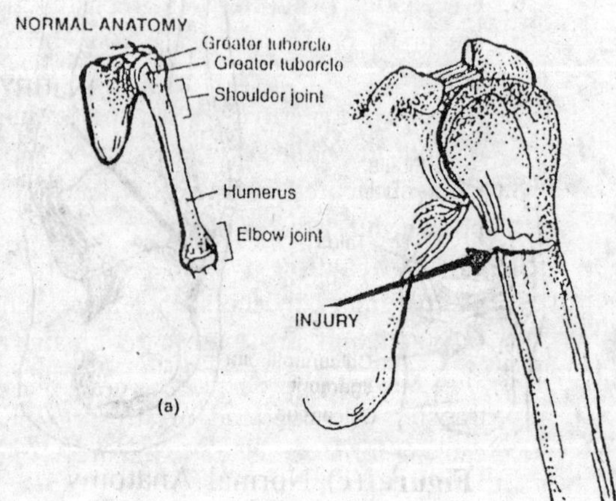

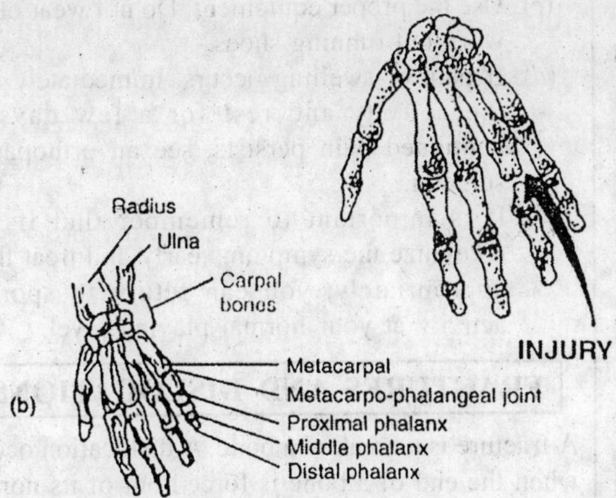

Types of Fractures

There are many kinds of fractures. Common types include simple, compound, multiple, comminuted, greenstick, spiral, stress complicated fractures.

1. **Simple Fracture:** In a simple fracture, a bone breaks, but the skin over it doe not.
2. **Compound Fracture:** In a compound fracture, both the bone and skin break, and there is danger of infection.
3. **Multiple Fracture:** Multiple fracture means there is more than one fracture in a bone.
4. **Comminuted Fracture:** Comminuted fracture means the bone has splintered, or shattered, usually owing to a crushing injury.
5. **Spiral Fracture:** A spiral fracture results when a bone is broken by a twisting force.
6. **Greenstick Fracture:** In a greenstick fracture, the break occurs only part way through the bone.
7. **Impacted Fracture:** When the broken ends of both the bones driven into one another.
8. **Communicated Fracture**–When the bone is broken into several pieces.
9. **Stress Fractures:** A stress fracture is an overuse injury. It occurs when muscles become fatigued and are unable to absorb added shock. Eventually, the fatigued muscle transfers the overload of stress to the bone causing a tiny crack called a stress fracture.

Doctors can detect a fracture in several ways. Usually, there is pain, soreness, or tenderness in a fracture area. Swelling and discolouration also occur. Sometimes, there is a movement of the bone under the skin and obvious deformity. Crepitus often signals a broken bone. Crepitus is a harsh grating sound caused when the broken ends of the bone rub together. In some cases, only an X-ray reveals a fracture. Fractures require medical treatment. The injured part of the body should be immobilized until skilled help available.

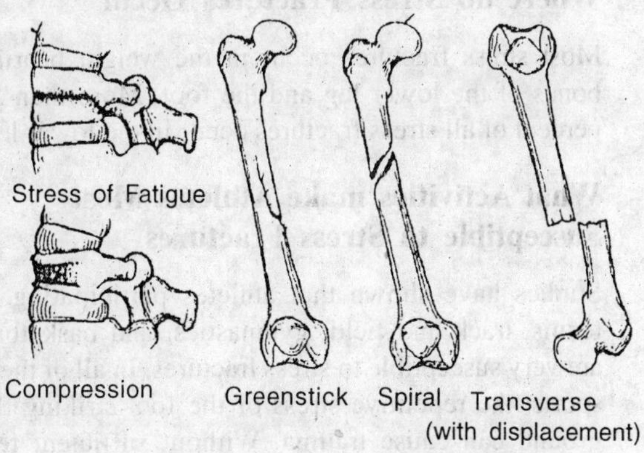

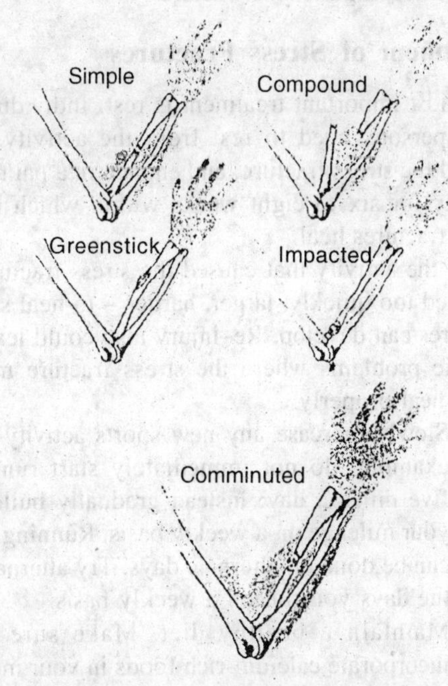

Causes of Stress Fracture

Stress fractures often are the result of increasing the amount or intensity of an activity too rapidly. They also can be caused by the impact of an unfamiliar surface (a tennis player who has switched surfaces from a soft clay court to a hard court), improper equipment (a runner using worn or less flexible shoes); and increased physical stress, a basketball player who has had a substantial increase in playing time.

Where do Stress Fractures Occur

Most stress fractures occur in the weight bearing bones of the lower leg and the foot. More than 50 percent of all stress fractures occur in the lower leg.

What Activities make Athletes Most Susceptible to Stress Fractures

Studies have shown that athletes participating in tennis, track and field, gymnastics, and basketball are very susceptible to stress fractures. In all of these sports, the repetitive stress of the foot striking the ground can cause trauma. Without sufficient rest between workouts or competitions, a sportsperson risk developing a stress fracture.

Treatment of Stress Fractures

The most important treatment is rest. Individuals / sportspersons need to rest from the activity that caused the stress fracture, and engage in a pain-free activity for six to eight weeks within which most stress fractures heal.

If the activity that caused the stress fracture is resumed too quickly, larger, harder – to-heal stress fractures can develop. Re–injury also could lead to chronic problems where the stress fracture might never heal properly.

(*a*) Slowly increase any new sports activity. For example, do not immediately start running five miles a day; instead gradually build up your mileage on a weekly basis. Running also can be done on alternate days. Try alternating the days you run on a weekly basis.

(*b*) Maintain a healthy diet. Make sure you incorporate calcium-rich foods in your meals.

(*c*) Use the proper equipment. Do not wear old or worn out running shoes.

(*d*) If pain or swelling occurs, immediately stop the activity and rest for a few days. If continued pain persists, see an orthopaedic surgeon.

(*e*) It is important to remember that if you recognize the symptoms early and treat them appropriately, you can return to sports / activity at your normal playing level.

FRACTURES AND DISLOCATIONS

A fracture is a break in a bone. A dislocation occurs when the end of a bone is forced out of its normal position in a joint. Fractures and dislocations frequently result from sports accidents subject to many understandable reasons.

Signs of fractures and dislocations include pain, an unusual position of a joint or bone, and tenderness and swelling around the injury. The victim may also experience a grating sensation, caused by fragments of broken bone rubbing together. The victim may be unable to use a hand or a foot.

One should keep the victim quiet and treat for shock. Whenever possible, the injured person should not be moved until expert help arrives. Improper handling of an injured bone or joint may seriously damage arteries, muscles, or nerves. It may also increase the severity of the fracture or dislocation.

If you have to move the victim before help arrives, apply a splint to the injured area. The splint prevents broken or dislocated bones from moving. You can make a splint from any material that will support the injured part without bending. For fractures of the arm or leg, the splint should be long enough to prevent movement of joints above and below the injury. Pad the splint surfaces that touch the body. Do not try to correct any deformities before splinting. Do not push bone fragments back into an open wound.

Use strips of cloth to tie the splint above and below t he point.of injury. Do not tie the splint so tightly that it interferes with blood circulation. Blueness or swelling in fingers, for example, indicates that a splint has been tied too tightly to an arm.

A person who may have suffered a broken neck or other spinal injury should not move. A person may receive such an injury by diving into shallow water, falling from a considerable height, or striking the head in a sporting accident. Moving such person may cause permanent paralysis or even death.

DISLOCATION

The term dislocation usually refers to the movement out of normal position of the bones of a joint. When bones become dislocated they do not meet properly at the joint. This usually results in pain and swelling.

Sometimes in dislocation the bones of a joint are pulled out of place only slightly, **doctors call this a sub luxation or incomplete dislocation**. In other cases, the bones become completely separated from each other. This is a complete dislocation. A doctor corrects a dislocation by manipulating the bones to return them to their normal position, **this procedure is called reducing the dislocation.** Some dislocated joints may return to their normal position naturally. In simple dislocation, the patient has no external wound. A compound dislocation is one accompanied by a wound opening from the body surface. **When a dislocation occurs in the same joint many times, doctors say it is habitual.**

Causes of Dislocation

In sports causes of dislocation vary from game to game and situation to situation. However, some of the main reasons may be a direct blow to the part concerned i.e. knee, wrists, shoulder, ankle etc. Pulling or jerking on a particular joint may also cause dislocation. Some time dislocation is caused due to powerful muscle contraction particularly knee cap dislocation. Cutting moves on the fields or courts also causes dislocation in the different joints. In such moves sports persons change direction suddenly that causes bones in the different joints to rotate which results in dislocation. Dislocation sometime may be the end result of severe sprain in a particular part. Poor muscle conditioning may also be the cause of dislocation.

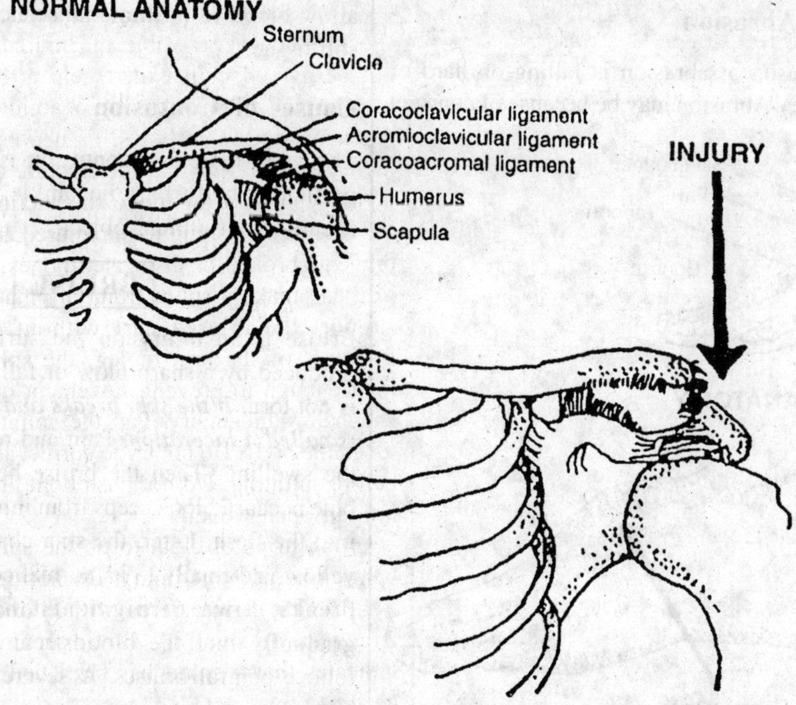

Preventive Measures of Dislocation

Some of the preventive measures in dislocation may be as under:

1. Sportspersons / individuals must build their overall strength and muscle tone with a long term conditioning/fitness prgramme according to the need of their game or sport.
2. Adequate warm up should be done before game/match or any physical activity.
3. One must wear protective devices/ equipment during contact sports.
4. Irregular surfaces should be avoided for running or track events.

ABRASION

Abrasion is a scraped skin or mucous membrane, which is normally a minor injury. It may become serious if it spreads to a large area or if foreign particles get mixed in it. Symptoms and signs of abrasion are that skin looks scraped or irritated and starts bleeding. Abrasion causes immediate pain, which lasts for short period.

Causes of Abrasion

The main reason of abrasion is falling on hard or rough surfaces. Abrasion may be because of constant irritation of skin by ill fitted shoes; rough fabric, seams in clothing or other parts of sports equipment such as helmets and pads etc.

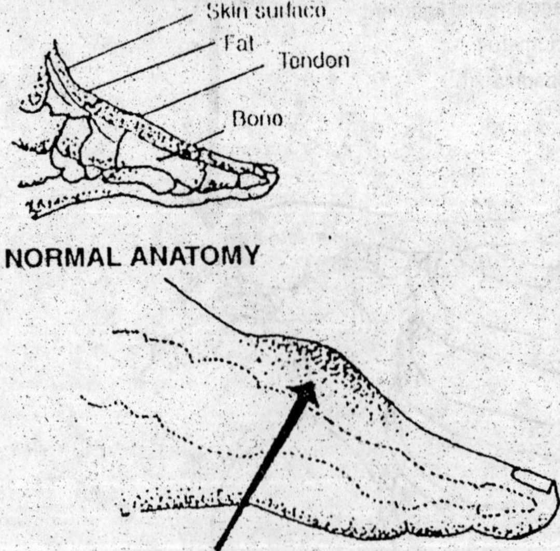

Preventive Measures

Some of the preventive measures to avoid abrasion are that one must wear protective clothing/ uniform including long sleeves,high socks, elbow and kneepads and specially designed uniform for a particular sports/ game. One must also wear good quality and well fitted footgear to help avoid falls and prevent abrasion. Irritating fabric and poorly placed seams in uniforms or sports cloths should be avoided. A combination of cotton and synthetic sports clothing are recommended. To prevent the abrasion, quality of playing fields should be good and poor-quality playing fields should be avoided.

CONTUSION

Contusion is bruising of skin and underlying tissues of the body parts due to a direct blow. Contusion causes bleeding from ruptured small capillaries that allow blood to infiltrate muscles, tendons or other soft tissue.

Causes of Contusion

The main reason of contusion is direct blow to a particular body part i.e. ankle, elbow, arm etc. usually from a blunt object.

BRUISE

Bruise is an injury on the surface of the body produced by a sharp blow or fall. Usually the skin is not torn. *If the skin breaks and bleeds, the injury is called a laceration.* Pain and redness occur with the swelling. Then the bruise becomes black and blue because blood seeps from injured blood vesseis into the flesh. Later, the skin changes to greenish-yellow and finally to its normal colour as the blood breaks down to pigments that are absorbed gradually into the bloodstream. Ice packs help relieve painful bruises. A severe bruise should be treated by a doctor.

TENNIS ELBOW/LATERAL EPICONDYLITIS

Lateral Epicondylitis or Tennis Elbow is a common cause of pain along the outside aspect of the elbow. Causes include direct trauma to the area as result of a fall, sports accident, or work related injury versus overuse as seen in repetitive lifting, carrying, or performing fine manipulations of the hand. Patients complain of point tenderness over the bony prominence along the outside of the elbow- the lateral epicondyle. The pain aggravated by activities involving extension of the wrist. These include lifting a suitcase shaking hands, turning door knobs, etc. Another common cause for this condition is hitting backhand tennis shots with the wrist in slight extension.

A diagnosis is made readily by focal tenderness along the prominence or lateral epicondyle and into the origins of the extensor muscles of the wrist. Resisted wrist extension also reproduces the patient's pain. X-ray examinations are usually unremarkable in this condition.

Treatment is directed at relieving the offending cause of pain through rest, combined with ice, anti inflammatory medication and a stretching and strengthening programme for the wrist extensors. Other treatments include a wrist brace to assure rest and a tennis elbow or counter fore brace worn around the proximal forearm to take pressure off the origin of the muscles.

In rare circumstances when patients do not respond to activity modification, and conservative methods, surgical intervention is indicated.

TREATMENT FOR SIMPLE SPORTS INJURIES

Approach to Doctor

Listen to your body. Several signs will indicate to you when you should see your doctor. You must approach your doctor in case of the following:

- if pain is severe or persists.
- Inability to move the injured part of your body.
- The injury does not appear to be healing.

Immediate Care of Injuries

The immediate care of common sports injuries (sprains, strains, contusions, etc,) consists of a four-step programme that should be followed as soon as an injury occurs, whether or not you go to physician. The four part programme is called RICE, and stands for REST, ICE, COMPRESSION, and ELEVATION.

Rest

As soon as an injury occurs, it is important to stop the activity immediately. Prolonged delay in stopping the activity could cause further damage to the injured part. When a body part has become injured, the body reacts with an inflammatory process, which causes swelling, redness, local increase of heat in the area, pain, and malfunction. The degree of each of these depends upon the severity of the injury.

Ice

Put ice on the Injured part as soon as possible after the injury. Ice or cold, specifically, controls swelling by constricting the blood and lymph vessels, decreases muscle spasm (which often accompanies injury), and decreases some of the discomfort and pain caused by the inflammation. By reducing the swelling that collects around the injured area, the rehabilitation time will be lessened and you will be able to return to your sport more quickly. The ice should be applied for 20-30 minutes. It could be in the form of an ice bag chemical packs, frozen vegetables, can of soda, snow etc. It should be applied every hour for the next several hours.

Compression

Compression also helps to limit swelling in the injured area. The compression should be applied concurrently with the cold treatment (a wet elastic bandage). After the ice treatment, a dry elastic wrap or tape should be applied comfortably firm not too tight to cut off circulation, or too loose to allow further swelling. If lack of sensation or numbness is felt, the wrap is probably too tight. The use of sponge pads around bony prominences (ankle bones) will insure even pressure around the injured part. The wrap should be loosened while going to bed, but worn continuously until the swelling has subsided (about 48-72 hours).

Elevation

The fourth part of treatment is to elevate the injured part while being compressed. In elevating, support should be placed under the entire limb. The height should be above the level of the HEART to help drain the excess fluid from the injured area. While sleeping the compression wrap should be loosened and the foot of the bed or mattress raised by some suitable object (for injuries to the lower extremity) or the head of the bed or mattress raised for the upper extremity injuries.

RICE should be continued for at least 48-72 hours. Under no circumstances during this time should any form of heat be applied, including excessive time in hot showers or baths. That would just increase the swelling and inflammation. When you are sure that the swelling has stopped, give yourself an extra day of RICE. During the acute (first 72 hours) stage of the injury, no other activity should be performed. Your body has been injured and will need all the help it can to heal the injury. This means optimal healing conditions proper nutrition, your normal amount of sleep, and a positive attitude. The same amount of effort you placed in your sport/ athletic endeavours should be placed in your rehabilitation programme.

PREVENTION OF SPORTS /ATHLETIC INJURIES

The risk of injury accompanies participation in almost all sporting activities. As the number of participants in both competitive and recreational sports has increased, there has been a corresponding increase in the number of injuries. Sports/ Athletic injuries can have profound, long lasting effects on sportsperson/athletes. Injuries, particularly those not properly cared for, may develop into conditions that can last a lifetime. Some of these conditions are chronic Tennis Elbow, Runner's Knee or osteoarthritis. Great Indian Cricketer Sachin Tendulkar had to be out of the game for about a year due to Tennis Elbow.

Except for unforeseen circumstances such as injuries that occur from high forces generated in sports/athletics(broken bones, dislocated joints) the athlete / sportsperson or those responsible for the sportsperson's/ athlete's health training can reduce the risk of injury from any of these factors. Which are given below:

Lack of Pre-participation Screening / Medical Checkup

A pre-participation physical and medical examination should be done on all trainees/ athletes prior to the start of their season or activity and which should include:

- A thorough medial history should be collected.
- Body measurements (bp, ht, wt) should be recorded.
- Medical exam (circulo- respiratory check, abdominal, pelvis check, etc.).
- Lab tests – hematocrit, urinalysis etc. should be done.
- Orthopaedic exam (consisting of Body build, Posture, Flexibility, % body fat, strength, and Maturation) should be conducted.

If any problems is/ are found, the trainee/ athlete is given some remedial exercises or limitations of activity may be known to him. The sportsperson / trainees should not be allowed to participate until the deficiency has been made up or corrected.

Poor Coaching or Coaching error

The coach/ physical educator is responsible for the structure and administration of the physical training programme and the trainee's /athlete's conduct on the playing field/ court. Most sports/ athletic programmes do not have the services of a physician or expert trainer at the games and practices and therefore the coach/ physical educator must also assume these roles. Unfortunately, the quality and control of coaches is difficult. But some of the important qualifications, which a coach should have, include:

- Certification / qualification and training.
- Basic first aid training.
- Technique instruction, fundamentals
- Knowledge of the psychosocial aspects of sport
- Continuing education courses and clinics

Lack of Conditioning / Fitness

A conditioned trainee/ athlete, enhances his/ her performance, decreases the risk and severity of injury to occur, and may be able to return to activity sooner after an injury than a non conditioned trainee/ athlete. *The idiom "get in shape to play sports,not play sports to get in shape" has good sound medical research behind it.*

Sportspersons/ Athletes must be conditioned to be able to stand the physical demands of their sports. The fitness components of conditioning consist of *cardiovascular endurance, body composition, flexibility, strength and power, muscular endurance, speed and agility.* Each of these components must be addressed completely to condition the sportsperson / athlete. Conditioning is a series of biological adaptations. For example, the trainee / athlete does not attain high levels of strength all at once. The athlete/ trainee stresses the muscles and becomes a little stronger. The process is repeated over and again until the desired effects are reached. This is a long-term process and consists of an off season programme, pre-season programme, and competition season programme. The coach must have an artist's feel for maximizing this rate of biological adaptation. Failure to move in a systematic and progressive path may result in over conditioning and overuse injuries or under training which does not utilize the athlete's/ trainee's true potential. The coach is critical to the conditioning process. Overuse injuries may be divided into four general categories : *training errors, anatomical factors, equipment problems and surface problems.*

Training errors consist of mistakes committed by the sportsperson/ athlete such as too great an increase in training mileage, persistent high intensity training without alternate easy days, or too great an increase in intensity without recovery time.

Anatomical factors include functional leg length discrepancy, quadriceps and hamstring insufficiency, poor flexibility and poor patella mechanics (q - angle –15 degrees).

Equipment problems have been discussed later in this section.

Surface problems consist of problems dealing with the ground/ leg interactive forces. These include too hard/ too soft, or an unyielding surface, some direction running, or too much up or downgrades or uneven terrains.

The conditioning programme should also start with a proper **warming up** to allow the body to adapt gradually to the on coming activity. The warming up consists of preliminary stretching just the immediately stressed muscles (legs). Jogging – to increase the body's inner core temp and warm the muscles up. Then complete body stretching- slow static stretches holding each stretch for at last 10 seconds and several repetitions on each body part.

Sport specific warm up activities should then be performed, such as volleying the ball in tennis, practice swings in cricket, or warm up weights in weight training. After the exercise period, a cooling down period should be allowed for and then finish off with the gentle stretching of the previously active body parts.

Improper use of Equipment

This is a subject that is on everyone's mind but often overlooked. We all want to "*look good*" when we work out and it is difficult to workout without seeing manufacturer's labels and brand name exposure in all sporting events and locations. Equipment includes the sneakers (light canvas shoe with soft rubber sole) we wear, cotton /nylon shorts we put on; wool / cotton socks on our feet, gloves, helmets or prescription braces.

Equipment should be worn if required or needed. This includes mouth pieces, shin pads, orthotics, or eye protection. The equipment should be carefully cleaned and maintained. Injury may occur if the equipment breaks down or improperly fits. A running shoe that still looks good after running 50 miles a week for one year may be internally broken down allowing for increased shock throughout the body. Missing parts or lack of properly sized equipment (hand-me-downs) are common problems in large families or sports organizations. The correct footwear is critical for sports. A pair of tennis sneakers (shoes) is not appropriate for the vertical forces in running. Running shoes are not appropriate for the lateral and front back shear forces in tennis. Previous injuries require preventive measures such as ankle braces, orthotics (artificial support), or proper sized grip for racquet sports.

If the equipment cannot be repaired properly it should be thrown out, not handed down. The equipment should be used properly and not used as a weapon (helmets, sticks).

Psycho – Social Considerations

The psychological aspect of the sportsperson / athlete must also be taken into effect in preventing injuries. Be aware of the "*injury proned*" sportsperson / athlete who is labelled as such due to many reasons. This may be due to the *lack of self confidence or inadequate preparation* for the activity. The athlete may be afraid of *re-injury*, or those that may not have "*mind set*" of competitive athlete/ trainee. Communication between the coach/ trainer and the affected sportsperson/ athlete is critical. The athlete/player *not concentrating* completely on the game should not be allowed to participate. Any diversions could cause an injury to occur. Contracts can be made up between the player/ athlete and coach / trainer that outlines both parties *responsibilities and expectations.*

Inadequate First Aid Care

The delay of the immediate recognition and care of injuries could have long lasting effects. An emergency action plan should be initiated at all sports/athletic practices and events. This includes.

- A first responder
- First aid supplies
- Access to the emergency medical system
- Follow- up care

Inadequate Rehabilitation

Once an injury has been recognized and properly treated (RICE or perhaps even surgical intervention) the next step is to rehabilitate the injured part to a point that allows the player/ athlete safe return to the sport. The athlete/ player often feels that the day the caset or sling is removed, the athlete / player is able to return back to the sport. Atrophy (wasting away) of the affected part or side often accompanies any injury and must be taken into consideration. If the service of a trainer or therapist is not used a home programme must be initiated. When the affected side is returned to the pre-injury state the athlete may initiate the gradual return to the activity.

Premature Return to Activity

An athlete's/player's premature return to practice or a game after injury places the athlete at a greater risk of re-injury or injury to another body part or other player. The determination for return should be made as objective as possible and include full pain-free range of motion, normal or average strength and power, functional stability performance of the skills of the sport, relative freedom from over all pain, psychological readiness to return to the sport without excessive emotional concerns, and biological readiness. Biological healing often takes longer to heal than clinical evaluation.

Sports related injuries require specialized care to promote optimum healing. Whether you are a jogger or tennis player, a professional soccer player or marathon runner, a child or senior citizen or even a musician or actress, trauma to the muscles and joints can limit or prevent your participation in these activities. To provide proper diagnosis and prevent future injuries, one must keep above and the following summarized points/ tips always in mind.

Basic Steps to Reduce the Risk of Sports Injuries

Sportspersons/athletes/players/Students / trainees/ individuals can reduce their risk of injury by following the basic steps, which are given below:

1. Overall conditioning is essential; it can help sportspersons/athletes avoid injury, and it also

enhances rehabilitation and shortens the "*down time*" of sportspersons / athletes.

2. Every student / sportsperson/athlete should receive a pre- participation physical examination, including a general medical examination and an orthopaedic examination.
3. Athletes/ sportspersons should work with coaches and sports/athletic trainers/experts round the year to ensure they maintain their condition with appropriate exercises and nutrition.
4. Sportspersons /athletes should focus on developing muscular strength and endurance, cardiovascular fitness and flexibility.
5. Good nutrition is a must. Incorporate the basic food groups that is grains, fruits and vegetables, dairy and meat / poultry / fish. Athletes / sportspersons diets should also be high in complex carbohydrates.
6. Sportspersons / athletes practising or playing in warmer climates should become acclimatized to high levels of activity in hot weather. Practice should be held early in the morning or late in the afternoon.
7. Limit workouts and practices to maximum two hours.
8. The night before an event, sportsperson/ athletes should hydrate with electrolyte fluids to reduce the risk of dehydration.
9. Fluid breaks should be offered at least every 45 minutes, and sportspersons / athletes should be entitled to unrestricted amounts of fluids to help prevent dehydration and other forms of heat- related illness.
10. All athletes/ sportspersons should use appropriate equipment that fits properly in practices as well as competitions.
11. Ice should be available on the sidelines of every game / match and practice injuries.
12. Every institute with a sports/ athletic programme should have a written emergency plan that is reviewed regularly and addresses every level of medical care.
13. Every institute should be encouraged to develop an Injury Protection Manual that documents how injuries will be handled.
14. The physical education / sports department should be encouraged to have a Medical Card for every sportsperson / athlete in the institute / college / department / university.
15. Physical educators/ coaches should be certified in first aid.

REHABILITATION

WHO estimate that more than 300 million people worldwide are disabled over 70% of whom live in the developing countries. Only about 1% to 2% of disabled persons in the developing world have access to rehabilitation and the majority of them are relegated to the margins of society. Over the past decade, WHO has been promoting community–based rehabilitation as a way to increase access to rehabilitation and promoting equalization of opportunities for the social integration of disabled persons into the community and society. This approach employs resources within the family and community, along with support from the referral services.

Rehabilitation has been defined as "the combined and coordinated use of medical, social, educational and vocational measures for training and retraining the individual to the highest possible level of functional ability". It includes all measures aimed at reducing the impact of disabling and handicapping conditions and at enabling the disabled and handicapped to achieve social integration. Social integration has been defined as the active participation of disabled and handicapped people in the main stream of community life.

Scope of Rehabilitation

Scope of Rehabilitation is very vast which cannot be covered fully in the preview of this book. However, some descriptions about this are given here. It involves disciplines such as physical medicine or physiotherapy, occupational therapy, speech therapy, audiology, psychology, education, social work, vocational guidance and placement services. The experts have identified the following areas of concern in rehabilitation.

(*a*) Medical rehabilitation – restoration of function.

(*b*) Vocational rehabilitation – restoration of the capacity to earn a livelihood.

(c) Social rehabilitation – restoration of family and social relationships.

(d) Psychological rehabilitation – restoration of personal dignity and confidence.

Rehabilitation is no longer looked upon as an extracurricular activity of the physician. The current view is that responsibility of the doctor does not end when the "temperature touches normal and stitches are removed." The patient must be restored and retrained "to live and work within the limits of this disability but to the hilt of his capacity". As such medical rehabilitation should start very early in the process of medical treatment.

Examples of rehabilitation are establishing schools for the blind, provision of aids for the crippled, reconstructive surgery in leprosy, muscle reeducation and graded exercises in neurological disorders like polio, change of profession for a more suitable one and modification of life in general in the case of tuberculosis, cardiac patients and others. The purpose of rehabilitation is to make productive people out of non productive people.

It is now recognized that rehabilitation is a difficult and demanding task that seldom gives totally satisfactory results; but needs enthusiastic cooperation from different segments of society as well as expertise, equipment and funds not readily available for this purpose even in affluent societies. It is further recognized that interventions at earlier states are more feasible will yield results and are less demanding of scarce resources. In this direction the Rehabilitation Council of India (RCI) that is a statutory body under the RCI Act, 1992 came into force on 31st. May 1993 (Introduced later in this section and Govt. of India also enacted "The persons with Disabilities (Equal Opportunities, Protection of Rights and full Participation) Act. 1995. Many hospitals and other organizations (Govt. and Non Govt. Social) have a rehabilitation department / institutions that work with disabled patients to help them return to normal life. There are two basic types of rehabilitation-therapy, physiotherapy and occupational therapy. Physiotherapy treats diseases or injuries. Occupational therapy helps overcome or reduce physical handicaps by teaching the patient various skills.

PHYSIOTHERAPY AND THERAPEUTIC EXERCISES

Introduction

Sports physiotherapy is the application of various physical methods in preventing, curing and rehabilitating sports injuries. Recovery is very important for sportsman. If there is insufficient recovery, sportsmen are prone to more injuries and performance is affected. Physiotherapy plays a vital role in quick recovery in athletes.

Exercise therapy is a means to accelerate the patient's recovery from injuries and diseases which affects the normal way of living. Physical therapy is the utilization of heat, light, water, electricity, massage, exercise and radiation for the main purpose of bringing about a healing and rehabilitative response. The process of recovery is delayed by inactivity and the muscular weakness which results from it, the repeated use of alternative patterns of activity makes it difficult when they are no longer needed e.g. limping after leg injury.

The main Goals of Treatment through Exercises

1. To promote activity whenever and wherever it is possible to minimize the effects of inactivity.
2. To correct the inefficiency of specific muscle or muscle groups and regain normal range of joint movement without delay to achieve efficient functional movement.
3. To encourage the patient to use the ability he has regained in the performance of normal functional activities and accelerate his rehabilitation.

General Rules for Exercises

1. Maintain general conditioning.
2. Maintain good body mechanics.
3. Exercise the affected part two to three times daily.
4. Execute all exercises smoothly to avoid pain.
5. Modify exercises if they cause pain, discomfort, or decrease in joint range.

6. Increase each exercise towards the ultimate goal of 10 repetitions per set.
7. Know the reason for a particular exercise and routine.
8. Be certain that full strength, endurance and flexibility are restored before resuming competition.

Importance of Physiotherapy

Physiotherapy is to promote physical rehabilitation. It is most suitable for all patients. Physiotherapy is no static art. Methods of treatment constantly change and many that were once prominent and popular have lost popularity. The use of electrical currents have gone out of fashion, massage is also looked at with cold scientific eye and does not emerge unscathed from the appraisal, and passive treatment of patients making no effort to help themselves are regarded as prolonging rather than cutting short invalidation. Yet in spite of all this most of the patients are referred for the physiotherapy than ever before.

Physiotherapy plays an important role in recovering from the injuries. The problems arising from loss of function are different for each patient, and the treatment is planned according to the individual's need. If the treatment is ineffective then it should be altered or discontinued. Physiotherapist must select the suitable techniques which suits to the abilities, disabilities and needs of the patient.

1. Physiotherapy gives relaxation to hypersonic muscles.
2. The normal range of joint movement is maintained by therapeutic exercises.
3. The tone and power of working muscles are maintained.
4. It reduces loss of muscular strength
5. It maintains the endurance of the muscles.
6. Neuromuscular co-ordination is improved by the repetition of exercises.
7. These exercises give confidence to the patient.
8. Therapeutic exercises build up weak muscles and the blood flow to the working muscles is also increased.
9. Normal joint movement and the extensibility of the muscle is maintained.
10. Fear, anger and excitement increases the muscular tension, physiotherapist does his best to reassure the patient's confidence and co-operation.

CLASSIFICATION OF THERAPEUTIC EXERCISE

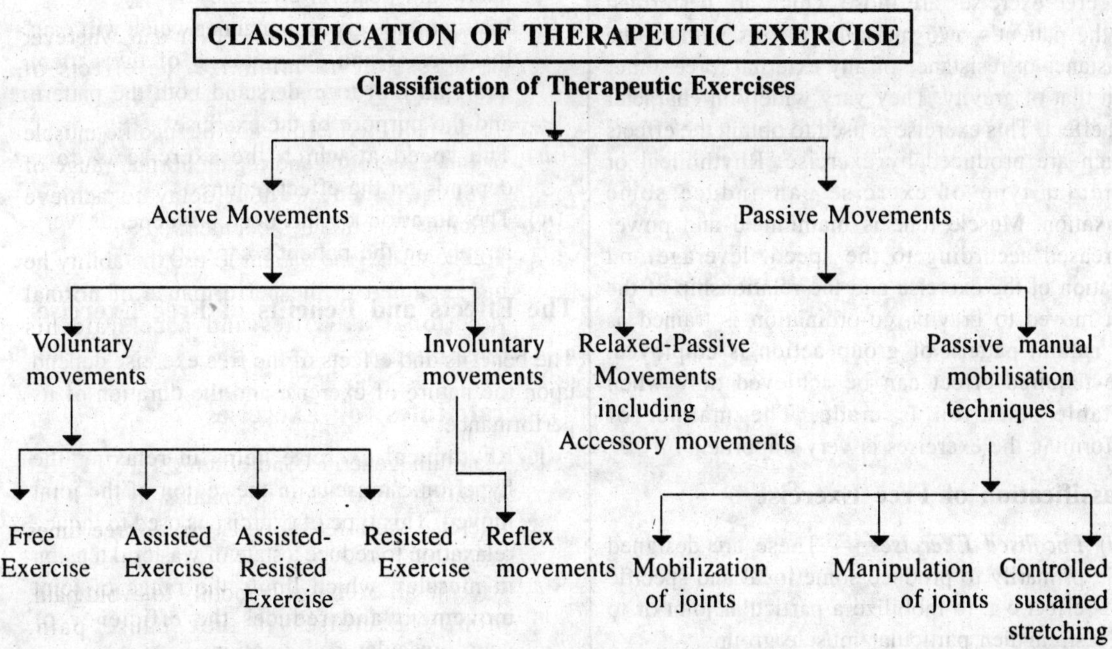

ACTIVE MOVEMENT

Active movement is executed by the athlete without assistance. Exercises in this category are those used for general conditioning and those used remedially for restoring function to an injured part.

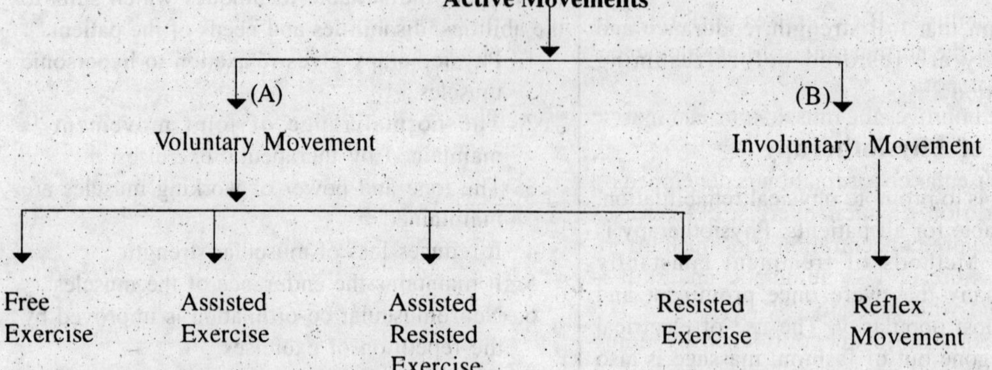

A. VOLUNTARY MOVEMENT

Movement performed or controlled by the voluntary action of muscles working in opposition to an external force.

Free Exercise

The working muscles are subject only to the forces of gravity acting upon the part moved or stabilized.

Free exercises are those which are performed by the patient's own muscular efforts without the assistance or resistance of any external force, other than that of gravity. They vary widely in character and effect. This exercise is used to obtain the effects which are produced by exercise. Rhythmical or pendular type of exercise can induce some relaxation. Muscle tone is maintained and power increased according to the speed, leverage and duration of the exercise and the relationship of the part moved to gravity, co-ordination is trained as the natural pattern of group action is employed. The required effect can be achieved only when suitable selection is made. The manner of performing the exercises is very important.

Classification of Free Exercise

(*i*) ***Localised Exercises*** — These are designed primarily to produce some local and specific effect e.g. to mobilize a particular joint or to strengthen particular muscle groups.

(*ii*) ***General Exercises*** — These are usually involved in the use of many joints and muscles all over the body and the effect is widespread e.g. as in running.

Technique of Free Exercise

(*i*) As a basis for movement, the starting position is selected and taught with care to insure the maximum postural efficiency.

(*ii*) Instruction is given in manner which will gain the interest and co-operation of the patient and lead him to understand both the pattern and the purpose of the exercise.

(*iii*) The speed at which the exercise is done depends on the effect required.

(*iv*) The duration of the exercise depends very largely on the patient's capacity.

The Effects and Benefits of Free Exercise

The benefits and effects of the free exercise depend upon the nature of exercise and the duration of its performance.

1. Rhythmical exercise helps in relaxing the hypertonic muscles in the region of the joint moved. This type of exercise is used to induce relaxation to reduce a state of wasteful tension in muscles, which limits the range of joint movement and reduces the efficiency of neuromuscular coordination.

2. Alternating and reciprocal contraction and relaxation of opposing muscles is required to sustain the movement and normal state of relaxation.
3. Joint Mobility – By exercises performed in full range, the normal range of joint movement is maintained.
4. Exercise improves the muscle tone and muscle power.
5. Neuromuscular co–ordination is developed by the repetition of such exercises. Exercises which require concentration and much effort, become more or less automatic and skill is developed with practice.
6. The patients build up confidence by doing the objective exercises and activities.

Exercises can be used to increase respiration, to increase both the local as well as the general circulation and to provide work for the heart muscles.

Assisted Exercise

Assisted exercise is movement of an injured part by the athlete, but with the assistance of another person. The magnitude of assisting force must be sufficient only to augment the muscular action and must not be allowed to act as a substitute. As the power increases assistance must decrease in the same proportion.

Technique

The programme planning should ensure that weak muscles exert their maximum effort and assistance only augments their effort.

(*i*) Starting position – Stability for the body as a whole ensures that the patient's whole attention is concentrated on the pattern of movement and the effort required to perform.

(*ii*) Pattern of Movement – This must be well known and understood bythe patient.

(*iii*) Fixation – Adequate fixation of the bone of origin of the prime movers improves their efficiency. For the movement to be transferred to neighbouring joints to compensate for the inefficiency of the weak muscles, movement in these joints must be controlled by manual pressure or by other means like fixation, so that the movement is pivoted at the required joint.

(*iv*) The part moved should be supported throughout to reduce the load on the weakened muscles by counter balancing the effects of gravity force. The advantage of manual support is that it can be adjusted according to required movement.

(*v*) Effort should be made to reduce tension in antagonistic muscles.

(*vi*) Preliminary stretching of the weak muscles to elicit the myotatic (stretch) reflex provides a powerful stimulus to contraction.

(*vii*) The force should be applied in the direction of the movement.

(*viii*) The movement should be smooth throughout.

(*ix*) The repetitions should be according to the understanding of the condition which has caused the weakness.

(*x*) The co-operation of the patient is essential.

Effects and Benefits of Assisted Exercises

(*i*) The muscles which have difficulty in performing movement unaided carry out the action with assistance and thus gradually gain strength and hypertrophy, provided they are made to carry out maximum effort of which they are incapable.

(*u*) It helps in neuro- muscular re-education. The memory of the pattern of coordinated movement is stimulated by the correct performance of a movement which the patient is unable to achieve without assistance. These exercises may be helpful in training coordination.

(*iii*) Confidence in the ability to move is established.

(*iv*) The range and control of effective joint movement can be increased by assisted exercises.

Assisted – Resisted Exercise

This type of exercise constitutes a combination of assistance and resistance during a single movement.

Resisted Exercise

Resisted exercise is movement that the athlete performs against a resisting force.

External force is applied to oppose the movement in order to counteract force of muscular contraction. Tension is increased within the muscles by the resistance and the muscles respond by an increase in their power and hypertrophy. This results in increase of tension in the muscle, which results in development of greater power and efficiency.

Technique of Resisted Exercise

(*i*) Starting position should be comfortable and stable so that whole concentration is on the pattern of movement and the efforts are made to overcome the resistance.

(*ii*) Pattern of movement should be such which should allow contraction of the muscle in full range of movement.

(*iii*) Stabilization of the bone of origin improves movement efficiency.

(*iv*) Preliminary stretching of movement improves myotatic (stretch) reflex.

(*v*) The resisting force may be applied to resist the contraction of the working muscles by manual pressure, weights, springs etc. and the pressure is exerted in the direction of the movement. Magnitude will vary according to the purpose and requirement.

(*vi*) The movement should be smooth and controlled.

(*vii*) Repetition will vary according to condition of the individual patient.

Resistances

(*a*) Resistance by the physiotherapist is applied manually in the line of the movement, and the hand is placed on the surface of the skin in the direction of the movement.

(*b*) The patient can resist his own movement by using his own body weight.

(*c*) Resistance by weights is simple and effective method of resisting active exercise. Resistance by weights is also known as progressive resistance exercise.

(*d*) Resistance by weight and pulley circuits allows the force exerted by a weight to act in any direction therefore the muscles need not work against the resistance of both gravity and the weight. This is useful to give resistance of weak muscles.

(*e*) Resistance by springs and other elastic substances. It is stretched or compressed according to the type of spring used.

(*f*) Resistance by water increases with the speed and the surface area of the part moved.

Effects and Benefits of Resisted Exercise

1. They help to build up weak muscles and restore the balance of muscle power.
2. They improve the blood circulation.
3. Heat is produced with the strenuous muscular activity which stimulates the heat regulating centre causing vaso-dilatation of the skin.
4. A general rise in blood pressure frequently anticipates exercise.

B. INVOLUNTARY MOVEMENT

Reflex Movement

Reflex movement is involuntary and may be defined as the motor response to sensory stimulation. These reflex movements are concerned with the repetition of movement patterns which have become automatic.

The reflex Arc

The reflex arc is the pathway of impulses which give rise to reflex activity. It consists of two neurons, an efferent neuron which leads from sensory receptor organ to the Central Nerous System (CNS) and an efferent neuron leading from the CNS to the affected organ (muscle fibres). Most of them consist of a chain of neurons in which one or several connecting neurons lie between the afferent and efferent neurons. Reflex activity can be stimulated by various means to facilitate movement or the maintenance of posture.

Stretch Reflex

This is a spinal reflex activated by stretching a muscle. When an innervated muscle is stretched it responds by contracting and developing tension to counteract the stretching force. This is a good means of promoting activity in muscle when voluntary effort is ineffective. Tension in a contracting muscle is increased by the application of a resisting force and the quality of the contraction is improved.

Righting Reflex

These reflexes are responsible for maintenance and restoration of equilibrium.

Postural Reflexes

These reflexes are concerned with maintenance of posture.

Effects and Benefits of Reflex Movements

1. The initiation of reflex movement provides a means of promoting activity of the neuromuscular mechanism when voluntary effort is ineffective.
2. Normal joint movement and the extensibility of muscles is maintained by this type of movement when spastic paralysis makes voluntary movement impossible.
3. Circulation is improved by the contraction of muscles and movement of joints achieved during these movements.
4. Temporary relaxation of spastic muscles is obtained following repeated movement.
5. Postural reflexes are conditioned to reproduce a satisfactory pattern of posture by repeated use of these patterns.

PASSIVE MOVEMENTS

When the muscles are inactive or relatively slow, movement produced by the application of external force is known as passive movement and that resulting from the contraction of muscles is active movement.

Passive movement is the exercise of an affected part by another person or by a device, without effort by the athlete.

These movements are produced by an external force during muscular inactivity or when muscular activity is voluntarily reduced as much as possible to permit movement.

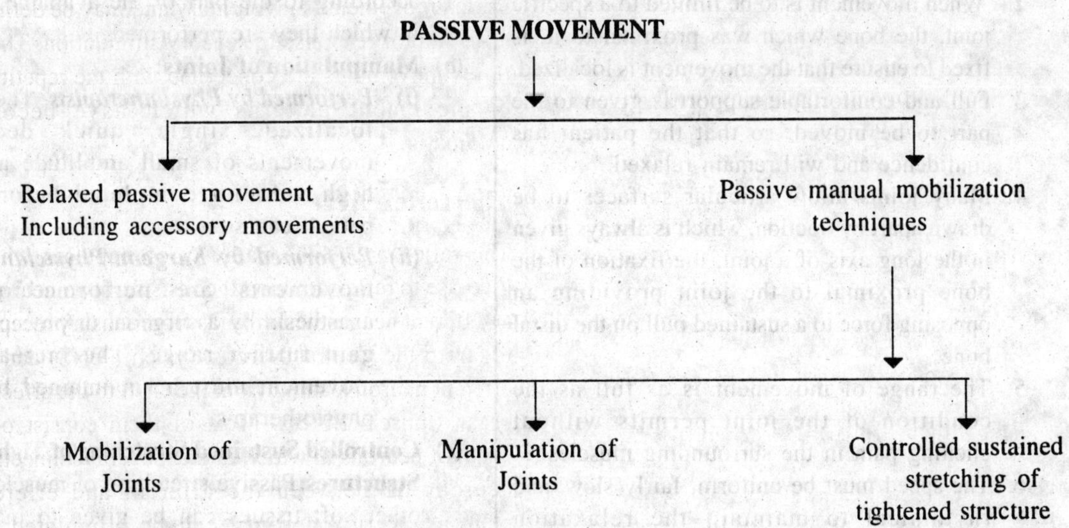

Relaxed–Passive Movements Including Accessory Movements

(a) ***Relaxed Passive Movements*** – These are movements performed accurately and smoothly by the physiotherapists. A knowledge of the anatomy of joints is required. The movements are performed in the same range and direction as active movements. The joint is moved through the existing free range and within the limits of pain.

(b) ***Accessory Movements*** – These occur as part of any normal joint movement but may be limited or absent abnormal joint conditions. They consist of gliding or rotational movements which cannot be performed in isolation as a voluntary movement but can be isolated by the physiotherapist.

Principles of Giving Relaxed Passive Movements

1. A patient is taught to relax and then he is provided a suitable starting position which ensures comfort and support. The physiotherapist will inspire confidence and co-operation in maintaining relaxation through the movement.
2. When movement is to be limited to a specific joint, the bone which was proximal to it, is fixed to ensure that the movement is localized.
3. Full and comfortable support is given to the part to be moved, so that the patient has confidence and will remain relaxed.
4. Many joints allow articular surfaces to be drawn apart by traction, which is always given in the long axis of a joint, the fixation of the bone proximal to the joint providing an opposing force to a sustained pull on the distal bone.
5. The range of movement is as full as the condition of the joint permits without eliciting pain in the surrounding muscles.
6. The speed must be uniform, fairly slow, and rhythmical to maintain the relaxation throughout the movement. Duration depends upon the condition.

Effects and Benefits of Relaxed Passive Movements

1. Adhesion formation is prevented and the present free range of movement maintained.
2. When active movement is not possible, because of muscular inefficiency, these movements may help to preserve the memory of movement patterns by stimulating the receptors of kinesthetic sense.
3. They help to maintain extensibility of muscle when full range of movement is impossible.
4. The rhythm of continued passive movements can have a soothing effect and induce further relaxation and sleep.
5. Accessory movements are performed to increase lost range of movement and to maintain joint mobility.

Passive Manual Mobilization Techniques

(*a*) **Mobilization of Joints:** These are usually small repetitive rhythmical oscillatory, localized accessory, or functional movements performed by the physiotherapist in various amplitudes within the available range, and under the patient's control. These can be done very gently or quite strongly, and are graded according to the part of the available range in which they are performed.

(*b*) **Manipulation of Joints:**

(*i*) ***Performed by Physiotherapists:*** These are localized, single, quick decisive movements of small amplitude and of high velocity completed before the patient can stop it.

(*ii*) ***Performed by Surgeon/Physician:*** The movements are performed under anesthesia by a surgeon, or physician to gain further range. The increase in movement must be maintained by the physiotherapist.

(*c*) **Controlled Sustained Stretching of Tightened Structures:** Passive stretching of muscles and other soft tissues can be given to increase range of movements. Movement can be gained by stretching adhesions in these structures or by lengthening of muscle due to inhibition of the tendon protective reflex.

Effects and Benefits

1. The slow stretch produces a relaxation and lengthening of the muscles. Steady and sustained stretching is used to over come spasticity pattern of limbs.
2. A steady and prolonged passive stretch can over come the resistance of shortened ligaments.

DOPING

There is growing tendency, in modern times of using 'Dopes' by the sports person to be super-human being and to better one's performance on the field. Having adopted every known diet and physiological and psychological preparation in order to excel in a given event, it is perhaps inevitable that some athletes should then be tempted to seek a 'wonder drug' that will give them a competitive edge over others. When particularly fine performance is achieved, there is also a strong temptation for the less successful competitors to hint that some form of 'doping' was responsible. A strict control of drug usage is thus vital to the atmosphere of an international contest, protecting the hard won victory from jealous criticism while at the same time ensuring punishment of dishonest participants.

Concept

Doping is an old phenomenon. The main idea of doping is to improve the physical and mental side of the athletes. Theoretically doping is quite straight forward, but practical application is quite difficult. Often, the dividing line between permissible forms of medical treatment and doping is extremely fine. An athlete may report to the team physician complaining that he has difficulty in sleeping in a strange environment, it seem reasonable enough to prescribe a barbiturate sedative, yet traces of the drug may persist on the following day, with beneficial effects on the performance of an over-excited competitor. A footballer may be given an injection of local anesthetic to allow him to move his ankle freely after a minor sprain; however, the cocaine derivative used for such treatment may have general effects on the body; persistent traces of the drug can lead to the disqualification on the day of competition. There also seems little point in denouncing a drug procedure that cannot be detected. Equally there are no sure way of proving re-transfusion of stored blood, deliberate starvation, or dehydration. Much must thus be left to the sense of fair play and sportsmanship of the athlete, coach and attending physician. The wise athlete is his own policeman. He knows that most of the drugs are of no practical value, and many have dangerous side–effects. He also realizes that symptoms such as pain and fatigue are warning that his body has reached the limit of its capacity, attempts to surpass this limit by the use of drugs may cause permanent injury.

Meaning of Doping

Doping may be defined as the use of chemical substances, foreign to the body, to improve athletic performance.

Doping is the use of substances or the employment of means in an attempt to augment artificially the performance of an athlete, during, either participation or preparation.

This is rather broader concept of doping than the simple use of drugs- it could encompass other artificial means of trying to change the outcome of a race, for instance a programme of deliberate starvation, or dehydration, the transfusion of the athlete's own stored blood.

Blood Doping

Blood doping or blood boosting or blood transfusion is the injection of either whole blood or packed red blood cells (RBC's) into the participant the day prior to competition in the hope of increasing the blood volume and its oxygen carrying capacity, and thus improving endurance performance. Blood doping may be the injection of an individual's, own blood which was withdrawn several weeks prior to reinjection. Training continues and this apparently allows time for the body to regenerate new RBC's in which to restore the normal haemoglobin level. The ergogenic effects from the blood doping is considered to be unethical.

1. It causes infections of the blood.
2. Blood doping leads to intravascular blood clotting.
3. When attempted by an untrained and physician it leads to mismatch blood transfusion.

The Prevention of Doping

Methods for the prevention of doping fall into three broad categories – control by governmental or inter governmental legislation, regulation by athletic association and gentle persuasion.

1. Regular weight records should be maintained
2. The trainer must explain the effects of drugs rationally rather than emotionally. All types of drugs have no place in sports because of both immediate and long-term harmful effects.
3. All drug addicts should have the knowledge of physiological harmful effects of the drugs on human body.
4. Sports associations make various types of spot checks to ensure that their rules are observed.
5. The testing of the urine of winners is required.
6. The innocent athletes should not be disgraced and the guilty should be disqualified.
7. A list of prohibited drugs should be distributed to all team physicians before the competition, and in the medical centre at the competition site and the drugs are marked with a special colour coding.
8. The pharmaceutical companies label their products with chemical rather than high sounding trade marks.
9. To make random spot checks on the urine of competitors at unannounced times during their preparations, but it is quite expensive.
10. To keep a close and regular check on the weights of top athletes, and make careful examination of any who show a surprising gain or loss.
11. Any athlete caught using these drugs must be disqualified.

Some Other Useful Matters

Structural Classification of Muscles

The arrangement of the fibres and the method of attachment vary considerably among the different muscles. These structural variations form the basis for a classification of the skeletal muscles:

1. **Longitudinal:** This is a long strap like muscle whose fibres lie parallel to its long axis. Two examples are the rectus abdominus on the front of the abdomen, and the sartorius which slants across the front of the thigh.
2. **Quadrate or Quadrilateral:** Muscles of this type are four sided and are usually flat. They consist of parallel fibres. Examples include the promoter quadratus on the front of the wrist and the rhomboid muscle between the spine and scapula.
3. **Triangular or Fan Shaped:** This is a relatively flat type of muscle whose fibres radiate from a narrow attachment at one end to a broad attachment at the other. The pectoralis major on the front of the chest is an excellent example.
4. **Fusiform or spindle shaped:** This is usually a rounded, which tapers at either end. It may be long or short, large or small. Good examples are the brachialis and brachio radialis muscles of the upper extremity.
5. **Penni form or feather like:** In this type of muscles series of short parallel fibres extends diagonally from the side of a long tendon, giving the muscle as a whole the appearance of a wing feather e.g., extensor digitorium longus and tibialis posterior muscles of the leg.

6. **Bipenni form:** This is a double penniform muscle. It is characterized by a long central tendon with the fibres extending diagonally in pairs from either side of the tendon. It resembles a symmetrical trail feather.
   Example : Flexor hallucis longus and rectus femoris of the leg and thigh respectively.
7. **Multipenniform:** In this type of muscle there are several tendons present, with the muscle-fibres running diagonally between them. The middle portion of the deltoid muscle of the shoulder and upper arm is a prime example of a multipenniform muscle.

Effects of Training on Muscular system

Muscles act as biochemical machine that convert potential (chemical) energy of fuel substances into Kinetic (mechanical) energy. During short and fast bursts of extreme muscular activity e.g., 100 m sprint, glycolysis act as mode of energy production in the muscles. On the other hand, during long bouts of exhaustive exercise, as in long distance running for marathon, aerobic oxidation of fats meet energy need of the muscles. It is a well-known fact that excellent sports performances directly depend on muscle potential and function, which in turn is wholly dependent on whole body system. The body system moves according to one's own pattern of practice movement. Thus, every change in function is followed by an adaptive change:

(*a*) **Muscle Fibre Changes:** Though the number and type of fibre is genetically determined, the aerobic training may change their proportions by increasing intermedially type of red muscle fibre. If the slow twitch fibre types are experimentally stimulated at a steady low frequency over extended periods as in long distance running, the fibre becomes predominantly slow twitch type. On the contrary, as might be expected quick bursts of muscle activity promote development of fast twitch type.

(*b*) **Proportion of active muscles:** Many fibres are not able to contract and they are known as dormant/inactive fibres. Extensive training improves transmission of nerve impulses and thereby cause dormant fibres to become active.

(*c*) **Lactic acidosis Tolerance:** Brief periods of exercise as in sprinting, squash etc. causes transitory accumulation of lactic acid in muscles which results in fatigue. A trained and practising sportsman can tolerate 200mg of lactic acid per 100 ml of blood. Thus recovery after a strenuous activity is fast.

(*d*) **Muscle/body Metabolism:** The regular physical exercise as in athletes is reflected in a slightly elevated basal metabolic rate (BMR). Training of muscles causes increase in the size and number of mitochondria, myoglobin and haemoglobin content and thereby increased oxidative capacity. The increased oxidative capacity of the trained muscles has greater ability to use non-carbohydrates for energy. Increased metabolic rate causes burning of fat and content of muscle protein (myosin and actin) increases.

(*e*) **Increase in size of fibres and connective tissue:** The individual muscle fibres increase in thickness as a result of strength training. Growth of total muscle is due mainly to the increases in fibre size as muscle fibres are not created through exercise but they are enlarged. Training causes additional stress on connective tissue of muscles and makes them thicker and tougher as exercise multiplies tendons and ligaments.

(*f*) **Replenishment to muscles:** Improved cardiovascular functioning causes the more and more blood being supplied with training and the muscle fibre becomes more active and efficient.

(*g*) **Posture:** Regular training tones up muscles, improves the body shape by increasing the physical, physiological and biochemical potential of muscles.

(*h*) **Less injury to muscle fibres:** Trained muscles are less prone to injury during strenuous and vigorous exercises like, stretching, jumping, punching etc.

Effects of Training on Respiratory system

Respiration is the biochemical process of dehydrogenation of organic nutrients; particularly carbohydrates such as glucose, in the protoplasm of cell, liberating chemical energy and carbon-di-oxide.

As a result of exercise, the demand for oxygen increases. In response to this demand for more oxygen, the rate and depth of breathing are immediately increased. Emotional and environmental factors before exercise and competition also influence the rate of breathing. Following adaptation changes occur in the respiratory system due to training:

(*a*) **Lung volumes:** Vital capacity, breathing capacity and total lung capacity increases.

(*b*) **Ventilatory efficiency:** Trained athletes have significantly lower values of breathing equivalent (B.E.), which is the amount of air ventilated through the lungs for one litre of oxygen consumption. The efficiency is increased mainly because of the trained respiratory musculature.

(*c*) **Maximum minute ventilation:** The amount of air ventilated at the maximum effort, increases with training. Normally, the maximum minute ventilation is about 70-100 litres per minute. In case of a trained athlete minute ventilation increases to 120 litres per minute. In highly trained endurance athletes, the volume has been found even upto 180 litres/minute.

(*d*) Increase in pulmonary ventilation with training is caused partially by increase in the maximal oxygen uptake, which leads to an increased production of carbon dioxide and due to a higher level of lactate.

(*e*) Ventilation is reduced at sub-maximal exercise.

(*f*) **Tidal volume:** Tidal volume is increased with training.

(*g*) **Breathing frequency:** Breathing frequency is reduced with training. This leads to extraction of more oxygen from the inspired air.

(*h*) **Diffusion capacity:** Diffusion of oxygen through the alveoli membrane is increased. The increase is mainly due to increase in the number of pulmonary capillaries and increased area of alveoli.

(*i*) **Second wind:** Second wind may fail to appear in case of trained athletes.

Effects of Training on Circulatory Systen

Circulatory sys0tem consists of Heart, Blood, Veins Arteries and Capillaries. Heart is the chief organ o circulatory system. Heart performs the function o supplying blood to the muscles and organ according to their need. The circulatory systen collects waste products generated during exercise and passes to the excretory organs for discharging them out of the body.

(*a*) **Cardiac Output:** Cardiac out put in case o trained athlete, increases by 40-60% o maximal capacity. During rest it is around litres/min whereas, while exercising, i increases up to 40 litres/minute.

(*b*) **Stroke volume:** Stroke volume increase progressively from rest to moderate work an then it levels off at about 30 to 40% of th maximum aerobic power.

(*c*) **Hypertrophy of the heart/Bradicardia:** As a result of training, the size of the heart changes Heart size (size of right ventricle) increase due to endurance training and the strengt training causes increase in the thickness o ventricle walls thereby increasing th efficiency of heart.

(*d*) **Heart Rate:** Heart rate increases linearly wit increasing oxygen consumption in bot trained and untrained sports persons. The hear rate of a trained athlete is consistently lowe than that of an untrained athlete at any give work load.

(*e*) **lood Pressure:** Blood pressure increase during exercise as the requirement of bloo by the muscles is increased. The pressur exerted on the walls of the blood vessel increases as the heart pumps more and mor blood to meet the requirement of muscles.

(*f*) Pulse becomes normal in the shorter duratio after the cessation of activity in case of traine athletes.

(*g*) New capillaries are formed within the muscl fibres. The additional capillaries increase th supply of oxygen to tissues.

(*h*) Latent capillaries become active and star functioning.

(*i*) Blood cholesterol level is decreased.

(*j*) The quantity of R.B.C's increases with regular training.

Preventive Measures to Avoid Sports Injuries on the Play Field

Sports injuries are preventable to a large extent, and paying attention to some simple guidelines can make sports participation more safe and enjoyable. By adopting the following measures, sports injuries can be avoided on the play field.

(*a*) **Pre-participation Physical Examination (PPE):** The primary objective of P.P.E. is detection of underlying medical problems that may limit competition or place a person at 'Increased risk' for example weak heart, asthma, trauma induced headaches. Another primary objective is detection of physical deficiencies that may place the participant at increased risk injury e.g. unrehabilitated ankle sprain or ligament instability of the knee or shoulder.

(*b*) **Warming up:** Proper warm up before participating in any activity is essential. Warm up should last from 10 to 20 minutes. Whole body exercise should be done. Exercise like jogging, rotation of joints, jumping exercises and stretching should be done with correct technique to prevent injuries.

(*c*) **Progression:** Regardless of the type of activity, always begin at a low intensity and progress within own individual limitations to higher intensities. Doing too much in a day to achieve success fast could result in acute or chronic sports injury.

(*d*) **Protective clothing and equipment:** It is important to wear proper clothing and use correct equipment while playing. Using too heavy equipment or too light equipment during practice may cause injury to the body during competition. All prescribed guards and pads should be worn before the game to prevent injury to the sensitive body organs.

(*e*) **Individual Differences:** Load should be given according to the individual who is participating. Same load can not be given to a novice and a trained athlete. This may lead to injuries. Similarly girls and boys should be given different load. Exercises, which are not recommended for girls, should be avoided. Certain exercises produce adverse effects on the physiology of human beings. These should be avoided.

(*f*) **Cool down:** Cooling down after the participation in big muscle activity must not be neglected. It should last from 10 to 15 minutes. When the body reaches higher stage of activity, the physiological functions should be brought to rest gradually.

Process of Attaining Super Compensation in Sports Training

After the termination of Physical activity, the recovery process starts. The recovery process is the direct result of fatigue and is also as complex as fatigue. Unless the fatigue crosses a certain limit, the adaptation will not take place. During recovery, the various, tissues, organs, systems, substances, etc., which were depleted or affected during training are again restored or normalized. The pace of recovery is, however, different for different organs, tissues, substances etc. This is called the heterochronicity of recovery process. The recovery, however, does not end with the achievement of the pre activity level of substances, tissues etc. It overshoots the pre activity level. This is called overcompensation or supercompensation. This happens only when the level is optimum. The state of supercompensation is a temporary phase, which lasts for a few hours after which it again disappears and under compensation phase of a few hours occurs. In a pendulum like fashion, the phases of over and under compensation follow each other but with progressively diminishing amplitude till everything comes back to a stable pre activity level. The state of overcompensation or super-compensation is a phase of increased performance capacity for the training and competition demands, which caused supercompensation. The phase of supercompensation, in the initial stages of training, is a temporary and bio-chemical reaction to load. But if the load is repeated regularly for a number of days then a more stable adaptation takes place, which can last for several days. In other words, continuous and regular training leads to stable adaptation or increase in performance.

Ergogenic Aids

Some form of stimulating beverages and dietary helps have been in common usage amongst the sportsmen, since ancient times. The Roman gladiators believed that raw ox meat and testes give better results in the field. Five important ergogenic aids are -

(*i*) **Anabolic Agents:** They are synthetic chemicals designed to have effects similar to a natural steroid produced in the body, the hormone testosterone. Natural testosterone provides anabolic (building) and androgenic (musculinizing) effects. Anabolic agents are misused in sports to increase muscle strength and bulk and to promote aggressiveness and as a result increases athletic performance.

(*ii*) **Stimulants:** Stimulants are drugs, which increase alertness and reduce fatigue and may increase competitiveness and hostility. They are used because they can produce a psychological and physical stimulus, which may improve athletic performance.

(*iii*) **Beta-Blockers:** Drugs commonly used for heart disease to lower blood pressure and decrease the heart rate. They may also be used in the treatment of migraines and to tremors. In sports such as shooting or archer, where a steady arm or trigger finger is important, beta-blockers might be used to slow the heart rate and steady the nerves.

(*iv*) **Narcotic Analgesics:** They are powerful analgesics and are mainly used for management of severe pain. They produce a sensation of euphoria or psychological stimulation, a false feeling of invincibility and illusions of athletic process beyond the athlete's inherent ability.

(*v*) **Diuretics:** Diuretics have important therapeutic indications for the elimination of excess body fluids from the tissues in certain pathological condition and for management of high blood pressure. Diuretics are sometimes misused by competitors for two main reasons, namely: to reduce weight quickly in sports where weight categories are involved and to reduce the concentration of drugs by passing urine.

Bad Effects of Doping on Sports Persons

Winning in sports at all costs does not permit the philosophy of sports to degenerate merely into a competition amongst laboratories, scientists and athletes. Increased use of drugs in sports to gain an upper edge threatens the safety, health and longevity of athletes while preventing the original intent of sports.

(*i*) **Effect of Stimulants:**

(*a*) Aggressiveness, anxiety and tremors, which can lead to poor judgement, placing the individual at greater risk of injury.

(*b*) Dehydration and decreased circulation.

(*c*) Increased heart rate and blood pressure.

(*ii*) **Effect of Narcotic Analgesics:**

(*a*) The narcotic analgesics may increase the pain threshold so that the athlete may fail to recognize it, thus leading to more serious injury.

(*b*) Can cause physical and psychological dependence leading to many problems associated with addiction withdrawal.

(*c*) Dose related respiratory depression.

(*iii*) **Effects of Anabolic Agents:**

(*a*) Masculinization (features like males) among females.

(*b*) Increased aggressiveness, mood swings, depression, abnormal menstrual cycles, excessive hair growth on the body, in females.

(*c*) Deepening of voice in females.

(*d*) Acne, reduction in the size of testicles in males, decreased sperm production.

(*e*) Potential for kidney, liver dysfunction.

(*f*) Premature aging enlargement of prostate gland. These effects may be permanent with prolonged use.

(*g*) In adolescents, premature closure of the growth centres of the long bones may occur, resulting in stunted growth.

(*iv*) **Effects of Diuretics:**

(*a*) May cause dehydration, muscle weakening.

(*b*) A drop in blood pressure.

(*c*) Cardiac irregularities caused by electrolytic imbalance.

(*v*) **Effects of Beta Blockers:**

(*a*) Can cause heart failure.

(*b*) Asthma

(*c*) Depression

(*d*) Sleep disorders

(*e*) Sexual dysfunction

Causes of Shin Splint

Shin splint is a vague terms used to describe pain in the lower leg that often results from participation in various athletic activities, including running.

Causes: Two types of this condition exist, named for the location of the pain. Anterior shin splints occur in the front (anterior) portion of the shinbone (tibia). Anterior shin splints are due to muscular imbalances, insufficient shock absorption, toe running, or excessive pronation of the foot.

Tightness in the opposing (posterior) leg muscles places unnecessary strain on the anterior muscles and contribute to shin splints.

Insufficient shock absorption occurs as a result of running on the hard surfaces. This increases stress on all the body muscles and since legs bear most of the body weight, it may lead to stress in the anterior shin muscles.

Toe running occurs when the athlete lands only on the balls of the feet, without the normal heel contact. This inefficient method places the sole in muscles in continuous contractions.

Pain from posterior shin splints is felt on the inside part of the leg, along the tibia.

Excessive pronation contributes to both anterior and posterior shin splints. Though some pronation is necessary for normal joint function, too much produces an extremely unstable foot that may lead to injury.

Rehabilitation of shin splints

- Aspirin is a very effective anti-inflammatory medication and can be used in relieving pain from shin splints.
- Ice massage also is helpful in treating shin splints. Immediately after running, firmly massage tender areas with ice for 10 to 15 minutes. Icing should be done always after running and never before.
- A reduction in daily mileage and a change in running course may also be beneficial to the runner. By reducing mileage by 50 percent for at least a week and avoiding hills and hard running surfaces, shin splints can be prevented and minimized.
- Use of shoes with good quality mid sole prevents the elevation of pain due to shin splints.
- Proper weight raining exercises to strengthen the anterior and posterior lower leg muscles helps in preventing shin splints.
- Stretching exercises during recovery help in reducing pain due to shin splints.
- Strengthening and stretching exercises should be done only in the absence of pain.

Causes and Treatment of Athlete's Foot

Athlete's foot is an infection caused by fungi. These fungi are quite opportunistic and often find ideal conditions existing on the feet, especially between the toes and on the soles, due to sweat and moisture caused by heavy socks and tennis or jogging shoes. The fungi, tend to remain in the outer surface of the skin. These superficial skin infections can become bothersome. However, if treated early, the fungus can be eradicated quickly. The means by which fungus infections are acquired and transmitted are not entirely known.

All types of fungus infections have a tendency to be more severe under conditions of poor hygiene, heat and humidity. It is therefore highly recommended that proper foot bathing and drying, are essential to help control athletes foot.

Treatment of athlete's foot has advanced markedly over the past years. There are several oral antifungal medication containing Griseofulvin, or Ketocanozole. The best treatment, however, is to maintain good hygiene and proper cleaning of the feet.

Preventive measures can be summarised as follows:

1. Keep the feet dry.
2. Avoid occlusive footwear or synthetic stocking, rubber soled shoes or plastic in soles.
3. Use cotton and wool socks, and change them one to three times per day.
4. Use dry spray or powders.
5. Alternate pairs of sneakers if available.
6. Disinfect shower rooms and locker rooms daily.

Causes and Treatment of Tennis Elbow

Tennis elbow is part of a generalized problem found in many areas of the body basically through overuse or degeneration, the origin of a muscle may tear. Because the muscle continues to be used, the tear propagates, and symptoms worsen. The muscles that turn up (supinate) the palm and those that extend the fingers and wrist take their origin from the outside (lateral) aspect of the elbow. If these tear, any attempt to extend the wrist or fingers may be painful.

A typical history of tennis elbow may start from a backhand swing with a tennis racket. Normally the forearm should provide the force needed to hit the ball. However, if the wrist slaps at the ball (such as in table tennis), the player may tear the wrist extensors from the origin at the elbow or tear the fibres nearby. Each succeeding swing only causes the symptoms to worsen and to delay healing.

Treatment: Treatment consists of resting the area, reducing the inflammation, and once the injury heals, strengthening the area so that future damage will not occur.

Resting the area may simply mean stopping the offending actions. However, if the pain is considerable, splitting of the wrist may be necessary. This stops the wrist from moving and allows the wrist muscles to rest completely.

Anti-inflammatory medication, such as ibuprofen, may help the process. After the acute inflammation improves, the extensors and supinators of the forearm need to be strengthened.

Effects of Endurance Training on the Cardio-respiratory System

The cardio respiratory system provides a means by which oxygen is supplied to the various tissues of the body. Without oxygen the cells within the human body cannot possibly function, and ultimately death will occur. Thus the cardio respiratory system is the basic life support system of the body.

The improvement in the cardio respiratory system through endurance training occurs because of increased efficiency of co-ordinative function of four components-(a) the heart (b) the lungs (c) the blood vessels and (d) the blood.

Effects on Heart: The heart becomes capable of adapting to the increased demand through several mechanisms. Heart rate shows a gradual adaptation to an increased work load by increasing proportionally to the endurance training and will plateau at a given level for about 2 to 3 minutes. The resting heart decreases with endurance training. The rate of oxygen consumption can be estimated by taking the heart rate.

(*a*) The stroke volume increases while exercise heart rate is reduced at a given standard exercise load. The heart becomes more efficient because it is capable of pumping more blood with each stroke.

Cardiac Output = Increased stroke volume x Decreased heart rate.

Because the heart is a muscle, it will hypertrophy to some extent.

(*b*) **Blood flow:** The amount of blood flowing to the various organs increases, due to endurance training. In skeletal muscles, there is increased capillarisation.

(*c*) **Blood:** Endurance training increases the total blood volume, with a corresponding increase in the amount of haemoglobin.

(*d*) **Lungs:** As a result of training, some changes occur in lung volumes and capacities. The volume of air that can be inspired in single maximal ventilation is increased. The diffusion capacity of the lungs is also increased, facilitating the exchange of oxygen and carbon di oxide. Pulmonary resistance to air flow is also decreased.

EXERCISE

1. Which of the following phenomenon causes removal of blood from the injured area?
   (*a*) Muscle contraction
   (*b*) Gravity
   (*c*) Respiration
   (*d*) All of the above

2. Which of the following forms of energy, has the highest velocity?
   (*a*) Cosmic waves
   (*b*) X-rays
   (*c*) Short-wave diathermy
   (*d*) They are all equal

3. Which of the following forms of energy has the highest frequency?
   (*a*) Cosmic waves
   (*b*) X-rays
   (*c*) FM radio waves
   (*d*) Short wave diathermy

4. The method of heat transfer that involves the cooling of one object with the subsequent heating of another object through the circulation of air or water is–
   (*a*) radiation (*b*) evaporation
   (*c*) conduction (*d*) convection

5. The measure of the number of heat units required to raise a unit of mass by 1°C is termed–
   (*a*) calorie (*b*) thermal capacity
   (*c*) specific heat (*d*) change of state

6. Which of the following modalities has the greatest likelihood of frostbite?
   (*a*) Ice immersion
   (*b*) Reusable cold packs
   (*c*) Ice massage
   (*d*) Ice bag

7. Which of the following is a contradiction for the use of a paraffin bath?
   (*a*) No range of motion
   (*b*) Chronic condition
   (*c*) Pain
   (*d*) Skin conditions.

8. In which of the following modalities convection is used as its method of heat transfer?
   (*a*) Ice bag (*b*) Whirlpool
   (*c*) Hot packs (*d*) Infrared lamp.

9. Which of the following is not a local effect of cold application?
   (*a*) Decreased rate of cell metabolism
   (*b*) Decreased muscle spindle activity
   (*c*) Decreased nerve conduction velocity
   (*d*) Decreased viscosity of fluids in the area

10. Which of the following modalities has the greatest dept of penetration?
    (*a*) Moist heat pack
    (*b*) Hot Whirlpool
    (*c*) Infrared lamp
    (*d*) Ice bag.

11. Which of the following is not a local effect of heat application?
    (*a*) Increased rate of cell metabolism
    (*b*) Increased elasticity of soft tissue
    (*c*) Increased muscle tone
    (*d*) Decreased muscle spasm.

12. Which of the following would be the modality of choice to cause physiochemical changes within the tissues?
    (*a*) High voltage pulsed stimulation
    (*b*) Interferential stimulation
    (*c*) Low-voltage alternating current
    (*d*) Low-voltage direct current.

13. Which of the following is contradiction of ultrasound?
    (*a*) Scar tissue (*b*) Infection
    (*c*) Warts (*d*) Trigger points

14. Reflection of ultrasonic energy occurs least between–
    (*a*) water and soft tissue
    (*b*) soft tissue and fat
    (*c*) soft tissue and bone
    (*d*) soft tissue and air

15. When applying intermittent compression to an extremity, the pressure in the appliance should not exceed–
(*a*) the athlete's diastolic blood pressure
(*b*) the athlete's systolic blood pressure
(*c*) the difference between the athletes diastolic and systolic blood pressure
(*d*) the athlete's resting heart rate.

16. "Petrissage' technique of massage involves–
(*a*) pounding of the skin
(*b*) pinching of the skin
(*c*) kneading of the skin
(*d*) stroking of the skin

17. "Effleurage" technique of massage involves–
(*a*) kneading of the skin
(*b*) pounding of the skin
(*c*) stroking of the skin
(*d*) none of the above.

18. "Tapoment" of the skin involves–
(*a*) stroking (*b*) kneading
(*c*) pounding (*d*) friction

19. Immediate treatment provided to an athlete upon a sports injury is–
(*a*) short wave diathermy
(*b*) cryotherapy
(*c*) contrast bath
(*d*) whirlpool

20. Which of the following instruments measures the heart action?
(*a*) Electrocardiogram
(*b*) Sphygmomanometer
(*c*) Electroencephalograph
(*d*) Electromyograph

21. Green Stick fracture occurs owing to the–
(*a*) lack of strength
(*b*) forceful muscular contraction
(*c*) non-ossification of bone
(*d*) old age.

22. The degree of chronic fatigue may be assessed through–
(*a*) observation method
(*b*) clinical method
(*c*) introspection method
(*d*) all of the above.

23. The drugs that develop calmness are known as–
(*a*) diuretics (*b*) sedatives
(*c*) narcotics (*d*) none of the above

24. Energy requirements depend upon–
(*a*) age (*b*) sex
(*c*) physical activity (*d*) all of the above

25. Which of the following is not a fat soluable vitamin?
(*a*) Vitamin A (*b*) Vitamin C
(*c*) Vitamin D (*d*) Vitamin E

26. Prevention of sudden outbreak of a disease includes–
(*a*) adequate waste management
(*b*) health Education
(*c*) clean water supply
(*d*) all the above

27. Tendonitis is the–
(*a*) inflammation of tendon
(*b*) tearing of tendon
(*c*) strain
(*d*) muscle pull

28. Acclimatization is the–
(*a*) physiological adaptation to environment]
(*b*) constant exposure to climate
(*c*) exposure to high altitude
(*d*) all of the above

29. The drug that stimulates the central nervous system is–
(*a*) amphetamine (*b*) anabolic steroid
(*c*) anabolism (*d*) adrenalin

30. Increase in the blood lactate is due to–
(*a*) anaerobic threshold
(*b*) anaerobic
(*c*) aerobic potential
(*d*) absence of oxygen

31. The cardiovascular endurance capacity is–
(*a*) overall body endurance
(*b*) stamina
(*c*) aerobic power
(*d*) none of the above

32. What is cardiac hypertrophy?
(*a*) Changes in heart size

(*b*) Due to training the size (volume) of heart increases
(*c*) Normal thickness in the ventricular wall
(*d*) It is an Athletic heart.

33. Name the gadget used for treating chronic sports injuries?
(*a*) Short wave diathermy
(*b*) Infra red rays
(*c*) Ultra-violet rays
(*d*) Ultrasound diathermy

34. The upper two chambers of the heart are known as–
(*a*) ventricles (*b*) arteries
(*c*) veins (*d*) auricles

35. The voluntary muscles are controlled by–
(*a*) nerves (*b*) brain
(*c*) heart (*d*) muscles

36. Example of slow twitch muscle is–
(*a*) chest muscles (*b*) hip muscles
(*c*) soleus (*d*) trapezius

37. Example of fast twitch muscle is–
(*a*) cluteus maximus
(*b*) hamstrings
(*c*) medial gastrocnemius
(*d*) lateral gastrocnemius

38. What is the percentage of muscles in the body?
(*a*) 40% (*b*) 60%
(*c*) 80% (*d*) 100%

39. In case of sprain, the immediate treatment recommended is–
(*a*) hydrotherapy
(*b*) cryotherapy
(*c*) heat therapy
(*d*) none of the above.

40. Which of the following is not a local effect of heat application?
(*a*) Increased rate of cell metabolism
(*b*) Increased elasticity of soft tissue
(*c*) Increased muscle tone
(*d*) Decreased muscle spasm.

41. Which artery supplies the blood to posterior and hind limbs?
(*a*) Renal (*b*) Gastric
(*c*) Iliac (*d*) Hepatic

42. Which vein drains blood from liver?
(*a*) Renal (*b*) Iliac
(*c*) Hepatic (*d*) Gastric

43. One complete heartbeat consisting of one systole and one diastole lasts for–
(*a*) 0.72 sec (*b*) 0.8 sec.
(*c*) 0.85 sec. (*d*) 1 min.

44. What is known as the pacemaker of heart?
(*a*) Pericardium
(*b*) AV node
(*c*) SA node
(*d*) Both AV and SA node

45. The amount of blood flowing from the heart over a given period of time is known as–
(*a*) stroke volume (*b*) cardiac output
(*c*) heart rate (*d*) blood pressure

46. Which of the following properties is not possessed by slow twitch fibres?
(*a*) Red fibres
(*b*) High myoglobin
(*c*) Slow action potential
(*d*) High haemoglobin

47. Number of fibres per neuron in slow twitch muscle is–
(*a*) 10-180 (*b*) 300-800
(*c*) 150-300 (*d*) 100-250

48. Number of fibres per neuron in fast twitch muscle is–
(*a*) 10-180 (*b*) 300-800
(*c*) 150-300 (*d*) 100-250

49. What is not possessed by fast twitch muscles in comparison to slow twitch muscles?
(*a*) Less resistant to fatigue
(*b*) High AT Pase activity
(*c*) Less myosin crossbridges
(*d*) Fast contraction speed

50. Elite male and female distance runners possess–
(*a*) more of slow twitch fibres
(*b*) more of fast twitch fibres
(*c*) more of intermediate twitch fibres
(*d*) 50% ST and 50% FT fibres

51. Sliding Filament theory was proposed by–
(*a*) Huxely (*b*) Hudson
(*c*) Sanderson (*d*) Denahue

52. According to Huxely's sliding filament theory, the number of phases of contraction are–
(*a*) two (*b*) three
(*c*) four (*d*) five

53. Which of the following stages is not a phase in sliding filament theory?
(*a*) Rest (*b*) Excitation
(*c*) Expansion (*d*) Relaxation

54. In which type of muscular contraction there is no change in the length of the muscle despite tension?
(*a*) Concentric (*b*) Eccentric
(*c*) Isometric (*d*) Isokinetic

55. In which type of contraction, the muscle lengthens in its original length while producing tension?
(*a*) Concentric (*b*) Isometric
(*c*) Eccentric (*d*) Isokinetic

56. Arm stroke during free style swimming is an example of–
(*a*) isokinetic contraction
(*b*) isometric contraction
(*c*) eccentric contraction
(*d*) concentric contraction

57. The condition where there is lack of adequate blood flow to active muscles is called–
(*a*) ischemia (*b*) spasm
(*c*) torn issue (*d*) haemorrhage

58. During expiration which of the muscles are not active?
(*a*) Rectus abdominus
(*b*) Adductor
(*c*) Oblique muscles
(*d*) External intercoastals

59. The average energy expenditure of an individual engaged in normal daily activity is–
(*a*) 2000-4000K Cal
(*b*) 3500-6000K Cal
(*c*) 1800 to 2700K Cal
(*d*) 1500-3000 K Cal

60. One ATP can give energy upto–
(*a*) 5.7-6.9 K. Cal (*b*) 2-4 K Cal
(*c*) 5-8 K Cal (*d*) 6-8 K Cal

61. Which system is not a part of the aerobic system for producing ATP?
(*a*) Aerobic glycolysis
(*b*) Krebs cycle
(*c*) Electron transport cycle
(*d*) Phosphogen system

62. One mole of glycogen in aerobic system provides how many moles of ATP?
(*a*) 39 (*b*) 34
(*c*) 30 (*d*) 32

63. ATP is stored in–
(*a*) muscle (*b*) gall bladder
(*c*) pancreas (*d*) liver

64. Discomfort or decreased efficiency resulting from prolonged or excessive exercise is known as–
(*a*) spasm (*b*) ischemia
(*c*) fatigue (*d*) tiredness

65. Lactic acid is a by-product of–
(*a*) aerobic glycolysis
(*b*) anaerobic glycolysis
(*c*) both
(*d*) none of the above

66. Due to which characteristic of muscle it tends to return to original shape and length after contraction or extension?
(*a*) Excitability (*b*) Contractibility
(*c*) Extensibility (*d*) Elasticity

67. The nervous system communicates with muscle via which junctions?
(*a*) Tendons (*b*) Myoneural
(*c*) Synapse (*d*) All of the above

68. Which muscles contract only when stimulated by nervous system?
(*a*) Skeletal muscles
(*b*) Smooth muscles
(*c*) Cardiac muscles
(*d*) All of the above

69. Which muscles are called striated?
(*a*) Skeletal
(*b*) Cardiac
(*c*) Smooth
(*d*) Smooth and Cardiac

70. The connective tissue which ensheaths both the tendons and the muscle is–
(*a*) perimysium (*b*) endomysium
(*c*) fascicles (*d*) epimysium

71. The primary function of sarcoplasmic reticulum is to–
(*a*) store Calcium ions
(*b*) help in contraction
(*c*) store Mg^{2+} ions
(*d*) its empty with no functions.

72. In skeletal mucles, the light areas are called–
(*a*) I-bands (*b*) A-bands
(*c*) T-tubules (*d*) Z-line

73. A sacromere is an area–
(*a*) between two I-bands
(*b*) between two Z-lines
(*c*) between two A-bands
(*d*) between I and A bands

74. Myosin heads are called–
(*a*) A-bands (*b*) I-bands
(*c*) Cross bridges (*d*) Z-lines

75. Thin myofilaments do not compose of which one of the following proteins?
(*a*) Actin (*b*) Troponin
(*c*) Tropomyosin (*d*) Myosin

76. Calcium from sacroplasmic reticulum fills the binding sets of which protein molecules?
(*a*) Troponin (*b*) Tropomyosin
(*c*) Actin (*d*) Myosin

77. Which element acts as the "on and off' switch of skeletal muscle?
(*a*) Mg^{2+} (*b*) Ca^{2+}
(*c*) Na^{+} (*d*) Cl^{-}

78. If a muscle fibre is stimulated so rapidly that it does not relax at all between stimuli, a small sustained contraction occurs called–
(*a*) ischemia (*b*) fatigue
(*c*) tetanus (*d*) exhaustion

79. Calcium in smooth muscles attached to which protein?
(*a*) Actin (*b*) Troponin
(*c*) Tropomyosin (*d*) Calmodulin

80. Which smooth muscle is stimulated by nervous stimulation?
(*a*) Visceral smooth muscle
(*b*) Unitary smooth muscle
(*c*) Multiunit smooth muscle
(*d*) All of the above

81. Which of the following is not a pathway of air during respiration?
(*a*) Pharynax (*b*) Trachea
(*c*) Diaphragm (*d*) Bronchi

82. Mark the correct passage of air during respiration–
(*a*) nasal cavity → pharynx → trachea → bronchi → alveoli
(*b*) nasal cavity → trachea → pharynx → bronchi → alveoli
(*c*) nasal cavity → trachea → pharynx → alveoli → bronchi
(*d*) trachea → pharynx → bronchi → alveoli → nasal cavity

83. The substance which reduces surface tension in alveoli in order to avoid the collapse is–
(*a*) blood (*b*) oxygen
(*c*) surfactant (*d*) alkali

84. What is the average total surface area of our lungs?
(*a*) 65 sq. mt (*b*) 72 sq. mt
(*c*) 75 sq. mt (*d*) 79 sq. mt

85. What is the percentage of oxygen bound to haemoglobin in blood?
(*a*) 90.8% (*b*) 92.5%
(*c*) 95% (*d*) 98.5%

86. Apneustic and Oneumotoxic centres of respiration are located in which area of brain?
(*a*) Medulla (*b*) Cerebrum
(*c*) Cerebellum (*d*) Pons

87. Rhythmicity centre of respiration is located in–
(*c*) Medulla (*d*) Cerebrum
(*c*) Cerebellum (*d*) Pons

88. Which of the following mechanisms is not responsible for increased respiratory rate during heavy exercise?
(*a*) increased CO_2
(*b*) increase in body temperature
(*c*) epinephrine release
(*d*) impulses from the cerebral cortex

89. Muscles at the back of the humerus are–
(*a*) quadriceps (*b*) biceps
(*c*) triceps (*d*) intecostals

90. The muscle which is the strongest in human body is–
(*a*) quadriceps (*b*) rectus femoris
(*c*) sternomustoid (*d*) triceps

91. In which type of fracture does the bone split along its length?
(*a*) Impacted (*b*) Depressed
(*c*) Green stick (*d*) Longitudinal

92. Which muscle is located on the upper back?
(*a*) Brachioradialis (*b*) Pectineus
(*c*) Soleus (*d*) Trapezius

93. Soleus muscle is located in–
(*a*) lower leg (*b*) forearm
(*c*) trunk (*d*) upper leg

94. Mark out the correct pair–

(*a*) Study of cells	I. Osteology
(*b*) Study of muscles	II. Cytology
(*c*) Study of bones	III. Myology
(*d*) Study of organs	IV. Splanchnology of Viscera

95. Which of the following is not an electrical modality?
(*a*) Ultraviolet light (*b*) Lasers
(*c*) TENS (*d*) Ultrasound

96. Light energy having a wavelength greater than 730mm is termed–
(*a*) infrared energy (*b*) ultra sound
(*c*) ultraviolet (*d*) TENS

97. Which of the following ergogenic aids is not a stimulant?
(*a*) Amphetamines (*b*) Caeffine
(*c*) Cocaine (*d*) Morphine

98. Match the cause of fracture with their correct examples–

(*a*) Direct Blow	I. Person falling and landing on hands suffering a broken arm
(*b*) Indirect blow	II. Person playing football or skiing is susceptible to this injury
(*c*) Twisting Forces	III. Person who receives an electric shock can suffer fracture
(*d*) Muscle Contractions	IV. Person hit by a piece of flying rock and bone is broken at the point of impact.

99. Fractures where small fragments of bones are detached at the sites of muscle insertions are–
(*a*) avulsion fractures
(*b*) march fractures
(*c*) segmental fractures
(*d*) communicated fractures

100. Fractures where the bone is broken in two or more places and may heal slowly, due to the poor blood supply of smaller fragments is–
(*a*) epiphyseal fractures
(*b*) greenstick fracture
(*c*) segmental fracture
(*d*) stress fracture

101. The anterior ten pair of ribs joint to a bony plate called–
(*a*) diaphragm (*b*) intercoastals
(*c*) sternum (*d*) trachea

102. What is the total number of rules surrounding and protecting the lungs and heart in the thoracic cavity?
(*a*) Ten (*b*) Twelve
(*c*) Thirteen (*d*) Fourteen

103. Trachea splits into two bronchi. The right bronchus divides again into–
(*a*) two bronchi (*b*) two alveoli
(*c*) three bronchi (*d*) four alveoli

104. Left lung has–
(*a*) one lobe (*b*) two lobes
(*c*) three lobes (*d*) four lobes

105. The total surface area covered by alveoli in lungs of man are–
(*a*) 80-90 m^2 (*b*) 70-90 m^2
(*c*) 120-180 m^2 (*d*) 150-170 m^2

106. Breathing centre is located in–
(*a*) cerebrum (*b*) cerebellum
(*c*) spine (*d*) medulla

107. The lung capacity of an average man is–
(*a*) $3dm^3$ (*b*) $4dm^3$
(*c*) $5dm^3$ (*d*) $6\ dm^3$

108. What is the tidal volume of air a man can breathe in or out?
(*a*) $400cm^3$ (*b*) $450cm^3$
(*c*) $500cm^3$ (*d*) $550cm^3$

109. Even after forced expiration the air which remains in lungs and cannot be expelled is called–
(*a*) vital capacity
(*b*) residual air
(*c*) expiratory reserve volume
(*d*) tidal volume

110. The air which is expelled from body as unchanged room air is called–
(*a*) dead space air (*b*) residual air
(*c*) vital capacity (*d*) tidal volume

111. Which is the major inhibitory (neurotransmitter in brain?
(*a*) GABA (*b*) Serotonin
(*c*) Acetylcholine (*d*) Dopamine

112. Which chemical mimics action of acetylcholine?
(*a*) Curare (*b*) Botulinum toxin
(*c*) Nicotine (*d*) Atropine

113. Which of the following neurotransmitters blocks action of acetylcholine?
(*a*) Atropine (*b*) Muscarine
(*c*) Nicotine (*d*) Eserine

114. Which major neurotransmitter is synthesized from choline and mitochiondrially derived acetyl co-enzyme A?
(*a*) GABA (*b*) Acetylcholine
(*c*) Dopamine (*d*) Norepinephrine

115. The function of Achilles Tendon is–
(*a*) to flex foot towards knee
(*b*) to connect gastroenemius muscle to heel
(*c*) to raise leg
(*d*) to bend knee

116. The heart is surrounded by a sac like–
(*a*) endosarc (*b*) perisac
(*c*) pericardium (*d*) endocardium

117. Which enzyme facilitates the conversion of glucose to Glucose 5 phosphate?
(*a*) Aldolase (*b*) Enolase
(*c*) Glucokinase (*d*) Pyruvate Kinase

118. Which of the enzymes is not present in mitochondrial matrix?
(*a*) Enzymes of TCAcycle
(*b*) Pyruvate dehydrogenase
(*c*) Adenylate Kinase
(*d*) Oxidative enzymes

119. The number of ATP generated through Kreb's cycle is–
(*a*) 28 ATP (*b*) 24 ATP
(*c*) 22 ATP (*d*) 26 ATP

120. The number of ATP generated through glycolysis is–
(*a*) 6 ATP (*b*) 8 ATP
(*c*) 4 ATP (*d*) 10 ATP

121. What is the average minimum duration for the complete resynthesis of muscle glycogen after exercise?
(*a*) 1-2 hrs. (*b*) 24 hrs.
(*c*) 48 hrs. (*d*) 72 hrs.

122. Which is the most common site of fracture?
(*a*) Wrist (*b*) Forearm
(*c*) Hand (*d*) Ankle

123. Which mechanism of fracture is responsible for spiral fractures?
(*a*) Compression (*b*) Tension
(*c*) Angulation (*d*) Torsion

124. Hairline fracture is also called–
(*a*) infraction fracture
(*b*) torus

(c) greenstick fracture
(d) impacted fracture

125. Which of the following is not a complete fracture?
(a) Spiral fracture
(b) Oblique fracture
(c) Transverse fracture
(d) Avulsion fracture

126. Partial or complete tear of ligament substance is called–
(a) sprain (b) strain
(c) cartilage tear (d) dislocation

127. Which therapeutic modality is an integral part of non-surgical management of redicular pain from lumbar spine disorders?
(a) Epidural steroid injections
(b) Corticosteriod injections
(c) Botulinum toxin
(d) TENS

128. Which chemical is used in the treatment of muscle and joint inflammatory reactions?
(a) Cortisone
(b) Botulinum
(c) Epidural steroid injections
(d) None of the above

129. Which deep heat modality is the therapeutic application of high radiofrequency electrical currents?
(a) Shortwave diathermy
(b) Microwave diathermy
(c) Ultrasound
(d) TENS

130. Which modality uses high-frequency acoustic vibration above the human audible spectrum?
(a) TENS (b) Laser
(c) Ultrasound (d) Conversion

131. Which of the following is a conductive heating modality?
(a) Fluidtherapy
(b) Immersion
(c) Radiant heat therapy
(d) Hydrotherapy

132. Which therapeutic modality is the most commonly used forms of elctroanalgesia?
(a) Laser (b) EMS
(c) TENS (d) Deep heat

133. Which of the following is not a trans-cutaneaus or percutaneous electrical stimulation modality?
(a) IFC (b) EMS
(c) PENS (d) TENS

134. Which therapeutic modality is used to produce muscular contraction?
(a) TENS (b) Ultrasound
(c) IFC (d) EMS

135. Which ergogenic aid involves producing more red blood cells and haemoglobin?
(a) Blood doping (b) Erythropoietin
(c) Both of these (d) None of these

136. Which cryogenic aid is a CNS stimulant?
(a) Human growth hormone
(b) Anabolic steriod
(c) Amphetamine
(d) Leucine

137. Which ergogenic aid increases fat metabolism?
(a) Leucine (b) DHEA
(c) Diuretics (d) Carnitine

138. Which ergogenic aid stimulates endogenous steroid production?
(a) Proteins (b) Phosphate
(c) Ephedrine (d) Yohimbine

139. Cryotherapy refers to–
(a) Ultrasound (b) Cold therapy
(c) TENS (d) EMS

140. Biceps muscles are located in–
(a) upper limb (b) abdomen
(c) lower limb (d) back

141. The shape of pectoralis major is–
(a) diamond (b) rhomboid
(c) fan-shaped (d) triangular

142. The valve of heart guarding the atrioventricular opening on the right side is–
(a) bicuspid valve
(b) tricuspid valve
(c) mitral valve
(d) both bicuspid and tricuspid valve

143. The stroke volume of an average adult is–
(*a*) 70 ml (*b*) 80 ml
(*c*) 85 ml (*d*) 90 ml

144. Inner lining of squamous endothelium of artery and veins is–
(*a*) tunica intima (*b*) tunica media
(*c*) tunica externa (*d*) pericardium

145. What is the correct sequence of blood circulation?
(*a*) Heart → arteries → arteioles → capillaries
(*b*) Arteries → heart → arterioles → capillaries
(*c*) Heart → arterioles → arteries → capillaries
(*d*) Heart → capillaries → arterioles → arteries

146. Which muscles constitute two-fifth of our body weight?
(*a*) Voluntary muscles
(*b*) Involuntary muscles
(*c*) Smooth muscles
(*d*) Non-straited muscles

147. Goblet cells produce–
(*a*) enzyme (*b*) harmone
(*c*) mucin (*d*) HCl

148. During histochemical analysis the fibres which stain black are–
(*a*) slow twitch type
(*b*) intermediate twitch type
(*c*) fast twitch type
(*d*) all of the above.

149. Slow twitch fibres are also called–
(*a*) slow oxidative type
(*b*) slow grey type
(*c*) intermediate objective type
(*d*) intermediate red fibres

150. Slow twitch fibres have a higher concentration of ____ than fast twitch fibres–
(*a*) haemoglobin (*b*) fibres
(*c*) tendon (*s*) myoglobin

151. Stanozolol, the drug which was misused by the Canadian Athlete Ben Johnson in 1988 Olympic Games is–
(*a*) narcotic analgesic
(*b*) anabolic steroid
(*c*) opiate
(*d*) diuretic

152. Onset of blood lactate accumulation (OBLA) is also known as–
(*a*) aerobic threshold
(*b*) anaerobic threshold
(*c*) lactation
(*d*) both (*a*) & (*b*)

153. Which of the following is a narcotic?
(*a*) Cocaine (*b*) Marijuana
(*c*) P. C. P. (*d*) Morphine

154. Heart rate is defined as–
(*a*) Quantity of blood pumped away by heart in one minute
(*b*) Number of systolic contractions per minute
(*c*) Number of diastolic contractions per minute
(*d*) Number of heart contractions per minute

155. During heavy exercise the supply of blood increases towards–
(*a*) brain (*b*) skeletal muscle
(*c*) skin (*d*) kidneys

156. Which of the following is carried by the blood?
(*a*) Enzymes (*b*) Oxygen
(*c*) Hormones (*d*) All of the above

157. Increase of muscle mass following resistance work, particularly heavy weight training is called–
(*a*) osteoporosis
(*b*) muscular Atrophy
(*c*) muscular Hypertrophy
(*d*) hyperplasia

158. Anabolic steroids affect directly–
(*a*) heart (*b*) muscles
(*c*) lungs (*d*) brain

159. F. I. M. S. stands for–
(*a*) Federation of Indian Medicine and Surgery

(*b*) Federation International Medicine and Sports
(*c*) International Federation of Medico-Sportive
(*d*) Federation of International Medico-Sportive

160. Fibre type having greater number of mitochondria and high concentration of myoglobin is–
(*a*) slow twitch (*b*) fast twitch
(*c*) medium type (*d*) both (*a*) and (*b*)

161. Fibres with small cross sectional area are–
(*a*) faster twtich (*b*) slow twitch
(*c*) both (*a*) and (*b*) (*d*) none of the above

162. Drugs that increase muscle bulk and extra power for muscle contraction are–
(*a*) caffeine
(*b*) androgenic steroids
(*c*) cortico Steroids
(*d*) betablockers

163. Softness of bones is known as–
(*a*) osteoporosis (*b*) osteomalacia
(*c*) osteoblast (*d*) osteoclast

164. "Cryo therapy" is the first aid treatment given for–
(*a*) bleeding wound (*b*) sprain
(*c*) dislocation (*d*) all of the above

165. Sports injuries can be minimized by–
(*a*) massage (*b*) sauna bath
(*c*) steam bath (*d*) none of the above

166. Knee cartilage injuries are commonly associated with–
(*a*) swimming (*b*) rowing
(*c*) boxing (*d*) football

167. Rehabilitation of sports injuries is done using–
(*a*) hydrotherapy
(*b*) corrective exercises
(*c*) cryotherapy
(*d*) none of the above

168. W. H. O.'s concept of health focuses on–
(*a*) health as a sense of total well being
(*b*) freedom from disease
(*c*) physical health
(*d*) mental health.

169. Immediate symptom of sprained ankle is–
(*a*) bleeding (*b*) odeama
(*c*) dislcoation (*d*) all of the above

170. Chronic sports injuries are treated using–
(*a*) diathermy (*b*) infrared
(*c*) ultra violet (*d*) ultrasound

171. Shoulder dislocation injuries are commonly associated with–
(*a*) rowing (*b*) basketball
(*c*) volleyball (*d*) judo

172. Rehabilitation of sports injuries is done using–
(*a*) calisthenics
(*b*) corrective exercises
(*c*) freehand exercises
(*d*) all of the above.

173. Contrast bath is recommended for–
(*a*) reducing dislocated joint pain
(*b*) reducing swelling
(*c*) treatment of wound
(*d*) none of the above

174. The common injury in basketball is–
(*a*) medical meniscus damage
(*b*) damaged medial ligament of the ankle
(*c*) damaged lateral ligament of the ankle
(*d*) all of the above.

175. Which of the following does not belong to the category of dope?
(*a*) Ergogenic aids (*b*) Caffeine
(*c*) Nicotine (*d*) All of the above

176. The first treatment recommended for long distance exhausted athlete is–
(*a*) artificial Respiration
(*b*) massage
(*c*) cryotherapy
(*d*) all of the above.

177. For complete treatment of sports injuries, one should depend upon–
(*a*) physiotherapy
(*b*) corrective exercise therapy
(*c*) both of the above
(*d*) conditioning.

178. In case a sports person gets nausiatic feeling, he is advised to–
(*a*) sit (*b*) lie down
(*c*) stand (*d*) all of the above.

179. Which of the following is associated with rickets–
(*a*) knock knee (*b*) pigeon chest
(*c*) odeama (*d*) abrasion

180. Sprain is an injury to–
(*a*) ligament (*b*) muscle
(*c*) bone (*d*) connective tissue.

181. Disease or injury affecting the wall of a blood vessel is–
(*a*) abdominal wound (*b*) stress fracture
(*c*) black eye (*d*) haemorrhage

182. Break in a bone as a result of injury of pathological weakness is called–
(*a*) severe bleeding (*b*) dislocating
(*c*) fracture (*d*) abrasion

183. Stress fracture is common among–
(*a*) young children (*b*) adults
(*c*) older people (*d*) women

184. Stress fracture is common among–
(*a*) dancers and Athletes
(*b*) factory workers
(*c*) women
(*d*) general population

185. The quickest and most effective way to stop bleeding is–
(*a*) direct pressure on the wound
(*b*) cryotherapy
(*c*) hydrotherapy
(*d*) tourniquests

186. Which of the following is more severe?
(*a*) Sprain
(*b*) Strain
(*c*) Both (*a*) and (*b*) are equally severe
(*d*) Abrasion

187. Which of the following comes under the category of wound?
(*a*) Abrasion (*b*) Lacerations
(*c*) Both (*a*) and (*b*) (*d*) Tennis elbow

188. Wound caused by a sharp object such as knife, razor or broken glass is–
(*a*) punctured wound (*b*) incised wound
(*c*) laceration (*d*) abrasion

189. Which of the following is NOT a spinal injury?
(*a*) Fracture (*b*) Dislocation
(*c*) Slipped Dics (*d*) Laceration

190. What type of first aid should be given to a person suffering from heat stroke?
(*a*) Have the patient lie down in a cool place.
(*b*) Let him stay in the sun for some more time
(*c*) Give him a glass of cold water
(*d*) Surround the patient

191. Full form of CPR is–
(*a*) Cardiopulmonary Rehabilitation
(*b*) Cardiopulmonary Retention
(*c*) Cardiopulmonary Resuscitation
(*d*) None of the above

192. Diuretics–
(*a*) increase the body's output of urine
(*b*) decrease the body's output of urine
(*c*) increase the size of muscle fibre
(*d*) causes weight gain.

193. Athlete's foot is caused by–
(*a*) virus (*b*) bacteria
(*c*) fungus (*d*) none of the above

194. "Shin Splint" occurs in–
(*a*) upper leg (*b*) lower leg
(*c*) abdomen (*d*) back

195. Which of the following is hard tissue?
(*a*) Tendon (*b*) Catilage
(*c*) Bone (*d*) Muscles

196. What should be the duration of Sauna bath initially?
(*a*) 6-8 minutes (*b*) 5-10 minutes
(*c*) 15 to 30 minutes (*d*) 1 hr. to 2 hr.

197. A typical fibre in the adult man may have a diameter of–
(*a*) 30-50 mm (*b*) 50-70mm
(*c*) 70-90 mm (*d*) 60-70 mm

198. The process of regeneration ATP is catalyzed by the enzyme–

(*a*) creatine
(*b*) phosphokinase
(*c*) phosphate
(*d*) creatine phosphokinase

199. The primary muscle substrate immediately available for ATP synthesis is–
(*a*) glucose (*b*) fructose
(*c*) glycogen (*d*) none of the above

200. In which of the following , does the reactions of energy synthesis take place?
(*a*) Nucleus (*b*) Cell sap
(*c*) Cell (*d*) Mitochondria

201. Pulmonary artery pumps the blood from–
(*a*) left Ventricle (*b*) left Auricle
(*c*) right Auricle (*d*) right Ventricle

202. Chronic injuries are treated with–
(*a*) X-rays (*b*) ultraviolet rays
(*c*) infrared rays (*d*) ultrasound

203. "Hydrotherapy" is given using–
(*a*) ice (*b*) water
(*c*) wax (*d*) heat

204. An example of injury caused by macrotrauma is–
(*a*) stress fracture (*b*) sprain
(*c*) tedinitis (*d*) flat feet

205. Stress fractures result when–
(*a*) osteoclastic activity is greater than osteoblastic activity
(*b*) osteoblastic activity is greater than osteoclastic activity
(*c*) osteoclastic and osteoblastic activities are equal
(*d*) the body reaches the stage of resistance

206. Which of the following tissues has the best potential to reproduce itself following an injury?
(*a*) Epithelial tissue
(*b*) Muscular tissue
(*c*) Nervous tissue
(*d*) Connective tissue.

207. Which of the following inflammatory mediators inhibit blood clotting?
(*a*) Histamine (*b*) Heparin
(*c*) Kinins (*d*) Leukotrienes

208. What can an athletic trainer do to decrease an athlete's perception of pain?
(*a*) Provide Psychological comfort
(*b*) Provide a distraction from the pain (talking etc.)
(*c*) Both (*a*) and (*b*)
(*d*) None of the above.

209. What is the percentage of water in human body?
(*a*) 50% (*b*) 60%
(*c*) 70% (*d*) 80%

210. Which of the following has the highest percentage of water in it?
(*a*) Gastric Juices and Saliva
(*b*) Gastric Juices
(*c*) Blood
(*d*) Muscle tissues

211. What is the percentage of water in the muscle tissues–
(*a*) 75% (*b*) 90%
(*c*) 85% (*d*) 80%

212. Water in the muscles is responsible for–
(*a*) flexibility (*b*) strength
(*c*) suppleness (*d*) endurance

213. How much water is expelled by the human body per day at regular temperatures?
(*a*) 3 gallons (*b*) 1 gallon
(*c*) 2 gallons (*d*) 4 gallons

214. All of the following are excitable tissues except–
(*a*) muscle fibre
(*b*) miniscule cartilage
(*c*) sensory nerves
(*d*) secretor cells.

215. Running barefoot may cause–
(*a*) amoebiasis
(*b*) tuberclosis
(*c*) hook worm infection
(*d*) ascariasis

216. The main function of WBC is to–
(*a*) transport substances
(*b*) remove dead cells
(*c*) increase blood circulation
(*d*) fight against bacteria

217. The stretch reflex is usually applied in polymetrics by–
(*a*) jumping (*b*) slow Stretching
(*c*) fast Walking (*d*) none of the above

218. Sliding filament theory of muscle contraction was given by–
(*a*) Huxley (*b*) Newton
(*c*) Darwin (*d*) Pythagoras

219. Which of the following branches helps in diagnostic teaching and coaching in sports?
(*a*) Kinesiology (*b*) Biomechanics
(*c*) Mechanics (*d*) Anthropometry

220. The best known special massage is–
(*a*) epithelial tissue massage
(*b*) peripheral tissue massage
(*c*) connective tissue massage
(*d*) muscular tissue massage

221. The type of massage used primarily as a therapeutic massage or remedial massages and is not a means of increasing athletic performance is–
(*a*) pounding
(*b*) effleurage
(*c*) connective tissue massage
(*d*) epithelial tissue massage

222. Weight of the Heart in humans is–
(*a*) 200 gms. (*b*) 400 gms.
(*c*) 220 260 gms (*d*) 300 gms.

223. Biggest Artery in the human body is–
(*a*) femoral artery
(*b*) aorta
(*c*) internal carotid artery
(*d*) facial artery

224. The outer most layer of the heart is called–
(*a*) myo cardium (*b*) endo cardium
(*c*) peri cardium (*d*) none of the above

225. Normal pulse rate range (h/m) in the adult human being is–
(*a*) 80-90 (*b*) 70-80
(*c*) 60-80 (*d*) 60-100

226. The volume of blood is ________ of total body weight–
(*a*) 1/2 (*b*) 1/3
(*c*) 1/4 (*d*) 1/12.

227. Protein Present in the matrix of cartilage is known as–
(*a*) casein (*b*) actin
(*c*) chondrin (*d*) ossien

228. Adrenalin hormone is produced by–
(*a*) the pituitary gland
(*b*) the kidneys
(*c*) the adrenal glands
(*d*) none of the above.

229. Testosterone hormone is–
(*a*) produced by women's ovaries
(*b*) produced by men's testis
(*c*) involved in digestion
(*d*) none of the above.

230. If a muscle is injured after a vigorous workout, one can exercise after–
(*a*) 12 hrs. (*b*) 24 hrs.
(*c*) 36 hrs. (*d*) 48 hrs.

231. Jogging on the spot–s
(*a*) tightens muscles
(*b*) strengthens few muscles
(*c*) strengthens all the muscles except the hamstring
(*d*) weakens muscles.

232. The word "muscle" in Latin means–
(*a*) mouse (*b*) mass
(*c*) mesh (*d*) strong

233. Isometric Exercises can raise the blood pressure to–
(*a*) 150/95 mm of Hg
(*b*) 180/95 mm of Hg
(*c*) 200/100 mm of Hg
(*d*) 300/250 mm Hg.

234. Blood gets de-oxygenated in–
(*a*) muscles (*b*) nerves
(*c*) lungs (*d*) heart

235. Front muscles of the thigh are known as–
(*a*) gluteal muscles (*b*) trapezius
(*c*) quadriceps (*d*) soleus.

236. Largest muscle in the human body is–
(*a*) trapezius (*b*) gluteus maximus
(*c*) soleus (*d*) pectoralis major.

237. Muscles convert–
(*a*) chemical energy into electrical energy
(*b*) electrical energy into chemical energy
(*c*) mechanical energy into chemical energy
(*d*) chemical energy into mechanical energy

238. Main element of human bone is–
(*a*) potassium (*b*) calcium
(*c*) phosphorus (*d*) iron

239. The skeleton of the baby consists almost entirely of–
(*a*) bones (*b*) cartilages
(*c*) tendons (*d*) ligaments

240. The structure which serves as a store for oxygen in the fibre is–
(*a*) myoglcbin (*b*) adipose tissue
(*c*) sarcoplasm (*d*) sarcolemm

241. The muscle fibre is covered by a thin membrane called–
(*a*) cell sap (*b*) sarcolemma
(*c*) myoglobin (*d*) none of the above

242. Gain in the strength takes place due to strengthening of–
(*a*) sarcoplasm (*b*) myoglobin
(*c*) sarcolemma (*d*) adipose tissue

243. The increase in the size of a muscle is due to increase in–
(*a*) sarcolemma (*b*) sarcoplasm
(*c*) myoglobin (*d*) mitochodria

244. Which blood "corpuscles" are called "Bacterial Scavengers"?
(*a*) W. B.S.'s (*b*) R. B. C.'s
(*c*) Platelets (*d*) None of the above

245. Which blood cells are formed in the lymphatic glands?
(*a*) R. B. C.'s (*b*) W. B. C.'s
(*c*) Platelets (*d*) None of the above

246. Volume of air breathed per minute is around–
(*a*) 5 litres (*b*) 7 litres
(*c*) 9 litres (*d*) 11 litres

247. Volume of air breathed per minute is also known as–
(*a*) respiratory minute volume
(*b*) minute volume
(*c*) respiratory capacity
(*d*) respiratory reserve volume

248. Volume of air that enters and leaves the lungs in ordinary quiet breathing is called–
(*a*) tidal air volume
(*b*) respiratory quotient
(*c*) respiratory minute volume
(*d*) total lung capacity

249. Ratio of the volume of CO_2 expired to the volume of oxygen used in a given time is known as–
(*a*) total lung capacity
(*b*) respiratory quotient
(*c*) tidal volume
(*d*) respiratory minute volume

250. In a trained athlete, the minute volume of the heart–
(*a*) decreases (*b*) increases
(*c*) remains same (*d*) none of the above

251. Central Nervous System consists of–
(*a*) brain and spinal column
(*b*) ibs and vertebral column
(*c*) brain and neurons
(*d*) dendrites and axons

252. Central Nervous System controls the–
(*a*) external messages
(*b*) internal environmental changes
(*c*) external environmental changes
(*d*) none of the above

253. Automatic Nervous System controls the–
(*a*) internal organs
(*b*) external environmental changes
(*c*) internal environmental changes
(*d*) external organs

254. Role of "Axon" is to carry the impulses–
(*a*) away from the nerve
(*b*) towards the brain
(*c*) towards the heart
(*d*) towards the nerve cell

255. The role of "Dendrite" is to collect the impulses from other neurons and carry them–
(*a*) towards the heart
(*b*) towards the spinal cord
(*c*) towards the brain
(*d*) towards the nerve cell

256. Glands situated on the upper lobes of kidney are–
(*a*) thymus (*b*) adrenal
(*c*) pituitary (*d*) hypothalamus

257. Diabetes is caused by the deficiency of–
(*a*) fructose (*b*) sugar
(*c*) insulin (*d*) hormones

258. Exercise causes increase in the weight of–
(*a*) pituitary
(*b*) pituitary and thyroid
(*c*) thyroid
(*d*) thymus

259. Which blood cells have no nucleus?
(*a*) WBC's (*b*) RBC's
(*c*) Platelets (*d*) Thrombocytes.

260. Which of the following is an example of exocrine glands?
(*a*) Adrenal gland (*b*) Salivary gland
(*c*) Thymus gland (*d*) Pineal gland

261. Which of the following is an example of connective tissue?
(*a*) Bone (*b*) Cartilage
(*c*) Blood (*d*) All the above

262. "Heparin" is found in–
(*a*) bone (*b*) blood
(*c*) cartilage (*d*) all of the above

263. Which of the following is required for clotting of blood?
(*a*) Iron (*b*) Calcium
(*c*) Sodium (*d*) Phosphorus

264. The end product formed in blood clotting is–
(*a*) fibrinogen (*b*) fibrin
(*c*) prothrombin (*d*) calcium

265. Which of the following is essential for fast healing of a wound?
(*a*) Fats (*b*) Protein
(*c*) Minerals (*d*) Carbohydrates

266. What is the normal value of cholesterol in the body of a healthy adult person?
(*a*) 50-180 mg. per 100ml. of plasma
(*b*) 60-100 mg. per 100 ml. of plasma
(*c*) 70-90 mg. per 100 ml. of plasma
(*d*) 60-190 mg. per 100 ml. of plasma

267. If by mistake you touch a hot iron bar, you immediately withdraw your hand. Name the most important tissue(s) involved in this process–
(*a*) epithelial tissue (*b*) nervous tissues
(*c*) connective tissue (*d*) both (*b*) and (*b*)

268. Fat is abundant in–
(*a*) lymphatic (*b*) a reolar tissue
(*c*) adipose tissue (*d*) liver tissue

269. Which of the following is the basic unit of muscles?
(*a*) Cells (*b*) Nucleus
(*c*) Myofibrils (*d*) Both (*a*) and (*b*)

270. Name of the proteins present in the muscle fibres–
(*a*) actinic (*b*) myositis
(*c*) both (*a*) and (*b*) (*d*) none of the above

271. Which of the following is a basic unit of nervous tissue?
(*a*) Cell (*b*) Proton
(*c*) Neuron (*d*) Myofibril

272. Which of the following is a simple gland?
(*a*) Exocrine gland
(*b*) Endocrine gland
(*c*) Both (*a*) and (*b*)
(*d*) None of the above.

273. Which of the following attaches skeletal muscle to bone?
(*a*) Ligament (*b*) Tendon
(*c*) Actin (*d*) Myosin

274. Ligament connects–
(*a*) bone to bone
(*b*) bone to muscle
(*c*) blood to cartilage
(*d*) cartilage to muscle

275. Which muscle in the body is called "throwers muscle"?

(a) Quadriceps
(b) Hamstrings
(b) Rectus Abdominus
(b) Pectoralis major

276. The respiration of the cell is controlled by–
(a) lisosome (b) nucleus
(c) golgi bodies (d) mitochondria

277. Which of the following is called the "Master Gland"?
(a) Pituitary (b) Hypothalamus
(c) Thyroid (d) All of the above

278. The blood gets oxygenated in–
(a) lungs (b) muscles
(c) liver (d) heart

279. Gluteus maximum muscle is situated in–
(a) upper back (b) lower leg
(c) hips (d) upper arm

280. The controlling centre of the cell is–
(a) mitochondria (b) nucleus
(c) golgi (d) mitosis

281. Which gland regulates the rate of metabolism in the body?
(a) pituitary (b) thyroid
(c) parathyroid (d) gonads

282. Thermoregulation in human beings is controlled by–
(a) skin (b) blood
(c) both (a) and (b) (d) none of the above

283. Which of the following enzymes is secreted by salivary gland?
(a) Ptyline (b) Amylase
(c) Both (a) and (b) (d) None of the above

284. Which of the following is the largest gland?
(a) Lungs (b) Kidney
(c) Liver (d) Thyroid

285. Human movement is caused when–
(a) all the muscle groups involved are relaxed
(b) all the muscle groups involved are contracted
(c) some of the muscles relax while the other contract
(d) none of the above

286. How many chromosomes are there in the human body?
(a) 23 pair (b) 23 only
(c) 24 pairs (d) 22 pair

287. The information is passed from one organ to another organ via–
(a) synapse (b) motor and plates
(c) soma (d) dendrites

288. The longest muscle in the body is–
(a) gracilis (b) deltoid
(c) sartorius (d) pectoralis major

289. Type of Energy used in playing football is–
(a) Kinetic Energy (b) Electrical energy
(c) Tehrmal Energy (d) Muscular Energy

290. Pulmonary vein drains blood into–
(a) Right Atrium (b) Left Atrium
(c) Right Ventricle (d) Left Ventricle

291. The Oeophagus in situated between–
(a) stomach and intestine
(b) pharynx and larynx
(c) stomach and pharynx
(d) intestine and larynx

292. Stimulation of Sympathetic nervous system will cause–
(a) decreased heart rate
(b) increased heart rate
(c) alternate increase and decrease in heart rate
(d) no effect on heart

293. The gland that secretes harmone is–
(a) pituitary (b) pancreas
(c) thyroid (d) all of the above

294. The endocrine gland found in the brain is–
(a) pancreas (b) pituitary
(c) thyroid (d) none of the above

295. Which of the following harmones is secreted by pancreas?
(a) Insulin (b) Growth Harmone
(c) Thyroxin (d) All of the above

296. The rate of atrophy is accelerated through the stimulation of–
(a) golgi tendon organs

(*b*) phasic stretch receptors
(*c*) actin and myosin filaments
(*d*) blood flow

297. The healing process begins with–
(*a*) inflammation (*b*) coagulation
(*c*) phagocytosis (*d*) repair phase

298. The process that limits the amount of warm blood entering the area is known as–
(*a*) vasoconstriction
(*b*) vasodilation
(*c*) both the above
(*d*) coagulation

299. The event of mechanical and chemical irritation of nerve endings is a sign of–
(*a*) heart attack (*b*) soreness
(*c*) pain (*d*) loss of function

300. Increased blood flow and increase in the rate of cell metabolism indicates–
(*a*) redness (*b*) swelling
(*c*) pain (d) heat

ANSWERS

1	2	3	4	5	6	7	8	9	10
(*a*)	(*d*)	(*d*)	(*d*)	(*b*)	(*b*)	(*d*)	(*b*)	(*d*)	(*d*)
11	**12**	**13**	**14**	**15**	**16**	**17**	**18**	**19**	**20**
(*c*)	(*b*)	(*b*)	(*b*)	(*c*)	(*c*)	(*c*)	(*c*)	(*b*)	(*a*)
21	**22**	**23**	**24**	**25**	**26**	**27**	**28**	**29**	**30**
(*c*)	(*b*)	(*b*)	(*d*)	(*b*)	(*d*)	(*a*)	(*a*)	(*a*)	(*b*)
31	**32**	**33**	**34**	**35**	**36**	**37**	**38**	**39**	**40**
(*c*)	(*c*)	(*a*)	(*d*)	(*b*)	(*c*)	(*c*)	(*a*)	(*b*)	(*c*)
41	**42**	**43**	**44**	**45**	**46**	**47**	**48**	**49**	**50**
(*c*)	(*c*)	(*b*)	(*c*)	(*b*)	(*d*)	(*a*)	(*b*)	(*c*)	(*a*)
51	**52**	**53**	**54**	**55**	**56**	**57**	**58**	**59**	**60**
(*a*)	(*d*)	(*c*)	(*c*)	(*c*)	(*a*)	(*a*)	(*b*)	(*c*)	(*a*)
61	**62**	**63**	**64**	**65**	**66**	**67**	**68**	**69**	**70**
(*d*)	(*a*)	(*a*)	(*c*)	(*b*)	(*d*)	(*b*)	(*a*)	(*a*)	(*d*)
71	**72**	**73**	**74**	**75**	**76**	**77**	**78**	**79**	**80**
(*a*)	(*a*)	(*b*)	(*c*)	(*d*)	(*a*)	(*b*)	(*c*)	(*d*)	(*c*)
81	**82**	**83**	**84**	**85**	**86**	**87**	**88**	**89**	**90**
(*c*)	(*a*)	(*c*)	(*c*)	(*d*)	(*d*)	(*a*)	(*a*)	(*b*)	(*b*)
91	**92**	**93**	**94**	**95**	**96**	**97**	**98**	**99**	**100**
(*c*)	(*d*)	(*d*)	(*b*)	(*d*)	(*a*)	(*d*)	(*d*)	(*a*)	(*c*)
101	**102**	**103**	**104**	**105**	**106**	**107**	**108**	**109**	**110**
(*c*)	(*b*)	(*c*)	(*b*)	(*a*)	(*d*)	(*c*)	(*b*)	(*b*)	(*a*)
111	**112**	**113**	**114**	**115**	**116**	**117**	**118**	**119**	**120**
(*a*)	(*c*)	(*a*)	(*b*)	(*b*)	(*c*)	(*c*)	(*c*)	(*b*)	(*b*)
121	**122**	**123**	**124**	**125**	**126**	**127**	**128**	**129**	**130**
(*c*)	(*a*)	(*d*)	(*a*)	(*d*)	(*a*)	(*a*)	(*a*)	(*a*)	(*c*)
131	**132**	**133**	**134**	**135**	**136**	**137**	**138**	**139**	**140**
(*b*)	(*b*)	(*b*)	(*d*)	(*c*)	(*c*)	(*d*)	(*d*)	(*b*)	(*a*)

141	142	143	144	145	146	147	148	149	150
(*d*)	(*b*)	(*a*)	(*a*)	(*a*)	(*a*)	(*c*)	(*a*)	(*a*)	(*d*)
151	**152**	**153**	**154**	**155**	**156**	**157**	**158**	**159**	**160**
(*b*)	(*b*)	(*d*)	(*d*)	(*b*)	(*d*)	(*c*)	(*b*)	(*d*)	(*a*)
161	**162**	**163**	**164**	**165**	**166**	**167**	**168**	**169**	**170**
(*b*)	(*b*)	(*b*)	(*d*)	(*a*)	(*d*)	(*b*)	(*a*)	(*b*)	(*a*)
171	**172**	**173**	**174**	**175**	**176**	**177**	**178**	**179**	**180**
(*d*)	(*b*)	(*b*)	(*d*)	(*c*)	(*a*)	(*c*)	(*a*)	(*b*)	(*a*)
181	**182**	**183**	**184**	**185**	**186**	**187**	**188**	**189**	**190**
(*d*)	(*c*)	(*a*)	(*a*)	(*a*)	(*a*)	(*c*)	(*b*)	(*d*)	(*a*)
191	**192**	**193**	**194**	**195**	**196**	**197**	**198**	**199**	**200**
(*c*)	(*a*)	(*c*)	(*b*)	(*c*)	(*b*)	(*b*)	(*d*)	(*c*)	(*d*)
201	**202**	**203**	**204**	**205**	**206**	**207**	**208**	**209**	**210**
(*a*)	(*c*)	(*b*)	(*b*)	(*b*)	(*a*)	(*b*)	(*c*)	(*c*)	(*a*)
211	**212**	**213**	**214**	**215**	**216**	**217**	**218**	**219**	**220**
(*a*)	(*c*)	(*b*)	(*b*)	(*c*)	(*c*)	(*a*)	(*a*)	(*b*)	(*c*)
221	**222**	**223**	**224**	**225**	**226**	**227**	**228**	**229**	**230**
(*c*)	(*c*)	(*b*)	(*d*)	(*c*)	(*d*)	(*d*)	(*c*)	(*b*)	(*d*)
231	**232**	**233**	**234**	**235**	**236**	**237**	**238**	**239**	**240**
(*c*)	(*a*)	(*d*)	(*a*)	(*c*)	(*b*)	(*d*)	(*c*)	(*b*)	(*a*)
241	**242**	**243**	**244**	**245**	**246**	**247**	**248**	**249**	**250**
(*b*)	(*c*)	(*b*)	(*a*)	(*b*)	(*b*)	(*a*)	(*a*)	(*b*)	(*a*)
251	**252**	**253**	**254**	**255**	**256**	**257**	**258**	**259**	**260**
(*a*)	(*c*)	(*c*)	(*a*)	(*b*)	(*b*)	(*c*)	(*b*)	(*b*)	(*b*)
261	**262**	**263**	**264**	**265**	**266**	**267**	**268**	**269**	**270**
(*d*)	(*b*)	(*b*)	(*b*)	(*b*)	(*a*)	(*d*)	(*c*)	(*c*)	(*b*)
271	**272**	**273**	**274**	**275**	**276**	**277**	**278**	**279**	**280**
(*c*)	(*c*)	(*b*)	(*a*)	(*d*)	(*d*)	(*b*)	(*a*)	(*c*)	(*b*)
281	**282**	**283**	**284**	**285**	**286**	**287**	**288**	**289**	**290**
(*b*)	(*c*)	(*b*)	(*c*)	(*c*)	(*a*)	(*a*)	(*c*)	(*a*)	(*b*)
291	**292**	**293**	**294**	**295**	**296**	**297**	**298**	**299**	**300**
(*c*)	(*b*)	(*d*)	(*b*)	(*a*)	(*a*)	(*a*)	(*a*)	(*b*)	(*d*)

UNIT-III

JOINTS AND THEIR MOVEMENTS-PLANE & AXIS JOINTS (ARTICULATIONS)

Joints are the connections between adjacent bones. They may allow free movement, slight movement or no movement at all.

e.g : Hip joint, knee joint etc.,

On the basis of anatomical structure the articulation between the bones of the skeleton are classified as

1. Fibrous joints
2. Cartilagenous joints
3. Synovial joints

Fibrous Joint

It firmly joins skeletal elements with fibrous connective tissue.

Cartilagenous Joint

It firmly joins skeletal elements with cartilage.

Synovial Joint

It is freely movable joint enclosed by joint capsule that contains synovial fluid.

One of the functions of this skeletal system is to permit body movement. It is not the rigid bone that allows movements but the articulation or joints between the bones.

The study of joint is "Arthrology" the joint of the body may be classified according to structure or function. The classification of joints is as follows:

1. Synarthrosis : immovable joints
2. Amphiarthroses : slightly movable joints
3. Diarthroses : Freely movable joints

Kinds of Synovial Joints

Synovial joints are classified into 6 main types:

1. **Gliding joint:** Gliding joint allows only side to side back and front movement, with some slight rotation. This is the simplest type, the articulating surface can be nearly flat e.g., Inter carpal inter torsal joint.
2. **Hinge joint:** The structure of the hinge joints permit bendings in only one plane. Much like the hinge of the door e.g., Knee joint, elbow joint and joints between phalanges.
3. **Pivot joint:** The movement in a pivot joint is limited to rotation above as central axis. In this type the articular surface on one bone is conical or rounded and fit into a depression on another bone e.g., Axis and Atlas that enables rotational movements of the head.
4. **Condyloid:** A condyloid articulation is structured so that an oval, convex articular surface of one bone fits into an elliptical. This permits angular movement into two directions as in an up and down and side to side, motion. It does not permit rotational movement e.g., Meta carpal, phalanges joint.
5. **Saddle Joint:** This is an articular process of a saddle shape joint. It has a concave surface in one direction and a convex surface in another. This unique articulation is a modified condyloid joint. It allows a wide range of movement e.g., carpo and meta corpo joint (thumb).
6. **Ball and socket joint:** These are formed by the articulation of a rounded convex surface with a cup like cavity. This type of articulation provides wide range of movement of all the synovial joint e.g., hip joint and : shoulder joint.

Shoulder Joint

The shoulder joint is a ball and socket joint. This joint is formed by the articulation of spherical head of the humerus with the small, shallow, somewhat pear - shaped glenoid fossa of the scapula. The shallow glenoid fossa is deepened by a cap of cartilage, the glenoid labrum attached firmly to the inner surface of the fossa and the head of the humerus fits into the cup. The humeral head is also covered with cartilage and the cartilage on the head is thicker at the centre. The articular capsule attached to the rim of the glenoid fossa and to the anatomical neck of the humerus.

The most prominent ligaments are coraco acromial ligaments; Gleno - humeral ligament, coraco humeral ligament. The muscles involved are deltoid, subcapularies supraspinatus, Infraspinatus, Teres major, Teres Minor, Biceps Brachi, Triceps Brachi and Coraco Brachialis., The possible movements are flexion, extension, abduction, adduction, circumduction, inward rotation and : outward rotation.

(*a*) **Flexion:** A foreward upward movement of humerus in a plane at right angle to the plane of the scapula. This movement occurs around lateral axis through sagittal plane.

(*b*) **Extension:** The return movement from flexion or when two adjacent bones, i.e., the humerus and scapula going away from each other around lateral axis and through sagittal plane.

(*c*) **Abduction:** A sideward upward movement in the plane parallel with the plane of the scapula. This movement occurs around sagittal axis and through frontal plane.

(*d*) **Adduction:** The return movement from abduction or when the humerus comes closer to the midline around sagittal axis through frontal plane.

(*e*) **Outward Rotation:** A rotation of the humerus around its mechanical axis so that when the arm from its normal resting position, turns laterally, this movement is done around vertical axis through horizontal plane.

(*f*) **Inward Rotation:** A rotation of the humerus around its mechanical axis so that the arm from its normal resting position turns, medially, this movement occurs around vertical axis through horizontal plane.

Elbow Joint

The elbow joint is a double hinge joint. The articular surfaces are :

(*i*) Ulnar notch of ulnar against the spool - like process trochlea of humerus, where most of the weight is borne and

(*ii*) The proximal saucer like surface of the radius against capitulum of humerus. The joint capsule is strengthened on all four sides by bands of ligaments like anterior, posterior, ulnar and radial collateral ligaments. The synovial membrane not only lines the capsule, but also it extends into proximal radio-ulnar articulation, cover the olecranon radio _ ulnar articulation, cover the olecranon process, coronoid process and also line the annular ligament. The possible movements are flexion and extension.

Movement of Elbow Joint

(*a*) **Flexion:** This is forward upward movement of the forearm through the sagittal plane around lateral axis. In .other words, the forearm comes close to humerus. This reduces the angular distance at elbow joint.

(*b*) **Extension:** This is return movement from flexion or foreward downward movement of the forearm through the sagittal plane around lateral axis. In otherwards the angular distance between forearm and humerus increases.

Hip Joint

The hip joint is formed by the head of the femur fitting into the deep cup shaped acetabulum of the hip bone (pelvis). The head of the femur is completely covered with hyaline cartilage except for a small pit near the centre known as fovea capitis. Hyaline cartilage also lines the horse-shoe shaped surface of the acetabulum. The articular capsule which attaches to the rim of the acetubulum (glenoid labrum) and below the direct margin of anatomic neck of the femur. The articular capsule is made up of longitudinal and circular fibres.

The external ligaments are supported by iliofemoral ligament, pubofemoral and ischio femoral ligaments. It is lined with an extensive synovial membrane. Muscles involved are Hamstrings; Rectus femoris, Quadriceps and sartorius. Movements of the hip joints are flexion, extension, abduction, adduction, circumduction, inward rotation and outward rotation.

1. **Flexion:** A foreward upward movement of the femur through sagittal plane around lateral axis; here femur reduces the angular distance with pelvis.
2. **Extension:** The return movement of flexion. This movement is done around lateral axis and sagittal plane. Here femur increases the angular distance with pelvis.
3. **Abduction:** A side movement of the femur around the frontal plane so that the thigh moves away from the midline of the body.
4. **Adduction:** The return movement from abduction; in this movement the plane is frontal and the axis is sagittal.
5. **Outward Rotation:** A rotation of the femur around its longitudinal axis so that the knee is turned outward.
6. **Inward Rotation:** An inward rotation of the femur around its longitudinal axis so that the knee is turned inwards.

Knee Joint

The knee joint is a hinge joint between the femur and tibia, the fibula has no share in it. The upper end of the tibia is broad and the articular surface is depended by a band of fibro cartilages, the *medial* and lateral menisci. Anterior and posterior cruciate ligaments connect the tibia and femur inside the joint and cross each other. The anterior cruciate ligament passes posteriorly and laterally. The posterior cruciate ligament passes anteriorly and medially. These ligaments stabilize the knee during the rotation that occurs in walking. Medial collateral ligament and lateral ligaments give strength and stability to the joint. The ligamentum patellae, the tendon of the quadriceps make up a large part of the front region side of the joint. The popliteal ligaments give additional support laterally and posteriorly.

The muscles involved are Hamstrings, quadriceps and Gastronemius, movements of the knee joints are flexion and extension.

(*a*) **Flexion:** When the reduction of angle is taking place between 2 bones e.g., tibia and femur at the posterior direction through sagittal plane around lateral axis.

(*b*) **Extension:** When there is an increase in the angle or when the 2 bones i.e., femur and tibia going away from each other through sagittal plane around lateral axis.

FUNDAMENTAL AXIS AND PLANE

Axis

It can be defined as any imaginary point or line around which movement takes place. Axis are of three types:

(*a*) **Sagittal axis:** It is an imaginary line passing from the anterior to posterior direction.

(*b*) **Lateral axis:** It is an imaginary line passing laterally from one side to other.

(*c*) **Vertical axis:** It is an imaginary line perpendicular to the ground.

Plane

It is an imaginary surface through which a movement takes place.

Planes are of three types :

(*a*) **Horizontal plane:** It is an imaginary surface which divides the body into superior and inferior part.

(*b*) **Sagittal plane:** It is an imaginary surface which divides the body into right and left lateral aspect.

(*c*) **Frontal plane:** It is an imaginary surface which divides the body into anterior and posterior aspects

Conclusion

1. Every movement has one axis and one plane.
2. Axis is always held at right angle to their corresponding plane.
3. When there is vertical axis, movement takes place in horizontal plane.

4. When there is lateral axis, movement takes place in sagittal plane.
5. When there is sagittal axis, the movement takes place in frontal plane.

MUSCULAR ANALYSIS OF MOTOR MOVEMENTS

The anatomical analysis of the movement should include an examination of the skeletal - joint action, an account of the muscle participation, and an identification of the neurological mechanisms involved. It should attempt to give specific answers to these questions.

1. Which joints are involved and what are their exact movements in the motor skill?
2. Are any of the joints used to the limit of their range of motion?
3. Which muscles are responsible for the joint actions, and what is the nature of their contraction?
4. Do any of the muscle groups exert maximal or near maximal effort?
5. Which neuromuscular mechanisms are likely to help or hinder the action, and what is the nature of their involvement?
6. Which anatomical principles contribute to maximal efficiency and accuracy in the performance of the motor skill?
7. Which principles are directly related to the avoidance of injury?

To facilitate answering these questions the technique being analysed should be divided into units or phases. Each phase is treated as a separate movement and should have a logical beginning and ending in terms of the muscle and joint movement. The golf drive, for instance, might have four phases, the stance, the preparatory phase, the downswing or force phase ending with the ball contact, and the follow through. The phases for walking, a repetitive or cyclical movement, are often separated into swing and support phases, with the support phase further subdivided into the restraining and propulsive phases. The standing long jump was divided into the preparatory phase, unsupported phases, and landing and recovery phases.

Skeletal Joint Actions

For each phase of the technique and for each joint participating in the phase, the precise joint action should be identified and recorded as was done for the same analysis of the force phase of the standing long jump. If it seems desirable to measure the ranges of motion of these joint actions, they can be measured directly using elgons or indirectly on sequential motion pictures of the technique.

Muscle Participation

The muscular action is identified for each joint movement and recorded next to the joint actions. This implies identifying not only the muscles that are contracting, but also their precise function in the movement, the kind of contraction they are undergoing (concentric, eccentric or static) and an estimate of the force of their contraction (strong, medium, mild). The method of identification of the muscle participation can vary from the relatively simple but least reliable to more complex laboratory procedures. The technique that requires no equipment relies on subjective judgement of the actions of a muscle based on the muscle's attachments, together with the relation to the joint in question. This method must be used with caution, however, as its validity is questionable. To make it worthwhile, assumed muscular actions should be verified whenever possible by referring to related EMG research reports.

There is one experimental technique that is available to everyone. This is palpation and inspection of superficial muscles. In spite of the limitations of this method and its subjective nature, it is recommended for students as it is a valuable learning experience. Students should be cautious, however, about applying their findings to sports skills which in most cases are performed under circumstances that differ widely from those under which basic movements are executed.

The most reliable laboratory method of investigating muscular action in present use is electromyography. Evidence of muscle participation and relative quantification of that participation is possible with this methodology.

CHART FOR ANATOMICAL ANALYSIS OF A MOTOR SKILL

Name of Joint	Starting Position	Observed Joint Action	Forece for Movement	Main Music Groups Active	Kind of Contraction	Force of Contraction
Metatarsal phalangeal	Extended	Hyper Extension	Muscle	Extensors/ flexors	Concentric	Strong
Ankle	Dorsiflexed	Plantar flexion	Muscle	Planter flexors	Concentric	Strong
Knee	Flexed	Extension	Muscle	Extensors	Concentric	Strong
Hip	Flexed	Extension	Muscle	Extensors	Concentric	Strong
Pelvis	Decreased tilt	Increased tilt	Muscle	Spinal Extensors	Concentric	Moderate
Lumbar spine	Flexion	Extension	Muscle	Spinal Extensors	Concentric	Moderate
Thoracic spine	Slight flexion	Extension	Muscle	Spinal Extensors	Concentric	Moderate
Cervical spine	Hyper extended	Flexion	Gravity	Spinal Extensors	Eccentric	Mild
Shoulder girdle	Upward tilt	Upward rotation	Muscle	Upward rotation	Eccentric	Moderate
Shoulder joint	Hyper extension	Flexion	Muscle	flexors	Concentric	Strong
Elbow	Extended	- - -	Muscle	Extensors	Static	Mild
Radioulnar	Pronated	- - -	Muscle	- - -	- - -	- -
Wrist	Extended	- - -	Muscle	Extensors	Static	Mild
Phalanges	Extended	- - -	Muscle	Extensors	Static	Mild

The recording of isokinetic contraction is another technique for making precise evaluations of muscular and joint performance. It requires the use of an electromechanical device designed specifically for this purpose. This method is discussed.

Neuro Muscular Considerations

The muscle response patterns of well learned motor skills involve the integrated action of many reflexes and the inhibition of others. After repeated viewings of the performance live or in film, the student should name and discuss the reflexes that could be acting at various points in each phase. The reflexes that should be considered are spindle reflexes, Golgi tendon organ reflex, joint reflexes, cutaneous responses, labyrinthine reflexes, neck reflexes, and visual righting reflexes, for each reflex, the receptors involved should be identified, the expected action due to the reflex described, and the actual results explained. In the standing long jump :

1. Reflex : Labyrinthine head righting reflex is present.
2. Time : Preparation for take off.
3. Evidence : As the trunk move farther forward the head and neck become more hyper-extended.

1. Reflex : Stretch reflexes in exten-sors of hip, knee and ankle are present.
2. Time : Early preparation for take off (crouch).

3. Evidence : The stretch reflexes are activated in the extensors as flexion occurs in the hips, knees and ankles. The result is facilitation of contraction of the extensors.

KINEMATICS

Kinematics is the study of the geometry, pattern (or) form of motion with respect to time. Kinematics may be described as appearance of motion or shape of motion.

Kinematics deals with the bodies as how far a body moves, how fast it moves, and how consistently it moves.

Linear kinematics deals with the kinematics of linear motion or translation. Linear kinematics involves the study of the shape, form, pattern and sequencing of linear movement.

Distance and Displacement

Distance and Displacement are quantities of kinematics. Units of distance and displacement are millimetre (mm) is 1/1000 m, centimetre (cm) is 1/100 m and kilo metre (km) is 1000 m.

Distance

When a body moves from one location to another, the length of the path that the body follows is the distance. (e.g.) : when a runner completes a 2 laps around a 400 m track, the distance that the runner has covered is equal to (400+400) 800 m.

Displacement

Displacement is change in position. Displacement is measured in a straight line from the starting position to final position. e.g., on a completion of a lap around the 400 m track, the displacement is zero because the starting and finishing positions are the same.

Speed and Velocity

Speed and Velocity are qualities of distance and displacement respectively.

Speed is defined as the distance covered divided by the time taken to cover it.

$$\bar{s} = \frac{l}{\Delta t}$$

$\bar{s}$ = Average speed

l = length of path

Δ = Delta (or) change in time

t = time

Velocity (V) is the change in position or the displacement that occurs during a given period of time.

$$V = \frac{d}{\Delta t}$$

V = Velocity

d = displacement

t = change in time (Δ^{-delta})

Acceleration

Acceleration is defined as the rate of change in velocity (or) the change in velocity occurring over a given time interval, with t representing the amount of time elapsed during the velocity assessment.

$$\bar{a} = \frac{\Delta v}{\Delta t}$$

Δv = change in velocity

Δt = change in time

For example, if a runner increases its velocity by 1m/ s each second, its acceleration is 1 m/s^2. A common unit of acceleration is m/s^2.

According to the direction and value of final velocity the acceleration can be divided into two types:

1. Positive acceleration
2. Negative acceleration

Positive Acceleration

The acceleration is determined as positive by two factors:

1. The final velocity (V_2) will be greater than initial velocity (V_1)
2. Positive direction.

Angular Kinematics

Angular Distance and Angular Displacement

When a rotating body moves from one position to another, the angular distance through which it moves is equal to the angle between its initial and final positions. (eg) a gymnast performing a forward giant circle on the horizontal bar shows the gymnast with his body in a momentary handstand position at top of the bar.

The angular displacement that a rotating body experiences is equal in magnitude to the smaller of the two angles between the body's initial and final positions. (eg.) initial and final positions is 350 when measured counter clockwise and 10 when measured clockwise. The magnitude of the angular displacement is, therefore 10. The direction of the angular displacement can be clockwise or counter clockwise.

Angular Velocity

Angular velocity is defined as the angular distance covered per unit time.

Angular speed & Angular velocity

The average angular speed of a body obtained by dividing the angular distance through which the body moves by the time taken.

$$\overline{\sigma} = \frac{\emptyset}{t}$$

Where $\overline{\sigma}$ = average angular velocity obtained in similar fashion by dividing the angular displacement by the time taken.

$$\overline{\varpi} = \frac{\theta}{t}$$

Where $\overline{\varpi}$ = average angular velocity and θ = angular displacement, specifying the direction.

Units of Angular Distance

1. **R.P.M:** Regulation Per Minute
2. **Degree:** One regulation is divided in 360 (i.e) a degree is a part of 360 equal parts of a regulation (or) circle.
3. **Radian:** A radian is an angle which is made by an arch of a circle the length of which is equal in length to the radius of that circle

   π radian = 180

   $\therefore$ 1 radian = 180 +227/ (since π = 22/7)

   hence , r = 57.29 (r = radius)

Relationship between linear and angular motion (equation)

$V_l = V_r \times r$ ....(1)

$d_l = D_r \times r$ ... (2) n

Where, V_l = linear velocity ....m/sec

v_r = angular velocity ... rot / sec

r = radius of the rotation ... Radian or metre

D_l = Kinear distance .... (metre)

D_r = Angular distance ... radian

Linear and Angular Kinematics

This chapter began with a reference to the close relationship between the quantities used in the description of linear motion and those used in the description of angular motion.

A much more precise figure for the number of degrees in a radian can be obtained by considering how many times an arc of a length equal to the radian can be divided into the circumference of a circle.

$$\frac{\text{Circumference}}{\text{Radius}} = \frac{2\pi r}{2} = 2\pi$$

From this it can be seen that 2π rad must be equal to 360°, or 1 rev. By simple division it can be determined that

1rad = 57.3 = 016 rev.

Negative Acceleration

The acceleration is determined as negative by the two factors:

1. The final velocity (V_2) will be less than initial velocity (V_1)
2. Negative direction

Projectiles

A projectile is a body in free fall that is subject only to the forces of gravity and air resistance.

Four primary mechanical purposes are used in projecting.

1. To project an object or the body for maximum horizontal distance.
2. To project an object or the body for maximum vertical distance.
3. To project an object for maximum accuracy.
4. To project an object for maximum accuracy when the speed of the projectile enhances the projectiles effectiveness.

Trajectory

The flight path of an object or the body is trajectory. Three factors influence the trajectory of a projectile:

1. **The angle of projection:** The angle of the projected object or body from the ground or projected surface in angle of projection. Three types of shape of trajectory are determined depending on the angle of projection.
   (*a*) Vertical trajectory
   (*b*) Oblique trajectory
   (*c*) Horizontal trajectory.

(*a*) **Vertical trajectory:** If the angle of projection is perfectly vertical (90 degree to the horizontal), the trajectory is also perfectly vertical. In vertical trajectory, the projectile follow the same path, Straight up and then straight down again.

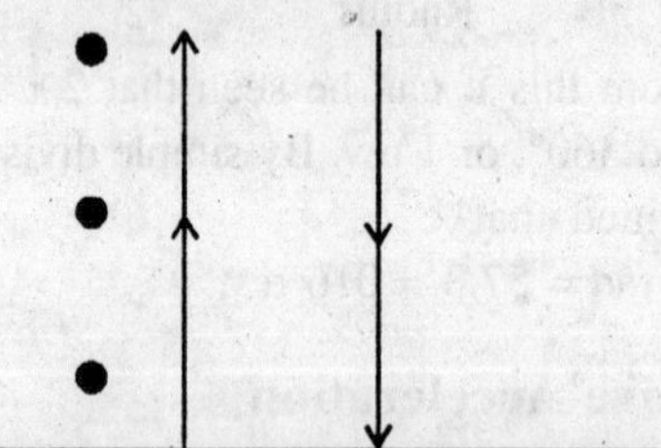

(*b*) **Oblique trajectory:** If the angle of projection is oblique (at some angle between 0 and 90 degree) the trajectory is parabolic, which means shaped like a parabola.

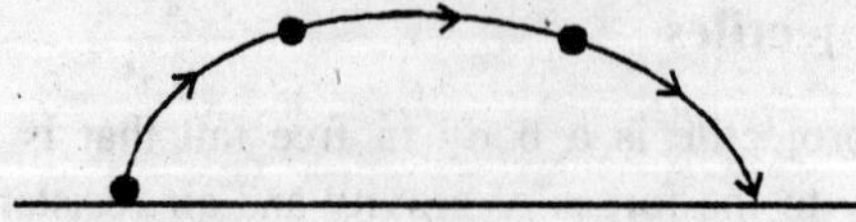

(*c*) **Horizontal trajectory:** If the angle of projection is zero, the trajectory is like horizontal.

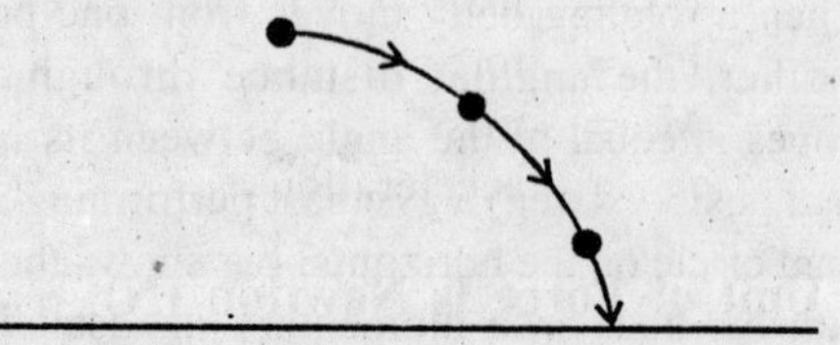

2. **The projection speed:** The magnitude of projection velocity is projection speed.
3. **The projection height:** It is the maximum vertical height attained by the object above the point of projection during its flight.

Range of Projectile

The range of projectile is the product of the horizontal velocity at release and the time of flight.

$$R = \frac{V^{2\pi} \sin 2\theta}{g} = 2\pi$$

R = Range of projectile
θ = The angle of release
V = initial velocity
g = gravitational force (9.81N)

LINEAR KINETICS

Kinetics Means a Complete Study of Force

(*a*) **Inertia**: Inertia means resistance to action or to change. The mechanical definition is resistance to acceleration is the tendency of a body to maintain a motionless state or a state of constant velocity.

For example,

1. 150 kg weight bar lying motionless on the floor has a tendency to remain motionless.
2. A skater gliding on a smooth surface of ice has a tendency to continue gliding on a straight line with a constant speed.

(*b*) **Force:** Force is a push or a pull acting on a body, a body's state of being "at rest" or in motion can be changed by the action of some other body.

Force may also be defined as the product of a body's mass and the acceleration of that body resulting from the application of the force.

F = ma
F = force
M = mass
A = acceleration

Unit of Force is Newtion (N)

Characteristics of force

All forces have four unique properties

1. Magnitude, how much force is applied.
2. Direction, the way the force is applied.
3. Point of application, where the force is applied on the body.
4. Line of action, the straight line extending through the point of application and extending indefinitely along the direction of the force. Forces can be identified as internal (or) external forces.

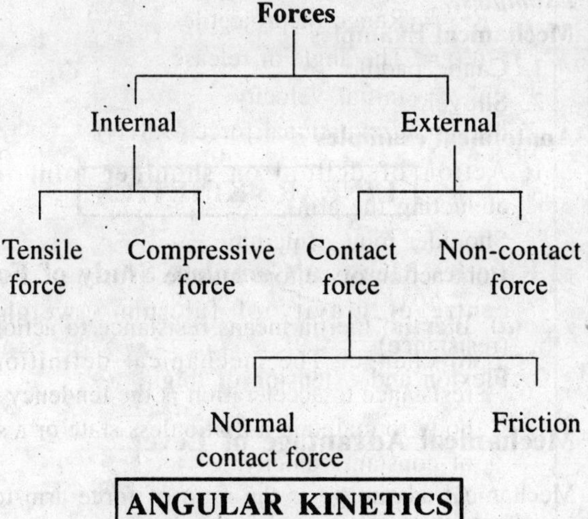

ANGULAR KINETICS

Angular kinetics is the study of the action of forces in angular motion.

Centre of a Gravity (CG)

According to Newton's law of gravition all bodies are attracted to one another with a force which is gravitional force. Gravity is the natural force that pulls all objects towards the centre of the earth. The gravitional pull always occurs through the centre of weight of an object.

A unique point is associated with every body, around which the body's mass is equally distributed in all directions. This point is known as the 'centre of mass' or the mass centroid of the body.

The centre of mass may also be referred to as the centre of gravity (CS), the point about which a body's weight is equally balanced in all directions.

For an adult man in a normal standing or lying position, the centre of gravity is said to be placed at 57% his total height. For an adult women, due to light arms, narrow shoulders and heavier pelvis, the centre of gravity is said to be at the height of 85%.

The centre of gravity for an individual is at the point of rest of the illium between belly and back approximately 1 inch below the level, when one is standing or lying.

The centre of gravity constantly change during a movement. It always shifts in the direction of movement or additional weight, while standing, when one moves both the hands up, the centre of gravity also moves up 3 to 4 inches.

Locating the Centre of Gravity (Methods of Finding out)

1. Balance method
2. Suspension method
3. Mannikin method
4. Reaction board
5. Segmental method

LEVER

Definition 1

Lever is a simple machine consisting of a rigid bar like body that may be made to rotate about an axis.

A lever is a rigid bar that rotates about an axis or fulcrum which is a point of support or axis about which a lever may be made to rotate.

In the human body, the bone acts as the rigid bar, the joint is the axis or fulcrum, and the muscles act as a force.

Definition 2

A lever is a mechanical device used to produce a turning motion about a fixed point called as axis.

Parts of a Lever

1. Fulcrum or the axis
2. Force (or) power
3. Weight (or) resistance
4. Force arm - the distance between fulcrum to the point of application of force.
5. Weight arm - the distance between fulcrum to the centre of weight.

Types of Lever

Depending upon the positions of the parts of levers, they can be classified into 3 types. They are

1. First Class Lever

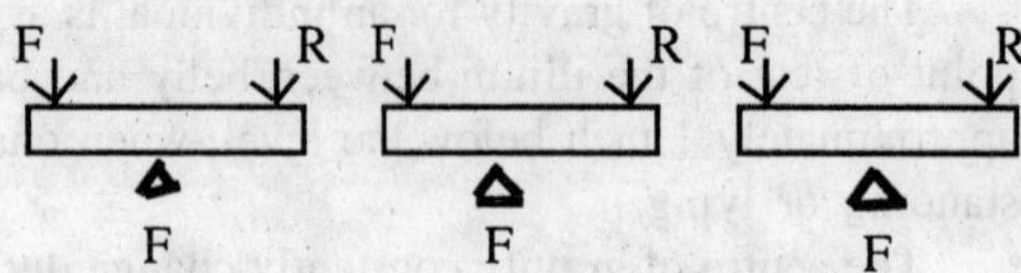

In a first class lever, the applied force and resistance may be at equal distance from the axis or one may be further away from the axis than the other.

***e.g., :* 1. Mechanical examples :**

(*a*) See saw
(*b*) Common balance
(*c*) Scissors
(*d*) Crow bar
(*e*) Cutting pliers

Anatomical Examples

1. Flexion and Extension of skull:

The atlanto occipital joint - fulcrum
the skull- weight (resistance)
neck muscles - force.
Extension of forearm (put the shot)
Elbow joint – fulcrum
Weight (resistance) – CG of the forearm
Force – contraction of triceps muscles.

2. Second Class Lever

In a second class lever, the applied force and resistance are on the same side of the axis, with the resistance closer to the axis. In a second class lever, the force arm is always longer than the weight arm. If weight is shifted near the fulcrum, the mechanical advantage will be greater.

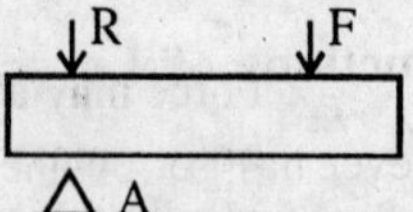

Examples:

Mechanical examples :

1. Wheel barrow
2. Lug nut wrench
3. Nut cracker

Anatomical examples :

1. Body raising on toes
2. Opening of lower jaw

3. Third Class Lever

In the third class lever, the force and resistance are on the same side of the axis, with the applied force closer to the axis.

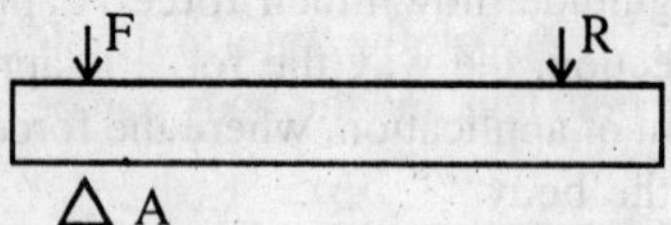

In third class lever, weight arm is always longer than force arm. So if force is shifted nearer to weight, the advantage can be increased.

Examples:

Mechanical Examples :

1. Canoe paddle
2. Shovel

Anatomical examples :

1. Action of deltoid on shoulder joint in abducting the arm
   Shoulder joint - fulcrum
   Contraction of deltoid muscle - force
   centre of gravity of fulcrum - weight (resistance)
2. Flexion and extension of thigh

Mechanical Advantage of Lever

Mechanical advantage is the ratio of force arm to weight (Resistance) arm for a given lever.

Mechanical advantage = Force arm (FA) / Weight arm (WA)

Force arm (FA) is the distance between the applied force and the fulcrum. The weight arm (WA) is the distance between the weight and the fulcrum.

Here A, the FA is longer than B. So mechanical advantage is greater in the situation A. While a weight is lifted using a Crowbar.

Functions of Levers

A lever has got 3 functions :

(*a*) Balancing

(*b*) To gain force advantage

(*c*) To gain speed advantage.

POSTURE

Posture is the correct alignment of the body segments. The good standing posture can be ascertained by plumb line test. In the plumb line test, the string passes even with ear lobe, centre of the shoulder, middle of the hip, slightly behind patella, and in front of the intermalleolue. The weight even on both legs and the body can be moved readily in any direction.

There are two types of posture :

1. Static posture (sitting, standing)
2. Dynamic posture (walking, running)

Values of Good Posture

1. **Hygienic value :** Since the body is erect and straight all internal organs are suspended properly they can function efficiently and perfectly.
2. **Economic value :** By the way of good posture one can get job opportunity and earn his livelihood.
3. **Social value :** Good posture is always attractive and there by get respect from the society.
4. **Spiritual value :** The spirit is uplifted with physical uplift of the trunk. The glory of the raising sun is never seen by one walking with protruding head and abdomen and flat feet.

Posture Deviation (Bad/Poor Posture)

Posture Deviation	
Structural	**Functional**
Bone modifications (conditions cannot be rectified without surgery)	Soft tissues such as muscular, ligaments (corrected through exercises and induction procedures)

Causes of bad posture

The following are causes for had posture :

1. Injury
2. Disease

3- Habit

4. Muscular (or) nervous weakness
5. Mental attitude
6. Heredity
7. Improper clothing

BAD POSTURE

1. **Round Shoulder:** In this, the scapulas are held in an abducted position. There is an increased thoracic curve. The arms and shoulder are held forward by continuous contraction of the pectoralis major and minor, while the trapezius rhomboid and leavator muscles are relaxed to permit the scapula to move forward. This gradually tends to make the anterior muscles permanently shorter, while lengthening the posterior muscle.
2. **Kyphosis:** Kyphosis, the convexity of the thoracic spine is increased. The sternum is depressed and the rib cage is lowered resulting in a decrease in the thoracic volume.
3. **Lordosis:** Lordosis is an increased posterior convexity of the normal lumbar curve. (exaggerated lumbar curve caused by a forward tilt of the pelvis) accompanied by a forward tilt of the pelvis.
4. **Flat back:** Flat back involves abnormal decrease in the normal lumber curve and more than normal tilt of the pelvis. In this condition the hamstrings are shortened while the hip flexors and the ligaments are lengthened. .
5. **Scoliosis:** The lateral curvature of the spine is called scoliosis. The muscles on the concave side of the curve would be stronger than those of the convex side. Majority of the curves are thoracic lumber in location.
   The scoliosis may be functional or postural. In this the curve can be disappeared when the subject hangs by his hand.
   If poor posture continues, the conditions become structural or resistant. In this case correction is extremely difficult and complex.

Correct Posture is Important Because

1. It aids the functioning of the organic systems.
2. It reduces strain on muscle, ligaments and tendons.
3. It increases the attractiveness of the person and influence selfconcept and psychological implications.

Correcting Posture

Correcting posture is a task for physical educators because the deviations sometimes grow out of poor habits, ignorance about correct posture and psychological problems.

1. Motivating for correct posture.
2. Leading through a corrective exercise programme.

The programme must consist of selected exercises related to required strength endurance, tone and flexibility to opposing muscle groups.

It has been demonstrated that the following is a successful corrective produce:

Correctly identify the postural deviation (or) incorrectness and inform the individual of its nature and the importance of correcting it.

Attempt to identify the basic causes of the deviations / incorrectness and control the cause.

Motivate the individual to correct the deviation

Prescribe an exercise programme designed to correct the condition.

Periodically evaluate the effects of the programme.

Guidelines for Correct Posture

1. The weight - bearing segments should be correctly and vertically aligned, so that the line of gravity passes through them.
2. The extension of the weight bearing joints should be an easy extension not by strain, tension, or excessive rigidity.
3. The feet should be placed apart to form a base of support over which the body can be balanced.
4. With respect to inward and outward rotation, the patella and feet should be pointed straight forward.
5. Little forward tilt of the pelvis.
6. The spinal column, naturally exhibit three curves, a convex cervical curve, a concave thoracic curve and convex lumber curve, when viewed from the rear, the spinal column should be straight.
7. The abdominal wall, is composed mostly with muscle tissue, should be kept in good tone and care should be taken to keep the wall straight to provide support to internal organs.
8. Many people have a tendency to abduct the shoulder girdles. The condition commonly known as chest and rounded shoulders should be avoided.
9. In good, erect posture, the neck should be held straight, but not rigid and the neck muscles are not unnecessarily stressed.

The posture can be tested by the following methods:

1. New York state posture rating test
2. Woodruff body alignment posture test.
3. Cureton's posture measurement.

LAW OF MOTION

Most human movement is a complex combination of the basic forms of motion. In general all motion may be described as translation (line motion) and rotation / some combination of these two:

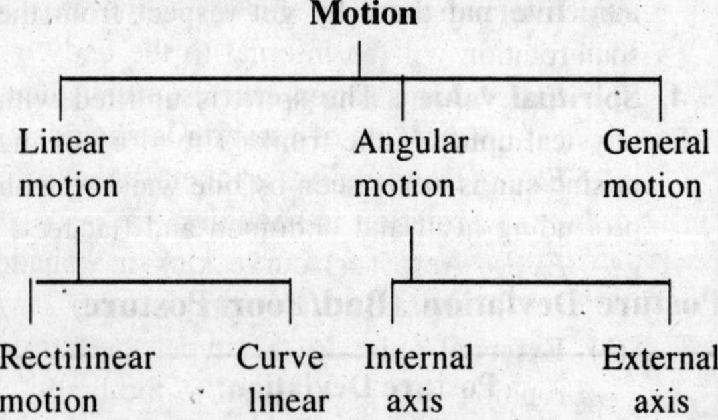

1. Linear Motion/ Translation

Linear motion is a motion along a line that may be straight or curved. In linear motion, all parts of the body are moving in the same direction at the same speed. Linear motion is also referred to as translatory motion or translation. Linear motion may be described as "Rectilinear" and "Curvilinear".

Rectilinear Motion: When a body moves in a linear motion if the line is straight, the motion is rectilinear.

Ex.1. Vertical, 100 mts run in straight line.

Curvilinear motion: When a body moves in a linear motion. If the line is curved, the motion is curvilinear.

Ex.1. In long jump. The path of athlete's body's flight in the air from take off board to landing.

Ex.2. Basket ball- shooting

Ex.3 Kabaddi - chain movement.

2. Angular Motion (Rotation)

Angular motion is rotation around a central imaginary linen known as the axis of rotation. Angular motion (or) rotation takes place when a body moves along a circular path about some line, in space so that all parts of the body travel through the same angle, in the same direction in the same time.

In angular motion or rotation, each and every body will have an axis of rotation. The body will rotate around the axis of rotation.

Ex: Giant cycle on a bar in gymnastics somersault in mid-air gymnastics.

The axis of rotation can be divided according to its position into two types:

(*a*) Internal axis

(*b*) External axis

(*a*) **Internal axis:** In this type, the axis of rotation will be internal to the body.

Ex 1: Arms raised exercise - calisthenis the axis of rotation is shoulder.

Ex 2: Bowling in cricket the axis of rotation is shoulder.

Ex 3: Aero (or) curve kick in kabaddi the axis of rotation is hip.

(*b*) **External axis:** In this type, the axis of rotation will be external to the body.

Ex. Rotation is horizontal bar in gymnastics. Horizontal bar is the axis (out side the body).

3. General Motion

When a body performs both the linear and angular motion, it is said to be in general motion.

EQUILIBRIUM

When all parts of a body are at rest or are moving with the same constant velocity, the body is said to be in a state of equilibrium.

Definition: "Equilibrium is a static of balance between two opposing forces of effects" - Dictionary of Science.

Types or Stages of Equilibrium

There are three types of equilibrium.

1. Static (or) stable equilibrium
   The equilibrium at rest is called static equilibrium. e.g., Centre of gravity height.
2. Unstable Equilibrium
   e.g., Base
3. Dymanic (or) Neutral Equilibrium
   e.g., Horizontal
   Principle Derived from the concept of Equilibrium

1. To start quickly in one direction keep centre of gravity as high as possible as near (close) to the edge of the base in the direction of movement.
   e.g., Crouch start i.e., start posture for sprint.
2. For greater stability or immobility increase the area of the base and lower the C.G. as much as is possible.
   e.g., Wrestler wrestling - spread limbs to have greater stability.
3. To stop quickly at rapid motion, spread the base and drop the centre of gravity as low as constant with the subsequent movement.
   e.g., In basket ball, dribbling stopping.
4. In all arm support activity the centre of gravity of the body be as nearly as possible over the point of support on the line of support or on the base of support.
   e.g., Hand stand, in gymnastics.
5. Movements of the body when suspended in the air or when hanging by arms or legs follow a definite pattern of movement which tends to maintain equilibrium or body balances.

e.g., Long jump - hang style – Hip forward spiking in volley ball - Arching.

There are two conditions:

(*a*) When the body is free in the air, if the head and feet move up or forward the hips move to down or to backward direction respectively.

(*b*) When the either hand or feet are supported if one moves up, the hip moves down and vice-versa. .

Note:

When the body is in the air, the centre of gravity follows a path where any movement of limbs does not effect it or change the path.

Factors Influencing Equilibrium

A body's ability to maintain equilibrium is increased by the following factors:

1. Increasing body mass.
2. Increasing friction between the body and the surface or surfaces contacted.
3. Increasing the size of the base of support.
4. Horizontal distance of the centre of gravity near the edge of the base of support.
5. Vertical distance of the centre of gravity as low as possible.

Force

Force is a push or a pull acting on a body. A body's state of being "at rest" or in motion can be changed by the action of some other body.

Force may also be defined as the product of a body's mass and the acceleration of that body resulting from the application of the force.

Spin

Spin is turning around an axis which passes through the centre of the object. Spinning objects also generate lift called magnus force.

Magnus Force

The lift force created by spin magnus effect.

The deviation in the trajectory of a spinning object towards the direction of spin resulting from the magnus force.

The spin can be classified into two types based on the axis of rotation.

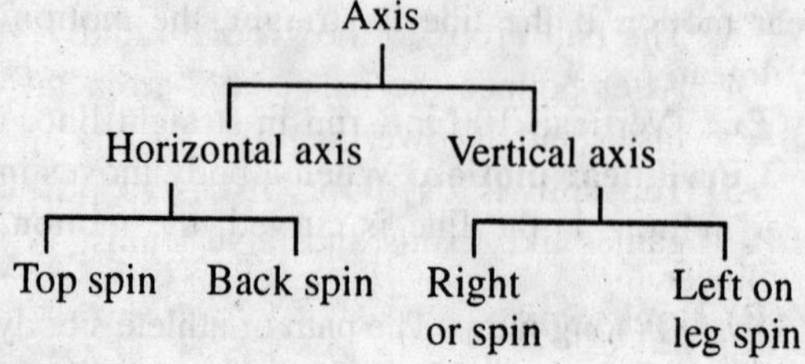

Horizontal axis

It is the rotation around in any axis and is the result of an application of the off centre force.

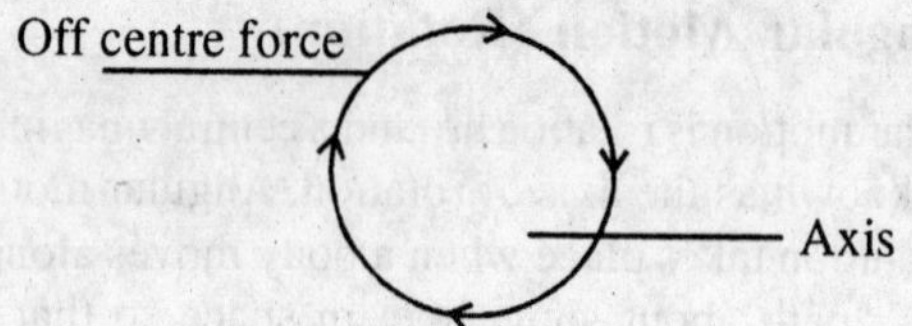

(A) Top Spin

In top spin, the ball rotates around on horizontal axis. Here the top of the ball rotates in the same direction as that of the ball.

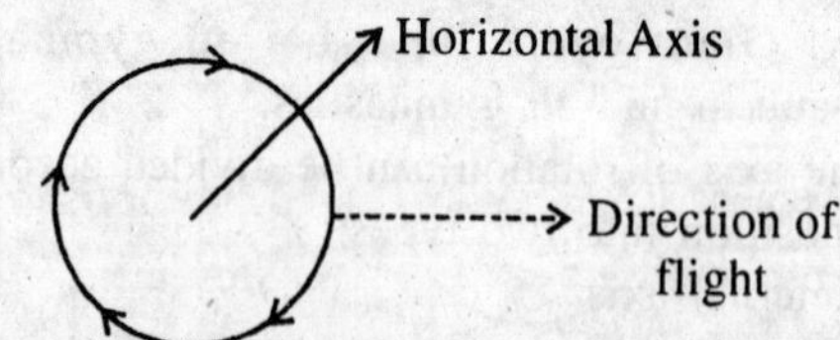

The top of the ball travels forward, down ward, back ward and upward.

The magnus force created by top spin

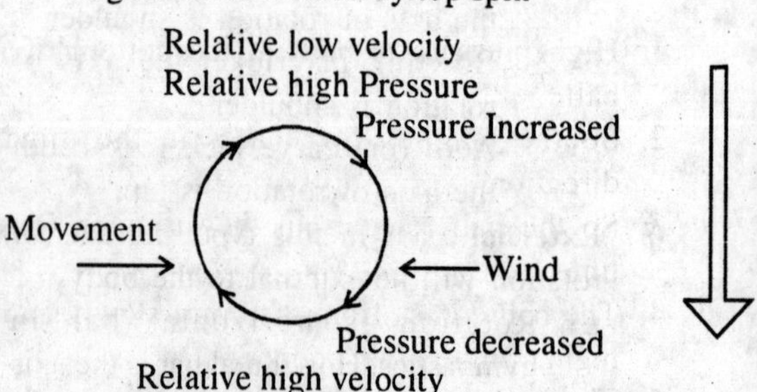

Effect of Top Spin

1. High pressure is built on top of the ball.
2. So the magnus force acts in the down ward direction.

3. The ball drops to the ground rapidly.
4. After bounce the ball comes from the count faster and at lower angle.
5. Top spin is used for offensive purpose in games like tennis and table tennis.

(B) Back Spin

In back spin, the ball rotates around a horizontal axis. Here the top of the ball rotates in the opposite direction to the direction of flight.

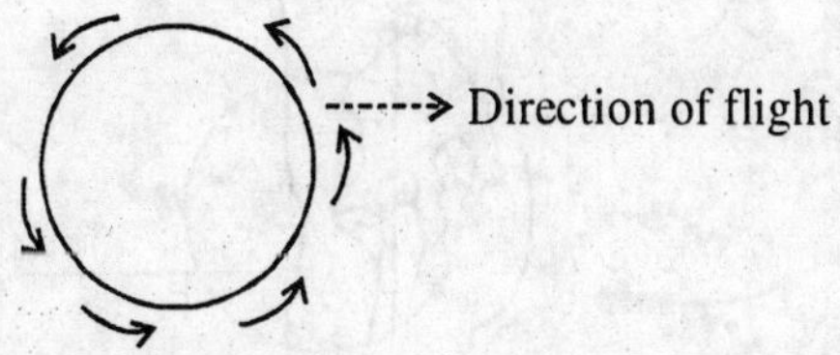

The top of the ball travels backward, downward, forward and upward.

The magnus force created by back spin

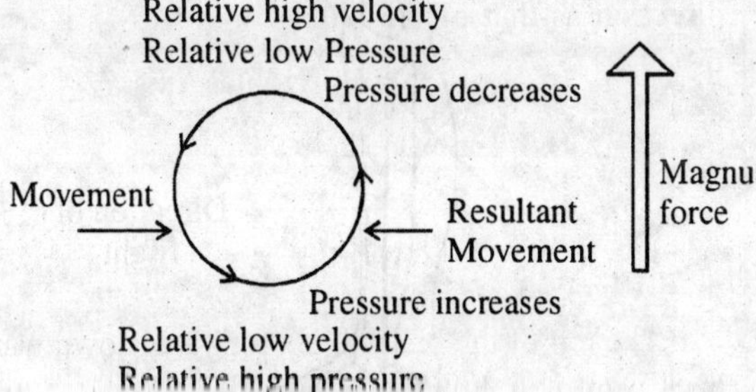

Effect of Back Spin

1. High pressure is built at the bottom of the ball.
2. So the magnus force acts in the upward direction.
3. So the ball remains in the air for a longer time.
4. The ball comes from the court slowly and at higher angle after bounce.
5. The ball does not bounce forward it is used for defensive purpose.

NEWTON'S LAWS OF MOTION

Sir Isaac Newton discovered many of the fundamental relationships that form the foundation for the field of modern mechanics.

(*i*) **Law of Inertia:** Newton's first law of motion is known as the law of intertia. This law states the following:

"A body will maintain in a state of rest or constant velocity unless acted on by an external force that changes the state."

In otherwords, a motionless object or body will remain motionless unless there is a net force (external force) acting on it. Similarly, a body travelling with a constant speed along a straight path will continue its motion unless acted on by a net force that alters either the speed or the direction of the motion. When we kick a foot ball which is at rest or motionless, that ball would move far distance the reason for that is an external force have acted on it. After travelling some distance, the ball will stop its movements. The reason for that is an external force (air resistance, .air friction, ground friction, and gravitational force) have acted on it.

(*ii*) **Law of Acceleration:** Newton's second law of motion is an expression of the inter relationships among force, mass and acceleration. This law, known as the law of acceleration, may be stated as follows for a body with constant mass.

"A force applied to a body causes an acceleration of that body of a magnitude proportional to the force, in the direction of the force, and inversely proportional to the body's mass".

When a ball is thrown, kicked, or struck with an implement, it tends to travel in the direction of the line of action of the applied force similarly, the greater the amount of force applied, the greater the speed the ball has. The formula that explains the quantitative relationships among as applied force, a body's mass and the resulting acceleration of the body is.

$$F = ma$$

$$a = \frac{F}{M}$$

Thus if a 1 kg ball is struck with a force of 10N, the resulting acceleration of the ball is $10m/s^2$ .If the ball has a mass of 2kg, the applications of the same 10N force results in an acceleration of only $5m/s^2$.

(*iii*) Law of Reaction: The third of Newton's law of motion is called law of reaction.

"For every action, there is an equal and opposite reaction".

When one body exerts a force on a second, the second body exerts a reaction force that is equal in magnitude and opposite in direction on the first body.

When a person pushes with a hand against a rigid wall the wall pushes back on the hand with a force that is equal and opposite to that exerted by the hand on the wall.

Researchers have studied the reaction force are generated by the ground for every foot ball during running. That reaction force are generally two to three times the runner's body weight.

Example: Take off in high jump.

TYPES OF A GOOD POSTURE

Broadly there are two types of postures :

(*a*) *Inactive posture* - when a person is sleeping or having rest and body requires minimum muscular efforts, and

(*b*) *Active posture* - where integrated muscular activity is required.

Active posture may be static or dynamic. Static posture is one where the body is passive, not active or changing stance and forces are acting in equilibrium. Dynamic posture is one where the body is in motion, active and changing its stance. Postural positions whether inactive or active (static and dynamic), can be broadly classified in four categories :

1. Standing position or posture.
2. Sitting position or posture.
3. Lying position or posture, and
4. Walking posture.

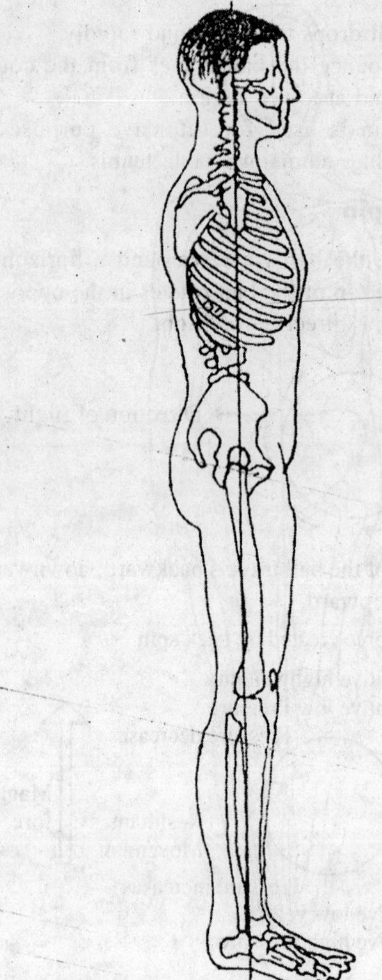

Standing Position or Posture

Standing position of an individual is generally considered as the basic posture from which all his other postures stem. Erect standing posture is to literally static, it in reality is movement upon a stationary base. The application of the principles of stability to a standing position i.e, balanced and free from muscular and ligamentous strain, would be that the line of gravity of the centre of the head, chest, abdomen (trunk) and pelvis fall in a straight line. In standing position weight should be equally distributed between the ball of the foot and the heel.

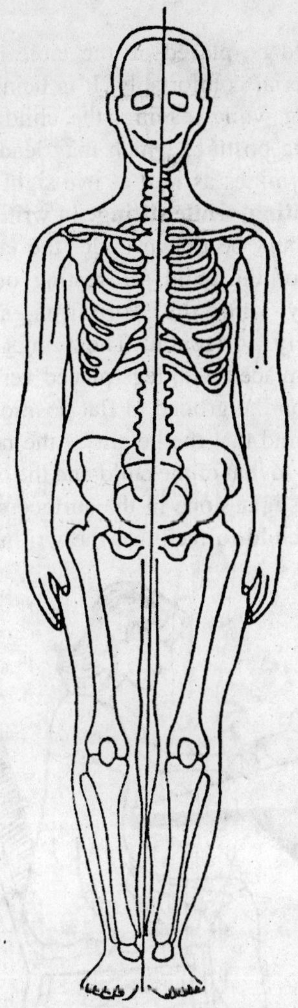

Static erect posture should be deliberately avoided except for short periods, otherwise it will produce undue muscular strain and stress, resulting in excessive fatigue. In case one has to stand for a longer duration, the effort should be made to shift the weight from one foot to another periodically. This will avoid undue neuro- muscular stress and strain being caused to the extensor muscles of any one leg. This can be done either by moving one leg sideways and lateron moving the other one similarly, or by moving one leg backward and the other forward and changing their position frequently. In this way brain's equilibrium centre adjusts the tension of the postural muscles enabling them to function automatically so as to readjust the body balance accordingly. Good standing posture is a position of extension of weitht fearing joints. This should be an easy extension and should not be accompanied by stress or strain of any kind.

Sitting Position or Posture

There are three types of sitting posture

(*i*) Simple Sitting.

(*ii*) Reading, While Sitting, and

(*iii*) Writing, While Sitting

(*i*) **Simple Sitting:** The simple sitting position is one in which a person occupies a position wherein the muscles involved in the process experience minimum stress and strain.

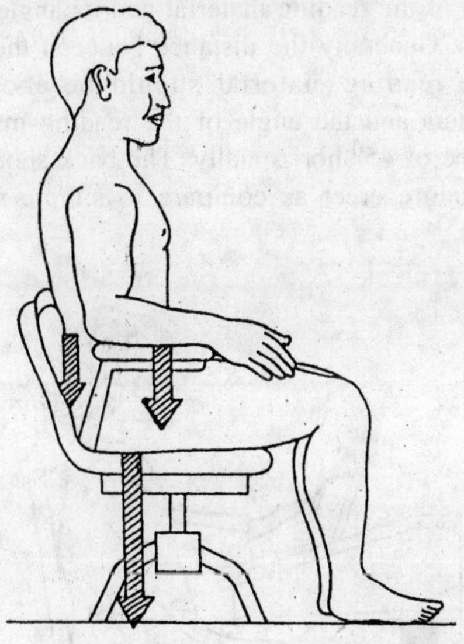

In simple sitting position, the parts of the body, head, shoulder and hips should be well placed in proper alignment with each other. The trunk, including the head and shoulders, should be in a natural, upright and relax position. Specially, kyphosis (outward curvature) of the lumbar spine should be avoided by maintaining the natural curves of the spine. The thighs should be placed horizontally, legs placed vertically and the feet resting on the ground in flat position. The hands flexed a little at the elbow, should rest on the thighs.

Frequent changes of position are important for preventing fatigue and the chair should allow the person to move about instead of restraining him in rigid sitting position. The weight of the sitter should be supported over a large area so as to equally distribute the pressure. The height of the seat should be designed to prevent when the foot is flat on the ground and the knee is bend at the right angle. Chair should also have a back rest, providing support to the lumbar region of the spine. The defective sitting posture has immense adverse effects on the natural curve of the spine, resulting in spinal deformities.

***(ii)* Reading, While Sitting:** The reading posture is almost similar to the simple sitting position. The only point to be kept in mind is the distance of the reading material and its angle from the eyes. Generally the distance between the eyes and the reading material should be about 30 centimeters and the angle of the reading material should be of 45^0 horizontally. The back should be a little more erect as compare to simple sitting position.

Efforts should be made to have proper lighting arrangement so that the light falls on the reading material from the back of the person reading. Appropriate furniture should be used for sitting, it should not be too high or too low, nor too inclined. Hands should be placed on the table holding the reading material comfortably. It is being generally observed that while reading, the children assume faulty reading postures which may lead to various posture deformities as well as eye sight problems.

***(iii)* Writing, while sitting:** In writing posture, the chair should be drawn under the table so that the elbows of the child are resting on the table comfortably and the forearms should be approximately horizontal. The things should be horizontally placed with legs placed vertically, and feet resting on the ground in flat position. It has to be kept in mind that the height of the table should be according to that of the child and the chair. There should be a slight slope in the surface of the table towards the child to facilitate the writing process.

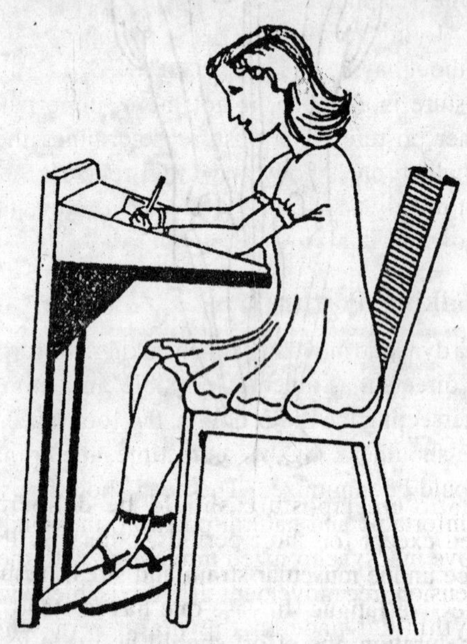

In this posture the child has to have a little forward inclination as compared to the reading posture. For proper writing posture, undue bending of the neck, forward or sideways should be avoided.

Lying Position or Posture

The best lying posture is one in which all the body segments are placed in such a position so as to exert minimum stress and strain. As one generally lies down to have rest or to relax, the best posture for this purpose is to lie down flat, keeping back on the floor or the bed, with legs fully stretched forward,feet a little apart in a comfortable position, arms straight to the side of the body. This posture is almost similar to one in shavasana in Yoga and is considered best for relaxation. The bedding should be firm if not hard. Spring and sponge mattresses are highly undesirable as they make the body sink out of alignment. High pillows cause tension in the muscles of the neck and impede proper circulation of the blood to the head. While sleeping it is not good to sleep on one's back, nor it is proper to sleep always on the same side, whether right or left. It has been observed that sleeping on one's side with knees drawn up a little, in a comfortable position, is considered as a good lying position while sleeping.

Lying posture is being generally neglected without having any proper knowledge about it. This posture is as much, if not more, important as any other posture. This posture determines the degree to which one's body and mind relaxes. Sleeping is not merely an act, it is an event, it rejuvenates both body and mind to face another day.

Walking Posture

In a dynamic movement like walking, the force should be directed, as much as possible, in a straight line, intersecting the major joints, the foot, knee, hip and the shoulders. At the same time, the spinal curve should be minimized. The head should be held in a comfortable and natural position, the hands should move in a synchronized movement with the legs, in a tension free movement. It is advisable to walk with rhythmical pace in the manner in which one experience minimum stress and strain. The leg moving forward should be in the line of direction, with heel touching first followed by toe pointing towards the direction of the movement, and the weight of the body will be shifted to the toes along with the outer edge of the foot.

Importantce of a Good Posture

No body can deny the significance and importance of a good posture in our daily life. Good appearance and good posture of an individual conveys good impression of his well being. It reflects the alertness, activeness, agility and wholesomeness of an individual's personality. Good posture allows the minimum or economical use of energy, effort and time whereas poor posture results in excessive utilisation of energy. There is a definite relationship between good posture and good health. God posture enables an individual to follow good health habits so as to lead a healthy life.

It has been observed that an individual who possess good posture is more agile, has better flexibility and has coordinated, rhythmical and graceful movements. Good posture also makes it possible to attain such positions which are conducive to efficient movements. Such posture further helps in developing the strength, physical fitness and athletic ability in an individual. If the body is well balanced and well aligned, the centre of gravity of each segment will fall in a straight vertical line and the weight bearing segments will be in a proper alignment, thereby providing stability and support with minimum stress and strain while standing as well as while in motion. Good posture enables an individual to feel relaxed, comfortable and at ease while efficiently performing different kinds of movements necessary for daily living. To maintain good posture one exerts much less muscular affort as compared to a bad posture. Poor or bad posture adversely affects the body segments and joint structures, and prolonged postural strain on the same is definitely injurious to these structures. By assuming balanced posture, our body exerts less pressure on different organs of the body and as a result, the person feels less fatigued. Good postural patterns permit and encourage normal functioning of the vital physiological processes, particularly those of respiration, circulation and digestion.

Bad or poor posture may casue psychological problems, emotional disturbances and generate feelings of inferiority in an individual. By attaining good posture one can avoid such psychological problems. A person having good posture is able to draw attention towards him and is able to gain social acceptability, recognition and social efficacy easily. The esthetic appeal of erect posture and poise cannot be denied. Good posture also improves his economic efficiency as he is full of confidence and is able to properly interact with people. He is also able to perform his duties more effectively and efficiently, thereby improving his employment prospects.

Causes of a Poor Psoture

The causes of poor posture can broadly be classified into two categories:

(*i*) Acquired – due to some accident or disease.
(*ii*) Congenital – present at birth or hereditary.

The deformities caused due to poor posture can be of two types :

(*i*) Functional divergence, and
(*ii*) Structural divergence.

The main causes of poor posture are listed below :

1. **Injury:** When a bone, ligament, or muscle is injured, it is likely to weaken the support at that point and throw the framework out of balance. When such condition exists, it is not possible to have a perfect posture. Even after the injury has fully healed, the habit developed during the injury may still persist, and the faulty posture may continue for a long time.
2. **Disease:** Posture is greatly affected by the disease that weaken the bones or the muscles or cause the joints to lose their strength or mobility. The example of this kind of disease are, rickets caused due to faulty nutrition of bone, and tubercular disease of joints or vertebrae. Poliomyelitis may cause weakening or distorting of motor nerve cells in the spinal cord, and thereby causing partial or complete loss of function in certain muscle groups. This type of loss of power in muscle groups upsets the body control and balance and also cause other kinds of defects.
3. **Habit:** Habits of posture, whether good or bad, are acquired in the same way as the habits of walking, speaking or sitting i.e., by practising a certain type of coordination so many times that the act becomes unconscious and habitual. In case of school and college students though the bones, joints, ligaments and muscles are in normal condition, but due to faulty and wrong habits, their coordination is disturbed, causing poor posture. Wrong habits of posture are also caused by occupation and environment as well.
4. **Weakness:** It is not possible to assume and maintain erect posture without expenditure of some energy. Such efforts, therefore, require some strength and endurance. Experiments have shown that slumped or slouched position of body can be maintained with quite less metabolic energy as compared to the erect position. The muscular weakness and lack of viability is thus responsible for such faulty postures.
5. **Mental attitude:** The posture is the manner is which we carry or hold our body and it is bound to reflect our mental attitude. Feelings of happiness, confidence and satisfaction help in maintaining a balanced and erect posture, whereas depression and feeling of sadness pose hurdles in maintaining proper posture.
6. **Heredity:** Heredity is another factor which is responsible for poor or defective posture. Hereditary defects like kyphosis and other genetic defects may cause poor posture.
7. **Improper clothing:** The type of dress one wears also has impact on individual's posture. For example wearing tight fitted dress, tight shoes, high heel shoes etc. will result in adopting poor posture. Such improper clothing makes one uncomfortable and may lead to faulty posture.
8. **Improper diet or malnourishment:** Improper diet or malnourishment may result in various diseases due to deficiencies of vitamins and minerals e.g. rickets etc. which result in adopting faulty and poor posture.
9. **Chronic fatigue:** Due to continuous work, lack of rest and sound sleep, body tends to develop fatigue, and such condition becomes chronic with persistence of such condition. Without proper relaxation, rest and sleep the body and the mind become over worked and inefficient. Such conditions put undue stress upon muscles thereby causing postural deviations.

10. **Over load:** One may develop round shoulders and deformities of spine like kyphosis and scoliosis by continuously lifting and carrying heavy weight on shoulders and the upper back. Everyday example of overloading can be observed as we find school children carrying heavy school bags on their back.
11. **Imitation:** Due to over exposure of the children to the popular media like TV, net work etc. there is general tendency among children to imitate their favourite heroes, models, stars, teachers, friends etc. Such imitation may distort their natural posture and may cause postural deviations.
12. **Unhygienic conditions:** It is very common to find crowded class rooms with improper sitting arrangements, improper furniture, improper and insufficient lighting arrangements etc in our country. Such unhygienic conditions result in postural deviations.
13. **Inappropriate time tables:** Improperly planned school curriculum puts extra stress upon the children, e.g. during long practical hours they have to maintain a static and most of the time bent posture which may be a factor causing postural defects.
14. **Lack of exercise:** Exercises tone up the spinal nerves and abdominal organs, improves appetite and digestion, promotes flexibility and co-ordination, reduces mental strain, provides energy, improves the physical ability and efficiency. Lack of exercises has several adverse effects which may lead to postural deformities and defects.
15. **Lack of awareness:** Many people are unaware regarding the concept of proper posture and continue to follow wrong or faulty postures. This becomes their permanent habit and a life style which leads to postural defects and deformities.
16. **Obesity:** Obesity or undue body overweight puts extra stress and strain on the muscular as well as skeletal structure of the body which may result in postural deviations.
17. **Poverty:** Lack of essential and basic facilities due to poverty is another important factor which may lead an individual to adopt bad or faulty posture.
18. **Occupation:** Certain occupations require sitting, standing or working in an imbalanced or improper posture constantly for log hours, which may result in postural defects and deviations.

Preventive and Remedial Measures of a Poor Psture

The appropriate remedial action should be started as soon as possible. Immediate attention is required as bad posture exerts unusual and atypical stress on the soft tissues, muscles and ligaments of the body segment. Time to time screening of body posture will go a long way in preventing postural defects. It must be remembered that the means of correcting postural deviations must be based upon medical diagnosis and recommendations. As ignorance regarding the basic concept of posture is one of the major causes for postural divergencies, proper knowledge regarding the importance of posture and appropriate guidance for correcting the same is necessary so as to develop a postural sense regarding body mechanics in the mind of an individual.

Whenever faulty posture is caused due to any disease, the disease must be treated first before anything else is attempted. If faulty posture is due to an injury, the injury must be treated and allowed to heal. In general, the cause or the reason must be removed or cured before any measures for improvement of posture can be effectively implemented. The treatment of patients with severe injury or disease may often require surgical operations.

As general muscular weakness is also one of the common causes of poor posture, an active childhood involving vigorous exercise, by engaging in games, sports and developmental exercises, is perhaps the best preventive measure that can be undertaken. The type of activity or game selected is equally important. Proper attention should be given while preparing time tables for schools, colleges etc. The time table must provide for extra curricular and recreational activities along with intermittent rest intervals. An hour in the gymnasium will not cure bad posture when many hours are spent in the environment that caused it. This highlights the necessity of improving hygienic condition and making environment conducive to healthy living. Some cases of faulty posture are due to fatigue, mental strain, improper digestion and assimilation of food, malnutrition or similar causes. Rest and proper nutrition are equally as important as a programme of corrective activities. Govt. and Non - Govt. Organisations should make sincere effords to elevate the standard of living of poor people and new drives or programmes like mid-day meals, free education, free vaccination and free health check-ups should be launched.

Due care should be taken to identify the cause of each individual's shortcomings, and corrective procedures in line with best educational and orthopaedic practice should be instituted. Postural defects which cannot be corrected by an individual's own efforts are known as resistant or structural defects and all such cases should be referred to a physician or orthopaedic surgeon. Coaches and physical education teachers make a valuable contribution when they recognize postural defects and deformities and make appropriate remedial suggestions.

Common Postural Deformities

There are a number of postural deformities which may either be acquired or may be congenital. Each type of postural deviation has its own peculiar causes and effects. Each postural deformity, therefore, demands and requires proper attention and specific treatment for correcting the same. It is, thus necessary to know about various major postural deformities. In this part of chapter four major postural deformities, alongwith their causes, prevention and remedial measures, have been dealtwith.

MUSCULAR SYSTM

Introduction

The human body contains more than 650 individual muscles anchored to the skeleton, which provide pulling power so that you can move around. These muscles constitute about 40% of our total body weight. The muscle's points of attachment to bones or other muscles are designated as origin or insertion. The point of origin is the point of attachment to the bone to which the muscle is anchored. The point of insertion is the point of attachment to the bone the muscle moves. Generally, the muscles are attached by tough fibrous structures called tendons. These attachments bridge one or more joints and the result of muscle contraction is movement of these joints. The body is moved primarily by muscle groups, not by individual muscles. These groups of muscles power all actions ranging from the threading of a needle to the lifting of heavy weights.

Contractions that really move bones, like those used in working, lifting an object or chewing food, are called isotonic contractions (iso-means same and tonic means tone or pressure or tension). In isotonic contraction the tension. within a muscle remain the same but the length of the muscle changes thus produce movement or do work.

Contractions that counter opposing forces, but do not move, are called isometric contractions. In isometric contractions muscle length remains the same but muscle tension increases. You can feel isometric contraction by pushing your arms against a wall and feeling the tension increases in your arm muscles. Isometric contractions 'tighten' a muscle, but they do not produce movement or do work.

Types of Muscles

The muscular system provides mobility and support to the body. There are three types of muscle. tissue : *Skeletal, smooth,* and *cardiac*. These vary in structure according to their function. Skeletal muscles are striated muscles that serve to move body parts. Smooth muscles are found in internal organs, while cardiac muscle is present only in the heart. Muscle filaments and filaments similar to those found in muscles are responsible for most of the movements of protoplasm in the body.

Skeletal Muscle

These muscles are attached to the bones. They move the bones of the arms, legs, fingers and other part of the skeleton. They are also called voluntary muscles.

The fibres that make up a skeletal muscle have alternate light and dark crossbones called striations.

Skeletal muscle is under voluntary control and is responsible for voluntary movements of body parts. Skeletal muscle is also called **striated muscle** because its composition results in a striped appearance. Each muscle fibre is formed by the fusion of embryonic muscle cells, or **myoblasts,** into a multinucleate structure called a **syncytium.** This syncytium is surrounded by a **sarcolemma,** similar to the plasma membrane of a uninucleate cell. A striated muscle fibre is composed of a bundle of 1,000 or more *myofibrils,* banded fibres formed from units called **sarcomeres**. Sarcomeres are bounded by **Z–lines** thin structures that extend across each myofibril. Within the myofibril, filaments of **actin** alternate with thick filaments of **myosin.**

The mechanism of muscle contraction known as the **sliding filament theory,** proposed by Hanson and Huxley, suggests that progressive forming and breaking of bridges between polarized actin and myosin filaments pull the Z- lines closer together. Hydrolysis of ATP is required for both relaxation and contraction in skeletal muscle. After death of the individual, as ATP disappears from the body, the muscles lose their ability to either contract or relax, and become stiff, a condition known as **rigor mortis.**

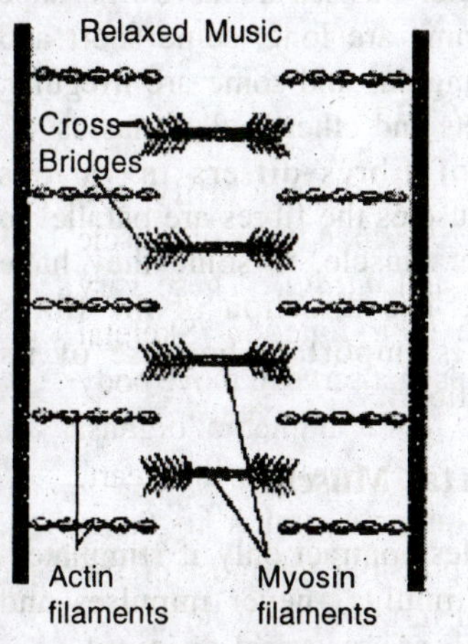

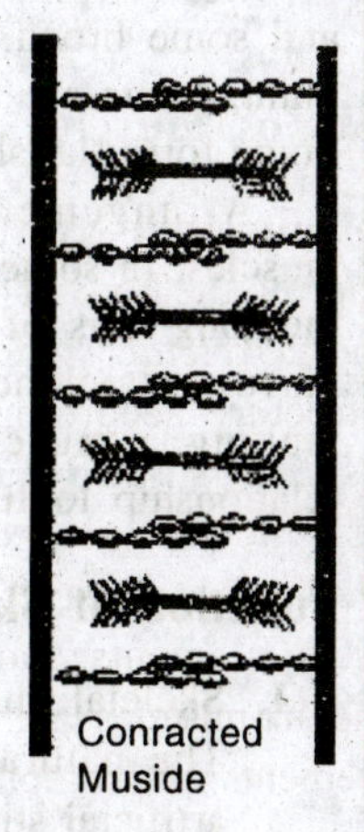

A skeletal muscle contracts in response to signals from a motor neuron. As seen in the muscle contraction, the "head" of the thick filament (myosin filament) attaches to the thin filament (actin filament) and "pulls" it towards the middle. In a muscle at rest, the myosin filaments are not able to attach to the actin filaments because the points of attachment are blocked by a filament of a protein called tropomyosin. The globular protein complex called *troponin* is able to bind to actin, calcium, and the fibrousprotein tropomyosin. Troponin and troponmyosin normally block the attachment sites on actin, making actin unavailable for myosin to bind with. The only way myosin can attach to the actin filaments is if the binding sites are uncovered.

Nerves attach to the muscle at a modified postsynaptic area of the sarcolemma called a*motor end plate*. Nervous impulses sent to a group of motor end plates called a motor unit result in the release of calcium into the cytoplasm of the muscle cell. Calcium reacts with the actin-troponin-tropomyosin complex, causing the attachment site to become uncovered. The myosin filaments are then able to bind with the actin filament and contraction occurs. Unlike smooth muscles, where the strength of contraction depends upon the degree of depolarization, striated muscle response is an all or non ephenomenon; the force of contraction is proportional to the number of fibres stimulated.

Skeletal muscles responsible for movement of the limbs can be classified according to their function. Those, which cause the joint to close up, are *Flexors*. Their opposite or antagonistic muscles are called *extensors*, which cause the joint to stretch out. For example, biceps in the arm are flexors, while triceps extending from the shoulder to the elbow are extensors. *Adductor* muscles move a limb towards the body while *abductors* move it away from the body.

The point of attachment of a flexor or extensor on the moving bone is called the *insertion*, and the point of attachment on the stationary bone is the origin. Voluntary skeletal muscles are attached to bones either directly or by means of straps of connective tissue called *tendons*. Ligaments, flexible bands of connective tissue that hold muscles and tendons in place, hold movable joints together.

Smooth Muscle

These muscles are found in most of the body's internal organs. Smooth muscles do not have alternate light and dark cross bands called striations as in the case of skeletal muscles. Smooth muscles in the walls of the stomach and intestines move food through the digestive system. Smooth muscles also control the width of the blood vessels and the size of the breathing passages. In such cases, the smooth muscles contract and relax automatically. We do not control them; therefore they are called involuntary muscles.

Smooth muscle provides the contractile force for movement in internal organs under control of the involuntary or autonomic nervous system. Smooth muscle is responsible for movement of the food through the digestive tract, the flow of blood through blood vessels, and the emptying of urine from the urinary bladder.

Smooth muscle is composed of long spindle-shaped cells, each with a single nucleus. Smooth muscle tissue is usually arranged in sheets, with the cells in electrical contact with one another through structures called *gap junctions*. Gap junctions are involved in propagating (sending) an action potential generated in the membrane of one smooth muscle cell to all the other muscle cells in the sheet of tissue. The extent of contraction depends upon how much the cell is depolarized.

Cardiac Muscle

This muscle is found only in the heart. It has features of both skeletal muscle and smooth muscle. Cardiac muscle has striations like skeletal muscle. But like smooth muscle, it contracts automatically and rhythmically without tiring. Cardiac muscle helps the heart to beat an average of 72 times a minute without rest throughout our lifetime.

Cardiac muscle, or heart muscle, is a striated muscle that occurs only in the heart. The heartbeat is controlled by non contractile cells in the heart called *Purkinje fibres*. These cells have no contractile proteins and are specialized for electrical conduction. The heart beat is initiated by electrical activity of the pacemaker or sinoatrial node (S.A.) in the wall of the right atrium. How heart cells keep up their rhythmic contraction is not known, but heart cells in culture continue to beat, and even single heart cells beat rhythmically, independently of other muscle cells or external innervation.

An electrical impulse spreads from the sinoatrial (S.A) node to all parts of the atrium and then to the atriom ventricular node, which is located adjacent to the partition between the two ventricles. From here, the impulse spreads through the ventricles and triggers simultaneous contraction of the ventricles.

As in smooth muscle, cardiac muscle cells are joined by gap junctions, structures that contain tiny pores through which electrical currents and calcium can pass from one cell to another. Although the heart beats regularly without nervous intervention, there is a main nerve to the heart, the tenth cranial nerve, or *vagus*. The vagus nerve contains branches of both the sympathetic and autonomic nervous systems. The sympathetic activity speeds the heart rate, and the autonomic slows it. Cardiac muscle has many mitochondria, as would be expected from its constant activity.

Structure of Skeletal Muscles

Skeletal muscles are organs, which are made up of skeletal muscle tissue plus important connective and nervous tissue components. Skeletal muscles differ in size, shape and arrangement of fibres. They range from very small strands such as muscle of middle ear to large masses such as the muscle of the thigh. Some skeletal muscles are narrow in shape and some broad. Some are long, some short and blunt. Some are triangular and some are irregular. Some form flat sheets and others bulky masses.

Arrangement of fibres differs in various muscles. In some muscles the fibres are parallel to the long axis of the muscle, in some they have narrow attachment. The direction of the fibres making a muscle is important because of its relationship to function.

Function of Skeletal Muscles

1. Skeletal muscles contract only if stimulated. The natural stimulus never impulses and artificial stimuli are electrical or injury.

2. Skeletal muscles contract in different types such as isotonic contraction, isometric contraction, twitch contraction etc.
3. Skeletal muscles contract according to graded strength.
4. Skeletal muscles produce movement by pulling on end bones of joints.
5. Muscles, which move apart, do not be over that part but go close to it.
6. Skeletal muscles always act in groups rather than singly.
7. Bone act as levers and joints as fulcrums of these levers.

Classification of Skeletal Muscles

The following is the classification of skeletal muscles according to some of the body parts :

1. **Upper Arm:** The major muscles that move upper arm are:
   - Pectoralis major
   - Latissimus dorsi
   - Deltoid
2. **Lower Arm:** The main muscles that move lower arm are:
   - Biceps
   - Triceps
   - Brachialis
3. **Leg Thigh:** The major muscles that move the thigh are:
   - Gluteus maximus
   - Iiopsoas
   - Rectus femoris
   - Adductor longus
4. **Lower Leg**
   - Quadriceps femoris
   - Hamstring muscles
   - Sartorius
5. **Foot:** The main muscles that move the foot are:
   - Tibialis anterior
   - Gastrocnemius
   - Soleus
6. **Head**: The muscles which move the head are :
   - Sternocleidmastoid
   - Splenius Capitis
   - Longissimus capitis
7. **Chest:** The main muscles that move the chest wall are:
   - External intercostals
   - Internal Inter-Costals
   - Diaphragm
8. **Shoulder:** The muscles which move the shoulder are:
   - Trapezius
   - Pectoralis
   - Serratus anterior
9. **Hand:** The muscles which move the hand are:
   - Palmaris longus
   - Flexor Carpis Radialis
   - Flexor carpi ulnaris
   - Extensor Carpi Radialis Loungus
   - Extensor carpi radialis brevis
10. **Abdominal wall:** The muscles which move the abdominal wall are:
    - External oblique
    - Internal oblique
    - Transversalis
    - Rectus abdominis
11. **Pelvic:** The muscles which move the pelvic floor are:
    - Levator ani
    - Coccygeus
12. **Trunk:** The muscles which move the trunk are:
    - Iliopsoas
    - Sacrospinalis
    - Iliopsoalis lumborm
    - Longissimus dorsi
13. **Facial expression and mastication:**
    - Occipio frontalis
    - Orbicularis oculi
    - Orbicularis oris
    - Masseter
    - Temporal

MUSCLE EXERCISE

Prior to strength training, warm up and flexibility exercises should be performed. Warm up should include at least 5 minutes of aerobic activity to provide increased blood oxygen levels and increased body temperature. Both of these factors will increase the effectiveness of the strength – training workout.

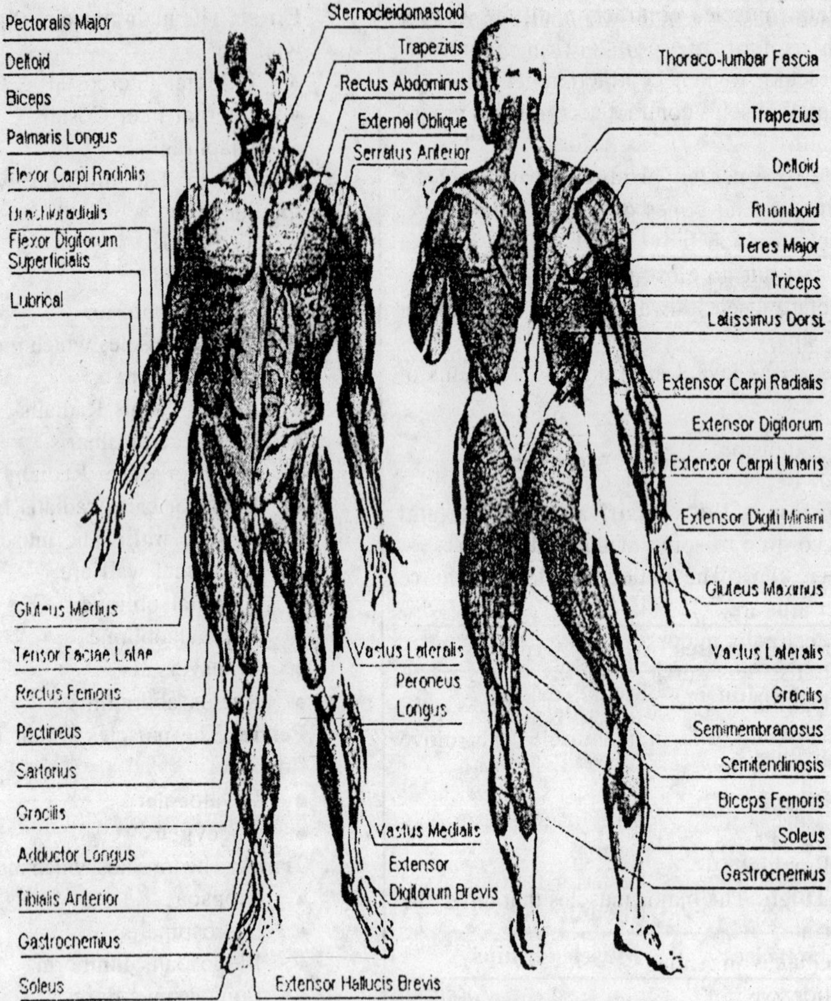

Exercise sessions should be organized so that the larger muscle groups are exercised first, followed by the smaller muscle groups.

The order of groups should be as follows:

- Abdomen
- Hips and lower back
- Upper Legs
- Calves
- Chest
- Upper back
- Shoulders
- Triceps
- Biceps
- Waist
- Neck

(A) **Chest Exercises**	**Muscle Groups**
Bench Press	Pectorals Triceps, Anterior Deltoids
Inclined Fly	Outer/Inner Pectorals, Anterior Deltoids
Inclined Press	Upper/Outer Pectorals, Triceps, Anterior/medial Deltoids Pectorals.

Declined Press	Lower / outer pectorals, Triceps, Anterior Deltoids pectorals.
Push up	Friceps, Anterior Deltoides.
Cable Crossover	Upper/Lower Pectorals
Pec Dec	Pectorals, Anterior Deltoids

(B) Back Exercises	Muscle Groups
Shrugs	Trapezius
One Arm Row	Trapezius, Latissimus Dorsi
Pull-ups	Biceps, Rhomboids
Back Extension	Erector Spinae
Roman Bench	Erector Spinae
Seated Row	Erector Spinae, Latissimus Dorsi, Biceps
Lateral Pull down	Latissimus Dorsi, Biceps

(C) Shoulder Exercises	Muscle Groups
Overhead (Military)	Medial deltoid, Triceps Press
Lateral Raises	Anterior /Medial Deltoid
Front Raises	Anterior /Posterior Deltoid
Prone Fly	Posterior Deltoid, Rhomboids

(D) Arm Exercises	Muscle Groups
Barbell Curl	Full Biceps/Forearms
Dumbbell Preacher Curl	Upper/Outer Biceps
Standing Dumbbell /Low Cable	Inner Biceps
Seated Hammer curls	Outer Biceps/ Forearms (Nrachialis)
Seated Inclined Dumbbell Curls	Lower Biceps
Triceps Kickback /Dip	Triceps Lateral Head
Triceps Seated Over Head Ext	Triceps Medial Head
Triceps Lying Extension	Triceps Long Head

(E) Lower Body	Muscle Groups
Squat	Gluteus Maximus, Quads, Hamstrings Erectors
Front Lunge	Gluteus Maximus, Quads, Hamstrings
Calf Heel Raise	Gastrocnemius, Soleus
Hip Extension	Gluteus Maximus
Hip Aduction	Aductors, Outer Thigh
Hip Aduction	Adductor, Inner Thigh
Leg Press	Gluteus Maximus, Quads, Hamstrings
Leg Extension	Quads
Leg Curl	Hamstrings

(F) Abdominal	Muscle Groups
Upper Crunches/ Inclined Sit- up	Upper Abdomen
Lower Crunches/ Leg Raises	Lowe Abdomen
Side Crunches	Outer Obliques
Crunch machine	Abdomen, Hip Flexor

RESPIRATORY SYSTEM

Introduction

Respiration is a physical process by which living organisms take in oxygen from the surrounding medium and emit carbon dioxide. The term respiration is also used to refer to the liberation of energy, within the cell, from fuel molecules such as carbohydrates and fats. Carbon dioxide and water are the products of this process, which is sometimes called cellar respiration to distinguish it from the physical process of breathing. Oxygen is supplied to the tissues and their carbon dioxide is removed by the combined action of the cardiovascular and respiratory systems. Not only do these two systems have a close spatial relationship in the thoracic cavity, they also have such a close functional relationship that they are often considered jointly under the heading cardiopulmonary. A disorder that affects the lungs has direct and pronounced effects on the heart, and vice versa. Furthermore, the respiratory system works closely with the urinary system to regulate the body's acide base balance. Changes in the blood pH, in turn, trigger autonomic adjustments of the heart rate and blood pressure. Thus, the cardiovascular, respiratory, and urinary systems have an especially close physiological relationship.

Thus respiration includes the movement of air into and out of the lungs, the exchange of gases between the air and the blood, the transport of gases in the blood, and the exchange of gases between the blood and tissues.

Types of Respiration

1. *Internal Respiration* – Exchange of gases between the blood and cells.
2. *External Respiration* – Exchange of gases between the blood and lungs.

Functions of the Respiratory System

The major functions of the Respiratory system are to :

- Exchange oxygen and carbon dioxide between the air and blood.
- Regulate blood pH (acid- base balance)
- Produce sounds
- Move air over the sensory receptors that detect smell.
- Protect against some microorganisms.

Organs of the Respiratory System

The main organs of the respiratory system are the nose, pharynx, larynx, trachea, bronchi and lungs. These organs draw in air exchange gases with the blood, and expel the modified air.

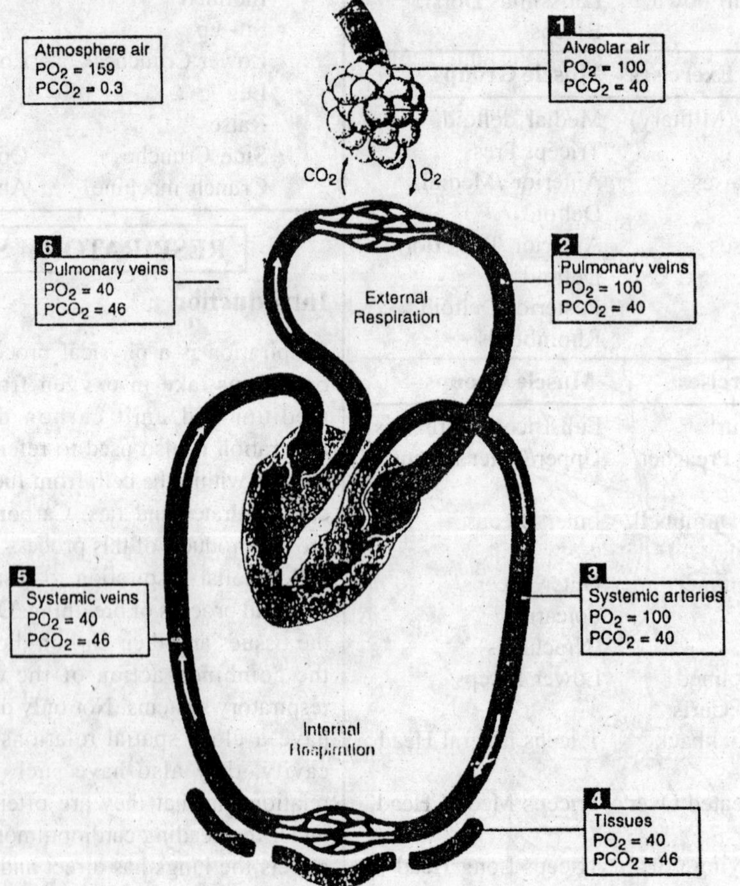

1. The conducting division of the respiratory system consists of those passages that serve for airflow, mainly from the nostrils through the bronchioles.
2 The respiratory division consists of the alveoli and other distal gas- exchange regions.
3 The airway from the nose through the larynx is often called the upper respiratory tract.
4 The regions from the trachea through the lungs compose the lower respiratory tract.

The Nose

The nose has several functions : It warms, cleanses, and humidifies inhaled air, detects odours, and serves as a resonating chamber to modify the voice. The external, protruding nose is supported by a frame work of done and cartilage. The interior half is supported by cartilages. The inside dilated chamber has guard hairs that block the inhalation of large particles.

The Pharynx

The Pharynx or throat is a muscular funnel extending 13 cm (5in) from the internal nostrils choanae) to the larynx. Air continues through the pharynx.

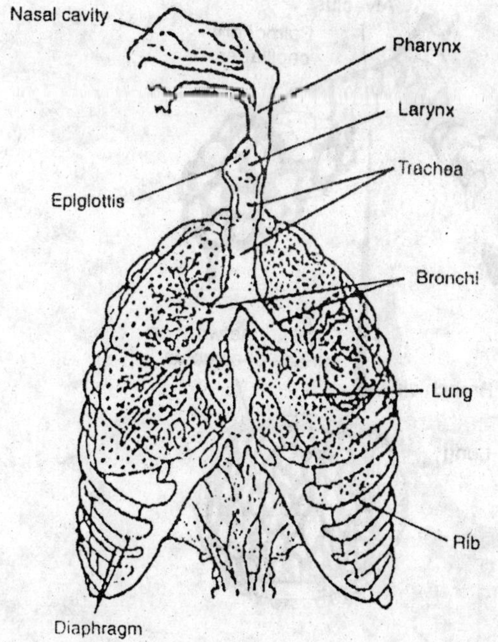

The Larynx

The Larynx or voice box is a cartilaginous chamber. Its basic function is to keep food and drink out of the airway, but it has evolved the additional role of producing sound. The superior opening of the larynx, the glottis, is guarded by a flap of tissue called the epiglottis. During swallowing, the extrinsic muscles of the larynx pull it upward towards the glottis, and the epiglottis directs food and drink into the oesophagus. The vestibular folds play a greater role in keeping food and drink out of the airway. The framework of the larynx consists of nine cartilages. These are the epiglottic, thyroid, and cricoid cartilages(allsingle)and the arytenoids, corniculate, and cuneiform cartilages (all paired).

The walls of the larynx are quite muscular. Deep intrinsic muscles operate the vocal cords. Superficial extrinsic muscles connect the larynx to the hyoid bone and elevate the larynx during swallowing. The interior wall of the larynx has folds. The superior pair is the vestibular folds, or false vocal cords. The inferior pair is the true vocal cords. The intrinsic muscles control the vocal cords by pulling on the corniculate and arytenoid cartilages. As air passes through the cords, high pitched sound occurs when the cords are pulled (tightly stretched) and lower- pitched sounds occur when the cords are more relaxed. The force of air through the cords determines loudness.

The Trachea

The trachea or windpipe is a rigid tube, 12 cm in length, with C- shaped cartilage rings to keep it from collapsing during inhalation. The larynx and trachea are lined with epithelium which provides a mucociliary escalator for removal of debris trapped in the mucus.

The Lungs

Human beings like other land animals breathe through their nostrils in noses and with the help of lungs. A pair of lungs is located in the airtight thoracic cavity, which is bounded by a convex, muscular and elastic sheet, called diaphragm.

Respiration by lungs is called pulmonary respiration.

Functionally, the lungs are elastic bags resembling rubber balloons. They lack any muscle, which may allow them to expand or contact by themselves. The lung respond passively to the pressure changes within the thoracic cavity due to contraction or relaxation of muscles of ribs and movement of diaphragm during inspiration and expiration.

Each lung is a conical organ with its broad, concave base resting on the diaphragm. The lung receives the bronchus, blood vessels, lymphatic vessels and nerves through its hilum. The left lung is divided into two lobes and the right into three lobes.

The Bronchial Tree

The bronchial tree is a system of highly branched air tubes, and begins with the primary bronchi that enter each lung from the trachea. Each primary bronchus divides into secondary (lobar) bronchi that enter each lobe of the lung. The next subdivision is that of tertiary bronchi that each supplies a bronchopulmonary segment. Tertiary bronchi gives rise to bronchioles, which lack cartilage but have smooth muscle in their walls. The portion ventiiated by each bronchiole is a primary lobule. Each bronchiole divides into 50-80 terminal bronchioles. Each terminal bronchiole gives off smaller respiratory bronchioles that divide into alveolar ducts ending in alveolar sacs. Alveoli bud form the walls of respiratory bronchioles, alveolar ducts, and sacs.

Alveoli

To compensate for high metabolic rates and oxygen needs, each human lung has an immense surface area (80 square metres) for gas exchange. An alveolus consists mostly of alveolar cells, which are thin to allow for rapid gas diffusion through them. Also present within the lumens of the alveoli are alveolar macrophages (dust cells) that are the last line of defence against inhaled matter. Each alveolus is surrounded with a basket of capillaries. Pulmonary circulation has a very low blood pressure to prevent the alveoli from filling with fluid. The osmotic uptake of water overrides filtration and keeps the alveoli dry.

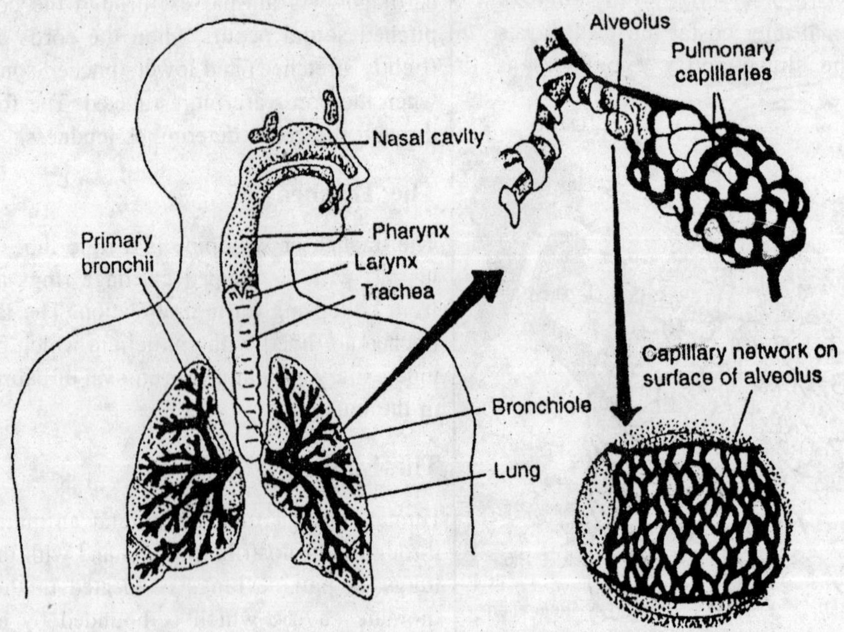

The Pleurae

The surface of each lung is covered by visceral pleura; the chest cavity is lined with parietal pleura. Between the two is the potential space of the pleural cavity containing pleural fluid. The pleura and pleural fluid serve to reduce friction during chest expansion, to create a pressure gradient, and to prevent infections through compartmentalization.

MECHANISM OF RESPIRATION

The process of breathing in is inspiration and breathing out is expiration. Several of the gas laws of physics are highly relevant to understanding respiratory function.

1. **Pressure and Flow:** The pressure that drives respiration is atmospheric (barometric) pressure. Air moves into the lungs because the volume of the lungs is increased, thus dropping intrapulmonary pressure. During expiration, the intrapulmonary pressure is above atmospheric pressure, so air leaves the lungs.
2. **Inspiration:** Changing the volume within the lungs is accomplished by stimulation of the diaphragm by the phrenic nerves, which cause a downward contraction, and stimulation of the external inter costal muscles to raise the ribs. The chest cavity expands, and the parietal pleura cling to it. The visceral pleura attached to the lungs are carried along, due to intrapleural pressure. The lungs expand. Another force, which expands the lungs, is warming of the inhaled air. As the inhaled air warms, it helps to expand the lungs.
3. **Expiration:** Inhalation requires muscular effort, thus burning calories and ATP. Exhalation, on the other hand is a passive process. Expiration is due to relaxation of he diaphragm and external intercostals muscles that, because of elastic recoil, return to their original position. When this occurs, air pressure is greater inside the lungs (in a now smaller volume) than outside the body, and air leaves the lungs. To force a deeper expiration, the internal intercoastal muscles contract and depress the ribs.
4. **Resistance to Airflow:** One factor that affects resistance to airflow is pulmonary compliance- the ease with which the lungs expand. The lungs normally expand easily, but compliance may be reduced by airway obstruction or degenerative lung diseases. Airflow is also affected by the diameter of bronchioles. During bronchoconstriction, the diameter of bronchioles is decreased, reducing compliance. During bronchodilation compliance is restored to normal.

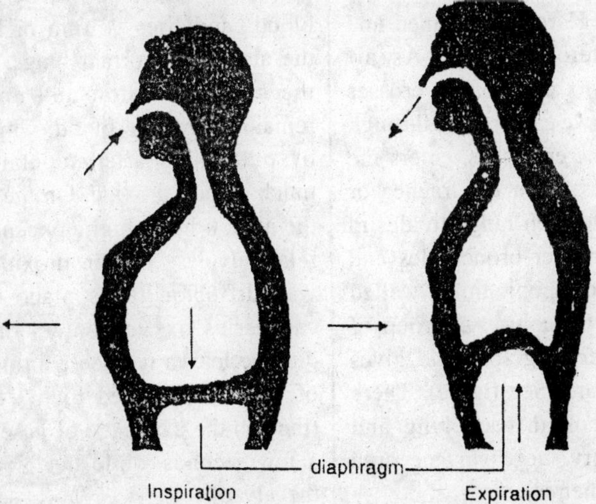

5. **Alveolar Surface Tension:** Alveoli have a thin film over the surface of their epithelium that could potentially cause them to collapse if not for the presence of surfactant. Surfactant reduces surface tension within the alveoli, also reducing the chance that the alveoli will collapse and " stick" to themselves during ventilation. Premature infants often have a deficiency of pulmonary surfactant and experience great difficulty in breathing.
6. **Alveolar Ventilation:** Not all the air that enters the lungs reaches the alveoli to be available for gas exchange. Dead air is air in the lungs that can not exchange gases with blood; in the conducting division, it is called anatomic dead space. Physiologic (total) dead space is the sum of anatomic dead space and any pathological dead space that may exist. In healthy people the anatomic and physiologic dead spaces are identical. Alveolar ventilation rate gives the most directly relevant measure of the body's ability to get oxygen to the tissues.
7. **Gas Exchange and Transport:** Composition of Air: Air is a mixture of gases, each of which contributes a share of the total atmospheric pressure called its partial pressure. Partial pressures are important because they determine the rate of diffusion of a gas, and therefore strongly affect the rate of gas exchange between the blood and alveolar air.

PARTIAL PRESSURE OF RESPIRATORY GASES AT SEA LEVEL

		Partial pressure (mmHg)			
Gas	**%in dry air**	**Dry air**	**Alveolar air**	**Venous blood**	**Diffusion gradient**
Total	100.00	760.0	760	760	0
H_2O	0.00	0.0	47	47	0
O_2	20.93	159.1	104	40	64
CO_2	0.03	0.2	40	45	5
N_2	79.04	600.7	569	573	0

In normal breathing through the nose, air travels through devious nasal passages that are lined with ciliated mucous epithelium. Here it is cleaned and warmed. Sensory cells detect odours. As air continues through the pharynx or throat, it crosses the path of food. This is why we can breathe through the mouth. The air passes the epiglottis, enters the larynx or voice box ad goes down the trachea or windpipe. A bronchus runs to each lung, divides in tree- like manner to give smaller bronchioles and finally deposits the air in microscopic thin – walled air sacs or alveoli (singular àlveolus). A group of alveoli appears like a cluster of grapes and gives the lungs a sponge-like texture (See figure). There are about 150 million alveoli in each lung and altogether they cover a very large surface area (approximately 100 square metres).

The alveoli are lined by a layer of moist flat epithelial cells and surrounded by networks of blood capillaries. A film of lecithin (a lipid) lines the alveoli of normal lungs. It functions to lower the surface tension and enables the alveoli to remain open. The blood, which flows to the lungs by pulmonary artery contains little oxygen and much carbon dioxide. On the other hand, the air in the alveoli has a high concentration of oxygen and relatively less carbon dioxide. Therefore, a two–way diffusion takes place through the cells of capillaries oxygen enters the blood and carbon dioxide leaves it since enormous breathing surface of lungs is exposed to the external environment (the air) the exchange of gases is completed within a few seconds while the blood is passed through the alveoli.

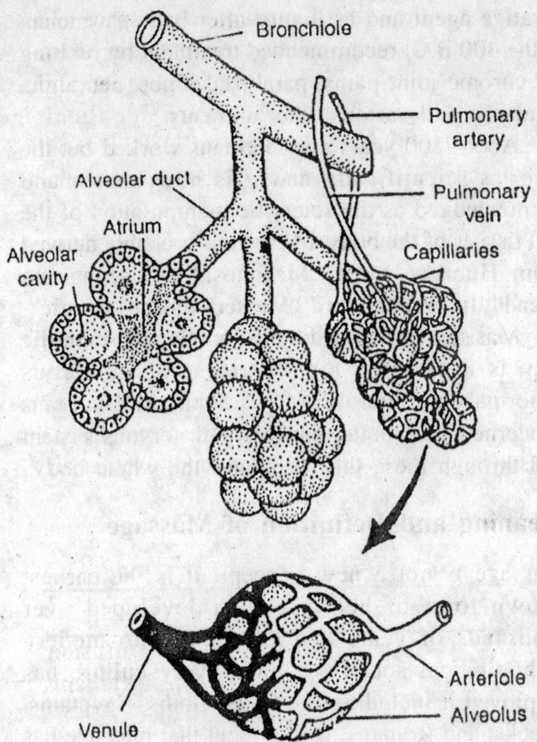

The alveoli and associated capillaries of lungs

NEURAL CONTROL OF RESPIRATION

The principal nervous normal type centre for controlling the rate and depth of respiration is in the respiratory section of the vagus nucleus in the medulla oblongata. The cells of this nucleus are sensitive to the acidity of the blood, which reflects higher and lower concentrations of carbon dioxide in the blood plasma. When the acidity of the blood is high, as is usually caused by an excess of carbon dioxide, the respiratory centre stimulates the respiratory muscles to greater activity. When the carbon dioxide concentration is low, breathing is depressed.

NON–RESPIRATORY AIR MOVEMENTS

Air movements such as yawning, sneezing, coughing laughing, and crying are considered non respiratory air movements. Sneezing is triggered (caused) by irritants in the nasal cavity and coughing is caused (triggered) by irritants in the lower respiratory tract.

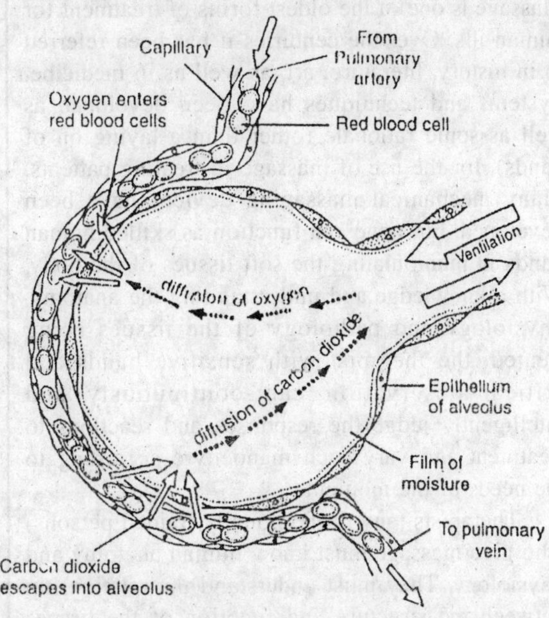

Gaseous exchange in the alveolus

MEASUREMENTS OF VENTILATION

A spirometer is used to measure expired breath. Four spirometric measures such as tidal volume, inspiratory reserve volume, cxpiratory rcscrvc volume, and residual volume, are called respiratory volumes. Others are known as respiratory capacities and calculated by adding two or more of the respiratory volumes.

Our respiratory and circulatory systems become adapted and modified for life in oxygen deficient environments. For example persons living at the altitudes of 3000m (10000ft) or more have large lungs, more highly branched capillary systems and a faster heartbeat than people living at lower altitudes. Moreover, the blood of high- altitude dwellers contains 30 percent more red cells than the blood of person living at sea level. Hence, they are able to make efficient use of the one third less oxygen, which is available.

MASSAGE

Introduction

Massage is one of the oldest forms of treatment for human ills. Over the centuries it has been referred to in history, literature, art, as well as in medicine. Systems and techniques have been developed as well as some rationale (other than a laying on of hands), for the use of massage in treating patients. Many mechanical massaging devices have been developed, but none can function as skilled human hands in manipulating the soft tissues of the body. With a knowledge and understanding the anatomy, physiology and pathology of the tissues being treated, the therapist with sensitive hands and critical observation can continuously and intelligently judge the responses and reactions to treatment and vary each manoeuvre according to the needs of the moment.

Therapists (any professionally trained persons) who give massage must know human anatomy and physiology. They must understand the relationship between the structure and function of the tissues being treated and the total function of the patient. They must know pathology, so that they can understand how to use massage to obtain the effects that are desired to alleviate the pathological condition being treated. They must be skilled in the proper manipulations of tissues, so that they can accomplish this aim and at the same time not cause further damage to the tissues or harm to the patient. Many physical therapists, physicians, and patients are convinced by clinical experience that massage has therapeutic value if basic principles are followed and the massage is skillfully done.

Brief History of Massage

The art of massage was used in the prehistoric times for their curative effects. The Chinese used such methods of curing as early as 300 B.C. There is also record of such use by Indians from the earliest times. Even the Japanese, Greeks, Egyptians, Turks and Romans were familiar with such benefits derived from massage and active movements. Among Greeks, massage was much used both as curative agent and as luxury after bath. Physician, in the 400 B.C. recommended treatment by rubbing for chronic joint pains, paralyzed limbs, neuralgic, headache and various other ailments.

About 200 years ago Germans worked out the theories scientifically and it is now known and acknowledged as the scientific manipulation of the soft tissues of the body. Massage is probably derived from Hebrew word "Maschesal" meaning "to knead". In French word "Masser" means "to rub".

Massage performed by the hands in a scientific way is useful for the treatment of numerous abnormal conditions. Primarily, it affects the organs concerned i.e., joints, muscles and nervous system and through these they influence the whole body.

Meaning and Definition of Massage

Massage is not a new concept. It is the earliest known form of healing-touch-developed over thousands of years and surviving into modern technological society. Almost every culture has employed it including the Celts, Goths, Egyptains, Greeks, and Romans. It is evident that massage has been with man from the beginning.

Massage stimulates circulation and the nervous system's response. It also helps strengthen muscle and skin tissue while relaxing stressed areas of the body. Massage aids in breaking down adipose (fatty) tissue. But there are beautifying effects of massage. Massage indirectly improves muscle tone and stimulates the circulatory system, leaving you with, healthy skin. Massage combined with proper diet and active exercise can only further enhance your total well-being.

Massage is a form of treatment in the earliest medical records and its use continues down through history. The main object of massage is to dispense the worn out matters formed in the muscles and not expelled by exercise. It causes the used matter to dispose of and so remove fatigue.

Massage is the scientific mode of treating certain forms of diseases by systematic manipulations.

Massage is a procedure which is usually done with the hands, such as friction kneading manipulations, rolling, and percussion of external tissues of the body in a variety of ways, either with a curative, palliative, or hygienic object in view.

John S, Coulter said, "Generally accepted meaning of the word, massage includes a great number of manipulations of the tissues and organs by the body for therapeutic purposes."

Gertrude Beard defined massage as the term used to designate certain manipulations of the soft tissues of the body ; these manipulations are most effectively performed with the hands and are administered for the purpose of producing effects on the nervous, muscular, and respiratory systems and the local and general circulation of the blood and lymph.

Massage acts as a mechanical cleanser as it increases the inter- change of tissue fluids emptied into the blood capillary and lymphatic network, removing the products of fatigue and inflammation.

When circulation is impaired, fresh blood is unable to reach and nourish the tissues, and waste products collect. This causes a decreased exchange of fluids within the tissues, leading to fatigue and a general imbalance within our body system. Massage increases the tone of muscles being treated by passively increasing the contracting power of the muscles bringing about a deep sense of relaxation, massage also improves circulation, helps maintain fluid balance, and relieve excess tension.

Massage has been in practice since ancient days and found in almost all cultures. The basis of massage is touch and the tools are fingers and hands. Massage is a powerful manoeuvre for psychosomatics and regulation of psychosomatics is quite important for competition.

Massage Helps

1. To supply oxygen to muscles.
2. To maintain fluid balance.
3. To remove waste products
4. To prepare an athlete for competition.
5. To support training programme.

Comfortable environment is very essential for massage. Massage surface, patients position and comfort, masseur's posture and clothing all are important for effective massage.

Guidelines for Massage

1. Massage should be rhythmic.
2. Hands should always be in contact with body
3. Should not apply force but body weight can be used to apply pressure
4. Should not talk too much during massage
5. Should be fully relaxed while giving massage.
6. Breathing should be deep and slow.

TYPES AND BENEFITS OF MASSAGE

Stroking

It is used mainly to warm ups, soothe, and prepare the body for deeper movements. It can be done with the fingers, whole hand, and forearm, The heels of the feet are also good to use when stroking inner and outer legs. The direction of the muscle fibres should follow with long consistent strokes on the skin's surface. Stroking can be done with varying degrees of pressure and in a circular motion. Strokes are to be directed towards the heart, aiding blood flow and the lymphatic system.

Benefits :

1. Locally stimulates circulation and metabolic interchange. Helps in relieving stiffness.
2. Stroking is a good move for exploring the body.
3. It soothes, warms and relaxes the muscles.
4. Relieves excessive muscular tension.
5. Improves circulation and relieves tension and fatigue.
6. Increases Lymphatic drainage.
7. Soothes and relaxes fatigued muscles.
8. Helps slumped tired organs by releasing and stretching out the muscles.
9. Soothes and warms up.
10. It may aid in breaking down the adipose tissue (fat)

Pinching

It is just what is sound like. But it should always be done gently to avoid bruising. For harder pinching squeeze tissue between the fingers. For lighter pinching squeeze the tissue between palm and fingers, pulling muscle tissue slightly away from the bone.

Benefits :

1. It improves circulation and stimulate sluggish muscles.
2. It stretches muscle fibres.
3. Stretches and indirectly increases the muscle's ability to contract.

Rolling

Rolling is like a light pinch gliding along the skin's surface without breaking contact. It is done with or against the grain of muscle fibres. Lift up, pulling away from the bone, and slightly pinch the tissue. Let the thumb give support and drag while the finger, walk and droll the muscle. It can be done with one hand or with both hands side by side, and is good to use when working with smaller muscle groups.

Benefits :

1. Rolling stimulates circulation and passively strengthens weak muscles.
2. Aids in the relief of excessive muscular tension.
3. It indirectly improves muscle contractility.
4. It helps in relieving tiredness and stiffness.
5. Those who do distance running like to use this movement when their legs start to cramp. Five minutes of rolling helps restore muscle strength and redistribute lactic acid build – up.
6. It relieves muscles spasm in calves.

Friction

Friction movements are best done with four fingers, but can be done with just the thumb or the palm of the hand. They are circular movements that go deep into the muscle not just surface rubbing. Apply fingers with moderate to deep pressure and actively separate muscle fibres as one makes circles with a relaxed, rhythmic motion. Use fingers for making small circles and whole hand for larger ones. Elbows and forearms are also good to use when making larger circles (especially on legs and thighs). Friction is especially good to use around joints, shoulder blades, and the soles of the feet because it stretches tendons and ligaments.

Benefits :

1. It is effective in breaking down scare tissue and waste deposits.
2. Friction movements stimulate circulation and metabolic interchange.
3. It stretches muscle tissue, limbering up joints.
4. It is good for tired hands especially for writers.
5. It stimulates circulation and tissue fluid interchange.
6. It relieves stiffness of the organ as it redistributes lactic acid build–up.
7. It maintains joint mobility and muscle power.
8. Friction movements stretch and strengthen muscle fibres.
9. It breaks up waste deposits, stimulates the reflex points affecting all body systems.

Percussion

Percussion movements are series of brief, brisk, rapidly applied contacts of the hand or hands in alternating movements. These movements are striking, slicing, hacking, chopping movements done in a rapid rhythmic motion. They are used mostly on the fleshier parts of the body and serve to stimulate nerve endings and the circulatory system, dispersing metabolic waste products. While doing massage remember always to keep your wrists loose. Following are the different percussion movements.:-

(i) **Slapping:** It is done with an open hand and the flat surface of the fingers. It can be used on all body parts. Start with the head to down wards, alternating the hands in a rhythmic motion.

(ii) **Hacking:** This movement is done with the pinkie side of the hand (or outer edge of the palm of the hand) and can be done hard or soft:

(i) ***Hard hacking*** : In this, fingers should be held together and kept relaxed as body contact is made with the outer edge of the palm. Alternate hands with a slicing rhythmic motion.

(*ii*) ***Soft Hacking*** **:** Keep the fingers slightly separated and relaxed. As the pinkie finger strikes the other fingers will follow naturally.

(*iii*) **Tapping :** Tapping can be done with the tip of the fingers if nail length permits. Separating the fingers slightly, apply alternating strokes to the fleshier parts of the body.

(*iv*) ***Cupping*** **:** It is done with fingers held together in a half fist. (The hand should work like a cup) Cupping can be effective in loosening mucous membranes and relieving congestion when applied to the chest and rib cage.

All the percussion movements should be executed firmly and strongly, but should not be painful. Be careful not to bruise or rupture the capillary beneath the surface of the skin. Avoid performing any of these movements on bone protuberances, glands or on the abdominal region.

Benefits :

1. It stimulates circulation as it aids in the relief of stiff and tense organs.
2. It disperses metabolic waste products.
3. It stimulates the reflex zones of all body systems.

Vibration

It is just what it sounds like. Executed with the fingers or the palm of the hand, vibration is best described as a rapid shaking or trembling movement on the skin surface without breaking contact. It is important to keep the shoulders and neck relaxed at all times. Following are the movements of vibration:

1. Vertical vibration is stationary vibration moving up and down on the skin's surface without breaking contact.
2. Horizontal vibration is stationary vibration moving sideways on the skin's surface without breaking contact.
3. Running vibration is any of the movements used while gliding along the skin's surface. The pressure should be deep while moving hand continuously vibrates.

By using any vibration, one should vibrate for three seconds and take rest for two seconds. With the practice the rhythm will become natural.If the hands are weak, one hand can be placed over the other for support.

Benefits :

1. It stimulates the local nerve responses loosening stiff joints and stretching scar tissue.
2. It is also very soothing and relaxing.
3. It aids in dispersing metabolic waste products.
4. It relieves excessive muscular tension
5. It maintains the circulation and tissue fluid interchange.

Raking

Raking is one of the easier movements that can be done on almost any part of the body especially on the neck and larger muscles. Deep contact is made by hooking the finger tips into the soft tissue while pulling and gliding along the skin's surface. A variation of the movement is done by alternating the fingers in any order while pulling them towards the palm of the hand. This movement is effective when the muscle is not contracted.

Benefits :

1. It passively stretches and warms muscles.
2. It is useful for treating localized tensions in the neck and shoulder areas.

Petrissage

Petrissage is progressive picking up and rolling pressure movement as one pushes with one hand and pulls with other in an alternating pattern. The hands should glide vertically along the muscle, without breaking contact.

Benefits :

1. It is good for bed -ridden, as it helps in stretching and strengthening the muscles.
2. It helps to remove waste products as it increases the circulation and indirectly tones the muscles.
3. It increases the lymphatic drainage.

Centring

Centring allows the movements to come naturally and without an effort. It is integral part of massage that underlies every technique. Centring needs concentration and breath : be still, relax, focus your attention on your breath and wait as you feel calm.

Pressure Therapy

Pressure therapy is to perform pressure on specific areas of the body. The location of specific areas (points) may vary in each person as they are more sensitive to touch. Pressure is applied to release energy blocks within these points or channels. By stimulating the points, circulation is improved, helping to maintain energy balance and general good health. Stationary vertical pressure means pressure without movement at a 90 degree angle. It is best applied with thumbs and can also be experimented with palms, elbows and heels of the feet. When using thumb light pressure is applied with ball of the thumb and hard pressure is applied with the tip. Pressure is applied gradually and the point should be held until stimulation is felt. If nothing is felt, try changing the degree of the angle. When you feel the change, hold briefly and move on to the next point. It should be effortless, use your body weight whenever possible rather than muscle, lean into the points being effected instead of pushing.

Benefits :

1. It is beneficial in relieving symptoms due to cold coughs and asthma.
2. It helps in alleviating the menstrual discomfort.
3. It helps in clearing the sinus congestion and relieve headaches.
4. It is good for hearing and tired eyes.
5. It relaxes body tension and improves circulation.
6. It aids in the relief of the stiffness in the body.
7. It helps to maintain the good health of internal organ systems.
8. It releases blocks within the urinary bladder channel and gall bladder points.
9. It relieves arthritis of the knees.
10. It helps in digestion by working the stomach, spleen, liver channels.

CONTRADICTIONS OF MASSAGE

Do not massage when there is an indication of :

1. A person suffering from acute pain in abdomen. One should not massage the abdomen immediately after meals.
2. A person with unstable cardiac conditions.
3. A person suffering from any disease of bones, muscles skin.
4. A person effected by virus.
5. A person having unhealed fracture. After the bone has healed one may massage the fractured site.
6. A person having unhealed acutely ruptured muscles.
7. A person suffering from bacterial acutely inflammatory, or serve localized arthritis.
8. A person in pain due to infection.
9. Haemorrhage.
10. A person having feeling of vomiting.

PRINCIPLES OF MASSAGE

Nowadays massage plays an important role in medial treatment. To obtain satisfactory results from the use of massage one must have knowledge of the effects of massage and an understanding of principles.

1. A definite uniform rate should be established for all movements.
2. Massage movements should be slow, gentle and rhythmical.
3. Duration of the massage will vary according to the size of the area to be treated.
4. The massage should not be limited to the diseased or injured area only (affected part of the body).
5. Massage treatment should be given according to the age and size of the patient.
6. As the condition of the treated tissue changes it is necessary to make a change in the duration of the massage, because massage is "a means to an end".
7. The duration of massage should vary according to pathology, the size of the area, the age of the patient, the rate of speed of movement and any change in the signs and symptoms.

8. The frequency of the application will depend upon pathological condition that is to be treated.
9. The type of massage movement will depend upon the pathology of the tissues.
10. It is essential that therapist have good scientific knowledge of massage and of its physiological effects and should also observe carefully the effects of the treatment.

EFFECTS OF MASSAGE

The effects of massage have been described and classified in several different ways. These effects might be classified as physical, physiological and psychological. A purely physical effect can be demonstrated by stroking superficial veins and, with direct pressure, removing the blood from the portion of vein which is stroked.

Effect of massage on skin

(*i*) Massage increases the temperature of skin by 2° C to 3°C.
(*ii*) Massage produces a direct effect on the superficial layers of the epidermis.
(*iii*) With the improved circulation, the openings of the sebaceus and sweat glands directly improves the functions of these glands.
(*iv*) Women show higher increase in temperature of skin than men.
(*v*) Massage to a particular part of the skin for some weeks, a definite improvement in the texture and appearance of the skin can be noted.
(*vi*) The use of massage is to achieve better cosmetic results.
(*vii*) Massage opens the pores of skin and skin becomes soft.

Effects of the Massage on Circulation of Blood

1. Massage increases nutrition of the tissues and removes the products of fatigue.
2. Deep massage increases the blood flow and systolic stroke volume.
3. Massage assists arterial circulation.
4. The rate of heart beat or the stroke volume also increases.
5. All the smaller vessels become visible because of the blood flow created through them.
6. Massage increases the circulation of blood.
7. More capillaries are open with an increased rate of blood flow.
8. The heart rate also increases.
9. The red blood cells count increases after massage
10. Abdominal massage increases the haemoglobin and red cells of the circulating blood.
11. Massage increases oxygen capacity of the blood.

Effects of Massage on Nervous System

1. Massage produces little changes in the nerve itself.
2. The pain caused by vigorous massage gradually lessens, when the massage continues for some time compared with that caused at the beginning of the treatment.
3. It relieves certain types of pains.
4. Massage affects the central nervous system and also the sensory nerves.
5. Massage affects the reflex control of circulation.

Effects of Massage on Muscles

1. Massage causes relaxation of the muscles.
2. Massage increases the muscle tone.
3. Massage produces an actual increase in the size of the muscles structures.
4. The muscles become firmer and more elastic.
5. The muscles are strengthened and grow by massage.
6. Massage improves the nutrition of the muscles and promotes their development.
7. Massage makes the muscles stronger.
8. Massage helps the muscles to perform more exercises.
9. Muscles fatigued by work can be restored much more rapidly by massage than by rest of the same duration.

Some Other Useful Matters

Newton's Law of Motion

Everything that moves is governed by laws of motions formulated by Sir Isaac Newton. These laws describe things move and make it possible to predict the motion of an object.

Newton's First Law : The law of Inertia states that a body at rest will remain in rest and a body in motion will remain in motion at the same speed and in the same direction unless acted on by some outside force.

Example :

1. Once an object is in motion it will take less force to maintain its speed and direction (ie. momentum). For example, it takes an individual more effort to start pedalling a bicycle to set it underway than it does to maintain speed once the bicycle is moving.
2. The heavier the ball and the faster it is moving, the more the force that is required to stop it or to absorb its momentum.

Newton's Second Law : The law of acceleration states that a change in velocity (acceleration) of an object is directly proportional to the force producing it and inversely proportional to its mass.

Example :

It shot putting, the athlete who is stronger and thus able to expend more force will toss the 12-pound shot farther than an athlete who possess less strength. Also, an athlete will find more force is needed to propel a 16-pound shot than a 12-pound shot.

Newton's Third Law: The law of action and reaction states that for every action there is an equal and opposite reaction.

Example :

1. Bouncing on a trampoline or springing from a diving board are examples of the law of action and reaction.
2. The water pushes the swimmer forward with a force equal to the force exerted by the swimmer on the backward thrust of the strokes.

Mechanical Principles of Running

The speed of running is governed by length of the stride and the frequency of the stride. Better runners have a greater stride length per given pace than poorer runners. In running, as in walking, the forces recruited to produce and control the movement are the internal muscular forces of gravity, normal reaction, friction and air resistance. There is no optimal speed in running because the energy needed to run is proportional to the square of the velocity. Therefore, whether the run is an easy jog or a full-speed sprint, economy of effort is a highly definable objective. To achieve this it is essential for the runner to observe the principles that apply to efficient running.

1. In accordance with law of inertia, a body remains at rest unless acted upon by a force. The force required to overcome inertial is greatest at take off and least after acceleration has ceased. The problem of overcoming inertia decreases as the speed increases.
2. Greater the power of the leg drive, the greater the acceleration of the runner.
3. The force for the run is provided through the upward and forward ground reaction force in response to the downward, backward drive of the foot. In most efficient run, vertical movements of the centre of gravity are reduced to a minimum.
4. The more completely the horizontal force is directed straight backward, the greater its contribution to the forward motion of the body. Lateral motions are inefficient and detract from forward propulsion.
5. Since a long lever develops greater speed at the distal end than does a short lever, the length of the leg in the driving phase should be as greater as possible when speed is a consideration.
6. Proper warm up ensures little resistance due to internal forces i.e., forces produced due to muscles, tendons, ligaments etc.

7. By flexing the free leg at the knee and carrying the heel high under the hip, the leg is moved more rapidly as well as more economically. This high knee lift increases as speed increases.
8. The force of air resistance can be altered by shifting the centre of gravity. A forward lean will work to counter act a head wind. A tail wind often enhances performance.

Postural Defects

1. **Kyphosis:** Also called hunchback. A back with a hump, or a person whose back is humped. The condition is an abnormal backward curvature of the upper portion of the spine.
   Corrective measures: Emphasis should be given on maintaining correct posture while sitting, standing and reading. Modern surgical techniques and medicines can correct many of the causes of Kyphosis.
2. **Lordosis:** Lordosis is an aggravated lower spinal curvature characterized by inverse letter 'c'. Chest is drawn out and the lower abdomen protrudes further.
   Corrective measures: Too much emphasis should not be given for maintaining correct posture. Lying supine on flat, hard bed.
3. **Scoliosis:** It is a lateral curvature of the central part of the spine and happens mostly in children from birth and young adult up to age 15.
   Corrective measures: In simple cases, a cast is applied from chest to the waist to reduce curvature.
4. **Flat feet:** Flat feet can usually be revealed by a simple test of making a footprint on level earth hard-packed sand.
   Corrective measures: Proper arch supports in side the shoes. Especially for over weight and those who have to stand a great deal of the time.

Corrective and Therapeutic Exercise

Corrective and therapeutic exercises are those prescribed and supervised by persons specialized in doing so for the cure and prevention of certain physical defects. For many people with poor posture or other physical deformities among sports person, corrective and therapeutic exercises are a part of the rehabilitation programme. These exercises can be generally classified as follows-

(*a*) **Passive exercises**-Accomplished by a therapist or mechanical device with no active muscle contraction of the involved part by the patient.

(*b*) **Active assistive exercise** - Exercises accomplished by active contraction by the patient with the assistance of the therapist or a mechanical device.

(*c*) **Active exercise** - Accomplished by the patient without assistance or resistance.

(*d*) **Resistive-Active exercise** - Accomplished by the patient against resistance either manual or mechanical.

Stretching exercise - Exercises involving forced motion, either passive or active.

Role of Biomechanics in Sports

All movements performed by athletes in different sports disciplines are basically mechanical movements and are governed by certain laws of mechanics. The science of sports biomechanics is an applied form of mechanics which studies the movements of the athlete from the mechanical point keeping in view the biological constraints.

This takes into consideration the conditions under which these movements are performed and also mechanical aspects of loco motor apparatus. There are many tasks in the field of sports, which the sports biomechanics accomplishes.

Some of these are as follows :

(*a*) Development of new techniques, which are more efficient than the existing techniques.

(*b*) Evaluation of existing techniques for learning and training process.

(*c*) Qualification of various motor abilities.

(*d*) Development of biomechanical principles for general orientation.

(*e*) Prevention of injuries.

(*f*) Designing of equipment.

Kinematics and Kinetics

Kinematics - It is a subdivision of dynamics where human motion is studied without regard to the forces acting on it. Various tasks of biomechanics in sports are dealt with using kinematic procedures, which involve the evaluation of distance, time, angles, velocity and acceleration in a movement. In kinematical analysis, high speed films usually in the range of 100-200 pictures per second or frames per second are taken by movie film camera or high speed camera during training and competitions. For example, in jumps, the time at take off, velocity of the body, centre of gravity, angle of trunk etc. are the parameters, which are analyzed.

Kinetics - It is another subdivision of dynamics where forces are studied which cause either motion or change in motion. The most important parameters are force-time characteristics, specially the ground reaction force. The quantification of force and force-time curves serve as criterion for evaluation of technique in many sports movements as jumps, throws, weightlifting etc. Force platforms and different force transducers are used to measure force of different body parts.

Muscle Classification

Muscle groups can be classified by the number of articulations crossed by the muscle. A muscle can affect the movement of each articulation that it crosses.

The simplest is the 'uniarticulate' (one joint) muscle. When the muscle shortens, it can produce motion in that single articulation, similarly, when the uniarticulate muscle is stretched, it is stretched to accommodate only the range of movement (ROM) of that single articulation.

The bi articulate or multi articulate muscle crosses two or more muscle articulations. When it shortens, it tends to pull the two body attachments towards the centre of the muscle and therefore tends to produce motion in all the articulations that it crosses e.g., muscles in the lower extremity that are used for locomotion.

Similarly, those muscles that cause or help cause motion are the 'agonists' (movers). Those muscles that can perform the movement opposite to the movement being done are called the antagonist. This relationship enables the body to perform the variety of movements of which it is capable.

Analysis of Floating Service in Volleyball

Force applied in striking the ball is maximized through sequential transfer of momentum from large segments to less massive segments.

The efficiency of imparting force to the volleyball is judged in terms of speed, distance, and direction of the ball after it is hit.

(*i*) The ball will move only if the force applied by hand is of sufficient magnitude to overcome the ball's inertia. The ball should be hit with optimum force so that it crosses over the net overcoming resistance due to air.

(*ii*) The body's internal resistance will decrease with warming up and it also decreases the chances of injury due to hyperextension of back and shoulder muscles while serving in volleyball.

(*iii*) In volleyball, the aim is to give correct direction to the ball. Thus, the point at which the ball is hit by the hand of the server will decide in which direction the ball will go.

(*iv*) Linear velocity is imparted to the ball as a result of the angular velocity of the arm. To impart more speed to the ball it must be hit with more force and with full stretched arm.

(*v*) Optimum summation of internal force is needed if maximum force is to be applied to move the ball. For maximum velocity of each contributing body segment to occur impact with the ball. The slower or heavier segments of the body i.e., legs hips, torso must start to move first and the lightest and smaller ones last. It is preferable for the slower segments to begin their forward movements while the faster segments like elbow, wrist and finger are still completing the backing.

(*vi*) When the ball is hit in its line of centre of gravity it will result in linear motion.

(*vii*) The ball will move in rotatory motion if the force applied is not in line with its centre of gravity.

Analysis of Backhand Stroke in Tennis

(*i*) The force applied to the ball must be great enough to overcome not only its mass but also all restraining forces e.g. wind resistance, friction between racket and the ball.

(ii) Backhand stroke involves great flexibility/stretchability of the back and shoulder muscles. Greater the range of movement, more will be the force applied to the ball through the racket.

(iii) To provide accurate direction to the ball, a step forward diagonally and shifting the body weight forward while flexing at the forward knee takes place. The rotation of pelvis and spine also helps.

(iv) Ball contact with the racket takes place when the racket is parallel to the ground and facing the opposite court.

(v) Linear velocity is imparted to ball as a result of the angular velocity of the racket and the arm. The linear velocity at the end of the segment (arm) is the product of the angular velocity and the length of the segment (arm). Thus, for a given angular speed, the linear speed imparted to the tennis ball with a tennis racket is much greater than that of a ball hit with a hand. On the other hand, more force is needed to move the longer lever.

(vi) Optimum summation of internal force is needed if maximum force is to be applied to move an object. For maximum velocity of each contributing body segment to occur at the impact, the big lower muscles begin their forward movement and later comes the role of smaller muscles which help in giving accuracy while hitting the ball.

Analysis of off Spin Bowling in Cricket

(i) The ball will moves only if the force applied be of sufficient magnitude to overcome the ball's inertia. The force applied should be sufficient enough to overcome the wind resistance, internal resistance and the friction between hands of the bowler and the ball.

(ii) In off spin bowling, the accuracy with which ball is thrown depends upon accurate judgement of the distance and direction of the bowlers target.

(iii) The bowler imparts maximum force to the ball by using the law of summation of forces. The big muscles are involved first and then the force is transformed to the smaller but faster muscle i.e., wrist and fingers.

(iv) Angular motion of the arm gives linear motion to the ball. The distance which is travelled by the ball in the air before first bounce depends upon at what angle was it released from hand of the bowler.

(v) The bowler shifts his body weight to the forward leg. The rotation of pelvis and spine helps in imparting maximum force to the ball at the time of release.

(vi) The force is applied away from the ball's centre of gravity and off spin occurs on the ball as a result of turning given by the fingers.

(vii) Off spin bowling is more accurate than fast.

(viii) In off spin bowling the ball turns to the right side.

Analysis of Backstroke in Swimming

(i) The arms should be able to move the whole body backward by applying minimum force. The force should be great enough to pull the body against the water resistance.

(ii) Water does not provide equal reaction force as is applied by the swimmer by his arms. Hence body is propelled linearly to a lesser distance due to division of force.

(iii) Optimum summation of internal force is needed if maximum force is to be applied while swimming. The maximum number of segments that can safely be employed should be moved through the largest possible range of motion for maximum force production while swimming.

(iv) The direction in which the swimmer moves is determined by the direction of the force 'applied' to it. If the swimmer arms and legs move away from the direction of the predetermined pathway, it will increase the friction and the component of force will be wasted.

(v) The Buoyant force of the water keeps the swimmer afloat. Fat people can float easily as compared to thin and muscular people, because they have mechanical advantage as compare to others. Females have mechanical advantage to float because of more fat.

EXERCISE

1. Which of the following planes of the body divides it into upper and lower parts?
(*a*) Saggital (*b*) Transverse
(*c*) Frontal (*d*) Vertical

2. How many bones are there in the carpus of human beings?
(*a*) 8 (*b*) 9
(*c*) 10 (*d*) 11

3. What type of bones perform the function of giving strength?
(*a*) Long bones (*b*) Irregular bones
(*c*) Flat bones (*d*) Short bones

4. Density of bones is greater in–
(*a*) men (*b*) women
(*c*) both (*a*) and (*b*) (*d*) none of the above

5. Which of the following is responsible for limiting the range of movements of joint?
(*a*) Tendons (*b*) Ligaments
(*c*) Both (*a*) and (*b*) (*d*) Muscle fibres

6. "Zygomatic" bone is present in–
(*a*) upper extremities (*b*) lower extremities
(*c*) vertebral column (*d*) skull

7. Flexion at elbow is brought about by–
(*a*) biceps (*b*) triceps
(*c*) both (*a*) and (*b*) (*d*) none of these

8. Strongest ligament of the hip joint is–
(*a*) pubofemoral (*b*) ileofemoral
(*c*) ischiofemoral (*d*) none of these

9. Which type of lever is most effective elevation of arm?
(*a*) Third class (*b*) Second class
(*c*) First class (*d*) None of these

10. Which muscle is involved in the elevation of arm?
(*a*) Deltoid (*b*) Biceps
(*c*) Triceps (*d*) Quadriceps

11. The following bones form the Elbow joint except–
(*a*) scapula (*b*) radius
(*c*) ulna (*d*) humerus

12. Main bones in forearm are–
(*a*) humerous-femur
(*b*) radius-ulna
(*c*) ulna-phalanges
(*d*) wrist bones -phalanges

13. On "Set" command the sprinter is in–
(*a*) stable equilibrium
(*b*) unstable equilibrium
(*c*) neutral equilibrium
(*d*) none of the above

14. An athlete covering 100m distance in 10 seconds , ran at a speed of–
(*a*) 10 m/s (*b*) 100 m/s
(*c*) 20 m/s (*d*) 1000 m/s

15. The forces acting on a runner near the end of a race are–
(*a*) weight (*b*) friction
(*c*) air resistance (*d*) all of the above

16. Which of the following is not a type of joint?
(*a*) Fibrous (*b*) Ossified
(*c*) Cartilagenous (*d*) Synovial

17. The study of the joint is called–
(*a*) osteology (*b*) arthrology
(*c*) ornithology (*d*) odonotology

18. Freely movable joints are also known as–
(*a*) synerthrosis (*b*) amphiarthroses
(*c*) diarthroses (*d*) fibrous

19. Which of the following is not a synovial joint?
(*a*) Hinge (*b*) Pivot
(*c*) Fibrous (*d*) Gliding

20. The structure of which joint permits bending in only one direction?
(*a*) Pivot (*b*) Hinge
(*c*) Gliding (*d*) Ball and Socket

21. The shoulder joint is a type of–
(*a*) ball and socket joint
(*b*) hinge joint
(*c*) saddle joint
(*d*) condyloid

22. Knee joint is an example of–
(*a*) gliding joint (*b*) pivot joint
(*c*) hinge joint (*d*) saddle joint

23. Hip joint is a–
(*a*) pivot joint
(*b*) hinge joint
(*c*) saddle joint
(*d*) ball and socket joint

24. Joint in the phalanges and metacarpals are–
(*a*) pivot (*b*) saddle
(*c*) hinge (*d*) condyloid

25. Imaginary line perpendicular to ground is called–
(*a*) vertical axis (*b*) sagittal axis
(*c*) lateral axis (*d*) none of these

26. Every movement has–
(*a*) one axis
(*b*) one plane
(*c*) one axis and one plane
(*d*) none of the above

27. Imaginary surface which divides the body into anterior and posterior aspects is–
(*a*) horizontal plane (*b*) sagittal plane
(*c*) frontal plane (*d*) none of these

28. An imaginary line passing from anterior to posterior direction is–
(*a*) sagittal axis (*b*) vertical axis
(*c*) sagittal plane (*d*) frontal plane

29. The knee joint is a hinge joint between–
(*a*) femur and tibia
(*b*) femur and fibula
(*c*) humerus and tibia
(*d*) humerus and fibula

30. Units of distance and displacement are–
(*a*) m/s (*b*) m
(*c*) m/s^2 (*d*) radian

31. What is a change in position?
(*a*) Speed (*b*) Displacement
(*c*) Distance (*d*) Velocity

32. Which of the following is not a quantity of linear kinematics?
(*a*) Speed (*b*) Velocity
(*c*) Angular velocity (*d*) Displacement

33. The flight path of an object is–
(*a*) velocity (*b*) projectile
(*c*) speed (*d*) trajectory

34. Which of the following is not the shape of trajectory determined by angle of projection?
(*a*) Vertical (*b*) Frontal
(*c*) Horizontal (*d*) Oblique

35. Parabolic trajectory is–
(*a*) vertical (*b*) oblique
(*c*) horizontal (*d*) none of these

36. If the angle of project is 300, the trajectory is–
(*a*) oblique (*b*) horizontal
(*c*) vertical (*d*) parabolic

37. The movement at Atlanto occipital joint is an example of–
(*a*) first class lever (*b*) second class lever
(*c*) third class lever (*d*) none of these

38. Raising of body on toes is an example of–
(*a*) first class lever (*b*) second class lever
(*c*) third class level (*d*) none of these

39. Canoe paddle and shovel are examples of–
(*a*) first class lever (*b*) second class lever
(*c*) third class level (*d*) none of these

40. In which type of lever, the force and resistance are on the same side of the axis, with the applied force closer to the axis?
(*a*) First Class lever
(*b*) Second class lever
(*c*) Third class level
(*d*) None of these

41. Increased posterior convexity of the normal lumbar curve refers to–
(*a*) round shoulder (*b*) kyphosis
(*c*) lordosis (*d*) scoliosis

42. What is the lateral curvature of the spine called?
(*a*) Flat back (*b*) Lordosis
(*c*) Kyphosis (*d*) Scoliosis

43. Which of the muscles is not involved in the flexion of wrist joint during throwing?
(*a*) Flexor carpiradials
(*b*) Flexor digitorum

(*c*) Teres major
(*d*) None of them

44. What is the forward inclination of the shoulder girdle called?
(*a*) Scoliosis (*b*) Round Shoulder
(*c*) Kyphosis (*d*) Lordosis

45. Which of the following is pressure manipulation technique?
(*a*) Pinching (*b*) Clapping
(*c*) Pounding (*d*) Kneading

46. Isotonic muscle contraction is also called–
(*a*) AROM (*b*) Static
(*c*) RST (*d*) PROM

47. The exercise suggested in patients who cannot exercise actively is–
(*a*) AAROM (*b*) AROM
(*c*) PROM (*d*) RST

48. Exercise done on patients with weak muscles and when joint pain limits movement are–
(*a*) AROM (*b*) AAROM
(*c*) PROM (*d*) RST

49. The movement of joints in the coronal plane but moving away from median plane is called–
(*a*) flexion (*b*) extension
(*c*) adduction (*d*) abduction

50. If one straightens one's legs, the knees undergo–
(*a*) felxion (*b*) abduction
(*c*) adduction (*d*) extension

51. The movement of the forearm in which the palm faces anteriorly is called–
(*a*) supination (*b*) pronation
(*c*) protraction (*d*) retraction

52. Upward movement of joints is–
(*a*) opposition (*b*) retraction
(*c*) supination (*d*) elevation

53. The movement of hand where the thumb touches the 5th finger is–
(*a*) protraction (*b*) pronation
(*c*) opposition (*d*) dorsiflexion

54. The circular motion combining flexion, extension, abduction and adduction are–
(*a*) circumduction (*b*) pronation
(*c*) supination (*d*) retraction

55. The massage where shearing stresses are created below the skin–
(*a*) effleurage (*b*) petrissage
(*c*) topetement (*d*) deep friction

56. The massage where the focus of pressure is moved by the hands gliding over the skin is–
(*a*) effleurage (*b*) traction
(*c*) petrissage (*d*) topetement

57. Percussion-oriented massage involving striking of soft tissues with repetitive blows, using both hands in a rhythmic, gentle and rapid fashion is–
(*a*) petrissage (*b*) tapotement
(*c*) deep friction (*d*) traction

58. Which eastern massage applies forces through digital pressure to cure imbalances of energy?
(*a*) Shiatsu
(*b*) Acupunture
(*c*) Acupressure
(*d*) Both acupuncture and acupressure

59. Which technique is used in the treatment of fractures?
(*a*) Traction (*b*) Effluerage
(*c*) Petrissage (*d*) Tapotement

60. Which technique of manipulation is an indirect myofascial technique with an emphasis on relative position of a joint or body part as an essential component of treatment?
(*a*) Articulatory technique
(*b*) Indirect positional technique
(*c*) Counterstrain
(*d*) Direct thrust

61. Biceps is an example of–
(*a*) flexor muscle (*b*) extensor muscle
(*c*) adductor muscle (*d*) abductor muscle

62. Triceps is an example of–
(*a*) flexon muscle (*b*) extensor muscle
(*c*) adductor muscle (*d*) abductor muscle

63. Considering the neck articulations, which of the following muscles is not responsible for flexion?

(a) Longus capitis
(b) Rectus capitis anterior
(c) Sterno cleidomastoid
(d) Splenus capitis

64. Which of the following cervical articulation muscles is responsible for extension?
(a) Sternocleidomastoid
(b) Longus Colli
(c) Longus capitis
(d) Trapezius

65. Which of the following elbow articulation is not responsible for flexion?
(a) Brochiolis (b) Triceps brochii
(c) Biceps brochii (d) Brochio radialis

66. Which of the radioulnar articulations is not responsible for pronation?
(a) Quadratus (b) Carpi radialis
(c) Anconeus (d) Biceps bronchii

67. Which of the following knee articulations muscles is not responsible for medial or internal rotation?
(a) Popliteus (b) Sartorius
(c) Gracilis (d) Gastro enemius

68. Which of the following ankle articulation joints is responsible for dorsal flexion?
(a) Soleus (b) Plantaris
(c) Tibialis anterior (d) Gastroenemius

69. Distance is–
(a) scalar quantity
(b) vector quantity
(c) same as displacement
(d) measured in m/s

70. Average velocity $\overline{v}$ is equal to–
(a) $\frac{d}{t_2 - t_1}$ (b) $\frac{V_f - V_i}{t_2 - t_1}$
(c) $\frac{1}{t_2 - t_1}$ (d) $\frac{\Delta Q}{t}$

71. To convert a quantity from radians to degree, multiply by–
(a) 3.14 (b) 57.3
(c) 0.0175 (d) 360

72. To convert from degrees to radians one multiplies by–
(a) 57.3 (b) 3.14
(c) 0.0175 (d) 2 p

73. The angle between two body segments is called–
(a) absolute angle (b) relative angle
(c) right angle (d) none of these

74. Average angular velocity ϖ is equal to
(a) $\frac{\Delta Q}{\Delta t}$ (b) $\frac{\Delta W}{\Delta t}$
(c) $\frac{V_T^2}{r}$ (d) $W^2 r$

75. Linear acceleration is equal to–
(a) radius × angular displacement
(b) radius × angular velocity
(c) radius × angular acceleration
(d) ¡ × omega

76. Newton's first law of motion is known as –
(a) Law of acceleration
(b) Law of inertia
(c) Law of action reaction
(d) Law of momentum

77. The vertical motion of a projectile is given by which law of motion?
(a) Law of inertia
(b) Law of acceleration
(c) Law of action-reaction
(d) None of these

78. Angular interpretation of Newton's second law is mathematically represented as–
(a) $\Sigma T_a = 1_a \infty a$
(b) $\Sigma T_a \Delta t = (H_f - H_i)_a$
(c) $T = F \times r$
(d) $1_a = \Sigma m_i r_i^2$

79. What are also called moments of force ?
(a) Inertia (b) Acceleration
(c) Trajectories (d) Torques

80. The point were the entire mass or weight of the body may be considered to be concentrated is–
(*a*) centre of mass (*b*) centre of gravity
(*c*) torque (*d*) lever

81. The cartilage which serves to cushion the impact of large forces on bone ends is called–
(*a*) fibrous cartilage (*b*) hyaline cartilage
(*c*) notch (*d*) fossa

82. Function of long bones in the body is to–
(*a*) give strength
(*b*) give protection
(*c*) act as lever
(*d*) provide surface area for muscle attachment

83. The specific function of tarsal bone is–
(*a*) protection (*b*) gives strength
(*c*) act as lever (*d*) none of the above

84. Example of synovial joint is–
(*a*) suture
(*b*) knee joint
(*c*) inter vertebral disc
(*d*) shoulder joint

85. What type of muscles are capable of resisting fatigue in a long duration activity?
(*a*) Deltoid (*b*) Fast twitch
(*c*) Slow twitch (*d*) both (*b*) and (*c*)

86. Muscles which cause the joints to bend are called–
(*a*) flexors (*b*) extensors
(*c*) abductors (*d*) adductors

87. Force generation but fibre lengthening is also known as–
(*a*) eccentric contraction
(*b*) concentric contraction
(*c*) isotonic contraction
(*d*) isometric contraction.

88. "Kyphosis" is also called–
(*a*) hollow back (*b*) round back
(*c*) lateral back (*d*) back curve

89. "Hunch back" is also known as–
(*a*) back pain (*b*) scoliosis
(*c*) lordosis (*d*) kyphosis

90. Side ward curvature of the spine is called–
(*a*) knock knee (*b*) kyphosis
(*c*) scoliosis (*d*) lordosis

91. The path of an object projected into free air space is known as–
(*a*) speed (*b*) abnormal curve
(*c*) velocity (*d*) parabola

92. Duration is a measure of–
(*a*) distance (*b*) displacement
(*c*) force (*d*) time

93. "Speed" is indicated in–
(*a*) Km/sec^2 (*b*) Cm/hour
(*c*) Newton (*d*) Km/hr.

94. First law of motion is also called–
(*a*) Law of action and reaction
(*b*) Law of conservation of energy
(*c*) Law of inertia
(*d*) Law of transference of momentum.

95. Mechanics is the branch of physics that deals with bodies–
(*a*) at rest
(*b*) in motion
(*c*) Both (*a*) and (*b*)
(*d*) none of the above.

96. The branch of mechanics that describes the cause of force is–
(*a*) kinetics (*b*) kinematics
(*c*) biomechanics (*d*) fluid mechanics

97. The branch of mechanics, which deals with the force that produces or changes the state of motion is–
(*a*) kinematics (*b*) statistics
(*c*) biomechanics (*d*) kinetics

98. Endo skeleton involves–
(*a*) covering of skin, hair, nails
(*b*) bones and cartilages
(*c*) bones only
(*d*) none of the above

99. Exo skeleton involves–
(*a*) covering of skin, hair, nails
(*b*) bones and cartilages
(*c*) long bones only
(*d*) short bones only

100. Study of joints is called–
(*a*) kinesiology (*b*) biology
(*c*) anthropometry (*d*) arthrology

101. Largest bone in the human body is–
(*a*) tibia (*b*) femur
(*c*) fibula (*d*) humerus

102. Metacarpals and phalanges are examples of–
(*a*) saddle joint (*b*) hinge joint
(*c*) condyloid joint (*d*) gliding joint

103. Carpo metacarpal joint is an example of–
(*a*) condyloid joint
(*b*) ball and socket joint
(*c*) saddle joint
(*d*) gliding joint

104. Movements possible in Condyloid joint are–
(*a*) flexion and extension
(*b*) circumduction only
(*c*) flexion, extension, abduction, adduction
(*d*) flexion, extension, abduction, adduction and circumduction

105. Which of the following is an example of uniaxial joint?
(*a*) Condyloid
(*b*) Saddle
(*c*) Hinge
(*d*) Condyloid and saddle both.

106. Which of the following is an example of bi-axial joint?
(*a*) Hinge (*b*) Pivot
(*c*) Both (*a*) and (*b*) (*d*) None of the above

107. Number of bones in the Axial skeleton are–
(*a*) 60 (*b*) 80
(*c*) 40 (*d*) 20

108. Number of Bones in the Appendicular skeleton are–
(*a*) 120 (*b*) 180
(*c*) 126 (*d*) 116

109. Imaginary line passing laterally from one side to other is called–
(*a*) sagittal axis (*b*) sagittal plane
(*c*) vertical axis (*d*) lateral axis

110. Side ways bending of trunk is an example of movement in–
(*a*) frontal plane and sagittal Axis
(*b*) sagittal plane and sagittal axis
(*c*) frontal plane and transverse axis
(*d*) sagittal plane and lateral axis

111. Bending forward of the trunk is an example of movement in the–
(*a*) frontal plane (*b*) transverse plane
(*c*) sagittal plane (*d*) longitudinal axis

112. A forward upward movement of the foot at the ankle joint is–
(*a*) planar flexion (*b*) dorsi flexion
(*c*) inversion (*d*) eversion

113. Bending of head towards right or left side of the shoulder is–
(*a*) extension (*b*) flexion
(*c*) lateral flexion (*d*) lateral extension

114. Newton's second law of motion is also known as–
(*a*) Law of inertia
(*b*) Law of Action reaction
(*c*) Law of momentum
(*d*) Law of gravitation

115. Lever System prevalent in human arm is–
(*a*) class III (*b*) class II
(*c*) class I (*d*) none of the above

116. Osteology is the study of–
(*a*) muscles (*b*) bones
(*c*) joints (*d*) nerves

117. Study of muscles is called–
(*a*) osteology (*b*) anthropology
(*c*) myology (*d*) anthropometry

118. Total number of bones in the human skull are–
(*a*) 20 (*b*) 21
(*c*) 22 (*d*) 23

119. How many Carpal Bones are there in the wrist?
(*a*) 6 (*b*) 7
(*c*) 8 (*d*) 9

120. Boxer's muscles are–
(*a*) trapezius
(*b*) sterno cliedo ,astoid

(c) abdominal
(d) deltoid

121. "Neck Joint" is an example of–
(a) pivot joint (b) hinge joint
(c) saddle joint (d) condyloid joint

122. "Trapezius" muscles help in–
(a) pushing the neck backward
(b) punching
(c) raising the leg forward
(d) none of the above

123. The force experienced by a spinning ball as it moves through the air is called–
(a) tensila force (b) magnus force
(c) compressive force (d) contract force

124. Shortest bone in the human body is–
(a) phalenge (b) metatarsal
(c) innominate bone (d) tarsal.

125. Which of the following has maximum percentage in the composition of bone?
(a) Calcium sulphate
(b) Calcium phosphate
(c) Chloride
(d) Fluoride

126. Total number of bones in the cranium are–
(a) 7 (b) 8
(c) 9 (d) 10

127. "Thoracic vertebrae" consists of–
(a) 7 bones (b) 12 bones
(c) 5 bones (d) 8 bones

128. "Sacrum" Vertebrae consists of–
(a) 5 bones (b) 6 bones
(c) 4 bones (d) 3 bones

129. "Lumbar" Vertebrae are–
(a) 6 in number (b) 7 in number
(c) 5 in number (d) 4 in number

130. A bone which is formed by the replacement of cartilage is known as–
(a) long bone (b) short bone
(c) sesamoid bone (d) replacing bone.

131. A Bone which is formed by the transformation of connective tissue is called–
(a) replacing bone (b) investing bone
(c) sesamoid bone (d) flat bone

132. Bones cells are also called–
(a) osteoblasts (b) osteocytes
(c) osteoclasts (d) osteoporosis

133. Technique of ossification of bones of right hand is used to determine–
(a) height
(b) age
(c) weight
(d) equilibrium ability

134. "Hamstring" muscle–
(a) extends knee (b) flexes knee
(c) extends elbow (d) flexes elbow

135. Synovial joints are–
(a) slightly movable (b) freely movable
(c) both (a) and (b) (d) none of the above

136. The vertical axis passes–
(a) perpendicular to the ground
(b) horizontal to the ground
(c) both (a) and (b)
(d) none of the above

137. The law of gravity is an example of a law of motion studied in the body of knowledge called–
(a) chemistry (b) physics
(c) mechanics (d) all of the above

138. Flat feet is also known as–
(a) plantar fascitis (b) pes planus
(c) morton's neurama (d) metatarsalgia

139. In isometric contraction, the muscle–
(a) shortens
(b) lengthens
(c) neither shortens nor lengthens
(d) shortens as well as lengthens

140. The scapula bone is situated in–
(a) leg (b) hip
(c) upper back (d) arm

141. "Latissimus Dorsi" is situated in–
(a) lower leg (b) thigh
(c) back (d) upper arm

142. "Lordosis" is also called–
(a) round back (b) hollow back
(c) lateral back (d) back curve

143. Parabola is–
(*a*) the path of an object projected into free air
(*b*) path of an object formed with air resistance
(*c*) path of the object falling vertically down
(*d*) none of the above

144. The terms rest and motion are studied under–
(*a*) biochemistry (*b*) anatomy
(*c*) biomechanics (*d*) none of the above

145. In which type of lever, the weight is in between force and fulcrum?
(*a*) type I (*b*) type II
(*c*) type III (*d*) all of the above

146. The movements around ball and socket joints are–
(*a*) flexion and extension
(*b*) rotation and circumduction
(*c*) hyper extension
(*d*) all of the above

147. Which of the following is an example of Hinge joint?
(*a*) Hip joint (*b*) Elbow joint
(*c*) Ankle joint (*d*) All of the above.

148. At the time of release of discus–
(*a*) centripetal force is more than centrifugal force
(*b*) centrifugal force is more than centripetal force
(*c*) centripetal and centrifugal forces becomes zero
(*d*) none of the above.

149. The sternum is located in–
(*a*) foot (*b*) palm
(*c*) chest (*d*) skull

150. Which of the following is a ball and socket joint?
(*a*) Hip joint
(*b*) Shoulder joint
(*c*) Both (*a*) and (*b*)
(*d*) None of the above.

151. During abduction the arm moves–
(*a*) towards the body
(*b*) away from the body
(*c*) in front of the chest
(*d*) none of the above

152. In which type of lever, the force is in between weight and fulcurn?
(*a*) Type I (*b*) Type II
(*c*) Type III (*d*) All of the above

153. Synovial joint is–
(*a*) slightly movable (*b*) freely movable
(*c*) both (*a*) and (*b*) (*d*) none of the above

154. Which of the following is a fibrous joint?
(*a*) Joints of the skull
(*b*) Joints of the fingers
(*c*) Joints of the ribs
(*d*) All of the above

155. The terms "anterior and posterior" are synonymous with–
(*a*) frontal and back (*b*) verbal and dorsal
(*c*) lateral and medial (*d*) none of the above

156. Study of bones is called–
(*a*) osteoporosis (*b*) osteoclast
(*c*) osteology (*d*) arthrology

157. The bone cells which are involved in building of bone are–
(*a*) osteoblasts (*b*) osteoclasts
(*c*) osteocytes (*d*) none of the above

158. The skeleton of thorax is made up of–
(*a*) cartilage (*b*) bone
(*c*) both (*a*) and (*b*) (*d*) none of the above

159. Which of the following is joint of reciprocal innervation?
(*a*) Pivot joint (*b*) Saddle joint
(*c*) Condyloid joint (*d*) Hinge joint

160. Carpal joint is the example of–
(*a*) pivot joint
(*b*) condyloid joint
(*c*) hinge joint
(*d*) ball and socket joint

161. The point where the force which moves the lever is applied is called–
(*a*) point of resistance
(*b*) moment of the force
(*c*) point of effort
(*d*) load arm

162. The lever where fulcrum lies between the effort and the load is called–
(*a*) Lever of first class
(*b*) Lever of second class
(*c*) Lever of third class
(*d*) None

163. Friction force is a–
(*a*) tensila force (*b*) compressive force
(*c*) contract force (*d*) non-contact force

164. The contractile element of muscles are–
(*a*) sarcolema (*b*) myofibrils
(*c*) epimysium (*d*) none of these

165. The Area Located in the Centre of the Sarcomere containing both actin and Myosin is called–
(*a*) I Band (*b*) Z Band
(*c*) A Band (*d*) None of these

166. Sprint in which running speed is gradually increased from jogging to striding and finally to sprinting is called–
(*a*) decceleration sprint
(*b*) acceleration sprint
(*c*) sprinting sprint
(*d*) none of these

167. The excitory chemical transmitter at the neuromuscular junction are–
(*a*) acetycholine (*b*) norepinephrine
(*c*) dopamine (*d*) all of these

168. The inhibitory transmitter in the brain is called–
(*a*) gamma-Aminobutyric acid (GABA)
(*b*) glycine
(*c*) serotonin
(*d*) none of these

169. The inhibitory transmitter in the spinal cord is called–
(*a*) dopamine (*b*) glycine
(*c*) serotonin (*d*) none of these

170. Protein involved in muscular contraction is called–
(*a*) actin (*b*) myosin
(*c*) both (*d*) none of these

171. The electrical activity developed in a muscle or nerve cell during activity or depolarization is called–
(*a*) resting membrane potential
(*b*) action potential
(*c*) both
(*d*) none of these

172. A complex chemical compound which when combined with inorganic phosphate forms ATP is called–
(*a*) adenosine phosphate
(*b*) adenosine diphosphate
(*c*) both
(*d*) none of these

173. A complex chemical compound formed with the energy released from food and stored in cells, particularly muscles is called–
(*a*) adenosine phosphate
(*b*) adenosine diphosphate
(*c*) adenosine triphosphate
(*d*) none of these

174. A neuron that conveys sensory impulses from a receptor to the Central Nervous System is called–
(*a*) afferent nerve (*b*) efferent nerve
(*c*) both (*d*) none of these

175. Any activity which is performed in the presence of oxygen is called–
(*a*) anaerobic (*b*) aerobic
(*c*) aerobic anaerobic (*d*) none of these

176. Anaerobic Exercises are those–
(*a*) which are performed in the presence of oxygen
(*b*) which are performed in the absence of oxygen
(*c*) which are performed in the high altitude with the help of oxygen
(*d*) none of these

177. A compound that promotes tissue building is called–
(*a*) caffeine (*b*) amphetamine
(*c*) anabolic steroid (*d*) none of these

178. A Synthetically structured drug which produces stimulation of the C.N.S. is called–

(a) caffeine (b) amphetamine
(c) anabolic steroid (d) none of these

179. Lack of sufficient red blood cell or haemoglobin is called–
(a) anaemia (b) hydrophobia
(c) pyria (d) none of these

180. ATP-PCSYSTEM is–
(a) an aerobic energy system in which carbohydrate is broken down and ATP is produced–
(b) an anaerobic energy system in which fat is broken down and ATP is produced
(c) an anacrobic energy system in which ATP is manufactured when phosphocreatine is broken down
(d) none of these

181. Contraction (Systole) and Relaxation (Diastole) of the heart is called–
(a) ventrical cycle (b) cardiac cycle
(c) atrial cycle (d) none of these

182. The shortening of a muscle during contraction is called–
(a) eccentric contraction
(b) concentric contraction
(c) isometric contraction
(d) none of these

183. The lengthening of muscle during contraction is called–
(a) eccentric contraction
(b) concentric contraction
(c) isometric contraction
(d) none of these

184. Contraction in which tension is developed, but there is no change in the length of the muscle is called–
(a) eccentric contraction
(b) isotonic contraction
(c) isometric contraction
(d) none of these

185. Contraction in which the muscle shortens with varying tension while lifting a constant load is called–
(a) concentric contraction
(b) isotonic contraction
(c) isometric contraction
(d) none of these

186. Awareness of the body position is called–
(a) aesthetic sense (b) balance
(c) kinesthetic sense (d) none of these

187. Amenorrhea is an–
(a) abnormal cessation of mensuration
(b) beginning of mensuration
(c) cessation of mensuration after the age of 45
(d) none of these

188. The portion of oxygen used to resynthesize and restore ATP and PC in muscle following exercise is called–
(a) alactacid O_2 debt (b) lactic O_2
(c) both (d) none of these

189. That portion of recovery O_2 use to remove accumulated Lactic acid from the blood is called–
(a) alactacid O_2 debt (b) lactacid O_2
(c) both (d) none of these

190. ATP is stored in–
(a) liver (b) muscle
(c) nerve cell (d) none of these

191. The immediate source of energy is–
(a) ATP (b) carbohydrate
(c) fat (d) none of these

192. The removal and Examination of tissue from the Living cell is called–
(a) M.R.I. (b) biopsy
(c) X-ray (d) none of these

193. A state of discomfort or decreased efficiency result from prolonged or excessive exercise is called–
(a) oxygen debt (b) second wind
(c) fatigue (d) none of these

194. A phenomenon characterized by a sudden distress of fatigue during early in the exercise to a more comfortable, less stressful feeling later in exercise is called–
(a) oxygen debt (b) second wind
(c) fatigue (d) none of these

195. A heat illness caused by fatigue resulting from prolonged exposure to environmental heat–
(*a*) heat cramp (*b*) heat exhaustion
(*c*) heat illness (*d*) heat stroke

196. Incapacitation from excessive environmental heat–
(*a*) heat cramp (*b*) heat exhaustion
(*c*) heat illness (*d*) heat stroke

197. Heat illness characterized by painful muscular contraction, caused by prolonged exposure to environmental heat–
(*a*) heat illness (*b*) heat stress
(*c*) heat cramp (*d*) none of these

198. An often fatal illness characterized by high body temperature, hot dry skin or unconsciousness caused by excessive exposure to environmental heat is called–
(*a*) heat cramp (*b*) heat stroke
(*c*) heat illness (*d*) none of these

199. A series of chemical reactions occurring in mitochondria, in which electron combine with O_2 to form water and ATP is resynthesized is called–
(*a*) hydrogen transport system
(*b*) electron transport system
(*c*) krebcycle
(*d*) none of these

200. A protein compound that speeds up chemical reactions–
(*a*) glycogen (*b*) enzyme
(*c*) myoglobin (*d*) none of these

201. The area in the centre of a band, where the cross bridges and action are absent–
(*a*) Z-Line (*b*) H-Zone
(*c*) I-Band (*d*) None of these

202. The cell membrance of a muscle fibre is called–
(*a*) sarcomere (*b*) sarcolema
(*c*) sarcoplasm (*d*) none of these

203. The smallest functional unit of a muscle fibre is called–
(*a*) sarcomere (*b*) sarcolema
(*c*) sarcoplasm (*d*) none of these

204. A nerve that conveys impulse from a receptor to the central nervous system is called–
(*a*) motor nerve (*b*) sensory nerve
(*c*) both (*d*) none of these

205. The amount of air inspired or expired per breath is called–
(*a*) lung volume (*b*) tidal volume
(*c*) vital capacity (*d*) none of these

206. The amount of O_2 required or consumed over and above resting level during recovery phase of an activity is called–
(*a*) high aerobic capacity
(*b*) high anaerobic capacity
(*c*) both
(*d*) none of these

207. Aerobic capacity contributes to–
(*a*) endurance development
(*b*) strength development
(*c*) agility development
(*d*) power development

208. Lactic acid is a by-product of–
(*a*) aerobic glycolysis
(*b*) anaerobic glycolysis
(*c*) both
(*d*) none of these

209. Red muscle fibre have–
(*a*) high aerobic capacity
(*b*) high anaerobic capacity
(*c*) both
(*d*) none of these

210. The final path way for aerobic metabolism are–
(*a*) krebs cycle
(*b*) electron transport system
(*c*) both
(*d*) none of these

211. The major food fuel during exercise of short duration is–
(*a*) fat (*b*) protein
(*c*) carbohydrate (*d*) none of these

212. The major food fuel during exercise of long duration is–
(*a*) fat (*b*) protein
(*c*) carbohydrate (*d*) none of these

213. White or pink muscle fibre have–
(*a*) high aerobic capacity
(*b*) high anaerobic capacity
(*c*) both
(*d*) none of these

214. The concept of O_2 debt was originally developed by–
(*a*) Hillary Kreb (*b*) Hill
(*c*) Mc. Loy (*d*) None of these

215. Portion of connective tissue which covers each muscle fibre or cell is called–
(*a*) epimysium (*b*) endimysium
(*c*) fasciculli (*d*) none of these

216. The muscles cells are grouped together to form muscle bundles called–
(*a*) fassiculli (*b*) endomysium
(*c*) epimysium (*d*) none of these

217. Perimysium is–
(*a*) connective tissue which covers each muscle fibre
(*b*) a connective tissue which covers the muscle bundle or group of muscle cell
(*c*) both
(*d*) none of these

218. A connective tissue which covers entire muscle fibre is–
(*a*) endomysium (*b*) perimysium
(*c*) epimysium (*d*) none of these

219. During an aerobic exercise energy to working muscles is supplied by–
(*a*) phosphogen system
(*b*) lactic acid system
(*c*) both
(*d*) none of these

220. A warming-up serves to–
(*a*) decrease in heart rate
(*b*) increase in body and muscle temperature
(*c*) increase in lung volume
(*d*) none of these

ANSWERS

1	2	3	4	5	6	7	8	9	10
(*b*)	(*a*)	(*c*)	(*a*)	(*b*)	(*d*)	(*c*)	(*b*)	(*a*)	(*a*)
11	**12**	**13**	**14**	**15**	**16**	**17**	**18**	**19**	**20**
(*a*)	(*b*)	(*b*)	(*a*)	(*d*)	(*b*)	(*b*)	(*c*)	(*c*)	(*b*)
21	**22**	**23**	**24**	**25**	**26**	**27**	**28**	**29**	**30**
(*a*)	(*c*)	(*d*)	(*d*)	(*a*)	(*c*)	(*c*)	(*a*)	(*a*)	(*b*)
31	**32**	**33**	**34**	**35**	**36**	**37**	**38**	**39**	**40**
(*b*)	(*c*)	(*d*)	(*b*)	(*b*)	(*b*)	(*a*)	(*b*)	(*c*)	(*c*)
41	**42**	**43**	**44**	**45**	**46**	**47**	**48**	**49**	**50**
(*c*)	(*d*)	(*c*)	(*c*)	(*d*)	(*a*)	(*c*)	(*b*)	(*d*)	(*d*)
51	**52**	**53**	**54**	**55**	**56**	**57**	**58**	**59**	**60**
(*b*)	(*d*)	(*c*)	(*a*)	(*d*)	(*a*)	(*b*)	(*c*)	(*a*)	(*c*)
61	**62**	**63**	**64**	**65**	**66**	**67**	**68**	**69**	**70**
(*a*)	(*b*)	(*d*)	(*d*)	(*b*)	(*d*)	(*d*)	(*c*)	(*a*)	(*a*)
71	**72**	**73**	**74**	**75**	**76**	**77**	**78**	**79**	**80**
(*b*)	(*c*)	(*b*)	(*a*)	(*c*)	(*b*)	(*b*)	(*a*)	(*d*)	(*b*)
81	**82**	**83**	**84**	**85**	**86**	**87**	**88**	**89**	**90**
(*b*)	(*b*)	(*b*)	(*b*)	(*c*)	(*a*)	(*a*)	(*b*)	(*d*)	(*c*)

91	92	93	94	95	96	97	98	99	100
(d)	(d)	(d)	(c)	(b)	(b)	(d)	(b)	(a)	(d)
101	**102**	**103**	**104**	**105**	**106**	**107**	**108**	**109**	**110**
(b)	(c)	(c)	(d)	(d)	(c)	(b)	(c)	(d)	(a)
111	**112**	**113**	**114**	**115**	**116**	**117**	**118**	**119**	**120**
(c)	(b)	(c)	(c)	(a)	(b)	(c)	(c)	(c)	(d)
121	**122**	**123**	**124**	**125**	**126**	**127**	**128**	**129**	**130**
(a)	(a)	(b)	(d)	(b)	(b)	(b)	(a)	(c)	(d)
131	**132**	**133**	**134**	**135**	**136**	**137**	**138**	**139**	**140**
(b)	(b)	(b)	(b)	(b)	(a)	(c)	(b)	(a)	(c)
141	**142**	**143**	**144**	**145**	**146**	**147**	**148**	**149**	**150**
(c)	(b)	(a)	(c)	(b)	(d)	(b)	(b)	(c)	(c)
151	**152**	**153**	**154**	**155**	**156**	**157**	**158**	**159**	**160**
(b)	(c)	(b)	(a)	(b)	(c)	(a)	(c)	(b)	(b)
161	**162**	**163**	**164**	**165**	**166**	**167**	**168**	**169**	**170**
(c)	(a)	(c)	(b)	(c)	(b)	(d)	(a)	(a)	(a)
171	**172**	**173**	**174**	**175**	**176**	**177**	**178**	**179**	**180**
(b)	(b)	(c)	(a)	(b)	(b)	(b)	(b)	(a)	(c)
181	**182**	**183**	**184**	**185**	**186**	**187**	**188**	**189**	**190**
(b)	(b)	(a)	(c)	(b)	(c)	(a)	(a)	(b)	(b)
191	**192**	**193**	**194**	**195**	**196**	**197**	**198**	**199**	**200**
(a)	(b)	(c)	(b)	(b)	(c)	(c)	(b)	(c)	(b)
201	**202**	**203**	**204**	**205**	**206**	**207**	**208**	**209**	**210**
(b)	(b)	(b)	(b)	(b)	(d)	(a)	(b)	(a)	(b)
211	**212**	**213**	**214**	**215**	**216**	**217**	**218**	**219**	**220**
(b)	(c)	(b)	(b)	(b)	(a)	(b)	(c)	(c)	(b)

UNIT-IV

LEARNING PROCESS

These are the definitions of learning by scholars.

1. **Skinner:** "Learning includes both acquisition and retention."
2. **Pressy:** "Learning represents experience that leads to a change or adjustment in performance and to the acquisition of new ways of behaving."
3. **Gates:** "Learning is modification of behaviour through experience."
4. **Crow and Crow:** "Learning involves the acquisition of habits, knowledge and attitudes."
5. **J.P. Guilford:** "We may define the term very broadly by saying that learning is any change in behaviour, resulting from behaviour." In this definition, a distinction between change in behaviour, due to maturity and change in behaviour due to learning is unavoidable though both these activities occur simultaneously.
6. **Garrett** - "Learning is that activity by virtue of which we organise our responses with new habits." Thus, the element of organization in learning is one the importance of which cannot be over emphasized. Guilford too, has written that the meaning of learning is, inevitably, an organization of behaviour. Thus, in learning to ride a cycle we have to organise the learning of turning the pedal, balancing the handle, etc., in order to be reasonably safe with the vehicle. It is another matter that a person does not learn this organization at the outset and that he may take much longer time to learn to balance the handle than the time he may take to learn to turn the pedal. But his learning of the art of cycling will be completed only when he accomplishes this organization.
7. **R.S. Woodworth:** The learning of a new acting is an addition to the person's store of experiences. Clarifying the statement further, Woodworth says that reinforcement too, is an indispensable element of the act of learning because this activity forms only successful responses and weeds out the unsuccessful responses.
8. **To quote Woodworth:** "An activity may be called learning insofar as it develops the individual in any way, good or bad and makes his environment and experiences different from what it would otherwise have been."
9. **Gardner Mulphy:** The persons, who stress external behaviour consider learning to be a change of behaviour while those who lay emphasis on internal changes are convinced that learning is change in the perspective of the individual. Combining these two view, Gardner Murphy wrote that, "From this point of view it would be legitimate to regard learning as a modification, both of behaviour and of the way of perceiving."
10. **Hilgard:** Many examples may be presented from every day life like, memorizing a poem, working at the typewriter, manipulating knife and fork, etc. The following definition of learning given by Hilgard is an essence of all the foregoing definitions offered by other psychologists, "Learning is the process by which an activity originates or is changed through reaching to an encountered situation, provided that the characteristics of the change in activity cannot be explained on the basis of native response tendencies, maturity or temporary status of the organism." Despite the fact that this definition is unsatisfactory because of the shortcomings, it may serve its purpose for the time being.

Different Types of Learning

1. Motor Learning
2. Perceptual Learning
3. Manual Skill Learning
4. Conceptual Learning
5. Appreciational Learning
6. Associate Learning
7. Attitudinal Learning

Motivation

Motivation is the first requisite of efficient learning. It may be defined as "the means of developing proper attitudes in the learner towards the activity". According to another definition "Motivation is the name for the psycho physiological processes that lays the foundation of goal seeking activity." In education we are interested in modifications brought about in the behaviour of the learner but all individuals do not learn the same thing and at the same rate in a given situation. It is also observed that certain aspects of the material learned last for a longer time than the other aspects. Sometimes we want to learn something but are unable to do so. All these differences are due to the fact that different learning processes are differently motivated and different aspects of a given situation do not motivate us to the same extent. Thus the basic problem of all teaching is to arouse adequate motivation that can lead to the achievement of desired goals. All individual always works much below his working capacity and reason his Achievement Quotient (A.Q) is never hundred percent. The simple learning from its proper goals by adequate motivation. A teacher who can do this will find that the output of work will be multiplied many times and that learning will not be only speeded up but will be better retained and better liked. In the field of physical education, a number of devices and methods are available which may be utilized by a teacher to help in motivating the efforts of his students.

Motivation is of two types:

(*i*) ***Intrinsic Motivation:*** This type of motivation involves the making of the subject matter of study interesting and meaningful. Every activity may be some-what interesting and have some intrinsic worth. The teacher by making the good or bad points of taking part in an activity clear, can motivate the students. By explaining the meanings of the subject in detail in the case of general education, he can create interest, attention and love for the subject among his students. Such a situation when the student knows the meaning and real value of an activity motivates him to attend to that activity and thus helps in better learnings. This type of motivation works at an age when the students are able to understand the meaning of an activity. Teaching children who are immature and unable to understand the meaning of an activity has no meaning at all. For this reason intrinsic motivation has its limitations.

(*ii*) ***Extrinsic Motivation:*** As already stated, intrinsic motivation fails where mental maturity is lacking but there is no such precondition for extrinsic motivation. It works in all ages and in almost all cases since its application is based on certain inner tendencies (which motivate our behaviour). Examples of such tendencies are competition, assertion, curiosity, possession and status etc., such tendencies are utilized in the methods adopted for teaching.

Techniques of Motivation

Important extrinsic and intrinsic techniques of motivation are as follows:

1. **Reward and Punishment:** Student endeavours to do the best in order to get reward. He becomes pleased when he is given reward and greater enthusiasm on the part of the student is shown. Following things must be kept in mind while giving reward to an individual:
   (*a*) The nature or amount of reward should be according to the level of performance. Additional reward is always fatal for the future progress of an individual.
   (*b*) Individual must know the importance of reward. If reward is given to so many individuals at a time, the reward loses its validity.

(c) Reward should not be traditional or a routine activity. Different types of rewards should be given at different occasions.

(d) Reward should have some monetary or social value.

As far as punishment is concerned its fear leads an individual not to do unwanted jobs. The child comes to the class with full preparation in order to avoid punishment. Following things must be kept in mind before assigning any punishment.

(a) Punishment should not be regular. Such punishment can make the children habitual to them.

(b) Punishment should not be so severe. Such punishment can create hatred in the minds of children towards the whole system.

(c) Punishment should be given keeping in view the mental and physical resistance of children.

(d) Punishment should be judiciously distributed to all guilty persons.

Researches have made it clear that reward is better technique of motivation than punishment. Punishment is fatal to the psychological development of the organism also. So, punishment should be avoided as much as possible.

2. **Praise and Blame:** When child is praised at his successes, he is overjoyed. As a result he works better than before. Following points must be kept in view while using praise as a technique of motivation.

(a) If an organism is praised at every big or small successes randomly, he will be addicted to listening the words of praise. As a result no new behaviour is created as a result of praise.

(b) Weaker children should be praised even at their small bits of successes. While talented children should be praised only when they have really done something very unique.

(c) Praise technique should be applied according to changing ratio schedule, i.e., sometimes, it should be used and sometimes not and the subject must not know at what time this is to be given.

As far as blame is concerned, students are directly blamed for their failures and they are made ashamed. But excess use of blame as a technique of motivation may frustrate the child. Following points must be kept in mind before blaming the students on their failures.

(a) Positive efforts of a child must be praised first before him on his failure.

(b) Students should not be solely made responsible for their failure. Other related factors and conditions must also be included in the list of factors causing failures in life.

(c) The language of the blame should not be insulting for students. The self respect of every individual must be recognised.

3. **Success and Failure :** Success creates self confidence among individuals and possibility of more successes increases. Teacher creates such an environment in the class in which all the barriers in the way of success are removed. Failure can also work as a source of motivation especially the talented students accept the failure as a challenge for them. In order to use this technique in the classroom situation, the teacher presents such problems in the class which students are unable to solve. The bright students accept this challenge for future and thus they are motivated for work.

4. **Competition and Cooperation:** The feeling of competition is universal in humans. In the classroom situations weak students compare themselves with their own group and bright students compare their achievements with that of bright group students. In this way the whole class is motivated. In games and sports too competition works as the best motivator. Every sports person does harder and harder efforts to raise his performance level. Such type of competition is called individual competition. Team competition also works as a good motivating force. These two types of competitive feelings are aroused by the teacher in the class in order to motivate the pupils.

The utility of cooperation as a technique of motivation is very limited. Here students are asked to work with mutual cooperation so that every one in the group may get opportunity to develop. Project method of teaching is a good example of this technique.

5. **Knowledge of Progress :** It is a traditional method of motivating the students that they are regularly told about their progress on the basis of formative evaluation. When they come to know about their achievements, they work harder to raise this level due to the feed back obtained from the knowledge of the progress. Teacher and sports teacher should regularly evaluate the achievement of students and students should be informed immediately about this. If any delay is made in evaluation or its reporting, the teachers will not be able to give any feed back to his students. For this purpose regular tests should be conducted in the class and they should be evaluated with no delay. If evaluation and its reporting takes much time, students forget their mistakes or actual activities and as a result, they do not get any feed back from these.
6. **Novelty:** Researches have proved that monotony makes a man bored. In order to motivate such persons in their task novelty and change in the approach is essential. In the class room situation a teachers brings about novelty in his method of teaching at regular intervals. This makes the students come across to new experiences at every movement. Level of student must be kept in view while introducing novelty in the situation so that this novelty may not work as a bouncer.
7. **Aspiration Level:** Level of aspiration has a direct relationship with the objectives of life. An individual can achieve the objectives of his life when his aspiration level is high. A teacher tries to raise this level as much high as possible but it is always matched with the mental or physical potentialities of the pupils. If this level of aspiration is higher than physical or mental level, student will get frustrated at their successive failure. Contrary to this if this level is lower than the physical or mental level, it will reduce the activities of student and they will develop inferiority complex.

Theories of Motivation

1. **Instinct Theory:** This theory of motivation was propounded by an English psychologist McDougall. He pleaded that every human being has some innate powers or instincts. These instincts work as motives also and influence our behaviour. Under the influence of these instincts relationship between the object and the individual is established. Sentiments are aroused as a result of this. These sentiments organise an individual's emotional life and bring about stability in his behaviour. Thus sentiments are an important factor behind the force of motivation. He explained the importance of self respects regarding sentiments. An individual's character is evaluated in terms of the stability of his self respect. If organisation of moral sentiments is more stable than the sentiments regarding the self respect, the character of the person will be strong.
2. **Psychoanalytic Theory:** (By Freud, Young and Adler) According to them conscious plays-main role is controlling an individual's behaviour. As against unconscious mind there is the role of repression. Repression is the elimination of painful and unhealthy experiences from the conscious mind. Thus repression is a defence mechanism with the help of which an individual tries to adjust partially. This repression is necessary because as child grows many of his need and feelings are disliked by the people which were earlier liked. When these needs are eliminated from the conscious mind, they are collected into unconscious mind and affect human behaviour indirectly. Sometimes these repressed needs come to the conscious level also when they receive any stimulus from out side. Thus according to these psychologist

human behaviour is influenced by such motives also bout which he is totally unaware.

3. **Maslow's Need theory:** This theory has already been explained under the head of Maslow's Hierarchy of Needs.

4. **Social Theory :** This theory is of two type—

   (*a*) **Cultural Pattern Theory (by Mead & Benedict) :** According to this theory, behaviour of a person is influenced by the respective culture in which be lives. For example individuals of those castes which have strict controlling system on their members become foolish, dry and short tempered when they grow. On the contrary, the castes in which children are behaved affectionately, they manifest considerate behaviour when they grow. Thus behaviour is very much influenced by the pattern of rearing of a person. In the class room situation, a teacher can motivate his students by his own behaviour.

   (*b*) **Field Theory (by Kurt Levin):** According to this theory, the behaviour of an individual is not determined by his qualities or personality traits but all those forces which act between an individual and his environment. Thus there is a close relationship between an individual and his environment. In the class room situation a child can be motivated by creating an environment suitable to the child.

5. **Drive Theory :** This theory is somewhat similar to need theory of Maslow. According to this theory an individual is driven to act when certain biological needs create some inner tension which is called drive. Thus drive is the primary cause of motivation.

   The drawback of this theory is that it is helpless to explain why an individual, in the absence of inner drive behaves in a particular situation due to the effect of his environment as is explained by the social theory of motivation.

6. **Incentive Theory:** According to this theory, external incentives such as rewards, monetary benefits, promotion in the social status etc. can also motivate an individual to act in a certain direction.

7. **Expectancy Theory:** According to this theory an individual is not actually getting any reward or monetary benefits but the expectation of getting such a reward or benefits can motivate him to do the job in the best manner possible. In the field of games a sportsman can be motivated to perform his best by giving him some incentive not at present but in the future.

8. **Learning or behaviour Theory (Clark Hall):** According to this theory an individual's behaviour depends on the satisfaction or dissatisfaction of his needs. When his needs are satisfied, his psychological tensions are reduced and he retains the reaction of his learnt behaviour. When his organic needs are satisfied, he learns to link the social conditions with his primary needs and retains that particular behaviour.

9. **Motivation Hygiene Theory (Fredrick Herzberg):** This theory was indoctrinated in the field of industry and commence. First Herzberg interviewed farmers, account officers, nurses and house wives in Pistbarg University in 1966 and propounded this theory.

   According to this theory motives enhance the efficiency by providing comforts and satisfactions to the pupils. Motives keep them delighted by increasing their achievement on one hand and pupils get satisfied by their motives on the other. This is turn enriches learning. Since the effect of motives are positive and persists for a longer period of time, as a result motives develop the following feelings in the pupils.

   (*i*) Achievement
   (*ii*) Recognition
   (*iii*) Responsibility
   (*iv*) Advancement; and
   (*v*) Personal growth

   The above feelings are directly affected by hygienes factors. They are given further:

(*i*) Method of supervision
(*ii*) Condition of work
(*iii*) Inter-personal relations.
(*iv*) Social policy and administration.
(*v*) Status
(*vi*) Security

If level of these factors is low the individuals become unhappy. As a result learning outcomes fall. It can also develop negative attitude among the individual. Thus individuals can be motivated by raising the level of these six hygiene factors. This theory has direct application in the field of sports and education. The performance of Indian cricket team is low only because of low hygiene factors today. If organisational climate of the school is good, it will automatically increase the achievement of pupils. Therefore, good school administration is essential for all round development of pupils. If school administration is good pupils will automatically be motivated for higher achievement.

DIMENSIONS OF PERSONALITY

1. Physical Dimension: The physical body structure or the physique is the primary aspect or dimension of human personality and all other dimensions are subservient to it. No doubt that heredity has a very important role in the development of this aspect of personality, but heredity alone would be helpless if appropriate environment is not available, and vice–versa environment alone is not sufficient enough for development of physical aspect of personality as without genetic support, it would be without any base. It will be appropriate to suggest that genetics provide the plinth or base of personality and environment helps in raising a beautiful structure thereon.

The comments such as "he has got a wonderful personality" or "he is not having a good personality" are quite common. This common conception of personality reflects the importance attached to the physical dimension of personality by the society . We everyday hear that first impression is the last impression. This first impression, obviously, refers to one's physical appearance, i.e., the outward mask, and how one carries himself. Physique, i.e., the height structure and muscular framework, has profound effect on the onlookers. An individual possessing a well built physique tends to be more confident of himself . The manner or the way he carries himself, not only has aesthetic appeal, but is also a source of admiration for others. It has been generally observed that persons having weak, sick and deformed physique are not sure of themselves whereas persons having tall, robust and athletic built have commanding and effective appearance. Good physique and health do have positive relationship. A person having good healthy physique is able to mobilize all his resources to lead zestful and harmonious life. A healthy individual not only contributes to the welfare of the society but is an asset to it.

Physical dimension has attracted the attention of psychologists as well as physiologists from the time immemorial, almost since the start of our civilization. Classification of human beings on the basis of their physical built-up and structure is probably, the oldest type of classification in the history of our evolution.

Since early times there have been serious efforts to discover types of physique and to relate the same to various aspects of personality. *Naccarati* (1921) adopted a morphological index the ratio of height to weight, as the most satisfactory indicator of physical type, and gave three-fold classification :

1. *miscroplanchnics*, characterized by small trunks and development of the limbs in excess of the trunk (the thin, slender body build);
2. *macrosplanchnics* (*or megalosplanchnics*), denoted by large trunks, excessively developed (the short and fat body build); and
3. *normosplanchnics,* who show a harmonious development of physical constitution. **Hall** later on, classified persons into four types: *Muscular, thoracic, abdominal, and nervous.*

In the early twentieth century, *Kretchmer* in his book "Physique and Character" based his classification on three biological types according to physical structure, and using Greek terminology, described the same as :

1. Picknik (having round and fat bodies) who were good natured, happy sociable and easy going,
2. Athletic (having robust, well built, and balanced body) who were energetic, adjustable and social by temperament; and
3. Asthenic (having lean, thin long limbed, slender body structure) who were sensitive, imaginary, emotional and idealistic.

Berman suggested six body types on the assumption that one or two glands may have an ascendant function in a given individual :

1. *Thymocentric personality* marked by lack of inhibitory capacity, moral irresponsibility, criminality, and general incapacity to meet the demands of a taxing environment ;
2. *Thyroid personality*, having excessive activity, quick mentality, impulsiveness restlessness , and great energy;
3. *Adrenal personality*, having intense energy, vigour, and persistence in case of hyper adrenals, and in case of adrenal insufficiency revealing lack of energy, irritability, dullness, fatigability, and loss of appetite;
4. *Pituitary personality* which is of two types, one which tends to be masculine, and the other which tends to be feminine;
5. *Eidetic type personality*, who are perpetually restless, eternally unsatisfied, and who hold themselves aloof from others,
6. *Gonadocentric personality*, those lacking proper and normal development of masculinity.

In his book "the Varieties of Temperament" *Sheldon* based his classification on the temperamental and physical characteristics to provide three types of personalities :

1. *Endomorphic* (having round, fat, and soft bodies), who were fond of food, easy going, slow in reactions, and sociable.
2. *Mesomorphic* (having well developed, rugged and athletic body) who were adventurous, assertive, courageous, and having a liking for physical activity; and
3. *Ectomorphic* (having weak, fragile, and delicate body build) who were reserved, anxious pessimistic, and having inhibition towards physical activity.

2. Mental and Intellectual Dimension: A well built physical stature of an individual, devoid of mental and intellectual abilities, is just like a statue without life. The fact that human beings have been bestowed with higher mental and intellectual abilities, is an important distinguishing feature between them and other living organisms. Human personality loses its meaning if conceived without mind and intellect. Man is a psychophysical organism i.e. a mind and body unit and one part is incapable of effective survival without the other. It is the marvel of human intellect that has made it possible for us to explore the universe. Renowned psychologists, physiologists, scientists, philosophers, and leaders are known for their mental and intellectual abilities. Those of us who are more intelligent and mentally alert, react and respond quickly to any sort of stimulation, and understand the things in a better way, are always in an advantageous position in the society. Mental and intellectual capabilities of an individual help him in adjusting to new requirements, circumstances, and everchanging conditions of present day life in a most appropriate way. Importance of mental and intellectual dimension can never be over emphasized.

As with many other modern ideas it was the Greeks, especially *Hippocrats* who first introduced the concept of type on the basis of emotional or temperamental features of personality. He divided people into four types of temperamental personalities, on the basis of four fluids or "humours" i.e., black bile, yellow bile, blood and phlegm. As per his classification, predominance of any of these fluids gave an individual a unique and different type of temperament :

1. those who had predominance of black bile (melancholic) were considered bad tempered, depressed, dejected, and pessimistic;
2. those with yellow bile (choleric) were irritable, short tempered, strong and imaginative:
3. those having predominance of blood (sanguine) were light hearted, cheerful, and happy; and

4. those having predominance of phlegm (phlegmatic) were considered slow, cold indifferent, and unresolved.

Perhaps the best known and the most important classification of personality is given by *Jung*. He begins with the assumption of a fundamental life force or energy in human beings which tend to take one or the other of the two directions; either outward i.e. towards the external environment, or inward i.e. towards one's subjective life patterns. On this basis ,he divided the personality into two divisions extrovert and introvert. Each type, extrovert or introvert, is organized around one of the four-fold features : thinking , feeling, sensation or intuition. The extroverts have more self confidence, take more interest in others, are outgoing lively and realistic. They are very social and form friends quite easily. Actors, social and political leaders, etc. belong to this group. On the other hand, introverts are too self conscious, they are more interested in their own thoughts and ideas, are self centerd, shy, reserved, and lovers of solitude. They do not make friends easily and keep in background on social occasions. Philosophers, poets artists scientists etc. belong to this class. Doubting whether people can be divided into these two distinctive classes, it has been suggested that between these two extremes lie most of the people, who have been labelled as *Ambiverts*. The ambiverts are a mixture of both the extremes in a balanced manner. Ambiverts are neither out-going nor reserved to themselves, they are able to adjust themselves with any situation.

Sheldon, apart from providing classification on the basis of physique, also gave three types of personalities on the basis of temperament :

1. Vicerotonic (happy outgoing and lovers of food);
2. Somatotonic (assertive, bold and risk taking) and
3. Cerebrotonic (studious, tense, and introverted).

3. Social Dimension: Inherently, by nature man is a social being. He has learnt speaking, reading, writing and behaving with others from the society in which he lives. If he is isolated completely from the society, he will not be able to survive for long. Human beings are not only gregarious, liking to be in sight of his fellows, but also have an innate propensity to get themselves noticed, and noticed favourably. Man besides gratification of his biological needs and values, must fulfill such emergent social values as status, power, affection and good will. This is necessary in order that he may have a feeling of being at home in the social world. Sociological and psychological tendencies are intimately related to each other. Psychologically each individual is born with specific inherent attitudes, interest, tendencies, and capacities. In order to be an acceptable member of the society, he has to mould and modify his behaviour, learn and acquire various manners qualities and etiquettes, and has to follow the rules, customs and traditions of the society. The social interaction enables an individual to develop social attributes like tolerance, cooperation and fair play. It inculcates the spirit of service and sacrifice, and cultivates a sense of responsibility and duty besides providing social efficiency. It can thus be said that the essence of an individual's development is the development of the society.

An individual has to discipline all his wishes and desires and be prepared for sacrifices in order to live smoothly in the society. The real recognition of one's personality comes from the society in which he lives. The truth is that both, the individual and the society, are mutually inter-dependent and inseparable. One cannot exist without the other. Both develop each other integrally and harmoniously, with full sense of responsibility.

Undoubtedly sociability is a very important quality of human beings. The manner in which he interacts with other members of the society, how he influences their work and conduct, and how he himself is influenced by others is an important aspect of personality. Sociality or social dimension of personality has much wider implications than the other dimensions of personality. Social dimension is the sum of integration of those traits which categorize the typical reactions of one person towards other persons. Social dimension is, essentially, a matter of how one responds to himself and others.

The possibility of classifying people in terms of their principal social roles has been recognized since long. Theophrastus, a disciple of Aristotle, in the third century before Christian era, attempted to classify the role and status of individuals in society. In his book "Ethical Character" he has described three types. "the flatterer", "the boor", and "the coward". *Lateron*, *Thomas* and *Znnaiaecki* predicted three types of personality development :

1. the philistine, or a practical man, who over emphasizes the wish for security and safety,
2. the Bohemian, who inclines towards new experiences, is flighty, and has consistent interests which determine much of his behaviour; and
3. the creative man, who though relatively stable, possesses the capacity for modification of attitudes and wishes in terms of some goal or aim of a creative sort in the fields of art, religion, politics, economics etc.

Burgess, while attempting a sociological interpretation of personality, offered a classification of three types of personality :

1. the objective or direct, with such features as equability, enthusiasm, franknes, and aggressiveness,
2. introspective or indirect, marked by imaginative, sensitive, and inhibited forms of thinking, and
3. the psychopathic or perverse, categorized by eccentricity, egocentrism, emotional instability, and strong sense of inferiority.

Basing his analysis of personality on one's reactions towards society, **Spranger** suggested six categories :

1. *Theoretical* – metaphysician and pure scientists,
2. *Economic* – Typical business man.
3. *Esthetic* – sensuous gratification unreliable,
4. *Social* – interested in fellow beings and social movements ,
5. *Political* – desires power over others, and
6. *Religious* – either mystic or missionary type.

4. Emotional Dimension: Emotion is an all important factor in life and occupies a very prominent position in our daily life. A life devoid of emotions is insipid and unattractive. Love, affection, etc are not the only emotions by which our life is made worth living. Emotions make our life interesting as well as dull, happy as well as unhappy. These are present in each and every living organism at all the stages of development. Emotions are personal in nature, and differ from an individual to individual. A child is not born with innate emotional experiences but he learns to show different emotions by experience. Every person responds to the situations as a result of emotions differently. Every emotional experience involves many physical and physiological changes in our body. Emotions increase energy mobilization in our body. The effect of emotions on our body may be beneficial or harmful. According to ***Ruch***, " Emotions play a vital part in our motivational pattern. Life without emotions would be, virtually a life without motion." They determine as to what kind of personal and social adjustments an individual will make, not only as a child but also as an adult. They are responsible for finest human characteristics as well as for the most horrible and mean things of life. Dominance of unpleasant emotions is harmful to good personal and social adjustments and any interference with good emotional development will play havoc with an individual's adjustment in life. Since control over the life environment becomes increasingly difficult as we grow up, we should learn to control emotions and develop emotional tolerance – thc ability to accept and adjust to unpleasant emotional experiences. A well controlled person has the ability to quickly control shift on emotional reaction. On the basis of emotions, **Morgan and Gilliland** classified personality into four types :

1. Elated (happy and optimistic),
2. Depressed (pessimistic and emotional)
3. Irritable (short tempered), and
4. Unstable (Unbalanced and emotional).

PERSONALITY TRAITS

In every day life, no one, not even psychologists, doubt that underlying the conduct of a mature person there are characteristic dispositions or traits. We usually think of personality as being made up of traits. Psychologists have defined a trait as a mode of behaviour. Traits are not creations in the mind of the observer, nor are they verbal fictions; they are accepted biophysical facts, actual psychological dispositions . These are specific qualities of bahaviour or adjustive patterns, such as reactions to frustrations, ways of meeting problems, specific patterns, aggressive or defensive behaviour, and outgoing or withdrawing behaviour in the presence of others. The traits are outward signs of dynamic forces that act and interact in an infinite number of ways. That is why the integration of these traits or personality – is never the same in any two individuals. In the opinion of *Gordon Allport*, the personality traits are dynamic and flexible dispositions, resulting, at least in part, from the integration of specific habits, expressing characteristic modes of adaptation to one's surroundings." *M. A. May*, in his article "Problems of Measuring Character and Personality:" has concluded that "traits are only convenient names given to types or qualities of behaviour which have elements in common. They are not psychological entities, but rather categories for the classification of habits". An individual's patterns of behaviour are influenced by the sanctions and restrictions imposed by the social environment wherein he grows up. As he develops towards maturity, many characteristic traits tend to become a permanent habit, and his behaviour reflects inner adjustments towards life situations attained through varied experiences at home, in school, and in social set ups. These adjustments have direct influence on the kind of behaviour expected from him to the normal life situation.

Traits are a product of learning, though they are based on hereditary foundations. They are moulded mainly by child's training in the home and school, and by imitating a person with whom the child identifies himself. Later the child will emulate the traits of members of the peer group, developing characteristic methods of adjustment accepted and approved by that group. Traits continue in a relatively unchanged form over a period of time and can, however be modified with experience. Traits are not directly observable; they are inferred. We do not directly observe a trait in another person. We observe specific indictions, acts, and verbalizations, and from these we generalize and draw conclusions. If we see an individual lose his temper with slight provocation in several situations, we say that he has a trait of irritability. What we have observed, is in essence, a correlation, a functional consistency across situations. Traits are not at all times active, but they are persistent even when latent.

Each person is unique, not only by virtue of an inherited physiological organism which will not be exactly like that of anyone else, but more importantly, by virtue of his unique pattern of experiences which induce perceptions distinctively his own. Strictly speaking, no two persons have precisely the same trait. Though each of two men may be aggressive, the style and range of the aggression in each case will be noticeably different. In contrast to this position, it must be noted that all of us have certain experiences in common. This fact enables us to quite safely assume that certain common traits can also be identified in a population having a fairly uniform cultural milieu. However, in the strict sense of the definition of traits, only the individual trait is a true trait : (a) because traits are always in individuals and not in the community at large, and (b) because they develop and generalize into dynamic dispositions in unique ways according to the experiences of each individual . The common trait is not a true trait at all, but is merely a measurable aspect of complex individual traits.

Classification of personality Traits

In every personality there are traits of major significance and traits of minor significance. **Allport** was of the view that traits may exist at several levels, and classified the same as cardinal traits, central traits, and secondary traits :

(i) ***Cardinal Traits*** : Occasionally, some traits are so pervasive and so outstanding in life that they deserve to be called the *cardinal traits*. These are so dominant that there are few activities that cannot be traced. Directly or indirectly to their influence, these are so powerful that they permeate every aspect of an individual's life. No such trait can remain hidden for long; an individual is known by it, and may even become famous for it. Though pervasive and pivotal, a cardinal trait still remains within the personality; it never coincides with it.

(ii) ***Central Traits :*** Next in the hierarchy are a handful of distinguishable central traits. *Central traits* are those which are usually mentioned in careful letters of recommendations, in rating scale where the rater starts the outstanding characteristics of the individual, or in brief verbal descriptions of a person. These traits are the characteristics that are, although important, but not as all pervasive as cardinal traits, e g aggressiveness, kindness, etc.

(iii) ***Secondary Traits :*** On still lower pedestal, and less important level, are *secondary traits*, which are less conspicuous, less generalized, less consistent and less often called into play than central traits. They may escape the notice of all but close acquaintances. These traits are characteristics that emerge as situational preferences and behaviours.

Certain traits are readily observable; they appear in interpersonal contacts, in one's way of doing of a job, in response to questionnaires. *Cattell* has designated them as Surface traits. Cheerfulness, liveliness and quarrelsomeness are such traits. On the other hand are Source traits, which may be thought as underlying structures, expressed not directly but through the medium of surface traits. Source traits and surface traits are interchangeable means of personality description. A single surface trait may be a result of the action of one, two, or more underlying source traits. Source traits are thus, in part explanatory whereas surface traits are merely descriptive. Source traits have wider utility, stability, and meaning than surface traits. Source traits spring from influences that may be either in environmental objects and institutions – in which case they are called "*environmental mould traits*" or from sources within the constitution of an individual, in which case they are called "constitutional traits". Surface traits may be a combination of both these two. Both the source and surface traits are likely to vary with the cultural pattern and with the range of genetics and racial constitutions in the population. After examining 4500 traits, Cattell stated that there were 46 surface traits and 16 source traits, Lateron, he added three more source traits (zestfulness , excitability, and boorishness) in this list.

Cattell postulated that human behaviour is a result of interaction between external situations and an individual's traits. He has further divided personality traits into three categories on the basis of qualities of personality; temperamental traits (being persistently irritable, easy going, or bold), ability traits (such as intelligence and skill, while dealing complex situations) and dynamic traits (such as motivation, interest and attitude). He further sub-divided dynamic traits into attitudes, sentiments, and urges.

Functioning of the Traits

Two views have been put forward with regard to the functioning of the traits. According to one of them it can be said that behaviour of an individual is regulated from within and is independent of external environment i.e. a sincere person will be sincere in all the situations while dealing with other people. This approach may be referred as the *theory of "unitary"* or *general traits*. On the other hand, some psychologists while explaining the functioning of the traits lay emphasis on behaviour response while facing the demands of situation rather than upon any integration of traits within the individual. This view has been labelled as *the theory of "specificity"*of traits. On the basis of extensive investigations, Cattell has developed 16 Personality Factor Questionnaire to assess the dimensions of personality.

FACTORS AFFECTING DEVELOPMENT OF PERSONALITY: (HEREDITY AND ENVIRONMENT)

Our planet is inhabited by countless species, and all the species have some features unique to themselves which distinguish them not only from other species but within themselves also. Each living organism is born with a unique genetic code, a genetic blueprint , which is passed on to it from its parents. Many authors have termed this as Nature. Once born, every living organism is subjected to diverse environmental conditions, some favourable and some hostile, which influence its growth and development . This environment has been termed as Nurture.

Heredity

Human life starts from a single cell, the zygot, produced by the union of two germ cells, one each from the parents. It is this tiny cell which contains all that a child is to biologically inherit from his parents .Genes are very small units present on the chromosomes carried by this cell, it has 23 pairs of chromosomes. These genes are the most powerful indicators of what is being passed on to the child. Genes do not just orchestrate our growth before birth and then leave us alone. Instead, they are "turning on" and "turning off" in patterned ways throughout our life span and they are partly responsible for attributes and behaviour patterns that we carry with us through out our lives. Unique individual genetic make-ups cause us to develop and age in our own ways. The genetic make up or genotype determines our physiological and even some psychological peculiarities. These genotypes or the cluster of genes, transmit the sum total of the traits which we are to inherit from our parents. Heredity is the nature's process of passing on certain physical and mental characteristics from one generation to another. Heredity is the development potential one receives from its parents, which may be similar or dissimilar to the parents.

Environment

Environment, plays a very significant role in shaping one's personality. According to **Woodworth** "Environment covers all the outside factors that have acted on the individual since he began life." Soon after his birth, a child is exposed to complex external environment physical as well as social, or cultural.

Heredity Versus Environment

The natural question, that then, arises is whether it is the heredity (the nature) or the environment (the nurture) that plays the 'title' role in one's development. Psychologists like *Galton, Karl Pearson* and others hold the view that heredity is more important than the environment. On the other hand, *Locke, Watson* and others have completely divergent opinion and believe that environment alone is responsible for moulding and shaping human personality. To understand the implication of this controversy, let us examine the example of a plant's life cycle. The seed, on whose germination depends the emergence of the plant, has within it all the characteristics that the plant is to have : its type — whether it will be a bush or a tall tree, its shape and size, shape and structure of its leaves, shape, colour and even fragrance of its flowers the type and taste of its fruit and even the mode of dispersal of seeds for further propagation, are all encoded therein. In short, the seed contains the whole life story of the plant. But the climatic conditions of the place where it is sown, availability of water and sunlight, the composition of the soil, mineral and nutritional elements available in the soil, all influence (positively or negatively) to give shape to the final product, the plant, i.e., the expression of the traits within the seed is to some extent dependent upon the environment. Similarly, in case of human beings also, the environment, physical and social, in which a child is brought up, do influence and mould his personality characteristics.

In reality, it is to the Nature OR Nurture which influence the human development but it is the Nature AND Nurture combination which produce the end result – the human personality. Human characteristics do not fall into two mutually exclusive classes, one hereditary and other the environmental. The genetic constitution sets the limits and the general direction of development, and the environment works on it. The development of personality is a result of constant interaction of the organism and its environment. *Lefton* has very appropriately stated that "A person's genetic make-up is the foundation on which all his or her behaviours are built. Experiences in the environment act in collaboration with inheritance to shape day to day behaviour." Environment is incapable of changing the basic hereditary characteristics, what it does is to provide opportunities for full expression of these characteristics .We change in response to the environment. All the external physical and social conditions and events can affect us. From crowded living accommodations to stimulating social interactions, all do affect us. Developmental changes are generally the product of a complex interplay between "Nature"- the genetic endowment and the "Nurture" the environmental influences. *Ann Anastasi* had asserted many years ago that "instead of asking how much is due to genes and how much is due to environment, we should be asking how heredity and environment work together to make us what we are."

It is quite clear that genes do not determine anything; instead, they provide us the potentials that are realized or not, depending on the quality of our experiences. The development of personality characteristics is result of not only the genetic and environmental interaction but those are also interrelated. It will not be incorrect to say that they are intimately intertwined. How our genotypes are expressed depends on what kind of environment we experience, and how we respond to the environment depends on what kinds of genes we have. Growing up in a deprived environment can make a child with the genetic potential to be genius to perform as a poorly child with far less genetic potential.

The concept of gene environment interaction tells us that people with different genes react differently to the environments they encounter. The concept of gene–environment correlation also tells us that people with different genes, encounter different environments.

The gene–environment correlation can be of three types : passive, evocative and active.

1. **Passive correlations:** The kind of home environment that parents provide for their children is influenced in part by the parents own genotypes. For example sociable parents not only transmit their "social" genes, they create a very social home environment. Such children not only inherit genes, for sociability, but also receive environment that matches their genes and that makes them even more sociable. Such correlation between gene and environment is called passive correlation.
2. **Evocative correlations:** An individual's genotype also evokes certain kinds of reactions from other people. The smiling, sociable baby is likely to get more smiles and social stimulation than the withdrawn, shy baby does. The genetic make-up of an individual may affect the relations of other people, and hence affect the kind of social environment that one will experience.
3. **Active correlation:** An individual's genotype influence what kind of environment he will actively seek. The individual with a genetic predisposition to be extrovert is likely to seek out parties whereas those with genes for shyness may actively avoid large group activities and remain confined to themselves. *Scarr and McCartney* have found that the balance between these three types of correlations keep on shifting alongwith an individual's development.

To sum up, both heredity and environment are at work over the entire life span of an individual, although the relative contribution of these two forces change with age. Environmental forces determine whether we achieve our genetic potential, and heredity determines how we respond to environmental experiences. We are shaped by an incredibly complex interplay of hereditary and environmental influences from conception to death.

ROLE OF PHYSICAL ACTIVITIES IN THE DEVELOPMENT OF PERSONALITY

Physical activities and sports play an important role in the development of personality of an individual. The aim of physical education is to strive for optimum development of an individual in all spheres of life and thus, *physical activities play pivotal role in development of one's personality. Book Walters* clearly illustrates the role of physical education and physical activities in shaping up the personality of an individual. In his own words "The aim of physical education is the optimum development of the physically, socially, and mentally integrated and adjusted individual through guided instructions and participation in selected total – body sports rhythmic and gymnastic activities conducted according to social and hygienic standards".

As one participates in physical activities of his own volition, it provides a free, pleasurable, immediate natural expression of his innate desires. Such exercise unfolds the hidden talents and desire, and helps in shaping up the personality. Physical activities meet the basic needs of human beings, such as the sense of security, the sense of belonging, happiness, experience etc. Physical activities also provide recreation which go a long way in producing perfectly happy, satisfied and balanced individual, having pleasing and energetic personality, having zest for life experiences.

One of the primary and apparent aspect of one's personality is his physical appearance. Children as well as adults, boys as well as girls, all are very much concerned as to how they look. Adolescents spend quite some time before the mirror to put on their best appearance. Physical activities are conducive to the growth and development of the physique. Robust and athletic physique does enhance one's personality. Poise, grace, agility, and the manner one carries himself, have great impact on one's personality. An individual is able to develop appropriate neuro – muscular coordination for such movements through physical activities and rigorous training only. Workouts in gym are becoming a must for all the youngsters of today, who are becoming more and more conscious about their bulging biceps, broad shoulders, expanded chest, and trim waistline. Actors like Arnold Schwarzenegger and Sylvestor Stallone are their ideals, blowups are pinned up in each youngsters wardrobe quite prominently

All physical activities must be learned and that involves analytic thinking, analyzing and interpreting new situations. This, mental exercise enhances the intellectual abilities of the participants and broadens their mental horizon. One also learns to control and regulate one's emotions while participating in competitions as well as during practice sessions. Sports persons are not unduly disturbed by their emotions. They learn to take the successes and failures, achievements and disappointments as part of the game and accept the same in their stride. Unutilized energy, undoubtedly has harmful effect on one's personality makeup. Physical activities and sports provide an interesting and challenging outlet for such energy as well as for blowing out other emotional storms building within.

Participation in sports and other physical activities provides avenues for social interactions, and lays foundations for amicable relationships. Success in such activities also provides social recognition, status, social acceptance and respect. Sports team comprise athletes coming from different , and many times, diverse social, economical and cultural matrix. Physical activities and sports provide opportunities of interaction between athletes coming from different regions speaking different language, belonging to different caste and religions, and thus help an individual to develop multi-dimensional personality. The inculcation of qualities like honesty, sincerity, fair play, punctuality, dedication, obedience of rules, respect for elders, and moral values through sports is responsible for development of sound and ideal character, a very essential attribute of personality. One cannot succeed or achieve any goal unless one sincerely strives to achieve the same. In sports, one learns to make sincere efforts, which reflect positively in the development of an individual's personality. Group effort, loyalty to the team and strong ties are much in evidence in sports and physical activities. The varied experiences and opportunities provided by sport situations make valuable contribution in development of one's personality. Participation in physical activities and sports enables us to develop tolerant attitude towards other players as well as spectators. Participation in sports and physical activities provide many such situations where tolerance pays. Adherence to the code of descipline is fundamental not only to the learning of any physical activity, but also for effective participation in sports. Team spirit or joint efforts are the primary characteristics of any athletic endeavour. Cohesiveness is one of the pre-requisites for team's success. As a member of the team one learns the habit of adjustment in order to achieve the goal. Members of a sport team may be many , their role in the play field may be different, but it is their joint effort, cooperation and helping each other that produces the results. In the play fields as well as off the fields, a member of the team learns to adjust socially and emotionally with other team members. All these are attributes of a well developed personality.

Competitive situations are inherent in sports and physical activities. One learns to excel and out-beat the others while following the rules of the game. Unless the aim or the goal to be achieved is clear, the physical effort or the athletic endeavour would be directionless. To set realistic goals is one of the fundamental principles of sports. Setting realistic goal enables an individual to organise his way of living in different life situations in a better way. Aggression and hostility, to some extent, is necessary for any successful athletic endeavour. At the same time, too much or too less of the same, would hamper the performance and jeopardize the results. Similarly, fickle and temperamental behaviour is beyond comprehension of any sincere athlete. Participation in physical activities and sports trains an athlete to manage and control his aggression and temper, which help in the development of a balanced personality.

While making efforts to win, an athlete also learns to face failure. He learns to overcome and correct his mistakes and try again for success. Pessimistic and negative approach is alien to sport environment and an individual develops a positive outlook towards life, which leaves a permanent impression on his personality. Successful sport performance also contributes to self confidence of the athlete. He has to face many problems some on the play field and some off the field. Sport settings quite often pose many challenging situations. Through dedicated effort and foresight, an individual learns to solve the problems and to face the challenges of the life with full confidence. Perseverance and persistence are two important attributes of an athletic performance. These traits provide stability to an individual and are helpful in developing his personality.

INTEREST

Life will be colourless and barren unless one has something to work for. Boredom and depression are frequent companions of one who lacks personal goals and interests. A sense of direction and enthusiastic concern stabilizes one's life. It gives impetus and interest to daily activities and keeps one going when difficulties are encountered. Interest is not an activity. It is a permanent tendency or a mental structure which supplies sufficient motivating power to maintain the motor activity. Interest can be the cause of an activity and the result participation in the activity. Interest may refer to the motivating force. It compels us to attend to a person, a thing or an activity, or it may be the effective experience that has been stimulated by the activity itself. *Drever has defined interest by stating that "An interest is a disposition in its dynamic aspects"*.

Interest builds up either by past satisfaction or by an anticipated future satisfaction. It is important to note that even failure win hope leads to continued interest. Individuals develop different interests according to their disposition, attention, economic, social or political status etc. Acquired interest depends to a large extent on one's experience. A child's interest reflects the structure of his personality, particularly of the way previous experiences influence his perceptions of himself. While children pursue their interest in group activities, they simultaneously develop their social and technical skills. They find opportunities for outlets in creative expressions and social interaction while exploring their own interests. Interests lead to exploratory activities in many new fields. Such an understanding is quite helpful when interests are used in vocational guidance and classroom planning .

Likes and dislikes are often reflected through the interests one develops. The scope of likes and dislikes of an individual is modified by his abilities and the environmental opportunities. A high level of aptitude permits him to engage successfully in a number of activities. Similarly, the richer an individual's environment, the more opportunities he will have for a wide range of experiences. The needs and value system of an individual provides direction to his selection of takes. Only those activities that satisfy relevant needs will continue to be attractive. If the needs can be satisfied in only a small range of possibilities, interests become limited accordingly. Variation in interests reflects the influence of the individual's experience. Nowhere do differences in interests appear to strikingly as between the two sexes. Such differences begin to appear quite early in the children. Helping around the home, for example, appears as a definitely feminine preferences in the early childhood years, whereas boys prefer outdoor activities. At the age of about ten extremely feminine or masculine activities are almost unanimously disliked by the opposite sex. At this age the preferences and interests of the boys are characterized by anti-sissy, anti-work in home and anti-intellectual factors, more interested in aggressive outdoor plays, riding bicycles etc. On the other hand, interests of girls at this age are typically anti-physical activity and anti-aggressive. Sex differences indicate the part played by cultural influence in the development of interest. Most boys are expected (and taught) to identify with the masculine and the girls with the feminine roles. The distinctiveness of the experiences imposed by each of theses paths is highly influential in determining the basic interest patterns of each sex.

Interests need not be permanent at all the times. Any action or object which is not associated with fulfillment of any permanent need evokes only temporary interests. The moment the purpose is served or the need fulfilled, one loses interest in that thing or the work. On the other hand when the action or object is associated with fulfillment of permanent needs, it develops permanent interest which subsists to evoke constant response towards fulfilling the need. Interests are more than static qualities of the personality, more than favoured clusters of activities. Interest has important dynamic qualities. Interest is sometimes innate but mostly acquired. It is through the development of interest and the activities pursued in interest satisfaction that one explores and tests his skills and abilities. By this process one eventually acquires a realistic concept of his personal characteristics, capacities and abilities, and his strengths and weaknesses. Through this medium he learns about the characteristics of his social environment, resources available in his physical environment, and the means and skills through which his personality can reach a maximum of his life's need fulfillments.

ATTITUDE

Early psychologists had defined attitude simply as a tendency to seek or avoid something. Merely liking or disliking, approval and disapproval do not convey the real meaning of attitudes. *Stagner* has defined attitude in much broader sense. According to him, *"An attitude can be defined as the meanings that one associates with a certain object (or idea) and which influence his acceptance of it. An element of acceptance or avoidance is present in any attitude, but additional association are also involved."*

Lahey has defined, "*Attitudes as beliefs that predispose one to act and feel in certain ways.*" This definition suggests three basic components of attitude : beliefs, feelings and, dispositions to behave, Most of the attitudes are learnt directly from our experiences and we learn them from others. Many of the specific attitudes closely reflect the prevailing attitudes in our homes and communities. When members of a community have almost same attitude on a topic, anyone growing up in that community is almost sure to adopt it too. The religious and communal hatreds are such examples. Attitudes are learned by a process of interpretation, response and confirmation. The attitude retained is the one that is confirmed by experiences. Like any other response, attitudes are confirmed or modified through repeated trials. We may take the example of a child learning about dogs. Any child almost instantly reaches out and tries to touch almost any object, just to explore it. When he comes near a dog, he tries to touch it, treating it like any other toy he likes to play with. Here an attitude or belief is being tested and the same will be confirmed if it is followed by pleasant results, i.e., if the dog licks the child or plays with him and this conveys pleasant feelings to the child. But if the dog reacts and pounces at the child's fingers or barks loudly in protest, child may cry and move away. This will give unpleasant result and next time the child may not try to come near the dog and will try to avoid it. Behaviour of the child in both the situations shows a learned attitude. An attitude can be confirmed or contradicted by further experience. *We can say that attitudes are a realistic summary of experience that one likes what works out well and avoids what works out badly.* An attitude is generally build on previous attitude .A child growing up in a family, a neighbourhood, and a town tries on their outlooks and behaviours and finds that they work. He continuously responds in these ways and so on he has learned an attitude. Does this mean that attitudes can not be altered or changed? The answer to such a question is that the attitudes can be changed although the process is slow and change is generally partial. Among the attitudes hardest to alter are those rooted in emotional needs.

People conform to and up hold the systems of attitudes they have developed for themselves. Ordinarily any contradiction to their views will not immediately bring any change rather they will try to give meaning to such situations so that the same can be viewed according to their beliefs. We everyday see that we accept views and opinions of persons we respect more quickly than if the same view or opinion is expressed by adversary. This reflects our acceptance on one hand and rejection on the other hand.

LEADERSHIP AND ITS TRAINING IN PHYSICAL EDUCATION

Introduction

Leadership is an important element in directing functions of a group, an organisation or management. Wherever there is an organised group of people working towards common goals, some form of leadership becomes essential. "The power of leadership is the power of integrating." A leader stimulates what is best in a group, unites and concentrates scattering. A groups leader provides channel to the unutilized energy and creativity in the group. Marry Parker Follet has rightly expressed: "The leader is the person who influences the most, is not he who does great deeds, but he who makes us feel that I can do great deeds."

Meaning of Leadership

Leadership is the ability to build up confidence and zeal among people and to create an urge in them to be led. To be a successful leader one must possess foresight, drive, initiative, self-confidence and personal integrity. Different situations may demand different types of leaderships.

In the words of the great English Soldier Field Marshal Montgomery, "The capacity and will of an individual to rally men and women to a common purpose" is leadership. In other words, leadership is the act of influencing other people to cooperate towards some common goals which they come to find desirable. This act is performed by a very few in a society.

Definitions

The definitions of leadership given by some famous authors, experts and experienced heads of various organisation, profession, manage- ment and establishment are mentioned below:

1. "Leadership is the exercise of authority and making of decisions," states *Durlin. R.*
2. "Leadership is the ability to secure desirable actions from a group of followers voluntarily, without the use of coercion (force)," states *Alford and Beaty.*
3. "Leadership is the activity of influencing people to strive willingly for group objectives," expressed *George R. Terry.*
4. "Leadership is the initiation of acts which results in insistent pattern of group interaction directed towards the solution of mutual problem," stated *Hemphill, J.K.*

5. "Leadership is a process of influence on a group in a particular situation at a given point of time, and in a specific set of circumstances that stimulates people to strive willingly to attain organisational / group objectives and satisfaction with the type of leadership provided," viewed *Jame J. Cribbinb.*
6. "Leadership is an art, a science, or a gift by which a man is enabled and privileged to direct the thoughts, plans and actions of his fellowmen by honourable and legitimate means for noble and altruistic ends," expressed by *Frederic E. Wolf.*

In the above mentioned definitions of leadership, stress is laid on the capacity of an individual to influence and direct group efforts artfully in a systematic way towards the achievement of common goals of a group/organisation/ profession. Thus, we can say the leadership is the practice of influence that stimulates subordinates or followers to do their best towards the achievement of desired goals. Further, Frederick E.Wolf has rightly expressed that leadership is an art, because it is not every body's cup of tea to make everyone to follow the leader. It is a science because there is always systematic approach for developing the cultivating leadership. Considering leadership as a gift is very much true because it requires certain innate qualities.

Leadership is a dynamic process that caters to the needs of the members of the group. Further, it emerges in the interaction of individuals with one another. Without right leadership, no home, community, organisation, discipline, institution, profession and fnally nation can move on the path of progress. It means that the welfare as well as progress of society or a profession depends upon qualitative leadership. Therefore, the leader is said to "*give the lead*" he makes acceptable suggestions, shows the right path, acts as a model for others, give commands, which are respected and carried out. In all the cases, what a leader does affect others more than himself or herself. Without the cooperation of his followers, no leader can retain his position and prestige for a long duration. He may rule as a dictator for some time but his future certainly will be in dark. Therefore, he should not adopt dictatorial attitude.

Natrure and Characteristics of Leadership

An analysis of the definitions cited above explores the nature and characteristics of leadership as stated below :

1. Leadership is a personal quality.
2. It exists only with followers. It is implied that if there are no followers, there is no leadership.
3. It is the willingness of people to follow that makes a person a leader.
4. Leadership is a process of influence. It means that a good leader will always strive to influence the behaviour, attitude and beliefs of his subordinates.
5. It exists only for the realization of common goals.
6. It involves readiness to accept complete responsibility in all situations.
7. Leadership is the function of stimulating the followers to strive willingly to attain objectives of the profession/group.
8. Leadership styles do change under different circumstances.
9. Leadership is neither bossism nor synonymous with management.

Qualities of a Leader

Progress in any field depends upon the quality of professional leadership available. When any leader is striving to promote his profession, he is promoting himself directly or indirectly. Directly he is gaining stature and social recognition, and indirectly he gets the gains of profession through work. Leadership is not a quality which can be bestowed upon any person. One does not become a leader by accident. The responsibility of leadership comes on the shoulders of one who has his background of experience and training coupled with vital personal qualities, because these all add to the professional competence of the leader. One thing is certain that there are certain qualities which distinguish a leader from other individuals around. In general, the qualities that make the individual a leader can be mentioned, such as confidence, diligence, courage, will power and determination, foresightedness, mental alertness, logical reasoning and decision making, sense of morality and a strict code of ethics, discipli-narianism and dynamism. It implies that to be a successful physical education teacher / leader one requires a number of qualities. Though the qualities of a leader are innumerable yet the word "LEADERSHIP" itself contains the qualities of a great successful leader. Each letter of "leadership" can be abbreviated in the following manner:

L : Loyalty
E : Enthusiasm, Endurance, Engaging Personality.
A : Alertness, Adjustment, Ability to Coordinate Activities.
D : Discipline, Dutifulness, Dependabilty, Desire to Help Others.
E : Energetic, Earnestness.
R : Reliability, Right-thinking and Right judgement.
S : Sincerity, Sympathy, Self Control, Sacrifice Super Motor Capacity.
H : Health, Honey, Humour.
I : Intelligent, Industriousness, Impartiality, Interest in Teaching
P : Patience, Perseverance, Personality, Physical Skill, Public Relations.

In addition to the above stated qualities a few qualities such as knowledge of the child's growth and development, moral character, competence in writing and oral language, tactfulness, friendliness, tolerance and good temperaments would add extra strength to the popularity of one's leadership.

In brief, since physical education is a dynamic discipline the physical educators must be dynamic too. They should be able to theorize, analyze, organize, improvise, deputize, harmonize, supervise and if need be compromise. Such qualities would enable them to handle human beings in learning and competitive situations, build up their esteem and prestige in the society and shape the denstiny of the profession.

PERSONALITY

Personality is a dynamic organisation with in the individual of those physical systems that determine his unique adjustment to his environment. - ALLPORT.

Theories of Personality

A theory is an unsubstantiated hypothesis or speculation concerning reality which is not yet definitely known to be so. When the theory is confirmed it becomes a fact.

1. Freud's Concept of Personality

Sigmund Freud was born in Morevis (Czechoslovakia) on may 6th 1856 and died in London on September 23rd 1939. For nearly eighty years, he resided in Vienna and left that city only when he over ran Austria. He was a medico. In spite of his practice he found time for research and writing.

Freud's anatomy of personality built around the concepts of personality is related with the other two.

Id : It is the savage and immoral basic stuff of a man's personality. It consists of such ambitions, desires, tendencies and appetites of an individual as are guided by pleasure seeking principle. It knows no laws, follows no rules and considers only the satisfactions of its needs and appetites.

Ego : If the raw Id were left to its own devices, it would bring disastrous effects.

Super Ego : The super ego is the ethical moral arm of the personality. It is idealistic and does not care for realities. Perfection is its goal rather than pleasure. It is a decision making body which decides what is bad or good, virtue or vice according to the standard of society which it accepts.

All the above personality constituents - Id ego and super ego are inter related. Although each has its own function yet it can never exist alone.

Freud holds that the individuals who have a strong or powerful ego are said to have a strong balanced personality proper balance between super ego and Id.

If an individual has weak ego, he will have adjusted personality. The super ego is more powerful than ego. It does provide desirable out let for the repressed wishes and impulses. If Id defects ego, the pleasure seeking impulses try to dominate the ego and thus do not care for social or moral values. The person engages himself in unlawful or immoral activities resulting in a delinquent character.

Freud also tries to centre the personality, characteristics around sex. Sex is life energy. Sexual needs of individual are the basic needs which have to be satisfied for a balanced growth of the personality.

2. Jung's concept of Personality

Carl Gustav Jung was born is Kessuyl, Switzerland on 26th July 1875 and grew up in Base.

He was a psychiatric practitioner in mental hospital at Zurich. He died on 6th June 1961 at the age of 85 at Zurich. He had close relationship with Freud.

Jung divided all the human beings basically into two distinct types - INTROVERT and EXTROVERT according to their social participation and the interest which they take in social activities.

Qualities of Introvert and Extrovert

Introvert	Extrovert
(*i*) More theoretical	(*i*) Realistic and Practical
(*ii*) Afraid of external realities	(*ii*) Support theory with facts.
(*iii*) Absorbing in his own	(*iii*) Optimistic intellectual
(*iv*) Cool and aloof	(*iv*) Risk taker and change seeker.
(*v*) Better in writing than speaking	

Later on Jung further sharprned his two fold division by gripping sub types. In this process he took into consideration the four psychological functions.

1. Thinking
2. Feeling
3. Sensation
4. Intuition.

1. ***Feeling type:*** Helpful nature feel for others and admires others, more social feelings, go on suffering but do not express their feelings to others, day dreamer.
2. ***Thinking type:*** Theoretical, support theory with facts, realistic and practical, fluent in speech.
3. ***Sensation type:*** Good taste and enjoyment seeker, interested in athletics cool and aloof, better in writing than speaking, interested in books, magazines.
4. ***Intuition types:*** Concerned with probabilities than activities, not interested in external factors, moody and temperamental.

The classification has been criticized on the ground that in general such different types or classes as suggested by Jung do not exist. Most of us on the basis of typical characteristics prescribed for extrovert and introvert may belong to both of the categories. This brings complication and hence this type approach does not give any clear picture of the classification or description of personality.

3. Adler's concept of personality

Alfred Adler was born in Vienna in 1870 died in Aberdeen, Scotland in 1937. He was a medical practioner.

(*a*) Adler assumed that man is motivated primarily by social urges. In herently, man is a social being. He relates himself to other people; engages in co-operative social activities, places social welfare above selfish interest and acquires a style of life which is predominantly social in orientation.

(*b*) Adler's second major contribution to personality theory is the concept of creative self, self is a highly personalised, subjective system which interprets and makes meaningful experiences of the organism, creative self searches for experiences which will help in fulfilling the person's unique style of life. The concept of the self has played a major role in recent formulations required in personality.

(*c*) The third feature of Adler's psychology which sets it apart from classical psychoanalysis is its emphasis upon the uniqueness of personality. Adler considered person to be a unique configuration of motives, traits, interests and values. Every act performed by the person bears the stamp of his own distinctive style of life.

(*d*) The fourth concept of man is primarily a social and not a sexual creature. He is motivated by social and not by sexual interest. His ingenorities are not limited" to the sexual domain, but may extend to all facets of his being, both physical and psychological. He strives to develop a unique style of life in which the sexual drive plays a minor role.

Adler made consciousness the centre of personality which makes "him a pioneer in the development of an ego oriented psychology. Man is a conscious being, he is ordinarily aware of the reasons for his behaviour. He is conscious of his ingenorities and conscious of the goal for which he strives. He is a self conscious individual who is capable of planning and guiding his actions with full awareness of their meaning for his own self realisation.

Dimensions

Measuring personality is given as under:

(*a*) ***Observations:*** By observing a person in different situations over a period of time his personality can be judged. However it is only subjective and its accuracy depends upon the knowledge and ability of an observer.

(*b*) ***Ratings:*** By this method certain traits of personality are divided into several classes. A number of questions are developed and a 5 point ratings scale is used.

Example: The questions may be: How do you rate the personality of your coach? (*a*) Very superior (*b*) Superior (*c*) Average (*d*) Inferior (*e*) Very Inferior.

(*c*) ***Interview:*** Interviews are a popular and common method of judging personality. But the success of the interview depends on the experience and skills of the interviewer.

(*d*) ***Psychological Inventories:*** It is frequently used, it contains many questions (or) statements which have to be answered and finally the scores are calculated to understand the personality. Some of the popular inventories are 1. Cattell's 16 personality factor questionnaire: This questionnaire was developed by the psychologist Raymond Cattel. He has listed 16 major traits in his questionnaire which are as follows.

1. Reserved - outgoing
2. Less Intelligent - More intelligent
3. Affected by feelings - Emotionally stable
4. Submissive - Dominant
5. Serious - Happy go Lucky
6. Expedient - Conscientious
7. Timid - Venturesome
8. Tough minded. - Sensitive
9. Trusting - Suspicious
10. Practical - Imaginative
11. Forth right - Shrwed
12. Self assured - Apprehensive
13. Conservative - Experimenting
14. Group dependent - Self sufficient
15. Uncontrolled - Controlled
16. Relaxed - Tense.

Cattel also distinguished between surface traits and source traits. Surface traits is the observable behaviour and source traits are the underlying traits, from which the surface traits come. Eg. For source traits sensitive ego for surface traits: crying.

Eysenck Personality Inventory.

EPI of 57 questions and two major traits

(*i*) Introverson and Extroverson

(*ii*) Stability and instability.

The answers to 57 questions have to be answered in yes / no pattern. e.g.; Are you interested in your game? This was developed by a psychologist names "Hans Eysenck". According to Eysenck' dimensions the chloric type would be extroverted and unstable, the sanguine type would be extroverted and stable, the phlegmatic type would be Introverted and stable and finally the malancholic type would be introverted and unstable.

4. Minnesota Multiphasic Personality Inventory

The MMPI contains 586 questions presented in a true / false pattern. At first it was developed to study abnormal behaviour, but now it is widely used as a psychological test in a clinic setting. This was first used by 'CUBIN' in 1935.

Example:

1. My father was a good man T /F.
2. I work under a great deal of tension T/F.

California Psychological Inventory :

CPI has got 18 dimensions to measure like normal behaviour, self - control, etc.

5. Projective Technique

A psychological test that presents ambiguous results when the test taken. Test taker projects his / her personality in making a response.

Through projective technique you get information about unconscious motives and conflicts which subjects cannot report directly. Through this technique people are made to project their personality on to any stimuli or material. Some of the well known projective test are:

(*i*) **Rorscharch Ink blot test:** It was developed by a Swiss Psychiatrist named Herman Rorschach, people are presented with ambiguous stimuli like ink blots, vague drawings and may be asked to report what this stimuli look like to them (or) tell stories about them, because there is no one proper response. It is assumed that people project their own personality through them. There may be no single correct response to the Rorschach Ink blot shown in (a) some responses would clearly not be in keeping with the features of the blot. It could be a bat (or) a flying insect (or) the face of an animal to some persons. But responses like an ice cream cone may suggest personality problems. In 1921 it was first used. It has got 10 cards. 5 are in black and white and shades of grey. the other 5 are in a variety of colours. Subjects are given the card one by one and are asked. What they look like (or) what they could be. They can give one (or) several responses. They can hold the card upside down (or) side wards.

(*ii*) **Thematic Apperception Test: (TAT):** It was developed by the psychologist "Henry Murray" in Harward during 1930. It consists of drawings that are open to various Interpretations.

EFFECT OF SPORTS ON PERSONALITY

Sports allows the athlete to use his natural aggression, it builds character, it makes him a competitor, it promotes the development of leadership potential, sportsmanship and good citizenship. The other analysis might suggest that sports causes and increases hostility. It encourages cheating and a win at any cost, attitude, it is ego inflating and is generally damaging to the personality development within the limitations of present research data one cannot conclude that the effect of personality in one way. Warren Fraleigh gives that an individual undergoes the following circular process:

Participants in normal play activities - gain favourable self evaluation and group status - attain success and satisfaction from participation - seek more participation - develop more skill- obtain favourable self evaluation and status - reach more success - seek more - achieve high skill.

You can expect the athletes personality to be modified by the extent and nature of his athletic experiences. Further more since most personality traits are developed during youth, the age of the competitor is another factor. Younger athletes are more impressionable and susceptible (every weak to get - repoints) to external influences.

INDIVIDUAL DIFFERENCES

Differences between individuals that distinguish or separate them from one another and make one another a unique individual in oneself is named as individual differences.

Man and women differ from each other because of sex. No two individuals of either sex are alike in this world. Even twins are not exactly identical in all respects. Hence all persons differ from one another.

Catogeries of Individual Differences

1. **Physical Differences:** Height, complexion, size, form of the body, eyes, hair, facial expressions, speech, walk etc.
2. **Mental Differences:** Strong memory, weak memory, quick grasp, slow grasp, reasoning and thinking powers, power of imagination, creative expression, concentration etc. Based on this difference people are classified as genius, very superior, bright, normal, border line, moron, imbecile, and idiot.
3. **Motor ability differences:** Differences in reaction time, speed of action, steadiness, rate of muscular movement, resistance to fatigue etc.
4. **Difference in Achievement:** Difference in knowledge and intelligence.
5. **Emotional Differences:** Difference in love, affection, unstable emotions, anger, fear, etc.
6. **Difference in Interests and Aptitudes:** Differences in specific tastes, interests, attending social functions, picnics, excursions, social gathering, mechanical aptitude, scholastic, musical or artistic aptitudes etc.
7. **Differences in attitudes, beliefs and optinions:** Differences in attitude towards different people groups, objects, ideas etc. Differences in respect of belief opinions etc.
8. **Learning Differences:** Differences are found in the field of learning. Some learn easily and fast, some learn slow etc.
9. **Differences in social and normal development:** Differences in adjustability, unsocial or antisocial, differences in ethical and moral sense.

Reasons for Individual Differences

1. **Genetic Factor:** Each new individual starts with a new set of genes which are the carriers of traits of a person.
2. **Environmental Factor:** All influences and conditions under which a person lives, grows and develops and the training which one receives. Different environment has a different effect on a person, suitable environment helps in the development of inborn qualities while the absence of it hinders it.

INDIVIDUAL DIFFERENCES AND PHYSICAL EDUCATION

For physical education the individual differences in the matters of build up of body, height, motor ability etc. are important as the differences of intelligence is the most important item for general education.

Individual differences in the field of physical education

1. Keeping in view the natural differences of sex, there should be different programmes of physical education for boys and girls.
2. A class may be divided into three or four groups on the basis of motor ability and separate physical education programme can be conducted based on their ability.
3. Each child should be given some special training in the game or activity for which he has a special aptitude.
4. Each child should be allowed and encouraged to achieve attainments in training at his own speed.
5. There should be separate classes for children who have retarded physical growth or are physically handicapped.

Individual Differences in Motor Learning

In any learning situation, be it with children or adults, the teacher must provide for individual differences among the learners. The importance of considering individual differences in motor development, readiness, motivation, and reinforcement has already been discussed. However, other factors should be taken into consideration by the teacher when planning for learning.

Differences in social and economic backgrounds should be considered. Some individuals come from middle class families while others are disadvantaged. Differences in physical abilities among individuals in the learning situation may be pronounced. Differences in intelligence and preferred learning styles hold implication for the manner in which the skills are to be taught. Personality differences must also be considered. Some individuals are outgoing. Whereas others are shy and with- drawn, some individuals, are eager to try new skills, while others are intimidated by the prospect of learning something new.

While consideration of individuals differences is advocated, designing learning experiences to accommodate individual differences requires careful planning and commitment on the part of the physical educator. It is not an easy task to design learning experiences for a diversity of abilities, but it is not an impossible one. The physical educator should drive to help each individual to be the best he or she can be.

Motor Learning Concepts

In planning for motor learning the physical educaters must take into consideration a learner's level of readiness, development, individual characteristics, motivation, and need for reinforcement. At this point it will be helpful to consider additional concepts, factors and conditions that promote the learning of motor skills and improve performance.

1. Practice sessions should be structured to promote optimal conditions for learning.
2. Learners must understand the task to be learned.
3. The nature of the skill or task to be learned, should be considered when designing practice.
4. The nature of the task and the background of the learner should be considered in deciding to teach the skill by the whole or the part method.
5. Whether speed or accuracy should be emphasized in learning a skill depends on the requirements of the skill.
6. Transfer of learning can facilitate the learning of motor skills.
7. Feedback is essential for learning.
8. Mental practice can enhance the learning of motor skills.
9. Learners may experience plateau stage in performance.
10 Self-analysis should be developed.
11. The leadership provided determines to a great degree how much learning will take place.

GROUP DYNAMICS

Group dynamics is relatively a new concept in socio psychological field. Group dynamics is defined as a field of inquiry dedicated to advancing knowledge about the nature of groups, the laws of their development and their inter relations with individuals, other groups and larger institutions.

Group dynamics is that branch of knowledge that deals with the study of groups. It tries to answer most of the questions concerning the nature and working of groups. In education and educational psychology "Group Dynamics is the study of the forces exerted by the individual on the group or by the group on the individual"

Group

A group is said to be a collection or aggregate of two or more persons.

"The collection of two or more inter dependent individuals who usually feel, think and act together" - S.K. Mangal.

There are three kinds of groups :

1. **Primary group:** Family neighbourhood, peer groups and community. They are naturally stable, spontaneous, permanent and informal associations. There is enough scope for face to face contact, so it is called visible face to face groups.
2. **Secondary group:** This is called organised group. Here the members have come together for a certain purpose. They meet at a particular place and at a particular time. They are organised and controlled by rules and regulations. There is active interest among its

members. Eg. A class, a political party, teachers association, N.C.C. unit.

3. **Tertiary group:** These are organised groups. They are not stable and permanent. Eg. A group at a railway station or bus stand.

Group dynamics tells us what are the different centripetal and centrifugal forces that try to change the structure of the group. How does an influential member or a leader bring change in the composition or working of the group? What are the pressures that a group may exert in bringing uniformity of thinking, feeling acting among its members. If a change of membership or leadership occurs in group which other features of the group will change and which will remain stable? In general group dynamics tries to answer these types of questions related with the change that take place within the groups.

COHESIVENESS IN SPORTS

Anyone who has been involved in any team sport knows the value of cohesiveness. Coaches try to develop cohesiveness in their teams because they believe cohesive teams win more games. Surely you have heard spectators and sports announcers as well as coaches and players praise the unity, teamwork and cohesiveness of successful teams, especially when the teams win without individual superstars. Conversely lack of cohesion or team dissension is often cited when a team of talented individuals fails to meet expectations. Given the popularity of cohesiveness in sports talk it is not surprising that cohesiveness is a popular research topic. Many sport psychologists have examined the relationship between cohesiveness and team performance, and according to the results we can answer the question 'Do cohesive teams win more games?" with "yes" "no" and "may be".

Some evidence does indicate a positive relationship between team cohesiveness and team success. One of the most extensive and representative investigations in the sport cohesiveness literature, involving over 1,200 male intra mural basket ball players on 144 teams provides strong evidence that team cohesiveness and success are positively related. In the previous study of the overall investigation Martens and Peterson (1971) examined the influence of pre season cohesiveness on team success and reported that highly cohesive teams won more games than teams with low cohesiveness. In the third study Perterson and Martens (1972) looked at the influence of team success on post season cohesiveness and observed that successful teams were more cohesive than less successful teams.

Obviously, further research does not always clarify or help us to understand a phenomenon especially if the research is haphazard with no systematic progression that builds upon and extends previous work. As Carron (1982) notes to date the overall strategy of sport cohesiveness research can be described as a generally erratic "shotgun" approach, no overall conceptual model has emerged to integrate the findings in any meaningful way, and as with the sport personality research discussed in chapter 3, the findings are as diverse as the studies themselves. Although the sport cohesiveness literature is some what less diverse and more" cohesive" than the sport personality research, the absence of an intergrating framework and clear standard definitions and measures continues to be a major problem. '

Team Cohesiveness and Performance in Sports

Arron's conceptual system raises numerous research possibilities but so far sport cohesiveness research has focused almost exclusively on the cohesiveness / performance relationship. Conflicting findings on cohesiveness and performance are cited.

The first step in sorting out the literature is to consider the definition and measurement of cohesiveness in the research most of the sport cohesiveness studies used the same measure. The sport cohesiveness questionnaire (Martens Landers and Loy, 1972), thus providing a basis for comparing findings the Martens et al. Questionnaire includes two categories of items: (a) direct ratings of closeness or attraction to the group and (b) interpersonal attraction or friendship ratings. The direct items and friendship ratings are not highly related to each other and they often relate differently to team performance. When the research findings as sorted out by type of 'measure some consistency emerges most of the positive relationships involve direct cohesiveness ratings and most of the negative relationship are found with interpersonal attraction measures. All of the major studies reporting negative relationships used an inter-personal attraction measure Fielder 1954 Lander & Lueschen 1974 Lank 1969 Mc Grath 1962). In several studies with mixed results positive relationships were found when direct measurement were used but not when friendship ratings were used (Landers & Grwon 1971 Martens & Peterson, 1971 Widmeyer & Martens 1978).

A second approach to drafting the literature on cohesiveness and performance is to consider key mediating variables particularly the team factors from Curron's conceptual system of the team factors listed, the one .receiving the most attention and the one that seems to have the most impact on the sport cohesiveness / performance relationship is the nature of the group task. Positive cohesiveness / performance relationships are reported most often for team sports that require extensive interaction and cooperation among players, such as basket ball and volley ball with sports that require independent performances and little interaction, such as bouling and rifle teams, cohesiveness may relate negatively to performance.

Economics and Sports

We are all aware of the tremendous sums of money involved in the sports industry. In the United States alone, more than $ 100 billion a year is involved but we don't always consider the extent of the economic relationship, which involves more than gate receipts, player salaries and media contracts. When we include large corporations that manufacture sporting goods; clothing manufactures who produce athletic attire; architects, contractors and designers who build, remodel and design stadia resort sites; and concession owners and operators at sporting events, we can more fully appreciate how massive the sport industry actually is yet, even these considerations don't exhaust the extensive and complex economic web of the business of sport. The purpose of this learning experience is to examine the relationship between sport and economics.

Whether directly or indirectly, the economics of modern sport touches several levels of society. We can easily include agents, lawyers, media rèpresentatives, trainees, managers, athletes, scouts and maintenance personnel in this economics web. In addition, we cannot ignore sport gambling, ranging from legalized wagering through race and sports books and off-track betting, to consideration of bookies, gambling syndicates and part-time entrepreneurs who make illegal profits from sport.

For these reasons, it is clear that the economic of sport cannot be easily separated from legal, social (or) political consequences. Some of the more familiar aspects of economics are related to professional sport; several examples are the emergence of player's associations, collective bargaining, free agentry, and strikes. In recent years such issues have been resolved by the courts. Although these issues stemmed from some sort of "economic impasse" their solution has not been one of mere dollars and cents. The courts have interpreted some of these disagreements as a form of labour - management disputes requiring arbitration, whereas others have been interpreted as aspects of antitrust legislation.

Interestingly, economic considerations are not limited to professional sport. Amateur sport has also proved to be quite profitable, and although not frequently mentioned by the press, the university, or the community at large. Amateur sport is not immune from some of the same controversial issues that plague professional sport. For instance, the 1983 Super Bowl generated $60 million for the Los Angeles area. Further more, it has been estimated that the 1984 Olympic Games brought California $ 3 billion in revenue and created close to 70,000 jobs for the Los Angeles area. In addition, the 1984 Summer Olympics earned a profit, returning a substantial amount to the Los Angeles area and to the United States olympic committee. This profit is to be used to build stronger and better U.S. olympic teams in the future.

As an example, each invited team to the 1983 NCAA basket ball tournament received a minimum of $140,000 and making it to the regionals meant $ 420,000. Again, we see the complex and indirect ways in which sport and economics are inter related.

Conclusion

Obviously, the relationship between sport and economics has beneficial consequences for those involved; in some instances these benefits pass unknown to the public at large. Nevertheless, the community (or) the university profits in some way. Although the facts, figures, and events provide us with some interesting descriptive information, we might ignore the significance of the relationship between sport and 'economics without a deeper understanding of the impact that sport has on a particular community or university, usually a theoretical frame work helps us active the necessary understanding. Unfortunately, few researchers have used theoretical perspectives to study this relationship and thus most of our information is purely descriptive. Yet, despite the absence of a specific theory as a guide, we can still apply a few general concepts to understand the complex nature of this particular relationship. We see the complex and indirect ways in which sport and economics are inter related and this is what makes the topic so fascinating for sport scientists.

POLITICS AND SPORTS

Many people believe that politics and sport have nothing to do with each other. The purpose of this learning experience is to introduce us to the relationship between sport and politics.

Politics is the study of conflicts, power and policy. "Politics is about power - who gets it, how it is obtained, how it is used, and to what purpose it is put". As we can see from these definitions, power is a central element of politics.

Sport is a contest that results in winners and losers, it also represents a struggle for power. This struggle carries meanings about superiority and value. Winners are seen as superior and powerful and losers are viewed as inferior and powerless. Thus sport can be viewed as political because it conveys these meanings and symbols of power.

Several sports sociologists have suggested that sport and politics are inter-related because sport can be put to political use to gain, keep, demonstrate or increase power.

Based on this assumption about sport and power, research on politics and sport is categorized into 4 themes:

(*i*) Sport as a means of promoting nationalism.

(*ii*) Sport as a tool for political propaganda.

(*iii*) Sport as a means of fostering (or) sustaining existing social conflict and

(*iv*) Political decisions made about, for (or) in sport.

The Olympic Games the most vivid example of sport promoting nationalism.

Nationalism represents a devotion to national interests; it portrays the unity and independence of one nation above all others.

In the Olympics, athletes embody their own country's sense of independence and unity by representing them and competing in that country's name.

Throughout history, sport has been used to relay propaganda to the general public, such as demonstrating strength and superiority (or) serving as a rallying point or a visible medium for communicating national policies and ideological beliefs.

Sport is also a means of sustaining social conflict at international and national levels.

At the national level sustaining social conflict between the races or sexes takes more forms. For example, blacks and women are denied power or control over sport; we find few members of these groups in management or administrative positions in sport at all competitive levels.

Political decisions made about, for (or) in sport take place at the international, national and local levels.

At the international level we are all aware of the political decisions to prevent certain countries from participating in the olympic games.

National and local decisions, however, may not always be viewed as having political implications.

Sport legistation and litigation in sport also involve political decision making.

MEDIA AND SPORTS

Sport and the mass media has a very symbolic relationship in American Society. On one hand, the staggering popularity of sport is due to no small extent, to the enormous amount of attention provided to it by the mass media. On the other, the media are able to generate enormous sales in both circulation and advertising based upon their extensive treatment of sport. Media attention, fans, the flames of interest in sport and increased interest in sports warrants further media attention. This notion of symbiosis also provides a fruitful manner of approaching the history of the sport - mass media relationship.

The nature of the sport - mass media relationship has been distinctly shaped by the emerging contours of American capitalism since the 1830s. On one hand, much of sport and virtually all of the mass media have been organized as commercial enterprises throughout the history. Many of the specific developments in the sport-mass media relationship can be fathomed only through, the continued recognition that each of these institutions has been constituted of individual units first and foremost striving for economic profit in some level of competition with each other. On the other hand, sport emerges as an institution especially well suited culturally and ideologically, first, to the emerging industrial capitalism of the century, and second - and indeed far more so to the mature corporate capitalist society of the twentieth century.

The symbolic relationship between sports and the mass media is evident in the large chunks of broadcast .time allocated to sports coverage and the generous coverage of sports news in daily newspapers. Visitors from abroad commonly remark that the newspapers in United States, the bastion of capitalism, devote more space to sports affairs than to business news. In fact, many metropolitan dailies now carry more news about sports than any single subject. If a man from mass were to judge our interests from the space devoted to them in newspapers, he'd think that sport was our main pre occupation. It is estimated that about 30 per cent of the persons buying daily newspapers do so primarily for the sports section.

Intrusion of Television Into Sports

The link between television and sports is even stronger than with newspapers in the sense that television buys, supports, and controls sports events in subtle and not so substle ways. The rise in player salaries and in player employer benefits over the last decade is directly related to the entertainment value of the game, the money paid by TV rights. So many sports organizations have built their entire budget around television that if ever was withdrawn, the whole structure would collapse.

Corporate sport has clearly become a branch of the entertainment industry and thus must put on it good show to remain financially solvent. Evidently, the television audience agrees that big time sport is good entertainment. The total number of network devoted to sports has increased dramatically from 650 hours in 1961 to over 1,300 hours. Fortunately for sport, commercial money has been available to cover the escalating cost of television coverage.

Sports and television have become so inextricably linked that it is difficult to separate the two in the minds of many passive consumers of corporate sport. Television needs sport, therefore, as much as sports need television, since both function as powerful as specializers for the habit of passive consumption. Televised pro sports have become an advertising medium for macho related sports products like beer, cigars, cars and toiletries. Sports Watching has developed to such a high degree that many fans are now passive participants and super consumers of sport and sport related products.

Sports represent a particularly desirable form of programming for corporate sponsors because it is non controversial in the sense of politics or religion; sports coverage on television also delivers a desirable audience in terms of demographics young, mobile and upscale consumers. Moreover conversation about sports represents a social lubricant, as a contemporary lingoes franca within the business world. In certain respect television and sports have become two sides of the same coin. The financial support from television for sports has become so substantial that rules, format, and scheduling have been moulded and adopted to meet the commercial interests of television.

It is interesting to note that increasing popularity of television as a medium for sports coverage has not been at the expense of the sports page in the daily newspaper, in fact, television seems to have fed the appetite of the sports fan for more personalized coverage of their favourite teams in the local newspaper.

SOME OTHER USEFUL MATTERS

Sociological Factors Affecting Women Participation in Sports

In many societies women do not have an equal opportunity to participate in sport. It is necessary to tease out desired differences in role from culturally induced discrimination and look at other countries to see if we can learn from them.

- It is important to recognize that this is not fundamentally a sport issue, but a case of social inequality which also manifests itself in sport.
- The physiological difference between males and females are the source of sexual stereotyping, but cultured traditions and trends distort and exaggerate the male/ female roles in society to the extent that basic freedoms are denied.
- Where social inequality exists, the forces of a democratic society can press for reform. However, an additional problem exists when social inequality is justified on biological grounds and a policy is enacted which presumes women predisposition for certain sports.
- In Britain, for example, the resistance to women's soccer is based on traditional stereotyping and the conservative attitude. This does not appear to be the case in the United States where the game is played by both sexes. In the Soviet Union, the 'official' view is that women's soccer is physiologically harmful and morally degrading, and every effort is made to discourage it. The view that certain sports undermine femininity is the most difficult to overcome. It often has the support of many women.
- The differentiation of sex roles in society stems from the traditional notion of family life. This tradition recognizes the role of the woman as a wife and mother, where their leisure time is committed to home and family. The development of this stereotype affected the participation of women in sports and resulted in dominance by men.
- There are a large number of myths about the capacity of women to cope with sport. This attitude of the society delayed women's participation in sport like triple jump, pole vault, hammer throw etc. Even today the power sports are formidable for women, since it is wrongly believed that it can interfere with women's menstrual cycle, menopause and create reproductive problems, since ultimate responsibilities of the women is to give birth to a child and nurturing him/her and not just participation in sports.

Effects of Stress and Anxiety on Sports Performance

1. **Stress :** Stress and anxiety are often used inter changeably. Stress is defined by Selye (1976) as the non specific response of the body to any demand made on it. The sources of stress are referred as stressors:

   The body reacts to different kinds of stressors in the same way. During the alarm reaction stage the body tries to deal with a stressor. This is when breathing and heart rate quicken and adrenalin is released. During the resistance stage, a series of hormonal and chemical changes attempt to maintain homeostasis. The final stage is that of exhaustion, when the body can no longer put up any resistance to the stress and gets exhausted.

Psychological stressors do no have too powerful effect, but in the long period of time, the general health of the sports person falls and the performance decreases.

2. **Anxiety:** Optional arousal is necessary for best possible performance in sports. The unusual responses associated with physical performance are generated by our perceptions of the demands of the situation. It is more important to win in a competition game than in a recreation sports. It is important to come up to the expectations of our supporters and perform well in a competition match. Even the most confident of us has occasional doubts. These doubts can, if we dwell on them generate 'anxiety' a vague form of fear which involves bodily responses or stress reactions.

   Stress and anxiety cause performance deterioration. Optimum level of anxiety before, during and after the competition enables the sports person to be ready to perform. Too much of stress and anxiety causes muscle tension, nervousness, inability to concentrate, inability to make decisions, feeling overwhelmed, feeling out of control, trembling, nail biting, increased sweating etc. which deteriorates the performance.

Personality Factors Affecting Performance of Sports Person

I. Personal factors-Personal factors can be divided into-

(*a*) **Physique**- It means height, weight, physical appearance, and general health. The sports person's gain or loss in these physical factors influences his sports career.

(*b*) **Nervous system** - The emotional quotient, thinking and perception plays an important role in learning and assimilating skills in games and sports.

(*c*) **Mental factors** - Decision making time, anticipation and mental equilibrium plays an important role in different game situations.

II. Social factors : A child learns from home. The fundamental factors of personality are directed by home. A healthy and congenial atmosphere plays an important role in improving performance of sports person.

(*a*) **Parental attitude:** Parental attitude and behaviour with the sports person influences performance.

(*b*) **Socio-economic status**: It is important to consider social status and its relation with economic status of family.

Importance of Group Dynamics and Group Cohesion in Sports Performance

I. **Group process.** Most sports and activities take place within social context.

Some people derive satisfaction from training and competing alone, depending upon their own psychological and physical resources. Most are drawn to the activity because of the opportunity to join people who share their enthusiasm.

II. **Potential for success.** In general, most skillful individuals make the best team. Individual success of the players is highly correlated with overall success of the team, especially in sport involving great deal of interaction.

III. **Interaction:** High interaction games like basketball and football requires a lot of cooperation between players. High interaction may present coordination problems for players. If one player is being selfish or aggressive, or if a defence is not working together, overall team performance suffers.

IV. **Team cohesion:** Cohesion is the extent to which members of a team exhibit a desire to achieve common goals and group identity. But friendship groups can have negative effects. In sports it is important to take a less able player who interacts effectively with others, rather than a more skilful, but selfish one.

Relevance of Aggression in Sports

Aggressive behaviour is quite visible in sport. Not all aggressive behaviour in sport is violent and destructive. In fact, many forms of aggressive behaviour are accepted and even promoted; often aggression is a part of the game. The term aggression refers to a wide range of sport behaviours that causes confusion. Most aggressive behaviours in sport are neither clearly desirable nor clearly undesirable. Instead, most aggressive acts are seen as distasteful by some people and justifiable by others.

Aggression in any form of behaviour directed towards the goal of harming or injuring another living being who is motivated to avoid such treatment. This Barons definition raises several key points.

- First, aggression in behaviour. Aggression is not an attitude, emotion, or motive.
- Negative thoughts or wanting to hurt someone is not aggression.
- Accidental harm is not aggression, but acts that are intended to injure others are aggression, whether or not they are successful.
- Aggression involves living beings. According to Baron, kicking your dog is aggression, but kicking a hockey stick or bat is not aggression.

  Much aggression in sport is instrumental as participants use aggressive behaviours to get the ball, score points, or stop opponents.

Importance of Individual Differences in Skill Learning and Performance

The differences between the individuals that distinguish or separate them from one another and make one a unique individual in one self are called individual differences.

From the point of view of sports, we should know that individual difference exist between children in such physical and psychological characteristics as health, height, weight, speed, strength, flexibility neuro muscular co-ordination, endurance, attitudes, intelligence, emotional stability etc. Individual differences are very much responsible for making some children grow into fine sports person, while others remain even below average standard in this respect. Similarly, they are responsible for making some students intellectually gifted ones while others remain dull and drab. It does not mean that every student should have a different class or a different teacher and every sportsman should have a different group or different sports coach. Every student has to join one or the other class and every sports man has to join one or the other group of sports to enjoy. In fact, majority of students or sports person have average abilities and capabilities. But those who have exceptional qualities need individual attention and training. It is important to give sufficient opportunities to each and every individual to show his talent and potentialities.

Role of Feedback in Learning Skills of Games and Sports

A person trying to hit a softball or shoot in basketball wearing a blind fold with no one around to give an advice would probably not do very well. Many young athletes feel very much the same way, when learning skills, because they are seldom explicitly told what to do or whether they performed the skill correctly. Even though they can see, they are often not told what to look at, what to look for, or what their performance looked like. It is important for a coach to teach the skills correctly and with minimum of frustrations for himself and the athlete. A systematic approach is vital. Such an approach lets the athletes know how they are executing their skills and includes information about both the correct and the incorrect aspects of their performance.

This information they receive about their performance is called feedback.

1. Intrinsic feedback is the information athletes receive as a natural consequence of their performance. For instance, when players kick a soccer ball, kinesthetic feedback arising

from sensory receptors located in their muscles, tendons and joints provides them with knowledge about their kicking movement. Auditory feedback received through players ears enable them to hear the sounds associated with the kick itself. After the ball is kicked and on its way, visual feedback received through their eyes allows them to see the flight of the ball and provides knowledge about how far and how accurately the ball has travelled.

2. Augmented feedback is the information the athletes would not ordinarily receive as a natural consequence of their performance. It is provided by a source external to the athlete, such as coach, teammate, mirror or videotape system. Augmented feedback can be given verbally or through physical demonstration to correct the error.

Whether it is intrinsic or augmented, feedback can serve four functions.

(*a*) Information or knowledge
(*b*) Reinforcement
(*c*) Punishment, and
(*d*) Motivation.

Attention and Arousal

Attention: According to Valentine, 'Attention is not separate faculty. It denotes an activity or attitude of the mind'. In the words of Stuart, 'Holding of a sense impression in thought is generally called attending to it and attention is the name for the process.

Role of attention in attaining excellence in sports:

The coach or sports teacher who is associated with training the children for excellence in sports must be aware of using play way methods of attracting the attention of the child. Vast play grounds, magnetic nature, meaningful methods, colourful objects when used attract the attention of the pupil and effective learning takes place.

1. **Magazines:** Magazines available in the book shops and stores are the source of information regarding sports. There is a wide choice of reading which ranges from major activities like tennis and cricket to upcoming sports like the triathlon. Magazines contain pages of pictures, stories and news about particular sports.
2. **Books:** Successful books on sports are usually the life stories of current sports stars. At regular intervals, the histories of individual sports or their clubs are published in great details. Coaching and training information help to improve sports performance.
3. **Newspapers:** National and regional newspapers devote several pages to sports and employ a large number of sports journalists. The newspapers are good at building startup when they are successful. However, they carry critic columns which analyses the weaknesses of team/players. Today, newspaper play a major part in forming our views about sport. The way sports writers present sport, and the pictures they use, affect how we think about sports.
4. **Electronic Media:** Before television, the great advantage of radio was that it reported events live. The commentator described the action as it happened and the listeners felt they were there. In spite of television, radio still has its place today. Television is every man's choice, even today. Television has its own advantage. It shows talks, symposiums, live telecasts, expert views and also shows pictures and quiz on sports and thus considerably helps in sports awareness.
5. **Computer-CD ROMS and the Internet:** CD ROMS contain a wealth of information about a whole range of subjects. For example, one can find out every detail about the modern Olympic Game from just one disc. Through the internet, one can gather information on sporting subjects from around the world. Future developments, in this area are likely to be stunning.

With the current innovation in print as well as electronic media, sports awareness in spreading globally.

EXERCISE

1. Outstanding athletes usually possesss certain personality characteristics, such as–
(*a*) aggressiveness (*b*) neurotic
(*c*) ambivalence (*d*) submissiveness

2. Psycho-Sexual development takes place during–
(*a*) later childhood (*b*) adolescence
(*c*) young age (*d*) adulthood

3. The psychologist who has been most closely related with the study of achievement motivation is–
(*a*) Eclelland (*b*) Maslow
(*c*) Croom (*d*) Mc Gregor

4. The concept of mental age was given by–
(*a*) Stern (*b*) Galton
(*c*) Binet (*d*) Watson

5. The impulses that travel from CNS to muscle are called–
(*a*) efferent (*b*) afferent
(*c*) sensation (*d*) all of the above

6. Which one is the simplest form of Cognition?
(*a*) Conception (*b*) Perception
(*c*) Sensation (*d*) Affection

7. The functional division of spinal cord is–
(*a*) somatic motor (*b*) somatic sensory
(*c*) visceral motor (*d*) none of the above

8. The response defined as a result of training is called–
(*a*) conditioned stimulus
(*b*) unconditioned reflex
(*c*) conditioned reflex
(*d*) conation

9. Sports performance is the bi-product of–
(*a*) skill
(*b*) conditional ability
(*c*) total personality
(*d*) tactical ability

10. The first metamorphosis falls between the age of–
(*a*) 7-10 years (*b*) 3-5 years
(*c*) 11-14 years (*d*) 2-4 years

11. Which is the most effective method for encouraging self learning?
(*a*) Demonstration method
(*b*) Lecture method
(*c*) Observation method
(*d*) Task method

12. Body mind relationship was first promulgated by–
(*a*) Socrates (*b*) Plato
(*c*) Hitler (*d*) Homer.

13. Who said, 'I think therefore I am?'
(*a*) Discartes (*b*) Plato
(*c*) Aristotle (*d*) Rousseau

14. Who said, 'sound mind in a sound body?'
(*a*) Discartes (*b*) Rousseau
(*c*) Aristotle (*d*) Plato.

15. The hereditary factors of learning are–
(*a*) height and weight
(*b*) physical structure
(*c*) body composition
(*d*) all of the above

16. Autogenic training is a technique–
(*a*) to bring about relaxation in body
(*b*) to increase anxiety level
(*c*) to counter avoidance syndrome
(*d*) none of the above

17. The stress condition is–
(*a*) advantageous to the performer
(*b*) detrimental to the performer
(*c*) neither (*a*) nor (*b*)
(*d*) helpful in the development of strength

18. Violence associated with the competition sport is mainly due to–
(*a*) the very nature of the competitive sport
(*b*) the social tensions within the society
(*c*) the social backwardness
(*d*) identity of spectators with teams on racial, religious or national considerations.

19. The personal factors in learning are–
(*a*) heredity factors
(*b*) fitness factors
(*c*) psychological factors
(*d*) all of the above

20. Gestalt has propounded–
(*a*) theory of trial and error
(*b*) theory of conditioning
(*c*) theory of learning
(*d*) nione of the above

21. Feedback method–
(*a*) is helpful to the learner
(*b*) is detrimental to the learner
(*c*) is neither helpful nor detrimental
(*d*) none of the above

22. Learning of physical skills is concerned with–
(*a*) cognitive learning
(*b*) affective learning
(*c*) motor learning
(*d*) all of the above

23. Natural motivation is also known as–
(*a*) intrinsic (*b*) self assertion
(*c*) self actualization (*d*) extrinsic

24. Human psychology is confined to the study of–
(*a*) behaviour (*b*) mind
(*c*) soul (*d*) relationship

25. Which of the following is a law of learning?
(*a*) Law of readiness (*b*) Law of exercise
(*c*) Law of effect (*d*) All of the above

26. Mental development includes–
(*a*) external and internal organs
(*b*) reasoning and thinking
(*c*) ethical and moral
(*d*) emotional maturity

27. Through which of the following methods, desirable channels are provided for the release of emotional energy?
(*a*) Inhibition (*b*) Sublimation
(*c*) Catharsis (*d*) Repression

28. The rate of progress in learning slows down and reaches a limit beyond which further improvement seems impossible. It is known as–
(*a*). plateau (*b*) loss of interest
(*c*) boredom (*d*) difficult stage

29. The therapy of psychoanalysis was developed by–
(*a*) Skinner (*b*) Sigmund Freud
(*c*) Plato (*d*) Darwin

30. Which is the description of the methods of personality measurements?
(*a*) Rating scale.
(*b*) Interviews and observations
(*c*) Paper and pencil test
(*d*) All of the above

31. Eros refers to–
(*a*) life instincts
(*b*) energy
(*c*) aggressive and destructive urges
(*d*) judge for thought of ego

32. According to Freud's psychoanalytic theory, internalized parent is–
(*a*) ego (*b*) superego
(*c*) conscience (*d*) ego ideal

33. Which level of consciousness contains material that can be easily brought to awareness?
(*a*) Unconscious
(*b*) Conscious
(*c*) Preconscious
(*d*) Conscious and preconscious

34. The conflict where the boy feels rivalry with his father for the affection of the mother is–
(*a*) Oedipus conflict (*b*) Electra conflict
(*c*) Both (*d*) None

35. Which leadership style takes full charge of his team?
(*a*) Permissive (*b*) Autocratic
(*c*) Directive (*d*) Democratic

36. Encouragement by spectators is a–
(*a*) social incentive
(*b*) monetary incentive
(*c*) reward incentive
(*d*) social competitive incentive

37. Cognitive evaluation theory of motivation was propounded by–

(*a*) Thorndike (*b*) Kohler
(*c*) Pavlov (*d*) Deci

38. **Behaviour carried out with the intention of harming another person is called–**
(*a*) stress (*b*) tension
(*c*) aggression (*d*) anxiety

39. **According to Frieud, the typical moral arm of the personality is–**
(*a*) ID
(*b*) Ego
(*c*) Super Ego
(*d*) Both ego and superego

40. **The leader who allows complete freedom in decision making and does not participate in the group activities is called–**
(*a*) autocratic (*b*) democratic
(*c*) lassez faire . (*d*) none of the above

41. **Stress is–**
(*a*) advantageous to the player
(*b*) detrimental to his abilities
(*c*) both advantageous and detrimental as per the situation
(*d*) none of these

42. **Maslow places ______ needs at the bottom of hierarchy.**
(*a*) esteem (*b*) belongingness
(*c*) safety (*d*) physiological

43. **Which need is on top of the Maslow's hierarchy of needs?**
(*a*) Self-actualization (*b*) Esteem
(*c*) Belongingness (*d*) Safety

44. **ERG theory was given by–**
(*a*) Maslow (*b*) Alderfer
(*c*) Jung (*d*) McClellan

45. **Alderfer's theory categorizes needs into three categories. The most important is–**
(*a*) growth needs (*b*) relatedness need
(*c*) existence need (*d*) none of these

46. **Which of the following is an intrinsic motivator?**
(*a*) Pay (*b*) Promotion
(*c*) Feed back (*d*) Interest of play

47. **The two factor theory of motivation is given by–**
(*a*) Maslow (*b*) Jung
(*c*) Alderfer (*d*) Herzberg

48. **Reinforcement theory of motivation is given by–**
(*a*) Jung (*b*) Hezberg
(*c*) Skinner (*d*) Maslow

49. **Which law of learning states that things most often repeated are best retained?**
(*a*) Law of readiness (*b*) Law of exercise
(*c*) Law of effect (*d*) Law of recency

50. **The state of being first creates a strong almost unusable impression. This is–**
(*a*) law of primacy (*b*) law of intensity
(*c*) law of recency (*d*) law of effect

51. **Reaction time is a component of–**
(*a*) physical fitness
(*b*) motor fitness
(*c*) health related physical fitness
(*d*) none of the above

52. **The test that measures reaction time is–**
(*a*) standing broad jump
(*b*) sargent jumps
(*c*) shuttle run
(*d*) stick drop test

53. **These are the conditions related with stress except**
(*a*) hypertension (*b*) anemia
(*c*) mental illness (*d*) peptic ulcer

54. **Theory of conditioning was given by–**
(*a*) Aristotle (*b*) Pavolv
(*c*) Gestalt (*d*) Thorndike

55. **Psychological process of adaption which eventually leads to increase in performance capacity is known as–**
(*a*) principle of progression of load
(*b*) principle of continuity
(*c*) principle of differentiation
(*d*) none of the above

56. **Observing one's own behaviour through self-analysis is called–**
(*a*) developmental method
(*b*) clinical method

(*c*) introspection method
(*d*) rating scale method

57. The knowing aspect or awareness in psychology is known as–
(*a*) affection (*b*) conation
(*c*) cognition (*d*) none of the above

58. In born tendency for particular mode of behaviour in lower or higher animals is called–
(*a*) emotion (*b*) feeling
(*c*) instinct (*d*) sentiment

59. The best method for training of emotions in sports is–
(*a*) repression (*b*) redirection
(*c*) inhibition (*d*) sublimation

60. Proximo-distal growth means–
(*a*) development from spinal cord outwards
(*b*) no uniform growth and development
(*c*) growth from general to specific
(*d*) growth from head to the lower body parts

61. Cephalo-caudal growth means–
(*a*) growth from general to specific
(*b*) no uniform growth and development
(*c*) growth and development proceeds from birth to death
(*d*) growth is from head downwards

62. Surplus energy theory of play was propounded by–
(*a*) Mc. Dougal (*b*) Lazarus
(*c*) Karl Groose (*d*) Herbet Spencer

63. Who gave laws of learning?
(*a*) Watson (*b*) Mc. Dougali
(*c*) Carlus (*d*) Thorndike

64. Theory of learning was given by–
(*a*) Thorndike (*b*) Gestalt
(*c*) H. C. Buck (*d*) G. D. Sondhi

65. Achievement motivation is synonymous to–
(*a*) biofeedback theory only
(*b*) feedback theory
(*c*) neuro-biofeedback theory
(*d*) none of the above

66. Decreased performance in the beginning but gradual improvement is indicated by–
(*a*) concave graph
(*b*) convex graph
(*c*) concavo-convex graph
(*d*) none of the above

67. Increased performance in the beginning but gradual decline later is indicated by–
(*a*) concave graph
(*b*) convex graph
(*c*) both (*a*) and (*b*)
(*d*) none of the above.

68. The initial steep rise in the learning graph is an indication of quick progress and is technically known as–
(*a*) "end spurt'
(*b*) 'initial spurt'
(*c*) saturation point
(*d*) none of the above

69. What type of motivation is not applicable to young children?
(*a*) Intrinsic motivation
(*b*) Extrinsic motivation
(*c*) Achievement motivation
(*d*) None of the above

70. The 'trial and error' theory of learning was propounded by–
(*a*) Newton (*b*) Pavlov
(*c*) Thorndike (*d*) Homer

71. In the childhood, individual's behaviour is most influenced by–
(*a*) community (*b*) school
(*c*) peer group (*d*) family

72. The cause of frustration among sports person is–
(*a*) result of own performance
(*b*) normally due to mismatched level of aspiration and ability
(*c*) result of good performance
(*d*) natural outcome of competitive sports

73. The period of growth and development from 9 to 11 years is known as–
(*a*) early childhood (*b*) later childhood
(*c*) puberty (*d*) adulthood

74. The reason for lower performance in sports competition is–
(*a*) fear of failure (*b*) anxiety
(*c*) aggression (*d*) motivation

75. Individual differences are due to–
(*a*) environmental impact
(*b*) heredity impact
(*c*) heredity and environmental impact
(*d*) community impact

76. Cognitive learning is also called–
(*a*) mental learning (*b*) affective learning
(*c*) motor learning (*d*) all of the above

77. Introverts are interested in–
(*a*) themselves
(*b*) others
(*c*) themselves and others
(*d*) none of the above

78. During adolescence, the behaviour of a person is influenced by–
(*a*) family (*b*) peer group
(*c*) school (*d*) society

79. Concentration is the narrowest path of–
(*a*) Aggression (*b*) Arousal
(*c*) Activation (*d*) Attention

80. Whose name is associated with conditioned reflex learning?
(*a*) John Dewey (*b*) Arsitotle
(*c*) Rousseau (*d*) Pavlov

81. The personal feedback is facilitated through–
(*a*) television
(*b*) tape recorder
(*c*) kinesthetic knowledge
(*d*) all of the above

82. Concurrent feedback is provided to the learner–
(*a*) after the activity
(*b*) during the activity
(*c*) before the activity
(*d*) none of the above

83. Achievement motivation relates to–
(*a*) need of the person
(*b*) knowledge of the person
(*c*) experience of the person
(*d*) aptitude of the person

84. Terminal feedback is the information provi[illegible] to the learner–
(*a*) before the activity
(*b*) during the activity
(*c*) after the activity
(*d*) none of the above

85. Law of effect in learning was stated by–
(*a*) Pavlov (*b*) Thorndike
(*c*) Skinner (*d*) Gestalt

86. The Psychologists usually study on which of the following?
(*a*) Cats and dogs (*b*) Monkeys
(*c*) People (*d*) Pigeons and rats

87. How is psychology defined today?
(*a*) The science of behaviour and mental processes
(*b*) The science of human behaviour and mental processes
(*c*) The science of mind
(*d*) The study of motivation, emotion, personality, adjustment and abnormality.

88. Who is regarded as the "Father" of psychology?
(*a*) Sigmund Freud (*b*) Ivan Pavlov
(*c*) John B. Watson (*d*) Wundt.

89. When catching a ball, your hand knows that when to grasp it because–
(*a*) Your parasympathetic nervous system is active
(*b*) Alpha waves are being generated by your brain
(*c*) Participating muscles receive efferent signals from the brain
(*d*) Afferent signals inform your hand that the ball is about to make contact.

90. Body assumes a 'fight or flight' condition preparing for emergency situations, when the ________ nervous system is active.
(*a*) central (*b*) somatic
(*c*) sympathetic (*d*) parasympathetic

91. Emotion is defined as–
(*a*) feeling (*b*) disturbed
(*c*) fear of future (*d*) state of organism

92. A reliable psychological test means-
(*a*) accuracy of measurement
(*b*) forecasting behaviour
(*c*) consistency of measurement
(*d*) none of the above

93. The first test intelligence was developed by–
(*a*) Binet and Simon
(*b*) Pavlov and Watson
(*c*) Terman and Merril
(*d*) Maslow and McDougall

94. In developmental process the terms "gang-age" occurs during–
(*a*) early childhood (*b*) puberty
(*c*) infancy (*d*) later Childhood

95. Cognition deals with–
(*a*) learning (*b*) memory
(*c*) creativity (*d*) all of the above

96. Which is not a primary motive?
(*a*) Affection (*b*) Hunger
(*c*) Sex (*d*) Thirst

97. What processes are part of classical conditioning?
(*a*) Generalization (*b*) Discrimination
(*c*) Extinction (*d*) All the above.

98. Psychology is taught to the student of physical education because–
(*a*) it enhances performance
(*b*) it is related to behaviour
(*c*) it helps in learning
(*d*) it motivates athletes

99. In psychological testing, norm is defined as–
(*a*) record of performance
(*b*) unique performance of a team
(*c*) average performance of the team
(*d*) highest performance of athlete

100. What level of stress may enhance performance of athletes?
(*a*) Heightened
(*b*) Moderate
(*c*) Optimal
(*d*) None of the above.

101. That the things most recently learned are best remembered refers to–
(*a*) law of intensity (*b*) law of effect
(*c*) law of primacy (*d*) law of recency

102. Which is the lowest level of learning?
(*a*) Rate learning (*b*) Understanding
(*c*) Application (*d*) Correlation

103. Emotional stability, anxiety, sadness and built ability are attributes of which personality dimension?
(*a*) Extroversion (*b*) Agreeableness
(*c*) Bourgeoisies (*d*) Openness

104. Which of the following is not an attribute of agreeableness personality dimension?
(*a*) Altruism (*b*) Complexity
(*c*) Trust (*d*) Modesty

105. According to Frieud's Psychoanalytic theory, innate biological instincts and urges present at birth refer to–
(*a*) id (*b*) eros
(*c*) libido (*d*) thanatos

106. Conditional Response Theory of Learning was propounded by–
(*a*) Kohler (*b*) Pavlov
(*c*) Thorndike (*d*) Deci

107. Trial and Error Method of Learning was given by–
(*a*) Thorndike (*b*) Boaz
(*c*) Kohler (*d*) Pavlov

108. Which law of learning states that preparedness makes one learn more quickly and effectively than otherwise?
(*a*) Law of effect (*b*) Law of readiness
(*c*) Law of exercise (*d*) Law of effect

109. Which law of learning is also called the law of use and disuse?
(*a*) Law of exercise (*b*) law of readiness
(*c*) Law of effect (*d*) Law of intimacy

110. The law of effect is also known as–
(*a*) law of use and disuse
(*b*) law of satisfaction

(c) law of recency

(d) law of frequency

111. Motor skills are learnt best by–

(a) imitation (b) practice

(c) observation (d) memorization

112. Which of the following somato types has not been mentioned by Scheldon?

(a) Omomorph (b) Ectomorph

(c) Endomorph (d) Mesograph

113. The fastest period of growth in human beings is–

(a) childhood (b) adolescence

(c) infancy (d) puberty

114. What makes the foundation of physical education strong?

(a) Scientific facts

(b) Philosophical concept

(c) Chronological traditions

(d) Social practices

115. According to what type of age are children admitted to school?

(a) Mental age

(b) Anatomical age

(c) Chronological age

(d) Physiological age

116. What makes the administration and organisation of physical education most efficient?

(a) Infrastructure

(b) Highly qualified personnel

(c) Teacher's personality

(d) Technical knowledge and skills

117. Motor qualities are the foundation stone of–

(a) behaviour

(b) habits

(c) sports skill

(d) communication skill

118. Super-ego is known to represent one of the following aspect of personality.

(a) Psychological (b) Social

(c) Anthropological (d) Physical

119. Each instinct according to William McDougall, is said to have its corresponding.

(a) Reflex (b) Drive

(c) Tendency (d) Emotion

120. Man became a "homo sapien" animal because he developed.

(a) A high brain

(b) An upright posture

(c) A solid set-up

(d) A superior nervous system

121. Philosophy deals with–

(a) function of kind (b) social behaviour

(c) tone of wisdom (d) social traditions

122. How many schools of philosophy are there generally?

(a) Two (b) Three

(c) Four (d) Five

123. The Plato is father of–

(a) realism (b) pragmatism

(c) idealism (d) naturalism

124. The mental stress condition is

(a) advantageous to player

(b) detrimental to player

(c) neither advantageous nor detrimental

(d) none of the above

125. The period of growth and development from **11-14** years of age is known as

(a) adolescence (b) childhood

(c) puberty (d) youth hood

126. Factors influencing growth are

(a) heredity (b) nutrition

(c) exercise (d) all of the above

127. The age in the years, months and days is known as

(a) anatomical age

(b) chronological age

(c) psychological age

(d) none of the above

128. Pragmatists view reality as something which is–

(a) absolute (b) fixed

(c) experienced (d) none of the above

129. Under conditions of the stress the athlete's performance is likely to–

(a) be inferior to his normal

(b) be superior to his usual

(*c*) be of the same standard as his usual
(*d*) vary in quality relative to his usual

130. Conditioned response theory was put forward by–
(*a*) Thorndike (*b*) Pavlov
(*c*) Jung (*d*) McDougal

131. The consequences of participation in organised sport for both individuals and society are–
(*a*) positive (*b*) negative
(*c*) both (*d*) uncertain

132. Violence associated with competitive sports is mainly due to–
(*a*) very nature of competitive sports
(*b*) social tensions within the society
(*c*) social backwardness
(*d*) identity of spectators with teams on racial, religious or national considerations.

133. John Dewev is referred to as the father of–
(*a*) pragmatism (*b*) realism
(*c*) idealism (*d*) naturalism

134. Sociology deals with–
(*a*) functions of the body
(*b*) activities of the mind
(*c*) movements of the body
(*d*) behaviour of man in relation to society

135. Find out which is not the law of learning?
(*a*) law of readiness (*b*) law of effect
(*c*) law of reaction (*d*) law of exercise

136. Psychoanalytic theory has been originated by–
(*a*) Pavlov (*b*) Freud
(*c*) Gestalt (*d*) Thorndike

137. "Trial and error" method of learning was invented by–
(*a*) Thorndike (*b*) Jung
(*c*) Skinner (*d*) Wundth

138. The period of growth and development from 0-8 years of age is known as–
(*a*) infancy (*b*) childhood
(*c*) younghood (*d*) all of the above

139. Cognitive learning is also called–
(*a*) mental learning (*b*) affective learning
(*c*) motor learning (*d*) all of the above

140. The name of Pavlov is associated with–
(*a*) trial and error learning
(*b*) conditioned reflex learning
(*c*) learning by doing
(*d*) all of the above

141. The first 25 centimetre of small intestine is known as–
(*a*) perinium (*b*) endonium
(*c*) duodenum (*d*) jejunum

142. Digestive enzymes contained in pancreatic Juice are–
(*a*) amylase (*b*) lipase
(*c*) trypsin (*d*) all of the above

143. Saliva is secrecated in–
(*a*) stomach (*b*) mouth
(*c*) duodenum (*d*) small intestine

144. Gastric juice is secreted in duodenum.
(*a*) False (*b*) Partially false
(*c*) True (*d*) Partially true

145. Bile is situated in deuodenum.
(*a*) False (*b*) Partially false
(*c*) True (*d*) Partially true

146. Pancreatic fluid is secreted in duodenum.
(*a*) True (*b*) False
(*c*) Partially true (*d*) Partially false

147. Sucrose, maltose, lactose enzymes are produced in–
(*a*) duodenum (*b*) stomach
(*c*) mouth (*d*) small intestine

148. Trypsin, amylase and lipase enzymes are produced in–
(*a*) duodenum (*b*) mouth
(*c*) stomach (*d*) small intestine

149. Trypsin, amyelase and lips enzymes are produced in–
(*a*) duodenum (*b*) mouth
(*c*) stomach (*d*) small intestine

150. Peptic ulcer occurs on parts of the–
(*a*) stomach (*b*) duodenum
(*c*) both (*d*) none of these

151. The liver is the largest gland in the body.
(*a*) False (*b*) True
(*c*) Partially false (*d*) Partially true

152. The tidal air in an average normal individual is about–
(*a*) 800 ml (*b*) 1000 ml
(*c*) 500 ml (*d*) None of these

153. Liver is situated in the upper most part of the abdominal cavity on the right side beneath the diaphragm.
(*a*) True (*b*) False
(*c*) Partially true (*d*) Partially false

154. The function of liver is–
(*a*) the secretion of bile
(*b*) formation of urea
(*c*) maintenance of body temperature
(*d*) all of the above

155. The function of pancreas is–
(*a*) endocrine (*b*) exocrine
(*c*) both (*d*) none of these

156. Pharynx, laryns, trachas, bronchi and lungs are constituents of–
(*a*) circulatory system
(*b*) respiratory system
(*c*) digestive system
(*d*) none of these

157. The right lung has got three lobs and the left lung has two lobs.
(*a*) Truc (*b*) False
(*c*) Partially true (*d*) Partially false

158. The interchange of gases takes by diffusion are in the alveoli.
(*a*) False (*b*) True
(*c*) Partially false (*d*) Partially true

159. The cells which covers the surface of the body are called–
(*a*) muscular tissue (*b*) nervous tissue
(*c*) epithelial tissue (*d*) connective tissue

160. Columinar epithelium, ciliated epithelium and squamousepithellium are the varieties of–
(*a*) compound epithelium
(*b*) simple epithelium
(*c*) both of these
(*d*) none of these

161. The main function of epithelial tissue is–
(*a*) acts as a protective covering
(*b*) provide frame work to the body
(*c*) provide movements to the body
(*d*) none of these

162. The tissues which are specialized for contraction and by means of which movements are performed are–
(*a*) nervous tissue (*b*) connective tissue
(*c*) muscular tissue (*d*) none of these

163. Grey matter, white matter and neuroglia are the constituent of–
(*a*) muscular system
(*b*) circulatory system
(*c*) digestive system
(*d*) nervous system

164. The tissue which provides the frame work of the body are called–
(*a*) muscular tissue (*b*) nervous tissue
(*c*) connective tissue (*d*) none of these

165. Aeriolar tissue, elastic fibrous tissue, mucous tissue, adipose tissue, elastic tissue and fibrous tissue are the constituents of connectice tissue.
(*a*) True (*b*) False
(*c*) Partially true (*d*) Partially false

166. The tissue which are found in the wall of arteries and contains a large proportion of elastic fibres are called–
(*a*) fibrous tissue
(*b*) elastic tissue
(*c*) elastic fiberous tissue
(*d*) none of these

167. The lobes of the lungs are divided into different lobes by–
(*a*) bronchi (*b*) fiscula
(*c*) alveoli (*d*) none of these

168. External respiration is also called as pulmonary respiration.
(*a*) True (*b*) False
(*c*) Partially false (*d*) Partially true

169. Blood leaves the lungs at oxygen pressure of–
(*a*) 100 mm Hg (*b*) 120 mm Hg
(*c*) 150 mm Hg (*d*) None of these

170. The act of breathing which replaces the air in the alveoli with outside air is called–
(*a*) tissue respiration
(*b*) pulmonary respiration
(*c*) both
(*d*) none of these

171. The tissue cells which takes oxygen from rich haemoglobin to enable oxidation to go on and the blood receives in exchanges of waste products of oxidation is called–
(*a*) internal respiration
(*b*) external respiration
(*c*) both of these
(*d*) none of these

172. The total air capacity of lung is–
(*a*) 2-3 litres (*b*) 6-8 litres
(*c*) 4.5-5 litres (*d*) None of these

173. Maximal volume of air forcefully expired after maximal inspiration is called–
(*a*) tidal air (*b*) lung capacity
(*c*) vital capacity (*d*) none of these

174. The average vital capacity of normal man is–
(*a*) 3-4 litres (*b*) 3-6 litres
(*c*) 4-5 litres (*d*) None of these

175. The average vital capacity in normal woman is–
(*a*) 4-5 litres (*b*) 3-4 litres
(*c*) 4-6 litres (*d*) None of these

176. The rate of respiration beats/ min. in an adult individual is between–
(*a*) 20-40 (*b*) 20-30
(*c*) 10-20 (*d*) None of these

177. Metabolism is the word used to indicate–
(*a*) the exchange of gases in the lungs
(*b*) the chemical changes which takes place in the body
(*c*) the store of O_2 in the muscles
(*d*) none of these

178. The hormone which regulates the amount of water passed by the kidneys is–
(*a*) thyrotropic hormone
(*b*) gonadotropic hormone
(*c*) antidiuretic hormone
(*d*) none of these

179. Parathyroid glands are–
(*a*) two in numbers (*b*) three in numbers
(*c*) four in numbers (*d*) none of these

180. Parathyroid Glands lies–
(*a*) in the thorax
(*b*) on the upper pole of each kidney
(*c*) in the neck
(*d*) none of these

181. The Thymus gland lies–
(*a*) in the thorax
(*b*) on the upper pole of each kidney
(*c*) in the neck
(*d*) none of these

182. The adrenal gland lies–
(*a*) in the thorax
(*b*) on the upper pole of each kidney
(*c*) in the neck
(*d*) none of these

183. Adrenaline and non adrenaline are secreted by–
(*a*) thymus gland (*b*) adrenal gland
(*c*) parathyroid gland (*d*) none of these

184. The function of skin is–
(*a*) heat regulating organ
(*b*) organ of special sense
(*c*) protective function
(*d*) all of these

185. The function of kidney is to–
(*a*) act as reservoir
(*b*) discharge of urine of the bladder
(*c*) to secret urine
(*d*) none of these

186. Menopause period of a woman's life occurs at the age of–
(*a*) 20 to 25 years (*b*) 30 to 35 years
(*c*) 45 to 50 years (*d*) None of these

187. Puberty usually appears in the age of–
(*a*) 16 to 18 years (*b*) 10-14 years
(*c*) 20-25 years (*d*) None of these

188. No. of chromosomes received by a child from his parents are–
(*a*) 44 pairs (*b*) 22 pairs
(*c*) 23 pairs (*d*) 46 pairs

189. Out of the 23 pairs of chromosomes–
(*a*) 22 pairs are sex chromosomes
(*b*) 14 pairs sex chromosomes
(*c*) 1 pair is sex chromosomes
(*d*) none of these

190. Out of the 23 pairs of chromosomes–
(*a*) 22 pairs are autosomes
(*b*) 14 pairs are autosomes
(*c*) 1 pair is autosome
(*d*) none of these

191. One X from mother and one x from father, produces a female.
(*a*) false (*b*) true
(*c*) partially true (*d*) partially false

192. One Y from father and one x from mother, produces a male.
(*a*) False (*b*) True
(*c*) Partially true (*d*) Partially false

193. A Sensory nerve fibre which receives the impulse is called afferent nerve.
(*a*) True (*b*) False
(*c*) Partially true (*d*) Partially false

194. A nerve fibre which transmit impulse for action is called afferent nerve.
(*a*) True (*b*) False
(*c*) Partially true (*d*) Partially false

195. The sense of the position of the head in relation to the body is decided by–
(*a*) peripheral nerve (*b*) vestibular nerve
(*c*) both (*d*) none of these

196. The balance and gait may be permanently affected by any injury to the head.
(*a*) True (*b*) False
(*c*) Partially true (*d*) Partially false

197. The sound travels at the rate of–
(*a*) 343 m/s (*b*) 446 m/s
(*c*) 500 m/s (*d*) 450 m/s

198. The tissue which are found in the wall of arteries and contains a large proportion of elastic fibres are called–
(*a*) fibrous tissue
(*b*) elastic tissue
(*c*) elastic fibrous tissue
(*d*) none of these

199. The lobes of the lungs are divided into different lobes by–
(*a*) bronchi (*b*) fiscula
(*c*) alveoli (*d*) none of these

200. External respiration is also called as pulmonary respiration.
(*a*) True (*b*) False
(*c*) Partially false (*d*) Partially true

ANSWERS

1	2	3	4	5	6	7	8	9	10
(*a*)	(*b*)	(*a*)	(*c*)	(*a*)	(*c*)	(*b*)	(*c*)	(*c*)	(*a*)
11	**12**	**13**	**14**	**15**	**16**	**17**	**18**	**19**	**20**
(*c*)	(*b*)	(*a*)	(*d*)	(*d*)	(*a*)	(*b*)	(*d*)	(*d*)	(*c*)
21	**22**	**23**	**24**	**25**	**26**	**27**	**28**	**29**	**30**
(*a*)	(*c*)	(*a*)	(*a*)	(*d*)	(*b*)	(*c*)	(*a*)	(*b*)	(*d*)
31	**32**	**33**	**34**	**35**	**36**	**37**	**38**	**39**	**40**
(*a*)	(*b*)	(*c*)	(*a*)	(*c*)	(*a*)	(*d*)	(*c*)	(*c*)	(*c*)
41	**42**	**43**	**44**	**45**	**46**	**47**	**48**	**49**	**50**
(*c*)	(*d*)	(*a*)	(*b*)	(*c*)	(*d*)	(*d*)	(*c*)	(*b*)	(*a*)
51	**52**	**53**	**54**	**55**	**56**	**57**	**58**	**59**	**60**
(*b*)	(*d*)	(*b*)	(*b*)	(*a*)	(*c*)	(*c*)	(*c*)	(*d*)	(*a*)
61	**62**	**63**	**64**	**65**	**66**	**67**	**68**	**69**	**70**
(*d*)	(*d*)	(*d*)	(*a*)	(*b*)	(*a*)	(*b*)	(*b*)	(*a*)	(*c*)

71	72	73	74	75	76	77	78	79	80
(d)	(b)	(b)	(b)	(b)	(a)	(a)	(b)	(d)	(d)
81	**82**	**83**	**84**	**85**	**86**	**87**	**88**	**89**	**90**
(c)	(b)	(a)	(c)	(b)	(d)	(a)	(a)	(c)	(c)
91	**92**	**93**	**94**	**95**	**96**	**97**	**98**	**99**	**100**
(b)	(c)	(a)	(b)	(d)	(a)	(d)	(b)	(c)	(c)
101	**102**	**103**	**104**	**105**	**106**	**107**	**108**	**109**	**110**
(d)	(a)	(c)	(b)	(a)	(b)	(a)	(b)	(a)	(b)
111	**112**	**113**	**114**	**115**	**116**	**117**	**118**	**119**	**120**
(b)	(a)	(b)	(b)	(a)	(b)	(c)	(b)	(b)	(a)
121	**122**	**123**	**124**	**125**	**126**	**127**	**128**	**129**	**130**
(c)	(c)	(c)	(b)	(c)	(d)	(b)	(c)	(a)	(b)
131	**132**	**133**	**134**	**135**	**136**	**137**	**138**	**139**	**140**
(a)	(a)	(a)	(d)	(c)	(b)	(a)	(b)	(a)	(b)
141	**142**	**143**	**144**	**145**	**146**	**147**	**148**	**149**	**150**
(c)	(d)	(b)	(c)	(c)	(a)	(a)	(a)	(a)	(a)
151	**152**	**153**	**154**	**155**	**156**	**157**	**158**	**159**	**160**
(b)	(c)	(a)	(a)	(a)	(b)	(a)	(b)	(d)	(b)
161	**162**	**163**	**164**	**165**	**166**	**167**	**168**	**169**	**170**
(a)	(c)	(d)	(c)	(a)	(b)	(a)	(b)	(a)	(a)
171	**172**	**173**	**174**	**175**	**176**	**177**	**178**	**179**	**180**
(a)	(c)	(c)	(c)	(b)	(c)	(b)	(c)	(c)	(a)
181	**182**	**183**	**184**	**185**	**186**	**187**	**188**	**189**	**190**
(a)	(b)	(b)	(d)	(c)	(c)	(b)	(c)	(c)	(a)
191	**192**	**193**	**194**	**195**	**196**	**197**	**198**	**199**	**200**
(b)	(b)	(d)	(b)	(b)	(a)	(a)	(b)	(a)	(b)

UNIT-V

DEVELOPMENT OF TEACHER EDUCATION IN PHYSICAL EDUCATION

Physical Education took its place along side of other subjects in the curriculum of schools only after 1920. Earlier, physical training classes were held by Ex-army men or outstanding gymnasts who were designated Drill Masters. Their conduct was great with enthusiasm and strictness. They had no general educational qualifications.

When the British came to India in large numbers it was found necessary to start English schools for their children.

They started the school of physical training at the central Y.M.C.A Esplanade, Madras in 1920 by the late Shri Harry Crow Buck, the father of scientific physical education in India. It was the first step in the awakening of physical education in India. The school gradually gained in strength and in 1924 it was shifted to the Royapettah Y.M.C.A. In 1932 the school was permanently established at Saidapet in a campus of 70 acres. The Government of Madras gave financial assistance, since then the school changed its name to the Y.M.C.A College of Physical Education. Following the leadership of the Y.M.C.A. College, many other colleges were started in different parts of India by the other states to meet the great demand for leaders in physical education. Now 57 institutions offering professional education in physical education and sports sciences are there.

Till 1957 no college or university offered satisfactory training opportunities and facilities of a high level for physical education. The course offered lower and higher grade certificates and the post graduate diploma. The highest course was the one year post graduate diploma in physical education. It was rightly apprehended that the springing up of too many Institutions with little facilities would make no positive contributions to professional preparation.

In accordance with the recommendation of the Central Advisory Board of physical education and recreation, the first degree college was established by the ministry of education, New Delhi, in Gwalior in 1957. The college was named the Lakshmibai Physical Education College. B.P.E degree was offered in this college. Dr. P.M. Joseph, the arch - designer of physical education in India was appointed principal of the college. Following this the Govt of Punjab started a similar three-year degree course in physical education in Patiala in 1960.

Higher learning leading to a degree in physical education was initiated in three universities as detailed below.

1. Two year MPE in LNCPE, Gwalior, Madhya Pradesh, Jiwaji University.
2. One year MPEd at the Punjab Govt College of Physical Education Patiala Punjabi University.
3. Two-year MA at the University "of Physical Education Chandigarh, Punjab University.

Facilities for research work for Ph.D degree are available in the above universities. The Punjab Govt College of Physical Education deserves special mention. It is the only college giving degrees at all levels, for the certificate, the diploma, bachelors degree, masters degree and doctorate.

Other universities also gave opportunities for teacher education as detailed below :

Sai Netaji Subhash as National Institute of Sports, Patiala :

2 yrs Master's Degree course in coaching.
2 yrs Diploma course in sports medicine.
1 yrs. Diploma course in Coaching.

Lakshmibai National Institute of Physical Education, Gwalior :

3 yrs Bachelor of Physical Education (B.PEd)
2 yrs Master of Physical Education (M.PEd)
1 yr M.Phil in Physical Education.

LNCPE - Trivandrum :
3 yrs Bachelor of Physical Education (B.PE)
2 yrs Master of .Physical Education (M.PE)

Banaras Hindu University
B.Sc in Physical Education - 3 yrs.

Indira Gandhi Institute of Physical Education & Sports Sciences, New Delhi
B.Sc. in Physical Education, Health Education & Sports – 3yrs.

Bachelor's / Master's Degree in Physical Education (B.PEd / M.PEd / B.P.E / M.PE) courses are also conducted in the following universities and colleges:

Agra University
Alagappa University
Amaravathi University
Andhra University

Annamalai University
BPES - 3 yrs, MPEs - 2 yrs

Bangalore University
BPEd - 1 yr

Bharathiar University
BPEs - 3 yrs, MPEs - 2 yrs - MPEd - 1yr.

Government College of Physical Education - Patiala (Punjab).

Government College of Physical Education - Bangalore.

Dr. S.A.C.P.E. - Tiruchendur - Tamil Nadu.
Department of Physical Education - Pandicherry University.

Department of Physical Education - Chandigarh University - Punjab.

Professional Courses in Sports and Physical Education in India

They are as follows :

Netaji Subhash National Institute of Sports in Patiala.
Conducting 2 yrs Master's Degree in coaching in various specialization games.
2 yrs Diploma Course in Sports Medicine.
1 year Diploma course in Coaching.

Lakshmibai National Institute of Physical Education in Gwalior
3 yrs Bachelor of Physical Education (B.PEd)
2 yrs Master of Physical Education (M.PEd)
1 yr M.Phil in Physical Education.

LNCPE - Trivandrum :
3 yrs Bachelor of Physical Education (BPE).
2 yrs Master of Physical Education (MPE)

Indira Gandhi Institute of Physical Education and Sports Sciences.
3 yrs - B.Sc - Physical Education, Health Education and Sports.

Y.M.C.A. Chennai and Annamalai University Conducts
BPEd 1 yr course
MPEd 1 yr course,
MPhil 1 yr course
Bachelor of Physical Education – 3 yrs. course
Master of Physical Education - 2 yrs course.
BPEs - Three year course.
MPEs - Two year course.

Pondicherry University conducting MPEs - 2 yrs course.

Y.M.C.A. College, Chennai conducts,
M.PEd course
Certificate course in yoga.
Certificate course in Physiotheraphy
Certificate course in Asanas
Certificate course in Swimming
Certificate course in Athletics
Certificate course in Gymnastics

The following are the job opportunities for physical education professionals:

- Sports club directors
- Programme Manager
- Sports Manager
- Fitness Specialist
- Facilities Supervisor
- Physiologists
- Exercise Specialist
- General Manager
- Fitness Instructors
- Athletic Trainers
- Personnel Trainers.
- Nutritionist.
- Strength and conditioning coaches
- Psychologist.
- Athletic Director
- Associate and Assistant Director
- Sport Information Director
- Promotion or Marketing Director

Academic Advising Coordinator
Ticket Manager
Facilities and event Manager
Budget manager
Director of Public Relations facilities
Physical Director,
Physical Education Teacher
Aquatic Director.

PROFESSIONAL ETHICS: GENERAL

A teacher has to make a lot of preparation before the class reports for the activities so that the class may be properly managed. He should appear in a trim and suitable dress. He should check up the play area and see that all the markings are made and the necessary equipment kept ready.

SPECIFIC

(*a*) **Strength of the class:** In order that a class can be managed easily and taught well it must be smaller in number. Even though for class room work the number fixed is 40 to 45 pupils per class. Ideal number for physical education class shall be 25.

(*b*) **Place and Time:** Students reporting for physical activities should know the exact place where they have to report. In the same manner a definite time within which the students have to report should also be fixed because it takes time for the students to come to the play grounds from the class room. Teacher should say strictly for student sports uniform. .

(*c*) **Uniform:** Physical activities require easy and free movements of the body. So necessary suitable dress should be prescribed. It is recommended that sleeveless banians and shorts with proper foot - wear (canvas shoes with socks) will be an ideal dress for boys, with a shirt (or) a divided skirt with shirt and foot - wear will be a suitable dress for girls. Further, it is better to have uniformity in colour of the dress used by the students. The uniformity in dress has a great demonstrative value and it also develops group feeling among the students.

(d) **Class formation:** .

(*i*) The students should not be made to face the sun.

(*ii*) Shorter students should remain in front.

(*iii*) There should be enough room for every student to enable him to perform the activity without hindrance.

(*iv*) The teacher should be in a position to have a view of all the students.

Every student must be able to see the teacher from his place.

Formation: Generally line (or) rank formation, file or column formation, semi - circular formation, circular formation etc.

(*e*) **Roll - call:** The attendance of the students must be taken as quickly as possible. Several methods are adopted in taking the roll, they are as follows :

(*i*) Reading the name.

(*ii*) Calling roll numbers.

(*iii*) Painting or fixing numbers on walls or pegs.

(*iv*) Squad system.

(*f*) **Safety Measures:** There are activities which are dangerous in themselves through apparatus work, tumbling, body contact games etc. Safety measures are to be taken whenever tumbling and gymnastics are taught, mats have to be provided. While playing some of the body contact games themselves and their rules can be modified to suit the activities of the boys. Further care in play-area are; (i) it should be free from stones, thorns etc. (ii) must always keep the first - aid readily available.

(*g*) **Discipline:** Discipline forms a part of physical education activities. It is recognised by all that discipline in a school shall neither be dictatorial nor authoritative and discipline must come out of self control and out of the realisation of the individual's responsibility to the group or the society.

1. The personality of the teacher determines to a very large extent the discipline in a class. The teacher's dress, voice, pleasing manners and familiarity with the students will help in maintaining discipline in the class.

2. The teacher must select such types of activities that would be not only suitable to the class but also interesting. Boys would always like to engage in activities which give fun and pleasure to them. So the activities period must be fun and enjoyable.
3. The efficiency of the routine class work done by the teacher every time when the students come for the physical education class, goes a long way in bringing about discipline in the class. The insistence upon uniform etc. brings about good discipline.
4. Discipline is affected when students of unequal strength and ability are made to compete with one another. To avoid this, the teacher must divide the boys into homogeneous groups. i.e. groups of equal strength and ability, so that there will be keen competition. A teacher has to manage his class well so that his teachings and the boy's learning will be effective.

ETHICS OF A GOOD TEACHER

1. The teacher must have mastery over the lesson.
2. He should always avoid unnecessary and wasteful talk and arguments with the pupils.
3. He should take safety precautions.
4. He would always put in his best.
5. He should select activities suited to the age, sex, needs, interests and capacities of the students.
6. He must check up the physical arrangements and keep the equipment ready for the lesson.
7. He must always be punctual to the class and insist upon punctuality on the part of the students.
8. He must be suitably dressed.
9. He must cultivate a good speaking voice.
10. He should be considerate in his views and take into consideration the students view points.
11. He must be able to secure obedience in a congenial manner.
12. He must strive to impart the spirit of self - discipline on the part of the students.
13. He should adopt such disciplinary measures as are appropriate to the degree of conduct.
14. He should avoid passing sarcastic remarks as they may hurt the feelings of the students.
15. He should always recognise the sincere attempts of the students and show his appreciation of good performance.
16. He should use the whistle sparingly.

TRAINING LOAD AND PERIODIZATION

The principles and laws of development and achievement of top form provide the base for periodisation. It is obligatory to understand top form. The concept of sports form or top form was first propounded by famous Russian Scientist L.P. MATWEYEW in 1956. He was the first person to give theoretical base to periodisation. His basic concepts about sport form and periodisation in sports training are still valid today.

"The process of preparing the sportsman to give his best performance in a particular competition is called periodisation"

TOP FORM AND PERIODISATION

Top form is temporary phase of optimum performance. It cannot be maintained for a long period. Moreover in order to achieve top form at higher level of training state sports training has to aim at the development of various performance factors in a definite sequence during this period, obviously, top form is absent. Therefore we come across three phases of sport form i.e. :

(*a*) phase of development of training state;
(*b*) phase of advising and maintaining top form and
(*c*) temporary loss of form

The first phase of sport form is also called phase of base creation. In this phase the aim is to develop the base for achieving top form at high level, in preparatory period of periodisation. The various performance factors on which the performance depends develop in a sequential manner in this phase. The duration of this phase or of preparatory period depends on extent to which the performance factors are to be developed for a continuous and steady development of sports performance. This phase is obligatory.

The second phase of sport is called the form phase of achievement and maintenance of top form. The phase is obligatory if the aim is to participate successfully in a competition. From periodisation point of view this phase corresponds with competition periods. In the competition period the aim is not to develop phase further but to create inter relationship among the already developed performance factors, depending on the competition calendar, the competition period can be formulated to achieve top form for one or more competitors. The most common variations are single peak, double peak and triple peak competition period.

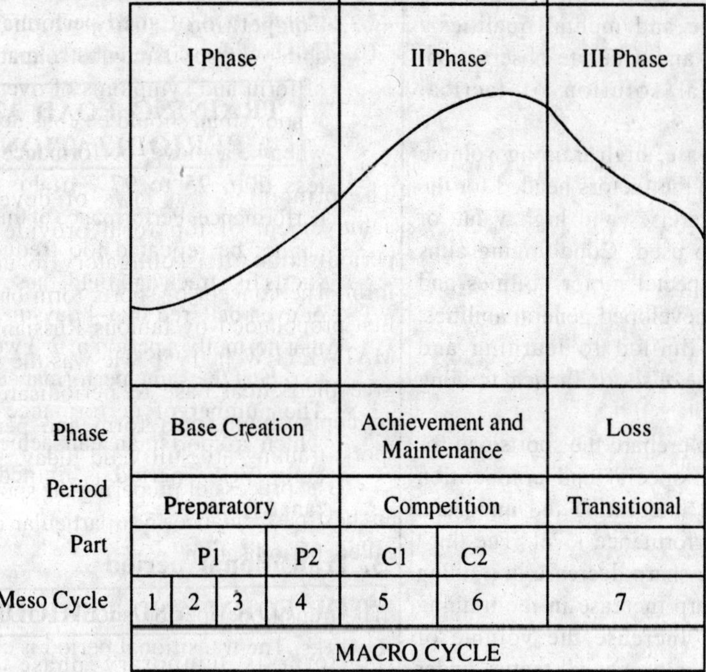

AIMS AND CONTENTS OF PERIODS

1. Preparatory period

It is normally the longest period. According to BERGER and MINOW (1987) its duration should be 2/3 to 3/4 of the total duration of the training cycle. The main aim of the preparatory period is to develop the various factors on which the performance depends. It prepares the sportsman for achieving top form at a high level in the competition period. The training period is characterized by high volume but medium intersity, preparatory period is normally divided into two (or) three phases depending upon its total duration. Each phase has definite aims and tasks. In single periodisation there are normally three phases which are discussed below :

Phase I: This phase has three principle objectives.

(*a*) To regain the previous training state.

(*b*) To condition the sportsman to take higher training loads in the next phase of preparatory and competitions periods.

(*c*) To develop those factors which form the base for the specific factors of performance. This phase is characterised by sharply increasing training volume whereas there is very less increase in training intensity. General exercises are used predominantly.

Technique training is mainly restricted to learning of new skills or the skills of other sports. Relearning, if needed is also started in this phase. The aim of technique training is not automatisation but skill acquisition up to the level of fine co ordination.

Tactical training is mainly limited to theoretical sessions to improve tactical knowledge and improvement of psychic and mental qualities / factors needed for quick and accurate observation, perception, and mental solution of tactical situations and tasks.

Phase II: In this phase, high training volume and load used to develop the factors needed for the performance. Special exercises and high value of general exercise are also used. Conditioning aims at the development of special motor abilities and maintaining the already developed general abilities. Technique training is limited to learning and perfection of the technique of sport. Tactical training is not an important task.

Phase III: It aims to prepare the sportsman for the competition through special and competition exercise developing and integrating the important factor to achieve the performance level. The third phase is characterized by sharp decrease in training volume on one hand sharp increase in the training intensity on the other. Increase the volume of tactical training and this improves all tactics under competition conditions.

2. Competition Period

Competition period is necessary for proper control and maintenance form for required time period, numbers and frequency of competition and their dates and performance level of the sportsman. It also depends to a significant extent on the individual peculiarities of the sportsman.

In order to develop specific motor abilities, skills and tactics optimum number of competitions is essential. Suitable competitions should be selected to achieve top form at the right time. For this 4 to 6 competitions in a sequence of increasing difficulty are necessary. The competition density and frequency may differ from sport to sport.

For effective formulation of the competition period the following ways may be taken into consideration:

1. Irrespective of the sport normal period of 4 - 6 weeks is needed for achieving top form. Hence the prepartory period must be about six weeks.
2. The stability of the top form is achieved after participating in a number of competitions.
3. Competition density which is beyond the ability of sportsman to tolerate leads to loss of form and symptoms of over load.
4. A sportsman should be considered in top form when he achieves performances which are not less than 95 to 97% of his personal best performance. Performance of this level or higher cannot be repeated too frequently. In some sports like track and field, these can be repeated or even bettered in 3-4 days in a row, but after that normally a period of 2-3 weeks is required to repeat the same performance.
5. The number of performance improvements which a sportsman can achieve in a single competition period is limited say normally range from 6-8.

3. Transitional period

The transitional period should not be more than 4-6 weeks. The transitional period is characterized by low training volume and low training intensity. General exercise with low intensity are used for recovery and relaxation. No competion in this period but to do sports and activities which are not related to the special sport.

TRAINING METHODS AND SPECIFIC TRAINING PROGRAMME FOR DEVELOP-MENT OF VARIOUS MOTOR QUALITIES

Training methods

In training there are different sets of methods for different training tasks. These are :

(i) Methods of conditioning
(ii) Methods of technique training
(iii) Methods of tactical training
(iv) Methods of intellectual development

DEVELOPMENT OF VARIOUS MOTOR QUALITIES

Speed-Development

1. **Mobility of Nervous System:** The rapid contraction and relaxation of muscle is possible when the motor centres in the central nervous system undergo rapid excitation and inhibition.

2. **Explosive strength:** The explosive strength, depends on muscle composition, muscle size and muscle co-ordination and metabolic process.

The sprinters have a very high proportion of fast twitch fibres (90%) and the endurance athletes have a very high proportion (90%) of slow twitch muscle fibres.

	Continuous Method	Interval Method	Repetition Method
(i) Characteristics	1. Continuous activity without pause recovery	1. Activity with pauses or intervals of complete recovery	1. Activity with pauses or interval of incomplete recovery
	2. Low Intensity	2. Medium to high intensity	2. Very high intensity
	3. Very high volume	3. Low to medium volume	3. Low volume
(ii) Variations	1. Slow continuous method	1. Intensive interval method	1. Competitions and trails
	2. Fast continuous method	2. Extensive interval method	2. Playing or combating at very high intensity but with pauses of complete recovery
	3. Changing pace method		3. Speed training
	4. Fartlek		4. Maximum strength training

Effects of basic methods of conditioning

Method	Physiological Effect	Training Effect	Psychic Effect
Continuous Method	Economy of Aerobic Metabolism Cardio Respiratory System Oxygen consumption	Basic Endurance General Endurance Strength Endurance Capillarisation Self-conquest	Will power Psychic Endurance Ability to Tolerance Pain and discomfort Muscle glycogen
Internal Method	Economy of Aerobic Metabolism Cardio Respiratory System Capillarisation Oxygen consumption	Basic Endurance General Endurance Strength Endurance	Psycho-physical Mobilisation Ability to improve dried will power

3. **Technique:** Good technique enables the sportsman to fully utilize his strength flexibility etc.
4. **Bio-chemical reserves and metabolic power:** The metabolic process of energy production must take place at a very high place.
5. **Psychic factors:** They are motivation, attention and concentration, ability to relax.

TRAINING FOR SPEED DEVELOPMENT

1. **Reaction ability:** The sportsman reacts repeatedly.
2. **Acceleration ability:** Acceleration ability improved by short sprints.
3. **Locomotor ability:** It is the ability to maintain maximum speed of motion for maximum duration possible.
4. **Movement Speed:** It is improved indirectly by improving technique, explosive strength.

ENDURANCE

Continuous method: In this method an exercise is done for long time without any break.

Slow continuous method: In this method the exercise is done for very long duration at a certain speed without any pause.

Fast continuous method: In this method the, work is done at a fast rate. Heart rate is between 160-180 beats per minute.

Variable pace method: In this method the exercise is done continuously but with changing pace (or) speed The heart rate ranges between 140 – 180 beats per minute.

Fartlek Method: In Fartlek the change of pace (or) speed is not pre planned. The place and surface on which sportsman is running also varies.

STRENGTH

Dynamic Concentric Method

(*i*) **Maximal resistance method:** The intensity is from 80% maximum effect: Improvement in maximum strength, improvement of explosive strength.

(*ii*) **Sub - Maimal resistance method:** Intensity: 50 - 80%

Dynamic Eccentric Method

Slow eccentric method: In this method the muscles are forced to contract eccentrically but with more than 100% of their force.

Reactive method (ployometric): In this method the muscles are first made to strengthen against resistance before contracting them maximally.

FLEXIBILITY

1. **Ballistic method:** The stretching movement is done with a swing hence the name ballistic method. The joints is stretched rhythmically to its maximum range.
2. **Slow stretch and hold method:** In this method the joint is slowly stretched to the maximum limit and held for 3 to 8 seconds and return to the original position.
3. **Post iso-metric method:** This method is based on the principle of proprioceptive neuromuscular facilitation. The muscle is first contracted isometrically for 6 - 7 seconds after this the muscle is gradually stretched to its maximum limit and is held in this position for 8 - 10 seconds. This procedure is to be repeated 4 - 8 times for each muscle groups.

CO-ORDINATION

1. **Physical exercise:** Through enough variations in physical exercise motor co ordination can be developed.
2. **General and specific exercise:** General co-ordinative abilities, general exercise and later special exercise should be used.
3. **The movement should be done correctly and consciously:** The execution of movement is made possible by control and regulation processes.
4. **Means for improving motor sense organs:** The co-ordinative abilities depend on the function and capacity of various sense organs.
5. **Accentuated development of co-ordinative abilities:** Through physical exercise several co-ordinative abilities can be improved.

DEFINITION : TECHNIQUE

Technique is defined as the motor procedure for tackling a motor task. The system of movements of body parts in a definite sequence is called motor procedure and these movements may take place simultaneously. Technique or motor procedure is basically a model and is presented in verbal, mechanical or physical mathematical form. The most common form of presenting the technique is verbal and physical. The physical aspect of technique is conveyed through demonstration and audio visual aids.

Aims of Technique

The general aim of technique in different groups of sports are :

1. **Endurance Sports:** In these sports, technique aims at ensuring high movement economy or reduction in energy expenditure. In endurance sports, one or two techniques have to be learnt. The movements are simple and can be learnt in a short period.
   Eg. Long distance running, cycling, rowing
2. **Sprints:** In Sprints, the technique is to ensure high movement frequency with high generation of force for short duration. In these sports also one or two movements are to be learnt.
   Eg. 100 mts. sprint
3. **Power Sports:** In power sports, the techniques aim at generating maximum force for imparting maximum speed to the body or to an implement. In these sports, normally one or two techniques have to be learnt. The movements are usually complex requiring much longer period of training for perfection.
   Eg. Shotput, high jump, weight lifting.
4. **Technical Sports:** The technique aims executing a movement or combination of elements with high quality; combined with grace and beauty.
   Eg. Gymnastics, diving, figure skating.
5. **Regulatory Sports:** In regulatory sports the techniques aim at regulating a system consisting of sportsman and equipment/ automobile/ animal. The force for movement is external and the sports man has to control and regulate it to get best results.
   Eg. Sailing, motor sport, equestrian
6. **Combat Sports:** In these sports, the aim of technique is to execute learned movements for tackling a task in consideration of situation and tactics. A large number of techniques are required to be learnt and mastered along with the variations.
   Eg. Boxing, judo, wrestling
7. **Team Games:** The technique aims at tackling a task in consideration of situation, opponent, teammate and their variations have to be mastered.
   Examples: Basketball, volleyball

Classification of Technique

The three classifications are determined by the nature of technique.

1. Single or multiple
2. Performance/Competition Situation
3. Constant or variable
   (*a*) Sports where single technique determines the performances, and which are based on a constant technical model, where the structure of competition is relatively constant. This includes most track and field events; swimming, bowling, shooting, archery, etc.
   (*b*) Sports where a multiplicity of techniques determine the total performance and where the structure of competition is relatively constant. Within each sport there exists a similarity of technical model between certain techniques, but each technique is identifiably quite separate. This includes artistic gymnastics, dance, figure skating, diving etc.
   (*c*) Sports where a multiplicity of technique may be demanded of a rapidly changing competition structure. In this category comes all team sports, combat sport, sports where there are exchanges with an opponent (such as racquet games).

The department of technical training must follow a different course for each classification.

TACTICS

Definitions

Tactics is the art of competing. Nature and types of tactical tasks is determined by the nature of competition in a sport.

In short, tactics may aim at regulation of motor actions or at regulation of movement execution or at the psychic state of opponent (or) the official. The means of tactics may be motor actions, gestures, behaviour or even language. Tactics may be used before or during the competition.

Aims of Tactics

(*a*) Sportsman must be taught to organise for the competition and to prepare competition plan or strategy.

(*b*) He should learn to perceive and analyse the competition situation quickly and effectively and should be able to quickly find a mental solution.

(*c*) He should be able to quickly select and apply the skills, which he has learnt, for the best tactical results.

(*d*) He should be able to compete in such a manner that he is able to outsmart his opponent.

(*e*) He should be able to implement his competition plan effectively even under most difficult conditions.

(*f*) He should be able to assess and analyse his own tactical behaviour as well as of his opponents.

Training for Tactics

Tactics can be achieved by accomplishing the following three things.

1. **Tactical Knowledge:** The tactical knowledge forms the basis of tactics. The sportsman must be given knowledge about the following things.

   (*a*) Rules and regulations of the game or sport

   (*b*) Knowledge about the tactical concept of the game or sport

   (*c*) A sportsman should also know .when and where a particular technique should be used to get the best tactical advantage.

   (*d*) A sports man must master the special tactical rules (or) fundamentals of his game or sport.

   (*e*) It is important for the sportsman to fully understand the inter relationship among fitness, skill, tactics and psychic factors for successful participation in a competition.

   (*f*) He should also know in which way and upto what extent the judges/ umpires, spectators etc. can be impressed by his peformance.

   (*g*) A sportsman must learn to observe and analyse his own tactical behaviour as well as the behaviour of the other sportsmen.

   (*h*) Last but not the least, the sportsman must know how to organize for the competition effectively.

2. **Tactical Skills:** Tactical skill is an automatised motor action aimed at a tactical task.

   There are highly automatised motor actions. In sports only the basic tactical actions should be acquired as a highly automatised skill.

   (*a*) ***Variations of tactical skills*** : There are the variations of a basic tactical skill. These are only semi-automatised, thereby enabling their variable applicability according to the competition situation.

   (*b*) ***Creative tactical skills :*** In sports quite frequently the situations demand that the tactical action should be done in an entirely new manner. They are called creative tactical actions as these are the product of creative tactical thinking. Creative tactical actions are the hall mark of outstanding sportsman.

3. **Tactical Abilities:** Tactical ability is the capacity of the sportsman to apply his physical and psychic abilities, technical and tactical skills according to the competition

situation for effectively tackling a tactical task.

Three important psychic aspects of tactical action (Barth, 1980) are :

(*a*) ***Special abilities of perception :*** These are the abilities which enable sportsman to have good orientation, differentiation of sensory input and perception of the situation.

Bastion (1981) gave valuable hints and guidelines for improving these functions of action regulation.

(b) ***Special intellectual abilities :*** These abilities enable the sportsman to correctly anticipate the situation and to think and decide quickly.

(c) ***Special volitional and emotional abilities :*** The first two types of tactical abilities cannot be fully utilised without special volitional (e.g.: motivation, interest) and emotional abilities. (e.g. temperament, ability to control one's emotional state).

Principles of tactical preparation

1. **Unity of theory and practice:** The tactical mastery are of physhic in nature and not effectively trainable through physical exercises. Tactical training essentially consists of a large amount of tactical work e g lectures, discussions, explanations etc. with the help of audio - visual and other teaching aids.
2. **Observation and perception of tactical tasks:** For high level of tactical mastery correct and quick observation and perception of tactical situation and tasks is of paramount importance. Through proper and systematic use of theoretical and practical problems the abilities and skills of the sportsman should be developed for quick and correct observation and perception of competition situations.
3. **Organisation for competition:** Tactical preparation must aim at developing abilities, skills and knowledge of the sportsman to organise for the competition.
4. **Forming competition plan:** The coach has to help the sportsman to learn and formulate the competition plan himself on the basis of his tactical organisation. It gives a sense of confidence and responsibility to the sportsman which is crucial for confident and determined effort in the competition.
5. **Competition qualities:** The sportsman must possess not only competition plan but also the competition qualities such as volitional, cognitive and emotional qualities to realise his competition plan under the competition, condition. These qualities can be best developed by participation in many competitions.
6. **Tactical evaluation:** Each sportsman must know the means and possibilities of correctly assessing the tactical behaviour of himself as well as others. The stress should teach the sportsman to assess and evaluate tactical behaviour systematically for driving guidelines and conclusions for improving his own tactical efficiency.
7. **New and unaccustomed situations:** Tactical actions and tactical behaviour are conscious creative activities. These are best developed by constantly exposing the sportsman to new and unaccustomed situations demanding problem solving through a creative effort. For this, constantly changing exercise pattern, conditions, increasing the difficulty progressively, adding some new elements during tactical training which are demanding in nature both physically and mentally should be excercised.
8. **Creative self effort** : Tactics is the product of creative self effort. Every sportsman must always try to find new solutions for old situations: The self effort should not be limited to doing tactical exercises on the field but it must extend to acquiring of new tactical knowledge, development of mental and social skills needed for tactics. Tasks of study, observation and analysis of tactical behaviour, formulation of tactical plan, are good for this purpose. Guidance and encouragement must be provided by the coach.

SHORT TERM AND LONG TERM TRAINING PLAN IN TRAINING METHODS

Spans of plans

Planning training programmes is not simply a question of planning a couple of weeks of training. Initial plans should encompass several years progression.

Long term

Ultra long term planning in detail is a waste of time. All programmes should be based on what has gone before. Long term programmes will be subject to changes due to factors which are more than likely out side the coach's control. Long term planning can not be detailed but may be recorded but as time passes plans laid for several years ahead should be more in the realms of organizing ambitions into realistic goals. Four years ahead would seem to be above the furthest a coach can realistically expect to plan.

Consideration

1. The talent of the athlete, should the coach be considering the Olympic Games as a possibility or should the sights be set a little lower?
2. The age of the athlete, with younger athletes consider the date of birth so that the year in which the athlete changes, age group can be determined. A youngster is likely to have a greater amount of success when at the older end of an age group than when at the other end.

The long term plans stretching years ahead should be more properly entitled targets or ambitions. All targets must be realistic but not set too low.

Annual

An athletes training programme should be designed to meet three objectives.

1. Preparation for an optimal improvement in performance.
2. Preparation for a competition peak.
3. Preparation for the major competitions within that peak.

Short term -micro cycles

These are the weekly or monthly cycles of training that include the athlete's day-to-day training sessions. Micro cycles must always be planned in the light of what has happened in the previous cycle as well as being progressive, they must also be continuous and readily modified. Weekly training programmes should be divided up into units. Often training sessions contain more than one unit of work. A session which involves work on skill acquisition (perhaps drills) followed by work on speed endurance, for example, contains two units of work. A strength training session is one unit as are session on all the other aspects of training the programme of a young athlete training two or three times per week should only contain four or five units of work. Over the years this can be built up to the theoretical maximum of seventeen units. A typical ten unit week could be broken down as follows :

Day one 2 units hard
Day two 2 units easy
Day three rest
Day four 2 units hard
Day five 2 units medium
Day six 2 units easy
Day seven Rest.

This allows the athlete to recover from the accumulated fatigue of consecutive days training.

PERIODISATION

The planning of a year's work for an athlete utilises Matveyev's six phases.

Phase one : preparation : 1

1. Analysis of previous year
2. Getting fit to train
3. Total body conditioning using strength mobility and endurance
4. Modification or consolidation of technique
5. Preparation for phase two.

Phase two : preparation : 2

1. Beginning and development of event specific training

2. Development of technique
3. Preparation for phase three.

Phase three : Competition preparation : 1

1. Development of competition specific conditioning.
2. Early competitions including possible selection for major competition peak.
3. Evaluation of early competition performance.

Phase Four : Competition preparation : 2

1. Consolidation of competition specific conditioning.
2. Preparation for competitive peak.
3. Final chance to make slight technical changes.

Phase five : Competition

The major competitive part of the year
Achievement of goals

Phase six : Transition phase :

1. Active rest and recuperation
2. Preparation for phase one.

Physical Education as a Profession

"*I admit that your vocation is laborious, but I utterly deny that it is tragic or deplorable, as you call it. To be a school master is next to being a king. In the opinion of the fools it is a humble task, but in fact it is the noblest of occupations*", said Erasmus (1456-1536).

Dorohthy Westly-Libson states that any field may be termed as a profession, if it has the characteristics or fulfills the criteria given below :

1. The performance of a service to the public.
2. The possession of a unique body of scientific knowledge, and technical skill.
3. The requirement of a highly specialised and usually formal preparation.
4. The regulation of standards of the admission to practice by members of the profession.
5. The organisation of practitioners into comprehensive professional groups that maintain high standards of conduct and ethics.

Abraham Flexner proposed the following criteria for a profession : "*It should be learned in character and definite in purpose, possessed of techniques, capable of being transmitted through an orderly and highly specialised educational discipline, and organised in a brotherhood with increasing elements of altruistic motivation*". The criteria include both the characteristics and the process of instruction in any profession and the requirement of a good professional.

Any fully developed profession can be tested to the following criteria :

1. **Pace with times.** Are the physical educators upto date in their acquisition of knowledge and skill ?
2. **Efficiency.** Are they efficient in their performance and service ?'
3. **Relevance.** Are the roles and services rendered by physical educators suitable to the needs and problems of the community and its structure ?
4. **Structure.** Are the activities and theories of physical education well organised and disciplined?
5. **Approach.** Are they honest, fair and dedicated to their profession?

In order to advance professionally, a teacher of physical education is expected to undertake the following activities :

1. Read professional literature regularly.
2. Become a member of the local, state national or international level professional organisation.
3. Attend professional meetings, seminars, conferences and conventions.
4. Render service to his professional groups by serving on committees and through articles or publications.
5. Conduct research studies which might contribute to organised, authentic data underlying physical education theory and practice.
6. Guide/supervise research projects of research scholars and then getting them published in journals, books or presenting them in conferences/seminars.
7. Continue professional growth through extension courses, correspondence work etc.
8. Write books of professional literature in desired/local language.

No doubt, presently physical education is proudly recognised as a worthy profession. A careful study of test criteria to test the strengths and weakness of any profession indicates that much remain to be accomplished. Perhaps, besides other factors, the most important professional handicaps still exist which need to be taken care of. The handicaps are as follow:

1. There is a lack of national policy of professional training and programmes. If any thing of this sort is in existence then there is overlapping.
2. Sufficient material, moral financial and legal support of the Govt. and public is not available to the professional organisation/s.
3. Collaboration between professional organisations and educational institutions is not sufficiently established in the matters of training, research and extension programmes.
4. Professional organisations such as sports associations, federations, national associations on physical education, sports, psychology, etc. are run either by the non-technical individuals or by the half baked professionals.
5. In schools or colleges a sound physical education programme is either lacking or is being misutilised.

The above mentioned drawbacks can be taken care of properly, provided the leadership in the field is competent, qualified and well established. The job becomes very difficult for the leadership to carry forward when many problems are created from within the profession itself. This trend prevails in every profession, and physical education is no exception to it. The only point is that physical education is not as much exposed to the public as other professions, consequently it faces more criticism than appreciation. To change the negative opinion of the public with regard to the profession, the physical education teachers have to be professionally well qualified and have to develop their professional competence to handle the conduct of physical education at various levels. Like any other well developed profession, physical education is also having many branches to look after, for instance theory of subject and practice of various skills of games and sports, teaching and training, coaching, research etc. This part is being misunderstood by the public. Only well qualified and well trained leadership can remove such doubts, omissions and commissions from the mind of the public.

BRIEF HISTORY OF LEADERSHIP TRAINING IN PHYSICAL EDUCATION

Historically, the revival of the Olympic Games in 1896 has given a new meaning to physical education and sports. In fact, the modern athletics/sports training began in 1850 and the period upto the turn of new century has been considered as a period of *Amateurs Approach*. There were hardly any professional competent physical educators or coaches to train sports persons/athletes for sports competitions. Now sports scientists could be traced during the period to think in terms of physiological or psychological training. Eye-brow startling endurance shown by *Spiridon Louis* in the marathon race in the First Modern Olympics had to be considered as an expression of the natural talent in the man rather than a result of any pre-planned systematic training programme. The period between 1900-1920 is termed the period of *Semi-professional Approach*. During this period the athlete and the trainer became somewhat aware to the need for systematic training. The real professional approach started after 1920, when professional trainers and systematically trained physical educators appeared on the scene. Before that, the processes and procedures of athletic training were never debated or discussed in a formal manner in science labs. Only experience hand was the guiding factor for both the athlete and the trainer. The age of *Scientific Approach* to the training for sports began in 1940 and during the period upto 1960 observed remarkable improvement in policies and practices, and methods and methodologies of training. Further, during the period 1960-1980 there was a lot of research undertaken to introduce new techniques of performing skills in different games and sports. It attributed not only towards the enhancement of human performance but also to attain recognition as a subject in the educational institution.

In the modern society there is a great emphasis on leadership; leadership is a basic trait of an individual's personality. A society seeks leadership constantly because under the guidance of a good leader nation can progress. Progress in any field is related to the quality of professional leadership. Leadership is often regarded as the important modifier of organisational behaviour. It can be superior strength, superior tact, superior intelligence, superior knowledge, superior will power, any or all of these may be the means to the attainment of leadership.

Leadership has double meaning; the dictionary meaning 'to-lead' shows the two different senses (a) "to excel, to be in advance, to be prominent" (b) "to guide others, to be head of an organisation, to hold command". The personal leadership is different from group leadership. A person is born with the talent for personal leadership but he learns group leadership in a society.

Progress in physical education is closely related to the quality of leadership provided. Leadership is a partly learned attribute. Progress cannot be achieved only by chance but through the concerted efforts of all concerned individuals under the leadership of a good leader. The basic function of a leader is to motivate and inspire his followers.

PROFESSIONAL QUALIFICATIONS AND PROFESSIONAL QUALITIES OF A PHYSICAL EDUCATIONIST

In accordance with the need of the hour and changing scenario in the world, the professional qualifications as well as training methods of physical education teachers have been changed. Unfortunately in India fate of physical education is determined not by any professional association but by various committees, councils and commissions set up by the Government on the advice of a few experts or non-professional bureaucrats. It might not be possible to refer to all those committees and commissions appointed in this regard, but it is possible to mention, whatever they stated in mandatory terms, which the professional teachers must need to have, such as :

1. The academic qualifications as well as professional qualifications of a physical education teacher should be as good as that of any other academic teacher in school/ college.
2. Those who have to teach post graduate classes must possess a Ph.D. Degree.
3. No doubt, physical education teacher is trained to look after / supervise all the games/ sports of an institution, but it is desirable that he should be specialised minimum in one game/sport.
4. To take up a coaching assignment, a teacher/ coach must have diploma, if possible, a degree in coaching from a recognised institution. Further, now it has been realised that to become a qualified and successful coach one should have a background of physical education.
5. A teacher of physical education must have knowledge of physiotherapy to detect and correct postural deformities of student/player to a considerable extent.
6. He should be able to seek cooperation from colleagues in order to implement and achieve programme / goals of physical education.
7. As a requirement of the profession, he must be able to conduct some research independently. So that he can make use of the findings to achieve his goals.
8. He should have the ability to speak and write for his profession. It would be his real contribution if he can write a few books, articles, journals etc. in English or regional language because literature is the backbone of any profession.
9. He should participate in state / national / international conferences and seminars in order to discuss results of policies and practices undertaken by him.
10. He must have creditable performance / achievement in any sport, that will help him in motivating students, also in writing regarding aspects of performance, stress, anxiety, tension, motivation etc.

11. He must have qualities of a good leader to take the people along from all walks of life for the achievement/promotion of profession.

Since physical education is itself a dynamic discipline, same is true for a physical education teacher. If he does not act to adopt this quality, then he is bound to face many serious problems while working for the uplift of his/her profession. Mere academic and professional qualifications will not be much helpful, personal qualities such as tactfulness, friendly, dynamic cooperative, etc. are equally important for desired results.

NEED AND IMPORTANCE OF LEADERSHIP IN PHYSICAL EDUCATION

Physical education is not an exception where qualitative leadership is required because leadership is a reflection on the profession and it reflects to indicate the nature and aspiration of the profession. It means physical education as a profession cannot progress without qualitative and striving leadership. Future of physical education is definitely related to the kind and quality of leadership it gets. Therefore, it is implied that the physical educators have a moral responsibility to uphold the professional ethics, i.e. to improve their own stature/worth and value, to improve the surroundings, to make their profession attractive and worthy of being adopted by others. Another major responsibility that lies on the shoulders of the leadership is to formulate the sound policies and practices in order to raise the academic and professional standard of the profession. The quality of leadership can be adjudged from the level of satisfaction it provides to the participants or students in particular and the society in general.

Leadership in physical education is very important so that he can lead and control the groups/ teams at play fields. He must be in a position to guide the students to detect their physical defects. A good leader can make his students understand psychologically regarding the complexes on the play grounds. He is able to find out the postural defects and remedial measures and know how to treat these defects with physical exercises. He must be conversant with physical activities in general and should have mastery over some games. He also develops confidence, sense of discipline and ability to take decisions. A good leader in physical education takes the teams for competition from one place to another. They organize practice matches for various teams/ groups. All players have the opportunity to lead the team. They enjoy while taking the teams for picnic and hiking etc. They are able to organize the sports meet in small groups and at the school/college level and have confidence.

SOME OTHER USEFUL MATTERS

Career in Sports

For career in sports and physical education one should have an interest in sports and games, a high level of physical fitness, mental and physical stamina, a competitive spirit, leadership qualities, organizing ability, resilience and will power to cope with injuries and set backs, self confidence, self discipline, mental toughness, dedication and perseverance. Some distinct career streams in sports and physical education are as professional players or participants, teaching or coaching children or adults. Physical education teachers in schools or colleges should have the ability to instill in young people the importance of good health and fitness habits. Through the medium of sports, a physical education teacher has to teach children the meaning of leadership, aggression and competition; and administration of sports events. Within each stream, there can be diversifications. Some players can get into writing, reporting, management etc., after their peak period is over. Coaches can also move from group teaching towards individual training and coaching, sports administration or towards setting up of sports facility, physical fitness camps etc.

Sports physiotherapy can be a specialization for a medically trained person or a physiotherapist. A nutritionist, who has trained to help sports persons according to the requirements of their life styles, is called sports nutritionist. Sports journalism can be taken up by ex-sports persons or by journalists with a keen interest and knowledge of sporting activities.

Fitness training : In sports and fitness fields, newer options have emerged as in the field of establishing and managing sports/ fitness infrastructure or training in fitness. Heightened awareness of fitness and the huge marketing campaigns of home exercise machines plus nutritional awareness have been factors leading to a boom in the fitness segment which physical instructors have been quick to cash in on. Personal trainers should aim to promote all the five components of optimal health-strength training, weight management, cardio vascular exercise, nutrition and flexibility training.

Professional Courses in Physical Education

Training in sports can be availed of through organized coaching or amateur playing, or as part of talent spotting and subsequent training. There is a separate faculty for at the university level department of physical education, which offers training to handle opportunities for training children and adults in various sports activities.

1. The bachelor of physical education (B.P.Ed/ B P E) is offered at two stages: after 10+2 when it is three year programme or after graduation degree, it is a one-year programme.
2. The B P. Ed. course can be followed up by the M.P.E. course, which is of two-year duration (some universities offer one year course after B.P.E.)
3. The one year Diploma in sports coaching available at the Netaji Subhash National Institute of sports is open to persons with a 3-year B.A./ B.Com/ B.P.E/ M.P.E.s/B. Sc. degree with sports achievements. The course is conducted at Patiala, Bangalore, Calcutta, Gandhinagar and other related organizations all over India.
4. There are innumerable short-term and advance coaching programmes. The two-year masters degree in sports coaching is meant for Graduates with Diploma in coaching from the National Institute of Sports, with 60% marks and above.
5. The two-year Diploma course in sports medicine, which is recognized by Medical Council of India (MCI), is offered to MBBS Graduates.

The LNIPE, Gwalior offers 3 years BPE, 2 years MPE and one year M.Phil. Course. Many other universities and colleges offer under graduate and postgraduate courses in physical education. Recently Kurukshtera University and Maharishi Dayanand University, Rohtak has revived the 1-year certificate course in Physical Education after 10+2.

Curriculum Planning in Physical Education

There are 3 basic principles, which should be considered in the development of curriculum in Physical Education.

1. **Analysis of the situation:** It is important to learn the features of the local situation as they change from time to time. A teacher might be having the greatest interest in track events wanting to develop the swimming programme but a situation with pool or without track facilities will make his hopes impossible. Other situational factors can be climate, state or district law, topographic variation, religious character and social philosophy of the community may condemn dance of all kinds. The teacher can make efforts in improving the situation by taking initiative of taking into confidence the local authorities and his or her department.
2. **The individual to be educated:** The next principle in planning curriculum is to study and apprise the individuals who are to be educated. Their characteristics, socio-economic status, individual differences, nutritional status etc. should be taken into consideration. Some of the past records can be obtained from the institutional records and registers. Others can be assessed from the data on the growth and development, characteristics and the needs of boys and girls.

3. **Aim of the programme:** Physical Education should aim to provide skilled leadership and adequate facilities which will afford an opportunity for the individual or group to act in situations which are physically wholesome, mentally stimulating and socially sound. Physical education curriculum should clearly state its aim, the general direction in which it proposes to go.
   In the formulation of an aim for physical education, it will be helpful to agree upon an aim of education in general. When this is done the aim of physical education should be in agreement with the aim of education.

Numerous factors affect the curriculum in physical education. However, there is a consensus for the need of a general uniformity in fixing the type of activities, which should form a curriculum in physical education for guiding the authorities and physical educators to work according to local conditions and special needs.

1. **Developmental Activities:** a) A Exercise tables, dands, baithaks and yogic exercises. b) Stunts, pyramids, weight training and conditioning exercises.
2. **Rhythmics:** Rhythm fundamentals, rhythmic exercises with apparatus like Lezium, dumbbells, hoops, rings, ribbons etc.
3. **Games, Sports and Athletics**: a) Major games like football, basketball, athletics, hockey, volleyball, kho-kho etc. b) Recreation games, minor games, lead up games.
4. **Formal Activities**: Drill and marching, calisthenics and mass P. T. exercises.
5. **Apparatus Activities**: Parallel Bar, vaulting, beam, ropes, horizontal bar, malkhamb etc.
6. **Combatives**: Wrestling, Boxing, Judo, Lathi etc.
7. **Aquatics:** Swimming, diving, water sports life saving drills.
8. Self testing Activities, Tests of physical fitness motor fitness.
9. **Camping and outdoor Activities:** Hiking, cross country, mountaineering, picnics, excursions etc.
10. **Special Activities:** Demonstration, ceremonial parades, National Anthem, Flag salutation, practical projects, sports quizzes, exhibitions, talks, work shops, visits to sports museums and stadiums.

Role of Age in Physical Education

Physical Education should aim to help pupil grow and develop normally and well and obtain optimum physical and mental health as well as total fitness.

(*a*) 6-9 years of age: Children are not fully-grown and physiological systems are also not grown to full. Children tend however, to be over active in this period. They switch over from one activity to other quickly are curious to learn and feel new things. They perform experiments with everything around them, wholesome physical activities would give them the opportunity to grow and learn. Activities like story plays, rhythmics, action songs, dramatization, imitations and variety of recreation games interest them most. Emphasis on too much rigidity should be avoided in this age.

(*b*) 10 to 14 years of age: The growth is rapid in this period. Neuro-muscular coordination increases. Group affinity becomes pronounced and dependence on parents decreases. There is a distinct preference for competitions. Adventurous and exploration activities should be given in this age. Mysterious activities, games involving thinking and recreation are best for maintaining rapid physical and mental growth.

(*c*) 15 to 18 years of age: This is a period of stress storm and strife. Sense of belongingness is very high. There is surplus energy in the body. This age group is best for nurturing talent, combatives, strength involving exercises. Group activities, rhythmics and activities involving big muscles can be given for all round development. Leadership qualities can be developed through excursions. Drill and marching help pupil to gain maturity in body and mind.

Principles of Construction of Timetable in Physical Education

Good timetable ensures proper, organized, disciplined and efficient working of the school. The following principles should be kept in mind while constructing the timetable in physical education.

(*a*) **Type of school:** Different types of schools have different needs. Thus it should be kept in mind whether the school is a co-education school, a rural, urban or a girls school.

(*b*) **Availability of time:** The education department prescribes daily timing of the schools. Duration of the periods depend upon total working hours of the school.

(*c*) **Importance of subject:** Time table should be flexible to make room for more periods being given to the subjects which are important and difficult with examination point of view.

(*d*) **Departmental rules:** The central board and education department prescribes syllabus for each subject, and class and also suggests as to how many periods should be allotted to different subjects. A timetable should be prepared accordingly.

(*e*) **Work load:** Timetable should be prepared with a view to avoid too much workload to same teachers and very low workload to others. Too much workload shows bias and can kill spirit and creativity of the teachers.

(*f*) **Variety:** Too long periods of the same subject would kill the interest of students. Refreshing variety should be given in between and within the academic subject periods.

(*g*) **School building and equipment:** While framing the time-table the space, provisions and the equipment available in the school should be kept in mind.

(*h*) **Climate:** Summer and winter season timetables should be different.

(*i*) **Flexibility:** Rigid timetable creates monotony and fatigue. There should be the provision of vacant periods in the timetable to enable the teachers to prepare their lessons.

Development of Teacher Education in Physical Education in India

1. **Pre-Independence Period:** Physical education under the British rule was mainly the result of private initiative. Institutions such as Hanuman Vyayam Prasarak Mandal, Amravati and then Gujarat Vyayam Prashak Mandal, Ahmadabad, Bharat Seva Mandel, Sarasvati and other similar institutions were established all over India. The YMCA College of Physical Education, Madras was established in 1923 under the leadership of late S. C. Buck. This step marked the beginning of developing leadership in the field by providing one year training courses in physical education.
2. **After Independence:** The education reforms came on war footing after independence to suit Indian conditions and to fulfil the need of developing indegenous games and sports. A separate division for Physical Education and recreation was created under the Union Ministry of Education.
3. Dr. Tarachand Committee (1948) recommended the training of teachers in the field of Physical Education in respect of organization, administration and recreation, establishment of training colleges in Physical Education and instituting post graduate courses in Physical Education.
4. Central Advisory Committee and Physical Education and Recreation (1950) contributed by propagating the National Plan of Physical Education and Recreation which contained guidelines to State Governments for starting teacher training programmes in Physical Education, syllabi in Physical Education for boys and girls in schools etc.
5. **All India Council of Sports (1954):** The council marked the beginning of broad-basing sports in the country by expanding sports facilities in rural areas, establishing sports clubs and sports bodies on a massive scale.
6. **National Discipline Scheme (1954):** Under this scheme, young and suitable persons both men and women were recruited under the Central Govt. and were put through a training programme after which they were qualified to work as N.D.S. instructors in schools.
7. **Lakshmibai National College of Physical Education (1957):** The Govt. of India established this college in order to develop leadership in Physical Education.

8. **National Institute of Sports (1961):** The institute was established at Patiala, Punjab to candidates in systems of scientific coaching. The sports Authority of India established similar centers at Bangalore, Calcutta, Gandhinagar, New Delhi, and Manipur also.
9. **National Sports Policy 1980:** The teacher education programme in Physical Education was revised in some states, to provide the right type of leadership required for implementation of the compulsory programme of Physical Education and sports.
10. **Sports Authority of India (1984):** S.A.I. was established to look after various courses/ schemes of teacher education and sports infrastructure. Certificate courses, post doctoral and post graduate courses are being conducted at different centres of S .A.I. all over India.

Ethics in Sports

There is a growing disregard of utility and ethical aspects in sports, particularly spectacular sports which attract a large number of people.

1. Traditionally sports have been linked to good health but this linkage is getting highly suspect now due to the fact that major sports tournaments enjoyed by millions of people are sponsored by manufacturers of liqour, cigarettes and junk-food, which are clearly harmful for health.
2. Sports and physical education is basically aimed at encouraging people of all ages to take up exercising and improve life style, increase productivity and life span. But now many keen lovers of glamorous sports do not believe in playing the game themselves. They are quite happy to watch the game without minimum effort to join the game, which provides healthy exercise. Couch potatoes are increasing in number and so does match fixing and betting in different sports all over the world, which is an evil.
3. Several news reports keep telling us about how many millions are being given to our sports heroes by various companies for endorsing their products and the sports star becomes even better known for his millions than for sporting skills. The rules of some sports have been changed to make room for telecasting of advertisements.
4. High commercial stakes have also led to increasing resort to drugs by sports persons to enhance their performance, reaching a peak in Seoul Olympics with the fastest man on earth turned out to be a drugged man.
5. Winning at all costs is a growing mania in many a sports. A form of war is permeating the minds and souls of many contestants, as can be seen in football and authorized in boxing. Contestants would not only maim their opponents but now seem willing to sell their soul to achieve' a win, no matter how tarnished. While more and more efforts are being put into organizing sports tournaments as million-dollar extravaganza, sadly the basic aspects of sports / are being neglected.

Guiding Principles for the Physical Education Programme for High School Students

1. Both boys and girls should be exposed to a well designed programme.
2. The means of giving training should be in progression i.e., from simple to complex training methods should be used.
3. Five class periods of physical education each week are recommended. Minimum of three class periods should be there even if the other periods are given more weightage due to academic constraints.
4. A large number of activities should be continued from grade seven through grade twelve in order for the student to progress efficiently from the elementary to the advanced skills.
5. Nearly all activities should be introduced at the junior high school level so that students may explore the field, and be able to participate in intramurals and in games with their parents and friends with some degree of effectiveness.

6. In grades 8 and 9, team sport activity should be heaviest for both boys and girls in 11 and 12 grades, dual and individual sports should be developed.
7. All students should be enrolled in physical education classes. Time should be scheduled for special education pupils and others handicapped by functional or structural disorders.
8. Assignment should take into consideration, the individual differences.
9. The pupil/teacher ratio for physical education classes should not be constant, but should vary depending upon activity.
10. The instructional programme should be scheduled to allow for maximum participation and adequate time for each pupil to have an opportunity to gain the satisfaction that comes from achievement.

Qualities of a Physical Education Personnel

There are many important characteristics that must be possessed by a physical education teacher. Some of the major factors which helps an individual succeed as physical education teacher are :

1. **Personality:** Personality is the sum total of an individual's responses to the social situations in which he finds himself. The fundamental basis of personality is character. This is more important for a physical education teacher because he will be copied most frequently by students. Self control acceptance to changing situations, patience, an unbiased attitude are the examples of qualities that a physical educator need to possess.
2. **Training:** Training here means education one receives in school from the view point of success in the instructional position. A person learns more and more and grows better and better from school to College/ University. Physical educationist should be academically sound and educated so that he can inculcate good qualities of head and heart among students.
3. **Experience**: A failure may teach one what to do and what not to do in specific position, or it may discourage one. Experience teaches one to modify ones approach, make optimum and worthy use of time and money and perform the best with limited resources. Experience avoids last minute hassles and develops better insight into the future goals and programmes.
4. **Health:** Maintaining the enthusiasm and handling the pressures associated with teaching physical education requires a satisfactory level of mental and physical health and physical fitness. A teacher can stay mobile, resist fatigue and work more productively if he maintains good personal hygiene and has sound mind in the sound body.
5. Fair play, courtesy, generosity, self control and friendly atmosphere should be developed.

EXERCISE

1. Y. M. C. A. College of Physical Education was started in 1920 by–
(*a*) Jawahar Lal Nehru
(*b*) Harry Crow Buck
(*c*) Dalhousie
(*d*) Lord Mountbatten

2. Y. M. C. A. College of Physical Education is situated at–
(*a*) Kolkatta (*b*) Bangalore
(*c*) Mumbai (*d*) Chennai

3. What is the number of physical education institutes offering professional education in the field?
(*a*) 50 (*b*) 57
(*c*) 63 (*d*) 48

4. Which was the first institute in India to propagate the cause of indigenous physical education?
(*a*) YMCA, Chennai
(*b*) L. N. C. P. E., Gwalior

(*c*) Hanuman Vyayam Prasarak Mandal, Amravati
(*d*) Punjab Govt. College of Physical Edcuation, Patiala

5. Which premier institute of physical education was given the status of "Deemed University'?
(*a*) LNCPE, Gwalior
(*b*) YMCA, Chennai
(*c*) Punjab Govt. College of Physcial Education, Patiala
(*d*) Govt. College of Physical Education, Bangalore

6. LNCPE, Gwalior was made a "Deemed University" in which of the following years?
(*a*) 1990 (*b*) 1995
(*c*) 1999 (*d*) 2002

7. .Sports Authority of India was established in–
(*a*) 1994 (*b*) 1956
(*c*) 1968 (*d*) 1984

8. In which year did the Govt. of India introduce sports talent search scholarship scheme ?
(*a*) 1965-66 (*b*) 1957-58
(*c*) 1975-76 (*d*) 1970-71

9. Which of the following is an apex body for promotion of sports in the country?
(*a*) LNCPE (*b*) NSNIS
(*c*) SAI
(*d*) Punjab State Sports Council

10. When did SAI take over the control of NSNIS, Patiala and LNCPE, Gwalior?
(*a*) April , 1967 (*b*) May, 1987
(*c*) August, 1991 (*d*) September, 1995

11. The Rural Sports Tournament Scheme was introduced by Govt. of India in–
(*a*) 1956-57 (*b*) 1991-92
(*c*) 1970-71 (*d*) 1980-81

12. When was Lakshmi Bai College of Physical Education established in Gwalior?
(*a*) 1967 (*b*) 1947
(*c*) 1957 (*d*) 1977

13. In 1953, who presented the first project for organized sports coaching in India?
(*a*) Jawahar Lal Nehru
(*b*) Raj Kumari Amrit Kaur
(*c*) Rajendra Prasad
(*d*) Sir Dorabji Jamshedji Tata

14. What is the minimum qualification to become a coach in India?
(*a*) NSNIS diploma (*b*) B. Ph. Ed.
(*c*) M. Ph. Ed. (*d*) M. Phil.

15. Which institute has trained the maximum number of coaches in India?
(*a*) LNCPE, Trivandrum
(*b*) NSNIS, Patiala
(c) LNCPE, Gwalior
(*d*) Indira Gandhi Institute of Physical Education of Sports Sciences

16. Most appropriately, physical education curriculum can be defined as–
(*a*) division of the subjects for study
(*b*) putting educational philosophy into action
(*c*) prescribed course of subjects for study
(*d*) none of the above

17. Curriculum construction in physical education depends upon–
(*a*) nature, needs and characteristics of individuals
(*b*) aim and objectives of physical education
(*c*) facilities, time available and financial resource
(*d*) all of the above

18. Which of the following should form the content of curriculum in physical education?
(*a*) Rhythmics
(*b*) Apparatus activities
(*c*) Combatives
(*d*) All of the above

19. Which of the following was the first to facilitate the introduction of modern physical education in schools?
(*a*) National fitness corps
(*b*) The plan of physical education and recreation
(*c*) N.C.E.R.T. syllabus
(*d*) National policy of education, 1986

20. National fitness corps (NFC) programme was framed in–
(*a*) 1965 (*b*) 1986
(*c*) 1972 (*d*) 1984

21. When was YMCA (Chennai) College of Physical Education formed?
(*a*) 1914 (*b*) 1896
(*c*) 1918 (*d*) 1928

22. Who was the first principal of YMCA (Chennai) College of Physical Education?
(*a*) C. A. Bucher (*b*) H. C. Buck
(*c*) G. D. Sondhi (*d*) B. P. Coubertin

23. When was Laxmi Bai National College, Gwalior of Physical Education (LNCPE), established?
(*a*) 1958 (*b*) 1957
(*c*) 1963 (*d*) 1961

24. In which year was Netaji Subhash National Institue of Sports, Patiala established?
(*a*) 1958 (*b*) 1959
(*c*) 1960 (*d*) 1961

25. Which of the following is not a regional centre of Sports Authority of India?
(*a*) Kolkata (*b*) Bangalore
(*c*) Chandigarh (*d*) Patiala

26. Which of the following is not a scheme/ programme by S. A I. for spotting talent?
(*a*) NSTC (*b*) SAG
(*c*) SPDA (*d*) SGFI

27. What does a time table indicate?
(*a*) Load of work on teachers only
(*b*) Working hours of the school only
(*c*) Location of class or teacher at a particular time
(*d*) All of the above

28. Physical education teachers need a time-table because–
(*a*) it helps them plan budget
(*b*) it ensures students attentiveness
(*c*) it ensures proper utilization of time and energy
(*d*) it helps them plan their household works

29. Which of the following factors affect time-table?
(*a*) Number of students
(*b*) Equipment available
(*c*) Climatic conditions
(*d*) All of the above

30. In a heterogeneous class a physical education teacher must take into consideration–
(*a*) height of the students
(*b*) age of the students
(*c*) equipment available
(*d*) all of the above

31. Chronic injuries are treated by–
(*a*) infrared (*b*) ultra theraphy
(*c*) ultrasonic (*d*) ultraviolet

32. Water therapy is also known as–
(*a*) electrotherapy (*b*) waxtherapy
(*c*) hydrotherapy (*d*) ice therapy

33. Swelling is reduced by–
(*a*) sauna bath (*b*) whirlpool bath
(*c*) contrast bath (*d*) all of the above

34. A muscle contracts, but no movement takes place, it is known as.
(*a*) isometric (*b*) isotonic
(*c*) isokinetic (*d*) none of the above

35. Which of the following is called a pressure manipulation?
(*b*) Stroking (*c*) Clapping
(*d*) Pounding (e) Kneading

36. In rehabilitation of sports injuries, one of the following method is used–
(*a*) corrective exercise
(*b*) hydrotherapy
(*c*) cryotherapy
(*d*) none of the above

37. Shortwave diathermy is used for–
(*a*) treatment of immediate injuries
(*b*) treatment of chronic injuries
(*c*) treatment of psychological problems
(*d*) all the above

38. Hydrotherapy means–
(*a*) therapy with vaseline
(*b*) therapy with wax

(c) therapy with water
(d) therapy with oil

39. For reducing swelling, recommended treatment is–
(a) contrast bath (b) ultrasound
(c) ultra-therapy (d) ultraviolet

40. Sprains are due to–
(a) broken born
(b) bone ends out of place
(c) stretched or torn joint ligaments
(d) none of the above

41. Fracture Means–
(a) broken bone
(b) bone ends out of the place
(c) stretching of tendons
(d) none of the above

42. Cryotherapy is also known as–
(a) ice therapy
(b) hydrotherapy
(c) electrotherapy
(d) none of the above

43. Lumbargo is also called–
(a) pain in the head
(b) pain in the abdomen
(c) pain in the low-back
(d) all of the above

44. Contrast bath is recommended for–
(a) reducing a dislocated joint
(b) reducing swelling
(c) treatment of wound
(d) none of the above

45. The common injury is basketball is–
(a) medial maniscus damage
(b) damage medial ligament of the ankle
(c) damage lateral ligament of the ankle
(d) all of the above

46. Electrical gadgets used for treating immediate sports injuries is–
(a) ultra-violet rays
(b) ultra sound
(c) shortwavediathermy
(d) infra-red rays

47. During training the sensation of vomiting is caused due to–
(a) accumulation of lactic acid
(b) adrenaline
(c) carbon dioxide
(d) all of the above

48. The first-aid treatment recommended for long distance exhausted athlete is–
(a) artificial respiration
(b) massage
(c) cryotherapy
(d) all of the above

49. Effleurage is always done–
(a) from distal to proximal ends
(b) across the muscles
(c) from proximal to distal ends
(d) around joints

50. How do sports injuries occur?
(a) Lack of knowledge
(b) Inadequate training, technique and equipment
(c) Carelessness
(d) All the above

51. A work in which the amount of oxygen taken in and used by the body is sufficient to provide the energy necessary for the performance of task is called as–
(a) aerobic work (b) anaerobic work
(c) full work (d) none of the above

52. A work in which the amount of oxygen that the body can supply is less than the amount necessary to perform the task is known as–
(a) anaerobic work (b) aerobic work
(c) half work (d) none

53. The ability of the total body to use oxygen for energy is called–
(a) oxygen consumption
(b) tidal volume
(c) both
(d) none of the above

54. Which measurement is recognized as the best measurement of a person's cardio-vascular fitness?
(a) Body weight (b) Pulse rate
(c) Vo_2 max (d) None of these

55. How can the maximal Oxygen consumption increase?
(*a*) An increase in the amount of haemoglobin in the blood
(*b*) An increase in the maximal cardiac output
(*c*) An increase in amount and/or size of capillaries
(*d*) All of the above

56. The target Zone heart rate ranges from **70** to **85%** of individual's maximal heart rate. It is–
(*a*) true (*b*) false
(*c*) both (*d*) none of these

57. Formula for calculating Critical Heart Rate is–
(*a*) resting heart rate + 09.60 (maximal heart rate-resting heart rate)
(*b*) resting heart rate –0.80 (maximal heart rate-resting heart rate
(*c*) resting heart rate –0.60 (maximal heart rate + resting heart rate)
(*d*) none of the above

58. Why does muscle pull occur?
(*a*) Insufficient warm up before game
(*b*) Mineral deficiency
(*c*) Muscle imbalance
(*d*) All of the above

59. What should be applied when muscle pull occur?
(*a*) Ice (*b*) Warm water
(*c*) Infrared Lamp (*d*) None of these

60. Tennis elbows can be developed by–
(*a*) only tennis players
(*b*) only badminton players
(*c*) both
(*d*) none of these

61. What would you do when tennis elbow is developed?
(*b*) Stop playing game
(*c*) Use crepe bandage
(*d*) Use of wrist band
(e) None of these

62. What are the causes of muscle cramp?
(*a*) Salt deficiency
(*b*) Any injury to muscle
(*c*) Hyper ventilation
(*d*) All of the above

63. What do you understand by the word tendinities?
(*a*) Fracture
(*b*) An inflammation of the tendon
(*c*) Both
(*d*) Tiredness

64. What is the immediate management for sprain, strain and tendon injuries?
(*a*) Using Ice packs (*b*) Use of hot water
(*c*) Infrared Lamp (*d*) None of these

65. Cryo-therapy means–
(*a*) cold-therapy (*b*) heat application
(*c*) infrared (*d*) none

66. The word "Effleurage" is related with–
(*a*) massage
(*b*) weight training
(*c*) sprint training
(*d*) endurance training

67. The movement performed by the trainee with no aid on the body part of the subject may be termed as–
(*a*) passive manipulation
(*b*) active manipulation
(*c*) resistive manipulation
(*d*) none of these

68. The movement performed by the individual with the help of weight acting against the direction of movement may be termed as–
(*a*) resistive manipulation
(*b*) assistive manipulation
(*c*) passive manipulation
(*d*) none of these

69. Ethyl chloride is used in athletics as a means of treatment in–
(*a*) cryo-therapy (*b*) thermo-therapy
(*c*) electro-therapy (*d*) none of these

70. Diathermy and ultra-sound methods are used for the treatment of injuries in–
(*a*) cryo-therapy (*b*) thermo-therapy
(*c*) electro-therapy (*d*) none of these

71. A normal human body has–
(*a*) one kidney (*b*) two kidneys
(*c*) three kidneys (*d*) none of these

72. Human kidneys are situated at–
(*a*) 12th thorasic to 3rd lumber segment
(*b*) 8th thorasic to 2nd lumber segment
(*c*) 10th thorasic to 3rd lumber segment
(*d*) None of these

73. The chief excretory organs of human body are–
(*a*) lungs (*b*) skin
(*c*) two kidneys (*d*) none of these

74. Proximal convoluted tubule (PCT) or Pars comoluta is about–
(*a*) 20 mm long (*b*) 35 mm long
(*c*) 14 mm long (*d*) None of these

75. Henless loop (pass recta) is–
(*a*) V Shaped loop (*b*) U shaped loop
(*c*) A shaped loop (*d*) None of these

76. The renal blood flow–
(*a*) decreases during exercise
(*b*) increases during exercise
(*c*) partially effected
(*d*) none of these

77. In 24 hours the total volume glomerular filtrate is about–
(*a*) 170 litres (*b*) 190 litres
(*c*) 260 litres (*d*) None of these

78. The pituitary glands colour is–
(*a*) reddish grey (*b*) white grey
(*c*) blue (*d*) none of these

79. The pituitary gland is situated at–
(*a*) base of the brain (*b*) neck
(*c*) heart (*d*) none of these

80. The thyroid gland is situated at–
(*a*) roof of the throat (*b*) heart
(*c*) base of brain (*d*) none of these

81. The blood flow in thyroid gland per minute is–
(*a*) 3.5-6 ml./gm (*b*) 4.5-7 ml/gm
(*c*) 2.5-4.5 ml/gm (*d*) None of these

82. In human body adrenal glands are–
(*a*) 3 in number (*b*) 4 in number
(*c*) 2 in number (*d*) None of these

83. The fatigue is the result of accumulation of–
(*a*) carbonic acid (*b*) sulphuric acid
(*c*) lactic acid (*d*) all of these

84. Antidiuretic hormone is secreted by–
(*a*) pituitary gland
(*b*) adrenal gland
(*c*) thyroid gland
(*d*) para thyroid gland

85. Humerus bone is situated at–
(*a*) upper limb (*b*) lower limb
(*c*) back (*d*) all of these

86. Redial and Ulna bones are situated at–
(*a*) upper limb (*b*) lower limb
(*c*) back (*d*) all of these

87. Absence of normal Anterio-Posterior curve is called–
(*a*) kyphosis (*b*) lordosis
(*c*) flat back (*d*) all of these

88. Elementary school children should be given–
(*a*) natural exercise
(*b*) naturalised exercise
(*c*) finer muscle exercise
(*d*) big muscle exercise

89. The thoracic cage (thorax) consists–
(*a*) 14 pairs of ribs (*b*) 12 pairs of ribs
(*c*) 10 pair of ribs (*d*) None of these

90. The lumber region vertebrae's consists of–
(*a*) 6 Vertebrae's (*b*) 5 vertebrae's
(*c*) 7 vertebrae's (*d*) None of these

91. The cervicle region vertebrae's consists–
(*a*) 6 vertebrae's (*b*) 10 vertebrae's
(*c*) 7 vertebrae's (*d*) None of these

92. The shoulder blade is also known as–
(*a*) sternum (*b*) scapula
(*c*) ribs (*d*) none of these

93. The collar bone is known as–
(*a*) ribs (*b*) clavicle
(*c*) sternum (*d*) none of these

94. The ball and socket joint are–
(*a*) shoulder joint (*b*) hip joint
(*c*) both of these (*d*) none of these

95. The bones of skull are united with–
(*a*) ball and socket joint
(*b*) hinge joint
(*c*) pivot joint
(*d*) none of these

96. The knee joint is a–
(*a*) ball and socket joint
(*b*) hinge joint
(*c*) pivot joint
(*d*) none of these

97. The Radial and ulnar are linked by–
(*a*) pivot joint
(*b*) ball and socket joint
(*c*) hinge joint
(*d*) none of these

98. Biceps muscles are situated at.
(*a*) upper limb (*b*) back
(*c*) lower limb (*d*) none of these

99. Deltoid muscle is situated at–
(*a*) shoulder (*b*) elbow
(*c*) knee (*d*) none of these

100. Throwers muscle is–
(*a*) deltoid (*b*) pectoralis major
(*c*) Biceps (*d*) None of these

101. The Rowing muscle is–
(*a*) deltoid (*b*) petoralis major
(*c*) latissimus dorsi (*d*) none of these

102. The strongest muscle of the body is–
(*a*) rectus femoris (*b*) soleus
(*c*) sternomustoid (*d*) biceps

103. Pectoralis major muscles are situated at–
(*a*) chest (*b*) elbow
(*c*) knee (*d*) none of these

104. The muscle used for bending hips is known as–
(*a*) quadriceps (*b*) triceps
(*c*) biceps (*d*) none of these

105. The number of vertebrae's in spinal cord are–
(*a*) 25 (*b*) 31
(*c*) 28 (*d*) None of these

106. The muscle situated at the back side of humerus is–
(*a*) biceps (*b*) triceps
(*c*) quadriceps (*d*) none of these

107. Cerebellum is a part of–
(*a*) digestive system (*b*) muscular
(*c*) brain (*d*) none of these

108. The transfer of oxygen from air to the tissue of the body and transfer of CO2 from tissue to outside air is called–
(*a*) digestion (*b*) respiration
(*c*) absorption (*d*) none of these

109. Lungs are part of–
(*a*) nervous system (*b*) digestive system
(*c*) respiratory system (*d*) none of these

110. The normal body temperature is–
(*a*) 98.4ºF (*b*) 88ºF
(*c*) 72ºF (*d*) None of these

111. The range of normal body temperature is–
(*a*) 82º-88º.2F (*b*) 96º-99ºF
(*c*) 70º-72ºF (*d*) None of these

112. Overheating of the body is due to–
(*a*) high external temperature
(*b*) physical activity
(*c*) inadequate sweating
(*d*) combination of all the above

113. Somatotropic, Thyrotropic, Adrenocorticotropic and Gonadotropic hormones are secracted by–
(*a*) anterior lobe of pituitary gland
(*b*) posterior lobe of pituitary gland
(*c*) both
(*d*) none of these

114. The hormone that controls the growth of the body is called–
(*a*) thyrotropic hormone
(*b*) somatotropic hormone
(*c*) gonadotrophic hormone
(*d*) none of these

115. Diarthosis is–
(*a*) freely movable joints
(*b*) slightly movable joints
(*c*) immovable joints
(*d*) none of these

116. Amphiarthrosis is–
(*a*) freely movable joints
(*b*) slightly movable joints
(*c*) immovable joints
(*d*) none of these

117. Synoarthrosis is–
(*a*) freely movable joints
(*b*) slightly movable joints
(*c*) immovable joints
(*d*) none of these

118. The knee joint is–
(*a*) diarthrosis (*b*) amphiarthrosis
(*c*) synoarthrosis (*d*) none of these

119. The system which converts food substance that body cells can use as a source of energy is called–
(*a*) nervous system (*b*) muscular system
(*c*) elementary system (*d*) none of these

120. The organs which produces bile is–
(*a*) heart (*b*) lung
(*c*) liver (*d*) none of these

121. The organs which stores and concentrates the bile before use is–
(*a*) lung (*b*) liver
(*c*) gall bladder (*d*) none of these

122. The heart is composed of–
(*a*) 1 Pump (*b*) 2 pumps
(*c*) 3 pumps (*d*) None of these

123. Blood vessels entering the heart are called–
(*a*) veins (*b*) arteries
(*c*) canal (*d*) none of these

124. The blood vessel leaving the heart is called–
(*a*) veins (*b*) arteries
(*c*) canal (*d*) none of these

125. The amount of blood that can be circulated each minute is known as–
(*a*) aerobic work (*b*) cardiac out put
(*c*) lung volume (*d*) none of these

126. The nutrient which combines with protein to make haemoglobin is–
(*a*) calcium (*b*) iron
(*c*) both of these (*d*) none of these

127. Nutrients which helps to make cementing materials that hold cells together is–
(*a*) vitamin D (*b*) vitamin B
(*c*) vitamin A (*d*) none of these

128. The traumatic joint twist that result in stretching or totally tearing stabilizing connective tissue is–
(*a*) muscle pull (*b*) strain
(*c*) sprain (*d*) fracture

129. Fracture in which the bone splits along its length is known as–
(*a*) green stick fracture
(*b*) impacted fracture
(*c*) longitudinal
(*d*) depressed fracture

130. The term cardiac cycle is associated with–
(*a*) digestive system
(*b*) respiratory system
(*c*) circulatory system
(*d*) none of these

131. The sex steroids contains–
(*a*) 17 carbon atoms (*b*) 10 Carbon atoms
(*c*) 21 Carbon atoms (*d*) None of these

132. Ventricle is a part of–
(*a*) brain (*b*) lung
(*c*) heart (*d*) none of these

133. The Radial artery is situated at–
(*a*) upper limb (*b*) lower limb
(*c*) back (*d*) none of these

134. Thyroxin is produced by–
(*a*) pancrease (*b*) sex gland
(*c*) thyroid gland (*d*) none of these

135. Insulin is produced by–
(*a*) sex gland (*b*) pancrease
(*c*) thyroid gland (*d*) none of these

136. Protein builds–
(*a*) nerve tissue (*b*) bone tissue
(*c*) muscle tissue (*d*) none of these

137. Vitamin D is rich in–
(*a*) milk (*b*) butter
(*c*) egg yolk (*d*) none of these

138. Sunlight is a source of–
(*a*) vitamin B (*b*) vitamin C
(*c*) vitamin D (*d*) none of these

139. Vitamin B6 is present in–
(*a*) liver (*b*) milk
(*c*) egg (*d*) none of these

140. Rickets occurs due to the deficiency of–
(*a*) vitamin A (*b*) vitamin B
(*c*) vitamin D (*d*) none of these

141. Osteophorosis disease occurs in–
(*a*) muscles (*b*) nerves
(*c*) bones (*d*) none of these

142. Carbohydrates helps in–
(*a*) body building (*b*) energy giving
(*c*) protective (*d*) none of these

143. Functions of vitamins and minerals are–
(*a*) body building
(*b*) protective and regulating
(*c*) energy giving
(*d*) none of these

144. Malaria disease is due to–
(*a*) parasites (*b*) bacteria
(*c*) virus (*d*) all of these

145. Dengue fever is caused by–
(*a*) parasites (*b*) bacteria
(*c*) virus (*d*) all of these

146. Typhoid is caused by–
(*a*) parasites (*b*) bacteria
(*c*) virus (*d*) none of these

147. Diabetes is due to disorder of–
(*a*) lung (*b*) heart
(*c*) pancrease (*d*) none of these

148. The name of thigh bone is–
(*a*) ulna (*b*) radial
(*c*) femur (*d*) tibia

149. Bones in skeleton consists of–
(*a*) 200 (*b*) 214
(*c*) 206 (*d*) 207

150. Measles are caused by–
(*a*) virus (*b*) parasites
(*c*) bacteria (*d*) none of these

151. Diphtheria is caused by–
(*a*) bacteria (*b*) parasites
(*c*) virus (*d*) none of these

152. Small Pox is caused by–
(*a*) virus (*b*) parasites
(*c*) bacteria (*d*) none of these

153. Tuberculosis is caused by–.
(*a*) virus (*b*) parasites
(*c*) bacteria (*d*) none of these

154. Biceps is–
(*a*) involuntary muscle
(*b*) voluntary muscle
(*c*) cardiac muscle
(*d*) none of these

155. The condition in which one cannot see distant objects clearly is known as–
(*a*) myopia (*b*) hypermetropia
(*c*) anaemia (*d*) none of these

156. The conditions in which one cannot see close objects very clearly is known as–
(*a*) myopia (*b*) hypermetropia
(*c*) anaemia (*d*) none of these

157. Tymphanic membrance is responsible for–
(*a*) hearing (*b*) circulation
(*c*) digestion (*d*) none of these

158. Physical growth is indicated by increase in height, weight and size of the body.
(*a*) right (*b*) wrong
(*c*) partial wrong (*d*) none of these

159. What is the percentage of Intracellular fluids of the body weight?
(*a*) 40% (*b*) 60%
(*c*) 50% (*d*) 70%

160. What percentage of body is formed by extra cellular fluid?
(*a*) 20% (*b*) 30%
(*c*) 40% (*d*) 50%

161. Dehydration is caused by–
(*a*) loss of blood
(*b*) loss of appetite
(*c*) loss of salt and water
(*d*) none of these

162. The minute structure of human body is–
(*a*) tissue (*b*) organ
(*c*) cell (*d*) none of these

163. The constructive activities, growth and cell repair are called as–
(*a*) anabolism(*b*) cytabolism
(*c*) both(*d*) none of these

164. The protoplasm of cell is composed of–
(*a*) nucleus (*b*) cytoplasm
(*c*) both of these (*d*) none of these

165. Actin and Myosin are connected with–
(*a*) bones (*b*) muscles
(*c*) both of these (*d*) none of these

166. Karyokinesis is associated with–
(*a*) urine formation (*b*) body movement
(*c*) cell division (*d*) none of these

167. The water balance of the body is maintained by–
(*a*) gall bladder (*b*) kidney
(*c*) liver (*d*) heart

168. The mucus membrane is found in–
(*a*) alimentary track (*b*) respiratory
(*c*) both of these (*d*) none of these

169. Synovial membrane lies in the–
(*a*) cavity of joint
(*b*) alimentary track
(*c*) genito urinary track
(*d*) none of these

170. Serous membrane is found in–
(*a*) chest (*b*) abdomen
(*c*) both of these (*d*) none of these

171. Cardiac muscles are–
(*a*) unstriated muscles
(*b*) striated muscles
(*c*) both
(*d*) none of these

172. Gastrocnemius muscle is–
(*a*) voluntary (*b*) involuntary
(*c*) both of these (*d*) cardiac

173. The shape of deltoid muscle is–
(*a*) spindle shaped (*b*) bipennate form
(*c*) triangular (*d*) rhomboid

174. Soleus muscles is–
(*a*) unipennate (*b*) bipennate form
(*c*) spindle shaped (*d*) rectangular

175. Pectoralis major is–
(*a*) fan shaped (*b*) spindle shaped
(*c*) rhomboid (*d*) tringular

176. Gastrocnemius muscle is–
(*a*) fan shaped (*b*) spindle shaped
(*c*) rhomboid (*d*) none of these

177. Sternomustoid muscle is found in–
(*a*) leg (*b*) abdomen
(*c*) neck (*d*) chest

178. Vastus medilis is located in–
(*a*) thigh (*b*) upper limb
(*c*) abdomen (*d*) none of these

179. Rectus Abdominus is located in–
(*a*) neck (*b*) thigh
(*c*) abdomen (*d*) none of these

180. The study of the structure of the body is called–
(*a*) physiology (*b*) anatomy
(*c*) biology (*d*) none of these

181. The study of the functions of the normal human body is called–
(*a*) physiology (*b*) botany
(*c*) anatomy (*d*) none of these

182. The study of the fine structures of the body is called–
(*a*) cytology (*b*) biology
(*c*) histology (*d*) none of these

183. The study of the cells is called–
(*a*) cytology (*b*) biology
(*c*) histology (*d*) none of these

184. The study of all living things is called–
(*a*) cytology (*b*) biology
(*c*) histology (*d*) none of these

185. The study of bone is called–
(*a*) osteology (*b*) anthrology
(*c*) myology (*d*) none of these

186. The study of joints is called–
(*a*) osteology (*b*) arthrology
(*c*) myology (*d*) neurology

187. The study of Muscles is called–
(*a*) osteology (*b*) arthrology
(*c*) myology (*d*) neurology

188. The study of organs of viscera is called–
(*a*) myology (*b*) neuorology
(*c*) splanchnology (*d*) none of these

189. The study of nerves and nerve structure is called–
(*a*) myology (*b*) neurology
(*c*) anthrology (*d*) none of these

190. A canal like structure lying next to the nucleus and involved in the secretory activities of the cell is–
(*a*) mitochondria (*b*) golgi apparatus
(*c*) ground cytoplasm (*d*) none of these

191. Small rod-like structure which are closely connected with catabolic, or respiratory, processes of the cell body is–
(*a*) golgil apparatus
(*b*) ground cytoplasm
(*c*) mitochondria
(*d*) all of the above

192. A minute dense part of the cytoplasm, lying close to the nucleus, and plays important role in cell division is–
(*a*) ground cytoplasm (*b*) cell membrane
(*c*) centrosome (*d*) none of these

193. Spinal Cord is a part of–
(*a*) digestive system (*b*) respiratory system
(*c*) urogenital system (*d*) nervous system

194. The central and Peripheral systems when grouped together are called–
(*a*) cerebrospinal nervous system
(*b*) respiratory system
(*c*) urogenital system
(*d*) nervous system

195. Trapezius muscle is located in–
(*a*) chest (*b*) lower back
(*c*) upper back (*d*) none of these

196. Latissimus dorsi is located in–
(*a*) chest
(*b*) lower back
(*c*) lateral part of trunk
(*d*) none of these

197. Brachioradialis is located in–
(*a*) forearm (*b*) upper arm
(*c*) lower leg (*d*) upper leg

198. Rectus femoris is located in–
(*a*) thigh (*b*) calf
(*c*) lower back (*d*) upper back

199. Pectineus is located in–
(*a*) trunk region (*b*) abdominal region
(*c*) thigh (*d*) chest

200. Soleus is located in–
(*a*) upper leg (*b*) lower leg
(*c*) fore arm (*d*) none of these

201. Gastrocnemius is located at–
(*a*) lower back (*b*) lower leg
(*c*) upper leg (*d*) none of these

202. Gracilis is located at–
(*a*) thigh (*b*) calf
(*c*) abdomen (*d*) none of these

203. What percent of skeletal muscles consists of the body weight?
(*a*) 10% (*b*) 20%
(*c*) 30% (*d*) 40%

204. The contractile element of the muscle is–
(*a*) sarcoplasm (*b*) epimysium
(*c*) perimysium (*d*) myofibril

205. The muscle fitness are contained in bundles by sheets of connected tissue called–
(*a*) perimysium (*b*) epimysium
(*c*) endomysium (*d*) none of these

206. Myofibrils consists of fine protein threads called–
(*a*) actin (*b*) myosin
(*c*) both of these (*d*) none of these

207. Nervous tissue consists of matters such as–
(*a*) grey matter (*b*) white matter
(*c*) neuroglia (*d*) all of the above

208. Muscle tone is purely a reflex process.
(*a*) True (*b*) False
(*c*) Partially true (*d*) Partially false

209. The problem faced by athlete at high altitude is–
(*a*) L.A.P.E. (*b*) H.A.P.E
(*c*) Both (*d*) None of these

210. Saddle joint is–
(*a*) amphiarthrosis (*b*) synoarthrosis
(*c*) diarthrosis (*d*) none of these

211. Elbow joint is–
(*a*) pivot joint (*b*) condyloid joint
(*c*) saddle joint (*d*) hing joint

212. Cornal joint is the union of–
(*a*) parital and temporal
(*b*) maxilla and zygomatic
(*c*) frontal and partial
(*d*) parital and oscipetal

213. Parital bone is situated at–
(*a*) chest (*b*) spinal cord
(*c*) lower leg (*d*) skull

214. Fast twitch muscle fibres are–
(*a*) white muscle fibres
(*b*) red muscle fibres
(*c*) both
(*d*) none of these

215. Slow twitch muscle fibres are–
(*a*) white muscle fibres
(*b*) red muscle fibres
(*c*) both
(*d*) none of these

216. The only class of food which contains nitrogen–
(*a*) fat (*b*) carbohydrate
(*c*) pritein (*d*) none of these

217. Monosaccharides is–
(*a*) fat (*b*) carbohydrate
(*c*) protein (*d*) none of these

218. Disaccharides is–
(*a*) fat (*b*) carbohydrate
(*c*) both (*d*) none of these

219. The fuel food of human body are–
(*a*) fat and protein
(*b*) protein and carbohydrate
(*c*) fat and carbodydrate
(*d*) none of these

220. The rich source of carbohydrate is–
(*a*) cereals (*b*) pulse
(*c*) wheat (*d*) none of these

221. The rich source of fat is–
(*a*) butter (*b*) potatoes
(*c*) fish (*d*) none of these

222. The rich source of protein is–
(*a*) barley (*b*) milk
(*c*) meat (*d*) none of these

223. The rich source of starch is–
(*a*) wheat (flour) (*b*) milk
(*c*) barley (*d*) all of the above

224. Water lost each day as urine is about–
(*a*) 1,200 ml (*b*) 5,000 ml
(*c*) 1,500 ml (*d*) 2,000 ml

225. Water lost each day by the skin is about–
(*a*) 800 ml (*b*) 900 ml
(*c*) 200 ml (*d*) None of these

226. Water lost each day in Expired air is about–
(*a*) 200 ml (*b*) 600 ml
(*c*) 400 ml (*d*) 300 ml

227. Fish liver, oils, milk and dairy products are rich source of–
(*a*) vitamin D (*b*) vitamin E
(*c*) vitamin K (*d*) vitamin A

228. Thyrocalcitonin (TCT) is secreted by–
(*a*) thyroid gland (*b*) parathyroid gland
(*c*) adrenal gland (*d*) pitutary gland

229. The average total weight of parathyroid is about–
(*a*) 140 mg (*b*) 160 mg
(*c*) 180 mg (*d*) 200 mg

230. Parathormone (PTH) is secreated by–
(*a*) thyroid gland (*b*) parathyroid gland
(*c*) adrenal gland (*d*) pituitary gland

231. A total calcium content of normal adult human is–
(*a*) 20-25 g. per kg of fat free body tissue
(*b*) 10-15 g per kg of fat free body tissue
(*c*) 40-50 g per kg of fat free body tissue
(*d*) 70-90 g per kg of fat free body tissue

232. The axis perpendicular to the ground and divides the body into the upper and lower halves is–
(*a*) the vertical axis (*b*) the frontal axis
(*c*) the saggital axis (*d*) none of these

233. The axis which passes horizontally from side to side and divides the body into front and back halves is–

(*a*) the vertical axis (*b*) the frontal axis
(*c*) the saggital axis (*d*) none of these

234. The axis which passes horizontally from front to back and divides the body into right and left halves is–
(*a*) the vertical axis (*b*) the frontal axis
(*c*) the saggital axis (*d*) none of these

235. Wheat oil, egg yolk, milk are rich source of–
(*a*) vitamin D (*b*) vitamin E
(*c*) vitamin K (*d*) none of these

236. Spinach, soya bean and pig's liver are rich source of–
(*a*) vitamin K (*b*) vitamin D
(*c*) vitamin E (*d*) vitamin A

237. The deficiency of vitamin K causes–
(*a*) rickets
(*b*) aneamia
(*c*) prolonged blood clotting time
(*d*) none of these

238. Heart, blood vessels and lymphatics combine to form–
(*a*) respiratory system (*b*) muscular system
(*c*) circulatory system (*d*) none of these

239. Arteries carries blood–
(*a*) to the heart (*b*) from the heart
(*c*) both (*d*) none of these

240. Veins carries blood–
(*a*) from the heart (*b*) into the heart
(*c*) both (*d*) none of these

241. The shape of heart is–
(*a*) round (*b*) cone
(*c*) triangular (*d*) shapeless

242. The adult heart weights about–
(*a*) 260-230 gms (*b*) 320-400 gms
(*c*) 150-200 gms (*d*) None of the above

243. The upper chamber of heart is called–
(*a*) ventricle (*b*) atrial
(*c*) both (*d*) none of these

244. The lower chamber of heart is called–
(*a*) ventricle (*b*) atrial
(*c*) both (*d*) none of these

245. The atrial and ventricles of each side communicate with one another by means of–
(*a*) Atrial opening
(*b*) Ventrial opening
(*c*) Antrio ventricarlar opening
(*c*) None of these

246. The valve which guards the antroventricular opening on the right side are called–
(*a*) Tricuspid valve (*b*) Mitral valve
(*c*) Both (*d*) None of these

247. The valve which guards the antroventricular opening on the left side are called–
(*a*) Tricuspid valve (*b*) Mitral valve
(*c*) Both (*d*) None of these

248. The outer covering of heart is called–
(*a*) Myocardium (*b*) Pericardium
(*c*) Endocardium (*d*) None of these

249. The middle muscular layer of heart is called–
(*a*) Pericardium (*b*) Myocardium
(*c*) Endorcardium (*d*) None of these

250. The inner lining of the heart is called
(*a*) Myocardium (*b*) Pericardium
(*c*) Endocardium (*d*) None of these

251. The aorta carries blood away from–
(*a*) Right ventricle (*b*) Left ventricle
(*c*) Right Atrium (*d*) Let Atirum

252. Normal pulse rate range (number of beats per minute) in adult individual is–
(*a*) 96-100 (*b*) 80-90
(*c*) 60-80 (*d*) None of these

253. The cardiac output in an adult individual is about–
(*a*) 4 litres (*b*) 5 litres
(*c*) 6 litres (*d*) None of these

254. The stroke volume in an adult individual is about–
(*a*) 70 ml (*b*) 80 ml
(*c*) 90 ml (*d*) None of these

255. Stroke volume in an average individual is about–
(*a*) 90 ml (*b*) 100 ml
(*c*) 70 ml (*d*) None of these

256. Heart failure is due to–
(*a*) excess of cardiac output
(*b*) lack of cardiac output
(*c*) both
(*d*) none of these

257. Pulmonary Oedema is due to the failure of–
(*a*) left side of heart (*b*) right side of heart
(*c*) both (*d*) none of these

258. The impure blood of the body enters into the heart through–
(*a*) inferior vena cava
(*b*) superior vena cava
(*c*) both
(*d*) none of these

259. The condition where the brain is deprived of blood for more the 3 to 4 minutes is called–
(*a*) cardiac arrest
(*b*) syncope
(*c*) congestive heart failure
(*d*) none of these

260. The number of ribs attached indirectly to the body of sternum is–
(*a*) five (*b*) two
(*c*) three (*d*) none of these

261. The average ratio in blood between Plasma and cell is–
(*a*) 45:55 (*b*) 55:45
(*c*) 60:40 (*d*) None of these

262. Erythrocytes, leucocytes and thrombocytes are present in–
(*a*) fat cells (*b*) nerve cell
(*c*) blood cells (*d*) none of these

263. Average R.B.C. count in each cubic millimeter is–
(*a*) 4,000,000 (*b*) 1,000,000
(*c*) 5,000,000 (*d*) None of these

264. The colour of the blood is red due to the presence of–
(*a*) myoglobin (*b*) actin
(*c*) myocin (*d*) haemoglobin

265. R.B.C. are produced in–
(*a*) bone marrow (*b*) heart
(*c*) lungs (*d*) none of these

266. The average life of R.B.C. is–
(*a*) 100 days (*b*) 200 days
(*c*) 120 days (*d*) None of these

267. The function of blood is–
(*a*) supply of oxygen
(*b*) carry of Nutrients
(*c*) both
(*d*) none of these

268. The donor of AB Group can donate blood to–
(*a*) A Group (*b*) B Group
(*c*) AB Group (*d*) None of these

269. O Group is called–
(*a*) universal recipient (*b*) universal donor
(*c*) both (*d*) none of these

270. AB Group is called–
(*a*) universal recipient
(*b*) universal donor
(*c*) both
(*d*) none of these

271. A Group donor can donate Blood to–
(*a*) A Group (*b*) AB Group
(*c*) Both Group (*d*) None of these

272. O Group patient can receive blood from–
(*a*) A Group (*b*) AB Group
(*c*) O Group (*d*) B Group

273. Average W.B.C. count in each cubic millimeter of blood is–
(*a*) 20,000 (*b*) 30,000
(*c*) 8,000 (*d*) None of these

274. Neutrophil, eosinophil, basophil are the constituents of–
(*a*) R.B.C (*b*) W.B.C
(*c*) Platlets (*d*) None of these

275. Antidiuretic hormone and oxytocic hrmone are secreated by–
(*a*) anterior lobe (*b*) posterior lobe
(*c*) both (*d*) none of these

276. The waste products which result from the combustion fat in the tissues are excreted–
(*a*) by the wings (*b*) by the skin
(*c*) by the kidney (*d*) all of the above

277. Metabolism is the word used to indicate–
(*a*) the exchange of gases in the lungs
(*b*) the chemical changes which takes place in the body
(*c*) the store of O_2 in the muscles.
(*d*) none of these

278. The function of W.B.C. is to–
(*a*) to carry oxygen
(*b*) protects the body from microorganism
(*c*) supply energy to body
(*d*) none of these

279. The average platlets counts in each cubic millimetre of blood is–
(*a*) 800,000 (*b*) 600,000
(*c*) 350,000 (*d*) None of these

280. The colour of blood plasma fluid is–
(*a*) red (*b*) pink
(*c*) straw (*d*) none of these

281. Fibrinogen is essential for–
(*a*) blood formation
(*b*) blood coagulation
(*c*) both
(*d*) none of these

282. The resting phase of cardiac cycle is called–
(*a*) systole (*b*) diastole
(*c*) both (*d*) none of these

283. The contractile or emptying phase of the cardiac cycle is called–
(*a*) systole (*b*) diastole
(*c*) both (*d*) none of these

284. The difference in pressure between systole and diastole is called–
(*a*) blood pressure (*b*) pulse pressure
(*c*) osmotic pressure (*d*) none of these

285. Factor maintaining blood pressure is–
(*a*) the viscosity of blood
(*b*) the pumping force of heart
(*c*) both
(*d*) none of these

286. Anemia is a deficiency caused due to–
(*a*) excess of HB in blood
(*b*) lack of HB in blood
(*c*) lack of protein
(*d*) none of these

287. The arterial blood contains–
(*a*) unoxygenated blood
(*b*) oxygented blood
(*c*) both
(*d*) none of these

288. The function of pulmonary artery is–
(*a*) to carry impure blood into the heart
(*b*) to carry oxygenated blood into the heart
(*c*) t carry oxygenated blood from the heart
(*d*) none of these

289. The function of pulmonary vein is–
(*a*) to carry unoxygenated blood into the heart
(*b*) to carry oxygenated blood into the heart
(*c*) to carry oxygenated blood from the heart
(*d*) none of these

290. The principle salivary glands are–
(*a*) parotid (*b*) submadibular
(*c*) sublingual (*d*) all of the above

291. Parotid glands is situated–
(*a*) in the base of brain
(*b*) slightly in front of ear
(*c*) lies beneath the tongue
(*d*) none of these

292. The submandibular glands are situated–
(*a*) slightly in front of the ear
(*b*) lies beneath the tongue
(*c*) lies each side beneath the jaw bone
(*d*) none of these

293. The sublingual gland are situated–
(*a*) slightly in front of the ear
(*b*) lies beneath the tongue
(*c*) lies beneath the jawbone
(*d*) none of these

294. The saliva is secreted by–
(*a*) submandibular glands
(*b*) parotid glands
(*c*) sublingual glands
(*d*) all the above

295. The Foods are liquefied and mixed with HCl and prepared for intestinal digestion in–

(*a*) oesophagus (*b*) stomach
(*c*) deodenum (*d*) none of these

296. Proteins are converted into peptones in stomach.

(*a*) True (*b*) False
(*c*) Partially true (*d*) Partially false

297. The digestion of fat commences in stomach.

(*a*) True (*b*) False
(*c*) Partially true (*d*) Partially false

298. The stomach acts as reservoir for a short time.

(*a*) True (*b*) False
(*c*) Partially true (*d*) Partially false

299. The length of small intestine is about 2.4 metres long in length.

(*a*) True (*b*) False
(*c*) Partially true (*d*) Partially false

300. The small intestine lies in

(*a*) umbilican region of abdomen–
(*b*) end of illium
(*c*) both
(*d*) none of these

ANSWERS

1	2	3	4	5	6	7	8	9	10
(*b*)	(*d*)	(*b*)	(*c*)	(*a*)	(*b*)	(*d*)	(*d*)	(*c*)	(*b*)
11	**12**	**13**	**14**	**15**	**16**	**17**	**18**	**19**	**20**
(*c*)	(*c*)	(*b*)	(*a*)	(*b*)	(*b*)	(*d*)	(*d*)	(*a*)	(*a*)
21	**22**	**23**	**24**	**25**	**26**	**27**	**28**	**29**	**30**
(*c*)	(*b*)	(*b*)	(*d*)	(*c*)	(*d*)	(*d*)	(*c*)	(*d*)	(*d*)
31	**32**	**33**	**34**	**35**	**36**	**37**	**38**	**39**	**40**
(*d*)	(*c*)	(*c*)	(*b*)	(*d*)	(*a*)	(*b*)	(*c*)	(*a*)	(*c*)
41	**42**	**43**	**44**	**45**	**46**	**47**	**48**	**49**	**50**
(*a*)	(*a*)	(*c*)	(*b*)	(*d*)	(*d*)	(*a*)	(*a*)	(*a*)	(*d*)
51	**52**	**53**	**54**	**55**	**56**	**57**	**58**	**59**	**60**
(*a*)	(*a*)	(*a*)	(*c*)	(*d*)	(*a*)	(*a*)	(*d*)	(*b*)	(*c*)
61	**62**	**63**	**64**	**65**	**66**	**67**	**68**	**69**	**70**
(*a*)	(*d*)	(*b*)	(*a*)	(*a*)	(*a*)	(*b*)	(*a*)	(*a*)	(*c*)
71	**72**	**73**	**74**	**75**	**76**	**77**	**78**	**79**	**80**
(*b*)	(*a*)	(*c*)	(*c*)	(*b*)	(*b*)	(*a*)	(*a*)	(*a*)	(*a*)
81	**82**	**83**	**84**	**85**	**86**	**87**	**88**	**89**	**90**
(*a*)	(*c*)	(*c*)	(*a*)	(*a*)	(*b*)	(*a*)	(*a*)	(*b*)	(*b*)
91	**92**	**93**	**94**	**95**	**96**	**97**	**98**	**99**	**100**
(*c*)	(*b*)	(*b*)	(*a*)	(*d*)	(*b*)	(*a*)	(*a*)	(*a*)	(*b*)
101	**102**	**103**	**104**	**105**	**106**	**107**	**108**	**109**	**110**
(*c*)	(*a*)	(*a*)	(*a*)	(*d*)	(*b*)	(*c*)	(*b*)	(*c*)	(*a*)
111	**112**	**113**	**114**	**115**	**116**	**117**	**118**	**119**	**120**
(*b*)	(*d*)	(*c*)	(*b*)	(*a*)	(*b*)	(*c*)	(*b*)	(*b*)	(*c*)
121	**122**	**123**	**124**	**125**	**126**	**127**	**128**	**129**	**130**
(*b*)	(*a*)	(*c*)	(*b*)	(*b*)	(*b*)	(*d*)	(*c*)	(*a*)	(*c*)

131	132	133	134	135	136	137	138	139	140
(a)	(c)	(a)	(c)	(b)	(c)	(c)	(c)	(a)	(c)
141	142	143	144	145	146	147	148	149	150
(c)	(b)	(b)	(a)	(b)	(b)	(c)	(c)	(c)	(a)
151	152	153	154	155	156	157	158	159	160
(a)	(a)	(c)	(b)	(a)	(b)	(a)	(a)	(d)	(b)
161	162	163	164	165	166	167	168	169	170
(c)	(c)	(a)	(c)	(b)	(c)	(b)	(b)	(a)	(a)
171	172	173	174	175	176	177	178	179	180
(b)	(a)	(c)	(b)	(d)	(a)	(c)	(a)	(c)	(b)
181	182	183	184	185	186	187	188	189	190
(a)	(d)	(a)	(b)	(a)	(a)	(c)	(c)	(b)	(b)
191	192	193	194	195	196	197	198	199	200
(c)	(c)	(d)	(a)	(c)	(b)	(a)	(a)	(c)	(a)
201	202	203	204	205	206	207	208	209	210
(b)	(a)	(a)	(d)	(a)	(c)	(c)	(a)	(c)	(c)
211	212	213	214	215	216	217	218	219	220
(d)	(c)	(d)	(a)	(b)	(c)	(b)	(c)	(c)	(a)
221	222	223	224	225	226	227	228	229	230
(a)	(c)	(a)	(c)	(d)	(a)	(a)	(a)	(d)	(b)
231	232	233	234	235	236	237	238	239	240
(d)	(d)	(b)	(c)	(a)	(d)	(c)	(c)	(b)	(b)
241	242	243	244	245	246	247	248	249	250
(c)	(a)	(c)	(c)	(c)	(a)	(d)	(b)	(b)	(c)
251	252	253	254	255	256	257	258	259	260
(b)	(b)	(b)	(b)	(c)	(b)	(c)	(c)	(c)	(a)
261	262	263	264	265	266	267	268	269	270
(b)	(c)	(c)	(b)	(a)	(c)	(a)	(c)	(b)	(a)
271	272	273	274	275	276	277	278	279	280
(a)	(c)	(c)	(b)	(b)	(b)	(b)	(c)	(c)	(c)
281	282	283	284	285	286	287	288	289	290
(b)	(b)	(a)	(a)	(b)	(b)	(b)	(a)	(b)	(d)
291	292	293	294	295	296	297	298	299	300
(b)	(c)	(b)	(d)	(b)	(c)	(b)	(a)	(a)	(a)

UNIT-VI

HEALTH AND HEALTH EDUCATION

Introduction

Health is a very important topic and so is health education. Healthy people constitute a healthy nation. It is necessary to explain the meaning of health as it is not merely absence of disease but much more. In this chapter apart from elaborating the meanings of health and health education, definitions of health and health education, and various dimensions of health, the objectives, the scope, principles and importance of health education have also been discussed.

MEANING OF HEALTH

The strength of a nation rests upon the health of its people and future of the health of the people depends, to a large extent, on what is done to promote, improve and preserve the health, as health is a fundamental human right. To be a good man is the first requisite to success in life and to be a nation of healthy citizens is the first condition to national prosperity. The natural question that arises is, *what health is ? and on what it depends ?*

The dictionary meaning of health is, *"freedom from disease, sound body and mind etc; that condition in which functions of body and mind are duly discharged"*. Earlier, health was considered as a condition of being '*hale*', i.e., *safe and sound.* A more searching and deep look in the subject would show that health is more than this. The implication of health is that, health may be a continuum along linear scale, from near death at one end to optimum health on the other. Opitmum health would be that level which would enable the individual to live life to the fullest. Health is the ability of the body to sustain adaptive efforts and is used to imply body power, vitality, and ability to resist fatigue. Health is some times considered as the total outcome of the organic, neuro-muscular, interpretive, and emotional development.

Health is man's greatest wealth, he who has health must cherish it with care, lest he should lose it. To this end he must have adequate knowledge of how to live healthy. Health is not merely absence of disease, it is positive quality of the living body, of which fitness for one's work and happiness are distinguishing marks. *Health is the way; there is no way to health. Let all the habits of living be health promoting.* The term health is not an abstract thing but a relative concept. In it we see a continuum of freedom from sickenss to better health, and positive health.

Health educationists are slowly evolving away from the view that health is merely the treatment and prevention of illness; to a more open ended view that emphasizes the individual's own responsibility for his own well being. It may be emphasized that health is neither static nor isolated from external circumstances, our health depends on the way we relate to our environment and to each other; where we live, the jobs we do, the food we eat, the water we drink and air we breath are all important. We are now coming to realise that health is extricably bound up with our minds, environment and ways of living. *Health is basic to learning, to happiness, to success, to effective citizenship, and to worthwhile living. In Ayurved 'Swasthya' (health) has been defined as a well balanced metabolism, a happy state of being, the senses and the mind. Swami Vivekananda has said, "a weak person who has weak body or weak mind can never be master of a strong soul". Aristotle has also stated that a sound mind lives in a sound body.*

Health is a state of physical, mental, emotional, and social well being. Good health enables people to enjoy life and to have the opportunity to achieve the goals they have set for themselves. The real purpose of health is to develop and maintain vigour and vitality, to acquire interests and habits in ways of living that are wholesome and to meet the demands put upon the individual efficiently, with energy and satisfaction. The concept of health has been very appropriately summed up by *J. F. Williams, "Health is that quality of life that enables an individual to live most and serve best."* Health can be achieved, maintained and improved by supplying the basic physical, mental, emotional and social needs in proper proportion. In fact health is the key to education, success, good citizenship and a happy life. Nowadays health and its maintenance is being considered as a major social investment and it is being felt that health involves individual, state and international responsibility.

DEFINITION OF HEALTH

"Health is a condition or quality of the human organism expressing the adequate functioning of the organism in given conditions, genetic and environmental."

– *W.H.O. Tech. Rep. (1957)*

"Health is the condition of the organism which measures the degree to which its aggregate powers are able to function."

– *Oberteuffer*

"Health is that state in which the individual is able to mobilize all his resources - intellectual, emotional, and physical, for optimum daily living."

– *Encyclopaedia of Health*

"Health means soundness of body or mind; that condition in which its functions are duly and efficiently discharged.

– *Oxford English Dictionary.*

"Health is a state of complete physical, mental and social well being and not merely an absence of diseases or infirmity."

Recently this definition has been amplified and it has been added, "attainment of a level of health that will enable every individual to lead a socially and economically productive life."

– *World Health Organisation*

"Health is considered as that condition, mental and physical., in which the individual is functionally well adjusted internally as concerns his body parts, and externally as concerns his environments."

– *Voltmer and Esslinger*

"Health is the condition of being sound in body, mind or spirit, especially freedom from physical disease or pain."

– *Webster*

"Health aims at making growth more perfect, life more vigorous, decay less rapid and death more remote."

– *Siddalingaiya*

"One's ideal of health should be the highest realisation of his physical, mental and spiritual possibilities rather than mere freedom from diseases and deformities."

– *W. A. Yeager*

"It is the quality of life that enables an individual to live most and serve best."

– *J. F. Williams*

"Health is a state of relative equilibrium of body form and function which results from its successful dynamic adjustment to forces tending to disturb it. It is not passive interplay between body substance and forces impinging upon it but an active response of body forces working towards readjustment."

– *Perkins*

Dimensions of Health

Authorities in the field of health have recognised three closely interwoven dimensions of health :

1. Physical dimension,
2. Mental dimension, and
3. Social dimension

However, recently it has been felt that few more dimensions of health can be added viz emotional, spiritual, vocational, educational, curative and preventive.

Physical Dimension

Physical dimension purely refers to the perfect functioning of the body externally as well as internally. *Externally* : having good physique, good appearance, good texture and complexion, attractive features, well structured and strong body parts and limbs, well groomed posture, graceful carriage and efficient movement. *Internally* : all systems of the human body, i.e., digestive, circulatory, respiratory,

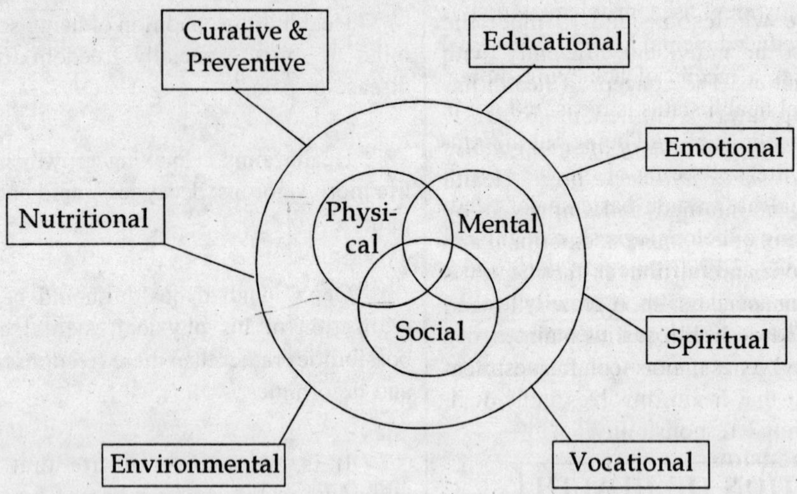

nervous, and excretory system, and sensory organs are functioning optimally. The pulse rate, blood pressure and body weight being in normal limits according to the age and sex. Physical dimension i.e. physical health means proper functioning of the systems and physical well being of the body, cumulative result being perfect and harmonious functioning of the human body.

Mental Dimension

Mental health is the balanced development of an individual's personality and emotional attitudes which enable him to live harmoniously with his fellow beings. *Sartorius has defined mental health as "a state of balance between the individual and the surrounding world, a state of harmony between oneself and others, a co-existence between the realities of the self and that of other people, and that of the environment.*" It is influenced by both biological and social factors. A good mental health implies that an individual has adjusted satisfactorily to his environment, home, work place, and other people of the society, so that he is realizing the maximum amount of happiness from living.

Generally mental ill health is the result of a combination of various psycho-bio-social factors. Some of the common causes of mental ill health are anxiety, tension, fear, insecurity, a sense of inequality and prejudices etc. However, mental health is not mere absence of mental illness. A mentally healthy person is free from internal conflicts, feels comfortable and secure about himself, accetps his short comings, has self respect, feels right towards others and is able to feel a part of the group, takes responsibilities, is able to meet the demands of life, is able to identify and face the problems as they arise, takes his own decision, sets reasonable goals for himself and has control over his emotions, fear and anger. Mental health can be summed up in the words of H.B. English, "Mental health is a relatively enduring state wherein the person is well adjusted, has a zest for living, and is attaining self actualisation or self reaslisation. It is a positive state and no mere absence of mental disorder."

Social Dimension

Social health is the ability to get along with one self and with others, to be independent but at the same time to realize how dependent one is on others. *Donald has defined social well being as "the quantity and quality of an individual's interpersonal ties and the extent of involvement with the community".*

Social health is concerned with helping an individual in making personal adjustment, group adjustment and adjustments as a member of the society. Sound social interaction at the early stage of life builds up correct attitude which go a long way in helping the child to adjust in the society.

Social maladjustment is a problem which is often reflected in reduced mental health. Thus social interaction becomes a means of achieving mental health. One's social health status is measured not in terms of personal feelings of well being but in terms of one's effect on the well being of others.

Each individual has certain basic social needs which include feeling of belongingness, recognition, self-respect and love, and fulfillment of these needs results in promoting social health. A socially healthy person possesses the desirable qualities of integrity, unselfishness, forgiveness, sense of fairness, co-operation etc.

Emotional Dimension

Emotions are the feelings which have great role in our life and lead to the modification of attitude, conducive to personal adjustment and well being. The environment we create by our behaviour, our attitudes, and our actions is the emotional environment and it greatly influences the personality of an individual. Emotion is an essential element in the adjustive nature of the life process.

Emotional health means emotional fitness and emotional control. A person can be called emotionally healthy if his emotions are always positive, and has full control over his emotions. On the other hand, a person who has no control over his emotions or is over powered with negative emotions can be called emotionally unbalance or emotionaly ill.

Spiritual Dimension

In the context of Indian culture, where people are having faith in divine powers, and another distinctive feature of human life, the presence of spiritual element (spiritual health) refers to that part of the individual which reaches out and strives for meaning and purpose in life. Man is a complex multi-dimensional being. He is not only having spirit, he also has mind, body and life. But these multiple sides of his nature are not contradictory. He is indivisible and nothing in him can be rejected. According to *Radhakrishnan, "the end of man is to let the spirit in him permeate his whole being, his soul, flesh and affections"*. Thus, with divine philosophy having great influence on our culture, spiritual health is very important dimension of health. Sound spiritual aspect results in developing man into a healthy human being.

Vocational Dimension

Vocational dimension is essentially a sub-domain of physical, mental and social health. The capacities or limitations of an individual, in relation to his working and occupation, to achieve the desired targets, play an important role in promoting physical, social, and mental health. Livelihood is a very serious problem being faced by an individual. Vocational health emphasizes upon the problem of livelihood and ensures the fulfillment of the economic needs of an individual. Man's progress in all fields depends upon his capacity to earn his livelihood and to meet his wants. Vocational satisfaction provides him social efficiency, social status, social prestige, emotional stability and mental relaxation. Vocationally satisfied individuals also contribute to the increase in production and national wealth. Vocational health is thus of great national importance as well.

Educational Dimension

Education is the consciously controlled process whereby changes in behviour are produced in the person, and through the person, in the group. It causes certain changes in one's behaviour and attitude enabling him to understand his responsibility to the society and the nation. Educational dimension of health, i.e., health education has heavy responsibility to discharge. Health education creates awareness regarding health rules, promotes health, builds up healthy environment and shows the path to follow towards the healthful living. Regarding the importance of educational dimension of health, *Ruth E. Grout states, "health education is the translation of what is known about health into desirable individual and community behaviour patterns by means of the educational process."*

Nutritional Dimension

Good nutrition is a basic component of health. It is of prime importance in the attainment of normal growth and development, and in the maintenance of health throughout life. There is a growing realization that adequate nutrition is a necessary step in improving the quality of life. The importance of malnutrition and under nutrition as an obstacle to social and economical development has brought nutritional health to the forefront of national and international concern.

Environmental Dimension

The internal environment of man himself and external environment which surrounds him reflect the health status of the individual, the society and the nation. Sanitation is one of the important aspects of environmental health. It is the quality of living that is expressed in clean home, clean neighbourhood and clean community. *Environmental sanitation can be defined as "the control of all those factors in man's physical environment which exercise or may exercise a negative effect on his physical development, health and survival."* Being a way of life, it must come from within the people. In the recent years, the subject of environment and its pollution has become a critical health area as much of the ill health in the country is due to defective and polluted environment. Understanding the environment is becoming more and more important as people have been placing ever larger demands on the environment and in the process bringing about ever more severe changes in it.

Curative and Preventive Dimension

This dimension deals with the study and application of curative medicine and preventive measures for the preservation of the health of an individual. The primary objective of curative medicine is the removal of disease. Over the years curative medicine has accumulated a vast body of scientific knowledge, technical skills, and machinery highly organised, not merely to treat disease, but to preserve life itself as far as it could be possible.

The main objective of preventive medicine is *prevention of disease and promotion of health.* It is applied to all healthy people. Modern preventive medicine can be defined as "*the art and science of health promotion, disease prevention, disability limitation and rehabilitation.*" In simple words preventive medicine is a kind of anticipatory medicine and measure. Scientific advances, improved living standards, and fuller education of the public, have opened up a number of new avenues for curative and preventive medicine.

MEANING OF HEALTH EDUCATION

Health education is rather an abstract term, meaning different things to different people. To some, it is a matter of public relations stating the activities of health department, and to many others it provides knowledge about health and diseases.

Anything that educates anyone in the matter of health, is health education, i.e. the education given for identifying the health needs and matching it with suitable adaptive behaviour can be termed as health education. In simple words, the entire process of involving people in learning about health and disease, making efforts for improving health and facilitating them to act appropriately for overcoming ailments and promoting a positive health, is health education.

According to W.H.O. Technical Report (1954), "*Health education, like general education, is concerned with changes in knowledge, feelings and behaviour of people. In its most usual forms, it concentrates on developing such health practices as are believed to bring about the best possible state of well being.*" It is apparent from this definition that health education is a process that helps people to find out their health needs, activates them for adopting suitable behaviour and building up right attitude for achieving and maintaining optimum health. Health education brings about changes in the knowledge and attitude of people and thereby effects the changes in their health *practices.* It is concerned with establishing changes in personal and group attitudes and behaviour that promote healthier living. *The object of health education is to "win friends and influence people"*, and it is an essential tool of community health. Briefly it is stated, that health education recognises three basic components:

(*i*) Unity of human beings in respect to their physical, mental, and social aspect.

(*ii*) The knowledge, attitudes, and practices are important to influence health behaviour.

(*iii*) The focus of health education on the individual, family and community.

All these components of health education are inter-dependent and constantly interact with each other.

Health educationists have recognised the importance of instilling in young and old alike, a body of health knowledge based on scientific facts, wholesome health attitude and desirable health practices. The art and science of engaging people in the process of learning, for the desired behaviour, for the preservation of health, is health education.

Health education is needed for all ages, both sexes, all classes of community, literate or illiterate, and in all parts of the world. Even in advanced countries, health education has assumed great importance due to ever changing conditions of life. Health education is thus, a never ending process.

DEFINITIONS OF HEALTH EDUCATION

"Health education, like general education, is concerned with changes in knowledge, feelings and behaviour of people. In its most usual forms it concentrates on developing such health practices as are believed to bring about the best possible state of well being."

– W.H.O. Technical Report (1954)

"Health education is a process that informs, motivates, and helps people to adopt and maintain healthy practices and life styles, advocates environmental changes, as needed, to facilitate this goal, and conducts professional training and research to the same end."

– Anne R. Somers

"Health education is concerned with the health related behaviour of people."

– Sophie

"Health education is a process that bridges the gap between health information and health practices. Health education motivates the person to take the information and do something with it, to keep himself healthier, by avoiding actions that are harmful, and practising those that are beneficial."

– President's Committee on Health Education, New York (1973)

"Health education is the sum of all those experiences in school, and elsewhere, that favourably influence habits, attitudes and knowledge related to individual, community and social health."

– Thomas Wood

"Health education is the translation of what is known about health into desirable individual and community behaviour patterns by means of the educational process."

– Ruth. E. Grout

"Health education aims at creating such a quality of life as may enable an individual to live most and to serve best."

– W.H.O" Expert Committee on Health Education

"Anything that educates anyone in the matter of health, is health education. It is concerned with the knowledge of all round healthy habits."

– Thomas Wood

OBJECTIVES OF HEALTH EDUCATION

After analysing the definition of health education as given by *Somers and adopted by National Conference on Preventive Medicine (U.S.A.), J.E. Park stated* three main objectives of health education:

(*i*) Informing people.

(*ii*) Motivating people.

(*iii*) Guiding into action.

Some other authors have also suggested similar objectives, however, naming the same differently i.e.

(*i*) Development of health knowledge.

(*ii*) Development of desirable health attitude.

(*iii*) Development of desirable health practices.

In order to overcome any confusion or ambiguity, if any, in the minds of readers/students with regard to the above stated twin sets of objectives, having been clubed, as given below :

1. **Informing People/Development of Health Knowledge:** The first objective of health education is to inform people or to develop health knowledge by presenting and interpreting scientific health data based on research and discoveries. Such information will help the individuals to recognise health problems and to solve them by utilising this valid information. It will also help in removing *ignorance, prejudice, blind beliefs and misconceptions regarding health and hygiene.*
2. **Motivating People/Development of Desirable Health Attitude:** Merely informing people about health is not enough. They must be motivated to the point that they want to apply this knowledge to every day living by favourably changing *their behaviour patterns, their attitudes, their habits and ways of living.* Individuals acquiring such healthful attitudes will tend to *transmit this knowledge to their famlies, community, society and nation, for healthful living.*
3. **Guiding into Action/Development of Desirable Health Practices:** Knowledge will be of little use unless it ensures good health practices and guides people to adopt and maintain healthy life styles. The health practices will determine, to a great extent, the health status of the person. Adopting harmful habits or practices will result in poor health whereas beneficial health habits will result in good and positive health.

To sum up, knowledge without incentive or motivation will not ensure desirable health attitudes and health practices. Thus these three objectives have close relationship and contribute to each other.

Ruth E. Grout has stated four objectives of health education :

- Optimum development of the individual with special reference to physical and emotional development.
- Betterment of human relationships, particularly from the stand point of health.
- Application of health facts and principles in respect of economic efficiency in the production and consumption of goods and services.
- Civic responsibility, especially in respect to health.

These objectives are discussed as under :

(*i*) **Opitmum Development of the Individual with Special Reference to Physical and Emotional Development:** Optimum development of an individual refers to the development of all the aspects of his personality. It is that state in which the individual is able to utilise and mobilize all his resources to lead an optimum and meaningful life. An individual, who is physically fit and emotionally stable, tend to lead a healthy life.

By engaging in physical activities apart from physical fitness, one is able to achieve maximum satisfaction in everyday life, better neuro-muscular coordination, better mental judgements and better emotional control. He can withstand fatigue and tolerate the stress and strains of daily life. Similarly, an emotionally stable person is able to control his emotions and channelise his energies in a positive direction. For the development of the healthy personality, emotional stability and wholesome emotional expression is essential. Physically developed person will tend to be emotionally satisfied and will accept challenges. These two aspects are just like two sides of a coin, each supplement and complement one another.

(*ii*) **Betterment of Human Relationship, Particularly from the Stand Point of Health:** Human relationship is a key to happiness and a successful life. A healthy person is very much expected to have good relations with his fellow beings. The objective of health education is the establishment and improvement of human relations through positive interaction between human beings, within family, and community at large. Health education contributes to the betterment of human relationships in many ways. A healthy person can easily identify himself with the group, he can think for betterment and welfare of the others, and try to cooperate and coordinate with others. Such a person is better adjusted in family, community and society, thus promoting much better human relationships.

(*iii*) **Application of Health Facts and Principles in Respect of Economic Efficacy in Production and Consumption of Goods and Services:** Each individual has to adopt some vocation, profession or trade, and has to be efficient in discharge of his functions. The economic efficiency, be it in production and consumption of goods or in providing services, has to be regulated and controlled by applying facts and principles of health, as any departure from the same might jeopardize the national health. Production and consumption has to be done in healthy and hygienic conditions. The basic facts and principles of health are not to remain confined to an individual's own personality but have to be reflected in the production and consumption of goods and services provided to the society, to ensure good health of the society. It is an objective of health education to educate the people on this important issue.

(*iv*) **Civic Responsibility, Especially in Respect to Health:** Another objective of health education is to contribute in cultivating a sense of civic responsibility in individuals. Health education aims to develop an individual in all aspects so as to produce a healthy, law abiding and useful citizens who possess all the civic qualities like co-operation, love, service to others, fellowship, sacrifice, sense of duty, sense of responsibility etc. Health education, through its service programmes, provide exposure to the individuals enabling them to imbibe a sense of duty, to spread the message of health. Such a healthy citizen can effectively play his role in the development of a healthy society as well as in the development of a healthy nation.

SCOPE OF HEALTH EDUCATION

Health education may be divided into three sections:

Although these three sections of health education have specific functions, but all of them serve the general purpose of educating the individuals regarding health education.

(*i*) **Healthful Living:** Healthful living covers the basic facts of health, hygiene and sanitary aspect of the environment where we live. This implies that environment or atmosphere has to be conducive to physical, social mental, and emotional health. Factors such as proper lighting, ventilation, proper water supply, adequate furniture and other such facilities at home, in school and at work place should be taken into consideration. The personality of the health instructor has a strong bearing on the health of the children too. A well balanced routine and schedule is also necessary for healthful living. There must be adequate time for rest, relaxation, play, work, and study. Even methods and modes have significant roll in imparting knowledge and conveying thoughts, and the same should be in accordance with good health practices.

(*ii*) **Health Services:** Health services comprise the activities designed to determine the health status of an individual. Health services are an important part of any health programme and should include health appraisal, counselling, examinations for disease and disability, protective measures of first aid, emergency care, mid-day meals, vaccinations and inoculations, and follow up procedures with remedial measures. The objective of health services is to help the individual in conserving, maintaining and improving his health. Health services also include periodical health check-ups, keeping of commutative records, and providing medical advice whenever demanded or required.

(*iii*) **Health Instructions:** Health instructions deal with the materials by which an individual is *helped to acquire health habits, learn health* skills, master health knowledge, and develop health attitudes. Health instructions provide knowledge regarding the structure and functioning of human body, the causes and methods of preventing certain disease, the factors contributing to and in maintaining good health, and the role of community in the health programmes. Such an instructional programme, if planned wisely and taught intelligently, will contribute to the development of sound health habits and healthy attitudes. Proper health instructions impress on each individual the responsibility for his own health and, as a member of a community, for the health of others. Health instructions promote understanding of health and the observance of desirable practices, and play a meaningful role in the lives of all people. Provision of health services and creating an environment for healthful living is not sufficient without health instructions.

PRINCIPLES OF HEALTH EDUCATION

1. Continuity of health programme is necessary to identify the problems, review the same from time to time and to find out its solution step by step.
2. Good human relations are of most importance in learning. The health educator must be kind, sympathetic and trust-worthy so that the people may rely on him and have faith in him.
3. Involvement of a local leader, teacher, well known personality, priest etc. in the health programme will lend credence to the programme and will go a long way to ensure its success.
4. This is a universal fact that people are not interested to listen those things which are not of their interest and therefore, health teaching and health programmes should be conducted in such a way that it relates to the interest of the people.
5. It is necessary to find out the real health needs of the people and only then people will gladly participate in the programme, i.e. programme should be need based.
6. Health education should not become an artificial situation or formal teaching - learning.
7. Health education programme should proceed from known to unknown. It is better to start from where people are and slowly be build up to avoid any clash of ideas and for better understanding.
8. It is important for health educationist to get into the culture of the community, and only thereafter, to introduce novel ideas with natural ease and a little caution as well.
9. Active participation is the key to learning. Through group discussions, workshops etc. positive and negative points should be discussed in detail and thoroughly dealt with.
10. A close study and application of relevant behavioural sciences is necessary for health education because these are concerned with individual, groups and society.
11. In health education, one must know the level of understanding, educational background, mental capacity and literacy of the people. One should use simple language so that they can understand it better.
12. Generally, it is difficult to demonstrate the beneficial effects of preventive and promotive health care. Therefore, to enable the people to understand the same, apart from reinforcement through repetitions at regular intervals, a close, friendly and sympathetic attitude of the teacher is must.
13. Success of any health programme depends on having a free flow of communication. It is necessary to get feed back and to get doubts cleared.
14. The health educator has to identify himself with the group by melting barriers, if any, and only thereafter meaningful interaction and exchange of ideas can take place.
15. It is necessary to motivate the people for participating in the health programme by providing appropriate incentives.
16. Health programme should be based on the well known principle of learning by doing,

and it should be practical oriented and positive in nature.

17. There has to be co-ordination and link between the people, teacher and the subject matter for effective results of the programmes.
18. A variety of teaching methods including audio-visual aids are essential not only for effective teaching of health but also for creating interest and involvement of the people.
19. Health education programme should be planned according to the needs, the resources available, and results to be achieved under the prevailing environmental conditions.
20. Health programme should deal not only with the problems of an individual but also of the family, community, society and nation as well.
21. Health education programme should be regularly evaluated through periodical appraisals. This will facilitate the instructor to carry out the programme with appropriate and suitable modifications.

IMPORTANCE OF HEALTH EDUCATION

Knowledge of health education assumes great importance in India, where most of the people are ignorant about the basic principles of health and hygiene. Because of this ignorance, they are unable to prevent the disease, most of which are preventable. There is an emergent need to remove this ignorance of masses. They are to be made aware of fundamental and basic principles of health and hygiene. Health education provides the scientific facts of community hygiene that could help in preventing and eradicating many diseases and remove ignorance. Health education programmes are basically of preventive and promotive nature. As prevention is better than cure, such programmes are very important in transmitting the knowledge, making the people aware of various dreaded diseases, occurrence of which could be easily avoided. In this way, health education can play an important role in eliminating many problems that adversely affect young people, adults, and society in general.

It is necessary for a prosperous country to have healthy citizens. Health education has a very significant role to play as it comprises health knowledge, health habits and health attitudes. It can improve the individual, family and community life for a bright and prosperous future.

Health education helps an individual to distinguish between good and bad health habits and encourages him to make good habits as enduring and lasting healthful behaviour. Health education is essential to assure that proper health habits are established early in life, as habits and behaviour adopted in childhood remain unchanged even in adult life. The good health habits instilled in children during their formative years reflect in their life, making them healthy, useful, and effective citizen of the country. In this way health education also contributes to national growth.

Many physical defects and ailments like hearing and sight problems, bad posture, malnutrition etc occur during early childhood. Health education plays an important role in checking, preventing and curing these defects and ailments by promoting intelligent health attitudes among children.

Health education is a comprehensive, qualitative and a dynamic process of education as:

1. It develops sound attitudes towards the importance of good health and safety practice at home and in the community.
2. It provides direct learning experience to encourage the practice of wholesome healthy habits in daily living.
3. It introduces students to the areas of health knowledge, enabling them to better understand and cope-up with individual and community health problems.
4. It introduces students to the basic mechanism and functions of human body.
5. It integrates many sources of health information in the biological, social and physical sciences so that they can be applied in a meaningfull way towards establishing a total health concept.
6. It helps students to achieve deeper insight into the nature of social relationships and family life.

7. It furnishes a setting for learning which enables the students to realize their fullest potentialities.
8. It encourages the development of responsibility and cooperation among students in observing environmental controls.
9. It establishes procedures for providing students with satisfactory heath counselling and guidance services.
10. It contributes to the education of physically challenged people, enabling them to make the most of educational opportunities available.

Health education has become increasingly important in the recent years due to the attention given by the print and electronic media with regard to the general concern about social - medical problems. Nowadays health is considered as a worldwide social goal. Health education is of great importance as its main aim is to achieve optimum health of an individual which include all the dimensions of health i.e. physical, mental, social, emotional and spiritual. Health education has become one of the most important disciplines of education. Health education is basic to learning, to happiness, to success, to effective citizenship, and to worthwhile living.

NUTRITION

Introduction

Nutrition is the science that deals with food and its uses by the body. We, like all other living things need food to live. Food supplies the energy for every action we undertake from eating banana to running a race. Food also provides material that our body needs to build up and repair its tissues and to regulate the functions of its organs and systems.

To keep our body cells running properly, they must be supplied with correct amount of food having required chemicals in ratio of the food. The chemicals in food, which our body needs, are called nutrients.

What we eat directly affects our health. A proper diet helps in prevention of certain illnesses and also helps in recovery from diseases/injuries. An inadequate or improper diet increases the risk of different diseases. Eating a balanced diet is the right way to have all the nutrients that our body needs.

BALANCED DIET

The balanced diet is the intake of appropriate types and adequate amounts of foods and drinks to supply nutrition and energy for the maintenance of body cells, tissues and organs and to support normal growth and development.

"A balanced diet is that which contains the proper amounts of each nutrient."

Functions of Diet

1. It provides energy for the various activities of the body.
2. It helps the body to grow and replace worn out tissues.
3. It has the chemicals, which help to control the body functions and protect the body from diseases.

Factors Affecting Diet

Diet depends on the following factors :

1. **Age, sex and body surface area:** Diet differs from age to age. Young ones need different types of food both in quality as well as quantity as compared to older people who need diet in less quantity and with lesser fats.
2. **Types and duration of activity:** Diet also depends on types of activity that we do and its duration. An athlete involving in vigorous training needs more caloric food as compared to office clerk. A sedentary person requires light food whereas a worker who does eight to ten hour hard work needs good diet.
3. **Eating habits and social customs:** Eating habits and social customs also affect the diet of an individual. Some individuals are habitual of eating fast food whereas others do not like it. Similarly, our social customs play an important role in food preparation. A section of society prefers nonvegetarian food whereas in other section of society only vegetarian food is served.

4. **Climatic factors:** Food is varied in different climates. As you have an experience of having different diet in summer and winter. Similarly, people living in different climatic zones have different foods.
5. **Health status and growth:** If you are in good state of health then you will have good diet whereas unhealthy individual cannot have similar diet. In growing age we give good food to the children. Sick individuals cannot have normal diet; usually they take light meal or as recommended by a doctor.
6. **Psychological considerations:** Some of the psychological factors affect the diet like how the food is cooked or what is the taste of food? If thc meal is tasty then everybody likes to have it.

Elements of Balanced Diet

There are hundreds of nutrients in the food. These are mainly grouped into six classes namely carbohydrates, proteins, fats, vitamins, minerals and water. Three nutrients, carbohydrates, proteins and fats supply us energy. Before details of these we must know about measuring unit of energy. The energy value of food is measured in heat units called calorie or kilo calorie. Calorie is the amount of heat required to raise the temperature of 1 gram of water by 1°. A Kilocalorie is equal to 1000 calories. A Kilocaloric is written as calorie with a capital C.

DAILY ENERGY REQUIREMENTS

Personal energy requirement = basic energy requirements + extra energy requirements

Basic Energy Requirements

- For every kg of body weight 1.3 calories of energy is required every hour. (An athlete weighing 50 kg would require 1.3 × 24 hrs × 50 kg = 1560 calories/day).

Extra Energy Requirements

- For each hour of training you require 8.5 calories of energy for each kg of body weight. (For a two hour training session a 50 kg athlete would require 8.5 × 2hrs × 50 kg = 850 calories)

An athlete weighing 50 kg who trains for two hours would require an intake of approx. 2410 calories (1560 + 850)

Energy Fuel

Like fuel for a car, the energy we need has to be mixed. The mixture that we require is as follows :

- 57% Carbohydrates (sugar, sweets, bread, cakes)
- 30% Fats (dairy products, oil)
- 13% Protein (eggs, milk, meat, poultry, fish)

The energy yield per gram is as follows: Carbohydrate - 4 calories, Fats - 9 calories and Protein - 4 calories.

What does a 50kg athlete require in terms of carbohydrates, fats and protein?

- *Carbohydrates* - 57% of 2410 = 1374 calories - at 4 calories per gram = *1374/4* = 343 grams.
- *Fats* - 30% of 2410=723 calories - at 9 calories per gram = 723/9 = 80 grams.
- *Protein* - 13% of 2410 = 313 calories - at 4 calories per gram = 313/4 = 78 grams.

  50kg athlete requires : 343 grams of Carbohydrates, 80 grams of Fat and 78 grams of Protein.

NUTRIENT BALANCE

Carefully planned nutrition must provide an energy balance and a nutrient balance. The nutrients are:

- **Carbohydrates:** our main source of energy.
- **Proteins:** essential growth and repair of muscles and other body tissues.
- **Fats:** a source of energy which is important in relation to fat-soluble vitamins.
- **Vitamins:** water and fat-soluble groups play important roles in many chemical processes in the body.
- **Minerals:** those inorganic elements occurring in the body and which are critical to its normal functions.
- **Water:** essential to normal body function - as a vehicle for carrying other nutrients and because 60% of the human body is water.

Carbohydrates

Carbohydrates are the main source of energy in all activities. They provide quick energy to the body and are not stored in the body for long. The ratio of carbohydrates is increased in endurance events/ activities. Carbohydrates i.e. CHO_2 are compounds of **carbon, hydrogen and oxygen**. Carbohydrates are of two types *(a) simple carbohydrates (b) complex carbohydrates.*

(a) *Simple carbohydrates contain vitamins and minerals.* Sugars are simple carbohydrates, which are used to provide energy immediately. These are called quick energy foods.

Sources of simple carbohydrates : They naturally occur in fruits, milk and milk products and vegetables (potatoes, carrots). They are also found in processed and refined sugars such as honey, jam, cakes, pastries, ice cream, table sugar, candy, syrups and regular carbonated beverages (drinks), jaggery (gur). Refined sugars provide calories, but lack in vitamins, minerals and fibres.

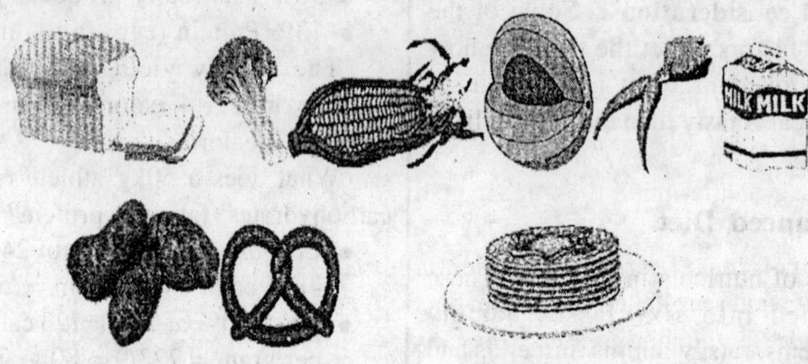

(b) *Complex carbohydrates are good source of minerals, vitamins and fibres.* Starches are complex carbohydrates that contain several sugar molecules combined together chemically. Their energy content is higher than sugar but is released more slowly.

Sources of complex carbohydrates : They are found in breads, cereals (wheat, bajra, rice), starchy vegetables and whole pulses (chana, moong, rajma).

Function of Carbohydrates

The primary function of carbohydrates is to provide energy to the body, especially the brain and nervous system. The body breaks down starches and sugars into substance called glucose that is used for energy by the body.

Recommendations

Nutrition experts recommend that 55 to 60% of our total calories should come from carbohydrates, preferably from complex carbohydrates (starches and naturally occurring sugars rather than processed or refined sugars).

To increase complex carbohydrates we should eat more fruits, vegetables whole grains, rice, bread and cereals and also more beans, dried peas and low fat milk.

Excess of carbohydrates are converted into fat by the liver and stored in adipose tissue.

It is recommended by the experts that processed and refined sugars should be used within the limits. *The consumption of excess sugar prior to exercise reduces performance and endurance.*

Proteins

Proteins are the basic structure of all living cells. These are complex organic compounds. **The basic structure of proteins is a chain of amino acids that contain carbon, oxygen, hydrogen and nitrogen**. The presence of nitrogen differentiates protein from carbohydrate and fat. There are two types of proteins (*a*) Non essential proteins (*b*) Essential proteins.

(*a*) **Non-essential protein** : The human body needs approximately 20 amino acids for the synthesis of its proteins. The body can make

only 13 of the amino acids that are known as the non-essential proteins or amino acids. In fact, they are essential but we do not have to get them from food we eat.

(*b*) **Essential proteins:** There are 9 essential amino acids. which are taken only from food and not made in the body. Thus, they are called essential proteins or amino acids.

If the proteins of a food supplied is enough of the essential amino acids it is called a complete protein food. If the proteins of a food does not supply all the essential amino acids, it is called an incomplete protein food.

(*i*) **Sources of Complete Proteins:** All meat and other animal products are sources of proteins. The best sources of complete proteins are eggs, milk, meat, poultry, beef and milk products.

(*ii*) **Sources of Incomplete Proteins:** Grains, fruits and vegetables are the sources of incomplete proteins as they lack one of the essential amino acids.

The plant protein can be combined to all of the essential amino acids and form a complete protein. For example complete plant proteins are rice and beans, milk and wheat cereal, and corn and beans.

(*iii*) **Functions of Proteins:** Protein is the main component of muscles, organs, and glands. Every living cell and all body fluid except urine and bile contain protein. The cell of muscles, tendons and ligaments are maintained with protein. Proteins are needed for growth and development of children and adolescents. Proteins are required for the formation of harmones, enzymes and haemoglobin.

It works as a source of energy in starvation (hunger) otherwise it is not a source of energy.

(*iv*) **Recommendations:** Protein requirements depend on the individual and daily activity. *Tissue growth whether due to growth, injury, weight training or pregnancy, affects protein requirements. During sickness, proteins are not only needed for repair work but are also used as an energy source.* Experts recommend that approximately 20% of the total daily calories should come from protein. Two or three servings of protein rich food will meet the daily needs of most adults.

In other terms, sedentary individuals need 0.8 g/kg/ b w/day (0.8 gram per kilo gram bodyweight per day). Athletes who participate in activities that demand different degrees of strength, speed and endurance may require up to 1.8 g/kg/bw/day.

It is important to note that exercise is the key for stimulating growth of new muscle tissue. Protein only supplies the materials.

(*v*) **Special Considerations:** High intake of proteins creates extra load on the body due

to disposal of nitrogen especially for kidneys and liver.
Dehydration can occur because of disposal of nitrogen, which may affect workout. It is, therefore, important to have adequate water when consuming increased level of proteins.

Fats

Like carbohydrates, fats also contain carbon, hydrogen and oxygen. They are the most concentrated source of energy in foods. One gram of fat provides double the energy provided by one gram of carbohydrates. Since our body can store fats, they work as energy banks and are called stored energy foods. The energy is provided when there is a need. If we eat more carbohydrates than required by our body the body converts the extra amount into fats and stores it. Our body mainly stores fats under skin and also in the regions of the kidneys and the liver.

Simple Fats

Consist of a glyceride molecule linked to one, two, or three units of fatty acids. According to the number of fatty acids attached, simple fats are divided into *monoglycerides* (one fatty acids), *diglycerides* (two fatty acids), and triglycerides (three fatty acids). *More than 95 percent of the stored fat in the human body is in the form of triglycerides.*

Based on the degree of hydrogen saturation, fatty acids are said to be *saturated or unsaturated.*

In saturated fatty acids the carbon atoms are fully saturated with hydrogens, therefore only single bonds like the carbon atoms on the chain (see Table). These saturated fatty acids are frequently referred to 'as saturated fats. The major sources of saturated fats are meats, cheese, and butter (Animal Origin).

In unsaturated fatty acids, the carbon atoms are not completely saturated with hydrogen, rather double bonds are formed between the unsaturated carbon atoms (see Table). These are generaly found in plant products.

Unsaturated fatty acids can be further classified as :

- Monounsaturated Fatty Acids, and
- Poly-unsaturated Fatty Acids

In monounsaturated fatty acids, only one double bond is found along the chain. Olive oil is the best example of triglycerides high in monounsaturated fatty acids.

In polyunsaturated fatty acids, two or more double bonds between unsaturated carbon atoms along the chain are available. Corn or cottonseed oils are high in polyunsaturated fatty acids.

Tables: Chemical structure of saturated and unsaturated fats.

Note: In general, saturated fats increase the blood cholesterol level, and polyunsaturated fats tends to decrease cholestrol.

Compound fats are a combination of simple fats and other chemicals. Examples of compound fats are *Phospholipids, Glucolipids,* and *Lipoproteines.* Phospholipids are similar to triglycerdies; *Glucolipids* are formed by a combination of carbohydrates, *fatty acids*, and *nitrogen*; and *Lipoproteins* are water soluble aggregates of protein with either *triglycerides, phospholipids*, or cholesterol. Lipoproteins transport fats (Cholestrol, triglycerides) in the blood and have a significant role in the development and prevention of heart disease. The total cholesterol / HDL-cholestrol ratio should be 4.5 and 4.0 or lower for men and women respectively. For the information of readers, HDL-cholesterol refers to High Density Lipoprotein chloesterol, also known as "*good cholesterol*" Whereas, LDL-cholesterol refers to Low-Density Lipoprotein Cholesterol, this type of cholesterol is not good for the heart, it increases proportionally with the amount of saturated fat and cholesterol intake in the regular diet. Total fat consumption on a daily basis should not exceed 30% of the total caloric intake, and less than half of the fat consumed should be in the form of saturated fat. The average intake of cholesterol also should be limited to less than 300 mg per day. The LDL-cholestrol can be further lowered by lossing excess body fat and using medication.

Derived Fats are a combination of simple and compound fats. Sterols are an example of derived fats.

MAJOR TYPES OF FATS LIPIDS

Unsaturated	Saturated
Sunflower oil	Beef
Olive Oil	Bacon
Rice Oil	Cheese
Nuts	Butter
Rapeseed Oil	Biscuits
Fish-Oil - Sardines	Crisps

(*a*) **Sources of Fats:** Saturated fats are found in foods from both animal and vegetable sources. Animal sources include meat, poultry and dairy products like milk, cream, cheese, butter and ice cream. Vegetable sources include palm, coconut oils. Monounsaturated fat is found in large amounts in foods from plants including peanut and olive oil. Polyunsaturated fats are found in foods from plants including sunflower, corn and soyabean and also fish oil.

(*b*) **Functions of Fats:** Fat is one of the three nutrients (along with carbohydrates and protein), which supplies calories (energy) to the body.

Fat is important for the proper functioning of the body. Fatty acids provide the raw materials, which help in the control of blood pressure, blood clotting and other body functions.

Fats are also an important energy source. When the body has used up the calories from carbohydrate, which occurs after the first 20 minutes of exercises, it begins to depend on the calories from fat.

Fats help in transportation of fat-soluble vitamins A, D, E and K. Fat maintains skin and hair.

(*c*) **Recommendations:** Experts recommend that saturated fat should be limited to 10% of the total calories for the day and remainder of the day's fat (ie. 20%) intake should be equal amounts of monounsaturated and polyunsaturated fat.

Today, many people are worried with the amount of fat in their diet. Diets those are high in fat lead to increase the risk of obesity (over weight) and heart disease. It is, therefore, recommended by the experts that fat intake should not exceed 30% of daily calories.

(*d*) **Special Considerations:** It is to be noted that fats are not easily digested. It also requires more oxygen for releasing energy, for example, if one litre of oxygen is required to release 5 K calories from carbohydrates whereas 3.7 litre of oxygen will be required to release the same amount of calories i.e. 5 K calories from fats.

Insufficient Fats Produce Fast Fatigue

Blood cholesterol is the most affected by the amount of fat we eat. We can reduce fat intake by choosing low fat or non-fat dairy products (cheese, milk and yogurt), lean meat, fruits, vegetables, whole grains and foods that are baked, boiled, steamed or roasted.

Vitamins

Vitamins are compounds of carbon that are absolutely essential for the normal working of the body. They are required in very small quantities. However, if our diet is lacking in any vitamin, we suffer from certain diseases called deficiency diseases.

Vitamins are obtained from food, except for vitamins D and vitamin K, which the body can produce. There are 13 vitamins needed by the body. The important ones are vitamins A, C, D, E, K and B complex (B_1 and B_2) Niacin (B_3) and B_{12}. These vitamins can be divided into two groups *(A)* fat soluble and *(B)* water soluble.

(A) ***Fat Soluble Vitamins:*** The fat-soluble vitamins, which include vitamin A, D, E and K are stored in the liver and in body fat.

(*i*) Vitamin A is found in milk, butter, egg, carrots, cod liver oil, tomatoes, pumpkin and green leafy vegetables. Vitamin A is needed for normal growth especially for keeping the eyes and skin healthy.

(*ii*) Vitamin D is found in cheese, butter, milk, green vegetables, fish liver oil and sunlight. Vitamin D is important for formation of strong bones and teeth. It is also known as the "Sunshine Vitamin".

(*iii*) Vitamin E is found in vegetable oils, butter, milk, whole grains, corn, nuts, seeds, spinach and other green leafy vegetables. Vitamin E is important to protect the cell membranes and also important in the formation of red blood cells (RBC).

(*iv*) Vitamin K is found in cabbage, cauliflower, spinach and other green leafy vegetables, cereals, soyabeans. Bacteria in the intestines normally also produce vitamin K. Vitamin K helps in the clotting of blood.

(B) ***Water soluble vitamins:*** The water soluble vitamins which include vitamin B_1, B_2, Niacin (B_3), B_{12} and vitamin C are not stored by the body.

(*i*) Vitamin B_1 also called thiamin is found in seafood, milk, meat, peas, cereals and green vegetables. Vitamin B_1 is important for growth and development. It is necessary for changing carbohydrates into energy.

(*ii*) Vitamin B_2 or riboflavin is found in yeast, egg, meat and peas. It is important for body growth and red blood cell production. It also helps in releasing energy from carbohydrates.

(*iii*) Vitamin B_3 or niacin is found in whole cereals, tomatoes, potatoes, meat and fish. It is important for healthy skin, digestion and nervous system.

(*iv*) Vitamin B_{12} is found in liver, milk, eggs and fish. Vitamin B_{12} is needed for forming red blood cells (RBCs) and for a healthy nervous system.

(*v*) Vitamin C is found in amla, citrus fruits, tomatoes, green leafy vegetables and potatoes. Vitamin C is needed for the maintenance of the ligaments, tendons, and other supportive tissue and strong blood vessels.

Special Considerations

(*i*) Vitamins are essential for metabolism of fats and carbohydrate.

(*ii*) Vitamins do not yield energy but act for repair and maintenance work.

DISEASE OCCURING IN HUMAN BEING DUE TO DEFICIENCY OF VARIOUS VITAMINS

Vitamin	Chemical Name	Diseases due to lack of corresponding vitamin
Vitamin-A	Retinal	Night blidness, terrar of infections, geropthalimia
Vitamin-B_1	Thamin	Beri-Beri
Vitamin-B_2	Riboflavin	Cracking in skin, appearance of red eyes, cracking in tongue etc.
Vitamin-B_3	Pantothenic acid	Hair to be whitened, mental stupidness etc.
Vitamin-B_5	Nicotinamide or Niacin	Plegra (Skin irritation)
Vitamin-B_6	Pyridoxi	Anaemia, Skin disease
Vitamin-B_7	Biotin	Paralysis, body ache, hair fall etc.
Vitamin-B_{12}	Cynocabalamin or Cabalamin	Anaemia (Megalycytic anaemia)
Vitamin-C	Ascorbic acid	Scurvey, Swalling or gems
Vitamin-D	Calciferol	Rickets (in children)
Vitamin-K	Filoqubonone	To delay in blood clotting

(*iii*) Water-soluble vitamins (B and C) are not stored; thus supplement of vitamin B and C is required.

(*iv*) Fat-soluble vitamins (A, D, E and K) can be stored in liver and fatty tissues.

(*v*) Vitamins do not increase physical work capacity; rather it is a psychological concept.

(*vi*) Vitamin E helps in recovery of muscle cramps.

(*vii*) During training fresh fruits and vegetables are recommended.

Minerals

Minerals contain elements needed by our body in small quantities. But these are essential for proper growth and functioning of the body. Their deficiency in our diet causes deficiency diseases. They are supplied in the form of salts by different foods. Some of the important minerals are mentioned below:

(*i*) Iron is important for the formation of haemoglobin which is the oxygen-carrying pigment found in red blood cells (RBC). Iron is found in meat, fish, liver, eggs, green vegetables, turnip, germinating wheat grains and yeast. Recommended daily allowance of iron is about 10 mg.

(*ii*) Calcium is needed for the formation of strong bones and teeth and also for clotting of blood and muscle contraction. Calcium is found in milk, milk products and green leafy vegetables. Daily recommended allowances of calcium are about 800 mg.

(*iii*) Phosphorus is required for the development of strong bones and teeth and also for making energy rich compounds in the cells from body. Phosphorus is available in meat, eggs, fish and whole grains. 750 mg. of phosphorus is recommended daily allowance.

(*iv*) Potassium is important for growth and keeping cells and blood healthy. It is available in green and yellow vege-tables. The recommended daily allow-ance of potassium is about 2000 mg.

(*v*) Sodium is needed for the proper functioning of the nervous system. It is found in common salt and also in meat and milk products. Daily-recommended allowances of sodium is about 500 mg.

(*vi*) Iodine is essential for proper thyroid function. Its deficiency causes a disease called goiter in which a gland in the throat swells up. Iodine is found in iodized salt, seafood and water.

(*vii*) Fluoride is important to make the enamel (polish) of the teeth hard and prevent dental cavities. It is available in coffee, spinach, onion and tea. Daily-recommended allowances of fluoride is 4 mg.

(*viii*) Copper is helpful in red blood cells, connective tissue and nerve fibres formation and functioning. It is found in grains, nuts and chocolate. Recommended daily allowances of copper is 3 mg.

(*ix*) Zinc is required for insulin production and also for functioning of male prostate, digestion and metabolism. It is available in meat, eggs and fish.

(x) Chloride is needed for muscle and nerve function and also for digestion. It is found in meat, milk products and fish. Daily-recom-mended allowances of chloride is 750 mg.

Special Consideration

(*i*) Minerals are essential in tropical climatic conditions and strenuous physical activity.

(*ii*) Supplementation of iron is must in females.

(*iii*) Supplements of calcium and phosphorus may be given to young athletes.

Water

Water is a nutrient that makes up almost 70 per cent of our body weight. Most of this water is in our cells. Some is between the cells and some in the blood. Life processes cannot occur without water. Water plays an important role in the body's molecules.

1. In the digestive system water helps to break down complex food molecules.
2. Water transports food, wastes, chemicals and gases throughout the body.
3. It carries waste products from the body through urine and sweat.
4. The body is cooled by the evaporation of water in the form of sweat from the skin.

We lose a lot of water every day as we sweat, breathe, cry or get rid of our wastes. The water in the food we eat replaces approximately half of this water. Vegetables and fruits contain large amount of water. The other half is replaced when we drink liquids. Normally we need 2.5 liter or 8 glasses of water every day to stay healthy. Athletes and sportspersons who are active in sports should drink enough water to replace the water they lose through sweating.

Water Loading

1. Drink at least eight glasses of water a day.
2. Drink regularly throughout the day; do not wait until you feel thirsty.
3. Carry a bottle of water with you as you commute.
4. Coffee and alcohol cause water loss. So never substitute tea, coffee, soft drinks or alcohol for water.
5. Always start the day with a glass of water. This helps the kidneys work more efficiently. Our body loses water during sleep, so drink a glass before going to bed.

6. Drink a glass of water half an hour before you eat.
7. In endurance events/activities start water loading at least two and half hour before the event.
8. Do not take chilled water, which takes longer time to absorb.
9. Headaches, stomach pains and fatigue are often caused by dehydration (lack of water). Drinking more water will help.
10. Increase your intake of varieties of salad, fruit and vegetables, which are high in water.
11. During intense and prolonged exercise sessions, drink required water. Drink enough fluids after activity/ exercise.

Special Consideration

An important indicator to use for hydration (state of water) is the colour of our urine. If urine is dark coloured or scanty it means there is a lack of water and we need more fluid. Urine should be clear coloured.

Proper water loading prevents many body ailments and infections. It prevents constipation.

NUTRITIONAL INTAKE

As we know that foods of various kinds supply different quantities of energy. The energy value of food is measured in heat units called calories or kilocalories. Calorie is the unit of heat used to express the energy value of food.

These nutrients, carbohydrates, fats and proteins, supply us with energy. The energy content or caloric value of different food items is given in table below:

CALORIC VALUE OF DIFFERENT FOOD ITEMS

Food	Quantity	Calories
1. Apple	1 medium	80
2. Bread	1 slice	65
3. Chapati	1	150
4. Rice	100 grams	550
5. Milk	1 cup	150
6. Butter	1 table spoon	100
7. Egg	1 boiled	80
8. Meat	50 grams	100
9. Carrot	1 medium	30
10. Potato	1 medium	145
11. Orange Juice	1 cup	120
12. Tomato	1 medium	50
13. Potato chips	1 small bag	135
14. Coka Cola	120 ml	100
15. Hamburger	1	250

How many calories do we need every day? As stated in the beginning this depends on the amount of energy a person uses and, also on person's age, body size, sex and daily activities.

When a healthy person takes in more calories than are used up each day, the excess energy gets stored in the body as fat and the person will gain weight. If a person consumes fewer calories than required, stored fat in the body will be broken down and weight will be lost. An overweight person must eat fewer calories and use up more calories by exercising in order to lose weight. Athletes and people involved in hard physical work require larger number of calories.

To remain healthy we need all the nutrients in the right amounts. No single food item contains all the nutrients. Thus, we need a combination of food items, *which is in other terms called balanced diet.* But a balanced diet is not the same for everyone. It depends on age, sex and the type of work that one carries out.

There are hundreds of food items, which we cannot eat. How do we know which one will give us the right balance of the nutrients we need each day? To make things easier, experts have divided food items into four groups as given in table on the top of next page.

Choosing a variety of food items from all four groups each day will help us stay healthy. Many people choose food on the basis of *whims* rather than on a scientific basis. Take the example of fruits. Do you know that expensive fruits such as pomegranates or grapes are not more nutritious than cheaper fruits such as guava, jamun or banana? Many people think that expensive almonds are more nutritious than the inexpensive groundnuts. *Selection of food should be on the basis of caloric value and not on the basis of price only.* The nutrients present and calories in 100 g of some fruits and dry fruits have been given in

MAJOR FOUR FOOD GROUPS

Food Groups	Food	Main Nutrients
I. Milk Group	Milk, cheese, ice-cream, paneer	Fats, proteins, minerals, water, carbohydrates
2. Vegetable/ fruit Group	Vegetables and fruits	Carbohydrates, vitamins, minerals, water
3. Cereal Group	Chapati, bread, rice, bajra, cornflakes, noodles	Carbohydrates
4. Protein Group	Meat, fish, chicken, beans, peas, nuts	Proteins, fats

Table from which you will see that price has no relation to the nutrition value. Compare banana with other fruits and you will understand why several sportspersons like to eat bananas when they are resting between games.

Similarly, cheaper vegetables like Methi (fenugreek), palak (spinach), sweet potato, carrots, brinjal, etc. provide us as much nutrition as the costly vegetables such as Shimla Mirch (Capsicum), French beans etc.

NUTRITION VALUE OF SOME FRUITS (PER 100 G)

Fruit	Protein (g)	Fat (g)	Carbohydrate (g)	Minerals (g)	Vitamins	Energy in Calories
Almond	20.8	58.9	10.5	2.9	A,B	655
Apple	0.3	0.3	13.4	0.3	A,B,C	50/
Banana	1.3	0.2	36.4	0.7	A,B,C	153
Grapes	0.5	0.3	- - - - -	0.6	C	17
Groundnut	26.7	40.1	20.3	1.9	A,B	541/
Papaya	0.5	0.1	6.5	0.2	A,C	28
Plum	0.8	0.1	12.8	0.4	C	56

EATING AND COMPETITION

What you eat on a day-to-day basis is extremely important for training. Your diet will affect how fast and how well you progress, and how soon you reach competitive standard. But once you are ready to compete, you will have a new concern: your competition diet. Is it important? What should you eat before your competition? When is the best time to eat ? How much should you eat? Should you be eating during the event ? And what can you eat between heats or matches? A lot of research has been done in this area and it is clear that certain dietary approaches can enhance competition performance. This discussion gives guidelines about eating and competing, which may help athletes to perform at their best during competition.

Eating Week Before the Competition

During the week before a competition you should fill up your glycogen stores so that you begin your competition with a full fuel supply. This is especially important if you are competing in an endurance sport or competing in a number of heats over a short period. The way to increase your glycogen stores is to taper training during the final week before a competition, and to increase carbohydrate intake. Eat plenty of complex carbohydrate foods, to help boost your glycogen stores. For the last three to four days try to eat a small meal or snack every two or three hours. Plan each meal around high- carbohydrate foods, for example baked potatoes, bread or pasta. Your total energy intake should remain about the same as usual. Eat smaller portions of high-protein foods such as meat, fish and eggs. Keep fat intake to a minimum and eat larger amounts of carbohydrate-rich foods (i.e. potatoes, pasta, cereals, etc). During these last few days you should, ideally, be getting 60-70% of your energy from carbohydrates.

Eating Before Competition

Your pre-competition meal should be *high in carbohydrate, low in fat, low in protein, low in fibre* (*i.e.* not too bulky and filling), *enjoyable and familiar.* Suitable types of food include: breakfast cereals, porridge bread, rolls and toast, fruit juice, fruit, rice cakes and plain crackers, boiled rice, potatoes, sweet potatoes, plain biscuits and carbohydrate drinks.

Pre-Competition Meal

Many competitors feel nervous on the day of the competition and do not want to eat. However, it is not a good habit/practice to avoid having a pre-competition meal. Your liver glycogen stores will be low and could adversely affect your performance in the last stages if you are competing in an endurance event. The liver can only store enough glycogen to last 12 hours, so if you eat nothing after the previous day's evening meal your liver glycogen stores will be considerably depleted (decreased). If you really do not feel like eating, try to have a liquid meal such as a carbohydrate drink, some fruit juice or commercial sports drink.

Eating Just Before the Competition

Studies have shown that eating a small amount (about 50 gms) of fast-absorbing carbohydrate just before exercise helps to delay fatigue and improve endurance.

Eating or Drinking During the Competition

If you are competing for more than an hour, you may find that taking extra carbohydrate during the event helps to delay fatigue and maintain exercise intensity, particularly during the later stages. If you take small amounts of carbohydrate at regular intervals during the competition, blood- sugar levels will be boosted and glycogen stores will not be depleted so rapidly. If you are competing in a tournament or match which involves intermittent, high- and low-intensity activity, and which lasts for over an hour, try to have some form of carbohydrate during the breaks.

Make sure you are well hydrated before the competition having your last drink about 15-20 minutes before the start. Drink at regular intervals (150 to 300 ml), ideally every 15 minutes or whenever you have a break during competition. Do not wait until you feel thirsty, you will already be dehydrated. Water is fine or you may prefer to use a commercial carbohydrate drink, as this will also refuel your glycogen stores.

Special Considerations

- Before training/competition exercise, carbohydrates provide the energy to sustain the workout. Athletes should take a carbohydrate drink or meal about two hours before competition/training. Fruits, cooked vegetables, sweet dish, cake and chicken may be included in such diet.
- Fats, meats, gas forming foods, greasy foods, highly seasoned foods and spicy foods should be avoided before competition.
- Diet of the athletes should not be different on the day of competition.
- Adequate fluids loading should be started at least 2.5 hour before competition.
- The experts do not recommend a large amount of concentrated glucose in less than hour before exercise.
- Caffeine in the form of coffee helps mobilization of free fatty acid. So it is recommended, but tablets of caffeine are not recommended.
- After competition diet must be rich in carbohydrates as well as proteins.
- During competition one should take fluids as and when required.

NUTRITIONAL TIPS

It is important to eat at regular intervals, ideally every 3-5 hours. This helps to keep blood sugar levels stable. Skipping meals or reducing your calorie intake does not help control weight in the long term.

Most of us do not drink enough water. Symptoms of dehydration include dizziness, lack of concentration, irritability and headaches. Aim to drink 6-8 glasses of water a day and you will stay well hydrated.

Your mother was exactly right when she forced you to eat up your greens. We should be eating 5 servings of fruit and vegetables a day for general health.

Beware the hidden fat foods, which are normally those tasty party foods. Quiche, sausages, pork pie, salami, and dips are some examples. Of course biscuits, cakes and desserts should also be kept to a minimum and only eaten as a special treat.

Bread, potatoes and pasta are all carbohydrate foods that have received bad press in the past. These foods do not make you fat on their own. However, if you have a big cheese sandwich, knob of butter on your potato (or have chips), or make a rich cream sauce for the pasta you will increase the amount of fat you are eating.

Dairy products are high sources of fat and cholesterol, but they do provide us with other beneficial nutrients. The best approach is to buy "low fat" versions of milk, cheese, yogurt etc, as they will provide you with all the nutrients without the fat element.

YOUR IDEAL WEIGHT

The most accurate assessment of your ideal weight takes into account the composition of your body

IDEAL WEIGHT TABLE

Height		Men		Women	
Feet & Inches	**Metres**	**Kg**	**Lbs**	**Kg**	**Lbs**
4'7"	1.40	...	...	40 - 53	88 - 116
4'9"	1.45	...	...	42 - 54	92 - 119
4'10"	1.50	...	...	43 - 55	94 121
4'11"	1.52	...	...	44 - 56	97 - 123
5'0"	1.54	...	...	44 - 57	97 - 125
5'1"	1.56	...	...	45 - 58	99 - 127
5'2"	1.58	51 - 64	112 - 141	46 - 59	101 - 130
5'3"	1.60	52 - 65	114 - 143	48 - 61	105 - 134
5'3 1/2"	1.62	53 - 66	116 - 145	49 - 62	108 - 136
5'4"	1.64	54 - 67	119 - 147	50 - 64	110 - 141
5'5"	1.66	55 - 69	121 - 152	51 - 65	112 - 143
5'6"	1.68	56 - 71	123 - 156	52 - 66	114 - 145
5'7"	1.70	58 - 73	127 - 160	53 - 67	116 - 147
5'7 1/2"	1.72	59 - 74	130 - 163	55 - 69	121 - 152
5'8"	1.74	60 - 75	132 - 165	56 - 70	123 - 154
5'9"	1.76	62 - 77	136 - 169	58 - 72	127 - 158
5'10"	1.78	64 - 79	141 - 174	59 - 74	130 - 163
5'10 1/2"	1.80	65-80	143 - 176	...	...
5'11"	1.82	66 - 82	145 - 180	...	...
6'0"	1.84	67 - 84	147 - 185	...	...
6'1"	1.86	69 - 86	152 - 189	...	...
6'2"	1.88	71 - 88	156 - 194	...	...
6'2 1/2"	1.90	73 - 90	160 - 198	...	...
6'3"	1.92	75 - 93	165 - 205	...	...

how much of your weight is lean body mass (muscle and bone) and how much is body fat. For optimum health, body fat should be no more than 20% of total body weight for men and 30% for women.

The table (on p. 295) is a guide to a healthy weight range for each height and sex group. The table does not take into consideration your age or your frame size. A person with a short physique ought to aim for an ideal weight at the lower end of the range, whereas a person of the same height but with a larger frame could quite satisfactorily weigh in at the top of the range.

PERSONAL HYGIENE

MEANING OF PERSONAL HYGIENE

The word '*Hygiene*' has been derived from *Greek* word '*Hygienos*' which means healthful. However, 'Hygiene is also termed as '*Hygia*' in *Greek*, which means the *goddess of health*.

In the modern times, it means "*the art of living*". It is true that a healthy mind lives in healthy body. It means that for proper and systematic working of the body it is essential to have proper hygiene. This type of hygiene is called personal hygiene. Hence personal hygiene means the study and application of preventive medicine and physiology for the preservation of the health of the individual. In other words personal hygiene means an individual can maintain his/her health by observing the principles of proper living, paying attention to his cleanliness, exercise, rest, sleep and proper ventilation in the house. Some times when a child in early life neglects the cleanliness, he may develop certain unhygienic habits. Such habits that are generally formed in the early childhood may take a serious turn and become very difficult to break in later life. Therefore, if the proper education is imparted to the children on personal hygiene and bad habits are checked in time, most of the diseases can be kept away, whereas its neglect may cause untold misery.

IMPORTANCE OF PERSONAL HYGIENE

Good habits serve as an instrument for the promotion of health and long life. Similarly for proper and systematic functioning of the different organs of the body, it is essential to have proper hygiene. So health and education have relative role for the longivity of life. Both of them go side by side. Education can not go on successfully unless the body is healthy. If good habits are developed among the children by education in the health-instruction class they shall lead to systematic education and successfull living. It has been rightly said that "*healthy body is a source of achieving the highest goal of life*". Therefore, we cannot ignore the importance of personal cleanliness and personal hygiene at home, in the class and institution.

Personal Hygiene Helps in

1. Developing healthy habits and attitudes.
2. Maintaining healthy atmosphere in the home, classroom and institution.
3. Encouraging the individual for reading of health literature.
4. Developing emotional stability.
5. Developing attractive personality.

Cleanliness

Personal cleanliness is one of the main ingredients of good health. It is a preventive measure against disease. So one must know how to keep himself clean and healthy. The habit of personal cleanliness must be cultivated in children so that they can keep themselves healthy. *Personal cleanliness includes: cleanliness of teeth, ears, nose, nails, skin, bowels habit, cleanliness, proper clothes etc.*

1. **Teeth:** Bad teeth result in developing various diseases such as pyorrohea and also causes a danger to the digestive system whereas healthy teeth contribute to a pleasing appearance and help in chewing and digestion of food. Diseased teeth and gums not only cause pain and discomfort in the oral cavity but also can lead to serious complications like heart dieases, joint pain, abdominal pain and

even cancer of mouth. Dental health is a matter of life long concern. Correct dental care can help to keep teeth for a long time. Neglect of teeth care is most likely to reflect on our general well being so we must take care of our teeth and in turn they will take good care of us. Teeth should be cleaned after every meal so that nothing is left stuck in the denture which can lead to severe pain, abscess, loss of tooth and disfigurement of face. So we must take measure to prevent them as it is well said "*prevention is better than cure.*" We must follow such rules regarding healthy teeth :

(*a*) Brush teeth daily after every meal especially after dinner.

(*b*) Brush teeth from up to downward direction and vice-versa.

(*c*) Don't eat sweet and sticky food in between meals. Children should avoid toffees, candies, chocolates etc.

(*d*) Avoid excessive consumption of alcohol, cigarettes, pan chewing to avoid mouth cancer.

(*e*) Consult dental surgeon regularly.

With proper personal and professional care one can keep natural denture throughout life.

2. **Ears:** Hygiene of ears is very essential. Ear is a sense organ because we hear things through ears, good hearing keeps one in active touch with people and events. Whereas poor hearing makes an individual dull and can lead to serious emotional disturbance. The ear is a delicate organ easily prone to injury. Students must learn the precautions to be taken to protect the ear in sports, specifically in swimming and diving. Do not put pins, needles or any sharp thing into the ears. Do not expose ears to loud noise, avoid hitting on ears don't put hydrogen peroxide in child's ear. Don't neglect cough or cold. Learn the early signs of deafness. Treat the illness early. If there is discharge or pain in ear, a doctor must be consulted.

3. **Eyes:** Eyes are the most important and valuable organs of the body. Every care is essential to retain their sight and keep them healthy. Poor nutrition may cause vision disturbances and inflammatory conditions of eyes and lids, so rich diet is to be taken for better sight. Proper eye hygiene includes good reading habits under lighting conditions and use of glasses when needed. One must practice and learn the following points to protect eyes :

   1. Wash eyes with fresh water.
   2. Protect the eyes from dust, smoke and bright sunlight and irritating vapours.
   3. Avoid rubbing eyes with dirty fingers.
   4. Use clean and separate towel or handkerchief.
   5. If eyes appear red, swollen or watery, consult doctor immediately.
   6. Games with bow and arrow, fire crackers, should be discouraged.
   7. Do not neglect eye strain consult doctor immediately.
   8. Disease of diabetes should be effectively treated as early as possible because it can lead to complications related with eye sight.
   9. Avoid stooping on book or close work.
   10. Eye sight should be got tested regularly.

4. **Nose and Throat:** Nose is another important sense organ responsible for giving the idea of smell, should be kept clean. It is through nose that one breathes and if nose gets stuffed, or disturbed we start breathing through mouth, in such case our respiratory system gets disturbed which can lead to serious lung diseases. Nose should therefore be kept clean, if some problem is experienced in this sense organ, a doctor must be consulted accordingly.

   Throat is also a vital organ of the body. It is connected with orther sense organs like ear, nose, tongue etc. If it is not kept clean may cause serious disorders. If there is some complaint, one should take medical advice.

5. **Nails and Fingers:** The nails are formed by the special horny cells of the epidermis and protect the finger tips of hands and feet. Since hands are used frequently for any work, the

nails get dirty very easily and this dirt in the nails becomes a source of infection for food when we touch it with hands. All this dirt may get into our mouth with food and make us sick. It is important to keep the nails of the fingers short, so that no dirt accumulates and chances of infection are reduced. Nails should not be bitten by teeth otherwise dirt of the nails may cause severe ailment of mouth and throat. One must develop the habit of cleaning the hands before cooking, handling and eating food. The nails of the toes be cut straight. The feet should be washed and dried properly before retiring to bed.

6. **Skin:** In order to avoid the dangerous effects of polluted atmosphere around us, one has to clean or wash the skin daily. If dirt is allowed to remain over the skin for a long time, it may cause skin diseases. By taking bath the body becomes fresh and remain active. During winter sun-bath may also be practised. Exposure of the body in the sun during winter provides vitamin D and K and improves vitality of the human body, which develops resistance against diseases. The best way to clean the skin or face is with soap and water, dry it with a soft towel by simple patting rather than rubbing. It is advisable to use cold creams in winter particularly when the skin is dry, but care should be taken in case of oily skin and skin with acne. One must avoid over exposure of skin or face to hot weather.
7. **Clothes:** One puts on different types of clothes according to various seasons. Clothes should be fit, clean and tidy, as clean dress adds something to one's personality. Preferably clothes should be washed regularly depending on the weather condition and occupation, and then dried in sun. Under clothes which are in direct contact with the body must be cleaned daily because they constantly come in contact with different body secretions and perspiration of skin. They should be made up of cotton as texture synthetic fibre may cause skin allergy. The clothes should be comfortable to the body and must not obstruct breathing and body development. Avoid wearing tight clothes.
8. **Hair:** Hair should be brushed or combed with personal brush/comb properly. For healthy hair, these should be washed with a good antiseptic soap or shampoo twice a week and then properly dried up. A gentle massage with oil will improve blood circulation and facilitate proper growth and lustre. The scalp is to be gripped lightly between fingers of both hand and gently moved forward, backward and from side to side over the bony skull. If dandruff is there then use anti dandruff shampoo. In case condition does not improve then consult doctor and follow his instruction carefully. The hair should be free from lice and any other infectious germs.
9. **Bowel:** The daily habit of emptying the bowel at regular time should be developed and intentional delay should be avoided. The child should be given proper training from the very beginning. A good nutritive diet with sufficient amount of roughage, plenty of water intake, regular exercise will help in cleaning the bowel. Frequent intake of junk and fried food should be avoided.

Therefore, one must develop good habit of keeping personal cleanliness up to the mark. Good habits are formed during childhood which last longer. If bad habits are nipped in the bud, it would be very beneficial in the long run for the individual as well as community. As Dr. Fielden said, "Life is like a house, give it good foundation and it shall give you good service for as long as you want it". So if we develop good habits in child to keep him healthy, he will help the society to give his best.

OCCUPATIONAL HEALTH

Introduction

Health is a basic human right. Health is man's natural condition, his birth right. It is the result of living in accordance with the natural laws pertaining to the body, mind, and environment. These laws relate to fresh air, sunlight, diet, exercise, rest and relaxation, sleep, cleanliness, elimination, right attitudes of mind, good habits and above all lifestyle. Health is not a static phenomenon, it fluctuates within a range varying from optimum function to various levels of dysfunction. It is multi dimensional physical, mental and social and each is influenced by numerous factors, medical and non-medical. In addition to these factors, the health of the workers is also influenced by the conditions prevailing in their work place. The aim of occupational health is to safeguard the health of the workers and to step up industrial production.

Now the trend is towards industrialisation. As industries develop in size and complexity, occupational health is a big problem. The national government has recognised the need for protecting the health of the workers. Occupational health is a field that is concerned with the health and welfare of workers in various professions. Health is very important for the development of the society, one's own self and for the country.

MEANING OF OCCUPATIONAL HEALTH

In the past we thought of occupational health entirely in relation to factories and mines, and it was known as 'industrial hygiene' or 'industrial health'. Modern concept of occupational health includes all types of employment commercial enterprises, service trades, forestry and agriculture and includes the subjects of industrial hygiene, industrial diseases, industrial accidents, toxicology in relation to industrial hazards, industrial rehabilitation and occupational psychology. *According to World Health Organisation (WHO), "occupational health should aim at the promotion and maintenance of the highest degree of physical, mental and social well-being of workers in all occupations; the prevention among workers of departures from health caused by their working conditions; the protection of workers in their employment from risks resulting from factors adverse to health; the placing and maintenance of the worker in an occupational environment adapted to his physiological and psychological equipment, and, to summarize, the adaptation of work to man and of each man to his job*". In modern occupational health, the emphasis is upon the people, the conditions in which they work and live, their hopes and fears and their attitudes towards their job.

Occupational health is the application of preventive medicine in all places of employment. Preventive medicine and occupational health have the same aim, "the prevention of disease and maintenance of the highest degree of physical, mental and social well being of workers in all occupations; the level of application of preventive measures are the same— health promotion, specific protection, early diagnosis and treatment, disability limitation and rehabilitation."

For the industrial production it is necessary to safeguard the health of the workers to provide a safe '*occupational environment*'. Occupational environment' is the sum of external conditions and influences which prevail at the work place. There are three types of interaction in a working environment (occupational environment):

(*a*) **Physical Agents:** In the working environment physical agents which may be adverse to health are heat, cold, humidity, air movement, heat radiation, light, noise and vibrations. These factors act in different ways on the health and efficiency of the workers. In an occupational environment the amount of working and breathing space, toilet, washing and bathing facilities are also important.

Chemical Agents: Some chemical agents cause disabling respiratory illness, injury to skin, some have a deleterious effect on blood and other organs of the body.

Biological Agents: The workers are exposed to bacterial and parasitic agents from the close contact with animals or their products, contaminated water, soil and food.

(*b*) **Man and Machine:** The unguarded machines, protruding and moving parts, poor installation of the plant, lack of safety measures are the causes of accidents. Working for long hours in un-physiological postures is the cause of fatigue, backache, diseases of joints, and muscles.

(*c*) **Man and Man:** In the modern occupational health, the emphasis is upon the workers, the conditions in which they live and work, their hopes and fears and their attitudes towards their job, their fellow-workers and employers, the human relationships amongst workers themselves and those in authority over them. The occupational environment of the workers cannot be considered with his domestic environment. Stress at work may disturb his sleep, just as stress at home may affect his work. Severe prolonged stress may produce serious physical or mental symptoms which do not allow man to work efficiently. Occupational health represents a dynamic equilibrium or adjustment between the industrial worker and his occupational environment.

SCOPE OF OCCUPATIONAL HEALTH

The scope of occupational health is vast because of the industrialization all over the world. This is due to emergence of new field of work, increase in population and overecrowding in the work place, which causes the problems of occupational health. So proper care / attention should be paid to safeguard the health of the workers. Accidents are a common feature in most of the industries. The main aim of occupational health is to prevent these accidents, the promotion and maintenance of the highest degree of physical, mental and social well being of workers in all occupations.

As industries develop both in size and complexity, this causes more occupational health problems. To solve these types of problems proper education should be given to the workers. Preplacement examination is the foundation of an efficient occupational health service. This will help in placing the right man in right job, so that they can perform their duties efficiently without detriment to his health. Proper training should be given to the workers, to those already working in the industry and to the new employed persons to prevent the occupational hazards.

It is the obligation of the society to protect the health of the workers engaged in different occupations because the worker is more important than the machine which he operates. To safeguard the health and welfare of the workers, factory laws have been framed to govern the conditions in industry. There are certain acts which lay down certain standards to which the employer must comply to ensure health and safety of workers.

PRINCIPLES OF OCCUPATIONAL HEALTH

Industrialization means a social and economic revolution in the culture of a nation, with the emphasis on mass production and community profit. Any such revolution is bound to carry with its hazards. There are certain principles to be followed to reduce such type of problems:

1. **Pre- Placement Examination:** It is done at the time of employment. It includes the worker's medical, family, occupational and social history; a thorough medical examination. The positive or negative results may either be totally rejected or the worker may be given a job suited to his physical and mental abilities. This will help in promotion of the workers.
2. **Periodical Examination:** Periodical examination is very necessary, because many diseases of occupational origin require months or even years for their development. The frequency and content of periodical medical examination depends upon the type of occupational exposure.
3. **Medical and Health Care Services:** Medical care should be provided to the worker and to his family also. Proper first aid services should be made available within the factory.
4. **Periodic Supervision:** Frequent visits should be made by the physician to check the working environment such as temperature, lighting ventilation, humidity, noise, air pollution and sanitation which affect the health of the workers and to study the various aspects of occupational physiology such as occurrence of fatigue due to night-work, shift work etc.
5. **Maintenance and Analysis of Records:** The worker's health record and occupational

disability record must be maintained to watch over the health of the workers and to improve the preventive measures.

6. **Health Education and Counselling:** The purpose of health education is to assist the worker in his process of adjustment to the working, home and community environment. It is given to the worker before he enters the factory. A worker is made aware of all the risks involved in the industry in which he is employed, the measures to be taken for personal protection and the correct use of protective devices like masks, gloves etc. Simple rules of personal hygiene like hand-washing, paring the nails, bodily cleanliness, and cleanliness of clothes should be impressed upon him.
7. **Periodical Checking of Machine:** All the machines, apparatus and equipments used in the factories should be checked periodically, to avoid accidents. If they need repair, to work properly, repair that or replace with the new one.
8. **General Maintenance:** It is a fundamental requirement for the elimination of occupational hazards. It includes general cleanliness, ventilation and lighting. The walls and ceilings, should be white washed at least once a year. To prevent accidents, the right thing should be in the right place. Inside and outside of the plant should also be kept clean and tidy.
9. **Harmful Material:** Harmful material should be substituted by a harmless one or one of lesser toxicity materials. Substitution is not always possible in the industries but it should be substituted to the fullest possible extent where possible.
10. **Protective Devices:** Workers should use the good quality of protective devices. They should know what kinds to use, and when and how to use, these devices. Protective devices such as gas masks, ear plugs, ear muffs, helmets, safety shoes, aprons, gloves, gum boots, barrier creams, screens and goggles should be provided by the factory owners.
11. **Environmental Monitoring:** Periodical environmental surveys should be done, especially sampling the factory atmosphere to "determine whether the dusts and gases escaping into the atmosphere are within the limits of permissible concentration. It should be done by joint collaboration of doctors and engineers.

FACTORS RESPONISBLE FOR OCCUPATIONAL HEALTH HAZARDS AND DISEASES

There are certain factors which cause occupational health hazards, but it depends upon the occupation of the worker. These are as follow:

Physical Hazards

(i) ***Heat and cold:*** In industries the common physical hazard is heat. The direct heat exposure causes burns, heat exhaustion, heat stroke and heat cramps. The indirect effects are, decreased efficiency and increased fatigue. Industries with local "Hot Spots" e.g. ovens radiate heat. Radiant heat is the main problem in glass and steel industries, heat stagnation is the problem in jute and cotton textile industry. High temperature is also found in mines, e.g., in the Kolar Gold mines of Mysore which is the second deepest mine of the world (11,00 feet), temperature as high as 150 degree F is recorded. Physical work under such conditions is very stressful and impairs the health and efficiency of the worker.

Working in cold causes chilblains, immersion foot, and frostbite as a result of coetaneous vasoconstriction.

(ii) ***Light:*** The workers may be exposed to the risk of poor illumination or excessive brightness. The effects of poor illumination are eye strain, headache, eye pain, congestion around the cornea and eye fatigue. Excessive brightness or 'glare' causes visual fatigue.

(iii) ***Noise:*** Noise is a health hazard in many factories / industries. Auditory effects consist of temporary or permanent hearing loss. Non-auditory effects consist of nervousness, fatigue, interference with communication by speech, decreased efficiency and annoyance. The degree of injury depends upon a number of factors such as intensity and frequency range, duration of exposure etc.

(*iv*) ***Vibration:*** Vibration usually affects the hand and arms. Exposure to vibration may also produce injuries of the joints, of the hands, elbows and shoulders.

(*v*) ***Ultraviolet Radiation :*** Ultraviolet radiation occurs mainly in welding. It mainly affects the eyes causing intense conjunctivitis (welder's flash). Redness of the eyes and pain are the symptoms. No permanent effect on the vision of the eyes occurs.

Chemical Hazards

All industries make use of chemicals. Chemical hazards are on the increase. These chemical agents act in three ways (i) Local action, *(ii)* Inhalation and *(iii)* Ingestion.

(*i*) ***Local Action:*** Some chemicals cause dermatitis, eczema, ulcers, and even cancer by primary irritant action. Some cause dermatitis by an allergic action. Some are absorbed through the skin and cause systemic effects.

(*ii*) ***Inhalation:***

(*a*) **Dusts** are produced in a number of industries - mines, foundry, quarry, pottery, textile, wood or stone working industries. Dust is released into the atmosphere during crushing, grinding, loading and unloading operations. Dusts have been classified into inorganic and organic dusts, soluble and insoluble dusts. The inorganic dusts are silica, mica, coal, abestos etc. The organic dusts are cotton, jute and the like. The soluble dusts dissolve slowly, enter the systemic circulation and are eliminated by body metabolism. The insoluble dusts remain, more or less, permanently in the lungs. The common dust diseases are silicosis and anthracosis.

(*b*) *Gases*: Exposure to gases is a common hazard in industries. Simple gases (e.g., oxygen, hydrogen) asphyxiating gases (e.g., carbon monoxide, cyanide gas, sulphur dioxide, chlorine, and anaesthetic gases e.g., chloroform, either etc.).

(*c*) ***Metals and other compounds***: The chief mode of entry of some of the metals is by inhalation as dust or fumes. The ill effects depend upon the duration of exposure and the dose or concentration of exposure.

(*iii*) ***Ingestion :*** Ingestion of chemical substances such as lead, mercury, arsenic, zinc, chromium, cadmium, phosphorus etc. can also be harmful. These are swallowed in minute amounts through contaminated hands, food etc. Much of the ingested material is excreted and only a small proportion reaches the general blood circulation.

Biological Hazards

In this the workers are exposed to parasitic agents at work place. Persons working among animal products e.g. hair, wool, hides and agricultural workers are specially exposed to biological hazards.

Mechanical Hazards

The mechanical hazards in the industry centre around machinery. Only few percentage of accidents occur due to mechanical causes.

Psychosocial Hazards

This is due to the worker's failure to adapt to the psychosocial environment. The capacity to adapt to different working environments is influenced by many factors such as education, cultural background, family life, social habits and worker's expectation from employment. Some of the psychosocial factors which may undermine both physical and mental health of the workers are such as frustration, lack of job satisfaction, insecurity, poor human relationships, emotional tension etc.

The two main effects on the health are:

(*a*) ***Psychological and behavioural changes:*** This includes hostility, aggressiveness, anxiety, depression, tardiness, alcoholism, drug abuse, sickness, absenteeism.

(*b*) ***Psychosomatic ill health:*** This includes fatigue, headache, pain in the shoulders, neck and back, hypertension, heart disease and rapid aging. The increasing stress on automation, electronic operations and nuclear energy causes psychological health problems in industry. Psychological hazards are more important than physical and chemical hazards.

OCCUPATIONAL DISEASES

Diseases arising out of or in the course of employment.

1. Diseases caused by physical factors

Due to Heat	Heat hyperpyrexia, heat exhausation, heat syncope, heat cramps, burns and coal effects such as prickly heat.
Due to Cold	Trench foot, frost bite, chilblains.
Due to light	Occupational cataract.
Due to pressure	Caisson disease, air ambolism, blast (explosion)
Due to noise	Occupational deafness
Due to Radiation	Cancer, leukaemia, aplastic anaemia
Due to mechanical factors	Injuries, accidents
Due to electricity	Burns

2. Diseases caused by chemical factors

Due to Gases	These cause gas poisoning.
Due to Dusts	Indrganic Dusts causes
Coal dust	— Anthracosis
Silica	— Silicosis
Asbestos	— Asbestosis, Lung cancer
Iron	— Siderosis
	Organic (Vegetable) Dusts
Cane fibre	— Bagassosis
Cotton dust	— Byssionosis
Tobacco	— Tobacossis
Grain Dust	— Farmer's lung
Due to Metals and their Compounds	Toxic hazards from lead, mercury, cadmium, manganese, chromium etc.
Due to chemicals	Acids, Alkalies, Pesticides

3. Diseases caused by Biological Factors	**Brucellosis, anthrax, actnomycosis, hydatidsis, tetanus, fungal infections, etc.**
4. Occupational Cancers	**Cancer of skin, lungs, bladder.**
5. Occupational Dermatosis	**Dermatitis eczema**
6. Diseases caused by Psychological Factors	**Industrial neurosis, hypertension, peptic ulcer etc.**

ENVIRONMENTAL POLLUTION

Introduction

Environment means whatever surrounds the individual. In other words, whatever surrounds the individual constitutes his environment. It is also known as external environment which includes the air, water, soil, noise, sun radiations, plants, deserts, rocks, buildings. etc. On the other hand, every one has internal environment which consists of his body, his internal systems and their functions. The body maintains balance between the external and the internal environment, but sometimes the state of balance is disturbed due to the environment pollution and diseases are caused. Environment is polluted when some foreign substances enter in it and affect the life of an individual. These foreign substances degrade the quality of water, air, noise and many other factors.

AIR POLLUTION

Truly speaking, there has never been pure air. Air is the closest component of environment for all lives. It provides oxygen for respiration, carries sound and smell and helps in maintaining the body temperature. The air may contain dust and smoke which when inhaled may cause sickness and death. Foreign substances have been present in the air at all times and at all places. The term air pollution is, therefore, applied when there is an excessive concentration of foreign matter in the external atmosphere which is harmful to man or his environment. Air pollution is a growing problem to health throughout the world. The problem of air pollution was first brought to a sharp focus when air pollution epidemics took place in Los Angeles (1948) and London (1952). In the London air pollution of 1952, many people became ill and some 4000 died within 12 hours.

Causes (Sources) of Air Pollution

The sources of air pollution may be classified into four broad categories :

1. **Industrial Processes:** Industries are a big source of Air Pollution specially, chemical and metallurgical industries, oil refineries. fertilizer factories, etc. All these have contributed significantly to air pollution.
2. **Combustion:** Industrial and domestic combustion of coal, oil and other fuel is another source of smoke, dust, and sulphur dioxide, carbon dioxide and so on. The London disaster was due to domestic coal burning.
3. **Motor Vehicles:** Motor vehicles are a major source of air pollution throughout the urban areas of the world. Motor vehicles including trucks, trains, aircrafts, two wheelers, three wheelers, light motor vehicles, tractors and other forms of transport, contribute to air pollution by emitting hydrocarbons, carbon monoxide, lead, nitrogen oxides and so on. These sources are more harmful when the engines are not adjusted and tuned properly. In addition diesel engines, when misused or badly adjusted, are capable of emitting black smoke and foul smelling fumes.
4. **Miscellaneous:** Use of insecticides and pesticides for crops and kitchen gardens and even at home burning of refuse and nuclear energy programmes also contribute to air pollution. Many harmful chemicals have already been identified as chemical pollutants. Some of them are carcinogenic agents, an agent that increases the chance of any cell becoming cancerous.

Air pollution is a global problem. It affects developing countries more because there is unplanned industrialisation and urbanisation. India is one of them. There are many contaminants (Pollutants) of air and some of them have been selected as indicators of air pollution. The important ones are sulphur dioxide, smoke, suspended substances, oxides of carbon and nitrogen, lead etc. The concentration of these substances is measured in the air and if they exceed the maximum permissible limits the air is labelled or termed as polluted and need immediate preventive measures.

Effects of Polluted Air

Air pollution affects health to a large extent. The respiratory system is the most affected system by air pollution. The common disease due to prolonged exposure to polluted air is chronic bronchitis. It is a chronic lung inflammation caused by the inhaled injurious substances. It is not a single disease but having a complex symptoms of various causes. The patient complains of chest pain, productive cough, fever off and on and general weakness.

Plants and animals are also very sensitive to air pollution. Sulphur dioxide, fluorine and lead affect the plants leading to stunted growth, burning of leaves and crop residues. Animals suffer from respiratory diseases by inhaling polluted air and by consuming contaminated food by the pollutants.

The depletion of ozone layer is another major problem of air pollution. If it is not checked, the increased ultra violet radiation would be a serious threat. Plants and animals would be affected adversely in many ways. Soil moisture would reduce significantly. Agricultural production can get a setback from reduced yields. The toxic gases slow down the process of photosynthesis.

Property and material are also affected by pollution. The pollutants can corrode metal, stone and marble. Taj Mahal of Agra has lost its lustre due to the pollution caused by a Mathura refinery. Ozone can cause rubber cracking. *The depletion of ozone layer is a very dangerous phenomenon for mother earth.*

The air pollution also affects the social and economic aspects of an individual/society. These are due to impairment of human, plant and animal health; corrosion of metal and building materials; cost of cleaning and repairing, unpleasant odours, cost of research and expenses due to adoption of technical measures to control pollution and administrative organisation. Air pollution also reduces visibility in towns.

Remedial Measures

The World Health Organisation published a document in 1968 "Research into Environment Pollution", which recommends certain remedial measures for the prevention of air pollution, as mentioned below :

1. **Containment**: Containment means we try to stop the release of toxic substances into the air by taking measures like providing enclosures, ventilation and air cleaning. Therefore, containment can be achieved by a variety of such engineering methods.
2. **Replacement**: This is related with replacing the products and technological processes causing air pollution with new products and processes. For example coal can be replaced by natural gas or electricity to prevent air pollution.
3. **Dilution**: The contaminants present in the air are diluted by vegetation and plantation. The establishment of "*green belts*" between industrial and residential areas is an attempt at dilution. However, this has got limited utility. When the atmosphere gets excessive amount of pollutants, this mechanism fails.
4. **Legislation**: Many countries have adopted legislation for control of air pollution. In India there is smoke "*Nuisance Act*" which is effective in big cities. The vehicles must be checked frequently for proper maintenance so that they cause minimum pollution.
5. **International Action**: To deal with air pollution globally, the World Health Organisation has established an International network of various centres and laboratories for controlling and study of air pollution. This net work consists of two international centres established at London and Washington, three regional centres at Nagpur, Tokyo and Moscow and other laboratories for air quality monitoring in big cities of the world. These centres will issue warnings of air pollution when and where needed.

OZONE LAYER

The air around us consists mainly of nitrogen and oxygen. It also contains small amounts of other gases, including carbon dioxide (which we breathe out and green plants absorb), hydrogen and ozone.

Some people wrongly think that ozone is the refreshing air we breathe in at the seaside. It is, in fact, a poisonous kind of oxygen. At ground level, the air contains very little ozone. But, 24 kms above the earth, there is a thin layer of it. This ozone layer blocks out most of the ultraviolet rays from the sun. If these rays reached the ground, they would kill all land animals and plants.

Gases called chlorofluorocarbons (CFCs), found in refrigerators, air conditioners, and many aerosol sprays, are rapidly destroying the ozone layer. Satellites have already detected a large 'hole' over the North pole. Many countries are passing laws to stop the production and use of CFCs.

In these conditions chlorine and other gases accumulate in the environment. The ultraviolet rays of the spring sun initiate the reactions and chlorine and other gases become active resulting in a hole in the ozone layer. The production of CFCs needs to be cut drastically if the ozone layer is to continue to shield the ozone.

If the ozone is depleted completely, the following effects may be realised:

- The size of eyes will be small, and may cause eye cataract.
- The size of nose will be longer.
- The height will be smaller.

- It may cause skin cancer.
- It may cause low yield of crops.

Save Ozone Layer : Save Earth

The ozone layer protects the life on earth from the damaging effects of sun's ultraviolet radiations.The depeletion of ozone layer is more susceptible towards infectious diseases and distrubances in marine food chain.

To Save the Ozone Layer-there are some Do's and Don'ts given below :

Do's

- Choose eco-friendly products by buying Refrigerators and Air conditioners which donot use C.F.C.s.
- Design the houses and offices to allow maximum natural air, light and heat to avoid artificial lighting and air conditioning facilities.
- Use and promote environment friendly products.

Don'ts

- Avoid using products like foam mattresses which are linked to ozone depleting substances (ODS).
- Reduce the consumption of plastics/Plastic Products.
- Avoid use of room freshners and chemical perfumes, most of which are not ozone friendly.

WATER POLLUTION

Water is polluted when some foreign substance is present in it which degrades its quality and makes it unfit or harmful for use. This foreign substance can be organic, inorganic, biological or some physical substance. This can be in the form of dissolved gases (e.g., hydrogen, sulphide, carbon dioxide, oxygen, ammonia, nitrogen); or dissolved minerals (e.g., salts of calcium, magnesium, sodium); suspended impurities (e.g., clay, silt, sand, mud) and microscopic plants and animals like worms or bacterials.

In simple words polluted water is impure water with some foreign substance which is detrimental to the health of human being, animals, and plants. When the quality of water changes it becomes less suitable for drinking purposes, agricultural activities, aquatic organisms or other purposes. Polluted water can cause various intestinal infections like cholera or dysentery or other diseases like jaundice.

Causes (Sources) of Water Pollution

The water pollution is mainly caused by the human activity, *i.e.,* urbanisation and industrialisation. The sources of pollution resulting from urbanisation and industrialisation are:

1. **Sewage:** It contains decomposable organic matter and pathogenic agents. Sewage is an important source of pollution in urban centres. The disposal of liquid waste in urban centres could not keep pace with growing population, especially in developing countries. Liquid waste comes from residential areas, industrial areas, institutions, hotels, hospitals, public buildings, commercial areas etc. The water contains human excreta, urine, detergents, chemicals, fruit skin and anything small enough to find its way into sewers. Normally liquid waste is discharged into nearby water bodies or disposed in open low lying areas with polluted water becoming breeding places for mosquitoes, worms and other harmful organisms. This leads to pollution of underground water. Its main effect is depletion of oxygen contents in the water.
2. **Industrial and Trade Wastage**: It contains tóxic agents ranging from metal salts to complex synthetic organic chemicals. Industrial waste is another major source of water pollution. Various industries iike chemicals, paper, tanneries, breweries, dyeing, textile, sugar, jute, oil refineries etc. produce millions of tons of industrial waste. Almost the entire waste is thrown into rivers, canals, or any other water body or in open low lying space. The discharge of this chemically

polluted water affects the underground water which is used directly through handpumps, wells and tubewells. This type of pollution affects the taste and smell of water. Industrial waste is a serious health hazard in big industrial cities. Chemical and toxic substances reduce the efficacy of purification system and damage the growth of plants.

3. **Agricultural and Related Activities**: The use of chemical fertilizers, pesticides, insecticide and herbicides is common in modern agricultural practices. These are frequently used to increase the productivity but they have proved harmful e.g. the use of D.D.T. as an insecticide has been banned in many countries. The excessive use of nitrogen and phosphrus has become a major agricultural pollution. The presence of such substances is responsible for depletion of dissolved oxygen which can cause death to fish and other aquatic life. When this water is consumed by animals or man, nitrates are reduced to toxic nitrates which can cause serious damage to respiratory and vesicular system. It often causes suffocation.
4. **Physical Pollutants**: It includes thermal pollution and radio-active substances. Disposal of hot water causes thermal pollution. The temperature of aquatic environment increases due to this hot water. This affects aquatic animals and plants adversely. Presence of radio-active substance has also been detected in many rivers. This is caused by processing of uranium, waste from research laboratories or hospitals where radioslopes or isotopes are used. Oil spills on coastal areas of lakes, seas and oceans. Even oceanic water is also polluted. Ship generated discharges of oil and petroleum products or leakage of large quantities of mineral oil cause marine pollution. During Gulf War in 1991 between U.S.A. and Iraq thousands of tons of oil was discharged in sea. These oil spills make the water poisonous and render it useless. Such leaks can cause ecological disasters.

Effects of Water Pollution

At present water pollution has become a major health hazard. Polluted water causes water borne diseases. In this form man is directly affected. The polluted water taken by land and aquatic animals is also harmful as man takes it indirectly through food chain. Water pollution causes huge economic loss to man. Huge money is being spent on water treatment to make it re-useable, to clean big rivers for the life of aquatic animals and for the use of agricultural activities.

Preventive Measures

While pollution seems to be inevitable consequence of modern industrial technology and comfortable life of human being, the problem now is to determine the level of pollution that permits economic and social development without presenting hazards to health. The pollution of water can be prevented to some extent if the following measures are taken by all individuals, society and Government.

1. **Treatment of Waste Water**: Two major sources of waste water have been identified. They are industries and urban population. Urban liquid waste is normally, known as 'sewage' and industrial waste as 'effluent'.

   (*i*) ***Sewage Waste Treatment:*** Domestic sewage is composed of human body waste and sullage which results from washing, laundry, food preparation, cleaning of kitchen utensils etc. Sewage contains pollutants in suspended, solid and solution form. It is unpleasant in appearance and hazardous in contents as it contains pathogenic germs.

   Sewage must be treated before it is thrown into some water body. It is essential to reduce the spread of communicable diseases caused by pathogenic germs present in sewage, surface and ground water. The treatment process includes three steps: i.e. collection, treatment, and re-use. Treatment is required to destroy pathogenic agents present in sewage and it is suitable for re-use, for whatever purpose.

(ii) ***Industrial Waste Water (Effluent) Treatment):*** Three types of pollutants are identified in industrial waste water.

(*a*) Floating pollutants e.g. oil, grease, fat and so on. They affect the growth of plants adversely.

(*b*) Suspended pollutants. They can be either organic or inorganic.

(*c*) Dissolved pollutants *e.g.*, acids, alkalis, heavy metals, insecticides etc. They can destroy aquatic life.

The industrial waste water is treated by methods such as dissolved air, floating chemical treatment, biological treatment, sedimentation, filtration and so on. In the cities having scarcity of water, there is need of effluent re-use in industry and effluent with no chemicals for irrigation. From concluding point of view it is stated that suitable policies should be formulated in order to prevent water pollution. It is hard fact that only legislative measures can help in solving water pollution problems.

2. **Population Control:** The Government of India is trying hard to control the population but the kind of Government is based on the vote banks. Perhaps this is the reason the Government is not following strictly the measures to control the Population. The over population in the country is bound to be deprived of basic education due to the paucity of funds and educational institutions. With the result the uneducated people do not understand their role in polluting the water in terms of the disposal of excreta of human beings as well as animals. Therefore it is the responsibility of the Government as well as people of the country to control the pollution so that within the available facilities they can improve their living standards by having proper facilities for the disposal of excreta urine and other disposals.

3. **Educative Measures:** Keeping in view the water pollution problems, the central and state universities, boards should make their earnest efforts to introduce syllabus in the schools, colleges and the university's courses with regard to the prevention of water pollution and consequences of polluted water. Also the social organisations, media, N.S.S. and N.C.C. camps should contribute to educate the public about the problem of water pollution and guide them for the prevention of pollution of water.

4. **Legislation**: Water pollution is global problem since the water of ocean, seas, rivers, canals is being polluted by one or the other way. Therefore National Government of countries of the world should pass a legislation to prevent the water pollution by a country or a particular industry or even individuals. In this respect Government of India accepted that water pollution is becoming a serious problem. To protect water from being polluted, in 1974 parliament passed the water (Prevention and Control of Pollution) Act. The Act seems to provide the legal deterrent against the spread of water pollution. The act is provided with constitutionwide powers for controlling pollution. Under this legislation no industry is allowed to establish unless the certificate by the owner is furnished with regard to the re-treatment of waste water of the industry and the centre and state waste boards are satisfied by the same.

NOISE POLLUTION

Noise pollution is another big environmental problem, especially in the big urban centres. Noise means excessive and unwanted sound. It can be defined as "an excessive", offensive, persistent or starting sound". In other words it may be defined as "wrong sound, in the wrong place, at the wrong time". In simple words noise pollution is unwanted and excessive sound forces into atmosphere without any consideration. Some of the psychologists have defined noise as under:

According to Harrel, "Noise is an unwanted sound which increases fatigue and under certain conditions it causes deafness."

In the words of J. Tiffen, "Noise is a sound which is disagreeable for the individual and which disturbs the normal way of an individual".

According to Blum, "Noise is a distracter and therefore, interferes with efficiency."

Causes (Sources) of Noise Pollution

The sources of noise are many and varied. These are automobiles, industries, aircrafts, radio's, T.V's amplifiers, industrial sources (small scale industries and the house hold industries). At present the religious places have became a big source of noise pollution through loud speakers.

The noise has two important characteristics:

1. Loudness or intensity.
2. Pitch or frequency.

1. The loudness or intensity depends upon the amptitude of the sound waves produced from the source.The loudness of the noise is measured in decibel (dB) units. One decibel is the smallest amptitude which can be heard by the human ear.

2. Pitch or frequency of sound is denoted as Hertz (hz). One hz is equal to one wave per second. There are many complicated instruments to measure noise level frequency, duration and other environmental factors which are specially useful in factories and other establishments where noise is a problem.

Effects of Noise Pollution

Noise is very harmful and serious health problem. The effects are serious and have far reaching consequences. Noise pollution affects a man in many ways such as annoyance, irritation, disturbance in sleep etc. are its simple effects. A constant exposure to noise can impair our hearing but sudden and severe exposure can cause deafness. It can also cause some psychological and physiological effects e.g. rise in blood pressure, mental tension, giddiness, and nausea are common. The latest research has found a relationship between noise level and heart disease. Doctors from Germany say that noise causes narrowing of arteries. According to Russian doctors continuous exposure to noise at a certain level (100 dB) causes pain in heart. Further surveys in this direction indicate that fairly large number of heart patients came from areas which are frequently and more exposed to noise pollution. Noise pollution can affect our efficiency also. It can change our habits and behaviour too.

Remedial Measures

To control the noise pollution there are three components of noise pollution such as source of medium of noise, and object affected by noise must be taken into consideration while adopting remedial measures. The most important medium is individual, society and Government. General awareness among masses is a powerful medium. People must be educated through various media about the ill effects of noise pollution.

The most effective method can be to put a check on the source points. Noisy machines should be located away from living places and the noise must be minimised by applying silencers to machines. The noise created by loudspeaker and other gadgets can be reduced by convincing the user. Effective prohibitory laws can be introduced, e.g., excessive noise has been recognised as a crime under section 268 of Indian Penal Code. The provisions made under motor vehicles Act can be effective if properly implemented. Similarly Factory Acts and Aircraft Act could be used to get rid of the problem.

Improvement in designing of machines banning pressure horns, improving roading system can go a long way in reducing a noise pollution.

At the receivers' end the pollution can be minimised by using ear plugs, ear muffs, noise helmets etc. Proper layouts of buildings, increased distance between source and receiver, planting trees and shrubs along roads etc. are also effective measures to control noise pollution.

COMMUNICABLE DISEASES

Introduction

A disease is a sickness that occurs when there is an upset or breakdown in the way the body usually functions. Most diseases make one feel sick or like something is not quite right with the body, but some diseases upset places in the body that one can not really feel, like blood, or one's internal organs. Symptoms are the changes that one can see or feel when one has a disease. Coughing can be a symptom of having a cold. People recover from some diseases in a short time. Others last a long time. Some leave permanent damage, other diseases can cause death.

Diseases that can be passed or transmitted from one person to another are called infectious or contagious, like the common cold. Illnesses like a heart attack or cancer are not contagious. If a person is around some one else who has an infectious disease, we say that person has been exposed. Very often, symptoms appear much later so the person never knows when he or she was exposed to the illness, that person has become infected.

A disease resulting from infection capable of being directly or indirectly transmitted from man to man, animal to animal from the environment through air, dust, soil water, food etc. to man and to animal.

There are many communicable diseases like Aids, small pox, measles, whooping cough, tuberculosis, viral hepatitis, hepatitis B, typhoid, malaria, rabies, tetanus etc.

HIV / AIDS

Ever since the initial identification of the Human Immuno Deficiency Virus (HIV) and Acquired Immune Deficiency Syndrome (AIDS) among the homosexual community of the developed nations in America and Europe in the late 1970's there has been an alarming rate of spread of the virus. This virus continues to spread around the world.

AIDS did not originate from India. But this fact cannot overshadow the profound status of HIV infection in the present Indian scenario. By the next decade, India will house nearly 50 million AIDS patients. In India the first case of HIV infection was officially reported from a clinic in Chennai in the summer of 1986. There has been a rapid spread of the disease across the nation ever since. The initial cases of HIV / AIDS were reported among commercial sex workers in Mumbai and Chennai and Intravenous Drug users (IDU) in the north-eastern states. In recent years it has spread from urban to rural areas and from individuals having "high-risk" behaviour to the general population. The estimated number of HIV / AIDS infected in the world in 2001 are 36 million and one out of 10 people is Indian who is affected by this virus.

Origin of HIV / AIDS

It may be said that the exact origin of AIDS will never be completely elicited. There are, however, certain facts that have led to a more or less general agreement as to the source of this epidemic. It is plausible to conclude that HIV is a pathogen new to the human race, probably resulting from an non-pathogenic, subhuman primate retrovirus, which made a species jump from African Primates (monkeys) to human. There is widespread evidence that many old world primates *e.g.* chimpanzees, mandrills, and African Green Monkeys, in sub-Saharan Africa have been infected with restroviruses similar to HIV for thousands of years, although they are non-pathogenic and do not cause debilitating illness.

What is AIDS?

AIDS stands for the Acquired Immune Deficiency Syndrome.

- **A.** *Acquired* means that it is something people acquire from outside. It is not inherited from parent like eye colour or blood type. It is transmitted through person's own behaviour or situation.
- **I.** *Immune* refers to the immune system, the body's defence mechanism against germs and infections (a weakened body defence system).
- **D.** *Deficiency* indicates a lack or weakening of (the immune system).

S. *Syndrome* refers to the presence of a group of signs and symptoms. When the body's defences are weakened, it is possible for many infections or diseases to simultaneously infect the body. The condition is referred to as a syndrome. It is a collection of signs and symptoms that are generally found together in a particular disease or diseases.

Currently the World Health Organisation and UNAIDS estimated that 8,500 persons will become infected with HIV each day while an estimated 4,000 persons will die from HIV / AIDS related deaths each day.

AIDS is a serious disorder of the Immune system. This system puts up a defence against any infections and protects the body from illnesses. AIDS is the condition where this system is under attack. The body's normal defences against infection break down and the body becomes vulnerable to infections and other diseases. Some of these infections would normally not affect healthy people. But when immune system is weaknened or depressed, they find an opportunity to flourish and so are called opportunistic infections.

AIDS was first identified in 1981 in the U.S.A. when previously healthy, homosexual men began to suffer and die on account of rare infections. After much debate and research, scientists identified a new syndrome and later termed it as AIDS.

What is HIV?

AIDS is caused by an organism called HIV.

H. Human indicates that the HIV only infects humans.

I. Immunodeficiency indicates that HIV causes the immune system to become weak and ineffective in defending the body against the germs. In this way, HIV leads to AIDS.

V. Virus is a disease causing parasite.

(*i*) AIDS is Acquired because it is caught from someone and is not inherited.

(*ii*) Immune and Deficiency because the virus destroys the body's defence system and as a result the person is more likely to get illness which the body would normally be able to fight off easily.

(*iii*) Syndrome describes the different signs and symptoms of the illness that result from the HIV infections. These signs and symptoms appear as multiple infection or illness.

Mode of Transmission

Diseases can be caused by pathogens. There are organisms or germs which can invade the body from outside, it can cause illness. Viruses, bacteria, fungi, and protozoa can be called the pathogens. All of these organisms are very small living creatures and can not be seen with the naked eyes.

A virus is a tiny organism which carries instruction for reproducing itself (called the genetic material). But it must invade a living cell (such as one in a person's body) to reproduce.

Concentration of viral load: There must be a sufficient quantity of HIV to allow infection to occur. If the concentration is too low then it is not possible for infection to take place.

Port of Entry: There must be a way for HIV to enter into the body. If HIV infected fluid does not have a path into another person's body then infection can not take place.

Body fluids like blood, semen, menstrual blood, vaginal fluid contain a high enough concentration of HIV / AIDS and can be exchanged.

Body fluids like sweat, tear, skin oils do not contain the virus to infect.

Fluids like cerebrospinal fluid, amniotic fluid, focal matter are not normally exchanged between persons. HIV / AIDS has been isolated from the body fluids or infected persons, including saliva and tears. However, only blood, semen, vaginal secretions, and breast milk have been implicated in transmission.

There are only three modes of transmission:

- Sexual Transmission.
- Blood Transmission
- Mother to Child Transmission.

(*a*) ***Sexual Transmission:*** The virus can be transmitted from an infected person to his or her sex partner (man to woman, woman to man and man to man). Sexual intercourse can damage the linings of sexual organs and can facilitate transmission of HIV / AIDS from the infected partner to the uninfected one by exchange of body fluids. It is easier for the virus to be transmitted if the uninfected partner is already suffering from some sexually transmitted disease because in this case the lining is already damaged. Due to the high rate of sexual transmission of the virus, sexual behaviour is the prime focus interrupting transmission. In India, sexual intercourse is the most frequent mode of transmission of HIV / AIDS.

(b) ***Blood Transmission:*** It occurs through the transfusion of infected blood or blood products or the use of blood contaminated needles, syringes or other skin piercing instruments. Recipients of a single unit of HIV infected blood have a virtually 100% probability of becoming infected.

Blood transfusion is a significant problem in areas where HIV infection is common and where HIV antibody screening of blood donors has not yet been introduced.

When blood is needed it should be obtained from a licensed blood bank. Licensed blood banks test blood for HIV and place a sticker on the blood unit indicating that it has been tested. Even though the bag has been tested for HIV, there is still a chance that it contains the virus if it was obtained from a patient in the window period. Blood received in the window period does not contain antibodies produced in response to HIV.

HIV can live between 30 seconds to one minute when exposed to air. When a needle pierces the skin and its contents injected, blood pressure and capillary action can push injected blood back into the bone and hub of the needle. How long HIV can live inside the needle depends on the conditions the needle is stored in.

(c) ***Mother to Child Transmission:*** Transmission of HIV / AIDS from an infected women to her foetus / infant may occur before, during and shortly after birth. The overall risk of HIV transmission from HIV infected women to her foetus in uterus or during delivery is about 30%.

The breast milk of mothers infected with HIV contains small amounts of the virus. Researchers have found that one third of babies born to HIV infected women become infected through milk, recent data confirms that some transmission may occur through breast feeding.

(d) ***It is observed that extra-marital sex*** is the primary mode of infection, 80% of AIDS patients identified, owed their extramarital sex to be the cause.

(e) Such rapid spread of the epidemic across the country today is also due to the labour migration and mobility in search of employment from economically backward to more developed regions.

(f) Low literacy levels leading to low awareness among the potential high risk group.

Non-Transmission of HIV/AIDS

The present attitudes towards AIDS are similar to the attitudes once seen towards syphils in the early 19th century. Myths and emotional hysteria can be generated due to misinformation about AIDS. Many myths about HIV today centre around the way in which it can be transmitted. There are only three routes of HIV transmission.

(a) **HIV/AIDS does not spread**

(i) Drinking water from the same glass as an infected person.

(ii) Swimming in pools used by people with HIV / AIDS.

(iii) Getting bitten by a mosquito that has already bitten an infected person.

(iv) Getting bitten by an infected person.

(v) Socialising or casually living with people with HIV / AIDS.

(vi) Caring and looking after people with HIV / AIDS.

(vii) Use of the same toilets as AIDS patients or people infected with HIV.

(viii) Shaking hands with people with HIV / AIDS.

(ix) Hugging or kissing a person with HIV / AIDS.

(*x*) Casual contacts such as sitting next to an infected person, or by coughing and sneezing, or from water, food, clothing, cups, glasses, plates, forks, spoons and other shared objects.

(*xi*) Receiving and reviewing literature from areas of the world where there is AIDS.

(*xii*) Donating blood.

(*xiii*) Bedbugs, flies, lice, and other insects and pests do not spread HIV / AIDS.

(*b*) **Identifying AIDS:** World Health Organisation (WHO) has listed a few signs that help in provisional diagnosis of AIDS.

Major Signs

(*i*) Weight loss greater than 10% of the body weight.

(*ii*) Continue fever for a period more than one month.

(*iii*) Chronic diarrhoea (for more than one month).

Minor Signs

(*i*) Persistent cough for a period longer than one month.

(*ii*) General itching dermatitis (skin irritation).

(*iii*) Recurrent Herps zoster (shingres)

(*iv*) Oropharyngeal candidiasis (fungus infection in the mouth / throat)

(*v*) Swelling of the lymph glands.

Cure for AIDS

So far there is No Cure For AIDS and a vaccine of prevention of infection may be far away. Even if there is a cure, the cost of the medicine would prevent it from being used in many developing countries.

Prevention of HIV / AIDS Infection

At present prevention is the only cure for AIDS. Since AIDS is a sexually transmitted disease, sexual behaviour is the prime focus of action for interrupting transmission. It is therefore important to have an information and education programme aimed at all men and women, to have facilities for detection and treatment of other sexually transmitted diseases and to have an environment which would promote condom use and frank information dissemination without stigmatization and discrimination against people known or suspected to have HIV/ AIDS. In India, prevention of sexual transmission is an immediate priority.

1. Safer sex activities for prevention

   (*i*) Sexual activities e.g. Hugging, kissing etc.

   (*ii*) Anything that does not involve the sharing of semen, vaginal secretion or blood.

   (*iii*) Long term mutually faithful relation-ship, be faithful to one's partner.

   (*iv*) Proper and consistent use of condoms.

2. For prevention of HIV / AIDS transmission through infected blood and blood products, include recruiting voluntary non-paid donors, screening all donated blood for HIV and educating health care workers to reduce unnecessary transfusions.

3. Preventing transmission at health care setting rests on careful attention to infection control procedure including proper sterilization of equipment, proper adherence to procedures based on "Universal Health Precautions", and provision of necessary supplies and equipment.

4. Preventing blood borne transmission among drug injectors should go hand in hand with efforts to prevent sexual transmission among them. These include reducing the demand for drugs, the use of drugs by injection and the sharing of injection equipment.

5. To screen blood and blood products, thorough testing of all blood samples for HIV should be done. This does not take into account blood screening done during the window period, where the person is already infected but his immune system has not produced antibodies against HIV. Their blood samples may or may not be free of HIV. In Bhutan, Indonesia and Thailand, all donated blood is now screened for HIV.

6. For preventing transmission from mother to child is to prevent sexual transmission of HIV to women of reproductive age. Secondary prevention would depend on the avoidance of child bearing by mothers who know or suspect that they are infected.

7. Counselling and contraceptive services should be made available for all men and women.

World Health Organisation (WHO) estimates that 16-17 million adults and children are infected with the HIV / AIDS virus in the world. Most of these will develop HIV related illnesses and ultimately AIDS. Therefore we need to plan for care of these patients at hospitals and at the home. They must receive treatment for common opportunistic infections such as tuberculosis, etc. As AIDS affects people in their most productive years, the economic impact on families with HIV infected members is enormous especially on children who may be orphaned. The impact of AIDS on society would include enormous health care costs, decimation of the work force and loss of skilled labour and educated professionals.

VIRAL HEPATITIS

'Viral hepatitis' is caused by two viruses, namely Hepatitis A virus (HA V) and Hepatitis B virus (HBV). A third form of hepatitis, referred to as non-A, non-B (NANB), has been found in all countries and is known as Hepatitis 'C'. There are three types of Hepatitis, A, B, and C.

Hepatitis A

It is an acute communicable disease caused by Hepatitis A virus (HA V). It is one of the most widespread infectious disease worldwide. It is common in places with poor standards of hygiene and sanitation. The virus attacks the liver and causes varying degrees of illness in patients.

The severity of infection is age related with symptoms being more common in adolescents, adults, and young children. Acute symptoms last for four weeks to three months, requiring total rest and occasionally hospitalisation. This causes disruption of daily activities and often leads to absence from work or school. Complete recovery can take as long as 6-12 months, with serious and occasionally fatal complications occurring in minority of patients. Hepatitis A can relapse in 20% of the cases that acquire the disease, and the symptoms may persist for up to six months.

Symptoms of Hepatitis A

1. It includes nausea, vomiting, yellowness in eyes, skin and urine (jaundice).
2. Diarrhoea, pale stool, abdominal pain and fatigue.
3. Fever and chills, lack of appetite, sore throat.

The frequency and severity of these symptoms, depends on the age of the person. This affects the young children more than adults. Two to five year olds develop jaundice with associated dark urine and pale stools.

Mode of Transmission

1. Hepatitis A virus is excreted in the faeces, and spread by faecal route.
2. Direct contact with an infected person's faeces or indirect contamination of food, water, hands and cooking utensils.
3. Raw or insufficiently cooked food (fruits, salads vegetables, seafood etc.).
4. Close contact with infected individuals within families, schools, day care centres and hostels.
5. Through contaminated needles and syringes or through contaminated blood products.
6. Poor standards of living, poor hygiene and sanitation.

The risk of early exposure is less among those living in an improved socio-economic environment. Any non-immune person exposed to the virus can develop hepatitis A. The children attending day care centres, schools etc, and individuals from upper socio-economic groups who are unlikely to have been exposed to the virus. The high risk of this virus is in travellers to highly endemic areas, food handlers, healthcare workers, school or day care employees and contacts with infected persons.

Prevention

1. Prevention is through human normal immunoglobulin (gamma globulin) prepared from pooled plasma of healthy blood donors.
2. Complete rest and treatment and diffusion of faeces.
3. The use of sodium hypochlorite.

4. By ensuring simple hygienic measures e.g., hand washing after defecation, before meals and after direct patient contact.
5. The sanitary disposal of excreta .to prevent faecal contamination of water, food and milk.
6. Boiled water should be advocated for drinking purposes.
7. Chlorination of water to destroy the virus.
8. Proper sterilization of syringes, needles, and other equipment.
9. Regular injections are required to maintain protection from this virus.

Hepatitis B

It is an acute systematic infection with serious disorder in the liver, caused by hepatitis B Virus (HBV) and transmitted usually by the parental route. Hepatitis B is endemic throughout the world including the remote areas and islands. Its prevalence varies from country to country and depends upon a complex mix of behavioural, environmental and host factors. It is lowest in countries or areas with high standard of living.

It is an acute infectious disease, and has world wide distribution. Infection is much higher in under developed areas of the world than in the developed countries. It is a DNA virus. Man is the only source of infection. Patients remaining HBS Ag positive for more than 6 months, following acute hepatitis B infection are called chronic carriers. The chronic carrier state may persist for years and may lead to chronic liver disease. This mainly contaminates blood and blood fractions and less frequently other secretions and excretions e.g., saliva, urine, semen. The period of communicability is usually several months, or as long as virus is present in blood.

It occurs at very early ages. High infection rates have been found in drug - abusers, prostitutes and homosexual population. Incubation period is 60 to 180 days; Lower doses of the virus results often in longer incubation periods.

Modes of Transmission

1. **Parental Route**: This is the most common route of spread of Hepatitis B. Traditionally Hepatitis B has been a hazard of (*a*) blood transfusion, (*b*) use of inadequately sterilized needles, syringes and other equipment during medical, surgical and dental procedures, and (*c*) exposure to infected blood. Transmission of Hepatitis B virus can take place in the family setting as a result of accidental percutaneous inoculation following the use of shared razors, toothbrushes, towels or by close contact.
2. **Vertical Transmission**: The Hepatitis B virus can get into the foetus from an infected mother. The mechanism of parental infections is uncertain. Hepatitis B virus can infect the foetus in uterus as a result of a leak of maternal blood into the body's circulation, or ingestion of accidental inoculation of blood.
3. **Other Routes**: Hepatitis B virus also exists in the variety of body secretions and excretions like saliva, semen and vaginal fluid. This clearly states that kissing or sexual intercourse may transmit infection.

Prevention

1. **Hepatitis B Vaccine ("H-B-Vax")**: The aim of this vaccination is to stimulate production of the surface antibody which is produced from the plasma of chronic carriers of hepatitis B virus. The immunization regimen consists of 3 doses of vaccine.
2. **Hepatitis B Immunoglobulin (HBIG)**: It is used for those acutely exposed to HBs AG - positive blood, for example (a) surgeon, nurses or laboratory workers (b) newborn infants of carrier mother, and (c) sexual contacts of acute hepatitis B patients. The HBVIG should be given as soon as possible after an accidental inoculation (ideally within 6 hours and preferably not later than 48 hours). At the same time the victim's blood should be drawn for HBs Ab testing. If the test is negative, vaccination should be started immediately and a full course given. If test is positive for surface antibody, no further action is needed.
3. **Positive-active Immunization**: The simultaneous administration of HBIG and hepatitis B vaccine is more efficacious than

HBIG alone. HBIG does not interfere with the antibody response to the hepatitis vaccine. This combined procedure is ideal both for prophylaxis of persons accidentally exposed to blood known to contain hepatitis B virus and for prevention of the carrier state in the newborn babies of carrier mothers.

4. **Other Measures**: No blood should be transfused until it is screened and blood donors tested positive should be rejected. Voluntary blood donors should be encouraged because purchased blood has shown a higher risk of post-transfusion hepatitis. The importance of adequate sterilization of all instruments and the practice of simple hygienic measures should be stressed among health workers. Finally people should be educated in terms of healthy living.

Hepatitis 'A' is different from Hepatitis 'B'.	
The Hapatitis A virus is transmitted mainly through contaminated food and water.	The Hepatitis B virus may be passed in through blood, sexual contact or from the infected mother to the new born.

Hepatitis C

Hepatitis 'C' is a slow killer. It is one of 40 new infectious diseases discovered since 1970, but has been around for decades, if not centuries. Before 1989, it was known as 'non-A, non-B hepatitis'.

There is a minute risk of catching the disease from implements that can carry blood (razors, tatoo pens, tooth-brushes etc.)

- It is also possible for mothers to pass it on to an unborn baby.
- The infection is also through sexual contacts.

Treatment is not always successful and depends on the virus 'geno type' or 'strain', but across the board 60% of patients will be cured when pegylated inter from is available.

One of the symptoms of Hepatitis C is debilitating tiredness which can lead to it being mistakenly diagnosed as chronic fatigue syndrome.

TUBERCULOSIS

Tuberculosis is a specific communicable disease caused by Mycotuberculosis or, more rarely by Mycobosis. It affects both pulmonary and extra-pulmonary tissues. The disease is usually chronic with varying clinical manifestations. The bovine form generally affects extrapulmonary organs, viz Intestine, bones, lymph nodes. Tuberculosis continues to be a major public health problem in India.

It can occur at any age but it is more prevalent in the older age than in the younger age group. Tuberculosis is communicable as long as bacilli are excreted by the infected host, and this period may extend weeks, months or even years. It is more prevalent among males than among females. Tuberculosis is often described as a social disease with medical aspects. It is due to poor quality of size, e.g., overcrowding, substandard housing, ignorance, low level of education, poor sanitation, poverty, large families etc. These are not specific but all these factors are inter-related and favour the spread of infection.

Mode of Transmission

Mainly droplet infection and droplet unuclei generated by an "open" case transmits tuberculosis. To transmit infection, the particles must be fresh enough to carry a viable organism. Cough is a prominent symptom of pulmonary tuberculosis. Coughing generates larger number of droplets of all sizes than speaking.

Two main sources of infection - the human and bovine.

(*i*) **The human Source**: In this the bacillary cases constitute by far the most important source of infection. The smere-positive patients are the real source of infection, and patients in whose sputum bacilli can be demonstrated by culture.

(*ii*) **Bovine Source**: Bovine tuberculosis is not a problem in India because milk is boiled before consumption.

The common source of tubercle bacilli is the sputum of the patients suffering from pulmonary tuberclosis.

Prevention

The basic principles of prevention and control are the same as far as any other infectious disease; these are:

(*i*) ***Early Detection of Cases:*** In the prevention of tuberculosis programme the basic principle is the early detection of cases i.e. identification of individual spreading the tuberculosis infection. In this case a patient whose sputum is positive for tubercle bacilli and such cases are the target of case - finding. Sputum examination by direct microscopy is considered the method of choice . Due to the reliability, cheapness and easiness, direct microscopic examination has become number one case-finding method. The examination of two consecutive specimens e.g., on the spot and overnight sputum, is sufficient to detect a large number of infectious cases. If tuberculosis is to be diagnosed early, facilities for microscopic examination of sputum should be available in all health institutions. In the early detection following are the check systems.

(*a*) Cough of about 3 or 4 weeks duration, continuous fever.

(*b*) Chest pain case finding should not be an end in itself. It is of little value as a control measure unless followed by chemotherapy.

(*ii*) ***Chemotherapy:*** It has completely revolutionised the treatment of pulmonary tuberculosis. The objective of chemotherapy is bacterial cure - i.e. to sterilize lesions quickly and completely, render the patients non-infectious and prevent the development of new cases in the community. The effects of chemotherapy are judged not by the anatomic healing of lesions, but mainly by the elimination of bacilli from the patients sputum. Chemotherapy should be easily available, free of charge to every patient detected. It should be adequate and applied to the entire pool of infectors in the community. Incomplete treatment puts the patients at risk of relapse and the development of bacterial resistance and the community at risk of infection with resistant organisms.

An anti-tuberculosis drug should satisfy the following criteria (a) it should be highly effective (b) it should be free from toxic side effects (c) It should be easy to administer (d) It should be reasonably cheap chemotherapy. Anti tuberculosis drugs are used in combination to increase therapeutic effectiveness and minimise the emergence of drug resistant strains. This requires the patient's full cooperation through preparation of the patient socially, economically and psychologically.

(*iii*) ***BCG Vaccination:*** BCG, known as bacille calmette Guerin, is harmless yet capable of conferring a stage of immunity when administered by vaccination. Recognition of value of BCG came in 1948 when it was accepted by tuberculosis workers from all over the world as a safe preventive.

The main aim of BCG vaccination is to induce a benign, artificial primary infection which will stimulate an acquired resistance. There are two types of vaccine - the liquid (fresh) vaccine and the freeze dried vaccine. Freeze - dried vaccine is a more stable preparation than liquid vaccine. BCG vaccination is now under way throughout the world as part of the WHO Expanded Programme on Immunization.

(*iv*) ***Chemoprophylaxis:*** Isoniazid has been tried in the chemoprophylaxis (termed as preventive treatment) of tuberculosis. It may be primary or secondary. Primary is giving the drug to persons who are unaffected to prevent the occurrence of infection in them. By secondary chemoprophylaxis is meant giving to already infected persons to prevent the development of the disease.

(*v*) ***Rehabilitation***: The people who need rehabilitation are those who are chronically ill and are still excreting tubercle bacilli. Those who had resection may require rehabilitation to suit their physical and mental abilities.

(*vi*) ***Surveillance***: It is an integral part of any effective tuberculosis programme. It is concerned with two aspects (a) Surveillance of the tuberculosis situation, e.g. by measuring the annual "infection rates" which will guide the epidemiologist and health administrator by indicating whether the TB problem is static, increasing, or decreasing; (b) surveillance of Central measures applied such as BCG vaccination and chemotherapy.

MALARIA

Malaria is a general term applied to a group of diseases caused by infection which specifies sporozoon parasites of the genus. Plasmodium is transmitted to man by certain species of infected, female Anopheles mosquito; and is clinically characterized by episodes of chills and fever with periods of latency, enlargement of spleen and secondary anemia.

It is one of the most widespread diseases. Malaria comprises three stages :

(*a*) Cold stage: This is characterized by sudden on set of fever and sensation of extreme cold. The patient desires to be covered with blankets. This stage lasts between 15 minutes to one hour.

(*b*) Hot Stage: The temperature may rise to 106" F. The patient feels burning hot and casts off his clothes. There is severe headache. This stage lasts for 2 to 6 hours.

(*c*) Sweating Stage: Fever comes down with profuse sweating. This stage lasts for 2 to 4 hours.

Malaria affects all ages. It is a seasonal disease and the maximum prevalence is from July to November. The length of time between the bite of an infected mosquito and the first attack of fever is usually not less than 10 days.

Mode of Transmission

1. *Vector Transmission:* A single infected vector, during her lifetime, may infect several persons. The mosquito is not infective unless the sporozoites are present in its salivary glands.
2. *Direct Transmission:* Malaria may be induced accidentally by hypodermic intramuscular and intravenous infections of blood or plasma, e.g. blood transfusion, malaria in .drug addicts.

Prevention

Traditionally, the measures for the prevention and control of malaria have been classified as:

(*a*) Protection against mosquito bites,
(*b*) Anti-larval measures,
(*c*) Anti-adult (mosquito) measures, and
(*d*) Control of the human reservoir.

In order to prevent malaria, following measures should be applied.

1. ***Measures to be applied by the individual:***

(*a*) Prevention of man / vector contact: using repellants, protective clothing, bed nets, screening of houses.

(*b*) Destruction of adult mosquitoes: use of domestic space sprays including aerosols.

(*c*) Destruction of mosquito larvae peridomestic sanitation, intermittent drying of water containers.

(*d*) Source reduction of mosquitoes: filling, small scale drainage, and other forms of water management.

(*e*) Measures against malarial parasites: chemoprohylaxis and chemotherapy.

2. ***Measures to be applied by the community:***

(*a*) Prevention of man / vector contact: usite selection and screening of houses.

(*b*) Destruction of adult mosquitoes: residual spraying or space spraying of insecticides.

(*c*) Destruction of mosquito larve: using larvicicles (chemical and biological).

(*d*) Source reduction: prevention of man made malaria, environmental sanitation, water management, drainage schemes.

(*e*) Measures against malarial parasities: presumptive treatment, radical treatment, mass drug administration.

RABIES

Rabies, also known as hydrophobia (fear of water) is an acute, highly fatal viral infection of the central nervous system. It is primarily a zoonotic disease of warm-blooded animals, particularly carnivores such as dogs, cats, jackals and wolves. It is transmitted to man usually by the bite of a rabid animal.

It is the only communicable disease of man which can be regarded as 100 percent fatal. Human rabies is an important public health problem in India. Dogs, particularly stray dogs, are mainly responsible for the urban rabies in India. Cats can also be a source of human infection. Wild-life rabies is an unidentified reservoir in many countries. The animals which spread rabies include a variety of animals - foxes, jackals, mongoose etc. These animals transmit the infection to domestic animals. Man may occasionally contract rabies from this cycle.

The saliva of rabid animals is the main source of infection for man. All warm blooded animals are susceptible to rabies. Rabies in man is a dead-end infection, and has no survival value for the virus. Men and children are more exposed to the risk of rabies than women. It commonly lasts from 1 to 3 months, but may vary from 10 days up to one year or longer. In no other communicable disease, the incubation period is so variable and dependent on so many factors *(a)* the site of the bite *(b)* severity of the bite *(c)* amount of virus injected *(d)* species of biting animal *(e)* protection provided by the clothing *(f)* treatment undertaken. Period tends to be shorter in severe exposures and bites on face, head and upper extremities and longer in ordinary bites and lower extremities. Bites by wild animals are more dangerous than bites by domestic animals.

The symptoms of the rabies in man are such as headache, sore throat, slight fever lasting 2 to 10 days, pain and tightening at the site of the wound. The patient does not like noise, bright light, or a cold drought of air. Mental changes include fear of death, anger, irritability and depression.

Mode of Transmission

1. **Bites:** Rabies is transmitted to man by the bite of a rabid animal. The virus is inoculated into the skin with the saliva of the biting animal. Man to man transmission, although rare, is possible.
2. **Licks:** Licks on abraded skin and scratches and on mucosa can also transmit the disease.
3. **Non-bite Routes:** Air borne transmission has been observed in nature in caves harbouring rabies infected bats.

Prevention

Prevention of human rabies may be considered under two heads:

Post-exposure Prophylaxis: Majority of persons requiring anti-rabies treatment are those who were bitten by a suspected rabid animal or exposed to the rabies virus. The post-exposure treatment includes the following :

1. ***Local Treatment of Wounds*:** Rabies can be prevented if all bite wounds and scratches are immediately dealt with appropriate local treatment. This treatment aims at removing and killing the virus by mechanical and chemical means. The local treatment consists of the following measures:
   - (*a*) Cleansing,
   - (*b*) Chemical Treatment
   - (*c*) Suturing,
   - (*d*) Antirabic Serum and
   - (*e*) A TS and Penicillin
2. ***Observe the animal for 10 days:*** The biting animal must be observed for at least 10 days from the day of bite to find out the symptoms of rabies. If the animal shows the symptoms of rabies, animal should be humanely killed, and its head removed and sent to a qualified laboratory for rabies examination. If the animal remains alive and healthy at the end of 10 days, there is no indication for antirabies treatment.
3. ***Indication for antirabies Treatment:*** Antirabies treatment should be started immediately.
   - (*a*) When the animal shows clinical sign of rabies.
   - (*b*) When the animal dies within the period of observation.

(c) Laboratory tests of the brain of the biting animal are positive, though clinical signs were not typical.

(d) If the biting animal cannot be traced or identified.

(e) All unprovoked bites from wild animals.

4. ***Anti-rabies Treatment:*** Vaccination remains the best prophylactic against rabies. The vaccine should always be given with the least possible delay after exposure to infection. The aim of vaccinations is to produce ecceptance in a peripheral nerve along which it will travel to the central nervous system.

The following vaccines which are currently in use can be placed in one of three classes.

(i) *Nervous Tissue (Brain) Vaccines:*

(a) Sheep Brain Vaccine.

(b) Suckling Mouse Brain Vaccine

(ii) *Avian Embryo Vaccines:*

(a) Inactivated Duck Embryo Vaccine.

(b) Inactivated Chick Embryo Vaccine.

(iii) *Cell Culture Vaccines:*

(a) Human Diploid Cell (HDC) Vaccine.

(b) Non-Human (animal)Cell Culture Vaccine.

Pre-exposure Prophylaxis: The immunization of man against rabies before exposure is recommended for certain high-risk group such as veterinarians, dog handlers, field naturalists, laboratory workers etc. For pre-exposure immunization only safer vaccines are recommended.

TETANUS

It is world-wide in occurrence. Tetanus is an important endemic infection in India. The natural habitat of the organism is soil and dust. The risk of acquiring the disease is pretty high between 5 to 40 years of age. Tetanus occurring in the new born is known as "neonatal tautens". Infants typically contract the disease at birth, when delivered in nonaspetic conditions - especially when the umbilical cord is cut with unclean instruments. Females are more exposed to the risk of tetanus especially during delivery or abortion. Its occurrence depends upon man's physical and ecological surroundings - the soil, agriculture, animal husbandry. The environmental factors such as unhygienic customs and habits e.g. application of dust or animal dung to wounds, ignorance of infection and lack of primary health care services.

The incubation period is usually 6 to 10 days. It may be short as one day or as long as several months.

Mode of Transmission

One gets infected through contamination of wounds with tetanus sores. The degree of accidents and injuries which may also lead to tetanus comprise a trivial pin prick, skin abrasion, puncture wounds, burns, human bites, animal bites, and stings, unsterile surgery,intra-uterine surgery, bowel surgery, dental extractions, injections, unsterile divison of umbilical cord, compound fracture,otitis melia, chronic skin ulcers, eye infections, gangrenous limbs.

Prevention

Prevention of tetanus can be done with the following:

1. ***Active Immunization:*** Tetanus can be prevented by active immunization with tetanus toxoid. Tetanus toxoid stimulates the production of the protective nutitoxin. Every individual in the community should be vaccinated regardless of age. Active immunization is done through combined vaccine (DPT) and monovalent vaccines. It is also recommended for all expectant mothers who were not satisfactorily immunized earlier. Complete course of immunization lasts for atleast five years. Neonatal tetanus can be prevented by immunizing mothers during pregnancy. No pregnant mother should be denied even one dose of tetanus toxoid, if she is seen late. All wounds must be thoroughly cleaned after injury - removal of foreign bodies, soil, dust, necrotic tissue. Tetanus may occasionally occur in spite of active or passive immunization or both.

2. ***Passive Immunization:*** Protection against tetanus can be achieved temporarily by an injection of human tetanus hyperimmune globulin (TIG) or ATS. It gives a longer passive protection upto 30 days or more compared with 7-10 days of horse ATS.
3. ***Active and Passive Immunization:*** Active and passive immunization can be given simultaneously in non-immune persons.
4. ***Antibiotics:*** Active immunization with tetanus toxoid is the best method of tetanus prevention but it is of no immediate use to a person who is non-immune and has sustained injury. For these reasons, antibiotics are provided in the prophylaxis against tetanus. Antibiotics alone is effective in the prevention of tetanus; it is not a substitute to immunization.

RECREATION

Introduction

In the modern world, a man is enjoying lot of luxuries provided by the advance technological development on one hand and facing lot of physical, mental emotional and social disturbances on the other hand. Advance technological development has provided all kinds of comforts in all walks of life, may it be home or any other work place, agriculture or industries. Consequently, it has reduced lot of dependence on each other, caused social problems, reduced physical work, caused physical problems, working on machines causes mental problems, and working in shifts allows meeting family members like strangers, cause emotional problems. Collectively all these factors affect family life, society and nation adversely in the long run. Further, the technological advancements in all spheres of life have created lot of free / leisure time after the working hours, at the same time the advancement in recreational gadgets like T.V., Cable T.V., Video-CD games, computer games have made the child least interested in physical activity resulting in so many physical, mental and emotional problems. To counteract both the aspects i.e. the utility of free time / leisure time in a constructive way and to make a child more physically active in order to allow his growth and development take place proportionately, active recreation activities, other than passive ones, are must.

MEANING OF RECREATION

Recreation carries different meaning to different individuals and it is applied to great variety of activities. Sometimes the term is applied to activities of young people and adults to differentiate those activities from that play of young children. Because of this diversity in the use of the word, it is desirable to understand clearly in the beginning to avoid confusion. In common usage, however, recreation has a more comprehensive\ meaning and it is not restricted to any particular age group and activity. *As Dr. .John H. Finely has pointed out, that the word "recreation" is broad enough to include 'play' in its every expression and also many activities that are usually not thought of as play - music, the drama, the craft, every free activity and especially creative activity for the enrichment of life"*.

Recreation means to regain lost vigour and get a sense of joy, refreshment and satisfaction. Recreation is life itself. Without recreation life is meaningless. The modern age is full of complexities, a man in order to survive has to do lot of physical and mental work, resulting in fatigue. Through recreation he can regain the lost vigour or energy. Recreation is concerned with those activities performed by an individual during leisure time or at hours not at work. Hence it is frequently referred to as leisure - time activity.

Recreation education is aimed at teaching people to utilise their free time / leisure time in a constructive manner. To achieve this aim and to have value as recreation, activities must be suited to his physical, mental, emotional and social needs. In other words, it implies a careful selection of activities for the utility of free time in healthy way.

DEFINITIONS OF RECREATION

Recreation may be considered as "Any form of leisure -time experience or activity in which an individual engages from choice because of the enjoyment and satisfaction which it brings directly to him".

(G.D. Butler)

Recreation may be defined as "An activity Voluntarily engaged in during leisure time and primarily motivated by the satisfaction of pleasure derived from it"

(Meyer and Brightbill)

ESSENTIAL CHARACTERISTICS OF RECREATION

Education is advocating that the recreation must have the following characteristics to benefit the participant to his fullest:

1. **Leisure Time:** To have recreation the activity must be engaged during one's free time. From this point of view, one can not leave during the working hours and engage in recreational activity.
2. **Enjoyable:** The activity engaged in must be enjoyable not boring one.
3. **Satisfaction:** The activity engaged in must bring immediate and direct satisfaction to the individual.
4. **Voluntary:** The individual must have chosen recreation activity of his / her own choice. There must be no compulsion.
5. **Constructive:** The recreational activity is constructive. It is not harmful to the participant physically, mentally, emotionally, socially or in any other way. It helps one to become a better integrated individual.
6. **Socially Acceptable:** The recreational activity is socially acceptable and individually beneficial to the participant/s.
7. **Non-survival:** Eating or sleeping are not recreational activities in themselves. One may engage in a picnic in which a dinner or lunch is involved, but other parts of the affair such as the social games and fellowship are important elements of recreational activity, without which it will remain no more recreational activity.

AIM OF RECREATION

Recreational education is aimed at *"Teaching People to utilise their free time in a constructive manner"*.

Objectives of Recreation

The field of recreation has many worth-while objectives. The American Association of Health, Physical Education and Recreation (AAHPER) states that this special field contributes to the satisfaction of basic human needs for creative self-expression; helps to promote total health - physical, mental, emotional and social; provides an antidote to the strains and tensions of life; provides an avenue to abundant personal and family living; and develops effective citizenship and vitalizes democracy.

One of the best statement of objectives was offered by the Commission on Goals for American Recreation. The objectives are as follows:

1. **Personal Fulfillment:** Recreation recognizes the need of people to become all that they are capable of becoming and contribute that recreation can make this goal.
2. **Democratic, Human Relations:** Recreation recognizes that it has goals that contribute to individuals as well as to the democratic society of which they are an integral part.
3. **Leisure Skills and Interests:** Recreation has the goal of meeting the interests of people and developing skills that will provide the incentive, motivation and medium for spending free time in a constructive and worthwhile manner.
4. **Health and Fitness:** Recreation recognizes the importance of contributing to reduce mental illness, stress and tension. It also has the goal to have physical activity in the modern society to make the people healthy and fit.
5. **Creative Expression and Aesthetic Appreciation:** Recreation attempts to provide the environment, leadership, material and motivation where – creativity, personal expression and Aesthetic appreciation on the part of the participant exists and develops.

6. **Environment for living in a Leisure Society:** Recreation plays an important role in encouraging such things as preservation of natural resources, construction of play grounds and recreation centres, and awakening the population to an appreciation of aesthetic and cultural values.

TYPES OF RECREATION

Some of the well established types of recreation are given below:

1. **Community Recreation:** It is sponsored by villages, towns and cities for their residents. It is controlled, financed and organized by the community.
2. **Industrial Recreation:** It is sponsored, conducted, administrated by the big industrial houses and other business establishments for its own employees.
3. **Therapeutic Recreation:** It is set up in hospitals, nursing homes and other establishments for the benefit of ill, and disabled patients. Its values are increasingly being recognised.
4. **Institutional Recreation :** School/college recreation is provided by the concerned authorities / boards / universities for the persons who are registered with them.
5. **Family Recreation:** It involves the activities a family which chooses to engage in during leisure time.
6. **Commercial Recreation:** It is found in such places as amusement parks, fun cities and so on. It is conducted for gaining profits.

NEED AND IMPORTANCE OF RECREATION IN THE MODERN SOCIETY

There are certain fundamental human needs which are required to be satisfied; there are objectives of education that need to be achieved; there are obligations of democratic society that need to be fulfilled; there is price of the technological advancement relished by the modern society that has to be paid; and there are factors / changes which have given rise to the wide spread recognition of the need and importance of recreation in the modern life. In the explanation given below, an attempt is made to point out why and how recreation is serving increasingly important functions in the life of the individuals, the community and the nation :

1. **Recreation-A Fundamental Human Need:** Among all the people and in all stages of history, man has found outlets for self expression and personal development in forms of recreation which have a striking similarity. Recreation is a common heritage of all people, although its expression takes varied forms. In all lands, play is the chief occupation of young child during his active hours. Through play the child attains growth and experience. It is nature's way of affording outlets to the great biological urge for activity and the means of acquiring skills needed in later life. As he grows older, other forms of activity make increasing demands on his time, energy and attention. In adult life the duties and responsibilities of earning a living, earning for family and maintaining a place in human society tend to relegate recreation to a place of minor significance on the margin of life. Yet the urge for recreation is so fundamental and universal that it can not be suppressed.
2. **Recreation Contributes to Human Happiness:** Happiness was recognized by our forefathers as a fundamental and worthy objective for every individual. In fact life would be incomplete and drab without recreation. The great leader of recreation Dr. Austin Fox Riggs has rightly expressed that "*The function of play is to balance life in relation to work, to afford a refreshing contrast to responsibility and routine, to keep alive the spirit of adventure and that sense of proportion which prevents taking oneself and one's job too seriously and thus to prevent the death of youth, and not infrequently the premature death of the man himself.*".

Among the needs for real living there should be *"beauty', knowledge and ideals; books, pictures and music; song, dance and games; travel, adventure and romance, friends, championships, and the exchange of minds"*. Recreation holds its place of importance in modern life because it has afforded and continues to afford opportunities for the attainment of these basic human needs which provide happiness.

3. **Recreation and Health:** Recreation which is vigours, which is carried on in the open air and which makes use of the fundamental muscles is the best known means of developing and maintaining healthy organs, certain forms of recreation cause increased circulation, greater respiratory activity, better elimination of wastes and improved digestion. It contributes to emotional stability by affording rest, relaxation and creative activity. Also gives tone to the body by a healthful stimulation of the nerve centres. The value of recreation has been characterized as an insurance policy against nervous disorders, which when collected in middle age, will reimburse hundred fold. Its contribution lies in its value in preventing illness by contributing to healthful, happy living. Recreation is also used increasingly in the mental rehabilitation of the individuals. People suffering from mental disorders have been found to react quickly to the stimulus of play, music in particular.

   Dr. William C. Menninger has said, "*Recreation has not only played an important part in the treatment programme of many mental illness but it has been a considerable factor in enabling former patients to remain well. Therefore, psychiatrists believe that recreative activity can also be valuable preventive of mental and emotional ill health*".

4. **Recreation and Character Development:** Recreation has been characterized as a force of tremendous consequence for the personal character and the national culture. Yet character development is not an objective specifically sought by persons engaging in recreation activities, it can be a natural by-product of participation in team games, drama, and music which require cooperation, loyalty and team play. Under recreation leaders of integrity and ability, people can be taught respect for rules, fair play, courage, an ability to subordinate the selfish interests of the individual to the welfare of the group and a capacity for team play. They also can be given valuable leadership experience. Recreation not only develops individual qualities, but it strongly influences the growth of social attitudes which affects the individual as member of group.

5. **Recreation and Crime Prevention:** Participation in wholesome recreation helps to build character. It acts as a safety valve for the prevention of crime and delinquency. Because recreational activities have a strong appeal for children and youth, delinquency is less likely to flourish in communities where opportunities for wholesome recreation are abundant and attractive. Children or young people engaged in recreation activities on the play ground cannot at the same time be robbing a bank, breaking into a home, involving in a gang raping or some other crime. The boy who goes to the play ground daily or who excels in some other co-curricular / social activity, and the girl who takes part in the composition for the drama play or who is a leader in the nature group are finding outlets for the normal desire for recognition, success, and achievement. They have little need to seek such satisfactions in unsocial ways. Most delinquent and criminal acts are committed during leisure hours and larger part of these acts are performed in order to get the means for the enjoyment of leisure. The police officials and prison authorities have testified from their experiences that much delinquency and crime result from inadequate recreation opportunities. As a result to avoid such things recreation plays an important role in the life of children, youngster, youth and adult.

6. **Recreation and Community Solidarity:** Many forces in modern society tend to separate people into distinct and often hostile groups, based on differences in their economic status, social position, race, creed, nationality, education or cultural background. Consequently, it grows suspicion, distrust, and dislike of our fellowmen and a lack of neighbourliness and unity of interest. Recreation affords a common ground / common platform where differences may be forgotten in the joy of participation or achievement. Recreation is essentially democratic. Interests and skill in sports, drama, or art are shared by all groups and classes. The young boy / girl/man / woman who excels in sports or any other activity is recognized regardless of his caste, colour, and creed by followers of these activities / group people.
7. **Recreation and Morale:** In periods of insecurity, depression and unusual strain man is more than ever in need of activity which brings satisfaction and sense of accomplishment. In different parts of the world people are facing earthquakes, floods, military invasions, and other larger scale disasters which lead to mental breakdown. During such times the value of recreation as means of building and restraining morale is highly appreciated. For example during world war II recreational activities played vital role. Comprehensive programme for men / women in the Armed Forces, leisure time activities for war workers and their families, and neighbourhood and community programme helped to sustain morale on the home front. The recreation services being provided for the Armed Forces, for the worker in war industries and for the morale of civilian groups are very definitely contributing to our war effort. Military leaders repeatedly testify to the morale value of such service.
8. **Recreation and Safety:** dequate provision for recreation, especially in the form of play grounds / swimming pools under the supervision of efficient leadership contribute definitely to the reduction of accidents. Recreation areas that are properly designed and carefully operated are remarkal safe. Recreation departments also contribute public safety by providing and supervising recreation areas by teaching skills that are essential to safe participation in injury prone recreation activities, and by enforcing safety regulations on public recreation areas. In the absence of safe recreation areas there is no safety in street recreation at a crowded place which may cause injuries.
9. **Recreation and Democracy:** Democracy and recreation are alike in spirit, and each tends to promote and strengthen the other. Democracy is committed to giving each individual the opportunity to grow fully, express himself freely and achieve an abundant life. Recreation, which represents activity freely chosen, offers the individual opportunity for genuine satisfaction, creative expression, and the development of his powers, helps him in attaining the objectives of democracy. It contributes to his effectiveness as a citizen in the modern democratic state.
10. **Recreation and Education:** In many respects the objectives, methods, and programmes of education and recreation are similar. But they are not identical. The fullest development of the individual is sought by both; but recreation affords immediate satisfactions, whereas education aims at a more distant goal. The element of compulsion is present in some aspects of education which is lacking in recreational experiences. Many activities, such as sports, music, drama, or arts are common to both programmes, but in education they represent areas in which skills; understanding and appreciation are to be acquired. In the recreation programme, however, the activities serve primarily as a means of using and enjoying skills and interests that have already been acquired. Yet educational growth is a part of every satisfying recreation experience.

The training for worthy use of leisure was one of the seven objectives of education. To achieve this objective, recreation provides opportunities to impart training and activities to use leisure time intelligently in a constructive manner. The early and continuous development of leisure attitude, habits, skills and knowledge, leads towards developing and educating judgement about recreation. The authorised educational institutions have realised that recreational programme affords an excellent medium for carrying on the learning process and for achieving objectives of education. Recreation therefore, plays an increasing role in the curriculum of formal education and in the extra curricular programme of an institution.

11. **Recreation and Economy:** Leaders in business and industry have long realized that the way in which their employees spend their leisure hours influences effectiveness on the job. In the welfare states of the world hundreds of dollars are being spent per year to care for one delinquent, whereas a playground, which may prevent children from becoming delinquents, can be operated at an annual cost of only a few dollars per child. The economy of providing playgrounds is clear. In other words, investment made in developing and providing recreational facilities is an investment in the welfare of human being, that pays dividends in dollars rupees as well as intangible returns.

From the concluding point of view, it is clear from above mentioned facts that why recreation has gained a place of importance in modern life and have pointed out several ways in which it contributes to an individual, community and Nation's welfare.

Factors/Recent Changes Respon- Sible for Affecting the Need for Recreatio

Recreation has already provided an outlet for self expression, for release of tension / stress, and for the attainment of satisfaction in life. During the last few decades, the marked and rapid changes that have taken place in our social, industrial, economic and political life, have increased the need of recreation and have greatly affected the life of the people. Some of these factors/ changes and their significance to create a need for organised recreation is discussed here briefly:

1. **The Growth of Cities:** The growth of cities made streets crowded and unsafe for play; vacant sites were built upon and the former recreational spaces were used for other purposes. Rivers, ponds, and lakes are polluted, forests cut down, and large areas closed to public use may be due to security threats. With the complexity of city life, neighbourliness disappeared and living became more artificial and stratified. People became largely dependent upon special agencies to provide opportunities for outdoor recreation. The rapid spread of population on the outskirts, especially in the metropolitan regions, eliminated many of the recreation places formerly available to the city inhabitants. Man, essentially by nature an outdoor animal, needs recreation spaces, facilities and leadership to compensate for the loss of natural resources.
2. **Changing Home Conditions:** Changes in the home as well as community have increased the leisure hours, resulting in the need for recreation to use free time properly. Physical labour saving devices such as washing and drying machines, food freezers, electricity, gas stoves and other kitchen gadgets, vacuum cleaners and advanced means of communication, to mention only a few have revolutionized house keeping methods. Before the introduction of all aforementioned facilities lot of time was consumed, that has been saved and used for other activities, including recreation. Another reason, the rapid increase in the number of multiple family dwellings that has not only reduced the back yard (the main play space) of the small children in many neighbourhoods but also reduced the opportunity for indoors of family recreation. The garage has replaced the garden

and automobile the family horse and buggy. The lack of indoor and outdoor space in many homes compels the children to seek elsewhere those experiences and values of cooperative and social activity which once they acquired at home. The play grounds, clubs, recreation centres etc. owe their popularity in part to changes in home conditions.

3. **Increase in Leisure:** When man worked 12-14 hours a day, six days a week the problem of the recreational use of leisure time, so essential today, was not in existence. For most people, time for recreation was very short and opportunities were very few. The growing tendency to include a provision for vacations with pay in labour contracts, day long work for 6-8 hours and five days work week have added appreciably to the leisure hours of large number of workers. Therefore, the acquisition of extensive periods of leisure which many people are not able to use intelligently, may create new social problems, such as too much drinking, gambling, rash driving and so forth. The new leisure presents, a direct challenge to each society to provide for the recreation needs and to plan intelligently to meet the increasing demands of the future to over come the social problems created by the abundant leisure time.

4. **Specialisation and Automation in Industry:** The changes in working conditions have resulted owing to technological inventions. The development of highly automatic machinery and specialisation of work in both industry and business are well known. No doubt, the demands upon the worker's physical and mental powers are less than before, but the nervous tension is greater. What is more, the degree to which the workers are controlled by the machine or the industrial system tends to develop nervous stress which is not beneficial to the individual or to society. The present advancement in automation indicates the dire need to save both (individual and society) from those effects of automation which may cause psychological imbalances. Because man is not a machine and by nature he is not used to long hours of repetitive task, the urgent need of today is the development and maintenance of a well-balanced physique by the people after their working hours. Psychologists have repeatedly claimed that for people whose energies are used mechanically, recreation becomes absolute necessity. Recreation, with its freedom of spirit and action, provides an antidote for this unhealthy tendency of mechanical life.

5. **Population Changes:** The growth in population has resulted in an unprecedented demand for play grounds and recreation programmes for children, youths, and adults. Further, this demand is likely to increase in years to come. A redistribution of population has also been taking place. Not only people have moved from the village to the city, creating serious problems for the metropolitan areas but also the people of poor states moving towards rich one for earning their livelihood. Such large scale mobility removes people from their adapted accustomed environment, tends to deprive them of the feeling of belonging, and creates a sense of instability that affects both children and adults. A well balanced recreation programme helps families become adjusted in their new community setting.

6. **The Rising Economy:** The rapid and unprecedented rise in national income and resulting higher standard of living have materially affected the recreation scenario. The average family, unlike earlier generations, has an income that permits an appreciable expenditure for recreation during their leisure time. Also it makes possible to spend large amount of income for amusements, travel, hobbies, and sports.

7. **Technological Development:** The products of scientific progress have not only greatly increased the volume of leisure time but have greatly influenced its use. The remarkable development in automobile and construction

of hard surfaced high-ways perhaps has affected the recreational life of the people to a greater extent than any other technological development. It has facilitated the people to visit friends on holiday or to travel to more distant hobby places such as parks, beaches, resorts, forests, and camping during vacations. An appreciable increase in visitors to state or national recreational spots (parks and forests) can be attributed largely to the development of automobile which has become the outstanding means of vacation travel. Other areas such as motion pictures, record player, radio, television, video games, CD videos, internets and so on have contributed by the scientific developments that have revolutionised many of the recreation habits of the people.

8. **Other Factors:** The development of farm machinery, rural electrification, availability of advance telecommunication facilities and transport means have given the added time for recreation and access to the city recreation sources to the rural population. The introduction of music, drama, art, dance and sports into the curriculum of school / college has a far reaching significance for the recreation movement.

It is pertinent to mention here that no doubt the above mentioned factors are the indicators of any country's progress made in many areas of national interest on one hand, but on the other hand it is also inferred that to-day's youth has become more lethargic, inactive, showing no interest in maintaining health, interested in poor diet. Moreover educational inatututions are utterly failed in engaging the children / youth in worthwhile recreation programmes.

RECREATION PROVIDING AGENCIES

Recreation facilities, activities and programmes are provided by *numerous agencies,* many of which have been created to meet the demand for various types of leisure - time opportunities. All the agencies have their own scope, objectives and field of activities. Some of these agencies serve only their members, others benefit the entire community. Many of them are concerned with a single form of recreation, while others offer a wide variety of activities. Some agencies exist for the financial profit which results from providing the public with recreation; others cater to the need of individual and community life.

Many forms of recreation are essentially individual activities and are engaged in differently from any other recreation agency, for example, walking, reading hobbies, painting, sketching, gardening, creative writing, nature study, woodcrafts, clay crafts etc. Many of these activities are more enjoyable when engaged in with a group, but some individuals have not the desire to share with others. Further, in spite of the many aspects of modern living that demands to take people away from their homes, the home is doubtless the country's main recreation centre. To-day's home, apart from its living, dining and drawing room areas devotes, a large percentage of its space to recreational uses, for example back yard space for children, play rooms, gardening space, space for pets, space for television and computer, space for musical instruments, space for home library and so on. However, there are some unavoidable limitations of home recreation to provide those recreational facilities and opportunities which may be provided by the other agencies such as:

1. **Government Agencies:** These agencies belong to Central, State and Local Governments. The government agencies provide recreation to the people of all the section of the society through various offices or departments. The government agencies provide recreation through Extension Service, National Park Service, The Forest Service, Recreation Bureau, Deptt. of Youth Welfare, and Sports, State Forests and Parks, Tourism etc. The recreation services of these offices / departments comprise of :

   (*a*) The provision of areas and facilities that are available for informal or organised use;

   (*b*) The employment of leadership personnel that organize and conduct indoor and outdoor activities, specifically on properties under public ownership;

(*c*) The promotion and organization of community wise programmes and events usually in cooperation with other agencies; and

(*d*) The provision of materials and advisory services for the benefit of local individuals and organization.

Apart from the activities such as picnicking, boating, swimming, diving, there are many other sports activities, on beaches, hills, rinks, hiking, playing golf, tennis, organizing various sports competitions and so on. Other special facilities such as public library, and museum are also made available by the government agencies.

2. **Voluntary Agencies:** Recreation has a prominent place in the programmes of most voluntary agencies, which include the YMCA the YWCA, the Youth Organisation, the Clubs, Boy Scouts, Camp Fire, Girl Guides and many others. These agencies serve varying age groups such as children, young people and adults. They do not restrict their services to the members only. The cost of financing the facilities and programmes is largely met through contribution from individuals or community members. These agencies promote cultural, religious, educational, creative skills and values through auditoriums. Further, these agencies emphasize out of door activity and afford opportunity for participation in wide variety of projects, including games, athletics, community service, camping as well as other craft activities. Through their programmes strong appeals are made to boys and girls and bases are provided for the development of interests that carry over into later life.

3. **Private Agencies:** There are innumerable private agencies and organisations which provide recreation to their members only. These organisations do not depend upon community support. The most important agencies in this group are industries, religious establishments, sports organisations and other clubs.

Many big industrial and business houses especially those which employ large number of workers provide recreation facilities to their employees. In many cases these are open to the families of workers and in some case to the entire community. Similarly, a considerable number of insurance companies, banks, cooperative societies and other commercial organisations provide recreation facilities and programmes. After the world war-II, the value and use of recreation as a therapeutic factor 'in hospitals was realized. It has proved its great value in the treatment of both the physically and mentally challenged people. Most of the religious establishments encourage their members to participate in wholesome recreation activities, and many of them conduct programmes that promote good fellowship among their members and afford a wise use of their leisure time. The tremendous popularity of games and sports such as golf, tennis, boating, fishing, polo, hiking, track and field, basketball, water sports etc. has resulted in the formation of thousands of clubs and organisations devoted to one or more of these activities. Some of these groups, such as golf clubs, polo clubs, and the more exclusive athletic clubs are open only either to the wealthy people or to those who have attained prominence in particular sport. Many others, however, serve people with moderate income. Comparable to the sports organisation or clubs there are many other clubs which organise other activities. Few of them are mentioned here such as hobby clubs, chess clubs, social clubs, dancing clubs, folk dancing groups, orchestra clubs, discussion groups, and craft groups. These clubs conduct activities to meet different interests of the members and community people.

4. **Commercial Agencies:** The universal urge for recreation, relaxation, and release from the daily routine has been capitalized by commercial agencies. Unlike other agencies, the commercial agencies are primarily motivated by profits rather than service. These

agencies involve both kinds of recreation i.e" passive recreation and active participation in strenuous physical activities. The commercial agencies provide passive recreation through amusement and entertainment programmes such as radio, record players, television, musical instruments, theatre, night clubs, motion pictures, time out establishments, circus, fun cities, appu ghars, and so on. Whereas active recreation is provided through professional sports. So many clubs are being run by the commercial agencies such as athletic club, boxing club, basketball club, winter sports, bicycle racing, tennis and golf clubs and so on. People have realized the value of recreation and they are becoming most mobile in their life. During vacations, they travel to the far away places from their residential places and stay in hotels, motels, resorts, private camps and so on. Such kind of activities are being undertaken by the commercial agencies and in turn they derived huge amount of income.

NATURE AND TYPE OF RECREATION ACTIVITIES

The forms of recreation vary as widely as the interests of a single individual throughout his life time and are as diverse as the differences between people. The variety of recreation activities in which an individual engages in is almost endless. However, all forms of recreation have one common characteristic, i.e. each activity provides a gratifying outlet for some basic urge or need. In other words, recreation activities in their varied forms bring physical, mental, emotional, social and creative satisfactions to the individual engaging in them. Recreation activities are often grouped according to these major types of personality expressions, but such a grouping is not entirely satisfactory. Therefore, the classification of recreation activities shall be considered from the point of view of the individual participant and it desires entirely different approach. A classification of activities under such headings as physical, dramatic, rhythmic, social, arts and crafts, music, games and sports, dancing, nature and out door activities, literacy and language, collecting, service activities etc. etc. is convenient and useful. While making classification of recreational activities, the most important thing should be taken into consideration i.e. the recreational activities selected and classified should meet the basic and fundamental satisfactions of participants according to their age and gender. Further, consideration should be given to the space requirement, skill cost, reasons, nature of members taking part or form of organisation, and so-on. Although the grouping of recreational activities is must yet their limitations as well as values must be recognized.

For the better understanding of students and to help those who want to organize recreational activities, a brief grouping is given below, which may be developed further as per the requirement in the same direction:

1. **Games and Sports:**
   (*a*) Low organised games (Bull in the Ring, Cat and Mouse, Hide and Seek, Snow Games, Tag Games etc. etc.)
   (*b*) Individual and Dual Games and Activities (Badminton, Athletic Events, Hopscotch, Golf, Ring Tennis etc. etc.)
   (*c*) Gymnastic and Stunts (Apparatus Work, Calisthenics, Gymnastic Marching, Pyramid Building, Rope Jumping, Tumbling etc. etc.)
   (*d*) Group or Team Games (Basketball, Volleyball, Dodgeball, Kick-Ball, Tug of War, Net Ball, Touch Football, Water Polo etc.etc.)
   (*e*) Sports (Archery, Boating, Fencing, Diving, Jumping, Kite Flying, Motor Cycling, Pistol or Rifle shooting, Swimming, Track Events etc. etc.)
2. **Social Activities:** Card Games, Dating, Club Meetings, Entertaining, Birthday Parties, Christmas Celebrations, New Year's Celebrations, Valentine's Day Celebration, Pencil and Paper Games, Table Games, Caroms, Chess, Treasure Hunts etc. etc.
3. **Musical Activities:** Vocal and Instrumental, Items. It also includes Music Festivals, Television Concerts, Music Competitions,

Band Concerts, Composing Music, Listening Groups etc. etc.

4. **Arts and Crafts Activities:** Block Printing, Book Binding, Dying and Colouring, Fabric Decoration, Finger Painting. Furniture Refinishing. Poster Making, Knitting, Leather Craft, Modelling, Paper Craft, Home Decoration, Paper Folding and Cutting, Plastic Crafts, Toy Making etc. etc.
5. **Drama Activities:** Fashion Shows, Mask-Making, Fairs, Carnivals, Doll Fashion Shows, Mock-Trials, Musical Dramas and Comedies, One Act Play, Theatre Play, Story, Plays, Stage Lighting, etc. etc.
6. **Dance Activities:** Folk, Classic, Modern, Social, Acrobatic etc.
7. **Nature and Outdoor Activities:** Bee Culture, Astronomy, Bird Walks, Camping, Caring for Pets, Excursions, Fishing, Museums, Parks, Art Galleries, Mountain Climbing, Hiking, Hunting, Nature Study, Collection and Identification. Snow Tracking, Visiting Zoo, etc. etc.
8. **Literacy and Language Activities:** Debates, Discussion Clubs, Book Clubs, Creative Writing, Lectures, Poetry Groups, Public Speaking. Puzzles, Mental Games, Reading, Reciting, Study Groups, Writing Letters, Story Telling, Foreign Language Groups.
9. **Collection Activities:** Antiques, Autographs, Early Printings, Butterflies, Buttons, Firearms, Lamps, Music Instruments, Paintings, Pictures, Post Cards, Stamps, Tapestries, Toys, Wood Cuts, etc. etc.
10. **Social service activities:** Helping for the Conduct of a Hobby, Craft or Nature Project; Teaching Students Free of Cost, Transporting Aged or Handicapped to Recreation Centres, Assisting with the Recreation Programme at a Hospital, or Home for Aged, Helping in Orphan Homes.

Though the above given list of recreation activities is far from complete, yet indicates the wide variety of activities that give direct satisfaction to the participants by fulfilling their basic and fundamental needs.

SOME OTHER USEFUL MATTERS

Physical Fitness

Physical fitness means that the organic systems of the body are healthy and function efficiently so as to enable the fit person to engage in vigorous tasks and leisure activities. Beyond organic development, muscular strength and stamina, physical fitness implies efficient performance in exercise or work and a reasonable measure of motor skill in the performance of selected physical activities.

The American Alliance for Physical Education Recreation and Dance has classified the components of fitness into two categories.

1. The health related fitness components concern healthy life-style. These components include muscular strength, muscular endurance, cardio respiratory endurance, flexibility and body composition.
2. Motor-skill related physical fitness includes qualities such as strength and power, balance, agility and speed, which are conducive to better performance in sports and other physical activities.

The components of health-related and motor-skill related physical fitness do overlap, for example, cardiovascular function, strength, and flexibility. However, the degree of development of each varies with the two types of physical fitness.

First aid in Sports Injuries

(*a*) **Severe Bleeding.** A severe cut or wound is dangerous because of the possibility of great blood loss. The simplest and most effective way to stop bleeding is by direct pressure on the wound with a gauge or any clean cloth. If this is not available, close the wound with your hand or fingers. It is important to keep the pressure constant. Hold the dressing snugly by hand against the wound for a few minutes. If no blood soaks through, apply additional layers of gauze and bind firmly with tape or strips of cloth. If the bleeding occurs in an arm or leg, raising the limb (unless broken) also helps control bleeding.

(*b*) **Suffocation.** This is similar to being choked. Breathing is difficult or the person does not breath at all. Apply artificial respiration immediately when breathing has stopped from any cause for example after electric shock or apparent drowning. Quickly explore the mouth for any obstructions, chewing gum or displaced false teeth, for example that would interfere with the passage of air. Continue artificial respiration for hours if necessary.

(*c*) **Sunstroke/Heat stroke.** The symptoms of sunstroke or heat stroke are high fever, dizziness, headache, a dry hot skin, red face, and rapid pulse. If the heat stroke is severe, unconsciousness may result. Put the victim in a cool place and cover him with a sheet. Loosen all clothing. Apply cold water over the body quickly and in large quantity to reduce the high fever.

(*d*) **Fractures.** A fracture is a broken bone. When no break in the skin occurs it is called simple fracture. If the broken bone pierces the skin and is exposed, it is a compound fracture. The best treatment is to keep the victim lying down quietly and warmly covered until the doctor arrives. Splints should be put over the injury only if it is absolutely necessary to move him. In case of a spinal fracture, any attempt to lift or turn the victim may result in paralysis.

Occupational Hazards

Occupational dangers are present in many industries. Diseases may arise directly in a person as a result of an employment which necessitates the handling of poisons or toxic gases, or with which is associated air compression, excessive heat, vibration, dust laden air, inadequate lightening or the prolonged use of certain joints and muscles.

1. **Deafness:** High-speed machines produce loud noise; vibrating tools cause repetition of loud noises. As a preventive measure ears should be plugged with suitable earplugs, which will serve to deaden the sound and prevent on set of deafness.
2. **Blindness due to cataract:** In glass making the finishers are exposed to the glare and fierce heat of a temperature around 1500 degree centigrade, coming from the furnace of molten glass. Ten percent of the workers develop cataract. Similar cataracts have been found in tinplate and sheet-mill workers due to exposure to infrared rays. Blindness can be prevented by wearing glasses, which screen off the infrared rays and by inventing machinery for doing the work instead of men doing it in the industries.
3. **Raynaud's phenomenon:** There is an increased frequency in engineering practice to give workers power-driven tools for work such as hammering, chiseling, grinding and polishing. The vibration caused by tools results in Raynaund's phenomenon in which the fingers first become white and bloodless with a loss of sensation and later cyanosed and in rare circumstances may become gangrenous.

   Although the instances of Raynaud's phenomenon are less but still development of robots and automatic machines can save humans from proneness to this hazard.
4. **Injuries from X-rays:** Exposure to X-rays causes dermatitis and carcinoma of the skin. In the industries the workers can be saved from harmful effects of X-rays by putting an adequate layer of lead between themselves and the X-rays, in the form of gloves, aprons, screens and lead windows.

Communicable Diseases

Communicable diseases are transmitted by direct contact or through air, food, water and sometimes through vectors like mosquitoes, rats, dogs, etc.

1. **Cholera:** Caused by bacteria vibriocholerae, transmitted through contaminated water and food. It can be prevented by vaccination, boiling of drinking-water in infected localities.

2. **Tuberculosis:** Caused by bacteria transmitted through cow's milk or discharge from persons suffering from active stage of T.B. Affects bones and causes loss of weight. Treatment and prevention with streptomycin and avoiding contact with infected person.
3. **Diphtheria:** Caused by bacteria, transmitted through saliva and nasal discharge. Incubation period is 3 to 5 days. Prevention and treatment by immunization, vaccine and injection within 12 to 24 hours of the appearance of symptoms.
4. **Influenza:** Caused by virus, usually all epidemic, transmitted by air borne droplets through respiration. Symptoms are inflammation of respiratory tract, fever, chills and muscular aches. Prevention by attenuated live virus vaccine.
5. **Hepatitis:** Mostly caused by virus. Usually an infection or inflammatory disease of liver jaundice. Symptoms-yielding of skin, fever, weakness, lethargy, stomach pains, swelling in the liver area, yellow urine. Prevention includes eating clean, maintaining personal hygiene, drinking boiled water and taking adequate rest.

Components of School Health Programme

A school health programmme should include provision of a wholesome environment, the organization of a healthful school day/weak and the establishment of such teacher pupil relationship that give a safe, sanitary and favourable atmosphere for the best development of teacher-pupil relationship. Healthful school living covers the following topics:

(*a*) **Condition of the school environment:** School environment should be such which enables the child to live safely and happily during school hours.

(*b*) **Condition of the classroom experiences:** Sound sanitary features, furniture design, cross-ventilation and the adequate space in the classroom ensures rich classroom experience.

(*c*) **Condition of the school organization:** Provision of indoor halls for co-curricular activities, injury free environment, adequate safety provisions and round the year physical, mental, social activities are important for perfect health of children.

(*d*) **Health instructions**: Health instruction plans should emphasize upon the development of habits and attitudes. Health instructions should utilize the interests, needs and desires of the boys and girls in establishing knowledge, attitudes and skill for healthful living. Health instructions can be given on topics like food and nutrition, protection against disease, care of teeth, ears and eyes.

Recreation

Recreation is a combination of two words 'Re + creation' which means to create again. So recreation means 'the activation of lost energy of creation.' According to Hut Chinsun 'Recreation is a worthwhile socially accepted leisure experience that provides immediate and inherent satisfaction to the individual who voluntarily participates in an activity.'

Pre-requisites for set up of a recreation centre are:

(*a*) Indoor games such as carom-board, playing cards, chess, table-tennis, darts, bowling, billiards and snooker etc.

(*b*) Well organized library and reading room for people of all ages.

(*c*) A well furnished theatre and the persons who are interested in dramatic art should be given opportunity to display and develop their talent.

(*d*) A museum with the collection of artistic work and display of models and pictures.

(*e*) A cinema house for showing good movies, slides and pictures on general awareness and health improvement.

(*f*) A well equipped gymnasium.

(*g*) Grounds and equipment for out door activities and competitions in sport programmes, facility for training and supervision of activities.

(*h*) Separate provision for child play center. Safety and variety of activities should be provided at the centre.

(*i*) Provision of hall for shows, competitions, talks, displays etc.

Health Education

Physical education teachers are generally entrusted with the responsibility of teaching health habits and developing health attitudes that is why subjects like health, hygiene, sanitation, nutrition, anatomy, physiology, body mechanics, fitness, first aid the like are specifically included in the total professional programme of physical education teachers.

1. **School Environment:** A clean and healthy environment paves the way for improved learning. Proper ventilation and cleanliness in the school, college will contribute to the health of the students and also their attitude towards maintaining cleanliness at home and public places.
2. **Health Instruction:** School children can be given health instructions in health matters, particularly in personal hygiene. School curriculum should include health instruction methods for different age levels. Audio-visual aids can be used to impart health instructions.
3. **Health Services**: The health service generally covers:
   (*a*) **Medical examination and follow up work:** Dental examination, ENT examination, so that the teacher could carry out health appraisal of the students.
   (*b*) **Follow up programme:** This includes removal of the defects observed among students. These defects can be postural deformities, minor deafness, vision problems etc.

Principles of Dietry Manipulations

A balanced diet is required for optimum health. In sports, it is known that manipulation of diet can affect performance. An adequate diet, in terms of quantity and quality, before, during and after training and competition, can help maximize performance.

1. The optimal diet for most sports would have 60% to 70% of total energy required from carbohydrates (versus about 50% to 55% advocated for the general population) about 72% from protein, and the rest from fat.
2. Maintenance of energy balance (i.e. in take versus output) can be assessed by monitoring body weight.
3. In athletic events of high intensity and long duration, performance is limited by carbohydrate availability. It is therefore important to replenish muscle glycogen stores by early and adequate intake of carbohydrates (i.e. almost immediately after training/ competition).
4. Increased fluid intake is essential to avoid dehydration. These fluids may contain some carbohydrates and electrolytes.
5. Fat consumption should not be greater than 30 % of the total energy intake.

   Vitamin supplements are not necessary for athletes who are eating a diet adequate in quantity and quality. It can be concluded that athletes do not need to take special "performance boosters'. What is required is a sensible, well balanced diet, sufficient in quantity and quality.

Balanced Diet for a Long Distance Runner

The best diet for the athlete is the one that considers physiological, sociological, and psychological factors. Many different dietary patterns will provide good nutrition, but a wide variety of foods is the basis of an optimal diet. Correct nutrition plays an important part in long distance running, that make high demands on energy, both in competition, as well as in training. The importance grows with increases in the training volume and competitive distance. Besides the oxidative use of carbohydrates and fat metabolism, there could be even a demand for proteins under extreme loads in long distance running. The basic recommended balanced diet for long distance runners of inter-university level should consist of 15% proteins, 40% fat and 40% carbohydrates. The need for an adequate vitamin intake should also be observed, keeping in mind that there could be deficiencies in vitamin B 1' rather than C.

The following procedures of balance diet is recommended:

Pre-race

1. Never start the race with an empty stomach.
2. The last meal should be taken 2 to 3 hours before the competition (Carbohydrate and Protein emphasis).
3. Avoid large quantities of fluids before a heavy workload.

During the race

1. Fluid intake is particularly important. It should start from the 10km marks. The quantities depending on the temperature.
2. Runs over 20 km require an intake of carbohydrates, vitamins and minerals for marathon 100% gruel, 20 g glucose, the juice of two lemons and 1 g salt.

After the race

1. The restoration of body fluid balance.
2. The restoration of energy reserves, including the structure of proteins.
3. The race restoration is best achieved in the order of immediate fluid intake, followed by carbohydrates in the first two hours and proteins as from the fourth hour after the race.

Role of Proteins and Carbohydrates in Diet of a Long Distance Runner

Proteins: Proteins are made up of carbon, hydrogen, nitrogen, sulphur and phosphorus by their chemical composition. Proteins play an important role in the growth and repair of cells. They are the main body building nutrient. High quality proteins are generally animal proteins such as egg protein, milk protein, fish meat protein. Lower quality protein is found in plants such as nuts, lentils and beans. For an athlete who does not eat meat or animal products a wide variety of plant proteins must be eaten to obtain all the necessary amino acids for health. During training the long distance runner needs extra protein to create muscle tissue. There is also an increased need for extra calories in this situation and enough extra protein will usually be obtained simply by eating more food. If too much protein is taken, any amount over what the body actually needs will be converted for use as an energy source or stored as body fat. 15% of total diet should be protein in case of long distance runners.

Carbohydrates : The body gets the major part of its energy requirements from carbohydrates. Carbohydrates are chemical compounds containing carbon hydrogen and oxygen. Sugars and starches are the components of this item. The carbohydrates break down quickly and easily in the digestive system to form the basic fuel of glucose. Thus it is an important part of a long distance runner's diet. It should be taken from natural resources such as rice, corn, potatoes, beans and fruits, before, during and after the training. Carbohydrates should be taken throughout the athletic career as it is an essential and excellent energy food. The natural or complex carbohydrates enter the blood slowly and insulin levels are steady. This increases the amount of energy available from the carbohydrate, and reduces the amount stored as fat.

EXERCISE

1. Accumulation of lactic acid in the muscles–
(*a*) improves body's efficiency
(*b*) leads to fatigue
(*c*) does not have any effect on the body
(*d*) none of the above

2. Aerobic efficiency can be best improved by–
(*a*) speed training
(*b*) flexibility training
(*c*) endurance training
(*d*) balance training

3. Muscle types can be determined by–
(*a*) use of spectrophotometer
(*b*) use of biopsy
(*c*) use of calorimeter
(*d*) all of the above

4. For complete treatment of the sports injuries one should depend upon–
(*a*) physiotherapy only
(*b*) corrective exercise therapy only
(*c*) both the above
(*d*) none of the above

5. Concentric and eccentric contraction of muscles take place in–
(*a*) isometric method (*b*) isotonic method
(*c*) both the above (*d*) none of the above

6. The catabolism represents–
(*a*) series of biochemical reactions leading to release of energy
(*b*) series of biochemical reactions leading to storage of energy
(*c*) consumption of energy
(*d*) none of the above

7. Creatine Phosphate releases energy–
(*a*) directly
(*b*) with the help of glucose
(*c*) with the help of atp
(*d*) all of the above

8. The main postural deformity among young girls is–
(*a*) kyphosis (*b*) lordosis
(*c*) scoliosis (*d*) arousal

9. Renal glands produce–
(*a*) adrenalin (*b*) renin
(*c*) pepsin (*d*) none of the above

10. Which disease is also called 'lockjaw'?
(*a*) Tetanus (*b*) Rabies
(*c*) Leprosy (*d*) Measles

11. Which of the following diseases is called hydrophobia?
(*a*) Tetanus (*b*) Leprosy
(*c*) Rabies (*d*) Chickenpox

12. Which of the following is a viral disease affecting central nervous system?
(*a*) Chickenpox (*b*) Rabies
(*c*) Tetanus (*d*) Leprosy

13. Which of the following is the measles vaccine?
(*a*) DPT (*b*) Quinine
(*c*) MMR (*d*) TIG

14. Which disease is transmitted from infected mammals to man?
(*a*) Chickenpox (*b*) Malaria
(*c*) Rabies (*d*) AIDS

15. Which of the following is not a source of protein?
(*a*) Eggs (*b*) Meat
(*c*) Oil (*d*) Milk

16. How many calories are required per kg of body weight every hour?
(*a*) 1 Kcal (*b*) 1.3 Kcal
(*c*) 2 Kcal (*d*) 2.5 Kcal

17. Of the following , the rich source of cal-cium is–
(*a*) milk (*b*) nuts
(*c*) meat (*d*) eggs

18. A rich source of Vitamin A is–
(*a*) citrus fruits (*b*) banana
(*c*) grape-fruit (*d*) apricot

19. Citrus fruits are rich in–
(*a*) vitamin A (*b*) vitamin B
(*c*) vitamin C (*d*) vitamin D

20. Bread, cereals and rice provide with most of the–
(*a*) carbohydrates (*b*) proteins
(*c*) vitamins (*d*) minerals

21. Make correct pairs–

A.	Milk, Cheese , yogurt	1.	Carbohydrates
B.	Meat , Poultry, Fish	2.	Calcium and nuts
C.	Vegetable group	3.	Protein
D.	Bread, Rice, Cereal	4.	Vitamins

Codes :
(*a*) A-2, B-4, C-3, D-1
(*b*) A-2, B-3, C-4, D-1
(*c*) A-1, B-3, C-2, D-4
(*d*) A-1, B-4, C-3, D-2

22. Sunlight is a source of–
(*a*) vitamin A (*b*) vitamin B
(*c*) vitamin C (*d*) vitamin D

23. Nitrogen forms a part of
(*a*) proteins (*b*) vitamins
(*c*) fats (*d*) carbohydrates

24. Obesity doess not cause–
(*a*) infertility
(*b*) cancer
(*c*) diabetes
(*d*) ischaemic heart diesease

25. The source of acid rain is–
(a) nitrous oxide (b) nitric oxide
(c) CFCS (d) CO_2

26. Which of the water pollutants is a source of water borne diseases like cholera and gastroenteritis?
(a) Animal Waste (b) Sewage
(c) Fertilizers (d) Mercury

27. Poor illumination in industries is a cause of–
(a) physical hazard
(b) chemical hazard
(c) biological hazard
(d) mechanical hazard

28. Exposure to ultraviolet radiation is a–
(a) mechanical hazard
(b) physical hazard
(c) chemical hazard
(d) biological hazard

29. Chilbians , frost , bite are caused due to–
(a) physical agents
(b) chemical agents
(c) biological agents
(d) mechanical agents

30. Lung cancer is caused due to–
(a) physical agents
(b) chemical agents
(c) biological agents
(d) mechanical agents

31. Diseases like hypertension, industrial neurosis, peptic ulcer are of–
(a) physical origin
(b) chemical origin
(c) biological origin
(d) psychological origin

32. Which form of Hepatitis was initially called the serum hepatitis?
(a) Hepatitis A (b) Hepatitis B
(c) Hepatitis C (d) Hepatitis D

33. Which hepatitis virus spreads by direct contact?
(a) Hepatitis A (b) Hepatitis B
(c) Hepatitis C (d) Hepatitis D

34. HIV Virus causes–
(a) AIDS (b) hepatitis C
(c) hepatitis B (d) TB

35. Match the following

A. Cholera	1. Mycobacterium
B. Chickenpox	2. Vibrio Cholera
C. Tuberculosis	3. Mycobacterium leprae
D. Leprosy	4. Varicella virus

Codes :
(a) A-2, B-3, C-1, D-4
(b) A-2, B-4, C-1, D-3
(c) A-1, B-3, C-2, D-4
(d) A-3, B-4, C-1, D-2

36. Reye syndrome is associated with–
(a) cholera (b) AIDS
(c) leprosy (d) chickenpox

37. Which of the following is a disease caused by virus?
(a) Cholera (b) Tuberculosis
(c) Leprosy (d) Chickenpox

38. Which communicable disease is also known as Hansen's disease?
(a) Hepatitis A (b) Tuberculosis
(c) Rabies (d) Leprosy

39. Which of the following is a bacterial disease of skin and nervous system?
(a) Chickenpox (b) Measles
(c) Leprosy (d) Tetanus

40. Unhealthy eating patterns do not cause–
(a) anemia (b) AIDS
(c) dental Caries (d) obesity

41. Which nutrients are essential to growth and repair of muscle and other body tissues?
(a) Proteins (b) Minerals
(c) Roughage (d) Vitamins

42. The inorganic elements occurring in the body and which are critical to its normal functioning are–
(a) vitamins (b) proteins
(c) carbohydrates (d) minerals

43. An athlete weighing 50 kg who trains for two hours required an intake of approximately–

(*a*) 2410 Kcal (*b*) 2800 Kcal
(*c*) 3000 Kcal (*d*) 4500 Kcal

44. Sugar, sweets, bread and cakes are rich sources of–
(*a*) carbohydrates (*b*) fats
(*c*) proteins (*d*) roughage

45. Fuel used by the body while doing the exercise of severe intensity is–
(*a*) carbohydrate
(*b*) carbohydrate and fat equally
(*c*) less carbohydrate and more fat
(*d*) none of the above

46. Fatty acids are stored in the–
(*a*) upper most layer
(*b*) adipose tissue
(*c*) connective tissue
(*d*) none of the above

47. What type of fats are not hazardous to health?
(*a*) Polyunsaturated (*b*) Unsaturate
(*c*) Saturated (*d*) All of the above.

48. Deficiency of Vitamin D causes–
(*a*) beri beri (*b*) scurvey
(*c*) rickets (*d*) night blindness

49. Faulty bone development among children is caused due to–
(*a*) scurvy (*b*) rickets
(*c*) beri beri (*d*) typhoid

50. Total number of vitamins required by human body are–
(*a*) 10 (*b*) 11
(*c*) 12 (*d*) 13.

51. Two types of Vitamin D are–
(*a*) D_1 and D_2 (*b*) D_3 and D_4
(*c*) D_5 and D_6 (*d*) D_7 and D_8

52. 'Vitamin K' is essential for–
(*a*) normal coagulation of blood
(*b*) providing nourishment to body
(*c*) prevention of disease
(*d*) metabolism of the body

53. Ratio of carbohydrate, proteins and fats in the diet of an average individual should be–
(*a*) 4:1:1 (*b*) 1:4:4
(*c*) 3:2:2 (*d*) 4:4:1

54. Which of the following vitamins is responsible for controlling body weight?
(*a*) B_2 (*b*) B_5
(*c*) Vitamin C (*d*) Vitamin D

55. Which of the following minerals is responsible for body growth and keeping the body healthy?
(*a*) Vitamin C
(*b*) Vitamin D
(*c*) Vitamin K
(*d*) Vitamin B complex

56. Which of the following minerals keeps brain, nails and hair healthy?
(*a*) Potassium (*b*) Sulphur
(*c*) Phosphorus (*d*) Calcium

57. 'Ascorbic Acid' is also known as–
(*a*) Vitamin D
(*b*) Vitamin B Complex
(*c*) Vitamin C
(*d*) Vitamin K

58. Proteins form the major part of diet for–
(*a*) strength dominating sports
(*b*) endurance dominating sports
(*c*) both (*a*) and (*b*)
(*d*) neither (*a*) nor (*b*)

59. The chief source of Vitamin A is–
(*a*) egg (*b*) banana
(*c*) guava (*d*) carrot

60. 'Lumbago' is also called–
(*a*) pain in the head
(*b*) pain in the abdomen
(*c*) pain in the low-back
(*d*) all of the above

61. For endurance dominating sports, the diet should be rich in–
(*a*) protein (*b*) fat
(*c*) minerals (*d*) carbohydrates

62. The instrument used for estimation of body fat is–
(*a*) flexmometer (*b*) gonimeter
(*c*) dynamometer (*d*) skinfold caliper

63. Which of the following minerals is present in abundance in the milk?

(a) Mineral salts (b) Calcium
(c) Fat (d) Protein

64. For strength dominating sports, the diet should be rich in–
(a) carbohydrates (b) vitmains
(c) minerals (d) proteins

65. Carbohydrates are more suitable for energy production in the body because–
(a) they have more affinity to oxygen
(b) they are more dynamic
(c) they are more powerful
(d) they have CO_2 carrying capacity.

66. Which enzyme digests protein?
(a) Amylase
(b) Trypsin
(c) Lipase
(d) None of the above.

67. Which Vitamin is easily destroyed by heat and air?
(a) K (b) C
(c) D (d) A.

68. Which of the following Vitamins is water soluble?
(a) C and B complex
(b) D and K complex
(c) A and D complex
(d) B_1 and B_5 complex.

69. Which of the following Vitamins is fat soluble?
(a) B_1 (b) B_5
(c) C (d) D

70. Which of the following minerals form bones and teeth?
(a) calcium and phosphorus
(b) potassium and calcium
(c) sulphur and iron
(d) phosphorus and iron

71. Vitamin B1 is also known as–
(a) calcium (b) thiamine
(c) phosphorus (d) none of the above

72. Essential amino acids–
(a) can be synthesized in human body
(b) cannot be synthesized in human body
(c) both (a) and (b)
(d) none of the above

73. Process by which food is taken by the organisms is called–
(a) digestion (b) absorption
(c) assimilation (d) ingestion

74. Process in which absorption of soluble food is done by the wall of small intestine and then passed to the blood is–
(a) assimilation (b) ingestion
(c) digestion (d) absorption

75. Absorption of the fat takes place in–
(a) mouth (b) large intestine
(c) small intestine (d) liver

76. Carbohydrates are converted into sugar in the–
(a) duodenum (b) large intestine
(c) digestive tract (d) liver

77. 'Calcium' responsible for regulating the contraction response is present in–
(a) protoplasm (b) pancreas
(c) cytoplasm (d) intestine

78. Carbohydrates is an important component of diet especially for–
(a) sprinters
(b) boxers
(c) long distance runners
(d) chess players

79. Which of the following has greater food value?
(a) White eggs (b) Brown eggs
(c) Both (a) and (b) (d) Ducks eggs

80. Four important mineral nutrients required in large quantities by the humans are–
(a) Phosphorus, Calcium, Sodium and Magnesium
(b) Calcium, Sodium, Potassium and Manganese
(c) Iron, Calcium, Sodium, Phosphorus
(d) Phosphorus, Iron, Calcium, Sodium and Magnesium.

81. Which of the following is the richest source of Vitamin C?
(a) Banana (b) Apple
(c) Guava (d) Tomato

82. Necessary basic conditions for good health include–
(*a*) proper diet
(*b*) personal and domestic hygiene
(*c*) exercise and rest
(*d*) all the above

83. Which of the following diseases does not occur due to deficiency of vitamins?
(*a*) Night blindness (*b*) Scurvy
(*c*) Rickets (*d*) None

84. Carbohydrate loading mostly helps–
(*a*) marathon runners (*b*) boxers
(*c*) sprinters (*d*) power lifters

85. Which activity burns the maximum calories?
(*a*) Cycling (5.5. miles/hr)
(*b*) Squash
(*c*) Running (10 miles/hr)
(*d*) Swimming (20 yd/min.).

86. Which of the following enzymes digests fat?
(*a*) Trypsin (*b*) Lipase
(*c*) Both (*a*) and (*b*) (*d*) None of the above

87. Deficiency of protein results in–
(*a*) marasmus (*b*) hypertension
(*c*) anemia (*d*) gout

88. Sports Medicine field does not include
(*a*) nutri1tion and diet
(*b*) treatment and prevention of injuries
(*c*) conditioning and training
(*d*) grants for sports promotion

89. Renal glands produce–
(*a*) adrenalin (*b*) renin
(*c*) pepsin (*d*) none of the above

90. Chronic injuries are treated by–
(*a*) infrared (*b*) ultra theraphy
(*c*) ultrasonic (*d*) ultraviolet

91. Water therapy is also known as–
(*a*) electrotherapy (*b*) waxtherapy
(*c*) hydrotherapy (*d*) ice therapy

92. Swelling is reduced by–
(*a*) sauna bath (*b*) whirlpool bath
(*c*) contrast bath (*d*) all the above

93. A muscle contracts, but no movement takes place, it is known as–
(*a*) isometric (*b*) isotonic
(*c*) isokinetic (*d*) none of the above

94. Which of the following is called a pressure manipulation?
(*b*) Stroking (*c*) Clapping
(*c*) Pounding (d) Kneading

95. In rehabilitation of sports injuries, which of the following method is used?
(*a*) Corrective exercise
(*b*) Hydrotherapy
(*c*) Cryotherapy
(*d*) None of the above

96. Shortwave diathermy is used for–
(*a*) treatment of immediate injuries
(*b*) treatment of chronic injuries
(*c*) treatment of psychological problems
(*d*) all the above

97. Hydrotherapy means–
(*a*) therapy with vaseline
(*b*) therapy with wax
(*c*) therapy with water
(*d*) therapy with oil

98. For reducing swelling, recommended treatment is–
(*a*) contrast bath (*b*) ultrasound
(*c*) ultra-therapy (*d*) ultraviolet

99. Sprains are due to–
(*a*) broken born
(*b*) bone ends out of place
(*c*) stretched or torn joint ligaments
(*d*) none of the above

100. Fracture Means–
(*a*) broken bone
(*b*) bone ends out of the place
(*c*) stretching of tendons
(*d*) none of the above

101. Cryotherapy is also known as–
(*a*) ice therapy (*b*) hydrotherapy
(*c*) electrotherapy (*d*) none of the above

102. Lumbargo is also called–
(*a*) pain in the head
(*b*) pain in the abdomen

(*c*) pain in the low-back
(*d*) all of the above

103. Contrast bath is recommended for–
(*a*) reducing a dislocated joint
(*b*) reducing swelling
(*c*) treatment of wound
(*d*) none of the above

104. The common injury in basketball is–
(*a*) medial maniscus damage
(*b*) damage medial ligament of the ankle
(*c*) damage lateral ligament of the ankle
(*d*) all of the above

105. Electrical gadgets used for treating immediate sports injuries is–
(*a*) ultra-violet rays
(*b*) ultra sound
(*c*) shortwavediathermy
(*d*) infra-red rays

106. During training the sensation of vomiting is caused due to–
(*a*) accumulation of lactic acid
(*b*) adrenaline
(*c*) carbon dioxide
(*d*) all of the above

107. The first-aid treatment recommended for long distance exhausted athlete is–
(*a*) artificial respiration
(*b*) massage
(*c*) cryotherapy
(*d*) all of the above

108. Effleurage is always done–
(*a*) from distal to proximal ends
(*b*) across the muscles
(*c*) from proximal to distal ends
(*d*) around joints

109. How do sports injuries occur?–
(*a*) Lack of knowledge
(*b*) Inadequate training, technique and equipment
(*c*) Carelessness
(*d*) All the above

110. A work in which the amount of oxygen taken in and used by the body is sufficient to provide the energy necessary for the performance of task is called as–
(*a*) aerobic work (*b*) anaerobic work
(*c*) full work (*d*) none of the above

111. A work in which the amount of oxygen that the body can supply is less than the amount necessary to perform the task is known as–
(*a*) anaerobic work (*b*) aerobic work
(*c*) half work (*d*) none of these

112. The ability of the total body to use oxygen for energy is called–
(*a*) oxygen consumption
(*b*) tidal volume
(*c*) both
(*d*) none of the above

113. Which measurement is recognized as the best measurement of a person's cardio-vascular fitness?
(*a*) body weight (*b*) pulse rate
(*c*) Vo_2 max (*d*) none of these

114. How can the maximal oxygen consumption increase?
(*a*) An increase in the amount of haemoglobin in the blood
(*b*) An increase in the maximal cardiac output
(*c*) An increase in amount and/or size of capillaries
(*d*) All of the above

115. The target zone heart rate ranges from 70 to 85% of individual's maximal heart rate, it is–
(*a*) true (*b*) false
(*c*) both (*d*) none of these

116. Formula for calculating Critical Heart Rate is–
(*a*) resting heart rate + 09.60 (maximal heart rate-Resting heart rate)
(*b*) resting heart rate –0.80 (maximal heart rate-resting heart rate
(*c*) resting heart rate –0.60 (maximal heart rate + resting heart rate)
(*d*) none of the above

117. Why does muscle pull occur?
(*a*) Insufficient warm up before game
(*b*) Mineral deficiency
(*c*) Muscle imbalance
(*d*) All of the above

118. What should be applied when muscle pull occur?
(*a*) Ice (*b*) Warm water
(*c*) Infrared Lamp (*d*) None of the above

119. Tennis elbows can be developed by–
(*a*) only tennis players
(*b*) only badminton players
(*c*) both
(*d*) none

120. What would you do when tennis elbow is developed?
(*a*) Stop playing game
(*b*) Use crepe bandage
(*c*) Use of wrist band
(*d*) None

121. What are the causes of muscle cramp?
(*a*) Salt deficiency
(*b*) Any injury to muscle
(*c*) Hyper ventilation
(*d*) All of the above

122. What do you understand by the word tendinities?
(*a*) Fracture
(*b*) An inflammation of the tendon
(*c*) Both
(*d*) Tiredness

123. What is the immediate management for sprain, strain and tendon injuries?
(*a*) Using Ice packs (*b*) Use of hot water
(*c*) Infrared Lamp (*d*) None of these

124. Cryo-therapy means–
(*a*) cold-therapy (*b*) heat application
(*c*) infrared (*d*) none of these

125. The word "Effleurage" is related with–
(*a*) massage
(*b*) weight training
(*c*) sprint training
(*d*) endurance training

126. The movement performed by the trainee with no aid on the body part of the subject may be termed as–
(*a*) passive manipulation
(*b*) active manipulation
(*c*) resistive manipulation
(*d*) none of these

127. The movement performed by the individual with the help of weight acting against the direction of movement may be termed as–
(*a*) resistive manipulation
(*b*) assistive manipulation
(*c*) passive manipulation
(*d*) none of these

128. Ethyl chloride is used in athletics as a means of treatment in–
(*a*) cryo-therapy (*b*) thermo-therapy
(*c*) electro-therapy (*d*) none of these

129. Diathermy and ultra-sound methods are used for the treatment of injuries in–
(*a*) cryo-therapy (*b*) thermo-therapy
(*c*) electro-therapy (*d*) none of these

130. A normal human body has–
(*a*) one kidney (*b*) two kidneys
(*c*) three kidneys (*d*) none of these

131. Human kidneys are situated at–
(*a*) 12th thorasic to 3rd lumber segment
(*b*) 8th thorasic to 2nd lumber segment
(*c*) 10th thorasic to 3rd lumber segment
(*d*) None of these

132. The chief excretory organs of human body are–
(*a*) lungs (*b*) skin
(*c*) two kidneys (*d*) none of these

133. Proximal convoluted tubule (PCT) or pars comoluta is about–
(*a*) 20 mm long (*b*) 35 mm long
(*c*) 14 mm long (*d*) None of these

134. Henless loop (pass recta) is–
(*a*) V Shaped loop (*b*) U shaped loop
(*c*) A shaped loop (*d*) None of these

135. The renal blood flow–
(*a*) decreases during exercise

(*b*) increases during exercise
(*c*) partially affected
(*d*) none of these

136. In 24 hours the total volume glomerular filtrate is about–
(*a*) 170 Litres (*b*) 190 Litres
(*c*) 260 Litres (*d*) None of these

137. The pituitary glands colour is–
(*a*) reddish grey (*b*) white grey
(*c*) blue (*d*) none of these

138. The pituitary gland is situated at–
(*a*) base of the brain (*b*) neck
(*c*) heart (*d*) none of these

139. The thyroid gland is situated at–
(*a*) roof of the throat (*b*) heart
(*c*) base of brain (*d*) none of these

140. The blood flow in thyroid gland per minute is–
(*a*) 3.5-6 ml./gm (*b*) 4.5-7 ml/gm
(*c*) 2.5-4.5 ml/gm (*d*) None of these

141. In human body adrenal glands are–
(*a*) 3 in number (*b*) 4 in number
(*c*) 2 in number (*d*) None of these

142. The fatigue is the result of accumulation of–
(*a*) carbonic acid (*b*) sulphuric acid
(*c*) lactic acid (*d*) all of these

143. Antidiuretic hormone is secreted by–
(*a*) pituitary gland (*b*) adrenal gland
(*c*) thyroid gland (*d*) para thyroid gland

144. Humerus bone is situated at–
(*a*) upper limb (*b*) lower limb
(*c*) back (*d*) all of these

145. Redial and Ulna bones are situated at–
(*a*) upper limb (*b*) lower limb
(*c*) back (*d*) all of these

146. Absence of normal anterio-posterior curve is called–
(*a*) kyphosis (*b*) lordosis
(*c*) flat back (*d*) all of these

147. Elementary school children should be given–
(*a*) natural exercise
(*b*) naturalised exercise
(*c*) finer muscle exercise
(*d*) big muscle exercise

148. The thoraic cage (thorax) consists–
(*a*) 14 pairs of ribs (*b*) 12 pairs of ribs
(*c*) 10 pair of ribs (*d*) None of these

149. The lumber region vertebrae's consists of–
(*a*) 6 vertebrae's (*b*) 5 vertebrae's
(*c*) 7 vertebrae's (*d*) None of these

150. The cervicle region vertebrae's consists–
(*a*) 6 vertebrae's (*b*) 10 vertebrae's
(*c*) 7 vertebrae's (*d*) None of these

151. The shoulder blade is also known as–
(*a*) sternum (*b*) scapula
(*c*) ribs (*d*) none of these

152. The collar bone is known as–
(*a*) ribs (*b*) clavicle
(*c*) sternum (*d*) none of these

153. The ball and socket joint are–
(*a*) shoulder joint (*b*) hip joint
(*c*) both of these (*d*) none of these

154. The bones of skull are united with–
(*a*) ball and socket joint
(*b*) hinge joint
(*c*) pivot joint
(*d*) none of these

155. The knee joint is a–
(*a*) ball and socket joint
(*b*) hinge joint
(*c*) pivot joint
(*d*) none of these

156. The Radial and ulnar are linked by–
(*a*) pivot joint
(*b*) ball and socket joint
(*c*) hinge joint
(*d*) none of these

157. Biceps muscles are situated at–
(*a*) upper limb (*b*) back
(*c*) lower limb (*d*) none of these

158. Deltoid muscle is situated at–
(*a*) shoulder (*b*) elbow
(*c*) knee (*d*) none of these

159. Throwers muscle is–
(*a*) deltoid (*b*) pectoralis major
(*c*) biceps (*d*) none of these

160. The Rowing muscle is–
(*a*) deltoid (*b*) petoralis major
(*c*) latissimus dorsi (*d*) none of these

161. The strongest muscle of the body is–
(*a*) rectus femoris (*b*) soleus
(*c*) sternomustoid (*d*) biceps

162. Pectoralis major muscles are situated at–
(*a*) chest (*b*) elbow
(*c*) knee (*d*) none of these

163. The muscle used for bending hips is known as–
(*a*) quadriceps (*b*) triceps
(*c*) biceps (*d*) none of these

164. The number of vertebrae's in spinal cord are–
(*a*) 25 (*b*) 31
(*c*) 28 (*d*) None of these

165. The muscle situated at the back side of humerus is–
(*a*) biceps (*b*) triceps
(*c*) quadriceps (*d*) none of these

166. Cerebellum is a part of–
(*a*) digestive system (*b*) muscular
(*c*) brain (*d*) none of these

167. The transfer of oxygen from air to the tissue of the body and transfer of CO_2 from tissue to outside air is called–
(*a*) digestion (*b*) respiration
(*c*) absorption (*d*) none of these

168. Lungs are part of–
(*a*) nervous system (*b*) digestive system
(*c*) respiratory system (*d*) none of these

169. The normal body temperature is–
(*a*) 98.4°F (*b*) 88°F
(*c*) 72°F (*d*) None of these

170. The range of Normal body temperature is–
(*a*) 82°-88°.2F (*b*) 96°-99°F
(*c*) 70°-72°F (*d*) None of these

171. Overheating of the body is due to–
(*a*) high external temperature
(*b*) physical activity
(*c*) inadequate sweating
(*d*) combination of all the above

172. Somatotropic, thyrotropic, adrenocorticotropic and gonadotropic hormones are secreated by–
(*a*) anterior lobe of pituitary gland
(*b*) posterior lobe of pituitary gland
(*c*) both
(*d*) none of these

173. The hormone that controls the growth of the body is called–
(*a*) thyrotropic hormone
(*b*) somatotropic hormone
(*c*) gonadotrophic hormone
(*d*) none of these

174. Diarthosis is–
(*a*) freely movable joint
(*b*) slightly movable joints
(*c*) immovable joints
(*d*) none of these

175. Amphiarthrosis is–
(*a*) freely movable joint
(*b*) slightly movable
(*c*) immovable joints
(*d*) none of these

176. Synoarthrosis is–
(*a*) freely movable joint
(*b*) slightly movable
(*c*) immovable joints
(*d*) none of these

177. The knee joint is–
(*a*) diarthrosis (*b*) amphiarthrosis
(*c*) synoarthrosis (*d*) none of these

178. The system which convert food substance that body cells can use as a source of energy is called–
(*a*) nervous system (*b*) muscular system
(*c*) elementary system (*d*) none of these

179. The organs which produces bile is–
(*a*) heart (*b*) lung
(*c*) liver (*d*) none of these

180. The organs which stores and concentrates the bile before use is–

(*a*) lung (*b*) liver
(*c*) gall bladder (*d*) none of these

181. The heart is composed of–
(*a*) 1 Pump (*b*) 2 pumps
(*c*) 3 pumps (*d*) None of these

182. Blood vessels entering the heart are called–
(*a*) veins (*b*) arteries
(*c*) canal (*d*) none of these

183. The blood vessel leaving the heart is called–
(*a*) veins (*b*) arteries
(*c*) canal (*d*) none of these

184. The amount of blood that can be circulated each minute is known as–
(*a*) aerobic work (*b*) cardiac out put
(*c*) lung volume (*d*) none of these

185. The nutrient which combines with protein to make hemoglobin is–
(*a*) calcium (*b*) iron
(*c*) both of these (*d*) none of these

186. Nutrients which helps to make cementing materials that hold cells together is–
(*a*) vitamin D (*b*) vitamin B
(*c*) vitamin A (*d*) none of these

187. The traumatic joint twist that results in stretching or totally tearing stabilizing connective tissue is–
(*a*) muscle pull (*b*) strain
(*c*) sprain (*d*) fracture

188. Fracture in which the bone splits along its length is known as–
(*a*) green stick fracture
(*b*) impacted fracture
(*c*) longitudinal
(*d*) depressed fracture

189. The term cardiac cycle is associated with–
(*a*) digestive system (*b*) respiratory system
(*c*) circulatory system (*d*) none of these

190. The sex steroids contains–
(*a*) 17 carbon atoms (*b*) 10 Carbon atoms
(*c*) 21 Carbon atoms (*d*) None of these

191. Ventricle is a part of–
(*a*) brain (*b*) lung
(*c*) heart (*d*) none of these

192. The Radial artery is situated at–
(*a*) upper limb (*b*) lower limb
(*c*) back (*d*) none of these

193. Thyroxin is produced by–
(*a*) pancrease (*b*) sex gland
(*c*) thyroid gland (*d*) none of these

194. Insulin is produced by–
(*a*) sex gland (*b*) pancrease
(*c*) thyroid gland (*d*) none of these

195. Protein builds–
(*a*) nerve tissue (*b*) bone tissue
(*c*) muscle tissue (*d*) none of these

196. Vitamin D is rich in–
(*a*) milk (*b*) butter
(*c*) egg yolk (*d*) none of these

197. Sunlight is a source of–
(*a*) vitamin B (*b*) vitamin C
(*c*) vitamin D (*d*) none of these

198. Vitamin B6 is present in–
(*a*) liver (*b*) milk
(*c*) egg (*d*) none of these

199. Rickets occurs due to the deficiency of–
(*a*) vitamin A (*b*) vitamin B
(*c*) vitamin D (*d*) none of these

200. Osteophorosis disease occurs in–
(*a*) muscles (*b*) nerves
(*c*) bones (*d*) none of these

ANSWERS

1	2	3	4	5	6	7	8	9	10
(*b*)	(*c*)	(*b*)	(*c*)	(*b*)	(*a*)	(*c*)	(*b*)	(*a*)	(*a*)
11	**12**	**13**	**14**	**15**	**16**	**17**	**18**	**19**	**20**
(*c*)	(*b*)	(*c*)	(*c*)	(*c*)	(*d*)	(*a*)	(*d*)	(*c*)	(*a*)

21	22	23	24	25	26	27	28	29	30
(*b*)	(*d*)	(*a*)	(*b*)	(*b*)	(*b*)	(*a*)	(*b*)	(*a*)	(*b*)
31	**32**	**33**	**34**	**35**	**36**	**37**	**38**	**39**	**40**
(*d*)	(*b*)	(*a*)	(*a*)	(*b*)	(*d*)	(*d*)	(*d*)	(*c*)	(*b*)
41	**42**	**43**	**44**	**45**	**46**	**47**	**48**	**49**	**50**
(*a*)	(*d*)	(*a*)	(*a*)	(*c*)	(*b*)	(*a*)	(*c*)	(*b*)	(*d*)
51	**52**	**53**	**54**	**55**	**56**	**57**	**58**	**59**	**60**
(*a*)	(*a*)	(*a*)	(*b*)	(*d*)	(*b*)	(*c*)	(*a*)	(*d*)	(*c*)
61	**62**	**63**	**64**	**65**	**66**	**67**	**68**	**69**	**70**
(*d*)	(*d*)	(*d*)	(*a*)	(*a*)	(*b*)	(*b*)	(*a*)	(*d*)	(*a*)
71	**72**	**73**	**74**	**75**	**76**	**77**	**78**	**79**	**80**
(*b*)	(*b*)	(*d*)	(*a*)	(*b*)	(*c*)	(*c*)	(*a*)	(*c*)	(*a*)
81	**82**	**83**	**84**	**85**	**86**	**87**	**88**	**89**	**90**
(*c*)	(*d*)	(*d*)	(*a*)	(*c*)	(*b*)	(*a*)	(*d*)	(*b*)	(*d*)
91	**92**	**93**	**94**	**95**	**96**	**97**	**98**	**99**	**100**
(*c*)	(*c*)	(*b*)	(*d*)	(*a*)	(*b*)	(*c*)	(*a*)	(*c*)	(*a*)
101	**102**	**103**	**104**	**105**	**106**	**107**	**108**	**109**	**110**
(*a*)	(*c*)	(*b*)	(*d*)	(*d*)	(*a*)	(*a*)	(*a*)	(*d*)	(*a*)
111	**112**	**113**	**114**	**115**	**116**	**117**	**118**	**119**	**120**
(*a*)	(*a*)	(*c*)	(*d*)	(*a*)	(*a*)	(*d*)	(*b*)	(*c*)	(*a*)
121	**122**	**123**	**124**	**125**	**126**	**127**	**128**	**129**	**130**
(*d*)	(*b*)	(*a*)	(*a*)	(*a*)	(*b*)	(*a*)	(*a*)	(*c*)	(*b*)
131	**132**	**133**	**134**	**135**	**136**	**137**	**138**	**139**	**140**
(*a*)	(*c*)	(*c*)	(*b*)	(*b*)	(*a*)	(*a*)	(*a*)	(*a*)	(*a*)
141	**142**	**143**	**144**	**145**	**146**	**147**	**148**	**149**	**150**
(*c*)	(*c*)	(*a*)	(*a*)	(*b*)	(*a*)	(*a*)	(*b*)	(*b*)	(*c*)
151	**152**	**153**	**154**	**155**	**156**	**157**	**158**	**159**	**160**
(*b*)	(*b*)	(*a*)	(*d*)	(*b*)	(*a*)	(*a*)	(*a*)	(*b*)	(*c*)
161	**162**	**163**	**164**	**165**	**166**	**167**	**168**	**169**	**170**
(*a*)	(*a*)	(*a*)	(*d*)	(*b*)	(*c*)	(*b*)	(*c*)	(*a*)	(*b*)
171	**172**	**173**	**174**	**175**	**176**	**177**	**178**	**179**	**180**
(*d*)	(*c*)	(*b*)	(*a*)	(*b*)	(*c*)	(*b*)	(*b*)	(*c*)	(*b*)
181	**182**	**183**	**184**	**185**	**186**	**187**	**188**	**189**	**190**
(*a*)	(*c*)	(*b*)	(*b*)	(*b*)	(*d*)	(*c*)	(*a*)	(*c*)	(*a*)
191	**192**	**193**	**194**	**195**	**196**	**197**	**198**	**199**	**200**
(*c*)	(*a*)	(*c*)	(*b*)	(*c*)	(*c*)	(*c*)	(*a*)	(*c*)	(*c*)

UNIT-VII

SPORTS TRAINING

Meaning of Sports Training

The training is a process of preparing an individual for any event or an activity or job. Usually in sports we use the term sports training which denotes the sense of preparing sportspersons for the highest level of performance. But nowadays sports training is not just a term but it is very important subject that affects each and every individual who takes up physical activity or sports either for health and fitness or for competition at different levels. Hence, sports training is *the physical, technical, intellectual, psychological* and *moral preparation* of an athlete or a player by means of physical exercises.

According to Harre (1982) sports training is a process of athletic improvement, which is conducted on the basis of scientific principles through which systematic development of mental and physical efficiency, capacity and motivation enables athletes to produce outstanding and record breaking athletic performances.

Thus, we can say that sports training is the overall scientific and systematic channel of preparation of sportspersons for the highest level of sports performance. Sports training also consists of all those learning influences and processes that are aimed at enhancing sports performance.

Definition of Sports Training

Some definitions of sports training as given by the experts of this area are as under:

According to *Hardial Singh* (1993), sports training is a pedagogical process, based on scientific principles, aiming at preparing sportsmen for higher performances in sports competitions.

Harre (1986) said, "Sports training, based on scientific knowledge, is a pedagogical process of sports perfection which through systematic effect on psycho-physical performance ability and performance readiness aim at leading the sportsman to high and the highest performance. Through active and conscious interaction with the given demands in sports training, the sportsman's personality develops according to the norms and standards of socialist society."

According to *Matveyev* (1981) sports training is the basic form of an athlete's training. It is the preparation systematically organised with the help of exercises, which in fact is a pedagogically organised process of controlling an athlete's development (his sporting perfectioning).

Martin (1979) said, "sports training is a planned and controlled process in which, for achieving a goal, changes in complex sports motor performance, ability to act and behaviour are made through measures of content, methods and organisation."

In the broad sense sports training is the entire systematic process of preparation of athletes for the highest levels of athletic performance. It comprises all those learning influences and processes, including self tuition by the athlete, which are aimed at improving performance.

Aim of Sports Training

In the light of the meaning and definitions of sports training, the aim of sports training is to improve rapidly the sports performance of a sportsperson particularly in sports competitions, which is mainly based on his physical, psychological, intellectual and technical capacities and capabilities. In other words, the aim of sports training in competitive sports is to prepare the sportspersons for the attainment of highest possible sports performance in competition.

Objectives of Sports Training

Keeping in view the aim of sports training in competitive sports, the following objectives of sports training may be set to reach the aim

1. **Personality Development :** One of the main objectives of sports training is the all round development of personality of the sportsperson, because a good personality counts a lot in sports competition and attainment of highest possible performance. Various personality traits such as drive, assertion, determination, self-confidence, leadership, emotional maturity, trainability, conscience and mental toughness can be developed through sports training and education. These factors play an essential role in all round development of sportsperson and in achieving higher performance in sports competitions.
2. **Physical fitness Development:** Next important objective of sports training is to develop physical fitness level of the sportsperson. Physical fitness consists of mainly strength, speed, endurance, flexibility and other coordinative abilities. These abilities are essential prerequisites of high sports performance. Sports training should be concentrated mainly on the development of the kind of fitness that is needed for the specific sports event or game concerned. The development of desired level of fitness and its components takes several years of systematic training. This needs the use of different types of physical exercises and various types of training methods in sports training programme for sportspersons/trainees.
3. **Skill / Technique Development:** Another vital objective of sports training is the development of skills or techniques in a particular sport or event in which sportspersons intend to perform or execute. Good skill or technique helps the sportsperson to make economical and optimum use of his physical abilities or physical prowess.
   The sportspersons learn the skill or techniques and get a mastery over it under conditions specific to their sport or event. As the sportsperson develops his/her level of physical fitness he/she must also keep improving the standard of his/her skill or technique. Thus these two aspects of sports training i.e. development of physical fitness and development of skill or technique should also go hand in hand.
4. **Tactical Development:** The importance of tactics is gradually increasing due to neck-and-neck competition at national and international levels. Thus, it is very important aspect of any sports training programme particularly at higher level to include tactical training as a part and parcel of all other components of training programme. Because the sportsperson must acquire those skills and abilities that will enable him/her to win the games or event.
5. **Mental Training:** Mental training is an integral and important part of sports training. Nowadays, in the hi-tech competitive era higher demands are put on the mental faculties of sportspersons. They are under tremendous stress and pressure both internal and external. The sportspersons must be able to act and think for themselves during sports training and also in competition to perform better. This is an important objective of sports training to develop and train the sportsperson's intellectual faculties and improve their knowledge of sports training and learn its application in a unique way in training and competition.

Characteristics of Sports Training

Main characteristics of sports training are as follows:

1. **Sports Training is Performance Oriented:** Sports training is always performance oriented as it targets at achieving high performance in a given sports competition. Each and every aspect or process of sports training leads to improving sports performance whether it is a physical or psychological preparation or skill/ technique development or tactical and mental training.

2. **Sports Training is Individual Matter:** Sports performance is a result of various factors, may differ from person to person. Thus sports training is to a great extent an individual matter. But it does not mean that sports training should not be given in group. Rather sports training in groups is essential for mobilising performance potentials by providing necessary emotional basis. Group training is economical and important factor in-group education. It is essential to give due weightage to individual factors while planning load and frequency management in sports training.
3. **Sports Training is Planned and Systematic:** Sports training is always planned and systematic for achieving the highest performance in a given competition. Desired results in any sports/ events or game cannot be achieved without proper planning i.e. long term, intermediate and short term planning and also without systematic process. One cannot have mastery over tactical aspect of any sport/event or game without developing skills or technique first. So sports training is a planned and scientific process to achieve excellent performance.
4. **Sports Training is Scientific Process:** Nowadays sports training is a highly scientific process, which is based on sound scientific principles. It is also based on advances made in natural and social sciences. Knowledge from these sciences has to be put in use in the process of sports training to attain the highest performance. Thus, sports training itself becomes a science which play a vital role in today's sports.
5. **Sports Training is Educational Process:** Actually, sports training is a planned and systematic educational process through which education is imparted to sportspersons regarding various training methods, training process, rules and regulations and regarding his abilities and capabilities. Sports training is an educational process to develop all round personality of an athlete through various means and methods. Without developing sports personality, proper training and high performance are not possible.
6. **Coach as a Leader/Mentor in Sports Training:** Another important characteristics of sports training is the leadership role of the coach. The coach's role as a mentor covers all aspects and forms of sports training. The coach is responsible to control everything in training i.e. planning, implementation, assessment etc. In sports training, coach assists athletes to follow training programme properly, and he/she communicates effectively with his/her athletes/players on the various aspects of training and performance.
7. **Development and Exploitation Reserves of Sports Persons:** One of the main tasks of sports training is to develop the capacities and capabilities of sportsperson besides exploitation of his potentials. Some time sportspersons are unaware about their performance limits. Hidden potentials are tapped through training and sportspersons are educated about these reserves. Through sports training sportsperson scales new heights of his own performance and sets the higher target.
8. **Sports Training is Controlled Process:** This is one of the unique characteristics of sports training that each and every element of training is fully controlled. In sports training athlete/player has to be very disciplined, dutiful and committed to all aspects of training to realise the maximum benefit for better performance. His/her training is fully managed through daily training sessions to micro, meso and macro training.

Principles of Sports Training and Conditioning

The following are the basic principles of sports training and conditioning:

1. **Principle of Overload:** In sports training this is the foremost principle to make any improvement in different abilities of an individual. The overload is that any

improvement in fitness needs an increased training load that challenges the trainee's state of fitness. Loading causes fatigue and when loading ends, then recovery starts. If the training load is optimal (just less than maximum which is unknown), the trainee will be more fit after recovery than before the training load was applied.

2. **Principle of Individuality:** As no two individuals are identical in this world. Thus each trainee or athlete does not react in the same way to a training method or system rather he or she reacts in a little different way. Age and sex differences also affect the training programme.

   According to the principle of individualization the training programme should be prepared and planned as per the trainee's own ability, requirements and his/her potential. So one must not just copy a training programme of any other individual trainee. Trainee's physical, physiological and psychological make-up, his/ her age, experience in sports, skill level, past and present performance, training load capacity and rate of recovery, body build and gender differences must be considered by the coach/ trainer while planning a training programme for him/her. The training programme will be most effective and successful only if it is followed by trainee for whom it was planned.

3. **Principle of Progressive Development:** This progressive development refers to the general motor skills and fitness development, which are the main goals of the early part of the training year. If there is a more balanced general development at the early stage, then the greater level of performance can be achieved at the later stage.

   In training children and junior athletes/players more emphasis should be given to this principle because it is the first step of the systematic step approach in the sports training. In sports training there should be increase in the intensity, frequency and/or duration of activity step by step instead of linear increase over periods of time in order to improve.

4. **Principle of Specificity:** The principle of specificity is that the nature of the training load determines the training effect. The training must be specific to the desired effect. The training programme should be prepared in a specific way that it meets the specific demands of a specific event/activity/game. The training load should also be specific in terms of recovery and intensity. Intensity is the quality or difficulty of the training load.

5. **Principle of Specialization:** This principle refers to training programme, which develops the techniques and abilities required for a specific event or activity. A runner needs speed and endurance components. So he/she should develop running technique that uses the most efficient running pattern for the racing distance.

   A thrower needs strength in specific parts of the body, just as different specific motor skills are required for each throwing event. All such traits or factors are developed through specialized training programme and specialized specific training exercises.

6. **Principle of Continuity:** This principle refers to continuity in training programme. The training effect will reverse itself if there is no continuity and the fitness or conditioning level will fall if the loading does not continue. If the sports training does not become more challenging, the fitness level will stagnate (plateau). If the sports training ends the fitness level slowly comes down until it reaches the level needed to maintain normal daily activities.

   The training load must continue to increase if the trainee's general and specific fitness is to continue to improve. If load remains at the same level, the fitness rises for a time, then begins to fall. So there must be a progressive overload for the improvement of performances.

7. **Principle of Active Participation:** The principle of active participation means that for good results of sports training programme, trainee must be actively involved in this process by his/her own choice. The sports

training is a two-way process among the trainee and the coach. The trainee/s should fully understand the aim and objectives of his/her training programme. There must be regular evaluation of every sports training programme. The trainee should not be a passive participant and he/she should follow the coach's directive or dictate. The trainee must provide quality feedback, working with the coach to reach for excellent training effect.

8. **Principle of Variety:** In sports training different types of training methods and means should be involved to overcome the problem of boredom or staleness or stagnation.
9. **Principle of Periodisation:** Sports training programmes are developed through a series of training periods or cycles. Usually there are three training period such as Macro cycle, Mesocycle and Micro cycle. Macro cycle is a large or long cycle may be 4 to 12 months or even longer. Mesocycle is an intermediate or medium length cycle may be weekly cycle. Microcycle is small cycle may consists of 3 to 10 days.

TRAINING METHODS

Introduction

It is a fact that apart from other factors, the performance of an individual in any game and sports is mainly dependent upon physical, physiological and psychological factors. Individuals differ in physical abilities, mental abilities, physiological capacities and personality traits. The individuals not only differ from one another but also differ from one ability to another within their own self.

Exercise physiologist, sports scientists, physical educationists and sports training experts have been devising different means and methods to develop these human abilities and capacities. On the basis of various experiments, new methods have been designed to develop physical abilities of the individual. It is said that human capacities and capabilities are unlimited which seems to be true when we see the unthinkable performances of world-class sprinters, middle and long distance runners, throwers, swimmers etc. Physical fitness or conditioning of an individual besides other factors is the basis of such performances.

The decision to carry out a physical fitness programme cannot be taken lightly. It requires a lifelong commitment of time and effort. Exercise must become one of those things that you do without question, like bathing and brushing your teeth. Unless you are convinced of the benefits of fitness and the risks of unfitness, you will not succeed.

Patience is essential. Don't try to do too much too soon and don't quite before you have a chance to experience the rewards of improved fitness/ condition. You can't regain in a few days or weeks but you can get it back if you go for systematic training with appropriate training method (s).

VARIOUS SPORTS TRAINING METHODS

The basic components of physical fitness such as endurance, strength, speed and flexibility can be developed through different training methods that are described briefly as under but one must also know about the basics of related factors/elements.

- Continuous Training Method
- Interval Training Methods
- Repetition Method
- Competitive and Trials Methods
- Circuit Training Method
- Fartlek Training Method
- Weight Training Means/Method
- Plyometric Training Means/Method

Endurance

The objective of endurance training is to develop the energy production system(s) to meet the demands of the event. Endurance can be developed *using continuous and interval running.* It can be discussed as follows :

Anaerobic Endurance: Anaerobic means 'without oxygen'. During anaerobic work, involving maximum effort, the body is working so hard that the demands for oxygen and fuel go above the rate of supply and the muscles have to rely on the stored reserves of fuel. In this case waste products gather, the main one being lactic acid. The muscles, being hungry of oxygen, take the body into a state known as oxygen debt. The body's stored fuel soon runs out and activity ceases - painfully. Activity will not be resumed until the lactic acid is removed and the oxygen debt repaid. Fortunately the body can resume limited activity after even only a small amount of the oxygen debt has been repaid. Since lactic acid is produced the correct term for this pathway is lactic anaerobic energy pathway. The alactic anaerobic pathway is the one in which the body is working anaerobically but without the production of lactic acid. This pathway can exist only so long as the fuel actually stored in the muscle lasts, approximately 4 seconds at maximum effort.

Using repetition methods of relatively high intensity work with limited recovery can develop anaerobic endurance.

Aerobic Endurance: A sound basis of aerobic endurance is fundamental for all events. Aerobic means 'with oxygen'. During aerobic work the body is working at a level that the demands for oxygen and fuel can be met by the body's intake. The only waste products formed are carbon dioxide and water. These are removed as sweat and by breathing out.

Aerobic endurance is developed through the use of Continuous Running Training method (duration runs) to improve maximum oxygen uptake (VO_2 max) and Interval training to improve the heart as a muscular pump.

This can be achieved through different aerobic activities or exercises details of which are given later in this section.

Speed Endurance: Speed endurance is used to develop the co-ordination of muscle contraction in the climate of endurance. Repetition methods are used with a high number of sets, low number of repetitions per set and intensity greater than 85% with distances covered from 60% to 120% of racing distance. Competition and time trials can be used in the development of speed endurance.

Strength Endurance: Strength endurance is used to develop the athlete's capacity to maintain the quality of their muscles' contractile force in a climate of endurance. All athletes need to develop a basic level of strength endurance. Examples of activities to develop strength endurance are weight training, circuit training, Fartlek, running, hill running etc.

1. Continuous Training Method

Dr. Ernst Van Aaken, a German physician and coach, is credited with introducing and popularizing this system of training. Dr. Van Aaken's work in this area started in 1920's but received widespread support later. Continuous training became extremely popular during the latter part of the 1960 years. Continuous training, as the name implies, involves continuous activity, without rest intervals. This has varied from high intensity, continuous activity of moderate duration to low-intensity activity of an extended duration, i.e. long, slow distance, or 'LSD', training. The long-distance runner maintains a pace that is just below his racing pace, although this will depend on the competition distance and the distance of the training runs. This has been a very effective way of training endurance athletes without requiring high levels of work that are stressful and uncomfortable for the athlete. One advantage of this -type of training for the competitive runner is the constant pace at near-competition levels. Running at an even pace during a race appears to be the most efficient way, physiologically, to attain the runner's best time. Therefore, this type of training greatly aids the runner in preparing himself for actual competition. It is suggested by the sports training experts that slower-paced variations, such as LSD or Fartlek, be introduced periodically, e.g. twice per week, to give the athlete some relief from the exhaustive, high-intensity, continuous training.

LSD training is probably the most widely used form of endurance conditioning for the jogger who wants to stay in condition for health-related purposes, the athlete who participates in team sports and endurance-trains for general conditioning, and the athlete who wants to maintain his endurance conditioning during the off-season. This appears to be an excellent approach to general endurance conditioning, since it has been shown to be effective and can be performed at a comfortable level of work. For the middle-aged, or older, individual who is attempting to attain or maintain an acceptable level of physical fitness, this is also the most judicious way to train from a medical viewpoint. Vigorous exercise in the older individual is potentially dangerous and burst-types of activity should not be encouraged.

2. Interval Training Methods

Woldemar Gerschler a professor at the University of Freiburg in Germany and his athletes worked closely with Dr. Hans Reindell, a physiologist, and developed Interval Training Methods.

Gerschler's great contribution was his understanding of the importance of cardiovascular conditioning and his devising a training scheme that would maximize cardiovascular fitness. That is, he realized that strong legs alone do not make a great runner. He sought a system that would increase the heart's stroke volume, and hence its ability to deliver blood and oxygen to the legs. With Reindell's help, he devised interval training-relatively fast runs over relatively short distances repeated a number of times.

The name of the system comes from the "interval," or rest period, between the fast runs. Gerschler and Reindell considered this the most important part of the workout, and they controlled it carefully. Believing that the heart adapted and grew stronger during the interval, they would not allow runners to begin the next repeat until their pulse rate had returned to 120 beats per minute. If this did not occur within 90 seconds of the end of the previous repeat, the workout was too difficult and had to be adjusted. Otherwise, the heart would be overworked, leading to fatigue and exhaustion, rather than to the desired training effect.

Interval training involves alternating short bursts of intense activity with what is called active recovery, which is typically a less-intense form of the original activity.

The Purposes of Interval Training: The purposes of interval training are to:

- Improve anaerobic performance, hence speed.
- Adapt the body to racing conditions, including race pace and high levels of lactate in the muscles.
- Accomplish more overall work with less physiological strain in comparison with continuous running training method.

There are three types of interval training, all of which require the runner to run at or above race pace for a given time or distance. The first type, sustains bursts of speed during continuous running. The runner increases from a slower pace up to race pace for a fixed distance of time. After the time or distance has been reached, the runner slows back to the previous training pace. These bouts are repeated at regular intervals throughout the run. The second type .of interval, repeats, are simply repeat runs at or above race pace for a given distance or time. These intervals vary in distance and speed and may even include hill work. The third type of interval, formal intervals, is run on the track at a given distance with a specific goal time.

The Advantages of Intervals: Interval training utilizes the body's two energy-producing systems: the aerobic and the anaerobic. The aerobic system is the one that allows you to walk or run for several miles, that uses oxygen to convert carbohydrates from various sources throughout the body into energy. The anaerobic system, on the other hand, draws energy from carbohydrates (in the form of glycogen) stored in the muscles for short bursts of activity such as sprinting, jumping or lifting heavy objects. This system does not require oxygen, nor does it provide enough energy for more than the briefest of activities. And its byproduct, lactic acid, is responsible for that achy, burning sensation in your muscles that you feel after, say, running up several flights of stairs.

Interval Basics: Interval training allows you to enjoy the benefits of anaerobic activities without having to endure those burning muscles. In its most basic form, interval training might involve walking for two minutes, running for two, and alternating this pattern throughout the duration of a workout. The intensity (or lack thereof) of each interval is up to how you feel and what you are trying to achieve. The same is true for the length of each interval. For example, if it is your habit to walk 2 miles per day in 30 minutes, you can easily increase the intensity of your walk (as well as up its calorie-burning potential) by picking up the pace every few minutes and then returning to your usual speed. A great trick is to tell yourself that you'll run a particular distance, from the blue car to the green house on the corner, for example, and then walk from the green house to the next telephone pole.

When you first start interval training, each interval can be a negotiation with yourself depending on how strong or energetic you happen to feel during that particular workout. This helps to break up the boredom that often comes from doing the same thing day after day.

Before undertaking interval training a few simple rules should be understood:

- Undertake a period of continuous running before starting interval running.
- Consider the various elements of the session and ensure that they are within the scope of the athlete/ trainee.
- The length of longer work interval gives a better effect.
- The pace should be comfortable raising the athlete's heart rate to the required % of MHR.
- The number of repititions should reflect the condition and age of the athlete/trainee.
- The active rest interval should enable the athlete to bring the heart rate down to near 100-110 bpm.
- Improvements can be made by changing any of the above variables, however the coach should change only one variable at a time.
- All changes should be gradual in nature and take place over a period of time.
- Ensure the surface to be run on is flat and even. Normally the interval train-ing is done on track although it can be done on good quality grass playing fields. Roads are not a suitable surface.

3. Repetition Method

This may be regarded as exercises which correspond in part to the requirements of competition being repeatedly performed during a training session. The intensity characteristics (movement parameters, frequency, velocity) depend on the actual level of performance or aim and objectives of the training year. Breaks should be provided for complete recovery as far as possible.

4. Competitive and Trial Methods

Endurance capacity for a particular event should be developed entirely by means of competitions and trials. This means that the athlete concentrates on a competitive distance. The factors have to be adjusted in a way that the physiological and psychological effects as well as frequency and technique correspond ideally with the competitive conditions. Tactics and general conditions have to be trained as well.

Note: No direct ranking should be associated with the subdivision of the most import methods such as Continuous/Duration Method, Interval and Trial Methods. It is, as a rule, of endurance if one method or only one variant is exclusively applied as every method and any single variant has specific physiological, biochemical, and psychological reactions. The complicated and multi-faceted adaptations required can normally be achieved by a skilful combination of the main training methods and their variants. The application of methods and their respective roles are determined first and foremost by the requirements of the competitive event as by the actual aim and objectives of the endurance training period. Individual resistance to the stress of training has also to be considered along with the specific tasks to be tackled during single training session.

5. Circuit Traing Method

Circuit training method, was developed by *R.E.Morgan and G.T. Adamson in 1953 at the University of Leeds, England*. This type of conditioning involves almost all of the training factors. Circuit training can be designed to develop strength, power, muscular endurance, speed, agility and neuromuscular coordination, flexibility, and cardiovascular endurance.

Circuit training is formal type of training in which an athlete goes through a series of selected exercises or activates that are performed in sequence or in a circuit. Circuits can be set up inside gymnasiums, exercise rooms, or outside on courts and fields. There are usually six to ten stations in a circuit. The athlete performs a specific exercise at each station and then goes to the next station. The idea is to progress through the circuit as rapidly as possible, attempting to improve either by decreasing the total time it takes to complete the circuit or by increasing the amount of work done at each station, or both. The stations are distributed throughout the area earmarked to circuit training. The greater the distance between stations, the greater the degree of cardiovascular conditioning as the individual runs from one station to the next.

Advantages of Circuit Training Method: Circuit training method offers a number of unique advantages, which are as under:

1. It combines a number of different components of training, thus total fitness is emphasized.
2. It provides an interesting training environment for the athlete, and there are established times and levels to motivate the athlete to continue improving.
3. The circuit can be modified to fit the needs of anyone group or individual.
4. It can be adapted within the time constraints of the individual.
5. It can accommodate large groups of individuals at a relatively low expense.
6. In circuit training progression in all activities is assured.

Circuit training is an excellent way to simultaneously improve mobility and build strength and stamina. The circuit-training format utilizes a group of 6 to 10 strength exercises that are completed one after another exercise. Each exercise is performed for a specified number of repetitions or for a given time period before moving on to the next exercise. The exercises within each circuit are separated by brief, timed rest intervals, and each circuit is divided by a longer rest period. The total number of circuits performed during a training session may differ from two to six depending on your training level (beginner, intermediate, or advanced), your period of training (preparation or competition) and your training objective.

Planning of Circuit Training Method: Identify the possible exercises that can be performed with the available equipment. Identify on paper 3 to 4 circuits of 6 to 10 exercise. In each circuit try to ensure that no two consecutive exercises exercise the same muscle group. e.g. do not have press ups followed by pull ups. It is important to warm up with easy jogging and stretching exercises and to repeat this as a warm down after the session.

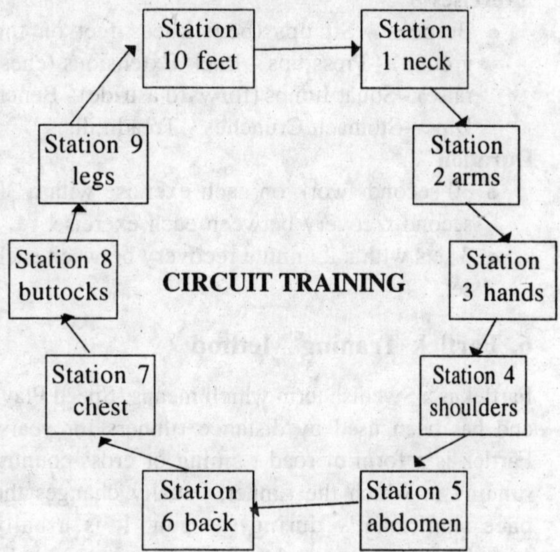

Arrangement of an exercise circuit, Ten exercises of a general nature are performed, with each exercise designed for a different group of muscles. After completing an exercise at one station, the exerciser performs the next exercise in the circuit.

Exercises

The following are some examples of circuit exercises :

- Arm
  - Press ups, Bench dips, Pull ups
  - Abdominals
  - Sit ups (lower abdominals), Stomach crunch (upper abdominals)
- Lower Back
  - Back extension chest raise
- Legs
  - Squat jumps, Compass jumps, Astride jumps, Step ups

- Arms and legs
  - Burpees, Treadmills, Squat thrusts, Skipping

Example Session

Exercises

- Press ups - Sit ups (bent knees feet on the ground) - Back Extensions (chest raise) - Squat Jumps (forward astride) - Stomach Crunches - Treadmills

Exercises-8

- Burpees - Sit ups (bent knees feet on the ground) - Press ups - Back Extensions (chest raise) - Squat Jumps (forward astride) - Bench Dips - Stomach Crunches - Treadmills.

Duration

- 30 seconds work on each exercise with a 30 second recovery between each exercise.
- 3 sets with a 2 minute recovery between each set.

6. Fartlek Traning Method

Fartlek is a Swedish term which means 'Speed Play' and has been used by distance runners for years. Fartlek is a form of road running or cross-country running in which the runner, usually changes the pace significantly during the run. It is usually regarded as an advanced training technique, for the experienced runner who has been using interval training to develop speed and to raise the anaerobic threshold. However, the 'average' runner can also benefit from a simplified form of Fartlek training, to develop self-awareness and to introduce variety into the training programme.

Fartlek is similar to interval training in that short fast runs alternate with slow running or jogging recovery intervals. However, in Fartlek the running is done on the road or on parkland or bush tracks. There is no predetermined schedule to follow, but instead the athlete will set her/his own interval lengths and pace in response to their own feeling of the workload. An advantage of Fartlek is that the athlete can concentrate on feeling the pace and their physical response to it, thereby developing self-awareness and pace judgment skills. Also the athlete is free to experiment with pace and endurance, and to experience changes of pace.

It is primarily a technique for advanced runners because it requires 'honesty' to put in a demanding workload, and also 'maturity' to not overdo the pace or length of the intervals. With these qualities, Fartlek makes for an excellent component of a distance runners training programme.

A 'mild' form of Fartlek can also be of benefit to the '*average runner*'. Particularly the road runner who normally trains over a variety of distance, at a fairly constant pace, and who may have done no or little specific speed training.

You can use this approach to develop more self-awareness, by concentrating on what you are feeling while running at the different paces. How fast a pace can you attain before your regular, easy breathing begins to be laboured? After slowing down, how long before your breathing and other responses return to normal? What happens to your stride length as you increase speed?

Fartlek for Games Players: For games players, the session should not just use running, but also jogging and walking to fit in with the demands of the sport. After all, no football player actually runs for the whole 90 minutes of a match, the pace is varied. Similarly, the direction of work should not always be straight ahead. This may be important for the track runner who has to cover the ground as quickly as possible in one direction, but the games player has to go forwards, backwards and from side to side. This must all be taken into account if the training session is going to copy accurately the pattern experienced in a match. Remember, if you are a games player, you are not training to be a better sprinter, you are training to be better at your game. Therefore, sprinting should not just take the form of back and forth shuttles but should make you change direction. This is where the imaginative element comes into play.

7. Weight Training Method/Mean

Weight training is doing exercise, using resistance (normally weights) to build muscle strength and endurance. In weight training one can use weights like Dumbbells, Bar Bells, Pulley Machines or simply one's own body weight as resistance.

Equipments in Weight Training: Various equipments have been used in weight training. The most popular are dumbbells. With proper technique most of the muscles in the body can be strengthened with the use of dumbbells. Advantage of dumbbells is the cheap, convenient and can be used in a small area.

Pulley Machines: Pulley Machines have revolutionarised weight training. Though they are bulky and one has to visit a gymnasium for a wide variety of pulley exercises the advantages are fabulous. The pulley system is the least injurious of the weight training methods. There are very few compressive stresses on the joints and the machines work on distraction principles.

Use of springs was very popular in the past. The variety of chest expanders, grip strengtheners and popular brands like Bull worker, provided isometric exercises. Isometrics were very popular in the past. Studies have shown that isometric exercises though very good for strength build up but can raise the blood pressure and proved to be hazardous.

Hydraulic Machines for weight training are used in sophisticated gymnasiums. Here the injury levels are very minimum, even when one is over training certain groups of muscles are using these for power building. Hydraulic machines are very useful because antagonistic muscles can be exercised on the same apparatus for example the machine that exercises the biceps muscles, also exercises the triceps. The only disadvantage of hydraulic is that it is very expensive.

Weight Training can also be performed with sandbags, weight cuffs and elastic bands, which are very portable and convenient outdoors.

Strength training can also be done using one's own body weight which is simple and convenient but over weight persons can cause injuries to their muscles and joints due to over loading by their own excess body weight.

Precautions: When one is performing any kind of weight training, one needs warm up and stretch the muscles which would be involved in the strength training. Always begin with lightweights and work towards higher weights. Cool down and stretch your muscles after the workout. If heavy weights are used, at least 48 hours rest is recommended between two workout sessions to give adequate rest to the building muscle.

Ten Golden Rules of Weight Training

1. Concentrate on the muscles while exercising. Focus your full mental awareness on the muscle group, which is being exercised.
2. Maintain a good rhythm during exercise. Lift slowly 2 seconds for the lift (Positive stroke) and 4 seconds for getting back to start position (negative stroke).
3. Knees and elbows should be soft during most exercises, which means that the knee and elbow joints are never fully extended to protect them from injury.
4. Exhale during the positive stroke or exertion and inhale during negative stroke.
5. Start light and then work your way up. Always begin with smaller weight.
6. Start with larger muscles and then work the smaller ones. Bench press before curls.
7. Rest between sets for 30 to 60 seconds and then begin the new set.
8. Rest for 48 hours between workouts to help muscles recover.
9. Take professional help to chalk out your programme and to teach you the correct technique.
10. Warm up and stretch before the workout and cool down after weight training.

Better performances can be the product of a number of factors. This product is primarily the outcome of efficient technique, the progression of speed and the growing competitive attitude on a sound basis of general endurance, all round strength and general mobility. The development of all round strength is best achieved via circuit training and then progressing this through strength training. Weight training is the most widely used and popular method of increasing strength.

Which Weight Training Exercises

The exercise must be specific to the type of strength required, and is therefore related to the particular demands of the event (specificity). The coach should have knowledge of the predominant types of muscular activity associated with the particular event, the movement pattern involved and the type of strength required. Exercises should be identified that will produce the desired development. Although specificity is important, it is necessary in every schedule to include exercises of a general nature - e.g. Power Clean, Bench Press, Back Squats, Sit Ups, Shoulder Press, Chest Press, Lat Pull downs, Lower Back Extensions, Triceps Press, Calf Raise, Bicep Curls, Leg Curls, Leg Extension, etc.

These general exercises give a balanced development, and provide a strong base upon which highly specific exercise can be built.

Amount of Weight (Volume)

The amount of weight to be used should be based on a percentage of the maximum amount of weight that can be lifted one time, generally referred to as one repetition maximum (lRM). The maximum number of repetitions performed before fatigue prohibits the completion of an additional repetition is a function of the weight used, referred to as repetition maximum (RM), and reflects the intensity of the exercise. A weight load that produces fatigue on the third repetition is termed a three repetition maximum (3RM) and corresponds to approximately 85% of the weight that could be lifted for 1RM.

Number of Repetitions

The number of repetitions performed to fatigue is an important consideration in designing a strength training programme. The greatest strength gains appear to result from working with 4-6RM. Increasing this to 12-20RM favours the increase in muscle endurance and mass.

One set of 8-12RM performed 3 days a week is a typical strength-training programme. The optimal number of sets of an exercise to develop muscle strength remains controversial. In a number of studies comparing multiple set programmes to produce greater strength gains than a single set, the majority of studies indicate that there is not a significant difference.

Handling heavy weights in the pursuit of strength will require a recovery of 3-5 minutes between sets, but only minimum recovery should be taken if strength endurance is the aim. The majority of athletic events are fast and dynamic, and therefore this quality must be reflected in the athlete's strength work.

Frequency of Training

This is really linked with recovery since the body must be allowed to recover from the strenuous demands of strength training. As a 'rule of thumb' 48 hours should elapse between sessions. If training strenuously, any athlete will find it extremely difficult to maintain the same level of lifting at each session, and the total weight lifted in each session would be better to be varied (e.g. a high, low and medium volume session) each week.

Safety in the Weight Training Room

Strength training is safe when properly supervised and controlled. The coach or teacher should make sure that their athletes are fully aware of the safety rules applying to the weight training room(s) they use. Weight training requires supervision to ensure sound technique in pursuit of safety and efficiency.

STRENGTH DEVELOPMENT

The common definition of Strength is *the ability to exert a force against a resistance.* The strength needed for a sprinter to explode from the blocks is different to the strength needed by a weight lifter to lift a 200 kg barbell. Therefore, it implies that there are different types of strength.

Types of Strength

The types of strength are:

- Maximum strength: *the greatest force that is possible to over come a resistance in a single maximum contraction.*
- Explosive strength: *the ability to overcome a resistance with a fast contractions.*
- Strength endurance: *the ability to express force over a longer period of time.*

Muscles Strength

A muscle will only strengthen, when it is worked beyond its normal operation, it is overloaded. Overload can be progressed by increasing the:

- Number of repetitions of an exercise.
- Number of sets of the exercise.
- Intensity - reduced recovery time.

Development of Strength

- ❑ Maximum strength can be developed with
  - Weight training
- ❑ Explosive strength can be developed with
  - Conditioning exercises
  - Medicine ball exercises
  - Plyometric exercises
  - Weight training
- ❑ Strength endurance can be developed with
  - Circuit training
  - Dumbbell exercise
  - Weight training
  - Hill running

Development of Maximum Strength

It is well known fact that weight training is the key factor in almost all sports and physical activities. This training method is frequently used to condition the athletes in general and to build muscle strength and endurance in particular. Keeping in mind the importance of this training method in various sports, an attempt has been made to describe briefly the different aspects of weight training in this section.

Development of Explosive Strength

(*i*) Medicine Ball Exercises: The ability to generate strength and power is a very important component for success in many sports, particularly in those involving explosive movements. Medicine ball training, in combination with a programme of weight training and circuit training, can be used to develop strength and power. Certain medicine ball exercises can also be used as part of a plyometric training programme to develop explosive movements. Medicine ball training is appropriate to all levels of ability, age, development and sport. To be most effective the programme should contain

exercises that match the pattern of movements of the sport.

(*ii*) Ploymetrics Training Means/method

Plyometrics: Speed and strength are integral components of fitness found in varying degrees in virtually all athletic sporting movements. Simply put the combination of speed and strength is power. For many years coaches and athletes have sought to improve power in order to enhance performance. Throughout this century and no doubt long before, jumping, bounding and hopping exercises have been used in various ways to enhance athletic performance. *In recent years this distinct method of training for power or explosiveness has been termed plyometrics.* Whatever the origins of the word the term is used to describe the method of training which seeks to enhance the explosive reaction of the individual through powerful muscular contractions as a result of rapid eccentric contractions.

Plyometric Exercises

The following are examples of lower body and upper body plyometric exercises.

Leg Ploymetrics

Bounds

How to Perform the Drill

- Jog into the start of the exercise.
- Push off with your left foot and bring the leg forward, with the knee bent and the thigh parallel to the ground.
- At the same time, reach forward with your right arm. As the left leg comes through, the right leg extends back and remains extended for the duration of the push-off.
- Hold this extended stride for a brief time, then land on your left foot.
- The right leg then drives through to a forward bent position, the left arm reaches forward, and the left leg extends backward.
- Make each stride long, and try to cover as much distance as possible.
- You should land on the sole of the foot (flat footed), allowing energy to be stored by the elastic components of the leg muscles, and immediately take off again.
- Keep the foot touch down time to the shortest time possible.

How Much

- One to three sets over 30 to 40 metres.
- Allow a full recovery between each set.
- Quality of bounding is far more important than quantity.

Hurdle Hopping

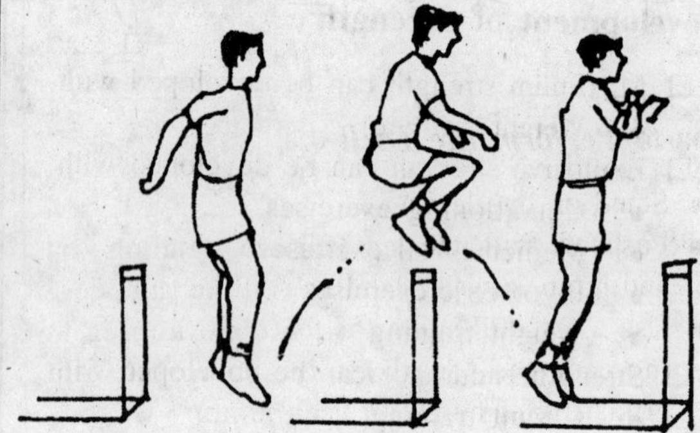

How to Perform the Drill

- Jump forward over the barriers with your feet together.
- The movement should come from your hips and knees.
- Keep your body vertical and straight, and do not let your knees move apart or to either side.
- Tuck both knees to your chest.
- Use a double swing to maintain balance and gain height.
- You should land on the balls of the feet, allowing energy to be stored by the elastic components of the leg muscles, and immediately take off again.
- Keep the feet touch down time between hurdles to the shortest time possible.

How Much

- One to three sets using 6 to 8 hurdles.
- Allow a full recovery between each set.
- Hurdles should set up in arrow, spaced according to ability.
- The height of the hurdles should be in the region of 12 and 36 inches high.
- Quality of hurdle hopping is far more important than quantity.

Single Leg Hopping

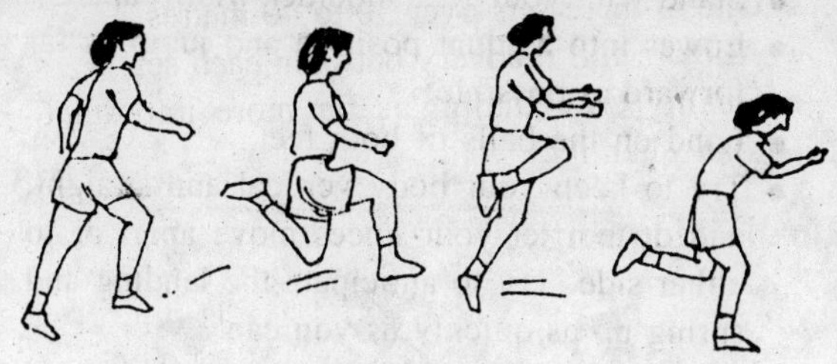

How to Perform the Drill

- Stand on one leg.
- Push off with the leg you are standing on and jump forward, landing on the same leg.
- Use a forceful swing of the opposite leg to increase the length of the jump but aim primarily for height of each jump.
- You should land on the ball of the foot allowing energy to be stored by the elastic components of the leg muscles, and immediately take off again.
- Keep the foot touch down time to the shortest time possible.
- Try to keep your body vertical and straight.
- Perform this drill on both legs.
- Beginners will use a straighter leg action whereas advanced athletes should try to pull the heel towards the buttocks during the jump.

How Much

- One to three sets over 30 to 40 metres.
- Allow a full recovery between each set.
- Quality of bounding is far more important than quality.

Box Jumps

How to Perform the Drill

- Assume a deep squat position with your feet shoulder width apart at the end of the row of boxes.
- Keep your hands on your hips or behind your head.
- Jump onto the box, landing softly in a squat position on the balls of the feet.
- Maintaining the squat position, jump off the box onto the ground, landing softly in a squat position on the balls of the feet.
- Jump onto the next box and so on.
- Keep the feet touch down time on the ground the shortest time possible.

How Much

- One to three sets using 6 to 8 boxes.
- Allow a full recovery between each set.
- The height of the box should be in the region of 30-80 cm.
- Quality of box jumping is far more important than quantity.

Depth Jumps

How to Perform the Drill

- Stand on the box with your toes close to the front edge.
- Step from the box and drop to land on then balls of both feet.
- Try to anticipate the landing and spring up as quickly as you can.
- Keep the feet touch down time on the ground in the shortest time possible.

How Much

- One to three sets using 6 to 8 boxes.
- Allow a full recovery between each set.
- The height of the box should be in the region of 30-80 cm.
- Quality of depth jumping is far more important than quantity.

Tuck Jumps

How to Perform the Drill

- Begin in a standing position.
- Jump up, grabbing both knees as they come up your chest.
- Return to the starting position landing on the balls of the feet.
- Try to anticipate the landing and spring up as quickly as you can.
- Keep the feet touch down time on the ground in the shortest time possible.

How Much

- 1 to 3 sets.
- Allow a full recovery between each set.
- 5 to 10 repetitions/set.
- Quality of Tuck Jumps is far more important than quantity.

Two legged Hops or Bunny Hops (see below)

How to Perform the Drill

- Stand with your feet shoulder-width -apart.
- Lower into a squat position and jump as far forward as possible.
- Land on the balls of both feet.
- Try to keep your body vertical and straight, and do not let your knees move apart or to either side. Try to anticipate the landing and spring up as quickly as you can.
- Keep the feet touch down time on the ground in the shortest time possible.
- Use quick double-arm swings and keep landings short.

How Much

- 1 to 3 sets.
- Allow a full recovery between each set.
- 5 to 10 repetitions/set.
- Quality of Bunny Hops is far more important than quantity.

ARM PLYOMETRICS

Chest Pass

How to Perform the Drill

- This drill requires a partner.
- Stand facing each other with your feet shoulder width apart and your knees slightly bent.

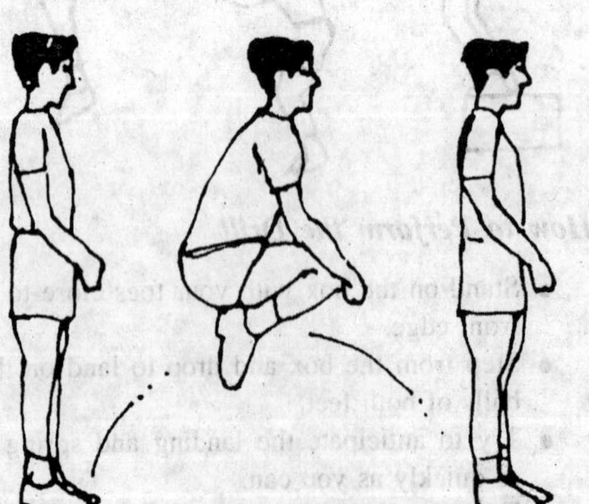

- Begin by holding the medicine ball with both hands at chest level, elbows pointing out.
- Pass the ball to your partner, pushing it off your chest and ending with your arms straight.
- Your partner catches the ball, allows the ball to come to the chest before passing it back to you.
- Try to anticipate the catch and return the ball as quickly as you can.
- Keep the catch time to the shortest time possible.

How Much

- 1 to 3 sets.
- Allow a full recovery between each set
- 10 to 20 repetitions/set.
- Quality of Chest Passes is far more important than quantity.

Incline Push up Depth jump

How to Perform the Drill

- Two mats, three to four inches high, placed shoulder width apart.
- A box high enough to elevate your feet above your shoulders when in a push-up position.
- Face the floor as if you were going to do a push-up, with your feet on the box and your hands between the mats.
- Push off from the ground with your hands and land with one hand on each mat.
- Push off the mats with both hands and catch yourself in the starting position.
- Keep the catch time to the shortest time possible.

How Much

- 1 to 3 sets.
- Allow a full recovery between each set
- 10 to 20 repetitions/set.
- Quality of Push Ups is far more important than quantity.

Power Drop

How to Perform the Drill

- This drill requires a partner.
- Lie supine on the ground with your arms outstretched.
- Your partner stands on the box holding the medicine ball at arm's length.
- Your partner drops the medicine ball into your hands.
- Catch the ball with elbows bent.
- Allow the ball to come towards your chest.
- Extend the arms to propel the ball back to the partner on the box.
- Keep the catch time to the shortest time possible.

How Much

- 1 to 3 sets.
- Allow a full recovery between each set
- 10 to 20 repetitions/set.
- Quality of the vertical toss is far more important than quantity.

Incline Chest Pass

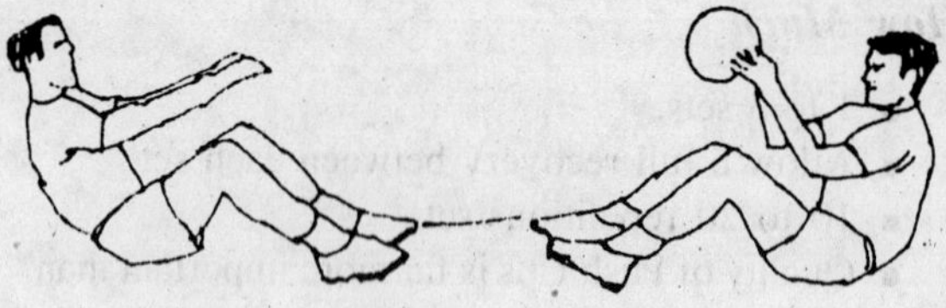

How to Perform the Drill

- Work with a partner and sit facing each other.
- Lean back at a 45 degree angle, keeping your abdominals tight.
- Begin by holding the medicine ball with both hands at chest level, elbows pointing out.
- Pass the ball to your partner, pushing it off your chest and ending with your arms straight.
- Your partner catches the ball, allows the ball to come to the chest before passing it back to you . Try to anticipate the catch and return the ball as quickly as you can.
- Keep the catch time to the shortest time possible.

How Much

l 1 to 3 sets.
l Allow a full recovery between each set.
l 10 to 20 repetitions/set.
l Quality of Chest Passes is far more important than quantity.

Vertical Toss

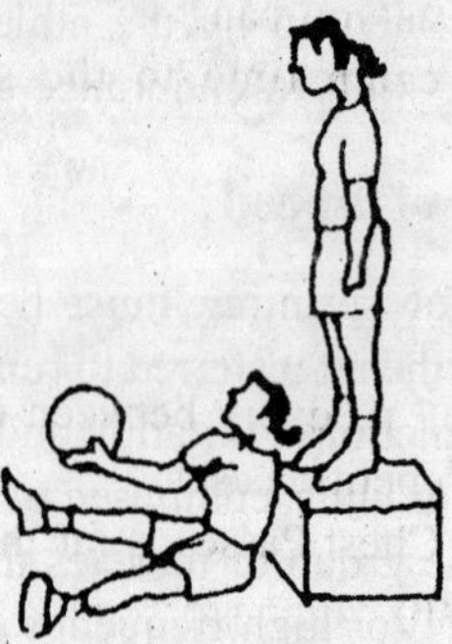

How to Perform the Drill

- This drill requires a partner.
- Sit in front of the box with your back to it, legs spread apart and straight.
- The other person stands on the box holding the medicine ball over you.
- Your partner drops the medicine ball into your hands.
- Catch the ball with elbows bent and toss it back over your head to the partner on the box.
- Keep the catch time to the shortest time possible.

How Much

- 1 to 3 sets
- Allow a full recovery between each set
- 10 to 20 repetitions/set
- Quality of the vertical toss is far more important than quantity.

Warm up

A thorough warm-up is essential prior to plyometric training. Attention should be given to jogging, stretching (static and ballistic), striding and general mobility especially about the joints involved in the planned plyometric session. A cooling down should follow each session.

Where to do it and what to wear

For bounding exercises use surfaces such as grass or resilient surfaces. Avoid cement floors because there is no cushioning. Choose well-cushioned shoes that are stable and can absorb some of the inevitable impact. All athletes should undergo general orthopaedic screening before engaging in plyometric training. Particular attention should be given to structural or postural problems that are likely to predispose the athlete to injury.

SPEED DEVELOPMENT

Speed is the quickness of movement of limb, whether this be the legs of a runner or the arm of the shot putter. Speed is an integral part of every sport and can be expressed as anyone of, or combination of, the following:

- Maximum speed
- Explosive strength (power)
- Speed endurance
- Factors influencing speed

Speed is influenced by the athlete's mobility, special strength, strength endurance and technique.

Development of Speed

The technique of sprinting must be rehearsed at slow speeds and then transferred to runs at maximum speed. The stimulation, excitation and correct firing order of the motor units, composed of a motor nerve (Neuron) and the group of muscles that it supplies, makes it possible for high frequency movements to occur. The whole process is not totally clear but the complex coordination and timing of the motor units and muscles most certainly must be rehearsed at high speeds to implant the correct patterns.

Flexibility and a correct warm up will affect stride length and frequency. Stride length can be improved by developing muscular strength, power, strength endurance and running technique. The development of speed is highly specific and to achieve it we should ensure that:

- Flexibility is developed and maintained all year round.
- Strength and speed is developed in parallel.
- Skill development (technique) is pre-learned, rehearsed and perfected before it is done at high-speed levels.
- Speed training is developed by using high velocity for brief intervals. This will ultimately bring into play the correct neuromuscular pathways and energy sources used.

Speed Work

It is important to remember that the improvement of running speed is a complex process, which is controlled by the brain and nervous system. For a runner in order to move more quickly, the leg muscles of course have to contract more quickly, but the brain and nervous system also have to learn to control these faster movements efficiently. If you maintain some form of speed training throughout the year, your muscles and nervous system do not loose the feel of moving fast and the brain will not have to re-learn the proper control patterns at a later date.

In the training week speed work should be carried out after a period of rest or light training. In a training session speed work should be conducted after the warm up and any other training should be of low intensity

Principles of Speed Improvement

The general principles for improved speed are as follows :

- Choose a reasonable goal for your event, and then work on running at velocities which are actually faster than your goal over short work intervals.
- Train at goal pace in order to enhance your neuromuscular coordination, confidence and stamina at your desired speed.
- At first, utilise long recoveries, but as you get fitter and faster shorten the recovery periods between work intervals to make your training more specific and realistic to racing. Also move on to longer work intervals, as you are able.
- Work on your aerobic capacity, conduct some easy pace runs to burn calories and permit recovery from the speed sessions.

- Work on your flexibility to develop a range of movement (range of motion at your hips will effect speed) and assist in the prevention of injury.

Speed Programme

For a number of sports acceleration and speed over a short distance (10-50m), is very important e.g. Football, Basket Ball, Softball, Cricket, Field Hockey, etc. A speed development programme can be framed according to need, level, and training state of the players.

FLEXIBILITY

Flexibility is the ability to perform a joint action through a range of movement. In any movement there are two groups of muscles at work:

1. Protagonistic muscles which cause the movement to take place.
2. Opposing the movement and determining the amount of flexibility are the antagonistic muscles.

Flexibility Training

The objective of flexibility training is to improve the range of stretch of the antagonistic muscles.

Flexibility plays an important part in the preparation of athletes by developing a range of movement to allow technical development and assisting in the prevention of injury.

Flexibility Exercises

The various techniques of stretching may be grouped as Static, Ballistic and Assisted. In both Static and Ballistic exercises the athlete is in control of the movements. In assisted the movement is controlled by an external force that is usually a partner.

PREPARING FOR COMPETITION

Build up Competition

These competitions are within the process of sports training i.e. these are part and parcel of sports training. These competitions are used for achieving top form during the competition period. These however, are also used to develop or stabilize a performance factor or factors (e.g) technical skill, tactics, conditions etc. These can also be used to assess the effect of training. Build up competitions are of high importance for the development of performance capacity and top form. These can also be had during the preparatory period.

Main Competition

This is the most important competition for a sportsman in a year or in a definite time period. Olympics, continental championship, world cup etc, fall in this category. Main competition is outside the sports training. Training is done in order to achieve top form in the main competition.

COMPETITION FREQUENCY

Participation in competitions is indispensable for the improvement of sports performance. The problem however, is to determine the optimum competition frequency as too many competitions have a negative effect on performances. Besides, it can give rise to the state of over load. The optimum frequency of competitions depends on several factors of training state.

In the performance training stage higher number of competitions is possible. In sports in which speed and explosive strength are primary determinants of performances, higher competition frequency is possible during the competition period. In these sports 1-2 competition in a weak is normal in competition period. But in endurance and strength endurance sports competition frequency is much lower. In these sports we find that the normal gap between two competitions is 1-2 weeks.

The frequency of competitions is markedly determined by individual competitors load tolerance. Exceptionally high competition frequency of famous long distance Ron Clarke (21 competitions in 56 days) and Henry Rono (more than 30 competitions in seven months) is well known and is a part of history. But such high competition frequency is only possible after a hard training for several years. But it can have negative effect on performance as was in the case of Henry Rona by the time he participated in his 30th competition.

It is risky to have too many competitions, but on the other hand too less competition will result in slower development of performance. It is therefore necessary to strive for optimum number of competitions in a year. In addition to this, the following suggestions are given.

One must participate in a competition only when he is adequately prepared for it physically, mentally, technically and tactically.

Competition should be in ascending order of difficulty.

Competition against a stronger or equally strong adversary or adversaries should not be avoided. The number and density of such competion, however, should be determined very carefully.

Competition density should be such that sufficient physical and psychic recovery is ensured. It should also ensure minimum disruption of training process, thereby ensuring optimum training volume during the competition period.

A special meso - cycle should be devoted exclusively for preparing a sportsman for the main competition.

Competition calendar should be such that it ensures optimum development of performance and achievement of top form in the main competition.

Psychological Preparation

Psychological preparation must start by giving important information about the competition to the sportsman. This enables the sportsman to be mentally prepared for the competition. Information about the following should be given to the sportsman.

Performance to be achieved.

Importance of the competition

Time and date of competition.

External conditions expected during competition (e.g) ground, weather, light conditions, audience etc.

Opponents, their performance level, strong and week points etc.

Referees, judges, umpires etc.

Anxiety and psychic symptoms of pre-start state.

Training state and performance of the sportsman himself.

Other information regarding the living conditions, food relevent social and political factors.

The optimum state of readiness for competition depends, to a great extent on the level of confidence.

Sportsman should be taught to use psycho-regulatory procedures.

Psychological preparation must continue as most of the sportsmen tend to get into the pre-start state which according to Ptini (1980) can be of three types i.e. :

(*i*) Optimum readiness
(*ii*) Start fever
(*iii*) Start apathy.

During this period psychological preparation should aim at achieving optimum readiness for the competition.

SPORTS TALENT IDENTIFICATION

The identification of talent through means and methods of sports medicinc, physiology bio-chemistry, however, has not proved to be satisfactory. These sciences are able to determine certain biological parameters (e.g) Vo. 2 muscle fibre distribution. Human performance capacity as a rule is more than the sum of its components and the modern science is not capable of satisfactorily recording and assessing it.

Identification of talent is made more complicated by the fact that it must also take into consideration the possibilities of development of the various performance prerequisites.

The trainability of performance pre-requisites depends basically on heredity and training activity.

The following are the Principles of Talent Identification :

1. Starting point is the structure of future performance : It is future oriented process. The aim is to find and develop talent for high performance several years ahead in the future.

(*i*) Prognosis of sport performance in a sport at a fixed time in the future.

(*ii*) Determination of the structure of prognostic performance.

(*iii*) Determination of the performance capacity and its structure essential to achieve prognostic performance.

2. It is long term process: Sports talent is a product of heredity and environment.

It is now generally believed that by about 13-14 years of age sports talent can be judged fairly accurately.

The process of talent identification therefore must begin in early childhood. It should be spread over a number of years.

The first step aims at locating children who are suitable for sports.

The second step comes after about four years training and aiming at finding children talent for a group of sports.

The third step is after about four years of advanced training stage and aims at identifying talent for a single sport (or) for one (or) two events.

The three steps for talent identification are presented in brief as below :

Step - 1

Aim screening of children for basic training stage.

(*i*) Health and physique.

(*ii*) General physical performance capacity.

(*iii*) Motives, interests, mental capabilities etc.

(*iv*) Interest of parents etc.

Step- 2

After 3 - 4 years of basic training advanced training stage

(*i*) Physique

(*ii*) Motor abilities

(*iii*) Performance

(*iv*) Cognitive, emotional and motivational factors and personality

(*v*) Ability to tolerate load.

Step - 3

High performance training stage

(*i*) Physique

(*ii*) Performance and the potential for performance

(*iii*) Talent indicators

(*iv*) Cognitive, emotional and motivational factors and personality traits.

(*v*) Experimentation by training for a limited period in a sport.

3. A wide range of factors must be considered:

Age chronological and biological

Performance and training stage (present and past)

Nature and duration of training in the past

Motivation, interest and attitude of the child and his parents.

Health

Socio-economical and living conditions

School – college results

4. It should become progressively more specific

The total personality of the child takes its final shape. The initial stages of training talent identification should be general in nature. The effort to spot talent for a specific sport (or) event should be made at a later stage.

5. Less trainable factors should be given more weightage

Most important among the less trainable factors are physique, height, speed, playing ability temperament etc.

While identifying talent in children less trainable factors should be given more weightage.

6. Talent indicators should be considered

Sports physiology can help in correctly identifying talent, completely identified in the laboratories. Talent must be based on performance in sports and physical activities.

(*i*) Performance level.

(*ii*) Rate of increase in performance.

(*iii*) Performance stability.

(*iv*) Ability to increase performance in a series of competitions.

(*v*) Ability to tolerate load.

LONG-TERM TRAINING PROCESS

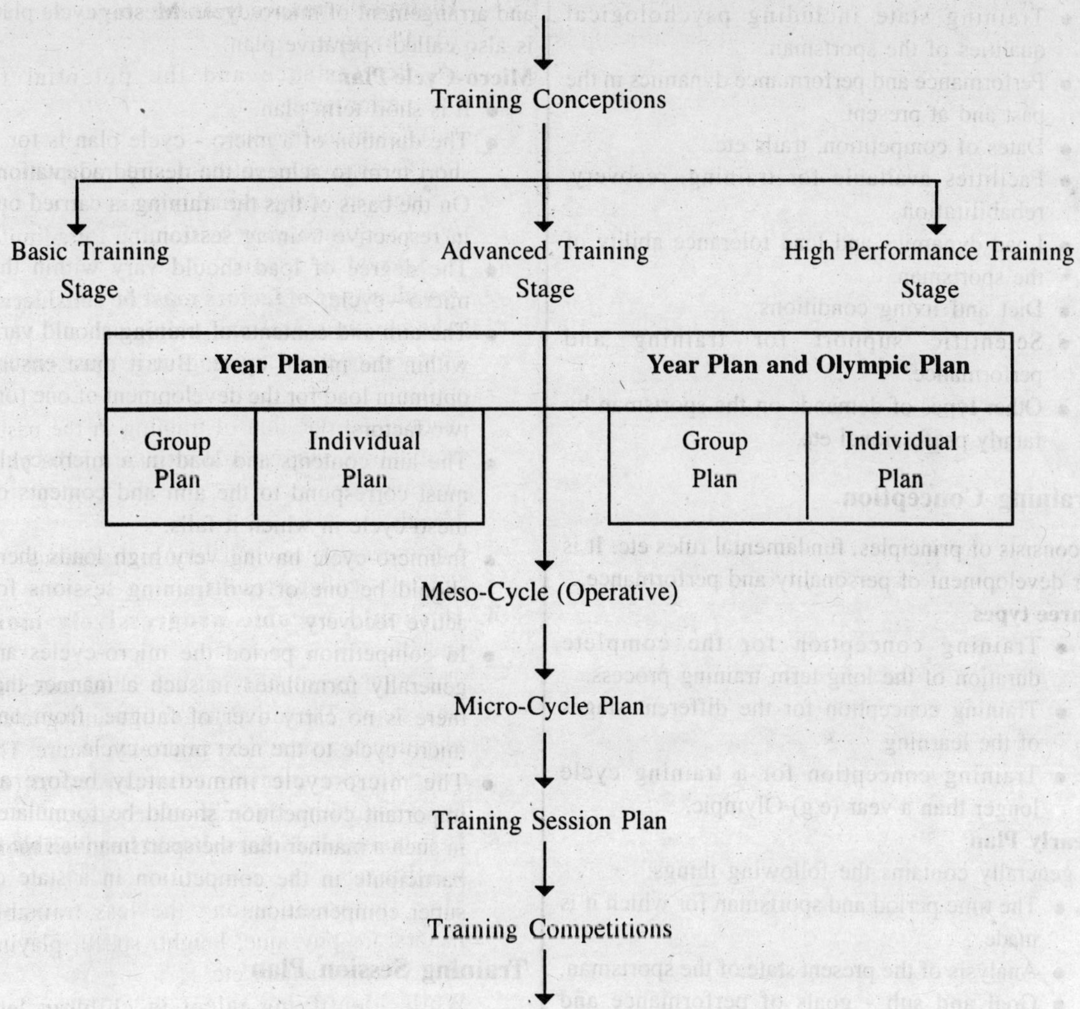

Yearly Plan

It is effective formulation.

The time period and sportsman for which it is made.

Analysis of the present state of the sportsman.

Goal and sub goals of performance and performance factors to be achieved at the end as well as at certain points during the total planned period.

Sequence of the development of performance factors.

Training Plan

It is a dynamic process. A plan when formed and implemented is continuously controlled and modified according to the effects and change in the personality and performance caused by training and other factors, planning, therefore, is an aspect of control and regulation of sports training.

Important Factors

- Time period available for training

- Training state including psychological qualities of the sportsman.
- Performance and performance dynamics in the past and at present.
- Dates of competition, trails etc.
- Facilities available for training, recovery, rebabilitation.
- Load dynamics and load tolerance ability of the sportsman.
- Diet and living conditions.
- Scientific support for training and performance.
- Other types of demands on the sportsman by family professional etc.

Training Conception

It consists of principles, fundamental rules etc. It is for development of personality and performance.

Three types

- Training conception for the complete duration of the long term training process.
- Training conception for the different stages of the learning.
- Training conception for a training cycle longer than a year (e.g) Olympic.

Yearly Plan

It generally contains the following things:

- The time period and sportsman for which it is made.
- Analysis of the present state of the sportsman.
- Goal and sub - goals of performance and performance.
- Factors to be achieved at the end as well as at certain points during the total planned period.
- Information about the training contents, proportions among different training elements, means, load indices (load dynamics) and so on.
- Sequence of the development of performance.
- Arrangement of meso-cycle.
- Dates of competitions, tests etc.
- Other relevant information.

Meso-cycle plan: These plans are made for carrying out training for 3 - 6 weeks. The aim and objectives are achieved through proper formulation and arrangement of micro-cycle. Meso - cycle plan is also called operative plan.

Micro-Cycle Plan:

- It is short term plan.
- The duration of a micro - cycle plan is for a short term to achieve the desired adaptation. On the basis of this the training is carried out in respective training session.
- The degree of load should vary within the micro - cycle.
- The aim and contents of training should vary within the micro- cycle. But it must ensure optimum load for the development of one (or) two factors.
- The aim contents and load in a micro-cycle must correspond to the aim and contents of meso-cycle in which it falls.
- In micro-cycle having very high loads there should be one or two training sessions for active recovery.
- In competition period the micro-cycles are generally formulated in such a manner that there is no carry over of fatigue, from one micro-cycle to the next micro-cycle.
- The micro-cycle immediately before an important competition should be formulated in such a manner that the sportsman is able to participate in the competition in a state of super compensation.

Training Session Plan

Training plans are divided into individual and group plans on the basis of the number of persons for which a plan is based. These plans are of different durations. Individual plans are more common in individual sports. These plans are necessary to ensure optimum development of sportsman. The group plans are more commonly used in team games and as such do not ensure optimum development of each individual.

The use of individual and group plan is primarily determined by the training state of the sportsman. In the initial stages of training, group training plans are generally used to ensure uniform type of training, facilitation training of large number of sportsman. It also helps in identification of talent.

FORMULATION OF A YEAR PLAN

1. **Performance prognosis and determination of performance structure:** This is first step for planning. It is structure determined in order to determine the performance capacity-required to achieve this performance.
2. **Determination of goal and sub-goals:** The goal of training is the performance to be achieved by the end of the year. The goals for the various performance factors also have to be determined.
   - The success of training plan depends heavily on correct analysis of performance at present and in the past.
   - Analysis of training in the past.
   - Present training state;
   - Talent
   - Time period available for training
   - Type of periodisation to be used.
   - Nature of sport and performance capacity
   - Age of sportsman
   - Infra-structure and facilities availability
   - Scientific support available
   - Competitions, their number and density
   - Personal qualities of sportsman and other demands on him by his family profession, living conditions etc.
3. **Determination of periods and arrangement of meso-cycles:** This is done in high performance training stage on the basis of periodisation to be used. The determination of periods and arrangement of meso-cycles results in the bifurcation of aim and contents, in gross form, of the periods and meso - cycles. This is done prior to the beginning of a meso - cycle by making a training and performance assessment of the previous meso - cycle.
4. **Determination of dates of tests, controls, competitions:** The dates of the importance for the competition, are fixed by the competition organisers and as such cannot be changed and have to be adjusted in the plan.
   The dates of tests and controls to check the performance also have to be determined and indicated in plan.
5. **Determination of load dynamic and load indices:** The load dynamic for the whole year has to be planned. This is done in consideration of the goals, sub goals, competition, calendar, periodisation, arrangement of meso-cycles etc. The optimum course of intensity and volume is determined. Planning, therefore, is a dynamic and continuous process.

SOME OTHER USEFUL MATTERS

Principles of Sports Training

Sports training is pedagogical process, based on scientific principles aiming at preparing sports person for higher performances in sports competitions.

Principles of sports training:

1. **Each person is an individual:** Each individual has his or her own particular talent, strength, and weakness. One type of training may not be helpful for all. The sports training programme should be according to one's strength and weakness and according to sports person.
2. **Set reasonable goals:** An athlete's goals should be based on what the athlete can do now (or has done recently). The athlete should move by steps and not by leaps. The purpose should be to attain higher pursuits of excellence without reaching the burnout.
3. **Have a master plan:** Every athlete needs a master plan. The plan sets goal and shows how the athlete will progress. A master plan looks at the total picture and takes the long view. It is like a competitive road map, provides direction and avoids distractions.
4. **Develop good mechanics:** Good performance mechanics should be developed early in an athlete's career. Good mechanics means easier, more effective training and competing. A noticeable characteristic of the world class athlete is a high level of technical skill.

5. **Variety:** A good training plan uses variety of training methods. The more predictable a training programme is, the duller it will be. This trait leads to stateliness in the athlete because challenges of training are decreased. Variety is essential to keep the interest and enthusiasm of athletes.

Rest is important: Rest is one of the most neglected needs of less successful or younger athletes. No rest no gain. Listening to the body and giving quality rest is important for performance enhancement.

List of Officials Required in Volleyball

In Volley Ball Officials required are:

(A) First Referee:

(*i*) Blows whistle during the match.
(*ii*) Gives signal for the service that begins the rally.
(*iii*) Blows whistle in case of foul or ball out of bounds.
(*iv*) Warning any team or member against misconduct or delay.
(*v*) First referee has the power to decide any matter involving the game including any matter not provided for in the rules.
(*vi*) Deciding whether or not the playing area is in good condition.
(*vii*) Performs the toss up for service and court.
(*viii*) Control's the team's warm up.

(B) Second Referee : He is the assistant to the first referee and may replace him or substitute for him and perform his duties in the event the first referee is unable to continue.

(*i*) He checks the player's position in their respective courts.
(*ii*) He supervises the behaviour of the members of each team, seated on the player's bench, and reports any misconduct to the first referee.
(*iii*) He controls the number of time-outs and substitutions.
(*iv*) He can signal other faults, without whistle even if they are not within his range of jurisdiction, but he may not insist on them to the first referee.
(*v*) He blows whistle on faults involving the positions of the team that receives the service.
(*vi*) He blows the whistle on faulty ball position in his side of the court.
(*vii*) He blows whistle with signal in case of penetrations in the opponents court, net touch, centre line cross, illegal attack hit or blocking by back line players and injury of a player.

(C) Scorer:

(*i*) The scorer keeps the score sheet according to the rules, making all recordings to control the game.
(*ii*) He awards the time outs and substitutions granted to each team and notifies the referee.
(*iii*) Records the data for match and teams before the match and secures the signatures of captains, and coaches.
(*iv*) During match, the scorer records the points record by each team and signals the scoreboard corrections.
(*v*) Announces the referees the change of courts as and when required.

(D) Linesmen:

(*i*) The linesmen record faults on the lines assigned to them. They use flags in signalling faults.
(*ii*) They use different signals for different faults like service fault, ball in, ball out nearest to them where the ball lords or the player commits any foul.

Role of Officials in Basketball

In Basketball the officials shall be

(A) Referee:

(*i*) The referee shall inspect and approve all equipments to be used during the game.
(*ii*) He shall recognize and designate other officials.
(*iii*) Checking the players for objects, which are dangerous for other players.
(*iv*) He shall administer a jump ball at the centre circle to start the game.
(*v*) If the officials disagree on any basket converted or not, he shall make the final decision.

(*vi*) He shall be the final authority in case of disputes.

(*vii*) He shall carefully examine the score sheet during, before and after the game.

(B) Umpire:

(*i*) Umpire shall help the referee perform his duties.

(*ii*) He shall be giving decisions on any faults and violations in his half during the game.

(*iii*) He shall consult the referee and inform him regarding any interruptions and act in co-ordination with the referee.

(C) Timekeeper:

(*i*) The timekeeper shall keep record of playing time and time of stoppage of game as provided in the rules.

(*ii*) The timekeeper shall note when each half is to start and shall notify the referee more than three minutes before this time so that he may notify the teams.

(*iii*) The time keeper shall indicate with a very loud signal the expiration of playing time in each half or a period.

(D) Scorer and Assistant Scorer:

(*i*) The scorer shall keep a record of the names and numbers of players who are to start the game and of all substitutes who enter the game.

(*ii*) He shall keep a chronological running summary of points scored and shall record the field goals and the free throws made.

(*iii*) He shall record the personal and technical fouls called on each player and shall notify the referee immediately about 5th foul of an individual player or seven fouls by a team.

(*iv*) He shall record time outs.

(*v*) He shall indicate number of faults committed.

(*vi*) He shall record the substitutions.

(*vii*) The assistant scorer shall operate the scoreboard. His duties shall not counter act or conflict with those of the other table officials.

(E) 30-Second operator: The 30-second operator shall operate the 30-second device (clock) as per the rules. He shall be very careful while restarting the 30-second clock.

Role of Officials in Football

(A) Duties of the referee: 01

(*i*) A referee shall be appointed in each game. His authority and duties granted to him by the laws of the game commence as soon as he enters the field of play.

(*ii*) The referee shall refrain from penalizing in cases where he is satisfied that, by doing so, he would be giving an advantage to the offending team.

(*iii*) Keeps a record of the game, acts as timekeeper and allows the full or agreed time.

(*iv*) The referee shall carry with him a pencil, cards, whistle and a coin on to the fields.

(*v*) A referee shall note down all fouls and infringements.

(*vi*) Signal for recommencement of the game after all stoppages.

(*vii*) A referee shall conduct the game absolutely fair and impartially.

(B) Lines Men: 02 : Line men will be assistants to the referee.

(*i*) They signal to the referee to indicate when the ball is out of play.

(*ii*) Which side is entitled to a corner-kick, goal kick or throw in.

(*iii*) When a substitution is required.

(*iv*) Linesmen shall signal "off side" using flags.

Role and Duties of Officials in Waterpolo

(A) Referees: 02

(*i*) Referees are responsible for controlling the game.

(*ii*) Each referee must carry a whistle with which to start and restart the game and to declare goals, goal throws, corner throws and infringement of the rules.

(*iii*) The referees must refrain from using whistle unnecessarily and apply advantage rules.

(*iv*) If the game has to be stopped, the referee must report his actions to the competent authority.

(B) Goal Judges: 02

(*i*) The Goal Judges must take up position opposite a referee and they must mutually agree upon ends. They stand directly level with the goal line and stay there for the whole game.

(*ii*) Goal Judges shall be responsible to the referee for the correct score of each team at their respective ends.

(*iii*) Goal Judges should exhibit the red flag to indicate to the referee that players are correctly positioned on their respective goal lines.

(C) Time Keepers: 01 or 02 : The time keepers must be fully acquainted with the rules of water polo and each must be provided with a water polo stop watch and a shrill whistle. The duties of timekeeper shall be:

(*i*) To record on the watch the exact periods of actual play and the intervals between periods.

(*ii*) To record the respective periods of exclusion of any player who may be ordered from the water.

(*iii*) To record the periods of continuous possession of the ball by each team.

(*iv*) The time keeper recording the 35 seconds shall reset the clock only when the ball is put into play.

(*v*) A time keeper must signal by whistle the end of each period independently of the referee. The last minute of any game and of an extra time shall be audibly announced.

(*vi*) The time keeper must be near to a referee.

(D) Secretaries: 01 or 02: Duties of the secretaries shall be :

(*i*) To maintain a record of all players, the scores, all major fouls (time, colour and cap number) and to signal the award of a third personal foul to any player by a signal with a red flag and a whistle immediately upon such award.

(*ii*) To control the periods of exclusion of players and to signal permission for reentry upon expiration of their respective periods of exclusion by raising the flag corresponding with the colour of the players cap.

(*iii*) To signal any improper entry.

Preparetion of Training Schedule for the Development of Speed Among Sprinters

A. Development of speed Training:

Reaction Exercises : Reaction-2-3 minutes-Recovery-2-3 minutes Recovery and so on upto a maximum of 10 exercises.

Note: Proper warm up to be performed before the start.

Drills:

(*i*) Starts are repeated maximum 10 times in competition form over 10-30 minutes.

(*ii*) 15 reaction runs at easy to medium speed.

(*iii*) Recovery 2-3 minutes.

(*iv*) For maximum speed.
- 6-8 reaction runs
- Recovery 2-3 minutes.

(*v*) Reaction from resting, sitting, lying position with response from acoustic/ visual signals.

(*vi*) Reaction speed ball games.

(*vii*) Relays.

B. Maximum speed Endurance:

(*i*) Extensive Aerobic Training (30-45 mins.) at aerobic threshold.

(*ii*) Continuous variable runs.
Duration = 25-30 mins.
Method = Fartlek at medium tempo, Heart Rate = 150-160 b/ min.

(*iii*) Maximum load according to interval method (Incomplete recovery) 3 × 5 X 40 m or 4 × 5 × 40 m sprints. Recovery 3 minutes between runs and 8-10 minutes between sets or 30 m flying starts and resistance runs.

- In the development of speed endurance, independent of the athletic type the specialization of event, the distance to improve the performance abilities are 150m, 200m, 300m and 400 m.
- Speed endurance development is through intensive and short programmes.
- For late developed athletes, speed endurance must be developed in range of 80-120 metres.

Process of Double Periodisation in Training of Sprinters of University Level

A sportsman who is undergoing regular training always possesses some sort of sport form but for achieving the desired success he must have the highest possible form, i.e. top form. Periodisation, therefore, is the systematic formulation of sports training for achieving top form in a competition at a definite time.

Double periodisation has 2 macro cycles in a year. In the double periodisation for sprinters the transitional period (active rest period) is kept at the end of the second macro cycle, because in this period of recovery, relaxation becomes necessary after about one year.

The university level sprinters come under the high performance group. Thus, the tendency to use double periodisation increases.

Macro cycle	I			II		
Periods	P	C	P	C	T	
Months	1	2	3	4	5	6
	7	8	9	10	11	12

P = Preparatory Period
C = Competition Period
T = Transition Period

In the double periodisation training of university level sprinters, the number of competitions will me more in number. The duration of macro cycle is considerably shorter.

(*a*) Preparatory Period in 1st Macro cycle Duration = 4-6 months. Means and methods of training = Specific, for example wind sprints, harness running etc.

(*b*) Competition Period in 1st Macro Cycle Duration 1-2 months. Means and Methods of Training = Weight training, Circuit training, Strength endurance etc.

(*c*) Preparatory Period in 2nd Macro Cycle Duration = 2-3 months. Means and Methods of Training: Specific methods e.g., Relay, Resistance Training-mud running, sand running.

(*d*) Competition Period in 2nd Macro Cycle Duration 2-3 months. Means and Methods of Training: Same as for 'b'.

(*e*) Transition Period in 2nd Macro Cycle Duration 3-4 weeks. Means and methods of Training: Fartlek training, swimming, interval training and other fast activities like Basketball, Handball etc.

Methods of Marking of Runway and Sector for Javelin Throw

1. First of all, the direction of throw should be determined.
2. A rope 2M at right angles to the direction of throw should be fixed on the ground and points x and y should be marked on the rope at a distance of 4 pleters in between. Draw Centre point through which the tape must pass when marking the sector lines upto scratch line which is 7cm in thickness.
3. Draw parallel lines from point x and y at right angle to the rope backward forming runways for the event.

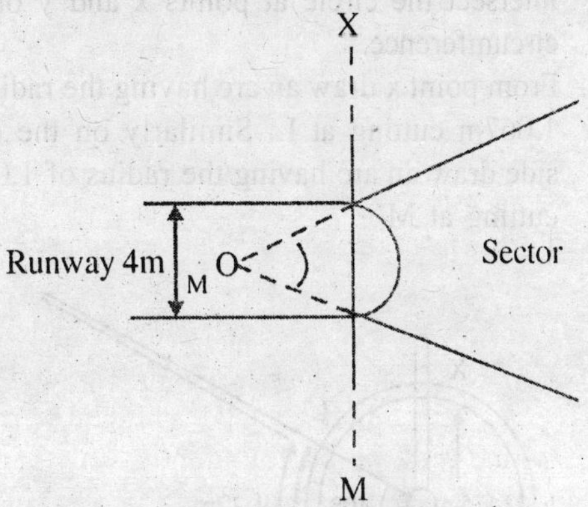

4. From points *x* and *y* draw an arc having raises of 8 metres cutting each other in between the parallel lines at point O. Point O will serve as centre to mark sector lines.
5. From point O, mark an arc cutting parallel lines at x and y. x y arc will serve as take off point for the event. From the central point O, draw lines passing through x and y points forming angle of 29°. Extend the two lines from points x and y, which are perpendicular to runway lines and are 75 cm in length. Their width will also be 7 cm.
6. The peg should be fixed at central point O to make the measurement of all the throws. Readings should be taken at the scratch line.

Fouls Associated with Javelin Throw:

1. Crossing the scratch line in the event of throwing the javelin.

2. A throw will be valid only if the javelin lands in the sector and either flat or on the tip.
3. No competitor should leave the runway unless and until the Javelin has landed on the ground.
4. Non-orthodox styles of throwing are not permitted.
5. The competitor can not touch the runway lines while running in between them.

Methods of Marking of Shot-put Circle

1. Mark a circle having a diameter of 2.135m. Draw the diameter at right angles to the direction of throw. This diameter will intersect the circle at points x and y on the circumference.
2. From point x draw an arc having the radius of 1.067m cutting at L. Similarly on the other side draw an arc having the radius of 1.067m cutting at M.

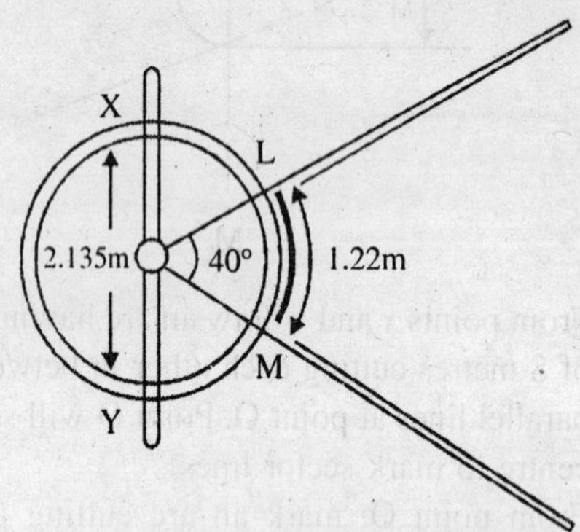

3. See the distance from either end of stop board i.e. L and M to X and Y should be 1.067m.
4. Draw lines from the centre of the circle, passing through points LandM. The lines will form a sector of 45°.
5. The diameter x and y should be extended 75 cm on both sides of the circle. This will form the rear half of the circle.

Fouls associated with shop put event:

1. Touching the area outside the circle after entering.
2. Stepping over or beyond the circle rim during the 'put'.
3. Leaving the circle before the shot has landed in the sector.
4. Shot falling outside the landing sector.
5. 'Throwing' the shot, instead of 'putting' it.
6. Stepping on the stop board in the event of 'putting'.

Methods of Marking of Standard Track

Procedure: Before the track is laid, there should be a thorough knowledge about the length and breadth of the ground. By calculating the area of the ground, we can get an accurate idea whether a Standard Track (400m) can be laid. We can also find out whether the space is available for officials, competitors, spectators, lanes, 100m dash or hurdle races in addition to the main track.

A general formula for calculating the straight or the curve for any track is as follows:

Let 't' be the total length of the track to be laid 's' the length of one straight and 'r' is the radius of the circle of which the curve is a part. In a complete track there are two straights and curves.

So, T = S+S+2 π (Circumference of a circle = p)

Now we want to lay 400m track where one straight (assumed) = 81.20 m.

Here 'T' = 400 m

S = 81.20 m

Putting the values in the formula, we get

400 m = 2 × 81.20 + πr

or 2 πr = 400-162.4

= 237.0m

237.60

Or $r = 2\pi$

237.60 × 7

Or $r = 2\pi$ 22 = 37.80 m.

Now this is running Distance Radius.

The curve radius will be = 3 + 80 - 0.30 m = 37.50 m

Therefore, the athlete running in the first lane keeps 30cm outward from the 1st land of the track.

Length = Straight + 2 x radius of the curves + 2 x width covered by lanes.

= 81.20 + 2 x 37.50 + 2 x 7.32

= 170.84 m (width of lanes = 1.22m)

Breadth = Distance (width) + 2 x width covered by lanes

= 75.0 + 14.64 = 89.64 m.

Thus the area required for the actual 400m track having lane width = 1.22 m and a total of 8 lanes is = 170.84 m by 89.64m.

Marking:

(*a*) Accurate marking along right lines is very essential for a standard track,

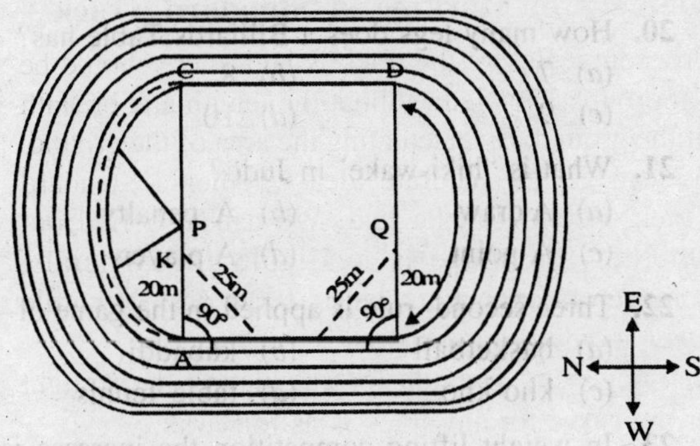

(*b*) Measure and mark a line AB, 81.20 m long.

(*c*) From B measure towards A, 15 m and put in a peg mark S and from B measure towards.

(*d*) Measure 20 m and put Peg 5. Having S as centre take 25m in the tape and draw arcs cutting s 1. Thus B S 1, is a right angle similarly right angle can be obtained at A.

(*e*) From point B extend a rope 75 m passing through Sl towards D. Similarly on the other side also.

(*f*) Check the distance A and B are 75 m. Also check up the distance diagonally between BC and AD. See they are equal.
Thus ABCD, rectangle is formed.

(*g*) Find the centres of lines A and BD 37.50m put in peg P and Q. with P and Q as centres describe two semicircles of 37.50 m radius.

(*h*) See that the steel wire moves freely on the pegs P and Q.

(*i*) Similarly the lanes at curves can also be drawn using Pand Q as centres. Join the curves to form straight lines and the lanes.

Notes:

1. Direction of track should be from north to south.
2. Staggers, hurdles and starting points can be marked on the track using different coloured line powder.
3. Ensure that there is no kink in the steel wire being used for marking.

EXERCISE

1. How many members are there in one team in the game of Rugby?
(*a*) 14 (*b*) 15
(*c*) 16 (*d*) 17

2. Total number of substitutes in a team of Rugby are–
(*a*) 7 (*b*) 8
(*c*) 9 (*d*) 10

3. The apparatus used in women Gymna-stics is–
(*a*) Parallel Bars, Balancing Beam, Vaulting Horse and Uneven Bar.
(*b*) Balancing Beam, Horizontal Bar and Uneven Bars
(*c*) Balancing Beam, Vaulting Horse, Uneven Bars and Floor
(*d*) All of the above

4. What is the duration of a round in Boxing?
(*a*) 1 minute (*b*) 2 minutes
(*c*) 3 minutes (*d*) 4 minutes

5. What is the duration of rest period in between the two rounds of a professional bout in Boxing?
(*a*) 20 seconds (*b*) 30 seconds
(*c*) 1 minute (*d*) 1.30 minutes

6. 'Going into the tank' in Boxing means–
(*a*) abusing the referee
(*b*) a boxer losing the fight deliberately
(*c*) throwing towel in the rink
(*d*) none of the above

7. How many cross lanes are there in Kho-Kho?
(*a*) 6 (*b*) 7
(*c*) 8 (*d*) 9

8. How may weight categories are in the game of Judo (Senior men)?
(*a*) 7 (*b*) 8
(*c*) 9 (*d*) 10.

9. Opening command to start the Judo bouts is–
(*a*) hajime (*b*) koka
(*c*) ippon (*d*) wazari

10. Highest penalty in Judo is–
(*a*) hanso ko-make (*b*) kei koku
(*c*) chui (*d*) shido

11. Highest point in Judo is–
(*a*) koka (*b*) ippon
(*c*) waza-ari (*d*) yuko

12. How many feathers are there in a shuttle cock?
(*a*) 14 to 16 (*b*) 15 to 17
(*c*) 17 to 19 (*d*) 21 to 24

13. What is the length of a standard swimming pool?
(*a*) 50 metres (*b*) 60 metres
(*c*) 70 metres (*d*) 80 metres

14. What is the depth of the water, in a standard size swimming pool?
(*a*) More than 1.8 metres
(*b*) Less than1.8 metres
(*c*) More than 2.0 meters
(*d*) More than 3 metres

15. Which of the following can not be the shape of a swimming pool?
(*a*) A type (*b*) L type
(*c*) U type (*d*) V type

16. What is the height of the net in tennis?
(*a*) 2 ft. (*b*) 3 ft.
(*c*) 4 ft. (*d*) 5 ft.

17. In cricket terminology 'trimmer' is referred to as–
(*a*). a delivery that knocks off the bails only
(*b*) a delivery that does not knocks off the bails
(*c*) a delivery that knocks off the bails but the bails fall back on to the stumps
(*d*) a delivery when the ball just touches the batsman and goes for a boundary.

18. How many bouncers can be bowled in one over in a test match in cricket?
(*a*) 1 (*b*) 2
(*c*) 3 (*d*) 4

19. What is the length of pitch in cricket?
(*a*) 21 yds (*b*) 22 yds
(*c*) 23 yds (*d*) 24 yds

20. How many legs does a Billiards Table has?
(*a*) 7 (*b*) 8
(*c*) 9 (*d*) 10

21. What is "hiki-wake' in Judo?
(*a*) A draw (*b*) A penalty
(*c*) A point (*d*) A player

22. Three second rule is applied in the game of–
(*a*) basketball (*b*) kabaddi
(*c*) kho-kho (*d*) table tennis

23. In weight lifting competition the increase is weight between two attempts must not be less than–
(*a*) 2.5 kg. (*b*) 5 kg.
(*c*) 10 kg. (*d*) 2 kg.

24. During the conduct of a penalty stroke in hockey, the umpire takes position over–
(*a*) centre line (*b*) 25 yrds
(*c*) striking circle (*d*) goal line

25. The height of the backboard of hockey goal is–
(*a*) 12 inches (*b*) 10 inches
(*c*) 18 inches (*d*) 24 inches

26. To take penalty stroke in hockey, any skill can be used except–
(*a*) push (*b*) flick
(*c*) scoop (*d*) hit

27. In soccer the penalty kick spot is marked at a distance of–
(*a*) 12 yards (*b*) 8 yards
(*c*) 10 yards (*d*) 16 yards

28. In hockey the corner hit is taken from the–
(*a*) back line (*b*) centre line
(*c*) side line (*d*) goal line

29. 'Round Robin" is a name given to–
(*a*) knock out tournament

(b) ladder tournament
(c) league type composition
(d) none of the above

30. The final event in "Decathlon" is always–
(a) javelin throw
(b) 1500 metre race
(c) 110 metre Hurdles
(d) 800 metre race

31. The ability to release maximum muscular force in the shortest possible time is called–
(a) muscular endurance
(b) muscular strength
(c) muscular power
(d) agility

32. Shortening of the muscle occurs during which type of contraction?
(a) Concentric contraction
(b) Eccentric contraction
(c) Isokinetic
(d) None of the above

33. Name the device used for recording muscular work–
(a) ergometer (b) electromyogram
(c) eergograph (d) all the above

34. Aerobic exercises contribute to the development of–
(a) speed (b) strength
(c) agility (d) endurance

35. Which of the following is test trainable?
(a) Flexibility (b) Endurance
(c) Speed (d) Strength

36. Which of the following is the longest cycle of training?
(a) Macrocycle (b) Microcycle
(c) Mesocycle (d) Weekly cycle

37. Duration of a macro-cycle is usually–
(a) 3-4 months to even 12 months
(b) 3-6 weeks
(c) one week
(d) 3-10 days

38. Mesocycle can be logically achieved in–
(a) one week (b) 2-5 weeks
(c) 3-6 weeks (d) 10 days

39. The first person to give a theoretical base to periodization was–
(a) Hardayal Singh (b) L. P. Matweyew
(c) Minow (d) Bastion

40. The shortest training cycle is the
(a) mesocycle (b) microcycle
(c) macro cycle (d) none of these

41. Continuous training method was introduced by–
(a) Dr. Ernst Van Aaken
(b) Woldemar Gerschler
(c) Reindell
(d) Morgan

42. LSD (low slow distance) training and can provide an athlete some relief from high intensity training–
(a) interval training (b) fartlek training
(c) speed training (d) weight training

43. Interval training methods was introduced by
(a) Morgan (b) Reindall
(c) Gerschler (d) Van Aaken

44. Circuit training was developed by–
(a) Morgan and Adamson
(b) Reindall
(c) Van Aaken
(d) Marlow

45. Dumb bells, Bar bells and Pulley machines are used in–
(a) weight training (b) speed training
(c) circuit training (d) strength training

46. Method of training for power or explosiveness is called–
(a) fartlek (b) circuit training
(c) plyometrics (d) strength training

47. Which of the following is not the technique of flexibility training?
(a) Static (b) Ballistic
(c) Assisted (d) Circuit

48. Speed endurance can be developed by the use of–
(a) circuit training
(b) running
(c) fartlek
(d) competition and time trial

49. Speed endurance cannot be developed with the help of–
(*a*) fartlek (*b*) interval training
(*c*) weight training (*d*) circuit training

50. The training method which increases the heart's stroke volume and hence its ability to deliver blood and oxygen to legs is–
(*a*) continuous training method
(*b*) fartlek
(*c*) interval training method
(*d*) weight training method

51. Which method of training utilizes both aerobic and anaerobic energy producing systems?
(*a*) Continuous (*b*) Fartlek
(*c*) Strength (*d*) Interval

52. The format of which training method utilizes a group of 6-10 strength exercises that are completed one after another?
(*a*) Continuous (*b*) Endurance
(*c*) Interval (*d*) Circuit

53. Which training method in Swedish means speed play?
(*a*) Circuit (*b*) LSD
(*c*) Fartlek (*d*) None

54. Which training method involves exercise using resistance to build muscle strength and endurance?
(*a*) Weight training
(*b*) Strength training
(*c*) Speed training
(*d*) Endurance training

55. Speed is not a combination of–
(*a*) maximum speed
(*b*) explosive strength (power)
(*c*) repetitions
(*d*) speed endurance

56. Overtraining causes–
(*a*) fatigue (*b*) rest
(*c*) recovery (*d*) tapering

57. Age and sex differences are considered in–
(*a*) principle of overload
(*b*) principle of specificity
(*c*) principle of individuality
(*d*) principle of periodization

58. Which principle of sports training refers to general motor skills and fitness development?
(*a*) Principle of overload
(*b*) Principle of individuality
(*c*) Principle of specificity
(*d*) Principle of periodization

59. Principle of specificity refers to–
(*a*) nature of training load
(*b*) age and sex difference
(*c*) training programme
(*d*) improvement is different abilities of an individual

60. Sports training programmes are developed through a series of training periods or cycles based on the principle of–
(*a*) continuity (*b*) periodization
(*c*) specificity (*d*) individuality

61. Interval training involves–
(*a*) high intensity training
(*b*) low intensity training
(*c*) high intensity with less intense training
(*d*) none of these

62. Strength endurance can be developed with–
(*a*) circuit training
(*b*) plyometric exercises
(*c*) conditioning exercises
(*d*) medicine ball exercises

63. Maximum strength can be developed with–
(*a*) Circuit training
(*b*) Plyometric exercises
(*c*) Conditioning exercises
(*d*) Weight training

64. In weight training, a typical strength training programme performed three days a week contains–
(*a*) one set of 12-20 RM
(*b*) 4-6 RM
(*c*) 8-12 RM
(*d*) 15-17 RM

65. What is the time for which the player must rest in between sessions of strength training?

(*a*) 24 hrs. (*b*) 12 hrs.
(*c*) 48 hrs. (*d*) 72 hrs.

66. Which of the following is not an example of circuit exercises for legs?
(*a*) Squat jumps
(*b*) Astride jumps
(*c*) Pull ups
(*d*) Step ups

67. Which of the following is not a type of interval training?
(*a*) Sustained burst of speed during continuous training
(*b*) Repeats
(*c*) Formal intervals
(*d*) Time trials

68. Overloading leads to–
(*a*) fatigue (*b*) adaptation
(*c*) recovery (*d*) rest

69. Which principle of training asks for a balance between stress and rest?
(*a*) Principle of Adaptation
(*b*) Principle of Overload
(*c*) Principle of Progression
(*d*) Principle of use/ disuse

70. Jogging swimming and cycling are a part of–
(*a*) continuous training
(*b*) weight training
(*c*) interval training
(*d*) fartlek training

71. Field games like rugby, hockey, soccer are covered under–
(*a*) speed play training
(*b*) weight training
(*c*) interval training
(*d*) continuous training

72. During interval training the work to rest ratio of a football match is–
(*a*) 1:1 (*b*) 2:1
(*c*) 3:1 (*d*) 4:1

73. If a muscle contracts and changes its length to produce force, the contraction type is–
(*a*) isotonic (*b*) isometric
(*c*) isokenetic (*d*) none of the above

74. Strength gain is fastest with–
(*a*) isotonic weight training
(*b*) isometric weight training
(*c*) isokinetic weight training
(*d*) none of the above

75. What type of training improves the speed at which a muscle shortens?
(*a*) Weight training
(*b*) Circuit training
(*c*) Stage training
(*d*) Plyometrics training

76. Which flexibility training methods tricks the receptor organs in the muscles and joints allowing the limbs to increase their range of movements?
(*a*) Active stretching
(*b*) PNF (Propriaceptor Neuromuscular Facilitation)
(*c*) Passive stretching
(*d*) Static stretching

77. Which phase of annual periodization aims at development of rebuilding of general abilities?
(*a*) Intensification (*b*) Accumulation
(*c*) Competitive (*d*) Peaking

78. Which of the following is the shortest phase of annual periodization?
(*a*) Accumulation (*b*) Intensification
(*c*) Transformation (*d*) Transition

79. What is the minimum weight for admission to competition and acceptance of a record in shot put?
(*a*) Men 6.085 kg Women 3 kg
(*b*) Men 7.00 kg Women 3.5 kg
(*c*) Men 7.260 kg Women 4 kg
(*d*) Men 7.5 kg Women 4.2 kg

80. The inside diameter of a throwing circle in shot-put is–
(*a*) 2.135 M ± 5 cm (*b*) 2.5 M ± 2.5 cm
(*c*) 2.60 M ± 3 cm (*d*) 2.78 M ± 4 cm

81. In a shortput event, how many practice throws are allowed?
(*a*) One (*b*) Two
(*c*) Three (*d*) Four

82. The angle of landing sector of shotput is–
(*a*) 60° (*b*) 90°
(*c*) 45° (*d*) 40°

83. The name of one of the famous athletic statue called "Discobolus" in Greek means–
(*a*) runner (*b*) winner
(*c*) discus thrower (*d*) javelin thrower

84. The diameter of the throwing circle in discus throwing is–
(*a*) 2.5 m (*b*) 1.75 m
(*c*) 2.00 m (*d*) 2.75 m

85. The angle of release of discus to achieve the greater distance is–
(*a*) 35° - 40° (*b*) 40° - 45°
(*c*) 25° - 30° (*d*) 45° - 60°

86. What is the minimum weight of discus or a competition and acceptance of a record?
(*a*) Men 1.5 kg Women 1.00kg
(*b*) Men 2 kg Women 1.00 kg
(*c*) Men 2.5 kg Women 1.5 kg
(*d*) Men 2.5 kg Women 2 kg

87. The maximum permissible slope of the ground within the throwing/ landing sector in discuss and shotput is–
(*a*) 1:500 (*b*) 1:750
(*c*) 1:800 (*d*) 1:1000

88. What is the time given to the player to throw the discus?
(*a*) One minute (*b*) Two minutes
(*c*) Three minutes (*d*) Four minutes

89. The Javelin was first introduced into modern Olympics in–
(*a*) 1908 (*b*) 1912
(*c*) 1904 (*d*) 1900

90. What is the minimum weight of Javelin?
(*a*) Men 500 gm Women 300 gm
(*b*) Men 500 gm Women 600 gm
(*c*) Men 800 gm Women 600 gm
(*d*) Men 800 gm Women 700 gm

91. The length of the runway in Javelin throw is–
(*a*) 33.5 m to 36.5 m
(*b*) 34-36 m
(*c*) 34.5 m to 37.5 m
(*d*) 40-45 m

92. The maximum allowance for the overall inclination of the landing sector in the throwing direction javelin throw shall not exceed
(*a*) 1:1000 (*b*) 1:100
(*c*) 1:10 (*d*) 1:10,000

93. What is the length of the Badminton court for singles and doubles?
(*a*) 13.44 m (*b*) 13.40 m
(*c*) 13.70 m (*d*) 13.55 m

94. The height or top of the net from the ground at the centre of the Badminton court is–
(*a*) 5 feet (*b*) 6 feet
(*c*) 5.1 feet (*d*) 5.5 feet

95. The number of feathers in a shuttle in Badminton is
(*a*) 10 feathers (*b*) 12 feathers
(*c*) 14 feathers (*d*) 16 feathers

96. The weight of the Badminton Racket is–
(*a*) four ounces (*b*) five ounces
(*c*) six ounces (*d*) seven ounces

97. The weight of the shuttle in a game of Badminton is–
(*a*) 4.70 – 5 gms (*b*) 4.8 – 6 gms
(*c*) 4 -8 gms (*d*) 4.74 to 5.50 gms

98. What is the number of line judges in a doubles match in Badminton?
(*a*) Four (*b*) Five
(*c*) Six (*d*) Seven

99. The length of the hockey field is–
(*a*) 100 yards (*b*) 50 yards
(*c*) 80 yards (*d*) 90 yards

100. The minimum length of the side boards of goal post is
(*a*) 2 feet (*b*) 4 feet
(*c*) 5 feet (*d*) 6 feet

101. Who among the following introduced the iso-kinetic method of training for the development of strength?
(*a*) Plato (*b*) J.J.Parrine
(*c*) B.P.Coubertin (*d*) Jacobson

102. Long term exercise programme made up of different activities and sports for developing all round fitness is known as–
(*a*) set training
(*b*) circuit training
(*c*) interval training
(*d*) cross training

103. Physical ability which enables a person to rapidly change body position and difference in a precise manner is called–
(*a*) speed (*b*) balance
(*c*) coordination (*d*) agility

104. 'Fartlek Training' is used best to develop–
(*a*) flexibility
(*b*) strength
(*c*) endurance
(*d*) neuromuscular coordination

105. Adaptation to training load at high altitudes is known as–
(*a*) thermoregulation
(*b*) super compensation
(*c*) acclimatization
(*d*) none of the above

106. Aerobic fitness is best achieved through–
(*a*) swimming
(*b*) circuit training
(*c*) short sprints
(*d*) long distance running

107. Progression method can equally be used in teaching the activities except–
(*a*) hammer throw
(*b*) mass physical training
(*c*) dance
(*d*) pole vault

108. Isometric exercise is the one in which muscle length is–
(*a*) constant (*b*) shortend
(*c*) lenthens (*d*) none of the above

109. 'Cybex' machine is based on the principle of
(*a*) isometric contraction
(*b*) isotonic contraction
(*c*) isokinetic contraction
(*d*) none of the above

110. The circumference of a ball in a water polo competition is–
(*a*) 0.68-0.71 m (*b*) 0.60-0.70 m
(*c*) 0.60-0.62 m (*d*) 0.72-0.74 m

111. Pushing against the stationary wall is an example of–
(*a*) eccentric exercise
(*b*) isometric exercise
(*c*) isotonic exercise
(*d*) isokinetic exercise

112. 'Supercompensation' means–
(*a*) fatigue
(*b*) second wind
(*c*) adaptation to load
(*d*) oxyzen debt

113. 'Stadiometer' is used to measure
(*a*) strength (*b*) weight
(*c*) height (*d*) stadium area

114. 'Fartlex' training is given for improving–
(*a*) strength (*b*) endurance
(*c*) flexibility (*d*) none of the above

115. 'Active flexibility' refers to
(*a*) muscular stretch without assistance
(*b*) muscular stretch with assistance
(*c*) stretching at maximum range
(*d*) none of the above

116. 'Micro cycle' involves training of
(*a*) one week (*b*) 6-8 weeks
(*c*) 8-10 weeks (*d*) 1-2 weeks

117. Leg strength can be best improved by–
(*a*) high jumps (*b*) depth jumps
(*c*) push ups (*d*) chin ups

118. 'Pyramid Training' was invented by
(*a*) Russians (*b*) Germans
(*c*) Swedish (*d*) Americans.

119. Who invented circuit training?
(*a*) Morgan and Adamson
(*b*) Aristotle
(*c*) Herbert Spencer
(*d*) C.A. Bucher

120. 'Fartlek Training' was first devised and adopted in

(*a*) USA (*b*) Sweden
(*c*) England (*d*) Switzerland

121. Basic principle of Fartlek training is–
(*a*) variation in space
(*b*) variation in pace
(*c*) variation in duration
(*d*) variation in place

122. 'Speed play' is also known as–
(*a*) weight training
(*b*) pressure training
(*c*) fartlek training
(*d*) interval training

123. The best season for doing 'Fartlek Training' is–
(*a*) racing season
(*b*) transition period
(*c*) competition period
(*d*) off season

124. The actual variables in interval method of training are–
(*a*) distance, time, repetitions, and recover period
(*b*) preparatory, transition and competition period
(*c*) distance, transition and Recovery period
(*d*) force, mass, acceleration.

125. Interval training is good for–
(*a*) off season
(*b*) mid season
(*c*) competition period
(*d*) none of the above

126. The schedules for interval training are prepared–
(*a*) annually (*b*) weekly
(*c*) monthly (*d*) quarterly

127. Who invented the method of weight training?
(*a*) Aristotle
(*b*) Herbert Spencer
(*c*) Fredrick Yahn
(*d*) Morgan and Adamson

128. Passive flexibility is due to–
(*a*) Muscular assistance
(*b*) External help
(*c*) Increase in strength
(*d*) Neither (*a*) nor (*b*)

129. Duration of 'macro cycle' is–
(*a*) 1 year plus (*b*) 2 months
(*c*) 2 weeks (*d*) 4 days

130. Best method to enhance explosive strength in lower extremities is–
(*a*) long distance running
(*b*) sand running
(*c*) bounding training and depth jumps
(*d*) mud running

131. Interval training is used for the development of–
(*a*) flexibility
(*b*) agility
(*c*) explosive strength
(*d*) endurance

132. The super compensation effect of training is due to–
(*a*) improper proportion between load and recovery
(*b*) proper proportion between load and recovery
(*c*) massage
(*d*) all of the above

133. The duration of a meso cycle is–
(*a*) 5 to 10 days (*b*) 4 to 6 weeks
(*c*) 4 to 6 months (*d*) 1 to 2 years

134. Best method to develop flexibility is
(*a*) ballistic method
(*b*) slow method
(*c*) slow stretching and holding method
(*d*) relaxation method

135. Fartlek is more closely related to
(*a*) jumpers
(*b*) throwers
(*c*) sprinters
(*d*) middle distance runners

136. After acquiring mastery of skills, stress is laid on
(*a*) development of motor components
(*b*) tactical training
(*c*) both (*a*) and (*b*)
(*d*) none of the above

137. Sprinting speed is best developed through–
(*a*) interval training
(*b*) weight training
(*c*) ins and outs
(*d*) continuous running

138. High altitude training at 8,000 ft–
(*a*) enhances performance
(*b*) deteriorates performance
(*c*) increases muscle strength
(*d*) none of the above

139. Abdominal muscles are best developed from–
(*a*) running
(*b*) abdominal crunch
(*c*) back hyperextension
(*d*) lateral bending

140. Circuit training is an effective method for developing–
(*a*) speed
(*b*) flexibility
(*c*) strength endurance
(*d*) agility

141. Plyometrics is also called–
(*a*) reflex phenomena
(*b*) reactive jumps
(*c*) agility training
(*d*) all of the above

142. Tactical training is done–
(*a*) after skills are mastered
(*b*) before skills are mastered
(*c*) both tactical training and technical training are done side by side
(*d*) all of the above

143. Overload in sports training relates to when–
(*a*) the oxygen is adequate to supply the need of the body
(*b*) the oxygen supplying mechanisms are not able to increase
(*c*) the intake of oxygen is insufficient to meet
(*d*) the supply of oxygen is more than required

144. Which of the following is a cyclic sport?
(*a*) Swimming (*b*) Rowing
(*c*) Football (*d*) Both (*a*) and (*b*)

145. Load intensity is–
(*a*) directly proportional to load volume
(*b*) inversely proportional to load volume
(*c*) same as load volume
(*d*) none of the above

146. The ability to overcome resistance is called–
(*a*) dynamic strength
(*b*) static strength
(*c*) relative strength
(*d*) strength endurance

147. Which of the following does not include the principles of sports training?
(*a*) Economy of movement
(*b*) Progression of load
(*c*) Cyclicity of training
(*d*) Continuity

148. Skill acquisition is mainly dependent upon–
(*a*) flexibility
(*b*) coordination ability
(*c*) muscular strength
(*d*) speed

149. Main consideration for effective periodization should be–
(*a*) base creation
(*b*) achievement of top form
(*c*) skill development
(*d*) development of tactical ability

150. Transition period aims at
(*a*) stabilization of performance
(*b*) super compensation
(*c*) recreation
(*d*) recovery

151. The first metamorphosis falls between the age of–
(*a*) 7-10 years
(*b*) 3-5 years
(*c*) 11-14 years
(*d*) 2-4 years

152. In selecting talent, the most important factor to be considered is–
(*a*) training state
(*b*) health
(*c*) interest and attitude
(*d*) all of the above

153. An efficient coach is he who–
(*a*) tells
(*b*) tells and demonstrates
(*c*) tells, demonstrates and explains
(*d*) tells, demonstrates, explains and inspires

154. While exercising on a Multigym the type of muscular contraction that occurs is–
(*a*) isotonic (*b*) isometric
(*c*) isokinetic (*d*) kinetic

155. What is the weight of a Football?
(*a*) 14-16 oz (*b*) 16-18 oz
(*c*) 18-20 oz (*d*) 20-22 oz

156. What is the duration of a Football game?
(*a*) 45-10-45 (min.) (*b*) 40-10-40 (min.)
(*c*) 35-10-35 (min.) (*d*) 45-2-45 (min.)

157. How many referees are required for a Football match?
(*a*) 4 (*b*) 3
(*c*) 2 (*d*) 1

158. The number of umpires required to conduct a Hockey match is–
(*a*) one (*b*) three
(*c*) four (*d*) two

159. In Hockey, the ball gets trapped in a goal keeper's pads, how does the game restart?
(*a*) With bully
(*b*) Centre hit
(*c*) Hit from the goal
(*d*) Toss.

160. How does the game of Hockey start?
(*a*) With a bully
(*b*) With forward pass
(*c*) With back pass
(*d*) None of the above

161. From what distance is the penalty stroke taken in Hockey?
(*a*) 6 yards (*b*) 8 yards
(*c*) 9 yards (*d*) 10 yards

162. What is the duration of one half in the game of Hockey?
(*a*) 34 minutes (*b*) 40 minutes
(*c*) 35 minutes (*d*) 30 minutes

163. Width of lanes in a standard track is–
(*a*) 1.22-1.25 m (*b*) 1.22 m
(*c*) 1.25 m (*d*) 1.21 m

164. What is the angle at which the throwing sector is marked?
(*a*) 40ºC (*b*) 45ºC
(*c*) 50ºC (*d*) 35ºC

165. Decathlon consists of–
(*a*) 6 track and 4 field events
(*b*) 4 track and 4 field events
(*c*) 3 track and 7 field events
(*d*) 7 track and 3 field events

166. The range of points awarded in 'Decathlon' is–
(*a*) 1-1200 (*b*) 1-1000
(*c*) 5-1000 (*d*) 12000

167. To break tie in the triple jumps competition–
(*a*) consider the next best performance
(*b*) provide an additional trial
(*c*) consider all the attempts
(*d*) adopt any one of the above

168. Number of flights in 110m (Hurdle) race is–
(*a*) 8 (*b*) 9
(*c*) 10 (*d*) 11

169. To break tie in long jump–
(*a*) consider the performance of the first attempt
(*b*) consider the performance of the last attempt
(*c*) consider the next best performance
(*d*) change the venue of competition

170. In 110m Hurdles, the number of strides performed between two hurdles is–
(*a*) 5 (*b*) 8
(*c*) 3 (*d*) 4

171. In 300m steeple chase, the number of Water jumps is–
(*a*) 6 (*b*) 7
(*c*) 8 (*d*) 9

172. The length of exchange zone in 4x100m relay is–
(*a*) 10 metres (*b*) 15 metres
(*c*) 20 metres (*d*) 30 metres

173. The weight of men's Javelin is–
(*a*) 600 gm (*b*) 800 gm
(*c*) 900 gm (*d*) 1000 gm

174. Distance of Marathon race is–
(*a*) 43.195 km (*b*) 42.195 km
(*c*) 41.185 km (*d*) 40.165 km

175. How many total jumps are there in 3000m steeple chase race?
(*a*) 34 (*b*) 36
(*c*) 35 (*d*) 33

176. How many time keepers should check the performance before a world record can be considered in the track events?
(*a*) 3 including one chief time keeper
(*b*) 2 including one chief time keeper
(*c*) 4 including one chief time keeper
(*d*) 5 including one chief time keeper

177. Events of the modern pentathlon are–
(*a*) Riding, Shooting, Fencing, Swimming and Cross Country Running
(*b*) Riding, Shooting, Fencing, Swimming and Kayaking
(*c*) Riding, Shooting, Fencing, Swimming and Canoeing
(*d*) 800m, Shot Put, Long Jump, 100m and Discuss

178. What is the width of lines in Athletics track events?
(*a*) 4 cm (*b*) 5 cm
(*c*) 6 cm (*d*) 7 cm

79. Dimensions of the volleyball Court are–
(*a*) 9m × 18 m (B × L)
(*b*) 10m × 20m (B × L)
(*c*) 11m × 21m (B ×L)
(*d*) 8m × 16m (B × L)

80. Width of the volleyball Net is–
(*a*) 1.80m (*b*) 1.20m
(*c*) 1.10m (*d*) 1m.

81. Height of Antena in volleyball is–
(*a*) 1.80m (*b*) 1.60m
(*c*) 1.40m (*d*) 1.20m

82. Height of the volleyball net for men is–
(*a*) 2.40 m (*b*) 2.41 m
(*c*) 2.42 m (*d*) 2.43 m

183. Height of the volleyball net for women is–
(*a*) 2.21 m (*b*) 2.22 m
(*c*) 2.23 m (*d*) 2.24 m

184. Height of the antenna above the net in volleyball is–
(*a*) 50 cm (*b*) 60 cm
(*c*) 70 cm (*d*) 80 cm

185. In volleyball, the distance of the attack line from centre line is–
(*a*) one metre (*b*) two metres
(*c*) three metres (*d*) five metres

186. According to the new rules, maximum points in the first 4 sets of a game in volleyball is–
(*a*) 15 (*b*) 14
(*c*) 25 (*d*) 24

187. Weight of a Volleyball is–
(*a*) 260-280 gms. (*b*) 200-250 oz
(*c*) 280-300 gms. d) 300-320 gms.

188. How many field players are there in one team in volleyball?
(*a*) 12 (*b*) 10
(*c*) 9 (*d*) 6

189. What is the width of boundary lines in volleyball?
(*a*) 6 cm (*b*) 5 cm
(*c*) 3 cm (*d*) 2 cm

190. Rotation in Volleyball takes place in the–
(*a*) clockwise direction
(*b*) anticlockwise direction
(*c*) both (*a*) and (*b*)
(*d*) zig-zag direction

191. How many substitutes are there in one team in volleyball?
(*a*) 6 (*b*) 5
(*c*) 4 (*d*) 3

192. "Which of the following is the correct duration of a Basketball match (for men)?
(*a*) 20-10-20 (in min.)
(*b*) 12-2-12, 10, 12-2-12 (in min.)
(*c*) Both (*a*) and (*b*)
(*d*) None of the above

193. What is the weight of a Basketball?
(*a*) 400-800 gm (*b*) 500-600 gm
(*c*) 567-650 oz (*d*) 567-650 gm

194. What is the thickness of backboard in basketball?
(*a*) 2 cm (*b*) 3 cm
(*c*) 4 cm (*d*) 5 cm

195. What is the L x B of the Backboard?
(*a*) 1.80 x 1.05 m (*b*) 1.05 x 1.80 m
(*c*) 1.00 x 2.00 m (*d*) 1.80 x 1.25 m

196. In basketball, what is the height of the Backboard from the ground?
(*a*) 2.85 m (*b*) 2.90m
(*c*) 2.35 m (*d*) 3.00 m

197. In basketball , what is the height of ring from the ground?
(*a*) 3.00 m (*b*) 3.50 m
(*c*) 3.05 ft. (*d*) 3.05 m

198. How many substitutes are there in the game of basketball, in one team?
(*a*) 4 (*b*) 5
(*c*) 6 (*d*) 7

199. What are the dimensions of a Basketball Court?
(*a*) 28 × 15 m (*b*) 28 × 15 yds
(*c*) 28 × 15 ft. (*d*) 26 × 15 m.

200. Events in 'power lifting' are–
(*a*) squad, bench press, dead lift
(*b*) squat, pullovers, curls
(*c*) dead lift, bench press, chin ups
(*d*) none of the above

201. The maximum weight of the ball in the game of hockey is–
(*a*) 150 gm (*b*) 160 gm
(*c*) 165 gm (*d*) 163 gm

202. What is the maximum weight of the hockey stick?
(*a*) 750 gm (*b*) 725 gm
(*c*) 700 gm (*d*) 737 gm

203. Each hockey team cannot have two teams of not more than ______ players–
(*a*) 11 players (*b*) 14 players
(*c*) 15 players (*d*) 16 players

204. What is the duration of hockey game?
(*a*) 60 minutes (*b*) 70 minutes
(*c*) 75 minutes (*d*) 80 minutes

205. During high jump, the arched back method of clearing the bar is called–
(*a*) fosbury flop (*b*) scissors
(*c*) western roll (*d*) straddle roll

206. Straddle Roll technique in high jump is also known as–
(*a*) western roll (*b*) fosbury flop
(*c*) scissors (*d*) belly roll

207. During Straddle Roll in High jumps the run up for top class athlete is angled at–
(*a*) 30° - 35° (*b*) 30° 40°
(*c*) 40° - 60° (*d*) 35° - 40°

208. In Olympic games the minimum length of the runway in high jump is–
(*a*) 15m (*b*) 18 m
(*c*) 20 m (*d*) 25 m

209. In high jump, the over all length of the cross bar is–
(*a*) 4 m ± 2 cm (*b*) 5 m ± 3 cm
(*c*) 4.5 m ± 2 cm (*d*) 4.25 m + 2.5 cm

210. For elite jumpers the length of the run up in long jump is–
(*a*) men 20-25 m women 30-35m
(*b*) men 35-45 m women 30-35 m
(*c*) men 40-45 m women 35-40 m
(*d*) men 35-40 m women 35-40 m

211. Which jumping technique is also called Running Air Technique?
(*a*) Hitch Kick (*b*) Hang technique
(*c*) Flipor Somersault (*d*) None of the above

212. The lateral inclination of the runway in long jump is–
(*a*) 1:10 (*b*) 1:100
(*c*) 1:1000 (*d*) 1:10000

213. The minimum distance between the take off board and the far end of the landing area in long jump is–
(*a*) 7 m (*b*) 8 m
(*c*) 10 m (*d*) 12 m

214. During triple jump, the minimum distance between the take-off board and far end of the landing area shall be–
(*a*) 15 m (*b*) 22 m
(*c*) 21 m (*d*) 25 m

215. The minimum length of the take-off board for men in triple jump is–
(*a*) 11 m (*b*) 12 m
(*c*) 13 m (*d*) 14 m

216. The length of the play field in football is–
(*a*) 80 – 120m (*b*) 90 – 120 m
(*c*) 90-110 m (*d*) 80-110m

217. Radius of the centre circle in a football field is–
(*a*) 8 yards (*b*) 10 yards
(*c*) 12 yards (*d*) 13 yards

218. Distance between the upright goal posts in football field is–
(*a*) 5 yards (*b*) 6 yards
(*c*) 7 yards (*d*) 8 yards

219. The number of extra players in a team in a game of football is–
(*a*) 3 (*b*) 4
(*c*) 5 (*d*) 6

220. What is the maximum weight of the ball in a football game?
(*a*) 350 gms (*b*) 375 gms
(*c*) 400 gms (*d*) 450 gms

221. The interval duration in each match of football is–
(*a*) 3 minutes (*b*) 4 minutes
(*c*) 5 minutes (*d*) 6 minutes

222. In football, the kick with the full instep is also called–
(*a*) low drive (*b*) lofted kick
(*c*) volley kicks (*d*) dribbling

223. The length of the kho-kho ground is–
(*a*) 25 m (*b*) 27 m
(*c*) 29 m (*d*) 31 m

224. The total number of players in a kho-kho team are–
(*a*) 8 (*b*) 10
(*c*) 12 (*d*) 14

225. In a kho-kho match, the duration of every team chase or defened is–
(*a*) 7 minutes (*b*) 9 minutes
(*c*) 11 minutes (*d*) 13 minutes

226. The weight of the ball in basket ball is–
(*a*) 600-650 gm (*b*) 500-550 gm
(*c*) 550-600 gm (*d*) 550-575 gm

227. What is the number of players on court in a basket ball match–
(*a*) 5 (*b*) 6
(*c*) 7 (*d*) 8

228. The Court measurement for basket ball field are
(*a*) 24 × 17 m (*b*) 28 × 15 m
(*c*) 25 × 15 m (*d*) 24 × 16 m

229. The dimensions of backboards in basket ball are–
(*a*) 1.85 × 1.20 m (*b*) 1.80 × 1.20 m
(*c*) 1.80 × 1.05 m (*d*) 1.85 × 1.05 m

230. The circumference of the ball in basketball game is–
(*a*) 72-75 cm (*b*) 75-78 cm
(*c*) 76-78 cm (*d*) 75.5-79 cm

231. The ball does not become dead in the basket ball when
(*a*) any goal is made
(*b*) any violation occurs
(*c*) a foul occurs while the ball is alive or in play
(*d*) ball is in flight on a free flow

232. The size of the boxing ring is
(*a*) 15 feet square (*b*) 17 feet square
(*c*) 19 feet square (*d*) 20 feet square

233. The number of steps provided in a boxing ring are–
(*a*) one (*b*) two
(*c*) three (*d*) four

234. For boxers upto and including 47 kg, the gloves weigh
(*a*) 200 gms (*b*) 225 gms
(*c*) 227 gms (*d*) 284 gms

235. Generally the upper age limit for a boxer to compete in National Championships is–

(*a*) 35 years (*b*) 37 years
(*c*) 38 years (*d*) 39 years

236. What is the duration of rounds in boxing?
(*a*) 2 minutes (*b*) 3 minutes
(*c*) 4 minutes (*d*) 5 minutes

237. What is the number of judges in a boxing contest?
(*a*) 5 (*b*) 4
(*c*) 3 (*d*) 2

238. In a game of cricket the tops of stumps are ____ inches above the ground–
(*a*) 25 (*b*) 26
(*c*) 27 (*d*) 28

239. The length of the bails in cricket is–
(*a*) 4 inches (*b*) 4 ¼ inches
(*c*) 4 ½ inches (*d*) $4\frac{3}{8}$ inches

240. The maximum length of cricket bat is–
(*a*) 38 inches (*b*) 39 inches
(*c*) 40 inches (*d*) 41 inches

241. The ball is not dead when–
(*a*) a batsman is out
(*b*) it strikes an umpire
(*c*) it reaches or pitches over the boundary
(*d*) the umpire calls 'over' or time

242. For any running event what is the minimum length of the track?
(*a*) 100 m (*b*) 200 m
(*c*) 300 m (*d*) 400 m

243. In races up to and including 400m, each competitor shall have a separate lane of width measuring–
(*a*) 1.22 to 1.25m (*b*) 1.20 to 1.25 m
(*c*) 1.8 to 1.20 m (*d*) 1.20 to 1.25m

244. For men, 110 m hurdle race, the height of the hurdle is–
(*a*) 0.840 m (*b*) 0.920 m
(*c*) 1.067 m (*d*) 1.11 m

245. For women 400m hurdle race, the height of the hurdle is–
(*a*) 1.067 m (*b*) 0.914 m
(*c*) 0.840 m (*d*) 0.762 m

246. In women 100m hurdle race, the distance from start line to first hurdle is–
(*a*) 13.72 m (*b*) 14 m
(*c*) 13 m (*d*) 15 m

247. The maximum distance covered in a marathon is–
(*a*) 40 km (*b*) 41.5 km
(*c*) 42.5 km (*d*) 42.195 km

248. What is the size of tennis court?
(*a*) 78 × 27 feet (*b*) 80 × 30 feet
(*c*) 77 × 25 feet (*d*) 79 × 30 feet

249. What s the maximum height of the net at the centre in a game of tennis?
(*a*) 2 feet (*b*) 2.5 feet
(*c*) 3 feet (*d*) 4 feet

250. What is the size of the ball in the game of tennis–
(*a*) 6.15 – 6.47cm (*b*) 6.35 – 6.67cm
(*c*) 6.40 – 6.72 cm (*d*) 6.42 – 6.74 cm

251. What is the maximum length of the frame of a tennis racket?
(*a*) 30 inches (*b*) 32 inches
(*c*) 35 inches (*d*) 37 inches

252. The 'playing surface' of the table tennis table is–
(*a*) 2.74 m × 1.525m (*b*) 2.70 m × 1.511 m
(*c*) 2.65 m × 1.4 m (*d*) 2.68 m × 1.415 m

253. The height of the playing surface in table tennis from the floor is–
(*a*) 70 cm (*b*) 76 cm
(*c*) 72 cm (*d*) 75 cm

254. What is the weight of the ball in a game of table tennis?
(*a*) 2 gm (*b*) 2.5 gm
(*c*) 3 gm (*d*) 3.5 gm

255. In table tennis, the period during which a ball is in play is called–
(*a*) rally (*b*) let
(*c*) point (*d*) obstruction

256. Which of the following games is not included in a Pentathlon?
(*a*) Long jump (*b*) Javelin throw
(*c*) Discus throw (*d*) High jump

257. In weight lifting, the lifter weighing 52 kg is categorized as–
(*a*) fly weight (*b*) feather weight
(*c*) light weight (*d*) middle weight

258. In weight lifting the lifters categorized middle weight weigh–
(*a*) 56 kg (*b*) 67.5 kg
(*c*) 90 kg (*d*) 75 kg

259. A national record in weight lifting is valid only if it exceeds the previous record by at least–
(*a*) 0.475 kg (*b*) 0.5 kg
(*c*) 0.7 kg (*d*) 1 kg

260. The length of a swimming pool to conduct Olympic games and world championships is–
(*a*) 25 mts (*b*) 30 mts
(*c*) 50 mts (*d*) 100 mts

261. Which of the following races in swimming does not start with a dive?
(*a*) Freestyle (*b*) Breast stroke
(*c*) Butterfly (*d*) Backstroke

262. What should be the minimum temperature of the water during race in swimming?
(*a*) 20°C (*b*) 24°C
(*c*) 30°C (*d*) 32°C

263. The length of the baton in a relay race is–
(*a*) 200-250 mm (*b*) 240-280 mm
(*c*) 280-300 mm (*d*) 300-320 mm

264. Word 'Tee off' is associated with which game?
(*a*) Polo (*b*) Snooker
(*c*) Golf (*d*) Billiards

265. In the water polo, the uniform distance between respective goal line is–
(*a*) 25 m (*b*) 30 m
(*c*) 35 m (*d*) 40 m

266. A state of decrease in performance capacity is due to–
(*a*) overload (*b*) under load
(*c*) both (*d*) none of these

267. The longest training cycle is called–
(*a*) micro cycle (*b*) macro cycle
(*c*) meso cycle (*d*) none of these

268. The shortest training cycle is called–
(*a*) meso cycle (*b*) macro cycle
(*c*) micro cycle (*d*) none of these

269. The training cycle which have normal duration of 3-6 weeks is called–
(*a*) macro cycle (*b*) micro cycle
(*c*) meso cycle (*d*) none of these

270. The training cycle which have normal duration of 3-10 days is called–
(*a*) micro cycle (*b*) meso cycle
(*c*) macro cycle (*d*) none of these

271. The ability to overcome or to act against maximal resistance is called–
(*a*) explosive strength
(*b*) maximum strength
(*c*) strength endurance
(*d*) none of these

272. The combination of strength and speed ability is called–
(*a*) explosive strength
(*b*) maximum strength
(*c*) strength endurance
(*d*) none of these

273. The ability to overcome resistance or to act against resistance under condition of fatigue is called–
(*a*) explosive strength
(*b*) maximum strength
(*c*) strength endurance
(*d*) none of these

274. Slow continuous, fast continuous, varied pace and Fartlek Method are the variations of–
(*a*) interval method
(*b*) repetition method
(*c*) continuous method
(*d*) none of these

275. Wind sprints, acceleration runs are the variations of–
(*a*) interval method
(*b*) repetition method
(*c*) continuous method
(*d*) none of these

276. The circuit training was first started, explained and studied by–
(*a*) Morgan and Adamson
(*b*) H. Clarke and D. Clarke
(*c*) Scholich
(*d*) None of these

277. Single periodisation has–
(*a*) one transitional period
(*b*) two transitional period
(*c*) three transitional period
(*d*) none of these

278. Double periodisation has–
(*a*) one transitional period
(*b*) two transitional period
(*c*) three transitional period
(*d*) none of these

279. For the speed work the intensity of load is measured in terms of–
(*a*) m/sec. or km. (*b*) m, km.
(*c*) Both (*d*) None of these

280. For the endurance work the intensity of load is measured in terms of–
(*a*) m/sec. or km. (*b*) m, km.
(*c*) Both (*d*) None of these

281. In low resistance work load the percentage of the maximum possible intensity should be–
(*a*) 70-80 (*b*) 30-50
(*c*) 80-90 (*d*) None of these

282. In medium resistance work load the percentage of the maximum possible intensity should be–
(*a*) 70-80 (*b*) 30-50
(*c*) 80-90 (*d*) None of these

283. In sub-maximum resistance work load the percentage of the maximum possible intensity should be–
(*a*) 90-100 (*b*) 75-85
(*c*) 30-50 (*d*) None of these

284. In multiple periodisation the number of the transitional period should be–
(*a*) one (*b*) two
(*c*) three (*d*) none of these

285. In single periodisation the number of preparatory period should be–
(*a*) one (*b*) two
(*c*) three (*d*) none of these

286. Performance deteriorating factors such as insufficient sleep, irregular daily routine, insufficient leisure time, use of alcohol and nicotine are the causes of–
(*a*) underload (*b*) over load
(*c*) both (*d*) none of these

287. Majors errors in training process such as rapid increase in load without stabilizing the adaptation and rapid increase of load after training breaks are the causes of–
(*a*) overload
(*b*) underload
(*c*) both
(*d*) none of these

288. The recovery phase can last for several days. The above statement is–
(*a*) true (*b*) false
(*c*) partially true (*d*) partially false

289. Factors affecting the pace of recovery are–
(*a*) nature of the load
(*b*) health and physical fitness
(*c*) sleep
(*d*) none of these

290. When the muscles are stretched first and then made to contract are called–
(*a*) eccentric – concentric contraction
(*b*) concentric – eccentric contraction
(*c*) both
(*d*) none of these

291. Iso-kinetic method for the development of strength was first introduced by–
(*a*) Gundlach (1967)
(*b*) J.J. Perrine (1968)
(*c*) Hettinger and Muller (1953)
(*d*) None of these.

292. Iso-metric method for the development of static strength was first advocated by–
(*a*) Gundlach (1967)
(*b*) J.J. Perrine (1968)
(*c*) Brunner (1967)
(*d*) Hettinger and Muller (1953)

293. For the development of strength endurance the intensity of work load should be–
(*a*) 80-100% (*b*) 75-80%
(*c*) 60-70% (*d*) 40-60%

294. For the development explosive strength along with maximum strength the intensity should be–
(*a*) 60-70% (*b*) 25-40%
(*c*) 30-50% (*d*) None of these

295. The ability to execute motor actions under given conditions, in minimum possible time is called–
(*a*) flexibility (*b*) agility
(*c*) endurance (*d*) speed

296. Reaction ability and acceleration ability are the forms of–
(*a*) flexibility (*b*) agility
(*c*) endurance (*d*) speed

297. The factor determining the various speed performance are–
(*a*) explosive strength
(*b*) mobility of nervous system
(*c*) muscle composition
(*d*) all of these

298. The ability to maintain the maximum locomotor speed for a long time is called–
(*a*) acceleration ability
(*b*) locomotor ability
(*c*) both
(*d*) none of these

299. The resistance ability against fatigue is called–
(*a*) strength
(*b*) endurance
(*c*) speed
(*d*) flexibility

300. The ability to resist fatigue caused by activities done at slow to moderate pace is called–
(*a*) basic endurance
(*b*) general endurance
(*c*) specific endurance
(*d*) none of these

301. The ability to resist fatigue caused by any particular sports activity is called–
(*a*) basic endurance
(*b*) general endurance
(*c*) specific endurance
(*d*) none of these

302. The ability to resist fatigue satisfactorily caused by various types of activities, may be aerobic or anaerobic or combination of both is called–
(*a*) basic endurance
(*b*) general endurance
(*c*) specific endurance
(*d*) none of these

303. Factors determining endurance may be due to–
(*a*) aerobic capacity
(*b*) anaerobic capacity
(*c*) various psychological factors
(*d*) all the above

304. Intensity can be measured in terms of–
(*a*) speed (*b*) distance/height
(*c*) speed(tempo) (*d*) all of these

305. Volume can be measured in terms of–
(*a*) duration (*b*) distance
(*c*) frequency (*d*) all of these

306. A state of decrease in performance capacity can be–
(*a*) due to overload
(*b*) due to underload
(*c*) both
(*d*) none of these

307. Increased excitability, obstinacy, tendency of hysteria, quarrelsome, oversensitive to criticism are the symptoms of overload
(*a*) True
(*b*) False
(*c*) Partially true
(*d*) Partially false

308. The somatic-functional symptoms of overload can be–
(*a*) loss of sleep
(*b*) loss of appetite

(*c*) loss of weight
(*d*) all of these

309. Intensity and volume of load, nature of load, health and physical fitness, nutrition, sleep, daily routine and total load are the factors affecting the pace of recovery–
(*a*) True (*b*) False
(*c*) Partially true (*d*) Partially false

310. Cinematography and measuring devices are–
(*a*) Bio-mechanical means of training
(*b*) Psychological means of training
(*c*) Both
(*d*) None of these

311. Ideomotor training, Autogenous training and psychotonic training are–
(*a*) natural means of training
(*b*) bio-mechanical means of training
(*c*) psychological means of training
(*d*) none of these

312. Weather conditions and altitude are–
(*a*) medical means of training
(*b*) natural means of training
(*c*) psychological means of training
(*d*) none of these

313. During conditioning in continuous method–
(*a*) intensity is kept high
(*b*) volume is kept high
(*c*) both
(*d*) none of these

314. Interval training includes–
(*a*) medium to high intensity
(*b*) low to medium volume
(*c*) both
(*d*) none of these

315. In repetition method–
(*a*) intensity is kept very high
(*b*) volume is kept low
(*c*) both
(*d*) none of these

316. Extensive interval training improves–
(*a*) basic endurance
(*b*) general endurance
(*c*) strength endurance
(*d*) all of these

317. Intensive interval training improves–
(*a*) speed endurance
(*b*) explosive strength
(*c*) maximum strength
(*d*) all of these

318. Repetition method helps to improve–
(*a*) speed ability
(*b*) maximum strength
(*c*) explosive strength
(*d*) all of these

319. Factors determining speed are–
(*a*) mobility of the nervous system
(*b*) explosive strength
(*c*) technique
(*d*) bio-chemical reserves and metabolic power.
(e) flexibility
(f) psychic factors
The above statement is.
(*a*) True (*b*) False
(*c*) Partially true (*d*) Partially false

320. Explosive strength, technique/co-ordination, metabolic power, flexibility are the factors determining–
(*a*) reaction ability (*b*) movement speed
(*c*) speed endurance (*d*) none of these

321. Explosive strength, technique/co-ordination, mobility of C.N.S., flexibility are the factors determining–
(*a*) acceleration ability
(*b*) reaction ability
(*c*) locomotor ability
(*d*) none of these

322. Functional capacity of sense organs are the factors determining–
(*a*) reaction ability (*b*) movement speed
(*c*) speed endurance (*d*) none of these

323. During competition period intensity is kept
(*a*) high (*b*) low
(*c*) both (*d*) none of these

324. During transitional period the intensity and volume is kept–
(*a*) high (*b*) low
(*c*) both (*d*) none of these

325. Ability to react quickly and effectively to a signal is called–
(*a*) coupling ability (*b*) reaction ability
(*c*) orientation ability (*d*) none of these

326. The ability to co-ordinate body part movement with one another in relation to definite goal oriented whole body movement is called–
(*a*) reaction ability
(*b*) orientation ability
(*c*) coupling ability
(*d*) none of these

327. The ability to perceive the externally given rhythm and to reproduce it in motor action is called–
(*a*) balance ability (*b*) rhythm ability
(*c*) adaptation ability (*d*) none of these

328. Ballistic method is one of the method of improving–
(*a*) strength (*b*) endurance
(*c*) flexibility (*d*) none of these

329. Endurance are classified as–
(i) Basic endurance
(ii) General endurance
(iii) Specific endurance according to.
(*a*) duration of activity
(*b*) nature of activity
(*c*) both
(*d*) none of these

330. Endurance are classified as–
(i) Speed endurance
(ii) Short time endurance
(iii) Medium time endurance
(iv) Long time endurance
according to
(*a*) Duration of activity
(*b*) Nature of activity
(*c*) Both
(*d*) None of these

331. Co-ordinative ability is mainly affected by coupling ability, rhythm ability, adaptation ability and differentiation ability–
(*a*) True (*b*) False
(*c*) Partially true (*d*) Partially false

332. Anaerobic capacity explosive strength, technique/co-ordination are the factors determining–
(*a*) movement speed (*b*) speed endurance
(*c*) locomotor ability (*d*) none of these

333. If an athlete wishes to run faster, he should
(*a*) move his arms faster
(*b*) keep his head bent forward
(*c*) raise the knee higher
(*d*) run on toes

334. Fartlek training method improves–
(*a*) endurance (*b*) speed
(*c*) strength (*d*) flexibility

335. Circuit training improves
(*a*) general physical and motor fitness
(*b*) speed
(*c*) endurance
(*d*) strength

336. Ability to release maximum muscular force in the shortest possible time is called–
(*a*) agility
(*b*) muscular power
(*c*) muscular strength
(*d*) muscular endurance

337. Muscle strength is improved by the movement done–
(*a*) against the gravity
(*b*) assisted by the gravity
(*c*) both the above
(*d*) none of the above

338. Pushing against the wall is an exercise of–
(*a*) isometric (*b*) isotonic
(*c*) isokinetic (*d*) polymetric

339. Arthur Lydiard's methods of training develops–
(*a*) strength (*b*) endurance
(*c*) agility (*d*) flexibility

340. Fartlek is more closely related to–
(*a*) jumpers
(*b*) throwers
(*c*) sprinters
(*d*) middle distance runners

341. After acquiring mastery of all skills, stress is laid on–
(*a*) development of motor components
(*b*) tactical training
(*c*) both (*a*) and (*b*)
(*d*) none of the above

342. Sprinting speed is best developed through–
(*a*) interval training
(*b*) weight training
(*c*) ins and out
(*d*) continuous training

343. To bring a sports person to peak performance in a shorter period of time we use–
(*a*) overload method
(*b*) critical method
(*c*) both the above
(*d*) none of the above

344. For endurance dominating sports, the diet should be rich in–
(*a*) protein (*b*) fat
(*c*) minerals (*d*) carbohydrates

345. High altitude training 8,000 feet–
(*a*) enhances performance
(*b*) deteriorates performance
(*c*) both (*a*) and (*b*)
(*d*) neither (*a*) or (*b*)

346. Which of the following does not belong to the category of dope?
(*a*) Ergogenic aids (*b*) Caffeine
(*c*) Nicotine (*d*) All the above

347. Interval training is an effective method for improving–
(*a*) endurance (*b*) flexibility
(*c*) speed (*d*) strength

348. For maximum adaptation to take place there should be–
(*a*) proper proportion between load and recovery
(*b*) improper proportion between load and recovery
(*c*) break in training
(*d*) none of the above

349. Name, from the following exercises which is considered harmful, to the body mechanics–
(*a*) Wrist rotation
(*b*) Knee rotation
(*c*) Neck rotation
(*d*) Shoulder rotation

350. Ergometry is a process by which we measure–
(*a*) brain activity (*b*) muscle potential
(*c*) lung capacity (*d*) cardiac output

ANSWERS

1	2	3	4	5	6	7	8	9	10
(*b*)	(*a*)	(*c*)	(*c*)	(*c*)	(*b*)	(*c*)	(*b*)	(*a*)	(*d*)
11	**12**	**13**	**14**	**15**	**16**	**17**	**18**	**19**	**20**
(*b*)	(*a*)	(*a*)	(*c*)	(*c*)	(*b*)	(*a*)	(*b*)	(*b*)	(*b*)
21	**22**	**23**	**24**	**25**	**26**	**27**	**28**	**29**	**30**
(*a*)	(*a*)	(*b*)	(*d*)	(*c*)	(*d*)	(*a*)	(*c*)	(*c*)	(*b*)
31	**32**	**33**	**34**	**35**	**36**	**37**	**38**	**39**	**40**
(*c*)	(*a*)	(*c*)	(*d*)	(*c*)	(*a*)	(*a*)	(*c*)	(*b*)	(*b*)
41	**42**	**43**	**44**	**45**	**46**	**47**	**48**	**49**	**50**
(*a*)	(*b*)	(*c*)	(*a*)	(*a*)	(*c*)	(*d*)	(*d*)	(*b*)	(*c*)
51	**52**	**53**	**54**	**55**	**56**	**57**	**58**	**59**	**60**
(*d*)	(*d*)	(*c*)	(*a*)	(*c*)	(*a*)	(*c*)	(*d*)	(*a*)	(*b*)
61	**62**	**63**	**64**	**65**	**66**	**67**	**68**	**69**	**70**
(*c*)	(*a*)	(*d*)	(*c*)	(*c*)	(*c*)	(*d*)	(*b*)	(*d*)	(*a*)

71	72	73	74	75	76	77	78	79	80
(*a*)	(*c*)	(*a*)	(*c*)	(*d*)	(*b*)	(*b*)	(*b*)	(*c*)	(*a*)
81	**82**	**83**	**84**	**85**	**86**	**87**	**88**	**89**	**90**
(*b*)	(*d*)	(*c*)	(*a*)	(*a*)	(*b*)	(*d*)	(*a*)	(*a*)	(*c*)
91	**92**	**93**	**94**	**95**	**96**	**97**	**98**	**99**	**100**
(*a*)	(*b*)	(*b*)	(*a*)	(*d*)	(*b*)	(*d*)	(*c*)	(*a*)	(*b*)
101	**102**	**103**	**104**	**105**	**106**	**107**	**108**	**109**	**110**
(*c*)	(*d*)	(*d*)	(*c*)	(*c*)	(*d*)	(*d*)	(*a*)	(*c*)	(*a*)
111	**112**	**113**	**114**	**115**	**116**	**117**	**118**	**119**	**120**
(*b*)	(*c*)	(*c*)	(*b*)	(*a*)	(*a*)	(*b*)	(*a*)	(*a*)	(*b*)
121	**122**	**123**	**124**	**125**	**126**	**127**	**128**	**129**	**130**
(*b*)	(*c*)	(*d*)	(*a*)	(*b*)	(*b*)	(*c*)	(*a*)	(*a*)	(*c*)
131	**132**	**133**	**134**	**135**	**136**	**137**	**138**	**139**	**140**
(*d*)	(*b*)	(*b*)	(*c*)	(*d*)	(*b*)	(*a*)	(*a*)	(*b*)	(*c*)
141	**142**	**143**	**144**	**145**	**146**	**147**	**148**	**149**	**150**
(*b*)	(*a*)	(*c*)	(*d*)	(*b*)	(*a*)	(*a*)	(*b*)	(*b*)	(*d*)
151	**152**	**153**	**154**	**155**	**156**	**157**	**158**	**159**	**160**
(*a*)	(*d*)	(*d*)	(*c*)	(*a*)	(*a*)	(*d*)	(*d*)	(*a*)	(*c*)
161	**162**	**163**	**164**	**165**	**166**	**167**	**168**	**169**	**170**
(*b*)	(*c*)	(*a*)	(*a*)	(*b*)	(*a*)	(*d*)	(*c*)	(*c*)	(*c*)
171	**172**	**173**	**174**	**175**	**176**	**177**	**178**	**179**	**180**
(*b*)	(*c*)	(*b*)	(*b*)	(*c*)	(*a*)	(*a*)	(*b*)	(*a*)	(*d*)
181	**182**	**183**	**184**	**185**	**186**	**187**	**188**	**189**	**190**
(*a*)	(*d*)	(*d*)	(*d*)	(*c*)	(*c*)	(*a*)	(*d*)	(*b*)	(*a*)
191	**192**	**193**	**194**	**195**	**196**	**197**	**198**	**199**	**200**
(*a*)	(*c*)	(*d*)	(*b*)	(*a*)	(*b*)	(*d*)	(*b*)	(*a*)	(*a*)
201	**202**	**203**	**204**	**205**	**206**	**207**	**208**	**209**	**210**
(*d*)	(*d*)	(*d*)	(*b*)	(*a*)	(*d*)	(*b*)	(*c*)	(*a*)	(*b*)
211	**212**	**213**	**214**	**215**	**216**	**217**	**218**	**219**	**220**
(*a*)	(*b*)	(*c*)	(*c*)	(*c*)	(*b*)	(*b*)	(*d*)	(*c*)	(*d*)
221	**222**	**223**	**224**	**225**	**226**	**227**	**228**	**229**	**230**
(*c*)	(*a*)	(*c*)	(*c*)	(*b*)	(*a*)	(*a*)	(*b*)	(*c*)	(*b*)
231	**232**	**233**	**234**	**235**	**236**	**237**	**238**	**239**	**240**
(*d*)	(*d*)	(*c*)	(*c*)	(*b*)	(*b*)	(*a*)	(*d*)	(*d*)	(*a*)
241	**242**	**243**	**244**	**245**	**246**	**247**	**248**	**249**	**250**
(*b*)	(*d*)	(*a*)	(*c*)	(*d*)	(*c*)	(*d*)	(*a*)	(*c*)	(*b*)
251	**252**	**253**	**254**	**255**	**256**	**257**	**258**	**259**	**260**
(*b*)	(*a*)	(*b*)	(*b*)	(*a*)	(*d*)	(*a*)	(*d*)	(*b*)	(*c*)

261	262	263	264	265	266	267	268	269	270
(*d*)	(*b*)	(*c*)	(*c*)	(*b*)	(*c*)	(*b*)	(*c*)	(*c*)	(*c*)
271	**272**	**273**	**274**	**275**	**276**	**277**	**278**	**279**	**280**
(*b*)	(*a*)	(*c*)	(*c*)	(*c*)	(*a*)	(*a*)	(*b*)	(*a*)	(*a*)
281	**282**	**283**	**284**	**285**	**286**	**287**	**288**	**289**	**290**
(*b*)	(*a*)	(*b*)	(*b*)	(*a*)	(*b*)	(*a*)	(*a*)	(*b*)	(*a*)
291	**292**	**293**	**294**	**295**	**296**	**297**	**298**	**299**	**300**
(*b*)	(*d*)	(*d*)	(*d*)	(*d*)	(*d*)	(*d*)	(*b*)	(*b*)	(*b*)
301	**302**	**303**	**304**	**305**	**306**	**307**	**308**	**309**	**310**
(*c*)	(*a*)	(*a*)	(*d*)	(*d*)	(*c*)	(*a*)	(*d*)	(*a*)	(*a*)
311	**312**	**313**	**314**	**315**	**316**	**317**	**318**	**319**	**320**
(*c*)	(*b*)	(*b*)	(*a*)	(*a*)	(*c*)	(*a*)	(*a*)	(*a*)	(*a*)
321	**322**	**323**	**324**	**325**	**326**	**327**	**328**	**329**	**330**
(*c*)	(*a*)	(*b*)	(*b*)	(*b*)	(*c*)	(*c*)	(*b*)	(*b*)	(*a*)
331	**332**	**333**	**334**	**335**	**336**	**337**	**338**	**339**	**340**
(*a*)	(*a*)	(*c*)	(*a*)	(*d*)	(*b*)	(*a*)	(*a*)	(*b*)	(*d*)
341	**342**	**343**	**344**	**345**	**346**	**347**	**348**	**349**	**350**
(*b*)	(*b*)	(*b*)	(*b*)	(*c*)	(*c*)	(*a*)	(*a*)	(*b*)	(*b*)

UNIT-VIII

RESEARCH

Introduction

Research is an art of scientific investigation. Different scholars define research in different ways. According to Redman and Mory, 'Research is a systematized effort to gain new knowledge." So, people regard research as a march from known towards unknown. It is actually a process of discovery. In common parlance research can be regarded as a search for the knowledge unknown. It is the search for the knowledge unknown. It is the search of specified particular subject. The basic instinct inherent in us, the inquisitiveness, make us curious to know the unknown. We always become curious to know the unknown facts and whenever we find something confronting us our inquisitiveness makes us probe and attain full and fuller understanding of the unknown. The new Penguin English Dictionary defines Research a scientific or scholarly investigation specially study or experiment aimed at the discovery, interpretation, or application of facts, theories or laws. It also calls research as careful or systematic searching or enquiry. So, analyzing the different definitions of Research we can assume that the method which man employs for obtaining the knowledge of whatever is unknown can be termed as Research.

Further, Research according to D. Slesinger and M. Stepehnson as mentioned in the Encyclopaedia of Social Science is "the manipulation of things, concepts or symbols for the purpose of generating, to extend, correct or verify in knowledge whether that knowledge aids in construction of theory or in the practice of an art". So, Research is an original contribution for enhancement and advancement of knowledge which already exists. Research is an academic activity and so, it should be used in a technical sense. According to Clifford Woody Research comprises defining and redefining problems; formulating hypothesis or suggested solutions; collecting, organising and evaluating data; making deductions and reaching conclusion, after which, careful testing is done to check whether it is fit to be formulated as law or hypothesis. So, we can conclude that research is a pursuit of truth with the help of observation, comparison, generalization and formulation of a theory. Thus, the term research refer to the systematic method comprising enunciating the problem, formulating a hypothesis, collecting the facts or data, analyzing the facts and reaching certain conclusions either in the form of solutions towards the concerned problems or in certain generalizations for theoretical formulations.

Research if will be started leads to progress in some fields of life. From the very creation of human habitation on the earth, man is curious to know more and more. So, it is a continuous search for revealing the mysteries of life. He wanted to establish truth by applying in cause and effect method. Advertisement is the sole nature of human activity. So, he devoted his time in education to make his research progressive.

In the modern age of science and technology, every year new products, new facts, new concept, new ways of doing things come into our lives due to ever - increasing significant research in the physical, the biological as well as social and psychological fields.

The word Research, if we analyse letter by letter, we get

R - Rational way of thinking
E - Expert and Exhaustive
S - Search for solution
E - Exactness
A - Analytical Analysis of Adequate Data
R - Relationships of facts
C - (*a*) Careful Observation
(*b*) Critical Observation
(*c*) Constructive Attitude
H - Honesty

The Research is:

- an attitude of enquiry
- an attempt to elicit facts and not mere theorizing
- a scientific method
- a friendly, welcoming attitude towards change
- a process of modifying the traditional steps and procedures which helps in proving new ideas, new techniques for new evolutions.
- a refined and systematic technique for obtaining sufficient solution of a problem.

NATURE AND SCOPE OF RESEARCH

1. Research is needed for the progress of the field of physical education.
2. It gives new dimensions to physical education and sports.
3. Research is needed for the development of new equipments and facilities.
4. It helps for the invention of new methods, technique and procedures.
5. Research helps to solve the critical problem.
6. It helps to dispel myths about many practices in physical education.
7. It helps to prevent athletic injury.
8. Research is useful for the development of scholarly knowledge.
9. It gives pride, prestige, respect, status and confidence to the physical educationists.
10. Research brings physical education equal with other disciplines.
11. Research is needed for professional betterment and all round progress.
12. The various methods of teaching should be adopted only through research. Ex: Part method whole method and part by whole method.
13. New inventions are made in class management size of class, grading and new records with the help of research.
14. The sub areas of physical education are being gradually developed by research. Ex : Competitive sports, sports psychology, sports medicine, anthropology.
15. Research is important for the growth of and development of exercise physiology, sports psychology, sports sociology, learning Health Education and sports journalism.
16. Research will record the progressive changes.
17. Due to research the norms are made in all the major games and field events for all age groups of both sexes.

TYPES OF RESEARCH

Types of Research Based on Purpose

1. **Basic (or) Fundamental or Pure Research:** It is designed to add an organized body of scientific knowledge and does not necessarily produce results of immediate practical value. It is used for advancement of knowledge. The goal of research is the development of theories by the discovery of broad generalization or principle, it is usually carried on in a laboratory situation sometimes with animals as subjects. This type of research has been the activity of psychologists rather than education. The main aim of the basic research is the discovery of knowledge solely for the sake of knowledge. It has little concern for the application of the findings or social usefulness of the findings. It may result in the discovery of new theory or development of the existing theory.
2. **Applied Research:** It is undertaken to solve an immediate practical problem and the goal of adding to scientific knowledge is secondary, it is a process for studying practical problem and finding a solution to it. The focus is to improve and modify the current practices. It is based on basic research. It is used for the purpose of applying or testing the theory and evaluating it's usefulness in solving problems.
3. **Evaluation Research:** The research done for the purpose of evaluating the success of a programme or a curriculum.
   Ex: Is CBSE syllabus better than I.C.S.E syllabus?
4. **Research and Development:** It is used for the development of effective products.
   Ex : Defence Research and Development Organisation (DRDO)

5. **Action Research:** It is focused on immediate and specific application and not on the development of theory or in general application. It's findings have local applicability to particular problem and universal validity. The research specialists are subsidized by universities, private or Government agencies and professional association.

Types of Research Based on Method

1. **Analytical Research:** Type of research that involves in depth study and execution of available information in an attempt to explain complex phenomena. It can be categorized in the following way. Historical, philosophical, review and meta- analysis.
2. **Historical Research:** It deals with events that have already occurred. It focuses on events, organisation institutions and people.
   (*a*) ***Philosophical Research:*** It is characterised by critical inquiry, problems dealing with objectives, curriculum, course content, requirement and methodology are some of the examples for philosophical research.
   (*b*) ***Review:*** A review is a critical evaluation of recent research on a particular topic.
   (*c*) ***Meta analysis:*** A quantitative means of analyzing the findings from numerous studies.
3. **Descriptive Research:** It is concerned with status. This research attempts to determine the current state of such things as knowledge, attitudes and behaviours related to specific issue. The forms of descriptive research is questionnaire, the interview, the normative survey, the case study, the job analysis, the documentary analysis, developmental studies and correlational studies.
   (*a*) ***The normative survey:*** The normative survey generally seeks to gather performance or knowledge data on a large sample from a population and to present the results in the form of comparative standards or norms.
   (*b*) ***The case study:*** The case study is used to provide detailed information about an individual (or) institution, community etc.
   (*c*) ***The job analysis:*** It is used to describe in detail the various duties, procedures, responsibilities, preparations, advantages and disadvantages of a particular job.
   (*d*) ***The documentary analysis:*** Type of descriptive research directed primarily at establishing the status of certain practices, areas of interest, usage of terms and space counts.
   (*e*) ***Development studies:*** It is concerned with interaction of learning or performance with maturation.
   (*f*) ***Correlational studies:*** The purpose of correlational research is to examine the relationship between certain performance variables.
4. **Experimental Research:** Traditionally regarded as the most scientific of all the approaches used, the researcher attempts to manipulate the influence of variable in order to arrive at cause, effect relationship, rather than rely upon existing data, examples of such approaches include the use of both controlled laboratory and field investigations.
5. **Qualitative Research:** Research method that involves intensive, long time observation in a natural setting. Precise and detailed recording of what happens in the settings interpretation and analysis of the data using description, namitives quotes, charts and tables.

FORMULATION AND SELECTION OF RESEARCH PROBLEM

Research Problem

Research problem is a matter difficult for settlement or solution, a question or puzzle propounded for solution.

The problem is a question, a felt need, an issue, which needs to be resolved, a difficulty.

It is the first - step for the discovery of new facts by following certain research procedures, Problems are infinite but it is very difficult to locate them for investigation. The selection of a good research problem is considered as a discovery in itself.

(*a*) Location of Research Problem (or) Sources of the Problem (or) Identification of the Problem

The identification of a research problem is a difficult but an important phase of the entire research process. It requires a great deal of time, energy and logical thinking on the part of the researcher. The following suggestions are designed to provide direction in the search for a research problem.

1. Personal experience of the investigator in the field of physical education is the main source for identifying suitable problem.
2. Many of the problems that arise in the classroom, the school or the community lend themselves to investigation.
3. **Systematically record unsolved problems:** Researcher's professional reading may point out several unsolved problems that could be taken as research topics, class discussions and critical thinking will provide many topics for research.
4. **Analyse literature in an area (or) subject field:** An analysis of the literature in a particular field is the most important source of research problem. Analyse the recommendations suggested in a dissertation, locate and read a review paper, review journals, research journals, term papers, or a recent text book.
5. By analysing throughly an area of special interest the researcher gets many unsolved problems.
6. **Consider corroboration of former studies:** (Study researches already completed) When the researcher reads the thesis already completed he may come across the recommendation heading from that he would be able to select some topic.

   Ex: If a study with the topic study of personality of women athletes and non athletes has been completed, similar study on men athletes and non-athletes could be undertaken by the new investigator.
7. **Examine controversial issues:** Controversy may exist concerning various practices in physical education and sports, controversy exist in warming up, intake of glucose, professionalism, and drugs in sports, thus the research scholar may face a multidimensional problem.
8. **Discussions:** Discussions in the classroom, with friends and experts, discussions in conferences and seminars will suggest many new problems. Consultation with faculty members and fellow research scholars also provide many research problems.
9. **Library Sources:** Various library sources such as books, encyclopaedias, journals; magazine and research abstracts provide idea for new problems.
10. Discover the interests of associations, clubs and society: Frequently various clubs and associations may express interest in expanding specific kinds of research.
11. Technical changes and curricular developments are constantly bringing forth new problems and new opportunities for research.

(*b*)Criteria in Selecting the Research Problem

Certain external and personal criteria are to be considered in the selection of research problem. External criteria have to do with such matters as novelty and importance for the field, availability of data and method and institutional or administrative cooperation.

Personal criteria involved are such considerations as interest training, cost and time etc.

A number of criteria in the form of conditions might be listed for the guidance in the selection of research problem:

1. **External Criteria:**

(*a*) **Novelty:** The research problem should be sufficiently original and new one. The investigator should not select a problem until he is sure that it really is a new problem which has never been investigated before successfully.

(*b*) **Significance of the problem:** While selecting problem, the researcher has to see whether the topic is significant to the profession and useful to the society. Every problem undertaken for investigation must offer something of practical value to physical education, the coaches and the athletes.

(*c*) **Availability of Data:** Availability of data is another most important factor affecting selection of problem, for example, if a research worker has taken a study with a topic, personality traits of Indian kabaddi players he should be able to get data from Indian kabaddi players, otherwise there is no meaning in selecting this topic.

(*d*) **Availability of techniques and apparatus:** One should have the appropriate apparatus or instrument and technique to conduct the research study. If the researcher has taken up a study with the topic, "A comparative study of blood pressure between hockey and foot ball players", the researcher should have spygmomanometer to measure the blood pressure. He also should know how to use the apparatus.

(*e*) **Availability of co-operation:** Researcher may require co-operation from various authorities, institutions and individuals. Investigator must make sure that necessary permission and co-operation will be available regarding research before selecting the research problem.

(*f*) **Aim and level of research:** The aim of research also influences the selection of the problem, the nature and scope of the study will be determined in the light of the levels like, master's degree, M.Phil degree and Ph.D.

2. **Personal Criteria:** The researcher should have a unique drive to do an authentic research work.

(*a*) **Interest towards the problem :** The problem should be interesting for the investigator himself. If investigator is not interested in it, he will not be able to face and overcome the obstacles which come at every step in research.

(*b*) **Researchers competence and knowledge**: Problem selected for investigation should be within the intellectual capacity and capability of the student. If the researcher does not have any knowledge about physiology, he should not select a topic from that area.

(*c*) **Courage and confidence:** The researcher should have courage and determination to carry out the study in spite of the difficulties that may be involved.

(*d*) **Time and financial factor:** The problem selected should be one that can be studied and completed in the allotted time. The researcher must consider carefully his own financial resources to carry out the study.

Based on the above criteria the researcher can modify or change his topic, and select the most suitable one.

Sampling Process and Techniques

There are various sampling techniques available for drawing a sample from the population. In deciding the sampling technique used for drawing a sample an investigator is concerned about two fundamental issues. These are representativeness of sample and minimisation of biases in the study. Further selection of sampling technique is done on the basis of characteristics of the population. Following are the different types of sampling techniques:

1. Simple Random Sampling

It is the most simple and widely used sampling technique. In this sampling technique each member of the population has the same probability of being included in the sample. In random sampling population is numbered from 1 to N and a series of numbers are drawn in a random fashion. Usually three methods are used to draw random samples. These are lottery method, Tappet's number method and computer based generation of random numbers. In a lottery method after preparing the chits from 1 to N corresponding to each population units, it is kept in a bowl. After mixing chits in the bowl, a chit is drawn without looking into the bowl. The number on the chit so drawn is noted. The chit is again replaced back to the bowl and another chit is drawn in a similar fashion. The population units corresponding to the numbers so drawn are included in the sample. The sample so drawn is a simple random sample.

Advantage of Random Sampling

(*a*) It is free from bias.
(*b*) It is more representative.
(*c*) It does not depend upon the prior knowledge of population.
(*d*) It facilitates the analysis of data which includes use of inferential, comparative, relationship and predictive statistics.
(*e*) It is easy to calculate the sampling error in this method.

Disadvantages of Random Sampling

(*a*) The selection of sample becomes difficult when the population units are widely dispersed.
(*b*) In many studies it is difficult to have a population which is completely catalogued.
(*c*) Random sampling is not suitable if the population is heterogeneous.
(*d*) Random sampling is subjected to more error for the same sample size than are found in stratified sampling.

2. Stratified Sampling

In stratified sampling the whole population is divided into number of homogeneous strata or groups and then from each stratum a proportionate sample is drawn using random method. The samples so obtained from each stratum together is known as stratified sample.

Process of stratification: The reliability of stratified sampling depends upon formation of strata. If a proper stratification is made even a small sample will be a representative sample.

Kinds of stratified sampling: There are three types of stratified sampling:

Proportional stratified sample: Under this method the number of units to be drawn from each stratum is in the same proportion as they stand in the population.

Random stratified sample: Under this method equal number of sample is drawn from each stratum randomly. This facilitates inter strata comparison.

Stratified weighted sampling: In this sampling an equal number of Units are selected from each stratum and averages are taken from each stratum but they are given weights in proportion to the size of the stratum in the whole population, this method is free from the defects of disproportionate sample and combines the advantages of the two stratified samples.

Advantage of Stratified Sampling

(*a*) It provides greater control over the sample as no portion of the population is left out being represented in the sample due to stratification.
(*b*) If stratum is perfectly homogeneous even a small sample would serve the purpose.
(*c*) Replacement of unit is possible in case of non response. If an athlete or subject refuses to co-operate with the investigator, this may be replaced by another individual from the same stratum.

Disadvantage of Stratified Sampling

a. Faulty stratification may lead to bias in the sample.
b. In stratified sampling a deliberate attempt has to be made to attain a proportionate sample.
c. In case of no clear cut strategies for stratification it is difficult to put a particular case in a stratum.
d. In the absence of information on proportion of population in each category drawing the sample becomes difficult.

3. Systematic Sampling

Systematic sampling is suitable when the list of sampling unit is available. Suppose that N units of the population are numbered 1 to N and sample of size n is to be selected such that (N/n) = k, k being an integer, systematic sampling then consists in selecting at random a unit from the first k units and then selecting every subsequent unit from the list. Systematic sampling is considered to be mixed sampling, which is partly probabilistic and partly non probabilistic.

Probabilistic because the first unit is selected at random from the first k units and non probabilistic because the other members in the samples are fixed on the choke of the first member. If a sample is to be drawn from the list of the students in college or from a telephone directory, systematic sampling would be suitable in such situations.

4. Sequential Sampling

In sequential sampling samples are drawn one by one. The idea is to draw the minimum sample required for drawing the conclusion about the hypothesis to be tested. Under this sampling plan a very small sample is taken and d and b, the two types of error are computed. On the basis of criteria involving a and b the decision of their accepting or rejecting the hypothesis is tested.

5. Cluster Sampling

Cluster sampling is essentially a simple random sampling. The only difference between cluster and random sampling is in the size of the basic unit being investigated. In cluster sampling an ultimate sampling unit in the population is a cluster of many.

Ex: A family, college team or university team may be an ultimate sampling unit in the experiment.

6. Multi-stage sampling

In multistage sampling the population is regarded as composed of a number of first stage (or primary) sampling units each of which, in it's turn, is made up of a number of third stage (or tertiary) units and so on until the ultimate sampling unit in which we are interested is reached. In this method, sampling is also carried out in stages. Initially, the first stage sampling units are sampled by some suitable random method.

Depending upon the nature of the study further stages may be added to get a sample of ultimate sampling units. In drawing a sample of class X boys in Madhya Pradesh first a sample of districts is drawn then a sample of school from each selected district is drawn and finally a sample of class X boys is drawn from each selected school.

Although multistage sampling introduces a flexibility into the sampling procedure, however, in general it is less efficient than some suitable single stage sampling.

7. Purposive Sampling

In this sampling, individuals are selected according to some purposive principle.

Ex : An observer who is to select a sample of students of height in the range of 5.4 to 5.8 from a college looks to the whole lot of students and then chooses students only from the required height group. It is normally claimed that the purposive sampling is more likely to give a representative sample. But in most cases it may involve some bias of unknown magnitude.

The advantage of this kind of sampling is that the investigator can pick up variables with objective in view. Further a small purposive sample can be a good representative on the other hand there is a lot of scope for subjectivity in this method. And also an investigator may not have full knowledge of the population which is one of the prerequisites in this method.

METHODS OF RESEARCH

It seems appropriate at this juncture to explain the difference between research method and research methodology. Research method may be understood as all those methods/techniques that are used for conduct of research. Research methods or techniques thus refer to the methods the researcher uses in performing research operation, in other words, all those methods which are used by the researcher during the course of studying his research problem are termed as research methods. Since the object of research, particularly the applied research, is to arrive at a solution for a given problem, the available data and the unknown aspects of the problem have to be related to each other to make a solution possible. Keeping this in view research methods can be put into the following three groups.

1. In the first group we include those methods which are concerned with the collection of data. These methods will be used where the data already available are not sufficient to arrive at the required solution.
2. The second group consists of those statistical techniques which are used for establishing relationship between the data and the unknowns.
3. The third group consists of those methods which are used to evaluate the accuracy of the results obtained.

Research methods falling in the above stated last two groups are generally taken as the analytical tools of research.

Research methodology is a way to systematically solve the research problem. It may be understood as a science of studying how research is done scientifically i.e. we study the various steps that are generally adopted by a researcher in studying his research problem along with the logic behind them. It is necessary for the researcher to know not only the research methods/ techniques but also the methodology. Researcher not only need to know how to develop certain indices or tests, how to calculate the mean, the mode, the median or the standard deviation or chi-square, how to apply particular research techniques, but they also need to know which of these methods or techniques, are relevant and which are not, and what would they mean and indicate and why. Researchers also need to understand the assumptions underlying various techniques and they need to know the criteria by which they can decide that certain techniques and procedures will be applicable to certain problems and others will not. All this means that it is necessary for the researcher to design his methodology for his problem as the same may differ from problem to problem.

For example: An architect, who designs a building has to consciously evaluate the basis of his decisions i.e. he has to evaluate why and on what basis he selects particular size, number and location of doors, windows and uses particular materials and not other and the like. Similarly, in research the scientist has to expose the research decisions to evaluation before they are implemented. He has to specify very clearly and precisely what decisions he selects and why he selects them so that they can be evaluated by others also.

From what has been stated above, we can say that research methodology has many dimensions and research methods do constitute a part of the research methodology. The scope of research methodology is wider than that of research methods. Thus, when we talk of research methodology we do not only talk of the research methods but also consider the logic behind the methods we use in the context of our research study and explain why we are using a particular method or technique and why we are not using others so that research results are capable of being evaluated either by the researcher himself or by others.

Why research study has been undertaken, how the research problem has been defined, in what way and why the hypothesis has been formulated, what data have been collected and what particular method has been adopted, why particular technique of analysing data has been used and a host of similar other questions are usually answered when we talk of research methodology concerning a research problem or study.

STATISTICAL TECHNIQUES

Parametric statistical tests assume that the data are essentially normally distributed following probability principles, for different statistical inferences.

Non-parametric statistical tests. This type of tests is applicable to non - normally distributed data also known as distribution free test which do not require normally distributed data.

Measures of Central Tendency

A measures of central tendency is a single figure (or) single score in a distribution.

Measures of central tendency has three parts.

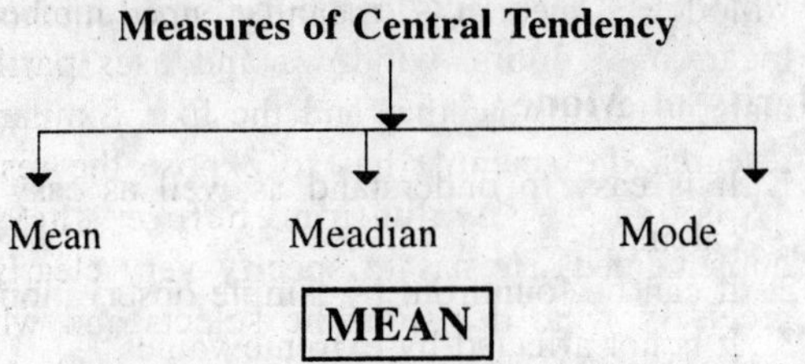

MEAN

Mean is an average, mean is defined as the central massing of the scores in a distribution.

Types of Mean

1. Arithmetic mean
2. Geometric mean
3. Hormonic mean

1. **Arithmetic mean:** A set of observation, if their sum is divided by the number of observation, mean is central massing of the scores and according to the distance of scores it will fill at the centre of the score, mean of the series one data is the single figure obtained by dividing the total value of various scores, or items, by their numbers. Mean for ungrouped data:

$$\text{Mean } \bar{X} = \frac{\Sigma x}{N}$$

Where

Σ = summation

X = raw score

N = Total number of score

Mean for grouped data :

$$\text{Mean } \bar{X} = A + \left(\frac{\Sigma\ fd}{N}\right) i$$

A = Assumed Mean

i = Class interval

N = Total number of score.

Merits of Mean

1. It is the simplest average to understand and easier to calculate.
2. It is affected by the value of each observation in the distribution.
3. It is defined by a rigid mathematical formula so the mean is the same for the distribution whichever way we calculate it.
4. It is a calculated value and not based on position in the distribution.
5. It provides good basis for comparison.
6. The mean is the most stable measures of central tendency that is why it is otherwise known as ideal average (or) sensitive mean.

Demerits of Mean

1. Since the value of mean depends upon each item of the series extreme items unduly affect, it may lead to a false conclusion.
2. By knowing the value of mean we cannot be able to judge the real fact.
3. It cannot be accurately calculated if one of the values is not known.
4. It cannot be located by observation (or) method.
5. It gives greater importance to the bigger items and lesser importance to the smaller items in the distribution.

Uses of Mean

1. It will help to find out the correct average of the group.
2. This will be used for further statistical calculation.
3. Mean enables the researcher to compare two (or) more groups.
4. When the scores are truncated the principles of mean will be used by finding out the average.

MEDIAN

Median is the mid point of the distribution in which 50% of scores, lie above the median and 50% of scores lie below the median.

$$\text{Ungrouped data median} = \left(\frac{n+1}{2}\right) \text{th score}$$

$$\text{Grouped data median} = L + \left(\frac{n/2 - cf}{fm}\right) i$$

L = Lower limit of the median step interval
cf = Cumulative frequency just below (or) above the median step interval.
f = frequency of the median step interval
i or c = class interval
N = Total number of scores.

Merits of Median

1. It is easy to calculate and easy to understand.
2. Since, it is the positional average the value of the mean can be computed even if the items at the extreme (or) unknown.
3. Median can some times be known by simple inspection.
4. We can be able to find out the median through graphical method.
5. It eliminates the effect of extreme item.

Demerits of Median

1. If the data is truncated the concept of median should not be used to find out average.
2. It is ill defined.
3. Since it is a positional average the value of median will not be depending upon every scores in the distribution.
4. For calculating median the data has to be arranged.
5. In case of even numbers of scores the value of median cannot be known in the simple observation.
6. If the number of items are large, it is very difficult to arrange the scores either ascending (or) descending.
7. It is not used for further statistical calculation.

Uses of Median

1. Median can be used to solve the immediate problem.
2. When the exact mid point of the distribution is needed, the concept of median is used.

MODE

Mode is defined as the value which occurs greatest number of times in a distribution. It is derived from the French word "La mode" meaning the fashion.

Mode = 3 median - 2 mean (grouped method).

Merits of Mode

1. It is easy to understand as well as easy to calculate.
2. It can be found out by simple observation.
3. It is not affected by extreme values.
4. It is very simple and precise.
5. It is the most representative average.
6. It can be used to describe the qualitative phenomenon.

Demerits of Mode

1. It is not based on all the scores.
2. It is ill defined.
3. It is not suitable for further statistical calculation.
4. When there are more than one mode, it is very difficult to find out exact average.
5. The value of mode is based upon the majority of the comes under specific category.

Uses of Mode

1. The concept of mode is used by the people in their daily life.
2. It is useful in industry and business.
3. Mode is used to solve the immediate problem.
4. Mode helps the manufacturers in deciding the models.

Measures of Variability

It is single score that indicates how the score are deviated from the measures of central tendency.

Ex : Range, mean deviation, standard deviation, quartile deviation.

Range

Range is the difference between the lowest and highest score.

Range is the measure of variability which measures maximum variation in the distribution.

$$R = X_H - X_L$$

Standard Deviation

Standard Deviation indicates the spread of the middle 68.26 percentiles of the scores taken from the mean.

$$S.D. = \sqrt{\frac{\Sigma x^2}{N}}$$

Grouped data method

$$S.D. = c\sqrt{\frac{\Sigma fd^2}{N} - \left(\frac{\Sigma fd}{N}\right)^2}$$

Raw score method (ungrouped)

$$S.D. = \sqrt{\frac{N\Sigma x^2 - (\Sigma x)^2}{N}}$$

Merits of Standard Deviation

1. It is rigidly defined.
2. It is based upon all the observation in the data.
3. The mean and standard deviation are considered as hard and clear with each other.
4. It is based upon the arithmetic mean.
5. Squaring the deviation makes all of them positive as such there is no need to ignore.

Uses of Standard Deviation

1. The standard deviation is the most reliable method of variability and it is used when the mean in the measures of central tendency spreads.
2. When the statistics need greatest, stability we use the concept of standard deviation.
3. It is the only one variability encountered in advanced statistics.
4. It is used when the co-efficients correlation and other statistics are to be computed.
5. Standard deviation is also used in construction of various test scales.

   T - scale

   H - scale

   6 - scale
6. The standard deviation provides the unit of measurement from the normal distribution.

Demerits

(*i*) It is very difficult to understand and calculate.

(*ii*) Since it is based upon all the observation, if any one of the observation is missed, the value of standard deviation changes.

Quartile Deviation

Quartile deviation indicates the spread of the middle 50% of the scores taken from median. Otherwise it is half of the difference between the first and third quartiles.

Merits

1. It is easy to calculate.
2. It is easy to understand.
3. It is not influenced by extreme values.
4. It ignores the first 25% and last 25% of the item.

Demerits

1. It will not give any idea of distribution of the remaining since it is a positional average, it is not used for further statistical calculation.

Uses of Quartile Deviation

(*i*) It should be used when the median is the measure of central tendency.

(*ii*) It is used when the standard deviation is disproportionate, all affected by widely scattered (or) extremely scattered (or) extreme scores.

HYPOTHESIS – FORMULATION, TYPES AND TESTING

Definition

A hypothesis is a tentative generalization the validity of which remains to be tested. It is most elementary stage, the hypothesis may be any guess, imaginative idea which becomes the basis for further investigation.

Importance of Hypothesis

By formulating hypothesis the researcher puts himself on the right track. Hypothesis is based on other experiences and one's own too serve as the torch light to the researcher. It makes him to decide what to look for and how to look for. He must keep on to the right track so as to reach the final goal, hypothesis gives right direction to the research.

Types of Hypothesis

Based on how they are derived, hypothesis is classified into two types.

(*i*) Inductive hypothesis

(*ii*) Deductive hypothesis.

An inductive hypothesis is a generalization based on observation. Such inductively derived hypothesis can be very useful but are of limited scientific value. They are derived from specific to general.

(*i*) Deductive Hypothesis

(*ii*) Deductive hypothesis are derived from theory. They contribute to the science of education by providing evidence that supports, expands (or) contradicts a given theory and by suggesting future studies. It is derived from general to specific.

Based on how they are stated hypothesis is classified into two types :

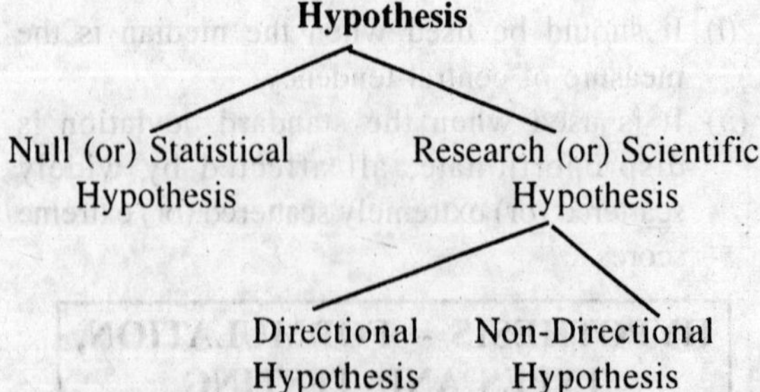

(*i*) **Null hypothesis:** A statistical or null hypothesis states that there is no relationship (or) difference between variables and that any relationship found will be by chance, not a true one.

Ex: There will not be any significant difference in fitness between basket ball players and foot ball players.

(*ii*) **Research Hypothesis:** Research hypothesis is staged in declarative form. A research hypothesis states an expected relationship or difference between two variables in other words, what relationship the researcher expects to verify through the collection and analysis of the data.

Ex: There will be significant difference in fitness between basket ball players and foot ball players.

WRITING RESEARCH REPORT

The findings of research must be reported so that the concerned people such as coaches, physical educationalists etc. could be aware of new professional field of knowledge.

A written format of a research work is known as thesis or research report. The success of a research scholar at any level mainly depends upon an orderly presentation of his thesis.

Research material collected by the research scholar during the long period of his study will have to be written in a professional manner for acceptance by his guide and finalised in form of research report.

Thesis report consists of three main sections:

(*i*) **Preliminary section (or) front material**

1. Fly leaf
2. Title page
3. Approval page
4. Vita
5. Acknowledgement
6. Dedication (optional)
7. Table of contents
8. List of tables
9. List of figures.

(*ii*) **The main body of thesis**

1. Introduction
2. Review of related literature
3. Methodology
4. Analysis and interpretation of results
5. Summary conclusions and recommendations.

(*iii*) **Reference section**

1. Bibliographies
2. Appendices
3. Index

A. Preliminary Section

1. **Fly Leaf:** It is an empty page
2. **Title page:**
   (*a*) Title of the study in the inverted pyramid form and in capital letters.
   (*b*) Name of the candidate (if desired previous background)
   (*c*) Name of the institution and university.
   (*d*) Degree to which report is submitted.
   (*e*) The month and year of presentation.
3. **Approval Page:** It is specified by the institution or university where the thesis is submitted. It can be in the form of certificate with the signature of the supervisor (or) in the following form.

$$\text{Approved} = \frac{\text{Signature of the advisor}}{\text{Typed name of the advisor}}$$

4. **Vita:** The vita gives the reader adequate background information about the scholar as given below.
   (*a*) Name of the author
   (*b*) Date of birth
   (*c*) Place of birth
   (*d*) Under graduate and graduate institutions attended
   (*e*) Degrees awarded with month and year.
   (*f*) Professional experiences
   (*g*) Awards and honours received
   (*h*) National, state, university and college Representation.
   (*i*) List of publications.
5. **Acknowledgement:** The research scholar acknowledges the guidance and assistance of his advisor and others who have helped him.
6. **Dedication (optional) personal information:** The research scholar dedicates the study to his/her near and dear.
7. **Table of contents:** In table of contents, chapter headings and subheadings, are given, it is typed in capital letters, double space between table of contents and chapter headings and single space between individual subheadings. Roman numerals for chapter and Arabic numberals for page numbers are given. Page numbers are typed in such a manner that the last number of page is in line with last letter of the word page.
8. **List of tables and figures:** If tables and figures are presented in the report a separate page is included, full titles of tables and figures with their corresponding numbers and page is cited.

B. Main Body of Thesis

1. **Introduction:** Normally it contains a short introductory statement leading to the problem. It should be followed by.
2. **Statement of the problem:** The entire study develops from the statement. The investigator should orient the reader to the importance and need of the study. The purpose of the study may itself be the statement on the problem. This should be stated concisely and dearly.
3. **Hypothesis:** The hypothesis which may be the assumption, an intelligent guess, or a speculation which is expressed in operational terms.
4. **Delimination:** It is the boundaries of the study the restriction like number and type of subjects participating, number and kind of variables and other factors are shown in deliminations.
5. **Limitations:** Limitation experienced by the scholar are also drawn back to the study– adequate instru-ments, duration, financial difficulties etc.
6. **Significance of the problem:** This deals with worthiness of the study. The scholar should state how can the results be used to improve some aspects of the profession.
7. **Operational definitions:** Important relevant terms in the study may be defined operationaly with proper references.

Review of Related Literature: The review of the related studies makes the reader familiar with the background of the study, it provides the investigator an insight into the problem. Previous research studies are abstracted and significant writings of authorities in the area under study are reviewed in this section.

Methodology: The procedure and methods adopted in the study are described in the following sub headings.

(*a*) Selection of subjects
(*b*) Selection of variables
(*c*) Tools used
(*d*) Administration of tests
(*e*) Data collection
(*f*) Experimental design and statistical procedure

Analysis and Interpretation of Data: In this chapter analysis and results are reported so as to draw the inferences of the study. The analysis of data are presented in tabulated form, in figures and pictorial presentation, discussions, findings are also presented in this Chapter.

Summary Conclusions And Recommendations: In summary, researcher briefly reviews the procedures, findings and entire development of the body. The conclusions are stated shortly and clearly in relation to hypothesis.

C. Reference Section

This section includes bibliography, appendix and index.

BIBLIOGRAPHY

It is a record of those sources and materials that have been used for study. The researcher may divide the bibliography into different sections. One for books, one for periodicals and journals and one for thesis.

APPENDIX

Appendices include questionnaires, copies of covering letters used, checklists, evaluation sheets, raw data and tests.

INDEX

If study is complex, of major importance and likely to be published in book or monograph form, the researcher also prepares an index in alphabetical order which follows the appendix.

Correlation

It refers to the relationship between the pairs of measures. Correlation analysis attempt to determine the degree of relationship between the variables.

It is a single score that indicates to what extent these variables are related. Coefficient of correlation is a quantitative value of the relationship between two (or) more variables either in a positive or negative direction is also called correlation.

Positive Correlation

The following are the example for the positive correlation. They are :

1. Intelligence and academic achievements
2. Height and shoe size.

From the above example we can be able to understand one variable increases proportionally the other variable also increase so there is positive correlation between two parallel variables.

Negative Correlation

1. Age of an automobile and trade value
2. Type spread in practice and number of typing errors.

From the above examples we can understand that one variable increases, the another variable tends to decrease. It shows there is negative relation between two variables.

There is a possibility having "o" as the correlation between two variables. That is known as no correlation exists between the two variables.

1. Relationship between the body weight and intelligence.
2. Relationship between the shoe size and monthly salary.

Formula for correlation

$$r = \frac{\sum xy}{\sqrt{\sum x^2 \sum y^2}}$$

Normal Curve : Definition

The normal curve is bilaterally symmetrical with a high concentration of scores at the centre and a slopping off towards the end.

Normal Probability Curve (or) Bell shaped curve (or) Curve of error (or) Gaussian Curve.

Normal Probability Curve

An understanding of normal probability curve is very important in the physical education students in research. This curve will give clear idea over reliability and it is also useful to arrive at conclusion through statistical result.

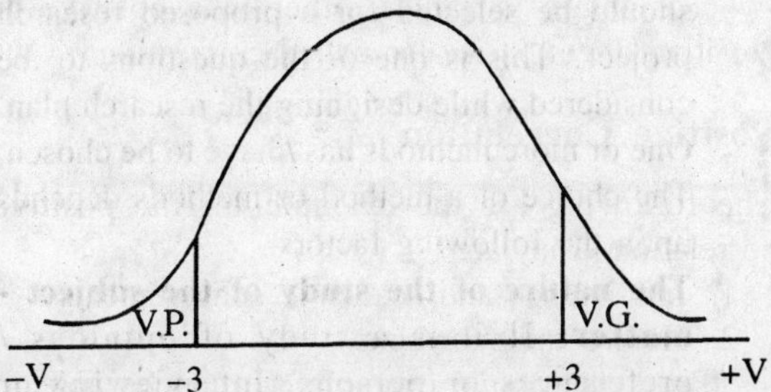

Whenever the data is collected from the homogenous group the obtained curve will be the normal curve in which all averages lie at centre of the curve and also the standard deviation is equally distributed on either side from the centre point.

CHI-SQUARE

The square of a standard normal variate is known as a chi-square variate with 1 degree of freedom.

Application of Chi-Square (χ^2)

Chi-square distribution has a large number of application in applied research but a few which are widely used are enumerated below :

1. To test the equal occurrence hypothesis.
2. To test the independence of attributes.
3. To compare the attitude in two different groups.

Chi-square test for equal occurrence Hypothesis: This test is meant for testing the significance of the discrepancy between theory and experiment and was developed by Prof. Karl Pearson in 1900, it enables us to find if the deviation of the experiment from theory is just by chance or is it really due to the inadequacy of the theory to fit the observed data?

It is a set of observed frequencies and frequency in the corresponding set of expected frequency.

't'-test : 't' - Ratio

t-ratio it is the standard error distance from the mean.

$$t = \frac{Dm}{\sigma_{Dm}}$$

Dm = mean difference

σ_{Dm} = standard error of mean difference.

$Dm = |m_1 - m_2|$

Uncorrelated data:

$$\sigma_{Dm} = \sqrt{\sigma^2_{m_1} + \sigma^2_{m_2}}$$

$$\sigma_{m_1} = \frac{\sigma_1}{\sqrt{N_1}}$$

$$\sigma_{m_2} = \frac{\sigma_2}{\sqrt{N_2}}$$

$$t = \frac{Dm}{\sigma_{Dm}}$$

$$\sigma_{Dm} = \sqrt{\sigma^2_{m_1} + \sigma^2_{m_2} - 2r\sigma_{m_1}\sigma_{m_2}}$$

$$\sigma_{m_1} = \frac{\sigma_1}{\sqrt{N_1}}$$

$$\sigma_{m_2} = \frac{\sigma_2}{\sqrt{N_2}}$$

$$Dm = |m_1 - m_2|$$

Z scale: The z scale consists of standard deviation distance of the scores from the mean value.

$$z = \frac{x - m}{\sigma}, \text{ m is the mean}$$

F - ratio: The ratio of true variance over error variance.

$$F = \frac{(ms)_b}{(ms)_w}$$

$(ms)_b$ = means square. (between the sets)

$(ms)_w$ = means square. (within the sets)

It is the formula used when more than two groups are tested. It will indicate if there is any overall significant difference among the means, it is used to upset or regret.

$$F = \frac{(ms)_b}{(ms)_w}$$

$$A = \sum x^2$$

$$B = \left(\frac{\sum x}{N}\right)^2$$

$$C = \frac{(\sum x_1)^2}{n_1} + \frac{(\sum x_2)^2}{n_2} + \frac{(\sum x_3)^2}{n_3}$$

$$+ - - - + \frac{(\sum x_1)^2}{n_i}$$

SUMMARY OF ANOVA TABLE

Sources of Variance	Sum score	Degree of freedom	M.S.	F
Total (SST)	A-B	N-1	$\frac{A-B}{N-1}$	
Between (SSB)	S-B	K-1	$\frac{C-B}{K-1}$	$\frac{(ms)_b}{(ms)_w}$
Within (SSW)	A-C	N-K	$\frac{A-C}{N-K}$	

DATA COLLECTION TOOLS AND TECHNIQUE

Meaning of Data

The search for answers to research questions calls for collection of data. Data are facts, figures and other relevant materials, past and present, serving as bases for study and analysis. Some examples of data are :

The types of loans secured by borrowers (for a credit survey)

1. **Choice of Methods of Data Collection:** Which of the above methods of data collection should be selected for a proposed research project? This is one of the questions to .be considered while designing the research plan. One or more methods has / have to be chosen. The choice of a method or methods depends upon the following factors.

   The nature of the study of the subject - matter: If it is a study of opinions / preferences or persons. Interviewing or mailing may be appropriate depending on the educational level of the respondents. On the other hand an impact study may call for experimentation and a study of behavioural pattern may require observation.
2. **The unit of enquiry:** The unit of enquiry may be an individual, household, institution or community. To collect data from households interviewing is preferable. Data from institutions may be collected by mail survey and studies on communities call for observational method.
3. **The size and spread of the sample:** If the sample is small and the area covered is compact, interviewing may be preferable but a large sample scattered over a wider area may require mailing.
4. **Scale of the survey:** A large scale survey may require mailing or interviewing through trained investigators.
5. **The educational level of respondents:** For a simple survey among educated persons concerned with the subject - matter of study,

a mail survey may be appropriate. But for a survey of less educated / illiterate persons like industrial workers, slum dwellers, rural people, interviewing is the only suitable method.

6. **The type and depth of information to be collected:** For collection of general simple factual and non-emotional data, interviewing or mailing is appropriate. For an in depth survey of personal experiences and sensitive issues, in depth interview is essential. For collection of data on behaviour, culture, customs, life style etc. observational method is required.
7. **The availability of skilled and trained man power:** In this case, even for a large general survey entailing many complicated questions, interviewing can be adopted.
8. **The rate of accuracy and representative nature of data required:** Interviewing is the most appropriate method for collecting accurate, data from a representative sample of population. Interviewing can achieve a higher response rate.

A researcher can select one or more of the methods keeping in view the above factors. No method is universal. Each method's unique feature should be compared with the needs and conditions of the study and thus the choice of the methods should be decided.

SOURCES OF DATA

The source of data may be classified into

(*a*) Primary sources

(*b*) Secondary sources

(*a*) Primary Sources: Provide direct description of the study by the person who was actually observing or witnessing the occurrence of the event or happenings.

Ex. Observation, interviewing, mailing etc.

(*b*) Secondary sources: These materials include publications written by authors who were not direct observers or participants in the events. Primary sources have to be preferred over secondary sources. The sources of information have been classified as direct and indirect sources.

Direct sources: Educational journals, books, monographs, year books and bulletins, thesis and government publication.

Indirect sources: Encyclopaedia, indexes, abstracts, directories, bibliographies, quotation and miscellaneous sources.

Data can be collected by following base:

1. **By observation:** Collection of information by way of investigators own observations, without interviewing the respondent.
2. **Through personal interviews:** The investigators follow a rigid procedure, seek answer to a set of pre consumed questions through personal interviews.
3. **Through telephone interviews:** This method of collecting information involves conducting interview of the respondents on telephone itself.
4. **By mailing questionnaires:** Questionnaires are mailed to the respondents with request to return after completing the same.
5. **Through schedules:** Data as collected by filling up the schedules by inumerators on the basis of replies given by the respondent.
6. **Execution of the project:** The researcher should see that the project is executed in a systematic manner.

TOOLS AND TECHNIQUE

Tools

The various methods of data gathering involve the use of appropriate recording forms. These are called tools or instruments of data collection.

They consist of observation schedule or observationnaire:

1. **Observation schedule or observationnaire:** This is a form on which observations of an object or a phenomenon are recorded. The items to be observed are determined with reference to the nature and objectives of the study. They are grouped into appropriate categories and listed in the schedule in the order in which the observer would observe them.

2. **Interview guide:** This is used for non-directive and depth interviews. It does not contain a complete list of items on which information has to be elicited from a respondent.
3. **Interview schedule and mailed questionnaire:** Both these tools are widely used in surveys. Both are complete lists of questions on which information is elicited from the respondents. The basic differences between them lies in recording response. While a schedule is filled out by the interviewer, a questionnaire is completed by the respondent.
4. **Rating scale:** This is a recording form used for measuring individuals attitude, aspirations and other psychological and behavioural aspects and group behaviour.
5. **Check list:** This is the simplest of all the devices. It consists of a prepared list of items pertinent to an object or a particular task. The presence or absence of each items may be indicated by checking 'yes' or 'no' or multipoint scale. The use of a check list ensures a more complete consideration of all aspects of the object, act or task.
6. **Opinionnaire:** This is a list of questions or statements pertaining to an issue or programme. It is used for studying the opinions of people. It is commonly used in opinion polls. People are asked to express their responses to the listed questions or reactions to the listed statements.
7. **Document schedule / data sheet:** This is a list of items of information to be obtained from documents, record and other materials. In order to secure measurable data, the items, included in the schedule are limited to those that can be uniformly secured from a large number of case histories or other records.
   For example: A study of annual returns and financial statements filed by joint - stock companies with registrar of joint - ' stock companies may include such items as age of the company, membership.
8. **Schedule for institutions:** This is used for survey of organisations like business enterprises, educational institutions, social or cultural organisations and the like. These data are gathered from their records, annual reports and financial statements.
9. **Inventories:** An inventory is essentially a list the respondent is asked to mark or check in a particular way".

Some example of inventories are:

1. Lists of interest: The respondents are asked to check those things that interest them a lot.
2. List of personality traits: People are asked to check which of these apply to them.
3. List of spare - time activities: One has to check the activity engaged most often.
4. Perceived effects of TV. (Stimulation of activities): The respondents may be asked to check 'true' or 'untrue' the following items.
   (*a*) I have copied the way the people dress on TV.
   (*b*) I have made things after they have been shown on TV.
   (*c*) I have purchased a particular brand after seeing its advertisement on TV.
   (*d*) I have gone to an art gallery after seeing it on TV and so on.

Inventories can be constructed with various purposes in mind or to test particular hypothesis. They invariably form part of a questionnaire/ schedule.

Some Other Useful Matters

Major Considerations in the Selection of a Good Research Problem in Physical Education

1. Selection of problem area should be closely related to professional work.
2. The research worker should take into consideration the availability of and personality characteristics of the faculty member under whose guidance he shall have to work.

3. Researcher must make sure that data shall be available within stipulated time and easily accessible.
4. Researcher must reflect on the availability of reference material, books and journals etc.
5. The researcher must spend enough time in establishing the significance of the research problem.
6. Possibility of the publication of the result. This is likely to add significant to the professional status of the research worker.
7. Researcher should take into account the risks, penalties, handicaps or costs of physical, financial, personal, social or professional character.
8. Researcher should be self-motivated and genuinely interested in the area of research.
9. The problem should be reasonably and sufficiently original so that it does not involve questionable duplication.
10. The nature and scope of the research study will be determined by the level of research like Master's degree, M. Phil. Degree or the PhD.

Guidelines in Selecting the Sample for Study

1. Define the universe of individuals, items or events in terms of its composition and characteristics.
2. Demarcate the sampling unit in terms of its geographical or social boundaries.
3. Determine the size of the sample in relation to the population, which it represents. The sample should neither be too large nor too small; it should be optimum. An optimum sample is one, which fulfills the requirements of efficiency, representativeness, reliability and flexibility.
4. Consider the financial aspects of the study while determining the size and type of the sample.
5. Control the systematic bias as much as possible. Sampling error can be controlled by increasing the size of the sample but doing so will have financial implications. Select a better sampling design, which has a smaller sampling error.
6. Make the sample truly representative of its population so that results from the sample study could be generalized. If a study on the personality structure of athlete is planned, the researcher should first of all clearly define the population of athletes in terms of game/sport, age, sex, achievement, status and such other characteristics, and then apply "random sampling technique to select the designed number of people as a sample for observation.

Different Tools Used for Data Collection in Research

1. **The Questionnaire:** A questionnaire is a form prepared and distributed to secure responses to certain questions. It is a systematic compilation of questions that are submitted to a sample of population from which information is desired.
2. **Interview:** Interview is a two-way method, which permits an exchange of ideas and information. Interviews vary in purpose, nature and scope. They may be confined to one individual or extended to several people who are closely associated with him as in a case study.
3. **Schedule:** Schedule is the name given to a list of questions to which responses are obtained from by the investigator in a face-to-face contact. It is the name usually applied to set of questions, which are asked by the interviewer from the interviewee. A schedule is different from a questionnaire in that it is administered personally to respondent or a group of respondents while the questionnaire is usually sent by mail expecting return of responses by mail.
4. **Opinionnaire:** Opinion polling or opinion gauging represents a single-question approach. The answers are usually in the form of 'Yes' or 'No'. It is a special form of inquiry used by the researcher to collect the opinions

of a sample of population on certain factors of the problem under investigation. These opinions, on different factors of the problems under study are further quantified, analyzed and interpreted.

5. **Sociometry:** Sociometry is a technique for describing social relationships that exist between individuals in a group.

It attempts to describe attractions or repulsions between individuals by asking them to indicate whom they would choose or reject in various situations.

Merits and Limitations of Means

Mean: The mean is considered as the first measure of central tendency. It is representative of the typical performance of individuals in a group.

Merits:

1. It is the simplest average to understand and easier to compute.
2. It is affected by the value of each observation or item in the distributions.
3. It is defined by a rigid mathematical formula with the result that every one who computes the average, gets the same answer.
4. Being determined by a rigid formula, it lends itself to subsequent algebraic treatment better than the median or mode.
5. It is relatively reliable in the sense that it does not vary too much when repeated samples are taken from the same population, at least not as much as some other kind of statistical descriptions.
6. The mean is typical in the sense that it is the centre of gravity balancing the values on either side of it.
7. It is a calculated value and not based on position in the series.

Limitations:

1. Since the value of mean depends upon each item of series, extreme items unduly affect it. The smaller the number of observation, greater is likely to be the impact of extreme scores.
2. It is not always a good measure of central tendency. The mean provides a 'characteristic' value, only when the distribution of the variable is reasonably normal (bell shaped). In case of a V-shaped distribution the mean is not likely to serve useful purpose.

Characteristics of a Normal Probability Curve

Normal probability curve was invented by De-Moivre in 1733. Later on Gauss and Laplace made improvements in the curve, thus, normal probability curve is also called Gaussian Curve or normal curve.

Characteristics of a normal probability curve are :

1. The curve is bell shaped.
2. The curve is bilaterally symmetrical i.e. if it is folded at the centre both parts superimpose each other.
3. The curve is asymptotic to the base.
4. The mean median, mode are equal and lie at the same point.
5. The normal probability curve is unimodal.
6. The base of the curve is measured in standard score units z.

$$z = \frac{X - M}{\sigma} = \sigma$$

7. For practical purposes the base is divided into 6 z units.
8. The total area under the curve is equal to N (Total Number of cases).
9. The area within M $\pm$ 1 σ is equal to 68.26 %.
10. The area within M $\pm$2 σ is 95.44 %.
11. The area within M $\pm$3 σ is 99.73 %.
12. The ordinates at equal distances from mean are equal.
13. Q_1 and Q_3 lie at equal distance from mean.
14. The maximum height of the ordinate at the centre is .3989.
15. The points of inflexion lie at $\pm$ 1 σ 1 from mean.
16. It is a mathematically defined curve in which ratio of height to the width at any point is given by

$$y = \frac{N}{\sigma\sqrt{2\pi}}\left(\frac{-X^2}{e^{2\sigma^2}}\right)$$

where N = Number of cases

σ = Standard deviation

π = 3.14 16 (a constant)

e = 2.7183 (a constant)

x = $x - M$ (Deviation from mean)

y = height of the ordinate

Characteristics of a Good Hypothesis

A good hypothesis should have the following characteristics:

1. It should be testable. An effective way of formulating a testable hypothesis would be to start conducting small prior studies on the subject.
2. A good hypothesis must be clearly stated, specified in unequivocal terms the relationship between dependent and independent variables.
3. A good hypothesis should be limited in scope and must be specific in its focus. Hypothesis of global nature are difficult to tackle in the sense that they require more time, more energy and more effort and involvement of a greater number of researchers.
4. Hypothesis must have consistency into the known facts. Many issues in behavioural field especially in physical education and sport are either controversial or have not been succinctly resolved. Under these circumstances it is natural for the hypothesis to be consistent with some available facts and inconsistent with others.
5. A good hypothesis should be stated in simple terms. The language used should be direct and clear. Vague, ambiguous and double meaning terms should not be used while stating hypothesis.
6. Hypothesis should be testable within reasonable time. It should be in such a manner that its testing can be completed within stipulated time except in special circumstances where extension of time limit is warranted.
7. Hypothesis should be set up in such a manner that it can be modified in the light of latest facts. Due to explosion in knowledge, theories and principles in almost all subjects are changing very fast. That is why a researcher must keep himself abreast of the newest.

Main Steps in Writing the Research Report

The main body consists of:

1. **Statement of the Problem:** Under this heading the researchers should state the problem in the opening paragraph, answering specific questions thereby highlighting the theoretical background of the problem.
2. **Significance or purpose of the problem:** Under this heading, the investigator should spell out the reasons for taking up such a study. How the problem is going to contribute to the body of knowledge. What specific purposes the study will give and who would benefit from the study.
3. **Assumptions:** Assumptions refer to the statement of the hypothesis in which the study is based. Clear assumptions indicate how well the investigator has searched literature and added something to it from his own empathies.
4. **Limitations:** Limitations underlie any controllable factors or circumstances which might have affected the results. The researcher delineates the constraints under which he completed the study, so that when the results are compared with any other study, there are no misgivings in the minds of the reader as to the correctness of the findings.
5. **Delimitations:** This denotes the scope of the study. The researcher must state clearly and logically, how and why it was necessary to delimit the study in terms of subjects, variables, geographical area etc. and definition of important terms. All difficult and important terms used in the study should be defined and explained exactly in the manner they have been used in the study.

EXERCISE

1. Research used for studying practical problems and finding a solution to it is–
   (*a*) basic research
   (*b*) applied research
   (*c*) experimental research
   (*d*) evaluation research
2. Research focused on determining how education works by testing conclusions related to theories of communication, learning, performance and technology is–
   (*a*) theoretical research
   (*b*) empirical research
   (*c*) interpretivist research
   (*d*) evaluation research
3. The type of research method involving in depth study and execution of available information in an attempt to explain complex phenomena is known as–
   (*a*) philosophical research
   (*b*) developmental research
   (*c*) analytical research
   (*d*) action research
4. Which of the following is a quantitative method of data collection?
   (*a*) Observation (*b*) Correlation
   (*c*) Interviews (*d*) Observation
5. The type of interview relying on the spontaneous generation of questions in the natural flow of interaction is–
   (*a*) informal interview
   (*b*) semi-structured interview
   (*c*) open-ended interview
   (*d*) focus-group interview
6. In which of the following methods of data collection, the investigator contacts third parties called witness capable of supplying the necessary information?
   (*a*) Direct personal interview
   (*b*) Indirect oral interview
   (*c*) Observation
   (*d*) Questionnaire
7. The questionnaire in which a sequence of questions is followed is called–
   (*a*) disguised
   (*b*) undisguised
   (*c*) un-structured
   (*d*) structured
8. Which method of research investigates the likelihood of a relationship between two variables and identifies associations rather than cause and effect?
   (*a*) Experimental design
   (*b*) Survey
   (*c*) Case studies
   (*d*) Correlation studies
9. The research method used to investigate cultures and population subgroups and seeks to describe and explain cultural behaviour is–
   (*a*) phenomenology
   (*b*) grounded theory
   (*c*) ethnography
   (*d*) action research
10. The research methods emphasizing on developing new knowledge and new theories about the topic being investigated is–
    (*a*) phenomenology
    (*b*) grounded theory
    (*c*) ethnography
    (*d*) action research
11. The number of elements in the obtained sample is called–
    (*a*) sampling frame (*b*) sampling unit
    (*c*) sample design (*d*) sample size
12. Sampling in which elements are grouped together because they share certain characteristics is–
    (*a*) cluster sampling

(*b*) systematic sampling
(*c*) stratified sampling
(*d*) simple random sampling

13. Which of the following is probability sampling?
(*a*) Purposive sampling
(*b*) Snowball sampling
(*c*) Cluster sampling
(*d*) Dimensional sampling

14. Which of the following is a non-probability sampling?
(*a*) Snowball sampling
(*b*) Stratified sampling
(*c*) Cluster sampling
(*d*) Simple random sampling

15. The sampling method chosen when the members of a special population are difficult to locate is–
(*a*) availability sampling
(*b*) purposive sampling
(*c*) snowball sampling
(*d*) dimensional sampling

16. Which of the following is not an advantage?
(*a*) Sampling saves time and money
(*b*) Sampling cannot be a substitute for census
(*c*) Sampling saves labour
(*d*) A sample coverage permits a higher overall level of adequacy than a full enumeration.

17. Controlled investigations that try to establish cause and effect between two or more variables with the purpose of predicting outcomes is–
(*a*) experimental design
(*b*) correlation studies
(*c*) survey
(*d*) case study

18. Focus group interviews are aimed at–
(*a*) homogeneous people with similar backgrounds
(*b*) heterogeneous people
(*c*) people living in the same area
(*d*) people of same religious groups

19. In testing of hypothesis, research and null hypothesis–
(*a*) exist together (*b*) one at a time
(*c*) are invalid (*d*) are same

20. Which of the following is not an average?
(*a*) Mean
(*b*) Median
(*c*) Mode
(*d*) Standard Deviation

21. The mean which stands for relative importance of the different items is–
(*a*) arithmetic mean
(*b*) weighted mean
(*c*) geometric mean
(*d*) harmonic mean

22. The middle value in a distribution refers to–
(*a*) mean (*b*) mode
(*c*) median (*d*) geometric mean

23. Which of the following is a positional average?
(*a*) Mean (*b*) Mode
(*c*) Median (*d*) Harmonic mean

24. Value in a series of observation which occurs with the greatest frequency is–
(*a*) mean (*b*) mode
(*c*) median (*d*) geometric mean

25. The formula 3 Median – 2 mean is used to compute–
(*a*) arithmetic mean (*b*) weighted mean
(*c*) median (*d*) mode

26. The Nth est of the product of N items or values is–
(*a*) arithmetic mean (*b*) weighted mean
(*c*) geometric mean (*d*) harmonic mean

27. The reciprocal of the arithmetic mean of the reciprocal of the individual observation refers to–
(*a*) weighted mean
(*b*) geometric mean

(c) median mean
(d) harmonic mean

28. The Arithmetic mean of a continuous series is measured by the formula–

(a) $\overline{X} = \frac{\Sigma x}{N}$ (b) $\overline{X} = \frac{\Sigma fx}{N}$

(c) $\overline{X} = A + \frac{\Sigma d x i}{N}$ (d) $\overline{X} = \frac{\Sigma fmi}{N}$

29. Which of the following is a measure of the variation of the items in a distribution?
(a) Mean (b) Dispersion
(c) Median (d) Mode

30. The simplest method of studying dispersion is–
(a) range
(b) quartile deviation
(c) mean deviation
(d) standard mean

31. The difference between the value of the smallest item and the value of the largest item included in the distribution is–
(a) range
(b) inter-quartile range
(c) mean deviation
(d) standard deviation

32. The difference between the third quartile and the first quartile is represented by–
(a) range
(b) inter-quartile range
(c) quartile deviation
(d) standard deviation

33. The average amount by which the two quartiles differ from the median is represented by the–
(a) range
(b) inter-quartile range
(c) quartile deviation
(d) mean deviation

34. The concept of standard deviation was introduced by–
(a) Karl Pearson (b) Fisher
(c) Gauses (d) Spearman

35. Root mean square deviation is also called–
(a) mean deviation
(b) standard deviation
(c) variance
(d) correlation

36. The square of the standard deviation is called–
(a) mean deviation
(b) quartile range
(c) inter-quartile range
(d) variance

37. Variance was introduced by–
(a) R A. Fisher (b) Pearson
(c) Tchebycheff (d) Spearman

38. The graphic method of studying dispersion is called–
(a) J curve
(b) S curve
(c) Lorenz curve
(d) Scatter diagram

39. Which of the following is not a method to ascertain whether two variables are correlated or not?
(a) Concurrent Deviation method
(b) Method of least squares
(c) Scatter diagram method
(d) Lorenz curve

40. Which statistical device helps in analyzing the covariant of two or more variables?
(a) Regression
(b) Median
(c) Standard Deviation
(d) Correlation

41. The least possible correlation between two variable is–
(a) –1.00 (b) –0.1
(c) –0.01 (d) –0.001

42. Which of the following is not a name for dispersion?
(a) Scatter
(b) Spread
(c) Regression
(d) Variation

43. Means + | σ covers–

(*a*) 68.27 % of the items
(*b*) 94.45 % of the items
(*c*) 99 % of the items
(*d*) 99.73 % of the items

44. In the positively skewed distribution, the value of–

(*a*) mean is maximum and mode least
(*b*) mean least and mode maximum
(*c*) mean least and median maximum
(*d*) mode least and median maximum

45. In a negatively skewed distribution the mean is–

(*a*) least
(*b*) maximum
(*c*) between mode and median
(*d*) coincides with mode and median

46. $\frac{Q_3 + Q_1 - 2\,Med}{Q_3 - Q_1}$ is –

(*a*) Karl Parson's Coefficient of skewness
(*b*) Bowley's Coefficient of skewness
(*c*) Kelly's coefficient of skewness
(*d*) Measure of skewness based on moments

47. First moment about origin measures–

(*a*) mean (*b*) variance
(*c*) skewness (*d*) kurtosis

48. Theoretical work on t-distribution was done by–

(*a*) Karl Pearson (*b*) Kelly
(*c*) Fisher (*d*) Gosset

49. The application of t-distribution to test difference between means of two independent samples is represented by the formula–

(*a*) $t = \frac{(\overline{X} - \mu)\sqrt{n}}{s}$

(*b*) $t = \frac{\overline{X}_1 - \overline{X}_2}{s} \times \sqrt{\frac{n_1 n_2}{n_1 + n_2}}$

(*c*) $t = \frac{\overline{d}\sqrt{n}}{s}$

(*d*) $t = \frac{r}{\sqrt{1 - r^2}} \times \sqrt{n - 2}$

50. Which of the following is method of testing the significance of the correlation coefficient in sample samples?

(*a*) t-test (*b*) z-test
(*c*) F-test (*d*) Chi-square

51. In observational research, there are no–

(*a*) variables
(*b*) standardized tests
(*c*) experimental tests
(*d*) statistical tests

52. What is the independent variable in experimental research?

(*a*) A variable which no body controls or changes
(*b*) The variable which is manipulated in an experiment
(*c*) The variable which is measured to see results of an experiment
(*d*) A variable which is held steady

53. F-ratio is used to compare–

(*a*) more than two standard deviations
(*b*) less than two means
(*c*) more than two means
(*d*) none of the above

54. Which of the following indicates consistency in performance?

(*a*) Validity
(*b*) Reliability
(*c*) Both (*a*) and (*b*)
(*d*) None of the above

55. The scope in research is indicated by–

(*a*) limitations of the study
(*b*) delimitations of the study
(*c*) definition and explanation of terms
(*d*) interpretation of research results

56. Hypothesis is also called–
(*a*) hunch of scholar
(*b*) tentative conclusion
(*c*) guess of the scholar
(*d*) all of the above

57. Research proposal is also called–
(*a*) abstract (*b*) summary
(*c*) synopsis (*d*) methodology

58. The principle of randomization is one in which a sample includes–
(*a*) total population
(*b*) part of the population which the researcher wishes to approach
(*c*) smaller portion of population in a systematic way
(*d*) a population other than the one for which investigations have been planned

59. The implications of experimental research are–
(*a*) what was
(*b*) what is
(*c*) what will be
(*d*) none of the above

60. Standard Deviation represents–
(*a*) central tendency of the data
(*b*) correlation of the data
(*c*) dispersion of the data
(*d*) probability

61. Value of which of the following can not be determined graphically?
(*a*) Mode
(*b*) Mean
(*c*) Median
(*d*) Standard deviation

62. Which measure of central tendency can be found only after arranging it properly?
(*a*) Mode (*b*) Mean
(*c*) Median (*d*) None of the above

63. Which measure of central tendency is capable of algebraic manipulations?
(*a*) Median (*b*) Mode
(*c*) Both (*a*) and (*b*) (*d*) Mean

64. The most unreliable and unstable average is–
(*a*) mode (*b*) mean
(*c*) median (*d*) none of the above

65. Which of the following instruments comes under the preview of Anthropometry?
(*a*) Ultrasound (*b*) Treadmill
(*c*) Dynamometer (*d*) Skin fold caliper.

66. The term which indicates 'relationship existing between parts of measures' is–
(*a*) standard deviation
(*b*) correlation
(*c*) degree of freedom
(*d*) range

67. Product moment coefficient of correlation measures which particular type of relationship between two variables?
(*a*) Linear (*b*) Curvilinear
(*c*) Parabolic (*d*) Circular

68. Which of the following is the best measure of variability?
(*a*) Range
(*b*) Standard Deviation
(*c*) Mean Deviation
(*d*) None of the above

69. 'Turtle pulse ratio' test is used to measure–
(*a*) motor educability
(*b*) physical fitness
(*c*) mental fitness
(*d*) motor fitness

70. 'Warners' skill test is for which of the following games?
(*a*) Basketball (*b*) Hockey
(*c*) Football (*d*) Volleyball.

71. Who among the following devised the test for hockey?
(*a*) Warner (*b*) Schmithel
(*c*) Petry (*d*) French

72. 'French' short services tests is for the game of–
(*a*) volleyball (*b*) tennis
(*c*) badminton (*d*) table-tennis

73. Who among the following devised the test for the game of Basketball?
(*a*) Broer-Miller (*b*) Schmithel
(*c*) Petry (*d*) Johnson

74. Who among the following devised the test for 'volleyball'?
(*a*) Petry (*b*) Johnson
(*c*) Broer-Miller (*d*) Warner

75. Broer-Miller devised the test for which of the following events?
(*a*) Table-tennis (*b*) Volleyball
(*c*) Basketball (*d*) Tennis

76. Who among the following gave the test for Volleyball?
(*a*) Johnson (*b*) Russel Lange
(*c*) Schmithel (*d*) Broer-Miller

77. 'Alignometer' is used to measure–
(*a*) size (*b*) strength
(*c*) posture (*d*) weight

78. Which of the following is used to measure static strength?
(*a*) Stadiometer (*b*) Ammeter
(*c*) Galvanometer (*d*) Dynamometer

79. Which of the following instruments is used to measure posture?
(*a*) Alignomotor (*b*) Scoliometer
(*c*) Both (*a*) and (*b*) (*d*) None of the above

80. Which of the following is measured by "Spring Scale Rig"?
(*a*) Strength (*b*) Endurance
(*c*) Flexibility (*d*) Mobility

81. Which of the following instruments measures 'height'?
(*a*) Spring scale rig (*b*) Dynamometer
(*c*) Stadiometer (*d*) Scoliometer.

82. "Quadrant jump" is a measure of–
(*a*) strength (*b*) agility
(*c*) skill (*d*) flexibility

83. Which of the following instruments measures lung capacity?
(*a*) Anemometer
(*b*) Wet spirometer
(*c*) Galvanometer
(*d*) Sphygmomanometer

84. Which of the following instruments measures the wind speed?
(*a*) Stadiometer (*b*) Galvanometer
(*c*) Anemometer (*d*) Ammeter

85. 'Sit and reach test' measures–
(*a*) abdominal strength
(*b*) shoulder flexibility
(*c*) hamstring and back flexibility
(*d*) hyperextension of the back

86. Harvard step test was constructed by–
(*a*) Harvard (*b*) Thomas Cureton
(*c*) Lucien Brouha (*d*) Sergent

87. Sergent Jump measures–
(*a*) explosive leg strength
(*b*) agility
(*c*) explosive arm strength
(*d*) flexibility

88. Goniometer measures–
(*a*) strength (*b*) power
(*c*) endurance (*d*) flexibility

89. "Ergograph" measures–
(*a*) muscular strength
(*b*) muscular endurance
(*c*) muscle length
(*d*) muscle size

90. Which of the following instruments is used to measure lean body weight?
(*a*) Galvanometer (*b*) Densitometer
(*c*) Anemometer (*d*) Goniometer

91. Which of the following is not a component of AAHPER youth fitness test?
(*a*) Pull ups
(*b*) Sit ups
(*c*) Standing broad jump
(*d*) German drill

92. Who among the following devised a test for motor ability?

(*a*) French (*b*) Smithel
(*c*) Warner (*d*) Barrow

93. Which of the following is not a criterion for selection of a research problem?
(*a*) Will the problem make a significant contribution?
(*b*) Is the problem of interest to the researcher?
(*c*) Consultation with faculty members
(*d*) Is the cost involved feasible?

94. Which of the following experimental designs involve single group?
(*a*) Repeated measures design
(*b*) Random group design
(*c*) Post test only random group design
(*d*) Factorial design

95. The experimental factors to be controlled in respect of the subjects are–
(*a*) randomization and physical ability
(*b*) age and sex
(*c*) motivation and interest
(*d*) all of the above

96. Whether or not a given source is genuine and admissible as evidence is found through–
(*a*) internal criticism
(*b*) external criticism
(*c*) both (*a*) and (*b*)
(*d*) none of the above

97. Which of the following is the most reliable measure of central tendency?
(*a*) Median (*b*) Mode
(*c*) Mean (*d*) None of the above

98. Which of the following is secondary source?
(*a*) Pictorial records
(*b*) Mechanical records
(*c*) Personal records
(*d*) Text books

99. Which of the following measures represents scatter of scores around median?
(*a*) Standard Deviation
(*b*) Average Deviation
(*c*) Quarlite Deviation
(*d*) None of the above.

100. Z-test method was given by–
(*a*) Spearman (*b*) Fisher
(*c*) Karl Pearson (*d*) Kelly

101. The chi-square was first used by–
(*a*) Fisher (*b*) Gosset
(*c*) Spearman (*d*) Karl Pearson

102. F-test is named after statistician–
(*a*) Fisher (*b*) Gosset
(*c*) Pearson (*d*) Kelly

103. Which test is also known as Variance Ratio test?
(*a*) F-test (*b*) Z-test
(*c*) T-test (*d*) Chi-square

104. In a symmetrical distribution–
(*a*) mean and mode coincide
(*b*) mean and median coincide
(*c*) mode and median coincide
(*d*) median, mean and mode coincide

105. Systematic sampling may be used instead of simple random sampling if the–
(*a*) popoulation list is in random order
(*b*) sample size is small
(*c*) popoulation is heterogeneous
(*d*) expected difference are small

106. External and Internal criticism is done in–
(*a*) experimental research
(*b*) survey method
(*c*) philosophical research
(*d*) historical research

107. Research means–
(*a*) to discover new ideas by scientific study
(*b*) to discover that is lost
(*c*) to discover something missing
(*d*) to search again

108. Research proposal means–
(*a*) research outline
(*b*) brief outline of the research work to be done
(*c*) research work itself
(*d*) abstract of the research

109. Experimental research aims at–
(*a*) what was?
(*b*) what is?
(*c*) what will be?
(*d*) none of the above

110. Equated group design is also called–
(*a*) random group design
(*b*) repeated measures design
(*c*) reverse group design
(*d*) parallel group design

111. Close form questionnaire contains questions that call for–
(*a*) free response
(*b*) check response
(*c*) descriptive response
(*d*) short response

112. The statistical measure which is generally applied for the determination of sampling error is–
(*a*) mean
(*b*) chi-square
(*c*) correlation
(*d*) standard deviation

113. In research, good hypotheses emerge from–
(*a*) discussion (*b*) literature
(*c*) observation (*d*) reasoning

114. Action research in physical education is concerned with–
(*a*) immediate classroom problems
(*b*) experimental studies
(*c*) correlation studies
(*d*) laboratory problems

115. The main purpose of a pilot study in physical education research is–
(*a*) to obtain funds for subsequent research
(*b*) to test and improve research plan
(*c*) to provide opportunities for students to get research experience.
(*d*) none of the above

116. The initial step in reviewing the literature is to–
(*a*) make a list of key words related to the study
(*b*) take notes on research articles
(*c*) check the preliminary sources
(*d*) study opinion articles to gain insight into the problems related to the study

117. Systematic sampling may be used instead of simple random sampling if the–
(*a*) population list is in random order
(*b*) sample size is small
(*c*) popoulation is heterogeneous
(*d*) expected difference are small

118. Experimental research method in physical education provides–
(*a*) detail study
(*b*) deep study
(*c*) systematic and logical study
(*d*) complete study

119. The test of significance used to comparing two means is–
(*a*) F-test
(*b*) Chi-square
(*c*) T-test
(*d*) None of the above

120. Hypothesis in research means–
(*a*) information gained from others
(*b*) intellectual guess temporarily accepted as true
(*c*) answer to the question
(*d*) none of the above

121. In statistics, a sample is considered small if its units are less than–
(*a*) 40 (*b*) 30
(*c*) 20 (*d*) 10

122. The highest possible positive correlation between two variables can be–
(*a*) 0.01 (*b*) 1.0
(*c*) -0.1 (*d*) +.001

123. Using short method, the standard deviation of a distribution can be calculated by using one of the following formulae Select–

(a) $\sqrt{\frac{\sum fx^2}{N}}$ (b) $\frac{\sum fx}{N}$

(c) $\sqrt{\sum fx^2}$ (d) $Si\frac{\sqrt{\sum fx^2}}{N}$

124. Analysis of variance is used when comparisons are made among–
(a) two groups
(b) more than two groups
(c) less than two groups
(d) no groups

125. A negative standard deviation indicates–
(a) a highly homogenous group
(b) a computational error
(c) a statistically significant result
(d) an unreliable measuring instrument

126. 95-(-15) is equal to–
(a) 110 (b) 80
(c) 94 (d) 15

127. Which of the following is the most reliable measure of variability?
(a) Range
(b) Quartile deviation
(c) Average deviation
(d) Standard deviation

128. The mid-point of the distribution is–
(a) median
(b) mean
(c) mode
(d) standard deviation

129. Test of significant used for comparing two means is–
(a) F test (b) t-test
(c) Chi-square test (d) None of the above

130. The 'T' test is used for–
(a) comparing three means
(b) comparing two means
(c) comparing four means
(d) more than four means

131. A continuous variable in the following is–
(a) body weight (b) time
(c) both of these (d) none of these

132. A discontinuous variable in the following is–
(a) body weight
(b) time
(c) score in basket ball game
(d) none of these

133. A variable has a numerical basis of grouping–
(a) True
(b) False
(c) Partially True
(d) Partially False

134. A variable which can not be subdivided by less than a whole number is–
(a) continuous variable
(b) discontinuous variable
(c) both
(d) none of these

135. The column in Frequency table indicated by F is–
(a) norms
(b) frequency column
(c) both of these
(d) none of these

136. The total of the frequency column is indicated by–
(a) N (b) F
(c) CI (d) None of these

137. A single score that represents all the scores in a distribution is called–
(a) measure of central tendency
(b) measure of variability
(c) both of these
(d) none of these

138. Mode, Median and Mean are measure of central tendency–
(a) True (b) False
(c) Partially true (d) Partially False

139. The score that appears most frequently when scores are ungrouped is known as–

(a) mean
(b) median
(c) mode
(d) none of these

140. The Median is the midpoint in a distribution above and below which lie 50 per cent of the scores is–
(a) true (b) false
(c) partially true (d) partially false

141. The mean may best be defined as the average–
(a) True (b) False
(c) Partially true (d) Partially False

142. The Formula for calculating mean is–

(a) $AM + \left(\frac{\sum fd}{N}\right) \times SI$

(b) $\sqrt{\frac{fd^2}{N} - \left(\frac{\sum fd}{N}\right)^2} \times SI$

(c) $\frac{Q_3 - Q_1}{N}$

(d) $\sqrt{\frac{N\sum X^2 - \left(\sum X\right)^2}{N}}$

143. The Formula for calculating median for ungrouped data is–

(a) $\left(\frac{N+1}{2}\right)^{th}$ score (b) $\left(\frac{N+2}{2}\right)$

(c) $\frac{N}{2}$ (d) None of these

144. The formula for calculating median for grouped data is–

(a) $1 + \left(\frac{\frac{N}{2} - CF}{fm}\right)xi$

(b) $Am + \left(\frac{\sum fd}{N}\right)xi$

(c) $\frac{N+1}{2}$

(d) None of these

145. The mode is a rough measure and may be quite inaccurate as a measure of central tendency in small groups–
(a) True (b) False
(c) Partially True (d) Partially False

146. The median is not affected by extreme scores in the distribution–
(a) True (b) False
(c) Partially True (d) Partially False

147. If one wishes to avoid the influence of extremely high or low scores on the measure of central tendency–
(a) the mean should be used
(b) the median should be used
(c) the mode should be used
(d) all the above

148. The most reliable of measures of central tendency is–
(a) mode
(b) median
(c) mean
(d) standard deviation

149. The point below which lie 25 percent of the scores and above which lie 75 percent of the scores is–
(a) Q_1 (b) Q_2
(c) Q_3 (d) None of the above

150. The 50th percentile is also known as–
(a) mean (b) median
(c) mode (d) none of these

151. The 0 and 100th percentiles are the lowest and highest scores in the distribution–
(a) True (b) False
(c) Partially True (d) Partially False

152. The measures of variability will be–
(*a*) the range
(*b*) the quartile deviation
(*c*) the standard deviation
(*d*) all of the above

153. The formula for calculating Quartile deviation is–

(*a*) $\frac{Q_4 - Q_3}{2}$ (*b*) $\frac{Q_3 - Q_1}{2}$

(*c*) $\frac{Q_3 - Q_2}{2}$ (*d*) None of these

154. The most reliable of the measures of variability is–
(*a*) mode
(*b*) standard deviation
(*c*) mean
(*d*) median

155. The formula for calculating the standard deviation is–

(*a*) $\sqrt{\left(\frac{\sum fd^2}{N}\right) - \left(\frac{\sum fd}{N}\right)^2} \times \text{SI}$

(*b*) $Am + \left(\frac{\sum fd}{N}\right) \times \text{SI}$

(*c*) $\frac{Q_3 - Q_2}{1}$

(*d*) None of these

156. The scatter or spread of the middle 50 per cent of the scores taken from median is–
(*a*) mode
(*b*) standard deviation
(*c*) quartile deviation
(*d*) none of these

157. The Formula for computing standard deviation from ungrouped scores–

(*a*) $\left(\frac{\sum fd^2}{N}\right) - \left(\frac{\sum fd}{N}\right)^2 \times \text{SI}$

(*b*) $\sqrt{\frac{N\sum X^2 - \left(\sum X\right)^2}{N}}$

(*c*) $Am + \left(\frac{\sum fd}{N}\right) \times \text{SI}$

(*d*) None of these

158. Quartile deviation is valuable when only the concentration of scores around the central tendency is sought–
(*a*) True
(*b*) False
(*c*) Partially true
(*d*) Partially False

159. The standard deviation is affected by extreme score in the distribution–
(*a*) True (*b*) False
(*c*) Partially true (*d*) Partially False

160. The principle of the normal curve is based upon the probable occurrence of an event when that probability depends upon chance–
(*a*) True (*b*) False
(*c*) Partially true (*d*) Partially False

161. In the normal probability curve, the mean the median and the mode are exactly in the centre of the distribution–
(*a*) True (*b*) False
(*c*) Partially true (*d*) Partially False

162. In the normal probability curve, the mean the median and the mode are numerically equal–
(*a*) True (*b*) False
(*c*) Partially True (*d*) Partially False

163. The formula for the standard error of mean is–

(*a*) $\sqrt{\frac{dist}{N}\, m_1^2 + m_2^2}$ (*b*) $\sqrt{\sigma\,\sigma}$

(*c*) Both of these (*d*) None of these

164. The standard error of a difference between two mean is–

(a) $\sqrt{\frac{dist}{N}}$ (b) $\sqrt{\frac{m_1^2 + m_2^2}{\sigma \sigma}}$
(c) Both of these (d) None of these

165. The ratio between the difference and its measure of reliability is known as–
(a) true difference (b) critical-ratio
(c) partial ratio (d) none of these

166. The larger the critical-ratio the greater is the statistical significance of difference–
(a) True (b) False
(c) Partially True (d) Partially False

167. The critical-ratio approach is applicable only–
(a) when the significance between the means of two independent samples is tested
(b) when the significance between the means of three independent samples is tested
(3) both of these
(4) none of these

168. The degree of relationship between two variables is known as–
(a) correlation (b) co-ordination
(c) both of these (d) none of these

169. The range of possible magnitude of correlation extends from–
(a) –1.00 from .00 to 5.00
(b) +1.00 through .00 to –1.00
(c) Both of these
(d) None of these

170. A perfect positive correlation indicates–
(a) +1 (b) 0
(c) Both of these (d) None of these

171. When the scores are arranged as ranks and number of cases are small the method designed for correlation–
(a) contingency co-efficient
(b) biserial correlation
(c) rank-difference method
(d) none of these

172. The co-efficient of multiple correlation has been developed for the purpose of indicating the degree to which values of one variable may correlate with two or more variables–
(a) True (b) False
(c) Partially True (d) Partially False

173. In normal curve when the concentration of scores is above or below the centre the distribution is known as–
(a) skewed (b) unskewed
(c) both of these (d) none of these

174. Skewness may be–
(a) positive (b) negative
(c) both of these (d) none of these

175. In normal curve when the concentration of scores is below the centre and it tails off towards the right then the skewness is–
(a) positive (b) negative
(c) both of these (d) none of these

176. In normal curve when the concentration of score is above the centre and it tails off towards the left when the skewness is–
(a) positive (b) negative
(c) both of these (d) none of these

177. If the distribution confirms to a normal curve, the deviation which indicates the spread of the middle 57.5 per cent of the scores taken from any measure of central tendency is–
(a) standard deviation
(b) mean deviation
(c) quartile deviation
(d) none of these

178. The quartile deviation is uninfluenced by the upper and lower 25 per cent of the scores–
(a) True (b) False
(c) Partially True (d) Partially False

179. The standard deviation is used as the measures of variability when the measure of central tendency is–
(a) mean (b) median
(c) mode (d) none of these

180. The mean will be lower than median in–
(a) negative skewness

(*b*) positive skewness
(*c*) both
(*d*) none of these

181. The mean will be higher than the median in–
(*a*) positive skewness
(*b*) negative skewness
(*c*) both
(*d*) none of these

182. The Z Scale consists of standard deviation distance of scores from the mean.
(*a*) True (*b*) False
(*c*) Partially True (*d*) partially False

ANSWERS

1	2	3	4	5	6	7	8	9	10
(*b*)	(*b*)	(*c*)	(*b*)	(*a*)	(*b*)	(*d*)	(*d*)	(*c*)	(*b*)
11	**12**	**13**	**14**	**15**	**16**	**17**	**18**	**19**	**20**
(*d*)	(*c*)	(*c*)	(*a*)	(*c*)	(*b*)	(*b*)	(*a*)	(*b*)	(*d*)
21	**22**	**23**	**24**	**25**	**26**	**27**	**28**	**29**	**30**
(*b*)	(*c*)	(*c*)	(*b*)	(*d*)	(*c*)	(*d*)	(*d*)	(*b*)	(*a*)
31	**32**	**33**	**34**	**35**	**36**	**37**	**38**	**39**	**40**
(*a*)	(*b*)	(*c*)	(*a*)	(*b*)	(*d*)	(*a*)	(*c*)	(*d*)	(*d*)
41	**42**	**43**	**44**	**45**	**46**	**47**	**48**	**49**	**50**
(*a*)	(*c*)	(*a*)	(*a*)	(*a*)	(*b*)	(*a*)	(*d*)	(*b*)	(*b*)
51	**52**	**53**	**54**	**55**	**56**	**57**	**58**	**59**	**60**
(*c*)	(*b*)	(*c*)	(*b*)	(*d*)	(*d*)	(*c*)	(*d*)	(*c*)	(*c*)
61	**62**	**63**	**64**	**65**	**66**	**67**	**68**	**69**	**70**
(*b*)	(*c*)	(*d*)	(*a*)	(*d*)	(*b*)	(*a*)	(*b*)	(*b*)	(*c*)
71	**72**	**73**	**74**	**75**	**76**	**77**	**78**	**79**	**80**
(*b*)	(*c*)	(*d*)	(*a*)	(*d*)	(*b*)	(*c*)	(*d*)	(*c*)	(*a*)
81	**82**	**83**	**84**	**85**	**86**	**87**	**88**	**89**	**90**
(*c*)	(*b*)	(*b*)	(*c*)	(*c*)	(*a*)	(*a*)	(*d*)	(*b*)	(*b*)
91	**92**	**93**	**94**	**95**	**96**	**97**	**98**	**99**	**100**
(*d*)	(*d*)	(*c*)	(*a*)	(*d*)	(*b*)	(*c*)	(*d*)	(*c*)	(*b*)
101	**102**	**103**	**104**	**105**	**106**	**107**	**108**	**109**	**110**
(*b*)	(*d*)	(*a*)	(*a*)	(*d*)	(*d*)	(*a*)	(*b*)	(*c*)	(*d*)
111	**112**	**113**	**114**	**115**	**116**	**117**	**118**	**119**	**120**
(*d*)	(*d*)	(*d*)	(*a*)	(*b*)	(*c*)	(*c*)	(*c*)	(*c*)	(*b*)
121	**122**	**123**	**124**	**125**	**126**	**127**	**128**	**129**	**130**
(*b*)	(*b*)	(*d*)	(*b*)	(*b*)	(*a*)	(*d*)	(*a*)	(*b*)	(*b*)
131	**132**	**133**	**134**	**135**	**136**	**137**	**138**	**139**	**140**
(*c*)	(*c*)	(*a*)	(*b*)	(*b*)	(*a*)	(*a*)	(*a*)	(*c*)	(*a*)
141	**142**	**143**	**144**	**145**	**146**	**147**	**148**	**149**	**150**
(*a*)	(*a*)	(*a*)	(*a*)	(*a*)	(*a*)	(*b*)	(*c*)	(*d*)	(*b*)

151	152	153	154	155	156	157	158	159	160
(*a*)	(*d*)	(*b*)	(*b*)	(*a*)	(*c*)	(*b*)	(*a*)	(*a*)	(*a*)
161	**162**	**163**	**164**	**165**	**166**	**167**	**168**	**169**	**170**
(*a*)	(*a*)	(*a*)	(*b*)	(*b*)	(*b*)	(*a*)	(*a*)	(*b*)	(*a*)
171	**172**	**173**	**174**	**175**	**176**	**177**	**178**	**179**	**180**
(*c*)	(*c*)	(*a*)	(*c*)	(*a*)	(*b*)	(*b*)	(*b*)	(*a*)	(*a*)
181	**182**								
(*a*)	(*a*)								

UNIT-IX

CONCEPT OF TEST

Tests have been proved to possess great utility in many spheres. Briefly, the utility and importance of tests can be observed in the following spheres:

1. **Guidance:** As has been indicated earlier, psychological tests are indispensable in all forms of guidance.
2. **Appointments:** Psychological tests are now-a-days resorted to for the appointment of appropriate individuals to posts in offices, factories and government services. It has the doubly beneficial effect of securing proper and desirable jobs for individuals according to their interests, inclination, intelligence and abilities, as well as ensuring that the highest levels of efficiency is achieved by the right man being in the right job. In this way, both the employees as well as the employer are benefited.
3. **Selection for Training:** An individual can benefit from training for some particular job only if he is initially in possession of the requisite intelligence, abilities and qualities, besides the necessary interest in the work involved. It is evident that the individual should be tested in respect of these qualities before any training is imparted to him. Hence, in all advanced nations of the world, all kinds of training institutes make use of psychological tests for selecting the required candidates. In India, for example, the recruitment to the Police Training Colleges, the Government. Teacher's Training Colleges, and other technical institutions is done only on the basis of psychological tests. In public schools the students who receive scholarships are selected on the basis of psychological tests in order to ensure that the scholarships are not wasted, as well they might be if they are provided to the wrong individuals. Psychological tests are further used for selection of candidates for National Defence Academy in the country. Such use of psychological tests for the selection of personnel in training school is constantly on the increase.
4. **Classification According to the Level of Intelligence:** Now-a-days, all educationists agree that the success of education depends upon the student being provided education of a kind that accords with his level of intelligence. Hence, individual students are classified and stratified according to their level of intelligence and different curricular and extra curricular programmes devised for the three categories of student, the brilliant, the average and the retarded. The classification is based on intelligence tests. It is not only on the field of education but also in various vocations, armed forces and industries that intelligence tests are used to classify individuals so that they can be given the proper kind of work that is within their capacity to perform with reasonable success.
5. **Prediction:** The term indicates the forecasting of success in the case of an individual. While guiding the individual, a psychologist can normally make fairly accurate predictions as to the degree of success that one is likely to achieve. The prediction is based upon psychological tests, the greater the capacity of a psychological test to assist in prediction, the greater is its validity and its reliability.
6. **Diagnosis:** Before giving any guidance, the directing psychologist makes a diagnosis of the problem present before him. He gives suggestions for alleviating a certain condition only after he has decided upon a diagnosis, since it is only upon diagnosing some

problem that he reaches the root causes. And psychological tests are essential for diagnosis, without them a proper diagnosis cannot be achieved.

7. **Research:** Psychological tests are of use even in the field of psychological research. Intelligence tests, interest inventories, personality tests, tests of mental bilities nd personality qualities help in research in these specific directions.

CONCEPT OF MEASUREMENT

Measurement is a process by which the developed abilities of the pupils are expressed in the quantitative form. The measurement is directly concerned with quantity. By measuring the content, skill and the results of abilities are expressed in numbers, scores, percentage and average, so that the provision of education of the pupils may be made according to their present achievement. By measurement, the variables, groups, capacities, time and distance etc. can be tested very conveniently. In short, according to Campbell, "Measurement is the assignment of numerals to objects or events according to rules."

Definition of Measurement

1. **J.P. Guilford:** "Measurement means the description of data in terms of numbers and this, in turn, means taking advantage of the many benefits that operate with numbers and mathematical thinking provide."
2. **Campbell:** Measurement is "assignment of numerals to objects or events according to certain rule is called measurement."
3. **Tyler:** He defined Measurement "as assignment of numerals, according to rules."
4. **Nunnally:** "Measurement consists of rules for assigning numbers to objects in such a way as to represent quantities of attributes."

Measurement and Evaluation

The term "measurement" and "evaluation" are often used interchangeably. However, in psychological, sociological and educational researches, these two terms connote two different meanings. "Measurement" refers to the process of assigning numerals to events, objects, etc. according to certain rules.

CONCEPT OF EVALUATION

Definition

1. By evaluation is meant appraisal or assessment with respect to some standard. Tuckman (1975) defines evaluation as, "a process wherein the parts, processes, or outcomes of a programme are examined to see whether they are satisfactory, particularly with reference to the programmes stated objectives our own expectations or our own standards of excellence. "Thus, evaluation involves a process of appraisal of an object or event with reference to some standard. The standard may be social, cultural or scientific. The standard may also be true or arbitrary. An investigator may measure the height of a child (which say, is 30°) and type him as short. A typist typing 80 words per minute may be described as a 'Grade A' typist. Description of the height of the child (which is 30^0) and the typing speed of the typist (which is 80 words per minute) are examples of measurement. However, when the child is said to be short or the typist is classified as a 'Grade A' typist, it means the performances of the typist and the height of a child are being compared with reference to some standard. A child is short because he is shorter than the general mean height of children of his age group and the typist is a 'Grade A' typist because his speed is faster than the average speed of most of the typists. Thus, the height of the child and the typing behaviour of the typist are being evaluated and not being measured."
2. In the words of Kothari Commission, "Evaluation is a continuous process, forms an integral part of the total system of education and is intimately related to educational objectives. It exercises a great influence on the pupil's study habits and the

teacher's methods of instruction and thus helps not only to measure educational achievements but also to improve it. The techniques of evaluation are means of collecting evidence about the students development in desirable directions."

Evaluation is an all exclusive and a global process in which data is collected from different persons at different times, from different sources using different techniques. The variety of information, sources and techniques make the process of evaluation more comprehensive. It covers the total personality of the student his cognitive, effective and psychomotor aspects and not only a few selected aspects of personality.

3. Sponsored by UNESCO in 1972 Inter-national Commission on Education stated that, "Real evaluation of a pupil's achievement should be based not on a single, summary examination, but on over-all observation of his work throughout a course of study. It should pay less attention to the volume of memorized knowledge and more to the development of his intellectual capacity, reasoning ability, critical judgement and proficiency in problem-solving."

Evaluation is a social and psychological process used in every field of life day by day. An individual evaluats the behaviours of other individuals. He also evaluates his own actions at regular intervals. A gardener evaluates his plants considering their beauty. A doctor evaluate his medicines by observing the behavioural changes in the patients. As a gardener and a doctor and other individuals evaluate their respective actions according to their results, similarly a teacher also evaluates his teaching on the basis of the behavioural changes occurred in the pupils. In the field of education, evaluation is linked with the learning objectives. Therefore, while evaluating his teaching, every teacher observes whether the behavioural changes which have occurred in the pupils are with reference to the pre-determined learning objectives. The teaching and testing going on side by side according to learning objectives is known as evaluation.

Chief Characteristics of Evaluation

1. **Comprehensive Process:** Evaluation is a comprehensive process. In it, not only cognitive aspect is evaluated as is done in essay type examination, it also evaluates the changes which occur in effective and cognitive aspects. It includes, all the changes which occur in all the aspects such as the physical, mental, social and moral aspects. Hence, evaluation is a comprehensive method to test the pupil. It includes both measurement and evaluation.
2. **Continuous Process:** Evaluation is a continuous process closely related to the learning objectives. The desirable learning experiences are created in the pupil in accordance with educational objectives and the behavioural changes which occur day-to-day are recorded. On the basis of this record, the ranking of pupils is made and they are upgraded to the next higher class.
3. **Social Process:** Evaluation is a social process. In this where all the aspects of personality are evaluated, it is also evaluated whether the teaching has been conducted according to the needs, ideals and norms of the society or not.
4. **Descriptive Process:** Evaluation is a descriptive process. In this is given the progress which occurs in all the aspects of the pupils.
5. **Cooperative process:** Evaluation is a cooperative process. The source of pupil's promotion is the pupil himself. As he writes in his answer books, so he gets the marks. In evaluation, the necessary material is collected by seeking essential cooperation of all the sources like teacher, pupils and parents. Then his progress is evaluated.
6. **Decisive Process:** Evaluation is a decisive process. After this, it is decided that-(*i*) whether any object or process is useful or not, (*ii*) to what extent the teaching is

successful according to the determined educational objectives, (iii) whether the learning experiences provided to the pupils in the class are effective or not, (iv) how far the teaching objectives have been achieved. If not achieved then whether the remedial instruction should be given or the teaching strategies are to be modified. Thus, evaluation measures the educational achievements. It also improves the teaching process.

Steps in Evaluation

Evaluation is a continuous process with the following steps:

1. Formulation and Definition of Educational Objectives.
2. Creating appropriate Learning Experiences through Educational Activities.
3. Evaluating on the basis of behavioural changes.

1. **Formulation and Definition of Education Objectives:** Teaching objectives are key to teaching. Hence for successful teaching, teaching objectives are determined while keeping five points in mind, otherwise the possibilities of failure of teaching enhance. These points are —
   (*i*) Teaching objectives should be determined keeping in mind the interests, attitudes, tendencies, abilities, needs and physical, mental, emotional and social aspects of personality of pupils,
   (*ii*) Keeping in view the social needs and ideals while determining the teaching objectives,
   (*iii*) Keeping in sight the nature and areas of contents while determining the teaching objectives.
   (*iv*) Take care of nursery, primary, middle and high levels of education while determining teaching objectives.
   (*v*) Having knowledge of educational psychology while determining educational psychology,

   When the above five things are achieved, then the teacher should make clear the areas in which what changes are to be brought about in the pupils in order to achieve teaching objectives. To make precise the specification of teaching objectives is to 'define' them.

2. **Creating appropriate learning experi- ences through educational activities:** The learning experiences mean those sources by which are predetermined objectives of teaching. It is the responsibility of the teacher to create teaching materials or conditions after determining and defining the teaching objectives so that the pupils get appropriate experiences of learning and in the end the teaching objectives are successfully achieved by those teaching experiences. The teacher should create an environment in which the pupils get appropriate experiences of learning from their own activities while living in that environment. For creation of appropriate educational environment the teacher should take care of the following points in the learning experiences—
   (*i*) They should be directly related to the teaching objectives.
   (*ii*) They should be meaningful and satisfactory for the pupils.
   (*iii*) They should be according to the interests of the pupils so that they may achieve determined objectives by keeping them maximum activated.
   (*iv*) They should be adequate.
   (*v*) They should be according to the maturity of the pupils.
   (*vi*) They should be the integral part of the behaviour of the pupils.

3. **Evaluating on the basis of behavioural Changes:** The ultimate aim of education is to bring a change in the behaviour of the pupils which occurs by teaching the pupils various school subjects. Change occurs in the various aspects of the personality of the pupils such as (i) Cognitive, (ii) Affective, (iii) Conative or Psychomotor. All the three aspects are tested by evaluation. These three aspects of behaviour are not separate, but are related to each other. All the three aspects are included in every behaviour, whether it is external or internal.

EVALUATION–APPROACH IN EDUCATION

The concept of evaluation approach is given by **B. S. Bloom.** His main emphasis was that testing should be based on teaching and both these activities should be objective – centred. Today teaching is organized by using the evaluation approach. Under this approach yearly plan and unit plan are prepared. The education process is considered as tri-polar process having three fundamental elements: 1. The educational objectives, 2. Learning experiences and 3. Change of behaviour.

The effectiveness and appropriateness of educational process is ascertained by evaluation approach. All the activities of teaching are evaluated in terms of student performances, which is known as change of behaviour. A criterion test is always objective-centred.

Meaning and Definition of Evaluation Approach

Quillen and Huna have defined the term evaluation approach in the following manner: "Evaluation is the process of gathering and interpreting evidences on changes in the behaviour of the students as they progress through school".

The evaluation approach is a new concept in the discipline of education. It has revolutionized the process of education. In it main emphasis has been laid on realizing the objectives of education in behavioural terms.

Teaching and testing activities are performed side by side in evaluation approach. The term evaluation does not confine only upto student achievement but it includes the total process of teaching and learning. All the activities of teachers and students are evaluated qualitatively and quantitatively. The evaluation of a student performances does not confine to cognitive domain, it also includes the affective and psychomotor domains. The total change of behaviour of student is evaluated. The term change of behaviour includes cognitive, affective and psychomotor behaviours. Three types of activities are done in the evaluation process.

1. How far have the teaching objectives been realized?
2. How far are the learning experiences?
3. What are the changes of behaviour that have occurred in the students?

B.S. Bloom has stated that education is tri-polar process.

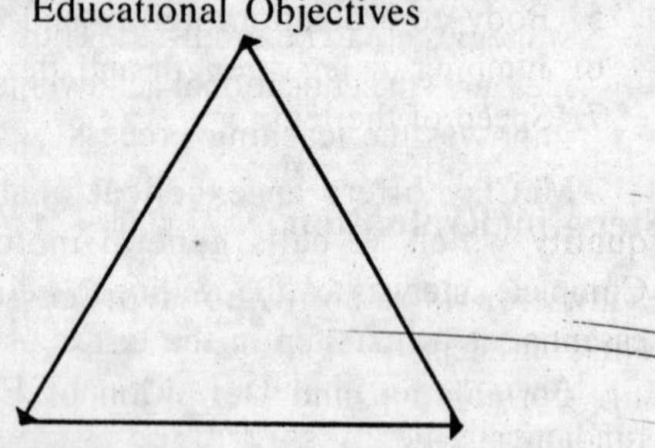

Steps in Evaluation Approach

The following are three steps used in evaluation approach

1. Educational objective.
2. Learning experiences.
3. Change of behaviour.

These three steps are closely related to each other and are performed in a sequence. The teaching and testing activities go side by side and these are objective centred. According to this approach, failure of the student is due to the inappropriateness of learning experiences of teaching. It is the main responsibility of a teacher to bring desirable changes among the students. Thus, the changes of behaviour are evaluated in terms of teaching objectives.

All the school subjects are taught to them for providing learning experiences. Other activities organized in the school, are meant for learning experience. These should be directly related to the teaching objectives.

CONSTRUCTION AND CLASSIFICATION OF TEST

Test Construction

The first step in the construction of an achievement test in physical education is to determine the quality to be measured. For example: The general athletic ability constitutes seven elements. They are:

1. Arm and shoulder girdle co-ordination
2. Arm and shoulder girdle strength
3. Hand - eye, foot eye, arm eye co-ordination.
4. Endurance
5. Body co-ordination, agility and control
6. Jumping or leg strength and flexibility
7. Speed of the legs.

McClay offers an excellent analysis of the quality which he calls general motor capacity. Complete analysis of the ability to be measured is essential as a first step in the test construction.

According to the age groups and following the fundamental bodily skills to be tested suitable test items should be selected.

1. Fundamental bodily skill
2. Selection of test items
3. Preliminary try-out
4. Securing reliability of simple test.
5. Securing an adequate criterion score
6. Experimental condition
7. Selecting the final patterns

Classification of test

The six types of tests presented have various qualities that are not mutually exclusive. For example: A criterion referenced test can be either standardized, or teacher made, knowing the qualities and characteristics attributed to each kind of test will enable the reader to better evaluate and construct tests.

1. **Standardized tests:** Tests that have been scientifically constructed and that may be accompanied by norms are called standardized tests. The validity, reliability of standardized tests have been established. Standardized tests are carefully developed and usually can be made available. Standardized tests have several characteristics.
   (*a*) They usually provide more psychometrically sound system.
   (*b*) They provide good tests when teachers do not have the time or skill to construct them.
   (*c*) They provide tests for a great variety of activities.
   (*d*) They serve several examples for format and content balance.
2. **Teacher made test:** More prevalent are teacher made tests. They are the work of teachers for their local purposes. They also have certain characteristics.
3. **Essay tests:** These tests require a written answer by the student that involve the organisation in information to be presented in logical paragraph form. Essay questions are usually general and test - the ability of students to write the material to be covered, numerous factors are characteristics of essay tests.
   (*a*) They may be constructed quickly.
   (*b*) They are difficult to grade objectively and reliably.
   (*c*) They usually require more time to answer.
4. **Objective tests:** Objective tests require a brief response to questions encompassing smaller pieces of information. They have certain chara-cteristics.
   (*a*) They may be quickly, efficiently and objectively graded.
   (*b*) They can be validated and revised.
   (*c*) They are reliable.
   (*d*) They encourage guessing.
   (*e*) They eliminate bluffing or evasion of an issue.
   (*f*) They clearly define the task to be done.
5. **Criterion referenced tests:** To interpret a student's score by comparing it to some predetermined standard, criterion referenced tests are used. They are unique in various aspects of function and construction.
   (*a*) They tend to encourage dosed, convergent thinking.
   (*b*) They establish minimum expectable learning essentials in a content area.
   (*c*) They reflect the proportion of what could (should) have been learned (percentages).
6. **Norm - referenced tests:** To interpret a students score by comparing it with scores of other students norms - referenced tests are

used. They are used and characterized in various ways.

(*a*) They reflect individual differences in the amount learned.

(*b*) They test to encourage open - divergent thinking.

(*c*) They reveal maximum achievement in a content area.

(*d*) They reflect the proportion of students who learned less than each other student.

(*e*) They are often used for summative evaluation at the compilation of a unit of instruction.

TEST EVALUATION

CRITERIA FOR SELECTING TESTS

Scientific Authenticity	Administrative Educational	Feasibility Applications
1. Validity		1. Tests in major recreational sports
2. Reliability	1. Economy	2. Sports skills
3. Objectivity	(Cost and Time)	3. Physical Fitness
4. Norms		4. Screeing Tests
5. Duplicate Form		5. Social Fitness
6. Standardized		

Hence the teacher should answer the following questions in order to select the`best and most useful tests.

1. Does the test measure the quality for which it is to be measured (validity)?
2. Can test be administered accurately (reliability and objecting)?
3. Can the test scores be interpreted in terms of relative performances (norms and standards)?
4. Is the best economical (economy)?

Criteria for Test Selection

(*a*) Scientific

(*b*) Administrative feasibility

(*c*) Educational applications

In order to make satisfactory selection of the test, teachers available should be least in terms of their scientific attributes. The three criteria are given above.

SCIENTIFIC

Validity

A test is valid if it measures what it proposes to measure. A test is designed to measure the ability of an individual. To serve a tennis ball it is important, that the test accompanies the (if a test is presented) measure of the volley ball then to be valid it must measure volleying ability and ideally, then to be valid it must measure it to such a degree that other influencing factors such as height and weight are individual to the results.

Method of Establishing Validity:

(*a*) **Subjective rating:** The subjective rating is given by the teacher to use in grading when used for establishing validity. They are given by atleast three judges and often tennis serve will provide an example. The techniques of the serve, execution force, accuracy and the like will be noted for each student by three judges; then same students are given a test. Then composite or average of three judge rating, compared to the objective service movement test score from each student and the assessments are available for each student. They are correlated and the result and coefficient of validity of the service placement test is the scores on the test range of the student is approximately calculated in the same order that the judges have evaluated them. If the coefficient is high, the service test will be said to be valid on the basis of the criterion of judges ratings.

(*b*) **Previously validated tests:** Some skills tests are already available. The test may be simplified, shortened, or revised in same way the old form of the test is administrated to a group and then the new form is given to the same group. If the Standing of the peoples in the group is similar, then the new test may be said to be measuring appreciably what old test was measuring.

(*c*) **Composite scores:** A composite score is achieved by administering complete tests, each supposedly related to the measurement area in question. The score are put into some types of comparable form such as t score and added to get one or total score (or) composite score. Other test (or) perhaps even some which were in the composite listing are correlated with the composite score each in turn in various combinations.

(*d*) **Tournament standing:** Some tests are designed for beginners others, for advanced players. Some for players and others for more developed players. A round robin or ladder tournament is conducted and then players are put in proper order of playing excellence. They are assigned some numerical value and it can be compared with various tests measuring the fundamental skills in the game.

(*e*) **Face validity (Empirical Judgment):** The 50 yards dash is considered to be a measure of running ability in speed of running also means excellence of running. The teacher considers the dash and arbitrarily says, that it is a measure of running. He concludes this on the basis of logic common sense judgment and so called true validity. That is to say that one can book. it a best and see inherently what it is measuring.

Reliability

A reliable test will yield the same scores for one pupil or numbers of pupils, regardless of the number of times teacher repeats it. A test is said to be reliable if it is dependable. The statistical technique used for asserting reliability is a correlation co-efficient. Four methods of establishing reliability:

(*a*) **Test - retest method:** Administer the test completely, one time and after a given period of time administer the test to the same pupil, usually, the second administration is on the next day or two and under very similar conditions and certainly before getting practicing and learning factors become influential in the result. The statistical techniques are used for this reliability co-efficient.

(*b*) **Parallel forms:** This type of reliability used generally with written test. The object is to construct two tests of similar difficulty and content. The students take both tests if they perform similarly on them. If two forms of the test really are parallel then the test may be considered reliable.

(*c*) **Split half: (odd and even):** The test is split in half and the two halves are compared statistically to arrive at reliability co-efficience, i.e. administrating the test and then correlate the total of even numbered trails with total number of odd trails. In a 10 trial test the 1, 3, 4, 5, 7 and 9. The trials totalled would provide the second score for the correlation problem.

This method requires the subsequent use of the Spearman Brown formula.

$$rx = \frac{nr}{1 + (n-1)r}$$

rx = stepped up co-efficient

n = proportion of increase in the test

r = split halves co - efficient

Split half co-efficient = 0.55

(*d*) **Rational equivalence:** By this method the reliability is established by determining the performance of pupils from item to item within the test.

Objectivity

Objectivity is the degree of uniformity with which various persons score the same test. If a instructor conducts currently and independently the result should be similar. For example in order to find out the objective in badminton test we need at least two examination. One gathers the first set of scores and the other collecting the second set of data from the same subject. If the two set of data agree, it would be concluded the test was objective. Objectivity in measurement is secured by the following means:

(*a*) Accurately shared and fully detailed instruction in measuring procedures.
(*b*) Simplicity of measuring procedures.
(*c*) The use wherever possible of mechanical tools of measurement.
(*d*) Reduction of results to mathematical scores.
(*e*) Maintenance of professional or scientific attitudes by testers.
(*f*) Selecting of intelligent measurement carefully framed.
(*g*) Supervision of measuring procedures by administrative officers, the statistical technique employed for ascertaining objective is a correlation, the correlation coefficient produced from the two sets of scores should be high the others is enhanced by clear test directions. Precise scoring methods and adherence to them.

Norms

A norm is a standard to which an obtained score may be compared. In other words a norm is a scale which permits conversion from a raw score to a score capable of comparison.

Duplicate Form

Boys and girls are interested in self testing activity and inclined to repeat and practice certain events which interest them and challenge their abilities and skills. Hence it would seem extremely desirable to provide atleast two forms of a test measuring a particular element of physical ability, these forms must be equivalent.

For example: Suppose we wish to measure skill in arm and shoulder co-ordination. To do this 10 to 15 single throwing tests have been used and arranged in order of difficulty from 1 to 15 test. 1.7 and 13 are selected for first form and 2.8, 14 for the second.

For example: In simple test like that in Chinning a number of things must be given consideration.

1. Size of the bar, 2. Distance of the bar from the ground, 3. Method of holding the bar that is front grasp or grasp (or) alternate grasp, 4. Whether or not the arms are down extended at full length on the down stroke, whether rest between chin is allowed etc.

Standard Directions

The directions which are given to the examiner and the student should be carefully worked as well as the exact method. Administrative phases, the directions should be printed and illustrations should be accompanied.

ADMINISTRATIVE

Economy

A test will be easily administered if it is economical and less time consuming. Generally the economic test will

1. Be easy to score
2. Be easy to interpret
3. Be easy to administer
4. Not consume more than 10 to 15 per cent of the total allocation of class teaching.

Educational Applications

A test must have following educational applications:

1. Test in major recreational sports
2. Sports skills
3. Physical fitness
4. Screening test
5. Social fitness

Concept and assessment of physical fitness, motor fitness, motor ability and motor.

Physical fitness: "Physical fitness is the ability to do the daily task with vigour and alterness, with undue fatigue, and with ample energy to engage in leisure pursuit and to meet emergency situations". - H. Harrison Clarke.

Health related physical fitness components:

1. **Cardio respiratory endurance:**
   Ability of the circulatory and respiratory system to efficiently adjust to and recover from exercise.
   Lab assessment: Tread Mill test. bicycle - ergometer test.
   Field assessment: Distance run, distance walk, step tests.
2. **Muscular endurance:** Ability of a muscle group to contract over an extended time against moderate resistance.
   Lab. assessment - Dynamometer,
   Field tests: Sit up, flexed arm hang, squat thrust, repeated bench press.
3. **Muscular strength:** Ability of a muscle or group of muscles to generate force in a single maximal effort.
   Lab test: Dynamometer, Tensometer, Cybex
   Field test: 1 Rm bench press, 1Rm leg press, 1 Rm squat.
4. **Body comparison:** Determination of the contribution of body fat and lean tissue to total body weight.
   Lab test: Skin folds, under water weighting.
5. **Flexibility:** Range of movement present at body joints.
   Lab assessment: Gonimeter, flexometer
   Field Assessment: Sit and reach, trunk extension splits.

Performance related physical fitness components:

1. **Agility:** Ability to make successive movements in different directions efficiently and rapidly.
   Lab assessment: Film analysis, EMG analysis.
   Field assessment: Shuttle run, line jumps, agility tests.
2. **Balance:** Ability to maintain equilibrium when one's centre of gravity and base of support are altered.
   Lab assessment: Film analysis, EMG analysis.
   Field Assessment : Stork stand, balance.
3. **Co-ordination:** Ability to effectively integrate the moments of the body parts.
   Lab assessment: Film analysis, EMG analysis
   Field Assessment: Ball catch, jump rope, jumping jack, wand leap.
4. **Speed:** Ability to perform rapidly successive movements over a short period of time in a single direction.
   Lab assessment: Electronic time devices.
   Field Assessment: Short distance sprint.
5. **Power:** Ability of a muscle or group of muscles to generate maximal force in a single effort.
   Lab assessment: EMG analysis, force platform
   Field assessment: Vertical jump, soft ball throw for distance
6. **Reaction time/movement:** Ability to respond rapidly to a Stimulus.
   Lab assessment: Electronic devices
   Field assessment: Reaction time strict test.

MOTOR ABILITY

Definitions of Motor Ability

"The immediate capacity of an individual to perform in many varied stunts or athletic events" - *Donald K. Mathews.*

"The present, acquired and innate ability to perform motor skills of a general or fundamental nature, explosive of highly specialised sports or gymnastic techniques" – *Barrow and McGee.*

Barrow motor ability test:

Purpose: To measure general or fundamental skills for the purpose of classification.

Level and sex: College men and high school boys.

Test items:

1. Standing broad jump
2. Zig - zag running,
3. Six pound medicine ball put.

Johnson Motor Educability Test: "Motor educability", a term popularised by McColy and referring to the "case with which an individual learns new motors skills".

Use of motor educability test:

(*i*) A method to place pupils in homogenous group 'for physical education classes.

(*ii*) Selecting prospective candidates.

Johnson test of motor educability: In 1932 Johnson proposed a test designed to measure "native neuromuscular capacity" and for homogeneous grouping of the pupils in physical education classes. The validity of the test is 69. The test consists of the following ten stunts.

1. Straddle jump
2. Stagger step
3. Stagger jump
4. Forward skip, holding opposite foot from behind.
5. Front roll
6. Jumping half turn, right or left
7. Back roll
8. Jumping half turn, right and left alternately,
9. Front and back roll combination
10. Jumping full turns.

SKILL TESTS

Modified Brady Volley Ball Test

Purpose: To find out overall volley ball playing ability.

Equipments: Volley balls

Markings

A target area is a line 5 feet long placed on the wall 11 feet above the floor from both ends of this line, lines extend towards the ceiling for atleast 4 feet. No restraining line is drawn on the floor.

Direction

The test consists of three 20 second trails. On the signal 'go' the subject throws the ball against the wall within the target and continuous until 'stop' signal is given if the subject loses the control of the ball, he should recover it and continue the volley.

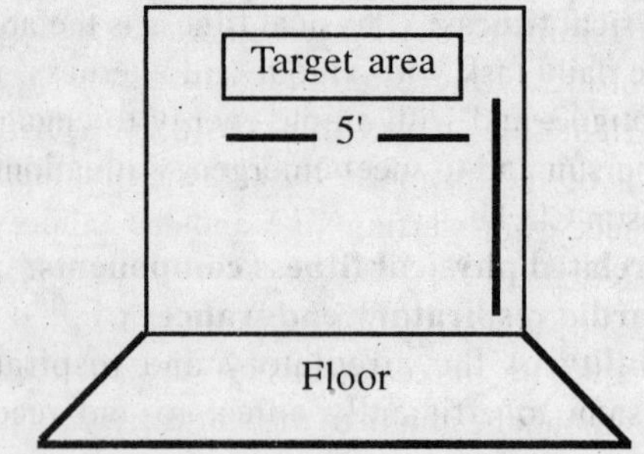

Scoring

The score is the number of legal volleys executed in three 20 second trials. The volley is counted only if the ball hits, in or above the target area clearly. If the scorer feels that the ball visibly comes to rest at contact, the volley is not counted.

KNOX BASKET BALL TEST

Purpose

To measure the basket ball playing ability.

Equipments

The equipments needed are seven obstacles (chairs may be used), a basket ball, a stop watch, and three tin cups, one painted blue, one red and one white.

direction

1. **Speed Dribble Test:** Four chairs are placed in a straight line so that the first one is 20 feet from the straight line and others 15 feet apart. The subject places the ball on the straight line and then stands back of it, with hands on knees with the signal, the subject picks up the ball and dribbles in a zig-zag manner up and down. Timing is taken from the signal to when the subject returns to the starting line. The score is the time in seconds.
2. **Wall Bounce Test:** A line is marked on the floor 5 feet from the wall and parallel to it. The subject stands behind this line and rebounds the basket ball from the wall fifteen times as quickly as possible using the chest pass.
   The score is the number of seconds from the signal 'go' until the ball hits the wall the fifteenth time.

3. **Dribble Shoot Test:** 3 chairs are arranged in a straight line diagonally from the basket to right side line of the court. The starting line is 65 feet from the basket; the first chair is 20 feet from starting line and the others are 15 feet apart.
   The subject dribbles, around the chair shoots until he makes a basket and dribbles back around the chairs to the starting line. The score is the time in seconds required to complete the test.
4. **Penny Cup Test:** A course is set up as follows: A signal line (B) is drawn 8 feet from and parallel to a starting line (A). A finish line 10 feet long is drawn 12 feet way from the signal line. Three tin cups pointed red, white and blue, are placed on this line one in the centre and one at each end.

The subject stands behind the starting line with his back to the cups and with a penny in his hand. At the signal, 'go' he pirots and runs toward the cups. As he crosses the "signal line", the tester calls out one of the 3 cups columns. The subject must drop his penny into the cup the tester called. The test is repeated four times. The score is the total time in seconds required to perform all the four trials.

Final Scoring

Scoring of the total knox test is the total number of seconds, required to perform each of the four tests. The probable range of scores is from 34 to 58. Low scores are the better score.

HEWITT TENNIS SERVICE PLACEMENT TEST

Purpose

To measure the tennis service ability.

Equipments

Tennis 25 tennis ball, and score cards.

Marking

Regislation size tennis court.

Direction

A ten minute warm up is permitted. The examiner stands behind the base line and serves 10 balls into the marked serve court, as shown in the figure. The ball should pass between the net and the 7 foot high rope. If this occurs, the trial score is the point value of the target area in which the ball lands. A ball travelling over the rope is scored 0.

Scoring

The test score is the sum of 10 trials. The validity of test ranges from 0.625 to 0.93. Using a criterion measure of round robin tournament ranking. Test-retest reliability is 0.94.

SPECIFICATIONS FOR HEWITT TENNIS SERVICE PLACEMENT TEST

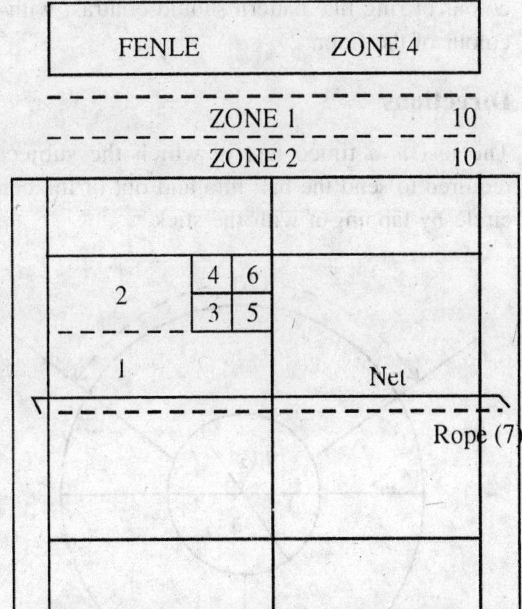

HOCKEY CHAPMAN BALL CONTROL TEST

Purpose

To measure ball control skills in hockey and more specifically the subjects ability to combine quickness in wrist and hand movements needed to manipulate the stick with ability to control the force element when contacting the ball.

Equipments

Hockey stick
Hockey ball

Markings

The target is placed on a gymnasium floor, the pattern made of self adhesive plastic, measures 9½ inches in diameter with an inner circle of measuring 4½ inches in diameter. The larger circle is divided into three equal segments of 120 degree lines 1/8 inch in width originality in the centre of the circle and extending to its outer edge are marked on the target to define the boundaries of segments. The colour of ring like pattern should contrast with the colour of the floor.

Directions

The test is a timed test in which the subject is required to send the ball into and out of the centre circle by tapping it with the stick.

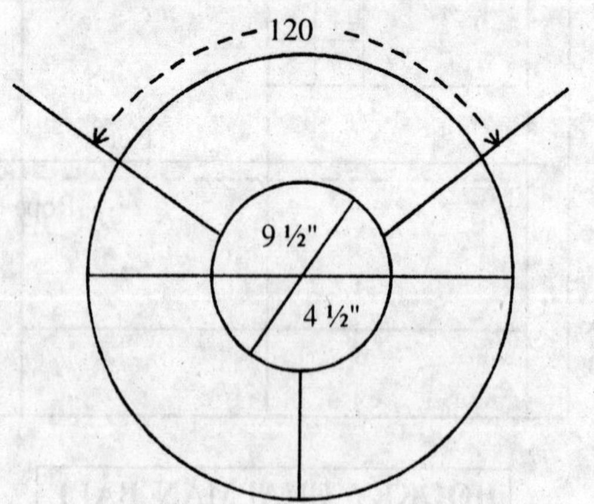

Scoring

A point is scored each time the ball is clearly tapped into (or) through the centre circle and each time it is tapped from the centre outside the larger circle provided it is sent out through a segment other than that through which it entered, no is awarded for a ball that is rapped while it is in the area between the two circles or with the rounded side of the stick. The total points scored on three 15 seconds trials is the subject score.

BADMINTON – THE FRENCH SHORT SERVE TEST

Purpose

To measure ability to serve accurately and low.

Equipment

Badminton racket
Shuttle cocks

Markings

Four concentric quarter circles are drawn on the right service court. A rope is stretched 20 inches above net and parellal to it. Markings 1½ inches wide in the form of archs are drawn on the floor at the distance of 22, 30, 38 and 46 inches from the midpoint of inter section of the centre line and the short service line of the right service court. The distance includes the width of the 2 inches line.

Directions

The subject stands in the service court diagonally opposite from the target. Twenty serves are attempted either consecutively or in groups of ten. The subject tries to send the shuttle between the net and the rope. The scorer nearer the centre of the left service court facing the target. The subject tries to hit the target area nearest the intersection of the centre line and short service line line shuttles which hit on a line are given, the higher point value.

Scoring

The zones are given point values of five, four, three two, one. Shuttle cocks that land on a line will score the higher value serves that fail to go between the rope and not that are out of the bounds of the right service court for doubles and that are not executed legally will score, zero. The final score is the total of values made on 20 services.

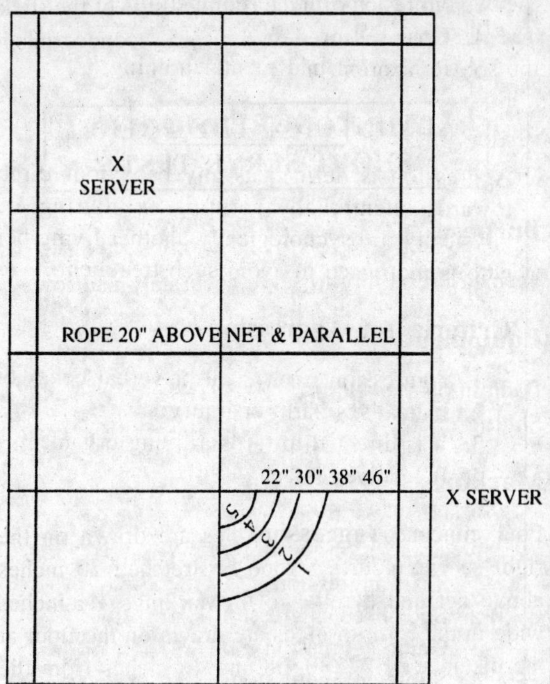

SPECIFICATION FOR THE SHORT SERVE TEST

Mcdonald Soccer Skill Test

Purpose

To measure the general soccer ability.

Equipment

Foot ball -3

Markings

A backboard 30 feet wide and 11½ feet high is placed. A restraining line is drawn 9 feet from the back board and parallel to it. Three soccer balls are used, one is placed on the restraining line the other two are located 9 feet behind this line in the centre of the area.

Directions

At the single the subject starts kicking the ball against the backboard as many times as possible in thirty seconds, any type of kicking may be used, rebounds may be retrieved in any manner including use of hands if a ball is out of control. The subject can use spare balls but should place it on the restraining line before kicking it.

Scoring

All the kicks both ground and fly balls that are hit on the back board from behind the restraining line are counted. The score is the number of legal kicks in the time period of 30 seconds. The best of four trials is recorded.

SPECIFICATION OF McDONALD TEST

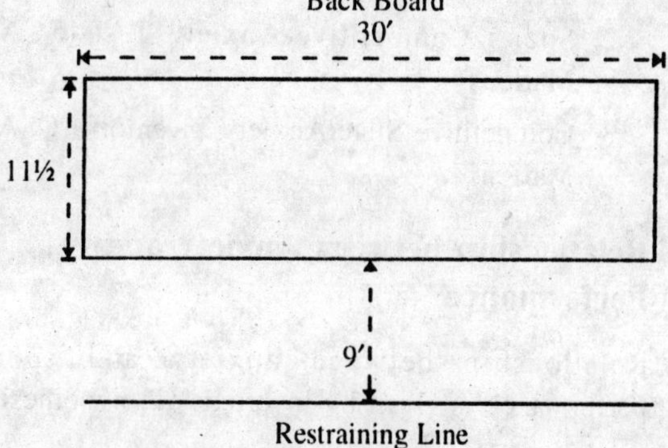

Testing psychological variables - compe-titive anxiety, aggression team cohesion, motivation, self concept.

Competitive Anxiety

Anxiety is a negative emotional state with feelings of nervousness, worry and apprehension associated with activation or arousal of the body.

Types of Anxiety

The researchers have studied and classified many types of anxiety. They are:

1. **State anxiety:** According to Spielberger state anxiety refers to an existing or immediate emotional state, characterised by apprehension and tension.

2. **Trait anxiety:** It is the predisposition to perceive certain situations as threatening and to respond to these situations with varying levels of state anxiety.
3. Competitive state anxiety
4. Competitive anxiety
5. Unconscious anxiety
6. Free floating anxiety
7. Cognitive anxiety
8. Somatic anxiety

Measuring Anxiety

For research purposes anxiety is measured using questionnaires, some of them are:

1. State Trait Anxiety Inventory (STAI) Spielberger
2. Sports Competitive Anxiety Test (SCAT) Martens
3. Competitive State Anxiety Inventory (CSAT) Martens

Relationship between Anxiety and Performance

Relationship between anxiety and sports performance is given by inverted "U" hypothesis.

Inverted "U" Hypothesis

Performance improves with increasing level of anxiety to an optimum point. Whereupon further increase in anxiety decreases the performance.

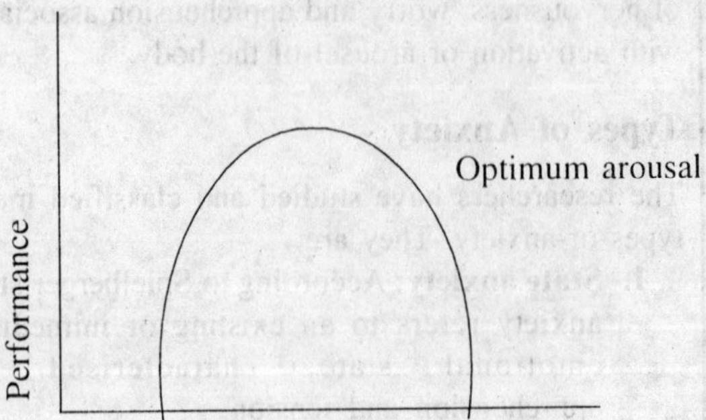

Methods of Reducing Anxiety

1. Motivation
2. Enough practice time
3. More exposure to competition
4. Goal setting
5. Relaxation and mental training

AGGRESSION

Aggression is defined as any behaviour directed towards intentionally harming or injuring either physically or psychologically another living being, who is motivated to avoid such treatment.

Criteria for Aggression

1. Aggression is physical or verbal behaviour
2. It involves harm or injury
3. It is directed towards a living organism
4. It involves intent.

Types of Aggression

1. Trait aggression
2. Socialised aggression
3. Game aggression
4. Strategic aggression
5. Situational aggression
6. Post game aggression
7. Instrumental aggression
8. Psychological aggression
9. Hostile aggression

Theories of Aggression

1. **Instinct theory:** The instinct can either be expressed directly by attacking another living being or displaced through catharsis, where aggression is released or blown off through socially desirable means such as sports.
2. Frustration aggression theory
3. **Social learning theory**
4. **Revised frustration aggression theory:** Competitive sports, differs from many activities in that it is usually conducted in the presence of fans and spectators.

When aggression is most likely to occur: Except certain situations to provoke aggressive behaviour, participants typically feel frustrated when they:

- Are losing
- Perceive unfair officiating
- Are embarrassed
- Are physically in pain or
- Are playing below their capabilities.

Controlling Aggression

Unfortunately, we cannot always control these situations. Stress management training can help students or athletes to deal with frustrating situations. Sports and exercise professionals have a moral responsibility to clearly distinguish between assertive behaviour and aggression with an intent to harm.

Sex Differences in Aggression

Sports psychologists believe that males are naturally more aggressive than females. In our culture aggression has traditionally been viewed as a desirable act for men, but not for women. Girls are taught not to be aggressive if so they may lose their feminity.

Team Cohesion

Carron (1982) defines cohesion as "A dynamic process which is reflected in the tendency for a group to stick together and remain united in the pursuit of it's goals and objectives".

The common thread was that cohesion consist of two basis of dimensions. Task cohesion and social cohesion. Task cohesion refers to the degree that group members work together to achieve common goals and objectives, whereas social cohesion reflects the inter personal attraction among group members.

The four major factors affecting the development of cohesion in sports and exercise settings:

1. Environmental factors
2. Personal factors
3. Team factors
4. Leadership factors

Components of Cohesion

1. Social satisfaction
2. Sociometric cohesion

Social satisfaction pertains to the group members satisfaction with the groups in terms of its ability to allow a person to obtain desired goals.

Sociometric cohesion refers to the amount of positive effect or liking among group members.

Haystrom and Selvins bi-dimensional model of cohesion.

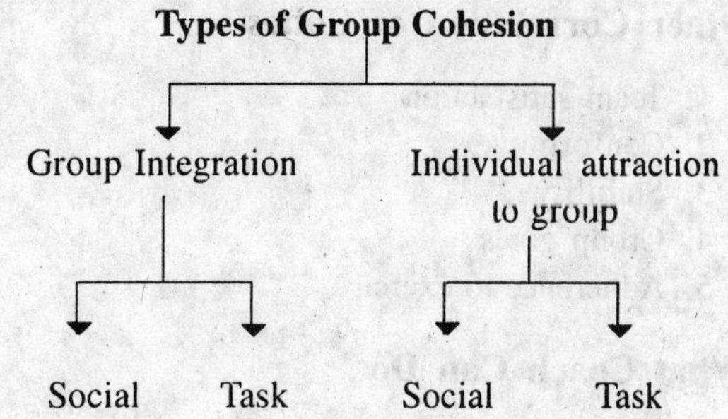

Measurement of Group Cohesion

There are numbers of ways of measuring group cohesion.

1. Sports cohesiveness questionnaire contains seven components:

a.	Inter personal attractiveness socio metric Measures	Socio Metric Measures
b.	Personal Power	
c.	Value of membership	Direct Measures
d.	Sense of belonging	
e.	Enjoyment	
	Direct measures	
f.	Team work	
g.	Closeness	

2. Sports cohesion instrument which measures both group goals and objectives and positive interpersonal relationship.
3. Group environment questionnaire.

Sample Questions

(Attract on group)

1. I do like the style of play of this team. (Task) (Strongly agree)
   (Strongly disagree)
   1 2 3 4 5 6 7 8 9
2. Some of my best friends are on this team. (Social) (Strongly agree)
   (Strongly disagree)
   1 2 3 4 5 6 7 8 9

Other Correlation of Cohesion

1. Team satisfaction
2. Conformity
3. Stability
4. Group goals
5. Adherence to exercise

What Coach Can Do

1. Explain individual rules in team success
2. Develop pride within sub units
3. Set challenging team goals
4. Encourage team identity .
5. Avoid formation of social checks
6. Stay in touch with team climate

What Group Members Can Do

1. Get to know teammates
2. Help the teammates whenever possible
3. Give team mates positive reinforcement
4. Be responsible
5. Resolve conflicts immediately
6. Give 100% effort at all times.

MOTIVATION

"Motivation is an urge to push towards a specific goal" – *Robert N. Singer.*

The origin of motivation lies in drives and needs of each individual.

Drives are of Two Types

1. Primary drives
2. Secondary drives

Some of the Types of Incentives

1. Social incentives
2. Monetary incentives
3. Reward incentives
4. Social competitive incentives

Intrinsic Motivation

This type of motivation is that which comes from within the person e.g., Expression of participation, joy:

Motivational Components of Sports

1. Biological motivation
2. Psychological motivation
3. Social motivation
4. Reinforcement motivation

Five Guidelines to Build Motivation

1. Both situations and traits motivate people
2. People have multiple motives for involvement
3. Change the environment to enhance motivation
4. Leaders influence motivation
5. Use behaviour modification to change undesirable participant motives.

Self Concept

Self knowledge is a useful thing. The better you understand yourself, the better the choice we can make in many contexts and the more accurately we can predict our reactions to many events and situations. In addition, several theories of personality suggest that the more accurate our self concept, the better the athlete performs.

Measuring Self-Concept

First make about 10 copies of the questionnaire given here. Next complete one copy yourself. The third step is to give copies (blank, of course except for your name in the space for it) to several people who know you well, good family members, romantic partners. There has to be at least five to ten people to provide ratings. Finally average their ratings on each dimensions and then compare these average

Example Questionnaire:

1. Cautious	1	2	3	4	5	6	7	1)	Adventurous
2. Insensitive	1	2	3	4	5	6	7	2)	Sensitive
3. Calm	1	2	3	4	5	6	7	3)	Anxious
4. Cooperative	1	2	3	4	5	6	7	4)	Uncooperative
5. Irresponsible	1	2	3	4	5	6	7	5)	Responsible
6. Composed	1	2	3	4	5	6	7	6)	Excitable
7. Sociable	1	2	3	4	5	6	7	7)	Shy
8. Suspicious	1	2	3	4	5	6	7	8)	Trusting
9. Imaginative	1	2	3	4	5	6	7	9)	Down to earth
10. Careless	1	2	3	4	5	6	7	10)	Careful

with your own ratings. The larger the difference the less accurate your-self concept.

Rate on each of the dimensions below circle on your no to indicate where he / she falls on dimension (4 is the middle of the scale).

ANTHROPOMETRIC MEASUREMENTS AND BODY COMPOSITION

Anthropometric Measurement

The oldest form of measurement, known as anthropometry, deals with the study of man, that is the study of body and mind and their inter relationship. It is the science of measuring the human body and its parts. It is used as an aid to study of human evolution and variation. Baron Quetelet a French Mathematician used the term anthropometry who is considered as father of anthropometry.

In the Egyptian sculpture, the length of the middle finger was considered a common measure of all body proportions. The early Greeks were experts in body proportions. Hippocrates the father of modem medicine believed that the body symmetry and proportion were related to health. W.H. Sheldon classified the somoto type as ectomorphy, mesomorphy and endomorphy. Sills introduced a fourth somoty type which is called omomorphy. Edward Hitchcock, a medical doctor, initiated yearly measurements of all students.

Anthropometric measurement is still practised today. The researchers usually focus their attention on elite athletes and dancers. They have added the body fat measures to the traditional measures of height, weight and girths.

Anthropometric Lab

It is a branch of study which deals with the body segments and measurements. The use of measuring instruments, classification of women by body types, relationship of somototype to various constitutional defects and diseases, ratial differences in skeletal and, muscle structure and the relationship between growth and strength and muscle hypertrophy are the areas of concern in laboratory research.

Anthropometry

The anthropometry laboratory should have the following instruments:

S. No.	Instruments	Use to measure
1.	Weighing machine	weight of the body
2.	Stadio meter	height of the body
3.	Measuring tape	to measure the length
4.	Skinfold caliper	body fat
5.	Anthropometer	to measure all the body segments

6.	Recumbent	difference in maximum and minimum length of the muscle.
7.	Sliding caliper	the muscles with (girth)
8.	Spreading caliper	Spreading change in size of the muscle.

Cricket Playing Skills :

1. **Batting:**

   Batting skills are given below:

   (*i*) Batting stance.
   (*ii*) Forward Defensive stroke.
   (*iii*) Backward-Defensive Stroke.
   (*iv*) Of drive, On drive and straight drive square drive etc.
   (*v*) Late cut.
   (*vi*) Leg glance.
   (*vii*) Hook shot.
   (*viii*) Lofted stroke.
   (*ix*) Sweeping.

   Batsmen's second important job is to run between the wicket.

2. **Bowling:**

   Following skills are required in bowling.

   (*i*) Fast bowling.
   (*ii*) Spin bowling-offbreak, leg break, top spin and googly.

3. **Fielding:**

   It consists of following sub jobs.

   (*i*) Stopping and throwing ball.
   (*ii*) Catching the ball- close in catches and high catches.

4. **Wicket keeping:**

   Following skills are required here.

   (*i*) Taking the ball into the gloves and savings the by runs.
   (*ii*) Stumping.
   (*iii*) Taking the catch from behind.

5. **Captaincy:**

   This is the most important skill needed to win a match.

'ootball playing Skills:

1. **Kicking:**

   (*i*) Instep kick
   (*ii*) Outstep kick
   (*iii*) Toe kick
   (*iv*) Chip kick
   (*v*) Punt kick
   (*vi*) Drop kick
   (*xii*) Scissors kick

2. **Passing:**

   (*i*) Short pass
   (*ii*) Long pass
   (*iii*) Through pass

3. **Trapping:**

   (*i*) Foot trap
   (*ii*) Thigh trap
   (*iii*) Belly trap
   (*iv*) Chest trap
   (*v*) Fore head trap

4. **Dribbling**
5. **Heading**
6. **Intercepting**
7. **Tackling**
8. **Goal keeping**
9. **Offensive Technique**
10. **Defensive Technique**

Hockey Playing Skills:

1. Hockey Grip
2. Hitting a ball such as hitting a moving or stationary ball or reverse hit.
3. Stopping a ball with a slanting or horizontal stick.
4. Push stroke --- fore hand or reverse push
5. Flick stroke--- forehand or reverse flick
6. Scoop stroke --- Push scoop or shovel scoop
7. Dribbling
8. Dodging
9. Interception
10. Tackling
11. Passing - short or long pass or through pass.
12. Taking a penalty corner
13. Defending a penalty corner
14. Taking a penalty stroke
15. Defending a penalty stroke
16. Goal keeping
17. Offending and Defending

Kabaddi Playing Skills:

1. **Raiding skills:**
   (*i*) Starting a raid.
   (*ii*) Movements during raid.
   (*iii*) Touching with feet- Sudden leg thrust, Squat leg thrust, Front kick,side kick, Aerokick, Swing kick, Mule kick, Toe kick etc.
   (*iv*) Touching with hand.
   (*v*) Withdrawal.
   (*vi*) Jumping.
   (*vii*) Falling

2. **Defensive skills:**
   (*i*) Holding - wrist catch, Over the shoulder catch, Trunk catch, Wrist and ankle catch, Single or double knee catch, Dive and catch etc.
   (*ii*) Offensive Tactics
   (*a*) Starting raid from one side
   (*b*) Employing pivoting and dodging
   (*iii*) Defensive Tactics
   (*a*) Chain formation
   (*b*) Pursuing
   (*c*) No cross play

SOME OTHER USEFUL MATTERS

Body Composition

Body composition is the ratio of lean body mass to fat body mass. Body composition consists of lean body mass and body fat. Lean body mass is made of structural and functional elements in cells, body water, muscle, bones and other body organs such as the heart, liver and kidneys.

Body composition Techniques

1. **Hydrostatic Weighing:** This technique is currently considered as 'Gold Standard' of body composition analysis. Hydrostatic measurements are based on the assumption that density and specific gravity of lean tissue is greater than that of fat tissue. Thus, lean tissue will sink in water and fat tissue will float.
2. **Height / Weight Tables:** This table was developed in 1953 to calculate the degree of individuals over or under weight status. There were many changes made to height/ weight table later on to meet the current requirements and to counter criticism. As on date the table gives no indication as to the degree of either obesity or leanness on an individual basis.
3. **Body Mass Index:** BMI has recently been used to quantify as individuals obesity level. It is derived from a ratio equation of height squared divided by weight.
4. **Skin Fold Measurements:** The best methodology for body fat estimation with skin fold measurement requires the use of a 'Caliper Device'. This device measures the thickness of substantial fat stores. The assumption is that substantial fat is proportional to overall body fat and thus by measuring several sites, total body fat may be calculated.
5. **Anthropometries measurement:** The anthropometries measurement (girth and length) is a quick, easy and inexpensive method to estimate body composition. Using a standard calibrated cloth tape, girth and length measurements are taken from specific points on the body. The methodology is based on the assumption that body fat is distributed on various sites on the body such as the waist; neck and thigh; Muscle tissue on the other hand is usually located at anatomical location such as the biceps, forearm and calf.

Sports Competition Anxiety Test

Sports Competition Anxiety Test (Martens, 1977)

1. **Test objective:** To measure individual differences in the construct of competitive sport anxiety; to measure competitive A (Anxiety) trait, which is defined as a construct that describes individual difference in the

tendency to perceive competitive situations as threatening and to respond to these situations with A (Anxiety) state reactions of varying intensity (Marten, 1977:36)

2. **Description:** The sport competitive anxiety test for children (SCAT-C) includes 15 questions with answer choices- hardly ever, sometimes and often. The student is given directions to choose the word that describes how he or she usually feel when competing in games and sports.
3. **Materials:** Test forms and pencils.
4. **Scoring:** Items 2, 3, 5, 8, 9, 12, 14 and 15 are scored using the following key.
   1 = Hardly ever
   2 = Sometimes
   3 = Often
   Items 6 and 11 are scored using the following
   1 = Often
   2 = Sometimes
   3 = Hardly Ever
   Items 1, 4, 7, 10 and 13 the remaining items, are not scored; they are included in the inventory as spurious items to direct attention to elements of competition other than anxiety.
5. **Validity:** The general approaches to construct validity included studies of group differences. High scorers on the SCAT-C were expected to manifest higher A states in stressful competitive situations than low scorers on SCAT-C.
6. **Reliability**: Test re-test reliability was determined for both sexes of grades 5 and 6 and 8 and 9. Within day reliability coefficients ranged from 0.85 to 0.93. Test-retest reliabilities ranged from 0.61 to 0.87.
7. **Comments:** The test is easy to administer in a group setting. However, the Martens monograph should be reviewed before using SCAT so that the theoretical framework generating this instrument is understood.

Miller-Wall-Volley Test in Badminton

The Miller Wall Volley test was developed in 1951 to measure the basic Badminton skill of 'clears' (shots hit high and deep into the opponents court) upon both men and women (Miller, 1951).

1. **Equipment:** A stopwatch, a sponge-end shuttlecock, badminton racket, marking tape or chalk.
2. **Test Area:** A wall measuring at least 10 feet in width and 15 feet in height is marked with horizontal lines, one inch wide and parallel to the floor. The first line is marked at the height of 7 feet 6 inches from the floor. A line is also marked on the floor at a distance of 10 feet from the wall.

3. Test Administration: A subject is allowed one minute practice of putting a sponge ended shuttlecock into play with a legal serve from behind the 10 feet restraining line after getting instruction from the tester. The subject is now asked to volley the shuttlecock against the wall above 7.5' line, as many times as possible in 30 seconds. The subject is required to start with a legal serve from behind the 10 feet restraining line. Three trials of 30 seconds each are given with at least 30 seconds interval between the trials.

4. Scoring: The sum of number of times the shuttlecock is volleyed against the wall during all the three trials provides the score of the test. The rebounds are counted only when shuttle cock is hit legally from behind the 10 feet restraining line and hits the wall above the 7.5' line.

Skill Test for Lawn Tennis

Dyer Tennis Skills Test : This test is used to measure tennis skill ability. It was developed in 1935 by J.T. Dyer on 736 women tennis players of 19 colleges.

1. **Equipment:** A Stopwatch, a back board, Tennis balls, Racket and a Measuring tape.
2. **Description and test administration:** The back board of 10 feet 15 feet or a wall of 15 feet wide and 10 feet high may be used. A horizontal line, 3 inches in width is marked at a height of 3 feet from the floor, which acts as a tennis net. Another line is marked on the floor at distance of 5 feet from the base of the wall that is restraining line. After giving a demonstration to the subjects through a trained helper, the tester asks the subjects to stand behind the restraining line with a racket

in his/her hand and two balls in the other hand. Extra balls are also provided at a distance as convenient to the subject. After asking the subject to be ready, the tester gives the signal 'start' and starts the stop watch, the subject drops the ball to the floor and plays it against the wall as rapidly as possible aiming to hit the wall above the 3 feet high net line for a maximum number of times. After 30 seconds, the tester gives the 'stop' signal and stops the stopwatch the subject stops volleying the ball. Each subject is given 3 trials. The tester needs. Three helpers, one for counting the number of balls hitting the wall, one for collecting the balls and one for checking the violations made at the restraining line.

3. **Scoring:** Each time the ball strikes the wall on or above the net line before the end of 30 seconds, scores one point. The sum of points achieved in all three trials, gives the final score.

McDonald Soccer Skill Test

In 1951, during his postgraduate study, McDonald constructed the soccer skill test for measuring accurate kicking, ball control and judgement of a moving ball in soccer. The test was constructed on college men and the validity coefficient of the test ranged from 0.63 to 0.94. The author has selected controlled kicking skill as the most fundamental skill element of soccer playing. He conducted the kicking test with a restraining line distance of 9 feet, 15 feet, 21 feet and 30 feet from the kickboard. However, the test with a nine feet retraining distance provided the highest validity coefficient and is in common use for soccer skill testing. Some details of the test are given below:

Equipment: A stopwatch, a soccer kickboard, three soccer balls, soccer field and marking powder.

Administration: The test field includes 11.5 feet high and 30 feet wide kickboard.

A horizontal restraining line is marked at a distance of 9 feet from the kickboard. Another line is marked at a distance of 18 feet from the kickboard. One soccer ball is placed on the 9 feet restraining line. Two extra balls are place on the 18 feet line. The subject (examinee) is instructed to make maximum number of kicks in 30 seconds by keeping the ball in his control while using any type of kick and ball control method. On the signal ready? Go! The timer starts the stopwatch and the subject starts kicking the stationary ball from or behind the restraining line and continues kicking the stationary ball from or behind the restraining line and continues kicking the rebounding ball as rapidly as control permits until the 30 seconds time limit expires (indicated by the timer). In case, the ball fails to rebound sufficiently, the subject has the option either to retrieve the same ball or to take one of the extra balls with the help of either hands or feet. After placing the retrieved or the extra ball on or just behind the 9 feet restraining line, the subject continues kicking the-ball again.

Scoring: The subject is given four 30 second attempt and the final test score is provided by the sum of kicks of the three best trials.

Brady's Volleyball Skill Test

Brady's Volleyball Skill Test Battery: Brady constructed a Volleyball skill test on 537 college men Volley ballers. The test-retest reliability coefficient reported is 0.92 while the validity coefficient has been reported to be 0.86. The test was constructed to measure general Volleyball playing ability of college men.

Equipment: Standard inflated Volleyballs, wall marking chalk, tape, stop-watch and pair of staircases for support to mark the target.

Test Target Dimensions: A target is marked on the wall with a good quality marking chalk. The target is bounded by a horizontal line of 5 feet length at a height of 11.5 feet from the floor/ground. The two ends of the horizontal line are extended upward towards the ceiling upto 3 to 4 feet high.

Test Administration: The subject/performer is asked to make a maximum number of volleys standing at any point in front of the target in one minute. He is specifically instructed that only the legal volleys will be counted, that is, the subject should perform real volleys and not the thrown balls, and the volleys must hit the wall within the boundaries of the target. If the ball is caught or gets out of control the subject is to be asked to repeat from the start. Two trials may be given and the best be considered. On the signal go! The ball is tossed against the wall at the target area and the stopwatch is started. On rebound, the ball is volleyed into the marked target consecutively for one minute till the stop signal is given.

Scoring: The number of real volleys in one minute gives the score of the test.

Schmithals-French Field Hockey Skill Test

The Schmithals-French Field Hockey Skill Test: In the beginning, the skill elements were selected with the help of three nationally best rated hockey umpires of USA (who were players and teachers of considerable experience) as to the frequency with which the skills were used in the game of field hockey. On the basis of the selection of the skills, tests were constructed in the following skills and combinations of skills.

(*i*) Dribble, dodge, circular tackle and drive the ball (bill control skill in hockey).

(*ii*) Drive for goal (straight to right, to left)

(*iii*) Fielding and drive

(*iv*) Push pass

(*v*) Drive for distance

(*vi*) Receiving the ball from team mate (left and right)

A series of inter-correlations was completed among all above mentioned six variables on the rationale given below:

(*a*) If two items correlate highly with each other, they are probably measuring the same skill; thus one of these two could be eliminated.

(*b*) If two items do not correlate, they are probably measuring two different skills and both might need to be retained.

On the basis of multiple correlations, it was determined that with which combination of skills, the test criteria correlated the most. The test criterion consisted of three separate subjective ratings by three national umpires classifying hockey players into five groups:

1. Superior
2. Above average
3. Average
4. Below average and
5. Inferior

The ratings of the instructor of each particular group involved was weighted so that the criterion consisted of twice the instructor's score plus the sum of the other two raters. The final regression (prediction) equation developed was:

$$X_0 = 0.38\,X_1 + 0.17\,X_2 + 0.48X_3 - 1.62$$

Where

X_0 = the test criterion, i.e. playing ability

X_1 = goal shooting left test

X_2 = dribble, dodge, circular tackle and drive test

X_3 = fielding and drive test

However, the dribble, dodge, circular tackle and drive test (Ball Control Test) was considered by the authors as the most economically administered and is generally used for evaluating Hockey Skill Testing even today.

Johnson Basic Basketball Skill Test

Johnson Basic Basketball Skill Test Items: To establish validity of the test battery, Johnson divided 180 high school basketball boys into two groups-' good' and-'poor'. The 'good' group of boys included those basketball players who represented in the school's basketball teams and the 'poor' group of boys included those basketball players who were not selected for representing their school's basketball squad. There were fifty boys in the first group ('good') and 130 in the second group ('poor'). A validity coefficient of 0.88 had been reported between test scores of both 'poor' and 'good' groups boys. The reliability and the validity coefficient of the basic test items battery have been reported by Johnson to be 0.93 and 0.84 respectively (Clarke and Clarke, 1987). Brief description of the three items constituting basic basketball skill testing in the Johnson Basketball Battery is given below:

(*i*) Johnson Field Goal Speed Test: The tester asks the basketball player (examinee) to stand in any position under the basket and is required to make maximum number of baskets in 30 seconds. The number of successful baskets thrown in 30 seconds provides the score for this test. This item measures the ability of the examinee to make successive field goals as quickly as possible under the stress of time.

(*ii*) Johnson Basketball throw for Accuracy (Passing Test): This test item measures the shoulder strength and the ability of consistent accurate throws. In this test either a rectangular (Clarke & Clarke, 1987) or a circular archery type target (Kirkendall et. al., 1987) is placed on a wall. The examinee, standing at a distance of 40 feet from the target, makes ten trials for hitting the ball in the centre of the target. For hitting, the examinee uses either the overhand or the hook pass method.

Scoring: For each hitting in the inner rectangle/circle or its line-three points are awarded; for each hitting in the middle rectangle or circle and its line-two points; and for each pass hitting in the outer circle/ rectangle and the line-one point is awarded. The total ten trials, score is used for evaluating basketball passing test item of the battery.

Position of Examinee, Tester and Recorder: The examinee stand just outside the forty feet line in front of the target; the tester stands 5 to 10 feet inside the 40 feet line on the right side of the examinee and the recorder stands on the right side of the target about 5 to 7 feet away from the target wall towards the tester.

(*iii*) **Johnson Basketball Dribble Test:** This test item has been designed with the purpose of measuring ball handling ability and agility level of the examinee.

The examinee is required to cover a maximum distance while dribbling around obstacles in 30 seconds. Four obstacles (chairs or hurdles) are arranged in a straight line at six feet apart. The first obstacle is 12 feet away from the starting line, which is 6 feet wide. The subject is asked to begin dribbling from one end of the starting line and is required to dribble for 30 seconds in a zigzag manner around the turnings at each obstacle point, approaching the first obstacle on the opposite side of the starting point and by turning about at the fourth obstacle.

Scoring: The score is equal to the number of zones covered in 30 seconds. The examinee gets one point on crossing each obstacle. However, two sides of the last obstacle and the starting line mark provide two separate points as they represent the boundaries of two zones each.

The above three Johnson basketball basic skill test items constitute the basketball skill test battery and the three scores added together constitute the Johnson basketball test battery score which may be compared directly among basket baller's score or after converting to T scores.

AAHPER Youth Physical Fitness Test

AAHPER Youth fitness test Table Youth fitness test items alongwith the elements tested by each items.

S. No.	Test Items Elements tested.
(*i*)	Pull-ups (boys) Muscular Strength (Dynamic) and Muscular or flexed Arm Hang Endurance of Arm and Shoulders. (Girls)
(*ii*)	Bent-Knee Sit-ups Muscular Strength and Endurance (Trunk).
(*iii*)	Shuttle Run Speed and Agility. (10x4 yards)
(*iv*)	Standing Broad Jump Explosive Strength of Legs.
(*v*)	50 Yard Dash Speed of Lower Extremities and explosive Strength.
(*vi*)	600- Yard Run-Walk Cardiovascular Endurance (10-12 years) 9 Min. Run-Walk or 1 Mile or 12 Min. run-Walk or 1.5 Mile Run-Walk (Age 13 and above)

The AAHPER Youth fitness test is to be conducted in two days as suggested below:

1st Day:

(*i*) Pull-ups or Flexed Arm Hang.
(*ii*) Bent-Knee Sit-ups.
(*iii*) Shuttle Run.

2nd Day:

(*i*) Standing Broad Jump (SBJ)
(*ii*) 50 Yard Dash.

(*iii*) 600 Yard Run-Walk (or 9 Min. Run-Walk or Mile Run-Walk for 10-12 year age groups or 12 Min. run-Walk or 1.5 Mile Run-Walk.

Very little equipment is required for the test.

The item wise administration procedure follows:

(*i*) Pull ups (boys only) and Flexed Arm Hang (girls only)

Equipment: A wooden or metal bar approximately 1.5 inches in diameter: piece of pipe or the rungs of a ladder may also be used and stopwatch (only for girls).

(*a*) **Pull ups (Boys) Test Administration:** The height of the bar should be such that when the subject hangs from it with fully extended arms, his feet do not touch the ground. The subject is asked to use an overhand grasp with the palms facing away from the body. From the hanging position, the pupil raises the body by the arm until the chin can be placed over the bar and then lowers the body to a full extension hang and repeats the pull ups as many times as possible. Only one trial is given unless it is obvious that the pupil has not had a fair chance. Neither swinging, nor kicking the legs nor knee raising is allowed.

Scoring : The maximum number of completed pull-ups is the score, which may be evaluated with the help of local norms (if available), or by comparison with other subjects tested.

(*b*) **Flexed-Arm Hang (girls only):** This test is almost similar to pull-ups (boys) except that the hanging-bar is adjusted at a height equal almost to the height of the subject. With the help of two assistants (one in front and one in back), the girl raises the body off the floor to position the chin above the bar, the elbows are flexed, chest is kept close to the bar and the subject holds this position as long as possible.

As soon as the subject takes the hanging position and the assistants helping the subject for body raising get away and do not touch the subject any more, the stopwatch is started. The stopwatch is stopped as soon as any of the following conditions is observed:

- The girl's head tilts backwards for keeping the chin above the bar.
- The girl's chin touches the bar.
- The girl's chin falls below the level of bar.

Scoring: The duration of time, which the girl holds the hanging position in the correct manner, recorded in seconds, is the score of this test item.

(*c*) **Bent-knee sit-ups (boy and girls) Equipment:** A mat for each subject or lying area on the floor and a stopwatch.

Test Administration: The subject is asked to lie on the back with the knees bent feet on the floor and heels not more than 12" from the buttocks. The angle at the knees should be less than 90°. The subject has to put the hands on the back of the neck with fingers clasped and has to place the elbows squarely on the mat. The subject's feet are to be held by an assistant or partner to keep them in touch with the surface. The subject is asked to tighten the abdominal muscles and bring the head and elbows forward as he or she sits-up finally to touch their elbows to the knees. The entire above process constitutes one sit-up. The subject is asked to return to the starting position and to sit-up again. After giving the above-mentioned demonstration to the subject, a signal 'Ready! Go'! is given to specific subject. At the signal 'go' the performer starts sit-ups and the timer starts the watch simultaneously. The performer continues performing the sit-ups at his/her best possible speed till the timer gives a stop signal after 60 seconds.

Scoring: The number of correctly performed sit-ups in 60 seconds is the score of this test. Only one effort is allowed to the subject unless the tester believes that the subject not had a fair opportunity. The following types of sit-ups are not counted for the score:

(*i*) If the subject does not keep the fingers clasped behind the neck.
(*ii*) If the subject brings both elbows forward in starting the sit-ups with pushing off the floor with the elbow.
(*iii*) If the subject returns to starting position with elbows flat on the surface.

(*d*) **Shuttle Run (boys and girls)**

Equipment : Two blocks of wood (2"x2"x4"), a stopwatch and marking powder. The subject should wear spikes or run bare foot.

Test Administration: 1\vo parallel lines are marked on the floor 10 yards apart or the width of the regular Volleyball court may be used for the test. The two wooden blocks are placed behind one of the lines. The subject is asked to start from behind the other line, places the block behind the starting line, runs, back and picks-up the second block to be carried back across the starting line. As soon as the second block is placed on the ground the timer stops the watch and records the time.

Scoring: Two trials are allowed to each subject with some rest in between. The time of the better of the two trials is recorded to the nearest 10th of a second as the score of the test item. Important Note: If two timers are available, it is preferable to ask two subjects to run at the same time from the opposite lines. This arrangement does not only save the time but also eliminates the need to return the block after each race.

(*e*) Standing Broad Jump (boys and girls) This test measures the power of legs in jumping horizontal distance and may be applied to children of both sexes aged seven years and above.

Equipment: Floor, mat or long jump pit may be used, measuring tape, marking tape/ chalk or a peg.

Test Administration: A demonstration of the standing Broad Jump is given to a group of subjects to be tested. The subject is then asked to stand behind the starting line with the feet parallel to each other. He is instructed to take off for the broad jump in the forward direction and jump as farthest as possible. The subject is given three trials.

Scoring: The distance between the starting line and the nearest point of landing provides the score of the test. The best (maximum distance) trial is used as the final score of the test.

(*f*) **50 Yard Dash (boys and girls)**

Equipment: Stopwatches (at least two) or a single stopwatch with a split second time.

Test Administration: Two lines are marked on the floor 50 yards apart. One line is used as a starting line and the other as the finish line. On the signal ready! Go! the subject start running at their best to reach the finish line at their earliest. The signal 'go' is accompanied with the downward sweep of the starter's arm to give the visual signal to the timer/timers who stand/stand at the finish line.

Scoring: The interval between the starting signal and the instant subject crosses the finish line is the score of the test. The time is recorded correct upto tenth of a second.

(*g*) 600 yard Run-walk or I-Mile Run-Walk or 1.5 Run Walk Test item (boys and girls)

Equipment: Track or marked area and stopwatch.

(*i*) **600 yard run-walk**

Test Administration: The subject is asked to take a standing start. At the signal ready! Go! the subject starts running the 600 yard distance. The test is usually performed on 10-12 subjects together by pairing off before the start of the event.

Walking is permitted but the performer is to cover the distance in the shortest period of time.

Scoring : The time taken to run 600 yards recorded in minutes and seconds is the score of this test item.

(*ii*) **One mile/1.5 mile run-walk:** This is similar to 600-yard run-walk. The performer has to run-walk one mile/1.5 mile in place of 600 yards and the time taken is recorded.

(*iii*) **9 Minute or 12 Minute run-walk:** At the signal ready! Go! the subject covers as much distance as possible in nine minutes or 12 minutes. If the track and running area is marked off every 200 yards, the tester can count the number of laps completed and additional incomplete lap distance covered in 9 to 12 minutes respectively. Although the tester has to encourage all the subjects to run the entire period of 9 or 12 minutes but interspersed walking is allowed and total distance covered exactly in 9 or 12 minutes is recorded correct upto one yard.

Difference between General Motor Ability and Motor Educability

General Motor Ability: It may be defined as motor fitness including neuro muscular coordination abilities or motor control by eye-hand coordination, eye-foot coordination and whole body movement coordination. Sometimes general motor ability is also defined as one's inherent potential to perform with best speed, agility, power, balance, coordination and quick reaction time. Thus, when we use the term general motor ability, we are talking about basic motor fitness and general body coordination skills needed in various sports, athletics and gymnastics activities.

A student with poor skills can be physically fit while student who may excel in a sport's skill, say, throwing, may not be physically quite fit.

Motor Educability: Physical educators often observe that some individuals learn skills more readily than others do. Different individuals have different inherent aptitude for motor learning in somewhat the same way as individuals have different aptitude for mental learning. Motor Educability may be defined as 'the ease and thoroughness with which one learns new motor skills'. Motor Educability is a psycho-physiological variable.

Barrow General Motor Ability Test for men: This is one of the most popular motor ability testing procedures for schoolboys and college students. Barrow (1954) selected 29-test items for the construction of a general motor ability test battery. These items were selected to measure eight factors of motor ability identified with the help of expert opinions. After testing 29 items, Barrow studied multiple correlation co-efficients of various combination of test items with the total performance score of 29 test items and found that the following two batteries, first consisting of six test items and the second consisting of only three items are highly correlated with 29 items because six or rather three test items also gave the same results. The first battery consisting of six items showed a correlation coefficient of 0.95 while the three item battery showed a correlation coefficient of 0.92 with the 29 item battery. The names of 3 item Barrow motor ability test are as enlisted below:

Barrow's 3 item Battery:

(*i*) Standing Broad Jump.

(*ii*) Medicine Ball Put (6 lbs).

(*iii*) Zig-Zag Run.

Equipment: Stopwatch, six pound medicine ball, measuring tape, five obstacles, 5 by 12 feet tumbling mat marked with a take-off line.

Test Administration: The three items may either be conducted in an athletic field area or in a gymnasium.

Test Item (I) Standing Broad Jump: This test measures the power of legs in jumping horizontal distance and may be applied to children of both sexes ages seven years and above.

Equipment: Floor mat or Ion jump pit may be used measuring tape, marking tape or a peg.

Test Administration: A demonstration of the standing broad jumps is given to a group of subjects to be tested. The subject is then asked to stand behind the starting line with the feet parallel to each other. He is instructed to jump as farthest as possible by bending knees and swinging arms to take off for the broad jump in the forward direction. The subject is given 3 trials.

Scoring: The distance between the starting line and the nearest point of landing provides the score of the test. The best (maximum distance) trial is used as the final score of the test.

Test Item (II) Zig-Zag Run: This test item measures primarily agility and secondarily the speed. The subject is given demonstration about the course of Zig-Zag running.

Then he/she is instructed to take the standing start position on the signal ready and to start running on the signal 'go' and that three laps are to be run and fast run is to be continued even after the finish line so as to slow down only after crossing the finish line.

The subject is specially informed that the obstacles are neither to be grasped while going around them and not to be misplaced in any way. If anybody fouls, then whole run is to be repeated.

After the signal ready? go!, the subject begins the Zig-Zag run, the timer starts the stopwatch.

Scoring and Evaluation: The final score is the time taken to run the three rounds of figure-of-eight. This time is to be evaluated with the help of norms of local population. If the norms are not available, then the comparative ranking of the persons tested may be assigned.

Test item (iii) medicine Ball Put: This test measures primarily arm and shoulder girdle strength and secondarily power, agility, arm and shoulder girdle coordination, speed and balance.

Test Administration: Before starting the test, the subjects are given the following instructions. The medicine ball is not to be thrown but to be put as will be demonstrated the subject is to stand between the two restraining lines and the ball is to be put straight down the -course. Each subject is to take three trials; fouls count a trial. However, in case of three continuous or more fouls the subject will be asked to reattempt until he makes a fair put.

After giving above instructions, the event is explained by giving a live demonstration. Then a subject is asked to take a position in the throwing area and put the medicine ball as explained and demonstrated, he is given three trials. .

Scoring and Evaluation: The maximum distance out of three trials of putting the medicine ball is the final score which is evaluated with the help of norms if available on the local population or the comparative ranking are assigned to the subjects tested. If the number is large enough the Mean, S.D. etc. are also computed and the norms are developed and used.

EXERCISE

1. Range of movement present at body joints refers to–
(*a*) muscular endurance
(*b*) muscular strength
(*c*) flexibility
(*d*) agility

2. The ability to effectively integrate the moments of the body parts is–
(*a*) agility (*b*) balance
(*c*) co-ordination (*d*) speed

3. Which of the following tests cannot measure coordination?
(*a*) Ball catch
(*b*) Jump rope
(*c*) Vertical jump
(*d*) Jumping jack

4. Which of the following is not measured using film analysis and EMG analysis?
(*a*) Agility (*b*) Balance
(*c*) Coordination (*d*) Speed

5. The ability to make successive movements in different directions efficiently and rapidly refers to
(*a*) agility (*b*) balance
(*c*) co-ordination (*d*) power

6. Which of the following tests is not a part of J. Johnson motor educabililty test?
(*a*) Back roll
(*b*) Front roll
(*c*) Vertical jump
(*d*) Stagger jump

7. Knox test is a skill test for–
(*a*) hockey (*b*) basketball
(*c*) volleyball (*d*) tennis

8. Chapman Ball Control test is used to test skills in–

(*a*) hockey
(*b*) basketball
(*c*) hewittest
(*d*) french short serve test

9. The father of anthropometry is–
(*a*) Baron Quetelet (*b*) Martens
(*c*) Spielberger (*d*) Carron

10. Optimal Arousal Theory of Anxiety was postulated by–
(*a*) Clark Hull (*b*) Carron
(*c*) Martens (*d*) Yuri Hania

11. Which theory of anxiety suggests that stress and anxiety will influence performance and that each athlete well respond is a unique way to competitive anxiety?
(*a*) Drive theory
(*b*) Inverted U-hypothesis
(*c*) Catastrophe theory
(*d*) Optimal Arousal theory

12. Which of the following tests is not test for measuring anxiety?
(*a*) STAI (*b*) SCAT
(*c*) BIDR (*d*) CSAI

13. Which of the following tests is used to measure aggression?
(*a*) SCAT
(*b*) BIDR
(*c*) GEQ questionnaire
(*d*) AMI

14. Which measurements of body composition are based on the assumption that density and specific gravity of lean tissue is greater than that of fat tissue?
(*a*) Hydrostatic weighing
(*b*) Body Mass index
(*c*) Electro biography
(*d*) Anthropometry

15. Which test for body composition is used to quantify an individual's obesity level?
(*a*) Height/Weight tables
(*b*) Body Mass Index
(*c*) Skinfold measurements
(*d*) Hydrostatic weighing

16. Which of the following measures of body composition uses the 'Caliper Device' to measure the thickness of substantiate fat stores?
(*a*) Body mass Index
(*b*) Hydrostatic weighing
(*c*) Skin-fold measurements
(*d*) Electrolipography

17. Which of the following is a test to measure balance?
(*a*) Qucik feet test
(*b*) 'T' drill test
(*c*) Stork stand test
(*d*) Lateral charge of direction test

18. Which of the following is not a test for agility?
(*a*) Illinois agility run test
(*b*) 'T' drill test
(*c*) Stork stand test
(*d*) Quick feet test

19. Which of the following test is not a test for Motor Ability?
(*a*) Larsen test
(*b*) Metheny-Johnson test
(*c*) Cozen's athletic ability test
(*d*) JCR test

20. Tests like SAT are used to measure–
(*a*) aptitude (*b*) intelligence
(*c*) achievement (*d*) performance

21. A piece of equipment used to measure units of work done by person is called-
(*a*) ammeter (*b*) ergometer
(*c*) galvanometer (*d*) manometer

22. Queens college step test is used to measure-
(*a*) cardiovascular (*b*) endurance
(*c*) flexibility (*d*) heart rate

23. What is the full form of AAHPERD?
(*a*) American and Australian, Health, Physical Education, Recreation and Dance
(*b*) American Association for Health, Physical Education, Recreation and Dance
(*c*) American Alliance for Health, Physical Education, Recreation and Dance
(*d*) None of the above

24. In which case we should not use test?
(*a*) When the number is small
(*b*) When variance is large
(*c*) When distribution is normal
(*d*) None of the above.

25. The evaluation which is undertaken during the course of training is called-
(*a*) sumamtive evaluation
(*b*) creative evaluation
(*c*) formative evaluation
(*d*) normative evaluation

26. The level of aspiration is ideal if the discrepancy between the set goal and actual performance comes-
(*a*) 50% (*b*) 40%
(*c*) 100% (*d*) 10%

27. The degree of consistency with which a measuring device may be applied is ascertained through-
(*a*) validity (*b*) reliability
(*c*) both the above (*d*) none of the above

28. McDonald soccer test involves-
(*a*) volleying the soccer ball against a back board
(*b*) volleying the soccer ball and also kicking a soccer ball for a distance
(*c*) volleying the soccer ball, kicking a soccer ball for a distance and dribble for speed
(*d*) kicking a soccer ball for a distance and dribble for speed

29. Which of the following is a motor educability test?
(*a*) J. C. R. test (*b*) I. O. W. A test
(*c*) Fleisman test (*d*) All of the above

30. AAHPERD Youth fitness test is for measuring–
(*a*) general motor ability
(*b*) motor fitness
(*c*) motor educability
(*d*) all of the above

31. The degree of uniformity with which various testers score the same test is found out through-
(*a*) validity (*b*) reliability
(*c*) objectivity (*d*) all of the above

32. Name the test to determine the cardiovascular efficiency-
(*a*) Harvard test
(*b*) Copers test
(*c*) Margaria step test
(*d*) bench test

33. Relaibility denotes-
(*a*) consistency of performance
(*b*) variability among groups
(*c*) inconsistency among subjects
(*d*) none of the above

34. In 2×2×2 factorial design, the number of treatment groups will be–
(*a*) 3 (*b*) 6
(*c*) 8 (*d*) None of the above

35. A treadmill is used for measuring–
(*a*) speed
(*b*) power
(*c*) work done in Running
(*d*) force

36. Which of the following tests does not measure performance ?
(*a*) I Q tests
(*b*) Otis Lennon
(*c*) Differential Aptitude test
(*d*) Wechsler

37. Measure of muscular talent is a test for–
(*a*) aptitude (*b*) intelligence
(*c*) achievement (*d*) diagnostic

38. The assignment of a number to express in quantative terms the degree to which a pupil possesses a given characteristic is called–
(*a*) test (*b*) measurement
(*c*) evaluation (*d*) none of these

39. Which of the following is a test for flexibility and balance?
(*a*) Ruler drop test
(*b*) 'T' drill test
(*c*) RAST
(*d*) Sit and Reach Test

40. Which of the following tests is used to measure reaction time?

(*a*) Ruler drop test
(*b*) SCAT
(*c*) Jumps Decathlon
(*d*) 5 Km predictor test

41. Interpretation of a student's score done by comparing it with scores of other students is done by–
(*a*) criterion referenced test
(*b*) norm-referenced test
(*c*) objective test
(*d*) essay test

42. Test used to measure cardio-respiratory endurance is–
(*a*) tread mill test (*b*) dynamometer
(*c*) tenso meter (*d*) cybex

43. Which of the following tests is not used to measure muscular endurance?
(*a*) Sit up (*b*) Flexed arm hang
(*c*) Squat thrust (*d*) Distance walk

44. Assessment of flexibility is done with the help of–
(*a*) dynamometer (*b*) tensometer
(*c*) gonimeter (*d*) cybex

45. Which of the following field test is not used to measure muscular strength?
(*a*) 1 Rm bench press (*b*) 1 Rm leg press
(*c*) 1 Rm squat (*d*) Flexed arm hang

46. Forward inclination of the shoulder girdle is known as–
(*a*) kyphosis (*b*) scoliosis
(*c*) lordosis (*d*) round shoulders

47. Tennis skill is measures by–
(*a*) Miller wall volley test
(*b*) Mc Donald's Test
(*c*) Dyers test
(*d*) All of the above

48. The ability to carry out daily task is–
(*a*) physical fitness
(*b*) fitness
(*c*) minimum muscular fitness
(*d*) cardio vascular fitness

49. "Miller wall volley test" is a test of
(*a*) badminton (*b*) squash
(*c*) volley ball (*d*) foot ball

50. The instrument used for estimation of body fat is–
(*a*) flexometer (*b*) goniometer
(*c*) dynamometer (*d*) skinfold caliper

51. Tournament standing serves as adequate standard for establishing–
(*a*) validity (*b*) reliability
(*c*) subjectivity (*d*) norms

52. Sargent jump measures–
(*a*) horizontal jumping ability
(*b*) vertical jumping ability
(*c*) both (*a*) and (*b*)
(*d*) neither (*a*) nor (*b*)

53. Which of the following terms has nothing to do with a test?
(*a*) Creativity (*b*) Validity
(*c*) Reliability (*d*) Objectivity

54. Ergometry is a process by which we measure–
(*a*) brain activity (*b*) muscle potential
(*c*) lung capacity (*d*) cardiac output

55. The major cause of bad posture in school children is–
(*a*) carrying a load of books
(*b*) bad habits of reading, sitting, standing, walking etc.
(*c*) muscle weakness
(*d*) tight dress

56. Pedograph is used for measuring a–
(*a*) kyphosis (*b*) flat foot
(*c*) scoliosis (*d*) lordosis

57. Kraus weber test is used for measuring–
(*a*) physical fitness
(*b*) motor educability
(*c*) minimum muscular strength
(*d*) skill ability in a sport

58. 'Copper's 12 minute run/walk test measures–
(*a*) speed
(*b*) cardio-respiratory endurance
(*c*) agility
(*d*) strength

59. Test-retest method is used for determining–
(*a*) validity (*b*) reliability
(*c*) objectivity (*d*) norms

60. Which of the following test measures cardio-respiratory function?
(*a*) Harvard step test
(*b*) J.C.R
(*c*) Oregen motor fitness test
(*d*) Kraus weber test

61. Which of the following is not a criteria of test selection?
(*a*) Classification of test
(*b*) Scientific authenticity
(*c*) Educational application
(*d*) Administrative feasibility

62. A test measures what is the purpose to measure is assessed by–
(*a*) validity (*b*) reliability
(*c*) objectivity (*d*) norms

63. Soccer skill is measured by–
(*a*) Miller wall volley test
(*b*) MC Donald's test
(*c*) Sports knowledge test
(*d*) All the above

64. Dyer test is associated with–
(*a*) tennis (*b*) badminton
(*c*) athletics (*d*) football

65. Physical fitness is the ability to–
(*a*) carry out daily task
(*b*) measure fundamental skills
(*c*) classify the groups
(*d*) none of the above

66. Tests are–
(*a*) designed to ascertain the quantity
(*b*) rendering service to the society
(*c*) appraisal of pupils programme
(*d*) instructional methodology

67. Wet spirometer is used for assessing–
(*a*) vital capacity (*b*) blood pressure
(*c*) pulse rate (*d*) flexibility

68. Twelve minutes run and walk test is used to assess–
(*a*) strength
(*b*) speed
(*c*) cardio-respiratory endurance
(*d*) none of the above

69. Types of muscle fibres are determined by–
(*a*) calorimeter
(*b*) biopsy
(*c*) spectrophotometer
(*d*) all of the above

70. Criteria of tests depends on–
(*a*) validity (*b*) reliability
(*c*) objectivity (*d*) all of these

71. Validity means–
(*a*) The test measures the quality for which it is to be used
(*b*) The test can be administered accurately
(*c*) Both of the above
(*d*) None of these

72. Reliability means–
(*a*) The test measure the quality for which it is to be used
(*b*) The test can be administered accurately
(*c*) Both of the above
(*d*) None of these

73. If test yields the same or approximately the same scores when administered twice to the same individual in same conditions it is called as–
(*a*) valid test (*b*) reliable test
(*c*) objective test (*d*) none of these

74. The sum of all the scores made by each individual on all the tests included in the experimental situation is known as–
(*a*) composite score
(*b*) standard score
(*c*) both of the above
(*d*) none of these

75. The reliability of objective written test is determined by–
(*a*) correlation between equivalent form of the test
(*b*) correlation between split halves test
(*c*) correlation between repeated test
(*d*) all the above

76. The direct measurement of fat deposits sub cutaneously is done by
(*a*) skin fold caliper
(*b*) harvard instrument

(*c*) both of the above
(*d*) none of these

77. How many skin fold are taken for measurement of fat in human body–
(*a*) Two (*b*) Three
(*c*) Four (*d*) None of these

78. The measurement of the size and proportion of the human body is called–
(*a*) anthropometry (*b*) plyometry
(*c*) corrective (*d*) none of these

79. When the digestive viscera dominates the body economy the body composition is–
(*a*) mesomorphy (*b*) endomorphy
(*c*) ectomorphy (*d*) none of these

80. When the cervical spine is curved forward but the head and chin are not dropped is called–
(*a*) cervical Lordosis
(*b*) poke neck
(*c*) both of the above
(*d*) none of these

81. When muscle, bone and connective tissue are dominating the body composition is–
(*a*) mesomorphy (*b*) endpmorphy
(*c*) ectomorphy (*d*) none of these

82. When the normal curve in the thoracic region is increased it is known as–
(*a*) thoracic kyphosis (*b*) forward head
(*c*) round shoulder (*d*) none of these

83. The Lumber Lordosis is also known as–
(*a*) hollow back
(*b*) flat back
(*c*) both of the above
(*d*) none of these

84. The flat back is also known as–
(*a*) lumbar lordosis (*b*) lumber kyphosis
(*c*) lordosis (*d*) none of these

85. A lateral deviation of the spine is present in–
(*a*) kyphosis (*b*) lordosis
(*c*) scoliosis (*d*) knock kness

86. Navicular Drop is connected with–
(*a*) foots function
(*b*) eye function
(*c*) ear function
(*d*) none of these

87. The range of possible movement around a joint is known as–
(*a*) speed (*b*) flexibility
(*c*) agility (*d*) none of these

88. Goniometer is used for–
(*a*) speed (*b*) agility
(*c*) both of the above (*d*) none of these

89. Electro goniometer is called as–
(*a*) elgon
(*b*) leighton
(*c*) both of these
(*d*) none of these

90. Scott and French test is used to measure–
(*a*) strength
(*b*) football skill
(*c*) trunk-hip flexibility
(*d*) none of these

91. Cable tension test is used to measure–
(*a*) Agility (*b*) Strength
(*c*) Both (*d*) None of these

92. Back and leg dynamometer is used for–
(*a*) vital capacity
(*b*) strength of back and leg
(*c*) speed of back and leg
(*d*) none of these

93. Jury of appeal committee shall consist–
(*a*) 3 or 5 person
(*b*) 3 or 5 or 7 person
(*c*) 7 or 9 person
(*d*) None of these

94. Person responsible for ensuring track runways, circle, landing area and all equipment are in accordance with rules is–
(*a*) the manager of the meet
(*b*) secretary
(*c*) the Technical Manager
(*d*) referee

95. At the conclusion of each event of track the result card shall be completed and signed by
(*a*) technical manager
(*b*) referee

(*c*) umpires
(*d*) judges

96. Timing recognized as official timing if taken in international events–
(*a*) By Hand Electrical Gadget
(*b*) By Photo finish Technique
(*c*) By Manually operated watches
(*d*) None of these

97. Person responsible for the functioning of the timing devices is–
(*a*) chief time keeper
(*b*) chief photo finish judge
(*c*) chief Referee
(*d*) none of these

98. In High jump the crossbar shall have a maximum thickness of–
(*a*) 19 mm (*b*) 29 to 31 mm
(*c*) 12 mm (*d*) None of these

99. Time shall be taken from the–
(*a*) sound of gun (*b*) flash/smoke
(*c*) whistle (*d*) none of these

100. If only two timings are available and they disagree–
(*a*) both shall be official timing
(*b*) longer time
(*c*) shorter time
(*d*) none of these

101. Standard width of the lane shall be–
(*a*) 1.20 mts.
(*b*) 1.22 mts.
(*c*) 1.22 to 1.25 mts.
(*d*) None of these

102. Direction of running shall be–
(*a*) right hand side (*b*) left hand side
(*c*) curve-running (*d*) none of these

103. 'In all sprint races a starter must use–
(*a*) standing start (*b*) elogonated start
(*c*) crouch start (*d*) none of these

104. Competitor making a false start in 100 mts be disqualified for–
(*a*) one false start
(*b*) two false start by anyone among the team
(*c*) three false start
(*d*) none of these

105. The height of the finish post shall be–
(*a*) 1.40 mts. (*b*) 1.22 mts.
(*c*) 1.30 mts. (*d*) none of these.

106. The following are the standard distance of hurdles race for men–
(*a*) 100 and 400 mts.
(*b*) 100 and 400 mts.
(*c*) 80 and 200 mts.
(*d*) 800 and 1.500 mts.

107. Height of hurdles for Men 110 mts. hurdles is–
(*a*) 1.67 mts. (*b*) 0.91 mts
(*c*) 0.84 mts. (*d*) 1.067 mts.

108. Height of hurdles race for women 100 Mts. is–
(*a*) 0.80 mt. (*b*) 0.91 mt.
(*c*) 0.76 mt. (*d*) 0.84 mt.

109. Weight of hurdles should be–
(*a*) not less than 10 Kg.
(*b*) 3 to 3.50 Kg.
(*c*) 8 to 9 Kg.
(*d*) None of these

110. The standard distance of steeplechase-race shall be–
(*a*) 300 mts. (*b*) 2000 mts.
(*c*) 3000 mts. (*d*) 1000 mts.

111. In 3000 mts. steeplechase race event included–
(*a*) 4 water jumps – 24 hurdles jumps
(*b*) 7 water jumps – 28 hurdles jumps
(*c*) 5 water jumps – 35 hurdles jumps
(*d*) none of these

112. In Steeplechase the water jump shall be–
(*a*) 2nd jump (*b*) 7th jump
(*c*) 4th jump (*d*) none of these

113. The standard distance of marathon race is–
(*a*) 26 kms. (*b*) 42 kms.
(*c*) 42.195 kms. (*d*) None of these

114. In field event if the tie remains it shall be resolved by–
(*a*) lowest performance
(*b*) second best performance and so on
(*c*) best of his all attempt
(*d*) none of these

115. Protest concerning the result shall be submitted within–
(*a*) 60 minutes
(*b*) 30 minutes before the announcement of the official result
(*c*) 45 minutes
(*d*) none of these

116. Which committee is responsible for a fair decision?
(*a*) Doping committee
(*b*) Technical committee
(*c*) Jury of appeal
(*d*) None of these

117. The wind velocity shall be measured by–
(*a*) the wind gauge
(*b*) official implements
(*c*) video camera
(*d*) none of these

118. The procedure of doping test includes the collection of–
(*a*) sugar sample (*b*) urine sample
(*c*) stool sample (*d*) blood sample

119. How many athletes may be used as substitutes in Relay race event?
(*a*) One athlete (*b*) Two athlete
(*c*) Three athlete (*d*) None of these

120. Landing area of high jump event should be in international events–
(*a*) not less than 5 ´4 mts.
(*b*) not more than 5 ×5 mts.
(*c*) 6× 4 ×.7 mts.
(*d*) none of these

121. Landing area of pole vault event shall be in international events–
(*a*) not less than 5 × 3 mts.
(*b*) not more than 6 × 4 mts.
(*c*) 6 × 4 × .7 mts.
(*d*) none of these 5 × 4 mts.

122. Long jump landing area shall be–
(*a*) 10 ×2.75 mts.
(*b*) 7 – 9 ×2.75 mts.
(*c*) 9 × .2.75 mts.
(*d*) None of these

123. Length and width of Plasticine indicator board shall be–
(*a*) 0.98 × 1.21. mts.
(*b*) 9.8 cm to 10.2 cm × 1.21 mts to 1.22. mts
(*c*) 1.22 mts to 1.25 mts.
(*d*) None of these

124. The angle of landing sector of shot put is–
(*a*) 45° (*b*) 40°
(*c*) 90° (*d*) 34.92°

125. Minimum weight of shot for acceptance of a record, (for men)–
(*a*) 7.26 kg. (*b*) 8 kg.
(*c*) 7.25 kg. (*d*) None of these

126. In discus competition each competitor shall be allowed–
(*a*) three trials (*b*) two trials
(*c*) eight trials (*d*) none of these

127. Inside diameter of the discus circle shall be–
(*a*) 2.135 mts. (*b*) 2.50 mts.
(*c*) 1.25 mts. (*d*) None of these

128. The thickness of Rim of discus circle shall be at least–
(*a*) 5 mm (*b*) 6 mm
(*c*) 7 mm. (*d*) 75 mm.

129. Minimum weight of discus for acceptance of record for men is–
(*a*) 1 kg. (*b*) 2 kg.
(*c*) 800 gms. (*d*) None of these

130. For women javelin competition weight of Javelin should be–
(*a*) 800 gms (*b*) 600 gms
(*c*) 825 gms. (*d*) None of these

131. Over all length of men's javelin is–
(*a*) 2.60 to 2.70 mts. (*b*) 2.20 to 2.30 mts.
(*c*) 2.65 to 2.75 mts. (*d*) None of these

132. The ten event which shall be held on two consecutive days is known as–
(*a*) pantaloon (*b*) decathlon
(*c*) heptathlon (*d*) none of these

133. The time between the finish of the last days event on the first day and the start of first event on second day should be

(a) 12 Hours. (b) 10 Hours.
(c) 24 Hours. (d) None of these

134. In walking event the sign for warning is given by–
(a) red sign (b) white sign
(c) green sign (d) yellow sign

135. First "Padamshree"in athletics is given to–
(a) P.T. Usha (b) Milkha Singh
(c) Bahadur Singh (d) None of these

136. Who was the winner of 100 mts. (men) in 1992 Olympic games?
(a) Carl Lewis (b) Ben Johnson
(c) Talt Mansur (d) Linford Christie

137. Person represented India in 6 Olympics from (1964 to 84) is–
(a) Ranjit Singh (b) Randhir Singh
(c) Milkha Singh (d) None of these

138. The first India women athlete to win a gold in Asian Games is–
(a) P.T. Usha (b) Shiny Abharam
(c) Kamaljit Sandhu (d) None of these

139. In which game the term rolling substitution is used?
(a) Volley Ball (b) Basket ball
(c) Foot Ball (d) Hockey

140. The term 'Yorker is used in–
(a) foot ball (b) table tennis
(c) tennis (d) cricket

141. To break tie in long jump–
(a) one additional trail is given
(b) average is taken
(c) next best performance is taken and so on
(d) last attempt is considered.

142. For women in 100m hurdles race the distance between hurdles is–
(a) 10m (b) 11m
(c) 8.5m (d) None of these

143. How many attempts a high jumper gets at each height?
(a) 3 (b) 4
(c) 2 (d) 5

144. Dimensions of kabaddi (men) court are–
(a) 12 m × 10 m (b) 12.5 × 10 m
(c) 11 m × 8 m (d) 10 m × 8 m

145. Which of the following games has no separate time keeper?
(a) Basket ball (b) Kabaddi
(c) Kho-Kho (d) Football

146. The main duty of the 'Marshal' in an athletic meet is to–
(a) discipline athletes
(b) supervise office
(c) conduct march past
(d) drive away unwanted people out of areas.

147. Umpires for the track events in an athletic meet are assistants to the–
(a) chief judge
(b) referee
(c) technical manager
(d) secretary

148. The width of the lines of a volley ball court should be–
(a) 8 cm (b) 5 cm
(c) 3 cm (d) 2cm

149. Time out for rest in volley ball has the duration of–
(a) 20 sec (b) 30 sec
(c) 40 sec (d) 60 sec

150. The decathlon event in athletics is completed within–
(a) 1 day (b) 3 days
(c) 2 days (d) None of the above

151. To break a tie in a running event–
(a) the race is re-run
(b) the tying athletes are eliminated
(c) the tie is not solved
(d) none of the above.

152. The size of the volley ball court is–
(a) 10 × 20 m (b) 9 × 20 m
(c) 9 × 18 m (d) 10 × 18 m

153. Dead ball is a term used in–
(a) hockey (b) foot ball
(c) soft ball (d) cricket

154. How many players constitute a kabaddi team?
(*a*) 10 (*b*) 12
(*c*) 16 (*d*) 14

155. In 'cricket an over' includes–
(*a*) 5 balls (*b*) 6 balls
(*c*) 7 balls (*d*) 8 balls

156. In Hockey for men, the total weight of the stick shall not exceed–
(*a*) 35 ounces (*b*) 40 ounces
(*c*) 28 ounces (*d*) 32 ounces

157. The size of the badminton court is–
(*a*) 44 × 20 feet (*b*) 44 × 22 feet
(*c*) 42 × 20 feet (*d*) 40 × 20 feet

158. The distance to be covered in men marathon race is–
(*a*) 50 km (*b*) 50 km 200 m
(*c*) 42 km 195 m (*d*) 48 km

159. The sector angle for discus throw circle is–
(*a*) 45° (*b*) 34.92°
(*c*) 30° (*d*) 40°

160. Court measurement for basketball is–
(*a*) 26 × 14 m (*b*) 25 × 15 m
(*c*) 28 × 15 m (*d*) 28 × 16 m

161. The height of the ceiling or the lowest obstruction from the floor shall be–
(*a*) 6 m (*b*) 7 m
(*c*) 9 m (*d*) 8 m

162. What is the distance between end line and free throw line?
(*a*) 5.8 m (*b*) 6.00 m
(*c*) 5.75 m (*d*) 5.50 m

163. The dimensions of backboard shall be–
(*a*) 1.75m × 1.20 m (*b*) 1.80 × 1.05 m
(*c*) 1.75m × 1.20 m (*d*) 1.85 × 1.05 m

164. What is the height of the Bottom of the board from the floor?
(*a*) 2.80 m (*b*) 2.75 m
(*c*) 2.88 m (*d*) 2.90 m

165. The diameter of the metal ring shall be–
(*a*) 2cm to 2.6 cm (*b*) 1.8cm to 2.0cm
(*c*) 1.6cm to 2.6cm (*d*) 1.6cm to 2.0 cm

166. The radius of the centre circle is–
(*a*) 3.60m (*b*) 1.80m
(*c*) 1.60m (*d*) 3.20m

167. What is the circumference of the basket ball?
(*a*) 75.9m to 78m (*b*) 74.0m to 77.9m
(*c*) 74.9m to 78m (*d*) 75m to 78.3m

168. How many points are awarded for a field goal?
(*a*) 2 (*b*) 4
(*c*) 1 (*d*) None of the above

169. A team must get the ball across the half court line in how many seconds?
(*a*) 10 seconds (*b*) 8 seconds
(*c*) 5 seconds (*d*) 24 seconds

170. A player has stopped the dribble. How long can the same player hold the ball when closely guarded?
(*a*) 3 seconds (*b*) 5 seconds
(*c*) 10 seconds (*d*) Indefinitely

171. How many seconds may a player stay in his own restricted areas?
(*a*) 3 seconds (*b*) 5 seconds
(*c*) 8 seconds (*d*) no time limit

172. When does the clock not stop during the game?
(*a*) When a player not stopping during the game.
(*b*) When a goal has not been scored.
(*c*) When a player commits a foul.
(*d*) When a substitute enters the game.

173. When may a substitute enter the game?
(*a*) When the ball is in play
(*b*) During the first period only
(*c*) Whenever requested by the coach
(*d*) When the ball is dead.

174. From which location on the floor is the ball put into play after a field goal?
(*a*) From anywhere along the end line
(*b*) From a specific spot on the end line
(*c*) Whenever requested by the coach
(*d*) When the ball is dead.

175. A player making a throw inside the basket hits the back of the backboard and the ball rebounded into court who gains possession of the ball?
(*a*) Ball is awarded to opponents for throw in at the end line

(*b*) Ball continues in play
(*c*) Ball is awarded to the same team for throw in at the end line
(*d*) Ball is awarded to the same players and the endline play is repeated.

176. Which way of advancing the ball is illegal?
(*a*) Throwing (*b*) Volleying
(*c*) Kicking (*d*) Batting

177. What is the penalty for violation?
(*a*) One free throw
(*b*) Two free throws
(*c*) Jump ball
(*d*) Opponents throw-in

178. A player makes a jump stop after receiving as pass, what is the player permitted to do?
(*a*) Pivot in any direction on the front foot
(*b*) Pivot in any direction on the back foot
(*c*) Pivot in any direction on either foot
(*d*) Pivot in any direction on both feet

179. How many fouls disqualify a player from the games?
(*a*) One technical foul
(*b*) Two disqualifying fouls
(*c*) Four personal fouls
(*d*) Five personal fouls

180. What is goal tending?
(*a*) Touching the net when the ball is in the air
(*b*) Giving up the ball without getting a shot
(*c*) Touching the backboard while the ball is in flight
(*d*) Affecting his down ward flight of the ball

181. An offensive player rebounds the ball near the basket what is the best option?
(*a*) Dribble away from the basket
(*b*) Pass to team-mate
(*c*) Shoot
(*d*) Set up a screen

182. The ball is temporarily out of play what is this called?
(*a*) Dead ball (*b*) Jump ball
(*c*) Time out (*d*) Delay of game

183. The interval time before each extra period is–
(*a*) 2 minutes
(*b*) 5 minutes
(*c*) 4 minutes
(*d*) no interval time is given

184. To whom does a substitute report before entering the game?
(*a*) Referee (*b*) Scorer
(*c*) Timer (*d*) Umpire

185. What is the key to successful rebounding?
(*a*) Jumping
(*b*) Arm and hand position
(*c*) Not fouling
(*d*) Positioning

186. Where should a player's eyes be focused when dribbling?
(*a*) Downward in order to control the ball
(*b*) Downward in order to see the feet of a defensive player
(*c*) Forward in order to pass to a team-mate
(*d*) Forward in order to alternate hands quickly

187. Which factor determines the actual trajectory of shot?
(*a*) Velocity
(*b*) Angle of release
(*c*) Direction
(*d*) Spin

188. What is the primary goal of players on offence?
(*a*) Dribble (*b*) Rebound
(*c*) Score (*d*) Pass

189. In which situation is the game forfeited?
(*a*) A team commits five team fouls
(*b*) A team is 10 minutes late to start the game
(*c*) One team fails to be ready within 30 seconds after a time out
(*d*) A team refuses to play after being instructed to do so

190. In which situation the game will default?
(*a*) One team fails to be ready within 30 seconds after a time out
(*b*) A team refuses to play after being instructed to do so

(c) A teams coach is disqualified
(d) The number of players of a team on the court is less than two.

191. How many time- outs are granted for each team in the fourth quarter of play?
(a) 1 (b) 2
(c) 3 (d) None of the above

192. A player jumps and attempts to shoot from the three point field goal area, then lands into the two points field goal area. If the shoot is counted, how many point will be given?
(a) 1 point (b) 2 point
(c) 3 point (d) None of the above

193. How many fouls committed by a player shall leave the game immediately?
(a) 2 (b) 3
(c) 5 (d) 6

194. Where is three seconds rule applicable?
(a) Opponent's restricted area
(b) Own restricted area
(c) At the centre circle
(d) At three point field goal area

195. What is the colour of the ring of the basket?
(a) White (b) Black
(c) Orange (d) Red

196. How many players are there in a team?
(a) 5 (b) 7
(c) 9 (d) 12

197. How many substitutions are allowed in a game per team?
(a) 3 (b) 4
(c) 5 (d) No limit

198. Duration of time in Basketball is–
(a) 20-10-20 minutes
(b) 20-5-20 minutes
(c) 10-2-10-15-10-2-10 minutes
(d) 15-2-15-15-15-2-15 minutes

199. Who is not sitting in the officials table?
(a) Timer (b) Scorer
(c) Coach (d) Commissioner

200. Duration of Time-out is–
(a) 30 seconds (b) 45 seconds
(c) 60 seconds (d) 120 seconds

201. The ball lodges in between ring and board in the course of play. What decision will you make?
(a) Side line throw (b) End line throw
(c) Jump ball (d) Free throw

202. A player throws from his own court to the opponents basket, the ball scored. What is the result?
(a) 2 points (b) 3 points
(c) 5 points (d) Violations

203. Which skill is related to the game of basketball?
(a) Smashing (b) Flicking
(c) Pivoting (d) Juggling

204. Which one is not related to the game of basketball?
(a) Four quarters
(b) 20-05-20
(c) 10-2-10-15-10-2-10
(d) 24 seconds

205. What type of tissue is bone marrow?
(a) adipose (b) connective
(c) areolar (d) cellular

206. In a good standing posture, the weight of the body should rest evenly on:
(a) the two legs (b) the two feet
(c) the two hip joints (d) the two toes

207. Active free movements are divided into:
(a) Passive forced and passive relaxed
(b) Rhythmic, agility and active holdings
(c) Assisted and restricted movements
(d) Cardiac and reflex movements

208. One deformity may lead to the development of another, knock knees may be a result of:
(a) flat-feet (b) bow legs
(c) genu legs (d) scoliosis

209. Which penalties are involved in the game of Hockey?
(a) Free hit (b) Penalty Corner
(c) Penalty Stroke (d) All the above

210. Which technical term is involved in the game of Hockey?
(a) Injector (b) Putting
(c) Let (d) Stick

211. Which positions are involved in the game of Hockey?
(*a*) Strikers (*b*) Linkers
(*c*) Stoppers (*d*) All the above

212. Hockey field length and breath is–
(*a*) 100 × 60 yards (*b*) 130 × 40 yards
(*c*) 60 × 60 yards (*d*) 60 × 100 yards

213. The height of the side board in goal post is–
(*a*) 12 inches (*b*) 16 inches
(*c*) 18 inches (*d*) 15 inches

214. The width of the leg-guard used by the goalkeeper is–
(*a*) 13 inches (*b*) 12 inches
(*c*) 18 inches (*d*) 10 centimetres

215. Stability of the spine is very important for all:
(*a*) jumping exercises
(*b*) lifting exercises
(*c*) vaulting exercises
(*d*) bending exercises

216. Where is FIH situated?
(*a*) Pakistan (*b*) Holland
(*c*) Belgium (*d*) France

217. The weight of the hockey ball is–
(*a*) 160-163 gs (*b*) 156-163 gs
(*c*) 100-150 gm (*d*) 169 gs

218. The weight of the hockey stick is–
(*a*) 26 oz (*b*) 30 oz
(*c*) 12-28 oz (*d*) 14-20 oz

219. Umpires shall blow the whistle to–
(*a*) signal a goal
(*b*) re-start the game after a penalty stroke in which a goal was not scored or awarded
(*c*) stop the game for any other reason and re-start after such a stoppage
(*d*) all the above

220. Which skill is involved in the game of hockey?
(*a*) Kicking (*b*) Bully
(*c*) Volley (*d*) All the above

221. Jumping jacks use arm and leg abduction and adduction along the:
(*a*) lateral plane (*b*) median plane
(*c*) horizontal plane (*d*) transverse plane

222. Who is called as hockey wizard?
(*a*) D. Pillay (*b*) Dhyan Chand
(*c*) Trikey (*d*) Samir Dad

223. What is the duration of play in the game of hockey?
(*a*) 30-5-30 (*b*) 20-5-20
(*c*) 35-5-35 (*d*) 45-5-45

224. The ball speed shall not be higher than the stick speed–
(*a*) 50% (*b*) 98%
(*c*) 100% (*d*) 60%

225. Specification of the shooting circle is–
(*a*) 15 mts (*b*) 16 yds
(*c*) 14 yds (*d*) 10 yds

ANSWERS

1	2	3	4	5	6	7	8	9	10
(*c*)	(*c*)	(*c*)	(*d*)	(*a*)	(*c*)	(*b*)	(*a*)	(*a*)	(*d*)
11	**12**	**13**	**14**	**15**	**16**	**17**	**18**	**19**	**20**
(*c*)	(*c*)	(*b*)	(*a*)	(*a*)	(*c*)	(*c*)	(*c*)	(*b*)	(*a*)
21	**22**	**23**	**24**	**25**	**26**	**27**	**28**	**29**	**30**
(*d*)	(*a*)	(*c*)	(*b*)	(*c*)	(*d*)	(*b*)	(*a*)	(*b*)	(*b*)
31	**32**	**33**	**34**	**35**	**36**	**37**	**38**	**39**	**40**
(*c*)	(*b*)	(*a*)	(*c*)	(*c*)	(*c*)	(*a*)	(*b*)	(*d*)	(*a*)

41	42	43	44	45	46	47	48	49	50
(*b*)	(*a*)	(*d*)	(*c*)	(*d*)	(*a*)	(*c*)	(*a*)	(*a*)	(*d*)
51	**52**	**53**	**54**	**55**	**56**	**57**	**58**	**59**	**60**
(*a*)	(*b*)	(*a*)	(*c*)	(*b*)	(*b*)	(*c*)	(*b*)	(*b*)	(*a*)
61	**62**	**63**	**64**	**65**	**66**	**67**	**68**	**69**	**70**
(*a*)	(*a*)	(*b*)	(*a*)	(*a*)	(*a*)	(*c*)	(*b*)	(*b*)	(*d*)
71	**72**	**73**	**74**	**75**	**76**	**77**	**78**	**79**	**80**
(*a*)	(*b*)	(*b*)	(*a*)	(*d*)	(*a*)	(*c*)	(*a*)	(*b*)	(*a*)
81	**82**	**83**	**84**	**85**	**86**	**87**	**88**	**89**	**90**
(*a*)	(*a*)	(*a*)	(*b*)	(*c*)	(*a*)	(*b*)	(*d*)	(*a*)	(*c*)
91	**92**	**93**	**94**	**95**	**96**	**97**	**98**	**99**	**100**
(*b*)	(*b*)	(*b*)	(*c*)	(*b*)	(*b*)	(*b*)	(*b*)	(*b*)	(*b*)
101	**102**	**103**	**104**	**105**	**106**	**107**	**108**	**109**	**110**
(*c*)	(*b*)	(*c*)	(*b*)	(*a*)	(*b*)	(*d*)	(*d*)	(*a*)	(*c*)
111	**112**	**113**	**114**	**115**	**116**	**117**	**118**	**119**	**120**
(*b*)	(*c*)	(*c*)	(*b*)	(*b*)	(*c*)	(*a*)	(*b*)	(*b*)	(*c*)
121	**122**	**123**	**124**	**125**	**126**	**127**	**128**	**129**	**130**
(*c*)	(*b*)	(*b*)	(*d*)	(*a*)	(*b*)	(*b*)	(*b*)	(*b*)	(*b*)
131	**132**	**133**	**134**	**135**	**136**	**137**	**138**	**139**	**140**
(*a*)	(*b*)	(*b*)	(*d*)	(*b*)	(*d*)	(*d*)	(*d*)	(*d*)	(*d*)
141	**142**	**143**	**144**	**145**	**146**	**147**	**148**	**149**	**150**
(*c*)	(*c*)	(*a*)	(*b*)	(*d*)	(*d*)	(*d*)	(*b*)	(*d*)	(*c*)
151	**152**	**153**	**154**	**155**	**156**	**157**	**158**	**159**	**160**
(*a*)	(*c*)	(*d*)	(*b*)	(*b*)	(*c*)	(*c*)	(*c*)	(*b*)	(*c*)
161	**162**	**163**	**164**	**165**	**166**	**167**	**168**	**169**	**170**
(*b*)	(*a*)	(*b*)	(*d*)	(*d*)	(*b*)	(*c*)	(*a*)	(*b*)	(*b*)
171	**172**	**173**	**174**	**175**	**176**	**177**	**178**	**179**	**180**
(*d*)	(*a*)	(*d*)	(*a*)	(*a*)	(*c*)	(*d*)	(*c*)	(*d*)	(*d*)
181	**182**	**183**	**184**	**185**	**186**	**187**	**188**	**189**	**190**
(*c*)	(*a*)	(*a*)	(*b*)	(*d*)	(*c*)	(*b*)	(*c*)	(*d*)	(*d*)
191	**192**	**193**	**194**	**195**	**196**	**197**	**198**	**199**	**200**
(*b*)	(*c*)	(*c*)	(*a*)	(*c*)	(*d*)	(*d*)	(*c*)	(*c*)	(*c*)
201	**202**	**203**	**204**	**205**	**206**	**207**	**208**	**209**	**210**
(*c*)	(*d*)	(*c*)	(*b*)	(*b*)	(*a*)	(*b*)	(*c*)	(*d*)	(*a*)
211	**212**	**213**	**214**	**215**	**216**	**217**	**218**	**219**	**220**
(*d*)	(*a*)	(*c*)	(*b*)	(*b*)	(*c*)	(*b*)	(*c*)	(*d*)	(*b*)
221	**222**	**223**	**224**	**225**					
(*c*)	(*b*)	(*c*)	(*b*)	(*b*)					

UNIT-X

MANAGEMENT

What is management?

There are various definitions of management. The following definition given by E.P.L. Breech has been widely accepted.

"A social process entailing responsibility for the effect and economical planning and regulation of the operations of an enterprise, in fulfillment of a given purpose or task, such responsibility involving:

(*a*) Judgement and decision on determining plans and in using data to control performance and performance against plans; and

(*b*) The guidance, integration, motivation and supervision of the personnel comprising the enterprise, and carrying out its operations."

A simpler definition has been suggested by Harold Koontz, which reads: "Managing is the art of getting things done through and with people in formally organized groups."

The first definition implies that management is a skill whereas the second definition specifies that it is an art. By combining the two views E.C. Eyre has suggested the following definition.

"Management is the art or skill of directing human activities and physical resources in the attainment of predetermined goals." An inherent implication of this definition is that management is about decisions and this view is universally accepted.

Finally, we can suggest a broad definition which goes like this:

Management can be defined as working with people to determine, interpret, and achieve organizational objectives by performing the functions of planning, organizing, staffing, leading and controlling. Thus management is the process of setting and achieving goals through the execution of five basic management functions that utilize human, financial and material resources.

If we analyze this definition we observe the following three points:

1. Firstly management and managers make conscious decisions to set and achieve goals. Decision making is a critical part of all management activities.
2. Secondly, management is getting things done through people. Once management acquired the financial and material resources for the organization, it works through the organizational members to reach the stated objectives.
3. Thirdly, to achieve the goals they set, managers must execute the five basic functions.

However, it is difficult to define the term 'administration'. The term is both a broad and a narrow one and is used to describe the activity of implementing policy decisions and also to describe the very top functions in public service, the most notable being that of the administration of the Indian Prime Minister.

It is perhaps safe to suggest that "administration is part of management and is rarely taken to be involved in policy-making decisions. It will certainly be very much concerned in the implementing of policy, but its freedom of action will be limited by the decisions of policy laid down by those charged with the laying down planning of general objectives.

Various definitions of management theory are neither constant nor universally accepted. This explains why the three terms - management, entrepreneurship and supervision carry different meanings to different people in different organizations.

Concept of Management

Management is a process of giving an order to the activities of planning, organizing and controlling, performed to determine and accomplish stated objectives with the use of human beings and other resources. It corrects disorganized human and physical resources into useful and effective results of all human activities, it is the most challenging, comprehensive, demanding, crucial and subtle. Management is the need of every type of human organization. All of us are affected by good or bad management practices. Managers affect the establishment and accomplishment of many social, economic and political goals in any country. Human efforts are made more productive by management. By combining isolated events and disjointed information into meanngful relationships, management brings order to endeavours. These relationships then work to solve problems and accomplish goals. There is no substitute for good judgement. Determining worthwhile goals and carefully selecting and utilizing resources efficiently and effectively by planning, organizing, actuating and controlling required time, good judgement, determination and lots of practice.

Management: Basic Resources are given in Outer Circle, and Functions of Management are shown by Arrows.

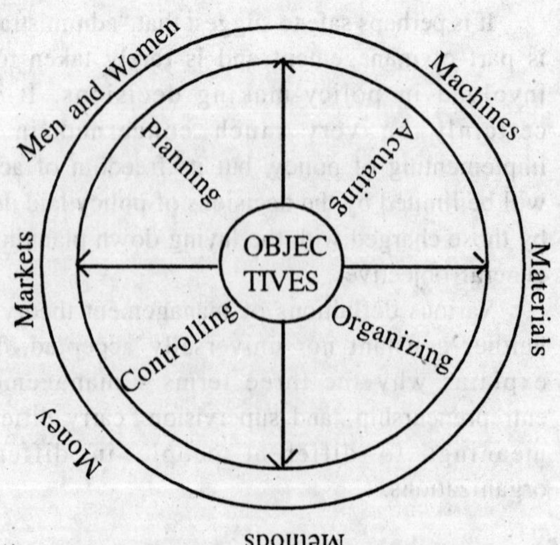

Principles of Management

Following are the principles of manage-ment:

(*a*) **Direction and Command:** Direction and command are the two basic principles of management. Unity of direction and unity of command are required so that people receive direction from only one supervisor.

(*b*) **Subordination of Individual Interest:** In order to manage an organization, subordination of individual interests must occur so that the general interest is best served.

(*c*) **Centralization:** In the process of management, centralization is desirable, especially centralization of decision making.

(*d*) **Order:** Order is supremo of Management. Order is essential for everything, and an orderly process and orderly appearance are required.

(*e*) **Turnover Reduction:** Employees should be adequately and fairly remunerated to reduce employee turnover and increase production.

(*f*) **Incentives and Rewards:** The emphasis is on performance, and standards and incentives rewards are used to maximise performance.

(*g*) **Specialization:** Division of work and specialization should characterize any enterprise, and management should be a separate function. Departmenta-lization is by process or place.

(*h*) **Authority:** Authority should be equal to responsibilities with enough authority granted to ensure success.

(*i*) **Discipline:** Discipline is required to ensure that the best interests of the organization are served.

ORGANIZATIONAL CHART OF SPORTS AUTHORITY OF INDIA

Established in 1984. Its main objectives address themselves to the effective and optimum utilization of various sports facilities and all matters pertaining to sports promotion and sports management. It makes available to N.S.S. and other organizations infrastructure and coaching facilities for preparing national teams. It controls physical education and sports academics in the country. (L.N.I.P.E. through) it provides sports science back up to the national team and sports federations as part of the national (effort) sports training facilities and procedures.

Intramurals and Extramurals

"Intra" means within murals mean organized within the confines of the school, college, or club. Objectives are:

1. Improve the physical efficiency of all students.
2. Evaluate their performance from time to time.
3. Instill their spirit of competition in the best tradition of sport and spirit of game.
4. To offer opportunities to all students irrespective of age, sex physical status etc to develop further sport and athletic skills acquired under instructional programmes.
5. To prepare a congenial climate for development of a healthy spirit of competition, sportsmanship and such other qualities of character.
6. To provide a sublimated outlet to morbid instinctive tendencies of aggressiveness, for self abasement through the medium of vigorous physical activity enabling students to maintain an optimal level of mental health.
7. To motivate students to take up responsible leadership positions such as team captains, game officials, managers etc.
8. To prepare a fertile ground for elite performance and sports excellence.
9. To afford opportunity to students to social interaction among themselves.
10. To act as an instrument of talent selection and grooming.
11. To satisfy students activity, interests and needs.
12. To provide optimal opportunity to greater number of students for acquiring the skill and art of organizing, administering and managing things on their own with least interference from superiors.
13. To use as a stepping stone for extramural programme having superior status to intramurals in terms of level of competition and organization.

Organization of Intramurals

1. Type of the institution (Residential non residential) or institution's variables.
2. Local and climatic conditions.
3. Facilities available (play ground, equipments, personnel and material)
4. Finance
5. Time at disposal
6. Co-operation and help that can be expected from the colleagues.
7. Activities in which students take major interest.

Intramurals offer great avenues for fair competition, personality development, leadership training, practical life experience and social interaction.

Units for Competition

The students have to be divided into several units for the purpose of competition. The unit must be equal in ability and strength.

In purely residential institutions - inter hostel basis or house basis, dormitory basis.

In partially residential institutions - students residing in the hostel will be divided into few teams on area basis etc.

In non residential institutions - on class basis among the particular grades. Primary, middle and senior section (high school stage)

On index basis subjunior, colts, junior and senior sections or ,base with age in college the units may be departmental basis class, faternity or study group, hostel etc.

Intramural Committee or Council

Comprising a chairman, a secretary, and assistant secretary, a treasurer and five executive members - to organize and conduct competitions.

1. To work out details of the programmes.
2. To schedule competitions and prepare draws.
3. To chart out rules and regulations of contests.
4. To entertain protests and decide contentious issues.
5. Chairman - senior Physical Education teacher assisted by class room teachers and Assistant

PET's, secretary - A junior teacher or senior students treasurer - custodian of finance.

Executive members: representatives of the staff, house masters, unit presidents, students, representatives, various team captains etc.

Extramurals

Extramural competitions are inter institutional competitions (representative teams/ athletes from various institutions or clubs separately for each game or sport. The major objectives of extramurals are

1. To provide opportunity to talented students to develop and exhibit their potential fully and achieve excellence.
2. To bring laurels to the institution by registering victory in highest number of events.
3. To develop brotherhood, fraternity and friendship among participating institutions.
4. To encourage social interaction among the teams.

The benefits of extramural competitions are

1. The standard of performance of participants will be improved.
2. Loyalty to the institution is developed.
3. There is ample scope for the development of leadership followership and sportsmanship qualities.
4. New acquaintance and friendship become possible.
5. Participants acquire a good knowledge of the places they visit.
6. Participants derive pleasure, fun and enjoyment through healthy competitions.

Drawbacks are:

1. Teams try to win by fair or foul means.
2. Unhealthy rivalry and jealousy are created.
3. Too much of time, money and energy are wasted.
4. There is too much strain on the part of students.
5. Some of the participants get swollen - headed and exhibit as false pride.

Organization of Extramurals

1. Depends on the basis of participant teams / individual, time and facilities available.
2. Need an organizing committee (PET & other faculty).
3. Subcommittees (reception, boarding, lodging, transport souvenir, ground and equipment etc.) Key factor is leadership both technical and administrative.

Concept of Techniques of Supervision

Supervision underscores guidance - with understanding in educational setting it is an ingenious technique of "improving instructions" as a systematic and continuous effort to provide "expert", supervision is primarily an attempt at studying and improving conditions that surround learning and people growth".

Several techniques are used for supervision in physical education each one being unique in its own way. The uses of the techniques are according to situations, person, occasion etc.

VISITATION

It is also called direct observation of physical education teacher personnel, facilities, and programme relationship between Physical Education teacher and head master, the teaching methods used etc.

Supervisory visits are of four types:

1. **Scheduled visit or inspection**: Inspection takes places once in three years or annually, the Regional Inspector of Physical Education announces to the school of his visit a few days in advance so the Physical Education teachers prepare the records, registers, plan for demonstration of activities etc. So that real problems can not be understood by the supervisor.
2. **Surprise check or unannounced visit**: They are targeted on a complaint, a critical situation or a reference from an important person or source and to ring upto the administration. These visits help the supervisor to see the institution in its natural environs, have

realistic assessment, such as, to know whether the prescribed syllabus is followed or not. If the tests and measurements are taken and recorded or not etc.

3. **Visit on request**: These visits are generally meant either to solve certain long standing specific problems, impart general guidance and advice on important matters. eg ; to assist in the organization of school sports meet, district sports meet, play day, laying out of play grounds and orienting new techniques and rules of games etc.
4. **Social visit or drop in visit:** The supervisor visits the school while having a supervisory schedule in neighbouring school or call on by Physical Education teacher or head of the institution, this type will improve social understanding between them.

CONFERENCE

Conferences in this types are: individual conferences and group conferences.

1. **Individual Conferences** between the visitor and a particular teacher or between the head of the institution and visitor helps the two individuals sort out problems, seek clarifications on important issues, discuss points disagreement and contention, and frankly exchange views on matters of personal and institutional interest.
2. **Group Conferences**: In faculty meetings with a visiting superior teachers should be encouraged to open up and communicate. (Staff meeting, orientation meetings, committee meetings etc) The staff members participate and express their views freely and frankly carefully planned, organized and recorded. Group conferences help participants to arrive at policy decisions conscientiously and pave way for follow-up-action.
3. **Working Conference**: Have a specific focus such as curriculum development, formulation of course, course content, improvement of theory, and activity practices at school, college, professional preparation, ethos, or formulation of professional code. It will be organized at local, regional, or national level and provide guidance to physical educators on matters of professional interest and importance of it.

DEMONSTRATION

Teaching by demonstration is a two-pronged strategy of improving instruction and teacher efficiency. Demonstration classes involving umpiring and officiating, arrangements, class formation, group organization, leadership training, demonstration of a skill or complicated activity etc.

BULLETINS

Supervisor shall prepare and print monthly, quarterly or half yearly bulletins and shall circulate them to schools. A bulletin may include articles on Physical Education teachers and other experts in the field. Ideas or suggestions of the supervisor for the implementation of an effective programme eg changes in rules of games and athletic events, new techniques and strategies etc. shall be informed to the Physical Education teachers through bulletins. Bulletins are of three types, they are:

A Suggestive bulletin is a recommendation from the supervisor eg : specific uniform for games etc.

Mandatory bulletins is the order from the higher authorities to be followed strictly.

A Personal bulletin is almost a personal letter rather than an official communication.

In conference section work shops are also added. They are practical work based interactive meetings of professional cadres - teachers, physical educators, scientists, engineers, medico's coaches etc. to discuss and debate scientific and professional concerns ' under the patronage of elite and enlighted brains. Workshops vary in duration from one day to two weeks or more. The weekend retreat work shop may be held for months in succession.

TOUR NOTES / REPORTS

Supervisors are required to submit tour notes to the superior authority for information and follow-up action. The report must contain a detailed description or the duties performed by the supervisor, observation on physical education programme, interaction with students and staffs, specific suggestions etc. The supervisor suggests constructive ways on account of the report.

In-Service Training

Refresher courses periodically conducted under the control of supervisor for physical education teachers. This training must be interesting, effective and objective oriented.

Professional Associations/Working Groups

They help to improve teacher education and solving professional problems. They organize seminars, symposia, conferences etc. Direct contact with experts, colleagues help the teachers to assimilate innovative ideas, on methods of teaching, management, organisation, research etc.

Organisation and Functions of Sports Bodies

Organisation refers to process of "setting up things" or otherwise an association of (group of) a number of individuals systematically united for some end or work.

An organisation has atleast four essential elements :

1. It involves more than one individual.
2. Each constituent unit (member) plays a definite role and makes a distinct contribution to its well being.
3. Functions of the organisation are well co-ordinated.
4. All its activities are directed towards the achievement of some goal.

Attributes of an Organisation

1. Identity - Uniqueness of its own way.
2. Instrumentality - helps to grow and coordinates the interests and skills
3. Activity programme - useful programmes
4. Membership - makes everlasting organisation
5. Jurisdiction - defines boundaries, functions and areas of operations.
6. Permanency - Existence in any matter
7. Division of labour - Assignment of jobs.
8. Hierarchy of authority - divides the powers and responsibilities according to the positions.
9. Formal rules and procedures. - Frame work of organisation.

TYPES OF ORGANIZATION

1. **Formal and informal Organization**

   Formal: Under the government authority (act of parliament) may be statutory body or simply registered. Job task hierarchy, communication net work, clearly delineated lines of authority and formal rules regulations and procedures are the hall marks of formal organizations eg Dept of university physical education, and athletic club.

   Informal: Based on the assumption of human activities, work abilities, responsibilities and relationships. They are temporary and transient formal constitutions, procedures and rules of working. They are formed on specific periods.

2. **Private and public sector organisation:**

   Private: Owned, fully funded by a family, a single person or group of private individuals, major objective in creating and running it may be some material advantage, money or honour / prestige or it may be simply a philanthropic venture temporarily one free from governmental controls monopolized by individual, whose every word is a law, function more efficiently, exercise economy and mean business. They create better facilities providing competent leadership and giving high incentives for excellence without sacrificing their commercial interests.

   Public sector organizations: Created and financed by the Government organizations consist of officials and bureaucrats who frame Governmental policies, execute Government decision and control administration within the frame work of the delegated authority. All departmental personnel are duly appointed, employees and their duties, functions and powers are clearly defined. Bureaucrats are nominated on various commissions, committees or income groups. They act as ex-officio members by virtue of their departmental set up. They are not sports autonomous bodies (societies). Central and state sport authorities, national and state councils, associations of universities etc. are the examples of semi governmental organizations. Government gives directions and guidelines. These are generally accountable to the government and come under public scrutiny and criticism. The Government organizations are rarely profit making agencies, aim is social welfare and service and service is helping people to grow, perform and excel in the field of their interest.

3. **Professional and consumer service organization:** The associations of physical education teachers, coaches, sports scientists, referees, umpires, technicians, sports officers etc. are examples. They are generally amateurish in functioning and their major objective is service. They subsist on their own funds but at times receive donations and grants from public and private sources. They hold periodic conventions, conferences, seminars, symposiaclinics, work shop etc. to discuss and debate wide ranging professional, academic, social and scientific issues.

   Consumer Service Organization: Sports goods manufacturers, skilled, semi - skilled or even non skilled individuals or technicians who provide mercenary services to educational institutions, players, athletes and officials in various ways.

4. **Sports Clubs Associations:** Voluntary organizations with certain specific common interests and objectives of sports development. A club is an association of like minded individuals generally formed for carrying out social, altruistic, recreation, sport activities. In general a typical club has a written constitution, specifying its aim and objectives composition, jurisdiction, office bearers and their functions, membership etc. Jawahar foot ball club, national badminton club are examples. In a specified geographical area sports clubs form into an association generally district (sport) association and it belongs in a hierarchical manner.

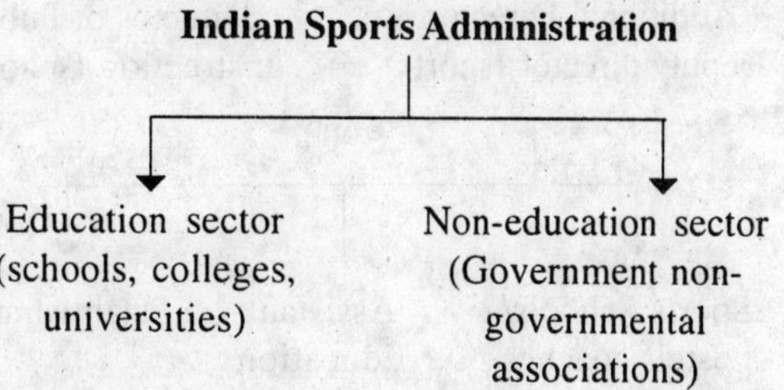

Education Sector

Education sector covers educational institutions where physical education and sport undoubtedly is the cradle of institutionalized sports but it does require complete renovation rejuvenation, and revamping.

Organizational Set-up of Sports Administration Educational Set-up

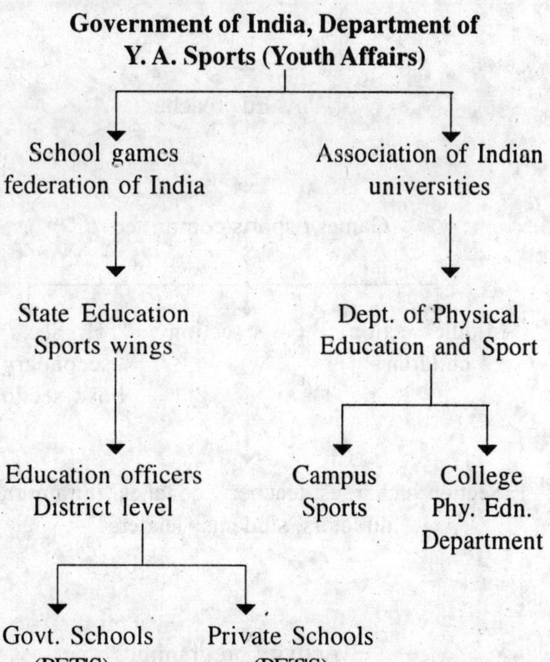

Organizational set-up of a typical state education sports wing

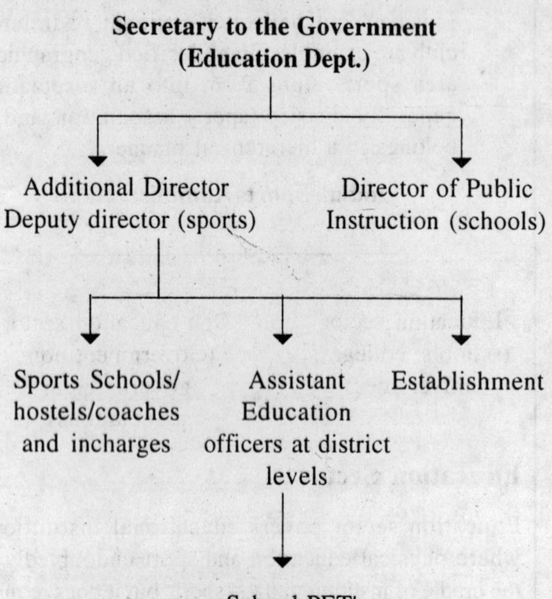

Organizational set up of physical education and sports in a school

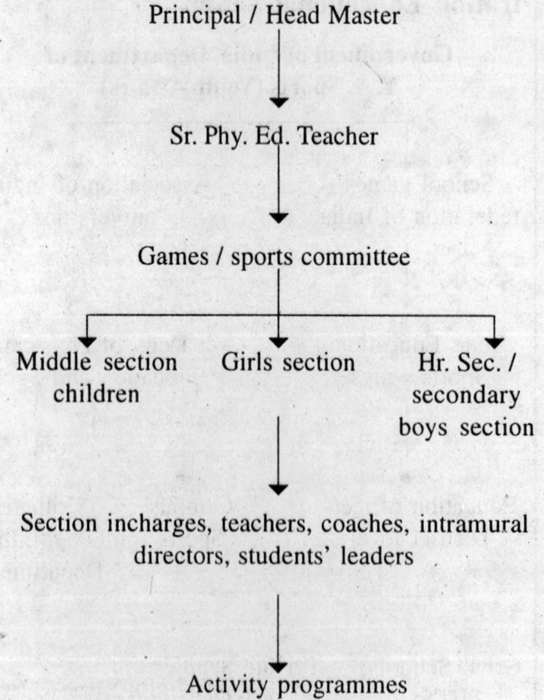

Organizational set up of a non-teaching department of physical education in a university : (Existing)

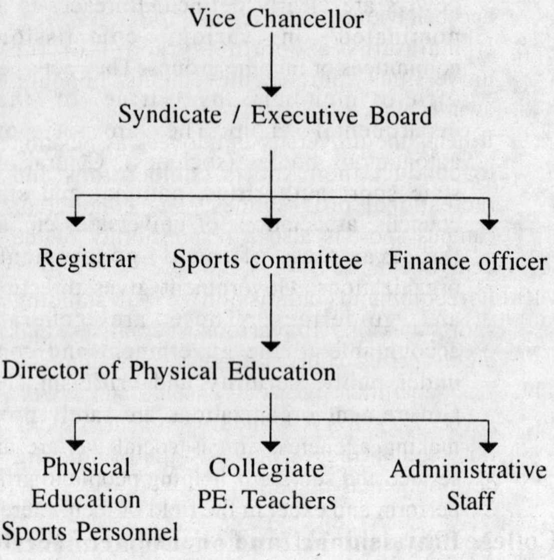

The functions are:

1. Within the limits and limitations of budgetary provisions and professional objectives, it formulates proposals and plans for the development of physical education and sports in the university.
2. It prepares the annual calendar of inter collegiate sports competitions and gets them organized with the help of physical education personnel from the department and affiliated colleges.
3. It supervise selection of university sports teams, arranges for their coaches and sponsors them for inter university competitions.
4. Within the frame work of laid down policies, it prepares the departmental budgets and operates it independently after it is duly approved.
5. It plans sports infrastructure and facilities and takes care of their maintenance and functionality.
6. Depending upon facility it hosts inter university sports competitions.

7. If appoints managers, coaches etc. for university teams and initiates follow up action on their reports on achievements, performance and behaviour of the teams.
8. It maintains a complete record of the universities sports achievements, honours, awards etc.
9. It helps the university employees association to conduct their sports competitions and recreational programmes. The conduct of campus sport is also a responsibility of the department.
10. It recommends admission of out standing sports persons to various specialised and highly prized courses against sports quota.
11. The department keeps a constant liaison with A.L.U, U.G.G, S.A.A and Department of sports for augmenting resources and formulating developmental plans.

College Physical Education Department: Functions:

1. To organize intramural sports competitions.
2. To prepare college teams to participate in inter collegiate competitions.
3. To host inter-collegiate competitions allotted to the college by university physical education department.
4. To conduct instruction classes if and when obligatory.
5. To prepare budget for the department and operate it after it is duly approved.
6. To get sport infrastructure constructed and be responsible for its care and maintenance.
7. To procure sports equipment, maintain its record and ensure its up keep.
8. To record sports achievements of the college and athlete and prepare annual report thereof.
9. To take care of athletic honour boards, trophies and cups won by the institution.
10. To look after sports hostels if established in the college.
11. To organize annual recreation fetes and sports festivals.
12. To provide health service and health supervision to the students and maintain their physico - medical record.

Organisational Chart of Physical Education Department of a college

Principal
↓
Director of Physical Education
↓
Assistant director of Physical Education
↓
Game Captains

Organisational Chart of Physical Education Programme of State

Governor
↓
Minister of Education
↓
Director of School Education
↓
Director of Collegiate Education
↓
Chief Educational Officer
↓
District Educational Officer
↓
Chief Inspector of Physical Education
↓
Regional Inspector of Physical Education
↓
Director of Sports and Youth Wings
↓
District Sports Officer
↓
Coaches

MANAGEMENT OF INFRASTRUCTURE, EQUIPMENTS, FINANCE AND PERSONNEL

Equipments

Need For the Equipment:

1. Equipment acts as an incentive to participants.
2. With equipment different kinds of activities could be taught and different skills could be acquired.

3. When various equipments are used properly, they develop neuro-muscular co-ordination. Equipments for an institution depend upon the finance available, strength of students, physical education periods, activities in the programme etc. If requirements could not be met due to financial difficulties, the physical education teacher should use other available equipments modifying them.

Type of Equipments:

1. Permanent (ex) goal post, bar, kho-kho post.
2. Temporary (or) destroyable or perishable net, ball, bats, racket etc.

Directions or Procedures for the Purchase of Equipment

1. Check what equipments are available in your department at the beginning of the year (previous stock).
2. Make a budget, without knowing the income and the strength of the student, you cannot make a purchase.
3. List the equipments purchased during the previous year.
4. List down the equipments, required to be purchased for the current year.
5. After preparing the list of things to be purchased during the year avoid over stocking the easily perishable equipment such as bladders, net etc.
6. If the order is large, quotation should be called for from various companies (Minimum from three firms).
7. Always purchase articles of high quality. Cheap articles get damaged at the earliest.
8. Select a good dealer and make your purchase regularly from him. As far as possible purchase equipment from a local dealer.
9. Place all order in writing.
10. It is always better to visit the sports company to select the articles required and purchase them. Place the initials or seal to see that the articles selected by you reach your school.
11. Check the equipment for correctness and quality after receiving them from the sports company. Damaged or unsatisfactory article should be returned with a note.
12. Stamp all the goods with the school seal to avoid loss.
13. Do not accept any free gift from dealer.
14. Settle the bills promptly.

Care and Maintenance of Equipment

1. Have a separate room for keeping the equipments with stands, shelves, cub boards boxes etc.
2. Keep the room clean and it is always better to have a good look.
3. Only authorized person should handle the equipment.
4. Keep a register for equipment.
5. Stamp all the equipments to prevent loss.
6. After use equipment should be cleared and properly stored in the correct place allotted to them.
7. Check all the equipments from time to time to prevent loss.
8. Minor repairs can be done if required.
9. All the goal post, net, basket ball board should be painted once in a year.
10. Leader balls should be kept clean. They should be inflated correctly and placed properly.
11. When the balls are not needed for play for a week or so, the air should be let off.
12. Rackets should be kept in press.
13. Hockey sticks and cricket bat should be seasoned.
14. Gymnastic mats should be kept clear and to dry the mats it should not be dragged but should be lifted and carried. Both sides of the mat should be used.

Need For a Gymnasium:

1. Gymnasium provides change of activities.
2. Protects the students from hot sun.
3. Activities can be conducted in the gymnasium during rainy season.
4. Disturbance and distraction from outside could be avoided.

5. It is easy to arrange light and to carry out the programme during night.
6. A large number of activities like rhythmic activities, gymnastics, indoor games of small area can be conducted without outside distraction.

Construction Size of the Gymnasium

For a high school minimum 100 f length to 60 f breadth. For a college 150 f length to 100 f breadth. The shape of the gymnasium is generally rectangular, the width and length being approximately in the ratio of 5:5.

It is always better to have a roof in the Gymnasium instead of terrace. The height of the roof must be from 15f to 22f.

Wall of Gymnasium: Wall must be hard and smooth. During construction provision must be made for hooks and cross beams on which apparatus can be hung like climbing ropes, roman rings, hanging malkhamb. The wall of the gymnasium may be painted light green.

Doors and Windows: Doors and window should open outward. If they open inward and project inside the floor, they may be dangerous for the participant. Glass windows and doors should not be used because they may be broken during activities.

Roof of the Gymnasium: Asbestos or tin sheet roofing is always better because they are cheaper and durable.

Floor: Wooden flooring is always preferred but it is so costly. So cement floor can be used. It should be smooth. It may be marked with different colours for various indoor games.

Apparatus: All apparatus must be of movable type, when the activities are over, they should be lifted by pulleys. By removing the apparatus, indoor games can be conducted.

PUPIL - TEACHER INTERACTION AND RELATIONSHIP

In a lesson with a positive climate pupils are supported in their learning by a teacher who cares about them and their learning.

A lesson with an effective learning environment has a positive climate. What is climate of a lesson? When we talk about the lesson climate we are referring to the prevailing mood of the lessons. Pupil and their learning are put at the centre of your lesson planning and delivery. The lesson has a relaxed but purposeful atmosphere. Pupils are expected to learn and to be on-task, supported by a caring, enthusiastic teacher. The teacher uses a positive teaching style, identifying and providing feed back on appropriate work, the positive reinforcement motivating pupils to learn and enhancing their self esteem. Thus, much of the interaction in the class is positive, creating effective inter-personal relationship.

You need to know pupils personally in order to build up a relationship with them. You and your pupils must develop mutual respect for each other, accepting each other and valuing each other's view points. All aspects of your teaching are important in showing you value pupils, including such aspects as questioning techniques. A teacher may, (ex) ask a question such as how can you get over a box putting your feet on it. If you only want and accept one possible answer 'a vault', you may discount an answer from a pupil which answers the question but is not the answer, you wanted. Hence, the pupil is not given the opportunity to make an effective contribution to the lesson.

You must not become too friendly with your pupils. We have seen some student teacher on their initial school experience adopting a friendly approach to their pupils and then they have not been able to establish their authority. You must maintain your status as a teacher so that your authority is not undermined and so that pupils do not lose respect for you. If you establish a good relationship with your pupils you can exert your authority when you need to.

The following are the components of good relationship :

1. Know your pupils.
2. Appreciate your pupils.
3. Acknowledge their efforts
4. Be a careful listener
5. Include pupils in decisions

6. Make some concessions when appropriate
7. Always show respect for pupils
8. Show honesty and integrity
9. Develop a sense of community, of belonging to the class.

As with all other aspects of your teaching you need to monitor your relationship with your pupils. You can do this by observing pupils' reaction to you and your lessons. If pupils get to class early, are enthusiastic, do things quickly and willingly, ask questions to enhance their learning, follow established rules and routines, treat pupils with respect, and help one another without being prompted, this suggests that you have or are establishing a good relationship with your pupils.

Equipment

Vaulting box, parallel bars, suspended horizontal bars, pair of roman rings, climbing rope, spring boards, mats etc.

Other special facilities:

1. Sanitary arrangement
2. Drinking water facilities
3. First aid kits
4. A store room to keep the equipment
5. A notice board
6. Office room
7. A small library with books for referring purpose.
8. Separate rooms for males and female for dressing.
9. Seating arrangements for spectators.

CONSTRUCTION OF A MULTI-PURPOSES SWIMMING POOL

Areas in a Swimming Pool

1. Area for beginners: The depth should be $2\frac{1}{2}$ to 4 feet. This should not be so steep or slanting.
2. Area for those who know swimming and who want to advance the swimming technique
3. Area for competition
4. Area for diving
5. Separate area for girls

Finance and Budget

Budget involves planning in advance, the income and expenditure expected for the year under physical education programme.

Guiding Factors for the Preparation of Budget

1. One has to see how much money was collected and spent during the last 3 years.
2. Is the same programme going to be continued for current year too?
3. Is there any thing new to be included for the current year?
4. What is the actual amount for the current year, work out the school expenses?

Rules of Utilisation

1. Every institution at such rates as fixed by the managements games fee approval should be obtained from the department of education.
2. Games fee should be collected with other special fees together at the beginning of the school.
3. The game fund for the institution shall consist of the game fees or any private person funding and other sources of income.
4. The head of institution shall maintain a separate account in local post office or bank.
5. A game committee or internal committee responsible for that headmaster as chairman, physical education teachers members of that.

Programme Planning in Personal

The required programme of physical education taught through regular instruction and practice, is usually arranged in the form of a syllabus. In the syllabus, activities are arranged class wise suited to different age -level and sex in a progressive and systematic way for mostly an academic year, syllabus provides a minimum of selected activities for each class which gives an opportunity to improve the skills of those activities progressively.

Educationists feel that a plan may restrict the child and teacher in learning and teaching the activities respectively. But at the same time in its absence a great deal of confusion may result. Hence a syllabus seems necessary for minimum requirement and to be used as a guide, though however the programme is left to the discretion of the teacher depending upon the situation.

PERSONAL

Voice

Record yourself reading a piece of text in a natural voice or having conversation with a friend. If you have not heard yourself on tape before, prepare for a shock. You may sound quite different from what you expect. Remember though that you hear your voice coming 'back' from your mouth whereas most people hear it coming 'forward'.

Clothes you Wear

Consider what you wear when you are teaching and what messages the various (out fits) might send to the pupils. You might like to compare what you wear with other PE staff, more widely, with other teacher in the school. There is no suggestion here that there is a right or wrong way to dress in school, but dress in an area of choice and you have some control over the messages sent. You may, also want you should wear in different school contexts, for example in PE lessons, in classroom lessons, at parents' evenings.

Methods and Techniques of Teaching

Method is a general way of guiding and controlling learning experiences. We must say that the choice of method in physical education for any teacher depends upon his personal experience, mental inclination and ability to pass on desirable experience to students.

1. **Lecture method:** This method is very widely used in the field of education especially in the classrooms where the teacher goes on speaking and the pupils go on listening to him.

   Lecture in physical education is used in a limited way. It is used only at places where the information is to be passed or regarding the history of game or where theoretical knowledge is to be imparted using lecture as a tool in teaching of physical activity. Lecture is a useful method only when it is combined with other methods of teaching.

2. **Command method:** It is a way by which the students are commanded to do an activity especially drill and marching or a start in athletics. In fact, command method itself is not a full fledged method because of the fact that an activity cannot be done or taught with command only unless it has been introduced, explained and demonstrated fairly well.
   Making children do set drills by using whistle or clapping or beating of the drum falls within the techniques of the command method. It is one man's commands which they have to follow. In this sense, this method is precise. Control of the morning assemblies, parades, march past etc. demand ample use of the command method.

3. **Project method:** This method denotes that problems have been presented to the students, areas have been demarcated and the school population is grouped. Now the students themselves should find the answers to their problems. Because of the nature of activities in physical education: In arranging camps, picnics, hikes and treks, perhaps this method may be of some use to the teachers of physical education. Whenever, the project method is used, the total work should be carefully planned; instructions and directions should be clearly given and the aim and objectives clearly defined.

4. **Discussion method:** In this method the teachers and students participate in discussion over a project or a problem. This is considered to be a democratic method. The discussion may be regarding a skill, the interpretation of rules and regulations of the game; officiating and coaching points etc. In this method the teacher gives maximum opportunity to the

students to open themselves up, put forward the problems and try to find the possible solutions.

This discussion method as such helps each and every individual to learn how to speak and find realistic solutions to the problems.

5. **Group directed - practice method:** This method is very effectively used. The class is divided into groups and each group has its group leader. Who is, of course, a bit better in the physical education activities than the others. The teacher gives instructions in a particular skill and asks the various groups to practice the skills under the directions of group leader. This method calls for sincere effort on the part of the students to practice skills faithfully. The teacher here becomes a 'supervisor' who goes on grinding the various groups by moving from place to place. This proves to be an effective method if adequate facilities of material equipment fields and courts are available.
6. **Demonstration method:** Here the teacher will demonstrate activity with a brief explanation. The students have to observe the teacher's demonstration and then perform the activity on the command of the teacher. This is the most highly recommended method of teaching.
7. **Imitation method:** This is adopted when an activity that was already taught or an activity which can be easily followed. In this case the teacher says "follow me" or "Do as I do". When the teacher leads an activity and then changes the movements, the boys perform the same by imitation.
8. **Oral method:** In this method the teacher merely explains the activity by words without any demonstration and expects the class to perform it (This method of teaching is not wholly desirable).
9. **Dramatization method:** In this method the pupil are made to perform the movements of animals, birds, motor cars, trains, aeroplane, soldiers, sailors etc. in story form. There is lot of scope for exhibiting the imagination of the pupils. This method is most suitable for the children of the elementary grades.
10. **At-will method:** In this method the students are given an opportunity to perform the activity taking their own time and rhythm. In other words this is a free form of exercising.
11. **Set - drill method:** This method will consist of a series of well - planned exercise of free arm type and exercise with light apparatus (dumb - bells, clubs, wands etc. These exercises are memorised and done rhythmically, not only for physiological effects but also for demonstrative values.
12. **Whole method:** This method is adopted whenever an activity is to be taught as a whole action without breaking it into its component parts. For example, the teaching of an athletic event like high jump which includes a series of movements (viz. approach, take - off, lay up and landing) is done by this method, even though each of these movements may be analysed and emphasised.
13. **Past method:** This is adopted whenever a particular activity is broken into its meaningful parts and taught. For example, the teaching of the individual skills in a major game.
14. **Observation and Visualization method:** Students whenever opportunity arises may be taken to the places where champion teams and athletes compete (e.g. state, national competition etc.). So that they can observe them in action and learn some of the finer tactics, strategies and techniques of the games and the events. Films preferably in slow motion, depicting the finer points, of the activity may be repeatedly shown with due comments so that effective learning may take place.

PRESENTATION TECHNIQUE

The immediate task before the teacher who is getting ready to face the class or a new teaching situation is anticipation, planning and preparation.

A. Planning

Planning is the next step after anticipation. It is better that the teacher must be warned about the mistakes that may be there on his part being a novice. Hence there should be over planning in better professional work through proper planning.

Principles of preparation: The third thing that occurs, before the class begins is the preparation. After anticipating and planning the teacher prepares. This means a plan resulting from anticipating some conditions and circumstances which lead towards preparation. There are two types of preparations namely:

1. **Personal preparation:** The modern physical education teacher should be careful about his dress and appearance on occasions other than in physical education classes. Clothes should be in appropriate style, shoes properly polished, skirts and blouses freshly laundered and head gear appropriately worn. Sometimes a beginning teacher forgets these things. But it must be kept in mind that what ever the teacher is going to wear that will have an effect on the student. A well-groomed appearance is always essential. He must have a commanding voice, pleasing manners and a sense of humour. He should avoid uncouth gestures and unnecessary mannerisms. He must be able to demonstrate the skill in a proper manner. In short a teacher shall always set an example to the students and must be a model to be followed.
2. **Technical preparation:** The teacher must be prepared more than a lawyer, a physician or a surgeon. He must have the technical knowledge and skill which are qualities to a professional service. Some of the guidelines that guide the physical education, refer to the child, some to the school, to the department, the teaching learning process, the programme of physical education and the required facilities.

The experienced teacher has come to learn that he is responsible for such preparation. The teacher should avoid negative comparison of the locality, the climate, the town, school etc. He should avoid statement of a complimentary nature, subject of conversation directed at a person, personal affairs, financial affairs, religious methods, political parties etc.

The teacher must arrange the subject matter to be taught in proper sequence. It is better for him to write the teaching notes or to have a clear mental picture of the subject to be taught. He must arrange for teaching aids, ground markings, essential equipment, proper safety measures etc. The formation of the class and the way in which it should be organised for the concerned activities must be pre-planned. So that easy handling of the class takes place.

B. Presentation

After making all preparation for handling a class, a teacher must be able to present the subject matter in the best way possible. Though there is no one best way of presenting a subject matter a teacher must bear in minds the common characteristics of good presentation. They are as follows.

1. Presentation must proceed from simple to complex and from known to unknown.
2. The presentation must be neither too fast nor very slow but must be adjusted to the pupil's level of understanding and skill.
3. Problems and situations shall be presented to the students to enable them to think and act.
4. For the better learning of the students, the teacher should always resort to improved techniques and tools.
5. Students must be made to-realize the importance of the part of the whole activity.

Having rated the characteristics of good presentation, let us deal with the steps in the way of presenting activity:

1. **Orientation:** Orientation to develop this insight, a part of day - to - day teaching. In presenting activities the teacher makes clear how they are means to a certain end. During orientation the students must get adequate but precise information with regard to the equipment to be used, surroundings of the

play field etc. Orientation should be neither too brief nor too long. It should be reasonably adequate. The orientation can be through test score for the perfection of skills. The orientation will make students understand what they are doing, why they are doing and how for they are succeeding.

2. **Verbal explanation:** In the beginning, the teachers are apt to talk too much. But whatever the talking teacher does should be brief, to the point and should be combined with observation directed towards finding at whether the students have grasped the meaning or not. The good teacher will always use black board for diagrams, charts for explaining the points, films for the description of the skills, thus making the teaching more effective and purposeful.

3. **The lecture:** Learning is a self - activity. Sometimes the teacher gives long speech for a lesson giving little opportunity to his students to question. Avoid lecturing if possible. If you can present a statement or talk on some pertinent topic, do so briefly and make it an interesting one. If you are to lecture, prepare it carefully. Make your points in logical order, use the vocabulary suitable to the age group, do sufficient informality to hold attention.

4. **Demonstration:** Demonstration means how something is done, as a technique in teaching, demonstration is always accompanied by directed observation. It is through orientation and verbal explanation that students are prepared for observing a demonstration. During demonstration further explanation may be added but this must be done skillfully. In demonstration like "watch me" or" do it like that" may be used for the students. A good demonstration is designed for a purpose by which pupils are helped to understand. It is a visual aid of learning, when the demonstration is for the purpose of showing a part of the activity.

   For example : Pivoting or goal shooting. A neat and smart demonstration is the key to practical learning in physical education.

5. **Exploration:** It is very difficult to break down the presentation into a separate technique for the purpose of discussion without over lapping or considerable repetition. Pupil should be given an opportunity to explore the activity or the skill which has been discussed, demonstrated and observed. Exploration be continued till there is progress in learning. Usually this period is very brief. Exploration follows closely a period of discussion, demonstration and observation. The teacher must observe the class as closely as Possible when the learning takes place. It is the mark of a good teacher. This is developed as a result of happy combination of professional preparation and personal dedication and experience.

6. **Recitation:** For centuries the most used teaching technique has been recitation in which the students recited or repeated facts they have been told or read and so memorised. Physical education teachers have depended upon this technique in the form of question and answer for determining, what the students know. Sometime the correct answer is not given by the student then the teacher goes on asking till the answer is found. The answer is mostly in "yes" or "no". This encourages guessing. It is better if all listen to your question. This will pave the way for good group discussion and the defensive role played by the student is minimised.

7. **Discussion:** The ability to lead discussion is of utmost importance in guiding the group process and thus creating a democratic learning climate. There is self expression on the part of the students by participating in physical education. In discussion, skill on the part of the teacher leads to the understanding of the concepts properly.

8. **Supervision:** Supervision means that the teacher is using directed observation in order to find out whether learning is taking place on all these occasions. Supervision also means that the teacher's observation is directed towards fulfilling his responsibility for safety and welfare of the students.

During supervising practice the treatment of the students towards one another and also how they respond to their leader, also rate the element of difficulty being caused to the learners. See what additional explanation, demonstration and discussion are necessary for the proper learning and modify your organization for presentation and your procedure accordingly. In supervision it is the duty of the teacher to rate the individual differences towards an activity.

9. **Evaluation:** No presentation is complete without an evaluation of the results. When presentation is finished, pupil have practised achievements are valued. The summary of the progress through a test, questionnaire or rating scale is made.

UNIVERSALITY OF MANAGEMENT

W.L. Mackenzie King rightly observed that "labour can do nothing without capital, capital nothing without labour, and neither can do anything without the guiding genius of management".

In fact, managers are needed in all types of organizations to make things happen. Management is needed not only in the business but also in all types of organized activities and in all types of organizations.

The functions of management must be performed by managers in all types of organizations, in all cultures of the world. From this emerges the concept of universality of management. Management functions must be executed by small business and large ones: public, semi-public and private organizations; manufacturing firms, service organizations, and retail concerns; and domestic, foreign and multinational firms. In other words, the functions of management are basically the same for any kind of organization. Although they may be applied differently by different managers – depending on variables such as the type of organization, culture, and types of employees – the functions remain the same. In all types of organizations managers operate by achieving goals through the coordinated efforts of other people.

Basically, an organization is a group of two or more persons that exists and operates to achieve clearly stated, commonly held objectives. Objectives are goals – targets to shoot for, states of being or places to be reached through plans and actions. In the words of Plunkett and Attner, "The objectives of an organization have to do with providing goods and services to its members or providing them to others outside the organization. In an organization it is quite possible that each member might do parts of jobs which each thought important to meet the objectives, while in actuality the members might be working in opposite directions. To prevent this from occurring and to ensure co-ordination of work to accomplish the objectives managers are needed."

Management is needed in organizations because without it people would go off on their own and work towards obtaining their own objectives independently of others. Without management in organization, effort would go waste. In short, management is needed for their different reasons :

1. **To reach objectives:** Management is needed to reach organizational and personal objectives. As one of the former presidents of the American Management Association said, "The basic function of management is to attain objectives through action taken by the members of the organization. Since dynamics are the forces which produce the action and motion, it follows that the dynamics of management are those forces which produce the action which is required. Those forces of management do not just happen. They must be given impetus by managers."
   The objective of most organizations, private and public – is to perform or provide a service. So the primary objective of an organization is to offer a profitable service. If profit is not made for a considerable period of time the organization will cease to exist.
2. **To maintain balance between conflicting goals:** Secondly, managers have to strike a balance among the conflicting objectives, goals, and activities of members of an

organization. Balance has to be maintained between such things as income and expenditure, individual and internal expenditures, the services offered versus the costs involved, and the demands of different groups having diverse interests.

Management has to reconcile the conflicting interests of diverse groups. It performs the function of stewardship on behalf of the owners, who strive to earn a satisfactory return on their investment. The return may be either profit (as in a business) or service (at different levels of government). It is equally vital to consider the best interests of the employees, who seek satisfactory wages and compensation, safe, healthy and comfortable work environment, and sufficient hours of paid holiday. It is also necessary to look into the interest of the general public, including consumers, government policy makers and administrators, creditors, suppliers, union leaders and trade associations. If management tends to favour one group at the expense of the others, it will tend to create an imbalance that will be detrimental to the long-term viability of the organization.

3. **To achieve efficiency and effectiveness:** The different ways of measuring the performance of an organization are in terms of efficiency or effectiveness. These two terms were introduced by P.F. Drucker in 1954.

   Efficiency refers to the ability to "get things done correctly". It can be measured or quantified as the ratio of output. An efficient manager is one who succeeds in achieving higher outputs (results, productivity, performance) relative to the inputs (labour, material, money, machinery, time) needed to achieve them. In other words, efficiency managers are those who can minimize the cost of the resources used to produce a fixed level of output. In a like manner an efficient manager is one who can maximize output from a fixed amount of resources (inputs).

Effectiveness is the 'ability to do the right things'; or to get things accomplished. This demands choosing the most appropriate objectives and the proper method of achieving the objectives . In other words, effective managers select the 'right things to do and 'right' method of getting them done.

According to Drucker, "effectiveness is the secret of success for any organization. For managers the pertinent question is not how to do things right, but how to find the right things to do, and concentrate resources and efforts on them. In the words of Drucker, "Management should concern itself with efficiency that is with doing better what is already being done. It should, therefore, focus on cost. But the entrepreneurial approach focuses on effectiveness, that is, on the decision what to do. It focuses on opportunities to produce revenue, to create markets and to change the economic characteristics of existing products and markets."

It may be added that a manager may be owner/operator/founder of an organization as well as someone hired to give it direction – to make decision and commit its resources (personnel, capital and equipment) to achieve the organization's objectives, and set in motion force for change, coordination and control in an organization.

SUPERVISION

What is supervision?

Supervision is one of the most important tasks of management. It has been defined as the direction, accompanied by authority, of the work of others." It is a compound of two words 'Super' and 'Vision' meaning superior power of perceiving. It means overseeing or superintending the work of others. Margarent Williamson defines supervision "as a process by which workers are helped by a designated staff member to learn according to their needs to make best use of their knowledge and skills and to improve their abilities so that they do their jobs more effectively and with increasing satisfaction to themselves and the agency."

The efficiency of an organization is judged by its achievements. Achievements are not possible without adequate supervision. The work which is not inspected, is not done' is an old saying. Inspection, overseeing and supervision arise in response to needs inherent in the functioning of an organization. Policy-making, programming, budgeting, and stuffing by themselves, may not necessarily lead to successful results unless there is someone to ensure that what has been programmed is actually being implemented.

Every organization public or private, provides for supervision as one of its most important tasks. Again supervision is inherent in the hierarchical nature of organizations, each level of which supervises the one below it and is, in turn, supervised by the one above it.

Supervision is more than inspection and investigation, the latter are mere parts of the process of supervision. Indeed, supervision is more than superintendence as an administrative task. It has an educative aspect also. A supervisor is supposed to teach the workers of the best ways of doing their work.

Phase of Supervision

There are three phases of a supervisor's jobs:

1. **Substantive Aspect:** A supervisor must know the technique and the know how of his work because he has to plan the work, assign duties to others and set standards of performance.
2. **Institutional Aspect:** A supervisor has to run the agency or unit under his charge according to the established rules and procedures and within the framework of policy. He should endure that the work is being well done and on time. He has the responsibility of see that all employees are regular and punctual in their duties and that there is proper the conservation of equipment and supplies.
3. **Personnel Aspect:** Authority alone cannot work out of others; hence, it is the job of the supervisor to create interest and enthusiasm among the workers. Real authority must flow from within.

Methods of Supervision:

Millet suggests the following six methods or techniques of supervision.

(*i*) **Prior Approval:** It is a common method of control by the headquarters over field establishments. It means that before taking any initiative or action outside the framework of policy, the field agencies must get prior approval or may not. This process usually causes delay and results in corruption. During emergency or crisis this system becomes inoperative.

(*ii*) **Service Standards:** Service standards mean fixing norms for performance. The top management can lay down certain targets or standards for the operating agencies to achieve. This will not only provide guide points to the operating agencies but shall also become a means for determining how effectively they have been doing the jobs assigned to them. In the words of Millet "Service standards are necessary in government in order to ensure that work is done promptly and properly". It may, however, be mentioned here that standards fixed must be fair, exact and concrete and must be judged objectively.

(*iii*) **Work Budget:** Budget allotments are a very powerful means of exercising supervision. Budget is not simply an array of figures it is a tool of control over administration. Budget allotments fix the magnitude of the work to be done in a given time and the operating agencies have to work within these allotments. The top management control becomes effective as these operating agencies are not given a free hand to spend money as and when they like.

(*iv*) **Approval of Personnel:** No agency of government is completely free to recruit staff. The superior staff is invariably appointed by the chief executive. Even in the case of subordinate personnel, the top management usually insists on its prior approval for all posts except the insignificant ones. In fact, this work is often entrusted to the central personnel agency of the department concerned.

(*v*) **Reports:** All subordinates offices submit progress reports to the headquarters. These reports may be monthly, quarterly, half-yearly or annually. Headquarters can come to know about the progress and take suitable action in case of deficient performance. These reports may be narrative or statistical, they may embrace the broad scope of all major activities, or may be confined to a few essentials, they may emphasize achievement or deficiencies in performance. The trouble with this method is that the returns and reports tend to multiply, thus entailing untold burden on the headquarters. Besides, in an administrative organization reports are occasionally sugar coated, information that will evoke a favourable reaction is played up and the lapses are glossed over. Without some standards guide forms, it is all too tempting for reporters to interject extraneous bits of information.

(vi) **Inspections and Evaluations:** Reporting as a supervisory technique is usually supplemented by some inspection practice. In whatever forms and whatever intervals, the written report submitted by the operating unit can never adequately replace the usefulness of personal first hand acquaintance with the work.

These are the basic features of supervisions:

1. Supervision and control is the job of every manager. He may be at the job or a "bottom manager". He has to guide, direct and control the lower staff, their work and production. It is pointed out supervisory management oversees the work of operators, while top and middle managers remain busy in overseeing the work of management members. Thus supervisors alone, of all management members, are concerned with directing and guiding non-management members of the organization. Because of their exclusive dealing with workmen, the supervisors are known as fist-line managers. These first-line managers are to be witnessed not only in the sphere of production, but in all other activities as well.
2. Supervision which is employee-oriented results in higher productivity than where supervision is production-oriented. Supervisors are in constant daily touch with operators and hold the key to effective direction of human beings. Through their influence on work environment and their adoption of wholesome attitude supervisors can tremendously contribute towards enlisting full support and collaboration of employees. On the contrary, supervisors may destroy the will to do and enthusiasm on the part of workers. Even the sincere efforts and splendid work of top management may go unrewarded if supervision is faulty.
3. They are to exercise leadership and communicative skill for obtaining the desired performance from the side of employees. Duty and authority for the work are delegated to them by the superior line executive, and supervisors remain accountable for performance to the delegator. The process of delegating managerial work is stopped with the supervisory level of management. Supervisors are also to see that the work is executed in the best possible manner by the operators. These supervisors provide employees with all necessary help or assistance in executing their jobs properly. For the provision of these facilities and assistance, supervisors are aided by a number of staff services like engineering, cost accounting, inspection, production, planning and personnel management.
4. The distinction between directing and supervision has been clarified by R.C. Davis, when he says, "Directing is defined as a function of instruction concerning the nature and requirements for the proper execution of a plan", while, "Supervision is the function of assuring that the work is being done in accordance with plan and instruction." This function involves overseeing and checking work while it is being done, to make certain that instructions are understood and the individual has the requisite ability to do the

work etc. Thus, supervision is the only control function that can result directly and immediately in corrective action for execution.

5. A supervisor is a first-line executive entrusted with the task of getting the work accomplished by the workers at the operative level in accordance with the standards which are predetermined and laid down by the top management. A supervisor thus, has certain assigned responsibilities for planning, organizing, directing and controlling the work of subordinates under him. His activities are concerned directly with the workers' activities for accomplishment of the original objectives.

6. Usually the supervisor performs the following functions:
   (*a*) He gives orders, issues instructions and enforces the rules. He arranges work and makes work assignments, determines procedures and prescribes methods. He makes arrangements for the supply of materials and tools for workers under him.
   (*b*) He explains the policies of the organization, and informs men about what is happening in the organization.
   (*c*) He hears complaints, grievances of his subordinates and helps them to solve the problems. As and when need be, he communicates it upward to the higher executive for solution.
   (*d*) He recommends promotions, transfers and pay increases for his subordinates.
   (*e*) He inspires workers and keeps them posted on how well they are doing their jobs.

7. A Government Act in the U.S.A defines the function of a supervisor. "Supervisors are those having authority to exercise independent judgement in hiring, discharging, disciplining, rewarding and taking other actions of a similar nature with respect to employees."

8. The supervisor works as a liaison between the management and the workers and holds the position of key-man. He performs the prescribed functions which concern the technical aspect of his responsibilities. Besides he owns certain implied responsibilities which require personal qualities. He has moral obligation towards the workers whom he supervises, and of course, his obligations towards management cannot be underestimated. We shall now see briefly his duties towards (1) workers, (2) towards management (3) towards his own functions and responsibilities, and (4) towards his parallel associates.

9. Supervisor helps in solving problems and to represent on their behalf to the higher authorities: To develop human relations with his subordinates. To inspire his subordinates and appreciate their good work. To present himself as an ideal before his subordinates. To listen to the suggestions of his subordinates and to give them suggestion. He is entrusted with the task of securing work accomplishment from employees in accordance with predetermined standards of performance, because supervisors are line executives with command authority. For such work accomplishments supervisors are expected to give orders, issue instructions, prescribe methods, determine procedures, explain company policies and inspire human beings.

10. The supervisor represents management ideas, thoughts and desires to working personnel, because the entire management duty in regard to work performance flows through supervisors. The supervisor forms the link between management and operators, and accordingly, has a two-fold obligation for satisfying the company as well as employee needs in the organization.

11. The relationship between a worker and his superior is the most important human relation in a workplace from the standpoint of the worker. Workers, therefore, want superiors who treat them as human beings, who understand their problems, and give consideration to their aspirations and social needs. The quality of

supervision is thus a major factor in influencing attitudes, building morale, satisfying the needs of the workers, and in stimulating their productivity.

12. Good supervisor has the responsibility:

(*a*) to work in cooperation and coordination with other supervisors.

(*b*) To consider and accept criticism and suggestions of his associates and modify his plans.

(*c*) To cooperate in transferring the workers from one department to the other.

(*d*) To provide necessary information to other departments when required.

(*e*) To consider for implementation, the new techniques adopted by other departments. Different periods of industrial history show the changing pattern of supervisory responsibilities.

13. The top management directing the middle-level management and the middle-level management directing the junior management or the first-line management. The superiors always oversee their juniors at work. This overseeing and guiding is an important executive and managerial function and thus according to Koontz and O' Donnell, supervision becomes a part of directing-an important function of manager.

14. Supervision refers to the direct and immediate guidance and control of subordinates in the performance of their tasks.

15. On the importance of supervision in management it is pointed out that he is the key man, the link between top management, as its direct representative and the workers. He is also the communication link between these two. As such, he can contribute a lot towards creating a healthy industrial climate by truthfully representing the ideas, thoughts and desires of the management to the operative workers. Simultaneously, he informs the management of the views, complaints, difficulties, problems etc. of the workers. This way he has two-fold obligation. As a human relations specialist, he tries to set the personal equation among the workers. From his point of view he is not only the key man at the operative level, but rather one of the many specialists contributing to the organization's effectiveness. His specialty being that of dealing with human relation problems.

16. Supervisor is a friend, philosopher and guide. The success of any enterprise depends on how far its goals, policies and targets are accomplished. Of course, this can be accomplished through the activities of the workers who are guided and controlled through supervision. In short, the first –line supervisor is the real executor of the plans, policies and programmes determined by the top management of the enterprise, and the success of it depends on the ability of the supervisor to translate them into actual performance level.

17. The function is performed by the first-level supervisors who may be called by any name. These first-level supervisors are located in all the functional areas of work of the organization-be it the superintendent in the accounts section or a foreman on the assembly line. They are the only executives who perform the function of controlling at the execution level, when the task is being done. Their's is the only control function which can result directly and immediately in corrective action.

18. The human relations in supervision are, very, important for the success of supervisors in obtaining the desired productive effort from their men. It means that management must give more consideration to the selection of the supervisory personnel, and to the development of leadership qualities in them of dealing effectively with human relations on the job. This requires constant training of supervisors in the field of human relations, which means application of methods of science to the study of people at work in order to influence and change their behaviour and attitude so as to make them more productive and effective.

19. Supervisor is a key management member. The supervisor is a manager, rather a key management member, who is required to undertake the doing functions of management. The actual work is accomplished under the direct care and control of the supervisor. All managerial efforts percolate through supervisors and are distilled into supervisory performance. Hence, for the selection of supervisors, the same considerations that are necessary in the case of other managers are upheld.

20. On the Job Training, through apprenticeship is rather indispensable for converting new candidates into successful supervisor. Supervisory candidates are placed Incharge of senior supervisor, who gives instructions, answers queries and explains the techniques of work. The job training becomes very effective in these cases where it is coupled with role playing. In the presence of candidates, senior supervisors play out different roles of supervision. Role playing demonstrates clear requirements and technicalities of the job supervision and prepares the candidates for acquiring insights into the problems of supervision.

21. *Supervisory Manuals* are also used by some companies for the purpose of giving a written account of supervisory duties. These manuals contain objectives and policies, rules and regulations, of the company as well as authority and organizational relationships of supervisory positions. Manuals, as position guides help supervisors in becoming familiar with their specialized field of work.

22. The principles of Supervision are:

(*a*) To be effective, a supervisor must be able to analyse his group and determine what courses of action will best help to achieve the group's goals and promote it's morale. It is important to the supervisor's success that his followers perceive him as effectively responding to the groups needs.

(*b*) The effectiveness of the supervisor must ultimately be judged in terms of the group's survival and its progress towards its goals. The effective use of supervision contributes to the achievement of the goals of the group undertaking. Effective supervision is a function of the characteristics of the supervisor, the group, the situation and the inter-relations among these factors. The effectiveness of the supervisor depends largely on how well he and his organization define his role and how completely they accept it.

23. Usually supervision is classified under the following heads:

(*a*) Autocratic or Authorization Supervision

(*b*) Free-rein or Independent Supervision

(*c*) Democratic Supervision

24. The supervisory techniques are of the following types:

(*a*) Consultative or Democratic technique;

(*b*) Authoritarian or Dictatorial technique; and

(*c*) Non-interfering of Free-rein technique.

25. According to S.S. Chatterji "Supervisor's attitude should be compatible with the job, in-consistent to exercise leadership and effect excessively close supervision at the same time. "Leadership implies mutual understanding and confidence between the leader and his followers." The leader must allow individual freedom and initiative for pursuing a common course of action. Experience of many companies and undertakings shows that general and loose supervision is more productive than close supervision, wherever supervisory leadership exists. The supervisory vision and attitude give tone to such leadership. The supervisor must demonstrate his impartiality and integrity of character in all decisions and actions, orders and instructions, words and examples."

Some Other Useful Matters

Principles of Management in Sports

A mechanism by which a defined human group pursues a determined set of objectives through systematic group efforts for their implementation most effectively and economically is called sports management. Principles of management in sports:

1. **Division of work:** Division of work should be according to the individual's area of specialization. This would ensure efficiency and save time.
2. **Authority and Responsibility:** Authority and responsibility both are inter related and work should not be superimposed rather the person should feel responsible for the task being assigned to him or her.
3. **Discipline:** Discipline in sports management means obedience, honesty, unbiased attitude and emphasizing spontaneous development of discipline.
4. **Unity of Command:** This principle requires that an employee should receive orders from one superior only. Otherwise, dual or multiple commands will create havoc in authority, discipline and order.
5. **Interest:** This principle demands that general interest must supersede individual interest and it is the duty of management to reconcile the staff when they are in conflict.
6. **Order:** This is the principle of arrangement relating to things and persons.
   Placement of right thing/person in right place at right time.
7. **Labour turn over:** Employee should be given the stability of tenure, so that he picks up book and tries his best to do justice with the work assigned to him, unnecessary labour turn over reflects bad management.
8. **Initiative:** 'Liberty to work and not freedom from work' should be the guiding principle. Initiative by the employees should be taken note of and employees should be left to take their own decisions and initiative in the welfare of organization or work.

Techniques of Supervision of Physical Education

Some of the techniques and procedures for supervision in sports and physical education are as follows:

Visit. Purpose of visit is to gain for the supervisor ample scope for establishing friendly contacts with the supervised. Visit should be planned methodically. The supervisor must state the purpose of the visit, fix dates, indicate the duration of his visit and give a plan of his work.

1. **Demonstration. Demonstration is an effective tool for stimul**ating teachers professional growth and giving them strength and confidence. Demonstrations should be carried out in the natural setting, so that the supervisor is able to understand pros and cons faced during the teaching learning process and is able to study the children's behaviour in depth.
2. **Conference.** The supervisor can help teachers from different schools by holding occasional conferences. The agenda of each conference should be well panned in advance to facilitate thoughtful and free discussion on matters of common interest to the participants.
3. **Orientation course.** Orientation programme is to familiarize teachers of one type of technique with the principles and methods of another technique, so that they may be properly equipped to impart instruction to pupils of the latter technique.

Responsibilities of Different Officials in an Intramural

The organization of intramural offers the best incentive for physical education activities in which the entire student body can participate in the properly classified grounds. There has to be clear-cut roles defined and duties assigned to the staff and volunteers in the organization of the intramural programme:

1. **Intramural Director:** The intramural director coordinates the activities into a unified programme that acts as a living link between the institution and the changing phases of student activities. The Director may be the head of the department of physical education or one of the staff members with special qualification and qualities for undertaking such a task.
2. **Staff Supervisor:** Each activity is under the supervision of a staff member who is not only highly skilled but also deeply interested in promoting and popularizing the particular activity.
3. **House Captain:** He heads a unit of competitors and helps to select the team for the various activities out of members of the house. He acts as a channel for the expression of student's views at the intramural committee.
4. **Unit Coach:** Each house may have a coach, for an activity, who coaches the team, arranges practice periods for participation and works out eligibility rules for inclusion in representative teams from his unit.
5. **Team Captain:** For each team a team captain is elected out of members of the team. He knits the members as a team and is responsible for conduct of the team on and off the field.

Functions of Sports Authority of India

Sports Authority is a national body committed to promoting sports and games in the country.

It was established in 1984 to foster new sports consciousness among the youth of the country. The late Prime Minister Smt. Indira Gandhi was its first president.

In order to ensure effective implementation of sports development programmes in different regions of the country, the regional centres of erstwhile Netaji Subhash National Institutes of Sports were restructured after the amalgamation with Sports Authority of India, six regional centres were set up.

SAI has a number of schemes/programmes viz. spotting and nurturing of young talent and adoption of schools, popularly known as National Sports Talent Contest (NSTC) Scheme, Special Area Games (SAG) Schemes, Sports Hostel Scheme, Sports Project Development Area (SPDA) etc.

Some of the functions of SAI are as follows:

(*a*) To promote and develop sports activities relating and incidental thereto and to draw up and implement plans for the promotion of sports and improvement of standards in the Country in Sports and games in keeping with the sports policy of the Government of India.

(*b*) To implement and carry out the existing schemes for the promotion of sports.

(*c*) To initiate, undertake, sponsor, stimulate and encourage research and development in sports and games and the related medicines, biomechanics, psychology and other allied sports sciences.

(*d*) To provide for education, training and facilities for imparting advance coaching in various games and sports.

(*e*) To coordinate amongst and to cooperate and liaise with state governments, State Sports Council, Indian Olympic Association or National sports federations or other similar national or international associations or bodies, in matters relating to sports and games and other allied subjects.

Essentials of an Efficient and Effective Financial Management in Sports

Preparation of the financial plan is the first task of promoters. Sports' managers, promoters and physical educationists who have to plan for generating finances for some sports promotion programme for educational institutions which have financial involvement for infrastructure have to explore the following essential aspects for an effective financial management:

(*a*) **Planning foresight:** The financial plan is expected to reflect the capital requirements of the company/institution. Foresight must be used in planning the scope of operation in order that the needs for capital may be estimated as accurately as possible.

(*b*) **Optimum use of funds:** It means that the financial plan be devised in such a way that adequate capital is not only procured but every 'penny' is properly used.

(*c*) **Mode of finance:** A fixed percentage of expenditure to be done on various aspect of the sports infrastructure, building, maintenance, emergency etc. should be decided for the smooth functioning of the institution.

(*d*) **External Influence:** External influences can be Government taxation policy, State of trade or business cycle i.e. boom, repression or recession, money market conditions etc.

Principles for Planning Facilities and Equipment in a Sport Organization

Facility management is a very important administrative responsibility. Physical education and athletics have more facilities than most other educational programmes.

Following are the general principle of planning facilities and equipment in a sports organization:

(*a*) Establishing a priority for use of facilities and equipment.

(*b*) Designing of equipment and facilities that are compatible with the unique characteristics of the community.

(*c*) Facility according to the age group.

(*d*) Facilities should be designed for efficient supervision.

(*e*) Physical education professional will have to persuade key officials to incorporate new concepts in facilities.

(*f*) Planning facilities for physically handicapped students.

(*g*) Proper maintenance and replacement of worn out equipment.

(*h*) The staff associated with provision of equipment and facilities should be alert and work in a coordinated manner for injury free participation.

(*i*) Building models of renovation and innovating new facilities.

(*j*) Planning for school should recognize the different types of activities in the programmes at each educational level.

Principles of Teaching Group Activities in Physical Education

Group activities of lower organization include minor games, relays, lead up games and such other games, which have flexible rules. Group activities are important for the learning, as it is essential to develop fundamental movements patterns among the youngsters before exposure to big muscle activities.

Principles of teaching group activities are as follows :

(*a*) Children should be familiarized with the game as a whole by using audio visual aids or by organizing matches for them to witness. Learning is facilitated when the concept of the game as a whole is clear in the mind.

(*b*) Extensive use of lead up games and minor games which involve repetition of the skill being taught facilitates learning and retention for long time.

(*c*) Proper supervision is necessary so that, while learning in groups, the necessary values are maintained and that the skill is learnt with correct technique in injury free environment.

(*d*) Introduction of drills is important. Each one should get the opportunity of handling the ball or the equipment.

(*e*) It is important to give sufficient time for learning the skill in a group. Too short a time or too long would harm the process of skill learning.

(*f*) Freedom of expression to the participants giving opportunity to the better skilled participants, captains, group leaders etc. can be helpful in making the experience of group learning wholesome.

Principles of Lesson Planning in Physical Education

The principles of lesson planning vary from activity to activity. Following are some of the principles common to all lessons:

(*a*) **Warming up:** It is necessary to do minor physical exercises like jogging, jumping and mobility exercises before doing any heavy or vigorous activity.

(*b*) **Harmonious development of human being:** A lesson plan should include the activities involving maximum body parts for the balanced development of difference muscles. Exercises of arms, legs, trunk, neck should be included.

(*c*) **Age and Sex:** Activities of the lesson plan should be selected according to age and sex of the participants. Same strength exercises cannot be given to girls and boys.

(*d*) **Progression**: The exercises, which are performed in the initial stages, should be simple, leading gradually to difficult ones.

(*e*) **Repetition Exercises**: Exercise done only once will have no developmental value. Variety of drills and games should be incorporated in the lesson plan for repetition and practice of the exercise.

(*f*) **Continuity:** Continuity of the lesson should be maintained. Too long gaps in between the exercises cause boredom and break the rhythm of learning.

(*g*) **Cool down:** The body should be brought back to normal by doing some light exercises in the end.

(*h*) Apart from above mentioned factors a lesson plan should take into consideration the time management, variety of activities and fun while learning, to make it lively and enjoyable especially for youngsters.

Procedure for Care and Maintenance of Equipment in Sports

Development of proper attitude, among all students, regarding their athletic equipment is the most important consideration in the care of equipment.

1. **Leather Balls:** The valuable part of any leather ball is stitching. Deflate the balls before stacking in between the seasons. Leather balls should be dired at room temperature. Apply dobbin to carried leather and saddle soap to fanned buff leather.
2. **Rubber balls:** Avoid direct sunlight, heat, grease and oil. Remove grease and oil with soda. Keep stock as little as possible. Dust the rubber goods with French chalk.
3. **Wooden equipment:** Avoid moisture, linseed oil is recommended whenever the finish of the wood fiddlers it. Javelin and vaulting poles should be stored in such a manner as to prevent warping. Store wooden equipment in a cool dry place.
4. **Iron equipment:** Nails, poles and iron pegs require anticorrosive paints.
5. **Synthetic frank/turfs:** Modern day tracks and turfs are very costly. It is important to keep the artificial grass turfs watered periodically. Synthetic tracks for athletic events should be maintained to prevent early wearing out. Only authorized people should be allowed to use the equipment and under the supervision of Physical Education teacher or coach.

Extramural

Extramural activities as play and sports bring together participants from several institutions like that of intramural activities together the participants within a single school. Extramural helps participants compete and excel and bring laurels to their club or organisation. People participate irrespective of caste, creed and colour and social qualities are inculcated among the children.

The principles of organising extramural competitions are:

(*a*) Individual player should not be exploited for the glory of town, school or club.

(*b*) A well balanced programme of games and sports should provide opportunities for participation in sports which may be carried over into later life.

(*c*) Greater employees should be placed upon extending opportunities for participation in sports and games to all students.

(*d*) The administration of all competitions should be unitedly controlled by properly constituted committees or officials.

(*e*) Students should be given the responsibilities as Marshalls, team captain, etc. to develop leadership qualities.

(*f*) Fair play, courtesy, generosity, self control and friendly atmosphere should be developed.

EXERCISE

1. 'Getting the right facts to the right people at the right time in the right way' is called–
   (*a*) game management
   (*b*) public relations in sports
   (*c*) motivation for sports
   (*d*) leadership in sports
2. The last link of the sports management chain is–
   (*a*) control and evaluation
   (*b*) finance and budget
   (*c*) public relations
   (*d*) none of the above
3. Funds for the sports programmes can be collected through–
   (*a*) aumni associations
   (*b*) donations/ gifts
   (*c*) funds from public sector undertakings
   (*d*) all of the above
4. Objectives of a national sports organisation may be–
   (*a*) to encourage the development of sports in the country
   (*b*) to organize the championships at national and regional level
   (*c*) to participate in international events from time to time be decided
   (*d*) all of the above.
5. The ability to see the enterprise/ sports organisation as a whole is called–
   (*a*) human skill
   (*b*) conceptual skill
   (*c*) mechanical skill
   (*d*) none of the above
6. The use of a particular method of teaching depends upon–
   (*a*) skill of the teacher
   (*b*) sex of the teacher
   (*c*) age of the teacher
   (*d*) none of the above
7. Biological sciences suggest–
   (*a*) physical exercises and balanced nutrition are interrelated
   (*b*) variety of activity sustains interest
   (*c*) games and sports are great social experience
   (*d*) playfield does not recognize the distinction of caste, language, creed, colour etc.
8. Freehand activity generally done in group is called–
   (*a*) plyometrics
   (*b*) callisthenics
   (*c*) drill and marching
   (*d*) weight training
9. Which of the following is not a principle of lesson planning?
   (*a*) Age and sex
   (*b*) Progression
   (*c*) Warming up
   (*d*) Teachers experience
10. Which of the following is a method for the classification of pupil?
    (*a*) Cozen method
    (*b*) YMCA method
    (*c*) Atlanta city method
    (*d*) All of the above
11. The Rajiv Khel Ratna Award Scheme was launched in–
    (*a*) 1991-92 (*b*) 1992-93
    (*c*) 1993-94 (*d*) 1994-95
12. The fund constituted to assist sports persons of yester years living in indignant circumstances is–
    (*a*) Rural Sports Programme
    (*b*) National Welfare Fund
    (*c*) National Sport Development fund
    (*d*) National Service Volunteer Scheme
13. The award given to coaches who have trained sports persons or teams making outstanding achievements in the year is–

(*a*) Arjuna Award
(*b*) Rajiv Gandhi Khel Ratna Award
(*c*) Dronacharya Award
(*d*) None of these

14. The Arjuna Award was instituted in–
(*a*) 1960 (*b*) 1961
(*c*) 1962 (*d*) 1963

15. The National Sports Festival for Women was started in–
(*a*) 1970 (*b*) 1974
(*c*) 1975 (*d*) 1976

16. Effective communication is essential in sports management to keep alive its–
(*a*) dynamics (*b*) characteristics
(*c*) principles (*d*) foundation

17. Blue Print of the competition plan is called–
(*a*) technique (*b*) tactics
(*c*) strategy (*d*) skill

18. The first step in planning process is–
(*a*) identification of target group
(*b*) determination of goals
(*c*) mobilization of resources
(*d*) provision of facilities

19. Which of the following is against the principles of Organisation?
(*a*) Proper decentralization
(*b*) Proper communication
(*c*) Overlapping of authority
(*d*) Delegation of power

20. Intramural programme creates in students the sense of–
(*a*) achievement (*b*) involvement
(*c*) humour (*d*) enjoyment

21. A leader must possess the following except–
(*a*) missionary zeal
(*b*) commitment
(*c*) persuasiveness
(*d*) selfishness

22. The basic functions of management are–
(*a*) planning and organisation
(*b*) directing and programme development
(*c*) personal management and financial management
(*d*) all of the above

23. Ambit within which the sports management must perform is generally referred to as–
(*a*) leadership in sports
(*b*) sphere of sports management
(*c*) evaluation in sports
(*d*) innovation in sports

24. Which of the following is the first step in a sports programme?
(*a*) Directing (*b*) Staffing
(*c*) Planning (*d*) Budgeting

25. Terms Administration and Management are–
(*a*) synonymous to each other
(*b*) entirely different from each other
(*c*) somewhat similar to each other
(*d*) all of the above

26. Sports management is–
(*a*) an art (*b*) a science
(*c*) both (*a*) & (*b*) (*d*) none of the above

27. The first step in planning process is–
(*a*) determination of objectives
(*b*) resource mobilisation
(*c*) constraints identification
(*d*) evaluation of alternatives

28. Which of the following does not come under the purview of constraint identification in sports management?
(*a*) Geographical (*b*) Physiological
(*c*) Economical (*d*) Social

29. Which of the following is the prime objective of planning in sports?
(*a*) Entertainment
(*b*) For physical fitness
(*c*) Development of oneness
(*d*) All of the above

30. The plan in which only the chief executive dictates, initiates and monitors is called–
(*a*) democratic plan (*b*) participative plan
(*c*) authoritarian plan (*d*) none of the above

31. Sports Talent Search Scholarship scheme was launched in–
(*a*) 1970-71 (*b*) 1975-76
(*c*) 1977-78 (*d*) 1980-81

32. Ex-Officio president of SAI is–
   (*a*) President of India
   (*b*) Prime Minister of India
   (*c*) Union Minister of Youth Affairs & Sports
   (*d*) Director General

33. Army Boys Sports Company (ABSC) scouts talent in the age group of–
   (*a*) 12-18 years
   (*b*) 8-14 years
   (*c*) 10-14 years
   (*d*) 14-18 years

34. The Society for National Institute of Physical Education and Sports (SNIPES) merged with SAI in–
   (*a*) 1982
   (*b*) 1983
   (*c*) 1985
   (*d*) 1987

35. SAI was established in–
   (*a*) 1985 (*b*) 1984
   (*c*) 1983 (*d*) 1982

ANSWERS

1	2	3	4	5	6	7	8	9	10
(*b*)	(*a*)	(*d*)	(*d*)	(*b*)	(*a*)	(*a*)	(*a*)	(*d*)	(*d*)
11	**12**	**13**	**14**	**15**	**16**	**17**	**18**	**19**	**20**
(*a*)	(*b*)	(*c*)	(*b*)	(*c*)	(*a*)	(*c*)	(*b*)	(*c*)	(*b*)
21	**22**	**23**	**24**	**25**	**26**	**27**	**28**	**29**	**30**
(*d*)	(*d*)	(*d*)	(*c*)	(*a*)	(*c*)	(*a*)	(*d*)	(*d*)	(*c*)
31	**32**	**33**	**34**	**35**					
(*a*)	(*b*)	(*b*)	(*d*)	(*a*)					

PHYSICAL TERMINOLOGIES

A

Abscissa: The horizontal, or x-axis of a graph.

Absolute Error (AE): Amount of error, dis-regarding plus and minus signs and divided by number of scores.

Absolute Strength: The measure of a person's strength with no consideration given to body size or maximum strength.

Academic Learning Time In Physical Education (Alt-Pe): Observational recording instrument developed by Siedentop and graduate students (1979, 1982) that entails time sampling in which a child is observed for a specified period of time and the child's activities during the time period are coded.

Acknowledgements: Section of a scholarly paper that credits individuals important to the development of the work.

Adaptive Testing: Practice of selecting test items that will best fit the ability level of each individual, also called tailored testing.

Agility: The accuracy and speed of changing direction while moving.

Agon: One of four classification categories of games that describes games in which competition is dominant.

Alea: One of four classification categories of games that describes games in which the player has no control over the outcome and in which fate or luck is dominant.

Alpha: A level of probability (of chance occurrence) set by the experimenter prior to the study; sometimes referred to as level of significance.

Alternate-forms Method: Method of establishing reliability involving the construction of two tests.

Alternative Format for Thesis And Dissertation Writing: Attempt to move away from the traditional format of thesis and dissertation writing to facilitate the publication of them.

Analysis of Covariance (Ancova): A combination of regression and ANOVA that statistically adjusts the dependent variable for some distractor variable called the covariate.

Analysis of Variance (ANOVA): Test that allows the evaluation of the null hypothesis between two or more group means.

Analytical Research: Type of research that involves in-depth study and evaluation of available information in an attempt to explain complex phenomena; can be categorized in the following way; historical, philosophic, review, and meta-analysis.

Analytic History: Type of historical research that focuses on how something occurred and why someone did something.

Analytic Narrative: A short interpretive description of an event or situation used in qualitative research.

Annotated Bibliography: List of resources that provides a brief description of the nature and scope of each article or book.

Anticipation Time: Motor behaviour task using a trackway with lights mounted at close intervals that turn on and off consecutively, simulating movement. The subject attempts to press a hand-held button when the last light turns on and off.

Antiquarianism: Collecting of old things; appropriate for historical research.

Applied Research: Type of research that has direct value to practitioners but in which the researcher has limited control over the research setting.

Attitude Toward Physical Activity (ATPA) Inventory: Kenyon's (1968) well-constructed attitude inventory based on the premise that attitude toward activity is relatively stable, and that positive attitudes are manifested by active participation or by watching others perform.

Avis Effect: A threat to internal validity where in subjects in the control group may try harder just because they are in the control group.

A Band : The area located in the center of the sarcomers containing both actin and myosin.

Acceleration Sprint: Sprint in which running speed is gradually increased from jogging to striding and finally to sprinting.

Acclimatization: Pertaining to certain physiological adjustments brought about through continued exposure to a different climate, e.g., changes in altitude and heat.

Acetylcholine (ACH) : A chemical substance involved in several important physiological functions such as transmission of an impulse from one nerve fiber to another across a synapse.

Acid: A chemical compound that gives up hydrogen ions (H^+) in solution.

Actin: A protein involved in muscular contraction.

Action Potential: The electrical activity developed in a muscle or nerve cell during activity or depolarization.

Active Transport: The movement of substances or materials against their concentration gradients by the expenditure of metabolic energy.

Adenosine Diphosphate (Adp): A complex chemical compound which when combined with organic phosphate (P_1), forms ATP.

Adenosine Triphosphate (ATP): A complex chemical compound formed with the energy released from food and stored in all cells, particularly muscles. Only from the energy released by the break down of this compound can the cell perform work.

Adipocyte: A fat cell; a cell that stores fat.

Adipose Tissue: Fat tissue.

Adrenocorticotropin Hormone (Atch); or Corticotropin : A hormone secreted by the anterior lobe of the pituitary gland that stimulates the production and release of the glucocorticoid hormones from the adrenal cortex.

Aerobic: In the presence of oxygen.

Aerotitis: Inflammation or disease of the ear.

Afferent Nerve : A neuron that conveys sensory impulses from a receptor to the central nervous system.

Alactic Acid Oxygen Debt: That portion on the recovery oxygen used to resynthesize and restore ATP + PC in muscle following exercise.

Aldosterone: A mineralocorticoid.

Alkaline: Pertaining to a base.

Alkali Reserve: The amount of bicarbonate (base) available in the body for buffering.

Alkalosis: Excessive base (bicarbonate ions) in the extracellular fluids.

All-or-None Law: A stimulated muscle or nerve fiber contracts or propagates a nerve impulse either completely or not at all; in other words, a minimal stimulus causes a maximal response.

Alveolar-Capillary Membrane: The thin layer of tissue dividing the alveoli and the pulmonary capillaries where gaseous exchange occurs.

Alveolar Ventilation: The portion of inspired air that reachers the alveoli.

Alveoli (Plural); Alveolus (Singular): Tiny terminal air sacs in the lungs where gaseous exchange with the blood in the pulmonary capillaries occurs.

Ambient: Pertaining to the surrounding environment.

Amphetamine: A synthetically structured drug closely related to epinephrine; it produces stimulation of the central nervous system.

Anabolic: Protein building.

Anabolic Steroid: A compound that promotes tissue-building, i.e. is conducive to the constructive process of metabolism (other processes of metabolism are called catabolic, meaning breaking down).

Anaerobic: In the absence of oxygen

Anaerobic Glycolysis: The incomplete chemical breakdown of carbohydrate. The anaerobic reactions in this breakdown release energy for the manufacture of ATP as they produce lactic acid (anaerobic glycolysis is known as the lactic acid system).

Anaerobic Threshold: That intensity of workload or oxygen consumption in which anaerobic metabolism is accelerated.

Anatomical Dead Space (DS): That volume of fresh air that remains in the respiratory passages (nose, mouth, Pharynx, larynx, trachea, bronchi and bronchioles) and does not participate in gaseous exchange.

Androgen: Any substance that possesses masculinizing properties.

Aneamia: A lack of sufficient red blood cells or haemoglobin.

Aneurysm: Blood-filled pouches that balloon out from a weak spot in the arterial wall.

Anthropometry: The measurement of the size and proportions of the human body.

Antidiuretic Hormone: (ADH; also called VASO PRESSIN): A hormone secreted by the posterior lobe of the pituitary gland that has the function mainly to promote water reabsorption from the collecting tubules of the kidney.

Apnea (Apneic): Cessation of breathing.

Aqueous: Pertaining to water.

Arteriovenous Oxygen Difference (a-VO2 diff.): The difference between the oxygen content of arterial and mixed venous blood.

Artery: A vessel carrying blood away from the heart.

Atherosclerosis: A disease of the arteries in which lipid (fat) material and cholesterol accumulate on the inside walls of the arteries.

Atpase: An enzyme that facilitates the breakdown of ATP, ATP is manufactured when phosphocreatine (PC) is broken down. This system represents the most rapidly available source of ATP for use by muscles. Activities performed at maximum intensity in a period of 10 seconds or less drive energy (ATP) from this system.

ATPS: Ambient Temperature Pressure Saturated.

Ateriovenutricular Node (AV NODE): A specialized area of tissue located in the right atrium of the heart from which the electrical impulse initiated by the sinoatrial node spreads throughout the heart.

Autonomic Nervous System: A self controlled system that helps in central activities such as those involving movement and secretion by the visceral organs, urinary output, body temperature, heart rate, adrenal secretion and blood pressure.

Axon: A nerve fiber.

B

Basic Research: Type of research that may have limited direct application but in which the researcher has careful control of the conditions.

Beta: The magnitude of committing a Type II error; it also refers to the coefficient representing the slope of the line in regression.

Biomechanics: The application of the physical laws of motion to the study of biological systems.

Blind Setup: Method of controlling a threat to internal validity in which the subject does not know if he or she is receiving the experimental or control treatment.

Body Composition Measurement: Assessment of the ratio of lean body weight (composed of muscle, bone, and other tissues) to internal and subcutaneous fat weight.

Broadness: A method of testing the validity of necessary and sufficient conditions in philosophic research in which the conditions must be narrow enough not to include illegitimate activities.

Barometeric (Atmospheric) Pressure (P): The force per unit area exerted by the earth's atmosphere.

At sea level, it is 14.7 pounds per square inch or 760 millimeters of mercury (mm Hg.).

Beta Oxidation: The series of reactions by which fat broken down from long carbon chains to two carbon units in preparation for entry into the Krebs Cycle.

Bicarbonate Ion (HCO3): A by product of the dissociation (ionizing) of carbonic acid.

Bioenergetics: The study of energy transformations in living organisms.

Biopsy: The removal and examination of tissue from the living body.

Black Bulb Thermometer: An ordinary thermometer placed in a black globe. The black bulb temperature measures radiant energy or solar radiation and is one of three temperatures used to compute the WBGT index.

Blood Doping: The removal and subsequent reinfusion of blood under taken for the purpose of temporarily increasing blood volume and the number of red blood cells.

Blood Pressure: The driving force that moves blood through the circulatory system. Systolic pressure is obtained when blood is ejected into the arteries; diastolic pressure is obtained when the blood drains from the arteries.

Bradycardia: A decrease or slowed heart rate.

Buffer: Any substance in a fluid that lessens the change in hydrogen ion (H^+) concentration which otherwise would occur by adding acids or bases.

C

Canonical Correlation: A correlational technique that can determine the relationship when there are two or more criterion variables and two or more predictor variables.

Case Study: Form of descriptive research in which a single case is studied in depth to reach a greater understanding about other similar cases.

Categorical Response: Type of closed question that offers the subject only two responses, such as "yes" or "no".

Categorical Variable: A kind of independent variable that cannot be manipulated because it is categorized by age, race, sex, and so on; also called moderator variable.

Cattel 16 Personality Factor (Pf) Questionnaire: Instrument that has frequently been used in research studies to assess personality traits.

Central Tendency (Measure of): A single score that best represents all the scores.

Central Tendency Error: Inclination of the rate to give an inordinate number of ratings in the middle of the scale, avoiding the extremes of the scale.

Cheffers' Adaptation of the Flanders' Interaction Analysis System (CAFIAS): Observational recording instrument developed by Cheffers (1972) that provides a device for coding behaviour through a double category system so that any behaviour can be categorized as verbal, nonverbal, or both.

Chi-Square: Technique that provides a statistical test as to the significance of the discrepancy between the observed and the expected results.

Chronicle: A listing of the happenings in time; used in historical research.

Classical Test Theory (CTT): A measurement theory built on the concept of observed scores being composed of a true score and an error score.

Closed Loop Theory: Theory of motor skill learning advanced by Adams (1971) in which information received as feedback from a movement is compared to some internal reference of correctness.

Closed Question: Category of question found in questionnaires or interviews that requires a specific response and that often takes the form of rankings, scaled items, and categorical response.

Coaches Behavioural Assessment Scale– (CBAS): Recording instrument developed by Smith, Smoll and (1977) to record the reactive and spontaneous behaviours of the coach to actions of players during games.

Coefficient of Correlation: A quantitative value of the relationship between two or more variables that can range from 0.00 to 1.00 in either a positive or negative direction; also called correlations.

Coefficient of Determination: The squared correlation coefficient; used in interpreting meaningfulness of correlations.

Cohorts: Problem in cross-sectional design that questions whether all the age groups are really from the same population.

Compound Symmetry: Antiquated assumption that a variable within a group must have equal variances, all correlations among variables must be equal, and the covariance matrices of all groups must be equal.

Concurrent Validity: Type of criterion validity in which a measuring instrument is correlated with some criterion that is administrated at about the same time, or concurrently.

Confirmatory Factor Analysis: A type of factor analysis that tests hypotheses about the structuring of variables with regard to the expected number of significant factors.

Constant Error (CE): Algebraic sum of plus and minus error divided by number of scores.

Construct Validity: Condition that is claimed (usually in educational settings) when a test adequately samples what was covered in course.

Context: In historical research, the total network of facts and meanings in the background of a subject.

Contingency Coefficient: Method of computing the relationship between dichotomus variables such as gender and race.

Contingency Table: A two-way classification of categories of occurrences and two or more groups that is used for computing the significance of the differences between observed and expected scores.

Control Variable: A factor that could possibly influence the results and that is kept out of the study.

Convergence: Consistency of results across two or more methodological techniques.

Convergent Validity: Correlations between measures of the same construct.

Correlation Research: Research that explores relationships among variables; sometimes involves prediction of a criterion variable.

Covariate: A distractor variable that is statistically controlled in ANCOVA and MANCOVA.

Cover Letter: The letter attached to a survey that explains the purposes and importance of the survey.

Cowell Social Adjustment Index: An early social behaviour rating scale developed by Cowell (1958) that involves teacher ratings of the degree to which students display certain behaviour traits.

Criterion Validity: The degree to which scores on a test are related to some recognized standard, or criterion.

Critical Theory: A value-based form of qualitative research that helps individuals make constructive choices.

Cronabach Alpha Coefficient: A technique use in estimating reliability of multiple trial test also called coefficient alpha.

Cross Sectional Study: Method of research in which samples of subjects from different age groups are secured in order to assess the effects of maturation.

Cross Validation: Technique to assess the accuracy of a prediction formula in which the formula is applied to a sample not used when the formula was developed.

Calcitonin: A hormone secreted by the thyroid gland that causes a decrease in the blood calcium level. It is thought that calcitonin may also be secreated from the parathyroid glands.

Calorie (cal): A unit of work or energy equal to the amount of heat required to raise the temperature of one gram of water through 1°C.

Calorimeter: Measures heat production in the human body.

Capillary: A fine network of small vessels located between arteries and veins where exchange between tissue and blood occurs.

Carboamino Compounds: The end product obtained from the chemical combination of plasma proteins and/ or haemoglobin (Hb) and carbon dioxide (CO_2)

Carbaminohemoglobin: A carboamino compound is formed in the red blood cells when CO_2 reacts with Hb.

Carbohydrate: Any of a group of chemical compounds including sugars, starches, and cellulose, containing carbon, hydrogen and oxygen only. One of the basic foodstuffs.

Carbonic Anhydrase: An enzyme that speeds up the reaction of carbon dioxide (CO_2) with water (H_2O).

Cardiac Cycle: Contraction (systole) and relaxation (diastole) of the heart.

Cardiac Output (Q): The amount of blood pumped by the heart in one minute; the product of the stroke volume and the heart rate.

Cardiorespiratory Endurance: The ability of the lungs and heart to take in and supply adequate amounts of oxygen to the working muscles, allowing activation that involve large muscle masses (e.g. running, swimming, bicycling) to be performed over long periods of time.

Cerebellum: That division or part of the brain concerned with co-ordination of movement.

Cerebral Cortex: That portion of the brain responsible for, mental functions, movement, visceral functions, perception and behavioral reactions, and for the association and integration of these functions.

Cerebral Thrombosis: A blood clot in the brain.

Cholesterol: A fat-like compound found in animal tissue that cause atherosclerosis.

Cholinesterase: A chemical that activates or breaks down acetylchotine.

Concentric Contraction: The shortening of a muscle during contraction.

Conditioning: Augmentation of the energy capacity of muscle through a exervise program. Conditioning is not primarily concerned with the skills performance as would be the case of training.

Cholesterol: A fat-like compound found in animal tissue that cause alterosclerosis.

Conduction: The transfer of heat between objects of different temperature in direct contact with each other.

Continuous Work: Exercises per formed to completion without test periods.

Convection: The transfer of heat from one place to another by the motion of heated substance.

Cortisol: A glucocorticoid.

Coupled Reactions: Two series of chemical reactions, one of which releases energy (heat) for use by the other.

Cross-Bridges: Extensions of myosin.

Cryogenic: Pertaining to the production of low temperatures.

D

Decision Accuracy: Approach used to validate criterion-referenced tests that assess the accuracy of classification of individuals to mastery and nonmastery categories.

Deductive Reasoning: Logical process in which the researcher moves from a theoretical explanation of events down to specific hypotheses about events.

Delimitation: A limitation, imposed by the researcher, in the scope of the study; a choice the researcher makes to effect a workable research problem.

Delphi Survey Method: Survey technique that uses a series of questionnaires in such a way that the respondents (usually experts) reach a consensus about the subject.

Dependent Test: A test of the significance of difference between means of two sets of scores that are related, such as when the same subjects are measured on two occasions.

Dependent Variable: Effect of the independent variable also called the yield.

Descriptive History: A method of constructing a "map" of past experience that locates in time and place a person, a trend, an event, or an organization by providing answers to particular questions.

Descriptive Research: Type of research concerned with status, including techniques such as surveys, case studies, and developmental research.

Developmental Research: Study of changes in behaviour across the life span.

Discriminant Validity: Evidence of validity demonstrated by weak correlations between measures of different constructs; also called divergent validity.

Discussion: Chapter or section of a research report that explains what the results mean.

Documentary Analysis: Type of descriptive research directed primarily at establishing the status of certain practices; areas of interest; and the prevalence of certain errors, usage of terms and space counts.

Domain-Referenced Validity: The degree to which a test measures essential component or objectives of a domain.

D Study: An approach employed in generalisability theory in which the researcher calculates generalisability coefficients for the various facts in the study.

Dual Publication: Occurrence of having the same scientific paper published in more than one journal or other publication; generally unethical.

Duration Method: Method of recording in observational research in which the researcher uses a stopwatch or other timing device to record how much time a subject spends engaged in a particular behaviour.

Dynamic Balance: The ability to maintain equilibrium while moving.

Dehydration: The condition that results from excessive loss of body water.

Density: The mass per unit volume of the object.

Diastole: The resting phase of the cardiac cycle.

Diastolic Volume: The amount of blood that fills the ventricle during diastole.

Diffusion: The random movement of molecules due to their kinetic energy.

Dopamine: An excitatory neurotransmitter chemical.

Dendrite: A nerve fibre.

Double Blind Study: An experimental protocol in which neither the investigator nor the subjects know which group is receiving a placebo and which group the real drug.

Douglas Bag: A rubber-lined, canvas bag used for collection of expired gas.

Drug: A chemical substance given with the intention of preventing or curing disease or otherwise enhancing the physical or mental disturbances of human or animals.

Dry Bulb Thermometer: A common thermometer used to record temperature of the air.

Dysmenorrhea: Painful menstruation.

Dyspnea: Laboured breathing.

E

Ecological Validity: The extent to which research emulates the real world.

Effect Size: A standardized value, the difference between the means divided by the standard deviation.

Eigen Values: The squared and summed correlations of each variable, or test, for a factor; the y-axis on a screen curve.

Electrogoniometer: Instrument used to measure flexibility.

Electromyography (EMG): Technique that uses skin or muscle electrodes to pick up electrical activity caused by muscle contraction during movement.

Empirical: Describes data or a study that is based on objective observations.

Endogenous Variable: A characteristic in path analysis whose variance is explained by exogenous variables, other variables within the model, or both.

Equally Likely Events: A concept of probability in which the chances of one event occurring are the same as the chances of another event occurring.

Error Score: In classical test theory, the part of an observed score that is attributed to measurement error.

Error Variance: The portion of the scores that is attributed to subject variability.

Expectancy: A threat to internal validity in which the researcher anticipates certain behaviour or results to occur.

Experimental Research: Type of research that involves the manipulation of treatments in an attempt to establish cause-effect relationships.

Exploratory Factor Analysis: Factor analysis performed for the purpose of identifying basic constructs, or factors, that underlie a set of measures.

Exogenous Variable: A characteristic in path analysis whose variance is explained by factors outside the model.

External Criticism: Phase of historical research process that establishes the authenticity of the sources.

External Reliability: The content of the data in qualitative research that determines the degree to which a study can be repeated.

External Validity: The generalisability of the results of a study.

Extraneous Variable: A factor that could affect the relationship between the independent and dependent variables, but that is not included or controlled.

Eccentric Contraction: The muscle lengthens while contracting (developing tension).

Ectomorpy: A body type component characterized by linearity, fragility, and delicacy of body.

Efferent Nerve: A neuron that conveys motor impulses away form the central nervous system to an organ of response such as skeletal muscle.

Efficiency: The ratio of work output to work input.

Electrical Potential: The capacity for producing electrical effects, such as an electric current, between two bodies (e.g., between the inside and outside of a cell).

Electrocardiogram (ECG): A recording of the electrical activity of the heart.

Electrolyte: A substance that ionizes solution such as salt (NaCl) and is capable of conducting an electrical current.

Electron: A negatively charged particle.

Electron Transport System (ETS): A series of chemical reactions occurring in mitochondria, in which electrons and hydrogen ions combine with oxygen to form water, and ATP is resynthesized. Also referred to as the respiratory chain.

Emboluis (singular); Emboli (plural): A clot of other plug transported by the blood from another vessel and forced into a smaller one, thus obstructing circulation.

Endocrine Gland: An organ or gland that produces an internal secretion (hormone).

Endomorphy: A body type component characterized by roundness and softness of the body.

Endomysium: A connective tissue surrounding a muscle fibre or cell.

Energy: The capacity or ability to perform work.

Energy System: One of three metabolic systems involving a series of chemical reactions resulting in the formation of waste products and the manufacture of ATP.

Engram: A memorized motor pattern stored in the brain; a permanent trace left by a stimulus in the tissue protoplasm.

Enzyme: A protein compound that speeds up a chemical reaction.

Epimysium: A connective tissue surrounding the entire muscle.

Epinephrine: A hormone secreted by the medulla of the adrenal gland that has effects on the heart, the blood vessels, metabolism, and the central nervous system.

Ergogenic Aid: Any factor that improves work performance.

Ergometer: An apparatus or device such as a treadmill or stationary bicycle used for measuring the physiological effect of exercise.

Estrogen: The female androgen.

Evaporation: The loss of heat resulting from changing a liquid to vapour.

Excitation: A response to a stimulus.

Excitatory Postsynaptic Potential (EPSP): A transient increase in electrical potential depolarization in a postsynaptic neuron from its resting membrane potential.

Exercise-Recovery: The performance of light exercise during recovery from exercise.

Expiratory Reserve Volume (ERV): Maximal volume of air expired from end-expiration.

Extracellular: Outside the cell.

Extrafusal Fibre: A typical or normal muscle cell or fibre.

Extrasystole: An extra heartbeat.

F

Factor Analysis: A statistical technique used to reduce a set of data by grouping similar variables into basic components (factors).

Factorial Anova: Analysis of variance in which there is more than one independent variable.

Family Resemblance Theory: Theory in philosophic research in which, in an attempt to unify components of a concept, the research recognizes that though the components lack specific shared characteristics, they share a system of overlapping features.

Field Work: A methodology common in qualitative research in which data are gathered in natural settings.

Fisher Z Transformation: Method of approximating normality of a sampling distribution of linear relationship by transforming coefficients of correlation to z-values.

Force Transducer: Device in biomechanical research that measures the forces exerted during motor performance, including the reactions between a runner's or jumper's feet and the ground as well as the forces exerted against equipment.

Forward Selection: Procedure used in multiple regression and discriminant analysis that enters the variables for prediction or discrimination among groups, in order of their importance.

Facilitated Diffusion: Diffusion that takes place with the help of a carrier substance.

Fasciculus (singular); Fasciculi (plural): A group of bundle of skeletal muscle fibres held together by a connective tissue called the perimysium.

Fast Twitch Fibre (FT): A muscle fibre characterized by fast contraction time, high anaerobic capacity, and low aerobic capacity, all making the fibre suited for high power output activities.

Fat: A compound containing glycerol and fatty acids. One of the basic foodstuffs.

Fatigue: A state of discomfort and decrease efficiency resulting from prolonged or excessive exertion.

Fatty Acid (Free Fatty Acid): The usable form of triglycerides.

Fibrillation: Irregularity in force and rhythm of the heart, or quivering of the muscle fibers, causing inefficient emptying.

Fibrinolysis: The dissolving of a blood clot.

Flaccid: Lacking muscular tonus.

Flexometer: An instrument used for measuring the range of motion about a joint (static flexibility).

Follicle-Stimulating Hormone (FSH): A hormone secreted by the anterior lobe of the pituitary gland that promotes growth of the ovarian follicle in the female and spermatogenesis in the male.

Foot-Pound: A work unit that is, application of a one pound force through a distance of one foot.

Fulcrum: The axis of rotation for a lever.

Functional Residual Capacity (FRC): Volume of air in the lungs at resting expiratory level.

G

Gain Score: The result of subtracting each subject's pretest value from the post test value.

Geisser/ Greenhouse Correction: A conservation approach to the adjustment of the epsilon estimate in repeated measures ANOVA that calculates adjusted degrees of freedom to find an F ratio to determine significance.

Generalisability Theory (G-theory): An extension of intraclass reliability that enables the researcher to identify sources of error in estimating reliability of scores on a test.

Gonimeter: Instrument used to measure the ranges of motion in a joint.

Goodness of Fit: Approach to philosophic inquiry in which the researcher, following exposure to a paradigm, attempts to determine whether some activity or object can be shown to properly fit as an instance of that paradigm (also a x^2 estimate used in confirmatory factory analysis).

Grounded Theory: A theory based on and evolving from data.

G-Study: An approach employed in generalisability theory that used repeated measure ANOVA to help identify the relative importance of different sources of variance that contribute to measurement error.

Gama-Aminobutyric Acid (GABA): An inhibitory neurotransmitter substance.

Gamma Motor Neuron: A type of efferent nerve cell that innervates the ends of an intrafusal muscle fibre.

Gamma System (Gamma Loop): The contraction of a muscle as a result of stretching the muscle spindle by way of stimulation of the gamma motor neurons.

Glucagon: A hormone secreted by pancreas and that causes increased blood glucose levels.

Glucocorticoids: A class of hormones secreted by the cortex of the adrenal gland, that promotes the increased synthesis of glucose from amino acids (glyconeogenesis), depress liver lipogenesis (formation of fat), mobilize fat in adipose tissues, maintain vascular reactivity, and inhibit the inflammatory reaction.

Glucose: A sugar.

Glycine: A simple amino acid, thought to be the main inhibitory transmitter in the spinal cord.

Glycogen: A polymer of glucose, the form in which glucose (sugar) is stored in the body, mainly in muscles and the liver.

Glycogenesis: The manufacture of glycogen from glucose.

Glycogen Loading (super-compensation) : An exercise diet procedure that elevates muscle glycogen stores to concentrations 2 to 3 times normal.

Glycogenolysis: The breakdown of glycogen to glucose.

Glycogen Sparing: The diminished utilization of glycogen that results when other fuels are available (and are used) for activity, if, for instance, fat is used to a greater extent than usual, glycogen is "spared", glycogen will thus be available longer before ultimately being depleted.

Glycolysis: The incomplete chemical breakdown of glycogen. In aerobic glycolysis, the end product is pyruvic acid; in anaerobic glycolysis (lactic acid system), the end product, is lactic acid.

Glyconeogenesis: The manufacturing of carbohydrates (glycogen) form noncarbohydrate sources such as fat and protein.

Golgi Tendon Organ: A proprioceptor located within a muscular tendon.

Growth Hormone (GH); also called Somatotropin (STH): A hormone secreted by the anterior lobe of the pituitary gland that stimulates growth and development.

H

Halo Effect: A threat to internal validity wherein raters allow previous impressions or knowledge about a certain individual to influence rating on all of that individual's behaviours.

Hardware: The mechanical units of a computer, such as the monitor, keyboard, disk drive, and printer.

High-Speed Cinematography: Most widely used measure in biomechanics in which a camera or cameras allow motion to be studied.

Historical Research: Type of research that deals with events that have already occurred.

Hydrostatic Weighing: Technique that measures body composition in which body density is computed by the ratio of an individual's weight in air and the loss of weight underwater.

Hypothesis: The anticipated outcome of a study or experiment.

Heart Attack: The blocking of blood flow to a portion of the heart muscle.

Heat: A form of energy.

Heat Cramps: Painful muscular contraction caused by prolonged exposure to environmental heat.

Heat Exhaustion: A condition of fatigue caused by prolonged exposure to environmental heat.

Heat Stroke: A disease caused by overexposure to heat and characterized by high body (rectal) temperature, hot, dry skin (usually flushed), and unconsciousness. It can be fatal.

Haematuria: Discharge of blood into the urine.

Haemoconcentration: Concentration of the blood.

Haemodilution: Dilution of the blood.

Haemodynamics: The study of the physical law governing blood flow.

Haemoglobin (Hb): A complex molecule found in red blood cells, which contains iron (haem) and protein (globin) and is capable of combining with oxygen.

Haemolysis: The rupture of a cell, such as the red blood cell.

High Density Lipoproteins (HDL): A specific kind of cholesterol found in the blood. Thought to be protective against coronary heart disease.

Hollow Sprints: Two sprints interrupt by a (hollow) period involving either jogging or walking.

Hormone: A discrete chemical substance secreted into the body fluids by an endocrine gland that has a specific effect on the activities of other cells, tissues, and organs.

Humidity: Pertaining to the moisture in the air.

Hydraulic Pressure: The force per unit area resulting from a vertical column of water of certain height.

Hypernatremia: Increased sodium concentration in the blood.

Hyperplasia: An increase in the number of cells in a tissue or organ.

Hypertension: High blood pressure.

hypertonic: Pertaining to a solution having a greater tension or osmotic pressure than one with which it is being compared.

Hypervolemia: An increased blood volume.

Hypotension: Low blood pressure.

Hypothalamus: That portion of the brain that exerts control over visceral activities, water balance, body temperature, and sleep.

Hypotonic: Pertaining to a solution having a lesser tension or osmotic pressure than one with which it is being compared.

Hypoxia: Lack of adequate oxygen due to a reduced oxygen partial pressure.

H Zone: The area in the centre of the band where the cross-bridges are absent.

I

Ilinx: One of four classification categories of games that describes games that are based on the pursuit of vertigo and that consist of an attempt to momentarily destroy the stability of perception.

Implications Approach: Method of philosophic research in which the researcher, following exposure to a paradigm, attempts to determine what a given phenomenon would or should be like if it were to conform to that paradigm; also called extra polations approach.

Independent Variable: The part of the experiment that the researcher is manipulating; also called the experimental or treatment variable.

Index of Discrimination: The degree to which a test item discriminates between persons who did well on the entire test and those who did poorly; also called item discrimination.

Inductive Reasoning: Logical process in which the researcher moves from specific observations through testing hypothesis to developing a general theory.

Inference: Generalisation of results to some larger group.

Internal Consistency: An estimate of the reliability of a set of scores that represents the consistency of repeated measures given on the same day; also called same-day test-retest method.

Internal Criticism: Phase of historical research process that establishes the credibility of a genuine artifact or document.

Internal Validity: The extent to which the results of a study can be attributed to the treatments used in the study.

Interobserver Agreement (IOA): Common way of estimating reliability among coders by using a formula that divides the number of commonly coded behaviours by the sum of the commonly coded behaviours and behaviours coded differently.

Intertester (Interrater) Reliability: The degree to which different testers can obtain the same scores on the same subjects; also called objectivity.

Interval Method: Method of recording in observational research, used when it is difficult to count individual occurrences, in which the researcher records whether the behaviour in question occurs in a certain interval of time.

Interval Scale: Scale of measurement that provides not only the order between scorers, but also the magnitude of the distance between them.

interview: Survey technique similar to the questionnaire except that subjects are questioned and respond verbally rather than in writing.

Intraclass Correlation: A correlation co-efficient, computed by analysis of variances, that is used in estimating test reliability.

Item Analysis: Process in analyzing knowledge test in which items are evaluated as to their suitability with regard to difficulty and discrimination.

Item Banking: The creation of large pools of test items that can be used for constructing tests that have certain characteristics with regard to the precision of estimating latent ability.

Item Characteristic Curve (ICC): Nonlinear regression for any item that increases from left to right, indicating an increase in the probability of a correct response with increased ability, or latent trait.

Item Difficulty: Analysis of the difficulty of each test item in a knowledge test determined by dividing the number of persons who correctly answered the item by the total number of people who responded to the item.

Item Response Theory (IRT): A theory that focuses on the characteristics of the test item and the examinee's response to the item as a means of determining the examinee's ability; also called latent trait theory.

I Band: That area of a myofibril containing action and bisected by a Z line.

Inert: Having no action.

Inhibitory Postsynaptic Potential (IPSP) : A transient decrease in electrical potential (hyperpolarization) in a postsynapticneuron from its resting membrance potential.

Inspiration Capacity (IC): Maximal volume of air inspired from resting expiratory level.

Inspiratory Reserve Volume (IRV): Maximal volume of air inspired from end-inspiration.

Insulin: One of the hormones secreted from the pancreas and that causes increased cellular uptake of glucose.

Intermittent Work: Exercise performed with alternate periods of relief as opposed to continuous work.

Interneuron (Internuncial Neuron): A nerve cell located between afferent (sensory) and efferent (motor) nerve cells. It acts as a "middleman" between incoming and outgoing impulses.

Interstitial: Pertaining to the area or space between cells.

Interstitial Fluid: The fluid between the cells.

Interval Sprinting: A method of training whereby an athlete alternately sprints 50 yards and jogs 60 yards for distances up to three miles.

Interval Training: A system of physical conditioning in which the body is subjected to short but regularly repeated periods of work stress interspread with adequate periods of relief.

Intrafusal Fibre: A muscle cell (fibre) that houses the muscle spindle.

Ion: An electrically charged particle.

Ischemia: Local and temporary deficiency of blood, chiefly due to the contraction of a blood vessel.

Isokinetic Contraction: Contraction in which the tension developed by the muscle while shortening at constant speed is maximum over the full range of motion.

Isometric (Static) Contraction: Contraction in which tension is developed but there is no change in the length of the muscle.

Isotonic: Pertaining to solutions having the same tension or osmotic pressure.

Isotonic Contraction: Contraction in which the muscle shortens with varying tension while lifting a constant load. Also referred to as a dynamic or concentric contraction.

J

Job Analysis: Type of case study that determines the nature of a particular job and the types of training, preparation, skills, and attitudes necessary for success in the job.

Jogging: Slow, continuous running. Also refers to all speeds of running.

Joint Receptors: A group of sense organs located in joints concerned with kinesthesis.

K

Kinesiology: The study of human movement dealing with the interrelationship of anatomy, neuromuscular physiology, and mechanics.

Kinesthetic Measurement: Measurement of one's ability to perceive body position and changes in force and degree of movement of the body and body parts. Method used in establishing construct validity in which the test scores of groups that should differ on a trait or ability are compared.

Kuder-Richardson (K-R) Method of Rational Equivalence: Formulas developed for estimating reliability of a test from a single test administration.

Kurtosis: Description of the shape of the curve of the distribution of data, for example, whether the curve is more peaked or flatter than the normal curve.

Kilocalorie (Kcal): A unit of work or energy equal to the amount of heat required to raise the temperature of one kilogram of water 1°C.

Kilogram-metres kg-m: A unit of work.

Kilojoules (KJ): Unit of energy.

Kinesthesis: Awareness of body position.

Krebs Cycle: A series of chemical reactions occurring in mitochondria, in which carbon dioxide is produced and hydrogen ions and electrons are removed from carbon atoms (oxidation). Also referred to as the tricarbocyclic acid cycle (TCA), or citric acid cycle.

L

Lakie Attitude Toward Athletic Competition Scale: Pencil and paper tests of sportsmanship developed by Lakie (1964) in which the responded is asked to indicate whether the course of action described is appropriate.

Language Analysis: Method of philosophic inquiry aimed at detecting contradictory or confusing ways in which terms are used.

Law: Generalisation about natural phenomena that describes what some "thing" is, often expressed mathematically.

Leniency: Tendency for observers to be overly generous in rating.

Likert Scale: Type of closed question that requires the subject to respond by choosing one of five scaled items with the assumption that there are equal intervals between items.

Limitation: A possible shortcoming or influence that either cannot be controlled or is the result of the delimitations imposed by the investigatory.

Linear Slide: A motor task in which a blind-folded subject attempts to move a near-frictionless handle down a trackway to some specified location or a certain distance.

Linear Structural Relations (Lisrel): A statistical approach used to establish relationships and examine the structural equations model.

Logical Validity: Condition that is claimed when the measure obviously involves that performance being measured; also known as face validity.

Logit: Probability of membership in a particular category occurring as a function of membership in other categories in multi-variate contingency tables.

Loglinear Model: A system that analyses multivariate contingency tables by transforming relative frequencies into logarithms.

Longitudinal Study: Research in which the same subject are studied over a period of year.

Lactacid Oxygen Debt: That portion of the recovery oxygen used to remove accumulated lactic acid from the blood following exercise.

Lactic Acid (Lactate): A fatiguing metabolite of the lactic acid system resulting from the incomplete break down of glucose (sugar).

Lactic Acid System (La System): An anaerobic energy system in which ATP is manufactured when glucose (sugar) is broken down to lactic acid. High intensity efforts requiring one to three minutes to perform draw energy (ATP) primarily from this system.

Lean Body Mass (Weight): The body weight minus the weight of the body fat.

Lever: A rigid bar (such as a bone) that is free to rotate about a fixed point or axis called a fulcrum (such as a joint).

Linear: Pertaining to a straight line.

Low Density Lipoproteins (LDL): A specific kind of cholesterol found in the blood, though to cause atherosclerosis.

Luteinizing Hormone (Lh) or Interstitial Cell Stimulating Hormone (Icsh): A hormone secreted by the anterior lobe of the pituitary gland that stimulates ovulation, formation of the corpus luteum, and hormone secretion in the female; and stimulates secretion by interstitial cells in the male.

M

Main Effects: Tests of each independent variable when all other independent variables are held constant.

Mainframe: A large computer.

Maxicon Principle: A method off controlling any explanation for the results except the hypothesis the researcher intends to evaluate. This is done by maximizing true variance, minimizing error variance, and controlling extraneous variance.

Maximum R2 Method: A multiple regression method in which the so-called best of all possible one-variable models is selected, as is the best two-variable model, the best three-variable mode, and so on until a predetermined criterion that ends the calculations is reached.

Mean: A statistical measure of central tendency that is the average score of the group.

Median: A statistical measure of central tendency describing the middle score in a group.

Meta-Analysis: A technique of literature review that contains a definitive methodology and the quantification of the results of various studies to a standard metric that allows the use of statistical techniques as a means of analysis.

Microcomputer: A small desktop computer.

Microform: A general term that encompasses microfilm, microfiche, and any form of data storage where the pages of a book, journal or newspaper are photographed and reduced in size.

Mimicry: One of four classification categories of games that describes games in which players make believe or try to make others believe that they are someone other than themselves.

Mode: A statistical measure of central tendency that is the most frequently occurring score of the group.

Motor Time (MT): The peripheral component of reaction time comprised of the interval between the first muscle action potential and the initiation of the movement.

Multiple Regression: Model used for predicting a criterion from two or more independent, or predictor, variables.

Multivariate Analysis of Covariance (Ancova): An extension of ANCOVA in which there are two or more covariates.

Multivariate Analysis of Variance (Manova): Analysis of variance wherein a combination of dependent variables is made that will maximally separate the levels of the independent variables.

Muscular Endurance: The ability to persevere in working against a submaximal resistance.

Maximal Heart Rate Reserve (HRR): The difference between the resting heart rate and the maximal heart rate.

Maximal Oxygen Consumption (max Vo2): The maximal rate at which oxygen can be consumed per minute, the power or capacity of the aerobic or oxygen system.

Medulla Oblongata: That portion or area of the brain continuous above with the pons and below with the spinal cord and containing the cardiorespiratory control centre.

Medullated Nerve Fibre: A nerve fibre containing a myelin sheath.

Membrane: A thin layer of tissue that covers a surface of divides a space of organ.

Menarche: The onset of menstruation.

Menses: The monthly flow of blood from the genital tract of women.

Menstruation: The process or an instance of discharging the menses.

Mesomorphy: A body type component characterized by a square body with hard, rugged, and prominent musculature.

Metabolic System: A system of biochemical reactions which cause the formation of waste products (metabolites) and the manufacture of ATP for example, the ATP-PC, lactic acid and oxygen systems.

Metabolism: The sum total of the chemical changes or reactions occurring in the body.

Metabolite: Any substance produced by a metabolic reaction.

Millimore: One thousandth of a mole.

Mineralocorticoids: A class of hormones secreted by the cortex of the adrenal gland, that function to increase the reabsorption of sodium from the distal tubules of the kidney. The most important mineralocorticoid is aldosterone.

Minute Ventilation: The amount of air inspired (V1) or expired (V) in one minute; usually it refers to the expired amount.

Mitochondrion (singular); Mitochondria (plural): A subcellular structure found in all aerobic cells in which the reactions of the Krebs cycle and electron transport system take place.

Moment (Moment Arm): The perpendicular distance from the line of action of the force to the point of rotation.

Motoneuron (Motor Neuron): A nerve cell, which when stimulated effects muscular contraction, most motoneurons innervate skeletal muscle.

Motor End-Plate: The neuromuscular or myoneural junction.

Motor Engrams: Memorized motor patterns that are stored in the motor area of the brain.

Motor Unit: An individual motor nerve and all the muscle fibers it innervates.

Mountain (Altitude) Sickness: A condition resulting from exposure to high altitude. Symptoms include nausea, vomiting, headache, rapid pulse, and loss of appetite.

Muscle Spindle: A proprioceptor located within an intrafusal muscle fiber.

Muscular Endurance: The ability of a muscle or muscle group to perform repeated contractions against a high ioad for an extended period of time.

Myelin Sheath: A structure composed mainly of lipid (fat) and protein that surrounds some nerve fibres (axoms).

Myocardial Contractility: The strength of ventricular contraction.

Myofibril: That part of a muscle fibre containing two protein filaments, myosin and actin.

Myoglobin: An oxygen-binding pigment similar to haemoglobin that gives the red muscle fibre its colour. It acts as an oxygen store and aids in the diffusion of oxygen.

Myosin: A protein involved in muscular contraction.

N

Narrative Technique: Method of recording in qualitative research in which the researcher records in a series of sentences the occurrences as they happen; also called continual recording technique.

Narrative Vignette: Component of qualitative research reports that gives detailed descriptions of an event, including what people say, do, think and feel in that setting.

Narrowness: A method of testing the validity of necessary and sufficient conditions in philosophic research in which the conditions must be broad enough that legitimate activities are not ruled out.

Negative Case Selection: Procedure used in theorizing in which the researcher looks for exceptions to the hypothesized construct that require either a reformulation of the hypothesis, a redefinition of the second variable.

Nominal Measure: Method of classifying data into categories such as gender, age, grade level, or treatment groups.

Nominal Scale: Scale of measurement in which the scores are classified by name.

Nonparametric Statistical Test: Any number of statistical techniques used when the data do not meet the assumptions required to perform parametric tests.

Normal Curve: Distribution of data in which the mean, median, and mode are at the same point (center of the distribution and ‡1s from the mean includes 68% of the scores ‡2s from the means includes 95% of the scores, ‡3s includes 99% of the scores.

Normal Science: An objective manner of study grounded in the natural sciences that is systematic, logical, empirical, reductive, and replicable.

Normative Survey: Survey method that involves establishing norms for abilities, performances, beliefs, and attitudes.

Null Hypothesis: Hypothesis that is primarily used in the statistical test for the reliability of the results that says that there are no differences among treatments (or no relationship among variables).

Neurosis: Death of a cell or group of cells in contact with living tissue.

Negative Energy Balance: A condition in which less energy (food) is taken in than is given, off; body weight decreases as a result.

Nerve Impulse: An electrical disturbance at the point of stimulation of nerve that is self-propagated along the entire length of the axon.

Net Oxygen Cost: The amount of oxygen, above resting values, required to perform a given amount of work. Also referred to as net cost of exercise.

Neuromuscular (Myoneural) Junction: The union of muscle and its nerve. Also referred to as the motor endplate.

Neuron: A nerve cell consisting of a cell body (soma), with its nucleus and cytoplasm, dendrites and axons.

Nitrogen Narcosis (Ruptures of the Deep): A condition affecting the central nervous system (much as does alcohol) due to the forcing (by pressure) of nitrogen into solution within the body; symptoms include dizziness, slowing of mental processes, euphoria, and fixation of ideas.

Nodes of Ranvier: Those areas on a medullated nerve that are devoid of a myeline sheath.

Nomogram: A graph enabling one to determine by aid of a straight edge the value of a dependent variable when the values of two independent variables are known.

Nonmedulated Nerve Fibre: A nerve fibre entirely devoid of a myolin sheath.

Norepinephrine: A hormone secreted by the medulla of the adrenal gland that has effects on the heart, the blood vessels, metabolism, and the central nervous system. Also the major neurotransmitter substance released at the ends of the sympathetic postganglionic fibres of the autonomic nervous system.

O

Oblique Rotation: A method in factor analysis in which the factors are redefined (and allowed to correlate) in order to make sharper distinctions in the meanings of the factors.

Observed Score: In classical test theory, an obtained score which is comprised of a person's true score an error score.

Observer Bias Error: Inclination of a rater to be influenced by his or her own characteristic and prejudices.

Omega Square (W2): A method of interpreting the meaningfulness of the strength of the relationship between the independent and dependent variables; the proportion of total variance that is due to the treatments.

One-Tailed t Test: Test that assumes that the difference between the two means lies in one direction only.

Open-Ended Question: Category of question in questionnaires and interviews that allows the respondent considerable latitude to express feelings and to expand on ideas.

Operational Definition: Observable phenomenon that enables the researcher to empirically test whether or not the predicted out comes can be supported.

Oral Presentation: Method of presenting a paper in which the author speaks before a group of colleagues at a conference following this format: introduction, statements of the problem, method, results, discussion, questions.

Ordinal Scale: Scale of measurement in which scores are classified by ranks.

Ordinate: The vertical, or y-, axis of a graph.

Original Position: Philosophic concept that describes the hypothetical situation in which all people seek fulfillment of their personal interests and desires.

Orthogonal Rotation: Technique in factor analysis designed to maximize the loadings of the tests, or variables, and minimize the relation among factors; also called varimax rotation.

Outlier: Unrepresentative score; a score that lies outside of the normal scores.

Overlap: A scientific model and the approaches used to test that model; also called perspective, tradition, and approach in historical research.

Obese (Obesity): Having excessive accumulation and storage of fatty tissue.

Osmosis: The diffusion through a semipermeable membrane of a solvent such as water from a lower to a more concentrated solution.

Osmotic Pressure: The force per unit area needed to stop osmosis.

Overload Principle: Progressively increasing the intensity of the workouts over the course of the training program as fitness capacity improves.

Oxidation: The removal of electrons.

Oxygen Debt: The amount of oxygen consumed during recovery from exercise, above that ordinarily consumed at rest in the same time period. There is a rapid component (alactacid) and a slow component (lactacid).

Oxygen Deficit: The time period during exercise in which the level of oxygen consumption is below that necessary to supply all the ATP required for the exercise, the time period during which an oxygen debt is contracted.

Oxygen Poisoning (Toxicity): A condition caused by breathing oxygen under high pressure. Symptoms include tingling of fingers and toes, visual disturbances auditory hallucinations confusion, muscle and lip twitching nausea, vertigo and convulsions.

Oxygen System: Anaerobic energy system in which ATP is manufactured when food (principally sugar and fat) is broken down. This system produces ATP most abundantly and is the prime energy source during long lasting (endurance) activities.

Oxygen Transport System: (VO2): Composed of the stroke volume (SV) the heart rate (HR), and the arterial-mixed venous oxygen difference (a-vO_2 diff.). Mathematically, it is defined, as Vo_2 = SV × HR × a-vO_2 diff.

Oxyhaemoglobin (HbO2): Hemoglobin chemically combined with oxygen.

Oxyhemoglobin (HBO2) Dissociation Curve: The graph of the relationship between the amount of oxygen combined with hemoglobin and the partial pressure of oxygen.

Oxytocin: A hormone secreted by the posterior lobe of the pituitary gland that stimulates milk ejection and contraction of the pregnant uterus.

P

Paradigm Crisis Phenomenon: Theory advanced by Kuhn (1970) that espouses that normal science does not really evolve in systematic steps the way scientific writers describe it.

Parameter Invariance: A postulate in item response theory that the item difficulty remains constant regardless of different populations of examinees and that examinee's abilities should not change when a different set of test items is administered.

Parametric Statistical Test: Test based on data assumptions of normal distribution and equal variance.

Path Analysis: Technique used to explain how certain characteristics relate to each other, with the hope of implying cause, by using correlations among all the variables to estimate the linkages among measures.

Pearson R: The most commonly used method of computing correlation between two variables; also called interclass or Pearson product moment coefficient of correlation.

Phenomenology: Method of philosophic research that designates those inquiries that focus on attempts to describe consciousness of experience.

Philosophical Research: Type of research characterized by critical inquiry in which the researcher establishes hypotheses, examines and analyzes existing facts, and synthesizes the evidence into a workable theoretical model.

Physical Estimation and Attaction Scale (Peas): Saonstroem's (1978) attitude inventory based on the theory that attitude toward activity is modifiable by participation in physical activity.

Pilot Study: A preliminary study done to validate the research methodology.

Placebo: Method of controlling a threat to internal validity in which a control group receives a "false" treatment while the experimental group receives the real treatment.

Plagiarism: Using ideas, concepts, writings, and drawings of others as your own; cheating.

Planned Comparison: Comparison among groups that are planned prior to the experiment, rather than as a follow-up of a test like ANOVA.

Population: The larger group from which a sample is taken.

Population Specificity: Phenomenon where by a regression equation that was developed with a particular samples loses considerable accuracy when applied to others.

Positive Correlation: When a small amount of one variable is associated with a small amount of another variable, and a large amount of one variable is associated with a large amount of the other.

Poster Session: Method of presenting research at a conference in which the author places summaries of his or her research on the wall or on a poster stand and answers questions from passers-by.

Post Hoc Comparison: Comparison made after obtaining significant difference in the ANOVA.

Power (Statistical): The degree to which the chances of rejecting a false null hypothesis are increased.

Power (Work): The change in work divided by the change in time, or the time rate of change of work; the product of force times distance divided by time.

Prediction Equation: A formula to predict some criterion (e.g. some measure of performance) based on the relationship between the predictor variable(s) and the criterion; also called regression equation.

Predictive Validity: Degree to which scores of predictor variables can accurately predict criterion scores.

Pre-Experimental Design: Three types of research designs that control very few of the sources of the sources of invalidity and that do not have random assignments of subjects to groups: one-shot study, one-group pretest-posttest design, and static group comparison.

Premotor Time (PMT): The central component of reaction time comprised of the time interval between stimulus presentation until the first action potential in the muscle is manifested.

Primary Source: Firsthand source of data in historical research in which there is only one person between the event and the researcher.

Probability: The odds that a certain event will occur.

Proportion of Agreement Index: Test of reliability in criterion – referenced measurements proposed by Hambleton and Novick (1973) to assess the consistency of correct decisions.

Proximity Error: Occurs when a rater considers behaviours to be more nearly the same when they are listed close together on a scale than when they are separated by some distance.

Pursuit Rotor: Motor behaviour task in which the subject attempts to keep a hand-held stylus on a small circle located on a rotating disk.

Parasympathetic: Pertaining to the craniosacral portion of the autonomic nervous system.

Parathormone (PTH): A hormone secreted by the parathyroid gland that causes an increase in the blood calcium levels.

Partial Pressure: The pressure exerted by the parathyroid gland that causes an increase in the blood calcium levels.

Partial Pressure: The pressure exerted by a single gas in a gas mixture or in a liquid.

Parietal Pleura: See Pleura'

Perimysum: A connective tissue surrounding a fasciculus or muscle bundle.

Periosteum: A fibrous membrance surrounding bone.

Peritonitis: Inflammation of the peritoneum.

pH: The power of hydrogen ion; the negative logarithm of the hydrogen ion concentration.

Phosphagen: A group of compounds; collectively refers to ATP and PC.

Phosphocreatine (PC): A chemical compound stored in muscle, which when broken down aids in manufacturing ATP.

Photosynthesis: The process whereby green plants manufacture their own food from carbon dioxide, water and energy from the sun.

Placebo: An inert substance having the identical physical characteristics of a real drug.

Plasma: The liquid portion of the blood.

Plasmolysis: The shrinking of a cell such as the red blood cell.

Pleural Cavity: The potential space between the parietal and visceral pleura.

Pneumothorax: The entrance of air into the pleural cavity.

Polycythemia: An increased production of red blood cells.

Ponderal Index: Body height divided by the cube root of body weight.

Positive Energy Balance: A condition in which more energy (food) is taken in than is given off; body weight increases as a result.

Postsynaptic Neuron: A nerve cell located distal to a synapse.

Power: Reference of work expressed per unit of time. For example, if one pound is raised one foot in one second, power is expressed as 1 foot-pound per cortex.

Premotor Area: The area of the brain just forward of the primary motor cortex.

Pressure: Force per unit area.

Primary Motor Cortex: That area of the brain (cortex) containing groups of motor neurons other that Beta cells.

Progesterone: A hormone secreted by the ovary that promotes further development of the uterus and mammary glands.

Proclactin or Lactogenic Hormone (LTH): A hormone secreted by the anterior lobe of the pituitary gland that stimulates secretion of milk after pregnancy.

Proprioceptors: Sensory organs found in muscles, joints, and tendons, which give information concerning movement and position of the body (kinesthesis).

Protein: A compound containing amino acids. One of the basic food-stuffs.

Proton: A positively charged particle.

Pulmonary Circuit: The flow of arterial blood from the heart to the pulmonary (lung) capillaries and of venous blood from the pulmonary capillaries back to the heart.

Pyramidal (Corticospinal) Tract: The area in which impulses from the motor area of the cortex are sent down to the anterior motorneurons of the spinal cord.

Pyruvic Acid (Pyruvate): The end product of aerobic glycolysis; the precursor of lactic acid (lactate).

Q

Qualitative Research: Research method that involves intensive, long-time observation in a natural setting; precise and detailed recording of what happens in the setting; interpretation and analysis of the data using description, narratives, quotes, and charts and tables. Can also be called ethnographic, naturalistic, interpretive, grounded, phenomenological, subjective and participation observational.

Quasi-Experimental Design: Research designs in which the experimenter tries to fit the design to more "real-world" settings while still controlling as many of the threats to internal validity as possible.

Questionnaire: Type of paper-and-pencil survey used in descriptive research in which information is obtained by asking subjects to respond to questions rather than by observing their behaviour.

R

Random Numbers Table: A table in which numbers are arranged in two-digit (or greater) sets so that any combination of rows or columns is unrelated.

Ranking: Type of closed question that forces the subject to place responses in a rank order according to some criterion.

Rating of Perceived Exertion (RPE): Self rating scale developed by Borg (1962) to measure an individuals perceived efforts during exercise.

Rating Scale: A measure of behaviour that involves a subjective evaluation based on a checklist of criteria.

Ratio Scale: Scale of measurement that has all of the properties of nominal, ordinal and interval measures, plus a true zero value that represents a complete absence of the characteristic.

Reader: Machine that enlarge microforms to make the information readable.

Reaction Time: Time elapsed from the presentation of a stimulus until the initiation of a response.

Reductionism: A characteristic of normal science that assumes that complex behaviour can be reduced, analyzed, and explained as parts that can then be put back together to understand the whole.

Relative Frequency: A concept of probability concerning the comparative likelihood of two or more events occurring.

Relative Strength: The measure of the ability to exert maximum force in relation to a person's size.

Reliability: The consistency and dependability of a measure.

Repeated Measures Anova: Analysis of scores on the same individuals on successive occasions such as a series of test trails; also called split-plot ANOVA or subject x trails ANOVA.

Research Hypothesis: Hypothesis deduced from theory of induced from empirical studies that is based upon logical reasoning and is predictive of the outcome of the study.

Research Proposal: A formal preparation that includes the introduction, review of literature, and proposed method for conducting the study.

Residual Score: The difference between the predicted and actual scores that represents the error of prediction.

Results: Chapter or section of a research report that describes what the researcher found.

Review: A research paper that is a critical evaluation of research on a particular topic.

Robust: Characteristic of a statistical test when it is relatively accurate even with fairly severe violations of the assumptions.

Round: Stage of the Delphi survey method in which respondents are asked their opinions and evaluations on various issues, goals and so on.

Rule of Context: A rule of internal criticism in historical research that maintains that a word must be understood in relation to the words that precede and follow it and not in the historian's own contemporary usage.

Rule of Omission: A rule of internal criticism in historical research that maintains that most historical sources are not accounts of complete scene. Also called free editing.

Rule of Perspective: A rule in internal criticism in historical research that requires the researcher to determine who left the record, relationship of a source to an event or group, and how the source collected the information.

Radiation: The transfer of heat between objects through electromagnetic waves.

Receptor: A sense organ that receives stimuli.

Reflex: An automatic response induced by stimulation of a receptor.

Relief Interval: In an interval training program, the time between work intervals as well as between sets.

Repetition: In an interval training program, the number of work intervals within one set. For example, six 220 yard runs would constitute one set of six repetitions.

Repetition Maximum (RM): The maximal load that a muscle group can cover a given number of repetitions before fatiguing. For example, a 10 RM load is the maximal load that can be lifted over 10 repetitions.

Repetition Running: Similar to interval training but differs in the length of the work interval and the degree of recovery between repetitions.

Residual Volume (Rv): Volume of air remaining in the lungs at end of maximal expiration.

Respiratory Exchange Ratio (R, RO): The ratio of the amount of carbon dioxide produced to the amount of oxygen consumed (Vco2/Vo2).

Resting Membrance Potential: The electrical difference between the inside and outside of the cell (i.e., across the cell membrance) at least.

Rest-Recovery: Resting during recovery from exercise.

Rest-Relief: In an interval training program, a type of relief interval involving moderate moving about, such as walking and flexing of arms and legs.

S

Sample: A group of subjects selected from a larger population.

Scaled Item: Type of closed question that requires subjects to indicate the strength of their agreement or disagreement with some statement or the relative frequency of some behaviour.

Scheme Theory: Theory of motor skill learning advanced by Schmidt (1975) as an extension of Adam's closed loop theory. The theory proposed to unify two more general explanations under one theoretical explanation.

Science: A process of careful and systematic inquiry.

Scientific Method of Problem Solving: Method of solving problems in which the following steps are used: developing a problem, defining and delimiting the problem, forming a hypothesis, gathering data, analyzing data, and interpreting the results.

Scree Curve: A method used in factor analysis to determine the number of important factors.

Secondary Source: Source of data in historical research in which there is more than one person between the event and the researcher.

Semantic Differential Scale: Scale used to measure affective behaviour in which the respondent is asked to make judgements about certain concepts by choosing one of seven intervals between bipolar objectives.

Semipartial Correlation: A technique in which one variable is partialed out from just one of two variables in a correlation.

Shrinkage: Tendency for the validity to decrease when the prediction formula is used with a new sample.

Significance: The reliability of or confidence in a statistic as to its likelihood of occurring again if the study were repeated.

Simple Structure: Research design in which the investigator wants each item to correlate highly on the one factor that item was designed to measure and load to a low degree on the other factors.

Sit-And-Reach: One of the oldest tests for measuring flexibility; from a sitting position the subject reaches as far forward (toward toes) as possible.

Skewness: Description of the direction of the hump of the curve of distribution of data the nature of the tails of the curve.

Software: The programs of instruction used to make computer function in the desired manner.

Spearman: Brown prophecy formula – Equation developed to estimate the reliability for the entire test when the split-half technique is used to test reliability.

Speculation: The basic component of the inductive process and the kept to developing theories; requires the researcher to go beyond the data and predict what will happen in the future.

Sphericity: An assumption with regard to repeated measures to the effect that they are uncorrelated and have equal variance.

Split-Half Technique: Method of testing reliability in which the test is divided in two and the two halves are correlated, usually by making the odd numbers one part and the even numbers the other part.

Sport Competition Anxiety Test (SCAT): Marten's (1977) sport-specific trait anxiety inventory that predicts trait anxiety in a sport context compared with general trait anxiety scales.

Spurious Correlation: Relationship in which the correlation between two variables is due primarily to the common influence of another variable.

Stability: A coefficient of reliability measured by the test-retest method on different days; also called test-retest method.

Stabilometer: Device for measuring balance consisting of a platform on which the subject attempts to stand, keeping the sides from tilting and touching the floor.

Standard Deviation: An estimate of the variability of the scores of group around the mean.

Standard Error of Prediction: The computation of the standard deviation of all of the residual scores of a population; the amount of error expected in a population; the amount of error expected in prediction; also called standard error of estimate.

Stanine: Type of standard score, derived from the word "standard" and "nine" because there are nine standard score units that have a mean of 5 and standard deviation of 2.

State Anxiety: An immediate emotional state of apprehension and tension in response to specific situation.

Static Balance: The ability to hold a stationary position.

Stepdown Technique: A procedure used as a follow up in multi-variate analysis to determine the actual differences among groups.

Step Test: Test used to measure cardiorespiratory fitness involving the measurement of pulse rate after stepping up and down on bench.

Step Wise Regression Method: Regression and discriminant analysis procedure similar to forward selection except at each step all of the dependent variables are evaluated to see if each still contributes to prediction or group separation. If one dependent variable does not it is stepped out (removed) from the linear combination. It is also used in multiple regression for predicting the criterion.

Stratified Random Sampling: Method of stratifying a population on some characteristic prior to random selection of the sample.

Subjective (Personalistic) Probability: Concept in probability regarding the subjective chances of occurrence of an event.

Sum of Squares: A measure of variability of scores; the sum of the squared deviations from the mean of scores.

Survey: Technique of descriptive research that seeks to determine present practices or opinions of a specified population; can take the form of questionnaire, interview, or normative survey.

Saline: A 0.9 per cent salt solution which is isotonic to the blood.

Salpigitis: Inflammation of a fallopian tube.

Saltatory Conduction: The propagation of a nerve impulse from one node of Ranvier to another along a medullated fibre.

Sarcolemma: The muscle cell members.

Sarcomere: The distance between two Z lines; the smallest contractile unit of skeletal muscle.

Sarcoplasm: Muscle protoplasm.

Sarcoplasmic Reticulum: A network of tubules and vesicles surrounding the myofibril.

Second Wind: A phenomenon characterized by a sudden transition from an ill defined feeling of distress of fatige during the early portion of prolonged exercise to a more comfortable, less stressful feeling later in the exercise.

Semipermeable Membrane: A membrance permeable to some but not all particles or substances.

Sensory Neuron: A nerve cell that conveys impulses from a receptor to the central nervous system. Examples of sensory neurons are those excited by sound, pain, light and taste.

Serotonin: An excitatory neurotransmitter chemical.

Serous Fluid: A water fluid secreted by the pleural.

Set: In an interval training program, a group of work and relief intervals.

Sino-Atrial Node (S-A Node): A specialized area of tissue located in the right atrium of the heart, which originates the electrical impulse to initiate the heartbeat.

Slow Twitch Fibre (ST): A muscle fibre characterized by slow contraction time low anerobic capacity, and high aerobic capacity, all making the fibre suited for low power output activities.

Soma: The cell body of a neuron.

Somatic: Pertaining to the body.

Somatotype: The body type or physical classification of the human body.

Spatial Summation: An increase in responsiveness of a nerver resulting from the additive effect of numerous stimuli.

Specific Gravity: The ratio of the density of an object to the density of water.

Specific Heat: The heat required to change the temperature of a unit mass of a substance by one degree.

Specificity of Training: Principle underlying construction of a training program for a specific activity or skill and the primary energy system(s) involved during performance. For example, a training program for sprinters would consist of repeated bouts of sprints in order to develop both sprinting performance and the ATP-PC system.

Speed Play (Fartlek Training): Involves alternative fast and slow running over natural surface. It is the forerunner of the interval training system.

Spirometer: A steel container used to collect, store and measure either inspired or expired gas volumes.

Spirint Training: A type of training system employing repeated sprints at maximal speed.

Starling's Law of the Heart: An increase in stroke volume in response to an increase in the volume of blood filling the heart ventricle during diastole.

Steady State: Pertaining to the time period during which a physiological function (such as Vo2) remains at a constant (steady) value.

Steroid: A derivate of the male sex hormones testosterone which has masculinizing properties.

Stimulus (singular); Stimuli (plural): Any agent, act or influence that modifies the activity of a receptor or irritable tissue.

Stpd: Standard Temperature Pressure, Dry.

Strength: The force that a muscle or muscle group can exert against a resistance in one maximal effort.

Stroke Volume (SV): The amount of blood pumped by the left ventricle of the heart per beat.

Sudomotor: Pertaining to activation of the sweat glands.

Sympathetic: Pertaining to the thoracolumber portion of the autonomic nervous system.

Synapse: The connection or junction of one neuron to another.

Synaptic Cleft: The gap or space between prosynaptic and postsynaptic neurons.

Systemic Circuit: The flow of arterial blood from the heart to the body tissues (such as the muscles) and of the venous blood from the tissue back to the heart.

Systole: The contractile or emptying phase of the cardiac cycle.

T

T Scale: Type of standard score that set the mean at 50 and standard deviation at 10 to remove the decimal found in z-scores and to make all scores positive.

Tallying Method: Method of recording in observational research in which the researcher records occurrence of clearly defined behaviour within a certain time frame; also called frequency counting method.

Tapping Board: Motor behaviour task in which a subject attempts to tap a metal stylus as quickly as possible back and forth between two circles mounted a certain distance apart.

Taxonomy: A classification system.

Tenacity: An unscientific method of problem solving in which people stick to certain beliefs regardless of the lack of supporting evidence.

Test-Retest Method: Method of determining reliability in which a test is given one day and then administered exactly as before a day or so later; also called stability.

Theorizing: Cognitive process of discovering abstract categories and the relationships among those categories.

Theory: Explanation of some aspect of practice that permits the researcher to draw inferences about future happenings.

Thurstone Type Scale: Scale used to measure affective behaviour in which the respondent expresses agreement or disagreement with each item, which has been rated by panel of judges and scaled with numerical value to reflect the most positive attitude.

Trait Anxiety: General tendency to be anxious.

Transferability: In qualitative research, the term analogous to external validity in experimental research.

Triangulation: Term borrowed from the field of surveying that refers to the use of more than one source of data to substantiate a researcher's conclusion.

True Experimental Design: Any design used in experimental research in which groups are randomly formed and that controls most sources of validity.

True Score: In classical test theory, the part of the observed score that represents the individual's real score and does not contain measurement error.

True Variance: The portion of the differences in scores that is (theoretical) real.

Truth Table: A graphic representation of correct and incorrect decisions regarding Type I and Type II errors.

Truth Value: In qualitative research, the term analogous to internal validity in experimental research.

T-Test: A statistical technique to assess difference between the two means could favour either group.

Type I Error: A rejection of the null hypothesis when the null hypothesis is true.

Type II Error: Acceptance of the null hypothesis when the null hypothesis is false.

Type III Error: Solving the wrong problem

Type IV Error: Solving a problem that is not worth solving.

Tachycardia: An increased or rapid heart rate.

Target Heart Rate (THR): A Predetermined heart rate to be obtained during exercise.

Target Organ: The cell, tissue or organ upon which a hormone has an effect.

Temperature: The degree of sensible heat or cold.

Temporal Summation: An increase responsiveness of a nerve, result from the addictive effect of frequent occurring stimuli.

Testosterone: The male sex hormone secreted by the testicles, it possess masculinizing properties.

Thermodynamics: The science of the transformation of heat and energy.

Threshold for Excitation: The minimal electrical level at which neuron will transmit or conduct an impulse.

Thrombus: A blood clot that remains at the point of its formation.

Thyroid-Stimulating HormonE (TSH): A hormone secreted from the anterior lobe of the pituitary gland that stimulates production and release of the thyrold hormones, thyroxin, and tridithyronine.

Thyroxin: A hormone secreted by the thyroid gland that causes an increase in metabolic rate.

Tidal Volume (TV): Volume of air inspired or expired per breath.

Tissue-Capillary Membrane: The thin layer of tissue dividing the capillaries and an organ (such as skeletal muscle); site at which gaseous exchange occurs.

Tonus: Resiliency and resistance to stress in a relaxed, resting muscle.

Total Lung Capacity (TLC): Volume of air in the lungs at end of maximal inspiration.

Training: An exercise program to develop an athletes skill of performance and energy capacities are of equal consideration.

Training Duration: The length of the training program.

Training Frequency: The number of times per week for the training workout.

Training Time: The rate at which the work is to be accomplished during a work interval in an interval training program.

Triglycerides: The storage form of free fatty acids.

Tropomyosin: A protein involved in muscular contraction.

Troponin: A protein involved in muscular contraction.

Twitch: A brief period of contraction followed by relaxation in response of motor unit to a stimulus (nerve impulse).

U

Univariate Technique: Statistical technique applied in the analysis of only one dependent variable.

User Generalisability: Concept in which the user (reader) evaluates the findings of the carefully described and interpreted study and asks what things apply to his or her situation.

V

Validity: Degree to which a test or instrument measurements what it purports to measure; can be categorized as logical, content, criterion and construct.

Variability: The degree of difference between each individual score and the central tendency score.

Variability of Practice: Motor skill learning advanced by Schmidt in which the practice of a variety of movement experiences facilities transfer to a new movement when compared to practicing a single movement.

Variable Error (VE): The standard deviation of the average constant error (CE) score.

Variance: The square of the standard deviation.

Veil of Ignorance: Philosophic concept that describes the hypothetical situation in which all people have limited knowledge of class position, status, economic worth, natural abilities, and assets.

Vasoconstriction: A decrease in the diameter of a blood vessel (usually an arteriale) resulting in a reduction of blood flow to the area supplied by the vessel.

Vasodilation: A decrease in the diameter of a blood vessel (usually an arteriale) resulting in an increased blood flow to the area supplied by the vessel.

Vasomotor: Pertaining to vasoconstriction and vasodilation.

Vein: A vessel carrying blood toward the heart.

Venoconstriction: A decrease in the diameter of a vein.

Ventilatory Efficiency: The amount of ventilation required per liter of oxygen consumed; i.e.VE/Vo2.

Very Low Density Lipoproteins (Vldl): A specific kind of cholesterol found in the blood that is thought to cause atherosclerosis.

Vital Capacity (VC): Maximal volume of air forcefully expired after maximal inspiration.

W

Wherry Doolittle Method: A multiple correlation technique used in the test selection.

Wave Summation: The varying of the frequency of contraction of individual motor units.

Wbgt Index: An index calculated from dry bulb, wet bulb, and black bulb temperatures. It indicates the severity of the environmental heat conditions.

Wet Bulb Thermometer: An ordinary thermometer with a watted wick wrapped around the bulb. The wet bulb temperature is related to the amount of moisture in the air. When the wet bulb and dry bulb temperatures are equal, the air is completely saturated with water and the relative humidity is equal to 100 per cent.

Y

Yates Correction for Continuity: Method of correcting 2 × 2 contingency table by subtracting 0.5 from the difference between the observed and expected frequencies for each cell before it is squared.

Z

Z Score: The basic standard score that converts raw scores to a mean of 0 with a standard deviation of 1.0.

Z Line: A portion band that defines the distance of one sarcomere in the myofibril.

Multiple Choice Questions

Note: *This paper contains **fifty** (**125**) objective type questions, each question carrying **two** (**2**) marks. Attempt. **all** the questions.*

1. Skinner propounded :
   (*a*) Feedback theory of learning
   (*b*) Gestalt theory of learning
   (*c*) Stimulus response theory of learning
   (*d*) Operant conditining theory of learning

2. Biological foundation of Physical Education involves
   I. Motor learning II. Sex characteristics
   III. Body type IV. Personality traits
   Find the correct combination:
   (*a*) I and II (*b*) II and III
   (*c*) III and IV (*d*) IV and I

3. Given below are two statements, one is labelled as Assertion (A) and other is labelled as Reason (R).

   Assertion (A) : Physical Education is an elective discipline.

   Reason (R) : Physical Education borrows principles from other allied fields.

   In the context of two statements, which one of the following is correct?
   (*a*) Both (A) and (R) are true and (R) is the correct explanation of (A).
   (*b*) Both (A) and (R) are true, but (R) is not the correct explanation of (A).
   (*c*) (A) is true, but (R) is false.
   (*d*) (A) is false, but (R) is true.

4. In skill learning the information processing model is comprised of four components. Arrange them in sequential order:
   I. Decision making II. Input
   III. Feedback IV. Output
   Codes:

(*a*)	I	II	III	IV
(*b*)	III	IV	II	I
(*c*)	II	I	IV	III
(*d*)	IV	III	I	II

5. Match List-I with List-II and select the correct answer from the codes given below:

List-I	List-II
I. 1936	1. London
II. 1948	2. Berlin
III. 1980	3. Seoul
IV. 1988	4. Moscow
	5. Los Angeles

Codes:

	I	II	III	IV
(*a*)	1	2	5	4
(*b*)	2	4	1	5
(*c*)	4	3	2	1
(*d*)	2	1	4	3

6. Which organ performs endocrine as well as exocrine functions in human body?
   (*a*) Liver (*b*) Kidneys
   (*c*) Pancreas (*d*) Gall bladder

7. Purpose of systemic circulation is
   (I) Supply of O_2 and nutrients to all parts of the body
   (II) Purification of blood
   (III) Bringing CO_2 and wastages from all parts of the body
   (IV) Removal of urine from blood
   Find the correct combination :
   Codes:
   (*a*) I and II (*b*) I and III
   (*c*) II and IV (*d*) III and IV

8. Given below are two statements, one is labelled as Assertion (A) and other is labelled as Reason (R).

   Assertion (A) : Skeletal muscles are called voluntary muscles.

   Reason (R) : Muscles are machines that convert chemical energy into mechanical work.

In the context of the above two statements, which one of the following is correct?
(*a*) Both (A) and (R) are true and (R) is the correct explanation of (A).
(*b*) Both (A) and (R) are true, but (R) is not the correct explanation of (A).
(*c*) (A) is true and (R) is false.
(*d*) (A) is false, but (R) is true.

9. Arrange the parts of large intestine (colon) sequentially:
I. Ascending colon
II. Sigmoid colon
III. Descending colon
IV. Transverse colon

Codes:

(*a*)	I	IV	III	II
(*b*)	II	III	IV	I
(*c*)	III	II	I	IV
(*d*)	IV	I	II	III

10. Match List-I with List-II and select the correct answer from the codes given below:

List-I	List-II
I. Soleus	1. Chest
II. Sartorius	2. Upper back
III. Trapezious	3. Lower leg
IV. Pectoralis	4. Across the thigh

Codes:

	I	II	III	IV
(*a*)	2	3	1	4
(*b*)	3	4	2	1
(*c*)	4	2	3	1
(*d*)	1	3	4	2

11. Find the correct answer.
Frontal plane divides the body into
(*a*) Front and back halves
(*b*) Left and right halves
(*c*) Upper and lower halves
(*d*) Inner and outer halves

12. Kinetics is the study of
(I) Velocity (II) Impulse
(III) Acceleration (IV) Force
Find the correct combination:
Codes:
(*a*) I and II (*b*) II and III
(*c*) II and IV (*d*) III and IV

13. Competition is defined as a process through which success is measured by :
(*a*) Determining who reaches certain level of excellence
(*b*) Comparing present performance with the past performance
(*c*) Standard of excellence set by those who have performed in the past
(*d*) Comparing the achievement of those performing the same activity under the same circumstances

14. Total movement structure of a squat jump involves the following phases:
I. Going down
II. Take-off
III. Moving up
IV. Landing
Proper sequence of these phases is :

(*a*)	IV	I	III	II
(*b*)	II	IV	I	III
(*c*)	III	II	IV	I
(*d*)	I	III	II	IV

15. Match List-I with List-II and select the correct answer from the codes given below:

List-I	List-II
I. Hinge joint	1. Wrist
II. Pivot joint	2. Hip
III. Ball and socket joint	3. Elbow
IV. Gliding joint	4. Neck

Codes:

	I	II	III	IV
(*a*)	1	3	4	2
(*b*)	2	1	3	4
(*c*)	3	4	2	1
(*d*)	4	2	1	3

16. Which of the following is a secondary law of learning?
(*a*) Law of readiness
(*b*) Law of recency
(*c*) Law of exercise
(*d*) Law of effect

17. Important Personality Theories are:
I. Maslow's Need Theory
II. Social Learning Theory

III. Trait Theory
IV. Attribution Theory

Codes:

(*a*) II and III (*b*) I and II
(*c*) III and IV (*d*) I and IV

18. Given below are two statements, one is labelled as Assertion (A) and other is labelled as Reason (R).

Assertion (A) : Team's performance goes down due to lack of cooperation.

Reason (R) : Group cohesion is the togetherness among group members striving for a common goal.

Find the correct answer :

(*a*) (A) is true, but (R) is false.
(*b*) (A) is false, but (R) is true.
(*c*) Both (A) and (R) are true and (R) is the correct explanation of (A).
(*d*) Both (A) and (R) are true, but (R) is not the correct explanation of (A).

19. Cognitive process consists of

I. Sensation II. Thinking
III. Perception IV. Problem solving

Identify the correct sequence:

Codes:

(*a*)	I	III	II	IV
(*b*)	II	IV	I	III
(*c*)	IV	I	III	II
(*d*)	III	II	IV	I

20. Match List-I with List-II and select the correct answer from the codes given below:

List-I	**List-II**
I. Inverted U hypothesis	1. Achievement
II. Aggression	2. Autocratic style
III. Leadership	3. Anxiety
IV. Motivation	4. Instrumental

Codes:

	I	II	III	IV
(*a*)	1	2	3	4
(*b*)	4	3	1	2
(*c*)	2	1	4	3
(*d*)	3	4	2	1

21. Development of maximum strength should start at the age of

(*a*) 8-10 years (*b*) 11-13 years
(*c*) 14-15 years (*d*) 16-18 years

22. Given below are two statements, one is labelled as Assertion (A) and other is labelled as Reason (R).

Assertion (A) : Physical education teacher should be highly skillful.

Reason (R) : Physical education teacher requires to demonstrate correctly the skill being taught.

Find the correct answer from the following:

(*a*) Both (A) and (R) are true and (R) is the correct explanation of (A).
(*b*) Both (A) and (R) are true, but (R) is not the correct explanation of (A).
(*c*) (A) is true, but (R) is false.
(*d*) (A) is false, but (R) is true.

23. While constructing time-table for physical education class, the factors to be considered are

I. Head of institution's preference
II. Convenience of parents
III. Availability of facilities
IV. Availability of Physical Education teacher

Codes:

(*a*) II and III (*b*) III and IV
(*c*) IV and I (*d*) I and II

24. Following food components do not produce heat and energy in the body:

I. Protein II. Vitamin
III. Fat IV. Minerals

Select correct answer from the codes given below:

(*a*) I and III (*b*) II and III
(*c*) III and IV (*d*) II and IV

25. Given below are two statements, one is labelled as Assertion (A) and other is labelled as Reason (R).

Assertion (A) : An obese person has BMI more than 30.

Reason (R) : BMI indicates the nutritional status of a person.

Find the correct answer from the following:

(*a*) Both (A) and (R) are true, but (R) is not the correct explanation of (A).
(*b*) Both (A) and (R) are true and (R) is the correct explanation of (A).
(*c*) (A) is true, but (R) is false.
(*d*) (A) is false, but (R) is true.

26. Health related fitness does not include
(*a*) Flexibility
(*b*) Speed
(*c*) Endurance
(*d*) Body composition

27. Match List-I with List-II and select the correct answer from the codes given below:

List-I (Vitamin)	List-II (Disease)
I. Vitamin-A	1. Pyorrhoea
II. Vitamin-B	2. Rickets
III. Vitamin-C	3. Beri-Beri
IV. Vitamin-D	4. Night blindness

Codes:

	I	II	III	IV
(*a*)	2	4	3	1
(*b*)	1	2	4	3
(*c*)	4	3	1	2
(*d*)	3	1	2	4

28. Incomplete recovery is vital in
(*a*) Continuous method of training
(*b*) Interval training
(*c*) Fartlek
(*d*) Cross country

29. Criteria for classification of competition are:
I. Level of competition
II. Age of competitor
III. Mode of organizing competition
IV. Training methodical aspect

Arrange the above criteria in proper sequence:
(*a*) I, II and III (*b*) II, III and IV
(*c*) II, IV and I (*d*) IV, I and II

30. Given below are two statements, one is labelled as Assertion (A) and other is labelled as Reason (R).

Assertion (A) : Selection of a sport is the first phase for identification of talent.

Reason (R) : Talent identification has three phases.

Find the correct answer from the following:

(*a*) Both (A) and (R) are true and (R) is the correct explanation of (A).
(*b*) Both (A) and (R) are true, but (R) is not the correct explanation of (A).
(*c*) (A) is true, but (R) is false.
(*d*) (A) is false, but (R) is true.

31. Long-term sport training process involves following stages:
I. Basic training
II. Training for high performance
III. Training for maintaining performance
IV. Advanced training

Arrange in proper sequential phases :

(*a*)	I	IV	II	III
(*b*)	I	II	III	IV
(*c*)	I	III	IV	II
(*d*)	I	II	IV	III

32. Match List-I with List-II and select the correct answer from the codes given below:

List-I	List-II
I. High performance	1. Tactical action
II. Organization of competition	2. Talent identification
III. Screening of children	3. Training stage
IV. Motor solution of competition task	4. Competition system

Codes:

	I	II	III	IV
(*a*)	1	3	4	2
(*b*)	3	4	2	1
(*c*)	4	2	1	3
(*d*)	2	1	3	4

33. Close form questionnaire contains questions that call for
(*a*) Descriptive response
(*b*) Free response
(*c*) Short response
(*d*) Check response

34. Hypothesis in research means

I. Intellectual guess
II. Brilliant guess
III. Intelligent guess
IV. Negative guess

Find the correct answer from the following:

(*a*) I, II, III (*b*) II, III, IV
(*c*) I, III, IV (*d*) I, II, IV

35. Given below are two statements, one is labelled as Assertion (A) and other is labelled as Reason (R).

Assertion (A) : External criticism establishes genuineness and authenticity of data.

Reason (R) : Research should get true data.

Find the correct answer from the following :

(*a*) (R) is true, but (A) is false.
(*b*) Both (A) and (R) are true.
(*c*) (A) is true, but (R) is false.
(*d*) Both (A) and (R) are false.

36. Identify the correct steps for relevant statistical procedure :

I. Mean values of two groups of data
II. Mean difference
III. Testing significance
IV. 't' value

Find the correct answer from the following :

Codes :

(*a*) II III IV I (*b*) I II IV III
(*c*) III IV I II (*d*) IV I II III

37. Match List-I and List-II and select the correct answer from the codes given below :

List-I	List-II
I. Standard deviation	1. $Q_3 - Q_1$
II. Mean	2. $\frac{\Sigma X^2}{N}$
III. 't' value	3. $Am + \frac{\Sigma fd}{N} Xi$
IV. Quartile deviation	4. $\frac{X_1 - X_2}{\text{Standard Error}}$

Codes:

	I	II	III	IV
(*a*)	1	2	3	4
(*b*)	4	1	2	3
(*c*)	2	3	4	1
(*d*)	3	4	1	2

38. Cooper's 12-minutes Run and Walk test measures :

(*a*) Agility
(*b*) Strength
(*c*) Speed
(*d*) Cardiorespiratory endurance

39. Performance related fitness involves

I. Power II. Basic endurance
III. Flexibility IV. Agility

Find the correct combination :

(*a*) I and II (*b*) III and IV
(*c*) II and III (*d*) I and IV

40. Given below are two statements, one of which is labelled as Assertion (A) and the other is labelled as Reason (R).

Assertion (A) : Johnson Basketball test is a standardized test.

Reason (R) : Johnson Basketball test evaluates Basketball playing ability.

Find out the correct answer from the codes given below :

Codes :

(*a*) Both (A) and (R) are true and (R) is the correct explanation of (A).
(*b*) Both (A) and (R) are true, but (R) is not the correct explanation of (A).
(*c*) (A) is true, but (R) is false.
(*d*) (A) is false, but (R) is true.

41. Four steps for preparing a standardized test are :

I. Preparation of preliminary form
II. Preparation of final form
III. Testing of validity
IV. Testing of reliability

Find out the correct sequence :

(*a*) I II IV III
(*b*) I III II IV
(*c*) III IV I II
(*d*) II I III IV

42. Match List-I and List-II and find out correct combination from the codes given below :

List-I	List-II
I. Obesity	1. Mesomorphy
II. Linearity	2. Endomorphy
III. Muscularity	3. Goniometry
IV. Flexibility	4. Ectomorphy

Codes:

	I	II	III	IV
(*a*)	2	4	1	3
(*b*)	4	1	3	2
(*c*)	1	3	2	4
(*d*)	3	2	4	1

43. Planning Physical Education lesson must emphasize on

(*a*) Body type of learner
(*b*) Efficiency of teacher
(*c*) Time of teaching
(*d*) Age of learner

44. Given below are two statements, one is labelled as Assertion (A) and other is labelled as Reason (R) :

Assertion (A) : Physical education teacher should be good in theory as well as practical skills.

Reason (R) : Physical education profession provides socio-economic status.

In the context of two statements, which one of the following is correct?

(*a*) Both (A) and (R) are true, and (R) is the correct explanation of (A).
(*b*) Both (A) and (R) are true but (R) is not the correct explanation of (A).
(*c*) (A) is true, but (R) is false.
(*d*) (A) is false, but (R) is true.

45. Match List-I and List-II and select the correct answer from the codes given below :

List-I	List-II
I. Intramural	1. Visitation
II. Finance	2. Competition
III. Supervision	3. Reappropriation
IV. Infrastructure	4. Layout

Codes:

	I	II	III	IV
(*a*)	2	3	1	4
(*b*)	3	2	4	1
(*c*)	4	1	3	2
(*d*)	1	4	2	3

46. Arrange the following phases of presentation technique in correct sequence :

I. Demonstration
II. Explanation
III. Practice and Supervision
IV. Feedback

Find the correct combination :

(*a*)	II	III	IV	I
(*b*)	I	II	III	IV
(*c*)	III	IV	I	II
(*d*)	IV	I	II	III

Directions (Qs. 47 to 50) : *Read the passage and answer the question that follow based on your understanding of the passage:*

Teaching offers many rewards, regardless of whether it takes place in a traditional or an alternative setting. Probably most important is that it offers an opportunity to help shape people's lives and promote a healthy life-style. Students select teaching as a career for many reasons. Each prospective teacher should take the time to list the reasons he or she has for choosing this career.

Many physical educators want to teach because of their love of children and their desire to help others. The conviction that involvement in a sound physical education program can have a significant impact on the quality of life of its participants motivates some individuals to enter the teaching profession. Prospective teachers who have been fortunate to reap the benefits of participation in a sound physical education program often express the desire to share with others the same benefits that they themselves have realized. Other individuals who had poor experiences while students in physical education enter the teaching profession because of the desire to improve the quality of physical education programs so that the benefits known to be associated with quality programs can be attained.

Certainly personal interest, likes, and dislikes influence one's decision to enter the teaching profession. Many choose to teach physical education because of their love for sport and perhaps the desire to transmit this love to others. The opportunity to be outdoors, to work out and stay physically fit, and to have fun are often given as reasons for entering the teaching profession.

The nature of the job attracts many individuals. In the school selling the long vacations, the informality of teaching in the gymnasium as compared to the classroom, and the security offered by tenure are some of the positive benefits that prompt some people to seek a teaching career.

47. Which of the following rewards of physical education teaching is the most important?
(*a*) Getting a job
(*b*) Promotion of healthy life style
(*c*) Enjoying the leisure time
(*d*) Improving the social contacts

48. What makes physical education teachers teach physical education activities?
(*a*) The love of children
(*b*) Monetary gains
(*c*) As a part of their job
(*d*) Devotion to profession

49. Which of the following influences the person to enter the teaching profession?
(*a*) Personal benefit (*b*) Social obligation
(*c*) Political pressure (*d*) Personal interest

50. The nature of physical education teaching job is
(*a*) Positive teaching
(*b*) Negative teaching
(*c*) Informality of teaching
(*d*) Formality of teaching

51. Select the correct option :
Flexion and extension occur around
(*a*) Medio-lateral axis
(*b*) Anterio-posterior axis
(*c*) Vertical axis
(*d*) Sagittal axis

52. Select the correct option :
Modern concept of Physical Education was started :
(*a*) After 1920
(*b*) After 1957
(*c*) In the last decade of nineteenth century
(*d*) After 1960

53. Select the correct option :
Cardiovascular system can be best trained for performance in endurance events by practicing in
(*a*) Ballistic exercises
(*b*) Yogic practices
(*c*) Aerobic exercises
(*d*) Anaerobic exercises

54. Select the correct option:
A behaviour where opponent is psychologically and / or physically harmed but the goal is to win is called
(*a*) Hostile aggression
(*b*) Assertive behaviour
(*c*) Instrumental aggression
(*d*) Violent behaviour

55. Select the correct option :
Carbohydrate loading used by athletes means
(*a*) Getting energy from the blood
(*b*) Storing energy in muscles
(*c*) Spending energy during hard physical workout
(*d*) Generating energy per unit of time

56. Select the correct option :
Common injury to the Basketball players is
(*a*) Head injury
(*b*) Interio lateral ligament injury of ankle
(*c*) Shoulder injury
(*d*) Lateral collateral ligament injury of hip

57. Select the correct option :
Somatotyping profile of (4, 4, 1) is considered as
(*a*) Endomorph Mesomorph
(*b*) Endomorphic Mesomorph
(*c*) Balanced Mesomorph
(*d*) Mesomorphic Endomorph

58. Which of the following type of research is designed to create and develop organised body of knowledge?
(*a*) Action research
(*b*) Contextual research
(*c*) Fundamental research
(*d*) Applied research

59. Purposive sample is a non-probability sample because it is
(*a*) selected without using any selection process
(*b*) chosen by throw of a dice
(*c*) not randomly selected
(*d*) selected at the last moment

60. During training the sensation of vomiting is caused due to
(*a*) Accumulation of lactic acid
(*b*) Adrenaline
(*c*) More oxygen intake
(*d*) Carbon dioxide

61. Building block of the body is
(*a*) Vitamins (*b*) Carbohydrates
(*c*) Proteins (*d*) Minerals

62. In the Olympic events, the gold medal awarded for the first place has the following ratio of gold.
(*a*) Silver gilt with 8 grams of fine gold
(*b*) Silver gilt with 7 grams of fine gold
(*c*) Silver gilt with 6 grams of fine gold
(*d*) Silver gilt with 10 grams of fine gold

63. Name the first Principal of YMCA college of Physical Education, Madras (Chennai) :
(*a*) P.M. Joseph (*b*) H.C. Buck
(*c*) G.D. Sondhi (*d*) A.K. Singh

64. All India Council of Sport was formed in
(*a*) 1954 (*b*) 1953
(*c*) 1952 (*d*) 1951

65. The first member of International Olympic Committee from India was
(*a*) G.D. Sondhi
(*b*) Raja Bhalinder Singh
(*c*) Sir Dorabji Tata
(*d*) P.M. Joseph

66. Harward Step Test measures
(*a*) Muscular efficiency of the knee muscles
(*b*) Cardio-respiratory efficiency
(*c*) Cardio-pulmonary index
(*d*) Respiratory pulmonary index

67. The term 'Hypokinetics' refers to that phase of physical education where amount of muscular activity is :
(*a*) Sufficient
(*b*) Insufficient
(*c*) More than required
(*d*) None of the above

68. Free hand exercises done generally in group are called
(*a*) Circuit training
(*b*) Callisthenics
(*c*) Drill and marching
(*d*) Weight training

69. Which of the following is against the principles of organization?
(*a*) Overlapping of authority
(*b*) Proper decentralization
(*c*) Delegation of power
(*d*) Proper communication

70. Getting the right facts to the right people at the right time in the right way is called
(*a*) Game management
(*b*) Public relations in sport
(*c*) Motivation in sport
(*d*) Leadership in sport

71. In which game pressure training method was first used?
(*a*) Hockey (*b*) Football
(*c*) Volleyball (*d*) Basketball

72. Weight training method was started by German gymnastic coach in the year
(*a*) 1810 (*b*) 1812
(*c*) 1820 (*d*) 1816

73. Traditional Schools of Philosophy include
I. Naturalism II. Progressivism
III. Pragmatism IV. Realism

Find the correct combination.
(*a*) I, II, III (*b*) II, III, IV
(*c*) III, IV, I (*d*) IV, I, II

74. Linear velocity depends on
I. Angular velocity directly
II. Radius of rotation inversely
III. Both angular velocity and radius of rotation directly
IV. Both angular velocity and radius of rotation inversely

Find the correct combination :

(a) I, II (b) I, III

(c) II, IV (d) III, IV

75. Factors associated with cohesion are

I. Team satisfaction

II. Individual performance

III. Team ranking in competition

IV. Social support

Find the correct combination.

(a) I, IV (b) II, III

(c) IV, III (d) I, II

76. The boycotts of Olympic Games due to political compulsion were

I. Montreal Olympic

II. Berlin Olympic

III. Moscow Olympic

IV. Rome Olympic

Find the correct combination.

(a) I, II (b) III, IV

(c) I, III (d) II, IV

77. Other than propulsive force the aerial motion of a body is influenced by

I. It's weight II. Spin

III. Elasticity IV. Air resistance

Find the correct combination.

(a) I, II, III (b) II, III, IV

(c) III, IV, I (d) IV, I, II

78. Median can be calculated with

I. $L_1 + \frac{i}{f}\left(\frac{N}{2} - C\right)$

II. $L_1 + \frac{L_2 - L_1}{f}(m - C)$

III. $L_1 + \frac{\frac{N}{2} - C}{f}(L_2 - L_1)$

IV. $L_2 + \frac{\frac{N}{2} - C}{f} \times i$

Find the correct combination.

(a) I, II, IV (b) II, III, IV

(c) I, III, IV (d) I, II, III

79. In Lakshmibai College of Physical Education, Gwalior, three years Bachelor Course and two years Master Course were started in

I. 1957 II. 1960

III. 1962 IV. 1963

Find the correct combination.

(a) I, IV (b) I, II

(c) II, III (d) III, IV

80. Motor educability depends on

I. Neuromuscular coordination

II. Consistency in efforts

III. Age of the subject

IV. Sex of the subject

Find the correct combination.

(a) I, IV (b) II, III

(c) I, II, III, IV (d) I, IV, II

81. Extramural competitions are more beneficial for

I. Champions

II. Beginners

III. Ordinary performer

IV. Skilled performer

Find the correct combination.

(a) I, IV (b) II, III

(c) III, IV (d) II, IV

82. Internal load is judged by

I. Load volume

II. Pulse rate

III. Load intensity

IV. Lactic acid concentration

Find the correct combination.

(a) I, IV (b) II, IV

(c) III, IV (d) II, III

83. Match List-I with List-II and select the correct option using the code given below :

List-I	List-II
I. Ludwig John	1. Educational gymnastics
II. John Dewey	2. Modern Olympic Games
III. P.H. Ling	3. Turnverein Movement
IV. Coubertin	4. Pragmatism

Codes:

	I	II	III	IV
(*a*)	1	3	4	2
(*b*)	2	1	3	4
(*c*)	4	2	1	3
(*d*)	3	4	1	2

84. Match List-I with List-II and select the correct option using the codes given below :

List-I	List-II
I. Stimulatory responses	1. Anabolic steroids
II. Drug increasing alertness	2. Narcotic analgesics
III. Psychological stimulation	3. Stimulation
IV. Testosterone hormone	4. Beta blockers

Codes:

	I	II	III	IV
(*a*)	1	3	4	2
(*b*)	3	4	2	1
(*c*)	4	1	3	2
(*d*)	4	2	3	1

85. Match List-I with List-II and select the correct option using the codes given below :

List-I	List-II
I. Oxygen storage in the muscle	1. Oxygen debt
II. Source of energy during all out sprint	2. Anaerobic metabolism
III. Rest period immediately after exercise	3. Myoglobin
IV. Excess oxygen consumed during recovery period	4. Recovery period

Codes:

	I	II	III	IV
(*a*)	1	2	3	4
(*b*)	2	4	3	1
(*c*)	1	4	2	3
(*d*)	3	2	4	1

86. Match List-I with List-II and select the correct option using the codes given below :

List-I	List-II
I. Leadership	1. POMS
II. Personality	2. SCAT
III. Group Cohesion	3. LSS
IV. Anxiety	4. GEQ

Codes:

	I	II	III	IV
(*a*)	1	3	2	4
(*b*)	3	1	4	2
(*c*)	4	2	3	1
(*d*)	2	4	1	3

87. Match List-I with List-II and select the correct option using the codes given below :

List-I	List-II
I. A non-parametric technique to compare obtained results with those to be expected	1. Z test
II. A statistical test to determine the significant difference between the sample mean and population mean	2. Correlation
III. A statistical technique to establish the relationship among variables	3. F-Ratio
IV. A test to assess the significant difference in the means of more than two groups	4. Chisquare Test

Codes:

	I	II	III	IV
(*a*)	4	1	2	3
(*b*)	4	1	3	2
(*c*)	1	3	4	2
(*d*)	3	1	2	4

88. Match List-I with List-II and select the correct option using the codes given below :

List-I	List-II
I. Frictional force	1. Body weight
II. Buoyant force	2. Banking
III. Gravity force	3. Stability
IV. Centrifugal force	4. Floating

Codes:

	I	II	III	IV
(*a*)	2	3	4	1
(*b*)	3	4	1	2
(*c*)	4	1	2	3
(*d*)	1	2	3	4

89. Match List-I with List-II and select the correct option using the codes given below :

List-I	List-II
I. Anabolic steroids	1. Slowing the neuromuscular cellular process
II. Amphetamines	2. Bringing the level to normal
III. Alcohol	3. Initiating the neuromuscular process
IV. Alkaline salts	4. Developing secondary male characteristics in female

Codes:

	I	II	III	IV
(*a*)	4	3	1	2
(*b*)	3	4	2	1
(*c*)	1	2	3	4
(*d*)	2	1	4	3

90. Match List-I with List-II and select the correct option using the codes given below :

List-I	List-II
I. Hockey	1. Ranji Trophy
II. Football	2. Agakhan Cup
III. Tennis	3. Subroto Cup
IV. Cricket	4. Davis Cup

Codes:

	I	II	III	IV
(*a*)	2	3	4	1
(*b*)	4	3	2	1
(*c*)	3	1	2	4
(*d*)	1	2	3	4

91. Match List-I with List-II and select the correct option using the codes given below :

List-I	List-II
I. Learning	1. Direction & intensity of effort
II. Components of motivation	2. Psychological core
III. Personality	3. Law of Effect
IV. Thorndike	4. Trial & Error

Codes:

	I	II	III	IV
(*a*)	1	2	3	4
(*b*)	4	1	2	3
(*c*)	2	3	4	1
(*d*)	3	4	1	2

92. Match List-I with List-II and select the correct option using the codes given below :

List-I	List-II
I. Reliability	1. Standard
II. Objectivity	2. Authenticity
III. Validity	3. Consistency in result
IV. Norms	4. Consistency in result with different tester

Codes:

	I	II	III	IV
(*a*)	3	4	2	1
(*b*)	3	4	1	2
(*c*)	4	3	2	1
(*d*)	2	3	4	1

93. Match List-I with List-II and select the correct option using the codes given below :

List-I	List-II
I. Basketball	1. Sudden death
II. Kabbaddi	2. Libero
III. Volleyball	3. Dead ball
IV. Wrestling	4. Lona

Codes:

	I	II	III	IV
(*a*)	3	4	2	1
(*b*)	3	4	1	2
(*c*)	2	4	1	3
(*d*)	1	4	3	2

94. Match List-I with List-II and select the correct option using the codes given below :

List-I	List-II
I. Bureaucratic Theory	1. Henry Fayol
II. Scientific Management Theory	2. Elton Mayo

III. Administrative Theory — 3. F.W. Taylor
IV. Human Relation Movement Theory — 4. Max Weber

Codes:

	I	II	III	IV
(*a*)	4	3	1	2
(*b*)	1	2	3	4
(*c*)	2	4	1	3
(*d*)	4	2	3	1

95. Match List-I with List-II and select the correct option using the codes given below :

List-I	List-II
I. Water Jump	1. Basketball
II. Diagonal excess	2. Hockey
III. 23 Metres	3. Steeple Chase
IV. 8 Seconds	4. 800 Metres

Codes:

	I	II	III	IV
(*a*)	3	4	2	1
(*b*)	4	3	1	2
(*c*)	2	1	3	4
(*d*)	3	4	1	2

96. Match List-I with List-II and select the correct option using the codes given below :

List-I	List-II
I. Circuit Training	1. Winter Bottom
II. Fartlek Training	2. Dr. Reindell and Greschler
III. Interval Training	3. Gosta Halmar
IV. Pressure Training	4. Morgan and Adamdson

Codes:

	I	II	III	IV
(*a*)	3	4	1	2
(*b*)	4	3	2	1
(*c*)	2	1	4	3
(*d*)	1	2	3	4

97. Match List-I with List-II and select the correct option using the codes given below :

List-I	List-II
I. Fosbury flop	1. Relay Race
II. Glide technique	2. Long Jump
III. Hitch Kick	3. Shot Put
IV. Snatch Baton Pass	4. High Jump

Codes:

	I	II	III	IV
(*a*)	4	3	2	1
(*b*)	4	2	1	3
(*c*)	3	2	4	1
(*d*)	3	2	1	4

98. Arrange the following phases of motor learning in order of sequence :

I. Phase of fine coordination
II. Phase of rough coordination
III. Phase of automatization

Codes:

(*a*) I, II, III (*b*) II, III, I
(*c*) II, I, III (*d*) III, II, I

99. Arrange the following mechanical phases of a 100 M sprint in order of their sequence of progression :

I. Retardation
II. Quick acceleration phase
III. Top speed phase
IV. Slow acceleration phase

Codes:

(*a*) I, II, III, IV (*b*) IV, II, III, I
(*c*) III, IV, I, II (*d*) II, I, IV, III

100. Arrange in correct sequential order the approaches adopted to study personality in sport :

I. Trait approach
II. Situation approach
III. Psychodynamic approach
IV. Interactional approach

Codes:

(*a*) I, III, IV, II (*b*) IV, II, I, III
(*c*) II, IV, III, I (*d*) III, I, II, IV

101. Arrange in correct sequential order the following statistical measures to analyse data :

I. F Ratio
II. Scheffee Post Hoc Test
III. Mean
IV. RSS, CF, TSS, SS_b, SS_w

Codes:

(*a*) III, II, IV, I (*b*) III, II, I, IV
(*c*) III, IV, I, II (*d*) IV, III, I, II

102. Arrange in correct sequential order the preventive measures of communicable diseases :

I. Disinfection II. Notification
III. Diagnosis IV. Isolation
V. Treatment VI. Immunisation
VII. Investigation

Codes:
(*a*) I, II, III, IV, V, VI, VII
(*b*) II, IV, I, III, VII, VI, V
(*c*) IV, III, II, I, VI, VII, V
(*d*) III, I, II, IV, V, VI, VII

103. Arrange the following institutes in chronological order of their inception in India :

I. YMCA College of Physical Education, Madras (Chennai)
II. Sport Authority of India, New Delhi
III. National Institute of Sport, Patiala
IV. H.V.P. Mandal, Amravati

Codes:
(*a*) I, II, III, IV (*b*) II, III, I, IV
(*c*) III, IV, II, I (*d*) IV, I, III, II

104. Arrange the following in the chronological order :

I. Modern Olympic Games
II. Asian Games
III. Commonwealth Games
IV. SAF Games

Codes:
(*a*) I, II, III, IV (*b*) IV, II, III, I
(*c*) IV, III, II, I (*d*) I, III, II, IV

105. Arrange the following events of the first day of Decathlon in proper sequence of their occurrence :

I. 400 m II. Shot Put
III. Long Jump IV. High Jump
V. 100 m

Codes:
(*a*) V, III, II, IV, I (*b*) I, IV, III, II, V
(*c*) V, IV, III, II, I (*d*) II, III, IV, V, I

106. Sequence of therapeutic modalities includes :

I. Cryo therapy II. Electro therapy
III. Massage therapy IV. Exercise therapy

Codes:
(*a*) I, III, IV, II (*b*) I, II, III, IV
(*c*) II, III, I, IV (*d*) I, III, II, IV

107. Given below are two statements, one labelled as Assertion (A), and the other as Reason (R).

Assertion (A) : Socialization takes place through participation in games and sports.

Reason (R) : Games and sports inculcate social habits.

Which one of the following statement is correct?
(*a*) (A) is true, but (R) is false.
(*b*) (A) is false, but (R) is true.
(*c*) Both (A) and (R) are false.
(*d*) Both (A) and (R) are true.

108. Given below are two statements, one labelled as Assertion (A), and the other as Reason (R).

Assertion (A) : Modern concept of health includes only a sound body with adequate fitness.

Reason (R) : Health is a state of complete well-being.

Which one of the following statement is correct?
(*a*) (A) is right, but (R) is wrong.
(*b*) Both (A) and (R) are right.
(*c*) (A) is wrong, but (R) is right.
(*d*) Both (A) and (R) are wrong.

109. Given below are two statements, one is labelled as Assertion (A), and the other as Reason (R).

Assertion (A) : Type-II error accepts the null hypothesis when it is false.

Reason (R) : This error is due to false interpretation of data.

Which one of the following statement is correct?
(*a*) (A) is right, but (R) is wrong.
(*b*) Both (A) and (R) are right.
(*c*) (A) is wrong, but (R) is right.
(*d*) Both (A) and (R) are wrong.

110. Given below are two statements, one is labelled as Assertion (A), and the other as Reason (R).

Assertion (A) : There exists a positive relationship between cohesion and performance in team sport.

Reason (R) : Assessment of task cohesion and social cohesion measures the relationship of cohesion and performance of a team.

Which one of the following statement is correct?

(*a*) (A) is right and (R) is wrong.
(*b*) (A) is wrong and (R) is right.
(*c*) Both (A) and (R) are right and (R) is the correct explanation of (A).
(*d*) Both (A) and (R) are right, but (R) is not the correct explanation of (A).

111. Given below are two statements, one is labelled as Assertion (A), and the other as Reason (R).

Assertion (A) : In normal standing position, the body weight is balanced by ground reaction force.

Reason (R) : The basic condition for maintaining equilibrium is – the resultant of all forces acting on a body must be zero.

Which one of the following statement is correct?

(*a*) (A) is right, but (R) is wrong.
(*b*) Both (A) and (R) are right.
(*c*) (A) is wrong, but (R) is right.
(*d*) Both (A) and (R) are wrong.

112. Given below are two statements, one is labelled as Assertion (A), and the other as Reason (R).

Assertion (A) : The main emphasis of the School Health Programme should be to educate children in matters of health and hygiene.

Reason (R) : To keep the children free from diseases.

Which one of the following statement is correct?

(*a*) Both (A) and (R) are right and (R) is the correct explanation of (A).
(*b*) Both (A) and (R) are right, but (R) is not the correct explanation of (A).
(*c*) (A) is wrong, but (R) is right.
(*d*) (A) is right, but (R) is wrong.

113. Given below are two statements, one is labelled as Assertion (A), and the other as Reason (R).

Assertion (A) : Recreation is a fundamental human need.

Reason (R) : Urge for recreation is universal.

Which one of the following statement is correct?

(*a*) Both (A) and (R) are right, but (R) is not the correct explanation of (A).
(*b*) Both (A) and (R) are right and (R) is the correct explanation of (A).
(*c*) (A) is wrong, but (R) is right.
(*d*) (A) is right, but (R) is wrong.

114. Given below are two statements, one is labelled as Assertion (A), and the other as Reason (R).

Assertion (A) : Playgrounds are known as the character building laboratories.

Reason (R) : Character building qualities are developed on playgrounds.

Which one of the following statement is correct?

(*a*) (A) is true, but (R) is false.
(*b*) Both (A) and (R) are true and (R) is the correct explanation of (A).
(*c*) (A) is false, but (R) is true.
(*d*) Both (A) and (R) are false.

115. Given below are the two statements one of which is labelled as Assertion (A), and the other as Reason (R).

Assertion (A) : Criterion reference test encourage closed convergent thinking.

Reason (R) : They establish the proportion of what could be achieved.

Which one of the following statement is correct?

(*a*) (A) is false, but (R) is true.
(*b*) Both (A) and (R) are true.

(*c*) (A) is true, but (R) is false.
(*d*) Both (A) and (R) are false.

116. Given below are the two statements, one of which is labelled as Assertion (A), and the other as Reason (R).

Assertion (A) : Norm is a standard set of scores with which an obtained score is compared.

Reason (R) : Norm is developed through logical experimentation.

Which one of the following statement is correct?

(*a*) Both (A) and (R) are true.
(*b*) (A) is true, but (R) is false.
(*c*) (A) is false and (R) is true.
(*d*) (A) is true and (R) is correct explanation of (A).

117. Make the correct choice from the Assertion (A) and Reason (R) given below :

Assertion (A) : Lymphatic vessels in the skin follow veins.

Reason (R) : Lymphatic vessels with viscera follow arteries.

Which one of the following statement is correct?

(*a*) Both (A) and (R) are true.
(*b*) Both (A) and (R) are false.
(*c*) (A) is false, but (R) is true.
(*d*) (A) is true, but (R) is false.

118. Make the correct choice from the Assertion (A), and the Reason (R) given below :

Assertion (A) : A carom player does not get injury in a competition.

Reason (R) : A player needs to warm up to avoid injury.

Which one of the following statement is correct?

(*a*) Both (A) and (R) are true and (R) is the correct explanation of (A).
(*b*) Both (A) and (R) are true, but (R) is not the correct explanation of (A).
(*c*) (A) is true, but (R) is false.
(*d*) (A) is false, but (R) is true.

119. Make the correct choice from the Assertion (A) and Reason (R) given below :

Assertion (A) : Competitions are indispensable for enhancement of sports performance.

Reason (R) : Competitions provide opportunity to the individual to prove his physical and psychic ability.

Which one of the following statement is correct?

(*a*) Both (A) and (R) are true and (R) is the correct explanation of (A).
(*b*) (A) is true but (R) is false.
(*c*) Both (A) and (R) are false.
(*d*) (A) is false, but (R) is true.

120. Make the correct choice from the Assertion (A) and Reason (R) given below :

Assertion (A) : Supervision is an expert technical service primarily concentrated with studying and improving conditions that surround learning and pupil growth.

Reason (R) : Supervision is a planned programme for a better teaching learning situation.

Which one of the following statement is correct?

(*a*) (A) is true, but (R) is false.
(*b*) (A) is false, but (R) is true.
(*c*) Both (A) and (R) are true and (R) is the correct explanation of (A).
(*d*) Both (A) and (R) are false.

Directions (Qs. 121 to 125) : *Read the passage and answer the questions that follow based on your understanding of the passage :*

What will our world be like in the future? What will physical education and sport be like in the twenty-first century? Recognising that change is ever present, certain trends and developments can be identified that lend themselves to a better understanding of the future of physical education and sport. These trends and developments include the wellness movement, the fitness movement, the educational reform movement and changing nature of education, the expending frontiers of the habitable universe and technological advances.

This decade is one of rapid technological advances. Many of these technological advances hold implications for the future of physical education and sport. Developments in computer technology combined with increasingly sophisticated research techniques have enabled us to widen the base of knowledge in physical education. Computer technology has facilitated biomechanical analysis of performance. Computer generated graphical representations of protypical sport performance will enhance the development of motor skills. Computers have also enabled researchers to better understand brain activity during learning, and subsequently design more effective instructional strategies; perhaps in the future physical educators will be able to predict with a great deal of certainty learning outcomes.

Developments in the field of communication hold promise for the future of physical education and sport, cable television is growing rapidly. The number of special interest programmes presented on cable television is increasing as well. Videotape equipment has become easier to use, and provides a valuable instructional tool for physical educators in all settings. Video cassette recorders are experiencing phenomenal growth; many individuals are investing in exercise videotapes so that they can work out in the privacy of their own home and at their convenience. In the future instructional tapes for different sport skills will help individuals learn at home at their own pace.

Developments in biotechnology hold implications for the future of physical education and sport. Today identification of fibre type proportion in muscles allows researchers to identify whether an individual has a greater potential to succeed in athletic events requiring explosive strength or endurance. Perhaps in the near future genetic engineering will be used to programme an individual's genes for success in certain sport activities.

Advances in technology have led to improvements in sport equipment, facilitating better performance by both skills and unskilled persons. Graphitecomposite tennis rackets have replaced metal and metal-composite tennis rackets, which replaced wooden rackets years ago. Pole vaulters using fibre-glass poles have attained heights previously only dreamed about by vaulters using wooden poles. Technology applied to the manufacturing of running shoes has led to increased comfort and fewer injuries for runners of all abilities. Grass fields are being replaced by artificial surface under tracts by allweather tracks, and open stadiums by domed arenas. There are numerous examples of how technology has affected physical education and sport, and the influence of technology on physical education and sport will continue in future.

121. Future of physical education and sport will depend on :

(*a*) Developing infrastructure
(*b*) Expending frontiers of the habitable universe
(*c*) Providing finances
(*d*) Increasing participation of younger population

122. Computer technology facilitates :

I. Biomechanical analysis
II. Genetic engineering
III. Graphic representation of protypical sport performance
IV. Sophisticated research techniques

Find the correct combination.

(*a*) I & II (*b*) I & III
(*c*) III & IV (*d*) II & IV

123. Genetic engineering will be used

(*a*) to retard growth of sportsperson
(*b*) to develop surgical techniques
(*c*) to find out genes for success
(*d*) to accelerate growth of young sportsperson

124. Match List-I with List-II and select the correct option using the code given below :

List-I	List-II
I. Improved sport equipment	1. Artificial surface
II. Muscle fibre typing	2. Computer
III. Understanding brain activity	3. Assessing potential of Marathon runner

IV. All weather tracts	4. Facilitation of performance of unskilled person		

Codes:

	I	II	III	IV
(*a*)	1	2	3	4
(*b*)	2	3	1	4
(*c*)	3	4	2	1
(*d*)	4	3	2	1

125. Wellness movement supports efforts directed toward
(*a*) Health promotion and disease prevention
(*b*) Fitness development
(*c*) Skill development
(*d*) Developing allround personality

126. India participated in Olympic Games for the first time in
(*a*) 1896 (*b*) 1900
(*c*) 1904 (*d*) 1924

127. Bones in human body are classified on the basis of
(*a*) Structure and Functions
(*b*) Location and Attachment
(*c*) Size and Shape
(*d*) Joint and Movement

128. Find the correct answer :
(*a*) Friction is a negative force for performance.
(*b*) Friction is a positive force for performance.
(*c*) Friction is negative as well as positive force for performance.
(*d*) Friction does not have any influence on performance.

129. Theory of insight learning was propounded by
(*a*) Thorndike (*b*) Pavlov
(*c*) Kohler (*d*) Cattell

130. First Teachers' Training College in India was started at
(*a*) Lucknow (*b*) Kandivali
(*c*) Chennai (*d*) Amravati

131. Aim of sports training is
(*a*) improvement of physical fitness.
(*b*) improvement of technical skills.
(*c*) improvement of tactical efficiency.
(*d*) improvement of sports performance.

132. One of the important research tool is
(*a*) Questionnaire (*b*) Library technique
(*c*) Hypothesizing (*d*) Survey

133. Test, Measurement and Evaluation are related with one another in the following way :
(*a*) Measurement and Evaluation are parts of test.
(*b*) Evaluation and Test are parts of measurement.
(*c*) Test and Measurement are parts of evaluation.
(*d*) Evaluation is a part of both Test and Measurement.

134. Basic function of Association of India Universities (AIU) is
(*a*) Purchase of equipment for Universities
(*b*) Planning of the Inter-University Competitions.
(*c*) Providing finance to develop sports facilities
(*d*) Appointment of Physical Education Directors for Universities

135. Sociological foundation of physical education discusses
I. Body type
II. Motor learning
III. Competition and Co-operation
IV. Socialization process
Find the correct combination.
(*a*) I and IV (*b*) II and IV
(*c*) I and III (*d*) III and IV

136. The digested food material in small intestine is absorbed in
I. Duodenum II. Vilus
III. Ilium IV. Villi
Find the correct combination :
(*a*) I and III (*b*) II and IV
(*c*) IV and III (*d*) II and I

137. Angular velocity depends on :
I. Radius of rotation directly.
II. Radius of rotation inversely.
III. Linear velocity directly.
IV. Linear velocity indirectly.

Find the correct combination :

(a) I and III (b) III and II

(c) II and IV (d) IV and I

138. Motivation consists of

I. Direction II. Intensity

III. Persistence IV. All of above

Find the correct combination.

(a) I and II (b) II and III

(c) I and III (d) IV

139. Micronutrients include :

I. Carbohydrate II. Minerals

III. Vitamins IV. Fat

Find the correct combination.

(a) I and II (b) II and III

(c) III and IV (d) IV and I

140. Interval training load depends on

I. Load volume

II. Heart rate

III. Load intensity

IV. Lactic acid concentration

Find the correct combination.

(a) I and II (b) I and III

(c) II and III (d) II and IV

141. Research problem involves the following characteristics :

I. Novelty II. Valuability

III. Feasibility IV. Simplicity

Find the correct combination :

(a) I, II, III (b) II, III, IV

(c) I, III, IV (d) I, II, IV

142. Criteria of a standard test involve

I. Reliability II. Complexity

III. Variability IV. Norm

Find the correct combination.

(a) I and II (b) II and III

(c) III and IV (d) IV and I

143. The primary goal of intramural competition is :

I. To provide opportunity for mass participation of students.

II. To participate in Inter-school competition.

III. To provide Intra-school competition experience.

IV. To improve sports performance for higher level of competition.

Find the correct combination.

(a) I and II (b) III and IV

(c) I and III (d) II and IV

144. Given below are two statements, one is labelled as Assertion (A) and the other is labelled as Reason (R).

Assertion (A) : Self expression is the aim of physical education according to Naturalism.

Reason (R) : Naturalism believes nothing beyond nature.

In the context of the two statements, which one of the following is correct?

(a) Both (A) and (R) are true and (R) is the correct explanation of (A).

(b) Both (A) and (R) are true but (R) is not the correct explanation of (A).

(c) (A) is true, but (R) is false.

(d) (A) is false, but (R) is true.

145. Assertion (A) : Internal respiration means the exchange of gases in cell through extracellular fluid.

Reason (R) : Pulmonary circulation means systemic circulation.

In the context of above statements, which one of the following is correct?

(a) Both (A) and (R) are true and (R) is the correct explanation of (A).

(b) Both (A) and (R) are true but (R) is not the correct explanation of (A).

(c) (A) is true, but (R) is false.

(d) (A) is false, but (R) is true.

146. Assertion (A) : Lowering centre of Gravity of the body increases degree of stability.

Reason (R) : Equilibrium has indirect relation with height of Centre of Gravity.

In the context of above statements, which one of the following is correct?

(a) (A) is true and (R) is false.

(b) (A) is false and (R) is true.

(c) Both (A) and (R) are false.

(d) Both (A) and (R) are correct.

147. Assertion (A) : Hostile aggression provokes one to harm others physically.

Reason (R) : Aggression is an intent to harm another person mentally and / or physically.

In the context of above statements, which one of the following is correct?

(*a*) (A) is true, but (R) is false.
(*b*) Both (A) and (R) are true, and (R) is the correct explanation of (A).
(*c*) Both (A) and (R) are true, but (R) is not the correct explanation of (A).
(*d*) (A) is false, but (R) is correct.

148. Assertion (A) : Before independence, there was not a single physical education college in India.

Reason (R) : Y.M.C.A. College of Physical Education was started in 1920 in Chennai.

In the context of above statements, which one of the following is correct?

(*a*) Both (A) and (R) are true and (R) is the correct explanation of (A).
(*b*) Both (A) and (R) are true but (R) is not the correct explanation of (A).
(*c*) (A) is true but (R) is false.
(*d*) (A) is false but (R) is true.

149. Assertion (A) : Person suffering from smallpox should be isolated.

Reason (R) : Isolation is a measure for prevention of infection.

In the context of above statements, which one of the following is correct?

(*a*) Both (A) and (R) are true and (R) is the correct explanation of (A).
(*b*) Both (A) and (R) are true, but (R) is not the correct explanation of (A).
(*c*) (A) is true, but (R) is false.
(*d*) (A) is false, but (R) is true.

150. Assertion (A) : For improvement of performance in long distance running, continuous training is effective.

Reason (R) : Continuous method of training improves basic endurance.

In the context of above statements, which one of the following statements is correct?

(*a*) Both (A) and (R) are true and (R) is the correct explanation of (A).
(*b*) Both (A) and (R) are true but (R) is not the correct explanation of (A).
(*c*) (A) is true, but (R) is false.
(*d*) (A) is false, but (R) is true.

151. Assertion (A) : 't' test is used to assess the significance of difference between two means.

Reason (R) : 't' test is a method used for inferential statistics.

In the context of above statements, which one of the following statements is correct?

(*a*) Both (A) and (R) are true but (R) is not the correct explanation of (A).
(*b*) Both (A) and (R) are false.
(*c*) Both (A) and (R) are true and (R) is the correct explanation of (A).
(*d*) (A) is true and (R) is false.

152. Assertion (A) : Lean Body Mass is the amount of body weight excluding body fat.

Reason (R) : Body composition involves components with which human body is formed.

In the context of above statements, which one of the following statements is correct?

(*a*) Both (A) and (R) are true but (R) is not the correct explanation of (A).
(*b*) Both (A) and (R) are true and (R) is the correct explanation of (A).
(*c*) (A) is true, but (R) is false.
(*d*) (A) is false, but (R) is right.

153. Assertion (A) : Management involves organizing, administering and supervising the work.

Reason (R) : Well began is half done.

In the context of above statements, which one of the following statements is correct?

(*a*) Both (A) and (R) are correct and (R) is the correct explanation of (A).
(*b*) Both (A) and (R) are correct but (R) is not the correct explanation of (A).
(*c*) (A) is true, but (R) is false.
(*d*) (A) is false, but (R) is true.

154. Arrange the following events in chronological order :

I. Foundation of L.C.P.E.
II. Starting of Y.M.C.A. College of Physical Education, Chennai.
III. Starting of academic department for Physical Education in Universities.
IV. Starting of M. Phil course in Physical Education.

Codes:
(*a*) I, II, IV, III (*b*) III, IV, I, II
(*c*) II, I, III, IV (*d*) IV, III, II, I

155. Arrange the following body parts in descending order :

I. Cell II. Tissue
III. Organ IV. System

Codes:
(*a*) I, II, III, IV (*b*) IV, III, II, I
(*c*) III, IV, I, II (*d*) II, I, IV, III

156. Arrange the following phases of take-off in proper sequence :

I. Absorption II. Active stretching
III. Take-off IV. Touch down

Codes:
(*a*) I, II, III, IV (*b*) IV, I, II, III
(*c*) III, IV, I, II (*d*) II, III, IV, I

157. Arrange the following in correct sequence for skill learning :

I. Associative Phase
II. Presentation stage
III. Automatization stage
IV. Cognitive stage

Codes:
(*a*) I, III, IV, II (*b*) II, IV, I, III
(*c*) III, I, II, IV (*d*) IV, II, III, I

158. Arrange the following sequence for First Aid Management in sprain :

I. Compression II. Ice
III. Rest IV. Elevation

Codes:
(*a*) II, III, IV, I (*b*) III, II, I, IV
(*c*) I, III, II, IV (*d*) IV, I, II, III

159. Arrange the following phases of periodization in correct sequence :

I. Preparatory phase
II. Transition phase
III. Competition phase
IV. Pre-competition phase

Codes :
(*a*) I, II, III, IV (*b*) I, III, IV, II
(*c*) I, IV, III, II (*d*) II, I, IV, III

160. Arrange the following phases of research in correct sequence :

I. Analysis of data
II. Drawing conclusions
III. Testing hypothesis
IV. Collecting data

Codes :
(*a*) II, III, I, IV (*b*) I, IV, III, II
(*c*) IV, I, II, III (*d*) III, II, IV, I

161. Arrange the following test in chronological order in respect of their origination :

I. Physical fitness
II. Motor fitness
III. Health Related fitness
IV. Motor Educability

Codes :
(*a*) I, III, IV, II (*b*) II, IV, III, I
(*c*) III, I, II, IV (*d*) I, II, III, IV

162. Arrange the following steps for managing a sports program :

I. Budgeting II. Directing
III. Planning IV. Staffing

Codes :
(*a*) II, III, I, IV (*b*) III, I, IV, II
(*c*) I, II, III, IV (*d*) IV, I, II, III

163. Match List-I with List-II and select the correct answer from the codes given below :

List-I	List-II
a. Educational Gymnastics	i. Ancient Olympics
b. Turner movement	ii. Rome
c. Gladiatorial combat	iii. Germany
d. Stade race	iv. Sweden

Codes:

	a	b	c	d
(*a*)	iv	iii	ii	i
(*b*)	iii	iv	i	ii

(*c*)	i	ii	iv	iii
(*d*)	ii	i	iii	iv

164. Match List-I with List-II and select the correct answer from the codes given below :

List-I	List-II
a. Aorta	i. Brings oxygenated blood to heart from lungs
b. Pulmonary vein	ii. Supplies oxygenated blood to heart muscles
c. Vena-Cava	iii. Brings deoxygenated blood to lungs
	iv. First artery to leave heart
d. Coronary artery	v. Brings deoxygenated blood to heart

Codes:

	a	b	c	d
(*a*)	i	ii	iii	iv
(*b*)	iii	iv	ii	v
(*c*)	iv	i	v	ii
(*d*)	iv	v	i	iii

165. Match List-I with List-II and select the correct answer from the codes given below :

List-I	List-II
a. Force of Gravity	i. Stability
b. Frictional force	ii. Rebound
c. Buoyant force	iii. Free fall
d. Elastic force	iv. Floating

Codes:

	a	b	c	d
(*a*)	iii	i	iv	ii
(*b*)	i	iv	ii	iii
(*c*)	ii	iii	i	iv
(*d*)	iv	ii	iii	i

166. Match List-I with List-II and select the correct answer from the codes given below :

List-I	List-II
a. Hinge Joint	i. Tarsal
b. Pivot Joint	ii. Ankle
c. Gliding Joint	iii. Elbow
d. Saddle Joint	iv. Head

Codes:

	a	b	c	d
(*a*)	iii	ii	iv	i
(*b*)	ii	iii	i	iv
(*c*)	iv	iii	ii	i
(*d*)	iii	iv	i	ii

167. Match List-I with List-II and select the correct answer from the codes given below :

List-I	List-II
a. B.M.I.	i. Leanness
b. Body composition	ii. Performance related fitness
c. Explosive strength	iii. Health related fitness
d. Pondoral Index	iv. Obesity

Codes:

	a	b	c	d
(*a*)	i	iv	iii	ii
(*b*)	iv	iii	ii	i
(*c*)	iii	ii	i	iv
(*d*)	ii	i	iv	iii

168. Match List-I with List-II and select the correct answer from the codes given below :

List-I	List-II
a. Penalty corner	i. Volleyball
b. Penalty spot	ii. Track & Field
c. Libero	iii. Hockey
d. Stop Board	iv. Football

Codes:

	a	b	c	d
(*a*)	ii	iii	iv	i
(*b*)	i	ii	iii	iv
(*c*)	iv	i	iii	ii
(*d*)	iii	iv	i	ii

169. Match List-I with List-II and select the correct answer from the codes given below :

List-I	List-II
a. F-test	i. Co-efficient of correlation
b. Measuring central tendency	ii. Standard Deviation

c. Test of correlation — iii. ANOVA

d. Measuring variability — iv. Median

Codes:

	a	b	c	d
(*a*)	i	iii	ii	iv
(*b*)	iii	iv	i	ii
(*c*)	iv	ii	iii	i
(*d*)	ii	i	iv	iii

170. Match List-I with List-II and select the correct answer from the codes given below :

List-I	List-II
a. Miller Volley test	i. Team cohesion
b. PACER	ii. Badminton
c. SCAT	iii. Cardiorespiratory endurance
d. Group Environment Questionnaire	iv. Anxiety

Codes:

	a	b	c	d
(*a*)	ii	iii	iv	i
(*b*)	iii	iv	i	ii
(*c*)	iv	i	ii	iii
(*d*)	i	ii	iii	iv

171. Match List-I with List-II and select the correct answer from the codes given below :

List-I	List-II
a. Three seconds rule	i. Football
b. Throw-in	ii. Hockey
c. Straight push	iii. Basketball
d. Service	iv. Badminton
	v. Baseball

Codes:

	a	b	c	d
(*a*)	i	ii	iii	v
(*b*)	ii	i	iv	iii
(*c*)	iii	i	ii	iv
(*d*)	i	ii	v	iv

Directions (Qs. 172 to 175) : Read the following passage and answer the question given below.

Burnout is becoming increasingly prevalent among teachers and coaches. Burnout can be defined as physical, emotional and attitudinal exhaustion. There are many causes of teacher burnout. Lack of administrative support, lack of input into the curriculum process, public criticism and the accompanying lack of community support are all factors contributing to burnout. Inadequate salaries, discipline problems too little time to do the evergrowing amount of work, large class sizes, and heavier teaching loads may also contribute to this problem. The lack of challenge, inadequate supervisory feedback and the absence of opportunities for personal and professional growth may also lead to burnout.

In the coaching realm burnout may be caused by competitive seasons that seem to go on without end, administrative and community pressures and time pressures. Teacher-coach role conflict occurs when a disparity exists between the expectations associated with being a teacher and a coach, this results in a multitude of simultaneous, somewhat diverse demands. The teacher-coach unable to satisfy these demands, experiences role conflict.

In both the teaching and coaching realms, personal problems may interact with professional problems to exacerbate burnout. Personal problems such as conflicts within one's family, money difficulties, or perhaps problems with relationships may cause additional stress for the individual. These stresses coupled with professional problems may hasten the onset of burnout.

The consequences of burnout are many and are often quite severe, affecting teachers as well as their students. The most critical impact of burnout may be on instruction. Burned out teachers may cope with the demands of teaching by sitting on the sidelines.

172. Which of the following is the prevalent cause of 'Teacher-burn out'?

(*a*) Lack of financial support
(*b*) Lack of administrative support
(*c*) Lack of political support
(*d*) Lack of family support

173. Which of the following is the most important cause of 'Coach-burn out'?
(*a*) Administrative and community pressure
(*b*) Parents pressure
(*c*) Participant's pressure
(*d*) Higher authority's pressure

174. Which role conflict leads to the burn out of a teacher-coach?
(*a*) Demands of the participants
(*b*) Demands of administration
(*c*) Demands of the parents
(*d*) Expectations of being a teacher-coach

175. Which of the following is the most dominant factor that leads to burnout in teaching and coaching?
(*a*) Political problems
(*b*) Social problems
(*c*) Personal problems
(*d*) Administrative problems

176. Select the correct option :
Flexion and extension take place around
(*a*) Medio-lateral axis
(*b*) Anterio Posterior axis
(*c*) Vertical axis
(*d*) Sagittal axis

177. Select the correct option Protraction and retraction take place in
(*a*) Hip Joint (*b*) Shoulder joint
(*c*) Elbow joint (*d*) Knee joint

178. Select the correct option :
Focus of physical education is
(*a*) Motion (*b*) Fitness
(*c*) Man (*d*) Man in motion

179. Select the most suitable option :
(*a*) Soccer is a game
(*b*) Soccer is a sport as well as a game
(*c*) Soccer is a sport
(*d*) Soccer is a play

180. Select that correct option :
During strenuous exercise, the major reason for onset of fatigue is
(*a*) O_2 debt
(*b*) Depletion of O_2
(*c*) Lactic acid formation
(*d*) Increase of CO_2 level

181. Which one of the following is not the part of Hydrotherapy?
(*a*) Wax bath (*b*) Cryotherapy
(*c*) Whirlpool bath (*d*) Contrast bath

182. Select the correct option :
Assessment of group cohesion is done through
(*a*) Observation during training and competition
(*b*) Performance tests
(*c*) Sociogram
(*d*) Knowledge based tests

183. Select the correct option :
Psychological core of personality is the most basic level of personality. It is
(*a*) Adjustment to environment
(*b*) Internal and constant
(*c*) Role related behaviour
(*d*) External & dynamic

184. Select the correct option :
National Fitness Corps was introduced in
(*a*) 1965 (*b*) 1966
(*c*) 1967 (*d*) 1968

185. In which of the following places, there is no centre of Sports Authority of India?
(*a*) Kolkata (*b*) Bangalore
(*c*) Patiala (*d*) Chandigarh

186. Which of the following is not related to the School Health Programme?
(*a*) Keeping health records
(*b*) Health education
(*c*) Controlling of diseases
(*d*) Health inspection

187. Solid gold medals were last given in Olympic Games in
(*a*) 1904 (*b*) 1908
(*c*) 1912 (*d*) 1920

188. Sunlight is a source of
(*a*) Vitamin A (*b*) Vitamin B
(*c*) Vitamin C (*d*) Vitamin D

189. Philosophical research is also known as
(*a*) Rational research

(*b*) Perceptual research
(*c*) Conceptual research
(*d*) Behavioural research

190. Sample may be big or small depends on
(*a*) Geographical area
(*b*) Demographic fluctuation
(*c*) Characteristics and traits of population
(*d*) Balance of births and deaths over time

191. When the 'Z' value is equal to or exceeds 2.58 one may safely conclude that the difference between the means is significant at
(*a*) 0.02 level (*b*) 0.01 level
(*c*) 0.001 level (*d*) 0.05 level

192. Kraus-Weber Test measures
(*a*) Minimum muscular strength
(*b*) Absolute muscular strength
(*c*) Maximum muscular strength
(*d*) Relative muscular strength

193. Metabolic adaptation is
(*a*) Adjustment of metabolic rate to enhanced of work load demand
(*b*) Metabolic rate suspension
(*c*) Metabolic impulsion
(*d*) Adaptation of metabolic ratio

194. Which of the following is an apex body for Olympic Games ?
(*a*) OCA (*b*) IOC
(*c*) ICC (*d*) FIFA

195. First step in Sport Management is
(*a*) Budgeting (*b*) Co-ordinating
(*c*) Planning (*d*) Directing

196. Blue print of the team competition plan is called
(*a*) Tactics (*b*) Skill
(*c*) Technique (*d*) Strategy

197. Kinematic parameters include
I. Inertia II. Velocity
III. Distance IV. Acceleration
Find the correct combination :
(*a*) I, II, III (*b*) I, III, IV
(*c*) I, II, IV (*d*) II, III, IV

198. Performance related fitness includes
I. leg explosive strength
II. Cardio-vascular endurance
III. Reaction ability
IV. Flexibility
Find the correct combination
(*a*) I, II (*b*) II, III
(*c*) I, III (*d*) II, IV

199. A first class lever can provide mechanical advantage in form of
I. Speed II. Strength
III. Balance IV. Coordination
Find the correct combination
(*a*) I, II, III (*b*) II, III, IV
(*c*) III, IV, I (*d*) IV, I, II

200. Biological basis of life includes :
I. Motor fitness II. Physical exercise
III. Intelligence IV. Food
Find the correct combination
(*a*) I, II (*b*) II, III
(*c*) I, III (*d*) II, IV

201. Development of group cohesion is based on
I. Team factors
II. Individual factors
III. Leadership factors
IV. Environmental factors
Find the correct combination :
(*a*) I, III, IV (*b*) I, II, III
(*c*) II, III, IV (*d*) IV, I, II

202. Personal sources of stress are
I. Event importance II. Trait anxiety
III. Self esteem IV. Uncertainty
Find the correct combination :
(*a*) I, II (*b*) II, III
(*c*) III, IV (*d*) IV, I

203. Professional ethics in physical education includes :
I. Moral values II. Judgement
III. Physical fitness IV. Sincerity
Find the correct combination :
(*a*) I, II (*b*) II, III
(*c*) I, IV (*d*) II, IV

204. Curve will be normal if
I. $\bar{X} > M < Z$
II. $(Q_3 - M) = (M - Q_1)$
III. Uni-mode
IV. Q.D. = $0.6745\ \sigma$

Find the correct combination :
(*a*) I, II, IV (*b*) I, II, III
(*c*) I, III, IV (*d*) II, III, IV

205. Evaluation measures :
I. Efficiency of efforts
II. Achievement level of target
III. Distance from goal
IV. Status of the subject

Find the correct combination
(*a*) I, II (*b*) II, III
(*c*) II, III, IV (*d*) I, II, III, IV

206. Progression of load proceeds
I. Linearly
II. Stepwise
III. Stimulus wise
IV. Circularly

Find the correct combination
(*a*) I, III (*b*) II, IV
(*c*) I, II (*d*) II, III

207. Intramural programme creates in students the sense of
I. Mass participation
II. Selfishness
III. Enmity
IV. Maximum involvement

Find the correct combination :
(*a*) I, II (*b*) II, IV
(*c*) III, IV (*d*) I, IV

208. Given below are two statements, one labelled as Assertion (A) and the other labelled as Reason (R) :

Assertion (A) : A runner runs without receiving any force from outside.

Reason (R) : Force is the cause of motion.

In context of the above two statements, which one of the following is correct?

Codes:
(*a*) (A) is right, but (R) is wrong.
(*b*) Both (A) and (R) are right.
(*c*) (A) is wrong, but (R) is right.
(*d*) Both (A) and (R) are wrong.

209. Given below are two statements, one labelled as Assertion (A) and the other labelled as Reason (R) :

Assertion (A) : The management of professional sports like football, baseball or basketball recruit players with very high pay.

Reason (R) : From the above statement one can deduce that players play for the sake of money only.

In context of the above two statements, which one of the following is correct?

Codes:
(*a*) (A) is right, but (R) is wrong.
(*b*) Both (A) and (R) are right.
(*c*) (A) is wrong, but (R) is right.
(*d*) Both (A) and (R) are wrong.

210. Given below are two statements, one labelled as Assertion (A) and the other labelled as Reason (R) :

Assertion (A) : Insulin is ineffective when taken by mouth.

Reason (R) : Insulin is destroyed in alimentary canal and size of molecule is too large for intestinal absorption.

In context of the above two statements, which one of the following is correct?

Codes:
(*a*) (A) is true, but (R) is false.
(*b*) (A) is false, but (R) is true.
(*c*) Both (A) and (R) are true.
(*d*) Both (A) and (R) are false.

211. Given below are two statements, one labelled as Assertion (A) and the other labelled as Reason (R) :

Assertion (A) : Strength of movement produced by a muscle depends upon how close to the joint it is attached.

Reason (R) : A muscle attached further away will produce a powerful movement than one attached to nearer the joint.

In context of the above two statements, which one of the following is correct?

Codes:
(*a*) (A) is false, but (R) is true.
(*b*) (A) is true, but (R) is false.
(*c*) Both (A) and (R) are false.
(*d*) Both (A) and (R) are true.

212. Given below are two statements, one labelled as Assertion (A) and the other labelled as Reason (R) :

Assertion (A) : Autocratic style of leadership is usually task oriented and tightly structured.

Reason (R) : Leadership style is responsible for effective decision making in sport.

In context of the above two statements, which one of the following is correct?

Codes:

(*a*) Both (A) and (R) are true and (R) is the correct explanation of (A).
(*b*) Both (A) and (R) are true, but (R) is not the correct explanation of (A) .
(*c*) (A) is truc, but (R) is false.
(*d*) (A) is false, but (R) is true.

213. Given below are two statements, one labelled as Assertion (A) and the other labelled as Reason (R) :

Assertion (A) : Physical Education is an integral part of education.

Reason (R) : Both education and physical education aim at the total development of personality.

In context of the above two statements, which one of the following is correct?

Codes:

(*a*) (A) is true, but (R) is false.
(*b*) (A) is false, but (R) is true.
(*c*) Both (A) and (R) are false.
(*d*) Both (A) and (R) are true.

214. Given below are two statements, one labelled as Assertion (A) and the other labelled as Reason (R) :

Assertion (A) : Health and safety skills can be taught in the school through First Aid and safety education.

Reason (R) : School age is the appropriate age to learn First Aid and safety education.

In context of the two statements, which one of the following is correct?

Codes:

(*a*) Both (A) and (R) are true and (R) is the correct explanation of (A).
(*b*) Both (A) and (R) are true, but (R) is not the correct explanation of (A).
(*c*) (A) is true, but (R) is false.
(*d*) (A) is false, but (R) is true.

215. Given below are two statements, one labelled as Assertion (A) and the other labelled as Reason (R) :

Assertion (A) : Osteophorosis disease occurs for the Basket Ball players due to overuse of joints.

Reason (R) : Over use of joints the synovial fluid is reduced in the joints.

In context of the two statements, which one of the following is correct?

Codes:

(*a*) Both (A) and (R) are true, but (R) is not the correct explanation of (A).
(*b*) Both (A) and (R) are true and (R)is the correct explanation of (A).
(*c*) (A) is true, but (R) is false.
(*d*) (A) is false, but (R) is true.

216. Given below are two statements, one labelled as Assertion (A) and the other labelled as Reason (R) :

Assertion (A) : Type – I error is rejecting the null hypothesis when it is true.

Reason (R) : Type – I error arises due to false interpretation of data.

In context of the above two statements, which one of the following is correct?

Codes:

(*a*) (A) is right, but (R) is wrong.
(*b*) Both (A) and (R) are right.
(*c*) (A) is wrong, but (R) is right.
(*d*) Both (A) and (R) are wrong.

217. Given below are two statements, one labelled as Assertion (A) and the other labelled as Reason (R) :

Assertion (A) : Agility is an essential component of motor fitness.

Reason (R) : Agility is determined by neuromuscular coordination.

In context of the above two statements, which one of the following is correct?

Codes:
(*a*) (A) is right, but (R) is wrong.
(*b*) (A) is wrong, but (R) is right.
(*c*) Both (A) and (R) are right.
(*d*) Both (A) and (R) are wrong.

218. Given below are two statements, one labelled as Assertion (A) and the other labelled as Reason (R) :

Assertion (A) : Muscular power is a measure of contraction speed of muscle.

Reason (R) : Muscular power is determined by the fibre type proportion of the muscle.

In context of the above two statements, which one of the following is correct?

Codes:
(*a*) (A) is right, but (R) is wrong.
(*b*) (A) is wrong, but (R) is right.
(*c*) Both (A) and (R) are right.
(*d*) Both (A) and (R) are wrong.

219. Given below are two statements, one labelled as Assertion (A) and the other labelled as Reason (R) :

Assertion (A) : Tactics is execution of movements with economy.

Reason (R) : It is regulation of one's action in line of preventing the opponent to regulate his action.

In context of the above two statements, which one of the following is correct?

Codes:
(*a*) (A) is right, but (R) is wrong.
(*b*) (A) is wrong, but (R) is right.
(*c*) Both (A) and (R) are right.
(*d*) Both (A) and (R) are wrong.

220. Given below are two statements, one labelled as Assertion (A) and the other labelled as Reason (R) :

Assertion (A) : Talent indicators are the products of heredity and environment.

Reason (R) : They are, the base of performance prognosis.

In context of the above two statements, which one of the following is correct?

Codes :
(*a*) (A) and (R) both are right.
(*b*) (A) and (R) both are wrong.
(*c*) (A) is right and (R) is wrong.
(*d*) (A) is wrong and (R) is right.

221. Make the correct choice from codes given below consulting the Assertion (A) and Reason (R) :

Assertion (A) : Management is the dynamic life giving element in every organization.

Reason (R) : It is the activating force that gets things done through people.

Codes:
(*a*) (A) is true, but (R) is false.
(*b*) (A) is false, but (R) is true.
(*c*) Both (A) and (R) are false.
(*d*) Both (A) and (R) are true and (R) is the correct explanation of (*a*).

222. Arrange the following mechanical phases of kicking a ball in order of sequence of progression :

I. Kicking — II. Stance
III. Back lift — IV. Follow through

Codes:
(*a*) II, III, I, IV — (*b*) III, I, IV, II
(*c*) I, IV, II, III — (*d*) IV, II, III, I

223. Arrange the following events in order of their first appearance in the process of historical development of games and sports :

I. Gladiatorial combat
II. Olympic Games
III. FIFA World Championship
IV. IPL

Codes:
(*a*) I, II, III, IV — (*b*) II, I, III, IV
(*c*) III, IV, II, I — (*d*) IV, III, I, II

224. Arrange the following sources of energy for muscular exercise in order of their sequence of availability :

I. Triglyceride — II. Glycogen
III. A.T.P. — IV. Phosphocreatine

Codes :
(*a*) I, III, IV, II — (*b*) II, I, III, IV
(*c*) IV, II, I, III — (*d*) III, IV, II, I

conditions. The greatest question that faces physical educators today is the future of physical education. What directions will physical education take under your guidance and leadership?

246. The students need to be included for programme planning and evaluation because

(*a*) Programmes are designed for the benefits of teachers

(*b*) Programmes are designed for the benefits of students.

(*c*) Programmes are designed for the benefits of institution.

(*d*) Programmes are designed for the benefits of Administration.

247. Contemporary physical educators are facing problems and challenges regarding :

I. Place of physical education in education.

II. Justification for requirement of physical education for all children.

III. Place of physical education in educational curriculum.

IV. Effective implementation of physical education programme.

Find out the correct choice :

(*a*) I, II, III (*b*) II, III, IV

(*c*) III, IV, I (*d*) IV, I, II

248. Benefits of physical education which appear to be unprovable due to mismanagement of physical education programmes, are

I. Character development

II. Social development

III. Service to education

IV. Physical fitness development

Find out the correct choice :

(*a*) I, II, IV (*b*) II, III, IV

(*c*) III, IV, I (*d*) II, I, III

249. Present leaders of physical education require to be

(*a*) Healthy

(*b*) Skillful

(*c*) Academically strong with communicational skill

(*d*) Moral and ethical

250. To develop readiness for change is essential for education and physical education, because

I. Change is inevitable

II. Readiness prepares for present

III. Readiness prepares for future

IV. Readiness develops self confidence

Find out the correct choice :

(*a*) III, I, II (*b*) I, III, IV

(*c*) IV, II, I (*d*) III, IV, II

ANSWERS

1	2	3	4	5	6	7	8	9	10
(*d*)	(*b*)	(*b*)	(*c*)	(*d*)	(*c*)	(*b*)	(*b*)	(*a*)	(*b*)
11	**12**	**13**	**14**	**15**	**16**	**17**	**18**	**19**	**20**
(*a*)	(*c*)	(*c*)	(*d*)	(*c*)	(*b*)	(*a*)	(*c*)	(*a*)	(*d*)
21	**22**	**23**	**24**	**25**	**26**	**27**	**28**	**29**	**30**
(*d*)	(*a*)	(*b*)	(*d*)	(*a*)	(*b*)	(*c*)	(*b*)	(*c*)	(*b*)
31	**32**	**33**	**34**	**35**	**36**	**37**	**38**	**39**	**40**
(*a*)	(*b*)	(*c*)	(*a*)	(*b*)	(*b*)	(*c*)	(*d*)	(*d*)	(*c*)
41	**42**	**43**	**44**	**45**	**46**	**47**	**48**	**49**	**50**
(*b*)	(*a*)	(*d*)	(*b*)	(*a*)	(*b*)	(*b*)	(*a*)	(*d*)	(*c*)
51	**52**	**53**	**54**	**55**	**56**	**57**	**58**	**59**	**60**
(*a*)	(*c*)	(*c*)	(*c*)	(*b*)	(*b*)	(*a*)	(*c*)	(*c*)	(*a*)
61	**62**	**63**	**64**	**65**	**66**	**67**	**68**	**69**	**70**
(*c*)	(*c*)	(*b*)	(*a*)	(*c*)	(*b*)	(*b*)	(*b*)	(*a*)	(*d*)

71	**72**	**73**	**74**	**75**	**76**	**77**	**78**	**79**	**80**
(*b*)	(*b*)	(*c*)	(*b*)	(*a*)	(*c*)	(*d*)	(*d*)	(*a*)	(*c*)
81	**82**	**83**	**84**	**85**	**86**	**87**	**88**	**89**	**90**
(*a*)	(*b*)	(*d*)	(*d*)	(*d*)	(*b*)	(*a*)	(*b*)	(*a*)	(*a*)
91	**92**	**93**	**94**	**95**	**96**	**97**	**98**	**99**	**100**
(*d*)	(*a*)	(*a*)	(*a*)	(*a*)	(*b*)	(*a*)	(*c*)	(*b*)	(*d*)
101	**102**	**103**	**104**	**105**	**106**	**107**	**108**	**109**	**110**
(*c*)	(*b*)	(*d*)	(*d*)	(*a*)	(*b*)	(*d*)	(*c*)	(*b*)	(*c*)
111	**112**	**113**	**114**	**115**	**116**	**117**	**118**	**119**	**120**
(*b*)	(*a*)	(*b*)	(*b*)	(*b*)	(*b*)	(*d*)	(*b*)	(*a*)	(*c*)
121	**122**	**123**	**124**	**125**	**126**	**127**	**128**	**129**	**130**
(*b*)	(*b*)	(*c*)	(*d*)	(*a*)	(*b*)	(*c*)	(*c*)	(*c*)	(*c*)
131	**132**	**133**	**134**	**135**	**136**	**137**	**138**	**139**	**140**
(*d*)	(*a*)	(*c*)	(*b*)	(*d*)	(*b*)	(*b*)	(*d*)	(*b*)	(*d*)
141	**142**	**143**	**144**	**145**	**146**	**147**	**148**	**149**	**150**
(*c*)	(*d*)	(*c*)	(*a*)	(*c*)	(*d*)	(*b*)	(*d*)	(*a*)	(*a*)
151	**152**	**153**	**154**	**155**	**156**	**157**	**158**	**159**	**160**
(*c*)	(*a*)	(*b*)	(*c*)	(*b*)	(*b*)	(*b*)	(*d*)	(*c*)	(*c*)
161	**162**	**163**	**164**	**165**	**166**	**167**	**168**	**169**	**170**
(*d*)	(*b*)	(*a*)	(*c*)	(*a*)	(*d*)	(*b*)	(*d*)	(*b*)	(*a*)
171	**172**	**173**	**174**	**175**	**176**	**177**	**178**	**179**	**180**
(*c*)	(*b*)	(*a*)	(*d*)	(*c*)	(*a*)	(*b*)	(*d*)	(*b*)	(*c*)
181	**182**	**183**	**184**	**185**	**186**	**187**	**188**	**189**	**190**
(*a*)	(*c*)	(*b*)	(*a*)	(*d*)	(*c*)	(*c*)	(*d*)	(*c*)	(*c*)
191	**192**	**193**	**194**	**195**	**196**	**197**	**198**	**199**	**200**
(*b*)	(*a*)	(*a*)	(*b*)	(*c*)	(*d*)	(*d*)	(*c*)	(*a*)	(*d*)
201	**202**	**203**	**204**	**205**	**206**	**207**	**208**	**209**	**210**
(*a*)	(*b*)	(*c*)	(*d*)	(*d*)	(*c*)	(*d*)	(*c*)	(a)	(*a*)
211	**212**	**213**	**214**	**215**	**216**	**217**	**218**	**219**	**220**
(*a*)	(*b*)	(*d*)	(*a*)	(*b*)	(*a*)	(*c*)	(*c*)	(*b*)	(*a*)
221	**222**	**223**	**224**	**225**	**226**	**227**	**228**	**229**	**230**
(*d*)	(*a*)	(*b*)	(*d*)	(*b*)	(*a*)	(*c*)	(*d*)	(*a*)	(*d*)
231	**232**	**233**	**234**	**235**	**236**	**237**	**238**	**239**	**240**
(*b*)	(*a*)	(*a*)	(*b*)	(*b*)	(*d*)	(*b*)	(*d*)	(*a*)	(*a*)
241	**242**	**243**	**244**	**245**	**246**	**247**	**248**	**249**	**250**
(*b*)	(*a*)	(*c*)	(*a*)	(*a*)	(*b*)	(*a*)	(*d*)	(*c*)	(*a*)